SOCIOLOGICAL THEORY

ORIGIN 1897

FOUNDERS Émile Durkheim, Robert Ezra Park, Ernest Burgess, Clifford Shaw, Walter Reckless, Frederic Thrasher

MOST IMPORTANT WORKS Durkheim, *The Division of Labor in Society* (1893), and *Suicide: A Study in Sociology* (1897); Park, Burgess, and John McKenzie, *The City* (1925); Thrasher, *The Gang* (1926); Shaw et al., *Delinquency Areas* (1925); Edwin Sutherland, *Criminology* (1924)

CORE IDEAS A person's place in the social structure determines his or her behaviour. Disorganized urban areas are the breeding ground of crime. A lack of legitimate opportunities produces criminal subcultures. Socialization within the family, the school, and the peer group controls behaviour.

MODERN OUTGROWTHS Strain Theory, Cultural Deviance Theory, Social Learning Theory, Social Control Theory, Social Reaction Theory, Labelling

© Pictorial Press/Alamy

Émile Durkheim

MULTIFACTOR/INTEGRATED THEORY

ORIGIN About 1930

FOUNDERS Sheldon and Eleanor Glueck

MOST IMPORTANT WORKS Sheldon and Eleanor Glueck: *Five Hundred Delinquent Women* (1934); *Later Criminal Careers* (1937); *Criminal Careers in Retrospect* (1943); *Juvenile Delinquents Grown Up* (1940); *Unraveling Juvenile Delinquency* (1950)

CORE IDEAS Crime is a function of environmental, socialization, physical, and psychological factors. Each makes an independent contribution to shaping and directing behaviour patterns. Deficits in these areas of human development increase the risk of crime. People at risk for crime can resist antisocial behaviours if these traits and conditions can be strengthened.

MODERN OUTGROWTHS Developmental Theory, Life Course Theory, Latent Trait Theory

© FayFoto/Boston

Sheldon and Eleanor Glueck

© Stock Montage

Karl Marx

CRIMINOLOGY IN CANADA

THEORIES, PATTERNS, AND TYPOLOGIES

SIXTH EDITION

LARRY J. SIEGEL
UNIVERSITY OF MASSACHUSETTS AT LOWELL

CHRIS McCORMICK
ST. THOMAS UNIVERSITY

NELSON

NELSON

Criminology in Canada: Theories, Patterns, and Typologies, Sixth Edition

by Larry J. Siegel and Chris McCormick

Vice President, Editorial Higher Education:
Anne Williams

Publisher:
Leanna MacLean

Marketing Manager:
Terry Fedorkiw

Developmental Editor:
Suzanne Simpson Millar

Photo Researcher:
Carrie McGregor

Permissions Coordinator:
Carrie McGregor

Production Project Manager:
Hedy Sellers

Production Service:
MPS Limited

Copy Editor:
Linda Szostak

Proofreader:
MPS Limited

Indexer:
Sonya Dintaman

Design Director:
Ken Phipps

Managing Designer:
Franca Amore

Interior Design:
Cathy Mayer

Cover Design:
Courtney Hellam

Cover Images:
© Philipp Nemenz/Getty Images
© Dennis Kitchen/Getty Images

Compositor:
MPS Limited

Library and Archives Canada Cataloguing in Publication

Siegel, Larry J., author
Criminology in Canada : theories, patterns, and typologies / Larry J. Siegel (University of Massachusetts at Lowell), Chris McCormick (St. Thomas University).
—Sixth edition.

Includes bibliographical references and index.
ISBN 978-0-17-653174-4 (pbk.)

1. Criminology—Textbooks.
2. Crime—Canada—Textbooks.
I. McCormick, Christopher Ray, 1956–, author II. Title.

HV6025.S54 2015
364.971   C2014-907982-6

ISBN-13: 978-0-17-653174-4
ISBN-10: 0-17-653174-2

This book is dedicated to my children, Julie, Andrew, Eric, and Rachel Siegel, and to my wife, Theresa G. Libby.
—*Larry J. Siegel*

For my students.
—*Chris McCormick*

Brief Contents

Contents

Preface

Writing a preface is the last thing, and one of the hardest things, to do in writing a book. It has to be an introduction but it can't say too much. It has to be inviting but also challenging enough to inspire more reading. Using interesting stories is a good way to begin each edition. For example, in the fifth edition of *Criminology in Canada*, I wrote about how former press baron Conrad Black renounced his Canadian citizenship in 2001 to take a seat in Britain's House of Lords. Success, it seemed, was his. Black's empire started to unravel, however, when Hollinger International began investigating illegal payments totalling $74 million that were made to Black and other executives.

A series of suits and countersuits followed between Black and Hollinger. And then, in 2005, video cameras recorded Black and his chauffeur removing 12 file boxes from Hollinger's headquarters, despite a court order that no evidence be removed. When Black was convicted, he was fined, ordered to pay $6 million in restitution, and told to report to a minimum-security prison to begin his six-and-a-half-year prison sentence for mail fraud and obstruction of justice. Black was convicted in a lengthy and highly publicized trial, which was covered by more than 300 journalists from the United States, Canada, Britain, and Europe.

While this case is a highly unusual one, it demonstrates that criminal acts capture public attention in a way that nothing else does. And yet, our ability to determine the validity of those news stories, television documentaries, and magazine articles is compromised because most of us have little independent knowledge of crime. Unless you hang out with cops (or criminals), what you know about crime is more than likely gleaned from the media.

Similarly, the third edition of *Criminology in Canada* began with the Pickton murders. Dozens of women had gone missing from Vancouver's Downtown Eastside in a series of slayings that had people convinced a serial killer was operating in their midst. Despite geographic profiling evidence confirming links between the cases, police failed to make the connection until more than 50 women had been murdered. If this case were used today, it would be updated to include reference to the more than 600 missing Aboriginal women, some from the infamous Highway of Tears in British Columbia.

The Pickton case made for a good introduction to the book because it was sensational, and yet it again illustrated the ambiguous role the media has in modern society. The media does a good job reporting crime, but they also seem to have an inordinate interest in notorious killers, serial murderers, drug lords, and sex criminals. It is not surprising, then, that many of us are more concerned about violent crime than about almost any other social problem. We worry about becoming victims of violent crime, having our houses broken into, or having our cars stolen. We alter our behaviour to limit the risk of victimization, and we question whether legal punishment alone can control criminal offenders. We are shocked by graphic news accounts of drive-by shootings, police brutality, and prison riots. We are fascinated by books, movies, and TV shows about law firms, clients, fugitives, and hardened killers. Yet these media do little to enlighten us as to the cause of criminal behaviour.

In contrast, this book addresses the question of why we behave the way we do. What causes one person to become violent and antisocial, while another channels his or her energy into work, school, and family? How do we explain the at-risk kid in a high-crime neighbourhood who successfully resists the temptation of the streets? What accounts for the behaviour of the multimillionaire who cheats on his or her taxes and engages in other fraudulent schemes? The former has nothing yet is able to resist crime; the latter has everything and falls prey to its allure. Is behaviour a function of personal characteristics, or of upbringing and experience? Is it influenced by culture or environment? Or is it a combination of all of these influences?

This text addresses some of these difficult questions through a typology-based approach. This means we look for patterns, so as to better predict behaviour and to learn how to control it. It might be looking at the role of gender, or the influence of social class. It might mean looking at opportunities for deviant behaviour, and the influence of peer groups. It might mean looking at the role of regulation in such disasters as the railcar explosion in Lac Megantic, Quebec, regulations which allowed a train carrying highly explosive oil to sit idle on a siding with no one on board, only to slip away during the night and coast downhill into the middle of a town where it derailed and exploded, killing almost 50 people. Such a disaster could have been predicted and thus prevented, if only our attention wasn't distracted by serial killers.

As a professor of criminology, I have taught thousands of students. To me, what is important is communicating my interests in crime, law, and justice to my students and inspiring them to explore their interests in the field. My goal has always been to help students understand a very broad field in a way that is easy to grasp. What could be more important or fascinating than a field of study that deals with such wide-ranging topics as the motivation for mass murder, the association between media violence and interpersonal aggression, the family's influence on drug abuse, and the history of organized crime? Criminology is a dynamic field, changing constantly with the release of major research studies, Supreme Court rulings, and governmental policy. Its dynamism and diversity make it an important and engrossing area of study. In this book, I have sought to find examples and cases that make the field come alive.

What makes criminology difficult, but also interesting, is the continuing debate regarding the nature and extent of crime, and the causes and prevention of criminality. Some people view criminals as society's victims who are forced to violate the law because of poverty and the lack of opportunity. Others view aggressive, antisocial behaviour as a product of mental and physical abnormalities that persist through the life course. Genetic, neurological, and physiological factors are also felt to influence criminality. Still another view is that crime is a function of the rational choice of greedy, selfish people who can be deterred only through the threat of harsh punishments. For these people, there can be no treatment—only punishment. As new research uncovers factors that affect crime, the debate over the nature and cause of crime develops.

Debate also continues over how the criminal justice system should best treat known criminals. Should they be punished by being locked up? Or should they be given a second chance and diverted into alternative justice programs? Should crime control policy focus on punishment or rehabilitation, or even on medical treatment? If the underlying cause is poverty, how can this situation be remedied? Many of these questions are tied to the current events we learn about through the media. When a group of teenagers were accused of luring Reena Virk to a secluded spot only to assault and then kill her, it fuelled the call for reforms to juvenile justice. When Melanie Carpenter was abducted in broad daylight from her place of work in Surrey, British Columbia, sufficient public alarm ensued that the dangerous offender legislation was amended. Similarly, when Georgina Leimonis was shot in a Toronto café, the public called for the deportation of violent criminals. Recent events involving the suicides of Amanda Todd and Rehtaeh Parsons have fuelled debate over cyber-bullying and sparked changes to cyber-crime and online activity. Because interest in crime and justice is so great and so timely, this text reviews these ongoing issues and covers the field of criminology in an organized and comprehensive manner. It is meant as a broad overview of the field, designed to whet the reader's appetite and encourage further and more in-depth exploration. Numerous students have told me that they kept this book throughout university, using it as

a criminology reference text beyond first year. That type of testimonial has inspired me to keep working to design this book to suit student needs, while meeting my interest in communicating my enthusiasm for a rich, growing field of study.

In this sixth edition, I have made every effort to make the presentation of material interesting, balanced, objective, and especially, as distinctly Canadian as possible. No single political or theoretical position dominates the text; instead, this text presents the many diverse views that are contained within criminology and that characterize its interdisciplinary nature. The multi-disciplinarity of the field ranges from biology to sociology, and includes history, economics, and psychology. The text analyzes the most important scholarly works and scientific research reports, while also presenting topical information on recent cases and events.

ORGANIZATION OF THE TEXT AND WHAT IS NEW IN THIS EDITION

The text is divided into three main sections or topic areas.

Section 1 provides a framework for studying criminology. Chapter 1 defines the field and discusses its most basic concepts: the definition of crime, the component areas of criminology, the history of criminology, criminological research methods, and the ethical issues that confront the field. Chapter 2 covers criminal law and its functions, processes, defences, and reform. In addition, the topic of wrongful convictions illustrates how mistakes can happen in even the most rationally organized system. Chapter 3 deals with the nature, extent, and patterns of crime, covering the various ways we learn about crime in our society: police statistics, victimization surveys, and the media. Criminologists attempt to reconcile these different sources to understand crime patterns. Chapter 4 is devoted to a new area of criminology: victimization. This chapter includes a discussion of the nature of victims, theories of victimization, and programs designed to help crime victims. A section on hate crime is especially relevant as we move into the twenty-first century after the events of 9/11.

- These introductory chapters lay out the basic issues that criminology deals with, highlighted by examples such as the Idle No More movement and other recent protests. Debates over criminalization are highlighted by issues like the necessity of self-defence in protests over shale gas development, and changes in the criminalization of euthanasia and marijuana. Updated provincial and national statistics on crime in general and youth crime specifically help show how patterns of crime are changing, while new victimization statistics allow for better international comparisons. Controversial issues in the news, such as the cyber-bullying of victim Amanda Todd, highlight the ongoing relevance of criminology to understand the world around us.

Section 2 contains five chapters that cover criminological theories: criminal choice (Chapter 5); biological and psychological views (Chapter 6); structural, cultural, and ecological theories (Chapter 7); social process theories that focus on socialization and include learning and control (Chapter 8); and theories of social conflict (Chapter 9). Of particular interest are the material on closed circuit television in Chapter 5, real cases of sleepwalking used as a defence in Chapter 6, early research done at McGill University in the 1920s in Chapter 7, and research on ethnicity and criminality in Chapter 9. Some of these cases are highly controversial, such as the case in Chapter 6 that discusses how a woman was given leniency after she stabbed her husband. Her defence? She was suffering from premenstrual syndrome.

- These chapters outline the theoretical issues that criminology deals with, and are highlighted in Chapter 5 by new material on surveillance and security, and in Chapter 6 by material on biological differences that predict criminality. Chapter 7 and Chapter 9 both discuss how racial profiling used by police has come under criticism, and Chapter 8 looks at interpersonal factors, such as the controversy surrounding Toronto's mayor and drug use. All these chapters deal with ongoing issues such as inequality and life chances. Chapter 9 continues to highlight how the risk of crime in a society increasingly oriented to mandatory minimum sentences connects the individual to wider social structures.

Section 3 is devoted to the major forms of criminal behaviour. Chapters 10 to 13 cover violent crime, common theft offences, white-collar and organized crimes, and public order crimes, including sex offences and substance abuse. Each of these chapters has been updated from the preceding edition, using where possible the latest criminal statistics provided by government studies and academic research. Throughout, recent Canadian research is highlighted and current topics keep the text fresh. Also updated in this edition is Chapter 14, which was added in the fifth edition to address crimes of the twenty-first century, including new and upcoming issues for our society, from transnational terrorism to cybercrime.

- These chapters on crime patterns and trends lay out current and controversial issues, and highlight the most recent information, such as statistics on patterns of violent crime in Chapter 10, including the major forms of murder, sexual assault, and family violence. Chapter 11, with its focus on property crime, discusses recent trends in crimes such as auto theft and computer-assisted crime,

while Chapter 12 highlights crimes of power, such as the train disaster at Lac-Mégantic, the Senate scandal, the recent economic collapse, and new efforts against organized crime. Chapter 13 also takes up the moral issues of the decriminalization of marijuana and euthanasia, while Chapter 14 looks at crimes of the twenty-first century, such as WikiLeaks and the Snowden affair, cyberterrorism, and environmental activism.

The text has been carefully structured to cover relevant material in a comprehensive, balanced, and objective fashion. With marginal notes and clearly defined learning objectives, lesson concepts are also easy to understand.

KEY FEATURES

Connections boxes are located in appropriate places throughout each chapter. These brief inserts link the material being currently discussed with relevant information located elsewhere in the text. Connections either expand on the subject matter or show how it can be applied to other areas or topics. In such a comprehensive book, these boxes help organize and coordinate the material for quicker learning.

Crime in the News is a special feature, where newspaper columns on crime and criminal justice are reproduced. Over a nine-year period, I wrote a biweekly column that sought to communicate criminological research in a popular format. The media is an important resource for our understanding of criminal justice, and it can be used proactively. For example, in Chapter 5, a column is reproduced that discusses research on red-light cameras. Despite being hailed as a way to deter red-light runners, the research actually shows that they increase the incidence of rear-end collisions, causing more accidents than they prevent. Why, then, are they so popular? Perhaps it is because insurance companies can collect higher premiums and the police can collect more fines.

- Each chapter now sports a new column, from prostitution in Chapter 1, wrongful convictions in Chapter 2, the discussion of crime patterns in the media in Chapter 3, and the coverage of domestic violence in the media in Chapter 4. As mentioned above, Chapter 5 looks at red-light cameras. Chapter 6 discusses new advances in forensic brain mapping, Chapter 7 looks at the London riots of 2011, Chapter 8 examines the cyber-bullying case of Amanda Todd, and Chapter 9 looks at racial profiling by police in Toronto. In the last section of the book, the crime in the media issue in Chapter 10 is whether duress can be a defence to murder, Chapter 11 discusses the topic of auto theft, and Chapter 12 looks at the explosion of the Deepwater Horizon oil well. Chapter 13 highlights the moral issue of euthanasia and assisted suicide, while Chapter 14 looks at the defence of necessity in environmental activism.

Famous Canadian Criminals and **Famous Canadian Court Cases** boxes use cases from our past to illustrate principles from the text. For example, Chapter 4 highlights the case of Angelique Lyn Lavallee, a battered woman in a violent common-law relationship who killed her partner late one night by shooting him in the back of the head as he left her room. This case ultimately resulted in a decision by the Supreme Court of Canada (1990) that set the legal framework for what has become known as the "battered wife syndrome" defence. Then Justice Minister Allan Rock also agreed to consider extending that principle to some pre-1990 cases. In this example, we see the origin of an important doctrine of Canadian criminal justice and consider the significance of gender in criminal cases.

- These exhibits have also been updated to include new information, such as in Chapter 1 where the ethical issues around Russel Ogden's research on assisted suicide at Simon Fraser University now makes reference to researchers at the University of Ottawa who interviewed Luka Magnotta in their research on sex trade workers. Police sought to subpoena their research notes, a move that the researchers resisted. In another example, The Famous Canadian Criminal exhibit in Chapter 3 on Karl Toft has been updated to include the case of a Saint John city councillor convicted of child abuse and molestation, while the exhibit in Chapter 12 profiles the infamous Senate scandals that have recently plagued the Conservative government.

Thinking Like a Criminologist asks you to apply reasoning from the chapter to a criminal justice question. For example, in Chapter 12, to deter property crime, various measures are discussed that could prevent theft from households and cars. These measures are based on ideas from Chapter 5 on rational choice theory. Can you think of other preventive measures after reading this chapter?

Each chapter has **Critical Thinking Questions**, designed to get students thinking about key issues in the chapter. These questions follow the popular **Thinking Like a Criminologist** section and are good preparation for essay questions on quizzes.

Each chapter has two additional boxes—**Comparative Criminology** and **Criminology Research**—in which broader questions address the relationship between crime and the wider society. Chapter 6, for example, discusses some issues concerning the relation between the media and violence. Are the media implicated in influencing violent behaviour? Do the media simply reflect norms already existing in society? These questions are still open for discussion. Chapter 4 examines gay bashing in some detail, and Chapter 9 highlights issues involving Aboriginal people and the criminal justice system.

Photos, charts, and figures are important pedagogical features for any text. Each chapter includes a chapter outline, a list of key terms contained in the chapter, and at least one boxed insert. These boxed features contain a detailed discussion or reading of an important and intriguing topic, issue, or program. A running marginal glossary provides concise definitions of key terms used throughout the text for quick reference. Public opinion polls discussed in the text also help situate current thinking on criminal issues, such as whether marijuana should be regulated, or euthanasia should be decriminalized.

As always, the effort has been made to update information, cite important new research as it appears, keep old features that work well, and work in new features to help communicate the material. As always, the effort is to highlight Canadian criminology, and to showcase Canadian cases. I hope you agree.

ANCILLARIES

About the Nelson Education Teaching Advantage (NETA)

The **Nelson Education Teaching Advantage (NETA)** program delivers research-based instructor  resources that promote student engagement and higher-order thinking to enable the success of Canadian students and educators. To ensure the high quality of these materials, all Nelson ancillaries have been professionally copy edited. Be sure to visit Nelson Education's **Inspired Instruction** website at www.nelson.com/inspired to find out more about NETA. Don't miss the testimonials of instructors who have used NETA supplements and seen student engagement increase!

Instructor Resources

All NETA and other key instructor ancillaries are provided in the *Instructor Resources* at http://www.nelson.com/siegelcriminology6e, giving instructors the ultimate tools for customizing lectures and presentations. Instructor materials can also be accessed through www.nelson.com/instructor.

- **NETA Test Bank**: This resource was written by Daniel Bear, Sheridan College. It includes over 1,700 multiple-choice questions written according to NETA guidelines for effective construction and development of higher-order questions. The Test Bank was copy edited by a NETA-trained editor. Also included are essay questions to promote critical thinking.

The NETA Test Bank is available in a new, cloud-based platform.

Nelson Testing Powered by Cognero® is a secure online testing system that allows you to author, edit, and manage test bank content from any place you have Internet access. No special installations or downloads are needed, and the desktop-inspired interface, with its drop-down menus and familiar, intuitive tools, allows you to create and manage tests with ease. You can create multiple test versions in an instant, and import or export content into other systems. Tests can be delivered from your learning management system, your classroom, or wherever you want. Nelson Testing Powered by Cognero for *Criminology in Canada* can be accessed through http://www.nelson.com/instructor. Printable versions of the Test Bank in Word and PDF formats are available through your sales and editorial representative.

- **NETA PowerPoint:** Microsoft® PowerPoint® lecture slides for every chapter have been created by Paul Hommersen, Sheridan College. There is an average of 47 slides per chapter, many featuring key figures, tables, and photographs from *Criminology in Canada*. Up to 50 percent of the slides also include talking notes in the Notes section to further support teaching. NETA principles of clear design and engaging content have been incorporated throughout, making it simple for instructors to customize the deck for their courses.
- **Image Library:** This resource consists of digital copies of figures, short tables, and photographs used in the book. Instructors may use these jpegs to customize the NETA PowerPoint or create their own PowerPoint presentations.
- **NETA Instructor's Manual:** This resource was written by Paul Hommersen, Sheridan College. It is organized according to the textbook chapters and addresses key educational concerns, such as typical stumbling blocks that students face and how to address them. Other sections of each chapter answer the following questions: How can I generate discussion in my course and assess my students? How can I engage my students? What can I do in the way of assignments and projects? And what can I do online?
- **DayOne:** Day One—Prof InClass is a PowerPoint presentation that instructors can customize to orient students to the class and their text at the beginning of the course.

- **Mind Tap:** MindTap for *Criminology in Canada* is a personalized teaching experience with relevant assignments that guide students to analyze, apply, and elevate thinking, allowing instructors to measure skills and promote better outcomes with ease. A fully online learning solution, MindTap combines all student learning tools—readings, multimedia, activities, and assessments—into a single Learning Path that guides the student through the curriculum. Instructors personalize the experience by customizing the presentation of these learning tools to their students, even seamlessly introducing their own content into the Learning Path.
- **The Cengage Criminal Justice Media Library:** The Cengage Criminal Justice Media Library offers an exciting collection of videos to enrich lectures. Qualified adopters may select from a wide variety of professionally prepared videos covering various aspects of policing, corrections, and other areas of the criminal justice system. The selections include videos from *Rims for the Humanities & Sciences,* Court TV videos that feature provocative one-hour court cases to illustrate seminal and high profile cases in depth, *A&E American Justice Series* videos, *National Institute of Justice: Crime File* videos, ABC News videos, and *MPI Home Videos.* Ask your Nelson Education sales representative for information on how to order the videos.
- **Crime Scenes 2.0: Interactive Criminal Justice CD-ROM (0-534-56831-9):** This interactive CD-ROM features six vignettes that allow students to play various roles as they explore all aspects of the criminal justice system. Exciting videos and supporting documents put students in the midst of a juvenile murder trial, a prostitution case that turns into manslaughter, and several other scenarios. This product received the gold medal in higher education and the silver medal for video interface from NewMedia Magazine's Invision Awards.
- **Careers in Criminal Justice Printed Access Card (ISBN-10: 0-495-59522-5; ISBN-13: 978-0-495-59522-9):** The Careers in Criminal Justice website is designed to help students investigate and focus on the criminal justice career choices that are right for them by offering extensive career profiling information and self-assessment testing. This insightful website includes over 70 Career Profiles and more than 25 video interviews with links and tools to assist students in finding a professional position. It also features a career rolodex, interest assessments, and a career planner with sample résumés, letters, interview questions, and more.

- **Nelson Criminology Dictionary (0-17-640608-5):** Written by Gary Parkinson and Robert Drislane, the *Nelson Criminology Dictionary* is a compact and inexpensive glossary of common criminological terms that students will encounter during their studies in criminology. More than 1,400 entries cover the main concepts and events that are used in criminology and criminal justice courses, making this dictionary an invaluable tool.

Student Ancillaries

 **MindTap:** Stay organized and efficient with MindTap—a single destination with all the course material and study aids you need to succeed. Built-in apps leverage social media and the latest learning technology. For example:

- ReadSpeaker will read the text to you.
- Flashcards are pre-populated to provide you with a jump-start—or you can create your own.
- Highlighting and note taking are compiled into your electronic notebook and link back to the MindTap Reader when it's time to study for the exam.
- Self-quizzing allows you to assess your understanding.

Visit http://www.nelson.com/student to start using **MindTap**. Enter the Online Access Code from the card included with your text. If a code card is not provided, you can purchase instant access at NELSONbrain.com.

About the Authors

LARRY J. SIEGEL was born in the Bronx in 1947. While living on Jerome Avenue and attending City College of New York (CCNY) in the 1960s, he was swept up in the social and political currents of the time. He became intrigued with the influence contemporary culture had on individual behaviour: Did people shape society or did society shape people? He applied his interest in social forces and human behaviour to the study of crime and justice. After graduating from CCNY, he attended the newly opened program in criminal justice at the State University of New York at Albany, earning both his M.A. and Ph.D. degrees there. After completing his graduate work, Dr. Siegel began his teaching career at Northeastern University, where he was a faculty member for nine years. After leaving Northeastern, he held teaching positions at the University of Nebraska–Omaha and Saint Anselm College in New Hampshire. He is currently a professor at the University of Massachusetts–Lowell. Dr. Siegel has written extensively in the area of crime and justice, including books on juvenile law, delinquency, criminology, criminal justice, and criminal procedure. He is a court certified expert on police conduct and has testified in numerous legal cases. The father of four and grandfather of three, Larry Siegel and his wife, Terry, now reside in Bedford, New Hampshire, with their two dogs, Watson and Cody.

Courtesy of Larry Siegel and Therese

CHRIS McCORMICK lives in Fredericton with his human family and two dogs, Rusty and Bussy, who were rescued from shelters in the United States by the National Brittany Rescue Association to now live a wonderful life in New Brunswick. Chris McCormick has degrees from Acadia, Queen's, and York Universities. He has taught at various institutions, including Acadia, York, and Bishop's University in Quebec, and Mount Saint Vincent, Dalhousie, and Saint Mary's University in Halifax, before moving to St. Thomas University to co-found the Criminology and Criminal Justice program. This is one of only five criminology programs in Canada, and is known for its strong social justice focus. Professor McCormick's teaching interests are in cultural studies, discourse analysis, and wrongful convictions. In addition, he has published in the areas of crime and media, corporate crime, and historical studies of crime and criminal justice in Canada. Between 2004 and 2013, he published *Crime Matters*, a biweekly column on crime and criminal justice issues in Fredericton, New Brunswick's city newspaper. Samples of this work in public scholarship are featured in chapters throughout the book. After all, it is not just what we do as academics that matters, but how we communicate it to others, our students, and our community. To paraphrase Karl Marx, the point is not just to understand the world but to make it better.

© Noel Chenier

ACKNOWLEDGMENTS

Many people helped make this book possible. I have attempted to incorporate the suggestions of those who reviewed this edition, including:

Joshua Barath, Georgian College

Raegan Carmichael, Simon Fraser University, University of the Fraser Valley

Linda Fisher, Douglas College

Glenn Hanna, University of Guelph/Humber

Hongming Cheng, University of Saskatchewan

Zachary Levinsky, University of Toronto Mississauga

The list of those who helped with material or advice includes those at Nelson Education Ltd. Many thanks, in particular, to Maya Castle, Lenore Taylor-Atkins, and Suzanne Simpson Millar for their assistance. I also thank Larry Siegel (University of Massachusetts at Lowell) for producing such a great text from which to work.

In addition, I also thank the various copy editors, research assistants, and editorial assistants whose contributions have enhanced the text over the years.

Chris McCormick
Department of Criminology
St. Thomas University
Fredericton, New Brunswick
2014

Concepts of Crime, Law, and Criminology

How is crime defined? How much crime is there, and what are the trends and patterns in the crime rate? How many people are victims of crime, and who is likely to become a crime victim? How did our system of criminal law develop, and what are the basic elements of crimes? What is the science of criminology all about? These are some of the core issues that will be addressed in the first four chapters of this text, providing a solid foundation for the chapters to come. Chapter 1 introduces the field of criminology: its nature, area of study, methodologies, and historical development. Concern about crime and justice has been an important part of the human condition for more than 5,000 years, since the first criminal codes were set down in the Middle East. And although the scientific study of crime—criminology—is considered a contemporary science, it has existed for more than 200 years.

Chapter 2 introduces one of the key components of criminology: the development of criminal law. Included in this discussion is the social history of law and the purpose of law, and how that purpose defines crime. The chapter also briefly examines criminal defences and legal reform using prominent Canadian examples. The final two chapters of this section create a picture of crime by reviewing the various sources of crime data. Chapter 3 focuses on the nature and extent of crime, while Chapter 4 is devoted to victims and victimization. Important and stable patterns in the rates of crime and victimization indicate that these are not random events. The way crime and victimization are organized and patterned profoundly influences how criminologists view the causes of crime.

Crime and Criminology

1

Learning Objectives

After reading this chapter, you will be able to:

1. Understand the scope of the field of criminology.
2. Be familiar with different parts of the "criminological enterprise."
3. Know the elements of what constitutes a crime.
4. Discuss the different views of crime.
5. Explain different methods and their use.

© Dan Riedlhuber/Reuters

The Idle No More movement of 2012, and ongoing, featured protests by First Nations peoples against environmental degradation and social inequality.

What people know about crime and criminal justice generally comes from media coverage of highly publicized cases. For example, in 2010, David Russell Williams was relieved as base commander at Canadian Forces Base (CFB) Trenton and charged with two counts of first-degree murder, two counts each of forcible confinement, breaking and entering, and sexual assault. He was subsequently sentenced to two life sentences for first-degree murder, two 10-year sentences each for sexual assault and forcible confinement, and 82 one-year sentences for burglary. He will serve a minimum of 25 years before parole eligibility and is not eligible for early parole under the so-called faint hope clause of the *Criminal Code of Canada* (CCC). A successful soldier and military commander, Williams was also a decorated military pilot who had flown Canadian Forces VIP aircraft for such dignitaries as Queen Elizabeth II and Prince Philip, the governor general, and the prime minister. And yet what we saw of him in the news was the endless parade of pictures he took of himself posing in trophy underwear and the recitation of details of his sordid crimes. He became a celebrity criminal.

Similarly, in 2003, a high-profile trial brought Maurice "Mom" Boucher, leader of the notorious Nomads chapter of the Hells Angels, into the public spotlight. In a police raid called Operation Hurricane, assets worth a total of $29 million were seized, including houses, bank accounts, narcotics, 28 vehicles, and 70 firearms, including a rocket launcher. Members of the Hells Angels faced charges of complicity to commit murder, gangsterism, and drug trafficking; after a lengthy trial involving more than 200 witnesses, they all pleaded guilty. Boucher had encouraged the murder of rival bikers as the Hells Angels sought to expand their territory. He also ordered the murder of two prison guards in an attempt to destabilize the **criminal justice system** and increase fear. For that order, he was convicted of murder and received two life sentences.

Such cases illustrate why crime and criminal behaviour have long fascinated people. Crime involves some that shock the conscience. In the mid-1990s, Karla Homolka and Paul Bernardo were convicted of murdering 14-year-old Leslie Mahaffy and 15-year-old Kristen French. In a controversial plea bargain, Homolka cooperated with the prosecution and testified against Bernardo. She was sentenced to 12 years in jail and was released on parole in 2005 amid great controversy. Bernardo received a life sentence for the two murders and was declared a dangerous offender for a string of rapes.

Details of Homolka's trial were subject to a publication ban in efforts to ensure a fair trial for Bernardo; however, this ban didn't prevent the public from learning details of the case. *The Washington Post* published a story, which Canadians could read in public libraries; *The Buffalo News* printed an article, and Canadians drove across the border to buy the newspaper. Details of the crimes were posted on the Internet faster than news lists and discussion groups could be shut down. Were the media sensationalizing the case, or were they simply responding to the public's need to know?

And in a last, more recent example, Robert Pickton was found guilty in December 2007 of six counts of second-degree murder for the deaths of women who disappeared from Vancouver's Downtown Eastside. In stories of the investigation, the public read about body parts discovered in buckets and freezers on Pickton's pig farm. He was charged in 20 other deaths, but in 2010 it was announced that the prosecution of those charges would likely not be pursued.

CONNECTIONS

For more examples of serial killers, see the Famous Canadian Criminals exhibit later in this chapter.

Such cases illustrate how criminal acts can be the work of strangers who prey on people they have never met, or how they can involve friends and family members in **intimate violence.** What compels a couple like Paul Bernardo and Karla Homolka to kidnap, sexually assault, and murder? They came from a community with tree-shaded parks, nice homes, and sports fields. They were seen as a young couple with a bright future. Could such outrageous behaviour be better understood if the crimes had been committed by teens who were the product of bad neighbourhoods and dysfunctional homes? Research indicates that habitually aggressive behaviour is often learned in homes where children are victimized and parents serve as aggressive role models—the learned violence then persists into adulthood.[1] Could someone who was considered normal ever commit such horrible crimes? Does their conviction and imprisonment deter others? Is it possible to deter the Picktons of our society who prey on vulnerable victims? Do the media have any responsibility in reporting such horrific crimes?

Such crime stories as these take their toll on the public. When Paul Bernardo was on trial for his crimes, about one-third of the Canadian population said that they did not feel safe walking alone in their own neighbourhood at night. This fear was more likely to be expressed by women than by men and was out of proportion to the actual risk of victimization. Although many Canadians thought crime had increased, overall rates of victimization had remained the same. Canadians were no more likely to be victims of assault, theft (either of personal or of household property), vandalism, or break and enter than they had been previously.

The public fear of crime is an important barometer of social health and how people feel about their communities. The public overestimation of the likelihood of crime in their own neighbourhoods, despite contradictory evidence from their

criminal justice system   The stages through which the offender passes, including police, courts, and corrections.

intimate violence   Crime that occurs in the context of familiarity, such as spousal abuse, child abuse, or elder abuse.

Robert Pickton was found guilty in December 2007 of six counts of second-degree murder in the deaths of women who disappeared from Vancouver's Downtown Eastside.

Concern about crime and the need to develop effective measures to control criminal behaviour has spurred the development of the study of **criminology**. This academic discipline is devoted to the study of crime patterns and trends, and the development of valid and reliable information regarding the causes of crime. **Criminologists** use scientific methods to study the nature, extent, cause, and control of criminal behaviour. Unlike media commentators, whose opinions about crime can be coloured by personal experiences, biases, and values, criminologists attempt to bring objectivity and scientific methods to the study of crime and its consequences. Because of the threat of crime and the social problems it represents, the field of criminology has gained prominence as an academic area of study.

This chapter introduces criminology: how it is defined, its goals, and its history. It also addresses such questions as the following: How do criminologists define crime? How do they conduct research? What ethical issues face those wanting to conduct criminological research?

own experience, points to the influence of other factors on the public's knowledge of crime. People do not rely on their experience when assessing the likelihood of being a victim of crime, but rather draw from such sources as the media. For example, even though victimization surveys often show only slight variations in personal victimization from year to year, many people often believe crime has increased in their neighbourhood.

Third-hand knowledge of crime has long-term effects, creating fear of crime, a negative view of the police and the courts, and an attitude favouring harsher punishments for offenders. The fear of crime skews the larger social agenda, resulting in people being more in favour of investing resources into reducing crime than into reducing poverty. In 2005, following the Boxing Day shooting on Toronto's Yonge Street that killed 15-year-old Jane Creba, 87 percent of residents said they believed that Toronto was becoming more violent, and 64 percent of residents said they would rather see an increase in policing and stricter penalties for crime than money spent on social programs. Furthermore, 76 percent of Toronto residents believed lenient judges were allowing gun crime to flourish in Canada's cities—and it didn't help that one of the suspects charged in the Boxing Day gunfight was out on parole at the time of the incident.[2]

CONNECTIONS

Experts have suggested a variety of explanations for bizarre violent episodes, such as serial homicide. Psychologists link violent behaviour to a number of psychological influences, including observational learning from violent TV shows, traumatic childhood experiences, mental illness, impaired cognitive processes, and a psychopathic personality structure. Chapter 6 reviews the most prominent of these explanations of violence.

WHAT IS CRIMINOLOGY?

Criminology is the scientific approach to the study of criminal behaviour. In their classic definition, criminologists Edwin Sutherland and Donald Cressey state:

> Criminology is the body of knowledge regarding crime as a social phenomenon. It includes within its scope the processes of making laws, of breaking laws, and of reacting toward the breaking of laws. ... The objective of criminology is the development of a body of general and verified principles and of other types of knowledge regarding this process of law, crime, and treatment.[3]

Sutherland and Cressey's definition includes the most important areas of interest to criminologists: the development of criminal law and its use to define crime, the cause of law violations, and the methods used to control criminal behaviour. Also important is the use of the scientific method in criminology. Criminologists use objective research methods to pose research questions (hypotheses), gather data, create theories, and test the validity of theories. They use every method of established social science inquiry: analysis of existing records, experimental designs, surveys, historical analysis, and content analysis.

criminology The scientific study of the nature, extent, cause, and control of criminal behaviour.

criminologist One who brings objectivity and method to the study of crime and its consequences.

An essential part of criminology is its nature as a multidisciplinary science. Few universities in Canada grant graduate degrees in criminology, but criminologists are also drawn from such disciplines as sociology, criminal justice, political science, psychology, history, geography, economics, and the natural sciences. Today, criminology's orientation is truly multidisciplinary—an integrated approach to the study of criminal behaviour. Criminology combines elements from many other fields to understand the connections among law, crime, and justice.

Criminology and Criminal Justice

In the late 1960s, research projects were developed to understand the way police, courts, and correctional agencies operated.[4] These academic programs, devoted to studying the criminal justice system, are concentrated in five university departments of criminology in Canada: Simon Fraser University in Burnaby, the University of Ottawa, the University of Montreal, the University of Toronto, and St. Thomas University in Fredericton. Students can also pursue this field in many community college programs and institutes for the study of criminal justice. The criminal justice studies program at Oshawa's University of Ontario's Institute of Technology is an example of such new developments in criminology studies.

Although the terms *criminology* and *criminal justice* may seem similar, they have major differences. Criminologists explain the etiology (origin), extent, and nature of crime in society, whereas criminal justice scholars describe and analyze the work of the police, courts, and correctional facilities, and how to better design effective methods of crime control.

Because both fields are crime-related, they do overlap. Criminologists must be aware of how the agencies of justice operate, and criminal justice experts design programs of crime prevention or rehabilitation through their understanding of the nature of crime. Thus, these two fields not only coexist, but also help each other to grow and develop.

Criminology and Deviance

Criminology is also sometimes confused with the study of **deviant behaviour**. However, deviance is more widely defined as behaviour that departs from social norms and is not always subject to formal sanction. Included within the broad spectrum of deviant acts is sunbathing in the nude, joining a nudist colony, or a woman going topless.

Crime and deviance are often confused, yet not all crimes are deviant or unusual acts, and not all deviant acts are illegal or criminal. For example, using recreational drugs, such as marijuana, may be illegal, but is it deviant? Most Canadians surveyed think that soft drugs should be allowed for individual use, and support for decriminalizing marijuana is high. For example, when Ross Rebagliati was threatened with losing his gold medal in snowboarding at the 1998 Winter Olympics after testing positive for marijuana, public surveys showed more concern with the high-handedness of officials than with Rebagliati's purported marijuana use. In 2010, 40,000 demonstrators rallied at the Ontario Legislative Assembly as part of the Million Marijuana March, a worldwide event held annually in over 200 cities to demand the full legalization of marijuana. In 2012, four British Columbia attorneys general called for the legalization of cannabis, arguing that the (then) 89-year-old law had failed.

Conversely, many deviant acts are not criminal even though they may be shocking. For example, suppose that a passerby observes a person drowning and makes no effort to save that victim. Although the general public would probably condemn such lack of action as callous and immoral, citizens are not required by law to be good Samaritans. In sum, many criminal acts, but not all, fall within the concept of deviance. Similarly, some deviant acts, but not all, are considered crimes.

The relationship between crime and deviance is illustrated in Figure 1.1, "Hagan's Varieties of Deviance." This model depicts the relationship between crime and deviance along three dimensions: the evaluation of social harm, the level of agreement about the norm, and the severity of societal response. As Figure 1.1 shows, the most serious acts of deviance are also the least likely to occur; however, strong agreement exists over the harmfulness of those acts and the need for a serious societal response.[5]

Two issues are of particular interest to criminologists: (1) How do deviant behaviours become crimes? (2) When should acts considered crimes be legalized? The first issue involves the historical development of law. Many acts that are legally forbidden today were once considered merely unusual or deviant behaviour. Thus, criminologists study the process by which crimes are created from deviance. For example, the sale and possession of marijuana was legal in Canada until 1923, when it was prohibited under federal law by simply adding marijuana to the law prohibiting opium.[6] Despite being criminalized, however, marijuana still enjoys widespread popularity: Health Canada estimates that 60 percent of Canadians between the ages of 20 and 44 have used marijuana, and the Canadian Addiction Survey reported that 70 percent of those aged 18 to 24 report using the substance.[7]

If marijuana use is widespread, criminologists will consider whether behaviours that were outlawed in the past have evolved into social norms and, if so, whether those behaviours should either be legalized or have their penalties reduced. This is called **decriminalization**.

> **deviant behaviour**   Behaviour that departs from or doesn't conform to social norms, but isn't defined as a crime by the law.
>
> **decriminalization**   Reducing the penalty for a criminal act, and its illegality.

FIGURE 1.1
Hagan's Varieties of Deviance

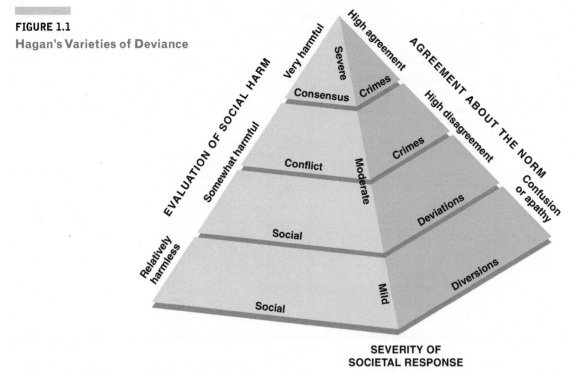

Source: The Varieties of Deviance, from Hagan, John. *The Disreputable Pleasures: Crime and Deviance in Canada*, 3rd ed. © 1991. Toronto: McGraw-Hill Ryerson Ltd., p. 13. This material is reproduced with permission of McGraw-Hill Ryerson Ltd.

CONNECTIONS

Some of the drugs considered highly dangerous today were once sold openly and considered medically beneficial. For example, the narcotic drug heroin, now considered extremely addictive, was originally named in the mistaken belief that its painkilling properties would prove *heroic* to medical patients. The history of drug and alcohol use is discussed further in Chapter 13.

On the one hand, then, we see how an illegal act is accepted and not seen as deviant. On the other hand, however, the line between behaviour that is considered deviant and behaviour that is outlawed can become quite controversial. For example, when does sexually expressive material cross the line from being merely suggestive to being pornographic? Can a line be drawn that separates sexually oriented materials into two groups, one that is legally acceptable and a second that is considered depraved or obscene? And, if such a line can be drawn, who gets to draw it? Many recent efforts have been made to control morally questionable behaviour and restrict the rights of citizens to freedom of their actions. In a very controversial case, a British Columbia man was charged with the possession of violent, pornographic stories involving children. He argued that the law violated his freedom of expression, and he was acquitted. On appeal, the case eventually went to the Supreme Court of Canada, which ruled that John Robin Sharpe was deprived of his right to freedom of expression when police seized his pornography because the stories were for his own personal use. This case is described in more detail in the following Famous Canadian Court Cases box, "*R. v. Sharpe* (2001)."

In sum, criminologists are concerned with the concept of deviance and its relationship to criminality. The shifting definition of deviant behaviour is closely associated with our concepts of crime. The relationship among criminology, criminal justice, and deviance is illustrated in Figure 1.2. These are also summarized in Concept Summary 1.1.

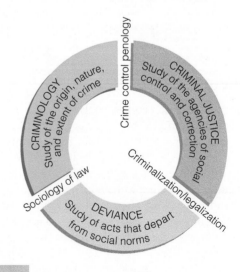

FIGURE 1.2

The Relationship among Criminology, Criminal Justice, and Deviance

Famous Canadian Court Cases
R. v. Sharpe (2001)

Parliament took less than six weeks to enact child pornography legislation in 1993, yet section 163.1 of the *Criminal Code of Canada* has been a source of relentless debate ever since. Though not the first case of its kind, the Sharpe case is noteworthy because it challenged the federal law against producing, dealing, and possessing child pornography.

John Robin Sharpe was arrested at the Canada–U.S. border in 1995 after customs officers found in his possession nude photos of underage boys and sexually explicit written material on several computer disks. Police later executed a search warrant at his Vancouver home. Among the materials seized were more than 500 photos of 91 different boys engaged in sexual activity and a collection of personal stories entitled *Kiddie Kink Classics*. Sharpe was charged with two counts each of possessing and distributing

child pornography, but he was acquitted by the British Columbia Supreme Court in 1999.

After the province's Court of Appeal upheld the ruling, Sharpe's case was tried before the Supreme Court of Canada, which had to decide whether child pornography laws violated the freedom of expression guarantee in section 2 of the *Charter of Rights and Freedoms*. In 2001, the Court attempted to strike a balance between the need to protect children from sexual exploitation and the need to protect fundamental rights and freedoms. Although section 163.1 of the *Criminal Code* was declared constitutional, exceptions were outlined in certain cases: for materials that have artistic, educational, or scientific merit and for purely personal materials that do not involve children in their production. Sharpe's case was retried, and he was found not guilty in relation to distribution but

convicted on possession, and received a four-month conditional sentence.

Sharpe was arrested again in 2003 for indecent assault against a man who came forward after police had issued a public appeal to those pictured in the seized photographs. In July 2004, at the age of 71, Sharpe was handed a prison sentence of two years less a day. Controversy regarding the Supreme Court ruling prompted the Liberal government to introduce legislation in December 2002 that would tighten the definition of *artistic merit* by introducing a standard of "contribution to the public good." However, the bill died on the ledger when the 2004 election was called.

SOURCES: Various media sources, 2002–2004; Robert Sharpe, Katherine Swinton, and Kent Roach, *The Charter of Rights and Freedoms*, 2nd ed. (Toronto: Irwin Law Inc., 2002).

CONCEPT SUMMARY 1.1

Criminology, Criminal Justice, and Deviance

Criminology explains the etiology (origin), extent, and nature of crime in society. Criminologists are concerned with identifying the nature, extent, and cause of crime.

Criminal justice refers to the study of agencies of social control that handle criminal offenders, specifically the police departments, courts, and correctional facilities. Scholars seek more effective methods of crime control and offender rehabilitation.

Overlapping areas of concern: Criminal justice experts cannot begin to design effective programs of crime prevention or rehabilitation without understanding the nature and cause of crime. They require accurate criminal statistics and data to test the effectiveness of crime control and prevention programs.

Deviance refers to the study of behaviour that departs from social norms. Included within the broad spectrum of deviant acts are behaviours ranging from violent crimes to joining a nudist colony. Not all crimes are deviant or unusual acts, and not all deviant acts are illegal.

Overlapping areas of concern: Under what circumstances do deviant behaviours become crimes? For example, when does sexual material cross the line from merely suggestive to obscene and therefore illegal? Or, if an illegal act becomes a norm, should society re-evaluate its criminal status? For example, debate continues regarding the legalization and/or decriminalization of abortion, recreational drug use, possession of handguns, and assisted suicide.

A BRIEF HISTORY OF CRIMINOLOGY

The scientific study of crime and criminality is a relatively recent development. Although written criminal codes have existed for thousands of years, they were restricted to defining crime and setting punishments. What motivated people to violate the law remained a matter of conjecture.

During the Middle Ages, people who violated social norms or religious practices were believed to be witches or possessed by demons. The prescribed method for dealing with the possessed was to burn them at the stake, a practice that survived into the 17th century. For example, between 1575 and 1590, the French Inquisition ordered 900 sorcerers and witches burned to death, and the Bishop of the German city of Trier ordered the deaths of 6,500 people. An estimated 100,000 people were prosecuted throughout Europe for witchcraft during the 16th and 17th centuries. Even those who questioned demonic possession advocated extremely harsh penalties as a means of punishing criminals and setting an example for others.

During the Middle Ages, the possessed were often burned at the stake, a practice that survived into the 17th century. This painting, The Trial of George Jacobs, August 5, 1692, by J.H. Matteson (1855), depicts the ordeal of the Salem patriarch, Jacobs. During the witch craze, he had ridiculed the trials, only to find himself being accused, tried, and executed.

CONNECTIONS

The English common law is the immediate antecedent of the Canadian legal system, except in Quebec, which inherited the Napoleonic Code from France. However, the influence of some of the earliest written codes, such as those of Hebrews and Babylonians, can still be detected. Chapter 2 traces the history of the law in some detail.

Classical Criminology

By the mid-18th century, social philosophers had begun to call for lawmakers to rethink the prevailing concepts of law and justice. They argued for a more rational approach to punishment, stressing that the relationship between crimes and their punishment should be balanced and fair. This view was based on the philosophy called **utilitarianism**, which emphasized that behaviour is purposeful and not motivated by supernatural forces. Rather than cruel public executions designed to frighten people into obedience or to punish those the law failed to deter, reformers called for a more moderate and just approach to penal sanctions. The most famous of these reformers was Cesare Beccaria (1738–1794), an Italian aristocrat whose writings described both a motive for committing crime and methods for its control.

Beccaria believed that people want to achieve pleasure and avoid pain. If crime provides pleasure to the criminal, pain must be used to prevent crime. Beccaria said that "in order for punishment not to be, in every instance, an act of violence of one or many against a private citizen, it must be essentially public, prompt, necessary, the least possible in the given circumstances, proportionate to the crimes, and dictated by the laws."[8]

utilitarianism A view that punishment should be balanced and fair, and that crime is a rational choice.

The ideas are referred to as **classical criminology**, which was characterized by several basic elements:

1. People will freely choose criminal or lawful solutions to meet needs or settle problems.
2. Criminal choices may be more attractive because they use less work for greater payoff.
3. People's choice of criminal solutions may be controlled by their fear of punishment.
4. If punishments are severe, certain, and swift, they will control criminal behaviour.

The classical perspective influenced judicial philosophy during much of the late 18th and the 19th centuries. Prisons began to be used as a form of punishment, and sentences were geared proportionately to the seriousness of the crime. Capital punishment was still widely used but began to be employed for only the most serious crimes. The byword was "Let the punishment fit the crime."

Then during the 19th century, a new vision of the world challenged the validity of classical theory and presented an innovative way of looking at the causes of crime.

19th-Century Positivism

Although the classical position held sway as a guide to crime, law, and justice for almost 100 years, during the late 19th century a new movement began that would challenge its dominance. **Positivism** developed as the scientific method began to take hold in Europe. This movement was inspired by new discoveries in biology, astronomy, and chemistry. If the scientific method could be applied to the study of nature, why not use it to study human behaviour? Auguste Comte (1798–1857) believed societies pass through stages that can be grouped on the basis of how people understand the world. People in primitive societies consider inanimate objects as having life (for example, the Sun is a god); in later social stages, people embrace a rational, scientific view of the world.

Positivism has two main elements. The first is the belief that human behaviour is a function of external forces that are beyond individual control. Some of these forces are social, such as the effect of wealth and class, while others are political and historical, such as war and famine. Other forces are more personal and psychological, such as an individual's brain structure and his or her biological makeup or mental ability. All of these forces operate to influence human behaviour.

The second aspect of positivism is its use of the scientific method to solve problems. Positivists would agree that an abstract concept, such as *intelligence*, exists because it can be measured by an IQ test. However, they would challenge such a concept as *ghosts* because it cannot be verified by the scientific method. The work of Charles Darwin (1809–1882) encouraged the view that all human activity could be verified by scientific principles.

Positivist Criminology

By the mid-19th century, scientific methods were being applied to understanding criminality. The earliest of these scientific studies were biological. For example, physiognomists, such as J.K. Lavater (1741–1801), studied the facial features of criminals to determine whether the shape of ears, noses, and eyes and the distance between them were associated with antisocial behaviour. Phrenologists, such as Franz Joseph Gall (1758–1828) and Johann Kaspar Spurzheim (1776–1832), studied the shape of the skull and bumps on the head to determine whether these physical attributes were linked to criminal behaviour. Phrenologists believed that external cranial characteristics dictate which areas of the brain control physical activity. Though their primitive techniques and quasi-scientific methods have been discredited, these efforts were an early attempt to apply a scientific approach to the study of crime (see Figure 1.3).

FIGURE 1.3

Early Positivists Believed the Shape of the Skull Was a Key Determinant of Behaviour

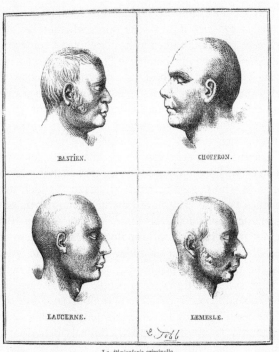

These drawings from the 19th century illustrate what were considered to be typical criminally shaped heads.

classical criminology The perspective that people freely choose crime, and that it can be reduced through the threat of criminal sanctions.

positivism A branch of social science that sees behaviour as a product of social, biological, psychological, and economic forces.

By the early 19th century, abnormality in the human mind was being linked to criminal behaviour patterns. Philippe Pinel (1745–1826), one of the founders of French psychiatry, claimed that some people behave abnormally even without being mentally ill. He coined the phrase *manie sans délire* (mania without delusion) to denote what eventually was referred to as a psychopathic personality. In 1812, an American, Benjamin Rush (1745–1813), described patients with an "innate preternatural moral depravity."[9] Another early criminological pioneer, English physician Henry Maudsley (1835–1918), believed that insanity and criminal behaviour were strongly linked: "Crime is a sort of outlet in which their unsound tendencies are discharged; they would go mad if they were not criminals, and they do not go mad because they are criminals."[10] These early research efforts shifted attention to brain functioning and personality as the keys to criminal behaviour.

Cesare Lombroso and the Criminal Man

In Italy, Cesare Lombroso studied the cadavers of executed criminals to scientifically determine whether law violators were physically different from people of conventional values and behaviour. Lombroso (1835–1909) was a physician who served much of his career in the Italian army. That experience gave him ample opportunity to study the physical characteristics of soldiers executed for criminal offences. Later, he studied inmates at institutes for the criminally insane.

Lombrosian theory can be outlined in a few simple statements. First, Lombroso believed that offenders are born criminals who engage in repeated assault- or theft-related activities because they have inherited criminal traits that impel them into a life of crime. This view helped spur interest in a **criminal anthropology**.[11] Second, Lombroso held that born criminals suffer from **atavistic anomalies** (or **traits**)—physically: that is, they are throwbacks to more primitive times when people were savages. Thus, criminals supposedly have the enormous jaws and strong canine teeth common to carnivores who devour raw flesh. In addition, Lombroso compared criminals' behaviour with that of people with mental illnesses and those who had certain forms of epilepsy. He concluded that criminogenic traits could be acquired through indirect heredity: from a "degenerate family with frequent cases of insanity, deafness, syphilis, epilepsy, and alcoholism among its members." For Lombroso, this indirect heredity is the primary cause of crime. Direct heredity—being related to a family of criminals—is the second primary cause of crime.

Lombroso's version of criminal anthropology was very popular in North America and Europe, and it was printed in articles and textbooks that adopted his ideas. He attracted a circle of followers who expanded on his vision of biological

determinism. By the turn of the 20th century, authors were already discussing the science of penology and the science of criminology.

CONNECTIONS

The theories of criminology that have their roots in Lombroso's biological determinism will be discussed in Chapter 6. Some criminologists believe that crime has both a biological and environmental basis and use the term *biosocial theory* to reflect the link among physical and mental traits, the social environment, and behaviour.

The Development of Sociological Criminology

At the same time that biological views were dominating criminology, another group of positivists were developing the field of sociology to scientifically study the major social changes taking place in 19th-century society.

Sociology was an ideal perspective from which to study society. After thousands of years of stability, the world was undergoing a population explosion: The population, estimated at 600 million in 1700, had risen to 900 million by 1800. People were flocking to cities in ever-increasing numbers. For example, Manchester, England, had 12,000 inhabitants in 1760 and 400,000 in 1850. The development of such machinery as power looms had doomed cottage industries and given rise to a factory system in which large numbers of people toiled for extremely low wages. The spread of agricultural machines increased the food supply while reducing the need for a large rural workforce; the excess labourers further swelled the cities' populations.

The foundations of sociological criminology can be traced to the works of L.A.J. (Adolphe) Quetelet (1796–1874) and Emile Durkheim (1858–1917).

CONNECTIONS

In Chapter 2, the historical development of laws and legal codes is discussed. In addition, the evolution of certain crimes is discussed, such as *breaking frames*, which was caused by developments such as industrial capitalism.

criminal anthropology Early efforts to discover a biological basis to crime through physical measurements, usually associated with Cesare Lombroso.

atavistic anomalies (or traits) The physical characteristics of "born criminals" that indicate they are throwbacks to primitive people.

L.A.J. Quetelet. Quetelet was a Belgian mathematician who began (along with André-Michel Guerry, from France) what is known as the cartographic school of criminology.[12] Quetelet made use of social statistics developed in France in the early 19th century (called the Comptes généraux de l'administration de la justice) and was one of the first social scientists to use objective mathematical techniques to investigate the influence of social factors, such as season, climate, sex, and age, on the propensity to commit crime. Quetelet's most important finding was that social forces were significantly correlated with crime rates, and that the same law-like mechanical regularity observed in the heavens and in nature also existed in the world of social facts.[13] Quetelet was a pioneer of sociological criminology. He identified many of the relationships between crime and social phenomena that still serve as a basis for criminology today.

Emile Durkheim. Emile Durkheim (1858–1917) was one of the founders of sociology and a significant contributor to criminology.[14] His definition of crime as "normal" has been more influential on modern criminology than has almost any other idea.

According to Durkheim, crime is normal because it has existed in every age, in both poverty and prosperity. It is virtually impossible to imagine a society in which criminal behaviour is totally absent, and people acted exactly alike. The inevitability of crime is linked to the human differences within society. Because people are so different from one another and use such a variety of methods and forms of behaviour to meet their needs, some will resort to criminality. Even if crimes were eliminated, human weaknesses and petty vices would then be elevated to the status of crimes. As long as human differences exist, crime is inevitable, serving as a symbolic reminder of moral boundaries.

Durkheim also argued that crime could be useful, and even healthy, for a society. The existence of crime implies that a way is open for social change and that the social structure is not rigid or inflexible. Put another way, if crime did not exist, it would mean that everyone would behave the same way and would agree totally on what is right and wrong. Such universal conformity would stifle creativity and independent thinking. Durkheim offered the example of the Greek philosopher Socrates, who, simply because he questioned the social order, was considered a criminal and sentenced to death for corrupting the morals of youth. When given the chance to flee to save his life, Socrates refused, saying that doing so would negate his ideal of standing up for what he believed. In addition, Durkheim argued that crime is beneficial because it calls attention to social ills. A rising crime rate can signal the need for social change and promote a variety of programs designed to relieve the human suffering that may have caused crime in the first place.

In *The Division of Labor in Society*, Durkheim described the consequences of the shift from a small, rural society, which he labelled *mechanical*, to the more modern *organic* society, characterized by a large urban population, division of labour,

and personal isolation. From this shift flowed **anomie**, or norm and role confusion, a powerful sociological concept that helps describe the chaos and disarray accompanying the loss of traditional values in modern society. Durkheim's research on suicide indicated that anomic societies maintain high suicide rates; by implication, anomie might cause other forms of deviance to develop.

The Chicago School and the McGill School

The primacy of sociological positivism was secured by research begun in the early 20th century by Robert Ezra Park (1864–1944), Ernest W. Burgess (1886–1966), Louis Wirth (1897–1952), Frederic Thrasher (1892–1962), and their colleagues in the sociology department at the University of Chicago. Known as the **Chicago School**, these sociologists pioneered research on the social ecology of the city and inspired a generation of scholars to conclude that social forces operating in urban areas create criminal interactions, thereby making some neighbourhoods almost natural areas for crime.[15] These urban neighbourhoods maintain such a high level of poverty that critical social institutions, such as the school and the family, break down. The resulting social disorganization reduces the ability of social institutions to control behaviour, and the outcome is a high crime rate.

The Chicago School sociologists and their contemporaries focused on the functions of social institutions and how their breakdown influences behaviour. They pioneered the ecological study of crime, which involves looking at crime in the context of where a person lives. Important works in the Chicago School tradition were *The Gang* (1927) by Frederic Thrasher, *The Ghetto* (1928) by Louis Wirth, *Gold Coast and Slum* (1929) by Harvey Zorbaugh, and *The Hobo* (1923) by Nels Anderson, a professor in the sociology department at the University of New Brunswick.

Less well known is the work of Carl Dawson and his colleagues at McGill University. Dawson, a native of Prince Edward Island and a graduate of Acadia University, studied at the University of Chicago before he went to Montreal to head McGill's social work and sociology departments. He and his students studied the processes of industrial development, transportation, poverty, ethnicity and immigration, housing, juvenile delinquency, welfare, and physiographic barriers to

anomie Rapidly shifting moral values produce normlessness, where the individual has little guide to what is socially acceptable, usually associated with Robert Merton.

Chicago School Early 20th century sociological research on the social ecology of the city and the study of urban crime.

mobility. This work constituted a significant contribution to early sociology and criminology in Canada.[16]

CONNECTIONS

The ecological approach of the Chicago School was applied to the study of crime in cities such as Chicago, New York, and Montreal. In particular, the Chicago School became known for the concentric zone model of deviance, in which crime is found to be higher in the more socially disorganized areas of a city. For a discussion of the application of this approach to Montreal, see Chapter 7.

During the 1930s, social psychologists argued that the individual's relationship to education, family life, and peer relations is the key to understanding human behaviour. In any social milieu, children who grow up in a home wracked by conflict, attend an inadequate school, and associate with deviant peers become exposed to pro-crime forces. One position was that people learn criminal attitudes from older, more experienced law violators; another view was that crime occurs when families fail to control adolescent misbehaviour. Each of these views linked criminality to the failure of socialization.

By the mid-20th century, most criminologists had embraced either the ecological or the socialization view of crime. However, these were not the only views of how social institutions influence human behaviour. In Europe, the writings of another social thinker, Karl Marx (1818–1883), had pushed the understanding of social interaction in another direction and sowed the seeds for a new approach in criminology.[17]

Conflict Criminology

Oppressive labour conditions prevalent during the rise of industrial capitalism convinced Marx that the character of society is determined by the way people develop and produce material goods. The most important relationship is between the owners of the means of production—the capitalist **bourgeoisie**—and the people who do the actual labour—the **proletariat**. The economic system determines all facets of human life as people's lives revolve around the means of production. Marx felt the exploitation of the working class would lead to class conflict and the end of the capitalist system.

Although Marx did not develop a theory of crime and justice, his writings were applied to legal studies by other social thinkers, including Ralf Dahrendorf, George Vold, and Willem Bonger.[18] Though these writings laid the foundation for a Marxist criminology, decades passed before Marxist theory had an important impact on the discipline. The Vietnam War, the development of an anti-establishment counterculture movement in the 1960s, the civil rights movement, and the women's movement were all important

events challenging the model of social consensus underlying the functionalism of the Chicago School. Young sociologists who became interested in applying Marxist principles to the study of crime began to analyze the social conditions that were felt to promote class conflict and crime. What emerged was the conflict-oriented radical criminology of the 1970s that indicted the economic system for producing the conditions that support a high crime rate. The radical tradition has played a significant role in criminology ever since.

Criminology Today

The various schools of criminology developed over 200 years. Although they have undergone great change and innovation, each continues to have an impact on the field. For example, classical theory has evolved into rational choice and deterrence theories, discussed in Chapter 5. Choice theorists argue that criminals are rational and use available information to decide whether crime is worthwhile, while deterrence theory says this choice is structured by the fear of punishment.

Criminal anthropology has also evolved considerably, as seen in Chapter 6. Although criminologists no longer believe a single trait or inherited characteristic can explain crime, some believe biological and mental traits interact with environmental factors to influence all human behaviour, including criminality. Biological and psychological theorists study the association between criminal behaviour and such traits as diet, hormonal makeup, personality, and intelligence.

Sociological theories, tracing back to Quetelet and Durkheim, maintain that individuals' lifestyles and living conditions directly control their criminal behaviour. Those at the bottom of the social structure cannot achieve success and, as a result, experience failure and frustration. This theory today is called the structural perspective, which is described in detail in Chapter 7.

Some sociologists who have added a social psychological dimension to their views of crime causation find that individuals' learning experiences and socialization directly control their behaviour. In some cases, children learn to commit crime by interacting with and modelling their behaviour after others they admire, while other criminal offenders are people whose life experiences have shattered their social bonds to society. This view, the social process perspective, is described in detail in Chapter 8.

The writings of Marx and his followers continue to be influential. Today, conflict criminologists still see social and political conflict as the root cause of crime. In their view, the inherently unfair economic structure of advanced capitalist

bourgeoisie   In Marxist theory, the owners of the means of production; the capitalist ruling class.

proletariat   In Marxist theory, the working class, who provide the labour in capitalism.

CONCEPT SUMMARY 1.2

The Major Perspectives of Criminology

CONCEPT SUMMARY 1.3

The Criminological Enterprise

CONCEPT SUMMARY 1.2

The Major Perspectives of Criminology

The focus is on *individual* factors (biological, psychological, and choice theories), *social* factors (structural and process theories), *political* and *economic* factors (conflict), and *multiple* (integrated) factors.

CLASSICAL/ CHOICE PERSPECTIVE	**Situational forces:** Crime is a function of free will and personal choice. Punishment is a deterrent to crime.
BIOLOGICAL/ PSYCHOLOGICAL PERSPECTIVE	**Internal forces:** Crime is a function of chemical, neurological, genetic, personality, intelligence, or mental traits.
STRUCTURAL PERSPECTIVE	**Ecological forces:** Crime rates are a function of neighbourhood conditions, cultural forces, and norm conflict.
PROCESS PERSPECTIVE	**Socialization forces:** Crime is a function of upbringing, learning, and control. Peers, parents, and teachers influence behaviour.
CONFLICT PERSPECTIVE	**Economic and political forces:** Crime is a function of competition for limited resources and power. Class conflict produces crime.
INTEGRATED PERSPECTIVE	**Multiple forces:** Biological, social-psychological, economic, and political forces may combine to produce crime.

CONCEPT SUMMARY 1.3

The Criminological Enterprise

These subareas constitute the field or discipline of criminology.

SUBAREA	Primary Focus
CRIMINAL STATISTICS	Gathering valid crime data
	Devising new research methods
	Measuring crime patterns and trends
SOCIOLOGY OF LAW	Determining the origin of law
	Measuring the forces that can change laws and society
THEORY CONSTRUCTION	Predicting individual behaviour
	Understanding the cause of crime rates and trends
CRIMINAL BEHAVIOUR SYSTEMS	Determining the nature and cause of specific crime patterns
	Studying violence; theft; and organized, white-collar, and public-order crimes
PENOLOGY	Studying the correction and control of criminal behaviour
VICTIMOLOGY	Studying the nature and cause of victimization

countries is the engine that drives the high crime rate. This effect occurs in two ways: First, the lack of resources causes the poor to commit crimes, such as prostitution; and second, the powerful are able to define the actions of the poor as crime. This view is discussed in more detail in Chapter 9.

Criminology, then, has had a rich history that still exerts an important influence on the thinking of its current practitioners. These major perspectives are summarized in Concept Summary 1.2.

WHAT CRIMINOLOGISTS DO: THE CRIMINOLOGICAL ENTERPRISE

Regardless of their background or training, criminologists are primarily interested in studying crime and criminal behaviour. As Wolfgang and Ferracuti put it:

> A criminologist is one whose professional training, occupational role, and pecuniary reward are primarily concentrated on a scientific approach to, and study and analysis of, the phenomenon of crime and criminal behaviour.[19]

Within the broader arena of criminology are several subareas that, taken together, make up the **criminological enterprise**. Criminologists may specialize in a subarea in the same way that psychologists might specialize in areas such as child development, perception, personality, psychopathology, or sexuality. Some of the more important criminological subareas are described in this section and are summarized in Concept Summary 1.3.

Criminal Statistics

The subarea of criminal statistics involves measuring the amount and trends of criminal activity. How much crime occurs annually? Who commits it? When and where does it occur? Which crimes are the most serious? Criminologists interested in criminal statistics try to create valid and reliable measurements of criminal behaviour. For example, they create techniques to use the records of police and court agencies. They develop paper-and-pencil survey instruments, and then use them with large samples of citizens to determine the percentage of people who actually commit crimes and the number of law violators who escape detection by the justice system. They also develop techniques to identify the victims

criminological enterprise The totality of criminology, which includes many fields, or subareas, of study.

of crime and establish more accurate indicators of the true number of criminal acts—how many people are victims of crime and what percentage report crime to police. The study of criminal statistics is a crucial aspect of the criminological enterprise because conducting research and creating criminological theories is dependent on reliable information.

CONNECTIONS

For an example of how statistics are used to measure patterns, see the Comparative Criminology box on international crime trends, later in this chapter.

Sociology of Law

Another subarea of criminology, the sociology of law, is concerned with the role that social forces play in shaping criminal law and, conversely, the role of criminal law in shaping society. Criminologists study the history of the law in an effort to understand how criminal acts, such as theft, rape, and murder, evolved into their present form. Criminologists might also join in the debate when a new law is proposed to control behaviour. For example, when the debate raged over the legality of Napster, an online service that let its 64 million members worldwide share music in violation of copyright law, criminologists would ask what role should the law take in curbing the public's access to media and culture? Should society curb actions that some people consider illegal, but by which no one is actually harmed? How is harm defined and by whom? When a company is denied profits, is it harmed? Is the behaviour that online shareware allowed any different from videotaping a documentary from the television or sharing a CD owned by a friend?

When most people are surveyed, they think that music file swapping should be legal. Recently, a Canadian court ruled that the music industry cannot force Internet service providers to identify online music sharers, and that using an online download service for personal use does not amount to copyright infringement.

Criminologists also participate in updating the content of criminal law. The law must be flexible and respond to changing times and conditions. Theft from automated bank machines, identity theft, and illegally tapping into satellite TV signals are acts that obviously did not exist when the criminal law on theft was originally formed.

The law must be flexible in responding to new versions of traditional acts. For example, Sue Rodriguez, who suffered from ALS (amyotrophic lateral sclerosis, or Lou Gehrig's disease), committed suicide in 1994, after losing her bid before the Supreme Court for legally assisted suicide. In looking at how the law should respond to these controversial issues, a commission called Dying with Dignity began hearings in 2010.

Although some believe that euthanasia is socially harmful, others are not quite so certain. Many Canadians felt great sympathy for Sue Rodriguez's plight, and before international media coverage of the issue, no law existed that banned second-party help in suicides. In response to the actions of Jack Kevorkian, the state of Michigan passed legislation making it a felony to help anyone commit suicide. Is assisted suicide the product of care and concern for human suffering, or is it a callous criminal act? Should a law be passed that a majority of the general public disapproves of—a condition that makes the law virtually unenforceable? Conversely, should criminal law be restricted to only those acts that are unpopular with the general public?

Theory Construction

Another area of criminological work is theory construction. For example, criminologists have long been intrigued by the reasons why people engage in criminal acts. Why, when they know their actions can bring harsh punishment and social disapproval, do they steal, rape, and murder? Why do people behave the way they do? Does crime have a social or an individual basis? Is it a psychological, a biological, a social, a political, or an economic phenomenon? Some criminologists have a psychological orientation and view crime as a function of personality, development, social learning, or cognition. Others investigate the biology of antisocial behaviour and study the biochemical, genetic, and neurological linkages to crime. Sociologists look at the social forces producing criminal behaviour, including neighbourhood conditions, poverty, socialization, and group interaction.

Understanding the true cause of crime remains a difficult problem. Criminologists are still unsure why, given similar conditions, one person elects criminal solutions to his or her problems while another conforms to accepted social rules of behaviour. Further, understanding crime rates and trends has proved difficult: Why do rates rise and fall? Why are crime rates higher in some areas or regions than in others? Why do some groups seem more crime-prone than others? Is it possible that crime is relative to societal standards and thus a social construction created by the media, politicians, and social alarmists?

Criminal Behaviour Systems

Similar to theory construction, this subarea of criminology involves research on specific criminal types and patterns, such as violent crime, theft crime, public-order crime, and organized crime. For example, Marvin Wolfgang's famous study *Patterns in Criminal Homicide* is considered a landmark analysis of the nature of homicide and the relationship between victim and offender.[20] Another study, Edwin Sutherland's analysis of business-related offences, helped coin a new phrase—**white-collar crime**—to describe economic crime activities.[21]

white-collar crime Crimes committed by those with power, such as embezzlement, false advertising, or stock market manipulation.

The study of criminal behaviour also involves research on the links between different types of crime and criminals, known as crime typology. Some typologies focus on the criminal, such as professional criminals, psychotic criminals, occasional criminals, and so on. Other typologies focus on the crimes, clustering them into such categories as property crimes, sex crimes, and so on.

Penology

The study of penology involves the correction and control of criminal offenders. Penologists formulate new strategies for crime control, and then help implement these policies. Some criminologists view penology as involving rehabilitation and treatment, providing behaviour alternatives for those convicted of law violations. This view portrays the criminal as someone whom society has failed; someone under social, psychological, or economic stress; and someone who can be helped if society is willing to pay the price. Others argue that crime can be prevented only through a strict policy of social control. They advocate such strict measures as capital punishment, mandatory prison sentences, and selective incapacitation for repeat offenders.

CONNECTIONS

In recent years, criminologists have devoted ever-increasing attention to the victim's role in the criminal process, looking at how individuals' lifestyles and behaviour may actually increase the risk that they will become crime victims. Living in a high-crime neighbourhood increases risk, as does associating with dangerous peers and companions. For a discussion of victimization risk, see Chapter 4.

Victimology

The last subarea of criminology considered here is victimology. This area of research is relatively recent. In the mid-20th century, two classic texts on the topic, one by Hans von Hentig and another by Stephen Schafer, first identified the critical role of the victim in the criminal process. These authors suggest that victim behaviour is often a key determinant of crime, that a victim's actions may precipitate or provide an opportunity for crime, and that the study of crime is not complete unless the victim's role is considered.[22]

The areas of particular interest in victimology include using victim surveys to measure the nature and extent of criminal behaviour, calculating the actual costs of crime to victims, creating probabilities of victimization risk, studying victim culpability or precipitation of crime, and designing services for the victims of crime. Victimology has taken on greater importance as more criminologists focus their attention on the victim's role in the criminal event.

A protestor participates at a 2013 Idle No More rally promoting justice and equality for First Nations people.

HOW DO CRIMINOLOGISTS VIEW CRIME?

As you will see in this text, criminology is multidisciplinary, drawing on biology, psychology, sociology, and other fields. In addition, professional criminologists align themselves with underlying philosophical perspectives: the consensus, conflict, and interactionist perspectives. Each perspective maintains its own view of what constitutes criminal behaviour and what causes people to engage in criminality. When biologists, psychologists, sociologists, historians, and economists bring these different perspectives to research, it affects how they define the nature and cause of crime itself. Criminologists' theoretical perspectives and conceptualizations of crime also affect their research orientations. This section discusses the three most common concepts of crime used by criminologists.

The Consensus View of Crime

This view holds that crimes are repugnant to all elements of society. Criminal law, with its definition of crimes and their punishments, is thought to reflect the values, beliefs, and opinions of society. The term *consensus* is used because it implies that general agreement exists among a majority of people on what behaviours should be outlawed by the criminal law and viewed as crimes. An example of a consensus crime is homicide.

Several attempts have been made to create a concise, yet thorough and encompassing, consensus definition of crime. Criminologists Edwin Sutherland and Donald Cressey have linked crime with criminal law:

> Criminal behavior is behavior in violation of the criminal law. ... [It] is not a crime unless it is prohibited by the criminal law [which] is defined conventionally as a body of specific rules regarding human conduct

In 1981, there were 88 residential burglaries per 1,000 households in the United States, compared with 41 per 1,000 households in England (including Wales). Ten years later, the U.S. rate had decreased to 54 per 1,000 households, but the English rate had increased to 68 per 1,000 households. By 2006, the divide had increased even further, with the United States at about 60 and England at about 100. Canada, on the other hand, was just slightly above the average, and below the United States.

The English experience is not unique. Crime rates appear to be increasing around the world even as they decline in Canada to rates not seen since the 1960s and 1970s. Asian countries now report an upswing in serious criminal activities. Cambodian officials are concerned with drug production/trafficking and human trafficking. Drugs produced in neighbouring countries are being trafficked into Cambodia for local consumption, and drug traffickers routinely use Cambodia as a transit country for distributing narcotics around the world. The trafficking of Cambodian women into Thailand for sexual activities and the presence of a large number of Vietnamese women in Cambodia who are engaged in prostitution are also major concerns. Even Japan, a nation renowned for its low crime rate, has experienced an upsurge in crime linked to its economy. Japan's economic bubble burst in 1990 and more than 15 years of economic stagnation has resulted in climbing numbers of reported crime.

Similarly, China, another relative safe nation, has experienced an upswing in violent crime. Chinese police handled almost 5 million criminal cases in 2005, and though this number was down slightly from the previous year, the decline comes after years of steady increases. And though crime declined in general, theft and robbery remain a serious problem, especially in public places such as railway stations, long-distance bus stations, and passenger docks. The Chinese Ministry of Public Security reports these trends:

- Criminals are targeting richer people and/or entities.
- Car theft is on the rise.
- Criminal cases happen more often in public spaces—meaning that the streets are becoming less safe than they used to be.
- The average age of criminals is lowering—more kids are involved in illegal activities.
- New types of criminal activities are emerging: blackmailing, cons, and prostitution via the Web.

Though these trends are alarming, making international comparisons is difficult because the legal definitions of crime vary from country to country. There are also differences in the way crime is measured. For example, in Canada, crime is measured by counting criminal acts reported to the police or by using victim surveys, whereas in many European countries, crime is measured by the number of cases solved by the police. Despite these problems, valid comparisons can still be made about crime across different countries using a number of reliable data sources. The United Nations Survey of Crime Trends and Operations of Criminal Justice Systems (UNCJS) collects cross-national data. The International Crime Victims Survey (ICVS) is conducted in 60 countries and managed by the Ministry of Justice of the Netherlands, the Home Office of the United Kingdom, and the United Nations Interregional Crime and Justice Research Institute. INTERPOL, the international police agency, collects data from police agencies in 179 countries. The World Health Organization (WHO) has conducted surveys on global violence. The European Sourcebook of Crime and Criminal Justice Statistics provides data from police agencies in 36 European nations.

International Crime Rates

What do these various sources tell us about international crime rates?

Homicide

Many nations, especially those experiencing social or economic upheaval, have murder rates much higher than the United States. Colombia has about 63 homicides per 100,000 people and South Africa has 51, compared with fewer than 6 in the United States. Even Mexico's rate is almost four times that of the United States. During the 1990s, there were more homicides in Brazil than in the United States, Canada, Italy, Japan, Australia, Portugal, Britain, Austria, and Germany taken together. The OECD reported in 2012 that Canada's rate was 1.8 homicides per 100,000 people.

Why are murder rates so high in nations such as Brazil? Law enforcement officials link the upsurge in violence to drug trafficking, gang feuds, vigilantism, and disputes over trivial matters in which young, unmarried, uneducated males are involved. Others find that local custom and practice underpin the homicide rate. India has experienced a shocking form of violence against women known as bride burning. A woman may be burned to death if her family fails to provide the expected dowry to the groom's family or if she is suspected of premarital infidelity. Many Indian women commit suicide to escape the brutality of their situation.

Rape

Violence against women is related to economic hardship and the social status of women. Rates are high in poor nations in which women are oppressed. Where women are more emancipated, the rates of violence against women are lower.

For many women, sexual violence starts in childhood and adolescence, and may occur in the home, school, and community. Studies conducted in a wide variety of nations ranging from the Cameroon to New Zealand found high rates of reported forced sexual initiation. In some nations, as many as 46 percent of adolescent women and 20 percent of adolescent men report sexual coercion at the hands of family members, teachers, boyfriends, or strangers.

Sexual violence has significant health consequences, including suicide, stress, mental illnesses, unwanted pregnancy, sexually transmitted diseases, HIV/AIDS, self-inflicted injuries, and, in the case of child sexual abuse, adoption of high-risk behaviours such as multiple sexual partners and drug use.

Some international comparisons of sexual violence reported in 2012 by the OECD show Australia's rate to be 92 per 100,000, the United States' to be 29, Mexico's to be 13, and Canada's just over 1. One difficulty in making any such comparisons is that sexual assault has a very low report rate.

Robbery

Countries with more reported robberies than Canada include the United States, England and Wales, Portugal, Spain, and Belgium. Countries with fewer reported robberies include Germany, as well as Middle Eastern and Asian nations. The OECD ranks Japan at the very bottom.

Vehicle Theft

Rates of vehicle theft tend to be higher, it seems, in wealthier countries, such as Australia, England and Wales, Denmark, Norway, Canada, France, Italy, and the United States.

Child Abuse

A World Health Organization report found that child physical and sexual abuse takes a significant toll around the world. In a single year, about 57,000 children under 15 years are murdered. The homicide rates for children aged 0 to 4 years are over twice as high as rates among children aged 5 to 14 years. Many more children are subjected to nonfatal abuse and neglect; 8 percent of male and 25 percent of female children up to age 18 experience sexual abuse of some kind.

How to Account for Different and Changing Rates?

Why are crime rates increasing around the world in some countries while going down in others? Why do some countries have high rates while others have lower rates? Crime control policies can result in increases in conviction and punishment, and help lower crime rates. Among western countries, the United States is notorious for increasing conviction rates, and instituting mandatory minimum sentences. However, get-tough-on-crime policies have been criticized in the United States for ignoring social factors such as unemployment, poverty, and lack of education. Canada is moving in the same direction; however, mandatory minimum sentences run the risk of being unconstitutional, and certainly undermine judicial discretion.

Crime rates may be spiralling upward abroad because nations are undergoing rapid changes in their social and economic makeup. In Eastern Europe, the fall of communism has brought about a transformation of the family, religion, education, and economy. These changes increase social pressures and result in crime rate increases. Some Asian societies, such as China, are undergoing rapid industrialization, urbanization, and social change. The shift from agricultural to industrial and service economies has produced political turmoil and a surge in their crime rates. For example, the island of Hong Kong, long a British possession but now part of the People's Republic of China, is experiencing an upsurge in club drugs. Tied to the local dance scene, ecstasy and ketamine use has skyrocketed, in sync with the traditional drug of choice, heroin.

Examining and comparing crime rates in different places has to take many factors into account, some economic, others political. But it does show us that crimes we experience at home are not unique to Canada.

Critical Thinking

While risk factors at all levels of social and personal life contribute to violence, people in all nations who experience change in societal-level factors—such as economic inequalities, rapid social change, and the availability of firearms, alcohol, and drugs—seem the most likely to get involved in violence. Can anything be done to help alleviate these social problems?

SOURCES: James Finckenauer and Ko-lin Chin, *Asian Transnational Organized Crime and Its Impact on the United States* (Washington, DC: National Institute of Justice, 2007); Dag Leonardsen, "Crime in Japan: Paradise Lost?" *Journal of Scandinavian Studies in Criminology and Crime Prevention* 7 (2006): 185–210; Karen Joe Laidler, "The Rise of Club Drags in a Heroin Society: The Case of Hong Kong," *Substance Use and Misuse* 40 (2005): 1257–1279; Virendra Kumar and Sarita Kanth, "Bride Burning," *Lancet* 364 (2004): 18–19; Etienne Knig, Linda Dahlberg, James Mercy, Anthony Zwi, and Rafael Lozano, *World Report on Violence and Health* (Geneva: World Health Organization, 2002); David P. Farrington, Patrick A. Langan, and Michael Tonry, *Cross-National Studies in Crime and Justice* (Washington, DC: Bureau of Justice Statistics, 2004); Pedro Scuro, *World Factbook of Criminal Justice Systems: Brazil* (Washington, DC: Bureau of Justice Statistics, 2003); "Comparisons of Crime in OECD Countries," *Civitas Crime* www.civitas.org.uk/crime/crime_stats_oecdjan2012.pdf.

According to the consensus view, crimes are behaviours believed to be repugnant to all elements of society. Do you agree with the artist's implied sentiment that spraying graffiti on a wall is not really a crime? Why do you think creating graffiti remains an outlawed behaviour?

which have been promulgated by political authority, which apply uniformly to all members of the classes to which the rules refer, and which are enforced by punishment administered by the state.[23]

This approach implies that the definition of crime is a function of the beliefs, morality, and direction of social authorities, and is applied uniformly to everyone in society. This statement reveals the authors' faith in the concept of an ideal legal system that can deal adequately with all classes and types of people. For example, laws banning burglary and robbery are directed at controlling the neediest members of society, while laws banning insider trading, embezzlement, and corporate price-fixing are aimed at controlling the wealthiest.

The consensus model of crime is accepted by many criminologists; however, they do argue over whether the law is applied uniformly.

The Conflict View of Crime

In contrast to the consensus perspective, the conflict view depicts society as a collection of diverse groups—owners, workers, professionals, students—who are in constant and continuing conflict. Groups able to assert their political power use the law and the criminal justice system to advance their economic and social position. Criminal laws are created to protect the haves from the have-nots. For example, contrast the harsh penalties exacted on the poor for their street crimes (burglary, robbery, and theft) with the minor penalties the wealthy receive for their white-collar crimes (securities violations and other illegal business practices). While the poor often go to prison for minor law violations, the wealthy are usually given lenient sentences for even the most serious

breaches of law. In fact, to this date, the financial institutions and their agents responsible for the 2008 economic meltdown have yet to face any penalties at all!

In the conflict view, the definition of crime is controlled by wealth, power, and position, and not by moral consensus or the fear of social disruption.[24] Crime is a political concept designed to protect the power and position of the upper classes at the expense of the poor. Even laws prohibiting such violent acts as rape and murder may have political undertones: Banning violent acts ensures domestic tranquility and guarantees that the anger of the poor will not be directed at the rich. A conflict theorist would see the following as crimes: violations of human rights, unsafe working conditions, inadequate childcare, inadequate opportunities for employment and education, substandard housing, pollution of the environment, price fixing, police brutality, assassinations, and war making.[25]

The Interactionist View of Crime

The third philosophical perspective is the interactionist view, which is based in the symbolic interaction school of sociology, associated with George Herbert Mead, Charles Horton Cooley, and W.I. Thomas.[26] This position holds that (1) people act according to their own interpretations of reality, according to the meaning things have for them; (2) they learn the meaning of a thing from the way others react to it, either positively or negatively; and (3) they reevaluate and interpret their own behaviour according to the meaning and symbols they have learned from others.

In this perspective, the definition of crime reflects the preferences and opinions of people who impose their definition of right and wrong on the rest of the population.

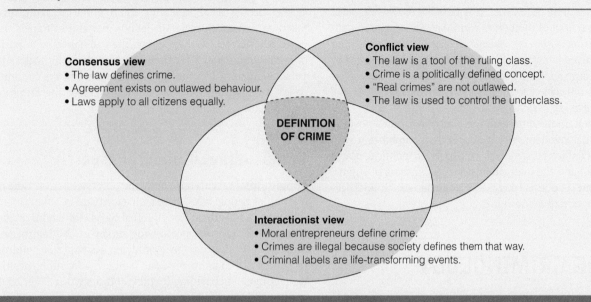

CONCEPT SUMMARY 1.4

The Definition of Crime Affects How Criminologists View the Cause and Control of Illegal Behaviour and Shapes Their Research Orientation

Consensus view
- The law defines crime.
- Agreement exists on outlawed behaviour.
- Laws apply to all citizens equally.

Conflict view
- The law is a tool of the ruling class.
- Crime is a politically defined concept.
- "Real crimes" are not outlawed.
- The law is used to control the underclass.

DEFINITION OF CRIME

Interactionist view
- Moral entrepreneurs define crime.
- Crimes are illegal because society defines them that way.
- Criminal labels are life-transforming events.

Criminals are individuals whom society chooses to label as outcasts or deviants because they have violated social rules. Crimes are outlawed behaviours because society defines them that way and not because they are inherently evil. As sociologist Howard Becker argued:

> The deviant is one to whom that label has successfully been applied; deviant behavior is behavior people so label.[27]

CONNECTIONS

Interactionists believe that society should intervene as little as possible in the lives of law violators lest they be labelled and stigmatized. Labelling theory, discussed in Chapter 8, is based on interactionist views and holds that the application of negative labels leads first to a damaged identity and then to a criminal career.

The interactionist and conflict perspectives both suggest that behaviour is outlawed when it offends people who maintain the social, economic, and political power necessary to have the law conform to their interests or needs. However, unlike the conflict view, the interactionist perspective does not attribute capitalist economic and political motives to the process of defining crime. Instead, interactionists see criminal law as conforming to the beliefs of crusaders **or moral entrepreneurs** who use their influence to shape the legal process in the way they see fit. Laws against pornography, prostitution, and drugs are motivated by moral crusades. Interactionists are

concerned with shifting moral standards, and crime has no meaning unless people react to it. The one-time criminal, if not caught or labelled, can simply "drift," or return to a normal way of life with little permanent damage, just as students who try marijuana do not view themselves as criminals or drug addicts. Only when prohibited acts are sanctioned do they become important, life-transforming events.

Defining Crime

The consensus view of crime dominated criminological thought until the late 1960s. Criminologists devoted themselves to learning why lawbreakers violated the rules of society, and the result was subcultural theory, for example. The criminal was viewed as an outlaw who, for one reason or another, flouted the rules defining acceptable conduct and behaviour. Then, in the 1960s, the interactionist perspective gained prominence. The rapid changes society was experiencing made traditional law and values questionable. Many criminologists were swept along in the social revolution of the 1960s and embraced the ideology that crimes reflected rules imposed by a conservative majority on nonconforming members of society. The result was labelling theory. And then, during the 1970s, more radical scholars gravitated toward conflict explanations of crime. These different perspectives are portrayed in Concept Summary 1.4.

moral entrepreneurs Interest groups or individuals who are in a position to promote their own values onto others.

Looking at underlying philosophical perspectives is important because criminologists' definitions of crime influence their thinking and research. Because of these perspectives, criminologists have taken a variety of approaches in explaining crime, its causes, and methods for its control. Considering these differences, it is possible to take elements from each school of thought to formulate an integrated definition of crime: *Crime is a violation of societal rules of behaviour as interpreted and expressed by a criminal legal code created by people holding social and political power. Individuals who violate these rules are subject to sanctions by state authority, to social stigma, and to loss of status.*

This definition starts with the consensus view's position that criminal law defines crimes, and then combines it with both the conflict perspective's emphasis on political power and control and the interactionist view's concepts of stigma. Thus, crime as defined here, is a political, social, and economic function of modern life.

DOING CRIMINOLOGY

Criminologists have used a wide variety of research techniques to measure the nature and extent of criminal behaviour. To understand and evaluate these patterns, it is important to develop some knowledge of the methods used to collect these data. This knowledge will provide some insight into how professional criminologists approach various problems and questions in their field.

Survey Research

Interviewing or questioning subjects is also called **cross-sectional research**, because it involves surveying people who come from a cross-section of the community. Most surveys involve sampling, in which subjects are selected as representative of a larger population. For example, a criminologist might interview a sample of 500 people drawn from the population of adult or young offenders under the supervision of Canadian correctional agencies. The sample represents the entire population of inmates, and, if done carefully, it will allow for generalizations to be made about the whole population. For example, because two-thirds of prison inmates were unemployed prior to incarceration, employment status might be related to criminal offending, and thus constitute a measure of "risk." Though surveys measure subjects at a single point in their lifespan, questions can also elicit information on subjects' prior behaviour and on their future goals and aspirations.[28]

Survey research can be designed to measure the attitudes and behaviour of participants. Self-report surveys, for example, ask participants to describe their criminal activity, and victimization surveys seek information from victims of crime. Surveys are also a good way to gather information on various groups that haven't come to the attention of police, such as drug addicts or youth in conflict with the law.

Such surveys have limitations. They don't show how subjects change over time, and they make it difficult to guard against people misrepresenting information or giving mistaken responses. Surveys of delinquents and criminals are especially suspect, as they rely on the willingness of a group of people not known for their candour about intimate and personal matters. Despite these drawbacks, surveys continue to be an extremely popular method of gathering criminological data.

Longitudinal (Cohort) Research

Longitudinal research involves the observation over time of a group of people who share a characteristic (a **cohort**). For example, the National Longitudinal Survey of Children and Youth (NLSCY) is a Canada-wide survey of children beginning in 1994 that has been studying a sample of children to collect information on their families, education, health, development, behaviour, friends, and activities. The 2008 survey cycle involved almost 36,000 respondents. Survey questions capture data on school experiences, arrests, hospitalizations, and family life (e.g., divorces and parental relations). The subjects might be given repeated intelligence tests and physical exams, and their diets could be monitored. Data could be collected directly from the subjects or without their knowledge from schools and police. If the research were carefully conducted, it might be possible to determine which life experiences, such as growing up in a broken home or failing at school, typically preceded the onset of crime and delinquency. While following a cohort over time is difficult, expensive, and time-consuming, the good news is that most people do not become serious criminals.

Another approach is to take a cohort of known offenders and look at their early life experiences by studying their educational, family, police, and hospital records; this format is known as a retrospective cohort study.[29] Here, criminologists could use the records of social organizations, such as hospitals, schools, welfare departments, courts, police departments, and prisons. School records contain data on academic performance, attendance, intelligence, disciplinary problems, and teacher ratings. Hospitals record incidents of drug

cross-sectional research Surveys that use data from all age, race, gender, and income segments of the population.

longitudinal research Research that tracks the development of a group of subjects over time.

cohort A sample of subjects whose behaviour is followed over a period.

use and suspicious wounds indicative of child abuse. Police files contain reports of criminal activity, arrest data, personal information on suspects, victim reports, and actions taken by police officers. Court records allow researchers to compare the personal characteristics of offenders with conviction rates and types of sentences. Prison records contain information on inmates' personal characteristics, adjustment problems, disciplinary records, rehabilitation efforts, and length of sentence served.

In one classic retrospective longitudinal survey that used court records to examine the effects of child abuse on a person's adult behaviour, Cathy Spatz Widom compared a group of approximately 900 people who were reported to have been abused, with a group of more than 600 people with no reported abuse. Interviewing the subjects 15 years after their cases had been heard in court, the research showed that when all possible factors were controlled, a connection existed between child abuse and juvenile delinquency. Being abused or neglected increased the likelihood of arrest as a juvenile by 53 percent and as an adult by 38 percent.[30]

CONNECTIONS

Cohort studies sometimes form the basis of critical criminological research, such as that conducted by University of Pennsylvania criminologist Marvin Wolfgang and his colleagues. Their findings have been instrumental in developing knowledge about the onset and development of a criminal career. Wolfgang's cohort research is discussed in Chapter 3.

Aggregate Data Research

Criminologists often make use of large databases gathered by government agencies and research foundations such as Statistics Canada, Correctional Services Canada, and so on. The most important of these sources are crime statistics compiled by the Canadian Centre for Justice Statistics and based on the Uniform Crime Reporting (UCR) system. The UCR is an annual report of the number of crimes reported by citizens to local police departments and the number of arrests made by police agencies.

Aggregate data can tell us about the effect of overall social trends and patterns on the crime rate. For example, to study the relationship between crime and poverty, criminologists might use data collected by Statistics Canada on income, the number of people on welfare, single-parent families in an urban area, and then cross-reference this information with official crime statistics from the same locality. The implication that crime is correlated with poverty is not simple to explain, but preliminary data would establish whether a pattern exists. For example, Theodore Chiricos conducted a review of research using aggregate data to study the relationship of unemployment to crime, and found the relationship to be a significant one.[31]

Experimental Research

In experimental research, criminologists manipulate events to see the effect on the subjects. True experiments have three elements: (1) a random assignment of subjects, (2) a control or comparison group, and (3) an experimental condition. For example, a sample of convicted offenders chosen at random might be asked to participate in a community-based treatment program. A follow-up could determine whether those in the community program were less likely to recidivate (repeat their offences) than were those who served time in prison.

For example, the Montreal Longitudinal-Experimental Study set out to examine the relationship between poor parenting skills and children's poor social skills and the development of delinquency. Researchers designed a study to assess the impact of parent skills training and prosocial skills training for disruptive students in a longitudinal-experimental study of boys considered to be at-risk. The study was done in 53 Montreal schools located in areas of low socio-economic status. Kindergarten teachers rated the behaviour of boys in their classes at the end of the school year, and the boys identified as being at-risk (i.e., disruptive, hyperactive, and aggressive) were randomly assigned to one of three groups: treatment, observation, or control. Parents were taught crisis management, non-abusive discipline, and positive reinforcement; while students were taught positive interaction, problem solving, and self-regulation.

The research confirmed that social intervention can positively affect the social development of disruptive boys because, as one would expect, the boys who received treatment adjusted better to school and were less aggressive. They also did better academically and reported committing fewer delinquent acts. Unfortunately, boys who did not receive treatment were twice as likely to have problems in school. Boys who received treatment still committed delinquent acts, such as trespassing and stealing small items, but at a much lower rate.

In a quasi-experiment, researchers may want to measure the effectiveness of a new law that sets a lower blood alcohol threshold for impaired driving, and survey how it is being enforced by the police. Researchers can compare one area's enforcement patterns to another, and because this offence is very sensitive to levels of police enforcement, it will show the effectiveness of law enforcement on drunk driving. If enforcement programs are weak, it will seem as if impaired driving is becoming less of a problem, despite drunk drivers accounting for about half of all fatal crashes. In one year, 7 percent of people surveyed said that in the past year, they had driven while over the legal alcohol limit.[32]

Another approach, the time-series design, would record impaired-driving arrest and fatality data before and after

Famous Canadian Criminals
Canada's Deadliest Serial Killers

The Pig Farmer

Robert Pickton began trial in 2006 on 27 cases of first-degree murder. He was charged in connection with the disappearance of more than 60 sex-trade workers. Beginning in 1983, women went missing from Vancouver streets in an area known for drug dealing, addiction, homelessness, and violence. Police wrapped up their $70 million investigation in late 2003 at Pickton's pig farm in Port Coquitlam, British Columbia. In 2007, Pickton was convicted of murder and sentenced to six concurrent life sentences. In a scary connection, one of Pickton's victims, Janet Henry, reported missing in 1997, was also victimized by Clifford Olson in the 1980s.

Canada's First Serial Killer?

Dr. Thomas Neill Cream, born in Glasgow and a graduate of McGill (1876), is estimated to have killed seven women in Great Britain and North America. Some think that he was Jack the Ripper, responsible for the murder of prostitutes. He worked occasionally as an abortionist, and at one point he was convicted of murder for adding strychnine to a patient's prescription.

Killer in the Making

Michael Wayne McGray, of Nova Scotia, pleaded guilty in 2000 to four counts of murder and implicated himself in 16 others. He testified that he found victims at random, driven by a "boiling urge" to kill. In 1991, he killed two gay men in Montreal, sparking fears of a serial murderer. As a child, McGray was violently beaten by his father, and he became a bully, killing local dogs and cats. He was later assaulted by guards in a reformatory. His criminal career eventually included sexual assault, break and enter, forgery, and dangerous driving. In 2010, while in custody, he allegedly killed his cellmate in Rocky Mountain Penitentiary.

A Deal with a Devil

Clifford Robert Olson had a criminal history that included break and enter, burglary, fraud, and theft. As a child, he also tormented neighbourhood dogs and cats. In 1978, he was charged with indecent assault in Nova Scotia, and then imprisoned for fraud in Saskatchewan. In 1981, he killed 11 children in British Columbia. Two weeks after the first murder, he raped a teen prostitute (Janet Henry), but police declined to press charges. In a widely criticized deal with the RCMP, Olson was paid $100,000 in exchange for information about the murders and the location of six bodies police had been unable to find. In 1996, he applied under section 745, the faint hope clause, to have his 25-year parole ineligibility period reviewed, but he was turned down.

The Terror of the Miramichi

Allan Legere, born in 1948, had a long history of crimes, including peeping through windows, theft, and possession of stolen property. In 1989, he escaped from custody, where he was being held for murder, and went on a six-month crime spree. Between May and November 1989, he beat four people to death in New Brunswick. His was the first trial in Canada to use DNA evidence to obtain a conviction in the absence of any other evidence.

The Scarborough Rapist

Paul Bernardo, with the help of his wife, Karla Homolka, was convicted in 1995 of killing teens Leslie Mahaffy and Kristen French. Both girls were held captive before being sexually assaulted and killed. Bernardo and Homolka were also implicated in the killing of Homolka's sister, Tammy. Bernardo pleaded guilty to more than 50 sexual assaults and was declared a dangerous offender. Police had interviewed him and obtained a forensic sample, but it was months before it was tested. His lawyer was later charged with obstruction of justice for concealing a set of videotapes Bernardo had made of his assaults.

He Did It for Money

Yves "Apache" Trudeau, 58, a former hit man for the Hells Angels, became a police informant after discovering the Hells Angels had put out a contract for his death. In exchange for placement in a witness protection program, Trudeau confessed to 43 murders and helped put 42 former associates behind bars. In 2004, Trudeau faced a number of new charges for sexually assaulting a minor, which revoked his parole. Automatically facing a life sentence, he returned to prison a marked man as a child molester and informant. In 2008, stricken with cancer and confined to a wheelchair, he was released on parole. Technically, he would not qualify as a serial killer because he did it for money.

---

changes in legislation. The effectiveness of the new law would be supported if a drop in the arrest and fatality rates coincided with the legislation's adoption.

Overall, criminological experiments are difficult and expensive to conduct, sometimes involve ethical issues, and often require long follow-up periods to verify results. However, those experiments that have been conducted have yielded important criminological data.

Observational and Interview Research

Sometimes criminologists focus their research on relatively few subjects, interviewing them in depth or observing them as they go about their activities. This research obtains the kind of in-depth data absent in large-scale surveys. For example, interviewing middle-class female drug abusers can provide insight into a group whose behaviour might not be

Crime in the News
The Arguments against Prostitution Continue

The idea of rights for prostitutes being debated in court seems inconceivable to some. But that is exactly what is happening right now.

The federal government is appealing a ruling by a lower Ontario court that the laws around prostitution are unconstitutional. The lower court in Justice Susan Himmel found the anti-prostitution provisions of the *Criminal Code of Canada* violate sex workers' constitutional right to security of the person by denying them an opportunity to pursue options for conducting their business more safely.

Those provisions make illegal the operation of brothels, living on the avails, and communicating for the purposes of prostitution. While prostitution is legal in Canada, those provisions effectively force sex trade workers to conduct hasty and furtive conversations on the street with prospective customers. Because this does not give them time to assess whether a "date" could be a problem, it makes the work more dangerous.

And, yes, the trading of money for sex and sex for money is legal in Canada. It just can't occur in the same place, be talked about in public, or benefit anybody else. So that means sex trade workers can't hire security guards, or secretaries to make appointments.

The provisions against the operation of brothels and living on the avails of prostitution were passed in the early 20th century. They did not stop the practice of prostitution, of course, but effectively decentralized

it, forcing it out into the bars and hotels. When those places were subject to enforcement, the trade was further decentralized onto the street.

These waves of enforcement have not been effective in eradicating prostitution, but rather have worked to make the problem worse, more visible, and more dangerous. Most people don't have a problem with prostitution unless they find condoms in their backyard or their daughters are propositioned by passing johns, but the government continues to act as if it is protecting the public by ruling on people's morality.

And what makes it worse is that history has a habit of repeating itself.

In the 1970s, the anti-solicitation provision of the *Criminal Code* was challenged and struck down on the basis that it was too vague. Left without a law to enforce, the police could do nothing, so they didn't. Municipalities entered the void and passed bylaws against prostitution, which were then also struck down by the courts.

The federal government then created a law against communication in 1985. This seemed to solve the problem until it was struck down on the basis of its unconstitutionality. In 1990, the Supreme Court of Canada held its nose and said that while freedom to communicate was constitutionally guaranteed, the law against communicating for the purpose of prostitution was a warrantable infringement.

So, let's get this straight, communication for the purpose of buying a hot dog

on the street is okay, but communication for the purposes of prostitution, even though the act is legal, is not. And yet the need to do so forces women to make deals that put them at risk. It sounds to me that Judge Himmel was right on track in striking down the three problematic sections of the *Criminal Code*.

The judge has been accused of playing politics, but it seems to me she did what judges should do—interpret the law and apply it if it is reasonable and refuse to be bound by it if it is not. And it appears the court of appeal is also going in that direction.

The five-judge panel is being told by federal lawyers that sex trade workers are not being placed at risk by laws that make it illegal for them to hire drivers or bodyguards, and to work in brothels. The government lawyers deny the law increases the risk of violence.

However, the justices have asked how it isn't participating in violence to prevent sex workers from taking measures to reduce threats to personal safety. One judge said the analogy is that a convenience store owner should not be allowed to install security cameras to protect a perfectly legal business.

That argument would sound silly, yet we have been too comfortable with moral hypocrisy for far too long.

SOURCE: Copyright Chris McCormick, published in the *Daily Gleaner* (Fredericton), June 16, 2011.

captured in a large-scale survey.[33] Or in a different example, Julian Tanner interviewed youths who lived on the street in Toronto. Using a technique called snowball sampling, each person interviewed introduces the researcher to more subjects. He interviewed 200 youths about their criminal activities and found that crime was related to the inability of the subjects to succeed in legitimate jobs.

Another common criminological method is the first-hand observation of criminals to gain insight into their motives and activities. This method may involve going into the field

and participating in group activities, such as William Whyte did in his famous study of a Boston gang, *Street Corner Society*.[34] Other observers conduct field studies but remain in the background, observing but not being part of the ongoing activity.[35]

Still another type of observation involves bringing subjects into a structured laboratory setting and observing how they react to a predetermined condition or stimulus. This approach is common in studies testing the effect of observational learning on aggressive behaviour, such as exposing subjects to violent films and observing their subsequent behavioural changes.[36] Research studying the relationship between explicit sexually violent pornography and attitudes endorsing interpersonal violence against women found that exposure to violent sexual material is related to a self-reported tendency to rape, the perception of rape victims as experiencing less trauma, and more callousness toward women in general.[37]

It can be seen then that criminology relies on many of the basic research methods common to other fields, including sociology, psychology, and political science.

ETHICAL ISSUES IN CRIMINOLOGY

As experts in the area of crime and justice, criminologists have a social responsibility. Their opinions can influence social policy in debates over gun control, capital punishment, and mandatory sentences. Although some criminologists argue for social service, treatment, and rehabilitation programs to reduce the crime rate, others suggest that only tough prison sentences can bring the crime rate down. Therefore, criminologists must be aware of the ethics of their profession and defend their work in the light of public scrutiny.

When criminologists choose a subject for study, they are guided by their scholarly interests, pressing social needs, and the availability of accurate data. As well, the direction

of criminological inquiry has been influenced by funding from institutions and government bodies, such as the departments of Health and Welfare, Canadian Heritage, and Justice. Private foundations also sometimes play an important role in supporting criminological research.

The availability of research money can influence the directions research takes. When governments provide research funds, they dictate the areas to be studied. For example, if funding is given for long-term cohort studies of criminal careers, other areas may be ignored, such as restorative justice. When research is hired out to consultants designed to satisfy the needs of government, it might not make for informed public debate.[38]

Other limits on research might also arise. For example, governments may be reluctant to fund research on fraud in government. If criminologists are too critical of the government's efforts to reduce or counteract crime, they may face barriers in being approved to receive future funding. This situation is made more difficult because criminologists typically work for universities or public agencies and are under pressure to attract research funding. Even when criminologists maintain discretion of choice, the direction of their efforts may not be truly objective.

Researchers might also find themselves at odds with official institutions. As shown by the Russel Ogden case, discussed below, the government has an interest in information for which the researcher might have pledged confidentiality. The resulting power imbalance can put the respondent's personal information at risk.

A second major ethical issue in criminology concerns the people who are to be the subjects of inquiries and study. Too

Famous Canadian Court Cases
The Russel Ogden Case

Russel Ogden, a graduate student at Simon Fraser University (SFU), conducted his criminology master's thesis on the topic of assisted suicides and euthanasia among persons infected with HIV/AIDS. In his proposal, approved by the SFU Ethics Committee, Ogden stated that he would offer his research participants absolute confidentiality. However, in 1994, Ogden received a subpoena to appear at a coroner's inquest, where he refused to reveal the identities of his research participants.

Ogden argued that the Wigmore criteria said the information he obtained was subject to researcher–participant privilege. He won his case and became the first

researcher to have researcher–participant privilege recognized in Canadian law. SFU changed their ethics policy, preventing any researcher from guaranteeing research participants absolute confidentiality.

Ogden incurred approximately $11,500 in legal expenses, but the university provided Ogden with only $2,000 on "compassionate grounds." Ogden sued the university but lost in 1998. The independent review board appointed to examine the case made the following three recommendations: that the university provide Ogden with a written apology and be reimbursed for his lost wages and legal fees, and that the university guarantee to provide

graduate students with a legal defence if their ethically approved theses are questioned by a third party. SFU's president accepted and complied with each of the recommendations.

In 2014, a Quebec Superior Court judge denied police access to a recorded interview with accused killer Luka Magnotta. University of Ottawa criminologists Chris Bruckert and Colette Parent had interviewed Magnotta in 2007 as part of their research on sex workers. In the first court decision on researcher–client confidentiality, the judge said the right is not absolute, and has to weigh the benefits against investigating serious crime.

often, criminologists have studied people who are poor and members of minority groups while ignoring white-collar, organized, and government crime, with unfortunate consequences. For example, if research on criminals shows a relationship between their criminal behaviour and their lower-than-average IQ scores—a conclusion reached in *The Bell Curve*—attention will focus on the criminality of one group while ignoring others. For example, although IQ can explain male crime, it cannot explain the difference in crime rates between women and men.[39] Perhaps the focus should be on the link between gender and crime, not IQ and crime. This type of research raises ethical issues for criminologists and the research they publish because of the potential social harm the research may cause to males in minority groups, whose members are, in general, more likely to be subject to aggressive policing.

Subjects can be misled about the purpose of the research. When Caucasian and non-Caucasian youngsters are asked to participate in a survey of their behaviour or take an IQ test, they are rarely told in advance that the data they provide may be used to prove the existence of significant racial differences in their self-reported crime rates. Should subjects be told the true purpose of a survey? Would such disclosures make meaningful research impossible? How far should criminologists go when collecting data? Is it ever permissible to deceive subjects when collecting data?

SUMMARY

Criminology is the scientific approach to the study of both criminal behaviour and society's reaction to law violations and violators. Criminology has a rich history in the utilitarian philosophy of Beccaria, the biological positivism of Lombroso, the social theory of Durkheim, and the political philosophy of Marx. In this multidisciplinary field, many practitioners originally trained as sociologists, psychologists, economists, political scientists, historians, and natural scientists. Included among the various subareas that make up the criminological enterprise are criminal statistics, the sociology of law, theory construction, criminal behaviour systems, penology, and victimology. Criminology and criminal justice are mutually dedicated to understanding the nature and control of criminal behaviour.

In viewing crime, criminologists use one of three perspectives: the consensus view, the conflict view, or the interactionist view. The consensus view is that crime is illegal behaviour defined by the existing criminal law, which reflects the values and morals of a majority of citizens. The conflict view is that crime is behaviour created so that economically powerful individuals can retain their control over society. The interactionist view portrays criminal behaviour as a relativistic, constantly changing concept that reflects society's current moral values. According to the interactionist view, criminal behaviour is behaviour so labelled by those in power; criminals are people society chooses to label as outsiders or deviants.

Criminologists use a variety of research methods, including cross-sectional surveys, longitudinal cohort studies, experiments, and observations. In doing research, criminologists must be concerned about ethical standards because their findings can have a significant impact on individuals and groups.

THINKING LIKE A CRIMINOLOGIST

You have been experimenting with various techniques to identify a sure-fire method for predicting violence-prone behaviour in delinquents. Your procedure involves brain scans, DNA testing, and blood analysis. Used with samples of incarcerated adolescents, your procedure has been able to distinguish with 80 percent accuracy between youths with a history of violence and those who are exclusively property offenders.

Your research indicates that your techniques could easily identify for special treatment potentially violence-prone career criminals in any group of youths. For example, children in the local school system could be tested, and those who are violence-prone could be carefully monitored by teachers. Those at risk for future violence could be put into special programs as a precaution.

Some of your colleagues argue that this type of testing is unconstitutional because it violates the subjects' *Charter* guarantee of being considered innocent until proven guilty. There is also the issue of error: Some kids may be falsely labelled as violence-prone. How would you answer your critics? Is it fair or ethical to label people as potentially criminal and violent even though they have not yet exhibited any antisocial behaviour? Do the risks of such a procedure outweigh its benefits?

KEY TERMS

anomie p. 11
atavistic anomalies p. 10
bourgeoisie p. 12
Chicago School p. 11

classical criminology p. 9
cohort p. 20
criminal anthropology p. 10
criminal justice system p. 3

criminological enterprise p. 13
criminologist p. 4
criminology p. 4
cross-sectional research p. 20

decriminalization p. 5
deviant behaviour p. 5
intimate violence p. 3

longitudinal research p. 20
moral entrepreneurs p. 19
positivism p. 9

proletariat p. 12
utilitarianism p. 8
white-collar crime p. 14

DOING RESEARCH ON THE WEB

Read more on the history of criminology by going to Nicole Hahn Rafter's take on biological theories of crime at www.albany.edu/museum/wwwmuseum/criminal/curator/nicole.html.

If you are interested in a career in forensics, go to www.forensics.ca/career_uni.php. The Canadian Society for Forensic Science can be found at www.csfs.ca.

To read more about the National Longitudinal Survey of Children and Youth, the latest research cycle is at www23.statcan.gc.ca/imdb/p2SV.pl?Function=getSurvey&SDDS=4450.

CRITICAL THINKING QUESTIONS

1. Beccaria argued that the threat of punishment controls crime. Are there other forms of social control? Aside from the threat of legal punishments, what else controls your behaviour?
2. What research method would you employ if you wanted to study drug and alcohol abuse at your school?
3. Would it be ethical for a criminologist to observe a teenage gang by hanging out with them, drinking, and watching as they steal cars? Should a criminologist who observes such behaviour report the incident to the police?
4. Can you identify behaviours that are deviant but not criminal? Can you identify crimes that are criminal but not deviant?
5. Do you agree with conflict theorists that some of the most damaging acts in society are not punished as crimes? If so, what are those acts?

NOTES

1. For a review, see Robin Malinosky-Rummell and David Hansen, "Long-Term Consequences of Childhood Physical Abuse," *Psychological Bulletin* 114 (1993): 68–79.
2. Cited in Chris McCormick, *Constructing Danger: Emotions and the Mis/Representation of Crime in the News,* 2nd ed. (Winnipeg: Fernwood, 2010).
3. Edwin Sutherland and Donald Cressey, *Principles of Criminology,* 6th ed. (Philadelphia: J.B. Lippincott, 1960), 3.
4. See Frank Remington, "Development of Criminal Justice as an Academic Field," *Journal of Criminal Justice Education* 1 (1990): 9–20.
5. John Hagan, *The Disreputable Pleasures: Crime and Deviance in Canada,* 3rd ed. (Toronto: McGraw-Hill, 1991), 13.
6. Patricia Erickson, *Cannabis Criminals: The Social Effects of Punishment on Drug Users* (Toronto: ARF, 1980); Edward Brecher, *Licit and Illicit Drugs* (Boston: Little, Brown, 1972), 413–416; Hagan, *The Disreputable Pleasures,* 27–30.
7. Sacco, *Deviance: Conformity and Control in Canadian Society;* "Marijuana Use Doubled over Past Decade: Study," *CBC News,* November 24, 2004; "The Canadian Addiction Survey: Substance Use and Misuse among the Canadian Population," *Correctional Service of Canada,* June 2006, 18, 1.
8. Cesare Beccaria, *On Crimes and Punishments* (originally published in 1764; Bobbs-Merrill, 1963).
9. Described in David Lykken, "Psychopathy, Sociopathy, and Crime," *Society* 34 (1996): 29–38.
10. See Peter Scott, "Henry Maudsley," in *Pioneers in Criminology,* ed. Hermann Mannheim (Montclair, NJ: Prentice-Hall, 1981).
11. Nicole Hahn Rafter, "Criminal Anthropology in the United States," *Criminology* 30 (1992): 525–547.
12. L.A.J. Quetelet, *A Treatise on Man and the Development of His Faculties* (Gainesville, FL: Scholars' Facsimiles and Reprints, 1969), 82–96.
13. Piers Beirne, "The Invention of Positivist Criminology: An Introduction to Quetelet's Social Mechanics of Crime," in *Crime and Society: Readings in Critical Criminology,* ed. Brian C. MacLean (Toronto: Copp Clark, 1996).
14. See, generally, Robert Nisbet, *The Sociology of Emile Durkheim* (New York: Oxford University Press, 1974), 209; Emile Durkheim, *Rules of the Sociological Method,* trans. S.A. Solvay and J.H. Mueller, ed. G. Catlin (New York: Free Press, 1966), 65–73; Emile Durkheim, *The Division of Labor in Society* (New York: Free Press, 1964 [1893]); Emile Durkheim, *Suicide: A Study in Sociology* (Glencoe, IL: Free Press, 1951).
15. Robert Park and Ernest Burgess, *The City* (Chicago: University of Chicago Press, 1925).
16. Marlene Shore, The Science of Social Redemption: McGill, the Chicago School, and the Origins of Social Research in Canada (Toronto: University of Toronto Press, 1987).
17. Karl Marx and Friedrich Engels, *Capital: A Critique of Political Economy,* trans. E. Aveling (Chicago: Charles Kern, 1906); Karl Marx, *Selected Writings in Sociology and*

Social Philosophy, trans. P.B. Bottomore (New York: McGraw-Hill, 1956). For a general discussion of Marxist thought, see Michael Lynch and W. Byron Groves, *A Primer in Radical Criminology* (New York: Harrow and Heston, 1986), 6–26.

18. Willem Bonger, *Criminality and Economic Conditions* (1916, abridged ed., Bloomington: Indiana University Press, 1969); Ralf Dahrendorf, *Class and Class Conflict in Industrial Society* (Palo Alto, CA: Stanford University Press, 1959).

19. Marvin Wolfgang and Franco Ferracuti, *The Subculture of Violence* (London: Social Science Paperbacks, 1967), 20.

20. Marvin Wolfgang, *Patterns in Criminal Homicide* (Philadelphia: University of Pennsylvania Press, 1958).

21. Edwin H. Sutherland, "White-Collar Criminality," *American Sociological Review* 5, 1 (1940): 2–10.

22. Hans von Hentig, *The Criminal and His Victim* (New Haven, CT: Yale University Press, 1948); Stephen Schafer, *The Victim and His Criminal* (New York: Random House, 1968).

23. Sutherland and Cressey, *Principles of Criminology*, 8.

24. Eugene Doleschal and Nora Klapmuts, "Toward a New Criminology," *Crime and Delinquency* 5 (1973): 607.

25. Michael Lynch and W. Byron Groves, *A Primer in Radical Criminology* (Albany, NY: Harrow and Heston, 1989), 32.

26. See Herbert Blumer, *Symbolic Interactionism* (Englewood Cliffs, NJ: Prentice-Hall, 1969).

27. Howard Becker, *Outsiders* (New York: The Free Press, 1963), 9.

28. Michael Gottfredson and Travis Hirschi, "The Methodological Adequacy of Longitudinal Research on Crime," *Criminology* 25 (1987): 581–614.

29. See, generally, David Farrington, Lloyd Ohlin, and James Q. Wilson, *Understanding and Controlling Crime* (New York: Springer-Verlag, 1986), 11–18.

30. Cathy Spaatz Widom, "Child Abuse, Neglect, and Adult Behavior," *American Journal of Orthopsychiatry* 15 (1989): 355–367.

31. Theodore G. Chiricos, "Rates of Crime and Unemployment: An Analysis of Aggregate Research Evidence," *Social Problems* 34, 2 (Apr. 1987): 187–212; see also "Poverty, Income Inequality, and Violent Crime: A Meta-analysis of Recent Aggregate Data Studies," *Criminal Justice Review* 18 (1993): 182.

32. "The Road Safety Monitor 2005: Drinking and Driving," Traffic Injury Research Foundation 2005.

33. Claire Sterck-Elifson, "Just for Fun? Cocaine Use among Middle-Class Women," *Journal of Drug Issues* 26 (1996): 63–76.

34. William F. Whyte, *Street Corner Society* (Chicago: University of Chicago Press, 1955).

35. Herman Schwendinger and Julia Schwendinger, *Adolescent Subcultures and Delinquency* (New York: Praeger, 1985).

36. For a review of these studies, see L. Rowell Huesmann and Neil Malamuth, eds., "Media Violence and Antisocial Behavior," *Journal of Social Issues* 42 (1986): 31–53.

37. Luis T. Garcia, "Exposure to Pornography and Attitudes about Women and Rape: A Correlational Study," *Journal of Sex Research* 23 (1986): 378–385; N.M. Malamuth and E. Donnerstein, "The Effects of Aggressive-Pornographic Mass Media Stimuli," in *Advances in Experimental Social Psychology*, ed. L. Berkowitz (New York: Academic Press, 1982), 104–136.

38. Don Clairmont, "In Defence of Liberal Models of Research and Policy," *Canadian Journal of Criminology* 41 (1999): 151–160.

39. See, for example, Michael Hindelang and Travis Hirschi, "Intelligence and Delinquency: A Revisionist Review," *American Sociological Review* 42 (1977): 471–486; Richard Herrnstein and Charles Murray, *The Bell Curve* (New York: Free Press, 1994); Alan Ryan, "Apocalypse Now?" in *The Bell Curve Debate: History, Documents, Opinions*, eds. Russell Jacoby and Naomi Glauberman (New York: Random, 1995), 21.

The Criminal Law and Its Process

Chapter Outline

Learning Objectives

After reading this chapter, you will be able to:

1. Understand the sources of the criminal law.
2. Be familiar with different functions of the law.
3. Know the elements of what constitutes a defence.
4. Discuss the legal rights of the individual.
5. Explain different cases and their significance.

The Supreme Court is Canada's highest court, the place of last appeal for those convicted of criminal offences and for those wishing to challenge the criminal law.

NEL

The criminal law controls the formal definition and content of crime. Developed over many generations, it incorporates historical traditions, moral beliefs, and social values, and is influenced by political and economic developments and conditions. The criminal law is a living concept, constantly evolving to keep pace with society. It governs the form and direction of almost all human interaction. Business practices, family life, education, property transfer, inheritance, the availability of certain drugs, and other common forms of social relations must conform to the rules set out by the legal code. Most important for our purposes, the law defines the behaviours that society labels as criminal. Consequently, students of criminology need to have a basic understanding of the law and its relationship to crime and deviance. This chapter will briefly review the nature and purpose of the law, chart its history, and discuss its elements relevant to Canadian society.

THE ORIGINS OF LAW

Crimes were recognized in many early societies.[1] In preliterate societies, common custom and tradition were the equivalents of law. Each group had its own customs created to deal with situations that arose in daily living, often long after the reason for their origin had been forgotten. Many customs eventually developed into formal or written law.

Early Legal Codes

One of the earliest surviving legal codes was developed in 2000 BCE in Sumer (part of present-day Iraq). It was later adopted by Hammurabi (1792–1750 BCE), king of Babylon, in his written laws, the **Code of Hammurabi**, preserved on basalt rock columns. Punishment was based on physical retaliation, or *lex talionis* ("an eye for an eye"). However, the severity of punishment depended on class standing: For assault, slaves would be put to death; freemen might lose a limb.

CONNECTIONS

Attitudes continually change regarding how to make punishments fit the crimes. See Chapter 5 for more about the view that crime and punishment should be closely aligned.

Babylonian laws were strictly enforced by judges. Burglary and theft were common in ancient Babylon, and local officials were expected to apprehend criminals. If they failed, they had to personally replace lost property; if murderers were not caught, the responsible official paid a fine to the deceased's relatives. Imagine holding police officers to such a standard today!

Another ancient legal code still surviving is the **Mosaic Code** of the Israelites (1200 BCE). According to tradition, God entered into a covenant or contract with the tribes of Israel in which they agreed to obey God's law in return for care and protection. This code is the foundation of Judeo-Christian moral teachings and also a basis for our present-day legal system. Its prohibitions against murder, theft, perjury, and adultery precede by several thousand years the same laws found today. A list of important legal documents would also need to include the Koran (652 BCE, Arabia), the primary sacred text of Islam.

Also surviving is the Roman law contained in the Twelve Tables (451 BCE), formulated in response to pressure from the lower classes, who believed that an unwritten code gave arbitrary and unlimited power to the wealthy. The laws deal with debt, family relations, property, and other daily matters. Other notable ancient lawgivers through the centuries were Confucius (551–479 BCE, China), Muhammad (570–632 BCE, Arabia), Solomon (873–933 BCE, Israel), and Lycurgus (9th century BCE, Greece).

Early Crime, Punishment, and Law

The early formal legal codes were lost during the Dark Ages, which lasted for hundreds of years after the fall of Rome. During this period, superstition and fear of magic and satanic black arts dominated thinking.

The regulation of crime during the early feudal period involved monetary payments as the main punishments for crimes. For example, the compensation (**wergild**) paid for killing a freewoman of child-bearing age was 24,000 denars; if the woman was past child-bearing age, the wergild was reduced to 8,000 denars.

Code of Hammurabi The first written criminal code, developed in Babylonia about 2000 BCE.

lex talionis Punishment based on physical retaliation ("an eye for an eye"), a precursor of more abstract forms of retribution used today.

Mosaic Code By tradition, the covenant between God and the tribes of Israel in which they agreed to obey his law in return for God's special care and protection.

wergild Under medieval law, the money paid by the offender to compensate the victim and the state for a criminal offence.

EXHIBIT 2.1

The Judgment of the Glowing Iron

After the accusation has been lawfully made, and three days have been passed in fasting and prayer, the priest, clad in his sacred vestments with the exception of his outside garment, shall take with a tongs the iron placed before the altar; and, singing the hymn of the three youths, namely, "Bless him all his works," he shall bear it to the fire, and shall say this prayer over the place where the fire is to carry out the judgment: "Bless, O Lord God, this place, that there may be for us in it sanctity, chastity, virtue and victory, and sanctimony, humility, goodness, gentleness and plentitude of law, and obedience to God the Father and the Son and the Holy Ghost." After this, the iron shall be placed in the fire and shall be sprinkled with holy water; and while it is heating, he shall celebrate mass. But when the priest shall have taken the Eucharist, he shall adjure the man who is to be tried ... and shall cause him to take the communion. Then the priest shall sprinkle holy water above the iron and shall say: "The blessing of God the Father, the Son, and the Holy Ghost descend upon this iron for the discerning of the right judgment of God." And straightway the accused shall carry the iron to a distance of nine feet. Finally his hand shall be covered under seal for three days, and if festering blood be found in the track of the iron, he shall be judged guilty. But if, however, he shall go forth uninjured, praise shall be rendered to God.

SOURCE: Fordham University, Center for Medieval Studies, "The Internet Medieval Sourcebook," http://www.fordham.edu/halsall/sbook.html (accessed May 8, 2005).

Guilt was determined by ordeals, such as having the accused place his or her hand in boiling water to see whether God would intervene and heal the wounds. It was also possible to challenge the accuser to a trial by combat. Exhibit 2.1 presents an ordeal called the judgment of the glowing iron, a method of proof used in early Germanic law. Settling trials by ordeal fell out of favour when the Catholic Church decreed that priests could no longer participate. Without the use of the ordeal in disputes, sometimes guilt could be disputed with the aid of **oath-helpers**, who would support the accused's innocence.

Despite reforms, until the 18th century, the systems of crime, punishment, law, and justice were chaotic. The law was controlled by the lords of the great manors, who tried cases according to local custom and rule. Although people generally agreed that theft, assault, treason, and blasphemy constituted crimes, penalties were often arbitrary and cruel, and included public flogging, branding, beheading, and burning. Peasants who violated the rule of their masters might have their teeth or eyes pulled out, while others were impaled or had their hands cut off; some were burned alive or plunged into boiling lead. Even simple wanderers and vagabonds were viewed as dangerous and subject to these extreme penalties.

Origins of Common Law

Because the ancient legal codes had been lost, law and crime were guided by superstition and local custom during the Middle Ages. Slowly, in England, a common law developed that helped standardize law and justice. This common law became the foundation for Canada's legal system.

Before the Norman Conquest in 1066, the legal system among the Anglo-Saxons in England was decentralized. Each county (shire) was divided into units of 100 families, and then further divided into groups of 10 called tithings, which were responsible for maintaining order among themselves and dealing with disturbances, fires, wild animals, and so on.

Petty cases were tried by courts of the hundred group. More serious and important cases could be heard by an assemblage of local landholders or by the local nobleman. If the act concerned spiritual matters, it could be judged in ecclesiastical courts, which were responsible for disciplining the clergy, ensuring church attendance and conformity to church rites, and controlling sexual morality and matrimonial disputes. In early Canadian society, various church courts enforced the moral rules of the faith. Between 1810 and 1880, for example, almost 8,000 people were excluded from Maritime Baptist churches for crimes ranging from fornication to usury.[2]

Crime and Custom. Crimes were viewed as personal wrongs, and compensation was paid to the victims. Even homicide could be settled by payment to the deceased's family, unless the crime was carried out by poison or ambush—in which case it was punished by death. If payment was not made, the victims' families would attempt to forcibly collect damages or seek revenge, and the result could be a blood feud between two families. Recognized crimes included treason, homicide, rape, property theft, assault, and battery. For treasonous acts, the punishment was death. Theft during the Anglo-Saxon era could result in slavery for thieves and their families, and if caught in the act of fleeing with stolen goods, the thief could be killed.

A scale of compensation existed for lesser injuries, such as the loss of an arm or an eye. Important persons, churchmen, and nuns received greater restitution than the general population, and they paid more if they were the criminal defendants. This scale became the precursor of the modern-day criminal fine. The criminal law was designed to provide an equitable solution to what was considered a private dispute.

The Norman Conquest. After the Norman Conquest, Anglo-Saxon justice was administered as it had been in previous centuries. The church courts handled acts that might be considered sin, and the local manorial courts dealt with

oath-helpers   During the Middle Ages, groups of 12 to 25 people who would support the accused's innocence.

most secular violations. However, to secure control of the countryside, William the Conqueror replaced the local tribunals with royal administrators, who dealt with the most serious breaches of the peace.

Because the royal administrators could not constantly be present in each community, a system was developed in which they travelled on a circuit, holding court in each county several times a year. When court was in session, the judge would summon a number of citizens who would, under oath, tell of the crimes and serious breaches of the peace that had occurred since the judge's last visit. The royal judge would then decide what to do in each case, using local custom and rules of conduct as his guide. If, for example, a local freeholder was convicted of theft, he might be executed if those before him had suffered that fate for a similar offence. However, if in previous cases the thief had been forced to make restitution to the victim, then that judgment would be rendered in the current case. This system, known as ***stare decisis*** ("to stand by decided cases"), meant that courts were bound to follow the law established in previously decided cases (precedent) unless the law was overruled by a higher authority, such as the king or the pope.

The current English system of law came into existence during the reign of Henry II (1154–1189). The Catholic Church's ban on trial by ordeal meant that a new method of deciding criminal trials needed to be developed. To fill the gap, British justices adapted a method that had long been used to determine real estate taxes. In the time of William the Conqueror, 12 knights in each district had been called before an inquest of the king's justices to give local tax information. These "12 free and lawful men of the neighbourhood" would view the land and testify as to who last had peaceful possession, and settle "claim jumping" disputes over land. Under King Henry II, these juries (from the Latin *jurati*, to be sworn), were local landholders whom judges called on to decide the facts of cases, investigate crimes, accuse suspected offenders, and even give testimony at trials.

At first, jurors were like witnesses, telling the judge what they knew about the case; these courts were known as *assise* or *assize* (from the Latin *assideo*, to sit together). By the 14th century, jurors had become the deciders of fact. Over the centuries, the English jury came to be seen as a check on the government, and royal prosecutors became representatives of the Crown and submitted evidence and brought witnesses to testify before the jury. Eventually, the accused in a criminal action was allowed to use witnesses to rebut charges, but not until the 18th century were witnesses required to take oaths. Few formal procedures existed, allowing the judge and the prosecutor to intimidate witnesses and jurors. However, developing routine judicial processes heralded the beginnings of the common law.

The great case that established the principle of jury independence, Bushell's case (1670), arose when a London jury acquitted William Penn, a leading Quaker and later the founder of Pennsylvania, of unlawful assembly in connection with his preaching in the street after a Quaker church was padlocked. The jurors were imprisoned by an angry royalist judge, and then were freed when the same judge said that a jury must reach a verdict based on the evidence, or else the jury would be nothing but a useless rubber stamp.

The Common Law

The **common law** is meant to apply to people without regard to social differences. When King Henry's judges began to apply a national law to replace laws in local jurisdictions, they took into account both local custom and Norman feudal law. As new situations arose, judges either invented new solutions or borrowed from European countries. During their gatherings, the circuit judges shared these incidents and discussed their decisions, developing an oral tradition of law. These cases, together with written decisions, filtered through the national court system (see Figure 2.1) and produced a fixed body of legal rule and principles. Thus, common law is judge-made law, case law derived from previously decided cases. Such crimes as murder, burglary, arson, and rape are common-law crimes—they were initially defined and created by judges.

Common Law and Statutory Law

The common law still is the law of the land in England, although it has been modified. For example, common law originally defined murder as the unlawful killing of another human being with malice aforethought.[3] For offenders to be found guilty, they must have (1) planned the crime and (2) intentionally killed the victim out of spite or hatred. However, this general definition proved inadequate, so over time English judges added other forms of murder: killing someone in the heat of passion, killing someone out of negligence, and killing someone in the course of committing another crime, such as during a robbery. Each form of murder was given a different title and a different degree of punishment. Thus, the common law was a constantly evolving legal code, based on legal decisions made from the ground up. (See Concept Summary 2.1 for a list of common-law offences.)

> ***stare decisis*** The principle that the courts are bound to follow the law established in previously decided cases (precedent) unless the law was overruled by a higher authority.
>
> **common law** Early English law that was developed by judges and incorporated Anglo-Saxon tribal custom, feudal rules and practices, and the everyday rules of behaviour of local villages. Common law became the standardized law of the land in England, and eventually formed the basis of criminal law in Canada.

FIGURE 2.1
Outline of Canada's
Court System

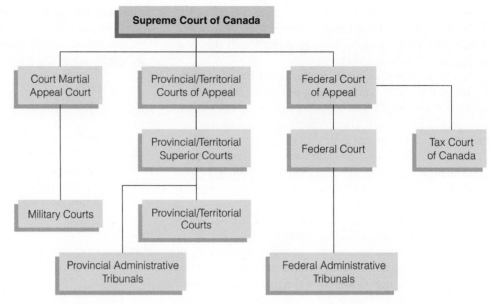

Source: *Canada's Court System*, Figure: Outline of
Canada's Court System, page 3. http://www
.justice.gc.ca/eng/dept-min/pub/ccs-ajc/page3.html.
Department of Justice Canada, 2005. Reproduced with
the permission of the Minister of Public Works and
Government Services Canada, 2014.

CONCEPT SUMMARY 2.1

Common-Law Crimes

Crimes against the Person
- *First-degree murder* is the unlawful premeditated killing of another person. Example: A man buys poison and pours it into coffee his wife is drinking, for the insurance benefits.
- *Voluntary manslaughter* is an intentional killing committed in mitigating circumstances. Example: A husband kills his partner who has been cheating on him, and their lover.
- *Assault* is unlawful touching, or the threat of such. Example: A student aims a gun at her friend and threatens to shoot; the friend believes the gun is loaded.
- *Rape* is unlawful sexual touching without consent. Example: After a party, a man offers to drive a female acquaintance home, but instead forces her to have sexual relations.
- *Robbery* is the wrongful taking of personal property from a person by violence or intimidation. Example: A man with a gun demands a passerby give him his wallet.

Inchoate (Incomplete) Offences
- *Attempt* is an intentional act for committing a crime that is more than mere preparation. Example: A bomb is planted in a person's car so it will detonate when turned on.
- *Conspiracy* is voluntary agreement to commit an act using means forbidden by law. Example: Two persons conspire to fake accidents to get reimbursement from insurance.

Crimes against Property
- *Burglary* is breaking and entering a dwelling house with the intent to commit a crime. Example: Someone breaks into and enters another's house without permission in order to steal.
- *Arson* is the intentional burning of a building. Example: A youth sets a house on fire for the excitement of watching the fire department arrive.
- *Theft* is taking personal property of another with the intent to keep it. Example: A shopper sees a diamond ring at the jewellery counter, takes it, and walks out of the store.

CONNECTIONS

Common-law practices still guide modern legal codes. For example, murder statutes still retain different degrees of seriousness, which are based on the intent of the murderer. The degrees of murder and other definitional issues are discussed in Chapter 10.

The creation of a new common-law crime can sometimes be traced back to a particular case. For example, an unsuccessful attempt to commit an illegal act was not considered a crime until the 1784 case of *Rex v. Scofield*, when the defendant was charged with trying to burn down a house he was renting. Being unsuccessful, Scofield argued that an attempt to commit a misdemeanour was not actually a crime. The court rejected the argument.[4] After *Scofield*, attempt became a common-law crime, and today criminal attempt (called **inchoate crimes**) is defined as a crime in section 24 of the *Criminal Code of Canada* (CCC).

inchoate crimes   Incomplete or contemplated crimes such as solicitation or criminal attempts.

The English Parliament also enacted supplementary legislation, creating statutory or written crimes. For example, in 1723, according to the *Waltham Black Act*, armed or disguised criminals would be punished with death if found guilty of offences against rural property, including the poaching of small game or arson.[5] The Act also allowed execution without a trial if the accused failed to surrender. The underlying purpose was Parliament's desire to control the behaviour of peasants whose poverty forced them to poach on royal lands. In the *Waltham Black Act*, then, the British ruling class created a mechanism for protecting its property and power.

Another example also illustrates how the law develops to protect the rights of the privileged. In 1812, the British government proposed a new capital offence, the *Frame Breaking Act,* which enabled people convicted of machine breaking to be sentenced to death (see Figure 2.2). Mill workers were upset by changes occurring in the workplace: wage reductions, the use of unapprenticed workers, and their own replacement by new weaving technology. The Army of Redressers, under the leadership of General Ned Ludd, broke into factories at night to destroy the new power looms. This event led to the term *Luddite,* which is used today to refer to someone who opposes technological change.

FIGURE 2.2
The British Parliament Acts against the Luddites

> # WHEREAS,
> Several EVIL-MINDED PERSONS have assembled together in a riotous Manner, and DESTROYED a NUMBER of
> # FRAMES,
> In different Parts of the Country :
> THIS IS
> ## TO GIVE NOTICE,
> That any Person who will give Information of any Person to Person thus wickedly
> ## BREAKING THE FRAMES,
> Shall, upon CONVICTION, receive
> # 50 GUINEAS
> ### REWARD.
> And any Person who was actively engaged in RIOTING, who will impeach his Accomplices, shall, upon CONVINCTION, receive the same Reward, and every Effort made to procure his Pardon.
>
> ☞ Information to be given to Messrs. COLDHAM and ENFIELD.
>
> Nottingham, March 29, 1812.

Statutory laws reflect existing social conditions that deal with issues of morality, such as gambling, sexual activity, and drug-related offences. For example, early in the history of Canada and the United States, narcotics such as heroin, opium, and cocaine were both legal to use and relatively easy to obtain.[6] However, public and governmental concern arose over the use of narcotics by Chinese immigrants who had come to Canada to build railroads and work in mines. By 1910, opium was criminalized in Canada.[7] Conversely, in the case of marijuana, the statutory law has changed in the opposite direction, toward decriminalization. As the use of marijuana became widespread among the middle class in the 1960s, attitudes and enforcement became more relaxed. As mentioned in Chapter 1, many Canadians are in favour of legalizing marijuana.

The Development of Law in Canada

Canada's unique legal system was not achieved overnight or without conflict.[8] The early Canadian criminal justice system was strongly influenced by the common law of England and by geographic, economic, political, and cultural factors. Before Confederation in 1867, Canada did not have a standard criminal justice system. The military was the first to maintain law and order, especially in naval ports, and the Hudson's Bay Company was using its employees to enforce its own penal code. And although an infrastructure for justice existed in Eastern Canada, in Western Canada law was being administered by circuit judges in log buildings. Canada's size and the pattern of westward settlement resulted in cases of frontier justice, but by the time the West was opening up, defendants were being taken to the more established parts of Canada for trial. The spread of law enforcement and the development of a legal system gradually became more sophisticated and professional.

Pierre Berton describes the stark difference between the American city of Skagway, Alaska, which was noted for its lawlessness, and the Canadian city of Dawson, Yukon, where crime and disorder were kept firmly in check by the North-West Mounted Police (NWMP).[9]

The *Police of Canada Act* (1868) created the Dominion Police, and the NWMP began in 1873. Initially given jurisdiction only in the Prairies, the force became the federal Royal Canadian Mounted Police (RCMP) in 1920. The NWMP was sent to protect the Aboriginal population from the Americans and to bring the Queen's justice to a dangerous territory. The NWMP was able to use criminal sanctions to repress political dissent, control the Aboriginal peoples, and maintain sovereignty.[10] Maintenance of order helped to encourage settlers, and in the process new markets were created for manufactured goods. The treatment of Aboriginal Canadians by the NWMP is seen by some as benevolent, especially in contrast to the situation in the United States.

CONNECTIONS

Recently, much debate has surrounded the treatment of Aboriginal peoples in the development of Canada. For more about this topic, see the discussion in Chapter 9.

Before Confederation, British common law was used for criminal prosecutions; after Confederation, crime control was centralized in the federal government through the *British North America Act.* The federal government was given the power to create criminal statute law, and the provinces and territories were responsible for its administration. Parliament codified the first criminal code in 1892, supplemented by municipal bylaws and provincial regulations. This centralization was significant because judicial precedent and legislative amendments had created substantial variation across the country. For example, incest was punishable by a severe prison sentence in some provinces and territories but was not even a crime in others.[11]

All existing statute law was eventually consolidated. Some offences prohibited in the 1892 CCC had their origin in 17th-century England; for example, offences against public order included inciting to mutiny, unlawful drilling (of soldiers), attending or promoting a prize fight, piracy, possessing a weapon at a public meeting, and pretending to practise witchcraft. Other previously included offences have since been repealed or amended, such as seducing a woman under promise of marriage, carnally knowing idiots, keeping a common bawdy-wigwam, injuring persons by furious driving, leaving holes in the ice unguarded, and abduction of heiresses.

A curious law in the CCC is section 163, offences tending to corrupt morals, where it is an offence to publish, distribute, or possess a crime comic. This section was passed in 1949 out of concern that juveniles were committing murders, robberies, and suicides. Batman and Robin were accused of encouraging homosexuality, and Popeye of using marijuana. This law is rarely enforced now, except against marijuana publications. Some other interesting laws still on the books in Canada are displayed in Table 2.1.

TABLE 2.1 Outdated Canadian Crimes

The *Criminal Code of Canada* includes laws defining the following activities as crimes. Some of them might surprise you.

- Duelling (section 71): It is an indictable offence to challenge or accept a challenge to fight a duel.

- Having a stink bomb (section 178): It is a summary offence for anyone except a peace officer to possess an offensive volatile substance.

- Trespassing at night (section 17): This is a summary, reverse onus offence, which means the burden of proof lies on defendants to show they have lawful excuse to loiter or prowl.

- Pretending to practise witchcraft (section 365): It is a summary offence to fraudulently pretend to use witchcraft or sorcery; it is legal to be a witch.

Gradually, the reforms taking place in Europe had an impact in Canada, manifested in the construction of prisons designed as places of punishment, the training of professional police, and the declining use of the death penalty.

CLASSIFICATION OF LAW

Law can be classified in ways that can help us understand its nature and purpose. Three of the most important classifications are (1) crimes and torts, (2) indictable and summary offences, and (3) *mala in se* and *mala prohibitum.* These classifications are briefly described here.

Criminal and Civil Law

Law can be divided into two broad, exclusive categories: the criminal law and civil law. Civil law includes such areas as property law (the law governing transfer and ownership of property) and contract law (the law of personal agreements). Of all areas of the civil law, **tort law** (the law of personal wrongs and damage) is most similar in intent and form to the criminal law.

A tort is a civil action in which an individual asks to be compensated for personal harm caused by the actions of another. The harm may be either physical or mental and includes such acts as trespass, assault and battery, invasion of privacy, libel (false and injurious writings), and slander (false and injurious statements). Someone can be sued for damages even if he or she has been acquitted of a criminal act, the reason being that the standards of evidence for a finding are lower in civil cases.

A tort may also occur when a behaviour is an indirect cause of injury, such as when it sets off a chain of events that leads to injury or death. In 1990, for example, the families of two youths who had attempted suicide sued the heavy-metal rock group Judas Priest and CBS Records, claiming that the group had put the subliminal message "Do it" in its *Stained Class* album to effect "mind control" over the band's fans. The group was vindicated because the youths were self-destructive before the album was released, having previously engaged in truancy and drug use.[12]

In a more recent case, in 2003, Wanda Young sued Memorial University and two social work professors for

tort law   The law of personal wrongs and damage, such as negligence, libel, and slander.

falsely labelling her a potential child sex abuser. A former student at the university, she had been covertly investigated and then cleared, but the labelling continued to compromise her employability. She sued for negligence and an absence of duty of care, and won an $880,000 award, which, however, was overturned on appeal. In 2005, the Supreme Court of Canada decided in *Young v. Bella, 2006,* that the jury was right in finding negligence and set aside the judgment of the appeal court.[13]

A person can be held both criminally and civilly liable for one action. For example, if one man punches another, the assailant can be both charged with criminal assault and sued by the victim, and perhaps required to pay monetary damages.

A key difference between the criminal law and civil law is that the state has the power to protect the public from harm by punishing individuals whose actions threaten the social order; whereas in civil law, the harm is considered private, and individuals are compensated for harm done to them by others.

In a criminal action, the state initiates legal proceedings by bringing charges and prosecuting the violator. The victim has a small role. If it is determined that the criminal law has been broken, the state can impose punishment, such as imprisonment, probation (community supervision by the court), or a fine payable to the state. Another major difference is the burden of proof required to establish liability. A criminal defendant's guilt must be proved beyond a reasonable doubt. However, in a civil case, a lower standard of proof is required, based on a balance of probabilities.[14]

Table 2.2 summarizes the differences and similarities between crimes and torts.

Montreal financier Earl Jones, the head of a Ponzi scheme that bilked investors of their savings, was convicted in 2010 of fraud worth $50 million.

TABLE 2.2 Comparison of Criminal and Tort Law

Similarities

Both criminal and tort law seek to control behaviour and both impose sanctions. Similar areas of legal action exist—for example, personal assault and control of white-collar offences, such as environmental pollution.

Differences

Criminal Law	Tort Law
Crime is a public offence.	Tort is a civil or private wrong.
The sanction associated with a criminal law is incarceration or death.	The sanction associated with a tort is monetary damages.
The right of enforcement belongs to the state.	The individual brings the action.
The government ordinarily does not appeal.	Both parties can appeal.
Fines go to the state.	The individual receives compensation for harm done.
The standard of proof is "beyond a reasonable doubt."	Guilt is established by a preponderance of the evidence.

Indictable and Summary Offences

Criminal laws can be further classified as either indictable offences or offences punishable on summary conviction. An **indictable offence** is a serious offence, such as murder (section 231), whereas a **summary offence**, such as loitering (section 179 on vagrancy), is a minor or petty crime. The main differences involve procedure and penalty. Summary offences, which have a six-month limitation period on prosecution, are heard in provincial or territorial court, and the maximum fine is $2,000, or a six-month jail term, or both.

Indictable offences have no limitation period on prosecution and can result in much more serious penalties if the defendant is found guilty.[15] Indictable offences involve a choice of trial by judge or jury, and section 625.1 of the *Criminal Code* includes the provision for a preliminary

indictable offence A serious offence, such as murder, which carries a serious penalty.

summary offence A minor offence whose penalty is a maximum six months in jail, or a fine.

inquiry to determine whether enough admissible evidence exists to result in a conviction in a full trial. Most preliminary inquiries are concluded in less than a day.

Figure 2.3 outlines the ordinary stages of how a case passes through the criminal justice system. An incident usually must be reported to the police, whereupon the police decide whether it is founded in fact. Charges may or may not be laid, but if they are, the prosecution then decides how the case will proceed. If the case makes it to court, then the defendant can either be found guilty or acquitted. At this

FIGURE 2.3

Flow through the Canadian Criminal Justice System

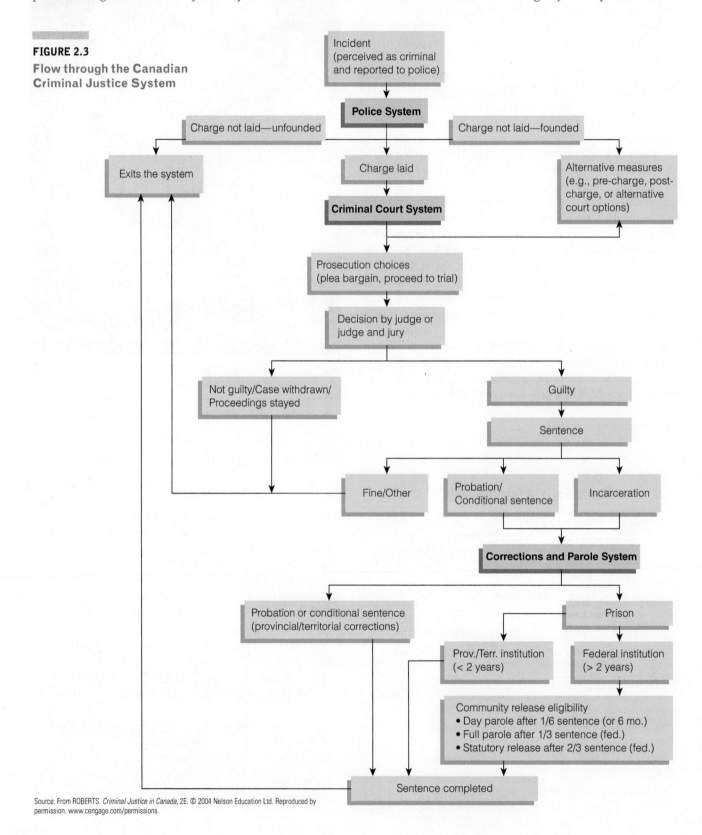

Source: From ROBERTS. *Criminal Justice in Canada*, 2E. © 2004 Nelson Education Ltd. Reproduced by permission. www.cengage.com/permissions.

point, a distinction can be made between criminal guilt and legal innocence, as sufficient evidence must exist to prove a case beyond a reasonable doubt. If the defendant is found guilty, various options are then available for the defendant and counsel to pursue.

Mala in Se and Mala Prohibitum

Criminologists also classify crimes as being either *mala in se* or *mala prohibitum*. **Mala in se** crimes are rooted in the core values inherent in our culture and are designed to control such behaviours as inflicting physical harm on others (assault, rape, murder), taking possessions that rightfully belong to another (larceny, burglary, robbery), or harming another person's property (malicious damage, trespass).

Mala prohibitum crime involves violations of laws that reflect current public opinion and social values that are more relative in nature. Actions are periodically designated as crimes to control behaviours that conflict with the functioning of society, such as drug use and possession of unlicensed handguns. Although linking *mala in se* crimes to an objective concept of morality is relatively easy, it is much more difficult if the acts are *mala prohibitum*. In adjudicating cases of obscenity, for example, the judge must take subjective community standards into account in deciding whether a particular behaviour violates that provision of the code. Although this provision sounds commonsensical, it has led to discrimination in the past. For example, in some cases, gay pornography was confiscated at the border, whereas heterosexual pornography was not.

FUNCTIONS OF THE CRIMINAL LAW

The criminal law is a written code defining crime and punishments, centralized under the jurisdiction of the federal government, which enables greater social control and perhaps higher respect for authority. From the consensus viewpoint (discussed in Chapter 1), the law reflects the interests of the majority. However, the conflict model sees the law reflecting the interests of the powerful.[16]

Regardless of which culture or jurisdiction created them or when, criminal codes have several distinct functions. The most important of these include (1) providing social control, (2) discouraging revenge, (3) expressing public opinion and morality, (4) deterring criminal behaviour, and (5) maintaining the social order.

Providing Social Control

The first and primary purpose of the criminal law is to control people's behaviour. It is a written statement of rules to which people must conform. Societies also have unwritten rules of conduct—ordinary customs and conventions, referred to as **folkways**, and universally followed behaviour called norms and morals, or **mores**. However, the criminal law formally prohibits behaviour believed to threaten societal well-being and behaviour that challenges the political authority. For example, the criminal law incorporates centuries-old prohibitions against the following behaviours harmful to others: taking another's possessions, physically harming another person, and damaging property. Similarly, the law prevents actions that challenge the legitimacy of the government, such as treason and collaborating with enemies. Whereas violations of mores and folkways may be informally enforced by any person, control of the criminal law is given to those in political power and administered and enforced by its agents.

Discouraging Revenge

The second function of the criminal law is that by delegating enforcement to others, the criminal law controls an individual's need to seek revenge or vengeance against those who have violated that individual's rights. By punishing people who infringe on the rights, property, and freedom of others, the law shifts the burden of retribution from the individual to the state. As Oliver Wendell Holmes stated, this punishment by the state prevents "the greater evil of private retribution."[17]

Although state retaliation may offend the sensibilities of many citizens, it is greatly preferable to a system in which people seek justice for themselves. If people took the law into their own hands, the risk would be arbitrary and excessive violence. In the Comparative Criminology box on page 43, we look at what happens when people act in self-defence, but the law doesn't agree.

Expressing Public Opinion and Morality

The third function of the criminal law is to reflect constantly changing public opinions and moral values. *Mala in se* crimes, such as murder and forcible rape, are almost universally prohibited, but the prohibition of legislatively created *mala prohibitum* crimes, such as traffic law and gambling violations, changes according to shifting social conditions and attitudes.

---

mala in se Crimes rooted in the core values inherent in our culture, deemed universal.

mala prohibitum Crimes defined by current public opinion and social values, subject to change.

folkways Customs with no moral values attached, such as not interrupting people who are speaking.

mores Customs or conventions essential to a community, which often form the basis of criminal law.

The criminal law codifies these changes in public sentiments. For example, if the government decides to criminalize membership in an organized gang, it will amend the *Criminal Code*. The government has the power to define the boundaries of moral and immoral behaviour through the criminal law. Nonetheless, it is difficult to control public morality through the law because of the problems associated with (1) gauging the will of the majority, (2) respecting the rights of the minority, and (3) enforcing laws that many people consider trivial or self-serving. (An example of how public sentiments change and can lead to changes in the criminal law is the case of Everett Klippert, detailed in Exhibit 2.2.)

The power of the law to express norms and values can be viewed in the development of the crime of **vagrancy** (the moving from place to place by a person who has no visible means of support and who refuses to work). While we understand vagrancy today as relating to homeless persons, the law is actually rooted in a different understanding. Historically, vagrancy laws were formulated in the 14th century after the bubonic plague had killed significant numbers of English peasants, threatening the labour-intensive feudal economy. The law was aimed at preventing workers from leaving their estates to secure higher wages elsewhere. The laws punished migration, thereby mooring peasants to the manors of the nobility and aiding wealthy landowners.[18] From a conflict point of view, vagrancy laws reproduce inequality in society.

However, in an opposing view, early English vagrancy laws were less concerned with maintaining capitalism than with controlling beggars and relieving the overburdened public relief and welfare systems.[19] These laws helped town officials deal with the threat to the community posed by vagrants, "Sabbath breakers," paupers, and the wandering poor. The current crime of vagrancy in Canada (section 179) is a summary offence and is restricted to controlling those who support themselves by crime and those who have been convicted of several sexual offences found loitering near playgrounds.

Deterring Criminal Behaviour

The criminal law's fourth social control function is its ability to deter potential law violators. The threat of punishment is designed to prevent crimes before they occur. For this reason, executions were held in public spaces during the Middle Ages, as warnings to people not to break the law. Although we don't have public executions today, the impact of criminal law is felt through news accounts of long prison sentences that perform the function of **general deterrence**. That is, people are less likely to commit crimes when they know they will be penalized. Clearly, such an idea is based on the assumption that crime is rational and thought out beforehand; it would not work for crimes of passion committed in the heat of the moment or for impulsive crimes.

The **specific deterrence** power of the criminal law is tied to the power it gives the state to sanction offenders. Whereas violations of folkways and mores are controlled informally through social disapproval, criminal law violators are subject to physical coercion and punishment, which are designed to prevent repeat offending. Today, the most common punishments are fines, community supervision or probation, and incarceration in prison. Canada last used the death penalty in 1962, and it was finally abolished in 1976.

EXHIBIT 2.2

The Decriminalization of Homosexuality in Canada

As a result of a case that went to the Supreme Court of Canada (*Klippert v. The Queen*, 1967 S.C.R. 822), Canadian legal history reached a turning point. The case was against Everett Klippert, a homosexual in a small community who was well known to the police. Klippert had previously pleaded guilty to four charges of acts of gross indecency, and his criminal record showed 18 similar convictions.

After Klippert's sentencing, the Crown applied to declare him a dangerous sexual offender. Two psychiatrists had testified that Klippert had never caused injury or pain to any individual, was unlikely to in the future, but would likely recommit the same offence with other consenting male adults. His sexual orientation was viewed by the psychiatrists as incurable. The judge declared Klippert a dangerous sexual offender. Klippert appealed to both the Northwest Territories Court of Appeal and to the Supreme Court of Canada. However, both appeals were unsuccessful.

In the Supreme Court decision, Chief Justice John Cartwright and Mr. Justice Emmett Hall dissented, indicating that they would have allowed the appeal. Their reasons formed part of the government's political decision to decriminalize homosexuality. Partly in response to Klippert's case, Pierre Trudeau made his now-famous comment that "the state has no place in the bedrooms of the nation," and homosexuality was decriminalized in 1969. The *Criminal Law Amendment Act, 1968–69*, amended the *Criminal Code* to exclude homosexuality between consenting adults (persons aged 21 years and older) from the provisions of the *Code* regarding acts of gross indecency.

---

vagrancy   A summary offence crime, meant to prohibit homelessness, begging, and loitering.

general deterrence   Measures, such as long prison sentences for violent crimes, aimed at convincing the potential law violator that the pains associated with crime outweigh its benefits.

specific deterrence   A punishment severe enough to convince convicted offenders never to repeat their crimes, which is based on the principle that an individual can be dissuaded from committing a crime if the cost outweighs the benefit.

Maintaining the Social Order

All legal systems are designed to support and maintain the boundaries of the social system. In medieval England, the law protected the feudal system by defining an orderly system of property transfer and ownership. Modern society is also supported and sustained by the criminal law, which reflects generalized needs and protects the economic and political system. Maintaining social order is the fifth function of the criminal law. In our society, by meting out punishment to those who damage or steal property, the law promotes the activities needed to sustain an economy that is based on the accumulation of wealth. For example, unless the law protected private capital, it would be impossible to conduct business through the use of contracts, promissory notes, credit, banking, and so on. Maintaining a legal climate in which capitalism can thrive is an underlying goal of the criminal law.

Historically, if one merchant cheated another, it was considered a private matter. Then in 1473, in the Carrier's case, an English court ruled that a merchant who held and transported merchandise for another was guilty of theft if he kept the goods for his own purposes.[20] Before the Carrier's case, the law did not consider it a crime for people to keep something that was already in their possession. Breaking with legal precedent, the British court recognized that the new English mercantile trade system could not be sustained if property rights had to be individually enforced. To this day, the substantive criminal law prohibits such business-related acts as fraud, embezzlement, and commercial theft.

THE LEGAL DEFINITION OF A CRIME

To fulfill the legal definition of a crime, several elements must be proved, including that a law defines the act as criminal.

For the state to prove that a crime occurred and that the defendant committed it, the prosecutor must show that the accused engaged in the guilty act, or **actus reus**, and had the **mens rea**, commonly called the intent to commit the act. The actus reus can be taking someone's money, burning a building, or a failure to act when there is a legal duty to do so, such as a parent's neglecting to seek medical attention for a sick child. The mens rea is the person's intent to commit

the crime at the time of the act. For most crimes, both the actus reus and the mens rea must be present for the act to be considered a crime. For example, if Sneaky Joe decides to kill Honest Ed and takes a gun and shoots him, Sneaky Joe can be convicted of the crime of murder because both elements are present: His shooting of Honest Ed is the actus reus; his decision to kill him is the mens rea. However, if Sneaky Joe only thinks about shooting Honest Ed but does nothing about it, the element of actus reus is absent, and no crime has been committed. Conversely, if he shoots him accidentally, the element of mens rea is missing, and the shooting is considered differently. Let us now look more closely at these issues.

Actus Reus

The actus reus is the criminal act itself. For an act to be illegal, the action must be voluntary. For example, one person shooting another could certainly be considered a voluntary act. However, if the shooting occurs while the person holding the gun is sleepwalking, he or she will not be held criminally liable because the act is not voluntary. But if the individual knows that he or she has such a condition and does not take precautions to prevent the act from occurring, the person could be held responsible for the criminal act. The central issue concerning voluntariness is whether the individual has control over his or her actions. For instance, in 1992, the Supreme Court of Canada upheld the acquittal of Kenneth Parks, who drove 23 km and stabbed his mother-in-law to death. The trial judge ruled that Parks had been sleepwalking, which is not a mental disorder as defined in law, and was thus acting involuntarily (non-insane automatism). Had he been found guilty, he could have been jailed for life.[21]

Mens Rea

To be a crime, the elements of a guilty mind must be present. In the legal sense, **intent** can mean carrying out an act intentionally, knowingly, and willingly. However, the definition also encompasses recklessness or negligence. Some crimes require specific intent, and others require general intent, and criminal liability varies. Most crimes require a general intent or the intent to commit the crime. Thus, when Wily Ann picks Honest Bill's pocket and takes his wallet, her intent is to steal. However, specific intent is the intent to accomplish a specific purpose. For example, burglary is the breaking and entering

actus reus An illegal act, such as taking money or shooting someone; also a failure to act, such as not taking proper precautions while driving a car.

mens rea The intent to commit the criminal act, needed for most offences except strict liability.

intent Carrying out an act intentionally, knowingly, and willingly.

of a dwelling house with the intent to steal. The break and enter requires a general intent; the theft is a specific intent.

Criminal intent also exists if the results of an action, though unintended, are certain to occur. For example, Kim wants revenge against her former boyfriend, John. She poisons the punch bowl at John's party, and several guests die as a result of drinking the punch. Kim killed the guests even though that was not the original purpose of her action. The law would hold that Kim or any other person should be substantially certain that the others at the party would drink the punch and be poisoned along with John.

The concept of *mens rea* also encompasses the situation in which a person intends to commit a crime against one person but injures another party instead. For instance, if Stan intends to kill Larry and shoots but misses and kills Jason instead, Stan is guilty of murdering Jason even though he did not intend to do so. This determination of criminal liability falls under the doctrine of **transferred intent**.

Mens rea is also found in situations in which harm has resulted because a person has acted negligently or recklessly. Negligence involves a person's acting unreasonably under the circumstances. For example, if a drunk driver hits a pedestrian, criminal negligence exists. In the case of drunk driving, the law maintains that a "reasonable person" would not drive a car when drunk and thereby unable to control the vehicle. This determination of criminal liability is known as **constructive intent**.

Strict Liability

Usually, both the *actus reus* and the *mens rea* must be present before a person can be convicted of a crime. However, several crimes do not require *mens rea*, because the person is guilty simply by doing what the statute prohibits; mental intent doesn't matter. The Crown needs only to prove the *actus reus* of the offence, unless the accused can show that he or she acted with due diligence or proper care. These offences are known as **strict-liability crimes**, or public welfare offences, and generally apply to statutes other than the *Criminal Code*. Health and safety regulations, traffic laws, and narcotic control laws are strict-liability statutes. For example, a person stopped for speeding is guilty of breaking the traffic laws regardless of whether he or she intended to exceed the speed limit. The underlying purpose of these laws is to protect the public; therefore, intent is not required. Offences of absolute liability cannot be defended against by showing that a person acted with due diligence. However, these offences usually violate the *Charter of Rights*.

CONNECTIONS

Many white-collar crimes, such as pollution of the environment, are considered strict liability. A person who is caught dumping toxic wastes is guilty of a crime, which proves that intent is usually not required. For an analysis of white-collar law enforcement, see Chapter 12.

CRIMINAL DEFENCES

When people defend themselves against criminal charges, they must refute the elements of the crime of which they have been accused. Several approaches can be taken to criminal defence. First, defendants may deny the *actus reus* by arguing that they were falsely accused and that the real culprit has yet to be identified. This is typical of wrongful conviction cases. Defendants may also claim that although they did engage in the criminal act they are accused of, they lacked the *mens rea* needed to be found guilty of the crime. If a person whose mental state is impaired commits a criminal act, that person may claim that he or she lacked the capacity to form sufficient intent to be held criminally responsible for the criminal actions. Excuse defences include, among others, ignorance, mental disorder, and intoxication.

Another type of defence is that of justification. Here, the individual usually admits to committing the criminal act but maintains the act was justified and should not be held criminally liable. Among the justification defences are necessity, duress, self-defence, and entrapment. Persons standing trial for criminal offences may also defend themselves by claiming either that their actions were justified under the circumstances or that their behaviour can be excused by their lack of *mens rea*. If either the physical or mental elements of a crime cannot be proved, the defendant cannot be convicted.

We will now examine some of these defences and justifications in greater detail and cite examples in some classic cases in which these defences were relevant.

Ignorance or Mistake

As a general rule, ignorance of the law is no excuse (CCC section 19). However, courts have recognized that ignorance can be an excuse if the government fails to make public the enactment of a new law, or if the offender relied on an official statement of the law that was later found to be incorrect. Ignorance or mistake can be an excuse if it negates an element of a crime. For example, if Honest Ed purchases stolen merchandise from Sneaky Joe but is unaware that the material was illegally obtained, he cannot be convicted of receiving stolen merchandise because he had no intent to do

transferred intent   An illegal yet unintended act results from the intent to commit a crime.

constructive intent   The finding of criminal liability for an unintentional act that is the result of negligence or recklessness.

strict-liability crimes   Illegal acts with no need for intent, or *mens rea*; they are usually acts that endanger the public welfare, such as illegal dumping of toxic wastes or speeding.

so. This situation is termed an honest *mistake of fact*, but it would be difficult to argue if the item Honest Ed purchased was a diamond ring for only $50.

A notable exception to the defence of ignorance is the law on "consent no defence" (CCC section 150), which says that a belief that a person is of legal age to consent to sex is not a defence unless the accused took all reasonable steps to ascertain the person's age.

In a classic example, the English case of *Tolson* (1889), a woman thought she had been widowed and so remarried, but her husband was alive and eventually resurfaced. Although she was convicted of bigamy, Tolson was acquitted on appeal because of honest mistake of fact. In another case, however, the defence of ignorance was rejected by the Yukon Court of Appeal in the 1965 *Ladue* case. The accused was charged with "indecently interfering with a dead human body" after initiating sexual activity with a deceased female. Ladue claimed that, in his intoxicated state, he believed the woman was merely unconscious.

Not Criminally Responsible on Account of Mental Disorder

In 2002, the Standing Committee on Justice and Human Rights examined section 16 of the *Criminal Code* and changed the former so-called insanity defence to one of mental disorder. Before 1992, a person could be found "not guilty by reason of insanity" (NGRI) and held indefinitely. However, in *R. v. Swain* (1991), the Supreme Court of Canada ruled that indefinite sentences were unconstitutional. Although section 16 exempts an accused from criminal responsibility, he or she is not acquitted. A verdict of "not criminally responsible on account of mental disorder" (NCRMD) will result in a disposition ranging from community living under supervision to detention in a psychiatric facility until fit for release.

A **mental disorder** is defined in section 2 of the *Criminal Code* as a "disease of the mind," and is determined by a trial judge. Mental disorder includes an illness, disorder, or abnormal condition that impairs the functioning of the mind, excluding self-induced states caused by alcohol or drugs, and transitory mental states, such as hysteria and concussion.

Everyone is presumed to be sane, and thus the burden of proving mental disorder rests on the accused. Sometimes, a person who was sane when he or she committed a crime becomes insane soon afterward. In that instance, the person receives psychiatric care until capable of standing trial, and is then tried on the criminal charge because the person actually had *mens rea* at the time the crime was committed. This defence traces its origins to the 18th century, the English common law, and the M'Naghten rule.

Fitness to Stand Trial. To be exempt from criminal responsibility, the accused must have had a mental disorder at the time of the offence that made it impossible to appreciate the nature of the act or to know that it was wrong. The accused must also be "fit to stand trial," which includes being able both to understand the proceedings against them and to instruct a lawyer. The percentage of individuals found unfit for trial is usually less than 1 percent of those charged.

A basic legal principle is that responsibility requires an operating mind, and the law exempts from criminal responsibility those who are incapable of making a rational choice because of mental disorder or immaturity. Experts agree that the law works well to balance the rights of people with mental disorders and the protection of society.

The M'Naghten Rule. In 1843, Daniel M'Naghten, believing Edward Drummond to be Sir Robert Peel, the prime minister of Great Britain, shot and killed Drummond, who was in fact Peel's secretary. At his trial for murder, M'Naghten claimed that he could not be held responsible because of delusions. The jury agreed and found him not guilty by reason of insanity.

Because of the importance of the people involved in the case, the verdict was not well received. The British House of Lords reviewed the decision and requested the court to clarify the law with respect to insane delusions. The court's response became known as the **M'Naghten rule**:

> To establish a defence on the ground of insanity, it must be proved that at the time of the committing of the act the party accused was labouring under such a defect of reason from disease of the mind, as not to know the nature and quality of the act he was doing; or, if he did know, that he did not know he was doing what was wrong.[22]

The M'Naghten rule maintains that an individual has a mental disorder if they are unable to tell the difference between right and wrong. The M'Naghten rule is a widely used test for legal mental disorder; however, over the years it has attracted much criticism. First, "disease of the mind" has never been properly clarified. Second, the rule does not cover situations in which people know right from wrong but cannot control their actions. Third, a defendant's psychological makeup is an issue best raised at the sentencing stage after guilt has been determined. Fourth, criminal responsibility is separate from mental illness. Criminal responsibility is not a trait or quality that can be detected by a psychiatric evaluation. Moreover, some offenders are erroneously judged

---

mental disorder A disease of the mind includes an abnormal condition that impairs functioning, excluding self-induced states caused by alcohol and transitory states such as hysteria.

M'Naghten rule In 1843, an English court established Daniel M'Naghten was not responsible for murder because delusions had caused him to act. The principle of criminal responsibility states that an accused cannot be held legally liable for their actions if they do not know what they are doing or cannot distinguish right from wrong.

by psychiatrists as having a mental illness. Conversely, some people who are found NCRMD because they had a mild personality disturbance in the past have been incarcerated in mental institutions far longer than they would have been imprisoned if they had been convicted of a criminal offence.

> ## CONNECTIONS
>
> One reason that mental disorder pleas are seldom successful is that the association between mental illness and crimes seems to be tenuous at best. For a discussion of this issue, see the sections in Chapter 6 on mental illness and crime.

Intoxication

The third defence that is possible to a criminal charge is intoxication. If, however, it is self-induced intoxication, which includes the taking of alcohol or drugs, such a defence is not possible to a general intent crime of violence, such as sexual assault and assault. Bill C-72, *An Act to Amend the Criminal Code (Self-induced intoxication),* was passed in 1995 and made people accountable for violent acts they committed while intoxicated. This change in the law creates a standard of care, and breach of this standard is criminal fault. However, there are two exceptions to this rule. First, an individual who becomes intoxicated by mistake, through force or under duress, can use involuntary intoxication as a defence. Second, voluntary intoxication is a defence when specific intent is needed, and the person could not have formed the intent because of his or her intoxicated condition. For example, if a person breaks into and enters another's house but is so drunk that he or she cannot form the intent to commit a robbery, the intoxication is a defence against theft but not against the break and enter.

In a classic intoxication defence case, *Otis* (1978), two men consumed a considerable amount of alcohol together. Otis, the accused, struck his friend about the face and head with a lamp and wine bottle. The victim experienced a massive brain hemorrhage and died. Although Otis was convicted of second-degree murder, the Ontario Court of Appeal ordered a retrial. This charge requires specific intent, and the Court ruled that the trial judge had not directed the jury to consider whether the accused had actually formed the intent to kill.

Duress

When a defendant commits an illegal act because the defendant or a third person has been threatened by another with death or serious bodily harm, this situation is called **duress**. This fourth defence, however, does not cover the situation in which defendants commit a serious crime, such as murder or sexual assault, to save themselves or others. The threat has to be immediate, and the accused cannot be a member of the group planning to commit the offence.

The defence of duress was successfully applied in the 1993 *Langlois* case, in which the accused was caught smuggling drugs into a penitentiary where he worked. After receiving several anonymous phone calls threatening him and his family, Langlois had followed an inmate's orders to pick up drugs and deliver them to motorcycle gang members inside the institution. Langlois claimed he did not alert authorities out of fear for his family's safety and doubt that police could offer adequate protection.

In a more recent case, a man named Soheil Biniaz was arrested and charged with trafficking after selling cocaine to an undercover police officer. He argued for an acquittal based

The conflict over the law and its limits starts with the individual protest and the officer enforcing the law, in this case over the anti-shale gas exploration protest in Rexton, New Brunswick.

© THE CANADIAN PRESS/Andrew Vaughan

duress   One of the grounds that excuse an accused from responsibility from an act, if it can be shown that the accused was forced or compelled by someone else to commit a criminal act.

On November 11, 1986, Stephen Kesler, his wife, and two daughters were working in their small drugstore in Calgary when two men entered. One demanded that Mrs. Kesler fill a pillowcase with drugs. The other man removed $150 from the cash register. Kesler attacked him and chased him from the store with a shotgun. Kesler shouted at the fleeing robber to stop, but when he continued to run, Kesler shot him fatally in the back. Kesler returned to the store to confront the other man, who was armed with a .22 rifle. Five shots were fired, and Kesler was hit in the shoulder. When the man fled, Kesler chased him and beat him with the butt of his shotgun. When police arrived, Kesler was charged with second-degree murder. He was eventually found not guilty (Grayson 1992). In a poll undertaken by Gallup in January 1985, just after the Kesler incident, 70 percent of respondents specified that such actions were "sometimes" justified.

In a more recent example, in 2010, Toronto grocer David Chan arrested a shoplifter and detained him for police. He was then charged with assault and forcible confinement. After considerable public debate, the charges were dropped.

The idea of going outside the law to enforce social order is not new. On the frontier, vigilantism was common in the absence of organized law enforcement. In Yukon, for example, in the mid-1890s, law was administered in an extra-legal process called the miners' meeting, an example of frontier justice. Anyone could air a grievance, criminal or civil, and the assembled parties reached a verdict and decided on the disposition in the case. The North-West Mounted Police subsequently put an end to this practice.

Palmer (1978) notes that in 19th century Ontario, people who violated certain standards of behaviour might be subject to various forms of "misrule." The offender might be seized, put on a donkey or wooden beam, and ridden about town or along a country road to the derision of the crowd. Physical beatings, tar and featherings, and even killings occurred. However, an escalating pattern of violence in the early 1800s led to a series of local bylaws outlawing these practices. Hundreds of such ritualized confrontations took place over the course of the 19th century and were common until the beginning of the 20th century.

It might be surprising to realize that Canadians and Americans are equally supportive of spontaneous vigilantism, even though Canada has a lower crime rate and high confidence in its police. When individuals identify with the established order but resort to means that break the law to uphold the established order, they are called vigilantes. Given that spontaneous vigilantes may be victims of crimes and that juries frequently acquit them, vigilantism might be seen as extra-legal, meant to repair a break in social custom. The police and juries are sometimes prepared to accept what some might feel to be excessive actions.

Ritualized confrontations were once means of maintaining social control, but such actions are not desirable in the 21st century. For example, Dobash and Dobash (1981) describe how misrules and charivaris were sometimes carried out against men who beat their wives. The intent was to set limits on the husband's right to discipline his wife. In France in the 18th century, rituals for men who beat their wives were restricted to the month of May. In England in the 19th century, wife beaters were subject to a parade of men, women, and children beating bells, kettles, and frying pans who proceeded to the house of the offending man, where they would chant rhymes and songs.

In Britain in 1500, and for at least 200 years, a woman could be subject to public ridicule if she was domineering or quarrelsome. Forced to wear a "scold's bridle," she would be paraded through the village. By the 20th century, such ritual shaming and confrontations had pretty much disappeared. Conflict resolutions have been appropriated by the state, which reserves to itself the right to try an accused and subject him or her to punishment if found guilty. Regulation and surveillance have become part of the monopoly of the state.

Existing law does not recognize the legitimacy of retribution carried out by individual citizens. However, a large proportion of Canadians report qualified support for vigilantism. Given the objective differences in crime rates between Canada and the United States, it is not surprising that more Americans than Canadians feel threatened by the circumstances in which they live. However, the Canadian support for going outside the law is surprising.

SOURCES: Russell P. Dobash and R. Emerson Dobash, "Community Response to Violence Against Wives: Charivari, Abstract Justice and Patriarchy," *Social Problems* 28 (1981): 563–78; J. Paul Grayson, "Vigilantism in Canada and the United States," *Legal Studies Forum* 16 (1992): 21–39; W. R. Morrison, *Showing the Flag: The Mounted Police and Canadian Sovereignty in the North, 1894–1925* (Vancouver: University of British Columbia Press, 1985); Bryan D. Palmer, "Discordant Music: Charivaris and Whitecapping in Nineteenth Century North America," *Labour* 3 (1978): 5–62; Thomas Stone, "The Mounties as Vigilantes: Perceptions of Community and the Transformation of Law in the Yukon," *Law and Society Review* 14, Fall (1979): 83–114.

on duress because he said he had been beaten, and he and his girlfriend had been threatened with death because of his gambling debts. Despite the duration of time during which he repeated the crime, the court agreed with his perception that he had no alternative, and acquitted him of the charge.[23]

Necessity

A fifth defence is the defence of necessity, which is applied in situations in which a person must break the law to avoid a greater evil caused by natural physical forces (storms, earthquakes, illness). This defence is available only when committing the crime is the lesser of two evils. For example, in the 1981 *Morris* case, the defendant was charged with assault and later acquitted by an Alberta Court. Morris admitted to grabbing his wife's neck during an altercation but argued that he immobilized his wife to prevent her from jumping from their moving vehicle.

However, as the famous English case *Regina v. Dudley and Stephens* indicates, necessity does not justify the intentional killing of another.[24] In that case, three sailors and a cabin boy had been shipwrecked and were floating in the open seas in a lifeboat. After nine days without food and seven without water, two of the sailors, Dudley and Stephens, killed and ate the cabin boy. Four days later, the sailors were rescued. The court acknowledged that the cabin boy most likely would have died naturally because he was in the weakest condition, but nevertheless judged the killing as unjustified.

In Canada, a similar situation involved Martin Hartwell, who piloted a plane that crashed in the Northwest Territories on November 8, 1972. Severely injured, he survived for 31 days in mid-winter until he was rescued. One passenger, a nurse, died on impact, and another, a pregnant woman needing surgery for a premature baby, was injured in the crash and died a few days later. A young boy suffering from acute appendicitis survived for three weeks, during which time he and the pilot ate corned beef, sugar cubes, snow, soap, and candles. During an inquest into events surrounding the crash, it was revealed that the pilot had survived by eventually resorting to cannibalism. Criminal charges were never brought against the pilot, but his actions would certainly have fallen under the defence of necessity.[25]

In a recent twist related to the protest against shale gas in Rexton, New Brunswick (see the photo above), a legal scholar has argued that necessity could be used by environmental activists in their illegal efforts against massive ecological destruction. This would be an important tool in a struggle with heavily outweighed opponents.[26]

Self-Defence

The sixth defence, self-defence, involves a claim that the defendant's actions were justified in response to the provocative behaviour of the victim to protect the defendant's person or property.

An individual is justified in using just enough force as is necessary against another to protect himself or herself against unprovoked assault (CCC section 34) and is not guilty of the harm done. This defence can excuse such crimes as murder, manslaughter, and assault; however, it has two main limits. First, defendants must have a reasonable belief that they are in danger of death or great harm, and that using force is necessary to prevent harm to themselves.

In a classic case, in 1990, the Supreme Court of Canada ruled that in the case of a battered woman, the threat need not be imminent if it is part of a pattern of domestic violence (*R. v. Lavallee,* S.C.C. 852). Angelique Lyn Lavallee was a battered woman in a volatile relationship, and killed her partner late one night by shooting him in the back of the head as he left her room after threatening her. The shooting occurred after an argument in which the appellant had been physically abused and was fearful for her life after being taunted with the threat that either she kill him or he would get her. This case created what has become known as the "battered woman syndrome," an area of law in which Canada is the world leader.

The second limit is that the amount of force used must be no greater than that necessary to prevent personal harm. For example, the accused in the 1998 *Berrigan* case stabbed and killed an unarmed man in the mistaken belief that the victim was drawing a gun from his pocket. Although Berrigan's violent response was not proportionate to the degree of force threatened by the victim, who was actually reaching for a cellphone, the British Columbia Court of Appeal allowed the accused to raise this defence.

In a separate case in 2007, the accused appealed his conviction to the Supreme Court. He alleged that he had been acting in self-defence when he shot and killed a police officer who had shot at him. The court rejected his argument that he had no other way to prevent injury to himself, such as surrendering. However, in an Alberta case in 2005, the court ruled that a man did act in self-defence when he pulled into traffic from a stoplight with an undercover officer hanging from the driver's window. The court agreed with the defendant that he thought he was being assaulted by a hooligan rather than being approached by the police.[27]

The rules concerning self-defence also apply to situations involving the defence of a third person. Thus, if a person reasonably believes that another is in danger of unlawful bodily harm from an assailant, the person may use the force necessary to prevent the danger. Using force to defend property from trespass or theft is allowable if the force is reasonable. In other words, the use of force should be a last resort after requests to stop interfering with the property or legal action have failed. This limit is based on the social policy that human life is more important than property.

Entrapment

The defence of **entrapment** allows the defendant to argue that law enforcement officers encouraged the commission

entrapment A criminal defence maintaining that the police initiated the criminal action.

of a crime, which would not have been committed had it not been for trickery, persuasion, or fraud on the officers' part. If law enforcement officers plan a crime, implant the idea in a person's mind, and pressure that person into committing the act, the person may plead entrapment. This plea is valid because the police cannot induce a person to break the law. However, if an officer simply provides an opportunity for the crime to be committed, and the defendant is willing and ready to act, then the situation is different. For example, if a plainclothes police officer poses as a potential customer and is approached by a prostitute, no entrapment has occurred. However, if the same officer approaches a woman and persuades her to commit an act of prostitution, the defence of entrapment is appropriate. Several Supreme Court cases have ruled that the police cannot randomly test a citizen's virtue.

In conclusion, a variety of defences can be used to justify an illegal act. They each apply to different circumstances and have varying results. Interestingly, in some cases, the defence is that no illegality is in fact involved, as in the Burnt Church fishing controversy of 2000. In a standoff between the Department of Fisheries and Oceans and fishers from the Burnt Church First Nation, the Mi'kmaq pressed for their demand to have their fishing rights recognized, rights that had been affirmed by the Supreme Court of Canada. Similarly, in 2006, the Supreme Court ruled that three New Brunswick men who had taken wood from Crown land to make furniture, build a home, and burn as firewood were exercising their Aboriginal rights, not stealing. That decision involved a consideration of historical treaty rights. In what follows, we look at the influence of the *Charter* on criminal cases.

THE CANADIAN CHARTER OF RIGHTS AND FREEDOMS

The Charter of Rights and Freedoms is the ultimate arbiter of law and legal rights in Canada. The *Charter* is included in the Constitution Act, which was repatriated from Britain in 1982 (see Table 2.3 for a sample of the legal rights that the Charter contains). All laws must uphold the rights guaranteed under the *Charter*. The impact of the *Charter* has been considerable.

Because the *Charter* guarantees rights to the individual that cannot be abridged except in unusual circumstances, these rights are said to be *inalienable*. For example, a person has a right to a lawyer, and appeals of convictions have been launched based on an accused person being denied access to legal advice. The prosecution must also give all the evidence gathered by the police to the defendant so that he or she can make a complete defence. This process, known as

---

TABLE 2.3 Constitution Act 1982—Canadian Charter of Rights and Freedoms—Legal Rights

Whereas Canada is founded upon principles that recognize the supremacy of God and the rule of law...

LIFE, LIBERTY AND SECURITY OF THE PERSON

7. Everyone has the right to life, liberty and security of the person and the right not to be deprived thereof except in accordance with the principles of fundamental justice.

SEARCH OR SEIZURE

8. Everyone has the right to be secure against unreasonable search or seizure.

DETENTION OR IMPRISONMENT

9. Everyone has the right not to be arbitrarily detained or imprisoned.

ARREST OR DETENTION

10. Everyone has the right on arrest or detention
    (a) to be informed promptly of the reasons therefore;
    (b) to retain and instruct counsel without delay and to be informed of that right; and
    (c) to have the validity of the detention determined by way of habeas corpus and to be released if the detention is not lawful.

PROCEEDINGS IN CRIMINAL AND PENAL MATTERS

11. Any person charged with an offence has the right
    (a) to be informed without unreasonable delay of the specific offence;
    (b) to be tried within a reasonable time;
    (c) not to be compelled to be a witness in proceedings against that person in respect of that offence;
    (d) to be presumed innocent until proven guilty according to law in a fair and public hearing by an independent and impartial tribunal;
    (e) not to be denied reasonable bail without just cause;
    (f) except in the case of an offence under military law tried before a military tribunal, to the benefit of trial by jury where the maximum punishment for the offence is imprisonment for five years or a more severe punishment;
    (g) not to be found guilty on account of any act or omission unless, at the time of the act or omission, it constituted an offence under Canadian or international law or was criminal according to the general principles of law recognized by the community of nations;
    (h) if finally acquitted of the offence, not to be tried for it again and, if finally found guilty and punished for the offence, not to be tried or punished for it again; and
    (i) if found guilty for the offence and if the punishment for the offence has been varied between the time of commission and the time of sentencing, to the benefit of the lesser punishment.

TREATMENT OR PUNISHMENT

12. Everyone has the right not to be subjected to any cruel or unusual treatment or punishment.

SELF-INCRIMINATION

13. A witness who testified in any proceedings has the right not to have any incriminating evidence so given used to incriminate that witness in any other proceedings except in a prosecution for perjury or for the giving of contradictory evidence.

INTERPRETER

14. A party or witness in any proceedings who does not understand or speak the language in which the proceedings are conducted or who is deaf has the right to the assistance of an interpreter.

SOURCE: *Constitution Act, 1982.*

disclosure, has become a fundamental principle of Canadian justice and is featured in the Famous Canadian Court Cases box. The principle of disclosure figured largely in the discussion of the wrongful conviction of Donald Marshall, in which it was found that the prosecution had evidence that could have been the basis for his release had it been known to the defence.

In the case of Donald Marshall and others who allege they have been wrongfully convicted, a special provision in the *Criminal Code* can be invoked by which the minister of justice can direct a new trial or appeal if it seems warranted. The Association in Defence of the Wrongfully Convicted (AIDWYC) has played a very important role in securing reviews of wrongful convictions, such as described in the Famous Canadian Criminals box.

The *Charter* has been criticized for doing too much to protect the rights of individuals and not enough to protect society. However, as can be seen in the Famous Canadian Court Cases box, the rights that have been protected are serious and fundamental to living in a democratic society. And although our society has occasional debates regarding whether certain procedural rights have been extended too far, a comparison with other countries can serve as an eye opener.

CHANGING THE CRIMINAL LAW

Governments routinely examine the substantive criminal law. Because the law reflects public opinion regarding various forms of behaviour, what was considered a crime 40 years ago may not be so considered today. Gambling, for example, has been almost totally legalized, leading to most criminal penalties having been removed. However, other new criminal laws have been created, and penalties have been toughened to conform to emerging social issues. Let's look at some examples.

Marijuana   The crime of possessing marijuana has been virtually decriminalized, evidenced by penalties reduced to a fine instead of a prison sentence. In May 1999, Health Minister Allan Rock allowed people to apply to use marijuana for medicinal purposes. However, because initially the drug could not be obtained legally, inevitably someone would be charged for growing marijuana. In 2000, an Alberta judge stayed a charge against Grant Krieger for cultivating marijuana; and, in 2001, it was announced that Canada would become the only country in the world with a government-regulated system for using marijuana as medicine. The health minister denied that allowing marijuana to be used for medicinal purposes was the thin edge of the wedge for legalizing marijuana. Most recently, several U.S. states have decriminalized and regulated the production and sale of marijuana, despite federal prohibitions. In Canada, the federal Health Department has now taken over the licensing of medical marijuana operations, putting an end to homegrown operations.

In 2003, the Supreme Court heard the case of *R. v. Clay*, who was convicted of drug possession and trafficking. It decided that Parliament has the constitutional right to prohibit possession despite evidence that marijuana doesn't harm and that its possession is essentially unenforceable. In 2004, the government reintroduced Bill C-10, *An Act to Amend the Contraventions Act and the Controlled Drugs and Substances Act*. This Bill died on the order paper.

The Canadian Centre for Justice Statistics (CCJS) reports that the rate of drug crimes decreased in 2012, but mainly because of a drop in cannabis-related charges, which comprise about two-thirds of all drug crimes reported by police. The overall rate of persons charged with cannabis possession had fallen probably due to uncertainty within law enforcement. Legislation introduced to decriminalize possession of small amounts of cannabis, together with recent court rulings questioning the constitutionality of laws on cannabis possession, resulted in the police reallocating resources toward more serious drug offences. Crime statistics are discussed more fully in Chapter 3.

Youth Justice   In 2003, the Youth Criminal Justice Act (YCJA) officially replaced the Young Offenders Act. The YCJA addressed various problems in the youth justice system, including the lack of a coherent youth justice philosophy, the highest youth incarceration rate in the Western world, the overuse of courts for minor cases that can be dealt with better outside the courts, sentencing disparities and unfairness in youth sentencing, the lack of reintegration after being released from custody, unfairness in transfers to the adult system, the blurring of serious and less serious offences, and insufficient recognition of the concerns and interests of victims.

Highlights of the Act include an end to transfers to adult court, lowering the age at which a youth can be tried as an adult to 14, reserving custody for violent offences, emphasis on alternative sentencing methods such as community programs, and imposition of mandatory supervision following release.

The government tried to introduce harsher sentences in 2006, arguing the need for general deterrence. However, while the Supreme Court disagreed, a series of high-profile violent youth crimes in 2007 continued to fuel public concern that the law was too lax. The *Nunn Commission* in Nova Scotia, for example, made 34 recommendations on how

> **disclosure**   A principle established in *R. v. Stinchcombe* (1991), where the prosecution must give all evidence gathered by police to the defendant in order to make a complete defence to the charges.

In the following cases, wrongful convictions occurred due to police tunnel vision, prosecutorial non-disclosure, eyewitness error, false confessions, and other systemic problems. In many cases, the intervention of the Association in Defence of the Wrongfully Convicted (AIDWYC) led to defendants' eventual exoneration. Section 690/696 of the CCC allows the minister of justice to use discretion in assisting people believed to have been wrongfully convicted. AIDWYC, founded in 1993, is dedicated to preventing wrongful convictions and reversing those that have already occurred. Presented here are a handful of cases of those who have been wrongly convicted in Canada.

David Milgaard was sentenced in 1970 to life imprisonment for the murder of Gail Miller, a crime for which Larry Fischer was eventually convicted. After years of lobbying and investigation, a new trial was ordered by the Supreme Court in 1992, and the charges were stayed. Milgaard was subsequently exonerated in 1997 by DNA testing arranged by AIDWYC and awarded $10 million in compensation. In this case, police ignored evidence of a serial rapist, perjured testimony was allowed, and a lack of disclosure to the defence could have exonerated Milgaard at the time of his trial.

Donald Marshall Jr. was sentenced in 1971 to life imprisonment for the murder of Sandy Seale, on the basis of police tunnel vision and the coercion of perjured testimony. After spending 11 years in prison, Marshall was acquitted by the Nova Scotia Court of Appeal and was eventually awarded more than $10 million. The inquiry into his case found systemic racism at every level of the justice system. Even at his initial appeal, Marshall was accused of being the author of his own misfortune.

Clayton Johnson was sentenced in 1993 to life imprisonment for murdering his wife after she was found at the base of the cellar stairs. In 1998, Johnson's case was referred to the Nova Scotia Court of Appeal after a reexamination of the forensic evidence, which was found to be faulty. The Crown dropped all charges; and in 2004, Johnson received $2.5 million for legal fees and compensation.

Thomas Sophonow was convicted twice and sentenced to life imprisonment for the 1981 murder of Barbara Stoppel. Both convictions were eventually overturned, and an acquittal was entered in 1985 by the Manitoba Court of Appeal. A key issue was eyewitness misidentification and improper police procedures, despite Johnson having had a solid alibi. DNA tests cleared him in 2000, and it was recommended that he be awarded $2.6 million.

Gregory Parsons was sentenced in 1994 to life imprisonment for murdering his mother, but the Newfoundland Court of Appeal ordered a new trial in 1996, and a stay of proceedings was entered in 1998 on the basis of DNA testing. An acquittal was eventually submitted instead, and Parsons received $650,000 in compensation.

Ronald Dalton was wrongfully convicted in 1989 of murdering his wife, who actually died while choking on food. He spent more than eight years in prison before being acquitted on retrial in 2000. Dalton tried to sue the pathologist who testified at his trial, and his case was the subject of an inquiry into Newfoundland and Labrador's justice system in 2003, along with the cases of Gregory Parsons and Randy Druken.

Guy Paul Morin was sentenced in 1992 to life imprisonment for murdering Christine Jessop. The Ontario Court of Appeal acquitted him in 1995 as a result of DNA testing. Morin and his parents received $1.25 million as a settlement. Morin's story was a classic case of police misconduct and tunnel vision, as attention focused on him to the exclusion of others because of his unusual behaviour.

Herman Kaglik, convicted in 1992 of sexual assault, spent almost five years in jail before being exonerated by DNA evidence. The Northwest Territories Court of Appeal entered an acquittal in 1998. The federal government paid him $1.1 million, the largest compensation package for wrongful conviction for an offence other than murder.

Steven Truscott, 14 years old, was sentenced to death in 1959 for the capital murder of his young friend despite police knowledge of a serial abductor working in the area at the time. Truscott's sentence was commuted to life imprisonment in 1960. In 2004, the minister of justice sent the case to appeal court for review; in 2007, his conviction was overturned; and, in 2008, he was awarded $6.5 million for the miscarriage of justice. Factors involved included poor police work and incompetent medical evidence.

SOURCES: injusticebusters, www.injusticebusters.com; ForJustice, www.forejustice.org; and Innocence Project, www.innocenceproject.org.

better to protect the public after a young offender awaiting trial on a series of charges killed a teacher's aide when he rammed her car with a stolen vehicle.

Assisted Suicide Assisted suicide has been a subject of legal debate in both Canada and the United States. In Michigan, a ban was passed to stop Dr. Jack Kevorkian from practising obitiatry, the act of helping people take their lives. A similar law in Canada was challenged in 1998, when a respirologist at Victoria General Hospital in Halifax was charged with ending the life of a terminally ill cancer patient after he had been taken off life support.[28] A Supreme Court of Canada decision in 1992 denied Sue Rodriguez the right to assisted suicide, which prompted the call for change in the criminal law.

assisted suicide The practice of seeking help from a physician in committing suicide; not legal in Canada.

I was surprised to hear the provincial government has reached an out of court deal with Erin Walsh. The settlement obviates the need to continue with his lawsuit and settles his claim of wrongful conviction once and for all.

With his failing health, the prospect of a lengthy trial would not have been attractive, especially after the announcement last week that there was no agreement admissibility of documents. That difficulty would have set the trial back months, and thus the decision on Walsh's $50 million lawsuit.

(Was the delay a move designed to reach an agreement?) If Walsh died before an agreement was reached, the lawsuit would be dead, too.

Erin Walsh had been charged for the shotgun killing of Chi-Chi Peters, a man he met while drinking with friends. He was quickly arrested, the trial took place within months, and the jury convicted him in an hour. He subsequently spent a decade in prison before being released on parole.

The settlement announcement last Friday states that both parties agreed that the prosecutor and the police acted in accordance with the law. However, we now know that a police report of an overheard jailhouse conversation that pointed to someone else as the killer was not disclosed to the defence. That was not an insignificant document to withhold. It could have been used to raise a reasonable doubt with the jury. On this basis of lack of disclosure, the New Brunswick Court of Appeal overturned the conviction and entered an acquittal in 2008.

(Was the Court of Appeal mistaken in thinking that there was a lack of disclosure?)

Thus, it is curious that another part of the announcement was that both parties agreed that all relevant documents were

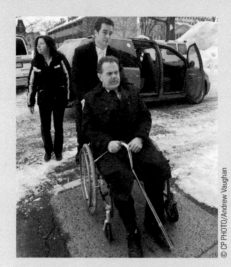

Erin Walsh was convicted in 1975 of a murder in Saint John, New Brunswick. In 2005, in possession of new evidence, he filed an appeal and was exonerated in 2008.

available to Mr. Walsh and his defence counsel at the 1975 trial.

This seems strange because in 2008, the federal Justice Minister ordered the conviction be reviewed in light of new evidence that someone else shot Peters. This new evidence was the undisclosed police report. It was uncovered by Walsh and raised doubts about the conviction.

(Was the Justice Minister mistaken in thinking that there was new evidence?)

The report in question was written by a Saint John police detective who overheard a jail cell conversation. One man asked another, "why did you shoot Peters," to which the other said, "you're going to help me, aren't you?"

The report was not disclosed to Walsh's lawyers by the former Crown prosecutor because he said he didn't think the defence could use it.

What of the claim that there was also other evidence which went missing? Statements that could have backed up Walsh's story that he was attacked by the other men, or that the man in the jail cell had bought ammunition for the shotgun the day before, or that forensic evidence disproved Walsh could have been the shooter?

We will never have answers to these questions because the case is closed, there is silence about the terms of the agreement, and there will not be a public airing of the issues at a trial.

Should a public inquiry be called?

Well, there have been some very important inquiries into wrongful commissions in Canada. They have disclosed police perjury, coercion of witnesses, misuse of jailhouse informants, forensic error, eyewitness misidentification, judicial bias, and prosecutorial misconduct.

I'm not sure there are any rocks that haven't been turned over.

What bothers me in this case is the unwillingness to put everything on the record. No, that's not true. What bothers me is the unwillingness to discuss what is already on the record. Not much digging is required to find out what seems obvious in this case.

Was there criminal conduct in this wrongful conviction? Probably not, given the legal requirements of the day. Was there moral misconduct? Well, now, that's an interesting question.

Unfortunately, that's one that's not likely to be answered. Not in a public inquiry anyway. The need for public legitimation seems pretty shallow, and there's no attempt to hide the fact.

SOURCE: Copyright Chris McCormick, published in the *Daily Gleaner* (Fredericton), October 22, 2009

Various jurisdictions have since approved assisted suicide, including the state of Oregon (in the United States), the Netherlands, Belgium, and Switzerland. In addition, palliative sedation is now used in many jurisdictions to provide continual sedation for a fatally ill person who is in chronic pain.

CONNECTIONS

Euthanasia and assisted suicide are discussed in more detail in Chapter 14, where issues surrounding the rightful connection between the law and morality are debated.

Famous Canadian Court Cases
Legal Rights and the *Charter*

Numerous high-profile cases in Canadian criminal justice history serve as glaring reminders of the disadvantaged position that individuals occupy when accused by the state. As a result, procedural protections have been put into place at all stages of the criminal process to safeguard individuals from injustice. The following cases show how enshrining legal rights in the *Charter* has substantially affected the criminal law.

R. v. Oakes

David Oakes was found guilty of unlawful possession of a narcotic in 1982, a time when section 8 of the *Narcotic Control Act* contained a reverse onus clause. Any person found to be in possession of illegal drugs was presumed to be trafficking unless the defence could prove otherwise. In 1986, the Supreme Court of Canada upheld the Ontario Court of Appeal's judgment on the basis it unreasonably interfered with the section 11 *Charter* right to be presumed innocent until proven guilty. This case is best known for its impact on section 1 of the *Charter*, as Oakes established the proportionality test, the basic framework of analysis that judges use to determine whether limitations on rights and freedoms are justifiable.

R. v. Swain

This *Charter* challenge involved sections 7 (right to life, liberty, and security of the person), 9 (right against arbitrary detention/imprisonment), and 15 (equality rights). Owen Swain was found not guilty of common and aggravated assault by reason of insanity. As such, he was subject to automatic and indefinite detention pursuant to section 542(2) of the *Criminal Code*. Both the trial judge and the Ontario Court of Appeal disagreed that the sentence infringed on Swain's constitutional rights; however, the Supreme Court of Canada overturned the sentence in 1991. Detaining an insanity acquittee indefinitely was deemed an unjustifiable *Charter* violation. Since 1991, section 672.54 of the *Criminal Code* has instructed courts to impose the least restrictive disposition possible after taking into account public safety concerns, the mental condition of the accused, and the goal of reintegrating offenders into society.

R. v. Stinchcombe

Suspected of wrongfully appropriating a client's property, lawyer William Stinchcombe was charged with criminal breach of trust, theft, and fraud. He was convicted after both the Crown and trial judge denied disclosure of witness statements that may have operated in his favour. In response, the Supreme Court of Canada established general disclosure principles respecting the section 11 *Charter* right to make a full answer and defence. Prosecutors are now obligated to provide the defence with all case information that might be relevant to the accused, even if it will not be presented in court. Despite the ruling, disclosure issues jeopardized Stinchcombe's retrial,

and in his third trial, no evidence was called by the Crown. Consequently, the 51-year-old Calgary man was found not guilty after a decade-long legal battle and two trips to Canada's highest court.

R. v. Askov

At stake in *Askov* was the section 11 *Charter* right to be tried within a reasonable time. The four accused in this case were charged with conspiracy to commit extortion and several other offences in 1983, but they were not tried until 1986 and the Ontario judge decided to stay the proceedings. In 1990, the Supreme Court of Canada recommended that delays not exceed six to eight months. This spurred the withdrawal or dismissal of 51,000 cases in Ontario alone, and created powerful incentives for officials to better allocate judicial resources, and for prosecutors to resolve cases in a more timely fashion.

SOURCES: "Case Summary *R. v. Stinchcombe*," Mapleleafweb, www.mapleleafweb.com; Connie Utrecht, "Lower BAC Will Increase Court Backlogs," *Canada Safety Council: Canada's Voice and Resource for Safety*, February 11, 2003; David Pomerant and Glenn Gilmour, "The Impact of *R. v. Stinchcombe* and the New Disclosure Policies of the Attorneys-General," A *Survey of the Preliminary Inquiry in Canada*, April 1993; Robert Sharpe, Katherine Swinton, and Kent Roach, *The Charter of Rights and Freedoms*, 2nd ed. (Toronto: Irwin Law, 2002); *R. v. Askov*, [1990] 2 S.C.R. 1199; *R. v. Oakes*, [1986] 1 S.C.R. 103, www.canlii.org/ca/cas/scc/1986/1986scc7.html; *R. v. Swain*, [1991] 1 S.C.R. 933, www.canlii.org/ca/cas/scc/1991/1991scc41.html.

Stalking Another concern worth discussing here is known as stalking. The Canadian federal government enacted a provision against criminal harassment in 1993, which prohibits and punishes acts defined as the willful, malicious, and repeated following and harassing of another person (see Exhibit 2.3). Stalking is not an insignificant event. A 2003 Ipsos poll showed that 10 percent of Canadians admitted to having stalked an ex-partner after a breakup, while 7 percent said they had sought revenge on a former partner. So while stalking is not a new concern, it involves the ongoing reconsideration of the law.

In 2005, the CCJS published *Family Violence in Canada*,[29] which, using material collected in the 2004 national victim-ization survey, said that 11 percent of women reported being stalked in the previous five years. About two-thirds of criminal harassment victims were female, and over 80 percent of all accused were male. The most common form of stalking is repeated calling or obscene calls; other forms include following, exhibiting threatening behaviour, harming pets, and damaging property.

> **stalking** The criminal offence of following or harassing a victim even though no actual assault or battery has occurred.

Most victims also know their stalkers. Victims said they were most often stalked by friends (23 percent), current or ex-intimate partners (17 percent), and to a lesser extent by neighbours or acquaintances. About one-quarter of all victims were stalked by strangers. The closer the relationship between the victim and stalker, the more likely the stalker would employ numerous methods and would continue for a longer time.

Risk factors for stalking include being young, female, Aboriginal, and single or divorced. Income level, educational status, and urban or rural residence did not affect the incidence of stalking.

Although stalking laws were originally formulated to protect women terrorized by former husbands and boyfriends, the laws have often been applied to people stalked by strangers or casual acquaintances. Critics claim the reaction to the perceived threat of stalking has been exaggerated and that stalking covers other behaviours that are already against the law, such as trespassing. However, others have argued that the gendered character of the crime has finally been recognized.

Cyberstalking refers to the use of the Internet, email, or other electronic communication devices to stalk another person. Some stalkers pursue minors through online chat rooms, establish relationships with them, and later make contact for the purpose of engaging in criminal sexual activities. Others harass their victims electronically, sending repeated, threatening, or harassing messages via email. A cyberstalker may trick others into harassing or threatening a victim by impersonating the victim and posting provocative messages on Internet bulletin boards and/or chat rooms. The stalker then posts the victim's name, phone number, or email address, in hopes that other chat participants will stalk or hassle the victim without the stalker's personal involvement.

Sex offender registration is a response to public concern about sexual predators moving into neighbourhoods. In 1996, the United States passed legislation requiring that the public be informed of the existence of convicted pedophiles in their midst.[30] New laws, such as California's so-called sexual predator law, were passed to keep sexually dangerous individuals in custody even after their sentences have been served. In 2001, Ontario became the first province to enact legislation (called Christopher's Law) to develop a sex offender registry, but no general policy was made regarding **community notification**. In 2004, the minister of public safety introduced draft legislation to create a sex offender registry, later proclaimed into law as the *Sex Offender Information Registration Act*, which requires released offenders to report to the police.

The Crown can already apply on conviction, before sentencing, to have an offender classified as a *dangerous offender* (CCC section 753). Such offenders can be held in jail indefinitely. In 2007, Canada had 349 dangerous offenders in the prison population. The Crown can also classify these offenders as long-term offenders (LTO), which places them under parole for 10 years, 25 years, or for the duration of their life. In 2006, the government proposed a Canadian version of the U.S. three strikes law, under which offenders who commit three sex or violent crimes will be declared a dangerous offender. In general, the number of offenders classified as dangerous or long-term has increased.

In 2000, in response to societal concerns about dangerous sexual predators, Canada launched a National DNA Databank, which enables judges to authorize the collection of DNA samples from convicted offenders. In 2004 and again in 2007, the databank was reinforced with legislation to include criminal harassment and those found NCRMD, to make it an offence to refuse DNA sampling, and to include retroactive offences. DNA was first used in an RCMP investigation in

cyberstalking The use of the Internet, email, or other electronic communication devices to stalk another person.

sex offender registration Requirement that released offenders register and report to the police, and keep them informed of their whereabouts, including any change of address.

community notification Legislation that requires convicted sex offenders to register with local police when they move into an area or neighbourhood.

1989, and the trial of Allan Legere (see the Famous Canadian Criminals box on page 22) was the first to use DNA evidence.

Following the 2004 murder of Holly Jones, police sought saliva samples from all men over age 16 in the area, a very controversial tactic. The Toronto police chief asked that DNA be obtained on arrest in the same way that fingerprints are.

Corporate Crime   In 2004, the minister of justice announced the passage of Bill C-45 regarding the criminal liability of corporations. Commonly referred to as the Westray bill, the legislation makes organizations criminally liable when senior officers commit, or do not stop, criminal actions within the organization or act in such a way as to constitute criminal negligence. The maximum penalty is $100,000. Canada now follows Australia, Britain, and the United States in developing legislation on workplace homicide.

Other future directions of the criminal law remain unclear. Crimes by corporations will certainly be given more attention. Other offences, such as recreational drug use, may be reduced in importance or removed entirely from the criminal law system, while legislation to restrict predators will likely be toughened. In addition, changing technology will require modification in the criminal law. For example, such technologies as automated teller machines and cellphones have already spawned a new generation of criminal acts involving theft of access numbers and cards and software piracy. As the information highway grows, as the nation's computer network advances, and as biotechnology produces new substances, the criminal law will be forced to address threats to the public safety that today are unknown. However, developments in technology, such as DNA testing and electronic monitoring, will change the way in which criminal investigation and punishment are carried out.

CONNECTIONS

The criminal law must be constantly modified to include areas that only a few years earlier were unknown. Chapter 13 contains sections on technological crimes, including the emerging areas of computer crime.

SUMMARY

The substantive criminal law is a set of rules that specifies the behaviour society has outlawed. The criminal law can be distinguished from the civil law on the basis that the former involves powers given to the state to enforce social rules, while the latter controls interactions between private citizens. The criminal law serves several important purposes: It represents public opinion and moral values; it enforces social controls; it deters criminal behaviour and wrongdoing; it punishes transgressors; and it banishes private retribution. It can also entrench the interests of the powerful and be used to resist social change. The criminal law used in Canada traces

its origin to the English common law, which was formulated during the Middle Ages when King Henry II's judges began to use precedents set in one case to guide their decisions.

In Canada's legal system, common-law crimes have been codified into the federal *Criminal Code*. Today, most crimes fall into the category of indictable offences—serious crimes usually punished by a prison term, or summary offences—minor crimes that carry a fine or a light jail sentence. Indictable offences include murder, rape, assault with a deadly weapon, and robbery; summary offences include simple assault and the possession of small amounts of drugs.

Every crime has specific elements. In most instances, these elements include the *actus reus* (guilty act), which is the actual physical part of the crime (for example, taking money or burning a building), and the *mens rea* (guilty mind), which refers to the state of mind of the individual who commits a crime—more specifically, the person's intent to do the act.

At trial, accused individuals can defend themselves by claiming to have lacked *mens rea* and, therefore, not being responsible for the criminal actions. One type of defence is excuse for mental reasons, such as mental disorder, intoxication, necessity, or duress. Another defence is justification by reason of self-defence or entrapment. Of all defences, mental disorder is perhaps the most controversial. In most cases, defendants using a mental disorder defence typically claim that they did not know what they were doing when they committed a crime or that their mental state did not allow them to tell the difference between right and wrong (the M'Naghten rule). Mental disorder defences can also include the claims that the offender lacked the substantial capacity to conform his or her conduct to the criminal law. Regardless of the mental disorder defence used, critics charge that mental illness is separate from legal responsibility and that the two should not be equated. Supporters counter that the mental disorder defence allows people who have mental illness to avoid penal sanctions.

The criminal law is undergoing constant reform. Some acts are being decriminalized—their penalties are being reduced—while other laws are being revised to make penalties for some acts more severe. The law must confront social and technological change.

THINKING LIKE A CRIMINOLOGIST

The Canadian Parliament is considering Bill C-210, an act to prevent the use of the Internet to distribute material that advocates, promotes, or incites racial hatred, violence against woman, or child pornography. The parliamentarians have asked you, a criminologist, to appear before the Justice Committee on Criminal Code Reform to identify whether legal controls are needed to control the use of the Internet. The fear is that unscrupulous entrepreneurs may use the Internet to sell undesirable material, such as pornography. Would you advise Parliament to control the Internet closely? What dangers might be presented by such an attempt at regulation? Is there a trade-off between individual rights and social security?

KEY TERMS

actus reus p. 39
assisted suicide p. 47
Code of Hammurabi p. 29
common law p. 31
community notification p. 50
constructive intent p. 40
cyberstalking p. 50
disclosure p. 46
duress p. 42
entrapment p. 44
folkways p. 37
general deterrence p. 38

inchoate crimes p. 32
indictable offence p. 35
intent p. 39
lex talionis p. 29
M'Naghten rule p. 41
mala in se p. 37
mala prohibitum p. 37
mens rea p. 39
mental disorder p. 41
mores p. 37
Mosaic Code p. 29
oath-helpers p. 30

sex offender registration p. 50
specific deterrence p. 38
stalking p. 49
stare decisis p. 31
strict-liability crimes p. 40
summary offence p. 35
tort law p. 34
transferred intent p. 40
vagrancy p. 38
wergild p. 29

DOING RESEARCH ON THE WEB

In "Criminal Injustice: Understanding the Causes, Effects, and Responses to Wrongful Conviction in Canada," by Myriam S. Denov and Kathryn M. Campbell in the *Journal of Contemporary Criminal Justice* 21 (3), 224–249 (2005), the authors discuss factors responsible for wrongful convictions in Canada. Search on Google News for "wrongful convictions" and find out whether any of these factors are discussed in news accounts.

CRITICAL THINKING QUESTIONS

1. What are the specific aims and purposes of the criminal law? To what extent is the criminal law aimed at controlling social harm?
2. What kinds of activities should be labelled criminal in contemporary society? Do you believe some acts that are now legal should be criminalized and some that are now criminal should be legalized?
3. Under common law, a person must have *mens rea* to be guilty of a crime. Would society be better off if criminal intent were not considered? After all, aren't we merely guessing about a person's actual motivation for committing crime?
4. When is it permissible to use force in self-defence? Considering that the law seeks to prevent crime, not promote it, should the permissible use of self-defence be tightened?
5. Should a person's past history of abuse be considered in judging criminal responsibility? Should the fact that a person was sexually abused as a child be used to defend his or her actions as an adult?

NOTES

1. The historical material in the following sections was derived from numerous sources. The most important include Rene Wormser, *The Story of Law*, rev. ed. (New York: Simon & Schuster, 1962); Jackson Spielvogel, *Western Civilization* (St. Paul, MN: West Publishing, 1991); Eugen Weber, *A Modern History of Europe* (New York: W.W. Norton, 1971); James Heath, *Eighteenth-Century Penal Theory* (New York: Oxford University Press, 1963); David Jones, *History of Criminology* (Westport, CT: Greenwood Press, 1986); Fred Inbau, James Thompson, and James Zagel, *Criminal Law and Its Administration* (Mineola, NY: Foundation Press, 1974); Wayne LaFave and Austin Scott, *Criminal Law*, 2nd ed. (St. Paul, MN: West Publishing, 1986); and Sanford Kadish and Monrad Paulsen, *Criminal Law and Its Processes* (Boston: Little, Brown, 1975).
2. Chris McCormick, "Matters of Record: Documenting Discipline in Nova Scotia Baptist Churches, circa 1800," paper presented to the 12th Church History Workshop, 2001.
3. Wayne LaFave and Austin Scott, *Handbook on Criminal Law* (St. Paul, MN: West Publishing, 1982), 528–529.
4. Caldwell 397 (1784), cited in LaFave and Scott, *Handbook on Criminal Law*, 422.
5. 9 George I, C. 22, 1723, cited in Douglas Hay, "Crime and Justice in Eighteenth and Nineteenth Century England," in *Crime and Justice*, vol. 2, eds. Norval Norris and Michael Tonrey (Chicago: University of Chicago Press, 1980), 51.
6. See, generally, Alfred Lindesmith, *The Addict and the Law* (New York: Vintage Books, 1965), Chapter 1.
7. A. Elizabeth Comack, "The Origins of Canadian Drug Legislation: Labelling versus Class Analysis," in *The New*

Criminologies in Canada, ed. Tom Fleming (Toronto: Oxford, 1985).

8. This section owes much to Alison J. Hatch for her excellent review: "Historical Legacies of Crime and Criminal Justice in Canada," in *Canadian Criminology: Perspectives on Crime and Criminality*, eds. Margaret A. Jackson and Curt T. Griffiths (Toronto: Harcourt Brace, 1995).

9. Pierre Berton, *Klondike: The Last Great Gold Rush, 1896–1899* (Toronto: McClelland and Stewart, 1981).

10. L. Brown and C. Brown, *An Unauthorized History of the R.C.M.P.* (Toronto: James Lorimer, 1973).

11. G.H. Crouse, "A Critique of Canadian Criminal Legislation," *Canadian Bar Review*, 12 (1934): 545–578.

12. William Henry, "Did the Music Say 'Do It'?" *Time*, July 30, 1990, 65; Doug Ireland, "Press Sins," *Village Voice*, March 20, 1990; Linda B. Deutschmann, *Deviance and Social Control* (Scarborough, ON: Nelson, 1994), 91.

13. *Young v. Bella,* [2006] 1 S.C.R. 108, 2006 SCC 3; also see "Wanda Young," at http://www.injusticebusters.com/04/ Young_Wanda.shtml, and "High Court Rules in Young's Favour," CBC, January 27, 2006.

14. For example, see *Brinegar v. United States*, 388 U.S. 160 (1949); *Speiser v. Randall*, 357 U.S. 513 (1958); *In re Winship*, 397 U.S. 358 (1970).

15. Richard Barnhorst, Sherrie Barnhorst, and Kenneth L. Clarke, *Criminal Law and the Canadian Criminal Code*, 2nd ed. (Toronto: McGraw-Hill Ryerson, 1992).

16. Curt T. Griffiths and Simon N. Verdun-Jones, *Canadian Criminal Justice*, 2nd ed. (Toronto: Harcourt Brace, 1994); for a good example of the conflict model, see, generally, R.S. Ratner and John L. McMullan, *State Control: Criminal Justice Politics in Canada* (Vancouver: UBC Press, 1987).

17. Oliver Wendell Holmes, *The Common Law*, ed. Mark De Wolf (Boston: Little, Brown, 1881), 36.

18. William Chambliss, "A Sociological Analysis of the Law of Vagrancy," *Social Problems* 12 (1964): 67–77; William Chambliss, "On Trashing Marxist Criminology," *Criminology* 27 (1989): 231–239.

19. Jeffrey Adler, "A Historical Analysis of the Law of Vagrancy," *Criminology* 27 (1989): 209–230; "Vagging the Demons and Scoundrels: Vagrancy and the Growth of St. Louis, 1830–1861," *Journal of Urban History* 13 (1986): 3–30.

20. *Carrier's case*, Y.B. 13 Edw. 4, f. 9, pl. 5 (Star Chamber and Exchequer Chamber, 1473), discussed at length in Jerome Hall, *Theft, Law and Society* (Indianapolis: Bobbs-Merrill, 1952), Chapter 1.

21. University of Montreal, *R. v. Parks* [1992] 2 S.C.R. 871 (S.C.C.), http://www.lexum. umontreal.ca/csc-scc/en/pub/1992/vol2/ html/1992scr2_0871.html (accessed May 22, 2005).

22. 8 Eng. Rep. 718 (1843).

23. *R. v. Biniaz,* British Columbia Provincial Court, March 9, 2006.

24. *Regina v. Dudley and Stephens,* 14 Q.B. 273 (1884).

25. "Canadian Rescue Pilot of Plane Lost a Month in Arctic," *New York Times*, December 10, 1972, 1; "Pilot Rescued after 32-Day Ordeal in Arctic," *The Globe and Mail*, December 11, 1972, A1; "Pilot Resorted to Cannibalism to Keep Alive, Statement Says," *Globe and Mail*, March 1, 1973, A1; "Bush Pilot Tells of Cannibalism," *New York Times*, March 2, 1973, 5.

26. "Eco-Terrorists facing Armageddon: The defence of necessity and legal normativity in the context of environmental crisis," Hugo Tremblay, *McGill Law Journal*, 58, 2, 2012.

27. *R. v. Boucher,* Quebec Court of Appeal, January 18, 2007; *R. v. Kravshar,* Alberta Provincial Court, November 7, 2005.

28. Brian Bergman, "The Final Hours," *Maclean's*, March 9, 1998, 46–49.

29. "Family Violence in Canada: A Statistical Profile, 2005," CCJS, 2005.

30. "Clinton Signs Tougher Megan's Law," CNN News Service, May 17, 1996.

The Nature and Extent of Crime

Learning Objectives

After reading this chapter, you will be able to:

1. Understand the various sources of information on crime.
2. Be familiar with how crime data is collected.
3. Know the compatibility of different information sources.
4. Discuss the large-scale factors that affect crime rates.
5. Explain different patterns of crime over time.

In 2005, Kelly Ellard was found guilty of second-degree murder in the death of Reena Virk, in Victoria, British Columbia.

© Reuters

How much crime is there? What are the patterns and trends in crime? Who commits crime? What is the nature of criminality? These are some of the most important questions in the study of criminology. Without such information, it would not be possible to formulate theories that explain the onset of crime or to devise social policies that facilitate its control or elimination. With knowledge, we have prediction and then control.

In this chapter, data collected on criminal offences are reviewed to provide a summary of crime patterns and trends. These topics are also discussed elsewhere in the book, particularly Chapters 11 to 14. This chapter addresses several questions: Are crime rates increasing? What factors influence crime rate trends? Where and when does crime take place? What social and individual patterns affect the crime rate? What effect do social class, age, gender, and race have on the crime rate? Finally, the chapter reviews the concept of criminal careers and what we can learn from available crime data regarding the onset, continuation, and termination of criminality.

The above questions address the issue of how to explain crime. However, the factors that *cause* criminal behaviour are different from those forces that affect what we *know* about crime. The causes of crime are discussed in more detail elsewhere, particularly Chapters 5 to 10. However, in terms of what we know about crime, it is important to state that a crime rate does more than reflect the simple facts of crime.

Crime rates are affected by five factors: (1) some crimes are **report-sensitive**, which means that the willingness of the public to report the crime determines whether we know about it; (2) **policing-sensitive** crimes reflect the level of police enforcement; (3) crimes are **definition-sensitive**, so a change in the law changes the rate; (4) **media-sensitive** crimes cause a feedback loop when they are publicized, changing the perceptions of the public and their willingness to report; and (5) of course, there are *real trends* in the number of crimes in society, which leads us to ask what causes crime.

In this first section of the chapter, we will look at the official statistics on crime and consider what they do and do not tell us about crime. In the second section, we will look at such factors as age and class, and briefly consider how they might be causes of crime.

THE UNIFORM CRIME REPORT (UCR)

The Canadian Centre for Justice Statistics (CCJS) has collected information on crime reported by the police every year since 1962 through the **Uniform Crime Report (UCR)** survey. This aggregate count is based on reports from 1,220 separate police detachments comprising 215 different police forces across Canada and represents crimes substantiated through police investigation. The UCR is an invaluable base from which to study crime in society. In 1984, the UCR was revised so that it could collect more detailed information, such as accused and victim characteristics (e.g., age, sex, alcohol and drug consumption, victim–offender relationship, and level of injury) and incident characteristics (e.g., location, time, secondary violations, and weapons). The revised version, the UCR2, gives the police and the public a more specific sense of how and why offences occur by using **incident-based data**. The CCJS has also collected detailed information on murders in the Homicide Survey since 1961.

In addition, a Crime Severity Index was created to reflect different rates in volume and seriousness of different crimes. Using data calculated back to 1998, it assigns a weight to different crimes, so that large changes in less serious crimes do not unduly affect the crime rate. Based on sentencing, murder will have a higher weight than that of mischief, for example.

Collecting the UCR

To compile the UCR, each month police agencies report to the CCJS the **incidence,** or number, of crimes known to them. This official crime count is taken from all complaints of crime received from victims themselves or from officers who discovered the infractions. This crime database represents only what the police know about crime, as some crimes are never detected and others are not reported to the police.

report-sensitive crimes   Crimes are sensitive to victims reporting them—if sexual assault is not reported, then it is unlikely that police will know about it.

policing-sensitive crimes   Crimes sensitive to law enforcement—drug crime is proactively investigated by police; otherwise, it would not be detected.

definition-sensitive crimes   Crimes sensitive to legislative activity—gambling has seen a loosening of criminal sanctions around gaming.

media-sensitive crimes   Crimes sensitive to media attention—youth crime, when covered in the media, increases public concern, which increases reports to police, which makes the news.

Uniform Crime Report (UCR)   An aggregate census based on reports from police, which is the basis for criminological research.

incident-based data   Compared with aggregate (UCR) crime data, incident-based data provides data on specific factors, such as the location of the offence and the relationship between the offender and the victim.

incidence   The number of crimes reported to the police in a given time period.

FIGURE 3.1

Police-Reported Crime Severity Indexes, Canada, 2002 to 2012

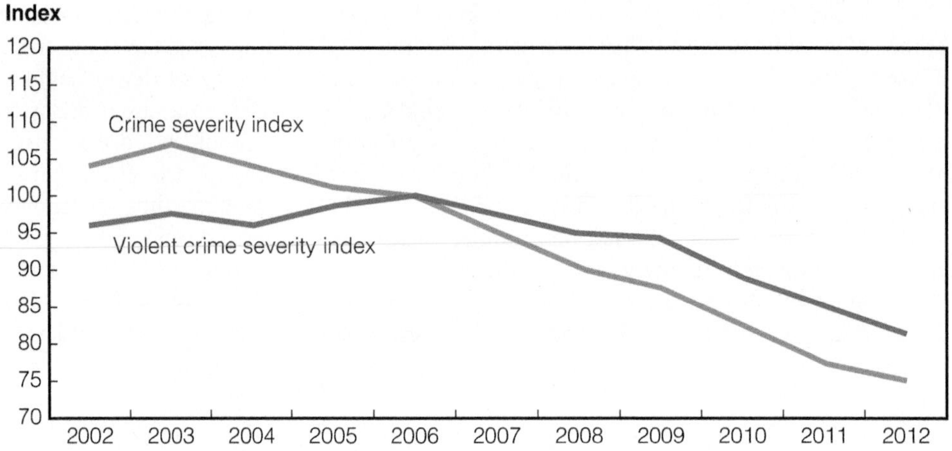

Index

Source: Statistics Canada, Chart 2, "Police-reported Crime Severity Indexes, 2002–2012," http://www.statcan.gc.ca/pub/85-002-x/2013001/article/11854-eng.htm (accessed July 28, 2014).

Note: The base index was set at 100 for 2006 for Canada.

Whenever complaints of crime are determined through investigation to be unfounded or false, they are eliminated from the count. The standard way to display the incidence of crime is to show all the crimes reported to the police that are felt to be **founded**—excluding false reports. Founded crimes are reported even if no one is arrested for the crime, if stolen property is recovered, or if a prosecution is undertaken.

The UCR uses several terms to express crime data. First, the *actual* number of crimes reported to the police and arrests made are expressed as raw figures (for example, 543 murders occurred in 2012). Second, the **percentage change** in the amount of crime between years is computed (for example, there were 55 fewer homicides than in 2011, for a decrease of 10 percent). The percentage change is important because it acts as a soft indicator of whether society is becoming more dangerous. In 2012, there were nearly 2 million criminal incidents, about 36,000 fewer than in 2011.

The third, and perhaps most important, way of expressing crime data is the crime rate per 100,000 people. Calculating the **crime rate** involves dividing the total crimes by the population, which enables changes in the population to be ignored when looking at changes in crime. For example, when the UCR indicates that the murder rate was 1.56 in 2012, it means that for every 100,000 people, less than 2 people were murdered that year. Out of a population of about 33 million people, 543 murders occurred. Therefore, the likelihood of a person being murdered is very low in Canada, as this is the lowest rate since 1966. The formula would look like the following:

crimes/population × 100,000 = rate

543 homicides/33 million population × 100,000 = 1.56

The result is a measure not weighted by the relative population. For example, Ontario has more murders than Newfoundland and Labrador; however, Ontario also has a greater population base, skewing the absolute number of crimes. When the population is factored in, Newfoundland and Labrador's murder rate is second only to Prince Edward Island, while Manitoba, Saskatchewan, and Alberta top the scales. The only jurisdictions with a higher murder rate were the Northwest Territories (11.53) and Nunavut (14.84).

Overall, the crime rate is currently at its lowest in decades.

Traditionally, the incidence of violent crime is low compared with the incidence of property crime committed in Canada. In 2012, Canada had about 415,000 violent offences, more than 1,900,000 property offences, approximately 343,000 other offences (such as counterfeiting), slightly more than 140,000 traffic offences, and an increase in drug offences at 109,000. In addition, there were 12,500 violations under the Youth Criminal Justice Act.

Historically, crime rates have increased moving from east to west across Canada. Little attempt has been made to measure this phenomenon. Hartnagel suggests that provinces and territories with a high rate of in-migration have higher rates of property and violent crime because geographic mobility produces weakened informal social control.[1] Large-scale changes in the economy combined with a rapid change in population have a destabilizing effect. When we look at the severity of crime, we see that the Atlantic provinces scored the lowest, on par with Ontario, followed by Quebec, the Prairies, and then the northern territories.

In 2009, the government began measuring crime using the Crime Severity Index (CSI), as shown in Figure 3.1. The CSI was introduced to compensate for the overall crime rate

founded   Crimes reported to police that are believed to be real; otherwise known as *actual*.

percentage change   An increase or decrease in crime rates over a period of years so that criminologists can tell whether society is becoming more dangerous.

crime rate   The number derived by calculating the ratio of crimes in the whole population expressed as per 100,000 people, providing the relative likelihood of crime occurring.

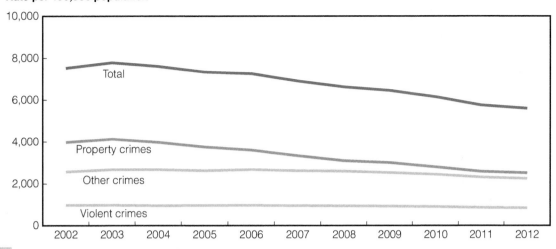

Rate per 100,000 population

FIGURE 3.2

Police-Reported Crime Rates, Canada, 2002 to 2012

Source: Statistics Canada, Table 1a, "Police-reported Crime, Canada, 2002–2012," http://www.statcan.gc.ca/pub/85-002-x/2013001/article/11854/tbl/tbl01a-eng.htm (accessed July 28, 2014).

being driven by high-volume, less-serious offences, such as minor thefts, mischief, and minor assaults. In calculating the CSI, each offence is assigned a weight, which is based on sentences handed down by criminal courts. The more serious the average sentence, the higher the weight for that offence. As can be seen from Figures 3.1 and 3.2, both the crime rate and the crime severity index have declined.

In addition to incidence and rate, police agencies report the total number of crimes that were **cleared**, which means that: (1) at least one person is arrested, charged, and turned over to the court for prosecution; or (2) some element beyond police control precludes the physical arrest of an offender (exceptional means), such as when a suspect dies or leaves the country. A case is considered to be "cleared otherwise" even if no charge is laid, as in the case of a young offender diverted to an alternative measures program. The clearance rate for violent offences is usually higher than for property crimes.

As we proceed through the system, the number of cases being dealt with gradually drops. This process is called **attrition**, or a **crime funnel**, illustrating how the number of crimes punished by the criminal justice system is lower than those committed or reported. For example, of all crimes committed in 2004, only 34 percent were reported. (See Figure 3.2.) The clearance rate was 69 percent for violent crimes and 20 percent for property crimes. About 16 percent of all cases reported to the police in 2003 and 2004 went to court, 58 percent resulted in a conviction, and 35 percent received a custodial sentence. Violent crimes are more likely to be solved because police devote more resources to them, and witnesses and the victim are more likely to be able to identify offenders because they are usually previously acquainted.

In other words, out of 100 crimes committed in 2004, 34 were reported, 15 were solved, 5 went to court, 3 resulted in a conviction, and 1 resulted in a prison sentence.

The Accuracy of the UCR

Despite the importance of the UCR and its wide use by criminologists, its accuracy has limitations. We will address the five main areas of concern: reporting practices, law enforcement practices, legal definitions, media practices, and methodological problems.

Reporting Practices. Many serious crimes are not reported to police by victims and do not become part of the UCR, which means that many crimes are report-sensitive. The reasons for not reporting vary. Some people do not have property insurance and therefore believe it is useless to report theft-related crimes. In other cases, the victim may fear reprisals from the offender, as in cases of domestic violence. The increase in levels of violence reported by women in recent years is probably due to an increase in the reporting of sexual assault and domestic violence. When the sexual assault law was changed in 1983, for example, the report rate went up. In some cases, people simply want to deal with the offence in their way, whether by forgetting it or taking revenge.

> **cleared** Refers to crimes that are determined to be founded, which are then solved or cleared away by the police; do not necessarily result in charges or convictions.
>
> **attrition** The number of cases decreases as they make their way through the criminal justice system; the number of cases investigated by police that result in convictions is a small percentage of the total.
>
> **crime funnel** The phenomenon in which, as cases move farther into the justice system, the number of cases being dealt with gradually drops.

Because of the difficulties posed by under-reporting, victimization surveys are used to measure the number of crimes not reported to the police. The 1993 General Social Survey (GSS) showed that crime reports ranged from a low of 10 percent for sexual assault to a high of 68 percent for attempted break and enter. The average report rate for all household offences was 42 percent. However, the 1999 GSS estimated that 22 percent of sexual assaults and 33 percent of household thefts were reported, and the report rate overall declined to 37 percent. In 2009, the overall rate of victimization dropped slightly to about 25 percent, and the report rate decreased from 34 to 31 percent. Usual reasons given for not reporting crime included the victim believing the incident was a private matter, that nothing could be done, that the victimization was not important enough, or that the offender would seek revenge.[2] Thus, UCR data significantly under-represent the total number of annual criminal events.

Victimization surveys are now used in many countries to complement UCR data. Similar to Canada's findings, the 2006 British Crime Survey (BCS) showed three times as many crimes were reported by victims in the survey as were reported to the police. The 2003 Scottish Crime Survey (SCS) showed that 49 percent of crimes in the SCS were reported to the police.[3] The United States uses the National Crime Victimization Survey to supplement its UCR data.

CONNECTIONS

Victimization surveys have become a vitally important way of measuring the dark figure of crime—crime not reported to police and thus not included in statistics. Victimization surveys are covered in more detail in Chapter 4.

Law Enforcement Practices. The ways in which police departments enforce and record criminal and delinquent activity also affect the validity of UCR statistics. In other words, some crimes are police-sensitive. This effect was recognized more than 40 years ago, when researchers found that the number of burglaries in New York City rose due to a change in the centralized crime reporting system.[4]

It might be appealing to try to improve a police department's public image by lowering the crime rate. Research published in 1983 found provincial and territorial differences in charge rates as a result of discretion on the part of the police.[5] However, such differences were probably more of a problem in the past than today.

Ironically, boosting police efficiency and professionalism may also increase crime rates. Higher crime rates may occur as departments adopt more sophisticated computer-aided technology and hire better-educated and better-trained employees. Crime rates are also affected by the way law enforcement agencies process UCR data. As the number of unsworn (civilian) police employees assigned to dispatching,

record keeping, and criminal incident reporting increased, so too did national crime rates. What appears to be a rising crime rate may be an artifact of improved police record-keeping ability.[6]

How law enforcement agencies interpret the definitions of crimes also affects crime rates. Some departments may define crimes loosely—for example, not reporting a trespass as a burglary, while others pay strict attention to guidelines. These reporting practices may help explain inter-jurisdictional differences in crime.[7]

In the past, arson has been seriously under-reported in the United States because many fire departments didn't report to the Federal Bureau of Investigation, and those that did defined as accidental or spontaneous many fires that were probably set by arsonists.[8] In a more contemporary example, in 2003, the CCJS noted that when the Toronto police implemented a new records management system, the transition had an effect on data quality.

In addition, the way in which police enforce the law affects the crime rate. Such crimes as prostitution, drug crime, traffic offences, and crime on the Internet are sensitive to the resources police devote to detecting the crime. Clearly, if the police go undercover, they will be able to arrest far more prostitutes, johns, and pimps than if they wait for someone to report the crime to them.

For example, Canada handed out only 25 convictions for cannabis possession between 1930 and 1946. Between 1962 and 1972, the number of cases exploded from 20 to 12,000 cases. In 2009, there were 48,981 cases, and in 2012, 57,429. The explosion of cannabis possession charges is largely due to police enforcement. Meanwhile public attitudes are overwhelmingly for decriminalization.

Some research shows that drug enforcement is higher in jurisdictions where forfeiture laws allow police to retain seized assets. Such laws were passed in the early 1980s in a conservative attempt to pay for the increased cost of enforcement and to deny criminals any benefit from the proceeds of crime. The research shows that legislation permitting police to keep seized assets raises drug arrests as a portion of total arrests by about 20 percent, and raises drug arrest rates by about 18 percent. This finding illustrates how police discretion in determining the allocation of police resources is affected by the payoff.[9]

It is difficult to know for certain the influence on crime statistics of variations in police charging practices.[10] Although the police have much discretion in deciding whether to lay charges, the Crown, screening agencies, and alternative measures programs also affect the laying of charges in different jurisdictions. Also, the development of zero-tolerance school violence policies has influenced the number of youths charged with non-sexual assault.

Legal Definitions. Changes to the law also affect crime rates. For example, amendments to the Criminal Code in 1990 broadened the definition of arson to include mischief or suspicious fires. Given that in almost half of fires with losses of more than $500,000, the cause was cited as unknown, what counts as a suspicious fire has some latitude. The result was an increase in arson statistics.[11] The arson rate varied between 30 to 40 incidents per 100,000 from 1978 to 1990, and then suddenly increased by 17 percent in 1990 because of a change in definition.

An arsonist is not always a lone pyromaniac who likes to watch fires; some fires are set to collect insurance money, while others are set for revenge. Sometimes in the case of insurance fraud, arson is difficult to investigate because of a high public tolerance for the crime.

An even more dramatic example of a definition-sensitive crime is sexual assault. Before 1983, a man could not be charged for sexually assaulting his wife; however, changes made to increase reporting also increased the number of men charged with the crime. Canada's sexual assault legislation was amended in 1988 to better deal with child sexual abuse, and again in 1991 to include the concept of consent. The overall result was that while the report rate is still very low, the situation has improved.

Other legislative changes that have affected criminal justice statistics are the *Young Offenders Act* (1984); *Dangerous and Impaired Operation* (1985), which allowed the police to take breath and blood samples; *Property Value Limits* (1985, 1995); and Bill C-68 (1997), which requires firearm owners to be licensed and to register their guns. We could also look at new terrorism and organized crime laws, hate crime laws, and juvenile crime legislation. Most recently, changes due to the *Youth Criminal Justice Act (YCJA)* divert youths who have committed non-violent crimes from the formal criminal justice system. As Figure 3.3 shows, the charge rate of youth crimes dropped, resulting in an apparently larger decrease in youth crime than was actually the case.

In one final example of a definition-sensitive crime, the Canadian *Criminal Code of 1921* made it illegal to have "care or control" of a vehicle while "intoxicated or under the influence of [a] narcotic."[12] In addition, in 1969, Canada introduced so-called breathalyser legislation, which criminalized impaired driving when the driver registers a blood alcohol content (BAC) limit of 80 mg of alcohol in 100 mL of blood. The law made it illegal to drive with more than the allowable limit, and made it mandatory for drivers to take a breath test via a breath analyzer device when requested to do so by the police. Individuals who test over the legal limit or who refuse to provide a breath sample can be charged with a *Criminal Code* offence.[13]

Media Practices. An additional factor to consider when looking at crime is the effect of the media. We often hear of random crimes committed in public by strangers against innocent victims, which encourages the perception that crime is random. We also hear cases where the victims are implicitly or explicitly blamed for the crime that happens to them. Despite victimization not being democratic, distorted media coverage sensitizes the public to fear crime, which then is transformed into police enforcement or legislative changes.

Similarly, the concern over youth crime shows that the public is being overexposed to a relatively infrequent type of crime. In 2007, the youth crime rate decreased 2 percent, and, as with most crime, the highest rates were in Saskatchewan and Manitoba. Despite youth crime being in decline, however, many Canadians felt that youth crime was out of control and that something needed to be done about it. Since the introduction of the YCJA in 2003, the proportion of apprehended youths formally charged with crimes dropped despite a 6 percent increase in the rate of youths cleared otherwise because of the new provisions of the YCJA.

Youth courts in Canada have heard fewer cases in recent years, evidenced by the overall caseload having declined 33 percent since 1991. Five offences typically account for half of the overall youth court caseload: theft, failure to comply with a disposition under the YCJA, common assault, break and enter, and possession of stolen property.

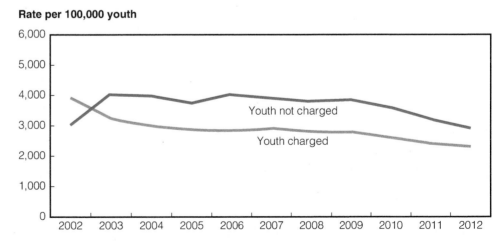

FIGURE 3.3

Youth Accused of Crime, by Clearance Status, Canada, 2002 to 2012

Source: Statistics Canada, Chart 17, "Youth accused of crime, by clearance status, Canada," http://www.statcan.gc.ca/pub/85-002-x/2013001/article/11854-eng.htm#a10 (accessed July 28, 2014).

Note: Youth not charged includes youth diverted from the formal criminal justice system through the use of warnings, cautions, and referrals to community programs.

Crime in the News
Perception and Reality Differ

Recently I listened to Michael Enright and his media-files team discuss the public's irrational fear of crime. They began with a recent Angus Reid poll, which found a disturbingly high percentage of Canadians believe crime has increased. Obviously it hasn't and, in fact, we haven't seen such a relative degree of safety since the 1960s. The panelists then discussed possible reasons for why people got it wrong.

The impression I came away with is that politicians distort issues to get votes, the media sensationalizes by leading with what bleeds, the police exaggerate crime to justify budget requests, and the public is too dim to see what is going on. I didn't learn anything new, and the most intelligent comment was actually a question, when Michael asked his panel, "Why are we more likely to believe we're in danger than to believe we're safe?"

Similarly, Lysiane Gagnon, writing in the *Globe* about a month ago, deplored the fact that Angus Reid also found there is a newfound enthusiasm for bringing back the death penalty. Speaking rhetorically, she asked, "Can it be that in just four years, Stephen Harper's government has managed to change the views of Canadians toward crime and punishment?" The remaining analysis should have been apparent from the title: "The view on crime is irrational." She lamented over the fact that Canadians seem to have adopted the hardline approach of the Conservatives, with over 60 percent supporting the death penalty for murderers, and 30 percent for convicted rapists. In 2004, support for the death penalty was much lower at 48 percent.

I have received several of the Conservatives' tough-on-crime flyers, have listened to the speeches and weighed the promises, but don't think it's as simple as being conned by the politicos. It's not that we buy into retributive discourses, but that we feel more anxious in the face of them. In environmental polls, for example, people feel less angst in times when they believe their governments are doing a good job. The parallel is that people are more afraid of crime when they don't believe the government is doing a good job. A similar counter-intuitive finding is that following a policy of covering news, "if it bleeds it leads" actually drives away media audience.

Sensationalistic, decontextualized reporting does affect a voyeuristic audience, but the more interested and empathetic are going to turn the channel. Sure, there is more and more correspondence in attitudes in Canada, the United States, and Great Britain now than in the past. Many people share tough-on-crime views such as the idea that mandatory, minimum prison terms are a deterrent to criminals, and long prison terms are a good method of fighting crime.

But many people also agree that rehabilitation and discretion are more effective than blind retribution. Criminologists know crime rates have been dropping since 1990.

However, the type of context we can provide when explaining the latest violent shooting or stabbing is difficult and runs counter to evolution.

As animals have evolved, we have had to be alert to danger. And the safer our surroundings become, the more sensitive our radar becomes. We are susceptible to messages of danger, and repeated messages become an "availability heuristic" for making sense of the world.

But how could we ever be expected to put crime news in context? Most of us don't know the true rate of risk, and so to be told we're irrational is not helpful, especially when continuously told what to fear. What we fear is how we feel, however irrational, and to be told otherwise misunderstands the underlying psychology.

To her credit, Ms. Gagnon quotes the pollster in charge of the Angus Reid survey, saying that when a government has a tough crime agenda, it actually feeds a population's fears. And she also quotes the head of the John Howard Society, saying "we are swept up in a miasma of underwear bombers, 9/11, and earthquakes in Haiti—with all this thrown together in a kind of disarticulated confusion.

I like that—disarticulated confusion. Sounds like a state of mind to me.

SOURCE: Copyright Chris McCormick, published in the *Daily Gleaner* (Fredericton), February 25, 2010.

Murder accounted for less than 1 percent of the cases heard in youth court, even though we are more likely to hear about it.[14]

One way to explain the discrepancy between the reality of dropping rates of youth crime and the perception that youth crime is out of control is media coverage. Violent youth crime is overrepresented in the media, while youth property crime is under-represented. The public gets the message that violent youth crime is a large problem. This message distorts perception, which in turn affects the reported rates of youth crime and the public's willingness to press charges, eventually resulting in pressure on politicians to change the law.

In a similar analysis, Bryan Hogeveen of the University of Alberta offers the analysis that media reports of debates in the House of Commons in the late 1990s created a new discursive category that emphasized protecting the public from risks associated with youth crime. The media coverage of public concern about young offenders was based on and showcased political debate and centred around the federal announcement that it would replace the *Young Offenders Act* with a tougher law that would be based on accountability.[15]

FIGURE 3.4
Crime as a Topic

Figure 3.4 begins to map out this relationship between crime and the media, by showing how the cyclical relationship between reporting crime, public sensitivity, political pressure, and police action generates more reports, which the public reads.

The CCJS *Juristat* series is an important source of data for the media because it presents complex information in a way that makes it appealing for the media to report without misrepresenting the facts.[16] The creation of UCR statistics was as much about providing journalists with information about crime as it was about measuring police workload.[17] Today, the media influence the timing and wording of press releases, the types of statistics used, and the types of information presented. The CCJS, the police, and the government employ information officers who provide the media with stories, as it is often beyond the scope of a reporter's ability to question the production of statistical knowledge.[18]

Methodological Problems. Methodological issues also raise questions about the accuracy of the UCR. Among the comments most often cited are the following:

- The definition of a crime can change.
- Non-violent crimes are under-reported.
- Cases are screened as unfounded and founded.
- The notation "cleared by charge" may not be made in the month the offence was committed.
- Reports can sometimes vary in accuracy and completeness.
- If an offender commits multiple crimes, only the most serious is recorded.
- Each act is listed as a single offence for some crimes but not for others.[19]

What does the future hold for the UCR? The changes made in the form of the Revised UCR will enable better analysis of incidents and the characteristics of accused persons and their relationships to victims. The changes made in the Crime Severity Index will better portray trends in the seriousness of crime overall.

SELF-REPORT SURVEYS

The limits of official statistics have led criminologists to seek alternative sources of information to measure crime patterns. As well, because official statistics don't record the personality, attitudes, and behaviour of individual criminals, and under-report such victimless crimes as substance abuse, criminologists have used **self-report surveys** to supplement and expand official data. (See Concept Summary 3.1.)

CONCEPT SUMMARY 3.1

Data Collection Methods

Uniform Crime Report (UCR)
- Data is collected from records of police departments across the nation.
- Strengths of the UCR are its measurement of homicides and arrests. It is a consistent, national sample.
- Weaknesses of the UCR are its omission of crimes not reported to police, its omission of most drug usage, and its reporting errors.

General Social Survey on Victimization
- Data is collected from a national survey of victims.
- Strengths of the GSS are its inclusion of crimes not reported to the police, its use of careful sampling techniques, and its regularity.
- Weaknesses of the GSS are its omission of substance abuse and its reliance on victims' memory and honesty.

Self-Report Surveys
- Data is collected by asking subjects to reveal their own behaviour and participation in delinquent or illegal acts.
- Strengths of self-report surveys are their inclusion of non-reported crimes, substance abuse, and offenders' personal information.
- Weaknesses of self-report surveys are their reliance on the honesty of offenders and their omission of offenders who refuse, or are unable, to participate and who may be the most deviant.

Self-report studies ask participants to reveal information about their law violations. For example, the criminologist can interview people who have been arrested or imprisoned. Subjects can also be telephoned at home or mailed a survey form. Most often, anonymous self-report surveys are administered to large groups through questionnaires. Self-reports are viewed as another mechanism to get at the dark figures of crime, those figures missed by official statistics.

self-report survey A research approach that requires subjects to reveal their own participation in delinquent or criminal acts.

The Focus of Self-Reports

Most self-report studies have focused on juvenile delinquency and youth crime.[20] First, the school setting makes it convenient to test thousands of subjects simultaneously, all of them with the means (pens, desks, time) to respond to a research questionnaire. Second, because school attendance is universal, a school-based self-report survey is an estimate of the activities of a cross-section of the community. Self-reports have also been used to examine the offence histories of prison inmates, drug users, and other groups.

Self-reports can assess the number and frequency of people who have committed illegal acts. They are particularly useful for assessing substance abuse, as most drug use goes undetected by police. Because most surveys also contain items measuring subjects' attitudes, values, personal characteristics, and behaviours, the data obtained from them can be used to test theories, measure attitudes toward crime, and measure the association between crime and family relations, educational attainment, and income.

Self-reports provide a broader picture of the distribution of criminality than do official data because self-reports can estimate the number of criminal offenders unknown to police, some of whom may even be serious or chronic offenders.[21] Self-reports also allow for evaluation of the distribution of criminal behaviour across racial, class, and gender lines to help determine whether official arrest data are truly representative of the offender population or whether they reflect bias, discrimination, or selective enforcement. For example, racial bias may be present if surveys indicate that people from different racial origins report equal amounts of crime, but the official data indicate that people who are members of minority groups are arrested more often than others. However, while self-reports can provide a significant amount of information about offenders that cannot be found in the official statistics, they are not used very often.[22]

One self-report study of 2,001 students aged 12 to 18 from 67 Alberta public and Catholic junior and senior high schools surveyed perceptions of youth crime, violence, and personal safety; victimization; delinquent behaviour; weapons possession at school; and their perceptions of police and the criminal justice system.

Another study, released in 2002, by Tanner and Wortley, surveyed 3,400 high-school students and 400 street youth in Toronto on issues ranging from their experiences of victimization and their perception of the city's youth crime problem to their participation in gangs.

In 2007, as part of the International Youth Survey, a study of more than 3,200 youth in Grades 7 to 9 revealed that 37 percent of Toronto students had sold drugs or had committed acts of violence or property crime. Violent behaviour was more prevalent among boys than girls, and over 40 percent of youth surveyed said they had been victimized at least once in the last 12 months.[23]

The Centre for Addiction and Mental Health and the University of Montreal released in 1998 the first national survey of alcohol and other drug use on university campuses, the Canadian Campus Survey (CCS). A new survey was done in 2004. A random survey collected responses from 6,282 undergraduate students from 40 Canadian universities. Heavy drinking was reported by 16 percent of respondents, and 32 percent reported having used cannabis in the past 12 months. Nine percent of students had used other illicit drugs during the previous year. This type of study demonstrates the value of self-report studies: they survey behaviour that is unlikely to be reported to the police and that has no victim in the traditional sense. Various other drug use surveys in Canada have been conducted by the Addiction Research Foundation and the Canadian Centre on Substance Abuse.

The 2002 Canadian Community Health Survey reported that three million people used marijuana or hashish at least once in the previous year. Seven percent reported using cannabis in 1989 and 12 percent in 2002. Although half said they used it only once a month, 10 percent reported they used it on a weekly basis, and 10 percent said they used it daily. The survey also collected data on the use of cocaine or crack, ecstasy, lysergic acid diethylamide (LSD), other hallucinogens, amphetamines (speed), and heroin. About 2 percent of people aged 15 or older reported using at least one of these drugs in the past year, up from 1 percent in 1994.

The Accuracy of Self-Reports

Though self-report data are useful, some methodological issues surround their accuracy. People will not candidly admit illegal acts. They have nothing to gain by doing so, and those who take the greatest risk are respondents who have official records who may also be engaging in the most criminality. Conversely, some people may exaggerate their criminal acts, may forget the acts, or may be confused about what is being asked. Most surveys contain questions on trivial offences—skipping school, running away, using a fake ID—lumped together with serious crimes, making it difficult to compare the groups. We cannot be certain how valid self-report studies are because we have nothing reliable to measure them against. Correlation with official reports is low because the inadequacies of those reports were largely responsible for the development of self-reports in the first place. Official statistics can show a declining youth crime rate, while self-report and survey data show the opposite.[24]

Various techniques have been used to verify self-report data.[25] The "known group" method compares incarcerated youths with "normal" groups to see whether the former report more delinquency. Another approach uses peer informants to verify a subject's answers. Yet another approach first asks youths whether they have ever been arrested or convicted of a delinquent act, and then checks the official record against their responses. Studies using this method have found a remarkable uniformity between self-reported answers and the official record. The conclusions are that (1) the problems of accuracy in self-reports are surmountable, (2) self-reports are more accurate than most criminologists believe, and (3) self-reports and official statistics are quite compatible.[26]

CONNECTIONS

Criminologists suspect that a few repeat juvenile offenders are responsible for a disproportionate share of serious adult crime. Results would be skewed if even a few of these chronic offenders were absent or refused to participate in a schoolwide self-report survey. For more about chronic offenders, see the discussion in this chapter.

The "Missing Cases" Issue

Although these findings are encouraging, questions remain about the validity of self-reports. Even if 90 percent of students voluntarily participate in a self-report study, researchers don't know whether the few who refuse to participate or who are absent that day make up a significant portion of the school's population of persistent high-rate offenders. School surveys also fail to count incarcerated youth and dropouts, whose numbers may include some of the most serious offenders. Some research suggests that the "missing cases" in self-reports may be more crime-prone than the general population.[27]

Self-reports are weakest in measuring substance abuse.[28] Drug users may significantly under-report the frequency of their substance abuse. For example, Gray and Wish found that less than one-third of juvenile detainees who tested positive for marijuana by urinalysis reported using it. A more recent study in a methadone clinic found a non-reporting user rate of 51 percent. However, the Validity Study conducted as part of the U.S. National Household Survey on Drug Abuse compared drug tests and self-reports in a general population and found a "truthfulness" rate of about 90 percent.[29] These findings illustrate a potential problem of self-report surveys, which perhaps are more likely in samples where anonymity is an issue.

Self-reports are a widely used measure of criminal behaviour, but their accuracy is limited in determining the behaviour of chronic offenders and persistent drug abusers.

CONNECTIONS

Self-report data are used as the standard measure of the nation's youth drug population. When reading the results of national drug use surveys in Chapter 13, keep in mind this research on the validity of self-report -surveys. Are heavy crack cocaine users likely to respond accurately to a self-report survey?

Victim Surveys

After the UCR and self-report surveys, a third source of crime data is surveys that ask people whether they have been victims of crime. Because many victims do not report their experiences to the police, such surveys are another method of getting at the dark figures of crime.

In Canada, telephone surveys are conducted to ask residents whether they have experienced crimes such as sexual assault, robbery, assault, break and enter, motor vehicle theft, household property theft, personal theft, and vandalism. They also examine the victim's experience of crime, the reasons victims decide not to report crimes to the police, and victims' perception of crime overall. Through such surveys, we find that many crimes are not reported to the police.

Many countries began victimization surveys in the 1960s or 1970s. They found the number of criminal victimizations was far higher than previously believed and that many victims failed to report crime to the police, fearing retaliation or official indifference. In Canada, the first victimization was conducted in 1988, and the first national study of violence against women was conducted in 1993. Now, international comparisons can be made with the International Crime Victimization Survey (see Figures 3.5, 3.6, and 3.7) and the World Crime Surveys, both under the auspices of the United Nations.

Surveys on criminal victimization in Canada have been conducted as part of the General Social Survey (GSS) every five years since 1988. The latest is to be conducted in 2014, but its results won't be published until 2015. In these surveys, all respondents were asked about their experiences with criminal victimization and their opinions on a variety of justice-related topics. These topics included their fear of crime and their perceptions about the performance of the police, criminal courts, and prison and parole systems.

Like the UCR and self-report surveys, victimization surveys may suffer from some methodological problems, so their findings must be interpreted with caution. Among the potential problems are the following:

- Overreporting owing to victims' misinterpretation of events. For example, a lost wallet is reported as having been stolen, or an open door is viewed as a burglary attempt.
- "Telescoping" events from the past, in which victims think that events happened more recently than they really did.
- Under-reporting owing to embarrassment of reporting crime to interviewers, fear of getting in trouble, or simply forgetting an incident.
- Inability to record the personal criminal activity of those interviewed, such as drug use or gambling; murder is also not included, for obvious reasons.
- Sampling errors that produce a group of respondents who are not representative of the population.
- Inadequate question format that invalidates responses. Some groups such as adolescents may be particularly susceptible to error because of the question format.[30]

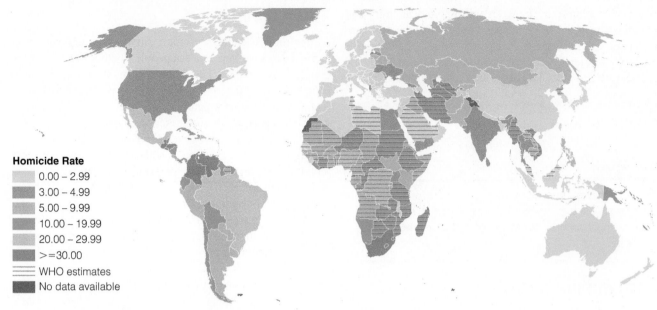

Homicide Rate

- 0.00 – 2.99
- 3.00 – 4.99
- 5.00 – 9.99
- 10.00 – 19.99
- 20.00 – 29.99
- >=30.00
- WHO estimates
- No data available

Note: The boundaries and names shown and the designations used on this map do not imply official endorsement or acceptance by the United Nations. Dashed lines represent undetermined boundaries. The dotted line represents approximately the Line of Control in Jammu and Kashmir agreed upon by India and Pakistan. The final status of Jammu and Kashmir has not yet been agreed upon by the parties. The final boundary between the Republic of Sudan and the Republic of South Sudan has not yet been determined. A dispute exists between the Governments of Argentina and the United Kingdom of Great Britain and Northern Ireland concerning sovereignty over the Falkland Islands (Malvinas).

FIGURE 3.5

Homicide Rates by Country

Source: United Nations, "Map 1.1: Homicide rates, by country or territory," *UNODC Homicide Statistics 2013.*

CONNECTIONS

Victim surveys provide indications of criminal incidents, and they describe the individuals who are most at risk for being hurt by crime and where and when they are most likely to become victimized. Data from crime surveys are used in Chapter 4 to draw a portrait of the nature and extent of victimization in Canada.

Are Crime Statistics Sources Compatible?

Are the various sources of criminal statistics compatible? Each has its own strengths and weaknesses, and although they are difficult to compare, they are complementary.

The UCR is carefully tallied and contains data on an extensive list of crimes, yet it omits the many crimes that victims choose not to report to the police. And the Crime Severity Index itself underscores the need to understand how cases are processed, for example, when it comes to youths and diversion (see Figure 3.8). The GSS does contain unreported crime and important information on the personal characteristics of victims, but it relies on personal recollections that flesh out the official picture of crime. Self-report

surveys can provide information on the personal characteristics of offenders—their attitudes, values, beliefs, and psychological profile—that is unavailable from any other source. Yet, at their core, self-reports rely on the honesty of criminal offenders and drug users, a population not generally known for accuracy and integrity.

Some criminologists believe that the data sources are more compatible than was first believed possible. Although their tallies of crimes are different, the crime patterns and trends they record are often quite similar.[31] For example, all three sources are in general agreement about the personal characteristics of serious criminals (such as age and gender), and where and when crime occurs (such as urban areas, night time, and summer months).

Other criminologists say that the data sources measure separate concepts (for example, reported crimes, actual crimes, and victimization rates). This debate underlines the fact that gathering information about crime and interpreting it is often problematic. Because each source of data uses a different method to obtain results, differences will inevitably occur among them. These differences must be carefully considered when interpreting the data on the nature of and trends in crime.[32]

The following section considers different ways of obtaining information about crime, to expand the idea that there are alternative sources of information to official crime statistics.

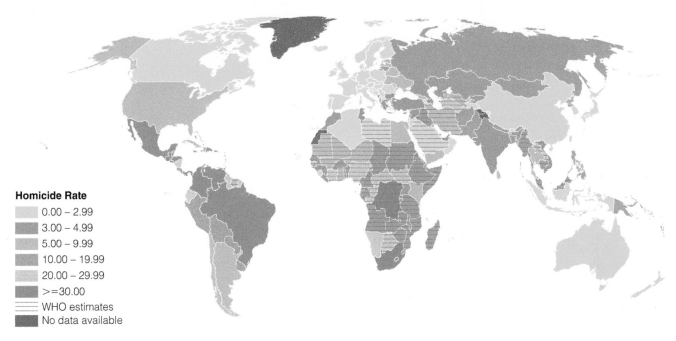

Homicide Rate

- 0.00 – 2.99
- 3.00 – 4.99
- 5.00 – 9.99
- 10.00 – 19.99
- 20.00 – 29.99
- >=30.00
- WHO estimates
- No data available

Note: The boundaries and names shown and the designations used on this map do not imply official endorsement or acceptance by the United Nations. Dashed lines represent undetermined boundaries. The dotted line represents approximately the Line of Control in Jammu and Kashmir agreed upon by India and Pakistan. The final status of Jammu and Kashmir has not yet been agreed upon by the parties. The final boundary between the Republic of Sudan and the Republic of South Sudan has not yet been determined. A dispute exists between the Governments of Argentina and the United Kingdom of Great Britain and Northern Ireland concerning sovereignty over the Falkland Islands (Malvinas).

FIGURE 3.6

Male Homicide Rate, by Country or Territory

Source: United Nations, "Map 1.5: Male homicide rate, by country or territory," *UNODC Homicide Statistics 2013*.

Alternative Sources of Information

Commissions of Inquiry. So far, three major sources of crime data have been discussed: police reports, self-reports, and victim surveys. Other sources of information exist, which are often overlooked in criminological inquiry but are very useful.

The commission of inquiry is unparalleled in its richness as a resource. Commissions of inquiry are appointed by provincial, territorial, or federal governments. They are quasi-judicial, which means they have broad-ranging powers of investigation similar to a court's. They cannot establish individual criminal liability, but they have a broader mandate than a court trial. The information revealed in a commission of inquiry might have been undiscovered or not investigated by the police and might not have been disclosed to victims or publicized in the media.

Some notable examples are the Commission on Systemic Racism in the Ontario Criminal Justice System (1995);[33] the Royal Commission on the Wrongful Incarceration of Donald Marshall Jr. (1989);[34] the commissions of inquiry into the wrongful convictions of James Driskell, David Milgaard, and others; the Report of the Task Force on the Criminal Justice System and Its Impact on the Indian and Métis People of Alberta (1991);[35] the Report of the Aboriginal

Justice Inquiry (1991);[36] the Report of the Saskatchewan Indian Justice Review Committee (1992); and the Report of the Commission of Inquiry into the Shooting Death of Leo LaChance (1993).[37] Other important inquiries include the Cohen Commission on hate crime (1965), the Arbour Commission on the closing of the Kingston Prison for Women (1996), the Gomery inquiry into the federal sponsorship program (2005), and the Miller inquiry into Kingsclear (1995; featured in the upcoming Famous Canadian Criminals box), the Arar Commission of Inquiry (2006), the Air India Commission of Inquiry (2007), and the Nunn Commission of Inquiry (2006), which made recommendations for reforming the youth criminal justice system.

The commissions of inquiry mentioned above add significantly to our knowledge of the treatment of Aboriginal peoples and members of ethnic minority groups in the criminal justice system. Inquiries have contributed to our knowledge of institutional child abuse, for example, in the Mount Cashel Orphanage Inquiry.[38] The children in the orphanage, run by the Irish Christian Brothers, were wards of the welfare system and were subject to extreme physical and sexual abuse, some known by the police as early as 1975.

In Nova Scotia, Chief Justice Stratton of New Brunswick was appointed by the minister of justice to hold an investigation into sexual and physical abuse at various provincial

Homicide Rate

- 0.00 – 2.99
- 3.00 – 4.99
- 5.00 – 9.99
- 10.00 – 19.99
- 20.00 – 29.99
- >=30.00
- WHO estimates
- No data available

Note: The boundaries and names shown and the designations used on this map do not imply official endorsement or acceptance by the United Nations. Dashed lines represent undetermined boundaries. The dotted line represents approximately the Line of Control in Jammu and Kashmir agreed upon by India and Pakistan. The final status of Jammu and Kashmir has not yet been agreed upon by the parties. The final boundary between the Republic of Sudan and the Republic of South Sudan has not yet been determined. A dispute exists between the Governments of Argentina and the United Kingdom of Great Britain and Northern Ireland concerning sovereignty over the Falkland Islands (Malvinas).

FIGURE 3.7

Female Homicide Rate, by Country or Territory

Source: United Nations, "Map 1.6: Female homicide rate, by country or territory," *UNODC Homicide Statistics 2013.*

FIGURE 3.8

Police-Reported Youth Crime Severity Indexes, Canada, 2002 to 2012

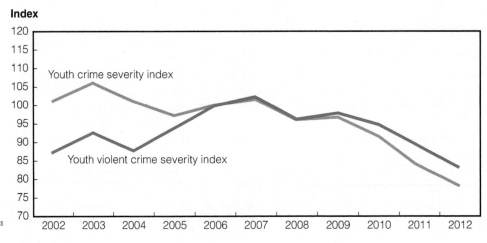

Source: Statistics Canada, "Police-reported Crime Statistics in Canada, 2012," *Canadian Centre for Justice Statistics, Uniform Crime Reporting Survey.* Catalogue no. 85-002-X, 2013.

Note: The base index was set at 100 for 2006 for Canada.

schools and training centres. The inquiry found "a conspiracy of silence and inaction," as those in positions of trust "turned a blind eye and deaf ears and ... chose not to implicate themselves or their co-workers."[39]

Many other commissions of inquiry could be mentioned, from the Krever inquiry into tainted blood to the Dubin inquiry on drug doping in professional sports. They are a fertile source of information on crime that otherwise might not be brought to light.

Explaining Crime Trends

What factors produce increases or decreases in the crime rate? How can the recent decline in the violence rate be explained? Numerous critical factors have been used to explain crime rate trends. For example, how can we account for the patterns we see in Figure 3.9?

Crime trends is a topic that attracts a lot of attention in criminology, as shown by the explanation from economist

Famous Canadian Criminals
A Man Who Abused Boys

In a province where a notorious child abuser, Karl Toft, was convicted in 1992 of sexual assault against 34 victims, there is now a case even more infamous.

Donnie Snook, a former Saint John, New Brunswick, city councillor and youth ministry leader pleaded guilty in 2013 to 46 charges, including sexual child exploitation, interference, and sexual assault. The charges also included making, possessing, and making available child pornography.

There were 17 victims, all protected by a publication ban on release of information that would identify them.

Just like Toft, Snook was in a position of trust and responsibility, which allowed him to commit his crimes with relative impunity. Snook took advantage of his position as a youth leader to exploit his victims.

As well as being a city councillor, he was director of the Saint John Inner City

Donnie Snook is escorted by two police officers.

© Cindy Wilson/*The Telegraph Journal*

Youth Ministry, which delivered a daily hot lunch program for disadvantaged youth. He

had also acted as a foster parent, a board member of the Boys and Girls Club, and was involved in other service activities. In 2003, he was awarded the YMCA Canada Peace Medal.

By pleading guilty to the charges, Snook avoided further trauma for the victims, all between the ages of 5 and 15 at the time of the offences. The crimes were said to have been committed between 2001 and 2013.

Pleading guilty would be a mitigating factor in his sentencing, and also saved several weeks spent prosecuting the case. He was sentenced to 18 years in prison, with credit for time served, and he would be eligible for parole after one-third of that time.

The Crown is appealing the sentence for giving too much credit for time served, and the defense is also appealing on the basis that the length of sentence is unreasonable.

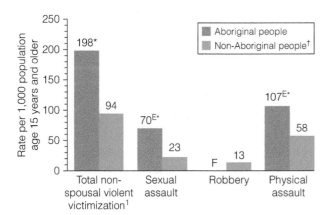

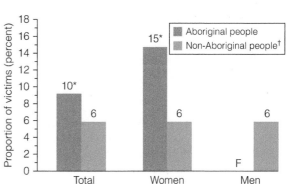

† . Reference category
* . Significantly different from reference category (p < 0.05)
F. Too unreliable to be published
1. Includes robbery and excludes all incidents of spousal sexual and physical assault. Includes incidents that occurred during the 12 months preceding the survey.

FIGURE 3.9

Spousal and Non-Spousal Violent Victimizations in Canada, 2009

Sources: Adapted from Statistics Canada, "*Violent Victimization of Aboriginal People in the Canadian Provinces, 2009*," by Samuel Perreault; *General Social Survey*, 2009; Catalogue no. 85-002-X, released March 11, 2009.

Comparative Criminology
The Politics of Statistics

In 1989, an inspector with the Metro Toronto Police Department said that Black people committed a disproportionate amount of the street crime in the Jane-Finch area. Although this area does have a high rate of crime, the fact that he linked it to an ethnic group provoked controversy. Similarly, in 1991, when a Metro Toronto police sergeant said Vietnamese and mainland Chinese immigrants committed a high percentage of crime in the Asian community, he was publicly reprimanded, despite himself being Chinese and the support he had in the Chinese community. In 1990, the Canadian Centre for Justice Statistics (CCJS) had proposed including statistics on the race of suspects and victims in its crime reports. The idea was quickly abandoned in the face of political pressure. Was this decision a matter of political correctness?

This debate over race is not new. The practice of assigning a racial category to offenders has a long history. Cesare Beccaria, for example, used a racial typology of criminals as part of his explanation for criminality.

So why does the criminal justice system not collect race statistics when it already collects statistics on identifiers, such as age and sex? Furthermore, Correctional Services notes the race of an inmate on its admission forms. Such information is integral to an informed analysis of crime patterns and a criminal's treatment. Statistics on the proportion of Aboriginal people in the criminal justice system, for example, show their extreme overrepresentation in prisons. In 2005–06, Aboriginal people represented 2.7 percent of the general population in Canada but 16.7 percent of the offenders in federal custody. Such disparities can alert us to socio-economic conditions on reserves and possible bias on the part of the justice system. The collection of these data shouldn't be abandoned just because it might be politically incorrect (Gabor 1994).

Statistics on race-related crime are routinely collected in the United States, where race is felt to be a strong predictor of criminal activity. The Federal Bureau of Investigation (FBI) reports that in 1999 29 percent of those arrested were Black, which is far higher than their proportion of the population. Black people are more likely to be arrested for murder (52 percent), robbery (54 percent), and being in possession of stolen property (43 percent). However, they are less likely to be arrested for arson (24 percent), vandalism (22 percent), and driving under the influence (10 percent).

Several reasons explain why the relationship between race and crime is underdeveloped in Canada (Hatt 1994; Johnston 1994; Wortley 1999). The first is found in the innate problem of crime statistics. Again, going back to the United States, 1986 FBI data indicate that 47 percent of violent crimes reported to the police were committed by Black persons. However, the National Crime Victimization Survey (NCVS) found that Black persons were responsible for only 24 percent of violent crimes, about half the official rate. Moreover, self-report surveys found no relationship between ethnicity and crime at all (Roberts 1994; Roberts and Gabor 1990). One conclusion that can be drawn from the official data then is that perhaps people are more likely to report to the police those crimes committed by members of ethnic minorities.

The second reason is the inherent difficulty of measuring race. Ethnicity is not homogeneous. Almost 12 million people identified themselves as being from multiple ethnic origins in the 2001 census, a full 38 percent of Canada's population. As Haggerty (2001) points out, there are real problems in categorizing ethnicity. Is ethnicity a matter of skin colour, country of origin, or self-identification?

The third reason that the relationship between race and crime is not studied more is the possibility that racial information will be used to justify racism. Wortley and Brownfield (1996) found that Black people report a higher rate of stops and searches by police. In a survey of Black, Chinese, and Caucasian residents of Toronto, Black people were most likely to describe experiences of discrimination (Wortley 1996). Forty-three percent of Black males reported having been stopped by the police, compared with 25 percent of Caucasian males, and 19 percent of Chinese males. Four out of 10 Black respondents reported that they had been treated unfairly, compared with 15 percent of Chinese and 10 percent of Caucasians. Between 1986 and 1993, the number of Caucasians incarcerated for drug trafficking increased 151 percent, while the number of Black people committed to detention increased 1,164 percent (Wortley 1999). Research also shows that Black people are less likely to be granted bail (Ontario 1995). The racialization of crime occurs when an ethnic group becomes identified with criminal activity. A 1995 Toronto survey found that 45 percent of people believed a relationship exists between ethnicity and crime. Furthermore, two-thirds of those people thought that Black people committed more crime (Henry, Hastings, and Freer 1996).

In the early 1990s, after University of Western Ontario professor Phillippe Rushton published work relating race and

Steven Levitt at the University of Chicago. He says that crime dropped sharply and unexpectedly in the 1990s because of four major factors: increases in the number of police, increases in prison incarceration, the decline in the use of crack cocaine, and the legalization of abortion in the 1970s. He concludes by saying that the real puzzle is not why crime fell in the 1990s, but rather, why crime did not begin falling earlier.[40]

Another factor that looks promising is the link between changes in parenting standards in the 1970s and delinquency 20 years later. Given that we know punitive parenting is linked to later abusive behaviour, is it surprising that more permissive parenting and declines in corporal punishment have not been linked to declines in youth crime,[41] or that corporal punishment in schools is

68 SECTION 1 | **Concepts of Crime, Law, and Criminology**

NEL

crime (1987, 1988), a debate ensued in the *Canadian Journal of Criminology* (Cernovsky and Litman 1993; Hatt 1994; Johnston 1994; Roberts and Gabor 1990; Rushton 1990, 1994). Julian Roberts and Thomas Gabor of the University of Ottawa wrote that the overrepresentation of certain ethnic minorities in crime statistics was misleading and should not be construed as support for a genetic theory of crime (Roberts and Gabor 1990). Rushton had proposed a theory that Black people were less intelligent and less law-abiding than Caucausians or Asians. Roberts and Gabor argued that a link exists between ethnicity and crime, but it was easily exaggerated and more often misunderstood. Black people are underrepresented in tax fraud and securities violations, and arrests for white-collar crimes are much higher for Caucasians.

When plans were underway to develop the incident-based UCR2 crime survey in the late 1980s, some people recognized the potential to significantly increase the amount of data available on crimes (Haggerty 2001). Specifically, crime could be traced to links with numerous contextual factors associated with the accused, including ethnicity. The Canadian police community was a strong advocate for introducing racial variables. Such data would make it possible to better control the criminality of certain ethnic groups and would reveal systemic racism within the criminal justice system. The common-sense demarcation of race chosen was European origin (Caucasian), South Asian, Black, East/Southeast Asian, Central and South American, and Aboriginal people. By 1991, police forces were providing the centre with data on racial origin, but the project was abandoned after objections were raised by

the prime minister's office, the privacy commissioner of Canada, the media, and academics. One fear was that the police would assign criminals to ethnic groupings already perceived as being criminogenic and thereby reinforce dominant stereotypes.

In fact, two commissions at the time advocated increasing the variety of statistics on the status of Aboriginal people in the criminal justice system (Alberta 1991; Saskatchewan 1993). And other reports, including one on racism in the criminal justice system in Manitoba (Manitoba 1991), were damning in their conclusion that racism was systemic. The Commission of Inquiry that looked at the shooting of Leo LaChance (Saskatchewan 1993) concluded that a major obstacle in the investigation in the case was that racism was not seen to be an issue. The 1989 Royal Commission into the Wrongful Conviction of Donald Marshall Jr. was unequivocal in its finding that racism played a part in his miscarriage of justice (Nova Scotia 1989). So perhaps solid grounds do exist for wanting to conduct research on the relationship among race, crime, and victimization.

SOURCES: Thomas Gabor, "The Suppression of Crime Statistics on Race and Ethnicity: The Price of Political Correctness," *Canadian Journal of Criminology* 36 (1994): 153–63; Ken Hatt, "Reservations about Race and Crime Statistics," *Canadian Journal of Criminology* 36 (1994): 164–66; J. Phillip Johnston, "Academic Approaches to Race–Crime Statistics Do Not Justify Their Collection," *Canadian Journal of Criminology* 36 (1994): 166–74; Scot Wortley, "A Northern Taboo: Research on Race, Crime, and Criminal Justice in Canada," *Canadian Journal of Criminology* 41 (1999): 261–75; Scot Wortley, "Justice for All? Race and Perceptions of Bias in the Ontario Criminal Justice System—A Toronto Survey," *Canadian Journal of Criminology* (October 1996): 439–67; Scot Wortley and David Brownfield, "The Usual Suspects: Race, Age, and Gender Differences in Involuntary Police Contact," 48th Annual Conference of the American Society of Criminology, Chicago, 1996; Julian V. Roberts, "Crime and Race Statistics: Toward a Canadian Solution," *Canadian Journal of Criminology* 36 (1994): 175–85; Julian V. Roberts and Thomas Gabor, "Lombrosian Wine in a New Bottle: Research on Crime and Race," *Canadian Journal of Criminology* 32 (1990): 291–313; J. Phillippe Rushton, "Population Differences in Rule-Following Behaviour: Race, Evolution and Crime," presented to the 39th Annual Meeting of the American Society of Criminology, 1987; J. Phillippe Rushton, "Race Differences in Behaviour: A Review and Evolutionary Analysis," *Personality and Individual Differences* 9 (1988): 1009–24; J. Phillippe Rushton, "Race and Crime: A Reply to Roberts and Gabor," *Canadian Journal of Criminology* 32 (1990): 315–34; J. Phillippe Rushton, "Race and Crime: A Reply to Cernovsky and Litman," *Canadian Journal of Criminology* 36 (1994): 79–83; Zack Z. Cernovsky and Larry C. Litman, "Re-analyses of J.P. Rushton's Crime Data," *Canadian Journal of Criminology* 35 (1993): 31–7; Thomas Gabor and Julian V. Roberts, "Rushton on Race and Crime: The Evidence Remains Unconvincing," *Canadian Journal of Criminology* 32 (1990): 335; Frances Henry, Patricia Hastings, and Brian Freer, "Perceptions of Race and Crime in Ontario: Empirical Evidence from the Toronto and Durham Region," *Canadian Journal of Criminology* (October 1996): 46–476; Kevin Haggerty, *Making Crime Count* (Toronto: University of Toronto Press, 2001); Alberta, *Report of the Aboriginal Justice Inquiry of Manitoba: The Justice System and Aboriginal People*, Chapter 13: Women (Winnipeg: Public Inquiry into the Administration of Justice and Aboriginal People, 1991); Nova Scotia, *Royal Commission on the Donald Marshall, Jr., Prosecution*, Vol. 1, Findings and Recommendations (Halifax: The Commission, 1989); Ontario, *Report of the Commission on Systemic Racism in the Ontario Criminal Justice System* (Toronto: Queen's Printer for Ontario, 1995); Saskatchewan, *Report of Commission of Inquiry into the Shooting Death of Leo LaChance* (Saskatchewan: Queen's Printer, Government of Saskatchewan, 1993).

inversely related to *social capital*, the level of community involvement?[42]

In what follows, we look at some major factors that have been linked to changes in the crime rate.

Age. The age distribution of the population has a great influence on violent crime trends. In general, young people are overrepresented for both property crimes and violent crimes compared with the proportion of their age group in the population.[43] So as a general rule, the crime rate follows the proportion of young males in the population. The postwar baby-boom generation reached their teenage years in the 1960s, when the crime rate began a sharp increase. Because both the victims and the perpetrators of crime tend to fall into the 18- to 25-year-old age category, the rise in crime reflected the age structure of society. With the gradual greying of society in the 1980s and a decline in the birth rate, it was not surprising that the overall crime rate stabilized between 1990 and 1995. Because the number of juveniles is likely to increase over the next decade (baby-boom-echo babies), criminologists fear this increase in the number of youth will signal a return to escalating crime rates.[44]

These trends are based on the assumption that the age-specific crime rate is a constant. However, rates of offending can also change for people at the same age but at different times. For example, people born in the early 1960s had a difficult time entering the legitimate job market in the 1980s, resulting in a heavier and more persistent involvement in criminal activity.[45]

Increases in youth crime are also influenced by bureaucratic processes. In some provinces and territories, a youth can be recommended for alternative measures only at the post-charge stage. Thus, trying to divert more youths from formal court processes might result in more charges being laid initially. In addition, the total number of cases is quite low, and any change calculated as a percentage will thus seem higher. When the effect of the media is factored in, especially its focus on sensationalism, it is easy for the public to get the general impression that youth crime, and especially crime committed by young women, is increasing in seriousness.[46]

Race. No simple relationship exists between race and crime (see the Comparative Criminology box). Any relationship that does exist is most likely a product of various factors, including lack of social opportunity, discrimination, and selective reporting and surveillance by the police. The Commission on Systemic Racism in the Ontario Criminal Justice System was established in 1992 after Black youths rioted, angered by the killing of a young Black man by the police. The commission examined whether criminal justice practices, procedures, and policies reflected systemic racism. The inquiry found that Black people have a disproportionate chance of being charged and imprisoned in Ontario compared with Caucasian people. When charged with drug trafficking, Black people are 27 times more likely than are Caucasian people to be held in pretrial detention, and 20 times more likely to be imprisoned when found guilty. Black people make up 3 percent of Ontario's population but 15 percent of the prison population. Defence counsel who represent members of racial minorities believe there are problems in the bail system and that police lay multiple charges on street-level addicts and drug dealers when they are members of a minority group.

Federal prison system statistics show that the percentage of the prison population that is Black is up to three times higher than the percentage of Black people in the population. For instance, nationally, Black people make up about 6 percent of inmates but 2 percent of the population. Aboriginal offenders represent less than 3 percent of the adult population but comprise about 17 percent of the people incarcerated. In addition, on conviction, Aboriginal offenders are more likely to be incarcerated, and the number of incarcerated Aboriginal offenders is increasing. Aboriginal people are more likely to be incarcerated if convicted, and Aboriginal women are more likely to be incarcerated than Aboriginal men. In Manitoba, Aboriginal women comprise 14 percent of the provincial population but 80 percent of the female jail population. The reconviction rate for Aboriginal men is also higher than for non-Aboriginal men (58 percent compared with 42 percent).[47] The statistical overrepresentation of certain ethnic groups isn't a surprise, but the causes are not clear.[48] What is clear is that racism in the criminal justice system has become an important issue.

Aboriginal People and Crime. In the 2001 census, almost a million people, or about 3 percent of the total population of Canada, identified themselves as being an Aboriginal person.[49] The 2009 GSS found that Aboriginal people were twelve-and-a-half times more likely to be victims of robbery or of physical or sexual assault than were non-Aboriginal people. Those aged 15 to 34 were more likely to experience a violent victimization, and to experience it from someone known to them. They were almost twice as likely to be victims of spousal violence and less likely to report it to the police. Aboriginal people were more likely to be victims of homicide than non-Aboriginal persons. Suicide among males was four times higher than the non-Aboriginal rate.[50]

Aboriginal people are more likely to have contact with police and for more serious reasons. For example, in 2004, they were more likely than non-Aboriginal persons to come into contact with the police as victims of a crime (13 percent compared with 7 percent), as witnesses to a crime (11 percent compared with 6 percent), and by being arrested (5 percent compared with 1 percent). In 2009, the GSS showed that Aboriginal people are less likely than non-Aboriginal people to believe that their police service was doing a good job of treating people fairly (47 percent versus 59 percent) and of enforcing the law (51 percent versus 60 percent). Aboriginal people were also less likely than non-Aboriginals to have confidence in their local police service (70 percent versus 84 percent). Exhibit 3.1 offers more information about Aboriginal people and crime.

The Economy. Debate remains over the effects the economy has on crime rates. Some criminologists believe that a poor economy actually helps to lower crime rates. Unemployed parents are at home to supervise children and guard their homes. And because a poor economy means people have less money to spend, there are fewer valuables around worth stealing. It also seems unlikely that law-abiding, middle-aged workers will suddenly turn to a life of crime if they are laid off during an economic downturn.

However, long-term periods of sustained economic weakness and unemployment eventually affect the crime rate. The recession that occurred in the late 1980s may have produced a climate of hopelessness in North America's largest cities, which saw increased violence rates between 1985 and 1990. Research shows that those people born in the 1960s had higher levels of criminal involvement due to more serious

EXHIBIT 3.1

Quick Facts: General Profile of the Aboriginal Offender

- In 2006, Aboriginal people numbered one million, about 3 percent of the Canadian population.
- In provincial and territorial jurisdictions, 22 percent of custodial admissions are for Aboriginal persons.
- About 18 percent of male inmates are Aboriginal people, as are 31 percent of female inmates.
- Aboriginal offenders are more likely to be under the age of 30.
- Aboriginal offenders are more likely to serve a higher proportion of their sentence before parole.
- Sixty-five percent of Aboriginal offenders have had prior convictions.
- Aboriginal offenders are more likely to be classified as medium and high security risk.
- In 2004, Aboriginal people were three times as likely to be victimized by crime as non-Aboriginal people.
- In 2004, the on-reserve rate of violence was three times higher than off-reserve.
- Almost 90 percent of Aboriginal people report being victims of childhood or adult violence.
- One-third of Aboriginal people under age 15 live in single-parent families.
- In Manitoba, 16 percent of 12- to 17-year-olds are Aboriginal persons, but make up 71 percent of that age group sentenced to custody.
- In 2007, Aboriginal people incarcerated in Saskatchewan were five times as likely to not have a diploma or a job.

SOURCES: National Crime Prevention Centre, *Aboriginal Canadians: Violence, Victimization and Prevention* (Ottawa: Department of Justice, 2001); Nathalie L. Quann and Shelley Trevethan, *Police Reported Aboriginal Crime in Saskatchewan* (Ottawa: Statistics Canada, 2000); "Victimization and Offending among the Aboriginal Population in Canada," *Juristat* 26, 3, 2006; *Corrections and Conditional Release Statistical Overview 2006*, Ottawa: Public Works; Incarceration of Aboriginal People in Adult Correctional Services, *The Daily*, July 21, 2009.

difficulties integrating into the job market in the early 1980s.[51] Inmates are more likely to have been unemployed at the time they committed their offence. Teenage unemployment rates are especially high in urban areas that contain large at-risk populations. Property crimes, such as arson and insurance fraud, also increase during times of economic recession.[52]

While such factors might be relevant within countries, some attempts have been made to discover economic reasons for a difference in reported crime rates across countries. Recent research correlates those differences with levels of development. By comparing data from victimization surveys with data in official records, some rates have been found to be strongly related to development: but it is not crime rates; rather people in richer countries report a higher percentage of crimes. The authors explain that the positive relation thought to exist between development and crime found by previous studies actually just reflects higher levels of reporting. The researchers conclude that development does not affect crime directly; however, they also suggest that reductions in inequality and increases in growth and education are associated with reductions in crime rates.[53]

Social Malaise. Other social problems also affect the crime rate. Increases in the number of single-parent families, in divorce and dropout rates, in drug abuse, and in teen pregnancies are significant. Cross-national research indicates that child homicide rates are greatest in those nations that have the highest rates of illegitimacy and teenage mothers.[54] This conclusion is very controversial because it neglects the social reasons for child poverty. As illegitimacy rates rise and social spending is cut, the rate of violent crime might trend upward. Furthermore, some research shows that legalized abortion in the early 1970s contributed to a lowering of the crime rate in the 1990s. This finding is controversial in itself, but when improving policing and prisons, plus a strong economy, can only account for half of the 30 percent crime rate decline, we need to look at other factors.[55]

A concept that has developed recently in discussions of the relationship between community well-being and crime is social capital. Factors such as length of residence, community structure, and access to formal organizations affect the well-being of a community. Conversely, communities with delinquent social networks, high rates of population turnover, and less access to community services will have higher crime rates.[56]

CONNECTIONS

In Chapter 14, social capital is discussed in terms of an integrated theory of criminality.

Culture and Crime Rates. Culture also makes a difference to crime rates. For example, Japan is a large industrialized country whose population is jammed into overcrowded urban areas, but its crime rate is extremely low compared with many Western countries. How can this difference be explained?

Cultural differences play an important role in controlling crime in Japan. In North America, individualism and self-gratification are emphasized, and success is defined by material goods and possessions. People are more willing to engage in confrontations, which increases the likelihood of violence. In Japan, honour is an important personal trait, and people are deeply loyal to historical traditions, which provide a sense of moral order. Networks of social groups create a strong commitment to social norms. An important cultural norm is patience when seeking change, a cooperative approach to decision making, respect for seniority and age, and concern for society at the expense of the individual. Japanese customs that subordinate personal feelings for the good of the group produce fewer violent confrontations, and violence is considered shameful.[57]

Nowhere are obedience and respect more important in Japan than in relationships with family members and friends.

The Japanese, then, are deterred from criminal behaviour not only by moral principles of right and wrong but also by the need to avoid embarrassment to self, family, and acquaintances. This fear of shame is the key to Japan's low crime rate.[58] In Japan's communitarian society, shameful acts are confronted in an effort to reintegrate offenders into society.

Although Japanese crime rates are low, what crime there is tends to involve organized criminal gangs. Youth in the *bosozoku* (hot-rodder) and "Yankee" gangs flout the conventional dress and speech codes so important in Japan. Members embrace an overtly macho behavioural code, featuring violence, reckless driving, and drug use. They may graduate into *yakuza* gangs, huge organized crime groups that are responsible for drug trafficking, extortion, gambling, and other criminal conspiracies. They are often hired by legitimate enterprises to settle labour disputes, close business deals, and collect debts. Although membership in traditional organized crime families is on the wane in North America, the number of Japanese *yakuza* members has increased sharply.[59]

Robbery rates have dropped in Canada to their lowest rate in 20 years. Of the 31,000 robbery offences in 2006, firearms were used 12 percent of the time. This photo shows a surveillance camera view of an armed bank robber in Vermont.

© AP Photo/Colchester Police

CONNECTIONS

The link among the economy, social malaise, and the crime rate is important for criminological theory. If crime rates are higher in poor or distressed regions, an association may exist between poverty and crime. This is the assumption made by the social structure theorists, who are discussed in Chapter 7.

Guns. Much controversy exists over whether the availability of firearms may influence the crime rate. In 2002, 21 percent of those charged with robbery with a firearm were youths. Numbers in the United States are even higher,[60] which suggests that in at least some areas, juvenile gun possession is all too prevalent and may in part be responsible for increasing violence rates.

In 2006, robbery increased 6 percent in Canada to about 31,000 offences, and firearms were used 12 percent of the time. Youths were charged in 12 percent of cases, and used firearms about 8 percent of the time. By 2012, youth crime had dropped 20 percent since 2009. Robbery itself had dropped to its lowest rate in 20 years. Firearm-related homicides, however, were up, but were still at their lowest rate in 50 years.[61]

CONNECTIONS

Bill C-68 was introduced to the legislature in 1995 as an attempt to control the problem of gun control. Gun control is discussed in more depth in Chapter 10.

The vast majority of violent crime is not committed with a firearm. In 2006, most violent crime (75 percent) was committed by physical force or threats. Weapons were used against 18 percent of victims of violent crimes, and a firearm was used against 2.4 percent of all victims. Police reported 8,105 victims of firearm-related violent crime in 2006, with robbery (49 percent) and assault (29 percent) the most common violations, representing about three-quarters of the total number of firearm-related violent victimizations. Attempted murder and homicide were much more likely to be committed with a firearm compared with robbery and assault. Approximately one-third of victims of attempted murder (36 percent) and homicide (31 percent) had a firearm used against them, compared with 14 percent of robbery victims and 1 percent of victims of assault. By 2012, while violent crime had decreased 26 percent since 2012, the use of firearms was up four percent over 2011. This was about 2000 incidents, for a rate of 6 per 100,000.[62]

Some debate surrounds the extent to which Canadians use firearms for self-protection. Some research shows that Canadians are three times more likely to use guns in self-defence than to commit violent crimes. However, other research shows that self-defence killings were outnumbered by the death of residents in the homes by 40 to 1. If a gun is available, it also increases the likelihood it will be used in a suicide.[63]

The gun control debate in recent years has focused on the effectiveness of the gun registry to prevent gun-related crime. In a 2006 news release based on research by Gary Mauser at Simon Fraser University, it was reported that of 5,194 homicides over a period of nine years, only 2.3 percent were committed with a registered gun.[64]

As can be seen in Figure 3.10, firearm-related crime has consistently decreased between 1998 and 2006, except for the use of handguns. Canada's homicide rate is lower than the rate in the United States, but higher than in Australia, England, and Wales.

Firearm-related crime varies considerably across the country, from a low in the east to a high in the west and north.

FIGURE 3.10

Homicides, by Most
Common Method,
Canada, 1982 to 2012

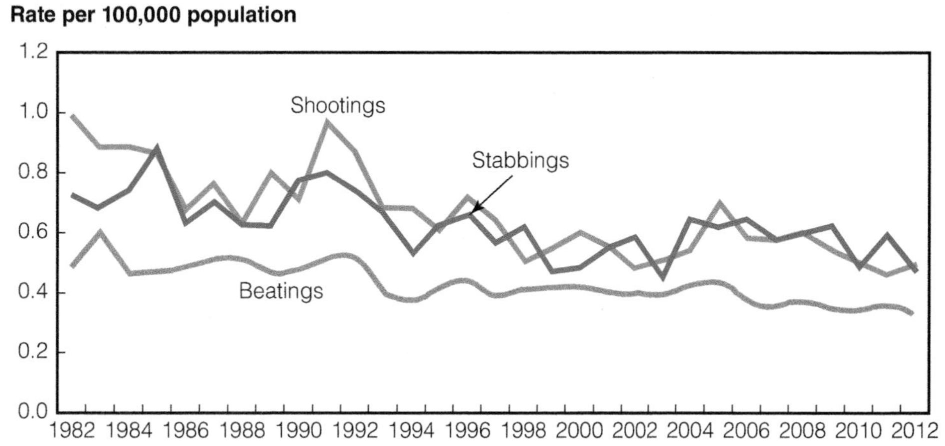

Rate per 100,000 population

Source: Statistics Canada, Chart 7, "Homicides, by most common method, Canada, 1982–2012," http://www.statcan.gc.ca/pub/85-002-x/2013001/article/11882-eng.htm (accessed July 28, 2014).

Persons convicted of a firearm-related violent offence were sentenced to an average of four years in prison, which is double the average sentence length for those convicted of a non-firearm violent offence.

Drugs.   Increasing drug use may affect crime rates. Groups and gangs involved in the urban drug trade recruit juveniles because they work cheaply, are immune from heavy criminal penalties, and are willing to take risks.[65] Because they arm themselves for protection, these drug-dealing kids present a menace that leads to other neighbourhood adolescents also arming themselves for protection. The result is an increasing spiral of violence. The criminalization of drugs creates an illegal drug trade that in turn makes for more gun-related violence.

The violent crime rate between 1980 and 1990 was due in part to the crack cocaine epidemic that swept North America's largest cities and the drug-trafficking gangs that fought over turf. These well-armed gangs did not hesitate to use violence to control territories, intimidate rivals, and increase their market share. In Washington, D.C., 21 percent of homicides were drug-related in 1985; by 1988, this figure had increased to 80 percent.[66] In Canada, in 2012, 95 homicides were gang-related, 80 percent of which were committed with a handgun. In 2012, 68 percent gang-related homicides were drug-related, compared to 11 percent on non-gang-related homicides. Many of these would be motivated by the "settling

of accounts." In 2005, in cases where it is known that alcohol or drugs was involved, police reported that a majority of accused (73 percent) and victims (57 percent) had consumed an intoxicant at the time of the homicide.[67]

In Canada, between 1992 to 2002, about 1 in 10 homicides involved trafficking or the settling of drug-related arguments. Marijuana and cocaine were most likely to be involved in these drug-related homicides, and young adults aged 18 to 24 had the highest drug-related offence rate. Among factors that can affect the rate of drug-related incidents are local police resources and enforcement priorities. Drug offences represent almost 10 percent of all adult criminal court cases, and the accused was found guilty in about half of all cases.[68]

Table 3.1 summarizes the relationship between drugs and crime in three separate ways.

CONNECTIONS

The drug–crime connection is a critical relationship for lawmakers. If drug use causes crime rates to increase, then an outright ban on drugs is warranted. If there is no drug–crime connection, efforts to legalize drug use might be justified. For sections about the drug–crime connection, see Chapter 13.

TABLE 3.1   Summary of the Relationship between Drugs and Crime

Drugs/Crime Relationship	Definition	Examples
Drug-defined offences	Violation of laws that prohibit or regulate the possession, use, distribution, or manufacture of illegal drugs	Growing marijuana; making methamphetamine; selling cocaine, heroin, or marijuana
Drug-related offences	Offences to which a drug's pharmacological effects contribute; offences motivated by the user's need for money to support continued use	Violence; stealing; prostitution
Drug-using lifestyle	The likelihood and frequency of involvement in crime is increased because drug users don't participate in the legitimate economy and are exposed to situations that encourage crime	Emphasis on short-term goals; learning criminal skills from other offenders

SOURCE: Adapted from the White House, "Drug Policy Information Clearinghouse Fact Sheet, 2000," http://www.whitehousedrugpolicy.gov (accessed May 10, 2005).

Justice Policy. Law enforcement experts suggest that reduction in crime rates may be attributed to aggressive police practices that target so-called quality-of-life crimes, such as panhandling, graffiti crime, petty drug dealing, and loitering. By showing that even the smallest infractions will be dealt with seriously, aggressive police departments may be able to discourage potential criminals from committing more serious crimes. This strategy has been called the broken windows approach, discussed elsewhere in this book, which attempts to reduce the incivilities experienced by neighbourhood residents. The issue is open to debate, but reducing fear among residents might enlist their help in fighting crime.[69]

Tough laws that target drug dealing and repeat offenders by imposing lengthy prison terms can have an effect on crime rates. The fear of punishment may inhibit some would-be criminals. Lengthy sentences also help boost the nation's prison population. It is possible that placing a significant number of potentially high-rate offenders behind bars helps stabilize crime rates. This process is called selective incapacitation.

CONNECTIONS

Although a great deal of debate continues over the impact that incarcerating criminals has on the crime rate, most scholars dispute the idea that locking them up can, on its own, bring crime rates down. New criminals are continually coming along to replace those behind bars. For more about this topic, see the sections in Chapter 5 on incapacitation.

What the Future Holds

While current conditions are always subject to change, prediction of future patterns is possible. Steffensmeier and Harer accurately predicted that violent crime would drop during the 1990s as baby boomers passed into middle age. They also predicted property crime rates would at first decline, then level off and begin rising toward the end of the decade as the baby-boom-echo kids born in the early 1980s began to hit their peak crime years. After the year 2000, both property and violent crimes were predicted to increase, although they have in fact decreased, as have youth crime rates.[70]

In 2002, the Canadian Police Survey on Youth Gangs had said the youth gang problem was growing, following increases in the U.S. youth gang population.

Of course, such predictions are based on population trends and can be thrown off by changes in the economy, justice policy, drug use, gun availability, gang membership, and other socio-cultural forces. For example, in 2000, it was predicted that the number of adults charged with drug offences would increase between 1998 and 2003. The CCJS reported that after nearly a decade of increases, the rate of drug crimes fell by 8 percent in 2003. However, by 2006, arrests for cocaine and drugs such as methamphetamine had increased, and over a million cannabis plants had been seized, a six-fold increase since 1993. Drug offences are notoriously subject to bias by the level of enforcement. However, outrage over crime also encourages residents to take actions to reduce crime, including assisting police, enforcing curfews, participating in Neighbourhood Watch, developing recreational facilities for youths, addressing poverty, and so on.

A particularly ambitious attempt to predict crime trends is seen in Table 3.2. The level of recorded crime is forecast to fall to 85 percent of its 1999 level by 2026, and to 81 percent by 2041.

CRIME PATTERNS

What do the various sources of criminological statistics tell us about crime? What is known about the nature of crime and criminals? What trends or patterns exist in the crime rate that can help us understand the causes of crime?

Criminologists look for patterns in crime to gain insight into the nature of crime. If crime rates are consistently higher at certain times, in certain areas, and among certain groups, this knowledge helps explain the cause of crime. For example, if criminal statistics show that crime rates are consistently highest in poor neighbourhoods in large urban areas, then crime may be a function of poverty and neighbourhood decline. If, in contrast, crime rates are spread evenly across the social structure, there would be little evidence that crime has an economic basis; crime might then be linked to socialization, personality, intelligence, or some other trait unrelated to class position or income. What, then, are the main traits and patterns in crime statistics?

The Ecology of Crime

A curious pattern is the relationship between crime and temporal and ecological factors, such as day, season, and climate; temperature; the density of the population; and geographical region.

Day, Season, and Climate. Most reported crimes occur during warm summer months. During the summer, teenagers, who, as a group, usually have the highest crime levels as a proportion of their age group, are out of school and have greater opportunity to commit crime. People spend more time outdoors, making themselves easier targets, and homes are left vacant, which makes them more vulnerable to property crimes.

In the past, in the days before direct deposit, crime rates might have been higher on the day that government social assistance cheques arrived, increasing such activities

TABLE 3.2 Actual and Forecast Rates of Specific Offences, 1999, 2026, 2041

	INCIDENTS PER 100,000			RATIO	
	1999 (actual)	2026	2041	2026/1999	2041/1999
Homicide, attempt	4	3	3	0.86	0.83
Assault and sexual assault, Levels 2 and 3	129	111	107	0.86	0.82
Robbery	92	75	72	0.82	0.78
Sexual assault, Level 1	74	67	64	0.91	0.87
Assault, Level 1	578	499	477	0.86	0.82
Other person	79	69	66	0.88	0.84
Total person	**955**	**825**	**789**	**0.86**	**0.83**
Break and enter	1,044	860	828	0.82	0.79
Other indictable property	645	531	515	0.82	0.80
Theft under	2,227	1,908	1,338	0.83	0.83
Other summary and hybrid property	1,416	1,187	1,138	0.84	0.80
Total property	**5,332**	**4,487**	**4,318**	**0.84**	**0.81**
Administration of justice	287	237	228	0.83	0.79
Public order, morals, weapons	331	278	267	0.87	0.83
Drugs	265	216	209	0.81	0.79
Criminal Code traffic	455	404	388	0.89	0.85
Miscellaneous	953	813	780	0.85	0.82
Total other	**2,283**	**1,949**	**1,872**	**0.85**	**0.82**
Total	**8,570**	**7,261**	**6,978**	**0.85**	**0.81**

SOURCE: Peter Carrington, "Population Aging and Crime in Canada, 2000–2041," *Canadian Journal of Criminology 43*, no. 3 (July 2001): 331–357. Reprinted with permission from University of Toronto Press (www.utpjournals).

as breaking into mailboxes and accosting recipients on the streets. Also, people may have had more disposable income on those days, and the availability of extra money may relate to behaviours associated with crime, such as drinking, partying, gambling, and so on.[71]

Temperature. Some crimes increase with a rise in temperature. Field studies indicate that the rates of some crimes (such as domestic assault) but not all (such as rape) continue to increase as temperatures rise. Research shows that a long stretch of hot and uncomfortable weather is related to an increase in the number of homicides, and Simon Fraser University criminal psychologist Ehor Boyanowsky recommends not arguing about finances or relationships at such times (seriously).[72] The correlation between temperature and assault is strong during the morning and evening hours: A person is four times as likely to be assaulted at midnight when the temperature exceeds 30°C than when the temperature is −20°C![73]

Population Density. Areas with low per capita crime rates tend to be rural, as large urban areas have by far the highest violence rates. These findings are also supported by victim data, which show higher victimization rates in urban areas than in rural areas. However, the relationship between size and criminality is not a simple one. Large urban areas tend to have higher rates of robbery and motor vehicle theft, while

small urban areas tend to have higher overall violent crime rates but lower homicide rates; rural areas tend to have lower rates of violent and property crime, but higher rates of homicide. Canada has one of the highest levels of urbanization in Western countries, with 8 out of 10 Canadians living in an urban centre with a population of 10,000 or more.[74]

Region. Definite differences are apparent in regional crime rates. Historically, Canada has had a pattern of crime rising from east to west, although this trend is beginning to change. For example, crime increased in Saskatchewan during the 1990s, while it declined in most other jurisdictions. Earlier in the chapter, it was suggested that internal migration has resulted in weaker social control in western provinces. For many years, southern American states also had significantly higher rates in almost all crime categories than were found in other regions of the country, indicating a southern subculture of violence. In the United States, large metropolitan areas have experienced the largest increases in crime; however, this is not the pattern in Canada. Smaller cities such as Winnipeg have higher crime rates than Toronto.[75]

What is apparent in Canada is that the rates of violent crime in general, and firearm-related violence in particular, are much higher in the West than in the eastern provinces. What causes this pattern and what can be done about it is difficult to say.

Social Class and Crime

A second crime pattern is the relationship between social class and crime. Traditionally, crime has been thought of as a lower-class phenomenon. People at the lowest rungs of the social structure would appear to have the greatest incentive to commit crimes. Those unable to obtain desired goods and services through conventional means may resort to theft or the selling of narcotics to obtain such goods; these activities are referred to as **instrumental crimes**. Those living in areas of poverty are also believed to engage in disproportionate amounts of **expressive crimes**, such as rape and assault, as a means of expressing their rage, frustration, and anger against society. Alcohol and other drug abuse help fuel violent episodes.[76]

In the United States, where perhaps the relationship between social class and crime has been studied the most, crime rates in inner-city, high-poverty areas are generally higher than those in suburban or wealthier areas; for example, the highest homicide victimization levels are in deteriorated inner-city areas.[77] Studies using arrest records have consistently shown that crime rates in lower-class areas are higher than in wealthier neighbourhoods. Surveys of prison inmates show that most prisoners were members of the lower class and were either unemployed or underemployed in the years before their incarceration.

However, an alternative explanation is that official crime rates are a function of law enforcement practices and do not represent actual criminal behaviour. Police may devote more resources to poor areas, and, consequently, apprehension rates there may be higher. Similarly, police may be more likely to formally arrest and prosecute lower-class citizens than those in the middle and upper classes, which may account for the lower class's overrepresentation in the official statistics and the prison population.

The third explanation is that crimes are class-related; that is, the rich are more likely to commit such crimes as tax fraud, while the poor are more likely to commit crimes important to them, such as welfare fraud. In the end, are any of us innocent?

CONNECTIONS

Crimes of power cause more harm to society than does street crime. This is discussed in Chapter 12.

Evidence for a Class–Crime Relationship. Using self-report data to test the class–crime relationship, early studies conducted in the 1950s did not find a direct relationship between social class and youth crime. They found that socio-economic class was related to official processing by police, court, and correctional agencies but not to the actual commission of crimes. In addition, factors generally associated with lower-class membership, such as broken homes, were found to be related to institutionalization but not to admissions of delinquency.[78]

For more than 20 years, self-report studies could not prove a class–crime relationship: If the poor possessed more extensive criminal records than the wealthy, it was because of differential law enforcement and not because of behaviour. The definitive work on this subject, a meta-review of 35 studies on the relationship between class and crime, concluded that little support existed for a lower class–crime connection.[79] In 1990, an update again found little evidence to support such a connection.[80] Consequently, official statistics probably reflect class bias in the processing of offenders from lower classes.

If a study includes trivial offences, such as using a false ID or drinking alcohol, these offences inflate the overall statistics. Youth often engage in such offences as petty larceny, drug use, and simple assault.[81] Those studies showing middle- and lower-class youths to be equally delinquent rely on measures weighted toward minor crimes (for example, using a false ID or skipping school); when serious crimes, such as burglary and assault, are used in the comparison, lower-class youths are more delinquent.[82]

A 2001 *Juristat* study on youth delinquency concluded that there was not a strong link between property crime and income. Furthermore, between 39 percent and 44 percent of children from all income groups reported having been involved in some or a lot of aggressiveness.[83]

The Class–Crime Controversy. However, the relationship between class and crime is an important one for criminological theory. If crime is related to social class, then such socio-economic factors as poverty and neighbourhood disorganization are a cause of criminal behaviour.

One difficulty is in how we measure class. So many different indicators are used that findings are ambiguous. For example, father's occupation and education are only weakly related to self-reported crime, while unemployment or being a welfare recipient is a much stronger correlate of criminality.[84]

The class–crime relationship may also be more complex than "the poorer a person is, the more crime he or she commits." Age, race, and gender may all influence the connection between class and crime.[85] Unemployment, racism, sexism, and unrealistic expectations can all create resentment.[86] It is not surprising that the true relationship between class and crime is difficult to determine.

instrumental crimes   Illegal activities resorted to by those unable to obtain desired goods through conventional means, such as theft or the sale of narcotics, to obtain such goods.

expressive crimes   Illegal activities with no instrumental purpose, such as shooting someone during the course of an argument.

CONNECTIONS

If class and crime are unrelated, the causes of crime must be found in factors experienced by members of all social classes—psychological impairment, family conflict, peer pressure, and school failure. Theories that view crime as a function of problems experienced by members of all social classes are reviewed in Chapter 8.

Recent evidence suggests that serious street crime and official crime is more prevalent among the lower classes, while less serious and self-reported crime is spread more evenly throughout the social structure.[87] Income inequality, poverty, and resource deprivation are all associated with the most serious violent crimes, including homicide and assault.[88] Nonetheless, although some crime rates may be higher in lower-class areas, poverty alone cannot explain why a particular individual becomes a chronic violent criminal; if it could, the crime problem would be much worse than it is now.[89]

As said above, different classes have different crimes, and thus different rates.

Age and Crime

The third crime pattern is the relationship between age and crime. Age is inversely related to criminality, which means that the older people are, the lower their likelihood of offending.[90] Regardless of economic status, marital status, race, sex, and so on, younger people are more likely (in terms of their proportion of the population) to commit (certain) crimes than are their older peers. This pattern has remained stable and persistent, and the age composition of the population is a key factor used in predicting crime trends.[91] Official statistics tell us that young people are arrested at a disproportionate rate to their numbers in the population, and victim surveys generate similar findings for crimes in which the age of the assailant can be determined.

Youth crime has caused a lot of concern, especially because youth commit some crimes at a much higher rate than their share of the population would warrant. Sensational cases in the media also exacerbate the problem. One such case is the trial of the killers of Reena Virk, described in the upcoming Famous Canadian Court Cases box.

Cases such as the savage beating and murder of Reena Virk, and the media spectacles that ensue, help explain people's exaggerated fears about youth violence. The circumstances surrounding this particular young woman's death thrust the issues of bullying and female violence into the public spotlight—not just in the small British Columbia suburb where this crime occurred, but also on national and international levels. In a similar way, the suicides of Rehtaeh Parsons and Amanda Todd also sparked public attention about cyber-bullying.

The Age–Crime Controversy. The inverse relationship between age and crime, called **aging out** or **desistance**, has been subject to debate; however, according to Hirschi and Gottfredson, the relationship between age and crime is constant and the age variable is actually irrelevant. Because all people, regardless of race, gender, class, family structure, domicile, work status, and so on, commit fewer crimes as they age, age is not an important factor in explaining crime. Even hard-core chronic offenders commit fewer crimes as they age. Differences in offending rates for groups (males and females or rich and poor) that exist at any point in their respective life cycles will be maintained throughout their lives.[92]

In a replication of Hirschi's research, Laub and Sampson studied a group of 500 delinquent men. From age 7 to 70, they committed 9,500 crime events and confirmed the classic age–crime pattern, even within a population characterized by serious, persistent criminal activity.[93]

CONNECTIONS

Hirschi and Gottfredson have used their views on the age–crime relationship as a basis for their general theory of crime. This important theory holds that the factors that produce crime tend to change little after birth and that the association between crime and age is a constant. For more discussion of their views, see Chapter 10.

Those who do not support the view of an inverse relationship between age and crime suggest that personal factors (gender and race) and social factors (lifestyle, economic situation, and peer relations) have a significant impact. Evolving patterns or cycles of criminal behaviour may be keyed to personal characteristics and lifestyle, including gender, race, and class. For example, the male-to-female crime ratio difference declines with age. The female homicide rate peaks between ages 25 and 29, doesn't fluctuate much, and is at a low rate throughout adulthood; in contrast, the male homicide rate is much higher, peaks between ages 8 and 25, and drops thereafter.[94]

The likelihood of a long-term criminal career is also determined by the age at which offending commences. People who involve themselves in criminality at a very early age (**early onset**) and who gain official records will be those most likely to become chronic offenders. Research shows

aging out Individuals reduce the frequency of offending as they age; also known as spontaneous remission, aging out occurs among all groups of offenders.

desistance The process by which crime rate declines with the perpetrator's age; synonymous with the aging-out process.

A member of the Indian Posse wears a bandana in his gang's colours.

that preschoolers (younger than age five) who are labelled as "troublesome" or "difficult" by parents are most likely both to become persistent offenders through adolescence and resistant to the aging-out process.[95]

Desistance is also influenced by criminal specialization. Crimes that provide significant economic gain, such as gambling, embezzlement, and fraud, are less likely to decline with maturity than are high-risk, low-profit offences, such as assault. People who are frequent cocaine and heroin users continue to commit criminal acts 10 years or more past the age when non-users have terminated their criminal activity.[96]

Two Classes of Criminals?   The population thus may contain different sets of criminal offenders: one or more groups whose criminality declines with age and another group whose criminal behaviour remains constant through their maturity.[97] The age–crime pattern may also undergo change, as a greater proportion of violent behaviour is concentrated among youthful offenders than it was 40 years ago.

In sum, some criminologists view the relationship between crime and age as constant, while others believe that it varies according to offence and offender. This difference has important implications for criminological research and theory. If age is a constant, then the criminality of any group can be accurately measured at any single point in time. If, however, the relationship between age and crime varies, then longitudinal studies that follow criminals over their life cycle would be needed to fully understand how their age influences their offending patterns.[98] Crime is also a type of social event that takes on different meanings at different times in a person's life.[99]

Various experiments have tried to deal with the problem of young offenders, such as boot camps and early intervention programs. In Scotland, the Freagarrach Project for persistent offenders (those who have committed more than five offences) was able to achieve a 20 percent to 50 percent reduction in repeat offences. These youths had an average of 18 offences against them. Close counselling, education, and

exercise, and a system of rewards achieved more significant results than a simple prison sentence would achieve.

In London, multisystemic therapy (MT) is a low-cost alternative to traditional mental health services aimed at reducing recidivism. The program appears to be successful in treating antisocial behaviour in young offenders. The program targets chronic, violent, and substance-abusing high-risk juveniles. Randomized, clinical trials found few repeat arrests, fewer self-reported offences, and reduced time spent in corrections facilities. The four-year recidivism rate was 22 percent for MT participants, compared with 87 percent for those with no treatment. Those who received treatment and were rearrested had committed less serious offences than those in a control group.[100]

In a 2005 study, researchers examined the long-term criminal activity of 176 youths who had participated in either multisystemic therapy (MST) or individual therapy, in the longest follow-up to date of MST. Arrest and incarceration data were obtained from 10 to 16 years later when the participants were about 29 years old. The results showed that MST participants had significantly lower recidivism rates than the individuals who had individual therapy (50 percent compared with 81 percent). Moreover, MST participants had 54 percent fewer arrests and 57 percent fewer days of confinement. This research suggests that MST is effective in reducing criminal activity among serious and violent juvenile offenders.[101]

Debates over the relationship between age and crime, and what to do about it, has sponsored new research in Canada, the United States, Sweden, and Britain.[102] Clearly, more research is required on this important topic. See Figure 3.11.

Why Does Aging Out Occur?   Despite the debate over the age–crime relationship, the overall crime rate does decline with age. Why does this phenomenon take place? One view is that a direct relationship exists between aging and desistance. As troubled youth mature, they are able to develop psychologically, acquiring a long-term life view able to resist the need for immediate gratification.[103] As well, teenage crime is fun, a social activity that provides adventure in an otherwise boring life. For many people, as they grow older, their sociological life patterns become inconsistent with criminality, so many delinquents literally grow out of crime.[104]

Wilson and Herrnstein argue that the aging-out process is a function of the natural history of the human life cycle. Deviance in adolescence is fuelled by the need for conventionally unobtainable money and sex and reinforced by close relationships with peers who defy conventional morality. At the same time, teenagers are becoming independent from parents and other adults who enforce conventional standards. Teens have a new sense of energy and strength and

early onset   Description of people who are deviant at a very young age and who are most likely to persist in crime, if their criminal career begins early in life.

Famous Canadian Court Cases
The Murder of Reena Virk

Reena Virk was a troubled 14-year-old whose struggle to gain the acceptance of peers ended in tragedy. The long history of harassment ended in 1997 with allegations that she was spreading rumours. She was lured by a group of teenagers to a muddy bank under a bridge in Saanich, Victoria, where she was brutally attacked and then drowned in a nearby waterway. A pathologist later testified that her injuries were so severe, it was as though she had been run over by a car.

A week after the incident, charges were laid against eight youths aged 14 to 17: seven girls and one boy. Six of the girls were accused of aggravated assault and convicted in 1998. These girls faced consequences ranging from a two-month conditional sentence to a year-long prison term. The only boy among the accused, Warren Glowatski, and the remaining girl, Kelly Ellard, were charged with second-degree murder for committing the second attack and the

Kelly Ellard

drowning. Glowatski insisted that Ellard was responsible for killing Virk but he was convicted in 1999 and sentenced to life in prison with no chance of parole for seven years.

Kelly Ellard's case attracted widespread media coverage and in 2000 she received a life sentence after being convicted in adult court of second-degree murder. However, this verdict was overturned in 2003 when the British Columbia Court of Appeal ruled that Ellard had been improperly cross-examined by the Crown and thus had been denied a fair trial. The Court released Ellard pending a retrial but revoked her bail after she was arrested for assaulting a 58-year-old woman in Vancouver. Ellard's second trial in 2004 resulted in a mistrial because of a deadlocked jury, but in 2005, she was found guilty of second-degree murder in her third trial.

SOURCES: "Ellard Admits Punching Virk," *CBC News*, July 7, 2004, www.cbc .ca/stories/2004/07/06/canada/ellard_ testify040706; "Second Trial Begins for Virk Murder Suspect," *CBC News*, June 14, 2004, www.cbc.ca/stories/2004/06/14/canada/ ellard040614; "The Murder of Reena Virk: A Timeline," *CBC News*, July 20, 2004, www .cbc.ca/news/background/virk.

FIGURE 3.11

Youths Accused of Crime, by Selected Offence, Canada, 2012

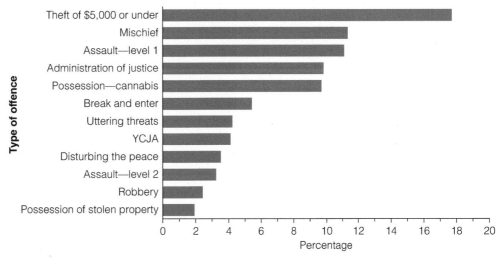

Source: Statistics Canada, "Police-reported Crime Statistics in Canada, 2012," Canadian Centre for Justice Statistics. Catalogue no. 85-002-X, 2013.

Note: Includes *Criminal Code* offences (excluding traffic offences) and other federal statute violations, such as drug offences and *Youth Criminal Justice Act* violations.

are involved with peers who are similarly vigorous and frustrated. Adulthood brings increasingly powerful ties to conventional society, such as a family. Adults also develop the ability to delay gratification and forgo the immediate gains that law violations bring.

When you're a teenager, you're rowdy. Nowadays, you aren't rowdy. You know, you want to settle down because you can go to jail now. [When] you are a boy, you can be put into a detention home. But you can go to jail now. Jail ain't no place to go.[105]

Aging out of crime is also influenced by the success or failure of interpersonal relationships. Children who are labelled antisocial by teachers, police, parents, and neighbours find they have little choice but to remain committed to their criminal careers.[106] However, if youths believe they have little chance of achieving success, money, and happiness through crime, they are more likely to desist.[107] Individuals are also influenced by their adult relationships. For example, people who maintain successful marriages are more likely to desist from antisocial behaviours than those whose marriages fail.[108]

Recent research by Sampson and Laub found that, for men, being married is associated with a reduction of 35 percent in the odds of committing crime compared with men who were unmarried.[109]

Even those who persist in a criminal career will eventually slow down as they age. Crime is too dangerous, physically taxing, and unrewarding; and its punishments are too harsh and long-lasting to become a long-term way of life for most people. The uniformity of maturational changes in the crime rate suggests to some that these changes must be part of a biological evolutionary process.[110]

CONNECTIONS

The belief that life events influence behaviour choices is at the core of life-course theories. These theories hold that as people and their social environment change, so do their criminal behaviour patterns. Theories of the criminal life course are discussed in Chapter 14.

Changing Demographics. The general decline in crime rates during the 1990s coincided with the decreasing proportion of persons aged 15 to 24. This age group has the highest rate for committing crimes and for being a victim of crime. In 2009, age-specific rates for those accused of crime were highest among 15- to 22-year-olds. In 2009, of 165,000 youths accused of committing a crime, 42 percent were charged, and 58 percent were dealt with by other means. Examples of those "other means" included the use of warnings, cautions, and referrals to community programs.

In 2009, the youth Crime Severity Index (CSI) showed that youth crime severity has generally been declining since 2001. However, the youth violent CSI was 10 percent higher than a decade earlier.

The changing age structure can explain only some of the change in crime rates. However, all types of crimes are expected to continue to decrease because of the aging of the population. Although an increase in the number of youths is forecast within a decade, the number of older adults will also increase, driving the crime trend downward.[111]

Gender and Crime

The fourth major crime pattern to be discussed here is the relationship between gender and crime. The three major forms of criminal statistics generally agree on the finding that crime rates are higher for males than for females. However, women are more at risk of committing, and being victimized by, certain crimes, as shown in Exhibit 3.2.

EXHIBIT 3.2

Quick Facts: Profile of Gender, Crime, and Victimization

The 2009 General Social Survey on victimization shows that:

- Women are more likely to be victims of sexual assault (34/1,000) than are men (15/1,000).
- Men are more likely to be victims of robbery (16/1,000) than are women (10/1,000).
- Men make up 87 percent of those accused of sexual offences, compared with women at 13 percent.
- Men are more likely to be victims of assault (94/1,000) than are women (67/1,000).
- Women and men report similar rates of victimization (112 and 125 incidents per 1,000).
- Total violent incidents for women (1,563/1,000) almost equal those for men (1,704/1,000).

The 2004 General Social Survey on victimization also shows that:

- Men are more likely to report victimization (38 percent) than women (26 percent).
- Women have more difficulty (33 percent) in daily activities after crime than men (17 percent).
- Women know their perpetrator (78 percent): (40 percent related, 38 percent friends).
- Men are more likely to be victimized by strangers, and less likely to be murdered by a spouse.

The 2008/09 Adult Criminal Court statistics show:

- Of all cases, 77 percent involved a male accused, while 17 percent involved a female accused.
- Males had the highest involvement in sexual assault (98 percent), being unlawfully at large (91 percent), weapons offences (91 percent), and break and enter (90 percent).
- Females had higher involvement than men in prostitution (31 percent), fraud (31 percent), and theft (30 percent).

The 2008/09 Youth Court Survey shows:

- Of most cases, 72 percent involved a male accused, while 21 percent involved a female accused.
- Males had a higher involvement than women in sexual assault (92 percent), other sexual offences (88 percent), drug possession (85 percent), attempted murder (82 percent), and weapons offences (82 percent).
- Females had a higher involvement than men in prostitution (44 percent), common assault (36 percent), and fraud (35 percent).
- Female inmates were most likely to be young, Aboriginal, single, unemployed, and have little education.

SOURCES: "Criminal Victimization in Canada," *Juristat* 25, 7, 2005; Criminal Victimization in Canada, 2009, by Samuel Perreault and Shannon Brennan, *Juristat*, Summer 2010; CCJS, Canadian Crime Statistics, Catalogue 85205XIE, 2002; CCJS, "Women in Canada," *Profile Series* (June 2001), Catalogue 85F0033MIE; Adult Criminal Court Statistics, 2008/2009 by Jennifer Thomas, *Juristat*, Summer 2010; Youth Court Statistics, 2008/2009, by Shelly Milligan, *Juristat*, Summer 2010.

Explaining Gender Differences: Biosocial Differences. How can the gender differences in the crime rate be explained? Early criminologists pointed to the emotional, physical, and psychological differences between males and females. They maintained that because females were weaker and more passive, they were less likely to commit crimes. The most widely cited evidence was contained in Cesare Lombroso's 1895 book, *The Female Offender*.[112] Lombroso argued that a small group of female criminals lacked typical female traits of "piety, maternity, undeveloped intelligence, and weakness." In physical appearance as well as in emotionality, delinquent females appeared more similar to men than to other women. Lombroso's theory became known as the **masculinity hypothesis**; in essence, a few masculine females were responsible for the handful of crimes committed by women.

Another early view of female crime focused on the dynamics of sexual relationships. Female criminals were viewed as either sexually controlling or sexually naive, either manipulating men for profit or being manipulated by them. The female's criminality was often masked, because criminal justice authorities were reluctant to take action against a woman.[113] Referred to as the **chivalry hypothesis**, Pollack's view was that much of the criminality of females is hidden because of our culture's generally protective and benevolent attitudes toward them.[114] In other words, when females offend, police are less likely to arrest, juries are less likely to convict, and judges are less likely to incarcerate.

Although these early writings are now seen as sexist and androcentric (male-centred), trait differences are a determinant of crime rate differences. For example, some criminologists link antisocial behaviour to hormones, arguing that male sex hormones (androgens) account for aggressive behaviour, and that gender-related hormonal differences explain the gender gap in the crime rate.[115]

Explaining Gender Differences: Socialization. By the mid-20th century, it was common for criminologists to describe gender differences in the crime rate as a function of socialization. Textbooks explained the relatively low female crime rate by citing the fact that in contrast to boys, girls were supervised more closely and protected from competition.[116] The few female criminals were seen as troubled individuals, alienated at home, who pursued crime as a means of compensating for their disrupted personal lives.[117] The streets became a second home to girls whose physical and emotional adjustment was hampered by a strained home life, such as absent fathers and overly competitive mothers.

Gender-based crime is influenced by socialization in that, traditionally, girls are both socialized to be less aggressive than boys are and supervised more closely by their parents. Girls are more likely to learn to respond to provocation by feeling anxious and depressed, whereas boys are encouraged to retaliate with aggression. Although females get angry as often as males, they are taught to blame themselves for harbouring negative feelings and are therefore much more likely than males to respond to anger with feelings of depression, anxiety, fear, and shame. Although females are socialized to fear that their anger will harm valued relationships, males react with moral outrage, looking to blame others for their discomfort.[118] Overall, women are much more likely to feel distressed than are men, experiencing sadness, anxiety, and uneasiness. The relatively few females who commit violent crimes report having home and family relationships that are more troubled than those experienced by male delinquents.[119]

Explaining Gender Differences: Feminist Views. In the 1970s, feminist writing revolutionized thinking on gender differences in the crime rate.[120] This writing, known as **liberal feminist theory**, focused attention on the social and economic roles of women in society and their relationship to female crime rates. The traditionally lower crime rate for women was explained by their second-class economic and social position. Some predicted that as women's social roles changed and their lifestyles became more like those of men, the crime rates would converge.[121]

Criminologists began to refer to the "new female criminal." The rapid increase in the female crime rate during the 1960s and 1970s, especially in traditionally male-oriented crimes (e.g., burglary and larceny), lent support to the convergence model. Support was also found in gangs, where police have seen increased recruitment of female members in the predominantly male world of street gangs. In addition, self-report studies indicated that (1) the pattern of female criminality, if not its frequency, is similar to that of male criminality, and (2) the factors that predispose male criminals to crime have an equal impact on female criminals.[122]

CONNECTIONS

Gender differences in the crime rate may be a function of androgen levels because these hormones cause areas of the brain to become less sensitive to environmental stimuli, making males more likely to seek high levels of stimulation and to tolerate more pain in the process. This issue is reviewed in greater detail in the discussion of the biosocial causes of crime in Chapter 6.

masculinity hypothesis The view that women who commit crimes have biological and psychological traits similar to those of men.

chivalry hypothesis The idea that low female crime and delinquency rates are a reflection of the leniency with which police treat female offenders.

liberal feminist theory An approach that focuses attention on the social and economic roles of women in society and their relationship to female crime rates.

CONNECTIONS

Critical criminologists view gender inequality as stemming from the unequal power of men and women in a capitalist society and the exploitation of females by fathers and husbands. Female crime patterns can be explained by these unequal power relationships. These views, referred to as Marxist or radical feminism, are considered more fully in Chapter 9.

Will gender differences in the crime rate eventually dissolve? Are gender differences permanent and unchanging? Some criminologists find that gender-based crime rate differences remain significant and argue that the emancipation of women has had relatively little influence on female crime rates.[123] They dispute the idea that increases in the female arrest rate reflect economic or social changes brought about by the women's movement. Many female criminals come from the socio-economic class least affected by the women's movement, and their crimes are more a function of economic inequality than of women's rights.

Also, the offence patterns of women differ from those of men, who are still committing a disproportionate share of serious crimes, such as robbery, burglary, murder, and assault.[124] In general, women commit fewer violent crimes overall, whether it is assaults, homicides, or sexual assaults. Younger women do commit more violent crimes proportionately, but it is doubtful that this shows gender convergence. As well, much international research has failed to find an association between economic development and female crime rates.[125] Little evidence suggests nations undergoing economic development experience increases in female violence.

Perhaps it is too soon for criminologists to write off "the new female criminal." After all, though male arrest rates are still considerably higher than female rates, the female rates seem to be increasing at a faster pace. It is possible that convergence has been delayed by a slower-than-expected change in gender roles; the women's movement has not yet achieved its full impact on social life.[126] One reason is that although women are expanding their economic role, they have not abandoned their conventional role of taking care of family and home; women today are being forced to cope with added financial and social burdens. If gender roles are truly equivalent, crime rates may eventually converge; these changes appear to be taking place now.

CONNECTIONS

The concept of relative deprivation refers to the fact that people compare their success with that of the people they are in immediate contact with. Even if conditions improve, people may still feel as if they are falling behind. A sense of relative deprivation, discussed in Chapter 7, may lead to criminal activity.

Criminal Careers

The fifth major crime pattern discussed here results from research on long-term offenders. Most offenders commit a single criminal act and on arrest discontinue their antisocial activity. Others commit a few crimes of a less serious nature. However, a small group of individuals accounts for a majority of all crimes committed. These persistent offenders are referred to as **career criminals** or **chronic offenders.** This research is significant because it addresses elements within a criminal's life that are related to crime, rather than factors that differentiate offenders from non-offenders.

Recent research shows that 60 percent of convicted offenders had at least one previous conviction. Among those recidivists, 28 percent had one prior conviction, and 72 percent had multiple prior convictions. The majority (62 percent) had been previously convicted at least once in youth court.[127] Almost two-thirds of people accused of homicide had a criminal record; among those, 73 percent had been previously convicted of a violent offence. These life-course persisters, as they are called, inflict much damage to society because they are responsible for such a large share of adult misconduct.

CONNECTIONS

More than 70 years ago, the Gluecks found that almost all of the reformatory inmates in their study of criminal careers had a background of serious antisocial conduct. Read about their research in Chapter 6.

Delinquency in a Birth Cohort.   The concept of the chronic or career offender is most closely associated with the research of Wolfgang, Figlio, and Sellin.[128] In their landmark study, *Delinquency in a Birth Cohort,* official records were used to follow the criminal careers of a cohort of 9,945 boys born in Philadelphia in 1945. The cohort members were followed from the time of their birth until they reached 18 years of age. Official police records were used to identify delinquents. About one-third of the boys (3,475) had some police contact. The remaining two-thirds (6,470) had none.[129] Their delinquent acts were weighted to allow the researchers to differentiate, for example, between a simple assault requiring no

career criminal   A person who repeatedly violates the law, devotes much of their life to criminality, and commits a large portion of the total crime in a community.

chronic offender   The small percentage of those who are arrested five or more times before age 18, who will become adult criminals, and are responsible for more than half of all serious crimes.

medical attention for the victim and a serious assault in which the victim needed hospitalization.

The best-known discovery was of the chronic offender. Fully 54 percent of the delinquent youths were repeat offenders, while the remaining 46 percent were one-time offenders. However, the repeaters could be further categorized as non-chronic recidivists and chronic recidivists. The former consisted of 1,235 youths who had been arrested more than once but fewer than five times and who made up 36 percent of all delinquents. The latter were a group of 627 boys arrested five times or more, who accounted for 18 percent of the delinquents and 6 percent of the total sample.

The chronic 6 percent were involved in the most dramatic amounts of delinquency, responsible for 5,305 offences, or 59 percent of all offences. Even more striking was the involvement of chronic offenders in serious criminal acts. Of the entire sample, they committed 71 percent of the homicides, 73 percent of the rapes, 82 percent of the robberies, and 69 percent of the aggravated assaults.

Wolfgang and his associates found that arrest and court experience did little to deter the chronic offender. In fact, punishment was inversely related to chronic offending: The more stringent the sanctions chronic offenders received, the more likely they were to engage in repeated criminal behaviour.

Birth Cohort II. The subjects who made up Wolfgang's original birth cohort were born in 1945. How have behaviour patterns changed in subsequent years? To answer this question, a new, larger birth cohort of 27,000 subjects (13,000 males and 14,000 females), born in Philadelphia in 1958, were followed until their maturity.[130] Although the proportion of delinquent youths was about the same as that in the 1945 cohort, those in the larger sample were involved in 20,089 delinquent arrests. Chronic offenders (five or more arrests as juveniles) made up 7.5 percent of the 1958 sample (compared with 6.3 percent in 1945) and 23 percent of all delinquent offenders (compared with 18 percent in 1945). Chronic female delinquency was relatively rare—only 1 percent of the females in the survey were chronic offenders.

Chronic male delinquents continued to commit more than their share of criminal behaviour. They accounted for 61 percent of the total offences and a disproportionate amount of the most serious crimes: 61 percent of the homicides, 76 percent of the rapes, 73 percent of the robberies, and 65 percent of the aggravated assaults. The chronic female offender was less likely to be involved in serious crimes.

As a group, the 1958 cohort was involved in significantly more serious crimes than was the 1945 group. For example, the violent offence rate (149 per 1,000 in the sample) was three times higher than the rate for the 1945 cohort (47 per 1,000 subjects).

In the 1945 cohort, chronic offenders dominated the total crime rate and continued their law-violating careers as adults. The newer cohort study showed that the chronic offender syndrome was maintained in the group of subjects born 13 years later than the original cohort and, if anything, the newer group was more violent than the first group. Finally, the efforts of the justice system seem to have little preventive effect on the behaviour of chronic offenders: The more often a person was arrested, the more likely he or she was to be arrested again. For males, 26 percent of the entire group had one violent-offence arrest; of that 26 percent, 34 percent went on to commit a second violent offence, while 43 percent of the three-time losers went on to a fourth arrest, and so on.

Chronic Offender Research. This effort to identify the chronic career offender has been replicated by other important research studies, such as Shannon's cohort approach to investigate career delinquency patterns.[131] West and Farrington's ongoing study of London youths has shown that a small number of recidivists continue their behaviour as adults and that arrest and conviction have little influence on their behaviour other than to amplify the problem that youths with multiple convictions as juveniles tend to have multiple convictions as adults. The most important childhood risk factors associated with chronic offending include a history of troublesomeness, a personality that reveres daring behaviour, a delinquent sibling, and a convicted parent. Farrington finds that the most chronic offenders could be identified by age 10 on the basis of personality and background features.[132]

In another study, a sample was followed through adulthood to age 30.[133] Seventy percent of the persistent adult offenders had been chronic juvenile offenders, who had an 80 percent chance of becoming adult offenders and a 50 percent chance of being arrested four or more times as adults. In comparison, subjects with no juvenile arrests had only an 18 percent chance of being arrested as an adult. The chronic offenders also continued to engage in the most serious crimes. Although they accounted for only 15 percent of the follow-up sample, the former chronic delinquents were involved in 74 percent of all arrests and 82 percent of all serious crimes, such as homicide, rape, and robbery.

The cohort follow-ups clearly show that chronic juvenile offenders continue their law-violating careers as adults, a concept referred to as the **continuity of crime**. Children who are disruptive and antisocial as early as age five are the most likely to exhibit stable, long-term patterns of disruptive behaviour through adolescence. They have measurable behavioural problems in such areas as learning and motor skills, cognitive abilities, family relations, and other areas of social, psychological, and physical functioning. Youthful offenders who persist are more likely to abuse alcohol, get

continuity of crime The view that crime begins early in life and continues throughout the life course. Thus, the best predictor of future criminality is past criminality.

into trouble while in military service, become economically dependent on their families or on society, have lower aspirations, get divorced or separated, and have a weak employment record.[134] Canadian research shows that aggressive children are more likely to feel unhappy and rejected.[135] Criminalizing their behaviour by lowering the age of criminal responsibility would do nothing to deal with the problems that might cause the behaviour in the first place.

Additional studies conducted in Europe, such as the Stockholm cohort project, with 15,117 male and female subjects, indicate that criminal career development in Sweden follows many of the same patterns found in American cohorts. Similarly, data from a sample of 411 males born in London found that the frequency of offending was predicted by early onset of antisocial behaviour, associating with deviant peers, personality traits such as a low level of anxiety, poor school achievement, and dysfunctional family relations. Those delinquents who persisted into adulthood (ages 21 to 32) exhibited low IQs, substance abuse, chronic unemployment, and a low degree of commitment to school.[136] Further analysis shows that the persistent offender group can be subdivided into high- and low-rate offenders, with the former committing two or three times as many offences as the latter.[137] Punishment does little to deter their behaviour and, if anything, prompts escalation of their criminal activities.

Correctional Services Canada reports that of 14,091 male offenders incarcerated in 1997, 54 percent had no term of previous federal incarceration, 17 percent had one term, 11 percent had two, 7 percent had three, and 10 percent had more than three. Women were far more likely to have had no previous term of federal incarceration (75 percent) and less likely to have more than three (4 percent). Of provincial and territorial inmates, 83 percent had at least one prior conviction. In a snapshot of inmates, it was found that 96 percent of those classified as high risk had previous convictions.[138]

In sum, research shows that a small group of offenders are responsible for a great deal of all crime. These youths begin their offending career at an extremely young age and persist into their adulthood.

Implications of the Chronic Offender Concept. The findings of the cohort studies and the discovery of the chronic offender is a puzzle for criminological theory. If relatively few offenders become chronic, persistent criminals, it is possible that they possess some individual trait that is responsible for their criminality. Most people exposed to troublesome social conditions, such as poverty, do not become chronic offenders; thus, it is unlikely that social conditions alone can cause chronic offending. So, what does?

Traditional theories of criminal behaviour have failed to distinguish between chronic and occasional offenders. They have concentrated more on explaining why people begin to commit crime and have paid scant attention to the reasons why people stop offending. The concept of the chronic offender has forced criminologists to consider the role of persistence and desistance in the onset of criminality and also in its termination. Why do most offenders "age out" of crime? Why do some persist into adulthood? Ongoing research efforts are now aimed at answering these critical questions.

The chronic offender concept has also raised questions about the treatment of known offenders: If we can identify chronic offenders, what should we do about them? How can chronic offenders be controlled if punishment actually escalates the frequency of their criminal activity? The chronic offender has thus become a central focus of crime control policy. Concern about repeat offenders has been translated into programs at various stages of the justice process.

Even more important has been the effect of the chronic offender on sentencing policy. Sentencing policies are increasingly designed to incapacitate serious offenders for long periods without hope of probation or parole. A mandatory sentence for violent or drug-related crimes is commonly known as a "three strikes and you're out" policy, and Canada has now adopted mandatory minimums for certain crimes, as discussed in Chapter 2. Whether such policies can be effective in reducing crime rates or are merely "get tough" measures designed to placate conservative voters remains to be seen.

SUMMARY

Canada has three primary sources of crime statistics: the UCR, which is based on police data accumulated by the CCJS; self-reports of criminal behaviour; and victim surveys. All three sources, pieced together, overlap to tell us about crime in Canada. Each data source has its strengths and weaknesses, and though quite different from one another, they agree on the nature of criminal behaviour.

The data sources show some stable patterns in the crime rate. Until the early 1990s, the amount of violent crime was increasing, only to go into two decades of decline. Some crimes are now at their lowest levels since the 1960s or 1970s. Ecological patterns show that some areas of the country are more crime-prone than others, certain seasons and times are more conducive to crime, and these patterns are relatively stable. Evidence also suggests a gender and age gap in the crime rate. Men usually commit more crimes than do women, and young people commit more crimes than seniors do. The crime data show that people commit fewer crimes as they age, but the significance and cause of this pattern is still not completely understood. A class pattern also exists in the crime rate. However, whether these are true differences or a function of discriminatory law enforcement remains unclear.

One of the most important findings of cohort research is the existence of the chronic offender, a repeat criminal responsible for a significant number of all law violations. Chronic offenders begin their career early in life and, rather than aging out of crime, persist in their criminal behaviour

Skinhead gangs continue to foster racial hatred and violence.

THINKING LIKE A CRIMINOLOGIST

An assistant deputy minister in the federal Department of Justice has asked for your professional advice on how to reduce the threat of young offenders becoming chronic offenders. Some of the more conservative members of the government believe that juvenile delinquents who are punished harshly are less likely to recidivate than are youths who receive lesser punishments, such as community corrections or probation.

The bureaucrat is unsure whether such an approach can reduce the threat of chronic offending. Can tough punishment produce deviant identities that lock youth into a criminal way of life? This would be counterproductive. Conversely, will a strategy stressing punishment have relatively little impact if these are serious chronic offenders? You find it difficult to offer advice because you remember a lecture given by the Minister of Corrections, John Edwards, at St. Thomas University in 1996, in which he described the profile of the federal offender. Ninety-seven percent are male, most are single, and 75 percent have committed serious violent offences. Two-thirds of the admissions have done provincial or territorial time, and most have records going back into their juvenile years. The average educational level of offenders is Grade 7, and 68 percent test below Grade 8 in language and mathematics. More than half claim to have been abused as children, and three-quarters have unstable job histories. Does punishment begin to get at these underlying issues?

into adulthood. The discovery of the chronic offender has led to the study of developmental criminology—why people persist, desist, escalate, or terminate their deviant behaviour.

This chapter shows that with the right tools, we can better understand the patterns of crime and the reasons crime occurs. However, we also need to be aware that crime statistics seldom portray at face value the reality they purport to describe. Crime statistics can be an artefact of reporting practices, police enforcement, changing legal definitions of crime, and media representations.

KEY TERMS

aging out p. 77
attrition p. 57
career criminal p. 82
chivalry hypothesis p. 81
chronic offender p. 82
cleared p. 57
continuity of crime p. 83
crime funnel p. 57
crime rate p. 56

definition-sensitive crimes p. 55
desistance p. 77
early onset p. 77
expressive crimes p. 76
founded p. 56
incidence p. 55
incident-based data p. 55
instrumental crimes p. 76
liberal feminist theory p. 81

masculinity hypothesis p. 81
media-sensitive crimes p. 55
percentage change p. 56
policing-sensitive crimes p. 55
report-sensitive crimes p. 55
self-report survey p. 61
Uniform Crime Report (UCR) p. 55

DOING RESEARCH ON THE WEB

The U.S. National Council on Child Abuse and Family Violence (NCCAFV) maintains a website with links to documents on child abuse and violence: www.nccafv.org.

In Canada, the National Clearinghouse on Family Violence maintains information on abuse and violence: www.phac-aspc.gc.ca/ncfv-cnivf/index-eng.php.

CRITICAL THINKING QUESTIONS

1. Would you answer honestly if a national crime survey asked you about your criminal behaviour, including drinking and drug use? If not, why not? Do you question the accuracy of self-report surveys?

2. How would you explain gender differences in the crime rate? Why do you think males are more violent than females?

3. Assuming that males are more violent than females, does that mean crime has a biological rather than a social basis (because males and females share a similar environment)?

4. The UCR reports that crime rates are higher in large cities than in small towns. What does that tell us about the effects of TV, films, and music on teenage behaviour?

5. What social and environmental factors do you believe influence the crime rate? For example, do you think a national emergency would increase or decrease crime rates?

NOTES

1. Timothy F. Hartnagel, "Crime among the Provinces: The Effect of Geographic Mobility," *Canadian Journal of Criminology*, October 1997: 387–402.

2. Rosemary Gartner and Anthony N. Doob, "Trends in Criminal Victimization: 1988–1993," *Juristat* 14, 1994; "Criminal Victimization in Canada, 2004," *Juristat* 25, 7, 2005.

3. *Crime in England and Wales, 2006/07*, London: British Home Office, 2007; Scottish Crime Survey 2003, retrieved from scotland.gov.uk. June 3, 2008.

4. Paul Tappan, *Crime, Justice and Corrections* (New York: McGraw-Hill, 1960); Daniel Bell, *The End of Ideology* (New York: Free Press, 1967), 152.

5. Jim Hackler and Wasanti Paranjape, "Juvenile Justice Statistics: Mythmaking or Measure of System Response," *Canadian Journal of Criminology* 25 (1983): 209–226.

6. Lawrence Sherman and Barry Glick, "The Quality of Arrest Statistics," *Police Foundation Reports* 2 (1984): 1–8; David Seidman and Michael Couzens, "Getting the Crime Rate Down: Political Pressure and Crime Reporting," *Law and Society Review* 8 (1974): 457; Robert O'Brien, "Police Productivity and Crime Rates: 1973–1992," *Criminology* 34 (1996): 183–207.

7. Duncan Chappell, Gilbert Geis, Stephen Schafer, and Larry Siegel, "Forcible Rape: A Comparative Study of Offenses Known to the Police in Boston and Los Angeles," in *Studies in the Sociology of Sex*, ed. James Henslin (New York: Appleton-Century-Crofts, 1971), 169–193.

8. Patrick Jackson, "Assessing the Validity of Official Data on Arson," *Criminology* 26 (1988): 181–195.

9. Brent D. Mast, Bruce L. Benson, and David W. Rasmussen, "Entrepreneurial Police and Drug Enforcement Policy," *Public Choice,* 104 (2000): 3–4.

10. Peter Carrington, *Factors Affecting Police Diversion of Young Offenders: A Statistical Analysis* (Ottawa: Solicitor General of Canada, 1998).

11. "Arson in Canada," *Juristat* 12, 1992.

12. *Criminal Code Amendment Act,* 1921 Can. Stat. Ch. 25, sec. 23.

13. Mark Asbridge, Robert E. Mann, Rosely Flam-Zalcman, and Gina Stoduto, "The Criminalization of Impaired Driving in Canada: Assessing the Deterrent Impact of Canada's First Per Se Law," *Journal of Studies on Alcohol,* 65, 2004: 450–459.

14. Jennifer Thomas, "Youth Court Statistics, 2003/04, *Juristat* 25, 4, 2005.

15. Bryan R. Hogeveen, "'If We Are Tough on Crime, If We Punish Crime, Then People Get the Message': Constructing and Governing the Punishable Young Offender in Canada during the Late 1990s," *Punishment & Society,* 7, 1, (2005): 73–89; also, Chris McCormick, "Youth Deviance and the Media: Mapping Knowledge and the Limits to Certainty," in *Youth at Risk and Youth Justice: A Canadian Overview,* John Winterdyk and Russell Smandych, eds., Oxford, 2012.

16. R.P. Ericson, M. Baranek, and J. Chan, *Visualizing Deviance: A Study of News Sources* (Toronto: University of Toronto Press, 1989); R.P. Ericson, M. Baranek, and J. Chan, *Negotiating Control: A Study of News Sources* (Toronto: University of Toronto Press, 1989); R.P. Ericson, M. Baranek, and J. Chan, *Representing Order* (Toronto: University of Toronto Press, 1991).

17. M. Maltz, "Crime Statistics: A Historical Perspective," *Crime and Delinquency* 23 (1977): 32–40.

18. A. Doyle and R. Ericson, "Breaking into Prison: News Sources and Correctional Institutions," *Canadian Journal of Criminology* 38: 155–190.

19. Leonard Savitz, "Official Statistics," in *Contemporary Criminology*, eds. Leonard Savitz and Norman Johnston (New York: Wiley, 1982), 3–15.

20. A pioneering effort in self-report research is A.L. Porterfield, *Youth in Trouble* (Fort Worth, TX: Leo Potishman Foundation, 1946); for a review, see Robert Hardt and George Bodine, *Development of Self-Report Instruments in Delinquency Research: A Conference Report* (Syracuse, NY: Syracuse University Youth Development Center, 1965). See also Fred Murphy, Mary Shirley, and Helen Witner, "The Incidence of Hidden Delinquency," *American Journal of Orthopsychology* 16 (1946): 686–696.

21. Franklyn Dunford and Delbert Elliott, "Identifying Career Criminals Using Self-Reported Data," *Journal of Research in Crime and Delinquency* 21 (1983): 57–86.

22. For example, see E. Vaz, "Middle Class Delinquency: Self Reported Delinquency and Youth Culture," *Canadian Review of Sociology and Anthropology* 2 (1965): 52–70; M. LeBlanc, "Middle Class Delinquency," in *Crime in Canadian Society*, eds. Robert A. Silverman and James J. Teevan (Toronto: Butterworths, 1975); I.M. Gomme, Mary E. Morton, and W. Gordon West, "Rates, Types, and Patterns of Male and Female Delinquency in an Ontario County," *Canadian Journal of Criminology* 26 (1984): 313–324.

23. "Youth Self-Reported Delinquency, Toronto, 2006," *Juristat* 27, 6, 2007.

24. Thomas Gabor, "Methodological Orthodoxy or Eclecticism? The Case of Youth Violence," *Canadian Journal of Criminology* 42 (2000): 77–83.

25. See, for example, Spencer Rathus and Larry Siegel, "Crime and Personality Revisited: Effects of MMPI Sets on Self-Report Studies," *Criminology* 18 (1980): 245–251; John Clark and Larry Tifft, "Polygraph and Interview Validation of Self-Reported Deviant Behavior," *American Sociological Review* 31 (1966): 516–523.

26. See, for example, Harwin Voss, "Ethnic Differences in Delinquency in Honolulu," *Journal of Criminal Law, Criminology and Police Science* 54 (1963): 322–327; Maynard Erickson and LaMar Empey, "Court Records, Undetected Delinquency

and Decision Making," *Journal of Criminal Law, Criminology and Police Science* 54 (1963): 456–459; H.B. Gibson, Sylvia Morrison, and D.J. West, "The Confession of Known Offenses in Response to a Self-Reported Delinquency Schedule," *British Journal of Criminology* 10 (1970): 277–280; John Blackmore, "The Relationship between Self-Reported Delinquency and Official Convictions amongst Adolescent Boys," *British Journal of Criminology* 14 (1974): 172–176; Clark and Tifft, "Polygraph and Interview Validation of Self-Reported Deviant Behavior"; Michael Hindelang, Travis Hirschi, and Joseph Weis, *Measuring Delinquency* (Beverly Hills, CA: Sage, 1981).

27. Terence Thornberry, Beth Bjerregaard, and William Miles, "The Consequences of Respondent Attrition in Panel Studies: A Simulation Based on the Rochester Youth Development Study," *Journal of Quantitative Criminology* 9 (1993): 127–158.

28. Minu Mathur, Richard Dodder, and Harjit Sandhu, "Inmate Self-Report Data: A Study of Reliability," *Criminal Justice Review* 17 (1992): 258–267.

29. Thomas Gray and Eric Wish, *Maryland Youth at Risk: A Study of Drug Use in Juvenile Detainees* (College Park, MD: Center for Substance Abuse Research, 1993); Udi E. Ghitza, David H. Epstein, and Kenzie L. Preston, "Nonreporting of Cannabis Use: Predictors and Relationship to Treatment Outcome in Methadone Maintenance Patients," *Addictive Behaviors* 32 (2006): 938–949; Lana D. Harrison, Steven S. Martin, Tihomir Enev, and Deborah Harrington, "Comparing Drug Testing and Self-Report of Drug Use among Youths and Young Adults in the General Population," DHHS Publication No. SMA 07-4249, Rockville, MD.

30. L. Edward Wells and Joseph Rankin, "Juvenile Victimization: Convergent Validation of Alternative Measurements," *Journal of Research in Crime and Delinquency* 32 (1995): 287–307.

31. Alfred Blumstein, Jacqueline Cohen, and Richard Rosenfeld, "Trend and Deviation in Crime Rates: A Comparison of UCR and NCVS Data for Burglary and Robbery," *Criminology* 29 (1991): 237–248. See also Hindelang, Hirschi, and Weis, *Measuring Delinquency*.

32. For a critique, see Scott Menard, "Residual Gains, Reliability, and the UCR–NCVS Relationship: A Comment on Blumstein, Cohen and Rosenfeld (1991)," *Criminology* 30 (1992): 105–115; David McDowall and Colin Loftin, "Comparing the UCR and NCVS over Time," *Criminology* 30 (1992): 125–133.

33. D. Cole and M. Gittens, *Report of the Commission on Systemic Racism in the Ontario Criminal Justice System* (Toronto: Queen's Printer for Ontario, 1995).

34. Nova Scotia, *Royal Commission into the Wrongful Incarceration of Donald Marshall, Jr.* (Halifax: Queen's Printer, 1989).

35. Alberta, Justice on Trial: Report of the Task Force on the Criminal Justice System and Its Impact on the Indian and Métis People of Alberta (Edmonton: The Task Force, 1991).

36. Manitoba, *Report of the Aboriginal Justice Inquiry* (Winnipeg: Queen's Printer, 1991).

37. Saskatchewan, Report of the Saskatchewan Indian Justice Review Committee (Regina: The Indian Justice Review Committee, 1992); Saskatchewan, Report of Commission of Inquiry into the Shooting Death of Leo Lachance (Regina: Saskatchewan Justice, 1993).

38. Michael Harris, *The Royal Commission of Inquiry into the Response of the Newfoundland Criminal Justice System to Complaints* (St. John's: Queen's Printer, 1991).

39. The Honourable Stuart G. Stratton, Q.C., *Report of an Independent Investigation in Respect of Incidents and Allegations of Sexual and Other Physical Abuse at Five Nova Scotia Residential Institutions*, June 30, 1995.

40. Steven D. Levitt, "Understanding Why Crime Fell in the 1990s: Four Factors That Explain the Decline and Six That Do Not," *Journal of Economic Perspectives* 18, 1 (2004): 163–190.

41. Joan E. Durrant, "Trends in Youth Crime and Well-Being Since the Abolition of Corporal Punishment in Sweden," *Youth & Society*, 31, 4 (June 2000): 437–455; also see Ronald L. Simons, Chyi-in Wu, Kuei-Hsiu Lin, Leslie Gordon, and Rand D. Conger, "Cultural Examination of the Link between Corporal Punishment and Adolescent Antisocial Behavior," *Criminology* 38, 1 (2000): 47–80.

42. Stephen S. Owen, "The Relationship between Social Capital and Corporal Punishment in Schools: A Theoretical Inquiry," *Youth & Society*, 37, 1 (2005): 85–112.

43. "Age of the Population," *Criminal Justice Indicators, 2005*, Statistics Canada 85-227-XIE.

44. Glenn Pierce and James Alan Fox, *Recent Trends in Violent Crime: A Closer Look* (Boston: National Crime Analysis Program, Northeastern University, 1992).

45. Valerie Pottie Bunge, Holly Johnson, and Thierno A. Balde, "Exploring Crime Patterns in Canada," Statistics Canada 85-561-MIE – No. 005, 2005.

46. Anthony N. Doob and Jane B. Sprott, "Is the 'Quality' of Youth Violence Becoming More Serious," *Canadian Journal of Criminology* 4 (1998): 185–194; Thomas Gabor, "Trends in Youth Crime: Some Evidence Pointing to Increases in the Severity and Volume of Violence on the Part of Young People," *Canadian Journal of Criminology* 7 (1999): 385–392.

47. Public Safety Canada, "The Recidivism of Federal Offenders," *Research Summary* 8, 4, 2003.

48. Donald J. Auger, Anthony N. Doob, Raymond P. Auger, and Paul Driben, "Crime and Control in Three Nishnawbe-Aski Nation Communities: An Exploratory Investigation," *Canadian Journal of Criminology* 10 (1992): 317–338; Carol LaPrairie, "The Role of Sentencing in the Over-Representation of Aboriginal People in Correctional Institutions," *Canadian Journal of Criminology* 32 (1990): 429–440.

49. "Victimization and Offending among the Aboriginal Population in Canada," *Juristat* 26, 3, 2006.

50. National Crime Prevention Centre, *Aboriginal Canadians: Violence, Victimization and Prevention* (Ottawa: Department of Justice, 2001).

51. M. Ouimet, "Explaining the American and Canadian Crime Drop in the 1990s," *Canadian Journal of Criminology* 44, 1 (2002): 33–50.

52. John McMullan and Peter D. Swan, "Social Economy and Arson in Nova Scotia," *Canadian Journal of Criminology* 31 (1989): 281–308.

53. Rodrigo R. Soares, "Development, Crime and Punishment: Accounting for the International Differences in Crime Rates," *Journal of Development Economics*, 73, 1 (2004): 155–184.

54. Rosemary Gartner, "Family Structure, Welfare Spending, and Child Homicide in Developed Democracies," *Journal of Marriage and the Family* 53 (1991): 231–240.

55. John Donohue and Steven Levitt, "The Impact of Legalized Abortion on Crime," National Bureau of Economic Research Working Paper, November 2000.

56. "Social Capital: Social Interactions and Determinants, and Outcomes/Consequences of Interactions," *Criminal Justice Indicators, 2005*, Statistics Canada 85-227-XIE.

57. Rosemary Gartner and Robert Nash Parker, "Cross-National Evidence on Homicide and the Age Structure of the Population," *Social Forces* 69 (1990): 351–371.

58. John Braithwaite, *Crime, Shame and Reintegration* (Cambridge: Cambridge University Press, 1989).

59. Koichiro Ito, "Research on the Fear of Crime: Perceptions and Realities of Crime in Japan," *Crime and Delinquency* 39 (1993): 392–395; Joachim Kersten, "Street Youths, Bosozoku, and Yakuza: Subculture Formation and Social Reactions in Japan," *Crime and Delinquency* 39 (1993): 277–295; Michael Vaughn and Nobuho Tomita, "A Longitudinal Analysis of Japanese Crime from 1926–1987: The Pre-War, War and Post-War Eras," *International Journal of Comparative and Applied Criminal Justice* 14 (1990): 145–160; Ted Westermann and James Burfeind, *Crime and Justice in Two Societies: Japan and the United States* (Pacific Grove, CA: Brooks/Cole, 1991).

60. Joseph Sheley and James Wright, *In the Line of Fire: Youth, Guns, and Violence in Urban America* (New York: Aldine de Gruyter, 1995).

61. "Crime Statistics in Canada, 2006," *Juristat* 27, 5, 2007.

62. Statistics Canada, "Study: Firearms and Violent Crime," *The Daily*, February 20, 2008.65: Thomas Gabor, "Canadians Rarely Use Firearms for Self-protection," *Canadian Journal of Criminology* 38 (1996): 217–220; Gary Mauser, "Do Canadians Use Firearms in Self-protection?", *Canadian Journal of Criminology* 37 (1995): 556–562.

63. Joseph Sheley and James Wright, *In the Line of Fire: Youth, Guns, and Violence in Urban America* (New York: Aldine de Gruyter, 1995).

64. "News Release," Garry Breitkreuz MP, December 7, 2006.

65. Alfred Blumstein, "Violence by Young People: Why the Deadly Nexus," *National Institute of Justice Journal* 229 (1995): 2–9.

66. Steven Dillingham, *Violent Crime in the United States* (Washington, DC: Bureau of Justice Statistics, 1991), 17; Bruce Johnson, Andrew Golub, and Jeffrey Fagan, "Careers in Crack, Drug Use, Drug Distribution, and Nondrug Criminality," *Crime and Delinquency* 41 (1995): 275–295.

67. "Homicide in Canada, 2005," *Juristat* 26, 6, 2006.

68. "Trends in Drug Offences and the Role of Alcohol and Drugs in Crime, 2002," *The Daily,* Statistics Canada, Monday, February 23, 2004.

69. J.Q. Wilson and G. Kelling, "Broken Windows: The Police and Neighborhood Safety," *Atlantic Monthly* (March 19, 1996), 29–38; and George L. Kelling and Catherine M. Coles, *Fixing Broken Windows: Reducing Order and Reducing Crime in Our Communities* (New York: Martin Kessler Books/Free Press, 1997).

70. Darrell Steffensmeier and Miles Harer, "Did Crime Rise or Fall during the Reagan Presidency? The Effects of an 'Aging' U.S. Population on the Nation's Crime Rate," *Journal of Research in Crime and Delinquency* 28 (1991): 330–339; James A. Fox, *Trends in Juvenile Violence: A Report to the United States Attorney General on Current and Future Rates of Juvenile Offending* (Boston, MA: Northeastern University, 1996).

71. Ellen Cohn, "The Effect of Weather and Temporal Variations on Calls for Police Service," *American Journal of Police* 15 (1996): 23–43.

72. E. Boyanowsky, "Violence and Aggression in the Heat of Passion and in Cold Blood. The Ecs-TC Syndrome," *International Journal of Law and Psychiatry*, 22, 3–4 (1999): 257–271.

73. R.A. Baron, "Aggression as a Function of Ambient Temperature and Prior Anger Arousal," *Journal of Personality and Social Psychology* 21 (1972): 183–189; Ellen G. Cohn, "Weather and Crime," *The British Journal of Criminology* 30 (1990): 51–64 (1990); Ellen Cohn, "The Prediction of Police Calls for Service: The Influence of Weather and Temporal Variables on Rape and Domestic Violence," *Journal of Environmental Psychology* 13 (1993): 71–83; Derral Cheatwood, "The Effects of Weather on Homicide," *Journal of Quantitative Criminology* 11 (1995): 51–70; Ellen Cohn and James Rotton, "Assault as a Function of Time and Temperature: A Moderator-Variable Time-Series analysis," *Journal of Personality and Social Psychology* 72, 6 (1997): 1322–1334; "Crime Goes Up with Temperature, Psychologist Finds," *Can West News*, July 21, 2006.

74. "A Comparison of Large Urban, Small Urban and Rural Crime Rates, 2005, *Juristat* 27, 3, 2007.

75. Valerie Pottie Bunge, Holly Johnson, and Thierno A. Balde, "Exploring Crime Patterns in Canada," Statistics Canada 85-561-MIE – No. 005, 2005.

76. Robert Nash Parker, "Bringing 'Booze' Back In: The Relationship between Alcohol and Homicide," *Journal of Research in Crime and Delinquency* 32 (1995): 3–38.

77. Victoria Brewer and M. Dwayne Smith, "Gender Inequality and Rates of Female Homicide Victimization across U.S. Cities," *Journal of Research in Crime and Delinquency* 32 (1995): 175–190.

78. F. Ivan Nye, James Short, and Virgil Olsen, "Socio-economic Status and Delinquent Behavior," *American Journal of Sociology* 63 (1958): 381–389; Robert Dentler and Lawrence Monroe, "Social Correlates of Early Adolescent Theft," *American Sociological Review* 63 (1961): 733–743. See also Terence Thornberry and Margaret Farnworth, "Social Correlates of Criminal Involvement: Further Evidence of the Relationship between Social Status and Criminal Behavior," *American Sociological Review* 47 (1982): 505–518.

79. Charles Tittle, Wayne Villemez, and Douglas Smith, "The Myth of Social Class and Criminality: An Empirical Assessment of the Empirical Evidence," *American Sociological Review* 43 (1978): 643–656.

80. Charles Tittle and Robert Meier, "Specifying the SES/Delinquency Relationship," *Criminology* 28 (1990): 271–301.

81. Delbert Elliott and Suzanne Ageton, "Reconciling Race and Class Differences in Self-Reported and Official Estimates of Delinquency," *American Sociological Review* 45 (1980): 95–110.

82. See also Delbert Elliott and David Huizinga, "Social Class and Delinquent Behavior in a National Youth Panel: 1976–1980," *Criminology* 21 (1983): 149–177. For a similar view, see John Braithwaite, "The Myth of Social Class and Criminality Reconsidered," *American Sociological Review* 46 (1981): 35–58, and Hindelang, Hirschi, and Weis, *Measuring Delinquency*, 196.

83. Jane B. Sprott, Anthony N. Doob, and Jennifer M. Jenkins, "Problem Behaviour and Delinquency in Children and Youth," *Juristat* 21, 4, 2001.

84. David Brownfield, "Social Class and Violent Behavior," *Criminology* 24 (1986): 421–439.

85. Douglas Smith and Laura Davidson, "Interfacing Indicators and Constructs in Criminological Research: A Note on the Comparability of Self-Report Violence Data for Race and Sex Groups," *Criminology* 24 (1986): 473–488.

86. Sally Simpson and Lori Elis, "Doing Gender: Sorting out the Case and Crime Conundrum," *Criminology* 33 (1995): 47–81.

87. Judith Blau and Peter Blau, "The Cost of Inequality: Metropolitan Structure and Violent Crime," *American Sociological Review* 147 (1982): 114–129; Richard Block, "Community Environment and Violent Crime," *Criminology* 17 (1979): 46–57; Robert Sampson, "Structural Sources of Variation in Race-Age-Specific Rates of Offending across Major U.S. Cities," *Criminology* 23 (1985): 647–673.

88. Chin-Chi Hsieh and M.D. Pugh, "Poverty, Income Inequality, and Violent Crime: A Meta-Analysis of Recent Aggregate Data Studies," *Criminal Justice Review* 18 (1993): 182–199.

89. Alan Lizotte, Terence Thornberry, Marvin Krohn, Deborah Chard-Wierschem, and David McDowall, "Neighborhood Context and Delinquency: A Longitudinal Analysis," in *Cross National Longitudinal Research on Human Development and Criminal Behavior*, eds. E.M. Weitekamp and H.J. Kerner (Stavernstr, Netherlands: Kluwer, 1994), 217–227.

90. Travis Hirschi and Michael Gottfredson, "Age and the Explanation of Crime," *American Journal of Sociology* 89 (1983): 552–584.

91. Darrell Steffensmeier and Cathy Streifel, "Age, Gender, and Crime across Three Historical Periods: 1935, 1960 and 1985," *Social Forces* 69 (1991): 869–894; John Laub, David Clark, Leslie Siegel, and James Garofolo, *Trends in Juvenile Crime in the United States: 1973–1983* (Albany, NY: Hindelang Research Center, 1987). On another note, for a comprehensive review of crime and the elderly, see Kyle Kercher, "Causes and Correlates of Crime Committed by the Elderly," in *Critical Issues in Aging Policy*, eds. E. Borgatta and R. Montgomery (Beverly Hills: Sage, 1987), 254–306, and Darrell Steffensmeier, "The Invention of the 'New' Senior Citizen Criminal," *Research on Aging* 9 (1987): 281–311.

92. Hirschi and Gottfredson, "Age and the Explanation of Crime"; Michael

Gottfredson and Travis Hirschi, "The True Value of Lambda Would Appear to Be Zero: An Essay on Career Criminals, Criminal Careers, Selective Incapacitation, Cohort Studies and Related Topics," *Criminology* 24 (1986): 213–234; further support for their position can be found in Lawrence Cohen and Kenneth Land, "Age Structure and Crime," *American Sociological Review* 52 (1987): 170–183.

93. John H. Laub and Robert J. Sampson, *Shared Beginnings, Divergent Lives: Delinquent Boys to Age 70* (Cambridge: Harvard, 2003).

94. Kyle Kercher, "Explaining the Relationship between Age and Crime: The Biological Versus Sociological Model," paper presented at the American Society of Criminology meeting, Montreal, November 1987; Alfred Blumstein, Jacqueline Cohen, and David Farrington, "Criminal Career Research: Its Value for Criminology," *Criminology* 26 (1988): 1–37; Sung Joon Jang and Marvin Krohn, "Developmental Patterns of Sex Differences in Delinquency among African American Adolescents: A Test of the Sex-Invariance Hypothesis," *Journal of Quantitative Criminology* 11 (1995): 195–220; Candace Kruttschnitt, "Violence by and against Women: A Comparative and Cross-National Analysis," *Violence and Victims* 8 (1994): 1–28; Josee Savoie, "Homicide in Canada, 2002," *Juristat* 23, 8, 2003.

95. David Greenberg, "Age, Crime, and Social Explanation," *American Journal of Sociology* 91 (1985): 1–21; Marvin Wolfgang, Robert Figlio, and Thorsten Sellin, *Delinquency in a Birth Cohort* (Chicago: University of Chicago Press, 1972); Lyle Shannon, *Assessing the Relationship of Adult Criminal Careers to Juvenile Careers: A Summary* (Washington, DC: U.S. Department of Justice, 1982); D.J. West and David P. Farrington, *The Delinquent Way of Life* (London: Heinemann, 1977); Donna Hamparian, Richard Schuster, Simon Dinitz, and John Conrad, *The Violent Few* (Lexington, MA: Lexington Books, 1978); Rolf Loeber, Magda Stouthamer-Loeber, and Stephanie Green, "Age at Onset of Problem Behaviour in Boys and Later Disruptive and Delinquent Behaviours," *Criminal Behaviour and Mental Health* 1 (1991): 229–246.

96. Darrell Steffensmeier, Emilie Andersen Allan, Miles Harer, and Cathy Streifel, "Age and the Distribution of Crime: Variant or Invariant?" paper presented at the American Society of Criminology meeting, Montreal, November 1987; Hilary Saner, Robert MacCoun, and Peter Reuter, "On the Ubiquity of Drug Selling among Youthful Offenders in Washington, DC, 1985–1991: Age, Period, or Cohort Effect?" *Journal of Quantitative Criminology* 11 (1995): 362–373.

97. Arnold Barnett, Alfred Blumstein, and David Farrington, "Probabilistic Models of Youthful Criminal Careers," *Criminology* 25 (1987): 83–107.

98. Peter Greenwood, "Differences in Criminal Behavior and Court Responses among Juvenile and Young Adult Defendants," in *Crime and Justice, An Annual Review of Research*, eds. Michael Tonry and Norval Morris (Chicago: University of Chicago Press, 1986), 151–189.

99. John Hagan and Alberto Palloni, "Crimes as Social Events in the Life Course: Reconceiving a Criminological Controversy," *Criminology* 26 (1988): 87–101.

100. Alison Cunningham, *One Step Forward: Lessons Learned from a Randomized Study of Multisystemic Therapy in Canada* (London, ON: Centre for Children and Families in the Justice System, 2002).

101. Cindy M. Schaeffer, and Charles M. Borduin, "Long-Term Follow-up to a Randomized Clinical Trial of Multisystemic Therapy with Serious and Violent Juvenile Offenders," *Journal of Consulting and Clinical Psychology*, 73(3) (2005): 445–453.

102. Travis Hirschi and Michael Gottfredson, "Age and Crime, Logic and Scholarship: Comment on Greenberg," *American Journal of Sociology* 91 (1985): 22–27; "All Wise after the Fact Learning Theory, Again: Reply to Baldwin," *American Journal of Sociology* 90 (1985): 1330–1333; John Baldwin, "Thrill and Adventure Seeking and the Age Distribution of Crime: Comment on Hirschi and Gottfredson," *American Journal of Sociology* 90 (1985): 1326–1329; Per-Olof Wikstrom, "Age and Crime in a Stockholm Cohort," *Journal of Quantitative Criminology* 6 (1990): 61–82.

103. Edward Mulvey and John LaRosa, "Delinquency Cessation and Adolescent Development: Preliminary Data," *American Journal of Orthopsychiatry* 56 (1986): 212–224.

104. Gordon Trasler, "Cautions for a Biological Approach to Crime," in *The Causes of Crime, New Biological Approaches*, eds. Sarnoff Mednick, Terrie Moffitt, and Susan Stack, 7–25 (Cambridge: Cambridge University Press, 1987).

105. James Q. Wilson and Richard Herrnstein, *Crime and Human Nature* (New York: Simon & Schuster, 1985), 126–147.

106. Charles Tittle, "Two Empirical Regularities (Maybe) in Search of an Explanation: Commentary on the Age/Crime Debate," *Criminology* 26 (1988): 75–85.

107. Neal Shover and Carol Thompson, "Age, Differential Expectations and Crime Desistance," *Criminology* 30 (1992): 89–105.

108. Erich Labouvie, "Maturing Out of Substance Use: Selection and Self-Correction," *Journal of Drug Issues* 26 (1996): 457–474.

109. Robert J. Sampson, John H. Laub, and Christopher Wimer, "Does Marriage Reduce Crime? A Counterfactual Approach to Within-Individual Causal Effects," *Criminology* 44, 3, (2006): 465–508.

110. Walter Gove, "The Effect of Age and Gender on Deviant Behavior: A Biopsychosocial Perspective," in *Gender and the Life Course*, ed. A. Ross, 131 (Chicago: Aldine, 1985).

111. Steven D. Levitt, "The Limited Role of Changing Age Structure in Explaining Aggregate Crime Rates," *Criminology* 37 (1999): 581–597.

112. Cesare Lombroso, *The Female Offender* (New York: Appleton Publishers, 1895/1920).

113. Otto Pollack, *The Criminality of Women* (Philadelphia: University of Pennsylvania, 1950).

114. For a review of this issue, see Darrell Steffensmeier, "Assessing the Impact of the Women's Movement on Sex-Based Differences in the Handling of Adult Criminal Defendants," *Crime and Delinquency* 26 (1980): 344–357.

115. Alan Booth and D. Wayne Osgood, "The Influence of Testosterone on Deviance in Adulthood: Assessing and Explaining the Relationship," *Criminology* 31 (1993): 93–118.

116. Darrell Steffensmeier and Robert Clark, "Sociocultural Versus Biological/Sexist Explanations of Sex Differences in Crime: A Survey of American Criminology Textbooks, 1918–1965," *American Sociologist* 15 (1980): 246–255.

117. Gisela Konopka, *The Adolescent Girl in Conflict* (Englewood Cliffs, NJ: Prentice-Hall, 1966); Clyde Vedder and Dora Somerville, *The Delinquent Girl* (Springfield, IL: Charles C Thomas, 1970).

118. John Mirowsky and Catherine Ross, "Sex Differences in Distress: Real or Artifact?" *American Sociological Review* 60 (1995): 449–468; for a review of this issue, see Anne Campbell, *Men, Women and Aggression* (New York: Basic Books, 1993).

119. Robert Hoge, D.A. Andrews, and Alan Leschied, "Tests of Three Hypotheses Regarding the Predictors of Delinquency," *Journal of Abnormal Child Psychology* 22 (1994): 547–559.

120. Freda Adler, *Sisters in Crime* (New York: McGraw-Hill, 1975); Rita James Simon, *The Contemporary Woman and Crime* (Washington, DC: U.S. Government Printing Office, 1975).

121. Timothy F. Hartnagel and Muhammad Mizanuddin, "Modernization, Gender Role Convergence, and Female Crime," *International Journal of Comparative Sociology* 27 (1986): 1–14.

122. David Rowe, Alexander Vazsonyi, and Daniel Flannery, "Sex Differences in Crime: Do Mean and Within-Sex Variation Have Similar Causes?" *Journal of Research in*

Crime and Delinquency 32 (1995): 84–100; Michael Hindelang, "Age, Sex, and the Versatility of Delinquency Involvements," *Social Forces* 14 (1971): 525–534; Martin Gold, *Delinquent Behavior in an American City* (Belmont, CA: Brooks/Cole, 1970); Gary Jensen and Raymond Eve, "Sex Differences in Delinquency: An Examination of Popular Sociological Explanations," *Criminology* 13 (1976): 427–448.

123. Darrel Steffensmeier and Renee Hoffman Steffensmeier, "Trends in Female Delinquency," *Criminology* 18 (1980): 62–85; see also Darrel Steffensmeier and Renee Hoffman Steffensmeier, "Crime and the Contemporary Woman: An Analysis of Changing Levels of Female Property Crime, 1960–1975," *Social Forces* 57 (1978): 566–584; Joseph Weis, "Liberation and Crime: The Invention of the New Female Criminal," *Crime and Social Justice* 1 (1976): 17–27; Carol Smart, "The New Female Offender: Reality or Myth," *British Journal of Criminology* 19 (1979): 50–59; Steven Box and Chris Hale, "Liberation/Emancipation, Economic Marginalization or Less Chivalry," *Criminology* 22 (1984): 473–478.

124. Meda Chesney-Lind, "Female Offenders: Paternalism Reexamined," in *Women, the Courts and Equality*, eds. Laura Crites and Winifred Hepperle, 114–139 (Newberry Park, CA: Sage, 1987).

125. Darrell Steffensmeier, Emilie Allan, and Cathy Streifel, "Development and Female Crime: A Cross-National Test of Alternative Explanations," *Social Forces* 68 (1989): 262–283.

126. Roy Austin, "Recent Trends in the Male and Female Crime Rate: The Convergence Controversy," *Journal of Criminal Justice* 21 (1993): 447–466.

127. Mikhail Thomas, Howard Hurley, and Craig Rimes, "Pilot Analysis of Recidivism among Convicted Youth and Young Adults: 1999/00," *Juristat* 22, 9, 2002.

128. Marvin Wolfgang, Robert Figlio, and Thorsten Sellin, *Delinquency in a Birth Cohort* (Chicago: University of Chicago Press, 1972).

129. See Thorsten Sellin and Marvin Wolfgang, *The Measurement of Delinquency* (New York: Wiley, 1964), p. 120.

130. Paul Tracy and Robert Figlio, "Chronic Recidivism in the 1950 Birth Cohort," paper presented at the American Society of Criminology meeting, Toronto, October 1982; Marvin Wolfgang, "Delinquency in Two Birth Cohorts," in *Perspective Studies of Crime and Delinquency*, eds. Katherine Teilmann Van Dusen and Sarnoff Mednick, 7–17 (Boston: Kluwer-Nijhoff, 1983). The sections that follow rely heavily on these sources.

131. Lyle Shannon, *Criminal Career Opportunity* (New York: Human Sciences Press, 1988); Lyle Shannon, *Assessing the Relationship of Adult Criminal Careers to Juvenile Careers* (Washington, DC: U.S. Department of Justice, 1998).

132. D.J. West and David P. Farrington, *The Delinquent Way of Life* (London: Heinemann, 1977); David Farrington and D.J. West, "Criminal, Penal and Life Histories of Chronic Offenders: Risk and Protective Factors and Early Identification," in *Integrating Individual and Ecological Aspects of Crime* (Stockholm: National Council for Crime Prevention, 1993).

133. See, generally, M. Wolfgang, T. Thornberry, and R. Figlio, eds., *From Boy to Man, from Delinquency to Crime* (Chicago: University of Chicago Press, 1987); Paul Tracy and

Kimberly Kempf-Leonard, *Continuity and Discontinuity in Criminal Careers* (New York: Plenum Press, 1996).

134. R. Tremblay, R. Loeber, C. Gagnon, P. Charlebois, S. Larivee, and M. LeBlanc, "Disruptive Boys with Stable and Unstable High Fighting Behavior Patterns During Junior Elementary School," *Journal of Abnormal Child Psychology* 19 (1991): 285–300; Jennifer White, Terrie Moffitt, Felton Earls, Lee Robins, and Phil Silva, "How Early Can We Tell? Predictors of Childhood Conduct Disorder and Adolescent Delinquency," *Criminology* 28 (1990): 507–535; John Laub and Robert Sampson, "Unemployment, Marital Discord, and Deviant Behavior: The Long-Term Correlates of Childhood Misbehavior," paper presented at the annual meeting of the American Society of Criminology, Baltimore, November 1990, rev. version.

135. Jane B. Sprott and Anthony N. Doob, "Bad, Sad, and Rejected: The Lives of Aggressive Children," *Canadian Journal of Criminology* 42 (2000): 123–134.

136. David Farrington and J. David Hawkins, "Predicting Participation, Early Onset, and Later Persistence in Officially Recorded Offending," *Criminal Behavior and Mental Health* 1 (1991): 1–33; Daniel Nagin, David Farrington, and Terrie Moffitt, "Life-Course Trajectories of Different Types of Offenders," *Criminology* 33 (1995): 111–139.

137. Susan Martin, "Policing Career Criminals: An Examination of an Innovative Crime Control Program," *Journal of Criminal Law and Criminology* 77 (1986): 1159–1182.

138. "A One-Day Snapshot of Inmates in Canada's Adult Correctional Facilities," *Juristat* 18, 8, 1998.

Victims and Victimization

4

Chapter Outline

Learning Objectives

After reading this chapter, you will be able to:

1. Understand the general characteristics of victimization.

2. Be familiar with different patterns of being a victim.

3. Know the theories of victimization.

4. Discuss the programs developed to assist victims.

5. Explain different approaches to prevent victimization.

Rehtaeh Parsons was a 15-year-old girl who lived in Cole Harbour, Nova Scotia. After an alleged sexual assault at a party, photos were circulated online by others. The police initially refused to investigate, and Rehteah killed herself, a victim of cyber-bullying.

Courtesy of Glen Canning

For many years, crime victims were not considered an important topic for criminological study. Victims were viewed as the passive receptors of a criminal's anger, greed, or frustration; they were people considered to be in the wrong place at the wrong time. In the late 1960s, several pioneering studies found that, contrary to popular belief, the victim's function is important in the crime process. Victims can influence criminal behaviour by playing an active role in the criminal incident—for example, when an assault victim insults and provokes his or her eventual attacker. Research efforts have found that victims also play an indirect role in the criminal incident—for example, when people choose a line of work or a lifestyle that takes them into high-crime areas.

The discovery that the victim plays an important role in the crime process has prompted the scientific study of the victim, or **victimology**. Victim studies have also taken on great importance because of concern for those who are injured in violent crimes or who suffer loss owing to economic crimes. The General Social Survey (GSS) indicates about one-quarter of Canadians annually are the victims of at least one crime. Of 7.4 million victimization incidents reported to the GSS in 2009, 31 percent were violent crimes (sexual assault, robbery, or physical assault), 36 percent were household crimes (break and enter, motor vehicle or household theft, or vandalism), while 34 percent were thefts of personal property. The advantage of using the GSS to measure victimization is that it enables us to count crimes not reported to the police, in this case 9,792,000 incidents!

In this chapter, the focus is on victims and their relationship to the criminal process. First, using available victim data, we analyze the nature and extent of victimization. We then turn to a discussion of the relationship between victims and criminal offenders, and we summarize the various theories of victimization. Finally, we look at how society has responded to the needs of victims and at the special problems they still face.

"Gutless politicians are only concerned for the rights of criminals," reads a protest sign outside a Just Desserts café in Toronto. The criticism became especially vehement after it was revealed that the suspect in a shooting at the café was an illegal immigrant convicted previously of violent offences. A public outcry demanded that "aliens" who commit crimes be deported.

PROBLEMS OF CRIME VICTIMS: LOSS AND SUFFERING

Being the target or a victim of rape, robbery, or assault can have considerable consequences.[1] The Insurance Bureau of Canada says that auto theft alone accounts for 13 percent of all property crime, and latest estimates put the total cost of auto theft claims at one billion dollars a year.[2] This includes $542 million for insurers to fix or replace stolen cars; $250 million in police, healthcare, and court-system costs; and millions more for correctional services.

However, property losses are only a small part of the toll that crime takes on victims.[3] Productivity losses due to injury, medical costs, psychological pain, and emotional trauma also take their toll. Then factor in insurance premiums, security, and surveillance costs. This figure does not include the cost of white-collar crime, tax evasion, or stock market manipulation. Other costs cannot be easily measured. Crime makes people feel unsafe and decreases their quality of life. The ripple effects are felt in a broad range of sectors, including health, social services, education, labour, and employment. Table 4.1 provides some international estimates of these costs.

victimology   The study of the victim's role in criminal transactions.

TABLE 4.1 Some International Estimates of the Costs of Crime

Cost of crime in Canada (2004) ($1,500/person)	
police, courts, corrections	$10 billion
with pain, suffering, lost wages, health, insurance costs	$46 billion
Cost of crime in the United States (1999) ($4,100/person)	$1 trillion
Cost of crime in Australia (2003) ($1,600/person)	$32 billion
Cost of crime in England and Wales (2000)	
cost of property	£19 billion
emotional and physical impact on victims	£18 billion
criminal justice system costs	£12 billion
costs in anticipation of crime	£5 billion
Total	£60 billion

SOURCES: Australian Institute of Criminology; (British) Home Office Research Studies; Department of Justice (Canada).

Victims are likely to suffer serious physical injury, often requiring medical treatment. And victims' suffering does not end when the attacker leaves the scene of the crime. They may suffer more victimization at the hands of the justice system. While the crime is still fresh in their minds, victims may be subjected to insensitive questioning by police, including innuendos or suspicion that they were in some way at fault. Victims may have difficulty learning what is going on in the case. In addition, their property is often kept for a long time as evidence and may never be returned. They may also lose wages because of time spent testifying in court.

CONNECTIONS

Some crimes are called victimless crimes, not because no one is hurt, but because an agreement exists between two parties. See Chapter 13 for more about this type of crime.

Time may be wasted when victims appear in court only to have their case postponed or dismissed. Furthermore, they may find that authorities are indifferent to their fear of retaliation if they cooperate in the offender's prosecution, and they may be fearful of testifying in court and being embarrassed by defence attorneys. Only a few courthouses have services on site to assist victims who are appearing in court as witnesses.[4]

After the criminal incident is over, the victim may suffer stress and anxiety, even when the physical traumas, financial losses, and justice process have been forgotten. For example, women who were sexually and physically abused as children are more suicidal as adults than are non-abused females.[5]

Those who suffered the pains of abuse also have significantly higher levels of homelessness; a history of physical and sexual abuse is especially common among homeless women, who may also display symptoms of mental illness.[6] The long-term emotional trauma suffered by women in the aftermath of spousal assault is also well documented.[7] Spousal abuse victims suffer an extremely high prevalence of depression, post-traumatic stress disorder, anxiety disorder, and obsessive-compulsive disorder. Symptoms include nightmares, hyperarousal, and repression of the abuse.

Many Canadians are victimized every year by robbery, and if the crime is marked by violence and loss of property, the psychological consequences can be as serious as post-traumatic stress disorder. Women generally suffer more than men, and seniors typically experience more distress than younger people. Virtually every victim experiences an emotional reaction, and up to a third of robbery victims suffer severe short-term trauma.

After six months, the effects diminish, but 5 percent to 10 percent of victims continue to suffer significant psychopathology. The effects last even longer for victims of domestic violence. Child abuse is also more pervasive than official statistics indicate, and children who are victims of physical assault will have problems, such as non-compliance, tantrums and aggression, serious intellectual deficits, language delays, and interpersonal problems.[8]

Male victims of violent attacks also suffer post-crime stress disorders. Viewing themselves from a male frame of reference, these victims express feelings of being weak and helpless. Whereas female victims internalize and blame themselves, males are more likely to externalize blame and express anger toward their attackers.[9] Often, men who have been incarcerated for violent crimes have themselves been subjected to multiple forms of abuse, as shown in research by John McKendy at St. Thomas University.[10]

Victims are more likely than non-victims to think that crime rates have increased, to worry about neighbourhood safety, and to experience a lower quality of life.[11] In short, the pain and suffering experienced by crime victims does not stop after the criminal incident is over. Many go through a fundamental life change, viewing the world more suspiciously and less as a safe, controllable, and meaningful place, becoming more likely to suffer psychological stress for extended periods.[12]

Some victims may find that the physical wounds received during a criminal incident haunt them for the rest of their lives, especially if they become physically disabled because of wounds sustained during episodes of violence. Many victims have no insurance, and specialized treatment costs add to the overload on an overburdened healthcare system.[13]

Hate crime adds a new dimension to victimization. Hate crimes are more likely to involve excessive violence and greater psychological trauma. They are seven times more likely to be directed against a person than are crimes in which hate isn't the motivating factor. They are twice as likely to involve physical injury and four times as likely to require hospitalization. The ensuing depression can cause intense feelings of vulnerability, and lead to physical ailments, learning problems, and interpersonal conflicts.[14]

The Perception of the Risk of Being a Victim

Consistently in national surveys, people's fears of victimization outstrip their actual likelihood of experiencing a crime. Such results raise questions about the public's perception of risk, as discussed by Rosemary Gartner and Anthony Doob of the University of Toronto.[15] The fact that the public overestimates the likelihood of crime, despite contradictory evidence from their own experience, points to the influence of extraneous factors in the public's knowledge of crime. People do not rely on their own experience in assessing the likelihood of being a victim of crime.

In fact, a study conducted in six urban public housing estates in eastern Ontario by Walter DeKeseredy and colleagues found that prior victimization is a negligible factor in women's fear of crime. Rather than viewing such fears as irrational, the authors look at how perceptions of neighbourhood disorder, routine activities, and neighbourhood satisfaction can predict women's perceptions of personal safety. Through a series of surveys and semi-structured interviews, they found that disorder and neighbourhood satisfaction

have an impact on perceptions of insecurity, and conclude that improving services (e.g., removing garbage, graffiti, vandalized items) may reduce fear as much as reducing crime.[16]

However, it is difficult to know whether fear is widespread. As Figure 4.1 shows, the public is not very concerned about their personal safety, walking alone after dark, or being home alone at night. The little concern they do express relates to using public transportation alone after dark.[17]

So if people have fears, the media likely helps to create a distorted expectation of victimization. For example, homicides, and especially sensational murders, tend to be covered far out of proportion to their occurrence.[18] Most murders are committed by someone known to the victim, but on television the murders most likely to be reported are random acts.[19] This depiction builds a fear of the unknown, and of strangers.

It is reassuring that the fear of crime seems to be decreasing,[20] yet we need to be conscious of how crime can be distorted in the media because it has an effect on demands for police services, the public's perception of the courts, and the programs that politicians develop to prevent and fight crime.[21]

As Thomas Fleming of Wilfrid Laurier University points out, prominent coverage in such media-driven murder cases as those of Clifford Olson, Paul Bernardo and Karla Homolka, and Robert Pickton create fear within the public out of proportion to their incidence.[22]

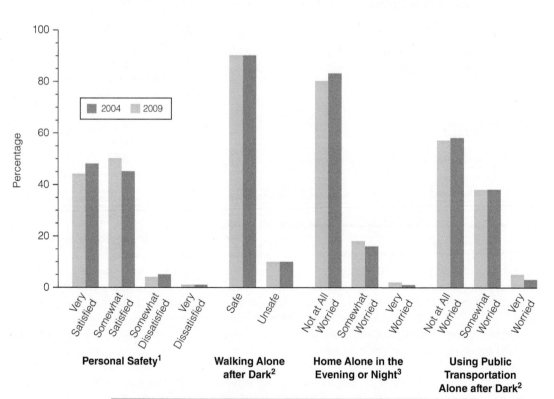

FIGURE 4.1

Self-Reported Feelings of Safety from Crime, 2004 and 2009

Sources: Adapted from Statistics Canada, "Criminal victimization in Canada, 2009," by Samuel Perreault and Shannon Brennan. Catalogue 85-002-X; *General Social Survey* 2009, released November 2009.

1. Responses of "no opinion" were excluded from analysis.
2. Based on responses of people who engage in these activities.
3. Based on responses of people who are home alone in the evening or night.

Problems of Crime Victims: Antisocial Behaviour

In the film *Never Talk to Strangers*, a psychiatrist played by Rebecca DeMornay suspects that her new boyfriend (Antonio Banderas) is a killer. As the bodies pile up, the audience begins to share her suspicions. In the film's surprise ending, we learn that DeMornay is the real killer. It seems her personality was irrevocably damaged when her father sexually abused her as a child and murdered her mother while she watched.

The association between early victimization and later criminality is not merely the subject of Hollywood films; victims of certain crimes are more likely to commit crime themselves. For example, in an analysis of juvenile court records, Cathy Spatz Widom found that child maltreatment was a significant predictor of future criminality. Having been abused or neglected increased the odds both of being arrested as a juvenile and of having at least one alcohol- or drug-related arrest in adulthood. The odds of adult arrest were 39 percent greater for maltreated adolescents than for their non-abused peers, a finding further confirmed by later research.[23] The phenomenon of child victims later becoming adult criminals is called the **cycle of violence**.[24]

The cycle of violence hypothesis is supported by research showing that young males are more likely to engage in violent behaviour if they were (1) the target of physical abuse and (2) exposed to interadult violence.[25] The association between victimization and future behavioural difficulties is not limited to males; research efforts have found that females exposed to family violence may be even more likely than their male counterparts to manifest behavioural and adjustment problems as they mature.[26]

And other research further supports the idea. A study by Jane Sprott (of Ryerson University) found that children who experience high levels of punitive parenting and lower parental nurturance exhibit more aggressive behaviour and are more likely to be involved in property offences.[27] A report on the correctional services system found that an extremely high percentage of Aboriginal offenders report early drug and alcohol use, physical abuse, parental absence or neglect, and poverty in their family backgrounds.[28] Compared with their non-Aboriginal peers, Aboriginal people are more likely to experience violence, especially from family members and on reserve.

Studies of family violence, such as the National Longitudinal Survey of Children, find significant numbers of children witness physical violence in the home, which is found to relate to both long-term behaviour problems such as aggression and to emotional problems such as anxiety.[29]

CONNECTIONS

Hollywood has frequently depicted women as psychopathic serial killers (*Friday the 13th, Black Widow, The Crush*). Are female serial killers common? No, women are rarely involved in multiple murders. Chapter 10 reviews serial murder in some detail.

The Nature of Victimization

Although criminologists depend largely on official statistics for information, victimization surveys are another important source for learning about the nature and extent of victimization. The surveys were originally conceived as a way to estimate the distribution of unreported crime, but can be used to estimate overall victimization patterns.

Victimization Surveys. In 1982, the first Canadian Urban Victimization Survey (CUVS) was set up to acquire information on the extent of crime, the impact of victimization, public perception of crime and the criminal justice system, and public knowledge of crime prevention and compensation programs.[30] The survey showed that many offences were not reported to the police. Robberies, for example, were estimated to occur at a rate of 993 per 100,000 population, compared with the official police rate of 108 per 100,000![31]

The next victimization survey was conducted in 1988 as part of the General Social Survey (GSS). A sample of people 15 years of age and older were asked about their knowledge of victim services, their perceived risk of victimization, and the number and kind of accidents and crimes they had been involved in during 1987. The survey results estimated 143 personal victimizations per 1,000 people and 216 household incidents of victimization per 1,000 people.[32] The last published GSS survey was conducted in 2009, and 2014 is the next cycle.

International patterns of victimization also show that Canadians are less likely to experience certain crimes compared with people in other countries, as shown in Figure 4.2. In 2012, among select countries, Canada had the highest car theft rate, and one of the lowest burglary rates. The Netherlands had the highest assault rate, while the highest rate of bribe-taking was in Azerbaijan.[33]

The patterns in victimization surveys are stable and repetitive, indicating that victimization is not random but rather is a function of personal and ecological factors. Studying these patterns informs us about the nature of victimization, which may lead to policies being created that might eventually reduce the victimization rate. Who are victims? Where does victimization take place? What is the relationship between victims and criminals? Do the report rates differ between a crime that is **acquaintance-related** and a crime that is **stranger-related**? Answers to these questions can come from

cycle of violence The phenomenon of child victims of abuse becoming adult criminals due to their early abusive experiences.

acquaintance-related crime A crime committed by an offender who has had a prior relationship with the victim; date rape is such a crime.

stranger-related crime A crime committed by an offender who has had no prior relationship with the victim, such as most incidents of carjacking.

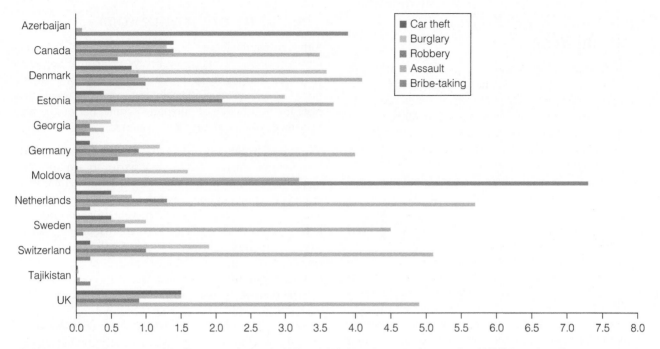

Victimization rates (percentages) for five types of crime in 2009 or 2010, in twelve countries; results of ICVS-based studies

---

FIGURE 4.2

Victimization Rates for Different Crimes

Source: Newsletter of the European Society of Criminology, 2012/3. "The International Crime Victims Survey," http://escnewsletter.org/node/108. Reprinted with permission from the European Society of Criminology.

crime victimization surveys. In the following sections, some of the most important patterns and trends in victimization are discussed.

CONNECTIONS

The importance of victimization is more apparent in the context of other sources of information about crime. Chapter 3 presents an overview of major issues related to the measurement of crime.

THE SOCIAL ECOLOGY OF VICTIMIZATION

The GSS survey data can tell us much about the social and demographic patterns of victimization: where, when, and how it occurs, and whether a victim's involvement in crime is random. Among the various factors we will look at are gender, age, social status, relationship between victim and offender, and patterns of repeat victimization.

In general terms, for example, the risk of personal injury increases moving from east to west across Canada, is higher for males than for females, and is lower for seniors than the young. Those living in urban areas have higher rates of theft, sexual assault, and robbery than do people living in rural areas. Some violent victimizations, such as robbery, are more likely to be committed by strangers and in public, while sexual assaults are more likely to be committed by acquaintances.

Victim Characteristics

Many social and demographic characteristics distinguish victims from non-victims. The most important of these factors are gender, age, social status, and relationship between victim and offender.

Gender. The GSS provides information on the background characteristics of the victims of crime, including gender. Gender is related to the risk of crime, the fear of crime, and a person's sense of control.

In 2009, men were more likely than women to be victims of robbery (16 per 1,000 versus 10 per 1,000) and assault (94 per 1,000 versus 67 per 1,000). Women were more likely to be victims of sexual assault (34 per 1,000 versus 7 per 1,000). The overall rate of victimization by gender has been quite similar over time, despite variations for individual crimes.

When men are victims of violent crime, the perpetrator is usually a stranger. Women are much more likely to be attacked by a relative than men are; about two-thirds of all attacks against women are committed by a husband, a boyfriend, a family member, or an acquaintance.[34] In two-thirds of sexual assaults, the victim knows her attacker.

Gender is a significant factor in such crimes as stalking, in which women account for the majority of victims.[35] Stalking is a gendered crime. Moreover, the way in which authorities deal with such crimes can be crucial. In the infamous Jane Doe case, the Metropolitan Toronto police failed to warn women that a serial rapist was committing crimes in a neighbourhood because they didn't want to alert the suspect. However, the result was that the serial rapist attacked again, and in 2000 Jane Doe sued the Toronto police for $4.5 million in damages.[36]

Risk is gendered and affects how women think about going about their everyday activities, as Wendy Chan of Simon Fraser University shows. Because women are more likely to think that crime has increased and to worry about being victimized, they tend to engage in defensive behaviours, managing their fear of crime by making decisions on where to walk, where to park, and whom to see.[37]

Age.   Age is also related to the risk of crime, although usually the focus is on how young people commit a greater proportion of certain crimes than do other age groups. For example, in 2003, youths 16 to 24 years represented 14 percent of the population but were responsible for 45 percent of property crimes and 32 percent of violent crimes.[38] In 2006, the overall crime rate reached its lowest point in 25 years, but the youth crime rate increased 3 percent. However, by 2012, the police-reported youth accused rate was down 7 percent from 2011, and more than 20 percent from 2009. The rate of youths accused of homicide in 2006 was the highest since 1961. In the case of homicide, these youths are especially likely to kill parents and other family members.[39]

However, we not only want to look at youth as perpetrators of crime but also as victims of crime. Statistics show that in 2009, the rate of violent victimization for those between the ages of 15 and 24 was 284 per 1,000, compared with those aged 25 to 34 (165), those 35 to 44 (114), those 45 to 54 (84), those 55 to 64 (39), and those 65 and over (19).[40] And for the specific crime of sexual assault, those aged 15 to 24 comprise 47 percent of the victims. The GSS victimization survey shows that youths face a much greater victimization risk than do older persons. Much of that crime is also intra-age (within the same age group). Seniors, who are thought of as being the helpless targets of predatory criminals, are actually much safer than are young people.

The association between age and victimization may be bound up in the lifestyle shared by young people. Adolescents often stay out late at night, go to public places, and hang out with kids who have a high risk of criminal involvement. Most adolescents aged 12 to 19 are attacked by offenders in the same age category, while a great majority of adults are victimized by adult criminals. Approximately 50 percent of victimizations occur in or around a private residence, about 30 percent at a public institution (such as a school), and about 20 percent in public places, such as a parking lot.

While victimization surveys such as the GSS generally do not look at those under 15 years of age, researchers often do. For example, Gelles and Straus found extensive physical violence in families, such as 16 percent of couples reporting a violent act toward a spouse, 50 percent of multi-child families reporting attacks between siblings, and 20 percent reporting incidents in which children attacked parents.[41] Children and youth are disproportionately targeted for sexual and physical assault, often by a family member. The general pattern is that youths are victimized out of proportion with their percentage of the population.[42]

Social Status.   The poorest Canadians are more likely to be victims of crime because they are more likely to live in areas that are crime-prone: inner-city, urban neighbourhoods. In 2009, households with incomes of less than $20,000 had a violent victimization rate of 147 per 1,000, compared with even the next highest income category (112 per 1,000). Incidents of robbery and physical assault were highest in this income category. The rate of victimization creeps up in the $100,000-and-over income group, but this higher rate could be due to increased reporting.

The 2009 GSS also reports that Aboriginal people had a higher rate of victimization compared with non-Aboriginal people for sexual assault (71 versus 23 per 1,000), physical assault (141 versus 78), theft of personal property (145 versus 107), and overall violent victimization (232 versus 114).[43]

Particularly disturbing is the finding that poverty increases the risk of child abuse. *The Canadian Incidence Study (CIS) of Reported Child Abuse and Neglect* documents child abuse cases involving neglect, emotional maltreatment, physical and sexual abuse, and exposure to domestic violence. Indirect measures of social status show that neglect was higher than average for those on social assistance, those who rent, and for those who had made two or more moves in the previous year. While poverty was not measured directly, "household risk factors" for substantiated cases showed that 24 percent of households depended on social assistance as their major source of income, 13 percent lived in public housing, 9 percent lived in unsafe conditions, 28 percent had moved at least once in the past 12 months, and 11 percent had moved two or more times.

The CIS also looked at "potential family stressors" by asking child welfare workers to complete a checklist of caregiver risk factors. For female caregivers, the problems most frequently noted were domestic violence (51 percent), lack of social support (40 percent), and mental health issues (27 percent). For male caregivers, the most frequent problems were lack of social support (33 percent), alcohol abuse (30 percent), and childhood maltreatment history (18 percent).[44]

Although people living in poverty are more likely to be the victims of assault, people who are wealthy are more likely to be the targets of break and enter, motor vehicle theft, theft of household property, and vandalism. Perhaps people who are affluent, who sport more expensive attire and drive better cars, attract the attention of thieves seeking lucrative targets. Victim data suggest that thieves choose their targets carefully. In contrast, Canada's poorest people are the targets of violence, an expressive crime.

Relationship. In addition to varying by age, gender, and social status, crimes also vary by the relationship between the victim and the offender. Although an increasing number of violent crimes are committed by strangers, a surprising number of violent crime victims are either related to or acquainted with their attackers. However, one problem with crime statistics is that they provide little information on crime victims, especially with regard to relationships. Victimization surveys and some changes in the Uniform Crime Report (UCR) are trying to rectify this omission (see Chapter 3 for more about the UCR).

The national survey of violence against women, for example, found that 30 percent of women currently or previously married had experienced at least one incident of abuse. The rate of assault among young women in the lowest income group was four times the national average and twice the national average.[45]

The 2009 GSS shows that the overall violent victimization rate was highest for those who are single, (231 per 1,000), compared with those who are married (62 per 1,000) or living common-law (137 per 1,000). In general, friends, acquaintances, or someone else known to the victim were the accused in over half of all violence, especially in sexual or physical assault, whereas perpetrators were more likely to be strangers in robbery incidents. Family-related violence has a high impact on victims, as does being victimized more than once (see Figure 4.3).

Homicide was more likely to be committed by a family member or acquaintance than by a stranger. This same pattern exists for sexual assault, non-sexual assault, criminal harassment, and abduction.

Women in relationships are more likely to experience violence than are men: They are four times more likely to be killed, three times more likely to suffer injury, five times more likely to need medical attention, and five times more likely to fear for their lives as a result of the violence. Approximately three-quarters of spousal homicides are against women, with young separated women at the highest risk. The rates are generally five times lower for men than for women. In recent years, spousal homicide rates have dropped. Several societal changes explain this decline, including more equality in relationships, changes in the law, and better training for the police and judges. In 2012, stranger homicides represented 16 percent of all solved homicides, and had decreased to its lowest point in 40 years, while intimate partner homicides remained stable.[46]

Most jurisdictions have policies on dealing with violence against women in relationships, such as registries of protection orders to ensure that police have access to information on peace bonds and restraining orders; improved rights and services for victims; funded transition houses, treatment, violence prevention, and public education programs.[47] When a spouse is killed, it is usually the woman; and when women kill, it is usually in self-defence. After Jane Stafford shot her sleeping common-law husband, the trial evidence indicated that he was domineering and abusive. He had threatened to kill all the members of her family, one by one, if she tried to leave him. On the night in question, he had threatened to kill her son.[48]

It is only within the last 15 years or so that the Canadian courts have come to realize that standards for assessing the violence of women compared with that of men must be different in some situations, as discussed in the Famous Canadian Criminals box. The case of Lyn Lavallee made Canadian history, as the court took into account the perspective of the victim as part of the defence to murder.

FIGURE 4.3

Emotional Consequences of Self-Reported Victimization Incidents, 2009

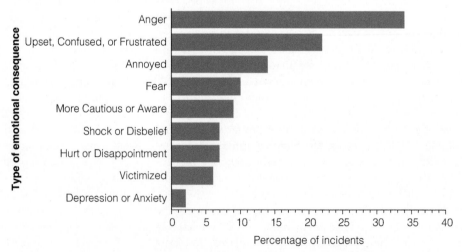

Note: Excludes all incidents of spousal sexual and physical assault. Excludes data from the Northwest Territories, Yukon, and Nunavut, which will be published at a later date.

Sources: Adapted from Statistics Canada, "Criminal victimization in Canada, 2009," by Samuel Perreault and Shannon Brennan. Catalogue 85-002-X; *General Social Survey* 2009, released November 2009.

Note: Excludes all incidents of spousal sexual and physical assault. Excludes data from the Northwest Territories, Yukon, and Nunavut, which will be published at a later date.

Angelique Lyn Lavallee was a battered woman in a violent common-law relationship. She killed her partner late one night by shooting him in the back of the head as he left her room. They had argued and she was fearful for her life. He had frequently abused her and she had concocted excuses to explain her injuries. A psychiatrist with experience in treating battered wives prepared a psychiatric assessment of the appellant that was used to support her claim of self-defence. The psychiatrist explained Lavallee's ongoing terror and her inability to escape the relationship, despite the violence that put her life in danger. He testified that when Lavallee shot her partner, it was the desperate act of a woman who believed that she would be killed.

Lavallee was acquitted on the grounds that she was psychologically trapped in an abusive relationship and that, to protect herself, she had the right to take steps that would not otherwise be tolerated. This conclusion differs from the traditional right of self-defence in that a woman can excusably kill her husband in self-defence even if no threat is imminent. Although the jury acquitted the appellant, its verdict was overturned by the Manitoba Court of Appeal.

Lavallee did not testify, but the statement she made to police on the night of the shooting was put into evidence. In it, she described a party with friends:

> Me and Wendy argued as usual and I ran in the house after Kevin pushed me. I was scared, I was really scared. I locked the door. Herb was downstairs with Joanne and I called for Herb but I was crying when I called him. I said, "Herb, come up here please." Herb came up to the top of the stairs and I told him that Kevin was going to hit me, actually beat on me again. Herb said he knew and that if I was his old lady things would be different; he gave me a hug.... He went outside to talk to Kevin, leaving the door unlocked. I went upstairs and hid in my closet from Kevin. I was so scared.... My window was open and I could hear Kevin asking questions about what I was doing and what I was saying. Next thing I know he was coming up the stairs for me. He came into my bedroom and said, "Wench, where are you?" And he turned on my light and he said, "Your purse is on the floor" and he kicked it. Okay, then he turned and he saw me in the closet. He wanted me to come out but I didn't want to come out because I was scared. I was so scared. He grabbed me by the arm right there. There's a bruise on my face also where he slapped me. He didn't slap me right then, first he yelled at me then he pushed me and I pushed him back and he hit me twice on the right-hand side of my head. I was scared. All I thought about was all the other times he used to beat me, I was scared, I was shaking as usual. The rest is a blank, all I remember is he gave me the gun and a shot was fired through my screen. This is all so fast. And then the guns were in another room and he loaded it the second shot and gave it to me. And I was going to shoot myself. I pointed it to myself, I was so upset. Okay, and then he went and I was sitting on the bed and he started going like this with his finger [the appellant made a shaking motion with an index finger] and said something like, "You're my old lady and you do as you're told" or something like that. He said, "Wait till everybody leaves, you'll get it then," and he said something to the effect of "either you kill me or I'll get you"— that was what it was. He kind of smiled and then he turned around. I shot him but I aimed out. I thought I aimed above him and a piece of his head went that way.

When the case was appealed to the Supreme Court, it said in its decision, "It is difficult for the layperson to comprehend the battered wife syndrome. It is commonly thought that battered women are not really beaten as badly as they claim; otherwise they would have left the relationship. Alternatively, some believe that women enjoy being beaten, that they have a masochistic strain in them." Luckily, we have left such views behind, and it is clear that the Supreme Court did not agree with these views.

As a consequence of that ruling, Justice Minister Allan Rock appointed a judge to review the cases of more than a dozen women convicted before 1990 of killing their abusive partners. This was a historic step. The federal government had the authority to release the women, shorten their sentences, or order new trials. And the 1990 Supreme Court of Canada ruling that set the legal framework for what has become known as the "battered wife syndrome" defence was a historic moment.

SOURCES: *R. v. Lavallee*, [1990] 1 S.C.R.: 852; "Ministers Respond to Self-Defence Review," Department of Justice News Release, Ottawa, September 26, 1997.

Repeat Victimization

Does prior victimization enhance or reduce the chances of future victimization? Certain patterns of behaviour encourage victimization, and people who maintain them become chronic victims who are constantly the target of predatory crimes.

Research shows that prior victimization is a strong predictor of future victimization.[49] Research also shows that households that have experienced victimization in the past are most likely to experience it again.[50] Offences that are more likely to be stranger-related, such as robbery, are not as likely to be repeat offences. This pattern is seen internationally.[51]

David Finkelhor and Nancy Asdigian identified three specific types of characteristics that increase the potential for victimization:

1. Target vulnerability. The victims' physical weakness or psychological distress makes them easy targets (e.g., drinking).
2. Target gratifiability. The victims' characteristics increase their risk because they have some quality or possession that an offender wants to obtain (e.g., leather coat).
3. Target antagonism. Some characteristics increase risk because they arouse anger, jealousy, or destructive impulses in the offender (e.g., dressing differently).[52]

What factors predict chronic victimization? It is a combination of personal and social factors. For example, repeat victimizations are most likely to occur in areas with high crime rates, but some personal characteristics are also important.[53] Kids who are shy, physically weak, or socially isolated may be prone to being bullied in the schoolyard. Kids who have themselves been abused may be more prone to bullying. Bullying then is a process that enhances chronic victimization. For example, boys who are bullied at school may become even more introverted after being victimized, increasing their chances for future victimization.[54]

Repeat victimization is also a function of rational choice and offender decision making. Offenders learn the weaknesses of victims, for example, when the abusive husband learns that his wife will not call the police. Or if the police do not respond to reported hate crimes, perpetrators learn they have little to fear from the law.[55] Victims of repeat victimization also are likely to believe that neighbourhood crime is increasing.

A study in British Columbia found that 18 percent of respondents had been victims of multiple offences. Furthermore, 18 percent of the sample accounted for 69 percent of the offences. The 6 percent of the respondents who had been victimized three times or more accounted for 30 percent of all incidents.[56]

CONNECTIONS

Efforts to understand the causes of the issues faced in Aboriginal communities today focus on those communities' wider relations with the dominant Caucasian society. Chapter 9 discusses issues of inequality and ethnicity in more detail.

THEORIES OF VICTIMIZATION

For most of its history, criminological theory has focused on the actions of the criminal offender, virtually ignoring the role of the victim. The resultant focus has been called *offenderology*.[57] However, then a number of scholars noted that the victim is not a passive target in crime but someone whose behaviour can influence his or her own fate. Crime is seldom random or gratuitous, but is an outcome of an interactional process that involves both victim and offender.

One of the first criminologists to comment on the role that victims play was Hans Von Hentig in the 1940s. He portrayed the crime victim as someone who "shapes and molds the criminal."[58] The criminal might be a predator, but the victim may have helped the offender by providing an opportunity for the crime to happen. Another pioneering **victimologist**, Stephen Schafer, focused on the victim's responsibility in the "genesis of crime" for provoking or encouraging the criminal.[59] These early works helped focus attention on the role of the victim in the crime problem. Today, several theories attempt to explain the causes of victimization, including victim precipitation theory, lifestyles theory, and routine activities theory.

Abuse committed at residential and mission schools for Aboriginal children run by religious orders gained national prominence during the 1980s. Children were physically, emotionally, and sexually abused by priests and nuns after the children had been forcibly taken from their families and transported hundreds of kilometres to schools in which they were not allowed to speak their own languages.

© Provincial Archives of Alberta, Photo Collection

victimologist A researcher who studies the role of victims in the crime process.

Victim Precipitation Theory

Is it possible that people cause their own victimization? According to the **victim precipitation** view, some people may initiate the confrontation that eventually leads to their injury or death. Victim precipitation can be either active or passive. This theory does not blame the victim or try to excuse the actions of the offender, but tries to explain why some people and not others become victims.

Active precipitation occurs when victims act provocatively, use threats or fighting words, or even attack first. This model of victim-precipitated crime was first popularized by Marvin Wolfgang in his 1958 study of criminal homicide. He defined the term *victim precipitation* as follows:

> "Victim-precipitated" is applied to those criminal homicides in which the victim is a direct, positive precipitator in the crime. The role of the victim is characterized by his having been the first in the homicide drama to use physical force against his subsequent slayer. The victim-precipitated cases are those in which the victim was the first to show and use a deadly weapon, to strike a blow in an altercation—in short, the first to commence the interplay or resort to physical violence.[60]

Examples of a victim-precipitated homicide include the death of an aggressor in a barroom brawl or a wife who kills her husband after he attacks and threatens to kill her. Wolfgang found that 26 percent of the 588 homicides in his sample could be classified as victim-precipitated. Clearly this theory applies more readily to violent crime than to property crime. In most cases where victims precipitate a violent confrontation, they are more likely than the person they targeted to suffer harm as a result.

Active Precipitation and Rape. Nowhere is the concept of victim precipitation more controversial than in the crime of rape. In 1971, Menachim Amir suggested that female victims often contribute to their attacks through a relationship with the rapist.[61] This statement is controversial because it diverts our attention (and blame) from the man to the woman. However, it focuses our attention on court cases in which the defendant is acquitted because the victim's actions are construed as consenting to sexual intimacy. Date rapes are rarely treated with the same degree of punitiveness as stranger rapes.[62]

Sometimes defendants are found not guilty because judges believe that a sexual assault was victim-precipitated, such as the case where the judge said, "The majority of rapes occur when the woman is drunk and passed out. A man comes along and sees a pair of hips and helps himself." Or the now famous *R. v. Ewanchuk* case where a judge explained his acquittal of a man who sexually assaulted a young woman who was being interviewed for a job in this way: "The complainant did not present herself in a bonnet and crinolines, she was the mother of a six-month-old baby, and along with her boyfriend shared an apartment with another friend."[63]

In another case, a mathematics professor wrote in a student newspaper that "a girl who had sexual intercourse with a large number of boys would not suffer as a result of an unwanted sexual encounter ... When a boy invites a girl to his bedroom ... she should consider it an invitation for sexual intercourse."[64]

Such cases clearly involve blaming the victim. Ezzat Fattah, one of the early pioneers in the discipline of victimology, says that we need to be aware that the interactions of victim and perpetrator involve unequal relations of power that are exploited by the aggressor.[65]

CONNECTIONS

Efforts to separate the causes of rape from the concept of victim precipitation have resulted in the modification of rape laws in Canada, including (1) banning testimony in court about the sexual history and reputation of the victim, and (2) banning the publication of the identity of the victim in the news media. Rape and the law are discussed in Chapter 10.

Passive Precipitation. **Passive precipitation** occurs when the victim exhibits some personal characteristic that unknowingly threatens or encourages the attacker. The threat can occur because of personal conflict, such as when two people are in competition over a job, promotion, love interest, or some other scarce and coveted commodity. Although the victim may never have met his or her attacker or even known of the attacker's existence, the attacker feels menaced and acts accordingly.[66]

For example, Sandy Welsh at the University of Toronto researches the causes and consequences of sexual harassment in the workplace, which is typically a gendered crime against women. Sexual harassment is a relatively new area of study: official complaints to the Canadian Human Rights Commission have been possible only since 1978. The more serious a complaint is, the more likely it is to be resolved because women must demonstrate they have suffered either physically or psychologically. The result is a double victimization because those victimizations deemed to be less serious are given less consideration by the authorities.

In another scenario, the victim may belong to a group whose mere presence threatens the attacker's reputation, status, or economic well-being. For example, hate crime violence may be precipitated when immigrant group members move into a community to compete for jobs and housing; similarly, the hiring of women in the workforce may be seen as a threatening

---

victim precipitation The view that a victim's behaviour or characteristics, such as verbal abuse, or openly displaying wealth, can act as the spark that ignites the subsequent offence.

active precipitation The aggressive behaviour of victims, which provokes a reaction.

passive precipitation The view that personal and social characteristics of victims make them attractive targets for predatory criminals.

---

act by insecure and emotionally unstable men. (See Exhibit 4.1 above for more factors that produce hate crimes.)

Dozens of organized hate groups are estimated to be operating in Canada. The Media Awareness Network and Hatewatch.org approximates that 500 hardcore hate sites are active on the Internet. The Internet enables these groups to reach and recruit more people than ever before, making it a medium that spreads hatred as easily as it spreads free speech. The Famous Canadian Court Cases box on page 105 looks at the issue of when the publication of free speech becomes a hate crime.

Recently, sentencing provisions in the Canadian *Criminal Code* were amended so that if a judge determined hatred was the motivation in an attack, it would be considered an **aggravating** rather than a **mitigating factor**, thus requiring

a more severe sentence (see Exhibit 4.2). When this bill was proposed in 1995, the justice minister was accused of promoting the special interests of homosexuals and had to defend the proposal by saying that he was not promoting a gay lifestyle.[67] In 2004, a new hate-crime bill passed the Senate, again, under vigorous opposition.

The first case to use the enhanced sentencing provision was the racially motivated murder of a Sikh cleric, Nirmal Singh Gill, in 1998. The Royal Canadian Mounted Police (RCMP) infiltrated a skinhead gang and collected evidence crucial to the prosecution. The five defendants were sentenced to 12 to 15 years incarceration.

Research indicates that passive precipitation is related to power; if members of the target group can establish themselves economically or gain political power in the community, their vulnerability will diminish. They become too formidable a target to attack and are no longer passive precipitators. For example, employed women in Canada are less likely to be homicide victims, whereas unemployed women suffer higher homicide victimization rates.[68] By implication, gaining economic power reduces the victimization risk for women.

In 2004, the federal government finalized a nationwide plan to combat racism, which included asking law enforcement agencies to establish hate crime units. Other initiatives were an educational campaign to promote antiracism and the funding of crime prevention programs, which were felt necessary in light of recent incidents across the country. B'nai Brith Canada reported more incidents of harassment and vandalism against Jews in 2003 than any year in the past two decades.

The concept of victim precipitation, whether active or passive, implies that, in some crimes, the offender's crime begins as a reaction to a victim's actions. The crime, as reaction, could not take place without action on the part of the victim. The victim's actions, which might consciously place him or her in harm's way, might also be inadvertent. Routine activities theory, discussed later in this chapter, will explore this idea further. One important point, however, is that modern crime prevention programs involve making targets harder to victimize, which requires that the programs be victim centred.

The Extent of Hate Crime. Until recently, Canada had no systematic method of collecting hate crime statistics. However, preliminary research shows that hate crime occurs

aggravating factor A circumstance that makes a crime more serious; for example, racism makes an assault more serious, resulting in a harsher sentence as a hate crime.

mitigating factor A circumstance that makes a crime less serious; for example, abused people react more when threatened, which may serve as a defence or may lead to a lighter sentence.

Crime in the News

Coverage of Domestic Violence in the News Leads to Some Observations

The media has not traditionally been a good source of information on family violence. Crimes were not covered, and victims were often blamed. This reflected societal attitudes to domestic violence and its treatment in the courts. In a recent study, news articles on men who killed their wives and then commit suicide were examined. The general conclusion is that coverage has improved, but still tends to mystify the problem.

The study used articles from the *Calgary Herald* from 2008 using the term "murder-suicide." Alberta has the highest rate of spousal homicide-suicide in Canada. This was compared to a second period a decade earlier to see if coverage had changed.

Research on domestic homicide often points out how news articles are framed to blame the victim or excuse the offender. Direct tactics involve using negative language to describe the victim, criticizing her actions such as her not reporting past incidences, or mentioning "consorting" with other men as contributing to her murder.

Indirect tactics include using sympathetic language to describe the perpetrator, and emphasizing mental, physical, emotional, and financial problems that might excuse his actions.

In 2008, there were two main cases covered extensively. One described the perpetrator as a loving family man who doted on his wife and young daughters but heard voices in his head and believed he was possessed by the devil. The second involved a woman who had restraining orders due to a troubled relationship. She had tried to break it off, but the period after the woman leaves is usually the most dangerous. She was said to be a caring, loving woman who never gave an indication of problems at home. However, the man lost jobs, drank frequently, made threats, and was physically violent. Authorities said it was a domestic dispute that went terribly wrong.

In these stories, the explanation is inexplicable: the man was loving and the couple seemed happy. Sometimes there were warning signs: the man had difficulties, or the couple had a history of conflict. And there was always an attempt to find an excuse: mental disorder, alcoholism, or unemployment.

In both cases, cognitive biases were used. Criticizing the victim, for example, by not calling the police is a "just-world bias," that good people do the right thing, and bad things happen to bad (incompetent) people. On the other hand, to focus on the (now) obvious warning signs is "hindsight bias." Both are ways of blaming in order to make ourselves feel safe.

The decade-old articles were short, either briefs or about 200 words. Police are the usual source, and the explanations include: domestic problems, depressed state, no concrete motive, and nobody knows.

In comparison, the lack of coverage, the paucity of detail, the reliance on official sources, and the absence of a context for explanation is striking. This was normal news coverage of domestic violence in the 1980s, a virtual silence compared to coverage 20 years later where there is an increased use of advocates as sources and a larger discussion of context.

The incidence of domestic violence has decreased over time in society, at the same time as newspaper articles about intimate partner violence have increased. The public is receiving more information about fewer cases, although there is still a tendency to mystify the nature of domestic violence.

In response, some researchers have worked to improve journalistic coverage. For example, the Rhode Island Coalition against Domestic Violence worked with reporters to develop a best practices handbook on news coverage of domestic violence murders. In comparing print coverage of domestic violence murders before and after, they found an increased tendency to label the murder of intimates as domestic violence, and more use of advocates as sources. As a result, murders that had previously been framed by police as unpredictable, private tragedies were more likely to be framed as social problems that required public intervention.

This example of action research shows the importance of naming interpretations and the possibility of changing them.

SOURCE: Copyright Chris McCormick, published in the *Daily Gleaner* (Fredericton), February 11, 2010.

---

primarily on the basis of race, religion, and sexual orientation. Julian Roberts at the University of Ottawa estimated that 60,000 hate crimes were committed annually in Canada.[69] Many jurisdictions now have established specialized hate/bias crime units.

Some organizations have tracked hate crimes on their own, such as the League for Human Rights of B'nai Brith, which, since 1982, has produced an annual report on the number of anti-Semitic incidents in Canada. But it was not until 1999 that the GSS measured self-reported hate crime victimization incidents at the national level. It found 272,732 incidents motivated by hate.[70] Whereas almost half (49 percent) of all hate crime incidents are assaults, fewer than one in five (18 percent) non–hate crime incidents are assaults. And whereas police-reported statistics indicate that in 30 percent of non-hate crimes the perpetrator is a stranger, in almost half (46 percent) of all violent hate crime incidents, the offender is a stranger to the victim. See Exhibit 4.3 on page 104 for the most recent statistics.

Hate/bias crime is slowly being recognized as a widespread and serious problem and as a new category of violent personal crime. This crime is displayed in violent

EXHIBIT 4.3

Quick Facts: Hate Crime in Canada

- Hate crime decreased by 5 percent in 2011, for a second year in a row, with 1,332 incidents, for a rate of 3.9 per 100,000.
- Incidents were motivated by race/ethnicity (52 percent), religion (25 percent), and sexual orientation (18 percent).
- Hate crimes motivated by sexual orientation showed the only increase, by 10 percent.
- Mischief is the most commonly reported non-violent offence.
- The 2004 GSS shows that 40 percent of incidents are reported to the police.
- Toronto, Montreal, and Vancouver account for 38 percent of all incidents, while Peterborough (17.9) and Hamilton (15.9) had the highest rates in 2011.
- Victims found it difficult to carry out daily activities in 40 percent of hate crime incidents compared with 23 percent of non–hate crime incidents in 2008.
- Incidents motivated by sexual orientation were more likely to be violent (46 percent), and homosexuals were more likely than other victims to suffer an injury.
- When the victim–accused relationship was identified, 77 percent of victims did not know their perpetrator, compared with 33 percent of victims of other violent crimes in 2008.
- Youths are more likely to be accused (60 percent), and to be male (88 percent).
- Hate crime is susceptible to reporting practices, both by the public and the police.

SOURCE: Statistics Canada, "Police-reported Hate Crimes, 2001," http://www.statcan.gc.ca/daily-quotidien/130711/dq130711a-eng .htm (accessed July 28, 2014).

acts directed toward a particular person or members of a group merely because the targets share a discernible racial, ethnic, religious, gender, or physical characteristic, or sexual orientation. Hate crimes can include the desecration of a house of worship or cemetery, harassment of a minority-group family that has moved into a previously all-Caucasian neighbourhood, or a racially motivated murder of an individual.

A number of conditions may influence hate crime offending, including

- economic recession, crime, unemployment blamed on members of minority groups;
- minority groups moving into an area being seen as a threat to a traditional way of life;
- the desire to alleviate boredom and create excitement;
- feelings of resentment for the economic or social success of minority groups;
- historical animosities transmitted from one generation to another; and
- belief that offenders' actions are condoned by the larger society or community.

Hate crimes usually involve convenient and vulnerable targets who are incapable of fighting back, for example, teenagers attacking vagrants and the homeless.[71]

The Roots of Hate. Why do people commit bias crimes? Hate crimes are generally spontaneous incidents motivated by the victims' walking, driving, shopping, or socializing in an area in which their attacker believes they do not belong.[72] Other reasons found for bias attacks are that the victim had moved into an ethnically distinct neighbourhood or had dated a member of a different racial or ethnic group. Although hate crimes are often unplanned, a majority of these crimes were serious incidents involving assaults and robberies.[73]

Although hate crimes are often mindless attacks directed toward minority-group members who have historically been the focus of past attacks, political and economic trends may cause violent attacks to be redirected against members of minority groups newly found to be a threat. For example, after the terrorist attacks of September 11, 2001, hate crimes against East Asian Americans had a short-term but significant increase. The CCJS reports that in the two months following 9/11, three times more hate crimes were committed than in any other two-month period. Hate crimes associated with terrorism are more likely to be violent.[74]

Lifestyle Theories

Some criminologists believe that people may become crime victims because they have a lifestyle that increases their exposure to criminal offenders. Both GSS and UCR data sources show that victimization risk is increased by such characteristics as being single, associating with young men, going out in public places late at night, and living in an urban area. Conversely, a person's chances of victimization can be reduced by staying home at night, moving to a rural area, staying out of public places, earning more money, associating with young women, or getting married. The important point is that crime is not a random occurrence but rather is, in part, a function of the behaviour and actions of its targets.

Criminality and victimization are bound in an association in which the probability of crime depends on the activities of the potential victim.[75] Crime occurs because victims have a lifestyle that places them in jeopardy: A person's chances of being robbed by a stranger are usually much greater in downtown Montreal at 2 a.m. than in a locked farmhouse in rural Manitoba.

The likelihood of victimization is greatest among groups with high-risk lifestyles. For example, teens may have the greatest risk of victimization because their lifestyle places them in an at-risk location—the neighbourhood high school. That's where the most criminal elements of the population, teenage males, congregate. In 2006, while only about 1 in 10 of youth crimes occurred on school property, assaults were the most prevalent offence (27 percent), and weapons were present in about 7 percent of school crimes.[76] In assaults against youths, the accused is usually an acquaintance,

Famous Canadian Court Cases
R. v. Keegstra

Responding to a spread of hate propaganda in Canada in the 1960s, the Cohen Commission concluded that hate propaganda posed a serious threat to society, and was responsible for 1970 *Criminal Code* amendments, such as section 319(2), which prohibits the communication of statements that willfully promote hatred against an identifiable group. A defence to this charge is when an accused can prove the objectionable statements are in fact true.

This law was disputed in a notorious case involving Alberta high-school teacher James Keegstra, who taught anti-Semitic material. His inflammatory depiction of Jews as a "treacherous" and "sadistic" people who "created the Holocaust to gain sympathy" caused him to be fired in 1982 after being confronted by parents and inspected by the school superintendent. Two years later, this clash with education officials had become a full-fledged battle with the criminal justice system when police charged him for violating Canada's anti-hate statutes.

Defence counsel unsuccessfully argued that section 319 of the *Criminal Code* is unconstitutional because it infringes on the rights to free speech and presumption of innocence. However, in 1990, the Supreme Court agreed that hate propaganda is protected under section 2 of the *Charter* because it constitutes expression. However, the justices were divided as to whether the anti-hate statute can be considered a reasonable limitation of rights and freedoms. By a margin of four votes to three, the Supreme Court decided that it was a reasonable limitation and upheld section 319.

SOURCES: Karen Mock, "Recognizing and Reacting to Hate Crime in Canada Today," Canadian Race Relations Foundation, www. crr.ca/EN/Publications/EducationalTools/ RecognizingandReacting.htm; *R. v. Keegstra*, [1990] 3 S.C.R. 697, www.canlii.org/ca/cas/ scc/1990/1990scc128.html; Robert Sharpe, Katherine Swinton, and Kent Roach, *The Charter of Rights and Freedoms*, 2nd ed. (Toronto: Irwin Law Inc., 2002); "Testing the Limits of Freedom of Expression: The Keegstra Case," *Human Rights in Canada: A Historical Perspective*, December 13, 1990.

---

especially in the case of male victims. Physical force was the most common weapon, and most took place in a public area.[77]

In Toronto in 2007, a report on school safety was commissioned after the shooting death of 15-year-old Jordan Manners at C.W. Jefferys Collegiate Institute. The School Community Safety Advisory Panel report described the Toronto District School Board, Canada's largest school system, as being rife with weapons and having unreported and widespread violence, harassment, and sexual assaults. The result was recommendations for an increased police presence in the schools and for education about guns and gangs, Internet safety, and drugs. In addition, an expanded anonymous safety tip-line service was instituted.

An adolescent's lifestyle continues to place him or her at risk after leaving the school grounds. Kids who hang out with their friends and get involved in the recreational pursuit of fun face an elevated risk for victimization. For example, their friends may give them false IDs so that they can go drinking; hanging out in bars places them at risk because many fights and assaults occur in places that serve liquor.[78]

Adolescents are not the only ones with high-risk lifestyles. Numerous studies have found that the homeless population is extremely vulnerable to physical harm because its members are constantly exposed to the criminal population in large urban areas. People who are homeless have a high victimization risk compared with the general population, and homeless victims are more likely to have a history of mental hospitalization, depression, and physical problems.[79]

Women working on the street are particularly vulnerable to predatory violence, especially since they face criminal prosecution themselves. Women who work for escort services don't turn up as murder victims at the same rate as street-involved women. Similarly, women who work in body-rub and massage parlours don't encounter the same kind of victimization from clients as do street prostitutes. When a conflict with a client occurs, he may use violence because he knows she is unlikely to report it to the police. Other high-risk professions include police officers, taxi drivers, security guards, bouncers, and retail business managers, as identified by John Lowman of Simon Fraser University.[80]

However, statistics on violence against street prostitutes suggest that they probably have the most dangerous form of work in Canada, as shown in the following quote from work by Lesley Ann Jeffrey at the University of New Brunswick and Gayle MacDonald at St. Thomas University.[81]

> I'm the only one left of all my friends. They are all dead from prostitution, being killed. And I'm the only one left, and I was left for dead. The cops had to cut the belt off my neck, and the person was charged with attempted murder, with attempt to kill. The cops had pictures of my body, with my face and everything. They told my mother they didn't think I was going to live. I have a speech impediment now, I stutter sometimes. And my jaw, both of them were broke, since that attack, too. And they took pictures and I was in the hospital four-and-a-half days on life

Hate crime is slowly being recognized as a widespread and serious problem, and in recent years criminologists have begun studying the issue. One group targeted for hate crimes is gay men and lesbian women.

A community survey at the 519 Church Street Community Centre in Toronto, conducted by Ellen Faulkner of Brock University, showed that 78 percent of respondents had experienced verbal assaults and 50 percent had been threatened with physical violence. Toronto's Wellesley Hospital created a program to help its emergency staff to be more sensitive and effective when caring for victims of gay bashing.

A New Brunswick study on discrimination and violence against lesbians, gays, and bisexuals found that 82 percent had been verbally abused; 34 percent had been chased or followed; 10 percent had been spat on; 19 percent had had their property damaged; 17 percent had had objects thrown at them; 18 percent had been punched, kicked, hit, or beaten; and 23 percent had been harassed or assaulted by the police.

A Nova Scotia study on homophobic abuse and discrimination found that 72 percent of gays and lesbians had been verbally abused because of their sexual orientation; 42 percent had been threatened with violence; 33 percent had been chased or followed; 9 percent had been spat on; 12 percent had had their property damaged; 25 percent had had objects thrown at them; 18 percent had been assaulted with a weapon, punched, kicked, or beaten; 16.5 percent had been harassed; and another 2 percent had been beaten by the police.

In a survey of homophobic violence reported in the *Gay Times* (1996), one in three gay men and one in four lesbians said they had been bashed in the previous five years. For those under age 18, the figures were even higher. Avoidance techniques were adopted, such as not holding hands or kissing in public (88 percent), avoiding telling people they are gay (65 percent), and avoiding looking "obviously gay" (59 percent).

- In 1985, Kenn Zeller was murdered in a Toronto park by five teenagers who had gone to the park to "beat up a fag."
- In 1989, a gay AIDS activist, Joe Rose, was murdered on a crowded Montreal bus by a gang of 15 youths who taunted him with shouts of "faggot" and stabbed him to death.
- In 1992, Daniel Lacombe was killed in Montreal by a group of young adults who had gone out to beat up gays.

- At least 14 gay men were murdered in Montreal between 1989 and 1994 as a result of homophobic violence.

The FBI reports that of the 17 murders reported among hate-motivated incidents, racial bias motivated 9 of the murders; sexual-orientation bias and ethnicity or national origin bias motivated 3 each; and religious bias motivated 2. In the Matthew Shepard case, which galvanized public attention in 1998, two men were tried and found guilty for luring a gay man from a bar, pistol-whipping him, and leaving him tied to a fence to die. The defendants tried to argue that his sexual advances provoked them into a homosexual panic and that they were just defending themselves.

In 1995, Scott Amedure was killed by Jonathan Schmitz after appearing on *The Jenny Jones Show*, a television talk show. On the show, Scott admitted to having a crush on Jonathan, who turned out to be homophobic. The show made a $25 million settlement with the victim's family.

Victor Janoff, in *Pink Blood: Homophobic Violence in Canada,* provides a comprehensive overview of queer bashing. He analyzes the impact of violence on gays and lesbians, and assembles evidence on the prevalence of homophobic violence in Canada. In an extensive series of interviews with police

---

support. They didn't know if I was going to live. I have scars here from life support and oxygen. There was not enough oxygen going to my brain, they put me in the round machine there, CAT scan it was, and I'm lucky to be alive now. And it's just like ... I'm jumping now ... I went from being left for dead, and all my other friends are dead, okay. And to me, I got to the point I didn't care if I died or not, but this person that did this to me got off because he ratted out another drug dealer.

The Equivalent Group Hypothesis. The lifestyle view suggests that victims and criminals share similar characteristics and that their lifestyle exposes them to increased levels of victimization risk. Similarly, the **equivalent group hypothesis** says that victims and criminals are not actually separate

groups, and the hypothesis is supported by research showing that crime victims self-report significant amounts of criminal behaviour.

In one study, the CCJS reported that half of all homicide victims 12 years and older had a criminal record, and 47 percent of this group had been previously convicted of a violent crime.[82] Many studies have shown that adolescents who engage in delinquent behaviour or join gangs also face the greatest risk of victimization. For example,

> **equivalent group hypothesis** The view that victims and criminals share similar characteristics, and their lifestyle exposes them to increased levels of victimization risk.

officers, community activists, victims, and prosecutors, Janoff details more than 300 incidents, including 85 homicides. In particular, he highlights the problem of the "homosexual panic defence."

This so-called defence is based on the idea that a homosexual proposition can cause a reaction akin to temporary insanity in a person who has latent homosexual tendencies or who has been abused. Usually, a homosexual advance is used as evidence of provocation in efforts to reduce the attacker's sentence, for example, from murder to manslaughter. The *Gay Times* reports that the defence of homosexual panic has been used in the United States at least 15 times in the past 10 years to reduce charges from murder to manslaughter.

In a recent case in British Columbia, the Crown accepted a plea bargain of manslaughter in a murder case, on the grounds that the defendant had been provoked by an aggressive homosexual assault. The court accepted the argument that a heterosexual man should react to an alleged advance with extreme violence. In another case, the Manitoba Court of Appeal said there can be no doubt that a homosexual advance may be provocation. However, in Alberta, in a case where the defendant alleged that the victim had reached toward the accused as if to grab him, the Court of Appeal decided it would be impossible for a jury to conclude that a heterosexual man's sensitivity to a homosexual approach should lead to anything more than annoyance.

Violence against homosexuals is on the rise in Australia, and since 1993 this defence has been used in 13 cases that resulted in death. Since 1990, the police have systematically recorded gay hate–related killings in New South Wales. Using data from the National Homicide Monitoring Program, the Australian Institute of Criminology has compared the victims and offenders in such homicides with other male homicides in New South Wales and found that the victims are generally older than other male homicide victims and are more likely to have been beaten to death. The offenders are much more likely to be younger than other homicide offenders and more likely to be unemployed (82 percent) and unmarried (77 percent). In a 1998 report on the "homosexual advance defence," the Criminal Law Division recommended that this defence be excluded through legislation because of its prejudicial basis.

SOURCES: L. Still, "Homophobe Who Killed Gay Handed Five-Year Sentence," *The Vancouver Sun*, June 29, 1995; D. Dahl, "Bias in the Criminal Justice System— The 'Homosexual Panic Defence,'" *The Vancouver Sun*, December 28, 1995; R. v. Ryznar, [1986] 6 WWR 210 (Man CA); R. v. Hansford (1987), 55 CR (3d) 347 (Alta CA) at 363; "Anti-Gay Crimes Are Reported on Rise in 5 Cities," *New York Times*, March 20, 1992; "Gay Discrimination Focus of Probe," *The Globe and Mail*, November 15, 1993; Jenny Mouzos and Sue Thompson, "Gay-Hate Related Homicides: An Overview of Major Findings in New South Wales," *Australian Institute of Criminology, Trends and Issues in Crime and Criminal Justice* 155 (June 2000); C. Petersen, "A Queer Response to Bashing: Legislating Against Hate," *Queen's Law Journal* 16 (1991), 237 at 246; S. Samis, "An Injury to One Is an Injury to All: Heterosexism, Homophobia and Anti-Gay/Lesbian Violence in Greater Vancouver," M.A. (Sociology) thesis, Simon Fraser University, 1994; Quebec Human Rights Commission; "Discrimination and Violence Encountered by Lesbian, Gay and Bisexual New Brunswickers," *New Brunswick Coalition for Human Rights Reform*, 1990; "Proud but Cautious: Homophobic Abuse and Discrimination in Nova Scotia," Nova Scotia Public Interest Research Group, 1994; Douglas Janoff, *Pink Blood: Homophobic Violence in Canada*, University of Toronto Press, 2005; Ellen Faulkner, *Anti-Gay/ Lesbian Violence in Toronto: The Impact on Individuals and Communities, Department of Justice Canada: Research and Statistics Division/Policy Sector.* TR1997-5e. (A Project of the 519 Church Street Community Centre Victim Assistance program, 519 Church Street, Toronto, Ontario: p. 40.)

young victims of school crime were likely to strike back at other students to regain lost possessions or recover their self-respect.[83] In another study, victims of violent assault were found to be those most likely to become offenders themselves.[84]

Similarly, an association has been found between participation in self-reported delinquent behaviour and personal victimization in such crimes as robbery and assault.[85] The conclusion is that, for personal victimizations, those most likely to be the victims of crime are those who have been most involved in crime.[86]

The criminal–victim connection may exist because the conditions that create criminality also predispose people to victimization. Both share similar lifestyle and residence characteristics. Some former criminals may later become targets because they are perceived as vulnerable:

Criminal offenders are unlikely to call the police, and if they do, who will believe them? Some victims may commit crime out of frustration; others may use violence as a means of revenge, self-defence, or social control. Some may have learned antisocial behaviour as a consequence of their own victimization experiences, as in the case of abused children.[87] Research cited in one study showed that more than 85 percent of female offenders had experienced physical and sexual violence both inside and outside the home, at the hands of parents, intimate partners, and strangers.[88]

Recent research looked at the question of the relationship between deviant lifestyle and victimization and whether it's affected by neighbourhood. The analysis looked at young males' drinking, drug use, and delinquency to determine whether the relationship between victimization and deviant lifestyle was influenced by neighbourhood. It was found that, among young males, deviant lifestyles led to being victimized, both around the same time and 18 months later. Being victimized by crime significantly increased deviant lifestyles, but not in the future. Furthermore, some evidence suggested that deviant lifestyle leads to crime victimization in low-crime neighbourhoods, although this indication was not statistically significant.[89]

The Proximity Hypothesis. **Lifestyle theory** implies that some people put themselves in jeopardy by choosing high-risk lifestyles, or that some people become victims because they are forced to live in close physical proximity to criminals and are targeted by criminals because they share similar backgrounds and circumstances.[90] Early research by Hindelang, Gottfredson, and Garofalo advanced the idea that association with and exposure to high-risk people in high-risk locations at high-risk periods increases the incidence of the risk of crime.[91] For example, people who reside in socially disorganized high-crime areas have the greatest risk of coming into contact with criminal offenders, irrespective of their own behaviour or lifestyle. Thus, according to the **proximity hypothesis**, victims do not encourage crime; they are simply in the "wrong place at the wrong time."[92] Thus, residents in lower-class areas may have little reason to alter their lifestyle or take safety precautions because personal behaviour choices do not, in fact, influence the likelihood of victimization.[93]

Thus, victimization is more dependent on where people live than how they live. People who live in close proximity to criminals are at greater risk of victimization than are people who reside in less risky areas but have attractive, unguarded homes.[94] Neighbourhood crime levels are more important for determining the chances of victimization than are individual characteristics. People who exhibit high-risk traits, such as unmarried males, will further increase their chances of victimization if they reside in a high-crime area.[95]

Recent research by Stephen Baron of Queen's University and colleagues on Gottfredson and Hirschi's model of the relationship between low self-control and criminality looks at intervening factors such as lifestyle and criminal events. Utilizing a sample of 125 homeless male street youths, the researchers explored how risky lifestyles and street youths' reactions to situations influenced their participation in violent behaviour both as offenders and victims. They found that lifestyle influenced the propensity to become involved in violence, and the way in which victims responded to aggression could mediate the effect of low self-control, and thus the likelihood of victimization.[96]

The Deviant Place Hypothesis. The **deviant place hypothesis** suggests that there are natural areas for crime, places in which crime flourishes regardless of precautions taken by residents. These areas are poor, densely populated,

highly transient neighbourhoods in which commercial and residential property exist side by side. The commercial property provides criminals with easy access to targets for theft crimes, such as shoplifting and larceny. Successful people stay out of these stigmatized areas; they are homes for "demoralized kinds of people" who are easy targets for crime: people who are homeless, people with addictions, people with mental disabilities, and seniors who are living in poverty.[97]

Both victim lifestyle and place of domicile interact to produce high crime and victimization. People who live in more affluent areas and take safety precautions significantly lower their chances of becoming crime victims. Similarly, people who can afford to leave dangerous areas do so.[98] More affluent people realize that criminal victimization can be avoided by moving to an area with greater law enforcement and lower crime rates. As residents leave inner-city, high-crime areas, those left behind suffer higher victimization rates.

Residents of poor areas who remain behind have a much greater risk of becoming victims because they live in areas with many motivated offenders; to protect themselves, they have to try harder to be safe than do people who are more affluent. People who take chances, who live in high-risk neighbourhoods, and who are law violators themselves share the greatest risk of victimization. Although victim behaviour cannot explain the onset of criminality, it can influence the occasion of crime. Although criminal motivation may be acquired early in life, the decision to commit a particular crime may depend on the actions and reactions of potential victims.

In recent research, social scientists use data from a national survey to examine criminal victimization among homeless people. Unsurprisingly, they find that homeless people are victimized disproportionately compared with those who are not homeless, and they also experience multiple forms of victimization. Also, disaffiliation from others, health problems, and traumatic events significantly increased the odds of being victimized.[99]

---

lifestyle theory   The view that the lifestyle of the victim is a factor in the likelihood of a crime being committed, such as the number of times the victim goes out or the people the victim associates with.

proximity hypothesis   The view that people become crime victims because they live or work in areas with large criminal populations.

deviant place hypothesis   The theory that suggests there are natural areas for crime, which are poor, densely populated, highly transient neighbourhoods in which commercial and residential property exist side by side.

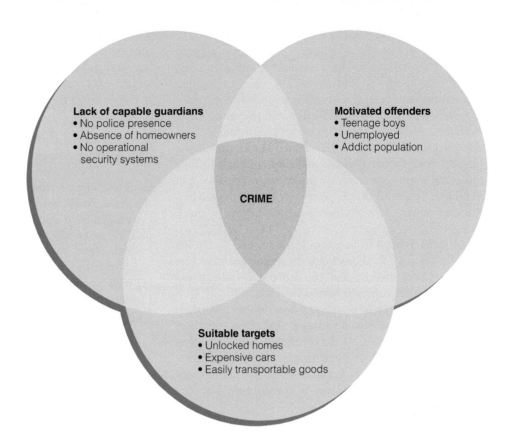

FIGURE 4.4
Routine Activity
Theory Posits the
Interaction of Three
Factors

Lack of capable guardians
• No police presence
• Absence of homeowners
• No operational
  security systems

Motivated offenders
• Teenage boys
• Unemployed
• Addict population

CRIME

Suitable targets
• Unlocked homes
• Expensive cars
• Easily transportable goods

Routine Activities Theory

An important attempt to formally describe the conditions that produce victim risk is Cohen and Felson's **routine activities theory**,[100] which assumed that the motivation to commit crime is constant. Some people will always be willing to break the law for gain, revenge, greed, or some other motive. Consequently, the volume and distribution of **predatory crime** are closely related to the interaction of three variables that reflect the routine activities of the typical Canadian lifestyle: the availability of **suitable targets** (such as homes containing easily saleable goods); the absence of capable guardians (such as police, homeowners, neighbours, friends, and relatives); and the presence of **motivated offenders** (such as a large number of unemployed teenagers). The presence of these components increases the likelihood that a predatory crime will take place: Targets are more likely to be victimized if they are poorly guarded and are exposed to a large group of motivated offenders (see Figure 4.4).

The routine activities approach can explain the rise in crime between 1960 and 1980, for example. The number of adult caretakers at home during the day (guardians) decreased because of increased female participation in the workforce; while mothers are at work and children are in daycare, homes are left unguarded. Similarly, the growth of suburbia and the decline of the traditional neighbourhood have led to a diminishing number of such familiar guardians

as family, neighbours, and friends. At the same time, the volume of easily transportable wealth increased, creating a greater number of available targets. In one study, burglary rates were linked to the proliferation of a commodity easily stolen and disposed of: television sets.[101] Finally, the baby-boom generation came of age from 1960 to 1980, providing an excess of motivated offenders, and the crime rate increased in predictable fashion. The implication of this theory is that crime is not a product of social disorder and anomie, but of prosperity, the economy, and changing participation in the labour force.

routine activities theory The view that crime is a normal function of the routine activities of modern living: a suitable, unprotected target will be identified as a target by motivated offenders.

predatory crime A violent, opportunistic crime, not usually familiar-related, such as stealing brand-name clothing from strangers.

suitable target According to routine activities theory, a target for crime that is relatively valuable, easily transportable, and not capably guarded.

motivated offenders The potential offenders in a population who exploit opportunities to commit crime.

Crime and Everyday Life. A core premise of routine activities theory is that the greater the opportunity to commit crime, the higher the crime and victimization rates. Accordingly, crime has grown as society has changed from a nation of small villages and towns to one of large urban environments. In a village, not only could thieves be easily recognized but the commodities they stole could also be identified long after the crime occurred. Cities provided a population mass that allowed predatory criminals to hide and evade apprehension. After the crime, criminals could blend into the crowd and disperse their loot; in the modern city, the public transportation system provides a quick escape.

As suburbs grew in importance, labour and family life moved away from the household, decreasing guardianship. The microwave, freezer, and automatic dishwasher freed adolescents from common household chores. Rather than help prepare the family dinner and wash dishes afterward, adolescents had the freedom to meet with their peers and avoid parental controls. As car ownership increased, teens had greater access to transportation and independence. Greater mobility makes it impossible for neighbours to know whether a teen belongs in an area or is an intruder planning to commit a crime.

Schools have also become larger and more complex, providing an ideal site for crime. Teachers might not know who belongs where, and spacious school grounds reduce teacher supervision. In the shopping mall, strangers converge in large numbers and youths hang out. The interior is filled with people, so drug deals can be concealed in the pedestrian flow. Stores have attractively displayed goods, encouraging shoplifting and employee pilferage. Substantial numbers of cars are parked in areas that make larceny and car theft virtually undetectable. Who notices people taking items from a car in a parking lot? In addition, shoppers can be attacked in parking lots as they walk in isolation to and from their cars.

These changes in the structure of society helped increase and sustain crime rates into the early 1990s. The upshot is that rather than change people, crime prevention strategies must reduce the opportunity to commit crime.

Moral Guardianship. Some criminologists believe that moral beliefs and socialization may influence the routine activities that produce crime. Even in the presence of criminal opportunities, people may refrain from crime if they are attached to conventional peers who have been socialized to hold conventional attitudes. The strength of social bonds may serve as a buffer, a form of moral guardianship, sufficient to counteract the lure of criminal opportunities.[102]

When Martin Schwartz and his associates studied date rape on college campuses, they found that men whose peer group supported emotional and physical violence against women were those most likely to engage in date rape (especially if they consumed alcohol on a weekly basis). Those who believed their peers would reject and disapprove of their behaviour were deterred from victimizing women. Peer rejection and disapproval may be forms of moral guardianship that can deter even motivated offenders from engaging in law-violating behaviour.[103]

Routine Activities and Lifestyle. Routine activities theory is similar to the lifestyle approach because it shows how routine living arrangements can affect victim risk: People who live in unguarded areas will be at the mercy of motivated offenders. Miethe and Meier argue that the two theories are in congruence, each relying on four basic concepts: (1) proximity to criminals, (2) time of exposure to criminals, (3) target attractiveness, and (4) guardianship.[104] For example, both routine activities theory and lifestyle theory would predict an increased risk of victimization for people (1) who live in high-crime areas (2) who go out late at night (3) carrying valuables, such as an expensive watch, (4) without friends or family to watch or help them.

Exhibit 4.4, *Rate Your Risk of Being Assaulted on the Street*, is a test that lets you assess your risk of being assaulted. It was developed by the Nashville (Tennessee) Police Department and includes questions on factors that affect assault rates. It reflects the idea that the routine activities people engage in can put them at relative danger from crime.

Testing Routine Activities Theory. Numerous attempts have been made to substantiate the principles of routine activities theory.[105] Personal characteristics increase the likelihood that people's routine activities will place them at a greater risk for victimization. These characteristics include being a youth, being a minority-group member, having a low socio-economic status, living in an urban area, and being a single parent. Maxfield found that victimization was most common in homes comprising a single parent and several children. Single parents may be less able to protect their families and themselves from the most common predatory criminals: other family members and former loved ones.[106] Note that this finding implies that going out of the home may not be the best predictor of risk, given the characteristics of violence in the family, especially for women and children.

Homes that are well guarded are the least likely to be burglarized.[107] Rape rates are high in areas where socio-economic distress results in divorce, unemployment, and overcrowded living conditions—factors that reduce the number of guardians and increase the number of potential offenders.[108] Some earlier research failed to find a relationship between property victimization and guardianship, seeming to provide weak support for routine activities theory.[109]

However, recent research has resulted in a different sentiment. Using survey data from 4,227 Seattle residents within 100 neighbourhoods, researchers looked at interrelationships between various dimensions of individual-level and neighbourhood-level guardianship. Using four

EXHIBIT 4.4

Rate Your Risk of Being Assaulted on the Street

The following test lets you rate your risk of being assaulted on the street. This test uses known risk factors taken from executive security courses, police detectives, and security consultants. Some of the questions may seem unusual but they are all factors that affect aggravated assault statistics.

1. How much do you travel outside of the city where you live in one year?
   - You travel under 1,600 km total.
   - You travel about 1,600 to 2,400 km in the U.S.
   - You travel in the U.S. more than 80,000 km.
   - You travel worldwide.
2. When you fly
   - You fly by commercial carrier.
   - You regularly fly using small, foreign-owned carriers.
   - You travel (fly, drive, etc.) with more than one suitcase and one carry-on type bag.
3. Security techniques
   - You go to conventions or seminars in other cities even occasionally.
   - You wear a convention badge while out of the meeting room itself on such a trip.
   - You regularly wear your last name visible when you work.
   - You (or other family members) open the door of your home for visitors without positive identification.
   - You never open your door to strangers when you are unarmed.
   - You only open a door when armed.
   - Your mailbox doesn't lock.
   - You have a solid door without a "peephole" or way to view who is outside.
   - You have a lock on your bedroom door.
4. How much cash do you carry?
   - You rarely carry any cash.
   - You carry $20 to $50.
   - You carry $50 to $400.
   - You carry over $400.
   - You separate the money you need from other large denomination bills.
5. Credit and bank cards
   - How many credit cards do you carry?
   - How many major oil credit cards [gas cards] do you carry?
   - How many major credit cards do you carry (MasterCard, Visa, American Express, Carte Blanche, Discover, etc.)?
   - You carry one or more ATM cards.
   - You carry secret code numbers to cards written down (even though you might hide them).
   - You never use outside ATM (anytime teller machines) after dark. (Leave this blank if the ATM is at a police sub-station.)
6. Sundry habits
   - How many acts of adultery have you committed (in the last two years)? Count each meeting during this marriage.
   - You are unmarried and you have dated a married person in the last year. How many dates have you had with this married person?
   - You are unmarried and you steadily cohabit with one person but you have dated on the sly in the last year.
   - Indicate your total number of partners.
   - You go to nightclubs and take home partners or go somewhere with them.
   - If so, are you male or female?
   - Do you ever use prostitutes?
   - Do you ever hitchhike or pick up hitchhikers?
   - Do you walk in public more than five times per month?
   - Do you generally walk at night with one or more companions?
   - Do you ever use cocaine, crack, uppers, downers, or narcotics away from home on any occasion?
   - Do you ever get drunk in public to the point where your speech is even slightly slurred or your balance is affected?
7. On the street
   - You visibly wear lots of gold chains when in public.
   - You wear rings, bracelets, or other jewellery worth over $2,000 while in public.
   - You wear an overcoat or full-length rain suit over a suit jacket in public.
   - You wear a natural fur in public.
   - Do you carry an umbrella or cane without necessity?
   - Do you walk with young children (age eight or under) or a dog?
8. Outings
   - Do you drive with any car door unlocked?
   - You have a remote starting device on your car.
   - You regularly commute by bus or subway.
   - You cannot change a car tire yourself and you drive.
   - You drive (more than once a month) with an eighth of a tank of gas or less.
   - You carry a tire inflator/puncture sealant screw-on canister in your car.
   - You frequent the same gas station.
   - You work at a gas station, bar, fast-food restaurant, or drive-in market.
   - You are going camping or partying in a boat in the next year.
   - There is no controlled access in and out of your work.
9. Other factors
   - You are a black male between the ages of 14 and 26.
   - You are over 60 years old.
   - You can run over 300 m without stopping to walk.
   - You are a first-degree black belt or higher in any martial art (Karate, Judo, Tae Kwon Do, Kung Fu, etc.).
   - You speak quietly when you talk.
   - You are considered calm but assertive when you talk.
   - You are afraid of guns and can't stand to touch one.
   - You are commissioned to or otherwise legally carry a handgun.
   - You always carry a handgun and you aren't commissioned or registered.
   - You know others illegally carry firearms where you drink or gamble.

SOURCE: © Ken Pence, PhD, Rate Your Risk, http://rateyourrisk.org.

dimensions of guardianship—physical (target hardening), personal (home occupancy), social (informal control), and natural (surveillance through environmental design)—the researchers expected that individual guardianship would be related more negatively to burglary as aggregate guardianship increased. Results showed that individual-level target hardening, place management, and natural surveillance reduced burglary when increases were made in neighbourhood-level target hardening, informal social control, and natural surveillance.[110]

Similar to other lifestyle theories, the routine activities view suggests that lifestyle plays an important role in victimization risk. Those who maintain a high-risk lifestyle by staying out late at night and participating in frequent activity outside the home also run increased chances of victimization.[111] This idea was corroborated in the Greater Vancouver Victimization Survey conducted by Statistics Canada.[112] Similarly, when Messner and Tardiff studied patterns of urban homicide, they found that lifestyles significantly influenced victimization: People who tended to stay at home were the ones most likely to be killed by family or friends.[113] Lasley found that youths in Britain who stayed out late at night and used excessive amounts of alcohol stood the greatest risk of becoming crime victims.[114] There is also a link between the developmental level of a society and the amount of theft that occurs, except for homicide, which is more conflict-linked.[115]

Because of the supporting research, and also because of its commonsensical approach, routine activities theory has become a very popular theory of victimization.

Is the Routine Activity Approach Valid? Not all criminologists, however, support this model.[116] According to routine activities theory, people who are affluent should have a lower victimization risk than people who are poor because they have the means to purchase security. Yet affluence allows people to increase activity outside the home, and wealth makes for a tempting target and for greater risk. Routine activities theory may explain why some people become victims, but it fails to explain whether others were first considered potential targets and then discarded, and, if so, why that decision was made. Furthermore, as in many criminological theories, the model does not explain why some people are not victimized despite the presence of risk factors.[117]

Some critics suggest that routine activities theory overemphasizes the victim and overlooks offender differences. Why do offenders choose to commit crime? Offender motivation is assumed to be rational, and offenders assumed to act from similar motives. However, all offenders are unlikely to perceive criminal opportunity or the risk of apprehension in a similar fashion. Other researchers have suggested that peer group pressure and cultural norms exert pressure on potential offenders, guide their motivation, and influence their choices; routine activities theory, they conclude, neglects to account for the factors that shape criminal choice.[118] And finally, the model is especially inadequate for measuring violence in the home committed by acquaintances. We cannot assume that women are less vulnerable because they spend more time with family members, given the high rates of assault and sexual abuse that occurs in families.[119]

CARING FOR THE VICTIM

The 2009 GSS shows a quarter of Canadians were victims of crime. These incidents are various, occur at the hands of both familiars and strangers in a variety of contexts, and have long-term consequences. In the aftermath of a crime, a victim will suffer financial problems, mental stress, and physical hardship.[120] In one study of 391 adult females, 75 percent had been victimized by crime at least once in their lives; 25 percent had developed post-traumatic stress syndrome, the symptoms of which lasted for more than a decade after the crime occurred.[121] The long-term effect of sexual victimization can include years of problem avoidance, social withdrawal, and self-criticism.[122]

Helping victims cope with crime, and ideally to avoid future crime, is the responsibility of all members of society. Law enforcement agencies, courts, and correctional and human service systems have come to realize that due process and human rights exist both for the defendant and for the victim of criminal behaviour.

The Government's Response

Internationally, governments are moving to address the needs of crime victims in several ways: allowing them to be present at all critical stages of the judicial proceedings, protecting witnesses and victims from intimidation, requiring restitution in criminal cases, setting up programs of victim compensation, expanding victim–witness programs, allowing or requiring the use of victim impact statements at sentencing, and funding victim compensation and assistance projects.

In Canada, the federal government has created new *Criminal Code* amendments, to develop policies to assist victims, and to conduct research on the effectiveness of existing programs.[123] The National Crime Prevention Strategy (NCPS), aimed at developing community-based responses to crime, was designed to increase public safety by developing sustainable approaches to crime prevention that deal with the root causes of crime. For example, the following projects in the Northwest Territories received $305,439 in funding:

- The Gwichya Gwich'in Band/Tsiigehtchic Charter Community project, Working Together—Strengthening the Community-Youth Action Program to develop positive youth activities by educating youth on drug and alcohol abuse, bullying, and violence.

- The Deline Justice Committee project, Out on the Land Program, to provide traditional and cultural activities for at-risk youth, encouraging healthy, crime-free lifestyles.
- The Native Women's Association of the NWT–Yellowknife Victim Service Program project, Youth for Change, to create youth awareness of family violence and its effects, preventative factors, and implementing a community awareness project.[124]

In addition to such research and social development programs, the following is a discussion of the most prominent forms of victim services in operation in Canada.

Victim Impact Statements

Section 735 of the *Criminal Code* allows victims to describe their physical injury, financial loss, and personal reactions to criminal victimization in a recorded statement that is introduced after conviction and before sentencing. Victim impact statements (VISs) are most often used in cases involving interpersonal victimization, but they can be used in conjunction with any offence, read aloud in court, and taken into consideration in sentencing.[125]

The *Corrections and Conditional Release Act* also permits these statements at parole hearings. Out of the hundreds of presentations made, the most frequently heard victim impact statements are from the families of murder victims and the victims of sexual offences.[126]

Differences exist in how each province and territory organizes and implements the use of the VIS. However, it is generally agreed that the VIS allows prosecutors and judges to experience the impact of crime more fully, and that composing and delivering a VIS helps victims recover from crime and reduce their feeling of powerlessness as participants in the criminal justice system.

Victims usually say they want the court (54 percent) or offender (39 percent) to understand the effect of crime, they believe their statement will affect the sentence (28 percent), they feel the statement will help them heal from the effects of the crime (18 percent), they were asked to give a statement (17 percent), or they wanted to have a voice (8 percent).[127]

However, in a study funded by the Victims of Crime Initiative conducted by University of Ottawa criminologist Julian Roberts, a survey of Ontario judges found that a victim impact statement had been submitted in only about 10 percent of cases.

Victim Compensation

One agenda of victim advocates has been to lobby for legislation creating crime **victim compensation** programs.[128] The first program was launched in Alberta in 1969; and in 1989,

the victim surcharge was created to collect revenue for provincial assistance programs. A 1994 Department of Justice study showed that only 15 percent of potential surcharges were actually imposed and only 3 percent collected, so Parliament amended legislation in 1999 to strengthen the surcharge, to increase the rate, and to impose the surcharge automatically.

As a result, the offender pays the surcharge, and the victim can apply for compensation to pay for damages. Each provincial and territorial compensation scheme is unique, however, and the amount of awards varies. In Ontario, for example, government funding exists for counselling, peer support networks, and educational campaigns. Compensation may be provided for medical and dental bills, loss of present and future wages, counselling, and, in some cases, for pain and suffering.

The 2005/06 Victim Services Survey, in a snapshot study of 628 victim service agencies, showed that the cost of providing formal services to victims of crime in Canada was $152.2 million. In addition, $93.2 million in compensation was paid to 11,437 applications. Compensation was paid for pain and suffering (44 percent), lost wages (23 percent), medical costs (20 percent), and for such expenses as child maintenance, counselling costs, and funeral and burial costs (13 percent).[129]

Over 400,000 victims of crime sought assistance from victim service agencies, which used the equivalent of nearly 1,800 paid full-time staff and 9,000 volunteers. Among these victims, 72 percent were victims of violent crime such as sexual and physical assaults. Of these, 47 percent had experienced violence by a spouse, former spouse, or intimate partner, and 26 percent had been victimized by another family member.

Court Services

A common victim program service involves helping victims and witnesses deal with the criminal justice system. This aid might involve explaining court procedures: how to be a witness, how bail works, or what to do if the defendant makes a threat. Transportation to court might be provided, along with counsellors who remain in the courtroom during hearings to explain procedures and provide support. Court escorts are particularly important for seniors, people with disabilities, victims of child abuse and assault, and those who have been intimidated by friends or relatives of the defendant.

Pretrial safety for victims is achieved through peace bonds, restraining orders, and provisions against communication with witnesses. Publication bans protect the victim's

> **victim compensation** Financial restitution to the victim of crime, usually provided by provinces and territories and funded by a surcharge levied in criminal cases.

identity and rape-shield provisions prohibit evidence about a victim's sexual history.[130] These services are funded in part by the victim fine surcharge.

Some provinces, such as Alberta, also have Aboriginal Court Worker programs, which help Aboriginal people involved in the justice system to obtain fair and culturally sensitive treatment in the justice system, before, during, and after court appearances. In 2003–04, Aboriginal people represented 4 percent of Alberta's adult population, but represented 39 percent of the provincially sentenced adult population in custody in Alberta, showing a clear need for such targeted assistance.[131]

Public Education

Some victim programs engage in public education to familiarize the general public with agencies that help crime victims. These include education programs that teach methods of dealing with conflict without resorting to violence, school-based programs that present information on spousal and dating abuse, and discussions of how to reduce violent incidents.[132] Some victim assistance projects seek to help victims learn about victim compensation services and related programs. For example, CAVEAT (Canadians Against Violence Everywhere Advocating Its Termination) developed its educational programs based on information from victims of violence and current research. Their crime prevention workshops and forums examine both prevention and response strategies, such as increasing awareness of issues, learning prevention skills, and developing early identification and intervention strategies.

Other programs help employers understand the plight of employees who have been victims of crime. Because victims may miss work or suffer post-crime emotional trauma, they may need to be absent from work for extended periods. If employers are unwilling to give them leave, victims may feel compelled to refuse to participate in the criminal justice process.

Crisis Intervention

Victim programs also make referrals to social services agencies to help victims recover from their ordeal by providing emergency and long-term assistance for transportation, medical care, shelter, food, and clothing. In addition, some programs provide **crisis intervention** to victims who feel isolated, vulnerable, and in need of immediate services. Some programs offer counselling at the service's office, while others do outreach in victims' homes, at the crime scene, or in a hospital. For example, after years of little regard being paid to the victims of sexual assault by the justice system, increased sensitivity to sexual assault victims has spurred the opening of crisis centres around the country. These centres typically feature 24-hour-a-day emergency phone lines and information

on police, medical, and court procedures. Some provide volunteers to assist the victim as their case is processed through the justice system. The growth of these services has been so explosive that services are now available in many major cities and college communities.[133] Most services maintain websites and provide emergency assistance, information, referral, crisis intervention, and counselling in a variety of settings.[134]

Victim–Offender Reconciliation Programs

In reconciliation programs, mediators facilitate face-to-face encounters between victims and their attackers in an attempt to create restitution agreements and possibly reconciliation between the two parties.[135] Included in these programs are alternative measures or diversion programs for young offenders and for adults in most provinces and territories. Charges are usually either stayed or not laid, providing that community service work is carried out. Although such programs were at first designed to handle routine misdemeanours, such as petty theft and vandalism, these programs now commonly facilitate restitution agreements in more serious incidents.

One of the first contemporary victim–offender mediation programs in the world was established in Kitchener, Ontario, in 1974. Today, Winnipeg has the largest victim–offender mediation program in North America and Europe. The continued growth of mediation programs is certain because restorative principles of sentencing have been incorporated into the Criminal Code (sections 717, 718). Unlike studies of victim participation in sentencing, evaluations of mediation programs indicate that they are successful and lead to victim and offender satisfaction.

In Canada, most alternative measures cases deal with non-violent offences, and pre-charge diversion programs, including mediation programs, are now the preferred path under the *Youth Criminal Justice Act*.[136]

CONNECTIONS

Reconciliation programs are based on the concept of restorative justice, which rejects punitive correctional measures and suggests that crime should be viewed as an interpersonal conflict that needs to be settled in the community through non-coercive means. The theoretical roots of the restorative justice concept can be found in Chapter 9's discussion of peacemaking criminology.

crisis intervention A form of program provided to victims of crime, many of whom are feeling isolated, vulnerable, and in need of immediate services such as counselling.

Victims' Rights in Europe

While Canada has taken steps to improve the rights of victims, the European Union (EU) has also moved toward increasing the role of victims in the justice process. At the forefront of this effort has been the Council of the European Union, the main decision-making body of the European Union. Its duties include passing laws, coordinating the broad economic policies of the member states, defining and implementing the EU's common foreign and security policy, concluding international agreements between the EU and international organizations, and adopting measures in the area of police and judicial cooperation in criminal matters.

In 2001, the Council agreed to implement the Framework Decision on the standing of victims in criminal proceedings. This decision is groundbreaking in that it sets out minimum standards for the treatment of victims of crime (and their families) and applies throughout the European Union. It highlights issues of concern, sets out principles that must be taken into consideration, and then lists a series of rights to which victims of crime are entitled in the course of criminal proceedings. European states are expected to modify their laws to conform to the Framework Decision.

Framework Principles

The Framework Decision stipulates that minimum standards must be drawn up for the protection of victims of crime—in particular, to secure access to justice and to compensate for damages, including legal costs. Underpinning these entitlements is the following series of principles:

- Victims of crime are entitled to a high level of protection.

- The laws and regulations of Member States should be made more consistent to achieve the main rights set out in the Framework Decision.
- The needs of crime victims should be addressed in a comprehensive and coordinated manner to avoid secondary victimization; thus, provisions are not confined to criminal proceedings.
- Cooperation between Member States should be strengthened through networks of victims' organizations.
- Suitable and adequate training should be given to people who come into contact with victims of crime.

Framework Provisions: Minimum Standards of Treatment

All victims of crime should

- be treated with respect
- have their entitlement to a role in criminal proceedings recognized
- have their right to be heard and supply evidence during proceedings safeguarded
- receive information on support; where and how to report an offence; their role in criminal proceedings; access to protection and advice; entitlement to compensation; and, information on the outcomes of their complaints, including sentencing and release of the offender
- have communication safeguards to minimize communication difficulties in criminal proceedings
- have access to free legal advice concerning their role in the proceedings and legal aid

- receive payment of expenses incurred as a result of participation in criminal proceedings
- receive reasonable protection, including protection of privacy
- receive compensation in the course of criminal proceedings
- receive penal mediation in the course of criminal proceedings where appropriate
- benefit from various measures to minimize the difficulties faced where victims are resident in another Member State, especially when organizing criminal proceedings

In addition, cooperation between Member States is to be encouraged; specialist services and victims' organizations should be promoted; training for personnel who come into contact with victims should be encouraged; and steps should be taken to prevent secondary victimization and to avoid placing victims under unnecessary pressure.

In addition to the Framework Decision, the EU Council adopted, in 2004, a directive that mandates each Member State have a national scheme that guarantees fair and appropriate compensation to victims of crime. The directive ensures that compensation is easily accessible in practice regardless of where in the EU a person becomes the victim of a crime. All Member States are required to guarantee fair and appropriate compensation to victims.

SOURCES: Council Framework Decision of 15 March, 2001, on the standing of victims in criminal proceedings: http://europa.eu.int/eurlex/pri/en/oj/dat/2001/l_082/l_08220010322en00010004.pdf; Proposal for a Council Directive on compensation to crime victims: http://europa.eu.int/eur-lex/en/com/pdf/2002/com2002_0562en01.pdf.

Victims' Rights

Just as the law guarantees that offenders have the right to counsel and a fair trial, society also has the obligation to ensure basic rights for law-abiding citizens.[137] These rights range from protecting citizens from violent crimes to providing victim compensation.

In 1985, the UN Declaration on *Basic Principles of Justice for Victims of Crime and Abuse of Power* set the framework for a victim's bill of rights. In 1986, Manitoba made world history by being the first jurisdiction to adopt that framework. In 1988, the provincial, territorial, and federal governments agreed on principles for the treatment of victims, including the following:

- Victims should be treated with courtesy and receive redress for crimes against them.
- Victims should receive information about their role in proceedings and be asked what assistance they need.
- Victims' and their families' safety should be ensured, and victims and their families should be given an opportunity to voice their views regarding the impact of the crime.
- Criminal justice system personnel should be sensitive to the needs of victims.[138]

Ontario's *Victim's Bill of Rights*[139] includes principles that support victims through the criminal justice process, improve information services, allow victims of sexual assault to be interviewed by officials of the same gender, make it easier for victims to sue assailants in civil actions, recognize emotional distress, make amendments to support child witnesses, and expand the Victims' Justice Fund.

Victim advocacy today is offered by an eclectic group of organizations, some independent, some government-sponsored, and some self-help. Advocates can be especially helpful when victims need, for example, to lobby police departments to keep investigations open and request the return of recovered stolen property. They can ask prosecutors and judges to help protect them from harassment and reprisals, such as making "no contact" a condition of bail. They can help victims make statements during sentencing, probation, and parole hearings. Victim advocates can also interact with the news media, making sure that reporting is accurate and that victim privacy is not violated.

SELF-PROTECTION

Although the public is generally satisfied with services provided by the police, fear of crime and concern about community safety sometimes prompt people to take an active role in community protection and citizen crime control groups.[140] However, attitudes supporting taking the law into your own hands are more conservative in Canada than in the United States. For example, a bumper sticker on a car from Texas reads: "Fight Crime. Shoot Back!" That sentiment would be unusual to see in Canada.

Leslie Kennedy says a significant number of crimes are not reported to police simply because some victims prefer to deal with the crime themselves.[141] Gartner and Doob report that many robbery victims and assault victims said they didn't report their victimization to the police because they "dealt with it another way."[142] In 2009, this response was the third most cited reason for not reporting a crime, after "incident not important enough" and "police couldn't do anything." Overall, only 31 percent of people report crime to the police.

One self-protection trend is **target hardening**, or making a home and business crime-proof through the installation of locks, bars, alarms, and other devices.[143] This approach is based on routine activities theory, and places the onus on the victim to prevent crime, such as by installing burglar alarms, participating in Neighbourhood Watch programs, engraving valuables with an identification number, building a fence, installing an intercom or phone to gain access, installing surveillance cameras or warning signs, and getting dogs to guard premises. People who fear crime are more likely to use crime prevention techniques, if they can afford it.

People who engage in household protection are less likely to become victims of property crimes;[144] for example, people who install burglar alarms are less likely to become burglary victims.[145] When such measures are effective in deterring crime, what sometimes occurs is crime **displacement**, in which crime moves to weaker targets.[146]

CONNECTIONS

Target hardening is based on the idea of rational deterrence, that making a crime difficult to complete will make it unattractive to the instrumentalist criminal. For more about rational choice and deterrence theory, see Chapter 5.

Fighting Back

Some people take self-protection to its ultimate end and are prepared to fight back. How successful is this strategy? Research indicates that victims who fight back often frustrate their attackers, but they also face increased odds of being physically harmed. For example, fighting back decreases the odds of a sexual assault being completed, but increases the victim's chances of receiving other injuries.[147] Robbery victims who fight back are less likely to be robbed but they are also more likely to be injured.

---

target hardening Making one's home and business crime-proof through the installation of locks, bars, alarms, and other devices.

displacement The effect when heavy law enforcement in one area drives crime to another, less well-enforced area, thus making this policing strategy ineffective overall.

Some research shows that the victims who escaped both serious injury and property loss were both those who used the most violent responses to crime, such as wielding a weapon, and those who used the least violent response, such as reasoning with their attackers. Those who fought back with their fists or who tried to get help were the most likely to experience both injury and theft.[148]

Self-protection in general, both forceful and non-forceful, reduced the likelihood of both property loss and injury, compared with non-resistance. In the past, it was thought resistance contributed to injury, probably due to confusion concerning the sequence of events. Recent research has found that injury followed self-protection in only 10 percent of the incidents, and such injuries were almost always relatively minor, so victim resistance appears to be generally a wise course of action.[149]

In the United States, where about one-third of households contain guns, armed victims are often ready and willing to use their guns against offenders.[150] Armed victims kill an estimated 1,500 to 2,800 potential felons each year in the United States.[151] Advocates say the risk of collateral injury is rare, victims should be encouraged to fight back, and that defensive gun use is associated with both lower rates of crime completion and injury.[152] In Canada, research done by Gary Mauser supports the view that Canadians do use guns for self-defence, up to 60,000 and 80,000 times per year.[153]

However, critics say that widespread gun ownership does not lead to a net deterrent effect, and that residential burglary rates actually increase with community gun prevalence.[154] Firearm ownership brings with it numerous problems, including accidental deaths, suicides, and the use of stolen guns in other crimes.[155] The issue of gun control will be discussed in depth in later chapters.

Members of minority groups are often incarcerated for minor offences, creating the impression in the public that dangerous offenders are left free to commit further offences.

Community Organization

Not everyone is capable of studying martial arts or wants to buy a handgun and do battle with predatory criminals. A better approach is for communities to organize against crime on the neighbourhood level. Neighbourhood patrol and block watch programs can organize local citizens in urban areas to patrol neighbourhoods, watch for suspicious people, lobby for improvements such as better lighting, report crime to police, conduct home security surveys, and serve as a source for crime tips as in Crime Stoppers.[156]

Although such programs are welcome additions to police services, little evidence exists that they have an appreciable effect on the crime rate, and their effectiveness is spottier in low-income, high-crime areas, which are most in need of crime prevention assistance.[157] Neighbourhood programs seem to have been more successful when they are part of

WHY ARE GUYS LIKE THIS OUT ON THE STREETS?

RELEASED AFTER SLITTING A MAN'S THROAT; NOW SUSPECTED OF MURDERING FIVE PEOPLE

BECAUSE GUYS LIKE THESE ARE CLOGGING UP THE JAILS:

SERVING MINIMUM MANDATORY SENTENCE FOR GROWING A POT PLANT IN HIS CLOSET

Reprinted with the permission of Pete Wagner

multi-issue community groups, rather than focusing solely on crime problems.

Another community-based program is National Night Out, an event involving citizens and law-enforcement agencies. Between the hours of 7 and 10 p.m., residents are urged to keep their porch lights on to warn criminals that neighbourhoods are fighting back against crime.

In Manitoba, civilians and the law are working on a partnership with ChildFind to establish an anonymous tip line to combat the sexual exploitation of children. Because intentionally viewing child pornography is illegal, staff at ChildFind who log on to child pornography sites, in hopes of identifying missing children, run the risk of prosecution. In British Columbia, Active Youth Network, comprising various youth-serving agencies, is working to facilitate improved communication and information sharing among those who work with high-risk youth.

In sum, community crime prevention programs, target hardening, and self-defence measures are flourishing across North America. They are a response to the fear of crime and the perceived shortcomings of police agencies in ensuring community safety. Along with private security, they represent attempts to supplement municipal police agencies and expand the war on crime to a personal, neighbourhood, and community concern.

SUMMARY

Criminologists now consider victims and victimization a major focus of study, with 28 percent of Canadian citizens being victims of crime each year, and the social and economic costs of crime in the billions of dollars. Like crime, victimization has stable patterns and trends. In general, victims of violent crime tend to be young, poor, single males living in large cities. Crime takes place more often at night, and in public places. However, many victimizations also occur

Victim Theories

Theory	Major Premise	Strengths
Victim Precipitation	Victims trigger criminal acts by their provocative behaviour. Active precipitation involves fighting words or gestures. Passive precipitation occurs when victims unknowingly threaten their attacker.	Explains multiple victimizations. If people precipitate crime, it follows that they will become repeat victims if their behaviour persists over time.
Lifestyle Theories	Victimization risk is increased when people have a high-risk lifestyle. Placing themselves at risk by going to dangerous places results in increased victimization.	Explains victimization patterns in the social structure. Males, young people, and people living in poverty have high victim rates because they have a higher-risk lifestyle than females, seniors, and people who are affluent.
Equivalent Group Hypothesis	Criminals and victims are one and the same. Both crime and victimization are part of a high-risk lifestyle.	Shows that the conditions that create criminality also produce high victimization risk. Victims may commit crime out of frustration or a need for revenge.
Routine Activities Theory	Crime rates can be explained by the availability of suitable targets, the absence of capable guardians, and the presence of motivated offenders.	Can explain crime rates and trends. Shows how victim behaviour can influence criminal opportunity. Suggests that victim risk can be reduced by increasing guardianship and reducing target vulnerability.
Proximity Hypothesis	People who live in deviant places are at high risk for crime. Victim behaviour has little influence over the criminal act.	Places the focus of crime on deviant places. Shows why people with conventional lifestyles become crime victims.

in the home, and women and female children are often the target of intrafamilial violence. Many women who are killed are the victims of their husbands.

Numerous theories of victimization exist. One view, called victim precipitation, contends that victims provoke criminals, sometimes just by their identity. Lifestyle theories suggest that victims put themselves in danger by engaging in high-risk activities. The routine activities theory maintains that a pool of motivated offenders exists and will take advantage of unguarded, suitable targets. The major theories of victimization are summarized in Concept Summary 4.1.

Numerous programs help victims by providing court services, economic compensation, public education, and crisis intervention. However, victims still complain about feeling victimized by the criminal justice system, whether being interviewed by unsympathetic police officers, being forced to wait for their court hearing in the same area of the courthouse as the defendant, not qualifying for legal aid, or not receiving compensation.

Rather than depend on the justice system, some victims have attempted to help themselves. In some instances, this self-help means communities organize for self-protection. In other instances, victims have armed themselves and fought back against their attackers. Evidence suggests that fighting back reduces the number of completed crimes but is also related to victim injury.

The development of victimology certainly adds to the complexity of studying the crime problem.

THINKING LIKE A CRIMINOLOGIST

The solicitor general of Canada has asked you to prepare a report on the relationship between physical abuse and criminal acts among adolescents ages 10 to 18. As a result of the self-report survey you conduct, you are able to provide the following information:

Adolescents experiencing abuse or violence are at high risk of immediate and lasting negative effects on health and well-being. Of the high-school students surveyed, an alarming one in five (21 percent) said they had been physically abused. Of the older students, ages 15 to 18, 29 percent said they had been physically abused. Younger students also reported significant rates of abuse: 17 percent responded "yes" when questioned whether they had been physically abused. Although girls were far less likely to report abuse than were boys, 12 percent said they had been physically abused. Most abuse occurs at home, it typically occurs more than once, and the abuser is usually a family member. More than half of those physically abused had tried alcohol and drugs, and 60 percent had admitted to a violent act. Non-abused children were significantly less likely to abuse substances, and only 30 percent indicated they had committed a violent act.

What is your interpretation of the association between abuse and delinquency? What recommendations would you make about current discussions to reform the *Youth Criminal Justice Act* to make it more responsive to underlying factors that affect youth crime?

KEY TERMS

acquaintance-related crime p. 95
active precipitation p. 101
aggravating factor p. 102
crisis intervention p. 114
cycle of violence p. 95
deviant place hypothesis p. 108
displacement p. 116
equivalent group hypothesis p. 106

lifestyle theory p. 108
mitigating factor p. 102
motivated offenders p. 109
passive precipitation p. 101
predatory crime p. 109
proximity hypothesis p. 108
routine activities theory p. 109
stranger-related crime p. 95

suitable target p. 109
target hardening p. 116
victim compensation p. 113
victim precipitation p. 101
victimologist p. 100
victimology p. 92

DOING RESEARCH ON THE WEB

Much attention is now given to victims: addressing their harm, helping them through the criminal justice process, developing bills of victim's rights, and so on. Increasingly, attention is now also being given to victims of non-traditional crimes, such as terrorism. Check out some of these initiatives, such as the UN Secretary-General's

Symposium on Supporting Victims of Terrorism, and some of the challenges they face.

CRITICAL THINKING QUESTIONS

1. Considering what we learned in this chapter about crime victimization, what measures can you take to better protect yourself from crime?
2. Do you agree with the assessment that a school is one of the most dangerous locations in the

community? Did you find your high school to be a dangerous environment?
3. Does a person bear some of the responsibility for his or her victimization if he or she maintains a lifestyle that contributes to the chances of becoming a crime

victim? That is, should we "blame the victim"?
4. Have you ever experienced someone precipitating crime? If so, did you do anything to help resolve the situation?

NOTES

1. Arthur Lurigio, "Are All Victims Alike? The Adverse, Generalized, and Differential Impact of Crime," *Crime and Delinquency* 33 (1987): 452–467.
2. "Top 10 Most Stolen Cars," Insurance Bureau of Canada, www.ibc.ca/en/Insurance_Crime/Top_Ten_Stolen_Cars.
3. Ted Miller, Mark Cohen, and Brian Wiersema, *The Extent and Costs of Crime Victimization: A New Look* (Washington, DC: National Institute of Justice, 1996).
4. Peter Finn, *Victims* (Washington, DC: Bureau of Justice Statistics, 1988); Alison Hatch Cunningham and Curt T. Griffiths, *Canadian Criminal Justice: A Primer* (Toronto: Harcourt Brace, 1997).
5. Susan Leslie Bryant and Lillian Range, "Suicidality in College Women Who Were Sexually and Physically Abused and

Physically Punished by Parents," *Violence and Victims* 10 (1995): 195–215.
6. Sally Davies-Netley, Michael Hurlburt, and Richard Hough, "Childhood Abuse as a Precursor to Homelessness for Homeless Women with Severe Mental Illness," *Violence and Victims* 11 (1996): 129–142.
7. See, generally, M.D. Pagelow, *Woman Battering: Victims and Their Experiences* (Beverly Hills, CA: Sage, 1981); Walter Gleason, "Mental Disorders in Battered Women," *Violence and Victims* 8 (1993): 53–66; Daniel Saunders, "Posttraumatic Stress Symptom Profiles of Battered Women: A Comparison of Survivors in Two Settings," *Violence and Victims* 9 (1994): 31–43.
8. Trevor Markesteyn, *The Psychological Impact of Nonsexual Criminal Offenses on Victims*, prepared for the Corrections

Branch, Ministry of the Solicitor General of Canada. Report No. 1992-21.
9. Elizabeth Stanko and Kathy Hobdell, "Assault on Men, Masculinity and Male Victimization," *British Journal of Criminology* 33 (1993): 400–415.
10. John McKendy, "Dialogue and the Risk of Responsibility," *Humanity & Society* 23 (1999): 238–253; see also, John McKendy, "Ideological Practices and the Management of Emotions: The Case of Wife Abusers," *Critical Sociology* 19 (1992): 61–80.
11. Alex C. Michalos and Bruno D. Zumbo, "Criminal Victimization and the Quality of Life," *Social Indicators Research* 50 (2000): 245–295.
12. Robert Davis, Bruce Taylor, and Arthur Lurigio, "Adjusting to Criminal Victimization: The Correlates of Postcrime

Distress," *Violence and Victimization* 11 (1996): 21–34.

13. James F. Anderson, Terry Grandison, and Laronistine Dyson, "Victims of Random Violence and the Public Health Implication: A Health Care or Criminal Justice Issue?" *Journal of Criminal Justice* 24 (1996): 379–393.

14. Derek Janhevich, *Hate Crime in Canada: An Overview of Issues and Data Sources* (Ottawa: Statistics Canada, 2001).

15. Rosemary Gartner and Anthony Doob, "Trends in Criminal Victimization in 1988–1993," *Juristat* 14 (1994).

16. Shahid Alvi, Martin D. Schwartz, Walter S. DeKeseredy, and Michael O. Maume, "Women's Fear of Crime in Canadian Public Housing," *Violence Against Women,* 7, 6 (2001): 638–661.

17. Samuel Perreault and Shannon Brennan,"Criminal victimization in Canada, 2009," Catalogue 85-002-X; *General Social Survey* 2009.

18. Paul Brantingham and Stephen Easton, "The Costs of Crime: Who Pays and How Much?" *Fraser Institute Critical Issues Bulletin* (1998).

19. "Murder Rate Down for Fourth Year in a Row—TV Coverage Up," *The Fraser Institute's National Media Archive*, 1996.

20. Sandra Besserer and Catherine Trainor, "Criminal Victimization in Canada, 1999," *Juristat* 20, 10, 2000.

21. For some interesting studies in this area, see Vincent F. Sacco, "The Effects of Mass Media on Perceptions of Crime," *Pacific Sociological Review* 25 (1982): 475–493; Julian V. Roberts and Michelle G. Grossman, "Crime Prevention and Public Opinion," *Canadian Journal of Criminology*, January (1990): 75–90; and "The Effect of Pretrial Publicity: The Bernardo Case," *Canadian Journal of Criminology*, July (1996): 253–270.

22. Thomas Fleming, "The History of Violence: Mega Cases of Serial Murder, Self-Propelling Narratives, and Reader Engagement," *Journal of Criminal Justice and Popular Culture* 14, 3 (2007): 277–291.

23. Timothy Ireland and Cathy Spatz Widom, *Childhood Victimization and Risk for Alcohol and Drug Arrests* (Washington, DC: National Institute of Justice, 1995).

24. Cathy Spatz Widom, *The Cycle of Violence* (Washington, DC: National Institute of Justice, 1992), 1; Cathy Spatz Widom, "The Cycle of Violence," *Science* 244 (1989): 160–166.

25. Steve Spaccarelli, J. Douglas Coatsworth, and Blake Sperry Bowden, "Exposure to Serious Family Violence among Incarcerated Boys: Its Association with Violent Offending and Potential Mediating Variables," *Violence and Victims* 10 (1995): 163–180.

26. Jerome Kolbo, "Risk and Resilience among Children Exposed to Family Violence," *Violence and Victims* 11 (1996): 113–127.

27. Jane B. Sprott, Anthony N. Doob, and Jennifer M. Jenkins, "Problem Behaviour and Delinquency in Children and Youth," *Juristat* 21, 4, 2001.

28. *Annual Report of the Correctional Investigator, 2002–2003* (Ottawa: Minister of Public Works and Government Services, 2003).

29. Canadian Centre for Justice Statistics, *Family Violence in Canada: A Statistical Profile 2004* (Ottawa: Statistics Canada, 2004).

30. Paul Rock, *A View from the Shadows: The Ministry of the Solicitor General of Canada and the Justice for Victims of Crime Initiative* (Oxford: Clarendon Press, 1986); Brian D. Maclean, "A Program of Local Crime-Survey Research for Canada," in *Crime in Society: Readings in Critical Criminology,* ed. Brian D. Maclean (Toronto: Copp Clark, 1996).

31. Solicitor General Canada, *Reported and Unreported Crimes: Canadian Urban Victimization Survey*, Bulletin 2 (Ottawa: Ministry Secretariat, 1984).

32. V.F. Sacco and H. Johnson, *Patterns of Criminal Victimization in Canada*, General Social Survey Analysis Services, Statistics Canada, Catalogue 11-612E, No. 2. (Ottawa: Ministry of Supply and Services, 1990).

33. The International Crime Victims Survey, 2012. http://escnewsletter.org/node/108.

34. Ronet Bachman, *Violence against Women* (Washington, DC: Bureau of Justice Statistics, 1994).

35. Statistics Canada, "Criminal Harassment," *The Daily*, November 29, 2000.

36. Elizabeth A. Sheehy, "Causation, Common Sense, and the Common Law: Replacing Unexamined Assumptions with What We Know about Male Violence against Women or from Jane Doe to Bonnie Mooney," *Canadian Journal of Women and the Law,* Project Muse, 2005.

37. Wendy Chan and George Rigakos, "Risk, Crime and Gender," *British Journal of Criminology* 42 (2002): 743–761.

38. Holly Johnson and Gary Lazarus, "The Impact of Age on Crime Victimization Rates," *Canadian Journal of Criminology* 31 (1989): 309–317.

39. William Meloff and Robert A. Silverman, "Canadian Kids Who Kill," *Canadian Journal of Criminology* (1992): 15–34.

40. "Criminal Victimization in Canada, 2004," *Juristat* 25, 7, 2005.

41. Murray Straus, Richard Gelles, and Suzanne Steinmentz, *Behind Closed Doors: Violence in the American Family* (Garden City, NY: Anchor Books, 1980); Richard Gelles and Murray Straus, "Violence in the American Family," *Journal of Social Issues* 35 (1979): 15–39; Richard Gelles and

Murray Straus, *Is Violence toward Children Increasing? A Comparison of 1975 and 1985 National Survey Rates* (Durham, NH: Family Violence Research Program, 1985).

42. "Children and Youth as Victims of Violent Crime," *Juristat* 25, 1, 2005.

43. Besserer and Trainor, "Criminal Victimization in Canada, 1999."

44. Nico Trocmé, Lil Tonmyr, Barbara Fallon, Cindy Blackstock, Bruce MacLaurin, Ken Barter, Joanne Daciuk, Daniel Turcotte, Caroline Felstiner, Richard Cloutier, and Tara Black, *The Canadian Incidence Study of Reported Child Abuse and Neglect* (Ottawa: Public Health Agency of Canada, 2005).

45. Walter S. DeKeseredy and Ronald Hinch, *Woman Abuse: Sociological Perspectives* (Toronto: Thompson, 1991); Karen Rodgers, "Wife Assault: The Findings of a National Survey," *Juristat* 14, 9, 1990.

46. Josée Savoie, "Homicide in Canada, 2002," *Juristat* 23, 8, 2003; Ruth Code, "Canada's Shelters for Abused Women," *Juristat* 23, 4, 2003; Tina Hotton, "Spousal Violence after Marital Separation," *Juristat* 21, 7, 2001; Valerie Pottie Bunge, "National Trends in Intimate-Partner Homicides, 1974–2000," *Juristat* 22, 5, 2002; Homicide in Canada, 2012, Statistics Canada.

47. Yasmin Jiwani, "The 1999 General Social Survey on Spousal Violence: An Analysis," The FREDA Centre for Research on Violence against Women and Children, August 2000; also, Daisy Locke, "Family Homicide," in *Family Violence in Canada: A Statistical Profile* (Ottawa: Statistics Canada, 2000), 39–44; Holly Johnson, *Dangerous Domains: Violence Against Women in Canada* (Scarborough, ON: Nelson Canada, 1996); and Robin Fitzgerald, *Family Violence in Canada: A Statistical Profile* (Ottawa: Statistics Canada, 1999).

48. *R. v. Whynot* (1983), 9 C.C.C. 449 (N.S.C.A.).

49. Janet Lauritsen and Kenna Davis Quinet, "Repeat Victimizations among Adolescents and Young Adults," *Journal of Quantitative Criminology* 11 (1995): 143–163.

50. Denise Osborn, Dan Ellingworth, Tim Hope, and Alan Trickett, "Are Repeatedly Victimized Households Different?" *Journal of Quantitative Criminology* 12 (1996): 223–245.

51. Jon Simmons and Tricia Dodd, *Home Office Statistical Bulletin: Crime in England and Wales, 2002/03;* Ron Melchers, "Do Toronto Police Engage in Racial Profiling?" *Canadian Journal of Criminology and Criminal Justice* 7 (2003): 347–366.

52. David Finkelhor and Nancy Asdigian, "Risk Factors for Youth Victimization: Beyond a Lifestyles/Routine Activities Theory Approach," *Violence and Victimization* 11 (1996): 3–19.

53. Graham Farrell, "Predicting and Preventing Revictimization," in *Crime and Justice: An*

Annual Review of Research, vol. 20, eds. Michael Tonry and David Farrington (Chicago: University of Chicago Press, 1995), 61–126.

54. Lauritsen and Quinet, "Repeat Victimizations," 161.

55. Graham Farrell, Coretta Phillips, and Ken Pease, "Like Taking Candy, Why Does Repeat Victimization Occur?" *British Journal of Criminology* 35 (1995): 384–399.

56. Alex C. Michalos and Bruno D. Zumbo, "Criminal Victimization and the Quality of Life," *Social Indicators Research* 50 (2000): 245–295.

57. A. Karmen, *Crime Victims: An Introduction to Victimology* (Pacific Grove, CA: Brooks/Cole, 1990).

58. Hans Von Hentig, *The Criminal and His Victim: Studies in the Sociobiology of Crime* (New Haven, CT: Yale University Press, 1948), 384.

59. Stephen Schafer, *The Victim and His Criminal* (New York: Random House, 1968), 152.

60. Marvin Wolfgang, *Patterns of Criminal Homicide* (Philadelphia: University of Pennsylvania Press, 1958).

61. Menachim Amir, *Patterns in Forcible Rape* (Chicago: University of Chicago Press, 1971).

62. Susan Estrich, *Real Rape* (Cambridge, MA: Harvard University Press, 1987), 69; L. Clark and D. Lewis, *Rape: The Price of Coercive Sexuality* (Toronto: Women's Press, 1977), 150.

63. "McClung Letter Throws Canadian Legal Circles into Turmoil," *The Globe and Mail*, March 1, 1999, A3.

64. Martin Yaqzan, "'Rape'—Yesterday and Today!" *The Brunswickan*, November 5, 1993; "Dispatch Case," *The Chronicle of Higher Education* (November 24, 1993), A34; "Date Rape Comments Cause Campus Furor: It's a Natural Outlet, Says Professor," *The Globe and Mail*, November 9, 1993, A4.

65. E.A. Fattah, "Some Recent Theoretical Developments in Victimology," *Victimology: An International Journal* 4 (1979): 198–213; see also, E.A. Fattah, "Canada's Successful Experience with the Abolition of the Death Penalty," *Canadian Journal of Criminology* 25 (1983): 421–431; E.A. Fattah, "Victimology: Past, Present and Future," *Criminologie* 33 (2000): 17–46.

66. Martin Daly and Margo Wilson, *Homicide* (New York: Aldine de Gruyter, 1988).

67. "Bill Won't Foster Gay Lifestyle, Rock Says," *The Globe and Mail*, November 18, 1994, A3; "Bill C-41 (Sentencing Reform) Passes Third Reading in House of Commons," Parliamentary press release, June 15, 1995.

68. Rosemary Gartner and Bill McCarthy, "The Social Distribution of Femicide in Urban Canada, 1921–1988," *Law and Society Review* 25 (1991): 287–311.

69. Julian V. Roberts, "Disproportionate Harm: Hate Crime in Canada," Department of Justice Canada, Working Document 1995-11e, 1995.

70. Derek E. Janhevich, *Hate Crime in Canada: An Overview of Issues and Data Sources*, Canadian Centre for Justice Statistics Catalogue no. 85-551-XIE, January 2001.

71. "Hate Crime in Canada," Canadian Centre for Justice Statistics Profile Series No. 17, 2008.

72. Mike McPhee, "In Denver, Attacks Stir Fears of Racism," *Boston Globe,* December 10, 1990, 3.

73. Jack McDevitt, "The Study of the Character of Civil Rights Crimes in Massachusetts (1983–1987)," paper presented at the annual meeting of the American Society of Criminology, Reno, NV, November 1989; see also, Jack Levin and Jack McDevitt, *Hate Crimes: The Rising Tide of Bigotry and Bloodshed* (New York: Plenum, 1993); Jack Levin and Jack McDevitt, *Hate Crimes: A Study of Offenders' Motivations* (Boston, MA: Northeastern University, 1993).

74. Derek Janhevich, *Hate Crime in Canada: An Overview of Issues and Data Sources* (Ottawa: Canadian Centre for Justice Statistics, 2001).

75. Lawrence Cohen and Marcus Felson, "Social Change and Crime Rate Trends: A Routine Activities Approach," *American Sociological Review* 44 (1979): 588–608; L. Cohen, James Kleugel, and Kenneth Land, "Social Inequality and Predatory Criminal Victimization: An Exposition and Test of a Formal Theory," *American Sociological Review* 46 (1981): 505–524; Steven Messner and Kenneth Tardiff, "The Social Ecology of Urban Homicide: An Application of the Routine Activities Approach," *Criminology* 23 (1985): 241–267.

76. "Youth Crime in Canada, 2006," *Juristat* 28, 3, 2008.

77. See, generally, Gary Gottfredson and Denise Gottfredson, *Victimization in Schools* (New York: Plenum Press, 1985), and "Children as Victims of Violent Crime," *Juristat* 11, 8, 1991.

78. Gary Jensen and David Brownfield, "Gender, Lifestyles, and Victimization: Beyond Routine Activity Theory," *Violence and Victims* 1 (1986): 85–99.

79. Less Whitbeck and Ronald Simons, "A Comparison of Adaptive Strategies and Patterns of Victimization among Homeless Adolescents and Adults," *Violence and Victims* 8 (1993): 135–151; Kevin Fitzpatrick, Mark La Gory, and Ferris Ritchey, "Criminal Victimization among the Homeless," *Justice Quarterly* 10 (1993): 353–368.

80. John Lowman, "Violence and the Outlaw Status of (Street) Prostitution in Canada," *Violence Against Women* 6, 9 (2000): 987–1011.

81. Leslie Ann Jeffrey and Gayle MacDonald, *Sex Workers in the Maritimes Talk Back* (Vancouver: UBC Press, 2006).

82. Josée Savoie, "Homicide in Canada, 2002," *Juristat* 23, 8, 2003: 10.

83. Joan McDermott, "Crime in the School and in the Community: Offenders, Victims and Fearful Youth," *Crime and Delinquency* 29 (1983): 270–283.

84. Simon Singer, "Homogeneous Victim–Offender Populations: A Review and Some Research Implications," *Journal of Criminal Law and Criminology* 72 (1981): 779–799.

85. Janet Lauritsen, John Laub, and Robert Sampson, "Conventional and Delinquent Activities: Implications for the Prevention of Violent Victimization among Adolescents," *Violence and Victims* 7 (1992): 91–102.

86. Gary Jensen and David Brownfield, "Gender, Lifestyles and Victimization: Beyond Routine Activities," *Violence and Victims* 1 (1986): 85–101.

87. Ross Vasta, "Physical Child Abuse: A Dual Component Analysis," *Developmental Review* 2 (1982): 128–135.

88. Elise Lake, "An Exploration of the Violent Victim Experiences of Female Offenders," *Violence and Victims* 8 (1993): 41–50.

89. Lening Zhang, John W. Welteb, and William F. Wieczorek, "Deviant Lifestyle and Crime Victimization," *Journal of Criminal Justice* 29, 2 (2001): 133–143.

90. Jeffrey Fagan, Elizabeth Piper, and Yu-Teh Cheng, "Contributions of Victimization to Delinquency in Inner Cities," *Journal of Criminal Law and Criminology* 78 (1987): 586–613.

91. M. Hindelang, M. Gottfredson, and J. Garofalo, *Victims of Personal Crime: An Empirical Foundation for a Theory of Personal Victimization* (Cambridge, MA: Ballinger, 1978).

92. James Garofalo, "Reassessing the Lifestyle Model of Criminal Victimization," in *Positive Criminology*, eds. Michael Gottfredson and Travis Hirschi (Newbury Park, CA: Sage Publications, 1987), 23–42.

93. Terance Miethe and David McDowall, "Contextual Effects in Models of Criminal Victimization," *Social Forces* 71 (1993): 741–759.

94. Terance Miethe and Robert Meier, "Opportunity, Choice, and Criminal Victimization: A Test of a Theoretical Model," *Journal of Research in Crime and Delinquency* 27 (1990): 243–266.

95. Robert Sampson and Janet Lauritsen, "Deviant Lifestyles, Proximity to Crime and the Offender–Deviant Link in Personal Violence," *Journal of Research in Crime and Delinquency* 27 (1990): 110–139.

96. Stephen W. Baron, David R. Fordeb, and Fiona M. Kaya, "Self-control, Risky Lifestyles, and Situation: The Role of Opportunity and Context in the General

Theory," *Journal of Criminal Justice* 35, 2 (2007): 119–136.

97. Rodney Stark, "Deviant Places: A Theory of the Ecology of Crime," *Criminology* 25 (1987): 893–911.

98. William Julius Wilson, *The Truly Disadvantaged* (Chicago: University of Chicago Press, 1987); Allen Liska and Paul Bellair, "Violent-Crime Rates and Racial Composition: Convergence over Time," *American Journal of Sociology* 101 (1995): 578–610.

99. Barrett A. Lee and Christopher J. Schreck, "Danger on the Streets: Marginality and Victimization Among Homeless People," *American Behavioral Scientist* 48, 8 (2005): 1055–1081.

100. Lawrence Cohen and Marcus Felson, "Social Change and Crime Rate Trends: A Routine Activities Approach," *American Sociological Review* 44 (1979): 588–608.

101. Lawrence Cohen, Marcus Felson, and Kenneth Land, "Property Crime Rates in the United States: A Macrodynamic Analysis, 1947–1977, with Ex-ante Forecasts for the Mid-1980s," *American Journal of Sociology* 86 (1980): 90–118.

102. Jon Gunnar Bernburg and Thorolfur Thorlindsson, "Routine Activities in Social Context: A Closer Look at the Role of Opportunity in Deviant Behavior," *Justice Quarterly* 18 (2001): 543–568.

103. Martin Schwartz, Walter DeKeseredy, David Tait, and Shahid Alvi, "Male Peer Support and a Feminist Routine Activities Theory: Understanding Sexual Assault on the College Campus," *Justice Quarterly* 18 (2001): 623–650.

104. Terance Miethe and Robert Meier, *Crime and Its Social Context: Toward an Integrated Theory of Offenders, Victims, and Situations* (Albany, NY: State University of New York Press, 1994).

105. See Messner and Tardiff, "The Social Ecology of Urban Homicide"; Philip Cook, "The Demand and Supply of Criminal Opportunities," in *Crime and Justice*, vol. 7, eds. Michael Tonry and Norval Morris, 1–28 (Chicago: University of Chicago Press, 1986); Ronald Clarke and Derek Cornish, "Modeling Offender's Decisions: A Framework for Research and Policy," in *Crime and Justice*, vol. 6, eds. Michael Tonry and Norval Morris, 147–187 (Chicago: University of Chicago Press, 1985).

106. Michael Maxfield, "Household Composition, Routine Activity, and Victimization: A Comparative Analysis," *Journal of Quantitative Criminology* 3 (1987): 301–320.

107. James Lynch and David Cantor, "Ecological and Behavioral Influences on Property Victimization at Home: Implications for Opportunity Theory," *Journal of Research in Crime and Delinquency* 29 (1992): 335–362.

108. David Maume, "Inequality and Metropolitan Rape Rates: A Routine Activities Approach," *Justice Quarterly* 6 (1989): 513–527.

109. James Massey, Marvin Krohn, and Lisa Bonati, "Property Crime and the Routine Activities of Individuals," *Journal of Research in Crime and Delinquency* 26 (1989): 378–400.

110. Pamela Wilcox, Tamara D. Madensen, and Marie Skubak Tillyer, "Guardianship in Context: Implications for Burglary Victimization Risk and Prevention," *Criminology* 45, 4 (2007): 771–803.

111. Terance Miethe, Mark Stafford, and Douglas Stone, "Lifestyle Changes and Risks of Criminal Victimization," *Journal of Quantitative Criminology* 6 (1990): 357–375.

112. R.R. Corado, R. Roesch, W. Glackman, J.L. Evans, and G.J. Leger, "Lifestyles and Personal Victimization: A Test of the Model with Canadian Survey Data," *Journal of Crime and Justice* 3 (1980): 129–139.

113. Messner and Tardiff, "The Social Ecology of Urban Homicide."

114. James Lasley, "Drinking Routines, Lifestyles and Predatory Victimization: A Causal Analysis," *Justice Quarterly* 6 (1989): 529–542.

115. Richard R. Benett, "Development and Crime," *The Sociological Quarterly* 32 (1991): 343–363.

116. Christopher Birkbeck and Gary LaFree, "The Situational Analysis of Crime and Deviance," *Annual Review of Sociology* 19 (1993): 113–137.

117. T.D. Miethe, M.C. Stafford, and J.S. Long, "Routine Activities/Lifestyle and Victimization," *American Sociological Review* 52 (1987): 184–194.

118. Leslie Kennedy and Stephen Baron, "Routine Activities and a Subculture of Violence: A Study of Violence on the Street," *Journal of Research in Crime and Delinquency* 30 (1993): 88–112.

119. Marcus Felson, *Crime and Everyday Life* (Thousand Oaks, CA: Pine Forge Press, 1994).

120. Patricia Resnick, "Psychological Effects of Victimization: Implications for the Criminal Justice System," *Crime and Delinquency* 33 (1987): 468–478.

121. Dean Kilpatrick, Benjamin Saunders, Lois Veronen, Connie Best, and Judith Von, "Criminal Victimization: Lifetime Prevalence, Reporting to Police, and Psychological Impact," *Crime and Delinquency* 33 (1987): 479–489.

122. Mark Santello and Harold Leitenberg, "Sexual Aggression by an Acquaintance: Methods of Coping and Later Psychological Adjustment," *Violence and Victims* 8 (1993): 91–103.

123. Alan Young, Victims of Crime Research Series. The Role of the Victim in the Criminal Process: A Literature

Review—1989 to 1999 (Ottawa: Department of Justice, 2001).

124. "Backgrounder: The National Crime Prevention Strategy at Work in the Northwest Territories. Building Safer Communities," http://www.publicsafety.gc.ca/cnt/cntrng-crm/crm-prvntn/strtg-eng.aspx.

125. John Howard Society of Alberta, "Victim Impact Statements, 1997," www.johnhoward.ab.ca/pub/C53.htm (accessed May 22, 2005).

126. "Use of Victim Impact Statements at Sentencing and Parole," retrieved from http://www.victimsweek.gc.ca/res/r58.html.

127. "Summative Evaluation of the Victims of Crime Initiative," publications.gc.ca/collections/Collection/J2-258-2004E.pdf.

128. Randall Schmidt, "Crime Victim Compensation Legislation: A Comparative Study," *Victimology* 5 (1980): 428–437.

129. "Serving Canada's Crime Victims: Results from the 2005/2006 Victim Services Survey," www.justice.gc.ca/eng/rp-pr/cj-jp/victim/rr07_vic4/p6.html.

130. A.C. Bowland, "Sexual Assault Trials and the Protection of 'Bad Girls': The Battle between the Courts and Parliament," in *Confronting Sexual Assault: A Decade of Legal and Social Change*, eds. Julian Roberts and R.M. Mohr (Toronto: University of Toronto Press, 1994).

131. "MLA Review of the Aboriginal Court Worker Program, 2006," retrieved from http://www.justice.gov.ab.ca/downloads/documentloader.aspx?id=47029.

132. Peter Jaffe, Marlies Sudermann, Deborah Reitzel, and Steve Killip, "An Evaluation of a Secondary School Primary Prevention Program on Violence in Intimate Relationships," *Violence and Victims* 7 (1992): 129–145; *Healthy Relationships: A Violence-Prevention Curriculum* (Halifax: Men for Change, 1994).

133. Vicki McNickel Rose, "Rape as a Social Problem: A By-Product of the Feminist Movement," *Social Problems* 25 (1977): 75–89.

134. Janet Gornick, Martha Burt, and Karen Pittman, "Structure and Activities of Rape Crisis Centers in the Early 1980s," *Crime and Delinquency* 31 (1985): 247–268.

135. Andrew Karmen, "Victim–Offender Reconciliation Programs: Pro and Con," *Perspectives of the American Probation and Parole Association* 20 (1996): 11–14.

136. *Canadian Youth: Who Are They and What Do They Want?* "Section 7. Justice," http://www.youth.gc.ca.

137. See Frank Carrington, "Victim's Rights Litigation: A Wave of the Future," in *Perspectives on Crime Victims*, eds. Burt Galaway and Joe Hudson (St. Louis: Mosby, 1981).

138. Alison Hatch Cunningham and Curt T. Griffiths, *Canadian Criminal Justice: A Primer* (Toronto: Harcourt Brace, 1997).

139. Ontario Ministry of the Attorney General, *Victim's Bill of Rights* (Toronto: Queen's Printer, 1996).

140. Pamela Wilcox Rountree and Kenneth Land, "Burglary Victimization, Perceptions of Crime Risk, and Routine Activities: A Multilevel Analysis across Seattle Neighborhoods and Census Tracts," *Journal of Research in Crime and Delinquency* 33 (1996): 1147–1180.

141. Leslie Kennedy, "Going It Alone: Unreported Crime and Individual Self-Help," *Journal of Criminal Justice* 16 (1988): 403–413.

142. Rosemary Gartner and Anthony Doob, "Trends in Criminal Victimization: 1988–1993," *Juristat* 14, 13, 1994.

143. Ronald Clarke, "Situational Crime Prevention: Its Theoretical Basis and Practical Scope," in *Annual Review of Criminal Justice Research*, eds. Michael Tonry and Norval Morris (Chicago: University of Chicago Press, 1983).

144. D.P. Rosenbaum, "Community Crime Protection: A Review and Synthesis of the Literature," *Justice Quarterly* 5 (1988): 323–395.

145. Andrew Buck, Simon Hakim, and George Rengert, "Burglar Alarms and the Choice Behavior of Burglars," *Journal of Criminal Justice* 21 (1993): 497–507; for an opposing view, see Lynch and Cantor, "Ecological and Behavioral Influences on Property Victimization at Home."

146. R. McNamara, *Crime Displacement: The Other Side of Prevention* (East Rockaway, NY: Cummings and Hathaway, 1994).

147. Alan Lizotte, "Determinants of Completing Rape and Assault," *Journal of Quantitative Criminology* 2 (1986): 213–217; Polly Marchbanks, Kung-Jong Lui, and James Mercy, "Risk of Injury from Resisting Rape," *American Journal of Epidemiology* 132 (1990): 540–549.

148. Caroline Wolf Harlow, *Robbery Victims* (Washington, DC: Bureau of Justice Statistics, 1987).

149. Jongyeon Tark and Gary Kleck, "Resisting Crime: The Effects of Victim Action on the Outcome of Crimes," *Criminology* 42, 4 (2004): 861–910.

150. Gary Kleck, "Guns and Violence: An Interpretive Review of the Field," *Social Pathology* 1 (1995): 12–45.

151. James Fyfe, "Police Use of Deadly Force: Research and Reform," *Justice Quarterly* 5 (1988): 157–176.

152. Gary Kleck, "Rape and Resistance," *Social Problems* 37 (1990): 149–162.

153. Gary Mauser, "Armed Self Defense: The Canadian Case," *Journal of Criminal Justice* 24 (1996): 393–406; see also, Gary Mauser, "Canadians Do Use Firearms in Self-Protection," *Canadian Journal of Criminology*, October (1996): 485–488; Gary Mauser, "Armed Self Defense: The Canadian Case," *Journal of Criminal Justice* 24 (1996): 393–406; Gary Mauser and Richard Holmes, "An Evaluation of the 1977 Canadian Firearms Legislation," *Evaluation Review* 16 (1992): 603–617; Gary Mauser and Michael Margolis, "The Politics of Gun Control: Comparing Canadian and American Patterns," *Government and Policy* 10 (1992): 189–209.

154. Philip J. Cook and Jens Ludwig, "The Effects of Gun Prevalence on Burglary: Deterrence vs Inducement" (May 2002). NBER Working Paper No. W8926. Available at SSRN: http://ssrn.com/abstract=310473.

155. Gary Green, "Citizen Gun Ownership and Criminal Deterrence: Theory, Research and Policy," *Criminology* 25 (1987): 63–81.

156. James Garofalo and Maureen McLeod, *Improving the Use and Effectiveness of Neighborhood Watch Programs* (Washington, DC: National Institute of Justice, 1988); Kevin D. Carriere and Richard V. Ericson, *CrimeStoppers: A Study in the Organization of Community Policing* (University of Toronto: Centre of Criminology, 1989); Dennis P. Forcese, *Policing Canadian Society* (Scarborough, ON: Prentice Hall, 1992).

157. Peter Finn, *Block Watches Help Crime Victims in Philadelphia* (Washington, DC: National Institute of Justice, 1986).

TWO

Theories of Crime Causation

An important goal of the criminological enterprise is to create valid and accurate theories of crime causation. Social scientists have defined theory as sets of statements that explain why and how several concepts are related. For a set of statements to qualify as a theory, we must be able to deduce some conclusions from it that are subject to empirical verification; that is, theories must predict or prohibit certain observable events or conditions.[*]

Criminologists collect vital facts about crime and interpret them in a scientifically meaningful fashion. By developing empirically verifiable statements, or hypotheses, and organizing them into theories of crime causation, criminologists identify the causes of crime, predict its occurrence, and develop methods for its control.

Since the late 19th century, criminological theory has pointed to various underlying causes of crime. The earliest theories generally attributed crime to a single underlying cause, such as atypical body build, genetic abnormality, insanity, physical anomalies, or poverty. Later theories attributed crime causation to multiple factors: poverty, peer influence, school problems, and family dysfunction.

In this section, theories of crime causation are grouped into five chapters. Chapters 5 and 6 focus on theories based on individual traits. These theories hold that crime is either a free-will choice made by an individual, a function of personal psychological or biological abnormality, or both. Chapters 7 through 9 investigate theories based in sociology and political economy. These theories portray crime as a function of the structure, process, and conflicts of social living.

---

[*] Rodney Stark, *Sociology*, 2nd ed. (Belmont, CA: Wadsworth, 1987), 618.

Choice Theory

Learning Objectives

After reading this chapter, you will be able to:

1. Understand the background of rational choice theory.
2. Be familiar with different crime prevention strategies.
3. Know the elements of general versus specific deterrence.
4. Discuss the logic and limits of incapacitation strategies.
5. Explain the policy implications of choice theory.

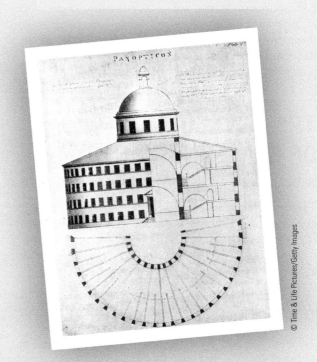

The Panopticon, designed by Jeremy Bentham, incorporated modern ideas of control through the observation of prisoners from a central guard tower.

© Time & Life Pictures/Getty Images

Crime data tell us that most offenders are young males who desist from crime as they mature, and that the bulk of adult offending is committed by relatively few persistent offenders. Why do these youths commit criminal acts? Furthermore, given that most young offenders age out or desist from crime, why do some continue to violate the law and risk apprehension, trial, and punishment well into adulthood?

To some criminologists, persistence is a function of personal choice. The decision to violate the law—commit a robbery, sell drugs, attack a rival, file a false tax return—is made for a variety of personal reasons, including greed, revenge, need, anger, lust, jealousy, thrill seeking, and vanity. The central issue is that the illegal act is a matter of individual decision making, a rational choice made after weighing the potential benefits and consequences of crime. The jealous suitor concludes that the risk of punishment is worth the satisfaction of punching a rival; the greedy shopper considers the chance of apprehension by store detectives so small that she takes a new sweater; the drug dealer concludes that the huge profits possible from a single shipment of cocaine outweigh the cost of apprehension. In the final analysis, people choose crime simply because they find it rewarding, satisfying, easy, or fun.

This chapter will review the philosophical underpinnings of **choice theory**, which first appeared as **classical criminology**, and the recent theoretical models that have developed. Because the central premise is that criminals are rational, their behaviour can be controlled or deterred by the fear of punishment. Desistence is thus explained by a growing and intense fear of punishment. These models include situational crime prevention, general deterrence theory, specific deterrence theory, and incapacitation. Finally, the chapter briefly reviews how choice theory has influenced policymaking in the area of criminal justice.

THE DEVELOPMENT OF CLASSICAL THEORY

Theories of crime based on the rational decision making of motivated criminals can trace their roots to the classical school of criminology. In Chapter 1, we saw that classical criminology was based on the works of Beccaria, Bentham, and other utilitarian philosophers. At its core are the following concepts:

- People choose all behaviour, including crime.
- A violation of another person is a violation of the social contract.
- Society must provide the greatest good for the greatest number.
- The law shouldn't try to legislate morality.
- People should be presumed innocent until proven guilty, with no torture.

- Laws should be written out with punishments prescribed in advance.
- Individuals give up some of their liberty in exchange for social protection.
- People are motivated by pain and pleasure.
- Punishment should be limited to what is necessary to deter people from crime.
- Punishment should be severe, certain, and swift.
- The law must be rational, transparent, and just, or is itself a crime.
- People's choices can be controlled by the fear of punishment.[1]

Beccaria saw people as egotistical and self-centred, needing to be controlled by the fear of punishment. However, he also believed that punishments must be proportional to the crimes; otherwise, people would not be deterred from committing more serious offences. For example, if both rape and murder were punished by death, a rapist would have little reason to refrain from killing the victim to eliminate the potential threat of the victim contacting the police and giving evidence in court.

Beccaria was one of those rare reformers to have an enduring influence on justice policy,[2] inspiring criminologists who believe that criminals choose to commit crime and that crime can be controlled by the judicious application of criminal punishments. The result was a foundation for criminal justice that is still with us today.

Beccaria's vision has had a powerful influence on events in the criminal justice system.[3] The belief that punishment should fit the crime and that people should be punished proportionately for their criminal acts was widely adopted throughout Europe and North America. In Britain, philosopher Jeremy Bentham (1748–1833) helped popularize Beccaria's views in his writings on **utilitarianism**. According to this theory, actions are evaluated by their tendency to produce advantage, pleasure, and happiness, and to avoid or prevent mischief, pain, evil, or unhappiness.[4] Bentham believed that the purpose of all law is to produce and support the total happiness of the community it serves. Because punishment is in itself harmful, its existence is justified only if it promises

choice theory The view that delinquent behaviour is a rational choice made by a motivated offender who perceives the chances of gain as outweighing any perceived punishment or loss.

classical criminology The theory that people have free will, choose to commit crime for reasons of greed or need, and can be controlled only by the fear of criminal sanctions.

utilitarianism A view that believes punishment of crime should be balanced and fair, and that even criminal behaviour is purposeful and reasonable.

to prevent greater evil than it creates. Punishment, therefore, has four main objectives:

1. to prevent all criminal offences
2. to convince the offender to commit the least serious crime possible
3. to ensure that a criminal uses no more force than is necessary
4. to prevent crime as cheaply as possible

The most stunning example of how the classical philosophy of Beccaria and Bentham was embraced in Europe occurred in 1789, when France's post-revolutionary government adopted these ideas in the *Declaration of the Rights of Man*:

> The law has the right to prohibit only actions harmful to society.... The law shall inflict only such punishments as are strictly and clearly necessary.... No person shall be punished except by virtue of a law enacted and promulgated previous to the crime and applicable to its terms.

Similarly, a prohibition against cruel and unusual punishments was incorporated into Canada's *Charter of Rights and Freedoms*, as section 12: "Everyone has the right not to be subjected to any cruel and unusual treatment or punishment."

The use of torture was largely abandoned in the 19th century, when criminals began to be incarcerated more frequently and prison sentences were structured to fit the severity of the crime. Although the proportionality demanded by Beccaria was often ignored by the legal system, the general theme of gearing punishment to deter crime was widely accepted.

By the end of the 19th century, the popularity of the classical approach began to decline; by the mid-20th century, this perspective was neglected by mainstream criminologists. During this period, positivist criminologists focused on the internal and external factors—poverty, low IQ, poor education, inadequate home life—believed to be the true cause of criminality. Because these conditions could not be easily curbed, the concept of punishing people for behaviours beyond their control seemed both foolish and cruel. Although classical principles still controlled the way police, courts, and correctional agencies operated, most criminologists rejected classical criminology as too simplistic an explanation of criminal behaviour.

CHOICE THEORY EMERGES

According to positivist criminology, if crime were caused by some social or psychological problem, such as poverty, then crime rates could be reduced by providing good jobs and economic opportunities. However, national surveys (such as Martinson's "What Works?") failed to uncover examples of rehabilitation programs that prevented future criminal activity.[5] Some went as far as suggesting that punishment-oriented programs could suppress future criminality much more effectively than those programs that relied on rehabilitation and treatment efforts.[6] Reviving classical concepts of social control and punishment seemed to make more sense than did futilely trying to improve entrenched social conditions or rehabilitate criminals using ineffectual methods.[7]

The classical approach began to enjoy a resurgence of popularity in the mid-1970s. Several criminologists produced books on the theme that criminals are rational actors who plan their crimes, fear punishment, and deserve to be penalized for their misdeeds. In *Thinking About Crime*, political scientist James Q. Wilson debunked the idea that crime is caused by poverty and can be altered by government programs. Instead, he argued, efforts should be made to reduce criminal opportunity by deterring would-be offenders and incarcerating known criminals.

According to Wilson, those people likely to commit crime lack inhibition against misconduct, value the excitement of breaking the law, have a low stake in conformity, and are willing to take greater chances than the average person. If they can be convinced that their actions will bring severe punishment, only the totally irrational will commit crime. This policy does have the advantage of restraining offenders and preventing their future criminality without having to figure out how to change their attitudes. Wilson said:

> Wicked people exist. Nothing avails except to set them apart from innocent people. And many people, neither wicked nor innocent, but watchful, dissembling, and calculating of their chances, ponder our reaction to wickedness as a clue to what they might profitably do.[8]

Unless we react forcefully to crime, those inclined to crime will get the message: "Crime pays."

Coinciding with the publication of Wilson's book was a conservative shift in public policy in many Western countries. Because these ideas focused blame on the individual rather than on social conditions, political decision makers embraced these ideas as a means of bringing the crime rate down. These views have helped shape criminal justice policy for the past two decades, even though declines in the crime rate probably occurred for other reasons.

Does Crime Pay?

Rational offenders are induced to commit crime if they perceive that crime pays more than they could earn from a legitimate job. Crime pays if the benefits of employment are lower than the expected benefits of theft. Does crime, in fact, pay?

To answer this question, Wilson and Abrahamse used a sample of incarcerated inmates to determine their perceived and actual "take" from crime. Wilson and Abrahamse divided the group into mid- and high-rate offenders in one of six crime categories: burglary, theft, swindling, auto theft, robbery, and mixed offences predominantly involving drug sales.

Using crime loss estimates derived from the National Crime Victimization Survey (NCVS), Wilson and Abrahamse found that mid-rate burglars on average earn about 32 percent of what they could have earned in a legitimate job. High-rate burglars, who commit an average of 193 crimes per year, earn roughly what they would have earned from a job (but they spend more time behind bars). Even if they were free (i.e., not incarcerated) for the entire year, high-rate burglars would earn about the same as if they had held a job for the same period. Research shows that criminals may be motivated to commit crime when they know of others who have made "big scores" and who are quite successful at crime. Though the prevailing wisdom is that crime does not pay, a small but significant subset of criminals actually enjoy earnings of close to $50,000 per year from crime, and their success may help motivate other would-be offenders.[9]

Crime profits are reduced by the costs of a criminal career: legal fees, bail bonds, the loss of family income, and the psychological cost of a prison sentence. Given these costs, most criminals actually earn little from crime. Would you be willing to become a high-rate robber if you knew that you would be spending half your life in prison for an annual salary of less than $15,000? If the average take is $300 for a gas station robbery and $2,500 for bank robberies, but the arrest rate is 80 percent, it doesn't seem appealing.[10]

If crime pays so little, why are there so many criminals? Criminals choose crime for numerous reasons, despite its relatively low payoff. One reason is that criminals tend to overestimate the money they can earn. In some cases, criminals' estimates were more than 12 times higher than a realistic assessment of their earning potential. For example, burglars estimated they could earn $2,674 per month from crime, while a more realistic figure is only $230!

In 1992, when three young men robbed a McDonald's restaurant in Sydney River, Nova Scotia, they had convinced themselves they could get $200,000 from the robbery. For a take that was only a fraction of what they had estimated, they killed three people and received long prison sentences.[11]

Some criminals believe they have no choice but to commit crime because legitimate work is unavailable. However, about two-thirds of the inmates reported having been employed before they were imprisoned. Rather than being excluded from the job market, criminals are more likely to be underemployed than to be unemployed.

Criminals are realistic, believing that eventually everyone is caught and punished. However, they are overly optimistic about getting away with each individual crime, and, being impulsive, they take the short-term view that each particular crime is worth the risk. Because research shows that only 7 percent of burglaries result in an arrest, and only 25 percent of those prosecuted are sent to prison, the expected cost of each burglary is less than five days; the rational choice then is whether the stolen goods will be worth five days in jail.[12] For an interesting case study of whether bank robbery is a rational choice, see the Famous Canadian Criminals box on page 129.

On the other hand, trying to reduce burglary by even 10 percent by increasing the severity of sentencing would increase prison costs by millions of dollars.[13]

From these roots evolved a more contemporary version of classical theory that is based on decision making, referred to as the rational choice approach to crime causation.[14]

The Concepts of Rational Choice

According to the rational choice approach, law-violating behaviour occurs when an offender decides to commit crime after considering both personal factors (need for money, revenge, thrills, and entertainment) and situational factors (how well a target is protected, the efficiency of the local police force). Before choosing to commit a crime, the reasoning criminal evaluates the risk of apprehension, the seriousness of expected punishment, the potential value of the criminal enterprise, and the need for criminal gain.

The decision to commit a crime, then, is a matter of personal decision making, which is based on weighing the available information. The decision to forgo crime may also be based on the perception that the economic benefits are no longer there or that the risk of apprehension is too great. For example, studies of residential burglary indicate that criminals will not target neighbourhoods well patrolled by police.[15] When police begin to concentrate patrols in a particular area of the city, crime rates tend to increase in adjacent areas that may be perceived by criminals as being safer, which is called **crime displacement**.[16]

Offence and Offender Specifications

Crime is both offence- and offender-specific.[17] **Offence-specific crime** refers to looking at the characteristics of particular offences; for example, burglary might involve evaluating the target's likely cash yield, the availability of a getaway car, and the probability of capture by police.

crime displacement An effect of crime prevention efforts, in which efforts to control crime in one area shift illegal activities to another area.

offence-specific crime An illegal act committed by offenders reacting selectively to characteristics of particular offences, assessing opportunity and guardianship; relevant to routine activities theory.

Edwin Alonzo Boyd, the son of a Toronto policeman, embarked on his career as a bank robber in 1949. He undertook this first robbery on his own, taking in just over $2,000. Sometimes he had a partner, Howard Gault, a former jail guard. Boyd's efforts were not always successful. In one robbery, the bank manager grabbed a gun and shot at Boyd, who had no choice but to run without the loot. Another time, Boyd was chased in his stolen car by a bank employee and just barely escaped.

Boyd was finally captured in 1951 and sent to Toronto's Don Jail, where he met "Tough Lennie" Jackson, another bank robber, and Willie "The Clown" Jackson, a small-time criminal. Lennie had a hacksaw blade hidden in his wooden leg, which they used to saw through the bars. Together with another bank robber, Steve Suchan, they slid through the window, landing in an exercise yard. They used bed sheets to make a rope that they threw to the top of

a wall, clambering up to make their way to freedom. They went on a 10-month bank-robbing spree that included the biggest cash haul in Toronto's history. It made exciting newspaper coverage. Willie Jackson was soon caught and sent back to the Don Jail.

It all came to an end in 1952, when two police detectives, Edmund Tong and Roy Perry, pulled over a car. Tong had been on the trail of the Boyd gang but didn't know the black Mercury contained Suchan and Lennie Jackson. As Tong approached the suspect vehicle, he was gunned down, and Perry was wounded in the arm.

In response to the public outrage, a manhunt was quickly mounted. Suchan and Lennie Jackson were captured in Montreal, but Boyd, who had had nothing to do with the murder, eluded capture for a while. He was arrested peacefully at his brother's house. The four were reunited in the Don Jail. Once again, they took advantage of Lennie's artificial foot by using it to

hide a piece of metal, a file, and hacksaw blades. They made a key to their cell door with the metal and file and used the hacksaw blades to cut through the bars. Rewards totalling $26,000 were posted for their capture. After a huge manhunt, police captured the gang in an abandoned barn near Yonge Street and Sheppard Avenue. All four were convicted on charges of armed robbery and auto theft. Leonard Jackson and Steve Suchan were executed by hanging for the murder of Edmund Tong.

Edwin Alonzo Boyd was sentenced to life in prison but was eventually paroled in 1966 and retired to a private life under a different name in British Columbia. He died in 2002. William Jackson also served a lengthy jail term in the Kingston Penitentiary, before being released.

SOURCES: Brian Vallee, *Edwin Alonzo Boyd* (Toronto: Doubleday, 1998); torontopolice .on.ca/d32/history; tv.cbc.ca/lifeandtimes/ bio1998/boyd.

Offender-specific crime refers to how criminals do not usually engage in random acts of antisocial behaviour. They analyze whether they have the appropriate skills, motives, needs, and fears. Criminal acts might be ruled out if offenders think they can reach a desired goal through legitimate means or if they are too afraid of getting caught.[18]

Note the distinction made here between crime and criminality.[19] Crime is an event; criminality is a personal trait. Criminals do not commit crime all the time, and even the most honest citizens may on occasion violate the law. Some high-risk people lacking opportunity may never commit crime, whereas given enough provocation or opportunity, a low-risk, law-abiding person may commit crime. What, then, are the conditions that promote crime and criminality?

Structuring Criminality. Many personal factors work together to condition people to choose criminality, such as the perception of economic opportunity: Offenders are more likely to desist from crime if they believe that (1) their future criminal earnings will be relatively low, and (2) attractive and legal income-generating opportunities are available.[20]

Fluctuations in the perceptions of risk over a person's lifetime also influence choices. Experienced criminals may desist

when they believe the risks are greater than the profit.[21] The veteran criminal knows when to take a chance and when to be cautious. Learning and experience are important elements in the choice of crime.[22]

Personality and lifestyle also help structure criminal choices. According to Agnew, people who choose crime over conformity share similar personal traits: They feel they can do what they want, they have less self-control than other people and seem unaffected by fear of punishment, and they are under stress or facing a personal problem that forces them to choose risky behaviour.[23]

Structuring Crime. The decision to commit crime is structured by the choice of (1) location, (2) target characteristics, and (3) the techniques available for its completion.

In choosing the place of crime, interviews with crack cocaine street dealers showed that they evaluated the

> **offender-specific crime** An illegal act committed by offenders who do not usually engage in random acts of antisocial behaviour, but who evaluate their skill at accomplishing the crime.

desirability of their "sales area" before setting up shop.[24] The middle of a long block was considered the best choice because they could see everything coming toward them from both directions; police raids could then be spotted ahead of time. Another tactic was to take buyers into spaces between apartment buildings or into back lots to do drug deals. Confederates could watch over the operation and come to the rescue if the buyer tried to "pull something."

Rational choice is also used in locating targets. Studies of professional and occasional criminals show that burglars check to make sure that no one is home before they enter a residence. Some call ahead, or ring the doorbell and claim they had the wrong address if someone answers. Some check to find out which families have star high-school athletes because those that do are sure to be at a game, leaving their houses unguarded.[25] In Waterloo, Ontario, recently, "obituary bandits" robbed homes when people were at funerals, after reading the death notices in newspapers. Others seek the unlocked door and avoid the one with a deadbolt; houses with dogs are usually considered off-limits.

Some burglars avoid freestanding buildings, which are more easily surrounded by police; others select targets with cash, such as bars, supermarkets, and restaurants.[26] Homemakers develop predictable patterns, which help burglars plan their crimes.[27] Burglars prefer working between 9 a.m. and 11 a.m. and in mid-afternoon, when parents are either working or dropping off or picking up kids at school. Burglars avoid Saturdays because families are at home, but Sunday during church hours is a prime time for weekend burglaries. Bank robbers choose city banks over country banks, because subway routes and areas with pedestrian traffic make escape easier.

Criminals learn techniques that help them avoid detection; for example, crack dealers learn how to stash crack cocaine in undisclosed locations so that they will not have to carry drugs on them. Females drawn into drug dealing tell how they have learned the trade in a businesslike manner:

> He taught me how to "recon" [reconstitute] cocaine, cutting and repacking a brick from 91 proof to 50 proof, just like a business. He treats me like an equal partner, and many of the friends are business associates. I am a catalyst ... . I even get guys turned on to drugs.[28]

In sum, rational choice involves shaping criminality and structuring crime. Personality, age, status, risk, and opportunity influence the decision to become a criminal; place, target, and techniques help to structure crime.

Rational Choice and Routine Activities

Rational choice theory dovetails with routine activities theory, which maintains that a supply of motivated offenders, the absence of capable guardians, and the presence of suitable targets determine crime trends.[29] **Routine activities**

theory provides a **macro perspective** on crime, predicting how change in social and economic conditions influences the overall crime and victimization rates. In contrast, rational choice theory provides a **micro perspective** on why individual offenders decide to commit specific crimes. These approaches overlap in saying that crime rates are a product of criminal opportunity: Increase the number of guardians, decrease the suitability of targets, or reduce the offender population, and crime rates should likewise decline; increase opportunity and reduce guardianship and crime rates should increase.

What are the connections between rational choice and routine activities?

CONNECTIONS

In Chapter 4, we discuss routine activities theory, which suggests that victimization is patterned, not random or accidental. This theory gives a macro perspective on some of the causes of crime.

Suitable Targets. Criminal choice is influenced by the perception of target vulnerability. As potential criminals go about their daily activities, they may encounter targets of illegal opportunity: an empty carport, an open door, an unlocked car, a bike left on the street. Corner homes, especially those near traffic lights or stop signs, are more likely to be burglarized. Secluded homes, such as those at the end of a cul-de-sac, surrounded by wooded areas, also make suitable targets.[30] Thieves also choose sites that are convenient, familiar, and located in easily accessible and open areas.[31]

Criminals are unlikely to travel long distances to commit crimes and are more likely to drift toward the centre of a

---

rational choice theory The view that crime is a function of a decision-making process, in which the potential offender weighs the potential costs and benefits of an illegal act.

routine activities theory The view that crime is a normal function of routine activities of modern living; offences occur when a suitable target is not protected by capable guardians.

macro perspective A large-scale view that takes into account social and economic reasons to explain how and why things happen; relevant to Marxism and functionalism.

micro perspective A small-scale view of events, looking at interaction to explain how and why things happen; relevant to interactionist studies of deviance and development.

city.[32] White found that "permeable neighbourhoods," those with a greater than usual number of access streets, are the neighbourhoods most likely to have high crime rates.[33] This fact might lend credence to the idea of having gated communities, where access is strictly controlled. Thieves may tend to choose open neighbourhoods because they offer more potential escape routes.[34] Robbers may be wary of people who are watching the community for signs of trouble, so robbery levels are relatively low in neighbourhoods where residents keep a watchful eye on their neighbours' property.[35] Here, we can see the influence of a routine activity on criminal choice: The more accessible the target, the more likely that crime will occur.[36]

Capable Guardians. The presence of **capable guardians** deters crime, because criminals tend to shy away from victims who are perceived to be armed and potentially dangerous.[37] In interviews conducted with career property offenders, Tunnell found that burglars will avoid targets if they feel police are in the area or if neighbours might be suspicious.[38] Communities with the reputation of employing aggressive crime-fighting police are less likely to attract offenders than areas with passive law enforcers.[39]

Guardianship can also involve passive or mechanical devices, such as security fences or burglar alarms, which improve guardianship and limit offender access to targets.[40]

Research has also shown that living in a cohesive community reduces the likelihood of victimization. Tightly knit communities have higher levels of informal guardianship, with members more active in intervening in public deviant or criminal activities. In a study of 19,000 respondents to national victimization surveys in 15 countries, and 10,000 respondents to city-level surveys in another 12 countries, community cohesion was found to reduce robbery and assault committed by strangers near the home.[41] Arguably, for the same reasons, Block Parent and Neighbourhood Watch programs also work to create cohesion and reduce crime.

Motivated Criminals. Crime rates also correspond to the number of **motivated criminals** in the population (that is, teenage males, drug users, unemployed adults). Rational offenders are less likely to commit crimes if they can achieve personal goals through legitimate means, so job availability reduces crime. In contrast, criminal motivation increases when the cost of living rises.[42] Criminal motivation can be reduced if offenders perceive alternatives to crime; in contrast, the perception of blocked legitimate opportunities increases criminal motivation.

Tunnell's career criminals said they committed crimes because they considered legitimate opportunities unavailable to people with their limited education and background. One offender told him:

> I tried to stay away from crime. ... Nobody would hire me. I was an ex-con and I tried, I really tried to get gainful employment. There was nobody looking to

hire me with my record. I went in as a juvenile and came out as an adult and didn't have any legitimate employment resumé to submit. Employment was impossible. So, I started robbing.[43]

Note how crime became the choice when legitimate alternatives were absent. In contrast, potential offenders who perceive legitimate alternatives, such as high-paying jobs, are less likely to choose crime.[44]

CONNECTIONS

Lack of conventional opportunity is a persistent theme in sociological theories of crime. The frustration caused by a lack of opportunity explains high crime rates in lower-class areas. The Chapter 7 sections on strain theories provide an alternative explanation of how lack of opportunity is associated with crime.

Interactive Effects. Motivation, opportunity, and targets are interactive. Motivated criminals will not commit crime unless they have suitable targets and the opportunity to exploit them. The presence of guardians will deter most offenders, rendering even attractive targets off-limits. These principles apply to crimes from shoplifting to bank robbery.[45] Exhibit 5.1 shows three basic approaches to crime prevention, depending on the level of intervention required.

EXHIBIT 5.1

Basic Approaches to Crime Prevention

- *Primary prevention.* Actions taken to reduce the occurrence of criminal acts (e.g., Neighbourhood Watch, Block Parents).
- *Secondary prevention.* Detecting early signs of high-risk individuals or situations before a crime takes place (e.g., Mothers Against Drunk Driving).
- *Tertiary prevention.* Intervention programs for youth or adult offenders to prevent further offences (e.g., community notification programs).

capable guardians In routine activities theory, the presence of police, homeowners, neighbours, and others, which can have a deterrent effect on crime.

motivated criminals The potential offenders in a population. According to rational choice theory, crime rates will vary according to the number of motivated offenders.

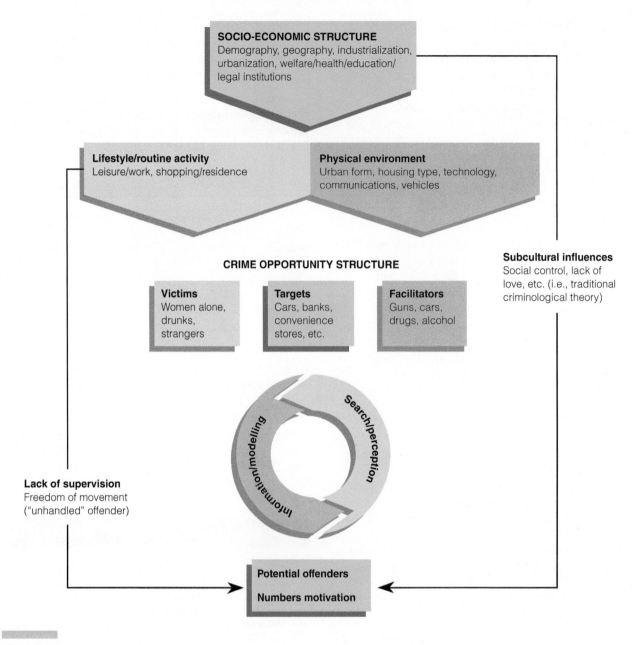

FIGURE 5.1

The Opportunity Structure for Crime

Source: Ronald Clarke, Situational Crime Prevention, in "Building a Safer Society: Strategic Approaches to Crime Prevention," Volume 19 of *Crime and Justice, A Review of Research*, ed. Michael Tonry and David Farrington, 103 (Chicago University of Chicago Press, 1995). Reprinted by permission.

Figure 5.1 illustrates the interrelationship among opportunity, routine activities, and environmental factors. Criminal opportunities, suitable victims, and targets abound in urban environments where facilitators (guns, drugs) are readily found. Environmental factors, such as physical layout and cultural style, may facilitate or restrict criminal opportunity. Motivated offenders living in these urban hot spots continually learn about criminal opportunities from peers, the media, and their own perceptions. This information may either escalate their criminal motivation or warn them of its danger.[46]

Warr found that kids who are attached to their parents and spend their weekends at home report little in the way of criminal motivation; lack of opportunity may reduce motivation.[47] Similarly, Hagan indicates that kids whose family relationships are strained, distant, and unrewarding are more likely to become attached to deviant peers, which in turn helps increase criminal motivation.[48]

In a national study of 1,700 youths aged 18 to 26, researchers found that adolescents who spend a great deal of time socializing with peers in the absence of authority figures (riding around in cars, going to parties) are also most likely to engage in deviance.[49] The presence of motivated peers combined with the lack of guardianship leaves more opportunity for substance abuse and dangerous driving. Participation in unstructured activities helps explain the association among crime rates and gender, age, and status: Teenage boys have the highest crime rate because they are most likely to engage in unsupervised socializing.

Opportunity combined with lack of guardianship increases criminal motivation.

Mapping.   Because crime is a rational choice and involves guardianship, opportunity, and motivation, it is predictable and can be mapped. If crime were random, there would be no pattern that could be mapped, as in Figure 5.2. Producing maps based on either police reports or calls for service enables the police to understand where the hot spots are and where enforcement would be most effective. A former Vancouver police officer, Kim Rossmo, developed a mathematical geographic profiling system that shows the probability of where an offender might live, which is based on the distance-delay concept: Offenders don't travel far from home, and the frequency of offending is in inverse proportion to the distance from home.[50]

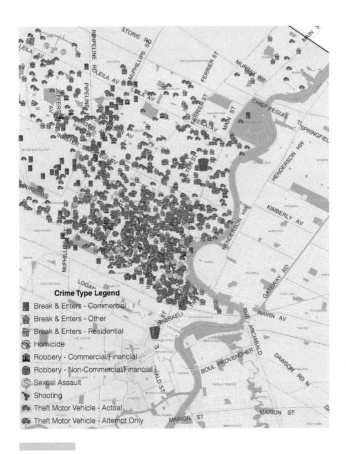

FIGURE 5.2

Crime in Winnipeg's District 3, over a One-Year Period, March 2010 to March 2011

Source: Reprinted with permission from the City of Winnipeg, CrimeStat.

IS CRIME RATIONAL?

Some crimes are the obvious product of rational and objective thought, especially when they involve an ongoing criminal conspiracy centred on economic gain. When prominent bankers in the United States savings and loan industry were indicted for criminal fraud, their elaborate financial schemes showed brilliant financial expertise. The stock market manipulations of Wall Street insiders, such as Boesky, Milken, and Martha Stewart, and the problems of Enron demonstrate an analysis of market conditions, interests, and risks separated only by degree from those of burglars. In 2008, when financial markets were manipulated and an economic collapse resulted, no one was ever charged with a crime.

CONNECTIONS

In Chapter 12, various criminal enterprises run by white-collar professionals and involving corporate interests are discussed. Learn how workers are exposed to risks, how consumers are sold faulty products, and how environmental pollution is a cost of doing business.

Are Street Crimes Rational?

Street crimes, such as prostitution and petty theft, are not random acts but are the product of the careful assessment of environmental, social, and structural factors. For example, serial killers target prostitutes because they think prostitutes are less likely to be missed than others.

Criminologists Clarke and Harris found that auto thieves are highly selective in their choice of targets. If they want to strip cars for their parts, thieves are most likely to choose Volkswagens; if they want to sell the cars or keep them permanently, they choose Mercedes; for temporary use, Buicks are top-ranked.[51] Vehicle selection is based on the cars' attractiveness and suitability for a particular purpose: German automobiles are selected for stripping because they usually have high-quality audio equipment that has good value on the second-hand market; thus, target selection is highly rational.

Studies of prostitutes suggest that these women make clear choices in their daily activities. For example, interviews with street-level sex workers in Brooklyn showed that despite increased competition, they still resisted sex practices that compromised their safety, such as sex without condoms, trading sex for drugs, or taking clients they considered too dangerous or distasteful.[52]

Similarly, some communities attempt to influence johns in their choice of soliciting. Some jurisdictions confiscate johns' cars, and others require men, after conviction, to attend "john school," where they learn more about the exploitation hidden in prostitution. Some put up signs, warning that areas are under video surveillance.

In another example, researchers found burglars used an average of four different methods for the disposal of stolen goods. The most common method was trading stolen goods directly for drugs: adults chose heroin, and juveniles chose cannabis. Other methods included selling to family and friends, fences, legitimate businesses, pawnbrokers, and second-hand dealers. Selling stolen goods was both profitable and low risk.

What was interesting was that many goods were stolen on commission and disposed of quickly, often in less than one hour. Burglars obtained 25 percent to 33 percent of the new price, earned an average income of $2,000 per week, and didn't seem to think they had much chance of being caught.[53]

Is Drug Use Rational?

Not surprisingly, recreational drug users report that they begin taking drugs when they believe that drugs will provide an enjoyable and exciting experience, which is facilitated when friends and family members encourage drug use and abuse substances themselves.[54]

Heavy drug users and dealers use specific techniques to avoid apprehension by police. They scope out the territory to make sure nothing is out of place that may be a potential threat, such as police officers or rival gang members.[55] One crack dealer told Jacobs:

> There was this red Pontiac sittin' on the corner one day with two white guys inside. They was just sittin' there for an hour, not doin' nothin'. Another day, diff'rent people be walkin' up and down the street you don't really recognize. You think they might be kin of someone but then you be askin' around and they [neighbours] ain't never seen them before neither. When ya' see strange things like that, you think somethin' be goin' on [and you don't deal].

Drug dealers are also careful about whether they should deal alone or in groups. Large groups draw more attention from the police but can offer more protection, and help divert the attention of police.

A study of female drug abusers, which looked at decision making, described one dealer who earned $50,000 per year, who said:

> I stayed within my goals, basically....I don't go around doing stupid things. I don't walk around telling people I have drugs for sale, I don't have people sitting out in front of my house. I don't have traffic in and out of my house....I control the people I sell to.[56]

However, some research shows that dealing drugs is more of a complement to a regular income than a replacement.

Dealers that sell on a daily basis sell on average only four hours a day, and earnings are generally low. For the occasional dealer, such as a university student, it is a way to make extra income, not unlike waiting tables.[57]

Can Violence Be Rational?

Although there is evidence that **instrumental crimes**, such as drug dealing and burglaries, are rational, is it possible that violent acts through which the offender gains little material benefit are the product of a reasoned decision-making process?

Hollywood likes to portray deranged people killing innocent victims at random, but people who carry guns and are ready to use them typically do so for more rational reasons. They may perceive that they live in a dangerous environment and carry a weapon for self-protection.[58] Some are involved in dangerous illegal activities, such as drug dealing, and carry weapons as part of the job.[59]

Even violent criminals are selective in their choice of suitable targets. For example, robbers choose victims who are vulnerable and do not pose any threat,[60] avoiding victims who may be armed and dangerous. Criminals are often scared off, wounded, or captured by armed victims.[61] Even serial murderers, outwardly the most irrational of all offenders, choose victims who are defenceless or cannot count on police protection: prostitutes, gay men, hitchhikers, children, hospital patients, seniors, and homeless persons. Rarely do serial killers target weightlifters or martial arts experts.[62]

Even the most violent interactions are motivated by rational thought and not unthinking rage. Even in apparently senseless killings among strangers, the real motive was revenge for a prior dispute or disagreement among the parties involved (or their families).[63] Homicides can be motivated by the offenders' desire to avoid retaliation from a victim they had assaulted or to avoid future prosecutions by getting rid of witnesses. Although some killings are the result of angry aggression, and violent acts appear to be irrational, they do involve calculation of risk and reward.

What Are the Seductions of Crime?

Last, as the focus of rational choice theory is on the opportunity to commit crime and on criminals' decisions to commit crimes because doing so is attractive, brings rewards,

> **instrumental crime** Illegal activity, such as the sale of narcotics, committed for the purpose of obtaining desired goods that are unable to be attained through conventional means.

excitement, prestige, and other desirable outcomes without lengthy work or effort,[64] it is also important to talk about the emotional component of crime.

Katz talks about the benefits to criminality, which he labels the **seductions of crime**.[65] These seductions of crime precede the commission of a crime and draw offenders into law violations. Someone challenges the badass with a bump or a stare, and the tough person beats up the challenger. Youths want to do something exciting, so they break into and vandalize a school building.[66] Shoplifting and vandalism are attractive because getting away with it is a thrilling demonstration of personal competence. Even murder can have an emotional payoff. Killers have life-or-death control over their victims.

Situational inducements created from emotional upheaval can also structure the decision to commit crime. When an individual is faced with humiliation or ridicule, such as being rebuked at a party because he or she is disturbing people, the person responds, "So, I'm acting like a fool, am I?" and attacks because of the public embarrassment.

People are most likely to be seduced by crime if they don't fear either losing the respect of their peers or suffering legal punishments.[67]

We have been speaking of crime in its usual sense, as predatory, unwanted behaviour. What do we do about violations that are nonetheless accepted by everyone involved? In 1994, the Government of Ontario implemented the *Ontario Tobacco Control Act*. This act fined merchants up to $25,000 for selling tobacco to minors; however, 60 percent of retailers remained willing to sell to minors. Similarly, in Alberta, fines were increased for retailers selling tobacco to minors: $3,000 for a first offence, $50,000 for a second. Under the *Prevention of Youth Tobacco Use Act*, those 17 years and under face a $100 fine if caught smoking in public, and their tobacco products can be confiscated.

Such research clearly demonstrates the principles of rational choice theory.[68] However, how can illegal acts be prevented? That is the challenge and the focus of the next section.

ELIMINATING CRIME

If crime is rational, then it can be controlled by convincing both current and potential offenders that the choice of crime is a poor one and that it will not bring rewards, but rather pain, hardship, and deprivation.

For example, jurisdictions with low incarceration rates also experience the highest crime rates.[69] Perhaps street-smart offenders know which areas offer the least threat and plan their crimes accordingly. Several potential strategies flow from this premise, discussed in Concept Summary 5.1. Depending on whether the object is crime prevention in

CONCEPT SUMMARY 5.1

Crime Control Strategies Based on Rational Choice

Situational Crime Prevention
- The aim is to deny the access of motivated offenders to suitable targets.
- Home security system signals guardianship; reward not worth risk apprehension.
- Problems are the extinction of the effect and displacement of crime.

General Deterrence Strategies
- The aim is to make potential criminals fear the consequences of crime.
- Operationalization involves mandatory sentences and aggressive policing.
- Problems are criminals who do not fear punishment; certainty of arrest and punishment are low.

Specific Deterrence Strategy
- The aim is to punish known criminals so that they will not repeat their offences.
- Operationalizations of this strategy are harsh prison sentences and stiff fines.
- A problem is that punishment may increase re-offending rates.

Incapacitation Strategies
- The aim is to reduce crime by incarcerating motivated offenders.
- Operationalizations are long prison sentences, placing more people behind bars.
- Problems are minor, non-dangerous offenders are locked up; very costly strategy.

general, or preventing a specific criminal from offending, the strategy is different. In the Comparative Criminology box on page 136, which strategy is being used?

The following sections discuss in detail each of these crime reduction or control strategies, which are based on the rationality of criminal behaviour.

SITUATIONAL CRIME PREVENTION

Because criminal activity is offence-specific, crime prevention and crime reduction should be achieved through policies that convince potential criminals to desist from criminal

seductions of crime   According to Katz, the visceral and emotional appeal that the situation of crime has for those who engage in illegal acts.

Comparative Criminology
Reducing Crime through Surveillance

Brandon Welsh and David Farrington have been using systematic review and meta-analysis to assess the comparative effectiveness of situational crime prevention techniques. Recently, they evaluated the effectiveness of closed-circuit television (CCTV) surveillance cameras and improved street lighting, techniques that are currently being used around the world.

They find that CCTV surveillance cameras serve many functions and are used in both public and private settings. CCTV can deter would-be criminals who fear detection and apprehension. They can also aid police in the detection and apprehension of suspects, aid in the prosecution of alleged offenders, improve police officer safety and compliance with the law (through, for instance, cameras mounted on the dashboard of police cruisers to record police stops, searches, and so on), and aid in the detection and prevention of terrorist activities. Nowhere is the popularity of CCTV more apparent than in Great Britain, where an estimated 4.2 million CCTV cameras, or 1 for every 14 citizens, are in operation. It has been estimated that the average Briton is caught on camera 300 times each day.

After reviewing 41 studies conducted around the world, Welsh and Farrington found that CCTV interventions (a) have a small but significant desirable effect on crime, (b) are most effective in reducing crime in car parks (parking lots), (c) are most effective in reducing vehicle crimes, and (d) are more effective in reducing crime in the United Kingdom than in other countries.

They found that effectiveness was significantly correlated with the degree of coverage of the CCTV cameras, which was greatest in car parks. However, the effect was most pronounced in parking lots that also employed other situational crime prevention interventions, such as improved lighting and security officers.

Notably, Welsh and Farrington found that CCTV schemes in the United Kingdom showed a sizable (19 percent) decrease in crime over the previous year, whereas CCTV schemes in other countries showed no desirable effect on crime. One reason was that all of the sites that used other interventions alongside CCTV were in England. It is possible that CCTV on its own is not sufficient to influence an offender's decision whether to commit a crime and thus needs to be buttressed by other methods, such as security fences or guards.

Another important issue is cultural context. In the United Kingdom, public support is high for the use of CCTV cameras in public settings to prevent crime. In America and other nations, the public is less accepting of surveillance technology and more apprehensive about its Big Brother connotations. Furthermore, in America, resistance to the use of CCTV in public places also takes the form of legal action and constitutional challenges under the U.S. Constitution's Fourth Amendment prohibition against unreasonable searches and seizures. In Sweden, surveillance cameras are highly regulated in public places, and in nearly all instances their use requires

a permit from the county administrative board. In Norway, there is a high degree of political scrutiny of public CCTV schemes run by the police.

The overall poor showing of CCTV schemes in countries other than Britain may be due in part to a lack of public support (and maybe even a lack of political support) for these schemes, which in turn may result in reduced program funding, the police assigning lower priority to CCTV, and negative media reactions. Each of these factors could undermine the effectiveness of CCTV schemes. In contrast, the British Home Office, which funded many of the British evaluations, wanted to show that CCTV was effective because it had invested so much money in these schemes.

Welsh and Farrington conclude that CCTV reduces crime in some circumstances. In light of the mixed results, future CCTV schemes should be carefully implemented in different settings and should employ high-quality evaluation designs with long follow-up periods.

Critical Thinking

Would you be willing to have a surveillance camera set up in your home or dorm for the purpose of preventing crime, knowing that your every move was being watched and recorded?

SOURCE: Brandon C. Welsh and David P. Farrington, *Making Public Places Safer: Surveillance and Crime Prevention* (New York: Oxford University Press, 2008).

---

activities, delay their actions, or avoid a particular target. Table 5.1 presents 15 techniques for preventing crime, from target hardening to facilitating compliance.

Criminal acts will be avoided if (1) potential targets are carefully guarded, (2) the means to commit crime are controlled, and (3) potential offenders are carefully monitored. Desperate people may contemplate crime, but only the truly irrational will attack a well-defended, inaccessible target and risk strict punishments. Crime prevention can be achieved by reducing the opportunities people have to commit particular crimes, a practice known as **situational crime prevention**.

Situational crime prevention was popularized in the early 1970s by Oscar Newman, who coined the term **defensible space** to signify that crime can be prevented or displaced through the use of residential architectural designs that reduce criminal opportunity, such as well-lit housing projects that maximize surveillance.[70] Situational variables, such as

situational crime prevention A method to eliminate or reduce particular crimes in narrow settings, such as increasing lighting and installing security alarms.

TABLE 5.1 Twenty-Five Techniques of Situational Prevention

Increase the Effort	Increase the Risks	Reduce the Rewards	Reduce Provocations	Remove Excuses
1. Target harden ■ Steering column locks and immobilisers ■ Anti-robbery screens ■ Tamper-proof packaging	6. Extend guardianship ■ *Take* routine precautions: go out in group at night, leave signs of occupancy, carry phone ■ "Cocoon" neighborhood watch	11. Conceal targets ■ Off-street parking ■ Gender-neutral phone directories ■ Unmarked bullion trucks	16. Reduce frustrations and stress ■ Efficient queues and polite service ■ Expanded seating ■ Soothing music/muted lights	21. Set rules ■ Rental agreements ■ Harassment codes ■ Hotel registration
2. Control access to facilities ■ Entry phones ■ Electronic card access ■ Baggage screening	7. Assist natural surveillance ■ Improved street lighting ■ Defensible space design ■ Support whistleblowers	12. Remove targets ■ Removable car radio ■ Women's refuges ■ Pre-paid cards for pay phones	17. Avoid disputes ■ Separate enclosures for rival soccer fans ■ Reduce crowding in pubs ■ Fixed cab fares	22. Post instructions ■ "No Parking" ■ "Private Property" ■ "Extinguish camp fires"
3. Screen exits ■ Ticket needed for exit ■ Export documents ■ Electronic merchandise tags	8. Reduce anonymity ■ Taxi driver IDs ■ "How's my driving?" decals ■ School uniforms	13. Identify property ■ Property marking ■ Vehicle licensing and parts marking ■ Cattle branding	18. Reduce emotional arousal ■ Controls on violent pornography ■ Enforce good behavior on soccer field ■ Prohibit racial slurs	23. Alert conscience ■ Roadside speed display boards ■ Signatures for customs declarations ■ "Shoplifting is stealing"
4. Deflect offenders ■ Street closures ■ Separate bathrooms for women ■ Disperse pubs	9. Utilize place managers ■ CCTV for double-deck buses ■ Two clerks for convenience stores ■ Reward vigilance	14. Disrupt markets ■ Monitor pawn shops ■ Controls on classified ads ■ License street vendors	19. Neutralize peer pressure ■ "Idiots drink and drive" ■ "It's OK to say No" ■ Disperse troublemakers at school	24. Assist compliance ■ Easy library checkout ■ Public lavatories ■ Litter bins
5. Control tools/weapons ■ "Smart" guns ■ Disabling stolen cell phones ■ Restrict spray paint sales to juveniles	10. Strengthen formal surveillance ■ Red light cameras ■ Burglar alarms ■ Security guards	15. Deny benefits ■ Ink merchandise tags ■ Graffiti cleaning ■ Speed humps	20. Discourage imitation ■ Rapid repair of vandalism ■ V-chips in TVs ■ Censor details of modus operandi	25. Control drugs and alcohol ■ Breathalyzers in pubs ■ Server intervention ■ Alcohol-free events

SOURCE: Center for Problem-Oriented Policing, "25 Techniques of Situational Prevention," found at http://www.popcenter.org/25techniques.

traffic flow, pedestrian walkways, and public lighting, become part of an environment that can enable or discourage crime.[71]

In 1971, C. Ray Jeffery wrote *Crime Prevention through Environmental Design*, in which he extended Newman's concepts and applied them to non-residential areas, such as schools and factories.[72] According to this view, such mechanisms as security systems, deadbolt locks, high-intensity street lighting, and Neighbourhood Watch patrols should be able to reduce criminal opportunity.[73] In 1992, Ronald Clarke published *Situational Crime Prevention*, which compiled the best-known strategies and tactics to reduce criminal incidents.[74] Today, crime prevention through environmental design (CPTED) is a well-accepted principle of situational crime prevention.[75]

In Canada, Patricia and Paul Brantingham of Simon Fraser University say that despite the claims of many programs, most situational crime prevention efforts have mixed success. Generic programs cannot address the diversity of

criminal behaviour and need to be targeted toward specific problems. The motive for stealing a car for a joyride is different from stealing a car for parts, so the prevention strategy should also be different.

For example, Welsh and Farrington compared the effectiveness of two forms of surveillance in preventing crime in public space: formal surveillance (CCTV) and natural surveillance (street lighting). They found that both are equally effective in reducing crime, especially property crimes. If CCTV and improved street lighting are targeted more narrowly on deterring property crimes, they will reduce the incidents of criminal activity to vehicles in parking lots. Furthermore,

defensible space The principle that crime prevention can be achieved through modifying the physical environment to reduce the opportunity individuals have to commit crime.

improved street lighting will reduce crime in public spaces with less public resistance than CCTV surveillance cameras.[76]

Sometimes, assuming the rational basis of crime might overestimate the extent to which people consider the legal consequences of their actions. For example, despite new laws in the 1990s making it easier for the police to deal with the buying and selling of sex, the overall volume of prostitution remained relatively unchanged because it just changed location. Unfortunately, this made prostitution much more dangerous as a result.

Also, sometimes the idea of the quick fix can be an illusion. Neighbourhood Watch programs are very popular, but their main effect is probably to improve people's attitudes about their neighbourhoods, not to reduce crime. For that, we might need more specific crime prevention strategies.

Crime Prevention Strategies

Several situational crime prevention efforts might reduce crime rates. One approach is to create an overall community strategy to reduce crime in general. For example, Felson suggests that such a strategy might include some or all of the following elements:

- uniform school-release schedules so that there is no doubt when students belong in school and when they are truant; combined with effective truancy control efforts
- after-school and weekend activities to keep children under adult supervision
- school lunch programs designed to keep students in school and away from shopping areas
- no-cash policies in schools to reduce the opportunity for students to either be targets or buy drugs or alcohol
- shopping areas and schools kept separate
- construction of housing to maximize guardianship and minimize illegal behaviour
- encouragement of neighbourhood stability so that residents will be acquainted with one another
- privatization of parks and recreation facilities so that people will be responsible for their area's security[77]

Felson's suggestions are designed to reduce crime by limiting the access that members of a highly motivated offender group (high-school students) have to tempting targets. Crime maps show that robberies and vandalism occur close to urban high schools. Some features of the total community strategy are designed to eliminate specific crimes (for example, by youths), but most features are designed mainly to reduce the overall crime rate.

An important point in any attempt to devise a crime prevention strategy, however, is that crime prevention policy and local practice should be based on using what works best. Systematic reviews of how policies work provide an evidence base that governments can use to develop new policy. Welsh and Farrington's Campbell Collaboration Crime and Justice Group is one such project that analyzes what works to prevent crime in four important areas: at-risk children, offenders, victims, and high-crime places. In their book, *Preventing Crime: What Works for Children, Offenders, Victims, and Places*, they discuss interventions that are effective in preventing crime: social-skills training for children, cognitive-behavioural therapy and incarceration-based drug treatment for offenders, face-to-face restorative justice conferences involving victims and offenders, prevention of repeat residential burglary victimization, hot-spots policing, closed-circuit television surveillance, and improved street lighting.[78]

Acting on evidence-based research into new crime prevention interventions needs to be initiated and can contribute to a safer society, both now and in the long run.

CONNECTIONS

Chapter 12 discusses many types of property crime, the total cost to society, and some tips on how to discourage it. For crimes of opportunity, especially, prevention measures are usually fairly inexpensive and uncomplicated.

Targeting Specific Crimes

So how do we apply the ideas of rational choice and routine activities theory into policies that can prevent crime? Can situational crime prevention be used to develop tactics to reduce or eliminate a specific crime problem, such as shoplifting in an urban mall or street-level drug dealing?

Crime prevention tactics in use today generally fall into one of four categories: (1) increasing the effort needed to commit the crime, (2) increasing the risks of committing the crime, (3) reducing the rewards for committing the crime, and (4) inducing guilt or shame for committing the crime. Some basic techniques and some specific methods that can be used to prevent auto crime are listed in Exhibit 5.2.

EXHIBIT 5.2

Neighbourhood Watch Tips on Vehicle Security

In Canada, vehicle thefts occur every eight minutes.

- Always lock the doors and roll up the windows tightly.
- Leave your valuables out of view and securely locked away.
- Park in well-lit areas with pedestrian traffic.
- Do not leave personal identification, such as credit card slips, in your vehicle.
- Do not hide spare keys—they can be found.
- Never put your name and/or address on your house or car keys.
- If you have a garage, use it. Lock both the vehicle and garage doors.
- Consider installing anti-theft devices.

Some tactics designed to increase the offender's effort include target-hardening techniques, such as installing unbreakable glass on storefronts, locking gates, and fencing yards. Crimes can also be made more difficult to commit through technological advances, such as having an owner's photo on credit cards to reduce the use of stolen cards. The development of new products also makes it more difficult to commit crimes. For example, the use of steering locks has helped reduce car theft in the United States, Britain, and Germany.[79] Installing a locking device on cars that prevents inebriated drivers from starting the vehicle significantly reduces drunk-driving rates.[80]

An excellent example of comprehensive crime prevention was developed at a Canadian bank. The bank has more than 400 branches, and one in four had been robbed the previous year, some more than once. Fourteen percent of the branches were considered at high risk. Based on interviews with convicted bank robbers, a robbery prevention program was instituted that centred on a target-hardening floor plan, robbery prevention procedures, and enhanced training for personnel. Robberies of the branches decreased 65 percent over a two-year period.[81]

Increasing the chances of apprehension is also important. Crime rates can be reduced by improving surveillance lighting, creating Neighbourhood Watch programs, controlling building entrances and exits, installing burglar alarms and security systems, increasing the number of private security officers, and modifying police patrols.[82] Research on gasoline drive-offs from convenience stores found that removing signs from store windows, installing brighter lights, and instituting a pay-first policy reduces the number of incidents of people driving off without paying.[83]

Target reduction strategies include such simple steps as making car radios removable, marking property so that it is more difficult to sell when stolen, and having gender-neutral phone listings. Caller ID and the consequent threat of exposure have resulted in significant reductions in the number of obscene phone calls.[84] Tracking systems similar to global positioning systems help police locate and return stolen vehicles.

Inducing guilt or shame might include such techniques as setting strict rules that embarrass offenders, such as publishing john lists in the newspaper to shame those arrested for soliciting prostitutes. Perhaps drunk drivers should be forced to have a large sign with the letter "D" placed on their car. This penalty for drunkenness hearkens back to the 17th century, when in Boston, for example, Robert Coles was "fyned ten shillings and enjoyned to stand with a white sheet of paper on his back whereon Drunkard shalbe written in great lres & to stand therewith soe longe as the Courte finde meete, fo abuseing himself shamefully with drinke."[85]

Research on the use of shaming against financial criminals is less encouraging. It suggests that potential damage to business prospects is more effective than shame. Eighty-eight percent of British executives in the *Times* 1000 largest companies survey said they would refuse to do business with people convicted of fraud. Thus, the inducement for corporate misbehaviour is not as easily corrected by shaming individuals.[86]

Crime Discouragers

The success of situational crime prevention may also rest on the behaviour of people whose actions directly influence the prevention of crime. Crime discouragers can be grouped into three categories: guardians, who monitor targets (such as store security guards); handlers, who monitor potential offenders (such as parole officers and parents); and managers, who monitor places (such as homeowners and doorkeepers). Crime discouragers have different levels of responsibility, ranging from highly personal involvement, such as homeowners protecting their house and parents controlling their children, to the most impersonal involvement, such as a stranger who stops someone from shoplifting in the mall (see Table 5.2).[87]

The concept of crime discouragement can be useful to plan situational crime prevention tactics. More effective crime reduction may occur if (1) managers are given tools to better monitor places, (2) guardians are better equipped to protect targets, and (3) handlers are allowed to exert greater control over offenders. For example, store clerks can enhance their discouragement role when provided with a mirror to watch merchandise and a button to summon supervisory help. A handler will become more effective if supplied with hidden cameras and eavesdropping devices. Managers given greater supervisory powers will help reduce crime by exerting better control over their charges.

Ramifications of Situational Prevention

Situational crime prevention can also produce unforeseen and unwanted consequences. Preventing crime from occurring in one locale might do little to deter criminal motivation, so crime is not prevented but displaced to alternative targets.[88] For example, a 2003 drug crackdown by Vancouver police spread drug activity from a concentrated area to a much wider area through the Downtown Eastside. Because enforcement does not address deeper issues, such as health, unemployment, and harm reduction, it cannot reduce crime overall.[89] There are six kinds of crime displacement:

1. *Temporal.* Offenders perpetrate crimes at times seen as less risky.
2. *Target.* Difficult targets are given up in favour of those easier to hit.
3. *Spatial.* Offenders move from high-target areas to less-protected areas.
4. *Tactical.* Tactics are changed to get around security measures.
5. *Perpetrator.* New offenders take the place of those who are apprehended.
6. *Type of crime.* Offenders take up another type of crime if one type is too difficult.[90]

> **target reduction strategies** Methods for reducing crime through the use of locks, bars, alarms, and other devices; based on the routine activities theory and its analysis of potential risk factors.

TABLE 5.2 Crime Discouragers

		TYPES OF SUPERVISORS AND OBJECTS OF SUPERVISION		
		A Guardians (monitoring suitable targets)	**B** Handlers (monitoring likely offenders)	**C** Managers (monitoring amenable places)
Level of Responsibility	1. Personal (owners, family, friends)	Student keeps eye on own bookbag	Parent makes sure child gets home	Homeowner monitors area near home
	2. Assigned (employees with specific assignment)	Store clerk monitors jewellery	Principal sends kids back to school	Doorman protects building
	3. Diffuse (employees with general assignment)	Accountant notes shoplifting	School clerk discourages truancy	Hotel maid impairs trespasser
	4. General (strangers, other citizens)	Bystander inhibits shoplifting	Stranger questions boys at mall	Customer observes parking structure

SOURCE: Marcus Felson, "Those Who Discourage Crime," in *Crime and Place*, eds. John Eck and David Weisburd, 59 (Monsey, N.Y.: Criminal Justice Press, 1995). Reprinted by permission.

Displacement assumes an equilibrium that might cause crime to spill over from one area to the next. However, this effect might not be the result of displacement, but the result of offenders casually drifting in and out of crime. The offender's willingness to commit crime must be accompanied by an opportunity. Therefore, the result may be a net preventive effect, as discussed by Thomas Gabor of the University of Ottawa.[91]

The problem of **extinction** also comes into play: Crime reduction programs may produce a short-term positive effect, but dissipate as criminals adjust to new conditions. Criminals learn to dismantle alarms or avoid patrols, or become motivated to try new offences they had previously avoided. For example, if every residence is provided with a burglar alarm system, motivated offenders might then turn to armed robbery, a riskier and more violent crime. However, some offenders are unlikely to turn to crimes they find morally repugnant, for example, from shoplifting to armed robbery.

Although displacement and extinction may be problems, a hidden benefit of situational crime prevention has been noted: **diffusion of benefits**.[92] Diffusion of benefits occurs when (1) efforts to prevent one crime cause the unintended prevention of another, and (2) crime control efforts in one locale reduce crime in other, non-target areas.

Crime control may deter criminals by causing them to fear apprehension. For example, video cameras set up in a mall to reduce shoplifting can also reduce property damage because would-be vandals fear being caught on camera.[93]

Another type of diffusion effect is called **discouragement**. By limiting one type of target, would-be lawbreakers may forgo other criminal activity because crime no longer pays. Drug enforcement programs that use municipal codes and nuisance abatement laws not only decrease drug dealing in targeted areas, but also reduce it in surrounding areas.[94]

GENERAL DETERRENCE

According to the rational choice view, motivated people will violate the law if left free and unrestricted. Rational offenders want the goods that crime provides without having to work for them and will commit crime if there is no fear of apprehension or punishment. The concept of **general deterrence** holds that crime rates are influenced and controlled by the threat of criminal punishment. If people fear apprehension and punishment, they will not risk breaking the law. An inverse relationship should thus exist between crime rates and the certainty, severity, and celerity (speed) of legal sanctions. If, for example, the punishment for a crime is increased

extinction   The phenomenon in which a crime prevention effort has an immediate impact that dissipates as criminals adjust to new conditions.

diffusion of benefits   An effect that occurs when an effort to control one type of crime has the unexpected benefit of reducing the incidence of another type of crime.

discouragement   The effect when efforts made to eliminate one type of crime also control other types of crime by limiting access to desirable targets and thereby reducing the value of the criminal activity.

general deterrence   A crime control policy that depends on the fear of criminal penalties, such as long prison sentences for violent crimes, aimed at convincing the potential law violator that the pains associated with crime outweigh its benefits.

and if the effectiveness and efficiency of the criminal justice system in enforcing the law are improved, then the number of people engaging in that act should decline.

The factors of certainty, severity, and celerity also influence one another. For example, if a crime, such as robbery, is punished severely but few robbers are ever caught or punished, then the severity of punishment for robbery will likely not deter people from robbing. However, if the certainty of apprehension is increased by modern technology, such as CCTV, or more efficient police work, even minor punishments might deter the potential robber.

In Western society, support has increased in favour of more punitive measures. This change reflects the middle-class view that no longer sees crime as affecting only the poor but as a problem affecting society as a whole. Harsher punishments, three-strikes-and-you're-out legislation, and mandatory minimum sentences are still, and increasingly, in favour, despite sometimes a lack of evidence on their effectiveness.[95]

Certainty of Punishment

According to deterrence theory, if the probability of arrest, conviction, and sanctioning increases, crime rates should decline. Rational offenders will realize that the increased likelihood of being punished outweighs any benefit they perceive from committing crimes.

Research does show an inverse relationship between crime rates and the certainty of punishment.[96] Evidence shows that people who believe that they will be punished for future crimes also say that they will not commit those crimes.[97] Some research says that if police could make an arrest in at least 30 percent of all reported crimes, the crime rate would significantly decline.[98] However, other research has found little relationship between the likelihood of being arrested or imprisoned and the corresponding crime rates.[99]

One reason for this ambivalent finding is that the punishment–crime association may be group-specific. For example, the arrest probability for Black people influences Black offence rates alone, while the arrest probabilities for Caucasian people affect Caucasian offending patterns.[100] Similarly, it is also crime-specific. The increased certainty of arrest helps lower the burglary rate.[101] And in Varma and Doob's analysis of the deterrence of tax evasion, they found the certainty of being caught was a stronger deterrent than the size of penalty.[102]

CONNECTIONS

In cases we will look at in Chapter 13, the rewards for engaging in corporate criminality are too great, and the oversight too minimal, for crimes not to occur.

However, in corporate crime, punishment is far from certain. Furthermore, the penalties are administrative, not criminal. When the Westray coal mine blew up in 1992, it was predictable and preventable. The safety violations that inevitably killed 26 miners resulted in 54 charges under the *Occupational Health and Safety Act*, all of which were eventually dropped. However, Australia, the United States, Britain, and now Canada have adopted changes to their criminal codes to make corporations more accountable for their actions. In the 1997 report into the Westray mine disaster, Mr. Justice Peter Richard said:

> The Government of Canada … should introduce in the Parliament of Canada such amendments to legislation as are necessary to ensure that corporate executives and directors are held properly accountable for workplace safety.[103]

A bill named after Westray, which criminalizes corporate inaction in cases of homicide, was passed in 2003. It has been used several times in court cases.

The Effect of Police Actions. If the increased certainty of apprehension and punishment deters criminal behaviour, increasing the number of police officers should be able to decrease the crime rate. Moreover, if these police officers are active and aggressive crime fighters, would-be criminals should be convinced that the risk of apprehension outweighs the benefits they can gain from crime. However, research is equivocal on whether an increase in police presence is an effective crime deterrent.[104] And crime rates are confounded by other factors, such as a decrease in the number of young males in the population.

Some police departments have conducted experiments to determine whether increasing police activities or allocation of services can influence crime rates. In 1988, for example, Edmonton implemented a Neighbourhood Foot Patrol, with constables assigned to 21 neighbourhoods. This initiative in community policing identified city areas by repeat calls for service and occurrence data. The result was that community and police satisfaction increased, and calls for service decreased.[105] Similar studies have found bike patrols to be effective, as police are more in contact with their surroundings and better able to patrol ball fields and parks to crack down on public drinking and vandalism. The key strategy is to pair crime prevention with program evaluation.[106]

In the classic experiment to evaluate the effectiveness of police patrols and the general deterrent effect of police activity, the Kansas City police department's 15 independent police beats or districts were divided into three groups.[107] The first retained a normal police patrol; the second (the proactive group) was supplied with two to three times the normal number of patrol forces; and the third (the reactive group) eliminated its preventive patrol entirely, and police officers responded only when summoned by citizens to a crime. Surprisingly, data indicated that variations in patrol techniques had little effect on residential or business burglaries, auto and auto accessory theft, robberies, or vandalism.

Other police departments have instituted **crackdowns**, sudden changes in police activity designed to increase the threat or actual certainty of punishment. Crackdowns can target specific neighbourhoods or specific offences and can even include efforts to decrease the signs of public disorder that create fear. Initial and residual deterrent effects vary, sometimes because of factors outside the scope of the crackdowns themselves. For example, targeting street-level narcotics dealers by using undercover agents and surveillance cameras in known drug-dealing locales may have an initial deterrent effect on controlling crime but may suffer diffusion over time, making the deterrent effect short-lived. Clearly, more research is needed in this important area of deterrence.[108]

These crackdowns illustrate what has become known as the broken-windows approach, first developed by George Kelling, in which the police deal with what the public sees as symptoms of crime, such as people urinating or sleeping in public, littering and loitering, creating graffiti, and being drunk in public.[109] In an example from Toronto, police took a zero-tolerance approach to crime, targeting such minor offences as panhandling and urinating in public. However, such approaches do not solve the underlying problems that cause the offences.[110] They may also be highly unpopular, such as the "stop and frisk" policies targeting minorities in various cities, and increase animosity against the police. Research shows that they are usually not very productive, either.

Severity of Punishment

The threat of severe punishments should also decrease the crime rate. Some studies have found that increasing sanction levels can control common criminal behaviours, for example, using an illegal, unauthorized descrambler to obtain pay cable television programs.[111] In one study, threatening letters were sent to violators who were using a descrambler and avoiding payments to the local cable company, which conveyed the message that illegal theft of cable signals would be criminally prosecuted. The letter did not indicate that the subject's personal violation had been discovered, but it was found that about two-thirds of the violators reacted to the threat by removing the illegal device.

However, an analysis of the deterrent effects of anti-drunk-driving laws found when the laws were toughened, the result was a short-term deterrent effect; however, because the likelihood of getting caught is low, the deterrent effect was small over the long term.[112] And in a study that evaluated the effect of mandating jail sentences for drunk-driving convictions, time series analysis indicated little deterrent effect.[113]

Research has also looked at the effect of firearm sentencing laws on violent crime rates. Some research efforts claim that these laws can lower crime rates, while others question their deterrent effect;[114] little evidence supports their ability to reduce crime in general.[115]

In sum, despite the hope of those espousing a law and order agenda, little evidence exists that increasing the punishments for specific crimes can alone deter their occurrence.

CONNECTIONS

The last execution in Canada happened in 1962. Read about this famous Canadian case of Arthur Lucas and Ronald Turpin, in Chapter 10.

The Special Case of Capital Punishment. If punishment severity can have a deterrent effect on crime, fear of the death penalty should significantly reduce murder rates. Capital punishment was abolished in Canada in 1976, and the last executions took place in 1962. However, not too long ago, half of Canadians would have liked capital punishment to be reinstated. Because of the perception that perpetrators of heinous crimes should face the death penalty, we will briefly look at the research to evaluate its effectiveness. Various studies testing the assumption that capital punishment deters violent crime can be divided into immediate impact studies, comparative research, and time series analysis.

If capital punishment is a deterrent, it should have the greatest impact after a well-publicized execution has taken place.[116] However, research shows that more homicides occurred during the 60 days following an execution than during those days preceding it, suggesting that the overall impact of executions might actually increase the incidence of homicide. That executions may increase the likelihood of murder has been labelled the **brutalization effect**.[117]

Some research indicates that in the short run, executing criminals can bring the murder rate down. Phillips studied the immediate effect of executions in Britain from 1858 to 1914 and found a temporary deterrent effect that was based on the publicity following the execution.[118] However, this finding is controversial and not well accepted in the field.

The second type of research, comparative research, compares the murder rates in jurisdictions that have abolished the death penalty with the murder rates of those jurisdictions that have the death penalty. Some research shows that homicide rates and execution risks move independently of each other and that the death penalty has no deterrent effect on violent crime rates,[119] while other research finds evidence that a deterrent effect of capital punishment exists.[120]

Research on 14 nations around the world found little evidence that countries with a death penalty have lower violence rates, but research has found evidence that homicide rates

crackdown The concentration of police resources on a particular problem area, such as street-level drug dealing, to eradicate or displace criminal activity.

brutalization effect The outcome of capital punishment having created an atmosphere of brutality, which reinforces the view that violence is an appropriate response to provocation.

decline after capital punishment is abolished.[121] This effect, called time series analysis, looks at whether the murder rate changes when death penalty statutes are eliminated. If the perception of execution is a deterrent,[122] each execution could prevent people from being victims of murder. However, it could be that life imprisonment is as effective.[123]

In sum, studies do not show capital punishment to have a deterrent effect.[124] The reason is probably that murder is often an expressive crime of passion involving people who know each other and who may be under the influence of drugs or suffering from poverty.[125] These factors may either prevent or inhibit rational evaluation of the long-term consequences of an immediate violent act. Murder is quite often a **conflict-linked crime** not committed during the course of another crime.

Perception and Deterrence

A core element of general deterrence theory is that people who believe that they are likely to be caught and severely punished will abstain from crime.[126] Some research supports this theory.[127] However, others have found little association between fear of future punishments and criminal activity,[128] especially for conflict-linked crime.

The certainty and not the severity of punishment seems to influence people.[129] People who believe they will be caught and subjected to criminal prosecution are less likely to engage in tax evasion.[130] The perceived risk of getting caught influenced active burglars, while the threat of severe punishments had relatively little effect.[131]

One criticism of this **perceptual deterrence** research is that it usually involves samples of non-criminals (such as college students) and crimes of minor seriousness (such as smoking marijuana). Experienced offenders, who are more criminally motivated and less committed to moral values, are less likely to be deterred by the perception that they will be punished in the future[132] and are the offenders least threatened by the idea of future punishment.[133] And prior sanctions actually lower the perception that crime is a risky undertaking, as criminals with the greatest number of prior convictions have the lowest fear of legal sanctions.[134] This finding shows the difficulty of basing studies solely on the general population.[135]

In sum, research measuring the perceptions of punishment shows (1) that the certainty of punishment has a greater influence on the choice of crime than does the severity of punishment, and (2) that people who believe they are certain to be arrested and punished for a crime are less likely to break the law regardless of the severity of the punishment.[136]

Informal Sanctions

The fear of **informal sanctions** may have a greater crime-reducing impact than the fear of formal legal punishments. Informal sanctions occur when significant others, such as parents, peers, neighbours, and teachers, direct their disapproval, anger, and indignation toward an offender. If this happens, law violators run the risk of feeling shame, being embarrassed, and suffering a loss of respect.[137] Can the fear of public humiliation deter crime?

Research efforts have established the influence of informal sanctions.[138] Social control is rooted in how people perceive negative reactions from interpersonal acquaintances (family, friends). Legal sanctions supplement informal control processes by influencing a small segment of criminally inclined persons.[139]

This effect also means that family and friends who don't react negatively to crime are facilitating it. For example, according to a study reported in *Science Daily*, if one's family and friends approve of speeding, then one is more likely to speed. Irrespective of age and gender, drivers who perceived their family and friends as approving of speeding, admitted to speeding more frequently.[140]

Evidence from Britain shows that efforts to control drunk driving by shaming offenders produced a moral climate that helped reduce the incidence.[141] And shaming works in the interaction with others who are familiar. Those fearful of being rejected by family and peers are reluctant to engage in crime.[142] Two factors seem to stand out: personal shame over violating the law and the fear of public humiliation if the deviant behaviour becomes public knowledge. People who will feel ashamed are less likely to commit theft, fraud, and motor vehicular offences. People have been found to be more likely to respond to anti-littering drives and anti-drunk-driving campaigns if the thought of being accused of littering or driving drunk makes them feel ashamed or embarrassed.[143] Women are much more likely to fear shame and embarrassment than are men, a finding that may help explain gender differences in the crime rate.[144]

Fear of shame and embarrassment can be a powerful deterrent to crime.[145] One study found that spouse abusers were more afraid of social costs, for example, loss of friends and family disapproval, than they were of legal punishments such as going to jail. The researchers found that in cases of wife assault, the potential for self-stigma and personal humiliation was the greatest deterrent to crime.[146]

---

conflict-linked crime or violence   An expressive crime or an act of expressive violence involving people who know each other and who may be under the influence of drugs.

perceptual deterrence   The view that the perceived risk of being caught or the threat of severe punishments can deter active criminal offenders.

informal sanctions   The disapproval of parents, peers, and neighbours directed toward an offender, which may have a greater crime-reducing impact than the fear of formal legal punishments.

The effect of informal sanctions may vary according to the cohesiveness of community structure and type of crime. Informal sanctions may be most effective in highly unified areas where everyone knows one another and the crime cannot be hidden from public view. The threat of informal sanctions may also have the greatest influence on instrumental crimes, which involve planning, and not on impulsive or expressive criminal behaviours or those associated with substance abuse.[147]

Public education on the social cost of crime that stresses the risk of shame and humiliation may be a more effective crime-prevention tool than legal punishments.[148]

Closed-Circuit Television (CCTV) and Public Surveillance

The debate over whether to mount closed-circuit television (CCTV) cameras in public places to deter crime has been eclipsed by their now widespread presence. CCTV systems can now be actively monitored (by a person watching in real time) or passively monitored (recorded). The main question now is whether such systems are effective.

The Scottish government's Central Research Unit analyzed CCTV surveillance in two cities, Airdrie and Glasgow. It concluded that 21 percent fewer offences took place in the two years after introduction of the cameras. Housebreaking, shoplifting, and theft from vehicles fell by 48 percent. Furthermore, it concluded that no displacement effect occurred to non-monitored areas.[149]

England's use of video surveillance goes back to 1986, and many countries are now increasing their use of CCTV. In the United States, a decade ago, about 75 percent of businesses used some form of CCTV to protect their premises.[150] The International Center for the Prevention of Crime estimates that delinquency in public areas can be reduced by up to 68 percent with the use of CCTV, but it needs to be used in conjunction with a quick response by the police, and video hard copies need to be stored for future prosecution.[151]

The type of surveillance (active or passive) also makes an important difference. Several Canadian studies show that unmonitored cameras are one of the least effective deterrents to robberies in banks and convenience stores. For example, the Peel Regional Police concluded that closed-circuit television is expensive to implement and is not a major deterrence.

Some legal and social issues surround the use of CCTV surveillance techniques. First is the notion that such techniques will damage the image of the police by creating a Big Brother mentality. This view is criticized by Sean Hier (of the University of Victoria) and his colleagues, who refer to it as the panopticon approach.[152]

Second, some fear that the recordings will be sold for their commercial value, violating the rights of those recorded on these tapes. Legal challenges have dealt with issues of privacy and the distinction between public and private places. The trend has been to allow surveillance as long as it does

not occur in truly private areas, and as long as its use has helped save money or lives.[153]

Video surveillance has been in use in Canada since 1992 by law enforcement agencies, banks, libraries, restaurants, and convenience stores, and at industrial sites, offices, apartment buildings, and public transit stations. In 1995, 70 percent of all bank robberies in Canada were video-recorded, and CCTV surveillance tapes captured 75 percent of all crimes investigated by law enforcement or private security. CCTV video cameras in commercial areas have also been instrumental in helping to find missing persons.[154]

In many provinces, the use of CCTV systems is controlled by *Freedom of Information and Protection of Privacy Acts*. Some fear that acceptance of video surveillance may be the first step in a series of more intrusive surveillance techniques (the panopticon approach). In 2001, the RCMP violated privacy laws when they set up a surveillance camera in Kelowna. The federal privacy commissioner said the $22,000 crime camera on the downtown street contravened federal law. However, police in Vancouver, London, Toronto, Winnipeg, and many other cities have or have already installed them.

Some have voiced a concern that once installed, CCTV systems will be used to serve a wide range of social-control functions, so-called *function creep*, whereby a camera system installed to watch for criminal behaviour may end up being used as a tool to monitor performance.[155] Because the state is indirectly behind most public-space CCTV systems, the systems permit the state to maintain a high degree of control over its population.[156]

In conclusion, a difference of opinion surrounds the effectiveness of CCTV surveillance. Such systems reinforce the traditional view that violence takes place in the public sphere. However, CCTV can be used as a tool to ensure the success of local economies by providing a safe place for

© Associated Press

The average person is caught on videotape up to a dozen times a day. And on this day, Conrad Black was caught illegally removing boxes from his office while under a court order not to do so.

businesses to set up and for consumers to gather. And, as Kevin Walby of Carleton University points out, it is no longer just the police who install CCTV, but also businesses and citizens.[157] The growing use of CCTV points to the need to develop adequate legal safeguards.[158]

New Developments in Surveillance. The average person is caught on videotape at least a dozen times a day. However, many other forms of surveillance are being developed that are potentially more invasive. A growing number of police departments use handheld wireless devices that contain records culled from motor vehicle registries, credit bureaus, and telephone directories. One private sector company in particular can provide information on 98 percent of the population. Broad searching through records and commercial files, called data mining, is very poorly regulated. In the push to acquire more information about people who might not even be suspected of committing crime, the public is becoming less compliant. In 2004, Canadian police chiefs proposed a surcharge on phone bills to pay for police wiretaps, but 88 percent of those replying to a poll by *The Globe and Mail* said no.

The ability now to track and monitor people is widespread, from cellphone tower dumps to automated license plate scanning equipment. A person's movements can be tracked and reconstructed should the need exist just with technology.

The 2004 Olympics saw an increase in the use of surveillance in the effort to detect and deter crime. Street-level cameras and speech recognition software, combined with helicopters, patrol boats, and mobile command centres, all created an extensive network of surveillance. At the 2014 Winter Olympics, Russia announced that it would monitor and record all communications, and save them for ten years.

Another development is radio frequency identification (RFID) chips implanted in commercial products, which can track their purchase and customer preferences. RFIDs can also be embedded subcutaneously for tracking purposes, for example, in the case of offenders under house arrest or pedophiles ordered to stay away from areas frequented by children.

The future can only be imagined.

General Deterrence in Review

Some experts believe that the purpose of the law and the justice system is to create a "threat system,"[159] and that the threat of legal punishment should deter lawbreakers through fear. Nonetheless, despite efforts to punish criminals and make them fear crime, little evidence supports the ability of fear of apprehension and punishment to reduce crime rates. How can this discrepancy be explained?

First, deterrence theory assumes that an offender is rational and weighs the costs and benefits of a criminal act before deciding on a course of action. However, some criminals are desperate people acting under the influence of drugs and alcohol or suffering from personality disorders. Surveys show that a significant portion of all offenders, perhaps up to 80 percent, are substance abusers.[160] Chronic offender research indicates that a relatively small group of offenders commit a significant percentage of all serious crimes. Some psychologists believe that members of this select group suffer from an innate or inherited emotional state that renders them both (1) incapable of fearing punishment, and (2) less likely to appreciate the consequences of crime.[161] The threat of future punishment likely has little deterrent effect on these people.

Second, many offenders are cut off from society, lacking the education and skills they need to be in demand in the modern economy.[162] Such desperate people are unlikely to be deterred from crime by fear of punishment because, in reality, they perceive few other options for success.

Third, as Beccaria's famous equation tells us, the threat of punishment involves not only its severity, but also its certainty and speed. Our legal system is not very effective. Only 10 percent of all serious offences result in apprehension (half go unreported and police make arrests in only about 20 percent of reported crimes). Police routinely do not arrest suspects in personal disputes, even when they lead to violence, as in the case of wife assault.[163] As apprehended offenders are processed through all the stages of the criminal justice system, the odds of their receiving serious punishment diminish. Thus, some offenders may believe that they will not be severely punished for their acts, and consequently have little regard for the law's deterrent power.

Only offenders who suffer the most severe sanctions are likely to fear future legal punishments. Adolescents as a group are responsible for a disproportionate amount of crime, but may be well aware that the juvenile court is generally lenient in the imposition of meaningful sanctions.

Research shows that even those accused of murder, the most serious of crimes, are often convicted of lesser offences and spend a relatively short time behind bars.[164] In 1995, the maximum penalty for murder for juveniles was extended to 10 years, far below that for adults. In making their "rational choice," offenders may be aware that the deterrent effect of the law is minimal.

Fourth, in such cases as white-collar crime, the rational deterrence of sanctions would seem to be most likely to have an effect because white-collar crime is rationally calculated and planned; however, the offenders are also likely to perceive their actions as acceptable within their subculture. In such an environment, the sanctions would seem unfair and deviant to the offender, not the criminal actions.

Sometimes, crime control measures designed to prevent crime will have perverse effects. In the Crime in the News exhibit, research is discussed that shows that red-light cameras actually increase collisions in intersections.

Crackdowns on crime are sometimes based on false perceptions. For example, a crackdown on jaywalking is based on the idea that jaywalking puts both pedestrians and motorists at risk. However, what's the evidence?

In 2002, Transport Canada found that most pedestrian fatalities occurred at intersections, and that many of those occurred on the crosswalk. People are injured by drivers forcing the light, or just not seeing them at all. And if you aren't safe on the crosswalk, maybe you're better off dodging traffic on your own.

We have ideas about safety and danger, but those ideas have to be tested by research. And sometimes crime control is not about safety, but politics and money.

Take the case of red light cameras, for example. Recently, many jurisdictions have placed cameras at intersections to photograph license plates as drivers speed through to beat the red light. Fredericton's mayor himself has called for such cameras.

The idea is that the cameras will act as a deterrent and make intersections safer. Calgary, for example, has been using intersection cameras for over 10 years, and statistics over time show the number of tickets being issued dropping, which must mean that the deterrent is working.

However studies done using insurance data instead of police statistics show an increase in rear-end collisions as people stop short to avoid being photographed as they pass through the red light.

This finding was confirmed by the U.S. Federal Highway Administration in its survey of 132 sites across seven jurisdictions in 2005. It is somewhat cynical, however, because it concluded that since the rear-end collisions are less costly, the result is a net benefit.

That study also said that the results could be improved by better education and dedicated flashing green turning lanes. Other research also points to the benefit of four-way red lights, and longer yellow light times.

In Canada, the Ontario Ministry of Transportation evaluated 68 sites in six cities pre- and post-introduction of cameras between 1995–2002. It found an increase in property damage accidents of 18.5 percent, and a 4.9 percent increase in fatal and injury rear-end collisions.

It found that rear-end collisions involving property damage alone increased 49.9 percent. On the other hand, there was a 12.7 percent decrease in collisions in camera-free intersections used as a control group. In fact, the non-camera intersections fared better than the camera intersections in every accident category.

Furthermore, one thing most studies miss is that red-light cameras and insurance claims both generate revenue. There is the direct cost of the ticket, the insurance companies can increase premiums due to tickets, and then, of course, there are the increased premiums due to rear-end collision insurance claims created by the introduction of the camera.

This increased cost to the consumer is not factored into the price of crime control. And, in fact, in the United States, some jurisdictions have been criticized for relying too much on insurance industry advice in deciding whether to introduce red light cameras. Crime control can be skewed in favour of increased revenue for the insurance industry, and for increased revenue by the police and municipal jurisdictions.

Jason Markusoff, writing in the *Calgary Herald* last week, says that this year it is expected that Calgary's traffic cameras will net an extra $4 million in fine revenue for the police, over and above the $39 million already budgeted for. Since cameras do not necessarily result in an increase in safety, and can in fact create their own problems, how can they be justified?

The mayor of Calgary has said he will ask any surplus to be turned over to the city, yet the police chief says he needs it for crime-fighting strategies. It's too bad that the crime rate is probably decreasing for reasons other than policing. However, there's not much money in saying that.

So, are red-light cameras good or bad? Well, I guess it's how you follow the money.

SOURCE: Copyright Chris McCormick, published in the *Daily Gleaner* (Fredericton), November 29, 2012.

SPECIFIC DETERRENCE

The general deterrence model focuses on future or potential criminals. In contrast, the theory of **specific deterrence** holds that criminal sanctions should be so powerful that known criminals will never repeat their criminal acts. For example, we hope the drunk driver whose sentence is a large fine and a week in the county jail will be convinced that the price to be paid for drinking and driving is too great to consider future violations; burglars who spend five years in a tough, maximum-security prison should find their enthusiasm for theft dampened. In principle, punishment works to prevent or reduce crime if a connection can be established between the planned action and its consequence.[165]

Does Specific Deterrence Deter Crime?

At first glance, specific deterrence does not seem to work, as a majority of known criminals are not deterred by their

specific deterrence A crime control policy suggesting that punishment be severe; that individuals can be prevented from committing a crime if cost outweighs benefit; see *utilitarianism*.

punishment. However, these people are already in a criminal career pattern. Chronic offender research indicates that a stay in a juvenile justice facility has little deterrent effect on whether a persistent delinquent will become an adult criminal.[166] It is no surprise, then, that most prison inmates have prior records of arrest and conviction before their current offence.[167] Convicted felons are often rearrested within three years of release from prison, and those who have been punished in the past are the most likely to recidivate.[168]

A pilot analysis of recidivism among convicted youth in Canada showed that 60 percent of the 57,000 convicted offenders between the ages of 18 and 25 had at least one previous conviction. Among recidivists, 72 percent had multiple prior convictions. The earlier the offender was convicted, the more likely he or she was to recidivate. The average number of prior convictions for offenders first convicted at age 19 was four, compared with eight for those convicted at age 12.[169]

However, research also shows that offenders sentenced to prison have no lower rates of recidivism than do those receiving community sentences for similar crimes. For example, white-collar offenders who received a prison sentence were as likely to recidivate as was a matched group of offenders who received an alternative sanction.[170]

Some research has shown that rather than reducing the frequency of crime, punishment increases reoffending.[171] It is possible that (1) punishment elicits defiance rather than deterrence, or (2) the stigma of apprehension helps lock offenders into a criminal career instead of convincing them to avoid one. Changes in drunk-driving legislation in Ontario imposed stiff sanctions, an automatic year-long suspension, a mandatory program, and a quadrupling of insurance premiums. However, the result has been an increase of people driving with suspended licences and no insurance. Research in Alberta on 514 incarcerated drunk drivers, however, did find that when the sentencing threshold was properly applied, a consistent deterrent effect resulted, even for chronic offenders. Shorter sentences were less effective, but sentences longer than six months did not produce additional benefits.[172]

In Ontario in 2007, tough consequences were created for street racing, but faced criticism because only a third were upheld at trial. Critics suggested that the new law duplicated previous laws and merely punitively increased the consequences by allowing roadside licence suspensions and car seizures.[173]

Some empirical research does indicate that in a few instances, offenders who receive harsher punishments than do their peers will be less likely to recidivate, or if they do commit crimes again, they will do so less frequently.[174] However, the consensus is that the association between crime and specific deterrent measures is complex, as the Criminology Research box shows.

CONNECTIONS

Hypothetically, experiencing punishment should deter future crime. However, punishment stigmatizes people and "spoils" their identity, a turn of events that may encourage antisocial behaviour. The two factors may cancel each other out, helping to explain why punishment does not substantially reduce future criminality. The effects of stigma and negative labels are discussed further in Chapter 8.

Pain versus Shame

If current efforts at specific deterrence are less than successful, should new approaches be attempted? In their two widely discussed works on specific deterrence, criminologists Newman and Braithwaite take opposing approaches to reforming criminals.

Newman embraces traditional concepts of specific deterrence.[175] However, he suggests society should return to the use of corporal punishment, and use electric shocks to punish offenders because the shocks are over with quickly, have no lasting effect, and can be adjusted to fit the severity of a crime.

Corporal punishment could be used as an alternative sanction to fill the gap between the severe punishment of prison and the non-punishment of probation. Electric shocks can be calibrated to fit the crime. For violent crimes in which the victim was terrified and humiliated and for which a local community does not want to incarcerate, a violent corporal punishment should be considered, such as whipping. In these cases, humiliation of the offender is seen as justifiably deserved. In sum, Newman embraces specific deterrence strategies if they are inexpensive, immediate, and individualized.

In 1994, when a young American boy was flogged in Singapore after he pleaded guilty to vandalizing property, an international debate was provoked over the value of corporal punishment. In Canada, we have generally moved away from corporal punishment as undesirable in a civilized society.

Braithwaite takes a radically different approach.[176] Braithwaite notes that countries such as Japan, in which conviction for crimes brings shame, have low crime rates. In Japan, prosecution of the criminal proceeds only when a breakdown occurs during the normal process of public apology, compensation, and forgiveness. In Japan, **reintegrative shaming** is used extensively as an alternative to humiliating offenders. Japan is the only nation with a sustained decline in the crime rate over the past 50 years (37 per 100,000 population compared with 699 per 100,000 population in the United States).[177]

reintegrative shaming A method of correction that encourages offenders to confront their misdeeds, experience shame, and then be reincluded in society.

Criminology Research
Does Capital Punishment Deter Murder?

According to deterrence theory, the death penalty—the ultimate deterrent—should deter murder—the ultimate crime. Most Americans approve of the death penalty, including, as Norma Wilcox and Tracey Steele found, convicted criminals who are currently behind bars. But is the public's approval warranted? Does the death penalty actually deter murder?

Empirical research on the association between capital punishment and murder can be divided into three types: immediate impact studies, comparative research, and time-series analysis.

Immediate Impact

If capital punishment is a deterrent, the reasoning goes, then its impact should be greatest after a well-publicized execution. Robert Dann began testing this assumption in 1935 when he chose five highly publicized executions of convicted murderers in different years and determined the number of homicides in the 60 days before and after each execution. Each 120-day period had approximately the same number of homicides, and homicides occurred on approximately the same number of days. Dann's study revealed that an average of 4.4 more homicides occurred during the 60 days following an execution than during the 60 days preceding it, suggesting that the overall impact of executions might actually be an increase in the incidence of homicide. Seventy years later, when Lisa Stolzenberg and Stewart D'Alessio examined the effect of the death penalty on the murder rate in Houston, Texas, they also found that even when executions were highly publicized in the local press, they still had little influence on the murder rate.

Comparative Research

Another type of research compares the murder rates in jurisdictions that have abolished the death penalty with the rates in those jurisdictions that employ the death penalty. Studies using this approach have found little difference in the murder rates of adjacent states, regardless of their use of the death penalty; capital punishment did not appear to influence the reported rate of homicide. Research conducted in 14 nations around the world found little evidence that countries with a death penalty have lower violence rates than those without; homicide rates actually decline after capital punishment is abolished, a direct contradiction to its supposed deterrent effect.

Time-Series Studies

Time-series studies look at the long-term association between capital sentencing and murder. If capital punishment is a deterrent, then periods that have an upswing in executions should also experience a downturn in violent crime and murder. Most research efforts have failed to show such a relationship. One test of the deterrent effect of the death penalty in Texas by Jon Sorenson and his colleagues found no association between the frequency of execution and murder rates during the years 1984 to 1997. Matt Breverlin used data gathered from 1974 to 2001 in all 50 states to demonstrate that the death penalty for juveniles has no statistically significant deterrent effect. His conclusion is that state-level economic conditions, population density, and incarceration rates have a much greater impact on the juvenile murder rate than the deterrent impact of the death penalty. These findings seem to indicate that

the threat and/or reality of execution has relatively little influence on murder rates. Although researchers are still uncertain why the threat of capital punishment fails as a deterrent, the cause may lie in the nature of homicide itself. Murder is often an expressive crime of passion involving people who know each other and who may be under the influence of drugs and alcohol. Those who choose to take a life in a crime of passion may be less influenced by the threat of punishment, even death, than those who commit crime for economic gain.

Rethinking the Deterrent Effect of Capital Punishment

In contrast to these results, some recent studies have concluded that executing criminals may, in fact, decrease the murder rate. Those who still maintain that an association exists between capital punishment and the murder rate believe that the relationship has been masked or obscured by faulty research methods. Newer studies, using sophisticated data analysis, have been able to uncover a more significant association. For example, criminologist Steven Stack has conducted numerous research studies that show the immediate impact of a well-publicized execution can lower the murder rate during the following month. James Yunker, using a national data set, has found evidence of a deterrent effect of capital punishment now that the pace of executions has accelerated. Economists Hashem Dezhbakhsh, Paul H. Rubin, and Joanna M. Shepherd performed an advanced statistical analysis on county-level homicide data to calculate the effect of each execution on the number of homicides that would otherwise have occurred.

Shame is a powerful tool of informal social control. Citizens in cultures in which crime is not shameful do not internalize an abhorrence for crime because when they are punished, they view themselves as merely victims of the justice system; their punishment comes at the hands of neutral strangers being paid to act. In contrast, shaming relies on the participation of victims. Imagine the deterrent effect of the "brank," shown in the picture on page 150.

Braithwaite divides the concept of shame into two distinct types. The most common form of shaming typically involves **stigmatization**. This form of shaming is an ongoing process of **degradation** in which the offender is branded as an evil person and cast out of society. Shaming can occur at a school disciplinary hearing or a criminal court trial. Harold Garfinkel called trials "degradation ceremonies."[178]

Using a variety of models (for example, the effect of an execution conducted today on reducing homicides in five years, and so on), they found that each execution leads to an average of 18 fewer murders. In another study, Shepherd claims that the reason some research has not found a deterrent effect is because capital punishment may have differing influences depending on where and how it is used. Calculating each state's murder rate separately and lumping all state data together masks the deterrent effect of the death penalty. Shepherd found that the use of capital punishment deterred murder in states that conducted more executions than the norm. In contrast, in states that conducted relatively few executions (one or two per year), the average execution was either followed by an increase in the murder rate or had no effect. Shepherd concludes that each execution has two opposing effects. It can contribute to a climate of brutal violence (i.e., the brutalization effect) that tells people it is okay to kill in revenge. It can also act as a deterrent and show potential criminals that the state is willing to use the ultimate penalty to punish crimes. However, only if a state routinely uses executions does the deterrent effect take place; only then do potential criminals become convinced that the state is serious about the punishment, so that the criminals start to reduce their criminal activity.

These efforts contradict findings that capital punishment fails as a deterrent. So, on the one hand, the most recent research indicates that the death penalty is being used more frequently, the tipping point may possibly have been reached, and the death penalty is now an effective deterrent

measure. On the other hand, capital punishment still carries significant baggage: since 1976, more than 100 people have been wrongfully convicted and sentenced to death in the United States. And, according to research sponsored by the Pew Foundation, a majority of death penalty convictions have been overturned, many due to "serious, reversible error," including egregiously incompetent defence counsel, suppression of exculpatory evidence, false confessions, racial manipulation of the jury, "snitch" and accomplice testimony, and faulty jury instructions.

After years of study, the death penalty remains a topic of considerable criminological debate.

Critical Thinking

Even if the death penalty is effective, it can, unquestionably, cause problems. For example, when Geoffrey Rapp studied the effect of the death penalty on the safety of police officers, he found that the introduction of capital punishment actually created an extremely dangerous environment for law enforcement officers. Because the death penalty does not have a deterrent effect, criminals are more likely to kill police officers when the death penalty is in place. Tragically, the death penalty may lull officers into a false sense of security, causing them to let down their guard—killing fewer citizens but being themselves killed more often. Given Rapp's findings, should we still maintain the death penalty?

SOURCES: Jeffrey Fagan, "Death and Deterrence Redux: Science, Law and Causal Reasoning on Capital Punishment," *Ohio State Journal of Criminal Law* 4 (2006): 255–320; Joanna Shepherd, "Deterrence versus Brutalization: Capital Punishment's

Differing Impacts Among States," *Michigan Law Review* 104 (2005): 203–253; Matt Beverlin, "A Study of the Deterrence Effect of the Juvenile Death Penalty," paper presented at the Southern Political Science Association annual meeting, New Orleans, 2005, 1–34; John Donohue and Justin Wolfers, "Uses and Abuses of Empirical Evidence in the Death Penalty Debate," *Stanford Law Review* 58 (2005): 791–845; Lisa Stolzenberg and Stewart D'Alessio, "Capital Punishment, Execution Publicity, and Murder in Houston, Texas," *Journal of Criminal Law and Criminology* 94 (2004): 351–380; Geoffrey Rapp, "The Economics of Shootouts: Does the Passage of Capital Punishment Laws Protect or Endanger Police Officers?" *Albany Law Review* 65 (2002): 1,051–1,084; Robert Dann, "The Deterrent Effect of Capital Punishment," *Friends Social Service Series 29* (1935); Thorsten Sellin, *The Death Penalty* (Philadelphia: American Law Institute, 1959); Walter Reckless, "Use of the Death Penalty," *Crime and Delinquency* 15 (1969): 43–51; Dane Archer, Rosemary Gartner, and Marc Beittel, "Homicide and the Death Penalty: A Cross-National Test of a Deterrence Hypothesis," *Journal of Criminal Law and Criminology* 74 (1983): 991–1,014; Jon Sorenson, Robert Wrinkle, Victoria Brewer, and James Marquart, "Capital Punishment and Deterrence: Examining the Effect of Executions on Murder in Texas," *Crime and Delinquency* 45 (1999): 481–931; Norma Wilcox and Tracey Steele, "Just the Facts: A Descriptive Analysis of Inmate Attitudes Toward Capital Punishment," *Prison Journal* 83 (2003): 464–483; Zhiqiang Liu, "Capital Punishment and the Deterrence Hypothesis: Some New Insights and Empirical Evidence," *Eastern Economic Journal* (Spring 2004); Steven Stack, "The Effect of Well-Publicized Executions on Homicide in California," *Journal of Crime and Justice* 21 (1998): 1–12; James Yunker, "A New Statistical Analysis of Capital Punishment Incorporating U.S. Postmoratorium Data," *Social Science Quarterly* 82 (2001): 297–312; Hashem Dezhbakhsh, Paul H. Rubin, and Joanna M. Shepherd, "Does Capital Punishment Have a Deterrent Effect? New Evidence from Postmoratorium Panel Data," *American Law and Economics Review* 5 (2003): 344–376.

Stigma and degradation may have a general deterrent effect, making people afraid of social rejection and public humiliation. However, as a specific deterrent, stigma can sometimes fail, because people who suffer humiliation at the hands of the justice system may choose to "reject their rejectors" by joining a deviant subculture of like-minded people who collectively resist social control, such as outlaw motorcycle gangs.

stigmatization An enduring label that taints a person's identity and changes him or her in the eyes of others.

degradation Shaming occurs when the offender is branded as evil and cast out of society through a ritual exclusion, such as a school disciplinary hearing or a criminal court trial.

The brank or scold's bridle was used in the 16th and 17th centuries. Also called a witch's bridle, it had a metal cage for the head and spikes to pierce the tongue. Some also had a bell, which would humiliate the "scold" as she was paraded through the streets in a cart. A scold was a troublesome woman who nagged her husband and wrangled with her neighbours. It was usually a husband who brought his wife to court, where a judge would decide if she were a public nuisance.

Braithwaite argues that crime control can be better achieved through a policy of reintegrative shaming. Here, disapproval is applied to the offenders' deeds, while they are cast as people who can be reaccepted by society. A critical element of reintegrative shaming occurs when the offenders begin to understand and recognize their wrongdoing and internalize shame. To be reintegrative, shaming must be brief and controlled, and then followed by "ceremonies" of forgiveness, apology, and repentance.

Ahmed and Braithwaite developed a shame-management measurement tool to assess how individuals manage their shame after wrongdoing. The study involved 1,401 students in Grades 4 to 7, and 978 of their primary caregivers. The results indicated the importance of shaming in managing school bullying, shaped in part by signals about what is acceptable. Children who are impulsive, who perceive their school as unable to control bullying, and whose families are enmeshed in conflict, are at a greater risk of becoming bullies. An adaptive strategy for handling shame, rather than a displacement strategy, can reduce the risk of bullying because it requires greater empathy with victims.

To prevent crime, society could encourage reintegrative shaming. For example, people interested in reducing domestic violence may mount a crusade to shame spouse abusers.[179] In early Canada, "rough justice" was often used to control the excesses of spousal abuse, a process that involved the whole community in shaming the individual involved. In addition, an effort could be made to create pride in solving problems non-violently, in caring for others, and in respecting the rights of women.

Reintegrative shaming can have a general deterrent effect and produce specific deterrence in individuals. Parents who use reintegrative shaming techniques in their child-rearing practices may improve parent–child relationships and ultimately reduce the delinquent involvement of their children.[180] Braithwaite and Mugford's research in Australia shows how offenders are brought together with victims so that they can experience shame, and with close family members and peers who help with reintegration.[181] Efforts like these can humanize a system of justice that today relies on repression and not forgiveness as the basis of specific deterrence.

In the next section, we look at efforts to rethink the nature and value of deterrence. The Famous Canadian Court Cases summarized on page 152 are particularly appropriate to consider because of some concern that deterrence as we have envisioned it is not tough enough on offenders.

RETHINKING DETERRENCE

So far, both specific and general deterrence strategies have not yielded the results predicted by choice theorists. Although a few studies have shown expected effects, there is still little conclusive evidence that formal sanctions can convince would-be criminals to forgo their intended behaviour or convince experienced offenders that crime does not pay.

Some criminologists argue that the concepts of specific and general deterrence should be considered interactive.[182] Most people have had experience with the direct effect of punishment (specific deterrence) and the indirect effect of the fear of punishment (general deterrence). In addition, they may have experienced punishment avoidance, either getting away with crime or knowing others who have escaped detection or have been punished, which is called vicarious deterrence. The total deterrent effect includes a combination of personal and vicarious experiences with punishment and its aftermath.

However, the two effects may cancel each other out. An experienced criminal may fear apprehension but know that the law's "bark is worse than its bite." For example, in a study of male offenders, only half said that their sentence would prevent them from reoffending.[183] A person with criminal friends will find the fear of punishment diminished when friends describe how easy it is to get away with crime.

INCAPACITATION STRATEGIES

If more criminals are sent to prison, the crime rate should decrease. Because most people age out of crime, the duration of a criminal career is limited. Placing offenders behind bars during their prime crime years should lessen their lifetime opportunity to commit crime. The shorter the span of opportunity, the fewer offences they can commit over their life course.

This idea seems logical, but does it work? For the past 20 years, the number of people held in prisons has grown significantly. Canada has an incarceration rate of 108 per 100,000, compared with 714 per 100,000 in the United States. Advocates of incapacitation suggest that this effort was responsible for the overall stabilization and actual decline in crime rates in the 1990s. Others suggest that this association is illusory and that a stable crime rate is actually controlled by the size of the teenage population, the threat of tough new mandatory sentences, a healthy economy, the initiation of tougher gun laws, the end of the crack epidemic, and the implementation of tough and aggressive policing strategies in large cities.[184]

If the crime rate drops as more and more people are sent to prison, it would appear that incapacitation works. However, crime rates may really be dropping because potential criminals now fear punishment and are being deterred from crime. What appears to be an incapacitation effect may actually be an effect of general deterrence.[185]

Research on the direct benefits of incapacitation has not shown that increasing the number of people behind bars or the length of their stay can effectively reduce crime. Numerous studies have set out to measure this effect of incarceration, and the results have not supported a strict incarceration policy. In a study using FBI data, if the prison population was cut in half, the crime rate would increase only 4 percent, and if prisons were eliminated, crime might increase 8 percent. As well, if the average prison sentence were increased 50 percent, the crime rate might be reduced by only 4 percent.[186]

A similar study of prison rates and incapacitation estimated that a 50 percent reduction in average time served would result in an increase in property and violent crime,[187] while other research suggested that a policy of mandatory prison sentences of five years for violent crime and three for property offences could reduce the reported crime rate,[188] perhaps by 6 percent to 17 percent.[189]

With these few exceptions, existing research indicates that the crime control effects of a strict incapacitation policy are modest at best.[190] The position of Canada's solicitor general is that incarceration is limited as a useful deterrent and that the best solution is to use alternative measures, such as conditional sentencing, and to try to return the offender to the community.

Incapacitation has attracted interest as a means to counteract the perceived dangerousness of sex offenders. This idea has emerged since the 1980s, in response to several high-profile cases involving the sexual assault and murder of young children. As Michael Petrunik of the University of Ottawa comments, favoured approaches are sex offender registration, community notification, peace bonds, and community surveillance.[191]

In May 2008, Canada gave royal assent to an omnibus anti-crime bill. The legislation includes five earlier bills that would toughen mandatory minimum sentences for gun-related crimes and strengthen bail rules for people awaiting trial on such offences, raise the minimum age of sexual consent to 16 from 14, toughen laws against drug-impaired driving, and make it easier to declare serious repeat offenders a danger to society and lock them up indefinitely—this in a year when crime in Canada reached a new 30-year low.[192]

The Logic of Incarceration

Why hasn't an incarceration strategy worked? There is little evidence that incapacitating criminals will deter them from future criminality, and even more reason to believe that they may be more inclined to commit crimes on release. The more prior incarceration experiences inmates had, the more likely they were to recidivate and return to prison within 12 months of their release.[193] Whatever reason they had to commit crime before their incarceration, a prison sentence didn't reduce those criminogenic forces. The criminal label precludes their entry into many legitimate occupations and solidifies their attachment to criminal careers.

The economics of crime suggest that if money can be made from criminal activity, someone will always be able to take the place of the incarcerated offender. New criminals will be recruited and trained, offsetting any benefit accrued by incarceration. Putting established offenders in prison may open new opportunities for competitors who were suppressed by the more experienced criminals. For example, the incarceration of organized crime members helped open drug markets to new gangs; the flow of narcotics into the country increased after organized crime leaders were imprisoned.

Incarceration may not work because the majority of criminal offences are committed by young adult offenders who are

Famous Canadian Court Cases
Effects of the *Charter* on Deterrence

The *Charter* attempts to balance power differentials between the government and the citizenry by defining and guaranteeing individual rights. However, some people argue that those rights interfere with the administration of justice, and offenders get off on technicalities.

Consider the section 8 *Charter* prohibition of unreasonable searches and seizures. The Supreme Court has ruled this provision protects property and an individual's reasonable expectation of privacy. This interpretation can compromise the principles of certainty, swiftness, and severity that are central to deterrence theory, and may reduce the odds of offenders being held accountable because a defendant can challenge the legality of searches and create lengthy court delays.

Numerous precedent-setting cases involving section 8 have been heard since the implementation of the *Charter*, such as the following:

- *R. v. Kokesch* (1990): Police confirmed suspicions that Kokesch was cultivating marijuana when officers conducted a perimeter search of his residence. Based on their observations, police obtained a search warrant and seized a number of plants from the defendant's home. Kokesch was acquitted because officers did not secure a warrant before initially trespassing on his property.
- *R. v. Wong* (1990): In the course of an illegal gambling investigation, police installed video cameras in a hotel room registered to Wong without prior judicial authorization. Officers eventually raided the room and seized profit lists, gambling paraphernalia, and a large sum of money. This evidence was admitted, but the Supreme Court ruled that this type of surveillance necessitates a warrant.
- *R. v. Dersch* (1993): Doctors withdrew some of the defendant's blood for medical purposes as he lay unconscious in hospital after a motor vehicle accident. When Dersch later refused a blood alcohol test, police requested a hospital report detailing the results of his blood work. Based on this information, a warrant was issued permitting officers to seize the initial blood sample. This evidence facilitated charges of impaired driving and criminal negligence causing death and bodily harm, but it was subsequently deemed inadmissible in court.

SOURCE: Robert Sharpe, Katherine Swinton, and Kent Roach, *The Charter of Rights and Freedoms,* 2nd ed. (Toronto: Irwin Law Inc., 2002).

---

unlikely to be sent to prison for a single felony conviction. Incarcerated criminals, aging behind bars, are already past the age at which they are at risk to commit crime. A strict incarceration policy may result in people being kept in prison beyond the time that they are a threat to society, while a new cohort of high-rate adolescent offenders is on the street.

Maintaining an incapacitation strategy is also expensive. Correctional services cost billions of dollars combined with the cost of policing, adult corrections, courts, legal aid, and criminal prosecutions.[194] Even if incarceration could reduce the crime rate, the costs would be enormous. At a time of cutbacks, should we be spending billions of dollars on this type of crime control strategy?[195]

Selective Incapacitation: Three Strikes and You're Out

A more efficient incapacitation model is suggested by the discovery of the chronic career criminal. If small numbers of people account for a relatively large percentage of the crime, then a policy of **selective incapacitation** could be an effective crime reduction strategy.[196] In a widely cited study of more than 2,000 inmates serving time for theft offences, Greenwood found that the selective incapacitation of chronic offenders could reduce the rate of robbery offences by 15 percent and the inmate population by 5 percent.

Chronic offenders can be distinguished on the basis of their offending patterns and lifestyle (for example, their employment record and history of substance abuse). Once identified, high-risk offenders would be eligible for sentencing enhancements that would increase the time they serve in prison.

Another concept receiving widespread international attention is the three-strikes-and-you're-out policy now used in many American states; persons convicted of three violent offences receive a mandatory life term without parole. This policy seems to offer an attractive solution to the problem of chronic offending by providing long (or life) sentences for repeat offenders. Some criminologists argue that such strategies, though attractive to the public, will not work, because (1) most "three-time losers" are at the verge of aging out of crime anyway, (2) current sentences for violent crimes are already severe, (3) an expanding prison population will drive up already high prison costs, (4) it creates racial disparity in sentencing, and (5) the police would be in danger because two-time offenders would violently resist a third arrest, knowing they face a life sentence.

In a meta-analysis of 50 studies dating from 1958 and involving 336,052 offenders, a prison sentence was found to

selective incapacitation The policy of creating enhanced prison sentences for the relatively small group of dangerous chronic offenders.

increase the likelihood of a repeat offence, compared with a community-based sanction. Also, lower-risk offenders tend to be more negatively affected by the prison experience. The conclusion was that prisons should not be used with the expectation of reducing criminal behaviour and that the use of incarceration has enormous cost implications. However, the researchers also suggested that the primary justification of prison should be to incapacitate offenders (particularly, those of a chronic, higher-risk nature) for reasonable periods and to exact retribution.[197]

POLICY IMPLICATIONS OF CHOICE THEORY

From the origins of classical theory to the development of modern rational choice views, the belief that criminals choose to commit crime has had an important influence on the relationship among law, punishment, and crime. When police patrol in well-marked cars, we assume that their presence will deter would-be criminals. When the harsh realities of prison life are portrayed in movies and TV shows, the lesson is not lost on potential criminals. Nowhere is the idea that the threat of punishment can control crime more evident than in the implementation of tough, mandatory criminal sentences to control violent crime and drug trafficking.

Despite their questionable deterrent effect, severe penalties, such as life imprisonment or capital punishment, are also viewed as effective means of restricting criminal choice. Many observers are dismayed because people who are convicted of murder sometimes kill again when released on parole. One study of 52,000 incarcerated murderers found that 810 had been previously convicted of murder and had killed 821 people following their previous release from prison.[198] About 9 percent of all inmates on death row in the United States have prior convictions for homicide; if they had been executed for their first offence, hundreds of people would be alive today.[199]

So although research on the core principles of choice theory and deterrence theories produces mixed results, little doubt remains that these models have had an important impact on crime prevention strategies.

The concept of criminal choice has also prompted the creation of justice policies referred to as **just desert**.[200] The just desert position can be summarized in these three statements:

1. Those who violate others' rights deserve to be punished.
2. We should not add to human suffering; punishment makes those punished suffer.
3. However, punishment may prevent more misery than it inflicts.

This utilitarian view is the key to the desert approach: Punishment is needed to preserve the social equity disturbed by crime; nonetheless, the severity of the punishment should be commensurate with the seriousness of the crime. These principles were laid out by Cesare Beccaria more than 200 years ago and still form a foundation of our criminal justice system.

Desert theory is also concerned with the rights of the accused. It alleges that the rights of the person being punished should not be unduly sacrificed for the good of others, as with deterrence. The offender should not be treated as more or less **blameworthy** than is warranted by the character of his or her offence. For example, if two crimes are equally serious, but if severe penalties are shown to have a deterrent effect only with respect to one, would it be fair to punish the person who has committed the crime more harshly simply to deter others from committing the crime? Conversely, imposing a light sentence for a serious crime would be unfair, because it would treat offenders as being less blameworthy.

In sum, the just desert model suggests that retribution justifies punishment because people deserve what they get for their past deeds. Punishment that is based on deterrence or incapacitation is wrong because it involves an assumption of offenders' future actions, which cannot accurately be predicted. Punishment should be the same for all people who commit the same crime. Criminal sentences that are based on individual needs or characteristics are inherently unfair, as all people are equally blameworthy for their misdeeds.

The influence of these views can be seen in sentencing models that give the same punishments to all people who commit the same type of crime.

SUMMARY

Choice theory assumes that criminals carefully choose whether to commit criminal acts. These theories are summarized in Concept Summary 5.2. However, people are influenced by their fear of the criminal penalties associated with being caught and convicted for law violations. The more severe, certain, and swift the punishment, the more likely it is to control crime. The choice approach is rooted in the classical criminology of 18th-century social philosophers Cesare Beccaria and Jeremy Bentham.

just desert   The philosophy of justice that asserts that those who violate the rights of others deserve to be punished, with severity commensurate with the seriousness of the crime.

blameworthy   The amount of culpability or guilt a person maintains for participating in a particular criminal offence.

Choice Theories

Theory	Major Premise	Strengths
Rational Choice	Law-violating behaviour is an event that occurs after offenders weigh information on their personal needs and the situational factors involved in the difficulty and risk of committing a crime.	Explains why high-risk youths do not constantly engage in delinquent acts. Relates theory to delinquency control policy. It is not limited by class or other social variables.
Routine Activities	Crime and delinquency are a function of the presence of motivated offenders, the availability of suitable targets, and the absence of capable guardians.	Can explain fluctuations in crime and delinquency rates. Shows how victim behaviour influences criminal choice.
General Deterrence	People will commit crime and delinquency if they perceive that the benefits outweigh the risks. Crime is a function of the severity, certainty, and speed of punishment.	Shows the relationship between crime and punishment. Suggests a real solution to crime.
Specific Deterrence	If punishment is severe enough, criminals will not repeat their illegal acts.	Provides a strategy to reduce crime.
Incapacitation	Keeping known criminals out of circulation will reduce crime rates.	Recognizes the role opportunity plays in criminal behaviour. Provides a solution to chronic offending.

The growth of positivist criminology, which stressed external causes of crime and rehabilitation of known offenders, reduced the popularity of the classical approach in the 20th century. However, in the late 1970s, the concept of criminal choice once again became an important perspective of criminologists. Today, choice theorists view crime as offence- and offender-specific. Research shows that offenders consider their targets carefully before choosing a course of action. By implication, crime can be prevented by convincing potential criminals that the risks of violating the law exceed the benefits.

Deterrence theory holds that if criminals are indeed rational, an inverse relationship should exist between punishment and crime. However, numerous factors confound the relationship. For example, if people do not believe they will be caught, even harsh punishment may not deter crime. Deterrence theory has been criticized on the grounds that it wrongfully assumes that criminals make a rational choice before committing crimes, ignores the intricacies of the criminal justice system, and does not take into account the social and psychological factors that may influence criminality. Research designed to test the validity of the deterrence concept has not indicated that deterrent measures actually reduce the crime rate.

Specific deterrence theory holds that the crime rate can be reduced if known offenders are punished so severely that they never commit crimes again. However, there is little evidence that harsh punishments actually reduce the crime rate. Incapacitation theory maintains that if deterrence does not work, the best course of action is to incarcerate known offenders for long periods so that they lack criminal opportunity. Research efforts have not provided clear-cut proof that increasing the number of people in prison and increasing prison sentences will reduce crime rates.

Choice theory has been influential in shaping public policy. The criminal law is designed to deter potential criminals and fairly punish those who have been caught in illegal acts. Some courts have changed sentencing policies to adapt to classical principles, and the correctional system seems geared toward incapacitation and special deterrence, testimony to the importance of classical theory.

THINKING LIKE A CRIMINOLOGIST

The solicitor general has issued a request for proposals for a national survey of sentencing practices. The government is interested in recommendations about criminal punishment. Specifically, do the length of criminal sentences and the way they are served have an impact on crime rates? What could be gained by either increasing punishment or requiring inmates to spend more time behind bars before their release? As a society, are we being too lenient or too punitive?

As someone who has studied choice theory, you have some ideas on how crime rates might be affected if we radically change the way we punished offenders. Initially, you favour selective incapacitation. However, you have come across research called "Deterrence and Homeless Male Street Youth" in the *Canadian Journal of Criminology* (1998), which causes you to question yourself. The research has found that although street youths fear legal sanctions, more serious offenders do not. Instead, their fear of punishment is reduced by their poverty. Drug use and association with criminal peers cause a lack of normative constraints. The more serious street youth offenders are immersed in a lifestyle in which crime, drugs, and criminal peers feed off one another, isolating them from conventional society. What would you propose with regard to sentencing for this group of offenders?

KEY TERMS

blameworthy p. 153
brutalization effect p. 142
capable guardians p. 131
choice theory p. 126
classical criminology p. 126
conflict-linked crime or violence
    p. 143
crackdown p. 142
crime displacement p. 128
defensible space p. 136
degradation p. 148
diffusion of benefits p. 140

discouragement p. 140
extinction p. 140
general deterrence p. 140
informal sanctions p. 143
instrumental crime p. 134
just desert p. 153
macro perspective p. 130
micro perspective p. 130
motivated criminals p. 131
offence-specific crime p. 128
offender-specific crime p. 129
perceptual deterrence p. 143

rational choice theory p. 130
reintegrative shaming p. 147
routine activities theory p. 130
seductions of crime p. 135
selective incapacitation p. 152
situational crime prevention p. 136
specific deterrence p. 146
stigmatization p. 148
target reduction strategies p. 139
utilitarianism p. 126

DOING RESEARCH ON THE WEB

Before you give your opinion regarding the Thinking Like
a Criminologist box, you might want to conduct an online
search to learn more about the structure of mental illness
and how it relates to crime.

CRITICAL THINKING QUESTIONS

1. If drug dealing is similar to any type of commercial
   sales, can it be controlled or eliminated in the same
   way a competitor is put out of business—for example,
   by driving down the price of goods and offering a
   much cheaper alternative? If so, what sort of legal alternative could you suggest?
2. If crime is rational, rather than motivated by uncontrollable psychological drives, would you want to live in a
   society in which crime rates are low because criminals
   are subjected to extremely harsh punishments, such as
   flogging for committing vandalism?

3. Why do arrests seem to have little effect on future
   domestic violence? Could it be that getting arrested
   increases feelings of strain and hostility, and does little
   to reduce the problems that led to domestic conflict in
   the first place? Explain how you think this works.
4. Is it possible to create a method of capital punishment
   that would actually deter murder, for example, by tel-
   evising executions? What might be some of the negative consequences of such a policy?

NOTES

1. Cesare Beccaria, *On Crimes and
   Punishments*, excerpted in Joseph E.
   Jacoby, *Classics of Criminology*, 2nd ed.
   (Prospect Heights, IL: Waveland, 1994):
   277–286; Francis Edward Devine,
   "Cesare Beccaria and the Theoretical
   Foundations of Modern Penal
   Jurisprudence," *New England Journal on
   Prison Law* 7 (1982): 8–21; Marcello
   Maestro, *Cesare Beccaria and the Origins of
   Penal Reform* (Philadelphia: Temple
   University, 1973).
2. Graeme Newman and Pietro Marongiu,
   "Penological Reform and the Myth of

Beccaria," *Criminology* 28 (1990):
325–346.
3. Bob Roshier, *Controlling Crime* (Chicago:
   Lyceum Books, 1989), 10.
4. Jeremy Bentham, *A Fragment on
   Government and an Introduction to the
   Principle of Morals and Legislation*, ed.
   Wilfred Harrison (Oxford: Basil Blackwell,
   1967).
5. Robert Martinson, "What Works?—
   Questions and Answers about Prison
   Reform," *Public Interest* 35 (1974): 22–54.
6. Charles Murray and Louis Cox, *Beyond
   Probation* (Beverly Hills, CA: Sage, 1979).

7. Ronald Bayer, "Crime, Punishment and the
   Decline of Liberal Optimism," *Crime and
   Delinquency* 27 (1981): 190.
8. James Q. Wilson, *Thinking About Crime*,
   rev. ed. (New York: Vintage Books, 1983),
   128, 260.
9. Pierre Tremblay and Carlo Morselli,
   "Patterns in Criminal Achievement: Wilson
   and Abrahamse Revisited," *Criminology* 38
   (2000): 633–660.
10. Frederick J. Desroches, *Force and Fear:
    Robbery in Canada* (Toronto: Nelson,
    1995).

11. Phonse Jessome, *Murder at McDonald's: The Killers Next Door* (Halifax: Nimbus, 1994).
12. Kevin Denny and Colm Harmon, "An Econometric Analysis of Burglary in Ireland," Centre for Economic Research, Working Paper Series, 2004.
13. Don Weatherburn, Jiuzhao Hua, and Steve Moffatt, "How Much Crime Does Prison Stop? The Incapacitation Effect of Prison on Burglary," *Contemporary Issues in Crime and Justice*, 93, 2006.
14. See, generally, Derek Cornish and Ronald Clarke, eds., *The Reasoning Criminal: Rational Choice Perspectives on Offending* (New York: Springer Verlag, 1986); Philip Cook, "The Demand and Supply of Criminal Opportunities," in *Crime and Justice*, vol. 7, eds. Michael Tonry and Norval Morris (Chicago: University of Chicago Press, 1986), 1–28; Ronald Clarke and Derek Cornish, "Modeling Offender's Decisions: A Framework for Research and Policy," in *Crime and Justice*, vol. 6, eds. Michael Tonry and Norval Morris (Chicago: University of Chicago Press, 1985), 147–187; Morgan Reynolds, *Crime by Choice: An Economic Analysis* (Dallas: Fisher Institute, 1985).
15. George Rengert and John Wasilchick, *Suburban Burglary: A Time and Place for Everything* (Springfield, IL: Charles C. Thomas, 1985).
16. John McIver, "Criminal Mobility: A Review of Empirical Studies," in *Crime Spillover*, eds. Simon Hakim and George Rengert (Beverly Hills, CA: Sage, 1981), 110–121; Carol Kohfeld and John Sprague, "Demography, Police Behavior, and Deterrence," *Criminology* 28 (1990): 111–136.
17. Derek Cornish and Ronald Clarke, "Understanding Crime Displacement: An Application of Rational Choice Theory," *Criminology* 25 (1987): 933–947.
18. Lloyd Phillips and Harold Votey, "The Influence of Police Interventions and Alternative Income Sources on the Dynamic Process of Choosing Crime as a Career," *Journal of Quantitative Criminology* 3 (1987): 251–274.
19. Michael Gottfredson and Travis Hirschi, *A General Theory of Crime* (Stanford, CA: Stanford University Press, 1990).
20. Liliana Pezzin, "Earnings Prospects, Matching Effects, and the Decision to Terminate a Criminal Career," *Journal of Quantitative Criminology* 11 (1995): 29–50.
21. Neal Shover, *Aging Criminals* (Beverly Hills, CA: Sage, 1985).
22. Ronald Akers, "Rational Choice, Deterrence and Social Learning Theory in Criminology: The Path Not Taken," *Journal of Criminal Law and Criminology* 81 (1990): 653–676.
23. Robert Agnew, "Determinism, Indeterminism, and Crime: An Empirical Exploration," *Criminology* 33 (1995): 83–109.
24. Bruce Jacobs, "Crack Dealers' Apprehension Avoidance Techniques: A Case of Restrictive Deterrence," *Justice Quarterly* 13 (1996): 359–381.
25. Paul Cromwell, James Olson, and D'Aunn Wester Avery, *Breaking and Entering: An Ethnographic Analysis of Burglary* (Newbury Park, CA: Sage, 1989).
26. John Gibbs and Peggy Shelly, "Life in the Fast Lane: A Retrospective View by Commercial Thieves," *Journal of Research in Crime and Delinquency* 19 (1982): 229–230.
27. George Rengert and John Wasilchick, *Space, Time and Crime: Ethnographic Insights into Residential Burglary* (Washington, DC: National Institute of Justice, 1989); see also George Rengert and John Wasilchick, *Suburban Burglary*.
28. Leanne Fiftal Alarid, James Marquart, Velmer Burton, Francis Cullen, and Steven Cuvelier, "Women's Roles in Serious Offenses: A Study of Adult Felons," *Justice Quarterly* 13 (1996): 431–454.
29. Ronald Clarke and Marcus Felson, "Introduction: Criminology, Routine Activity and Rational Choice," in *Routine Activity and Rational Choice* (New Brunswick, NJ: Transaction Publishers, 1993), 1–14.
30. Andrew Buck, Simon Hakim, and George Rengert, "Burglar Alarms and the Choice Behavior of Burglars: A Suburban Phenomenon," *Journal of Criminal Justice* 21 (1993): 497–507.
31. Ralph Taylor and Stephen Gottfredson, "Environmental Design, Crime, and Prevention: An Examination of Community Dynamics," in *Communities and Crime*, eds. Albert Reiss and Michael Tonry (Chicago: University of Chicago Press, 1986), 387–416.
32. Michael Costanzo, William Halperin, and Nathan Gale, "Criminal Mobility and the Directional Component in Journeys to Crime," in *Metropolitan Crime Patterns*, eds. Robert Figlio, Simon Hakim, and George Rengert (Monsey, NY: Criminal Justice Press, 1986), 73–95.
33. Garland White, "Neighborhood Permeability and Burglary Rates," *Justice Quarterly* 7 (1990): 57–67.
34. William Smith, Sharon Glave Frazee, and Elizabeth Davison, "Furthering the Integration of Routine Activity and Social Disorganization Theories: Small Units of Analysis and the Study of Street Robbery as a Diffusion Process," *Criminology* 38 (2000): 489–521.
35. Paul Bellair, "Informal Surveillance and Street Crime: A Complex Relationship," *Criminology* 38 (2000): 137–167.
36. James Massey, Marvin Krohn, and Lisa Bonati, "Property Crime and the Routine Activities of Individuals," *Journal of Research in Crime and Delinquency* 26 (1989): 378–400; note, however, that the findings here generally disagree with routine activities theory.
37. Gary Kleck and Don Kates, *Armed: New Perspectives on Guns* (Amherst, NY: Prometheus Books, 2001).
38. Kenneth Tunnell, *Choosing Crime* (Chicago: Nelson-Hall, 1992), 105.
39. Robert Sampson and Jacqueline Cohen, "Deterrent Effects of the Police on Crime: A Replication and Theoretical Extension," *Law and Society Review* 22 (1988): 163–188.
40. Marcus Felson et al., "Preventing Crime at Newark Subway Stations," *Security Journal* 1 (1990): 137–140.
41. Sandra Besserer, "Criminal Victimization: An International Perspective: Results of the 2000 International Crime Victimization Survey," *Juristat* 22, 4, 2002.
42. Simha Landau and Daniel Fridman, "The Seasonality of Violent Crime: The Case of Robbery and Homicide in Israel," *Journal of Research in Crime and Delinquency* 30 (1993): 163–191.
43. Tunnell, *Choosing Crime*, 67.
44. Angela Browne and Kirk Williams, "Exploring the Effect of Resource Availability and the Likelihood of Female-Perpetrated Homicides," *Law and Society Review* 23 (1989): 89–93.
45. John Z. Wang, "Bank Robberies by an Asian Gang: An Assessment of the Routine Activities Theory," *International Journal of Offender Therapy and Comparative Criminology* 46, 5 (2002): 555–568.
46. Ronald Clarke, "Situational Crime Prevention," in *Building a Safer Society: Strategic Approaches to Crime Prevention*, vol. 19 of *Crime and Justice: A Review of Research*, eds. Michael Tonry and David Farrington, 91–151 (Chicago: University of Chicago Press, 1995).
47. Mark Warr, "Parents, Peers, and Delinquency," *Social Forces* 72 (1993): 247–264.
48. John Hagan, "Destiny and Drift: Subcultural Preferences, Status Attainments, and the Risks and Rewards of Youth," *American Sociological Review* 56 (1991): 567–582.
49. D. Wayne Osgood, Janet Wilson, Patrick O'Malley, Jerald Bachman, and Lloyd Johnston, "Routine Activities and Individual Deviant Behavior," *American Sociological Review* 61 (1996): 635–655.
50. Brent Snook, David Canter, and Craig Bennell, "Predicting the Home Location of Serial Offenders: A Preliminary Comparison of the Accuracy of Human Judges with a Geographic Profiling System," *Behavioral Sciences and the Law* 20 (2002): 109–118.
51. Ronald Clarke and Patricia Harris, "Auto Theft and Its Prevention," in *Crime and Justice: An Annual Edition*, eds. Michael

Tonry and Norval Morris (Chicago: University of Chicago Press, 1992).

52. Lisa Maher, "Hidden in the Light: Occupational Norms Among Crack-Using Street-Level Sex Workers," *Journal of Drug Issues* 26 (1996): 143–173.

53. Richard J. Stevenson, Lubica M. V. Forsythe, and Don Weatherburn, "The Stolen Goods Market in New South Wales, Australia: An Analysis of Disposal Avenues and Tactics," *British Journal of Criminology* 41 (2001): 101–118.

54. John Petraitis, Brian Flay, and Todd Miller, "Reviewing Theories of Adolescent Substance Use: Organizing Pieces in the Puzzle," *Psychological Bulletin* 117 (1995): 67–86.

55. Bruce Jacobs, "Crack Dealers' Apprehension Avoidance Techniques: A Case of Restrictive Deterrence," *Justice Quarterly* 13 (1996): 359–381.

56. Patricia Morgan and Karen Ann Joe, "Citizens and Outlaws: The Private Lives and Public Lifestyles of Women in the Illicit Drug Economy," *Journal of Drug Issues* 26 (1996): 125–142.

57. Robert MacCoun and Peter Reuter, "Are the Wages of Sin $30 an Hour? Economic Aspects of Street-Level Drug Dealing," *Crime and Delinquency* 38, 4 (1992): 477–491.

58. Alan Lizotte, James Tesoriero, Terence Thornberry, and Marvin Krohn, "Patterns of Adolescent Firearms Ownership and Use," *Justice Quarterly* 11 (1994): 54–74.

59. Alan Lizotte, Marvin Krohn, James Howell, Kimberly Tobin, and Gregory Howard, "Factors Influencing Gun Carrying among Young Urban Males over the Adolescent-Young Adult Life Course," *Criminology* 38 (2000): 811–834.

60. Richard Felson and Steven Messner, "To Kill or Not to Kill? Lethal Outcomes in Injurious Attacks," *Criminology* 34 (1996): 519–545.

61. James Wright and Peter Rossi, *Armed and Considered Dangerous: A Survey of Felons and Their Firearms* (Hawthorne, NY: Aldine, 1983), 141–159.

62. Eric Hickey, *Serial Murderers and Their Victims* (Pacific Grove, CA: Brooks/Cole, 1991), 84.

63. Scott Decker, "Deviant Homicide: A New Look at the Role of Motives and Victim-Offender Relationships," *Journal of Research in Crime and Delinquency* 33 (1996): 427–449.

64. Christopher Birkbeck and Gary LaFree, "The Situational Analysis of Crime and Deviance," *American Review of Sociology* 19 (1993): 113–137; Karen Heimer and Ross Matsueda, "Role-Taking, Role Commitment, and Delinquency: A Theory of Differential Social Control," *American Sociological Review* 59 (1994): 111–131.

65. Jack Katz, *Seductions of Crime* (New York: Basic Books, 1988).

66. Bill McCarthy and John Hagan, "Mean Streets: The Theoretical Significance of Situational Delinquency among Homeless Youths," *American Journal of Sociology* 3 (1992): 597–627.

67. Bill McCarthy, "Not Just 'For the Thrill of It': An Instrumentalist Elaboration of Katz's Explanation of Sneaky Thrill Property Crime," *Criminology* 33 (1995): 519–539.

68. William O'Grady and Mark Ashbridge, "Illegal Tobacco Sales to Youth: A View from Rational Choice Theory," *Canadian Journal of Criminology* 42 (2000): 1–21.

69. George Rengert, "Spatial Justice and Criminal Victimization," *Justice Quarterly* 6 (1989): 543–564.

70. Oscar Newman, *Defensible Space: Crime Prevention through Urban Design* (New York: Macmillan, 1973).

71. Patricia Brantingham and Paul Brantingham, "The Relative Spatial Concentration on Criminality and Its Analysis: Toward a Revival of Environmental Criminology" (in French), *Criminologie* 27 (1994): 81–97; Paul Brantingham and Patricia Brantingham, "The Spatial Patterning of Burglary," *Howard Journal of Penology and Crime Prevention* 14 (1975): 11–23; Paul Brantingham and Patricia Brantingham, "How Public Transit Feeds Private Crime: Notes on the Vancouver 'Sky Train' Experience," *Security Journal* 2 (1991): 91–95; Patricia L. Brantingham and Paul J. Brantingham, "Situational Crime Prevention in British Columbia," *Journal of Security Administration* 11 (1988): 18–27; Paul Brantingham and Patricia Brantingham, "Situational Crime Prevention in Practice," *Canadian Journal of Criminology* 32 (1990): 17–40.

72. C. Ray Jeffery, *Crime Prevention through Environmental Design* (Beverly Hills, CA: Sage, 1971).

73. See also Pochara Theerathorn, "Architectural Style, Aesthetic Landscaping, Home Value, and Crime Prevention," *International Journal of Comparative and Applied Criminal Justice* 12 (1988): 269–277.

74. Ronald Clarke, *Situational Crime Prevention: Successful Case Studies* (Albany, NY: Harrow and Heston, 1992).

75. P.M. Cozens, G. Saville, and D. Hillier, "Crime Prevention through Environmental Design (CPTED): A Review and Modern Bibliography," *Property Management* 23, 5 (2005): 328–356.

76. Brandon C. Welsh, and David P. Farrington, "Surveillance for Crime Prevention in Public Space: Results and Policy Choices in Britain and America," *Criminology & Public Policy* 3, 3 (2004): 497–526.

77. Marcus Felson, "Routine Activities and Crime Prevention," in *Studies on Crime and Crime Prevention, Annual Review*, vol. 1, 30–34, National Council for Crime Prevention (Stockholm: Scandinavian University Press, 1992).

78. Brandon C. Welsh and David P. Farrington, *Preventing Crime: What Works for Children, Offenders, Victims, and Places* (New York: Springer, 2007).

79. Barry Webb, "Steering Column Locks and Motor Vehicle Theft: Evaluations for Three Countries," in *Crime Prevention Studies*, ed. Ronald Clarke, 71–89 (Monsey, NY: Criminal Justice Press, 1994).

80. Barbara Morse and Delbert Elliott, "Effects of Ignition Interlock Devices on DUI Recidivism: Findings from a Longitudinal Study in Hamilton County, Ohio," *Crime and Delinquency* 38 (1992): 131–157.

81. Brian R. Abraham and Peter J. Baldassaro Jr., "Leaving Robbers Barren," *Security Management* 45, 2 (2001): 42.

82. L. Blake and R.T. Coupe, "The Impact of Single and Two-officer Patrols on Catching Burglars in the Act," *British Journal of Criminology* 41 (2001): 381–396.

83. Nancy LaVigne, "Gasoline Drive-Offs: Designing a Less Convenient Environment," in *Crime Prevention Studies*, vol. 2, ed. Ronald Clarke, 91–114 (Monsey, N.Y.: Criminal Justice Press, 1994).

84. Ronald Clark, "Deterring Obscene Phone Callers: The New Jersey Experience," *Situational Crime Prevention*, ed. Ronald Clark, 124–132 (Albany, NY: Harrow and Heston, 1992).

85. Alice Morse Earle, "The Scarlett Letter," *Curious Punishments of Bygone Days* (Chicago: HS Stone & Company, 1896), text available online at www.gutenberg.org/files/34005/34005-h/34005-h.htm#Page_86.

86. Michael Levi, "Suite Justice or Sweet Charity? Some Explorations of Shaming and Incapacitating Business Fraudsters," *Punishment and Society* 2, 4 (2002): 147–163.

87. Marcus Felson, "Those Who Discourage Crime," in *Crime and Place, Crime Prevention Studies*, vol. 4, eds. John Eck and David Weisburd, 53–66 (Monsey, NY: Criminal Justice Press, 1995); John Eck, *Drug Markets and Drug Places: A Case-Control Study of the Spatial Structure of Illicit Drug Dealing*, Doctoral dissertation, University of Maryland, College Park, 1994.

88. Robert Barr and Ken Pease, "Crime Placement, Displacement, and Deflection," in *Crime and Justice: A Review of Research*, vol. 12, eds. Michael Tonry and Norval Morris, 277–319 (Chicago: University of Chicago Press, 1990).

89. Evan Wood et al., "Displacement of Canada's Largest Public Illicit Drug Market in Response to a Police Crackdown," *Canadian Medical Association Journal* 170, 10 (2004): 1551–1556; "Crackdown Hasn't Cut Drug Sales in Downtown Eastside," *Vancouver Sun*, May 11, 2004.

90. Keith Harries, *Mapping Crime: Principle and Practice* (Washington, DC: U.S. Department of Justice, Office of Justice Programs, National Institute of Justice, 1999).

91. Thomas Gabor, "Crime Displacement and Situational Prevention: Toward the Development of Some Principles," *Canadian Journal of Criminology* 32 (1990): 41–71.

92. Ronald Clarke and David Weisburd, "Diffusion of Crime Control Benefits: Observations of the Reverse of Displacement," in *Crime Prevention Studies*, vol. 2, ed. Ronald Clarke (New York: Criminal Justice Press, 1994).

93. David Weisburd and Lorraine Green, "Policing Drug Hot Spots: The Jersey City Drug Market Analysis Experiment," *Justice Quarterly* 12 (1995): 711–734.

94. Lorraine Green, "Cleaning Up Drug Hot Spots in Oakland, California: The Displacement and Diffusion Effects," *Justice Quarterly* 12 (1995): 737–754.

95. Anthony N. Doob and Carla Cesaroni, "The Political Attractiveness of Mandatory Minimum Sentences," *Osgoode Hall Law Journal* 39 (2001): 287–304; Carla Cesaroni and Anthony N. Doob, "The Decline in Support for Penal Welfarism," *British Journal of Criminology* 43, 2 (2003): 434–441.

96. R. Yeaman, *The Deterrent Effectiveness of Criminal Justice Sanction Strategies: Summary Report* (Washington, DC: U.S. Government Printing Office, 1972); see, generally, Jack Gibbs, "Crime Punishment and Deterrence," *Social Science Quarterly* 48 (1968): 515–530.

97. Daniel Nagin and Greg Pogarsky, "Integrating Celerity, Impulsivity, and Extralegal Sanction Threats into a Model of General Deterrence: Theory and Evidence," *Criminology* 39 (2001): 865–892.

98. Charles Tittle and Alan Rowe, "Certainty of Arrest and Crime Rates: A Further Test of the Deterrence Hypothesis," *Social Forces* 52 (1974): 455–462.

99. Robert Bursik, Harold Grasmick, and Mitchell Chamlin, "The Effect of Longitudinal Arrest Patterns on the Development of Robbery Trends at the Neighborhood Level," *Criminology* 28 (1990): 431–450; Theodore Chiricos and Gordon Waldo, "Punishment and Crime: An Examination of Some Empirical Evidence," *Social Problems* 18 (1970): 200–217.

100. Jiang Wu and Allen Liska, "The Certainty of Punishment: A Reference Group Effect and Its Functional Form," *Criminology* 31 (1993): 447–464.

101. Edwin Zedlewski, "Deterrence Findings and Data Sources: A Comparison of the Uniform Crime Rates and the National Crime Surveys," *Journal of Research in Crime and Delinquency* 20 (1983): 262–276.

102. Kimberly N. Varma, and Anthony N. Doob, "Deterring Economic Crimes: The Case of Tax Evasion," *Canadian Journal of Criminology* 40 (1998): 165–184.

103. "Mine Disaster Sparks Call for Corporate Liability in Criminal Code," *Edmonton Journal*, August 4, 1998; *The Westray Story: A Predictable Path to Disaster. Report of the Westray Mine Public Inquiry* (Halifax: Province of Nova Scotia, 1997).

104. David Bayley, *Policing for the Future* (New York: Oxford, 1994); Tomislav V. Kovandzic and John J. Sloan, "Police Levels and Crime Rates Revisited, A Country-Level Analysis from Florida (1980–1998)," *Journal of Criminal Justice* 30 (2002): 65–76; Steven Levitt, "Using Electoral Cycles in Police Hiring to Estimate the Effect of Police on Crime," *American Economic Review* 87 (1997): 70–91; Thomas Marvell and Carlisle Moody, "Specification Problems, Police Levels, and Crime Rates," *Criminology* 34 (1996): 609–646.

105. Joseph P. Hornick, Barry N. Leighton, and Barbara A. Burrows, "Evaluating Community Policing: The Edmonton Project," in *Evaluating Justice: Canadian Policies and Programs*, eds. Joe Hudson and Julian Roberts (Toronto: Thomson Educational Publishing, 1993).

106. S.G. Walker, C. Walker, C. Johnson, J. Sauvageau, and S. Williams, *You Can Do It: A Practical Guide to Evaluating Police and Community Crime Prevention Programs* (Ottawa: National Crime Prevention Centre, 2001).

107. George Kelling, Tony Pate, Duane Dieckman, and Charles Brown, *The Kansas City Preventive Patrol Experiment: A Summary Report* (Washington, DC: Police Foundation, 1974).

108. Michael Smith, "Police-Led Crackdowns and Cleanups: An Evaluation of a Crime Control Initiative in Richmond, Virginia," *Crime and Delinquency* 47 (2001): 60–68.

109. Lawrence Sherman, "Police Crackdowns," *NIJ Reports*, March/April 1990, 2–6; George L. Kelling and Catherine M. Coles, *Fixing Broken Windows: Restoring Order and Reducing Crime in Our Communities* (New York: Martin Kessler, 1997).

110. Lawrence Sherman, "Police Crackdowns," *NIJ Reports*, March/April 1990: 3; "Local Radar," *Canadian Living*, August 1997, 15; "Ontario May Try Tough 'Big Apple' Approach to Crime," *Halifax Daily News*, December 10, 1997.

111. Gary Green, "General Deterrence and Television Cable Crime: A Field Experiment in Social Crime," *Criminology* 23 (1986): 629–645.

112. H. Laurence Ross, "Implications of Drinking-and-Driving Law Studies for Deterrence Research," in *Critique and Explanation: Essays in Honor of Gwynne Nettler*, eds. Timothy Hartnagel and Robert Silverman (New Brunswick, NJ: Transaction Books, 1986), 159–171.

113. H. Laurence Ross, Richard McCleary, and Gary LaFree, "Can Mandatory Jail Laws Deter Drunk Driving? The Arizona Case," *Journal of Criminal Law and Criminology* 81 (1990): 156–167.

114. For a review, see Jeffrey Roth, *Firearms and Violence* (Washington, DC: National Institute of Justice, 1994).

115. Thomas Marvell and Carlisle Moody, "The Impact of Enhanced Prison Terms for Felonies Committed with Guns," *Criminology* 33 (1995): 247–281.

116. Robert Dann, "The Deterrent Effect of Capital Punishment," *Friends Social Service Series* 29 (1935).

117. William Bowers and Glenn Pierce, "Deterrence or Brutalization: What Is the Effect of Executions?" *Crime and Delinquency* 26 (1980): 453–484; John Cochran, Mitchell Chamlin, and Mark Seth, "Deterrence or Brutalization? An Impact Assessment of Oklahoma's Return to Capital Punishment," *Criminology* 32 (1994): 107–134.

118. David Phillips, "The Deterrent Effect of Capital Punishment," *American Journal of Sociology* 86 (1980): 139–148; Hans Zeisel, "A Comment on 'The Deterrent Effect of Capital Punishment' by Phillips," *American Journal of Sociology* 88 (1982): 167–169; see also Sam McFarland, "Is Capital Punishment a Short-Term Deterrent to Homicide? A Study of the Effects of Four Recent American Executions," *Journal of Criminal Law and Criminology* 74 (1984): 1014–1032; Steven Stack, "Publicized Executions and Homicide, 1950–1980," *American Sociological Review* 52 (1987): 532–540; for a study challenging Stack's methods, see William Bailey and Ruth Peterson, "Murder and Capital Punishment: A Monthly Time-Series Analysis of Execution Publicity," *American Sociological Review* 54 (1989): 722–743.

119. Karl Schuessler, "The Deterrent Influence of the Death Penalty," *Annals of the Academy of Political and Social Sciences* 284 (1952): 54–62; Thorsten Sellin, *The Death Penalty* (Philadelphia: American Law Institute, 1959); Walter Reckless, "Use of the Death Penalty," *Crime and Delinquency* 15 (1969): 43–51; Richard Lempert, "The Effect of Executions on Homicides: A New Look in an Old Light," *Crime and Delinquency* 29 (1983): 88–115; Derral

Cheatwood, "Capital Punishment and the Deterrence of Violent Crime in Comparable Counties," *Criminal Justice Review* 18 (1993): 165–181.

120. James Yunker, "A New Statistical Analysis of Capital Punishment Incorporating U.S. Postmoratorium Data," *Social Science Quarterly* 82 (2001): 297–312.

121. Dane Archer, Rosemary Gartner, and Marc Beittel, "Homicide and the Death Penalty: A Cross-National Test of a Deterrence Hypothesis," *Journal of Criminal Law and Criminology* 74 (1983): 991–1014.

122. Isaac Ehrlich, "The Deterrent Effect of Capital Punishment: A Question of Life and Death," *American Economic Review* 65 (1975): 397–417.

123. James Fox and Michael Radelet, "Persistent Flaws in Econometric Studies of the Deterrent Effect of the Death Penalty," *Loyola of Los Angeles Law Review* 23 (1987): 29–44; William B. Bowers and Glenn Pierce, "The Illusion of Deterrence in Isaac Ehrlich's Research on Capital Punishment," *Yale Law Journal* 85 (1975): 187–208.

124. William Bailey, "Disaggregation in Deterrence and Death Penalty Research: The Case of Murder in Chicago," *Journal of Criminal Law and Criminology* 74 (1986): 827–859.

125. Steven Messner and Kenneth Tardiff, "Economic Inequality and Level of Homicide: An Analysis of Urban Neighborhoods," *Criminology* 24 (1986): 297–317.

126. Donald Green, "Past Behavior as a Measure of Actual Future Behavior: An Unresolved Issue in Perceptual Deterrence Research," *Journal of Criminal Law and Criminology* 80 (1989): 781–804.

127. Donna Bishop, "Deterrence: A Panel Analysis," *Justice Quarterly* 1 (1984): 311–328; Julie Horney and Ineke Haen Marshall, "Risk Perceptions Among Serious Offenders: The Role of Crime and Punishment," *Criminology* 30 (1992): 575–594.

128. Raymond Paternoster, "Decisions to Participate in and Desist from Four Types of Common Delinquency: Deterrence and the Rational Choice Perspective," *Law and Society Review* 23 (1989): 7–29; idem, "Examining Three-Wave Deterrence Models: A Question of Temporal Order and Specification," *Journal of Criminal Law and Criminology* 79 (1988): 135–163; Raymond Paternoster, Linda Saltzman, Gordon Waldo, and Theodore Chiricos, "Estimating Perceptual Stability and Deterrent Effects: The Role of Perceived Legal Punishment in the Inhibition of Criminal Involvement," *Journal of Criminal Law and Criminology* 74 (1983): 270–297; M. William Minor and Joseph Harry, "Deterrent and Experiential Effects in Perceptual Deterrence Research: A Replication and Extension," *Journal of Research in Crime and Delinquency* 19 (1982): 190–203; Lonn Lanza-Kaduce, "Perceptual Deterrence and Drinking and Driving Among College Students," *Criminology* 26 (1988): 321–341.

129. Harold Grasmick and Robert Bursik, "Conscience, Significant Others, and Rational Choice: Extending the Deterrence Model," *Law and Society Review* 24 (1990): 837–861.

130. Steven Klepper and Daniel Nagin, "The Deterrent Effect of Perceived Certainty and Severity of Punishment Revisited," *Criminology* 27 (1989): 721–746.

131. Scott Decker, Richard Wright, and Robert Logie, "Perceptual Deterrence Among Active Residential Burglars: A Research Note," *Criminology* 31 (1993): 135–147.

132. Irving Piliavin, Rosemary Gartner, Craig Thornton, and Ross Matsueda, "Crime, Deterrence, and Rational Choice," *American Sociological Review* 51 (1986): 101–119.

133. Eleni Apospori, Geoffrey Alpert, and Raymond Paternoster, "The Effect of Involvement with the Criminal Justice System: A Neglected Dimension of the Relationship between Experience and Perceptions," *Justice Quarterly* 9 (1992): 379–392.

134. Eleni Apospori and Geoffrey Alpert, "Research Note: The Role of Differential Experience with the Criminal Justice System in Changes in Perceptions of Severity of Legal Sanctions over Time," *Crime and Delinquency* 39 (1993): 184–194.

135. Bradley R.E. Wright, Avshalom Caspi, Terrie E. Moffitt, and Ray Paternoster, "Does the Perceived Risk of Punishment Deter Criminally Prone Individuals? Rational Choice, Self-Control, and Crime," *Journal of Research in Crime and Delinquency* 41, 2 (2004): 180–213.

136. Harold Grasmick and George Bryjak, "The Deterrent Effect of Perceived Severity of Punishment," *Social Forces* 59 (1980): 471–491.

137. Harold Grasmick, Robert Bursik, and Karyl Kinsey, "Shame and Embarrassment as Deterrents to Noncompliance with the Law: The Case of an Anti-Littering Campaign," paper presented at the annual meeting of the American Society of Criminology, Baltimore, November 1990, 3.

138. Charles Tittle, *Sanctions and Social Deviance* (New York: Praeger, 1980).

139. For an opposite view, see Steven Burkett and David Ward, "A Note on Perceptual Deterrence, Religiously Based Moral Condemnation, and Social Control," *Criminology* 31 (1993): 119–134.

140. "Family and Friends Set the Speedometer," *ScienceDaily,* January 5, 2007, www .sciencedaily.com. releases/2006/12/061211124215.htm.

141. John Snortum, "Drinking-Driving Compliance in Great Britain: The Role of Law as a 'Threat' and as a 'Moral Eye-Opener,'" *Journal of Criminal Justice* 18 (1990): 479–499.

142. Green, "Past Behavior as a Measure of Actual Future Behavior," p. 803; Matthew Silberman, "Toward a Theory of Criminal Deterrence," *American Sociological Review* 41 (1976): 442–461; Linda Anderson, Theodore Chiricos, and Gordon Waldo, "Formal and Informal Sanctions: A Comparison of Deterrent Effects," *Social Problems* 25 (1977): 103–114; see also Maynard Erickson and Jack Gibbs, "Objective and Perceptual Properties of Legal Punishment and Deterrence Doctrine," *Social Problems* 25 (1978): 253–264.

143. Grasmick, Bursik, and Kinsey, "Shame and Embarrassment as Deterrents to Noncompliance with the Law"; Harold Grasmick, Robert Bursik, and Bruce Arneklev, "Reduction in Drunk Driving as a Response to Increased Threats of Shame, Embarrassment, and Legal Sanctions," *Criminology* 31 (1993): 41–69.

144. Harold Grasmick, Brenda Sims Blackwell, and Robert Bursik, "Changes in the Sex Patterning of Perceived Threats of Sanctions," *Law and Society Review* 27 (1993): 679–699.

145. Daniel Nagin and Raymond Paternoster, "Enduring Individual Differences and Rational Choice Theories of Crime," *Law and Society Review* 27 (1993): 467–485.

146. Kirk Williams and Richard Hawkins, "The Meaning of Arrest for Wife Assault," *Criminology* 27 (1989): 163–181.

147. Thomas Peete, Trudie Milner, and Michael Welch, "Levels of Social Integration in Group Contexts and the Effects of Informal Sanction Threat on Deviance," *Criminology* 32 (1994): 85–105.

148. Ronet Bachman, Raymond Paternoster, and Sally Ward, "The Rationality of Sexual Offending: Testing a Deterrence/Rational Choice Conception of Sexual Assault," *Law and Society Review* 26 (1992): 343–358.

149. "Does Closed Circuit Television Prevent Crime? An Evaluation of the Use of CCTV Surveillance Cameras in Airdrie Town Centre," *Crime and Criminal Justice Research Findings No. 8* (Edinburgh: The Scottish Office, Central Research Office, 1995).

150. Marcus Nieto, *Public Video Surveillance: Is It an Effective Crime Prevention Tool?* (Sacramento, CA: California Research Bureau, 1997).

151. International Center for the Prevention of Crime, "Crime Prevention Digest, 1997," www.crime-prevention-intl.org.

152. Sean P. Hier, Josh Greenberg, Kevin Walby, and Daniel Lett, "Media, Communication and the Establishment of Public Camera Surveillance Programmes in Canada," *Media, Culture & Society*, 29, 5 (2007): 727–751.

153. Robert D. Bickel, "Legal Issues Related to Silent Video Surveillance," paper presented to the Security Industry Association and the Private Sector Liaison Committee, 1999.

154. Nieto, "Public Video Surveillance: Is It an Effective Crime Prevention Tool?"

155. David H. Flaherty, "Investigation Report: Video Surveillance by Public Bodies," Investigation P98-012, March 31, 1998, Office of the Information and Privacy Commissioner for British Columbia, https://www.oipc.bc.ca/ investigation-reports/1259.

156. Roy Coleman and Joe Sim, "'You'll Never Walk Alone': CCTV Surveillance, Order and Neo-liberal Rule in Liverpool City Centre," *British Journal of Sociology* 51 (2000): 623–639.

157. Kevin Walby, "Little England? The Rise of Open-Street Closed-Circuit Television Surveillance," *Canada Surveillance & Society* 4, 1/2 (2006): 29–51.

158. Derek Lai, "Public Video Surveillance by the State: Policy, Privacy Legislation, and the Charter," *Alberta Law Review,* 45, 2007.

159. Ernest Van Den Haag, "The Criminal Law as a Threat System," *Journal of Criminal Law and Criminology* 73 (1982): 709–785.

160. Thomas Feucht, *Drug Use Forecasting* (Washington, DC: National Institute of Justice, 1996).

161. David Lykken, "Psychopathy, Sociopathy, and Crime," *Society* 34 (1996): 30–38.

162. Ken Auletta, *The Under Class* (New York: Random House, 1982).

163. David Klinger, "Policing Spousal Assault," *Journal of Research in Crime and Delinquency* 32 (1995): 308–324.

164. James Williams and Daniel Rodeheaver, "Processing of Criminal Homicide Cases in a Large Southern City," *Sociology and Social Research* 75 (1991): 80–88.

165. James Q. Wilson and Richard Herrnstein, *Crime and Human Nature* (New York: Simon & Schuster, 1985), 494.

166. Paul Tracy and Kimberly Kempf-Leonard, *Continuity and Discontinuity in Criminal Careers* (New York: Plenum Press, 1996).

167. Solicitor General of Canada (Correctional Services of Canada), *Basic Facts about Corrections in Canada* (Ottawa: Public Works and Government Services, 1997), 26.

168. Lawrence Greenfeld, *Examining Recidivism* (Washington, D.C.: U.S. Government Printing Office, 1985); Allen Beck and Bernard Shipley, *Recidivism of Prisoners Released in 1983* (Washington, DC: Bureau of Justice Statistics, 1989).

169. Mikhail Thomas, Howard Hurley, and Craig Grimes, "Pilot Analysis of Recidivism among Convicted Youth and Young Adults, 1999/00," *Juristat* 22, 9, 2002.

170. David Weisburd, Elin Waring, and Ellen Chayet, "Specific Deterrence in a Sample of Offenders Convicted of White-Collar Crimes," *Criminology* 33 (1995): 587–607.

171. Raymond Paternoster and Alex Piquero, "Reconceptualizing Deterrence: An Empirical Test of Personal and Vicarious Experiences," *Journal of Research in Crime and Delinquency* 32 (1995): 201–228.

172. Michael Weinrath and John Gartrell, "Specific Deterrence and Sentence Length: The Case of Drunk Drivers," *Journal of Contemporary Criminal Justice* 17, no. 2 (2001): 105–122; Canadian Press, "Drunk Driver Says It's No Wonder Suspended Drivers Hit the Road Illegally," May 31, 2004.

173. "Critics say police misusing new street-racing laws," CBC News, June 10, 2008.

174. Charles Murray and Louis Cox, *Beyond Probation* (Beverly Hills, CA: Sage, 1979); Perry Shapiro and Harold Votey, "Deterrence and Subjective Probabilities of Arrest: Modeling Individual Decisions to Drink and Drive in Sweden," *Law and Society Review* 18 (1984): 111–149; Douglas Smith and Patrick Gartin, "Specifying Specific Deterrence: The Influence of Arrest on Future Criminal Activity," *American Sociological Review* 54 (1989): 94–105.

175. Graeme Newman, *Just and Painful* (New York: Macmillan, 1983), 139–143.

176. John Braithwaite, *Crime, Shame and Reintegration* (Melbourne, Australia: Cambridge University Press, 1989).

177. John Braithwaite, "Shame and Criminal Justice," *Canadian Journal of Criminology* 42, 3 (2000): 281.

178. Harold Garfinkel, "Conditions of Successful Degradation Ceremonies," *American Journal of Sociology* 61 (1956): 420–424.

179. John Braithwaite, "Shame and Criminal Justice," *Canadian Journal of Criminology* 42, 3 (2000): 281.

180. Carter Hay, "An Exploratory Test of Braithwaite's Reintegrative Shaming Theory," *Journal of Research in Crime and Delinquency* 38 (2001): 132–153.

181. John Braithwaite and Stephen Mugford, "Conditions of Successful Reintegration Ceremonies: Dealing with Juvenile Offenders," *British Journal of Criminology* 34, 2 (1994): 129–171.

182. Mark Stafford and Mark Warr, "A Reconceptualization of General and Specific Deterrence," *Journal of Research on Crime and Delinquency* 30 (1993): 123–135.

183. Michele Peterson-Badali, Martin D. Ruck, and Christopher J. Koegl, "Youth Court Dispositions: Perceptions of Canadian Juvenile Offenders," *International Journal of Offender Therapy and Comparative Criminology* 45, 5 (2001): 593–605.

184. Andrew Karmen, *New York Murder Mystery: The True Story Behind the Crime Crash of the 1990s* (New York: New York University Press, 2000).

185. See, generally, Raymond Paternoster, "Absolute and Restrictive Deterrence in a Panel of Youth: Explaining the Onset, Persistence/Desistance, and Frequency of Delinquent Offending," *Social Problems* 36 (1989): 289–307; Raymond Paternoster, "The Deterrent Effect of Perceived Severity of Punishment: A Review of the Evidence and Issues," *Justice Quarterly* 42 (1987): 173–217.

186. David Greenberg, "The Incapacitative Effects of Imprisonment: Some Estimates," *Law and Society Review* 9 (1975): 541–580.

187. Isaac Ehrlich, "Participation in Illegitimate Activities: An Economic Analysis," *Journal of Political Economy* 81 (1973): 521–567; Lee Bowker, "Crime and the Use of Prisons in the United States: A Time Series Analysis," *Crime and Delinquency* 27 (1981): 206–212.

188. Reuel Shinnar and Shlomo Shinnar, "The Effects of the Criminal Justice System on the Control of Crime: A Quantitative Approach," *Law and Society Review* 9 (1975): 581–611.

189. Stephan Van Dine, Simon Dinitz, and John Conrad, *Restraining the Wicked: The Dangerous Offender Project* (Lexington, MA: Lexington Books, 1979).

190. For a review of this issue, see James Austin and John Irwin, *Does Imprisonment Reduce Crime? A Critique of "Voodoo" Criminology* (San Francisco: National Council of Crime and Delinquency, 1993).

191. Michael Petrunik, "The Hare and the Tortoise: Dangerousness and Sex Offender Policy in the United States and Canada," *Canadian Journal of Criminology and Criminal Justice,* 45, 1 (2003): 43–72.

192. "Politicians Can't Resist Being 'Tough on Crime': Despite Falling Crime Rate, Liberals and Tories Have Both Embraced Mandatory Minimums," *Toronto Star,* July 20, 2008.

193. John Wallerstedt, *Returning to Prison*, Bureau of Justice Statistics Special Report (Washington, DC: U.S. Department of Justice, 1984).

194. *Justice Spending in Canada* (Ottawa: Canadian Centre for Justice Statistics).

195. Figures from "Justice Spending," publications.gc.ca/Collection-R/Statcan/85-002-XIE/0039785-002-XIE.pdf; and from Corrections and Conditional release Statistical Overview 2006.

196. Peter Greenwood, *Selective Incapacitation* (Santa Monica, CA: Rand Corporation, 1982).

197. Paul Gendreau and Claire Coggin, *The Effect of Prison Sentences on Recidivism* (Ottawa: Solicitor General of Canada, 1999).

198. Stephen Markman and Paul Cassell, "Protecting the Innocent: A Response to the Bedeau-Radelet Study," *Stanford Law Review* 41 (1988): 121–170 at 153.

199. James Stephan and Tracy Snell, *Capital Punishment, 1994* (Washington, DC: Bureau of Justice Statistics, 1996), 8.

200. Andrew Von Hirsch, *Doing Justice* (New York: Hill and Wang, 1976).

Trait Theories

Chapter Outline

Learning Objectives

After reading this chapter, you will be able to:

1. Understand the background of trait theories.
2. Be familiar with the biological trait theory.
3. Know the elements of the psychological trait theory.
4. Discuss the implications of this approach.
5. Explain the social policy implications of trait theory.

Phrenology and craniometry sought to determine personality and criminality through an examination of the physical contours of the skull.

© Bettmann/CORBIS

TV shows and movies that portray violent criminals as mentally deranged and physically abnormal play an important part in our culture. The classic film is Alfred Hitchcock's *Psycho,* and since then, producers have made millions depicting the ghoulish acts of people who at first seem normal but turn out to be demented and dangerous. Through movies, we meet crazed babysitters (*The Hand That Rocks the Cradle*), frenzied airline passengers (*Turbulence*), disturbed roommates (*Single, White Female*), psychotic tenants (*Pacific Heights*), demented secretaries (*The Temp*), unhinged police officers (*Maniac Cop*), irrational fans (*The Fan, Misery*), abnormal girlfriends (*Fatal Attraction*) and boyfriends (*Fear*), unstable husbands (*Sleeping with the Enemy*) and wives (*Black Widow*), loony fathers (*The Stepfather*) and mothers (*Friday the 13th, Part 1*), maniacal children (*The Good Son*), and psychotic teenaged admirers (*The Crush*). No one is safe, when even the psychologists and psychiatrists who should be treating these people turn out to be demonic murderers themselves (*Silence of the Lambs, Dressed to Kill, Never Talk to Strangers*). Is it any wonder that we respond to a particularly horrible crime by saying of the perpetrator, "That guy must be crazy," or "She's a monster!"

However, real life can sometimes seem just as crazy. In 2004, a man whom police described as mentally ill loaded his car with weapons and headed to Toronto. He was unemployed and depressed, and he had diabetes and a hereditary heart condition. His plan was to shoot as many people as possible so that he would spend the rest of his life in jail. On arrest, he was charged with weapons-related offences and remanded for psychiatric examination. The only reason that he didn't go on his rampage was that a dog befriended him when he stopped for a rest in a park. He figured that if there was a nice dog in the area, there must be nice people, too.[1]

In 2008, Vince Li boarded a Greyhound bus in Brandon, Manitoba. As the riders watched *Zorro* on the television monitor, he pulled out a hunting knife and killed his seat companion. He had a history of menial jobs and had left his wife two years before. He often took unexplained bus trips and was urged by people who knew him to get help for paranoid schizophrenia. When he appeared before the judge to be remanded for psychiatric evaluation, he said, "Please, kill me." He was found not criminally responsible and was placed in a psychiatric institution without a criminal record.

CONNECTIONS

Some critics have called for the strict regulation of all media, believing them harmful to their mostly adolescent audience. Does watching all these aggressive, crazed people cause viewers to act violently themselves? The Criminology Research box later in this chapter (page 174) has more about media violence.

The view that criminals have physical or mental traits that make them abnormal is not new. Since the 19th century, criminologists have suggested that biological and psychological traits may influence behaviour. For example, low-birth-weight babies have been found to perform poorly in educational achievement later in life. Academic deficiency has been linked to delinquency and drug abuse, so it is possible that a condition present at birth will influence antisocial behaviour during later adolescence.[2]

These personal differences explain why, when faced with the same life situations, one person commits crime and becomes a chronic offender, while another attends school, church, and neighbourhood functions and obeys the laws of society. One person reacts to being cut off in traffic with road rage, while another barely notices. All people are aware of the law, but some are unable to control their urges and passions because they are impulsive and sensation-seeking.[3] The variations on this view of crime causation are referred to as **trait theories,** or constitutional theories.

Trait theorists do not suggest that a single biological or psychological attribute is adequate to explain all criminality. Rather, for each offender, a unique explanation accounts for his or her behaviour. Some have inherited criminal tendencies; others have nervous system (neurological) problems; some have a blood chemistry disorder that heightens their antisocial activity. What we want is to understand the basic influences on behaviour.

Trait theorists are not concerned with legal definitions of crime or explaining why people violate particular statutory laws, such as car theft or burglary. Instead, trait theorists focus on basic human drives that are linked to antisocial behaviour—aggression, violence, and impulsivity. They recognize that crime involves both personal traits, such as intelligence, personality, chemical, and genetic makeup on the one hand, and environmental factors such as family life, educational attainment, and neighbourhood conditions on the other. Although some people have a predisposition toward aggression, environmental stimuli can either suppress or trigger antisocial acts. Physical or mental traits are but one part of a large pool of factors that account for criminality.

Trait theories have gained prominence because of what is known about chronic recidivism and the development of criminal careers. If only a small percentage of all offenders go on to become persistent repeaters, it is possible that what sets them apart from the criminal population is an abnormal biochemistry, brain structure, or genetic makeup.[4] Even if criminals do 'choose crime,' the fact that some repeatedly make that choice could well be linked to their physical and mental makeup.

This chapter reviews the two major divisions of trait theory: the biological and the psychological.

trait theories   These approaches look at the combination of biological or psychological attributes that might explain criminality.

BIOLOGICAL TRAIT THEORY

Development of Biological Theories

Cesare Lombroso's work on the "born criminal" and identification of primitive atavistic anomalies was based on what he believed to be sound empirical research using established scientific methods. Raffaele Garofalo (1852–1934) also believed that certain physical characteristics indicate a criminal nature. For example, among criminals, "a lower degree of sensibility to physical pain seems to be demonstrated by the readiness with which prisoners submit to the operation of tattooing."[5] Enrico Ferri (1856–1929) believed that biological and organic factors cause delinquency and crime.[6] However, he also believed that criminals should not be held personally or morally responsible for their actions because social forces outside their control cause criminality.

CONNECTIONS

Biological explanations of criminal behaviour first became popular during the middle part of the 19th century with the introduction of positivism—the use of the scientific method and empirical analysis to study behaviour, discussed in Chapter 1.

Advocates of the inheritance school traced the activities of several generations of families believed to have an especially large number of criminal members. The most famous study of a "degenerate family" was Richard Dugdale's *The Jukes: A Study in Crime, Pauperism, Disease, and Heredity* (1875), which traced a family's history over 150 years. Dugdale claimed to have proved the existence of hereditary criminality, saying: "Fornication is the backbone of their habits, flanked on one side by pauperism, on the other by crime. The secondary features are prostitution, with its complement of bastardy, and its resultant neglected and miseducated childhood; exhaustion, with its complement intemperance and its resultant unbalanced minds; and disease with its complement extinction."[7] A later attempt at criminal anthropology was the **somatype** school developed by William Sheldon, which held that criminals manifest distinct physiques susceptible to particular types of delinquent behaviour (see Exhibit 6.1). Mesomorphs have well-developed muscles and are active, aggressive, and the most likely to become criminals. Endomorphs have heavy builds and are known for lethargic behaviour. Ectomorphs are tall, thin, less social, and more intellectual than the other types.[8]

Sheldon was a psychologist and physician, and arrived at his much-repeated finding that a correlation exists between body shape and criminality at a time when sociological approaches dominated criminology. It has been argued that Sheldon's work was popular because somatotyping was part of the antimodernist reaction against the dislocations of 20th-century life. Science may tell us what is true and false, but criminological ideas are also shaped by their social contexts.[9]

The work of Lombroso and his contemporaries is regarded today as faulty because they did not use control groups, and many of the traits they assumed to be inherited are not genetically determined. Many of the biological features they identified in criminals could have been caused by deprivation in surroundings and diet, or from environmental conditions such as poor nutrition or healthcare. The validity of these explanations of criminality became questionable; however, new theories were also developed.

Sociobiology. During the early 20th century, criminologists became concerned about the sociological influences on crime. The work of biocriminologists had been viewed as methodologically unsound,[10] but this situation changed:

> What seems no longer tenable at this juncture is any theory of human behaviour that ignores biology and relies exclusively on sociocultural learning.... Most social scientists have been wrong in their dogmatic rejection and blissful ignorance of the biological parameters of our behaviour.[11]

In the 1970s, Edmund O. Wilson published *Sociobiology*, and the biological basis for crime again emerged into the limelight.[12] **Sociobiology** differs from earlier theories of behaviour by stressing how biological and genetic conditions affect the perception and learning of social behaviours. Sociobiologists view the gene as the ultimate unit of life that controls all human destiny, while environment and experience are viewed as having an impact on behaviour. Most important, sociobiology holds that people are controlled by the innate need to have their genes survive. Consequently, they want to ensure their own survival and that of others who share their gene pool (relatives, fellow citizens). Even when people are altruistic and come to the aid of others, they are motivated by the belief that their actions will be reciprocated.

Sociobiologists view biology, environment, and learning as mutually interdependent factors. Problems in one area can be altered by efforts in another. In this view, people are biosocial organisms whose behaviours are influenced by physical as well as environmental conditions. For example, psychologists Wilson and Daly at McMaster University look at how the inequitable access to goods provokes antisocial behaviour and can help explain homicide rates.[13]

---

somatype   An idea used in a system developed for categorizing people on the basis of their body build, associated with the work of William Sheldon.

sociobiology   The branch of science that views human behaviour as motivated by inborn biological urges and desires. The urge to survive and reproduce motivates human behaviour.

EXHIBIT 6.1

Sheldon's Somatypes

In the 1940s, psychologist William Sheldon proposed the idea that body types were associated with personality characteristics. After studying 4,000 photographs of college-age men, and connecting body type and temperament, Sheldon identified three categories of human bodies: the endomorph, characterized by a preponderance of body fat; the mesomorph, characterized by a well-developed musculature; and the ectomorph, who had neither much muscle tissue nor much body fat. Ectomorphic people tend to be quiet, mesomorphs are energetic, and endomorphic people love to eat. In Sheldon's words, "the somatype is intended as a kind of identification tag ... a rather crude tool fashioned to reflect a basic structural orderliness which can be perceived in human life." For example, consider the following:

"Somatype 117—Walking Sticks—Fragile stretched-out creatures with the utmost surface exposure in proportion to mass.... This extremely rare somatype (incidence 2 per ten thousand), with his extreme predominance of surface over mass, seems caught in a predicament of biological overexposure, and for such an organism the ordinary circumstances of social life may amount to chronic overstimulation. Hebephrenic psychopathy may be one natural response to such a situation. The 117 is more common in the mental hospitals than in the general population, and his diagnosis is usually hebephrenic schizophrenia. But also he is encountered more frequently on college campuses than in the general population, and there the diagnosis is sometimes Phi Beta Kappa."

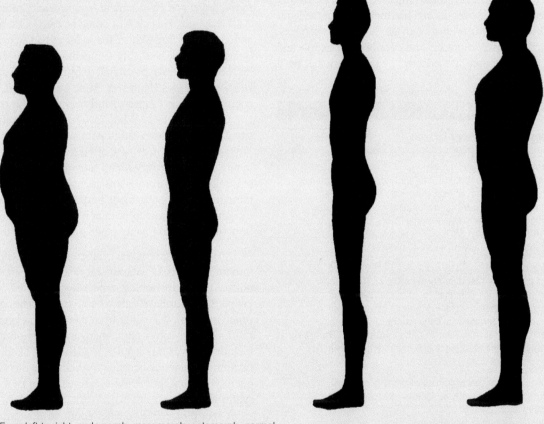

From left to right: endomorph, mesomorph, ectomorph, normal

SOURCE: William Sheldon, *Atlas of Men. A Guide for Somatyping the Adult Male at All Ages* (New York: Harper and Brothers, 1954).

Sociobiology has been criticized, but it revived interest in finding a biological basis for crime and delinquency.

Modern Biological Theories. Sociobiology has helped revive interest in the biological basis of crime. Rather than view the criminal as a person whose behaviour is controlled by biological conditions determined at birth, modern biological trait theorists believe that physical, environmental, and social conditions work together to produce human behaviour. Environmental forces can trigger antisocial behaviour in people biologically predisposed to deviance, or if conditions are right, mediate or offset the effects of biological predisposition. For example, perhaps chronic offenders suffer a biological or psychological condition or trait that renders them incapable of resisting social pressures and problems.[14]

Biological trait theory has several principles.[15] First, different genetic makeups mean that not all humans are born with equal potential to learn and achieve, which is called **equipotentiality**. Whereas sociological criminologists say that everyone is born equal and our behaviour is controlled by social forces such as parents, schools, neighbourhoods, and friends, biosocial theorists argue that no two people are alike (with rare exceptions, such as identical twins) and that the combination of human genetic traits and the environment produces individual behaviour patterns.

Another focus is the importance of brain functioning, mental processes, and learning. Although physical and social environments affect learning, people also learn through a process involving the brain and central nervous system.[16] Some biosocial theorists believe that learning is influenced by instinctual drives developed over history. **Instincts** are inherited and non-learned dispositions that activate behaviour patterns. For example, a drive to possess and control other people and things means that theft is motivated by the instinctual need

to possess goods. Rape and other sex crimes may be linked in part to an instinctual drive that males have to possess and control females.[17] However, such a theory doesn't legitimate rape as a natural act, or explain the cultural factors that exist as well.

The following subsections examine some of the more important sub-branches within biological criminology (see Concept Summary 6.1 for an overview).[18] First, we will review the biochemical factors believed to affect the learning of proper behaviour patterns. Then, we'll consider the relationship of brain function and crime, and current ideas about the association between genetic factors and crime. Finally, we will evaluate evolutionary views of crime causation.

Biochemical Conditions and Crime

Some trait theorists believe that biochemical conditions—both those that are genetically predetermined and those acquired through diet and environment—control and influence antisocial behaviour. This view of crime received national attention in 1979 when Dan White, the killer of San Francisco Mayor George Moscone and City Councillor Harvey Milk, claimed his behaviour was precipitated by an addiction to sugar-laden junk foods. However, Milk was the first openly gay councillor of San Francisco and responsible for the city's first gay rights ordinance. White, a former police officer also on city council, opposed Milk's political reforms. When White's "Twinkie defence" was supported by psychiatric evidence of hypoglycemia, the jury found him guilty of the lesser offence of diminished capacity manslaughter rather than first-degree murder. The story was made into the movie *Milk* in 2008.

Some of the more important biochemical factors that have been linked to criminality range from nutrition to hormones.

Nutritional Deficiencies. Biocriminologists maintain that minimum levels of vitamins and minerals are needed for normal brain functioning, especially in the early years of life. People with normal needs who are not receiving the appropriate nutrition will suffer from vitamin deficiency. This lack results in many physical, mental, and behavioural problems, including lower intelligence.[19] Alcoholics often suffer from thiamine deficiency because of their poor diets and consequently are susceptible to the serious, often fatal, Korsakoff's syndrome.[20]

A study of 261 homeless youth in downtown Toronto conducted by nutritionists at the University of Toronto found that over half of the youth had inadequate intakes of folate, vitamin A, vitamin C, magnesium, and zinc; in addition,

---

CONCEPT SUMMARY 6.1

Biosocial Theories of Crime

Biochemical
- Major premise is that crime is a function of diet, vitamins, hormonal imbalance, or food allergies.
- Strengths are that it explains irrational violence and how environment interacts with personal traits.
- The research focuses are diet, hormones, enzymes, environmental contaminants, and lead intake.

Neurological
- Major premise is that delinquents often suffer brain impairment, which is related to antisocial behaviour.
- Strengths are that it explains irrational violence and how environment interacts with personal traits.
- Research focuses are attention deficit disorder (ADD), ADHD, learning disabilities, brain injuries, and brain chemistry.

Genetic
- Major premise is that criminal traits and predispositions are inherited; the criminality of parents can predict the delinquency of children.
- Strengths are that it explains why only a small percentage of youth in high-crime areas become chronic offenders.
- Research focuses are twin behaviour, sibling behaviour, and parent–child similarities.

Evolutionary
- Major premise is that as the human race evolved, traits become ingrained; some of these traits make people aggressive and predisposed to commit crime.
- Strengths are that it explains high violence rates and aggregate gender differences in the crime rate.
- The research focuses of the theory are gender differences and understanding human aggression.

---

equipotentiality The concept that individuals are equal at birth and thereafter are influenced by their environment.

instincts The mechanism by which routine actions and behaviour are known automatically without being learned.

more than half of females had inadequate intakes of vitamin B12 and iron. Most youth got food from more than one source in the course of a day: 75 percent purchased food; about 50 percent obtained food from charitable meal programs; 47 percent to 75 percent received food from strangers or acquaintances; and about 10 percent stole food or took it from the garbage. When researchers compared the homeless youth with a sample of 114 domiciled youth, the homeless males had lower energy and nutrient intakes, and the homeless females had lower intakes of most nutrients.[21]

Similarly, a team of psychologists and nutritionists in Calgary were interested in how psychiatric symptoms such as depression, mood swings, and aggression might be improved by nutrient formulas containing vitamins, minerals, and essential fatty acids. This connection has been reported both in young criminal offenders and in adults with mood disturbance and other psychiatric disorders. The researchers found that the effect was quite large and suggested the need for broader clinical trials to administer nutritional supplements to children with these psychiatric symptoms.[22]

Sugar and Crime. Another suspected nutritional influence on behaviour is a diet especially high in carbohydrates and sugar.[23] For example, how the brain processes glucose was related to scores on tests measuring reasoning power.[24] High sugar intake levels have been associated with attention-span deficiencies.

Diets high in sugar and carbohydrates are also linked to violence and aggression. An experiment with 276 incarcerated youths was conducted to determine whether a change in the amount of sugar in their diet would have a corresponding influence on their behaviour.[25] In the experiment, several dietary changes were made: Sweet drinks were replaced with fruit juices, table sugar was replaced with honey, and breakfast cereals high in sugar were eliminated. These changes produced a decline of 45 percent in the number of assaults, thefts, fights, and incidents of disobedience within the institution.

Although research linking sugar intake to emotional, cognitive, and behavioural performance is impressive, some researchers have failed to find a link between sugar consumption and violence.[26] For example, one group of researchers had children described as sensitive to sugar follow a different diet for three consecutive three-week periods. One diet was high in sucrose, the second substituted aspartame (NutraSweet) as a sweetener, and the third relied on saccharin. Careful measurement found little evidence of cognitive or behavioural differences that could be linked to diet. If anything, sugar seemed to have a calming effect on the children, perhaps pointing to more situational factors that might cause excitement, such as a birthday party.[27]

In sum, although some research efforts allege a sugar–violence association in line with the "Twinkie defence," others suggest that many people who maintain diets high in sugar and carbohydrates are not violent or crime-prone, and that in some cases, sugar intake may actually reduce or curtail violent tendencies.[28]

Hypoglycemia. Research shows that abnormalities in the way the brain metabolizes glucose (sugar) can be linked to antisocial behaviours, such as substance abuse.[29] **Hypoglycemia** is a condition that occurs when glucose in the blood falls below levels necessary for normal brain functioning. The brain is the only organ that obtains its energy solely from the combustion of carbohydrates. Thus, when the brain is deprived of blood sugar, it has no alternative food supply to call on and its metabolism slows down. Symptoms of hypoglycemia include irritability, anxiety, depression, crying spells, fatigue, insomnia, nervousness, mood swings, phobias, temper outbursts, headaches, and confusion.

Hypoglycemia has been linked to outbursts of antisocial behaviour and violence. As early as 1943, murder was linked to hypoglycemia, while other studies have related assaults and fatal sexual offences to hypoglycemic reactions.[30] Hypoglycemia has also been connected with brain dysfunction and a syndrome characterized by aggressive and assaultive behaviour. A higher than normal prevalence of hypoglycemia has been found in studies of jail and prison inmate populations, and in groups of habitually violent and impulsive offenders.[31]

Hormonal Influences. Criminologist James Q. Wilson, in *The Moral Sense,* concludes that hormones, enzymes, and neurotransmitters are the keys to understanding human behaviour and that they explain gender differences in the crime rate. Males are biologically and naturally more aggressive than females, while women are more nurturing of the young and more important for survival of the species.[32] Hormone levels also explain the aging-out process, because as male hormones decline during the life cycle, violence decreases.[33]

Biosocial theorists are now evaluating the association between violent behaviour episodes and hormone levels, and the findings suggest that abnormal levels of male sex hormones (**androgens**) do, in fact, produce aggressive behaviour.[34] This link among hormonal changes, mood, and behaviour may explain why adolescents experience more intense mood swings, anxiety, and restlessness than do their elders.[35] Both hormonal activity and antisocial behaviour peak in adolescence,[36] and researchers believe that prepubertal development is a significant factor in peer-to-peer sexual harassment.[37]

Testosterone is the most abundant androgen, and research has found that prenatal exposure to unnaturally

---

hypoglycemia A biochemical condition, in this case a deficiency of sugar, which influences antisocial behaviour and criminality.

androgens Male sex hormones, which have been linked to criminality.

testosterone An androgen, or male hormone, which controls secondary sex characteristics and can alter behaviour.

Some recent experimental studies have shown that diet and crime are linked.

In Great Britain, Bernard Gesch and his associates studied the behaviour of 231 inmates at a maximum security prison. Half of the group received daily capsules containing vitamins, minerals, and essential fatty acids, such as omega-3 and omega-6, while a control group took placebo pills. Antisocial behaviour among inmates was recorded before and during distribution of the dietary supplements. Gesch found that the supplement group broke prison rules 25 percent less than those on the placebo. The greatest reduction was for serious offences—instances of fighting, assaulting guards, or taking hostages dropped 37 percent. There was no change in the control group.

In a 2003 Finnish study, 115 depressed outpatients being treated with antidepressants found that those who responded fully to treatment had higher levels of vitamin B12 in their blood at the beginning of treatment and six months later. Depression has been linked to antisocial activities. The researchers speculated that vitamin B12 deficiency leads to the accumulation of the amino acid homocysteine, which has been linked to depression.

In the United States, Carlos Iribarren and associates recently (2004) examined the relationship between omega-3 intake and hostility. Using a sample of 3,600 young adults living in urban environments, Iribarren and colleagues controlled for a wide range of factors and found that a higher consumption of the omega-3 fatty acid docosahexaenoic acid (DHA), or of omega-3-rich fish in general, was related to significantly lower levels of hostility.

Stephen Schoenthaler, a well-known biocriminologist, has conducted a number of studies that indicate a link between diet and aggressive behaviour. In some cases, the relationship is direct; in others, a poor diet may compromise individual functioning, which in turn produces aggressive behaviour. For example, a poor diet may inhibit school performance, and children who fail at school are at risk for delinquent behaviour and criminality.

The Link between Diet and School Performance

In one study of 803 New York City public schools, Schoenthaler found the academic performance of 1.1 million schoolchildren rose 16 percent after their diets were modified. The number of children identified as learning disabled fell from 125,000 to 74,000 in one year. No other changes in school programs for learning disabled children were initiated that year. In a similar experiment conducted in a correctional institution, violent and non-violent antisocial behaviour fell an average of 48 percent among 8,047 offenders after dietary changes were implemented. In both these studies, the improvements in behaviour and academic performance were attributed to diets containing more vitamins and minerals as compared with the previous diets. The greater amounts of these essential nutrients in the new diets were believed to have corrected impaired brain function caused by poor nutrition.

More recently, Schoenthaler conducted three randomized controlled studies in which 66 elementary school children, 62 confined teenage delinquents, and 402 confined adult felons received dietary supplements—the equivalent of a diet providing more fruits, vegetables, and whole grains. In this double-blind study, neither subjects nor researchers knew who received the supplement and who received a placebo. In each study, the subjects receiving the dietary supplement demonstrated significantly less violent and nonviolent antisocial behaviour when compared with the control subjects who received placebos. The carefully collected data verified that a very good diet, as defined by the World Health Organization, has significant behavioural benefits beyond its health effects.

Schoenthaler and his associates have also evaluated the relationship between nutrition and intelligence. These studies involved 1,753 children and young adults in California, Arizona, Oklahoma, Missouri, England, Wales, Scotland, and Belgium. In each study, subjects who were poorly nourished and who were

high levels permanently alters behaviour. Girls who were unintentionally exposed to elevated androgen levels during fetal development display a high long-term tendency toward aggression; boys prenatally exposed to steroids that decrease androgens displayed decreased aggressiveness.[38] In contrast, inmate studies indicate that testosterone levels are higher in men who committed violent crimes.[39] In 2001, the science journal *Nature* reported on a study showing that fish that watched two other male fish attack each other had higher levels of testosterone than fish that didn't watch the fighting. This finding indicates that the body's biology reacts to social behaviour and influences individual behaviour.

In animals, the relationship between testosterone and aggression is well established, but is more controversial in humans, influenced by culture, experience,[40] and time.[41] Hormone levels influence violent behaviour because areas of the brain become less sensitive to environmental stimuli. Males who possess high androgen levels are more likely to need excess stimulation and are more willing to tolerate pain in their quest for thrills. Androgens are linked, under stressful conditions, to emotional volatility. Some other physical reactions produced by hormones linked to violence include the need to seek unusually high levels of environmental stimulation and impulsive emotional responses to stressful environmental encounters.[42]

given dietary supplements showed a greater increase in IQ—an average of 16 points—than did those in the placebo group. The differences in IQ could be attributed to about 20 percent of the children who were presumably inadequately nourished prior to supplementation. The IQ research was expanded to include academic performance in two studies of more than 300 schoolchildren ages 6 to 14 years in Arizona and California. In both studies, children who received daily supplements at school for three months achieved significantly higher gains in grade level compared with the matched control group taking placebos. The children taking a supplement improved academically at twice the rate of the children who took placebos.

Schoenthaler concludes that parents of a child who behaves badly, or does poorly in school, may benefit from having the child's blood tested to determine whether concentrations of certain nutrients are below the recommended norms. If so, a dietary supplement may correct the child's conduct and performance. There is evidence that low levels adversely affect brain function, academic performance, intelligence, and conduct. When attempting to improve IQ or conduct, it is critical to assess all these nutrients and correct deficiencies as needed. If blood nutrient concentrations are consistently in the normal range, physicians and parents should consider looking elsewhere for the cause of a child's difficulties.

Schoenthaler finds evidence that vitamins, minerals, chemicals, and other nutrients from a diet rich in fruits, vegetables, and whole grains can improve brain function, basic intelligence, and academic performance, which are all variables that have been linked to antisocial behaviour.

Recent Initiatives to Use Diet to Fight Criminality

In 2008, researchers at the University of Oxford announced a study to be conducted whereby young male inmates would be given vitamin supplements to see if it would make them less impulsive. Controlled studies in Britain and Denmark show nutrition supplements were found to reduce assaults, thefts, and other offences among inmates in young offender institutions. Some inmates will be given a placebo while others will receive a daily dose of more than 30 vitamins and minerals, plus a dose of omega-3 fatty acids, which other studies have claimed can help to reduce aggression and mood swings. The researchers will monitor whether those receiving the supplements experience reduced levels of violence, drug-taking, and self-harm. The author of the project questions the legal assumption that criminal behaviour is entirely a matter of free will.

Critical Thinking

If this research is correct, should schools be required to provide a proper lunch for all children as a crime prevention strategy?

SOURCES: Jukka Hintikka, Tommi Tolmunen, Antti Tanskanen, and Heimo Viinamäki, "High Vitamin B12 Level and Good Treatment Outcome May Be Associated in Major Depressive Disorder," BMC Psychiatry 3 (2003): 17–18; C. Iribarren, J. H. Markovitz, D. R. Jacobs, Jr., P. J. Schreiner, M. Daviglus, and J. R. Hibbeln, "Dietary Intake of Omega-3, Omega-6 Fatty Acids and Fish: Relationship with Hostility in Young Adults—The CARDIA Study," European Journal of Clinical Nutrition 58 (2004): 24–31; C. Bernard Gesch, Sean M. Hammond, Sarah E. Hampson, Anita Eves, and Martin J. Crowder, "Influence of Supplementary Vitamins, Minerals, and Essential Fatty Acids on the Antisocial Behaviour of Young Adult Prisoners: Randomized, Placebo-Controlled Trial," British Journal of Psychiatry 181 (2002): 22–28; Stephen Schoenthaler, "Intelligence, Academic Performance, and Brain Function," California State University, Stanislaus, 2000; see also, S. Schoenthaler and I. Bier, "The Effect of Vitamin–Mineral Supplementation on Juvenile Delinquency among American Schoolchildren: A Randomized Double-Blind Placebo-Controlled Trial," Journal of Alternative and Complementary Medicine: Research on Paradigm, Practice, and Policy 6 (2000): 7–18.

Male sex offenders are sometimes treated with drugs that decrease testosterone,[43] such as the female hormones estrogen and progesterone.[44] Chemical castration is used in some American states, and surgical castration is used in some countries, although not in Canada. A problem with sex offenders is that most will have substance-abuse disorders, antisocial personality disorders, mood disorders, or psychological problems. The identification of the problem is not simple.

Researchers in Montreal were interested in the fact that individuals with lower socio-economic status (SES) report greater exposure to stressful life events and a greater impact of these events on their lives. Because this relationship between SES and health begins early in life, they performed a study of 217 children and 139 mothers. The researchers measured cortisol levels and cognitive function in the children and used phone interviews with the mothers to measure the children's symptoms of stress and depression. They found that children with low SES had higher cortisol levels, indicating stress, and which was also associated with their mother's extent of depressive symptoms. The researchers concluded that the study showed a neurobiological determinant to the association between socio-economic status and health that begins early in life.[45]

Other researchers have looked at female adolescent antisocial behaviour. Because cortisol levels in adolescent girls with conduct disorder (CD) were lower, it suggested that

Using the body to determine guilt or innocence of a criminal act goes back far in time.

In the Middle Ages, the accused would undergo a trial by ordeal, where they would be forced to hold a red hot iron bar. If the wound festered, they were guilty, but if the wound healed, it would show the intervention of God based on their innocence.

More recently, Inquisitors looked for signs on the bodies of accused witches. Cold spots, areas insensitive to pain, and other signs were seen as evidence of consorting with the devil, a carnal offense punishable by death.

In the 19th century, a surgeon named Lombroso was working on dissecting a criminal's corpse when he had a sudden revelation. There before him, he said, was revealed the nature of the criminal, in his large ears, deep-set eyes, and low forehead.

The development of criminal anthropology was based on the idea that criminals were less evolved and the evidence was in their physical features. He believed teachers could be trained to identify future criminals in children as young as five.

What is interesting in all of this is that the body is used as a sign of what is inside, and that through technology we can make the body reveal its truth.

What is a polygraph or lie detector, after all, but a machine that can divine the truth hidden inside the body by measuring physiological signals such as heart rate, sweating, and blood pressure?

Now a new machine has been developed that purports to determine who has committed a crime. Since the difference between the guilty and the innocent is that only the former has knowledge of the crime stored in their brain, "brain fingerprinting" technology is designed to detect it.

The technology is not designed to prove guilt or innocence, but rather is said to provide scientifically valid evidence that will help improve the speed and accuracy of investigations and parole hearings, reduce the cost of prosecuting innocent people, and allow law enforcement professionals to concentrate on suspects who have knowledge of crimes.

This is a forensic science technique to determine whether certain information is in a person's brain by measuring electrical brainwave responses to words, phrases, or pictures that are presented on a computer screen.

The idea is that the brain processes known information differently from the way it processes unknown information. Evidence of the guilty mind, so to speak, is revealed by an electroencephalograph.

The person being tested wears a special headband with electronic sensors, and views words, phrases, or pictures presented on a computer screen. These might be irrelevant, relevant, or information known only to the perpetrator and investigators, and not to the general public or to a person not at the scene of the crime.

The idea is to detect an electrical response to stimuli related to a crime, such as a murder weapon, victim's face, or knowledge of the internal workings of a terrorist cell.

Unlike a lie detector, it is not emotion-based, but rather works to detect knowledge of a crime. This technology has reportedly been tested in collaboration with the FBI and CIA, and used in several murder trials in the United States.

The technology is limited in that it cannot differentiate if a person was a witness or a perpetrator to a crime. It also cannot differentiate between a person who learned details of a crime from the media from one who actually committed an offence. It also would not be useful as a fishing expedition to find out if a person had done anything wrong if there was no evidence.

And now, the *Science News Examiner* reports that researchers at the University of Toronto have developed a technique that measures the intensity of infrared light absorbed in the brain to decode a person's decisions.

The person wears a fibre-optic headband that emits light into the pre-frontal cortex of the brain. They are asked questions and a computer decides the mental decision the person was making. Such futuristic technologies that purport to sense one's thoughts and intentions are liable to ignite debates over privacy and the marginal benefits relative to cost.

Talk about a naked body scan. But there were probably objections to the methods of the Inquisitors, too.

SOURCE: Copyright Chris McCormick, published in the *Daily Gleaner* (Fredericton), January 28, 2010.

---

antisocial behaviour was due to the lack of an inhibiting effect of the hormone.[46]

Premenstrual Syndrome (PMS). The onset of the menstrual cycle triggers excessive amounts of the female sex hormones, which are thought to cause antisocial, aggressive behaviour. During the 19th century, "disordered menstruation" was often introduced as a factor in defending women on serious charges, such as arson or homicide. Today, this condition is commonly referred to as **premenstrual syndrome (PMS),**[47] first popularized by Katharina

Dalton, whose studies indicated that females are more likely to commit suicide and be aggressive just before or during menstruation.[48]

> **premenstrual syndrome (PMS)** The biogenetic theory that several days prior to and during menstruation, females are beset by irritability and poor judgment as a result of hormonal changes, which places them at a greater risk for criminality.

Debate continues over any link between PMS and aggression.[49] Diana Fishbein, an expert on biosocial theory, says an association exists between elevated levels of female aggression and menstruation. She says that a significant number of incarcerated females committed their crimes during the premenstrual phase.[50]

Only a few criminal trials in Canada, Britain, and the United States have successfully used PMS as a mitigating factor in a woman's defence. The usual result has been the defendant being required to receive hormone injections as a condition of the sentence.[51]

The overwhelming majority of females who suffer anxiety and hostility before and during menstruation do not actually engage in violent criminal behaviour.[52]

Another mental disorder believed to be typically female is Munchausen's syndrome by proxy (MSBP), in which the mother either induces or fabricates illness in a child. The syndrome was identified in the late 1970s; however, there is little consensus as to what type of disorder it is.

Allergies. Allergies are excessive reactions of the body to foreign substances.[53] For example, hay fever is an allergic reaction caused when pollen cells enter the body and are fought or neutralized by the body's natural defences. The result is itching, red eyes, and active sinuses.

Neuroallergies affect the nervous system and are believed to produce enzymes that cause swelling of the brain and sensitivity in the central nervous system, which are linked to mental, emotional, and behavioural problems. Research indicates a connection between these allergies and hyperemotionality, depression, aggressiveness, and violent behaviour.[54]

Neuroallergy and cerebral allergy problems have been linked to hyperactivity in children. The foods most commonly involved in producing such allergies are cow's milk, wheat, corn, chocolate, citrus, and eggs, although about 300 other foods have also been identified as allergens. Corn is a suspected cerebral allergen, which has been linked to cross-national homicide rates.[55]

Environmental Contaminants. Dangerous quantities of copper, cadmium, mercury, and inorganic gases, such as chlorine and nitrogen dioxide, in the ecosystem influence behaviour and are linked to emotional and behavioural disorders, severe illness, or death.[56] The ingestion of food dyes and artificial colours and flavours has been linked to hostile, impulsive, and antisocial behaviour in youths.[57] Radiation from artificial lighting, such as fluorescent tubes and television sets, may be another important environmental influence on antisocial behaviour.[58]

Recent research studies have suggested that lead ingestion is linked to aggressive behaviours on both a macro and micro level. For example, areas with the highest concentrations of lead in the air also reported the highest levels of homicide.[59] Studies have linked lead to conduct problems and antisocial behaviour in hyperactive children.[60] A study of 900 Black youth found that lead poisoning was one of the most significant predictors of male delinquency and persistent adult criminality. Needleman tracked 300 boys from ages 7 to 11 and found that those who had high lead concentrations in their bones were much more likely to report attention problems, delinquency, aggressiveness, and poor language skills.[61]

High lead ingestion is also related to lower IQ scores, a factor linked to aggressive behaviour.[62] Lead has also been linked to attention deficit disorder. A study of 216 youths convicted in a juvenile court showed higher levels of lead in their bones than in the control group, with elevated lead levels leading to such antisocial activities as bullying, vandalism, truancy, and shoplifting. Some research indicates that there is a link between the decreased crime rates and the removal of lead from gasoline.

Neurophysiological Conditions and Crime

Some criminologists, looking at brain activity (**neurophysiology**), believe abnormalities acquired as early as the fetal stage may control behaviour throughout life.[63]

The relationship between neurological dysfunction and crime received a great deal of attention in 1968, when Charles Whitman killed his wife and his mother, barricaded himself in a tower at the University of Texas with a high-powered rifle, then killed 14 people and wounded 24 others before he was killed by police. An autopsy revealed that Whitman suffered from a malignant brain tumour, and had sought psychiatric treatment because he had experienced urges to kill.[64]

Since then, attention has focused on the association between impairment in brain functions, such as abstract reasoning, problem-solving skills, and aggressive behaviour.[65]

Neurological Impairments and Crime. Neurological functioning is measured in numerous ways, including visual awareness tests, short-term auditory memory tests, and verbal IQ tests. These tests can distinguish criminal offenders from non-criminal control groups.[66]

For example, the **electroencephalograph (EEG)** records the electrical impulses given off brain waves recorded by electrodes placed on the scalp.[67] Studies find that violent criminals have higher levels of abnormal EEG recordings than non-criminals.[68] In one study, a randomly selected group of 335 violent delinquents was divided into those

neurophysiology The study of brain activity that looks at neurological and physical abnormalities acquired during the fetal or perinatal stage, which are thought to control behaviour.

electroencephalograph (EEG) A device that can record the electronic impulses given off by the brain, commonly called brain waves.

CHAPTER 6 | **Trait Theories**

who were habitually violent and those who had committed only a single violent act. Sixty-five percent of the habitually aggressive offenders had abnormal EEG recordings, while only 24 percent of the one-time offenders had abnormal recordings.

Although 5 to 15 percent of the population have abnormal EEG readings, 50 to 60 percent of adolescents with known behaviour disorders display abnormal recordings.[69] These disorders include poor impulse control, inadequate social adaptation, hostility, temper tantrums, and destructiveness.[70] Studies of murderers have shown a disproportionate number manifest abnormal EEG recordings,[71] also leading to the conclusion that measures of abnormal brain activity are significantly associated with antisocial behaviour.

Fetal Alcohol Syndrome. Fetal alcohol syndrome (FAS), occurs when children are exposed to alcohol while in the womb and later experience developmental delays and often display crime-related behaviour. Half of all children with fetal alcohol spectrum disorder (FASD) are also diagnosed with ADHD, and these children are more likely to engage in disruptive school experiences. Common cognitive and behavioural problems are learning difficulties, poor impulse control, speech problems, and inability to foresee consequences. Half of young offenders appearing in provincial or territorial court are there because their mothers drank during pregnancy.[72] Some concern has been voiced about whether the condition is adequately recognized by the courts.[73]

Aboriginal youths are overrepresented in the criminal justice system and are more likely to have background histories of fetal alcohol disorders, substance abuse, childhood victimization, academic difficulties, and instability in the living environment.[74]

Minimal Brain Dysfunction. **Minimal brain dysfunction**, sometimes referred to as **MBD**, is related to an abnormality in cerebral structure. In its most serious form, MBD has been linked to serious antisocial acts, an imbalance in the urge-control mechanisms of the brain, and chemical abnormality. The category of minimal brain dysfunction includes behaviour patterns such as dyslexia, visual perception problems, hyperactivity, poor attention span, temper tantrums, and aggressiveness. One type of minimal brain dysfunction is manifested through episodic periods of explosive rage and is considered an important cause of such behaviour as spouse beating, child abuse, suicide, aggressiveness, and motiveless homicide.

Some studies measuring the presence of minimal brain dysfunction in offender populations have found that up to 60 percent exhibit brain dysfunction.[75] Researchers using brain-wave data have predicted with 95 percent accuracy the recidivism of violent criminals.[76]

Attention Deficit Hyperactivity Disorder. Many parents have noticed that their children do not pay attention to them—they run around and do things in their own way. Sometimes this inattention is a function of age; in other instances, it is a symptom of **attention deficit hyperactivity**

TABLE 6.1 **Symptoms of Attention Deficit Hyperactivity Disorder**

Lack of Attention
Frequently fails to finish projects
Does not seem to pay attention
Does not sustain interest in play activities
Cannot sustain concentration on schoolwork or related tasks
Is easily distracted

Impulsivity
Frequently acts without thinking
Often "calls out" in class
Does not want to wait his or her turn in lines or games
Shifts from activity to activity
Cannot organize tasks or work
Requires constant supervision

Hyperactivity
Constantly runs around and climbs on things
Shows excessive motor activity while asleep
Cannot sit still; is constantly fidgeting
Does not remain in his or her seat in class
Is constantly on the go like a "motor"

SOURCE: Adapted from American Psychiatric Association, *Diagnostic and Statistical Manual of Mental Disorders*, 4th ed. (Washington, DC: American Psychiatric Press, 1994); also online at http://web.cs.mun.ca/~jamie/dsm4.html.

---

disorder (ADHD), in which a child shows impulsivity, hyperactivity, and a developmentally inappropriate lack of attention. The various symptoms of ADHD are described in Table 6.1.

Between 3 percent and 5 percent of children, most often boys, are believed to have ADHD, and it is the most common reason children are referred to mental health clinics. ADHD is associated with poor school performance, grade retention, placement in special needs classes, bullying, stubbornness, and lack of response to discipline.[77] Suspected causes include neurological damage, prenatal stress, food additive and chemical allergies, and perhaps a genetic link.

Research now links ADHD, hyperactivity, and below-average written and verbal cognitive ability to the onset of a delinquent career. Youths who have both ADHD and MBD and grow up in a dysfunctional family are most vulnerable

---

minimal brain dysfunction (MBD) An abnormality in cerebral structure that causes maladaptive behaviour and is linked to antisocial acts and an imbalance in urge-control.

attention deficit hyperactivity disorder (ADHD) A condition in which a child shows a developmentally inappropriate lack of attention, impulsivity, and hyperactivity.

to chronic and persistent delinquency.[78] The relationship between chronic delinquency and attention disorders may be mediated by school failure: Kids who are poor readers are the most prone to antisocial behaviour; many poor readers also have attention problems.[79]

Although ADHD has historically been characterized as a childhood disease, it is a lifelong disorder affecting 2 percent to 6 percent of adults.[80] ADHD has a high likelihood of inheritance and is associated with high levels of substance abuse.[81] Early diagnosis and treatment of children with ADHD, usually with doses of stimulants such as Ritalin and Dexedrine, helps to control emotional and behavioural outbursts.

Other Brain Dysfunctions. Persistent criminality has been linked to dysfunction in the frontal and temporal regions of the brain, which regulate and inhibit human behaviour.[82] Brain lesions that occur in the neurological system can have permanent effects on behaviour, and clinical evaluation of depressed and aggressive psychopathic subjects showed 75 percent had dysfunction of the temporal and frontal regions of the brain.[83] Sex offenders, such as adult onset pedophiles, have often been shown to have suffered a brain injury. And in an analysis of uxoricide (wife homicide), Dutton found that most offenders had experienced traumatic childhoods and had personality disorders.[84]

Tumours, Injury, and Disease. The presence of brain tumours has been linked to psychological problems, including personality changes, hallucinations, and psychotic episodes. People with tumours are more prone to depression, irritability, temper outbursts, and even homicidal attacks. Previously docile people may undergo behaviour changes so great that they attempt to harm their families and friends; when the tumour is removed, their behaviour returns to normal.[85] In addition, head injuries caused by accidents have been linked to personality reversals marked by outbursts of antisocial and violent behaviour.[86]

A variety of central nervous system diseases, including cerebral arteriosclerosis, epilepsy, senile dementia, Korsakoff's syndrome, and Huntington's chorea, have also been associated with emotional disturbances dominated by rage and increased irritability.[87]

In a study of interaction between obstetrical complications and early family adversity, researchers looked at 849 boys from low socio-economic areas of Montreal. They found that such complications as preeclampsia and umbilical cord prolapse, coupled with the psychosocial factors of an adverse family environment, increased the risk of violence in the boys when they reached 16 to 17 years of age. It seems that neuropsychological deficits leading to behavioural problems are engendered by fetal brain damage, essentially rewiring the brain.[88]

Brain Chemistry and Crime. Neurotransmitters are chemical compounds that influence or activate brain functions. Abnormal levels of some neurotransmitters, including androgens, dopamine, norepinephrine, serotonin, monoamine oxidase, and GABA, have been linked with aggression. For example, people with histories of impulsive violence usually have a reduction in the function of the serotonin system. Studies of habitually violent Finnish criminals show that low serotonin levels are associated with poor impulse control and hyperactivity. Prozac, which is commonly prescribed for depression, is a serotonin enhancer. Low levels of certain chemicals in the brain are also linked to increased irritability, sensation seeking, and depression.[89]

Since the 1990s, doctors have prescribed selective serotonin reuptake inhibitors (SSRIs) to children with major depressive disorders. But in 2003, an advisory was issued that possible side effects included an increased risk of suicide, aggression, conduct problems, and hostility.[90]

Prenatal exposure of the brain to high levels of androgens can result in a brain structure that is less sensitive to environmental inputs. Affected individuals seek more intense and varied stimulation and are willing to tolerate more adverse consequences.[91] Such exposure results in a rightward shift in brain functioning and a lessening of cognitive and emotional tendencies. Interestingly, left-handers are disproportionately represented in the criminal population because the movement of each hand tends to be controlled by the hemisphere of the brain on the opposite side of the body.

Individuals with a low supply of the enzyme monoamine oxidase (MAO) engage in behaviours linked to violence and property crime, including defiance of punishment, impulsivity, hyperactivity, poor academic performance, sensation seeking and risk taking, and recreational drug use. Females have higher levels of MAO than males, which might explain gender differences in the crime rate.[92]

A deficiency of MAOA (a subtype of MAO) in abused children, especially boys, is a good predictor of future violence and criminality. In a study of 442 males in New Zealand, 37 percent had low levels of MAOA. Abused children with low MAOA activity (12 percent of the study) accounted for 44 percent of the violent crime connections. The researchers concluded that genetic characteristics moderate children's sensitivity to environmental insults, such as abuse, and help explain why not all victims of abuse grow up to victimize others.[93]

Because this linkage has been found, violence-prone people are treated with antipsychotic drugs that help control levels of neurotransmitters, sometimes referred to as *chemical straitjackets*. The brain can also produce natural opiates, chemically similar to the narcotics opium and morphine. Perhaps the risk and thrills involved in crime cause the brain to produce increased amounts of these natural narcotics. The result is an elevated mood state, which is perceived as an exciting and rewarding experience and acts as a positive reinforcer to crime.[94]

The brain then produces its own natural high as a reward for risk-taking behaviour. While some people achieve this high by rock climbing and skydiving, others engage in crimes of violence.

Criminology Research
Teenage Behaviour: Is It the Brain?

Teenagers and adults often don't see eye to eye, and new brain research is now shedding light on some of the reasons why so much conflict exists. Although adolescence is often characterized by increased independence and a desire for knowledge and exploration, it also is a time when the brain matures at different rates, and the resulting instability can result in high-risk behaviours, vulnerability to substance abuse, and mental distress.

Recent imaging studies in humans show that brain development and connectivity are not complete until the late teens or early twenties. It is becoming clear that the status of brain chemical systems and connectivity between brain regions make teenagers different from both the young child and the fully mature adult. In other words, as if you did not already know, there really is a big difference between the teenage and adult brains!

Brain Structure and Aggression

One area of teen brain functioning that has piqued the interests of neuroscientists is aggression. Adolescent aggressive behaviour can be divided into two types: proactive and reactive. Proactive aggressors plan how they're going to hurt and bully others. Reactive aggression, however, is not premeditated; it occurs in response to an upsetting trigger from the environment.

Research psychiatrist Frank Guido finds that aggressive teen behaviour may be linked to the amygdala, an area of the brain that processes information regarding threats and fear. Aggressive behaviour may also be associated with a lessening of activity in the frontal lobe, a brain region linked to decision making and impulse control. Reactively aggressive adolescents, most commonly boys, frequently misinterpret their surroundings, feel threatened, and act inappropriately aggressive. They tend to strike back when being teased, blame others when getting into a fight, and overreact to accidents.

Their behaviour is emotionally "hot," defensive, and impulsive. To find out why, Guido and his colleagues recruited two groups of male adolescents: one group diagnosed with "reactive-affective-defensive-impulsive" (RADI) behaviour and the other group without any history of mental illness or aggression problems. While being scanned by a brain imaging machine, both sets of teenagers were asked to perform tasks that involved reacting to age-appropriate, fear-inducing images. The tasks also tested the teenagers' impulsivity. The brains of RADI teenagers exhibited greater activity in the amygdala and lesser activity in the frontal lobe in response to the images than the brains of the teenagers in the control group.

Guido's research helps explain what goes on in the brains of some teenage boys who respond with inappropriate anger and aggression to perceived threats. It is possible that rather than having a social or environmental basis, antisocial behaviour is a function of how the brain influences decision making and impulse control.

Critical Thinking

1. If teen aggression is linked to brain chemistry and structure, what is the purpose of such crime-reducing policies as providing summer jobs for at-risk kids or providing counselling for those who have already violated the law?
2. Do you believe that crime declines with age because changes in the brain structure lessen in adulthood? Could differences between the teen brain and adult brain really explain age-related differences in antisocial behaviour or is something else to blame?

SOURCES: Society for Neuroscience News Release, November 5, 2007, "Studies Identify Brain Areas and Chemicals Involved in Aggression: May Speed Development of Better Treatment: www.sin.org/index.cfm?pagename=news_110507d; Society for Neuroscience News Release. "New Research Sheds Light on Brain Differences in Adolescents. Understanding Their Impulsive, Risk-Taking Behavior." November 6, 2007, www.sfn.org/index.cfm?pagename=news_110607b.

Arousal Theory. If obtaining thrills is a motivator of crime, adolescents may engage in shoplifting and vandalism simply because these acts offer the attraction of "getting away with it."[95] Is it possible that thrill seekers are people who have some form of abnormal brain functioning that directs their behaviour?

According to **arousal theory**, people's brains function differently in response to environmental stimuli. People generally seek to maintain a preferred or optimal level of arousal. Too much stimulation leaves them anxious; too little makes them feel bored. The way people's brains process sensory input, however, varies. Some nearly always feel comfortable with little stimulation, while others require a high degree of environmental input to feel comfortable. The sensation seekers seek out stimulating activities, which may include aggressive, violent behaviour patterns such as dangerous driving or road rage.[96]

The factors that determine a person's optimal level of arousal are not fully determined. Suspected sources include brain chemistry (serotonin levels) and brain structure. For instance, some people's brains have many more nerve cells with receptor sites for neurotransmitters.

CONNECTIONS

Jack Katz has written on the seductions of crime and how some people may be drawn into crime because it produces the natural high they crave. The seduction of crime is discussed in Chapter 5.

Genetics and Crime

Early biological theorists, believing that criminality ran in families, conducted research on deviant families, such as the Jukes and Kallikaks. Modern biosocial theorists are still interested in genetics and how heredity influences antisocial tendencies. Animals bred to have aggressive traits include pit bull dogs, fighting bulls, and fighting cocks. Genetic factors associated with human behaviour include extroversion, openness, agreeableness, and conscientiousness.[97] Human personality traits associated with criminality that may be heritable include aggression (psychopathy, impulsivity, and neuroticism) and psychopathology (such as schizophrenia).[98]

Richard Speck, the convicted killer of eight nurses in Chicago, was said to have inherited an abnormal XYY chromosomal structure (XY is the normal sex chromosome pattern in males), raising concern that all XYYs were potential killers and should be closely controlled.[99] However, neither Speck nor most violent offenders actually had an extra Y chromosome, so interest in the XYY theory dissipated.

Is it possible that the tendency for crime and aggression is inherited? Since the Speck case, numerous researchers have carefully explored the heritability of criminal tendencies using a variety of techniques, the most common being twin studies and adoption studies.

Twin Studies. If inherited traits cause criminal behaviours, twins should be quite similar in their antisocial activities. However, because twins are usually brought up in the same household and are exposed to the same set of social conditions, determining whether their behaviour is a result of biological, sociological, or psychological conditions is difficult. Trait theorists have tried to overcome this dilemma by comparing identical monozygotic (MZ) twins with fraternal dizygotic (DZ) twins of the same sex. MZ twins are genetically identical, while DZ twins have only half their genes in common. If heredity does determine criminal behaviour, the MZ twins should be much more similar in their antisocial activities than are the DZ twins.

Early studies on the behaviour of twins detected a significant relationship between the criminal activities of MZ twins and a much lower association between the criminal activities of DZ twins. Sixty percent of MZ twins shared criminal behaviour patterns (if one twin was criminal, so was the other), while only 30 percent of DZ twins were similarly related. This finding was viewed as evidence of a genetic basis to criminality.

More recently, Christiansen studied 3,586 male twin pairs and found a 52 percent similarity for MZ pairs and only 22 percent for DZ pairs, suggesting that MZ twins share a genetic characteristic that increases the risk of their engaging in criminality.[100] Genetic effects have been found to be a significant predictor of problem behaviours in children as young as three years old.[101] Although the behaviour of some twin pairs seems to be influenced by their environment, others displayed behaviour disturbances that could only be explained by their genetic similarity.[102]

However, the controversy over the heritability of crime persists, as not all research efforts have found that MZ twin pairs are more closely related in their criminal behaviour than are DZ or ordinary sibling pairs.[103] And, some experts have concluded that individuals who share genes are alike in personality regardless of how they are reared, with the environment inducing little personality resemblance in twin pairs.[104]

Adoption Studies. If the behaviour of adopted children is more similar to their biological parents than to their adoptive parents, the idea of a genetic basis for criminality would be supported. If, however, adoptees are more similar to their adoptive parents than to their biological parents, an environmental basis for crime would seem more valid.

Several studies indicate a relationship between biological parents' behaviour and the behaviour of their children, even with infrequent contact.[105] In the most significant study in this area, 1,145 male adoptees born in Copenhagen, Denmark, between 1927 and 1941 were examined; of these, 185 had criminal records.[106] After following up on 143 of the criminal adoptees and matching them with a control group of 143 non-criminal adoptees, Hutchings and Mednick found that the criminality of the biological father was a strong predictor of the child's criminal behaviour. When both the biological and the adoptive fathers were criminal, the probability that the youth would engage in criminal behaviour greatly expanded: 25 percent of the boys whose adoptive and biological fathers were criminals had been convicted of a criminal law violation; only 14 percent of those whose biological and adoptive fathers were not criminals had similar conviction records.[107]

A more recent analysis of Swedish adoptees found that genetic factors were highly significant. Boys who had criminal parents were significantly more likely to violate the law, while environmental influences were significantly less important. Nonetheless, having a positive environment, such as being adopted into a more affluent home, helped inhibit genetic predisposition.[108]

Evaluating Genetic Research. The findings of the twin and adoption studies give some support to a genetic basis for criminality. However, inadequate research designs and weak methodologies undermine the research. Newer, better-designed research studies provide less support than did earlier studies.[109]

The apparent genetic effect may actually be the effect of sibling influence on criminality, referred to as the contagion

> **arousal theory** The view that people with a high arousal level seek powerful stimuli to maintain an optimal level of arousal; often associated with violence, aggression, and sociopathy.

effect: Genetic predispositions and early experiences make some people, including twins, susceptible to the deviant behaviour displayed by antisocial siblings in the household.[110] Sibling pairs with warm relationships are more likely to behave similarly; siblings who maintain a close relationship also have similar rates of drug abuse and delinquency.[111]

These findings can be interpreted in a number of ways:

- Siblings in the same environment are influenced by similar social and economic factors.
- Deviant siblings may grow closer because of shared interests.
- Younger siblings who admire their older siblings may imitate the elder's behaviour.

What seems to be a genetic effect may actually be the result of warm and close sibling interaction. Contagion may explain the higher concordance of deviant behaviours found in identical twins as compared with fraternal twins or mere siblings. The relationship between identical twins may be more enduring than between other sibling pairs so contagion and not genetics explains their behavioural similarities. Accordingly, the contagion effect may also explain why the behaviour of twins is more similar in adulthood than adolescence. Youthful misbehaviour is influenced by friends and peer group relationships. As adults, the influence of peers may wane as people marry and find employment. In contrast, twin influence is everlasting; if one twin is antisocial, it legitimizes and supports the criminal behaviour in the co-twin. This effect may grow even stronger in adulthood because twin relations are more enduring than any other. What seems to be a genetic effect may actually be the result of sibling interaction with a brother or sister who engages in antisocial activity.

The genes–crime relationship is controversial because it implies that the propensity to commit crime is present at birth and cannot be altered. It thus raises moral dilemmas. For example, if genetic testing could detect a gene for violence, should a fetus be aborted?

Evolutionary Views of Crime

Recent biosocial research has focused on evolutionary factors in criminality.[112] As human beings have evolved, certain traits have become ingrained and responsible for some crime patterns. Jealousy, for example, is theorized to have developed in ancient times as a way to keep families intact. Women are said to benefit from jealousy because they can keep a provider attached to them, while for men it increases the likelihood that they will reproduce. Aggression is also favoured in evolution, especially for men who benefit from being pro-risk, while women benefit from being risk-averse. Similar behaviour has been observed in both humans and chimpanzees.[113]

Gender differences in the violence rate have been explained by the evolution of mammalian mating patterns.

Hypothetically, to ensure the survival of the gene pool, a male benefits from mating with as many suitable females as possible. In contrast, because of the long gestation period, females require a secure home and stable nurturing partner to ensure their survival. Because of these differences in mating patterns, the most aggressive males mate most often and have the greatest number of offspring. Unclear, however, is how the offspring survive despite the lack of a stable, nurturing father. Nonetheless, some believe the descendants of these aggressive males now account for the disproportionate amount of male aggression and violence.[114]

Two general evolutionary theories of crime are r/K theory and cheater theory.[115]

r/K Selection Theory. **r/K theory** holds that all organisms can be located along a continuum, which is based on their reproductive drives in relation to their environment. Those along one end (r-selection individuals) reproduce whenever they can and invest little in their offspring, while those along the other end (K-selection individuals) reproduce slowly and take care in raising their offspring. K-oriented people are more cooperative and sensitive to others, while r-oriented people are more cunning and deceptive. People who commit violent crimes seem to exhibit r-selection traits, such as a premature birth, early and frequent sexual activity, neglect as a child, and a short life expectancy.

This theory is based on the idea that natural selection favours different sets of adaptations. In environments with excess resources, rapid growth and early reproduction are favoured at the expense of competitive ability. In an environment with limited resources, competitive ability is important, even if the trade-off is slower growth and delayed reproduction. Populations subjected to the first set of forces of boom and bust are called opportunistic populations, in contrast with the more stable equilibrium populations that occur in more constant environments.

Cheater Theory. Cheater theory suggests that a subpopulation of men has evolved with genes that incline them toward extremely low parental involvement. Sexually aggressive, they use cunning to secure sexual conquests with as many females as possible. Because females would not willingly choose them as mates, these men use stealth to gain sexual access, such as mimicking the behaviour of more stable males. They use devious means for sexual domination, and their deceptive tactics spill over into areas where their talent for irresponsible, opportunistic behaviour supports their antisocial activities. Deception in reproductive strategies is thus linked to a deceitful lifestyle.

> **r/K theory** An evolutionary theory of crime that holds that K-oriented people are more cooperative and sensitive to others; r-oriented people are more cunning and deceptive.

Cheater males may be especially attractive to younger, less intelligent women, who begin having children at an early age. State-sponsored social assistance removes the need for potential mates to have the resources needed to be stable providers. The fleeting courtships that ensue produce children with low IQs, aggressive personalities, and little chance of proper socialization in father-absent families. Because the criminal justice system treats them leniently, sexually irresponsible men are free to prey on young girls. Over time, their offspring will supply an ever-expanding supply of cheaters who are both antisocial and sexually aggressive.

Needless to say, such evolutionary theories are controversial because they appear to suggest traditional sex-roles are biological rather than cultural.

Evaluation of the Biological Branch of Trait Theory

Biosocial perspectives on crime raise some challenging questions for criminology. If biology can explain the cause of street crime or suite crime, and if people who are poor or who are rich commit a disproportionate number of such acts, then by implication members of these groups are biologically different, flawed, or inferior.

Biological explanations for the geographic, social, and class patterns in the crime rate are problematic. However, biosocial theorists counter that their views are not deterministic. Rather than suggest that some people are born criminals, these researchers believe that some people carry the potential to be violent or antisocial and that environmental conditions can trigger their antisocial responses.[116] This theory would explain why some otherwise law-abiding citizens engage in a single antisocial act and why some people with long criminal careers often engage in conventional behaviour. It also explains why geographic and temporal patterns occur in the crime rate: People who are predisposed to crime may simply have more opportunities to commit illegal acts in the summer in Vancouver and Toronto than in the winter in Gander, Newfoundland.

According to the biosocial view, behaviour is a product of interacting biological and environmental events.[117] For example, girls who reach physical maturity at an early age are more likely to engage in delinquent acts, suggesting a relationship between biological traits (hormonal activity) and crime. However, the association may also have an environmental basis. Physically mature girls are the ones most likely to have prolonged contact with a crime-prone group: older adolescent boys.[118] Here, the combination of biological change, social relationships, and routine opportunities predicts crime rates.

The most significant criticism of biosocial theory has been the lack of adequate empirical testing using small, non-representative samples, such as adjudicated offenders in clinical treatment settings. Methodological problems make it impossible to determine whether findings apply only to offenders who have been convicted of crimes and placed in treatment or to the population of criminals as a whole.[119]

PSYCHOLOGICAL TRAIT THEORIES

The second branch of trait theory focuses on the mental aspects of crime, including the association among intelligence, personality, learning, and criminal behaviour.

In *The English Convict,* Charles Goring (1870–1919) used his biometric method to study the characteristics of 3,000 English convicts. He found little difference in the physical characteristics of criminals and non-criminals, but uncovered a relationship between crime and a condition that he called defective intelligence. Goring believed that criminal behaviour was inherited and could be controlled by regulating the reproduction of families exhibiting such traits as "feeblemindedness, epilepsy, insanity, and defective social instinct."[120]

Gabriel Tarde (1843–1904) used a different psychological approach as the forerunner of modern-day learning theorists.[121] Unlike Goring, who viewed criminals as having a mental impairment, Tarde believed people learn from one another through a process of imitation. Tarde proposed three laws of imitation to describe why people engage in crime. First, individuals in close and intimate contact tend to imitate one another's behaviour. Second, imitation spreads from the top down; consequently, youngsters imitate older individuals. Crime among young, poor, or low-status people is really their effort to imitate wealthy, older, high-status people (for example, through gambling, drunkenness, and accumulation of wealth). Third, new acts and behaviours are superimposed on old ones and either reinforce or discourage previous customs. For example, drug taking may be a popular fad among university students who previously used alcohol. However, students may find that a combination of both substances provides even greater stimulation, causing the use of both drugs and alcohol to increase. Tarde's ideas are similar to those of modern followers of **social learning theory**, who believe that criminality can be influenced by both interpersonal and observed behaviour, such as watching a movie or television.

The next section is organized along the lines of the predominant psychological views most closely associated with the cause of criminal behavior, outlined in Concept Summary 6.2. Some psychologists view antisocial behaviour from a psychoanalytic perspective, with a focus on early childhood experience and its effect on personality. In contrast, behaviourists stress social learning and behaviour modelling as the keys to criminality. Cognitive theorists analyze human thought and perception and how they affect behaviour. Other psychologists are concerned about the influence of personality or intelligence on behaviour.

CONCEPT SUMMARY 6.2

Psychological Trait Theories

Psychodynamic
- Major premise is that the development of the unconscious personality early in childhood influences behaviour for the rest of life; criminals have weak egos and damaged personalities.
- Strengths are that it explains the onset of crime and why crime and drug abuse cut across class lines.
- Research focuses are on mental disorders, personality development, and unconscious motivations and drives.

Behavioural
- Major premise is that people commit crime when they model their behaviour after others being rewarded for similar acts; behaviour is reinforced by rewards and extinguished by punishment.
- Strengths are that it explains the role of significant others in the crime process; shows how the media can influence crime and violence.
- Research focuses of the theory are the effects of the media on violence and the effects of child abuse.

Cognitive
- Major premise is that individual reasoning processes influence behaviour; reasoning is influenced by the way people perceive their environment.
- The strengths of the theory are that it shows why criminal behaviour patterns change over time as people mature and develop their reasoning powers; may explain the aging-out process.
- Research focuses of the theory are perception and cognition.

CONNECTIONS

Chapter 1 discussed how some of the early founders of psychiatry tried to develop an understanding of the criminal mind. Later theories suggested that mental illness and insanity were inherited and that deviants were inherently mentally damaged by reason of their inferior genetic makeup.

Psychodynamic Perspective

Psychodynamic (or psychoanalytic) psychology was originated by Sigmund Freud (1856–1939) and is still an important psychological theory.

According to **psychodynamic theory**, also called psychoanalytic theory, the human mind performs three separate functions. The conscious mind is the aspect that people are most aware of—everyday thoughts. The preconscious mind contains elements of experiences that are out of awareness but can be brought back to consciousness at any time—memories, experiences. The unconscious part of the mind contains biological desires and urges that cannot readily be experienced as thoughts. Part of the unconscious contains feelings about sex and hostility, which people keep below the surface of consciousness by a process called **repression.**

Psychodynamic theory also holds that the human personality contains a three-part structure. The id, the primitive part of people's mental makeup, represents unconscious biological drives for sex, food, and other life-sustaining necessities. The id follows the pleasure principle, requiring instant gratification without concern for the rights of others. The ego develops early in life, when a child learns that wants cannot be instantly gratified. The ego compensates for the demands of the id by helping the individual guide his or her actions to remain within the boundaries of social convention.

---

social learning theory   The view that behaviour is modelled on observation of social interactions, direct observation of those who are close, or indirectly through the media. Interactions that are rewarded are copied, while those that are punished are avoided.

psychodynamic (psychoanalytic) theory   The branch of psychology that holds that the human personality is controlled by unconscious mental processes developed early in childhood.

repression   A process identified in psychodynamic theory, in which the unconscious mind contains feelings about sex and hostility; most people keep these feelings below the surface of consciousness.

In the early morning hours of May 24, 1987, 23-year-old Kenneth Parks drove 23 km and attacked his parents-in-law with a kitchen knife as they lay sleeping. His mother-in-law was killed and his father-in-law seriously injured. Immediately after the incident, Parks went to the police station and told the police, "I just killed someone with my bare hands. Oh, my God, I just killed someone; I've just killed two people; my God, I've just killed two people with my hands; my God, I've just killed two people. My hands; I just killed two people. I killed them; I just killed two people; I've just killed my mother- and father-in-law. I stabbed and beat them to death. It's all my fault."

He claimed to have been sleepwalking during the crime. He had always been a deep sleeper and had a great deal of trouble waking up. Several members of his family also suffered from sleep problems, such as sleepwalking, adult enuresis, nightmares, and sleeptalking. The year before the incident had been particularly stressful. He had worked 10 hours a day as a project coordinator for Revere Electric. In addition, he had lost money betting on horse racing. When he stole $30,000 from his employer, he was dismissed and charged. His personal life suffered. His parents-in-law, with whom he got on well, were aware of the situation and supported him.

Kenneth Parks was charged with the first-degree murder of Barbara Ann Woods and the attempted murder of Denis Woods. At the trial, he presented a defence of automatism. The testimony of five expert witnesses called by the defence was not contradicted by the Crown. This evidence was that Parks was sleepwalking, and that sleepwalking is not a neurological, psychiatric, or other illness. At issue was whether sleepwalking should be classified as non-insane automatism, which would result in an acquittal, or as a "disease of the mind" (insane automatism), leading to a special verdict of not guilty by reason of insanity. The trial judge presented only the defence of automatism to the jury, who acquitted Parks of first-degree murder and then of second-degree murder. The judge then acquitted Parks of attempted murder. Two subsequent appeals upheld his acquittals.

The superego develops as a result of incorporating within the personality the moral standards and values of parents, community, and significant others. This moral aspect of personality passes judgments on their behaviour.

Human Development. The most basic human drive present at birth is eros, the instinct to preserve and create life, which is expressed sexually. Consequently, early in their development, humans experience the seeking of pleasure through the body. During the first year of life, a child attains pleasure by sucking and biting: the oral stage. During the second and third years of life, the focus of sexual attention is on the elimination of bodily wastes: the anal stage. The phallic stage occurs during ages four and five, as children focus their attention on their genitals. Males begin to have sexual feelings for their mother (the Oedipus complex) and girls for their father (the Electra complex). The latency stage begins at age six, and during this period, feelings of sexuality are repressed until the genital stage begins at puberty, which marks the beginning of adult sexuality.

If conflicts are encountered during any of these psychosexual stages of development, a person can become fixated. For example, an infant who does not receive enough oral gratification during the first year of life is likely as an adult to engage in smoking, drinking, or drug abuse, or to be clinging and dependent in personal relationships. Thus, in this perspective, the root of adult behaviour problems can be traced to psychological problems developed in the earliest years of life.

Psychodynamics of Abnormal Behaviour. According to the psychodynamic perspective, people who experience feelings of mental anguish and are afraid they are losing control of their personalities have a **neurosis**. Those people who have lost total control and who are dominated by their primitive id suffer from **psychosis**, with behaviour marked by bizarre episodes, hallucinations, and inappropriate responses. According to the psychodynamic view, the most serious types of antisocial behaviour, such as murder, might be motivated by psychosis, while neurotic feelings would be responsible for less serious delinquent acts and status offences, such as petty theft and truancy.

Psychosis takes many forms. The most common is **schizophrenia**, in which persons exhibit illogical and incoherent

> **neurosis**   A syndrome in psychodynamic theory whereby people suffer when they experience feelings of mental anguish and are afraid they are losing control of their personalities.
>
> **psychosis**   A syndrome in which people have lost total control and are dominated by their primitive id; their behaviour may be marked by bizarre episodes, hallucinations, and inappropriate responses to situations.
>
> **schizophrenia**   A psychosis marked by bizarre behaviour, hallucinations, loss of thought control, and inappropriate emotional responses; types of schizophrenia include catatonic (impairment of motor activity), paranoid (delusions of persecution), and hebephrenic (immature behaviour and giddiness).

TABLE 6.2 Violence, Psychosis, and Relationship to Victim of Stalkers

	Strangers	Acquaintances	Former Sexual Intimates
Serious violence	25%	28%	78%
Psychotic illness	75%	72%	12%
Total = 50	subtotal = 12	subtotal = 18	subtotal = 18

SOURCE: Reprinted from *The Lancet*, Frank R. Farnham, David V. James, and Paul Cantrell, "Association between Violence, Psychosis, and Relationship to Victim in Stalkers," p. 199, January 15, 2000, with permission from Elsevier.

thought processes and a lack of insight into their behaviour. They may experience delusions and hallucinate, for example, seeing themselves as agents of the devil, avenging angels, or the recipients of messages from animals and plants. David Berkowitz, the Son of Sam, exhibited these traits when he claimed that his killing spree began when he received messages from a neighbour's dog.

People who have paranoid schizophrenia also suffer complex delusions involving wrongdoing or persecution, and they think everyone is out to get them. In a study of 50 stalkers, psychotic illness was associated with the stalking of strangers (see Table 6.2). Almost three-quarters of those who stalked strangers and acquaintances had a psychotic illness, while only 20 percent of those who were former sexual intimates were psychotic. Although no relationship was found between serious violence and psychosis, a strong relationship was noted between violence and former sexual intimacy, as shown in Table 6.2.[122]

In 1994, Ralph Tortorici, brandishing a high-calibre rifle, walked into a classroom at the State University of New York and held the class hostage. In a dramatic example of the link between schizophrenia and crime, he was clearly delusional and psychotic. This sort of offender should be treated in a hospital, but he was committed to jail, where he eventually committed suicide. Today, prisons are criticized for not treating the mentally ill, just incarcerating them.

Canadian medical research shows that schizophrenia is also related to urban living: birth cohort studies indicate that the incidence of schizophrenia is twice as high in cities than anywhere else and the incidence increases with city size. Where a person is born and brought up is a larger contributing factor to risk than is genetic predisposition: it is said that 35 percent of schizophrenia cases would be prevented if people were not brought up in cities, compared with 5 percent of cases that would be prevented if people did not have parents or siblings who had the illness.[123]

CONNECTIONS

See the Famous Canadian Criminals box for an example of automatism, and the Famous Canadian Court Cases box later in this chapter (page 187) for an interesting case of criminality and paranoid schizophrenia.

Psychosis and Crime. Freud did not theorize much about crime, but he linked criminality to the unconscious sense of guilt a person retains because of an Oedipus complex or Electra complex. He believed that in criminals, especially youthful ones, guilt that existed before the crime is not the result of crime but its motive. It is as if the person is relieved to be able to fasten the unconscious sense of guilt onto something real and immediate.[124]

Psychologists have used psychoanalytic concepts to link criminality to abnormal mental states produced by early childhood trauma. Alfred Adler (1870–1937), the founder of individual psychology, used "**inferiority complex**" to describe the sense of inadequacy held by people who compensate for their feelings of inferiority by controlling others. Erik Erikson (1902–1984) identified the **identity crisis**— a period of serious personal questioning that young people undertake in an effort to determine their own values and sense of direction. Adolescents undergoing an identity crisis might exhibit out-of-control behaviour and experiment with drugs and other forms of deviance.

The psychoanalyst most closely associated with criminality is August Aichorn.[125] After examining many delinquents, he concluded that societal stress could not result in a life of crime unless a predisposition existed that prepared youths psychologically for antisocial acts. This mental state, called **latent delinquency**, is found in youngsters whose personality requires them (1) to seek immediate gratification (to act impulsively), (2) to consider satisfying their personal needs as more important than relating to others, and (3) to

inferiority complex   A term used to describe the sense of inadequacy held by people who compensate for their feelings of inferiority with a drive for superiority; controlling others may help reduce their sense of personal inadequacies.

identity crisis   A psychological state, identified by Erikson, in which youths face inner turmoil and uncertainty about life roles.

latent delinquency   The idea that a mental predisposition prepares youths psychologically for antisocial acts.

satisfy instinctive urges without consideration of right and wrong (that is, they lack guilt).

Psychodynamics of Criminal Behaviour.   Since this early work, psychoanalysts have viewed the criminal as an id-dominated person who suffers from the inability to control impulsive, pleasure-seeking drives.[126] Perhaps because criminals suffered unhappy experiences in childhood or had families that could not provide proper love and care, they suffer from weak or damaged egos that make them unable to cope with conventional society. Weak egos are associated with immaturity, poor social skills, excessive dependence on others, and being easily led by antisocial peers into crime and drug abuse. Some offenders have undeveloped super-egos and consequently commit crimes because they have difficulty understanding the wrongfulness of their actions.[127]

Personality conflict or underdevelopment may result in neurotic or psychotic behaviour patterns.[128] Offenders classified as neurotics have an unconscious desire to be punished for prior sins, and they may violate the law to gain attention or punishment from their parents. Imagine the politician, for example, who repeatedly texts explicit sexual pictures to female acquaintances—is that a desire for public humiliation?

And, in its most extreme form, criminality is viewed as a form of psychosis that prevents offenders from appreciating the feelings of victims or controlling their own impulsive needs for gratification.

Crime is a manifestation of feelings of oppression combined with the inability to develop the proper defence mechanisms to keep these feelings under control. Criminality actually allows troubled people to survive by producing positive psychic results: It helps them feel free and independent, gives them excitement and the chance to use their skills and imagination, provides them with positive gain, allows them to blame others for their predicament, and enables them to rationalize their sense of failure ("If I hadn't gotten into trouble, I could have been a success").

The psychodynamic model of the criminal offender depicts an aggressive, frustrated person dominated by events that occurred early in childhood.

Behavioural Theories

Behaviour theory maintains that human actions are developed through learning experiences. Rather than focus on unconscious personality traits or biological predispositions, behaviour theorists are concerned with what people do during their daily lives. The major premise is that people alter their behaviour according to the reactions they receive from others—rewards and punishments. Behaviour is constantly being shaped by life experiences, and crimes are learned responses to life situations that do not necessarily represent abnormal or morally immature responses.

Social learning theorists, such as Albert Bandura, argue that people are not actually born with the ability to act violently but learn through experiences to be aggressive.[129] These experiences include personally observing others acting aggressively to achieve some goal or watching stories in the media that show people being rewarded for their violent acts. People learn to act aggressively when, as children, they model their behaviour after the violent acts of adults. Later in life, these patterns persist in social relationships. The boy who sees his father repeatedly strike his mother is more likely to grow up to become a battering parent and husband.

Although mental or physical traits may predispose a person to violence, the activation of a person's violent tendencies is achieved by environmental factors. The specific forms that aggressive behaviour takes, its frequency, the situations in which it is displayed, and the specific targets selected for attack are largely determined by social learning. An adolescent who spends a weekend in jail for drunk driving may learn a lesson about not drinking and driving; another may find it an exciting experience to brag about to his friends.

This process of learning is called **behaviour modelling**. Studies of family life show that children who use aggressive tactics tend to have parents who use similar behaviours when dealing with others. A second influence on the social learning of violence is provided by environmental experiences. People who live in areas where violence is a daily occurrence are more likely to act violently than those who dwell in low-crime areas where conventional behaviour is the norm. A third source of behaviour modelling is the mass media, which commonly depicts violence graphically and as acceptable behaviour, especially for heroes who never face legal consequences for their actions. For example, David Phillips found that the homicide rate increases significantly immediately after a heavyweight championship prizefight, which models the acceptability of violent behaviour.[130]

What triggers violent acts? One idea is that a direct, pain-producing physical assault will usually trigger a violent response. Yet the relationship between painful attacks and aggressive responses is inconsistent. Whether people counterattack in the face of physical attack depends in part on their fighting skill and their perception of their attacker's strength. Verbal taunts and insults are also linked to aggressive responses. People who are predisposed to aggression by their learning experiences are likely to view insults from others as a challenge to their social status and to react with

> **behaviour theory**   The approach that human actions are developed through a variety of learning experiences over the course of a lifetime.
>
> **behaviour modelling**   In modern society, the process of learning aggressive acts from three principal sources: family members, environmental experiences, and the mass media.

"In *Alias Grace*, Margaret Atwood chronicles the life of Grace Marks, who, at sixteen years of age was accused along with James McDermott of murdering her employer and his lover. They were convicted in 1843, James was hung and Grace was confined to the Kingston Penitentiary. For a brief time she also received treatment at the Toronto Asylum."

So begins an essay by Dorothy Chunn and Robert Menzies on the institutionalization of criminally insane women in British Columbia's mental hospitals between 1888 and 1973. They look at the first 38 women to be transferred from judicial to psychiatric settings and how gender norms inform the ways in which these women are treated.

Confined for offences ranging from alcoholism to vagrancy, from killing their babies to killing their husbands, they are subject to abuse, hard work, poor diet, and indeterminate incarceration. They are treated with electroshock therapy, induced insulin comas, and lobotomy. Separated from their homes and families, their hopes of recovery are slim, but they can only ever be released if they demonstrate recovery.

The women are assumed to be suffering from biological and inherited tendencies that define their criminality. Most of the women they study came from the working class and ethnic minorities. Many had children and few had committed violent offences. In comparison, men who were institutionalized tended to be childless and had been incarcerated for crimes of violence. The women were more likely to be diagnosed with mood disorders, while the men were more likely to be diagnosed with paranoid schizophrenia.

Furthermore, even though the women were less likely than men to have a history of prior incarceration, they were institutionalized for terms as long as men's, were four times more likely to be administered drugs, and twice as likely to be given electroshock therapy.

Who are these women?

Olga Braun, a Doukhobor woman, was convicted of negligence in the death of her son, who was killed by a train in 1941. She spent 34 years in hospital and was eventually lobotomized. Jenny Albright, who killed her daughter in the course of a psychotic episode in 1902, effectively served a life sentence in hospital. Irma Wilinsky was arrested on vagrancy in 1946, and

violence. Still another violence-triggering mechanism is a perceived reduction in life conditions. Prime examples of this phenomenon are riots and demonstrations in poverty-stricken areas. Discontent produces aggression in members of lower-class groups who have been led to believe they can succeed but who cannot now succeed. This relationship is complex. For some individuals, no matter how deprived they are, they will not resort to violence. People's perceptions of their position have differing effects on their aggressive responses.

In summary, social learning theorists have said that the following four factors help produce violence and aggression:

1. An event that heightens arousal, such as being provoked through physical assault or verbal abuse.
2. Aggressive skills learned from observing others, either personally or through the media.
3. Expected outcomes, or the belief that aggression will be rewarded, either in money, reduced tension or anger, enhanced self-esteem, or the praise of others.
4. Consistency of behaviour with values, or the belief that aggression is justified and appropriate, given the circumstances of the current situation.

Cognitive Theory

One area of psychology that has received increasing recognition in recent years has been the **cognitive school**. Cognitive psychologists focus on how people perceive the world and solve problems. Pioneers of this school were Wilhelm Wundt (1832–1920), Edward Titchener (1867–1927), and William James (1842–1920). Today, the cognitive school has several subareas. For example, the moral development branch is concerned about the way people morally reason about the world, while the information-processing branch focuses on the way people process, store, encode, retrieve, and manipulate information to make decisions and solve problems.

Moral and Intellectual Development Theory. The moral and intellectual development branch of cognitive psychology is identified with Jean Piaget (1896–1980), who hypothesized that people's reasoning processes develop in an orderly fashion, beginning from birth.[131] At first, during the sensorimotor stage, children respond to the environment in a simple manner, seeking interesting objects and developing their reflexes. By the fourth and final stage, the formal operations stage, they have developed into mature adults who can use logic and abstract thought.

Lawrence Kohlberg applied the concept of moral development to criminology.[132] He found that people travel through stages of moral development, during which decisions

cognitive school (perspective) A theory that studies our perceptions of reality and of the mental processes required to understand the world we live in.

authorities wrote that she would likely remain institutionalized forever.

Pauline Boone, an Aboriginal woman from Prince Rupert, British Columbia, was committed for attempted suicide in the 1940s. She escaped but was brought back, contracted tuberculosis on the wards, and died. Her death certificate recorded her as an imbecile.

Louise Hamelin, a Doukhobor woman and mother of five, was arrested for public nudity and then transferred to the psychiatric institution in 1935. This arrest occurred during a period when the Doukhobors were rebelling against compulsory schooling, military service, and government registration. She was eventually released through the intervention of her husband and others in her community. Others were not so lucky.

Felicity Austen, a clairvoyant admitted in 1896, died after being injected with ether. Bertha Tailing, an Aboriginal woman from northern British Columbia, was sexually sterilized in 1935 for infanticide. Edith Olmstead, incarcerated for vagrancy, was given nitrous oxide, insulin, electroshock therapy, Largactil, and Ritalin. Adele Ross was administered insulin daily for two months to induce comas that lasted for hours.

It is obvious that the psychiatric profession benefitted from the incarceration of the criminally insane and perpetuated its power through decisions over whether or not to release the inmates. Many of these women committed crimes for which institutionalization in prison or a mental hospital was probably not the best solution.

Poverty, abuse, and lack of education were being treated through the prison and the hospital.

Women's criminality was seen through the lens of a patriarchal society, where prostitution and public drunkenness were deviant (women's) crimes. Moreover, because their crimes were perceived as an indication of their moral inferiority, caused by biological weaknesses, invasive treatment could be justified.

It was an age of moral control in the guise of science experimentation.

SOURCE: Based on Dorothy Chunn and Robert Menzies, "Out of Mind, Out of Law: The Regulation of 'Criminally Insane' Women inside British Columbia's Public Mental Hospitals, 1888–1973," *Canadian Journal of Women and the Law*, 10, 2, (1998): 306–337.

on issues of right and wrong are based on different reasoning, with serious offenders' moral orientation differing from that of law-abiding citizens. The following are Kohlberg's stages of development:

Stage 1: Obedience to power and avoidance of punishment.
Stage 2: Taking responsibility for self, meeting own needs, leaving to others responsibility for them.
Stage 3: Having good motives and concern for others, putting yourself in the other person's shoes.
Stage 4: Maintaining the rules of society and serving the welfare of the group or society.
Stage 5: Recognizing individual rights within a society with agreed-on rules—a social contract.
Stage 6: Assuming principles that apply to all humankind—justice, equality, and respect for human life.

As we can see, a person is classified at different levels of increasing abstraction, extending personal rights to others, and then to all society. In studies conducted by Kohlberg, criminals were found to be significantly lower in their moral judgment development than were non-criminals of the same social background.[133] Since Kohlberg's pioneering efforts, researchers have continued to show that criminal offenders are more likely to be classified in the lowest levels of moral reasoning (stages 1 and 2), while non-criminals are more likely to have reached a higher stage of moral development.

Research indicates that the decision not to commit crimes may be influenced by a person's stage of moral development. People at the lowest levels report that they are deterred from crime because of their fear of sanctions; those in the middle consider the reactions of family and friends; and those at the highest stages believe in a duty to others and universal rights.[134]

Does playing video games cause kids to act aggressively? Although laboratory observations suggest a media–violence link, there is less evidence that such an association occurs in the real world. Millions of kids play video games every day, yet few become violent criminals. It is possible, however, that playing violent video games can reinforce a predisposition to aggressive behaviour.

Krebs and Denton of Simon Fraser University advance Kohlberg's model with a new approach that is more attentive to how people make moral judgments to induce themselves and others to uphold systems of cooperative exchange that help them achieve their goals and advance their interests.[135]

Moral development theory suggests that people who obey the law simply to avoid punishment or who have outlooks mainly characterized by self-interest are more likely to commit crimes than are those who view the law as benefiting all of society and who sympathize with the rights of others. Higher stages of moral reasoning are associated with conventional behaviours, such as honesty, generosity, and non-violence.

Information Processing. When cognitive theorists who study information processing try to explain antisocial behaviour, they do so in terms of perception and analysis of data. When people make decisions, they engage in a sequence of thought processes. They first encode information so that it can be interpreted, search for a proper response, then decide on the most appropriate action, and, finally, they act on their decision.[136]

CONNECTIONS

The deterrent effect of informal sanctions and feelings of shame discussed in Chapter 5 may hinge on the level of a person's moral development. The lower the person's state of moral development, the less impact informal sanctions may have. If moral development increases, informal sanctions may be better able to control crime.

According to this approach, violence-prone people may be using information incorrectly when they make decisions. They may be relying on mental scripts learned in childhood that tell them how to interpret events, what to expect, how they should react, and the likely outcome of the interaction.[137] Hostile children may have learned improper scripts by observing how others react to events and by acting out their own parents' aggressive and inappropriate behaviour. Violence becomes a stable behaviour because the scripts that emphasize aggressive responses are repeatedly rehearsed as the child matures.

Violence-prone kids see people both as more aggressive than they actually are and as intending them ill when there is no reason for alarm. As these children mature, they use fewer cues than do most people to process information. Some use violence in a calculating fashion as a means of getting what they want; others react in an overly volatile fashion to the slightest provocation. Aggressors are more likely to be vigilant, on edge, or suspicious. When they attack victims, they may believe they are defending themselves, even though they are misreading the situation.[138]

Recent research on cognitive processes in sexual assault has found that rapists lack empathy toward their victims but

not toward the women who are sexually abused by other offenders. Their lack of empathy works as a refusal to recognize the harm they are inflicting.[139]

Information-processing theory has been used to explain date rape. Sexually violent males believe that when their dates say no to sexual advances, the women are really playing games and actually want to be taken forcefully.[140] This type of attitude is self-justifying, of course.

Treatment that is based on information processing acknowledges that people are more likely to respond aggressively to a provocation when thoughts intensify the insult or otherwise stir feelings of anger. Cognitive therapists teach explosive people to control their aggressive impulses by viewing social provocations as problems demanding a solution rather than as insults requiring retaliation. Problem-solving skills may include listening, following instructions, joining in, and using self-control. Treatment interventions that are based on learning social skills are relatively new, but this approach can have long-term benefits for reducing criminal behaviour.

Mental Illness and Crime

Each school of psychology has a unique approach to the concept of mental abnormality. Psychoanalysts view mental illness as a retreat from unbearable stress and conflict; cognitive psychologists link it to thought disorders and overstimulation; behavioural theorists might look to environmental influences, such as early family experiences and social rejection. Regardless of the cause of mental illness, is there a link between it and crime?

A recent survey of more than 6,000 adults in 14 countries found that mental ailments affect more than 10 percent of people in more than half the countries surveyed. Treatment rates ranged from 64 percent in developed countries to only 15 percent in developing countries. In Canada, 20 percent of children experience emotional problems requiring treatment, such as anxiety disorders and post-traumatic stress disorders. If mental illness is left untreated, the criminal justice system often becomes the avenue into the health system.[141]

Early research found that many offenders who engage in serious, violent crimes suffer from some sort of mental disturbance. A study of juvenile murderers found that many homicidal youths were hostile, explosive, anxious, and depressed.[142] Likewise, in a study of 45 males accused of murder, 75 percent could be classified as having some form of mental illness, including schizophrenia.[143] Abusive mothers have been found to have mood and personality disorders and a history of psychiatric diagnoses.[144] Substance abuse among people with mental illnesses is significantly higher than among the general population.[145] Furthermore, people with diagnosed mental illnesses appear in arrest and court statistics at a rate disproportionate to their presence in the population.[146]

However, people with mental illnesses may be more likely to withdraw or harm themselves than to act aggressively toward others.[147] Prisoners who had prior histories of hospitalization for mental disorders were less likely to be rearrested than were those who had never been hospitalized.[148] A 2001 study found that about 3 percent of violent offences could be attributed to individuals who had a disorder not related to substance use.[149] Raymond Corrado at Simon Fraser University found that 65 percent of offenders suffered from antisocial personality disorder, but only 5 percent from schizophrenic disorder.[150]

This research gives only tentative support to the proposition that mental disturbance or illness can be an underlying cause of violent crime. However, certain symptoms of mental illness are connected to violence, including the feelings that others are wishing the person harm, that one's mind is dominated by forces beyond one's control, and that thoughts are being put into one's head by others.[151] People who have other psychological disorders, such as substance abuse, psychopathy, and neuroticism, are most at risk for chronic criminal behaviour.[152]

Because people with mental illnesses are more likely to reside in deteriorated, high-crime neighbourhoods that are linked to violence,[153] their living in a stress-filled, urban environment may produce both symptoms of mental illness and crime.[154] A lack of resources may inhibit people who are mentally ill from obtaining the treatment that would result in reduced criminality. For example, in one study, treatment significantly reduced the probability of arrest (12 percent versus 45 percent).[155]

Personality and Crime

Personality can be defined as the reasonably stable patterns of behaviour, thoughts, and emotions that distinguish one person from another. Personality reflects a characteristic way of adapting to life's demands and problems. The way people behave is a function of how their personality enables them to interpret life events and make appropriate behavioural choices. The issue of whether crime can be linked to personality has always caused significant debate.[156] In their early work, the Gluecks identified the following personality traits, which they believed characterized antisocial youth:[157]

self-assertiveness	sadism
defiance	lack of concern for others
extroversion	feelings of being unappreciated
ambivalence	distrust of authority
impulsiveness	poor personal skills
narcissism	mental instability
suspicion	hostility
destructiveness	resentment

Several other research efforts have attempted to identify criminal personality traits.[158] Suspected traits include impulsivity, hostility, and aggressiveness.[159] Hans Eysenck identified two personality traits associated with antisocial behaviour: extroversion-introversion and stability-instability. Extreme introverts are overaroused and avoid sources of stimulation, while extreme extroverts are unaroused and seek sensation. Introverts are slow to learn and be conditioned; extroverts are impulsive individuals who lack the ability to examine their own motives and behaviours. Those with neuroticism are anxious, tense, and emotionally unstable.[160] People who are both neurotic and extroverted lack self-insight, are impulsive and emotionally unstable, and are unlikely to have reasoned judgments of life events. Whereas extrovert neurotics may act self-destructively—for example, by abusing drugs—more stable people will be able to reason that such behaviour is ultimately harmful and life threatening. Eysenck believes that the direction of the personality is controlled by genetic factors and is heritable.

In a recent study evaluating the most widely used measures of personality, the lack of agreeableness and conscientiousness seem to be most closely related to antisocial behaviours. *Agreeableness* involves the ability to use appropriate interpersonal strategies when dealing with others; *conscientiousness* involves a person's ability to control impulses, carry out plans and tasks, maintain organizational skills, and follow an internal moral code. Personality researchers now link antisocial behaviours to such traits as hostility, self-centredness, spitefulness, jealousy, and indifference to others. Law violators tend to lack ambition, motivation, and perseverance; have difficulty controlling their impulses; and hold unconventional values and beliefs. For example, kids who are low in conscientiousness will most likely have poor educational and occupational histories, which limit their opportunity for advancement; this blocked opportunity renders them crime-prone.[161]

Other personality deficits in criminals include hyperactivity, impulsiveness, short attention spans, conduct disorders, anxiety disorders, and depression. These traits make criminals prone to problems ranging from psychopathology and drug abuse to sexual promiscuity and violence.[162] As a group, people who share these traits are believed to have a character defect referred to as the antisocial, sociopathic, or psychopathic personality. Although these terms are often used interchangeably, some psychologists distinguish between sociopaths and psychopaths by suggesting that the former are a product of a destructive home environment, while the latter are a product of a defect or aberration within themselves.[163]

> **personality** The reasonably stable patterns of behaviour, thoughts, and emotions that distinguish one person from another; used to explain how psychological conflict or underdevelopment might result in neurotic or psychotic behaviour patterns.

The Antisocial Personality. Some, but not all, serious violent offenders may have a disturbed character structure commonly called **psychopathy**, **sociopathy**, or **antisocial personality**. Psychopaths have a low level of guilt and anxiety, and persistently violate the rights of others. Although they may exhibit superficial charm and above-average intelligence, this surface often masks a disturbed personality that makes them incapable of forming enduring relationships with others and continually involves them in such deviant behaviours as violence, risk taking, substance abuse, and impulsivity.

CONNECTIONS

The Glueck research is representative of the view that antisocial people maintain a distinct set of personal traits that makes them particularly sensitive to environmental stimuli. Once dismissed by mainstream criminologists, the Gluecks' views, reviewed in Chapter 10's section of life-course theories, still influence contemporary criminological theory.

From an early age, the psychopath's home life is filled with frustrations, bitterness, and quarrelling. Consequently, throughout life, he or she is unreliable, unstable, demanding, and egocentric. Psychopaths are risk-taking sensation seekers who are constantly involved in a variety of antisocial behaviours. They have been described as grandiose, egocentric, manipulative, forceful, and cold-hearted, with shallow emotions and the inability to feel empathy with others, remorse, or anxiety over their misdeeds. They are also able to rationalize their behaviour so that it appears warranted, reasonable, and justified.

Psychopaths are cold-blooded, planning their murders out carefully. Their acts are seldom spontaneous, and the psychopathic killer is more likely than others to use excessive force. The psychopath is at a higher risk of re-offending than the non-psychopath and will benefit the least from anger management. If psychopaths are not classified as dangerous offenders, the public is at serious risk when they are released.

Considering these personality traits, it is not surprising that studies show that psychopaths are significantly more prone to a criminal life and continue their criminal careers long after other offenders burn out or age out of crime. Psychopaths are continually in trouble with the law and therefore are likely to wind up in penal institutions. Some have estimated that up to 30 percent of all inmates can be classified as psychopaths or sociopaths, but a more realistic figure is probably 10 percent; not all psychopaths become criminals, and, conversely, most criminals are not psychopaths.

What Causes Psychopathy? Psychologists think a variety of factors contribute to the development of a psychopathic or sociopathic personality: an unstable parent, parental rejection, lack of love during childhood, and inconsistent discipline. Early childhood experiences seem important. Children who lack the opportunity to form an attachment to a mother figure in the first three years of life, who suffer sudden separation from the mother figure, or who see changes in the mother figure are the children most likely to develop sociopathic personalities. Psychopathy may also be related to personal traits. Children with ADHD are more likely to experience conduct problems in childhood.

Psychopaths may also suffer from lower than normal levels of arousal. If psychopathy is caused by damage to the frontal and temporal lobes, psychopaths may need greater-than-average stimulation to bring them up to comfortable levels (similar to arousal theory). Antisocial individuals are often sensation seekers who desire pleasure, an extroverted lifestyle, drinking, and a variety of sexual partners. The desire for this stimulation may originate in their physical differences.

Psychopaths have a low fear quotient that inhibits their fear of punishment. All people have a natural or innate fear of certain stimuli—spiders, snakes, fires, strangers. Psychopaths fall on the low end of the fearfulness continuum. Because the normal socialization process depends on the current punishment of antisocial behaviour, someone who does not fear punishment is more difficult to socialize.

Psychopaths also have ineffective coping mechanisms for dealing with negative stimuli and are less capable of regulating their activities. When facing the prospect of committing a criminal act, non-psychopaths may become anxious and afraid, whereas psychopaths feel no such fear. These reduced anxiety levels result in impulsive and inappropriate behaviour, apprehension, and incarceration. Psychologists have attempted to treat patients diagnosed as psychopaths by giving them adrenaline, which increases their arousal levels.

---

psychopathy A mental disorder, especially when manifested as antisocial behaviour. The term is often used interchangeably with *sociopathy* and *antisocial personality disorder*.

sociopathy A mental disorder characterized by lack of warmth and affection, inappropriate responses, and an inability to learn from experience. The term is often used interchangeably with *psychopathy* and *antisocial personality disorder*.

antisocial personality Synonymous with psychopathy, the antisocial personality is characterized by a lack of normal responses to life situations, the inability to learn from punishment, and violent reactions to non-threatening events.

Famous Canadian Court Cases
André Dallaire

The tale of André Dallaire's dramatic encounter with former Prime Minister Jean Chrétien began early one November morning in 1995. Aline Chrétien found a knife-wielding intruder in an upstairs hallway at 24 Sussex Drive. After retreating to the bedroom, she locked the door and Chrétien armed himself with a soapstone carving until RCMP officers arrested the trespasser.

The security breach was not only shocking but embarrassing for the Mounties. Dallaire had roamed the government property and its perimeter for more than three hours undetected by security. Although he likened himself to James Bond, this 34-year-old Montreal convenience store clerk's not-so-stealthy tactics included tripping alarms, waving at surveillance cameras, and hurling rocks at windows. Dallaire only paused in his mission

when Aline locked him out of the couple's bedroom, and he laid his knife on the floor and sat down to wait for the RCMP.

Dallaire was charged with break and enter, being unlawfully in a dwelling, possession of a weapon, and attempted murder. The motives of this would-be assassin were initially thought to be political. A sovereignty referendum had been held in Quebec just a week before the incident, and Dallaire had vanished from his home and job two days after the narrow separatist loss. In his statements to police, Dallaire described Chrétien as a traitor to Quebeckers and remarked that he would have acquired hero status for slaying the prime minister. Following a preliminary psychiatric evaluation, Dallaire was deemed fit to stand trial. However, acknowledging the defendant's history of mental health issues, a judge released Dallaire into the care of the Royal Ottawa Hospital while

awaiting trial. He was transferred to a group home when his condition stabilized.

At Dallaire's trial, a psychiatrist testified Dallaire had been in a paranoid schizophrenic state and his obsession with the referendum was delusional. Furthermore, the judge was assured that medication had absolved any threat Dallaire posed. The defendant expressed remorse in court and apologized to the Chrétien family. Although the Crown did not contest Dallaire's diagnosis, the prosecution did argue that a conviction for attempted murder was warranted, because the accused had purchased a knife and explored the crime scene in advance. The judge agreed with the Crown by staying the charge of being unlawfully in a dwelling house and finding Dallaire guilty but not criminally responsible for his actions on the remaining three counts.

Antisocial Personality and Chronic Offending. The antisocial personality concept jibes with what is known about chronic offending. Chronic offending is a continuum of behaviour; at its apex are the most extremely dangerous and predatory criminals. As many as 80 percent of chronic offenders exhibit sociopathic behaviour. Although sociopathic chronic offenders comprise about 4 percent of the male population and less than 1 percent of the female population, they are responsible for half of all the serious felony offences committed annually. Not all high-rate chronic offenders are sociopaths, but enough are to support a strong link between personality dysfunction and long-term criminal careers.

Research on Personality. Because maintaining a deviant personality has been related to crime and delinquency, numerous attempts have been made to devise accurate measures of personality and determine whether they can predict antisocial behaviour. Two types of standardized personality tests have been constructed. The first are projective techniques, such as the Rorschach inkblot test and the Thematic Apperception Test, which require a subject to react to an ambiguous picture or shape by describing what it represents or by telling a story about it. Clinicians interpret the responses and categorize them according to established behavioural patterns. Although these tests were not used extensively, some early research found that delinquents

and non-delinquents could be separated on the basis of their personality profiles.[164]

The second frequently used method of psychological testing is the personality inventory, such as the Minnesota Multiphasic Personality Inventory (MMPI).[165] This test requires subjects to agree or disagree with groups of questions in a self-administered survey. In one study, the MMPI was given to a sample of boys and girls in Grade 9 in Minneapolis; the scores had a significant relationship to later delinquent involvement.[166]

The MMPI and other scales used to predict crime and delinquency have proved inconclusive.[167] The Hare Psychopathy Checklist has also been used for diagnosing psychopathy. Although some law violators may suffer from an abnormal personality structure, many more offenders have personalities that are indistinguishable from the norm. Efforts to improve the MMPI have resulted in a new scale with, it is hoped, improved validity.[168] Interestingly, one problem with attempting to treat psychopaths is that they become better manipulators.

Are Some People Crime-Prone? Interest in the personality characteristics of criminals has been increasing. Because the most commonly used scales have not been very successful in predicting criminality, psychologists have turned to other measures, including the Multidimensional Personality Questionnaire (MPQ), to assess such personality traits as control, aggression, alienation, and well-being. Such scales can show how personality is linked to delinquency, and these measures are valid across genders, races, and cultures.[169] Adolescent offenders who are crime-prone respond to frustrating events with strong negative emotions. They feel stressed and harassed, and are adversarial, experiencing anger, anxiety, and irritability. They also have weak personal constraints and have difficulty controlling impulsive urges. Because they are both impulsive and aggressive, crime-prone people are quick to take action against perceived threats.

In research on the link between stalking and domestic violence, researchers found that both stalkers and abusers possessed traits such as emotional volatility, attachment dysfunction, substance abuse, and early childhood trauma. Other research has found a high correspondence between crime-prone individuals and risk-taking, low self-control, and offending behaviour.[170]

Evidence that personality traits predict crime and violence is important because it suggests that the root cause of crime is found in the forces that influence human development at an early stage of life. For example, Donald Dutton, a psychologist at the University of British Columbia, looked at the psychological profile of uxoricide (wife murder). He found that most perpetrators had traumatic childhoods and current personality disorders. The killing of the wife occurred when she tried to abandon the relationship, and was characterized by extreme violence and disorganized behaviour by the perpetrator. Dutton suggests that because the area of the brain involved in control of aggressive impulses matures during early development, improper attachment during this period may interfere with critical development. The biological impairment of the early trauma experience creates a specific rage response to abandonment and spousal homicide.[171]

If such an approach is valid, then rather than focusing crime control efforts on job creation and neighbourhood improvement, such efforts might be better focused on helping families raise children who are reasoned and reflective and enjoy a safe environment.

Intelligence and Crime

Early criminologists maintained that delinquents and criminals have below-average intelligence, which is a cause of their criminality. They believed criminals to be inherently substandard in intelligence and naturally inclined to commit more crimes than were more intelligent people. It was thought that if authorities could determine which individuals had low IQs, they might identify potential criminals before they could commit socially harmful acts.

Because social scientists had a captive group of subjects in juvenile training schools and penal institutions, they measured the correlation between IQ and crime by testing offenders. These inmates were used as a test group on which

numerous theories about intelligence were built, leading ultimately to the nature versus nurture controversy that continues today.

Canada's Experiment with Eugenics. In the 1920s, acting on the idea that IQ is related to delinquency, several provincial governments passed laws in an attempt to weed out undesirable characteristics, a practice known as negative eugenics. Alberta passed its *Sexual Sterilization Act* and created a Provincial Eugenics Board in 1928. This law was in force until 1972. British Columbia's law existed from 1933 to 1973. Ontario and Quebec only narrowly missed passing such laws under opposition by the Roman Catholic Church.

In 1965, Leilana Muir sued the Alberta government for her involuntary sterilization in 1959 and for falsely using this law to categorize her as a moron. She had been physically abused by her mother and abandoned at the Provincial Training School for Mental Defectives at the age of 11. The government in British Columbia sterilized at least 200 people, and Alberta's government sterilized almost 3,000 people whom they believed had "mental defects." In total, almost 5,000 people with disabilities were approved for sterilization. Female youths underwent tubal ligations or hysterectomies for "menstrual management," while males had vasectomies or were castrated.

The Eugenics Board acted arbitrarily and falsely—who can imagine approving such procedures for children? In 1997, when Muir sued again, she was awarded $750,000 in compensation, but the Alberta government refused to compensate the other victims. Finally, in 1999, it agreed to an $82 million settlement to 247 victims. The belief that mental illness, mental disability, and criminality were inherited was born from poorly constructed evolutionist thinking and has since been discounted.

Nature Theory. Nature theory argues that intelligence is largely determined genetically and that low intelligence as determined by a low IQ score is linked to criminal behaviour. When IQ tests were administered to inmates of prisons and juvenile training schools in the first decades of the 20th century, the nature position gained support because a large proportion of the inmates scored low on the tests. Henry Goddard concluded during his studies in 1920 that many institutionalized persons were "feebleminded" and that at least half of all juvenile delinquents were "mental defectives."[172]

In 1926, Healy and Bronner tested groups of delinquent boys in Chicago and Boston and found 37 percent were below normal, concluding delinquents were five to ten times more likely to have mental deficiencies than were non-delinquent boys.[173] Low IQ scores were seen to indicate potentially delinquent children and to prove a correlation between innate low intelligence and deviant behaviour. Criminologists accepted the idea that individuals with low IQs were predisposed toward delinquency because IQ tests were believed to measure the inborn genetic makeup of individuals.

Nurture Theory. The rise of cultural explanations of human behaviour in the 1930s led to the nurture school of intelligence. Here, intelligence is viewed as primarily sociological. Nurture theorists discredited the notion that persons commit crimes because they have low IQs. Parents with low IQs do not necessarily produce children who have low IQs[174] because environmental stimulation from parents, schools, and peer groups can improve a child's IQ level. Low IQs can also result from an environment that encourages delinquent and criminal behaviour, so low IQ scores among criminals may reflect the criminals' cultural backgrounds, not their mental ability.

Studies challenging the IQ–crime assumption began to appear as early as the 1920s. Slawson studied 1,543 delinquent boys in New York institutions and compared them with a control group.[175] Although 80 percent had lower scores in abstract verbal intelligence, they were normal in mechanical aptitude and nonverbal intelligence. He found no relationship among the number of arrests, the types of offences, and IQ.

In 1931, Edwin Sutherland evaluated IQ studies of criminals and delinquents and noted discrepancies in testing methods rather than differences in mental ability.[176] Sutherland's research all but put an end to the belief that crime is caused by low intelligence, and the IQ–crime link was all but forgotten in the criminological literature.

Rediscovering IQ and Criminality. Although the IQ–crime link had been dismissed by mainstream criminologists, it became an important area of study once again when Hirschi and Hindelang reexamined existing data and concluded that "the weight of evidence is that IQ is more important than race and social class" for predicting criminal and delinquent involvement.[177] Rejecting the notion that IQ tests are race- and class-biased, they concluded that major differences exist between criminals and non-criminals within similar racial and socio-economic class categories. Low IQ increases the likelihood of criminal behaviour through its effect on school performance because youths with low IQs do poorly in school, and school failure is highly related to delinquency and later to adult criminality.

Research conducted by international scholars[178] has found a direct IQ–delinquency link among samples of adolescent boys.[179] When Alex Piquero examined violent behaviour among groups of children in Philadelphia, he found that scores on intelligence tests were the best predictors of violent behaviour and could be used to distinguish between groups of violent and non-violent offenders.[180]

Other research supports these conclusions.[181] In *Crime and Human Nature*, James Q. Wilson said low intelligence leads to poor school performance, which enhances the chances of criminality.[182]

Although an evaluation of existing knowledge conducted by the American Psychological Association concluded that the strength of an IQ–crime link is "very low,"[183] in contrast, *The Bell Curve* comes down firmly on the side of an IQ–crime link, showing that people with low IQs are more likely to commit crime, get caught, and be sent to prison. Conversely, at-risk kids with higher IQs seem to be protected from becoming criminals. The authors conclude that criminal offenders have an average IQ of 92, about 8 points below the mean; chronic offenders score even lower than the "average" criminal. And it is not only low-IQ criminals who get caught; data show little difference in IQ scores between self-reported and official criminals.[184]

This debate will not be settled soon. Measurement is beset by many methodological problems. The criticism that IQ tests are race- and class-biased would certainly influence the testing of the criminal population, who are inundated with a multitude of socio-economic problems. Even if known offenders have lower IQs than does the general population, it is difficult to explain many patterns in the crime rate: Why are males more criminal than females? Why do crime rates vary by region, time of year, and even weather patterns? Why does aging out occur? IQ does not increase with age— why should crime rates fall with age? Such an approach has critical theoretical problems as well: Various issues that are ignored include the role of the police in enforcing the law, their use of discretion, and the ability of the law to reinforce social inequality. These issues are discussed in Chapter 9, "Social Conflict Theory."

SOCIAL POLICY IMPLICATIONS

For most of the 19th, 20th, and early 21st centuries, biological and psychological views of criminality have had an important influence on crime control and prevention policy. These views can be seen in primary prevention programs that treat personal problems before they manifest themselves as crime: family therapy organizations, substance abuse clinics, and mental health associations. Referrals to these resources are made by teachers, employers, courts, and social service agencies. If a person's problems can be treated before they become overwhelming, then future crimes might be prevented. Secondary prevention programs provide psychological counselling to youths and adults after they have violated the law. Attendance in such programs may be a mandatory requirement of a probation order, part of a diversionary sentence, or aftercare at the end of a prison sentence.

Comparative research shows that therapeutic and preventive treatment works. However, people with mental disorders continue to be incarcerated in correctional institutions. Yet prisons are not being used to warehouse offenders with mental disorders. The long-term trend in Canada has been to deinstitutionalize people who have mental illnesses,

© Schaefer Elvira/Shutterstock

Is it nature or nurture? Even if some aspects of intelligence are inherited, if children are raised in an environment that lacks economic resources and parental support, they will fail to maximize their intellectual potential. The mother pictured here is on social assistance, but attending university to better support herself and her child. Is it the responsibility of society to provide resources sufficient to enable all youth to achieve their rightful share of intellectual development?

to increase the use of medication, and to treat them in community clinics. The Supreme Court itself has reviewed how the better use of conditional sentencing can make healthcare a better solution than incarceration.[185]

CONNECTIONS

The law recognizes the psychological aspects of crime when it permits a plea of not criminally responsible on account of mental disorder (NCRMD) as an excuse for criminal liability or when it allows trial delay because of mental incompetence. See Chapter 2 for more about the NCRMD defence.

Biologically oriented therapy is also being used in the criminal justice system. Programs have altered diet, changed

lighting, compensated for learning disabilities, treated allergies, and so on.[186] More controversial has been the use of mood-altering chemicals, such as lithium and benzodiazepines, or the use of brain surgery, to control the behaviour of antisocial individuals.[187]

Some criminologists view biologically oriented treatments as a key to solving the problem of the chronic offender. They argue that inherited physical traits that cause disease have been successfully treated with medication after their genetic code has been broken; why not, then, a genetic solution to crime?[188]

Whereas such biological treatment is a relatively new phenomenon, it has become commonplace since the 1920s to offer psychological treatment to offenders before, during, and after a criminal conviction. For example, since the 1970s, pretrial programs have sought to divert offenders into non-punitive rehabilitative programs designed to treat rather than to punish. Based on some type of counselling regime, diversion programs are commonly used with first offenders and non-violent offenders. At the trial stage, judges often order psychological profiles of convicted offenders so that a treatment program can be planned. Should offenders be kept in the community? Do they need a more secure confinement to deal with their problems? If correctional confinement is called for, inmates are commonly evaluated at a correctional centre to measure their personality traits or disorders. Correctional facilities almost universally require inmates to participate in some form of psychological therapy, such as group therapy, individual analysis, or transactional analysis. Parole decisions may be influenced by the prison psychologist's evaluation of the offender's adjustment.

SUMMARY

The earliest positivist criminologists were biologists. Led by Cesare Lombroso, these early researchers believed that some people manifested primitive traits that made them born criminals. Biological views fell out of favour in the early 20th century, but in the 1970s, criminologists again turned to the study of the biological basis of criminality. For the most part, the effort has focused on the causes of violent crime.

Interest has been revived in several areas: (1) biochemical factors, such as diet, allergies, hormonal imbalances, and environmental contaminants (such as lead); (2) neurophysiological factors, such as brain disorders, EEG abnormalities, tumours, and head injuries; and (3) genetic factors, such as XYY syndrome and inherited traits. An evolutionary perspective holds that changes in the human condition that have taken thousands of years to evolve may help explain crime rate differences.

Biological and Psychological Theories

Theory	Major Premise	Strengths
Biological		
Biochemical	Crime, especially violence, is a function of diet, vitamin intake, hormonal imbalance, or food allergies.	Explains irrational violence. Shows how the environment interacts with personal traits to influence behaviour.
Neurological	Criminals and delinquents often suffer brain impairment, as measured by the EEG. Attention deficit hyperactivity disorder (ADHD) and minimum brain dysfunction are related to antisocial behaviour.	Explains irrational violence by pinpointing the medical and physiological basis for behaviour.
Genetic	Criminal traits and predispositions are inherited. The criminality of parents can predict the delinquency of children.	Explains why only a small percentage of youth in a high-crime area become chronic offenders.
Evolutionary	As the human race evolved, traits and characteristics became ingrained. Some of these traits make people aggressive and predisposed to commit crime.	Explains high violence rates and aggregate gender differences in the crime rate.
Psychological		
Psychodynamic	The development of the unconscious personality early in childhood influences behaviour for the rest of a person's life. Criminals have weak egos and damaged personalities.	Explains the onset of crime and why crime and drug abuse cut across class lines.
Behavioural	People commit crime when they model their behaviour after others they see being rewarded for the same acts. Behaviour is reinforced by rewards and extinguished by punishment.	Explains the role of significant others in the crime process. Shows how family life and media can influence crime and violence.
Cognitive	Individual reasoning processes influence behaviour. Reasoning is influenced by the way people perceive their environment and by their moral and intellectual development.	Shows why criminal behaviour patterns change over time as people mature and develop their moral reasoning. May explain the aging-out process.

Concept Summary 6.3 reviews the biological and psychological theories of criminal behaviour.

Psychological attempts to explain criminal behaviour no longer suggest that all criminals are insane or have mental damage. Today, there are three main psychological perspectives. The psychodynamic theorists say that aggressive behaviour is linked to personality conflicts developed in childhood. However, behavioural and social learning theorists believe criminality is a learned behaviour: Children who are exposed to violence and see it rewarded may become violent as adults.

In contrast, cognitive psychologists are concerned with human development and how people perceive the world. They see criminality as a function of improper information processing or moral development.

Psychological traits, such as personality and intelligence, have been linked to criminality, for example, to the psychopath, a person who lacks emotion and concern for others. The controversial issue of the relationship of IQ to criminality has been resurrected once again with the publication of studies purporting to show that criminals have lower IQs than do noncriminals. Psychologists have developed standardized tests with which to measure personality traits. One avenue of research has been to determine whether criminals and non-criminals manifest any differences in their responses to test items.

THINKING LIKE A CRIMINOLOGIST

In our culture, we believe that people should not be blamed for actions that are beyond their control. We think that a person cannot be legally responsible if he or she cannot meet certain tests. An obvious test of competence is cognitive; that is, whether the offender had criminal intent. Thus, the M'Naghten rule (1843) says that every person is to be presumed to be sane and that to establish a defence of not criminally responsible on account of mental disorder, it must be proved that, at the time of committing the act, the accused was suffering from a disease of the mind that meant he or she did not know the nature of the act being committed; or, if he or she did know the nature of the act, he or she had no knowledge that it was wrong. Used in this way, the definition seems overly restrictive and psychiatric. As a criminologist with expertise of trait theories of crime, do you think this description goes far enough in explaining aberrant behaviour?

KEY TERMS

androgens p. 167
antisocial personality p. 186
arousal theory p. 174
attention deficit hyperactivity disorder
   (ADHD) p. 172
behaviour modelling p. 181
behaviour theory p. 181
cognitive school (perspective) p. 182
electroencephalograph (EEG) p. 171
equipotentiality p. 166
hypoglycemia p. 167
identity crisis p. 180

inferiority complex p. 180
instincts p. 166
latent delinquency p. 180
minimal brain dysfunction (MBD)
   p. 172
neurophysiology p. 171
neurosis p. 179
personality p. 185
premenstrual syndrome (PMS)
   p. 170
psychodynamic (psychoanalytic)
   theory p. 178

psychopathy p. 186
psychosis p. 179
r/K theory p. 176
repression p. 178
schizophrenia p. 179
social learning theory p. 178
sociobiology p. 164
sociopathy p. 186
somatype p. 164
testosterone p. 167
trait theories p. 163

DOING RESEARCH ON THE WEB

You can read the report by Robert J. Sampson
and Stephen W. Raudenbush, "Disorder in Urban
Neighborhoods: Does It Lead to Crime?" at the National
Institute of Justice website: www.ncjrs.gov/txtfiles1/
nij/186049.txt.

To read another report linking collective efficacy to
violence, go to www.psc.isr.umich.edu/pubs/papers/
rr00-451.pdf.

CRITICAL THINKING QUESTIONS

1. What should be done with the young children of violence-prone criminals if, in fact, research could show that the tendency to commit crime is inherited?
2. After considering the existing research on the subject, would you recommend that young children be forbidden from eating foods that have a high sugar content?

3. Knowing what you do about trends and patterns in crime, how would you counteract the assertion that people who commit crime have a physical or mental abnormality? For example, how would you explain the fact that crime is more likely to occur in Western and urban areas than in Eastern or rural areas?

4. Aside from becoming a criminal, what other career paths are open to psychopaths?
5. Research shows that kids who watch a lot of TV in adolescence are more likely to behave aggressively in adulthood. This result has led some to conclude that TV watching is responsible for adult violence. Can this relationship be explained in another way?

NOTES

1. "Guilty Plea From Man Who Allegedly Planned Shooting Spree Rejected," Canadian Press, August 20, 2004; "Dog Ends Gunman's Plan for Shooting Rampage," *The Globe and Mail*, June 24, 2004; "Man Who Wanted to Kill Torontonians Ordered to Undergo Psychiatric Testing," Canadian Press, June 25, 2004; "Poor Health and a Messy Life Produced Mass-Murder Plot," *The Globe and Mail*, June 25, 2004.
2. Dalton Conley and Neil Bennett, "Is Biology Destiny? Birth Weight and Life Chances," *American Sociological Review* 654 (2000): 458–467.
3. For an example of research on the connection between road rage and trait theory, see Eric R. Dahlen, Ryan C. Martin, Katie Ragan, and Myndi M. Kuhlman "Driving Anger, Sensation Seeking, Impulsiveness, and Boredom Proneness in the Prediction of Unsafe Driving," *Accident Analysis & Prevention* 37, 2 (2005): 341–348.
4. Israel Nachshon, "Neurological Bases of Crime, Psychopathy and Aggression," in *Crime in Biological, Social and Moral*

Contexts, eds. Lee Ellis and Harry Hoffman (New York: Praeger, 1990).

5. Raffaele Garofalo, *Criminology*, trans. Robert Miller (Boston: Little, Brown, 1914), 92.

6. Enrico Ferri, *Criminal Sociology* (New York: D. Appleton, 1909).

7. Richard Dugdale, *The Jukes: A Study in Crime, Pauperism, Disease, and Heredity* (New York: Putnam, 1910); Arthur Estabrook, *The Jukes in 1915* (Washington, DC: Carnegie Institute of Washington, 1916).

8. William Sheldon, *Varieties of Delinquent Youth* (New York: Harper Bros., 1949); William Sheldon, *Atlas of Men: A Guide for Somatyping the Adult Male at All Ages* (New York: Harper and Row, 1954).

9. Nicole Rafter, "Somatyping, Antimodernism, and the Production of Criminological Knowledge," *Criminology* 45, 4 (2007): 805–833.

10. Lee Ellis, "A Discipline in Peril: Sociology's Future Hinges on Curing Biophobia," *American Sociologist* 27 (1996): 21–41.

11. Pierre van den Bergle, "Bringing the Beast Back In: Toward a Biosocial Theory of Aggression," *American Sociological Review* 39 (1974): 779.

12. Edmund O. Wilson, *Sociobiology* (Cambridge: Harvard University Press, 1975).

13. Margo Wilson and Martin Daly, "Competitiveness, Risk-taking and Violence: The Young Male Syndrome," *Ethology and Sociobiology*, 1985, 6: 59–73.

14. Anthony Walsh, "Behavior Genetics and Anomie/Strain Theory," *Criminology* 38 (2000): 1075–1108.

15. See, generally, Lee Ellis, "Introduction: The Nature of the Biosocial Perspective," *Crime in Biological, Social and Moral Contexts*, 3–18 (New York: Praeger, 1990).

16. See, for example, Tracy Bennett Herbert and Sheldon Cohen, "Depression and Immunity: A Meta-Analytic Review," *Psychological Bulletin* 113 (1993): 472–486.

17. See, generally, Lee Ellis, *Theories of Rape* (New York: Hemisphere Publications, 1989).

18. Leonard Hippchen, "Some Possible Biochemical Aspects of Criminal Behavior," *Journal of Behavioral Ecology* 2 (1981): 1–6; Sarnoff Mednick and Jan Volavka, "Biology and Crime," in *Crime and Justice*, eds. Norval Morris and Michael Tonry, 85–159 (Chicago: University of Chicago Press, 1980); Saleem Shah and Loren Roth, "Biological and Psychophysiological Factors in Criminality," in *Handbook of Criminology*, ed. Daniel Glazer, 125–140 (Chicago: Rand McNally, 1974).

19. Ulric Neisser et al., "Intelligence: Knowns and Unknowns," *American Psychologist* 51 (1996): 77–101.

20. Leonard Hippchen, ed., Ecologic-Biochemical Approaches to Treatment of Delinquents and Criminals (New York: Von Nostrand Reinhold, 1978), 14.

21. Valerie Tarasuk, Naomi Dachner, and Jinguang Li, "Homeless Youth in Toronto Are Nutritionally Vulnerable," *The American Society for Nutritional Sciences Journal of Nutrition* 135 (2005): 1926–1933.

22. Bonnie J. Kaplan, Jennifer E. Fisher, Susan G. Crawford, Catherine J. Field, Bryan Kolb, "Improved Mood and Behavior During Treatment with a Mineral-Vitamin Supplement: An Open-Label Case Series of Children," *Journal of Child and Adolescent Psychopharmacology* 14, 1 (2001): 115–122.

23. J. Kershner and W. Hawke, "Megavitamins and Learning Disorders: A Controlled Double-Blind Experiment," *Journal of Nutrition* 109 (1979): 819–826.

24. Richard Knox, "Test Shows Smart People's Brains Use Nutrients Better," *Boston Globe*, February 16, 1988, 9; Ronald Prinz and David Riddle, "Associations between Nutrition and Behavior in 5-Year-Old Children," *Nutrition Reviews Supplement* 44 (1986): 151–158.

25. Stephen Schoenthaler and Walter Doraz, "Types of Offenses Which Can Be Reduced in an Institutional Setting Using Nutritional Intervention," *International Journal of Biosocial Research* 4 (1983): 74–84; Stephen Schoenthaler and Walter Doraz, "Diet and Crime," *International Journal of Biosocial Research* 4 (1983): 85–94. See also A. Schauss and C. Simonsen, "A Critical Analysis of the Diets of Chronic Juvenile Offenders, Part I," *Journal of Orthomolecular Psychiatry* 8 (1979): 222–226; A. Hoffer, "Children with Learning and Behavioral Disorders," *Journal of Orthomolecular Psychiatry* 5 (1976): 229.

26. H. Bruce Ferguson, Clare Stoddart, and Jovan Simeon, "Double-Blind Challenge Studies of Behavioral and Cognitive Effects of Sucrose-Aspartame Ingestion in Normal Children," *Nutrition Reviews Supplement* 44 (1986): 144–158; Gregory Gray, "Diet, Crime and Delinquency: A Critique," *Nutrition Reviews Supplement* 44 (1986): 89–94.

27. Mark Wolraich, Scott Lindgren, Phyllis Stumbo, Lewis Stegink, Mark Appelbaum, and Mary Kiritsy, "Effects of Diets High in Sucrose or Aspartame on the Behavior and Cognitive Performance of Children," *The New England Journal of Medicine* 330 (1994): 303–306.

28. Dian Gans, "Sucrose and Unusual Childhood Behavior," *Nutrition Today* 26 (1991): 8–14.

29. Diana Fishbein, "Neuropsychological Function, Drug Abuse, and Violence, a Conceptual Framework," *Criminal Justice and Behavior* 27 (2000): 139–159.

30. D. Hill and W. Sargent, "A Case of Matricide," *Lancet* 244 (1943): 526–527; E. Podolsky, "The Chemistry of Murder," *Pakistan Medical Journal* 15 (1964): 9–14.

31. J.A. Yaryura-Tobias and F. Neziroglu, "Violent Behavior, Brain Dysrhythmia and Glucose Dysfunction: A New Syndrome," *Journal of Orthopsychiatry* 4 (1975): 182–188; Matti Virkkunen, "Reactive Hypoglycemic Tendency among Habitually Violent Offenders," *Nutrition Reviews Supplement* 44 (1986): 94–103.

32. James Q. Wilson, *The Moral Sense* (New York: Free Press, 1993).

33. Walter Gove, "The Effect of Age and Gender on Deviant Behavior: A Biopsychosocial Perspective," in *Gender and the Life Course*, ed. A.S. Rossi, 115–144 (New York: Aldine, 1985).

34. Alan Booth and D. Wayne Osgood, "The Influence of Testosterone on Deviance in Adulthood: Assessing and Explaining the Relationship," *Criminology* 31 (1993): 93–118.

35. Christy Miller Buchanan, Jacquelynne Eccles, and Jill Becker, "Are Adolescents the Victims of Raging Hormones? Evidence for Activational Effects of Hormones on Moods and Behavior at Adolescence," *Psychological Bulletin* 111 (1992): 62–107.

36. Alex Piquero and Timothy Brezina, "Testing Moffitt's Account of Adolescent-Limited Delinquency," *Criminology* 39 (2001): 353–370.

37. Loren E. McMaster, Jennifer Connolly, Debra Pepler, and Wendy M. Craig, "Peer to Peer Sexual Harassment in Early Adolescence: A Developmental Perspective," *Development and Psychopathology* 14 (2002): 91–105.

38. Albert Reiss and Jeffrey Roth, eds., *Understanding and Preventing Violence* (Washington, D.C.: National Academy Press, 1993), 118. This report by the National Research Council Panel on the Understanding and Control of Violent Behavior is hereafter cited as *Understanding Violence*.

39. L.E. Kreuz and R.M. Rose, "Assessment of Aggressive Behavior and Plasma Testosterone in a Young Criminal Population," *Psychosomatic Medicine* 34 (1972): 321–332.

40. Anne McIlroy, "Must Men Fight? Probably," *The Globe and Mail*, January 27, 2001.

41. Angela S. Book, Katherine B. Starzyk, and Vernon L. Quinsey, "The Relationship between Testosterone and Aggression: A Meta-Analysis," *Aggression and Violent Behaviour* 6 (2001): 579–599.

42. Lee Ellis, "Evolutionary and Neurochemical Causes of Sex Differences in Victimizing Behavior: Toward a Unified Theory of Criminal Behavior and Social Stratification," *Social Science Information* 28 (1989): 605–636.

43. For a general review, see Lee Ellis and Phyllis Coontz, "Androgens, Brain Functioning, and Criminality: The Neurohormonal Foundations of Antisociality," in *Crime in Biological, Social and Moral Contexts*, eds. Lee Ellis and Harry Hoffman, 162–193 (New York: Praeger, 1990). Also see Robert Rubin, "The Neuroendocrinology and Neurochemistry of Antisocial Behavior," in *The Causes of Crime, New Biological Appoaches*, eds. Sarnoff Mednick, Terrie Moffitt, and Susan Stack, 239–262 (Cambridge: Cambridge University Press, 1987).

44. J. Money, "Influence of Hormones on Psychosexual Differentiation," *Medical Aspects of Nutrition* 30 (1976): 165.

45. Sonia J. Lupien, Suzanne Kinga, Michael J. Meaneya, and Bruce S. McEwen, "Child's Stress Hormone Levels Correlate with Mother's Socioeconomic Status and Depressive State," *Biological Psychiatry* 48, 10 (2000): 976–980.

46. Kathleen Pajer, William Gardner, Robert T. Rubin, James Perel, Stephen Neal, "Decreased Cortisol Levels in Adolescent Girls with Conduct Disorder," *Archives of General Psychiatry* 58 (2001): 297–302.

47. For a review of this concept, see Anne E. Figert, "The Three Faces of PMS: The Professional, Gendered, and Scientific Structuring of a Psychiatric Disorder," *Social Problems* 42 (1995): 56–72.

48. Katharina Dalton, *The Premenstrual Syndrome* (Springfield, IL: Charles C. Thomas, 1971).

49. Julie Horney, "Menstrual Cycles and Criminal Responsibility," *Law and Human Nature* 2 (1978): 25–36.

50. Diana Fishbein, "Selected Studies on the Biology of Antisocial Behavior," in *New Perspectives in Criminology*, ed. John Conklin (Needham Heights, MA: Allyn & Bacon, 1996), 26–38.

51. Daniel J. Curran and Claire M. Renzetti, *Theories of Crime* (Boston: Allyn and Bacon, 1994); "Woman's Syndrome Brings Leniency," *Vancouver Sun*, February 10, 1987; "Should PMS Be a Woman's All-Purpose Excuse?" *London Times*, November 12, 1981, 12. See also J.C. Chisler and K.B. Levy, "The Media Construct a Menstrual Monster: A Content Analysis of PMS Articles in the Popular Press," *Women and Health* (1990): 89–104.

52. Fishbein, "Selected Studies on the Biology of Antisocial Behavior"; Karen Paige, "Effects of Oral Contraceptives on Affective Fluctuations Associated with the Menstrual Cycle," *Psychosomatic Medicine* 33 (1971): 515–537.

53. H.E. Amos and J.J.P. Drake, "Problems Posed by Food Additives," *Journal of Human Nutrition* 30 (1976): 165.

54. Ray Wunderlich, "Neuroallergy as a Contributing Factor to Social Misfits: Diagnosis and Treatment," in *Ecologic-Biochemical Approaches to Treatment of Delinquents and Criminals* (New York: Van Nostrand Reinhold, 1978), 229–253; Paul Marshall, "Allergy and Depression: A Neurochemical Threshold Model of the Relation Between the Illnesses," *Psychological Bulletin* 113 (1993): 23–39.

55. A.R. Mawson and K.J. Jacobs, "Corn Consumption, Tryptophan, and Cross-National Homicide Rates," *Journal of Orthomolecular Psychiatry* 7 (1978): 227–230.

56. Alexander Schauss, *Diet, Crime and Delinquency* (Berkeley, CA: Parker House, 1980).

57. C. Hawley and R.E. Buckley, "Food Dyes and Hyperkinetic Children," *Academy Therapy* 10 (1974): 27–32.

58. John Ott, "The Effects of Light and Radiation on Human Health and Behavior," in *Ecologic-Biochemical Approaches to Treatment of Delinquents and Criminals* (New York: Van Nostrand Reinhold, 1978), 105–183. See also A. Kreuger and S. Sigel, "Ions in the Air," *Human Nature* (July 1978): 46–47; Harry Wohlfarth, "The Effect of Color Psychodynamic Environmental Modification on Discipline Incidents in Elementary Schools over One School Year: A Controlled Study," *International Journal of Biosocial Research* 6 (1984): 44–53.

59. Paul Stretesky and Michael Lynch, "The Relationship between Lead Exposure and Homicide," *Archives of Pediatric Adolescent Medicine* 155 (2001): 579–582.

60. Oliver David, Stanley Hoffman, Jeffrey Sverd, Julian Clark, and Kytja Voeller, "Lead and Hyperactivity, Behavior Response to Chelation: A Pilot Study," *American Journal of Psychiatry* 133 (1976): 1155–1158.

61. Deborah Denno, "Considering Lead Poisoning as a Criminal Defense," *Fordham Urban Law Journal* 20 (1993): 377–400; Herbert Needleman, Julie Riess, Michael Tobin, Gretchen Biesecker, and Joel Greenhouse, "Bone Lead Levels and Delinquent Behavior," *Journal of the American Medical Association* 275 (1996): 363–369.

62. Ulric Neisser et al., "Intelligence: Knowns and Unknowns," *American Psychologist* 51 (1996): 77–101.

63. Terrie Moffitt, "The Neuropsychology of Juvenile Delinquency: A Critical Review," in *Crime and Justice: An Annual Review*, vol. 12, eds. Norval Morris and Michael Tonry, 99–169 (Chicago: University of Chicago Press, 1990); Terrie Moffitt, Donald Lyman, and Phil Silva, "Neuropsychological Tests Predicting Persistent Male Delinquency," *Criminology* 32 (1994): 277–300; Elizabeth Kandel and Sarnoff Mednick, "Perinatal Complications Predict Violent Offending," *Criminology* 29 (1991): 519–529; Sarnoff

Mednick, Ricardo Machon, Matti Virkkunen, and Douglas Bonett, "Adult Schizophrenia Following Prenatal Exposure to an Influenza Epidemic," *Archives of General Psychiatry* 44 (1987): 35–46; C.A. Fogel, S.A. Mednick, and N. Michelson, "Hyperactive Behavior and Minor Physical Anomalies," *Acta Psychiatrica Scandinavia* 72 (1985): 551–556.

64. R. Johnson, *Aggression in Man and Animals* (Philadelphia: Saunders, 1972), 79.

65. Jean Seguin, Robert Pihl, Philip Harden, Richard Tremblay, and Bernard Boulerice, "Cognitive and Neuropsychological Characteristics of Physically Aggressive Boys," *Journal of Abnormal Psychology* 104 (1995): 614–624; Deborah Denno, "Gender, Crime and the Criminal Law Defenses," *Journal of Criminal Law and Criminology* 85 (1994): 80–180.

66. Deborah Denno, *Biology, Crime and Violence: New Evidence* (Cambridge: Cambridge University Press, 1989).

67. Diana Fishbein and Robert Thatcher, "New Diagnostic Methods in Criminology: Assessing Organic Sources of Behavioral Disorders," *Journal of Research in Crime and Delinquency* 23 (1986): 240–267.

68. See, generally, David Rowe, *Biology and Crime* (Los Angeles: Roxbury Press, 2001).

69. Lorne Yeudall, "A Neuropsychosocial Perspective of Persistent Juvenile Delinquency and Criminal Behavior," *Annals of the New York Academy of Sciences*, 347 (1980): 349–355.

70. R.W. Aind and T. Yamamoto, "Behavior Disorders of Childhood," *Electroencephalography and Clinical Neurophysiology* 21 (1966): 148–156.

71. Z.A. Zayed, S.A. Lewis, and R.P. Britain, "An Encephalographic and Psychiatric Study of 32 Insane Murderers," *British Journal of Psychiatry* 115 (1969): 1115–1124.

72. Gideon Koren, Irena Nulman, Albert E. Chudley, and Christine Loocke, "Fetal Alcohol Spectrum Disorder," *Canadian Medical Association Journal* 11 (2003): 169–180; David Milne, "MDs Urged to Pursue Alcohol Screening of Pregnant Patients," *Journal of the American Medical Association* 3 (2003): 168–174.

73. L.N. Chartrand, and E.M. Forbes-Chilibeck, "The Sentencing of Offenders with Fetal Alcohol Syndrome," *Health Law Journal*, 2004.

74. Erika Y. Rojas, and Heather M. Gretton, "Background, Offence Characteristics, and Criminal Outcomes of Aboriginal Youth Who Sexually Offend: A Closer Look at Aboriginal Youth Intervention Needs," *Journal Sexual Abuse: A Journal of Research and Treatment*, 19, 3 (2007): 257–283.

75. D.R. Robin, R.M. Starles, T.J. Kenney, B.J. Reynolds, and F.P. Heald, "Adolescents Who Attempt Suicide," *Journal of Pediatrics*

90 (1977): 636–638; R.R. Monroe, *Brain Dysfunction in Aggressive Criminals* (Lexington, MA: D.C. Heath, 1978).

76. L.T. Yeudall, *Childhood Experiences as Causes of Criminal Behavior* (Ottawa: Senate of Canada, 1977).

77. Stephen Faraone et al., "Intellectual Performance and School Failure in Children with Attention Deficit Hyperactivity Disorder and in Their Siblings," *Journal of Abnormal Psychology* 102 (1993): 616–623.

78. Terrie Moffitt and Phil Silva, "Self-Reported Delinquency, Neuropsychological Deficit, and History of Attention Deficit Disorder," *Journal of Abnormal Child Psychology* 16 (1988): 553–569.

79. Eugene Maguin, Rolf Loeber, and Paul LeMahieu, "Does the Relationship between Poor Reading and Delinquency Hold for Males of Different Ages and Ethnic Groups?" *Journal of Emotional and Behavioral Disorders* 1 (1993): 88–100.

80. Elizabeth Hart et al., "Developmental Change in Attention-Deficit Hyperactivity Disorder in Boys: A Four-Year Longitudinal Study," *Journal of Consulting and Clinical Psychology* 62 (1994): 472–491.

81. Margaret Weiss and Candice Murray, "Assessment and Management of Attention-Deficit Hyperactivity Disorder," *Canadian Medical Association Journal* 3 (2003): 168–174.

82. Lorne Yeudall, "A Neuropsychosocial Perspective of Persistent Juvenile Delinquency and Criminal Behavior," Annals of the New York Academy of Sciences, 1980; F.A. Elliott, "Neurological Aspects of Antisocial Behavior," in *The Psychopath: A Comprehensive Study of Antisocial Disorders and Behaviors*, ed. W.H. Reid, 146–189 (New York: Brunner/Mazel, 1978).

83. Lorne Yeudall, Orestes Fedora, and Delee Fromm, "A Neuropsychosocial Theory of Persistent Criminality: Implications for Assessment and Treatment," in *Advances in Forensic Psychology and Psychiatry*, ed. Robert Rieber, 119–191 (Norwood, NJ: Ablex Publishing, 1987).

84. Donald D. Dutton, "The Neurobiology of Abandonment Homicide," *Aggression and Violent Behavior* 2 (2002): 407–421.

85. H.K. Kletschka, "Violent Behavior Associated with Brain Tumor," *Minnesota Medicine* 49 (1966): 1853–1855.

86. V.E. Krynicki, "Cerebral Dysfunction in Repetitively Assaultive Adolescents," *Journal of Nervous and Mental Disease* 166 (1978): 59–67.

87. C.E. Lyght, ed., *The Merck Manual of Diagnosis and Therapy* (West Point, FL: Merck, 1966).

88. "Obstetrical Complications and Violent Delinquency: Testing Two Developmental Pathways," *Child Development* 73, 2 (2002): 496–509.

89. M. Virkkunen, M.J. DeJong, J. Bartko, and M. Linnoila, "Psychobiological Concomitants of History of Suicide Attempts among Violent Offenders and Impulsive Fire Starters," *Archives of General Psychiatry* 46 (1989): 604–606; Matti Virkkunen, David Goldman, and Markku Linnoila, "Serotonin in Alcoholic Violent Offenders," *The Ciba Foundation Symposium, Genetics of Criminal and Antisocial Behavior* (Chichester, England: Wiley, 1995).

90. E. Jane Garland, "Facing the Evidence: Antidepressant Treatment in Children and Adolescents," *Canadian Medical Association Journal* 2 (2004): 170–174.

91. Lee Ellis, "Left- and Mixed-Handedness and Criminality: Explanations for a Probable Relationship," in *Left-Handedness: Behavioral Implications and Anomalies*, ed. S. Coren, 485–507 (Amsterdam: Elsevier, 1990).

92. Lee Ellis, "Monoamine Oxidase and Criminality: Identifying an Apparent Biological Marker for Antisocial Behavior," *Journal of Research in Crime and Delinquency* 28 (1991): 227–251.

93. "Gene Linked to Abused Children Who Become Violent," Associated Press, August 2, 2002; Erik Stokstad, "Violent Effects of Abuse Tied to Gene," *Science* 297, 5582 (2002): 752; A. Caspi et al., "Role of Genotype in the Cycle of Violence in Maltreated Children," *Science* 297, 5582 (2002): 851–854.

94. Walter Gove and Charles Wilmoth, "Risk, Crime and Neurophysiologic Highs: A Consideration of Brain Processes That May Reinforce Delinquent and Criminal Behavior," in *Crime in Biological, Social and Moral Contexts*, eds. Lee Ellis and Harry Hoffman, 261–293 (New York: Praeger, 1990).

95. Jack Katz, *Seduction of Crime: Moral and Sensual Attractions of Doing Evil* (New York: Basic Books, 1988), 12–15.

96. Lee Ellis, "Arousal Theory and the Religiosity–Criminality Relationship," in *Contemporary Criminological Theory*, eds. Peter Cordella and Larry Siegel, 65–84 (Boston, MA: Northeastern University, 1996).

97. For a general view, see Richard Lerner and Terryl Foch, *Biological-Psychosocial Interactions in Early Adolescence* (Hilldale, NJ: Lawrence Erlbaum Associates, 1987); Kerry Jang, W. John Livesley, and Philip Vernon, "Heritability of the Big Five Personality Dimensions and Their Facets: A Twin Study," *Journal of Personality* 64 (1996): 577–589.

98. David Rowe, "As the Twig Is Bent: The Myth of Child-Rearing Influences on Personality Development," *Journal of Counseling and Development* 68 (1990): 606–611; David Rowe, Joseph Rogers, and Sylvia Meseck-Bushey, "Sibling Delinquency and the Family Environment: Shared and Unshared Influences," *Child Development* 63 (1992): 59–67; Patricia Brennan, Sarnoff Mednick, and Bjorn Jacobsen, "Assessing the Role of Genetics in Crime Using Adoption Cohorts," *Genetics of Criminal and Antisocial Behavior*, 115–128; Gregory Carey and David DiLalla, "Personality and Psychopathology: Genetic Perspectives," *Journal of Abnormal Psychology* 103 (1994): 32–43.

99. T.R. Sarbin and L.E. Miller, "Demonism Revisited: The XYY Chromosome Anomaly," *Issues in Criminology* 5 (1970): 195–207.

100. See Sarnoff A. Mednick and Karl O. Christiansen, eds., *Biosocial Bases in Criminal Behavior* (New York: Gardner Press, 1977); David Rowe, "Genetic and Environmental Components of Antisocial Behavior: A Study of 265 Twin Pairs," *Criminology* 24 (1986): 513–532; David Rowe and D. Wayne Osgood, "Heredity and Sociological Theories of Delinquency: A Reconsideration," *American Sociological Review* 49 (1984): 526–540.

101. Edwin J.C.G. van den Oord, Frank Verhulst, and Dorret Boomsma, "A Genetic Study of Maternal and Paternal Ratings of Problem Behaviors in 3-Year-Old Twins," *Journal of Abnormal Psychology* 105 (1996): 349–357.

102. Michael Lyons, "A Twin Study of Self-Reported Criminal Behavior"; Judy Silberg, Joanne Meyer, Andrew Pickles, Emily Simonoff, Lindon Eaves, John Hewitt, Hermine Maes, and Michael Rutter, "Heterogeneity among Juvenile Antisocial Behaviors: Findings from the Virginia Twin Study of Adolescent Behavioral Development," in *The Ciba Foundation Symposium, Genetics of Criminal and Antisocial Behavior* (Chichester, England: Wiley, 1995).

103. Gregory Carey, "Twin Imitation for Antisocial Behavior: Implications for Genetic and Family Environment Research," *Journal of Abnormal Psychology* 101 (1992): 18–25.

104. David Rowe, *The Limits of Family Influence: Genes, Experiences and Behavior* (New York: Guilford Press, 1995), 64.

105. R.J. Cadoret, C. Cain, and R.R. Crowe, "Evidence for a Gene-Environment Interaction in the Development of Adolescent Antisocial Behavior," *Behavior Genetics* 13 (1983): 301–310.

106. Barry Hutchings and Sarnoff A. Mednick, "Criminality in Adoptees and Their Adoptive and Biological Parents: A Pilot Study," in *Biological Bases in Criminal Behavior*, eds. S.A. Mednick and K.O. Christiansen (New York: Gardner Press, 1977).

107. For similar results, see Sarnoff Mednick, Terrie Moffitt, William Gabrielli, and Barry

Hutchings, "Genetic Factors in Criminal Behavior: A Review," *Development of Antisocial and Prosocial Behavior* (New York: Academic Press, 1986), 3–50; Sarnoff Mednick, William Gabrielli, and Barry Hutchings, "Genetic Influences in Criminal Behavior: Evidence from an Adoption Cohort," in *Perspective Studies of Crime and Delinquency*, eds. Katherine Teilmann Van Dusen and Sarnoff Mednick (Boston: Kluver-Nijhoff, 1983), 39–57.

108. Michael Bohman, "Predisposition to Criminality: Swedish Adoption Studies in Retrospect," in *Genetics of Criminal and Antisocial Behavior*, eds. G.R. Bock and J.A. Goode (Chichester, England: John Wiley & Sons, 1995), 99–114.

109. Glenn Walters, "A Meta-Analysis of the Gene-Crime Relationship," *Criminology* 30 (1992): 595–613.

110. Marshall Jones and Donald Jones, "The Contagious Nature of Antisocial Behavior," *Criminology* 38 (2000): 25–46.

111. David Rowe and Bill Gulley, "Sibling Effects on Substance Use and Delinquency," *Criminology* 30 (1992): 217–232; see also, David Rowe, Joseph Rogers, and Sylvia Meseck-Bushey, "Sibling Delinquency and the Family Environment: Shared and Unshared Influences," *Child Development* 63 (1992): 59–67.

112. Lawrence Cohen and Richard Machalek, "A General Theory of Expropriative Crime: An Evolutionary Ecological Approach," *American Journal of Sociology* 94 (1988): 465–501.

113. "Sex, Lies, and Jealousy," *Toronto Star*, October 11, 2002, F05; Margie Wyle, "Are Humans Hard-Wired to Behave Aggressively?" *Toronto Star*, March 21, 2003, D04.

114. Lee Ellis, "The Evolution of Violent Criminal Behavior and Its Nonlegal Equivalent," in *Crime in Biological, Social and Moral Contexts*, eds. Lee Ellis and Harry Hoffman, 63–65 (New York: Praeger, 1990).

115. Lee Ellis and Anthony Walsh, "Gene-Based Evolutionary Theories of Criminology," *Criminology* 35 (1997): 229–276; Lee Ellis, "Sex Differences in Criminality: An Explanation Based on the Concept of r/K Selection," *Mankind Quarterly* 30 (1990): 17–37; Byron Roth, "Crime and Child Rearing," *Society* 34 (1996): 39–45.

116. Deborah Denno, "Sociological and Human Developmental Explanations of Crime: Conflict or Consensus," *Criminology* 23 (1985): 711–741.

117. Israel Nachshon and Deborah Denno, "Violence and Cerebral Function," in *The Causes of Crime, New Biological Approaches*, eds. Sarnoff Mednick, Terrie Moffitt, and Susan Stack, 185–217 (Cambridge: Cambridge University Press, 1987).

118. Avshalom Caspi, Donald Lyman, Terrie Moffitt, and Phil Silva, "Unraveling Girls' Delinquency: Biological, Dispositional, and Contextual Contributions to Adolescent Misbehavior," *Developmental Psychology* 29 (1993): 283–289.

119. Glenn Walters and Thomas White, "Heredity and Crime: Bad Genes or Bad Research," *Criminology* 27 (1989): 455–486.

120. Charles Goring, *The English Convict: A Statistical Study, 1913* (Montclair, NJ: Patterson Smith, 1972); Edwin Driver, "Charles Buckman Goring," in *Pioneers in Criminology*, ed. Hermann Mannheim (Montclair, NJ: Patterson Smith, 1970), 440.

121. Gabriel Tarde, *Penal Philosophy*, trans. R. Howell (Boston: Little, Brown, 1912).

122. Frank R. Farnham, David V. James, and Paul Cantrell, "Association Between Violence, Psychosis, and Relationship to Victim in Stalkers," *The Lancet*, January 15, 2000, 199.

123. "Schizophrenia Linked to Urban Living," *Canadian Medical Association Journal* 2 (2004): 170–174.

124. Sigmund Freud, "The Ego and the Id," in *Complete Psychological Works of Sigmund Freud*, vol. 19, 52 (London: Hogarth, 1948).

125. August Aichorn, *Wayward Youth* (New York: Viking Press, 1935).

126. David Abrahamsen, *Crime and the Human Mind* (New York: Columbia University Press, 1944), 137; see, generally, Fritz Redl and Hans Toch, "The Psychoanalytic Perspective," in *Psychology of Crime and Criminal Justice*, ed. Hans Toch, 193–195 (New York: Holt, Rinehart and Winston, 1979).

127. See, generally, D.A. Andrews and James Bonta, *The Psychology of Criminal Conduct* (Cincinnati: Anderson, 1994), 72–75.

128. Robert Krueger, Avshalom Caspi, Phil Silva, and Rob McGee, "Personality Traits Are Differentially Linked to Mental Disorders: A Multitrait-Multidiagnosis Study of an Adolescent Birth Cohort," *Journal of Abnormal Psychology* 105 (1996): 299–312; Seymour Halleck, *Psychiatry and the Dilemmas of Crime* (Berkeley, CA: University of California Press, 1971).

129. This discussion is based on three works by Albert Bandura: *Aggression: A Social Learning Analysis* (Englewood Cliffs, NJ: Prentice-Hall, 1973), *Social Learning Theory* (Englewood Cliffs, NJ: Prentice-Hall, 1977), and "The Social Learning Perspective: Mechanisms of Aggression," in *Psychology of Crime and Criminal Justice*, ed. Hans Toch, 198–236. (New York: Holt, Rinehart and Winston, 1979).

130. David Phillips, "The Impact of Mass Media Violence on U.S. Homicides," *American Sociological Review* 48 (1983): 560–568.

131. See, generally, Jean Piaget, *The Moral Judgment of the Child* (London: Kegan Paul, 1932).

132. Lawrence Kohlberg, *Stages in the Development of Moral Thought and Action* (New York: Holt, Rinehart and Winston, 1969).

133. Lawrence Kohlberg, K. Kauffman, P. Scharf, and J. Hickey, *The Just Community Approach in Corrections: A Manual* (Niantic: Connecticut Department of Corrections, 1973); Scott Henggeler, *Delinquency in Adolescence* (Newbury Park, CA: Sage, 1989), 26.

134. Carol Veneziano and Louis Veneziano, "The Relationship between Deterrence and Moral Reasoning," *Criminal Justice Review* 17 (1992): 209–216.

135. Dennis L. Krebs and Kathy Denton, "Toward a More Pragmatic Approach to Morality: A Critical Evaluation of Kohlberg's Model," *Psychological Review*, 2005, 112, 3, 629–649.

136. K.A. Dodge, "A Social Information Processing Model of Social Competence in Children," in *Minnesota Symposium in Child Psychology*, vol. 18, ed. M. Perlmutter, 77–125 (Hillsdale, NJ: Lawrence Erlbaum, 1986).

137. L. Huesman and L. Eron, "Individual Differences and the Trait of Aggression," *European Journal of Personality* 3 (1989): 95–106.

138. J.E. Lochman, "Self and Peer Perceptions and Attributional Biases of Aggressive and Nonaggressive Boys in Dyadic Interactions," *Journal of Consulting and Clinical Psychology* 55 (1987): 404–410.

139. Calvin M. Langton, and W.L. Marshall, "Cognition in Rapists. Theoretical Patterns by Typological Breakdown," *Aggression and Violent Behavior* 6 (2001): 499–518.

140. D. Lipton, E.C. McDonel, and R. McFall, "Heterosocial Perception in Rapists," *Journal of Consulting and Clinical Psychology* 55 (1987): 17–21.

141. "Stressed Parents at 'Loggerheads' with Children, Report Says," *Canadian Medical Association Journal* 164, 1 (2001): 84; "Justice System the Wrong Route to Help for Mentally Ill," *Canadian Medical Association Journal* 170, 9 (2004): 1381.

142. James Sorrells, "Kids Who Kill," *Crime and Delinquency* 23 (1977): 312–320.

143. Richard Rosner, "Adolescents Accused of Murder and Manslaughter: A Five-Year Descriptive Study," *Bulletin of the American Academy of Psychiatry and the Law* 7 (1979): 342–351.

144. Richard Famularo, Robert Kinscherff, and Terence Fenton, "Psychiatric Diagnoses of Abusive Mothers: A Preliminary Report," *Journal of Nervous and Mental Disease* 180 (1992): 658–660.

145. Richard Wagner, Dawn Taylor, Joy Wright, Alison Sloat, Gwynneth Springett, Sandy Arnold, and Heather Weinberg, "Substance Abuse among the Mentally Ill," *American Journal of Orthopsychiatry* 64 (1994): 30–38.

146. Bruce Link, Howard Andrews, and Francis Cullen, "The Violent and Illegal Behavior of Mental Patients Reconsidered," *American Sociological Review* 57 (1992): 275–292; Ellen Hochstedler Steury, "Criminal Defendants with Psychiatric Impairment: Prevalence, Probabilities and Rates," *Journal of Criminal Law and Criminology* 84 (1993): 354–374.

147. Marc Hillbrand, John Krystal, Kimberly Sharpe, and Hilliard Foster, "Clinical Predictors of Self-Mutilation in Hospitalized Patients," *Journal of Nervous and Mental Disease* 182 (1994): 9–13.

148. Carmen Cirincione, Henry Steadman, Pamela Clark Robbins, and John Monahan, *Mental Illness as a Factor in Criminality: A Study of Prisoners and Mental Patients* (Delmar, NY: Policy Research Associates, 1991). See also Carmen Cirincione, Henry Steadman, Pamela Clark Robbins, and John Monahan, *Schizophrenia as a Contingent Risk Factor for Criminal Violence* (Delmar, NY: Policy Research Associates, 1991).

149. Heather L. Stuart and Julio E. Arboleda-Flórez, "A Public Health Perspective on Violent Offenses among Persons with Mental Illness," *Psychiatric Services* 52 (May 2001): 654–659.

150. Raymond R. Corrado, Irwin Cohen, Stephen Hart, and Ronald Roesch, "Comparative Examination of the Prevalence of Mental Disorders Among Jailed Inmates in Canada and the United States," *International Journal of Law and Psychiatry*, 23, 5–6 (2000): 633–647.

151. John Monahan, *Mental Illness and Violent Crime* (Washington, DC: National Institute of Justice, 1996).

152. Howard Berenbaum and Frank Fujita, "Schizophrenia and Personality: Exploring the Boundaries and Connections between Vulnerability and Outcome," *Journal of Abnormal Psychology* 103 (1994): 148–158.

153. Eric Silver, "Extending Social Disorganization Theory: A Multilevel Approach to the Study of Violence among Persons with Mental Illness," *Criminology* 38 (2000): 1043–1074.

154. Stacy DeCoster and Karen Heimer, "The Relationship between Law Violation and Depression: An Interactionist Analysis," *Criminology* 39 (2001): 799–837.

155. Jeffrey Wanson, Randy Borum, Marvin Swartz, Virginia Hidaym, H. Ryan Wagner, and Barbara Burns, "Can Involuntary Outpatient Commitment Reduce Arrests among Persons with Severe Mental Illness?" *Criminal Justice and Behavior* 28 (2001): 156–189.

156. D.A. Andrews and J. Stephen Wormith, "Personality and Crime: Knowledge and Construction in Criminology," *Justice Quarterly* 6 (1989): 289–310; Donald Gibbons, "Comment—Personality and Crime: Non-Issues, Real Issues, and a Theory and Research Agenda," *Justice Quarterly* (1989): 311–324.

157. Sheldon Glueck and Eleanor Glueck, *Unraveling Juvenile Delinquency* (Cambridge: Harvard University Press, 1950).

158. See, generally, Hans Eysenck, *Personality and Crime* (London: Routledge & Kegan Paul, 1977).

159. Edelyn Verona and Joyce Carbonell, "Female Violence and Personality," *Criminal Justice and Behavior* 27 (2000): 176–195.

160. Hans Eysenck and M.W. Eysenck, *Personality and Individual Differences* (New York: Plenum, 1985).

161. Joshua Miller and Donald Lynam, "Personality and Antisocial Behavior," *Criminology* 39 (2001): 765–799.

162. David Farrington, "Psychobiological Factors in the Explanation and Reduction of Delinquency," *Today's Delinquent* (1988): 37–51; Laurie Frost, Terrie Moffitt, and Rob McGee, "Neuropsychological Correlates of Psychopathology in an Unselected Cohort of Young Adolescents," *Journal of Abnormal Psychology* 98 (1989): 307–313.

163. David Lykken, "Psychopathy, Sociopathy, and Crime," *Society* 34 (1996): 30–38.

164. Sheldon Glueck and Eleanor Glueck, *Delinquents and Nondelinquents in Perspective* (Cambridge, MA: Harvard University Press, 1968).

165. See, generally, R. Starke Hathaway and Elio Monachesi, *Analyzing and Predicting Juvenile Delinquency with the MMPI* (Minneapolis: University of Minnesota Press, 1953).

166. R. Starke Hathaway, Elio Monachesi, and Lawrence Young, "Delinquency Rates and Personality," *Journal of Criminal Law, Criminology, and Police Science* 51 (1960): 443–460; Michael Hindelang and Joseph Weis, "Personality and Self-Reported Delinquency: An Application of Cluster Analysis," *Criminology* 10 (1972): 268; Spencer Rathus and Larry Siegel, "Crime and Personality Revisited," *Criminology* 18 (1980): 245–251; see, generally, Edward Megargee, *The California Psychological Inventory Handbook* (San Francisco: Jossey-Bass, 1972).

167. Karl Schuessler and Donald Cressey, "Personality Characteristics of Criminals," *American Journal of Sociology* 55 (1950): 476–484; Gordon Waldo and Simon Dinitz, "Personality Attributes of the Criminal: An Analysis of Research Studies 1950–1965," *Journal of Research in Crime and Delinquency* 4 (1967): 185–201; David Tennenbaum, "Research Studies of Personality and Criminality," *Journal of Criminal Justice* 5 (1977): 1–19.

168. Edward Helmes and John Reddon, "A Perspective on Developments in Assessing Psychopathology: A Critical Review of the MMPI and MMPI-2," *Psychological Bulletin* 113 (1993): 453–471.

169. Avshalom Caspi, Terrie Moffitt, Phil Silva, Magda Stouthamer-Loeber, Robert Krueger, and Pamela Schmutte, "Are Some People Crime-Prone? Replications of the Personality-Crime Relationship Across Countries, Genders, Races and Methods," *Criminology* 32 (1994): 163–195.

170. "Interrelated Harms: Examining the Associations between Victimization, Accidents, and Criminal Behavior," *Injury Control and Safety Production* 8, 1 (2001): 13–28; Kevin S. Douglas and Donald G. Dutton, "Assessing the Link between Stalking and Domestic Violence," *Aggression and Violent Behaviour* 6 (2001): 519–546.

171. Donald G. Dutton, "The neurobiology of abandonment homicide," *Aggression and Violent Behavior*, 7, 4, July–August 2002, 407–421.

172. Henry Goddard, *Efficiency and Levels of Intelligence* (Princeton, NJ: Princeton University Press, 1920); Edwin Sutherland, "Mental Deficiency and Crime," in *Social Attitudes*, ed. Kimball Young (New York: Henry Holt, 1931), Chapter 15.

173. William Healy and Augusta Bronner, *Delinquency and Criminals: Their Making and Unmaking* (New York: Macmillan, 1926).

174. Joseph Lee Rogers, H. Harrington Cleveland, Edwin van den Oord, and David Rowe, "Resolving the Debate Over Birth Order, Family Size and Intelligence," *American Psychologist* 55 (2000): 599–612.

175. John Slawson, *The Delinquent Boys* (Boston: Budget Press, 1926).

176. Sutherland, "Mental Deficiency and Crime."

177. Travis Hirschi and Michael Hindelang, "Intelligence and Delinquency: A Revisionist Review," *American Sociological Review* 42 (1977): 471–586.

178. Deborah Denno, "Sociological and Human Developmental Explanations of Crime: Conflict or Consensus," *Criminology* 23 (1985): 711–741; Christine Ward and Richard McFall, "Further Validation of the Problem Inventory for Adolescent Girls: Comparing Caucasian and Black Delinquents and Nondelinquents," *Journal of Consulting and Clinical Psychology* 54 (1986): 732–733; L. Hubble and M. Groff, "Magnitude and Direction of WISC-R Verbal Performance IQ Discrepancies among Adjudicated Male Delinquents," *Journal of Youth and Adolescence* 10 (1981): 179–183.

179. Donald Lynam, Terrie Moffitt, and Magda Stouthamer-Loeber, "Explaining the Relation between IQ and Delinquency: Class, Race, Test Motivation, School Failure or Self-Control," *Journal of Abnormal Psychology* 102 (1993): 187–196.

180. Alex Piquero, "Frequency, Specialization, and Violence in Offending Careers," *Journal of Research in Crime and Delinquency* 37 (2000): 392–418.

181. Deborah Denno, "Sociological and Human Developmental Explanations of Crime: Conflict or Consensus," *Criminology* 23 (1985): 711–741; Christine Ward and Richard McFall, "Further Validation of the Problem Inventory for Adolescent Girls: Comparing Caucasian and Black Delinquents and Nondelinquents," *Journal of Consulting and Clinical Psychology* 54 (1986): 732–733; L. Hubble and M. Groff, "Magnitude and Direction of WISC-R Verbal Performance IQ Discrepancies among Adjudicated Male Delinquents," *Journal of Youth and Adolescence* 10 (1981): 179–183; Donald Lynam, Terrie Moffitt, and Magda Stouthamer-Loeber, "Explaining the Relation Between IQ and Delinquency: Class, Race, Test Motivation, School Failure or Self-Control," *Journal of Abnormal Psychology* 102 (1993): 187–196.

182. James Q. Wilson and Richard Herrnstein, *Crime and Human Nature* (New York: Simon & Schuster, 1985), 148.

183. Ulric Neisser et al., "Intelligence: Knowns and Unknowns," *American Psychologist* 51 (1996): 77–101.

184. Richard Herrnstein and Charles Murray, *The Bell Curve: Intelligence and Class Structure in American Life* (New York: Free Press, 1994).

185. Julian V. Roberts and Simon Verdun-Jones, "Directing Traffic at the Crossroads of Criminal Justice and Mental Health: Conditional Sentencing after the Judgment in Knoblauch," *Alberta Law Review* 39, 4 (2002): 788–809; "Comparative Examination of the Prevalence of Mental Disorders among Jailed Inmates in Canada and the United States," *International Journal of Law and Psychiatry* 23, 5–6 (2002): 633–647; Shirley Steller, *Special Study on Mentally Disordered Accused and the Criminal Justice System* (Ottawa: Canadian Centre for Justice Statistics, 2003).

186. Susan Pease and Craig T. Love, "Optimal Methods and Issues in Nutrition Research in the Correctional Setting," *Nutrition Reviews Supplement* 44 (1986): 122–131.

187. Mark O'Callaghan and Douglas Carroll, "The Role of Psychosurgical Studies in the Control of Antisocial Behavior," in *The Causes of Crime, New Biological Approaches*, eds. Sarnoff Mednick, Terrie Moffitt, and Susan Stack, 312–328 (Cambridge: Cambridge University Press, 1987).

188. Mednick, Moffitt, Gabrielli, and Hutchings, "Genetic Factors in Criminal Behavior: A Review," 47–48.

Social Structure Theories

7

Learning Objectives

After reading this chapter, you will be able to:

1. Understand the various structural factors.
2. Be familiar with the difference of structure versus trait theory.
3. Know the elements of social disorganization theory.
4. Discuss strain theory and its overlap with cultural deviance.
5. Explain how to evaluate policy initiatives based on this approach.

Homeless people often have to beg in public for money, and trade their self-respect in exchange.

In modern criminology, the motivation for crime is not seen to result simply from the flaws, failures, or free choices of individuals. Rather, a complete explanation of crime must consider the socio-cultural environments in which people are located.[1]

Sociology has been the primary focus used in criminology since early in the 20th century, led by Robert Ezra Park, Ernest W. Burgess, and their colleagues at the University of Chicago, who pioneered research on the social ecology of the city.

> **CONNECTIONS**
>
> As discussed in Chapter 1, sociological positivism can be traced to the works of Quetelet and Comte; the work of Durkheim will be reviewed here in the section on anomie theory.

Park applied anthropological methods of description and observation to urban life.[2] He was concerned about how neighbourhood structure develops, how isolated pockets of poverty form, and the social policies that could alleviate urban problems. Later, with Burgess, he studied the social ecology of the city and found that some neighbourhoods form **natural areas** of wealth and affluence, while others suffer poverty and disintegration.[3] Regardless of their race, religion, or ethnicity, the everyday behaviour of people living in these areas is controlled by the social and ecological climate.

Over the next 20 years, **Chicago School** sociologists carried out research that produced Harvey Zorbaugh's *The Gold Coast and the Slum,* Frederic Thrasher's *The Gang,* and Louis Wirth's *The Ghetto.*[4]

SOCIOLOGICAL CRIMINOLOGY

Sociologists look at how patterns of behaviour exist within the social structure. Criminologists look at how *criminal* patterns exist within society, how they can be predicted, and how they can be controlled. We look at social structure because explanations of crime as an individual-level phenomenon fail to account for consistent patterns in the crime rate. For example, if violence is related only to chemical or chromosome abnormality, how can we explain ecological differences and similarities in the crime rate? Similarly, much debate surrounds the effects of violent TV shows on adolescent aggression, yet adolescents in cities and towns with widely disparate crime rates, from St. John's, Newfoundland and Labrador, to Vancouver, British Columbia, all watch the same shows and movies. How can we explain crime rate differences in these areas? If violence has a purely biological or psychological origin, should it not be distributed more evenly throughout the social structure?

To answer these questions, sociology looks at social change and the dynamic aspects of human behaviour. It follows transformations in cultural norms and institutions and the subsequent effect they have on individual and group behaviour.[5] For example, in modern society, a reduction in the influence of the family has been accompanied by an increased emphasis on individuality, independence, and isolation. So, in turn, criminologists are interested in whether weakened family ties are linked to crime and delinquency.[6]

Rapid advances in technology and training have also influenced society. People who lack the requisite social and educational training have found that the road to success through upward occupational mobility has become almost impossible. Even today, in one of the most industrialized countries in the world, most children grow up to occupy the same social class position as their parents. Lack of upward mobility may make drug dealing and other crimes an attractive solution to socially deprived but economically enterprising people, especially when they are only marginally employed.[7]

> **CONNECTIONS**
>
> The association between crime and social class is confusing. Crime rates sometimes increase during periods of full employment and drop during periods of relatively high unemployment. Chapter 12 discusses a type of crime linked to employment: elite, or white-collar, crime.

Criminologists believe that understanding the dynamics of interactions between individuals and their families, peers, schools, and work is important to understanding the cause of crime.[8] Sociology is concerned with the benefits of positive human interactions and the costs of negative interactions. Crime is itself an interaction and therefore should not be studied without considering the interactions of all participants in a criminal act: the law violator, the victim, the law enforcers, the lawmakers, and the social institutions.

To summarize, concern about the ecological distribution of crime, the effect of social change, and the interactive

> **natural areas** Zones or neighbourhoods that develop as a result of social forces operating in urban areas, and become natural areas for crime.
>
> **Chicago School** Pioneering research on the social ecology of the city and urban crime developed in the early 20th century by sociologists at the University of Chicago.

nature of crime itself has made sociology the foundation of modern criminology. This chapter reviews sociological theories that emphasize the relationship between social status and criminal behaviour. In Chapter 8, the focus will shift to theories that emphasize socialization and its influence on crime and deviance; Chapter 9 covers theories based on the concept of social conflict, which are rooted in sociological, economic, and historical theories.

ECONOMIC STRUCTURE AND CRIME

All societies are characterized by stratification into social classes. These social classes are created by the unequal distribution of wealth, power, and prestige to their members. People within classes have similar possessions and share attitudes, values, norms, and lifestyles. In our society, it is common to identify people as upper-, middle-, and lower-class citizens. The upper class is reserved for a small number of exceptionally well-to-do families who maintain enormous financial and social resources, while the lower class consists of those people who live in poverty, including the working poor. The middle class are the managers, professionals, and white-collar workers.

A new shift is occurring in the distribution of poverty. For the first time, retired persons are better off than working-class people, with universal medical care and public and private pensions improving the lifestyle of most retirees. At the same time, a large proportion of Canada's children now live in poverty, a frightening reality for a country once designated by the United Nations as one of the best countries in which to live.

The Canadian census shows that almost 20 percent of Canadian children live in low-income households. This percentage hasn't changed since 1980. World Vision says that the people living in poverty are made up of new immigrants, Aboriginal people, and families headed by single mothers. Forty percent of these poor children live in urban centres, such as Toronto, Montreal, Ottawa, Winnipeg, and Vancouver.[9] Furthermore, although the proportion of children living in poverty dropped between 1990 and 2000, half of all food bank recipients were children. In 2004, the child poverty rate increased for the first time since 1996, when 16 percent of children were identified as living below the poverty line, 15 years after Parliament made a unanimous declaration to end child poverty.

When these children become adolescents, their legitimate opportunities are limited. As Baron and Hartnagel point out in their extensive survey of street youth, the resulting occupational strain is more likely to be solved through crime. Similarly, Bolland found in a survey of 2,468 inner-city adolescents that feelings of hopelessness increased violent

behaviour, substance use, sexual behaviour, and accidental injury.[10]

Inequality

Lower-class slum areas are scenes of inadequate housing and healthcare, disrupted family lives, underemployment, depression, and despair. Some people are driven to desperate measures to cope with their economic plight.

Members of the lower class are constantly bombarded with a flood of advertisements linking material possessions to self-worth, but they are often unable to attain desired goods and services through conventional means. Although they are members of a society that extols material success above any other, they are unable to satisfactorily compete for such success with members of the middle and upper classes.

The social problems found in lower-class areas have been described as an epidemic.[11] As neighbourhood quality decreases, the probability that residents will develop problems sharply increases. Adolescents in the worst neighbourhoods have the greatest risk of dropping out of school and becoming teenage parents, further limiting their mobility.

The disadvantages of lower-class citizens are particularly acute for members of racial minorities. Immigrants and Aboriginal people in Canada have lower income levels and a higher unemployment rate. Although many of the urban poor are Caucasian, members of minority groups are overrepresented within the poverty classes. Statistics Canada says that immigrants who arrived in Canada in the late 1990s have experienced a decline in income of 24 percent versus those who arrived 30 years earlier.

Economic problems are not the only issues faced by members of racial minorities. Aboriginal people, for example, have a much shorter lifespan than do Caucasians. A link has also been established between entrenched poverty and human immunodeficiency virus (HIV) infection. In Vancouver, Aboriginal people who are injection drug users are becoming HIV positive at twice the rate of non-Aboriginals.[12] Some people have also suggested that the concentration of poor, single-parent, and poorly educated Aboriginal people in large cities disadvantages them in ways that might account for their overrepresentation in the justice system.[13]

Low-income Aboriginal women are at least twice as likely to suffer physical or sexual assault by a partner as the national average. More than half have been assaulted by a partner, and one in eight has been raped by a partner. Policy implications of such findings are echoed in a report from Ontario that low incomes of people receiving welfare contribute to women staying in abusive relationships, giving weight to the relationship between poverty and victimization.[14]

A study of Native reserves in northern Manitoba found extensive lack of running water, plumbing, or sanitary septic systems on reserves, contributing to disease and deaths. Moving to southern cities is not always an option because of racism and lack of employment.

In this picture of a downtown Canadian city, we see the conditions in which some people live. Does this neighbourhood provide an enriched environment in which to grow up and escape poverty and crime, or a deprived one in which crime prospers?

In 1966, Oscar Lewis argued that the crushing lifestyle of slum areas produces a "culture of poverty" passed from one generation to the next.[15] The **culture of poverty** is marked by apathy, cynicism, helplessness, and mistrust of social institutions, such as schools, government agencies, and the police. This mistrust prevents people living in poverty from taking advantage of the meagre opportunities available to them. In 1970, Gunnar Myrdal described a worldwide **underclass** cut off from society, its members lacking the education and skills in demand in modern society.[16]

Are the Poor Undeserving?

Despite all our technological success, the fact that a significant percentage of citizens are either homeless or living in areas of concentrated poverty is an important social problem. Yet some view impoverished people as being in some way responsible for their own fate, believing that if they tried, they could "improve themselves."[17]

However, people living in poverty are more likely to experience high crime, poor schools, and excessive mortality. They have higher rates of unemployment, are more dependent on welfare, and are more likely to live in single-parent households. The burden of living in these high-poverty areas goes beyond merely being poor. Under these conditions, self-help and upward mobility are highly difficult. The barriers to getting ahead are not personal but systemic.

Adolescents residing in areas of concentrated poverty are more likely to suffer in their cognitive development, sexual and family formation practices, school attendance habits, and transition to employment.

People living in poverty confront obstacles far greater than the mere lack of financial resources: they are ill-prepared to take advantage of employment opportunities even in favourable labour markets. The fact that many of the underclass are children who can expect to spend all their life in poverty is probably the single most important problem facing the nation today.

---

culture of poverty The lower class culture, characterized by values and norms in conflict with conventional society.

underclass A world cut off from society, its members lacking the education and skills needed to survive, which becomes a breeding ground for criminality.

Unemployment and Crime

According to the social structure approach, crime is linked to economic deprivation. So what is the relationship between crime and unemployment? If people do not hold jobs, for example, they are more likely to turn to crime as a means of support. However, if jobs are available, crime rates should decrease. People who hold jobs should be less criminal than are people who are unemployed.

The crime rate has risen dramatically since the 1960s; this increase occurs even during prosperous times. There is little indication that changing market conditions cause offenders to renounce crime and choose legitimate earning opportunities. Crime rates are linked slightly to labour market conditions, but the relationship between them is one of many.

A routine activities theorist (as discussed in Chapter 5) might suggest that although joblessness increases the motivation to commit crime, it simultaneously decreases the opportunity to gain from criminal enterprise. During periods of economic hardship, potential victims possess fewer valuable items and tend to guard those valuables they do possess more closely. Parents who are unemployed may be at home to supervise their children, reducing the opportunity for the kids to commit crime. However, teenagers have higher crime rates than any other age group because they are not yet part of the workforce and are unlikely to be directly affected by employment rates.

When individual offenders are the unit of analysis, we find that unemployed individuals are more likely to commit crime. Surveys of adult inmates show that many were unemployed and underemployed before their incarceration, earning incomes below the poverty level. Unemployment may increase crime because it reduces people's stake in conformity. By severing attachments to co-workers and reducing parents' ability to be breadwinners, unemployment reduces the attachment people have to conventional institutions and their ability to exert authority over their children.

Numerous other possible explanations exist for the rather weak crime–unemployment association. It may be that only extremely high unemployment rates are associated with crime. Crime rates peaked in the 1930s during the Great Depression, and it is possible that only such a sustained period of economic chaos can affect crime rates. Recent short-term fluctuations in the economy may be of too short a duration to have a measurable effect.

The crime–unemployment relationship may also be offence-specific, having the greatest influence on opportunistic property crimes, such as burglary, and the least influence on violent assault crimes, which are more likely to be motivated by such factors as rage, jealousy, or substance abuse.

It is also possible to formulate the direction of the crime–unemployment relationship in a different way. Rather than joblessness motivating people to commit crime, criminal behaviour can exclude offenders from work. An early experience with delinquent behaviour and drug abuse may later result in unemployment as an adult. Hagan explains this relationship as social embeddedness: Early behaviour patterns become stable, lifelong habits and tendencies. Kids with early criminal experiences, whose friends are delinquent and whose parents are criminals, become embedded in behaviours that result in later unemployment. The chain of events runs from having criminal friends and parents, engaging in delinquency, and gaining police and court contacts to losing the opportunity for meaningful employment as adults. Embeddedness in a deviant lifestyle is contrasted with the establishment of roots in a conventional lifestyle: Youths who get early work experience, who make contacts, and who learn the ropes of the job market establish the groundwork for a successful career.

So, does an association exist between crime and unemployment? The data suggest that these two variables are interrelated in a variety of ways, and we turn now to social structure theory for an explanation.

BRANCHES OF SOCIAL STRUCTURE THEORY

The disadvantages of economic inequality have been viewed by many criminologists as a primary cause of crime, referred to here as **social structure theory**. These theories suggest that forces operating in deteriorated lower-class areas push many of their residents into criminal behaviour patterns. Unsupervised teenage gangs, high crime rates, and social disorder in poor areas are seen as major social problems. The Comparative Criminology box offers one sociologist's look at the "truly disadvantaged." The example is American, but that is where this approach began.

Lower-class crime is often the violent, destructive product of youth gangs and marginally employed young adults, which suggests that the social forces that cause crime begin to affect people while they are relatively young and continue to influence them throughout their life. Although not all youthful offenders become adult criminals, many begin their training and learn criminal values as members of youth gangs and groups.

Social structure theorists don't believe that crime is caused by psychological imbalance, biological traits, insensitivity to social controls, personal choice, or any other individual-level factor. People living in equivalent social environments behave in similar ways, and if the environment did not influence human behaviour, crime rates would be

social structure theory An approach that looks at the effects of class stratification in society.

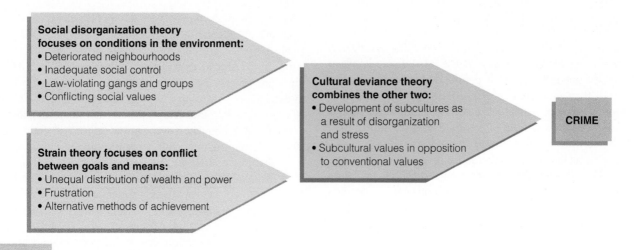

FIGURE 7.1
The Three Branches of Social Structure Theory

distributed equally across the social structure. Because crime rates are higher in lower-class urban centres than in middle-class suburbs, the social forces operating in urban areas must be influencing or controlling behaviour.[18]

Three independent yet overlapping branches are at work within the social structure perspective: social disorganization theory, strain theory, and cultural deviance theory, as outlined in Figure 7.1.

Social disorganization theory, the first branch, focuses on conditions within the urban environment that affect crime rates. A disorganized area is one in which institutions of social control, such as the family, commercial establishments, and schools, can no longer carry out their functions. Indicators of social disorganization include high rates of unemployment and of school dropouts, deteriorated housing, low income levels, and large numbers of single-parent households. Residents in these areas experience conflict and despair, and antisocial behaviour flourishes.

Strain theory, the second branch of social structure theory, holds that crime is a product of conflict between goals and means. Although social and economic goals are common, the ability to obtain these goals is class-dependent. Most people desire wealth, material possessions, power, and prestige; however, people in the lower class are less able to achieve these symbols of success through conventional means. Consequently, they feel anger, frustration, and resentment, which causes strain. Either they can accept their condition as socially responsible citizens, or they can choose an alternative means of achieving success, such as theft, violence, or drug trafficking.

Cultural deviance theory, the third variation of structural theory, combines elements of both strain and social disorganization. According to this view, unique lower-class cultures develop in disorganized neighbourhoods, creating a unique set of values in conflict with conventional social norms. Criminal behaviour is an expression of conformity to lower-class subcultural values and traditions, and not simply a rebellion against conventional society.

Each of these separate theories supports the view that socially isolated people, living in disorganized neighbourhoods, are the ones most likely to experience crime-producing social forces. We will now examine each branch of social structure theory in some detail.

SOCIAL DISORGANIZATION THEORY

Social disorganization theory links crime rates to neighbourhood ecological characteristics. Crime rates are elevated in highly transient, mixed-use neighbourhoods (residential and commercial properties exist side by side) or changing neighbourhoods, in which the fabric of social life has become frayed. These localities are unable to provide essential services, such as education, healthcare, and proper housing, and experience significant levels of unemployment, single-parent families, and families on welfare (see Figure 7.2).

social disorganization theory An approach that looks at neighbourhoods marked by culture conflict, lack of cohesiveness, transiency, and anomie.

strain theory An approach that looks at the conflict caused when people cannot achieve their goals through legitimate means, and are denied access to adequate educational opportunities and social support.

cultural deviance theory Criminal behaviour is in conformity to lower-class subcultural values that develop in disorganized neighbourhoods due to strain and values in conflict with conventional social norms.

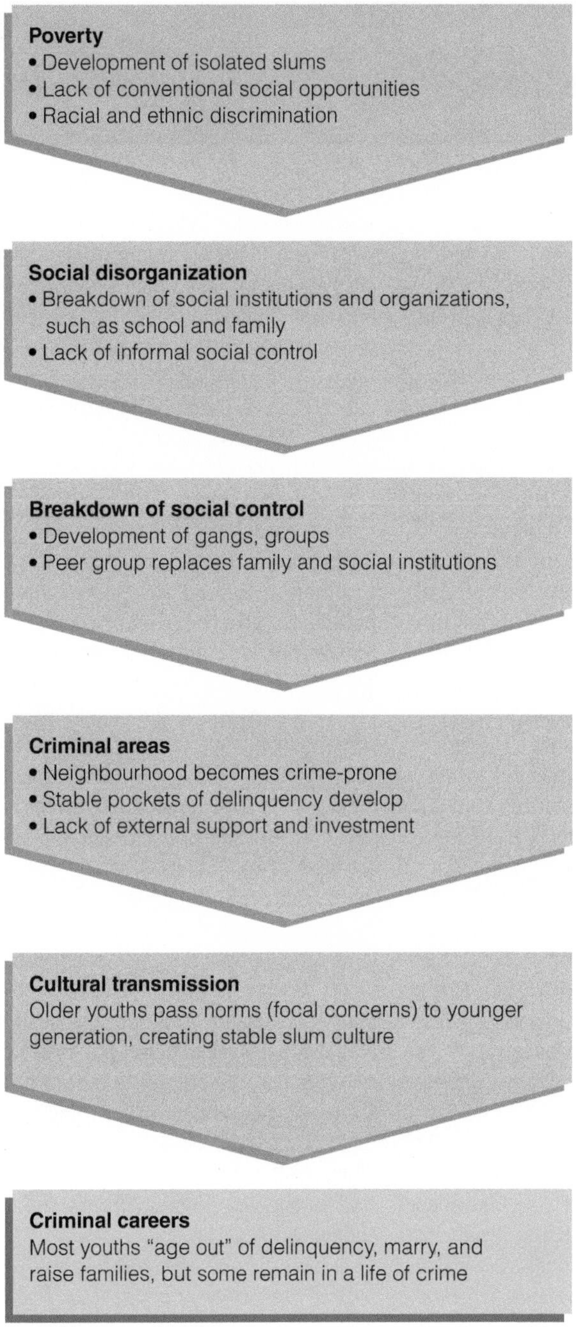

Poverty
- Development of isolated slums
- Lack of conventional social opportunities
- Racial and ethnic discrimination

Social disorganization
- Breakdown of social institutions and organizations, such as school and family
- Lack of informal social control

Breakdown of social control
- Development of gangs, groups
- Peer group replaces family and social institutions

Criminal areas
- Neighbourhood becomes crime-prone
- Stable pockets of delinquency develop
- Lack of external support and investment

Cultural transmission
Older youths pass norms (focal concerns) to younger generation, creating stable slum culture

Criminal careers
Most youths "age out" of delinquency, marry, and raise families, but some remain in a life of crime

FIGURE 7.2
Social Disorganization Theory

Social disorganization theory views crime-ridden neighbourhoods as ones from which residents are trying to leave at the earliest opportunity. Common sources of control, such as the family, school, business community, and social service agencies, are weak and disorganized. Personal relationships are strained because neighbours are constantly moving. Constant resident turnover weakens communications and blocks attempts at solving neighbourhood problems or establishing common goals.[19]

Concentric Zone Theory

Social disorganization theory was popularized by the work of two Chicago sociologists, Shaw and McKay, who linked life in transitional slum areas to crime. They began their research during the 1920s while working for a state-supported social service agency.[20]

During this time, Chicago was experiencing a transition that was also taking place in many other urban areas as a result of a late 19th-century population expansion, fuelled by a dramatic influx of foreign-born immigrants. Congregating in the central city, the newcomers occupied the oldest housing.

As the city core began to deteriorate, the wealthy, more established citizens became concerned about the moral fabric of society. The belief was widespread that immigrants from Europe were crime-prone and morally dissolute, and local groups were created for the purpose of "saving" the children of poor families from moral decadence.[21] It was popular to view crime as the province of inferior racial and ethnic groups, but this belief was rooted in the anxiety over social changes altering the face of 20th-century society: industrialization, urbanization, immigration, and increased geographic and social mobility.

Transitional Neighbourhoods. Shaw and McKay explained crime and delinquency within the context of the changing urban environment and ecological development of the city. They said Chicago had developed into distinct "natural areas," some affluent and others wracked by extreme poverty. So-called transitional areas had high rates of population turnover and were incapable of inducing residents to remain and defend the neighbourhood against criminal groups.

Low rents in these areas attracted newly arrived immigrants from Europe who congregated in these **transitional neighbourhoods**. Their children were torn between being assimilated into a new culture and abiding by the traditional values of their parents. Informal social control mechanisms that had restrained behaviour in the "old country" or in rural areas were disrupted in the city.

In transitional slum areas, successive changes in the composition of the population, the disintegration of traditional cultures, the divergent cultural standards, and the gradual industrialization of the area resulted in dissolution of neighbourhood culture and organization. The effectiveness of the neighbourhood as a unit of control and as a medium for the transmission of the moral standards of society was greatly diminished. High population turnover impeded the establishment of common values, and children had little access to the cultural heritages of conventional society, leaving them more susceptible to the

> **transitional neighbourhood** An area undergoing a shift in population and structure, usually from middle-class residential to lower-class mixed use.

Comparative Criminology
Bridging the Racial Divide in America

William Julius Wilson, one of the most prominent sociologists in the United States, has produced an impressive body of work that details racial problems and racial politics in American society. In 1987, he provided a description of the plight of the lowest levels of the underclass, which he labelled the *truly disadvantaged*. Wilson portrayed members of this group as socially isolated people who dwell in urban inner cities, occupy the bottom rung of the social ladder, and are the victims of discrimination. They live in areas in which the basic institutions of society—family, school, housing—have long since declined. Their decline triggers similar breakdowns in the strengths of inner-city areas, including the loss of community cohesion and the ability of people living in the area to control the flow of drugs and criminal activity. For example, in a more affluent area, neighbours might complain to parents that their children were acting out. In distressed areas, this element of informal social control may be absent because parents are under stress or, all too often, absent. These effects magnify the isolation of the underclass from mainstream society and promote a ghetto culture and behaviour.

Because the truly disadvantaged rarely come into contact with the actual source of their oppression, they direct their anger and aggression at those with whom they are in close and intimate contact, such as neighbours, businesspeople, and landlords. Members of this group, plagued by underemployment or unemployment, begin to lose self-confidence, a feeling supported by the plight of kin and friendship groups who also experience extreme economic marginality. Self-doubt is a neighbourhood norm, overwhelming those forced to live in areas of concentrated poverty.

In his important book *When Work Disappears*, Wilson assesses the effect of joblessness and underemployment on residents in poor neighbourhoods on Chicago's south side. He argues that for the first time in the 20th century, most adults in inner-city ghetto neighbourhoods are not working during a typical week. He finds that inner-city life is only marginally affected by the surge in the nation's economy, which has been brought about by new industrial growth connected with technological development. Poverty in these inner-city areas is eternal and unchanging and, if anything, worsening as residents are further shut out of the economic mainstream.

Wilson focuses on the plight of the Black American community, which had enjoyed periods of relative prosperity in the 1950s and 1960s. He suggests that as difficult as life was in the 1940s and 1950s for Black Americans, they at least had a reasonable hope of steady work. Now, because of the globalization of the economy, those opportunities have evaporated. Although in the past, racial segregation had the effect of limiting opportunity, growth in the manufacturing sector fuelled upward mobility and provided the foundation of today's Black American middle class. Those opportunities no longer exist as manufacturing plants have moved to inaccessible rural and overseas locations where the cost of doing business is lower. With manufacturing opportunities all but obsolete in the United States, many service and retail establishments, which depend on blue-collar spending, have similarly disappeared, leaving behind an economy that is based on welfare and government supports. In less than 20 years, formerly active Black American communities have become crime-infested slums.

The hardships faced by residents in Chicago's south side are not unique to that community. Beyond sustaining inner-city poverty, the absence of employment opportunities has torn at the social fabric of the nation's inner-city neighbourhoods. Work helps socialize young people into the wider society, instilling in them such desirable values as hard work, caring, and respect for others. When work becomes scarce, however, the discipline and structure it provides are absent. Community-wide underemployment destroys social cohesion, increasing the presence of neighbourhood social problems ranging from drug use to educational failure. Schools in these areas are unable to teach basic skills, and because desirable employment is lacking, few adults serve as role models. In contrast to more affluent suburban households where daily life is organized around job and career demands, children in inner-city areas are not socialized in the workings of the mainstream economy.

In *The Bridge over the Racial Divide: Rising Inequality and Coalition Politics,*

organized gangs that developed in these areas. Subcultural values developed, which were then passed down through succeeding generations through **cultural transmission**. Frederic Thrasher documents this well in his 1927 classic, *The Gang*.

Concentric Zones. Shaw and McKay noted that distinct ecological areas had developed in the city, composing a series of concentric circles or zones, which had significant differences in crime rates (see Figure 7.3). The heaviest concentration of crime appeared to be in the transitional inner-city zones, where large numbers of foreign-born citizens had recently settled. The zones farthest from the city's centre had correspondingly lower crime rates. Analysis of these data indicated a surprisingly stable pattern of criminal activity in the ecological zones over a 65-year period.

Shaw and McKay concluded that in transitional neighbourhoods, multiple cultures and diverse values, both conventional

> **cultural transmission** The cultural passing down of conduct norms from one generation to the next, which become stable and predictable.

Wilson expands on his views of race in contemporary society. He argues that despite economic gains, inequality is growing in American society, and ordinary families, of all races and ethnic origins, are suffering. Caucasians, Latinos, Black Americans, Asians, and Aboriginal Americans must therefore begin to put aside their differences and concentrate more on what they have in common—their aspirations, problems, and hopes. Mutual cooperation is needed across racial lines.

One reason for this set of mutual problems is the government tendency to aggravate rather than ease the financial stress placed on ordinary families. Monetary policy, trade policy, and tax policy are harmful to working-class families. A multiracial citizen's coalition could pressure national public officials to focus on the interests of ordinary people. As long as middle- and working-class groups are fragmented along racial lines, such pressure is impossible.

Wilson finds that racism is becoming more subtle and harder to detect. Caucasians believe that Blacks are responsible for their inferior economic status because of their cultural traits. Because even affluent Caucasians fear corporate downsizing, they are unwilling to vote for governmental assistance to the poor. Caucasians are continuing to be suburban dwellers, further isolating the poor members of minority groups in central cities and making their problems distant and unimportant. He continues to believe that the changing marketplace,

especially its reliance on sophisticated computer technologies, is continually decreasing demand for low-skilled workers, which affects Black Americans more negatively than other better-educated and affluent groups.

Wilson argues for a cross-race, class-based alliance of working- and middle-class Americans to pursue policies that will benefit them rather than the affluent. These policies include full employment, programs to help families and workers in their private lives, and a reconstructed "affirmative opportunity" program that benefits Black Americans without antagonizing Caucasians.

In his most recent work, *There Goes the Neighborhood,* Wilson, along with Richard P. Taub, assesses racial relations in four Chicago neighbourhoods. The picture he paints is bleak. He finds that racism is still an active part of people's lives though its motif is changing. People are unusually hostile when outsiders move into their enclave. If they have a choice, they move; if not, they are angry and sullen. In a Caucasian middle-class neighbourhood, people may be angry when Black and Latino newcomers arrive, believing they threaten property values and neighbourhood stability. Caucasians and Latinos are able to reach common ground on only one social issue: preventing kids from being bussed to a Black school district. People seem unfazed about using offensive racist language to express their feelings, and feel superior to other groups and races. Racism seems

to cloak social anxiety: people who are worried about jobs and healthcare tend to take their frustrations out on others. Wilson, as always, comes up with a prescription for positive change: strengthen neighbourhood social organizations and people will be less likely to flee. Race relations can be improved when people from diverse backgrounds come together to reach common goals, such as school improvement. Society as a whole must be willing to help out and repair inner-city neighbourhoods. Without such help, racial and class tensions spread throughout the city.

Critical Thinking

1. Is it unrealistic to assume that a government-sponsored public works program can provide needed jobs in this era of budget cutbacks?
2. What are some of the hidden costs of unemployment in a community setting?
3. How would a biocriminologist explain Wilson's findings?

SOURCES: William Julius Wilson and Richard Taub, *There Goes the Neighborhood: Racial, Ethnic, and Class Tensions in Four Chicago Neighborhoods and Their Meaning for America* (New York: Knopf, 2006); William Julius Wilson, *The Truly Disadvantaged* (Chicago: University of Chicago Press, 1987); William Julius Wilson, *When Work Disappears, The World of the Urban Poor* (New York: Alfred Knopf, 1996); William Julius Wilson, *The Bridge over the Racial Divide: Rising Inequality and Coalition Politics* (Wildavsky Forum Series, 2) (Berkeley: University of California Press, 1999).

and deviant, coexist. Kids growing up in the street culture often find that adults who have adopted a deviant lifestyle, such as the gambler, the pimp, or the drug dealer, are the most financially successful people in the neighbourhood. The kids then join with like-minded youths and form law-violating gangs and cliques, but because of their deviant values, slum youths come into conflict with middle-class norms, which are more in line with the legal code. Consequently, a **value conflict** occurs, and the result is a fuller acceptance of deviant goals and behaviour. Shut out of conventional society, neighbourhood street gangs become fixed institutions, recruiting new members and passing on delinquent traditions from one generation to the next.

Shaw and McKay's analysis found that even though crime rates changed, the highest rates were always in zones I and II (central city and transitional areas). The areas with the highest crime rates retained high rates even when, over time, families moved out to the suburbs and the ethnic composition changed (in this case, from German and Irish to Italian and Polish).

value conflict The clash of deviant values of teenage law-violating groups with middle-class norms, which demand obedience to the law.

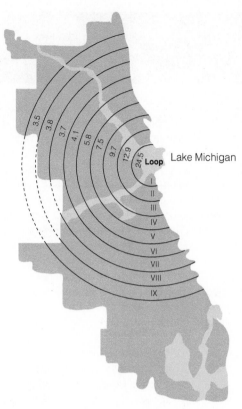

Note: Arabic numerals represent the rate of male delinquency

FIGURE 7.3

Shaw and McKay's Concentric Zone Map of Chicago Gangland

Source: Frederic M. Thrasher, *The Gang: A Study of 1,313 Gangs in Chicago* (Chicago: University of Chicago Press, 1927), p. 24.

The Legacy of Shaw and McKay. The social disorganization concepts originally articulated by Shaw and McKay have remained prominent within criminology for more than 75 years. The most important of their concepts is that crime is a result of the destructive ecological conditions in urban slums. Criminals are not, as some criminologists of the time believed, biologically inferior, intellectually impaired, or psychologically damaged. Crime is a constant fixture in a slum area regardless of the racial or ethnic identity of its residents. In a sense, criminal activity is a normal response to adverse conditions.

Because the basis of their theory was that neighbourhood disintegration and slum conditions are the primary causes of criminal behaviour, Shaw and McKay paved the way for the many community action and treatment programs developed in the past half-century. For example, Shaw was the founder of a very influential community-based treatment program, the Chicago Area Project.

However, some have faulted Shaw and McKay's assumption that neighbourhoods are essentially stable, while others have found their definition of social disorganization confusing.[22] The most important criticism is that the researchers used police records to calculate neighbourhood crime rates. Research indicates that police use discretion when arresting people and that social status is one factor that influences their decisions. Middle-class people might commit criminal acts that never show up in official statistics, while people in lower-class areas face a far greater chance of arrest and court adjudication.[23] Thus, the relationship between environment and crime rates may reflect a higher level of police enforcement.

These criticisms aside, the theory provides a valuable contribution to our understanding of the causes of criminal behaviour. By introducing a new variable—the ecology of the city—into the study of crime, the authors paved the way for succeeding generations of criminologists to focus on the social influences on criminal and delinquent behaviour.

CONNECTIONS

If social disorganization causes crime, why are the majority of low-income people law abiding? To explain this anomaly, some sociologists have devised theoretical models suggesting that individual socialization experiences mediate the effect of environmental influences. These theories will be discussed in Chapter 9.

The Social Ecology School

During the 1970s, theories with a more social psychological orientation developed critiques of social disorganization theory. However, the social disorganization tradition was kept alive by area studies showing that ecological conditions, such as substandard housing, low income, and unrelated people living together, predicted a high incidence of delinquency.[24]

In the 1980s, criminologists revived concern about the effects of social disorganization,[25] and **social ecologists** developed an approach that stressed the relation of community deterioration and economic decline to criminality while placing less emphasis on value conflict. Sampson and Groves produced a study using data from the 1982 British Crime Survey, and the social disorganization theory seemed to be vindicated.[26]

In the following sections, some of the more recent social ecological research is discussed in some detail.

Community Deterioration. Crime rates are associated with community-level indicators of social disorganization, including disorder, poverty, alienation, disassociation, and fear of crime. Neighbourhoods with deserted houses and apartments experience high crime rates, as abandoned buildings serve as a magnet for crime.[27] Areas where houses are in poor repair, boarded up, and burned out are also sites of the highest violence rates and gun crime.[28] In his now-classic research, Messner found that the percentage of people living in poverty and the percentage of single-parent homes are strongly related to neighbourhood crime rates.[29]

social ecologists Those whose approach looks at community-level indicators of social disorganization, such as disorder, poverty, alienation, and fear of crime.

In their update on this research almost 20 years later, Pratt and Godsey found that social support, institutional anomie, and general strain perspectives are important explanations of aggregate levels of crime. They show that the level of available social support is inversely related to homicide rates, that economic inequality has a direct relationship with homicide rates, and that low social support and high economic inequality interact together to influence homicide rates.[30]

Gangs flourish in deteriorated neighbourhoods, adding to the crime rate. Curry and Spergel found that gang homicide rates were associated with the percentage of neighbourhood residents living below the poverty line, the lack of mortgage investment in a neighbourhood, the unemployment rate, and the influx of new immigrant groups, factors usually found in disorganized areas.[31]

Furthermore, in a study of police charging practices in 447 Canadian communities, Schulenberg found that social disorganization theory was a strong predictor of crime rates.[32] Research conducted in Scandinavia and Great Britain also found that socially disorganized neighbourhoods experienced the highest amounts of crime and victimization.[33] Communities characterized by sparse friendship networks, unsupervised teenage peer groups, and low organizational participation had the greatest amounts of criminality.

This model, then, has the power to explain crime rates in countries with similar socio-economic conditions.[34]

Employment Opportunities.

The relationship between unemployment and crime is unsettled: crime rates sometimes rise during periods of economic prosperity and fall during periods of economic decline.[35] Yet high unemployment rates may have crime-producing effects in particular neighbourhoods or in areas wracked by poverty and social disorganization. Even though short-term economic trends may have little effect on crime, it is possible that long-term unemployment rates will eventually produce higher levels of antisocial behaviours.[36]

Neighbourhoods with few employment opportunities are the most vulnerable to predatory crime. Unemployment helps destabilize households, and unstable families are most likely to have children who put a premium on violence and aggression as a means of dealing with limited opportunity. Crime rates increase when large groups or cohorts of people of the same age compete for relatively scant resources.[37]

Limited employment opportunities also reduce the stabilizing influence of parents and other adults, who once counteracted the allure of youth gangs.[38] Even the most deteriorated neighbourhoods have a surprising degree of familial and kinship strength. Yet their social control capability can be neutralized by the consistent pattern of crime and neighbourhood disorganization that follows periods of high unemployment.

Community Fear.

Disorganized neighbourhoods suffer social and physical incivilities—rowdy youth, trash and litter, graffiti, abandoned storefronts, burned-out buildings, littered lots, strangers, drunks, vagabonds, loiterers, prostitutes, noise, congestion, angry words, dirt, and stench. The presence of such incivilities helps convince residents of disorganized areas that their neighbourhood is dangerous and that they face a considerable chance of becoming crime victims. Not surprisingly, when crime rates are actually high in these disorganized areas, fear levels undergo a dramatic increase.[39] Perceptions of crime and victimization produce neighbourhood fear.[40] People who report living in neighbourhoods that have high levels of crime and civil disorder become suspicious and mistrusting.[41] The Criminology Research box details the groundbreaking study of one early Canadian city's neighbourhoods.

Fear becomes most pronounced in areas undergoing rapid and unexpected racial and age-composition changes.[42] Fear can become contagious, as people talk of their personal involvement with victimization, spreading the word that the neighbourhood is getting dangerous and that the chance of future victimization is high.[43] People dread leaving their homes at night and withdraw from community life. Not surprisingly, people who have already been victimized are more fearful of the future than those who have escaped crime.[44]

When fear grips a neighbourhood, business conditions begin to deteriorate, population mobility increases, and a criminal element begins to drift into the area. Fear helps produce more crime, as people decrease their level of ownership and stay off the street, increasing the chances of victimization, producing even more fear, in a never-ending loop.

CONNECTIONS

The discussion of choice theory in Chapter 5 mentions that communities characterized by broken windows had higher crime rates.

Siege Mentality.

One unique aspect of community fear is the development of a **siege mentality**.[45] This mindset results in mistrust of critical social institutions, including business, government, and schools. When police ignore crime in poor areas, or when police are violent and corrupt, anger flares and people take to the streets and react in violent ways.

In 1992, after the Rodney King verdict acquitting four police officers in Los Angeles, California, people rioted as far away as Toronto, a city with much less conflict between members of minority groups and police. There has long been tension between the police and members of ethnic minorities in large Canadian cities, where immigration has swelled the numbers of the non-Caucasian population. Witness the riots in north Montreal, after the shooting of an ethnic youth, Fredy Villenueva, a city where the police used a crackdown on incivilities approach, distancing themselves and creating distrust.

siege mentality   A consequence and symptom of community disorganization, where fear causes the belief that the outside world is an enemy out to destroy the neighbourhood.

Carl Addington Dawson was born in 1887 in Augustine Cove, Prince Edward Island. He studied sociology at Acadia University in the 1890s, and then served as pastor of a Baptist church in Lockeport, Nova Scotia. Acadia was one of the first universities to offer courses in sociology, which was seen by urban reformers, settlement-house workers, and social-gospel ministers as a way to deal with the problems of urbanization and industrialization.

Dawson did not think that social reform was the best way to improve social conditions, but he believed that research and investigation of urban communities and their institutions would provide the insight to create a better society. Many churches were convinced that sin was not so much a product of an individual's shortcomings as it was a condition forced on that person by his or her position in society. The Baptists, for example, talked about improving the social environment as a way of preventing the production of criminals; they advocated prison reform, prohibition, and justice for Aboriginal people. They argued for inner-city missions, protection for children, and women's rights. Prohibitionists in Nova Scotia were motivated by a desire to eliminate the roots of human unhappiness and to create a society in which crime, disease, and **social injustice** would not exist.

Dawson had studied at Chicago and was brought to McGill University to research the problems of post-war Montreal. He was hired as the director of the School of Social Work, and then he became head of the first Canadian department of sociology in 1924. The new science of sociology gave the observer the opportunity to understand the forces that led to social fragmentation and social cohesion. Human ecology combined ideas borrowed from plant and animal ecology, physiology, and cultural anthropology. These areas of study became the framework within which all McGill sociology courses were taught, and the frame of reference for all research projects undertaken by Dawson and his students throughout the 1920s and 1930s.

Sociologists turned to biology for guidelines because they found suggestions for explaining the flux that characterized human society. Existence was a struggle for survival,

yet all beings were bound up in a web of relations with other beings and not because they were bound to the physical environment alone. Higher life forms succeeded the lower ones by "invading" an area and forcing the inhabitants to settle in a zone on the rim of their original habitat, which created instability.

Dawson saw society as an order that transcended its individual members, and the ultimate end of the evolutionary process was to establish an equilibrium and a harmonious social order. In keeping with his training, he chose not to focus on social pathology, but rather to investigate the broader structure of the city and the way in which it moulded the behaviour and institutions of its inhabitants. His research was in ordinary areas to ascertain through careful observation the social changes that were caused by advances in communication and transportation.

The city, he said, was an organism, with a centre of dominance—the business sector—around which were arranged a number of zones in concentric circles, their use and occupants varying with the value of the land and the distance from the centre. Each zone was divided into "natural areas," marked off from each other by natural or artificial boundaries and distinguished by their own characteristic institutions and populations. Inhabitants were "sifted" to these areas by a selective process, and their attitudes and behaviour were shaped by the areas. Dawson and his students looked at industrial development, transportation innovations, immigration, housing, labour organization, crime, juvenile delinquency, family disorganization, welfare work, and child labour. They plotted railroad property, industrial and commercial frontage, parks, boulevards, and physiographic barriers on maps of the city.

At the turn of the 20th century, only about one-third of the province's population were urban dwellers, but by 1928, Montreal had become the fifth-largest city in North America. Its port, industries, and services drew immigrants by the thousands every year. Electric streetcars, first introduced in 1892, contributed to the expansion of the city and enabled thousands of workers to move out of the city's inner core into the numerous residential neighbourhoods and

suburbs that were springing up all around the city. Although the main tendencies of expansion to radiate from the centre held true for Montreal, its topographic features distorted the concentric circles in a kidney shape around Mont Royal, as shown in Figure 7.4.

As the city grew, business institutions that had been located near the river encroached on the residential district, where the old walled town of Ville Marie had once stood. The St. Antoine district, on the verge of becoming a slum in the 1920s, had been created by the expansion of the business section. The area's more successful residents had already moved above the hill and to the west. The part of Montreal that experienced the most disruption as the business centre expanded was Dufferin district, a neighbourhood that lay in the city's transitional zone.

Robert Percy, a master's student who studied the area, found that the Dufferin district became a slum at the turn of the 20th century, when the commercial sector of Montreal expanded and a flood of Asian and European immigrants poured into the city. Its boundaries were invaded by machine shops, warehouses, and light manufacturing. The more successful English, Irish, Scottish, and French families who lived in the district departed, and their vacated homes were remodelled into flats and occupied by the less prosperous.

Although stable residential neighbourhoods were well equipped with churches and schools, Dufferin district did not have many such institutions, and rescue missions first made their appearance in Dufferin district in the 1890s. Constant noise, dirt, stimulation, vice, and despair characterized this disorganized physical environment.

Although the work of Carl Dawson and his students has been largely overlooked, it represents an important period in Canadian criminology: an attempt to apply scientific principles to the study of the natural organization of crime.

Muriel Bernice McCall and the Study of Social Disorganization

Muriel McCall was one of the first people to graduate from McGill with a master's degree in sociology. In her 1928 thesis, McCall says

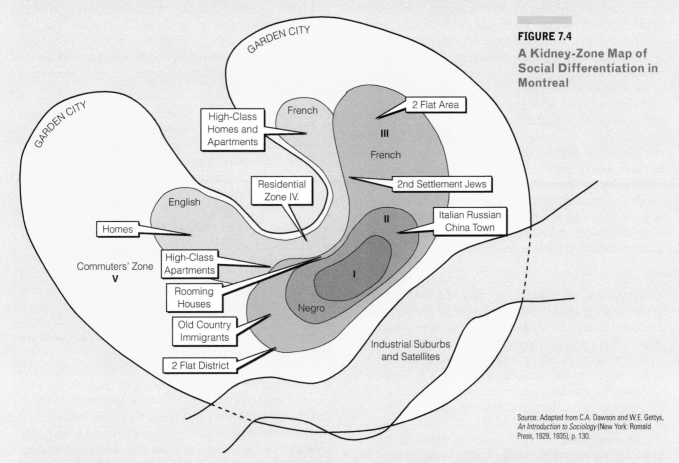

FIGURE 7.4
A Kidney-Zone Map of
Social Differentiation in
Montreal

GARDEN CITY

GARDEN CITY

GARDEN CITY

French

High-Class
Homes and
Apartments

2 Flat Area

III

French

Residential
Zone IV.

2nd Settlement Jews

English

II

Italian Russian
China Town

Homes

Commuters' Zone
V

High-Class
Apartments

Rooming
Houses

I

Old Country
Immigrants

Negro

2 Flat District

Industrial Suburbs
and Satellites

Source: Adapted from C.A. Dawson and W.E. Gettys,
An Introduction to Sociology (New York: Romald
Press, 1929, 1935), p. 130.

that the population of any great city is het-
erogeneous. In the area of transition, "they
are crowded together for the most part in
cheap boarding houses under most unsatis-
factory conditions. They are casual by nature
and by choice, preferring work as lackeys
and porters or even bootblacks to employment of a more permanent nature. Their
sense of moral right and wrong is practically
lacking. When they do enter into any legal
marriage relationship they regard it very
lightly. They are ready to air their troubles
on the slightest provocation and therefore
contribute a great deal of disintegration. . . .
[However,] the fourth zone is the habitat of
the upper middle and professional classes.
Private ownership of a home and restrictions upon how and where it shall be built
appear here for the first time. The homes in
Westmount and in Notre Dame de Grace are
homes of this kind. Small lawns appear in
front of the house and some attempt is made

to have the exterior of the home as attractive as the interior. There are children but
the families tend to be small and the care
of them is often left to nurse maids hired for
the purpose. Husband and wife are on an
equality of footing. Father has his club and
mother has hers. If they find it impossible
to get any enjoyment out of being together
there are always a multiplicity of other activities ready to claim them."

Critical Questions

1. How is the research of the Chicago
   School adapted to the particular circumstances of Montreal?
2. How is the study of crime rooted in the
   social conditions of the time?

SOURCES: I am indebted to Marlene Shore for
her excellent overview to this neglected period in
Canadian criminological history, in The Science
of Social Redemption: McGill, the Chicago

School, and the Origins of Social Research in
Canada (Toronto: University of Toronto Press,
1987). Carl Dawson, "Research and Social
Action," Social Welfare 5 (1923): 93–5;
S.D. Clark, "Sociology in Canada: An Historical
Overview," Canadian Journal of Sociology 1,
1975; V.A. Tomovic, "Sociology in Canada:
An Analysis of Its Growth in English Language
Universities, 1908–1972," Ph.D. thesis,
University of Waterloo, 1975; E.R. Forbes,
"Prohibition and the Social Gospel in Nova
Scotia," Acadiensis 1 (1971); John S. Moir,
"The Canadian Baptist and the Social Gospel
Movement, 1879–1914," in Baptists in Canada:
A Search for Identity Amidst Diversity, ed. Jarold
K. Zeman (Burlington: G.R. Welsh, 1980);
C.A. Dawson, "Human Ecology," in The Fields
and Methods of Sociology, ed. L.L. Bernard
(New York: Ray Lang and Richard Smith,
1934); C.A. Dawson, "The City as an Organism.
With Special Reference to Montreal," in
McGill University Publications 13 (1926);
Muriel Bernice McCall, "A Study of Family
Disorganization in Canada," M.A. thesis, McGill,
1928; Wilfrid Emmerson Israel, "The Montreal
Negro Community," M.A. thesis, McGill, 1928;
Margaret Millicent Wade, "A Sociological Study of
the Dependent Child," M.A. thesis, McGill, 1931.

Population Turnover. In our industrial society, urban areas undergoing rapid structural changes in racial and economic composition also seem to experience the greatest change in crime rates. Change, not stability, is the hallmark of inner-city areas. A neighbourhood's residents, wealth, and density are constantly changing. Some neighbourhoods may become multiracial, while others become racially homogeneous; some areas become stable and family-oriented, while in others, mobile, never-married people predominate.

As areas decline, residents flee to safer, more stable localities. Those who can't leave face an even greater risk of victimization. Because of racial differences, those left behind are all too often members of minority groups, who find themselves surrounded by an influx of new residents. High population turnover affects community culture because it interrupts communication and information flow.[46] A culture may develop that dictates to neighbourhood youth new standards of dress, language, and behaviour that are in opposition to those of conventional society. All these factors are likely to produce increasing crime rates.

Community Change. Social ecologists have charted the life cycles of urban areas, which begin with the building of residential dwellings, followed by a period of decline with marked decreases in socio-economic status and increases in population density. Later stages in this life cycle include changing racial or ethnic makeup, population thinning, and, finally, a renewal stage in which obsolete housing is replaced or upgraded, a process called gentrification. Areas undergoing such change experience increases in their crime rates.[47]

Communities go through cycles in which neighbourhood deterioration precedes increasing rates of crime and delinquency.[48] Those communities most likely to experience a rapid increase in antisocial behaviour contain large numbers of single-parent families and unrelated people living together. These areas have gone from having owner-occupied units to having renter-occupied units, and have an economic base that has lost semiskilled and unskilled jobs. These ecological disruptions strain existing social control mechanisms and inhibit their ability to control crime and delinquency.

Research shows that changing lifestyles in urban neighbourhoods, including declining economic status, increasing population, and racial shifts, are associated with increased neighbourhood crime rates, and even areas adjoining neighbourhoods undergoing racial change will experience corresponding increases in their own crime rates.[49] This phenomenon may reflect community reaction to perceived racial and class conflict. In changing neighbourhoods, adults support the law-violating behaviour of youths and encourage them to protect their property and way of life by violently resisting newcomers.

In his adaptation of Shaw and McKay's (1942) social disorganization theory, Siu Kwong Wong of Brandon University examined the role of family disorganization as a mediator of the effects of poverty, mobility, and ethnic heterogeneity on crime. Using Canadian municipal data from 1991, 1996, and 2001, he found that poverty influenced crime through an indirect effect through family disorganization. The link between poverty, family disorganization, and crime shows the importance of providing community supports to the family, especially through programs targeting families in poverty.[50]

Poverty Concentration. One aspect of community change is the concentration of poverty in deteriorated neighbourhoods. Although poverty rates or unemployment may not be direct causes of crime, the most deteriorated areas have much higher crime rates than more stable lower-class environments. Working and middle-class families flee inner-city poverty areas, resulting in a **concentration effect**, in which elements of the most disadvantaged population are consolidated in urban ghettos. As the working and middle classes move out, they take with them their financial and institutional resources and support. Businesses are disinclined to locate in poverty areas; banks become reluctant to lend money for new housing or businesses.[51] People who are members of minority groups living in these areas suffer race-based inequality, such as **income inequality**, **social injustice**, and institutional racism.[52]

Areas marked by concentrated poverty become both isolated from the social mainstream and more prone to the criminal activity of gangs.[53] The concentration effect contradicts Shaw and McKay's assumption that crime rates increase in transitional neighbourhoods. Today, the most crime-prone areas may be stable, homogeneous areas whose residents are "trapped" in public housing and urban ghettos.[54]

In his recent study, Marc Ouimet of the University of Ottawa compared social disorganization and opportunity theory for their ability to predict juvenile crime rates. He found

---

concentration effect The outcome when middle-class families flee inner-city poverty areas, taking with them institutional resources and support, which leads to the most disadvantaged people being consolidated in urban ghettos.

income inequality The differences in personal income that create structural inequalities in society, which may be at the root of crime.

social injustice The perception of unfairness, which leads to anger, especially where the poor and wealthy live in close proximity, and people can see how poorly off they are.

that social disorganization predicted where delinquents lived, while the opportunity theory helped explain where juvenile crimes are committed. Using neighbourhood-level data, he says, is ideal for social disorganization research.[55]

What this sort of research shows us is that individuals work within constraints and conditions that they do not choose, may not understand, and find difficult to control.

Weak Social Controls. Most neighbourhood residents share the common goal of living in a crime-free area. Some communities can regulate the behaviour of residents through the influence of community institutions, such as family and school. Other neighbourhoods, experiencing social disorganization, find that efforts at social control are weak. When community social control efforts are blunted, crime rates increase, further weakening neighbourhood cohesiveness in a never-ending cycle.

Neighbourhood agencies of social control operate on the primary level, with peers, families, and relatives exerting informal control through awarding approval and respect. Informal control mechanisms include criticism and ridicule.[56] Businesses, schools, churches, and organizations are part of the larger, secondary networks that communities can use to control crime.

Stable neighbourhoods are able to arrange for external sources of social control, such as additional law enforcement. The presence of police sends a message that the area will not tolerate deviant behaviour. Criminals and drug dealers avoid such areas and relocate to easier and more appealing targets.[57] This concept is described in Chapter 5 as "displacement."

As neighbourhood disadvantage increases, however, its level of informal social control decreases.[58] Because the population is transient in disorganized areas, interpersonal relationships remain superficial; social institutions, such as schools and churches, cannot work effectively in a climate of alienation and mistrust. In these areas, the absence of local political power limits access to external funding and police protection. Neighbourhoods need an injection of funds from the outside to rebuild properly.[59]

Social control is also weakened because unsupervised peer groups and gangs, which flourish in disorganized areas, disrupt the influence of neighbourhood control agents. Children who live in these neighbourhoods may want to attend school and other programs, but they may instead find themselves drafted into those gangs.[60]

Collective Efficacy. Communities that are cohesive and maintain high levels of social control develop collective efficacy—mutual trust and a willingness to intervene in the supervision of children and the maintenance of public order.[61] Cohesion among neighbourhood residents combined with shared expectations for informal social control of public space promotes collective efficacy.[62] Communities with high collective efficacy experience low violence rates and low levels of physical and social disorder (for example, drinking in the street, spray-painting graffiti, and breaking windows).

In contrast, neighbourhoods with low collective efficacy suffer high rates of violence and significant physical and social disorder. Local organizations designed to control crime, such as neighbourhood associations, may only be effective if they promote a sense of collective efficacy.[63] Moreover, spillover effects can extend beyond the geographic boundaries of a single neighbourhood. Collective efficacy can take three forms:

1. *Informal social control:* This form of social control works on the primary level and involves peers, families, and relatives exerting positive and negative reinforcement, such as awarding privileges or ridiculing lazy or disrespectful children.[64] In some neighbourhoods, neighbours practise informal social control through surveillance practices: for example, by keeping an eye out for intruders when their neighbours go out of town, which may reduce such crimes as street robberies.[65]

2. *Institutional social control:* Social institutions, such as schools and churches, cannot work effectively in a climate of alienation and mistrust. The positive impact that neighbourhood control agents can have is easily disturbed by the gangs found in disorganized areas. Children find that involvement with conventional social institutions, such as schools and afternoon programs, is blocked; they are instead at risk for recruitment into gangs and law-violating groups.[66] As crime flourishes, neighbourhood fear increases, which in turn decreases a community's cohesion and thwarts the ability of its institutions to exert social control over its residents.[67]

   While institutional social control includes businesses, stores, schools, churches, and social service and volunteer organizations,[68] recreation centres for teens also have been found to lower crime rates because they exert a positive effect, as compared with taverns and bars, which can destabilize neighbourhoods.[69]

3. *Public social control:* Stable neighbourhoods are also able to secure external resources and are better able to reduce the effects of disorganization and maintain lower levels of crime and victimization.[70] The police presence is typically greatest when community organizations and local leaders have sufficient political clout to get funding for additional law enforcement personnel,[71] and offenders relocate to other areas.[72]

In more disorganized areas, the absence of political power limits access to external funding and protection.[73] In these areas, fewer police are on patrol, they are less motivated, and their resources are stretched more tightly. These communities cannot mount an effective social control effort.[74]

Social Disorganization Theories

Theory	Major Premise	Strengths	Research Focus
Shaw and McKay's Concentric Zones Theory	Crime is a product of transitional neighbourhoods that manifest social disorganization and value conflict.	Identifies why crime rates are highest in slum areas. Points out the factors that produce crime. Suggests programs to help reduce crime.	Poverty; disorganization; gangs; neighbourhood change; community context of crime.
Social Ecology Theory	The conflicts and problems of urban social life and communities, including fear, unemployment, deterioration, and siege mentality, influence crime rates.	Accounts for urban crime rates and trends. Identifies community-level factors that produce high crime rates.	Social control; fear; collective efficacy; unemployment.

In areas where collective efficacy is sufficient, children are less likely to become involved with deviant peers and engage in problem behaviours. When social control is weak, there may be an overreliance on formal punishment, such as arrest and prosecution, to control offenders, a situation that helps destabilize neighbourhoods by putting many of its residents behind bars.

In an important extension of this research, Walter Dekeseredy (of Ontario's Institute of Technology) and his colleagues apply the collective efficacy model to domestic violence in Canadian public housing. Using data from the Quality of Neighbourhood Life Survey, they show that people who live in areas characterized by poverty and joblessness report higher rates of intimate partner violence than those living in more affluent communities. Community concerns about street crime in disorganized neighbourhoods and informal means of social control are not able to alleviate intimate partner violence in public housing.[75]

Social Altruism.   The inverse of communities that provide weak social controls are those that provide strong social supports for their members. Residents teach one another that they have moral and social obligations to their fellow citizens; children learn to be sensitive to the rights of others and respect differences.

People living in disorganized areas may also be able to draw on resources from their neighbours in more affluent surrounding communities, helping to keep crime rates down.[76] This phenomenon may explain, in part, why violence rates are high in poor neighbourhoods that are cut off from outside areas for support.[77]

Areas that place a greater stress on caring for fellow citizens seem, not surprisingly, less crime-prone. Social altruism, defined as contributing to charity, is inversely related to crime rates.[78] Crime rates are lower in altruistic areas, and well-funded charities help lower crime rates by providing a secure safety net for **at-risk** families.

The importance of social support, or altruism, can be illustrated in several ways. For example, recent research shows that social support is inversely related to aggregate rates of violent crime such as homicide.[79]

In another study, Vincent Sacco of Queen's University used data from the Canadian National Survey of Children and Youth to investigate the level of social capital found in students' relationships with parents, friends, and teachers. He concludes that the relationship between students' social connections and their feelings of vulnerability to criminal danger is an important one.[80]

In one final example, Carla Cesaroni, then of the University of Toronto, looked at how the Mennonite Central Committee created a program entitled Circles of Support, which helps reintegrate sex offenders back into the community. While ex-offenders join a circle as a means of self-protection because of the controversy that often attends the release of a high-profile sex offender, volunteers participate in the circles because of the perceived benefit to the community. She found that volunteers felt that benefit to the community was enhanced safety, which seems to be borne out by the fact that ex-offenders said they would have been much more likely to re-offend had it not been for the help of the circles.[81]

Taken in sum, the writings of the social ecology school show that (1) social disorganization produces criminality, and (2) the quality of community life, including change, fear, incivility, poverty, and deterioration, has a direct influence on an area's crime rate. It is not an individual property or trait that causes some people to commit crime but the quality and ambiance of the community in which they reside.

Concept Summary 7.1 provides an overview of social disorganization theory. But perhaps just as importantly, as

> **at-risk**   The susceptibility of people to criminal activity as a result of a "culture of poverty" passed from one generation to the next; marked by apathy, cynicism, and mistrust of social institutions.

disorganization can produce crime, altruism and efficacy can work to prevent it.

STRAIN THEORY

The personal component of a structural approach is that inhabitants of a disorganized inner-city area feel isolated, frustrated, and left out of the economic mainstream. What effect do these feelings have on criminal activities?

Criminologists who view crime as a result of lower-class frustration and anger are called strain theorists. They believe that although most people share similar values and goals, the ability to achieve personal goals is unequal because it is stratified by socio-economic class. Those in affluent areas feel less strain because educational and vocational opportunities are available. In socially disorganized areas, however, strain occurs because legitimate avenues for success are less open. To relieve strain, poor people may use deviant methods to achieve their goals, such as theft or drug trafficking, or even infanticide, as discussed in the Famous Canadian Criminals box later in this chapter. They may also reject socially accepted goals outright and substitute other, more deviant goals, such as being tough and aggressive (see Figure 7.5).

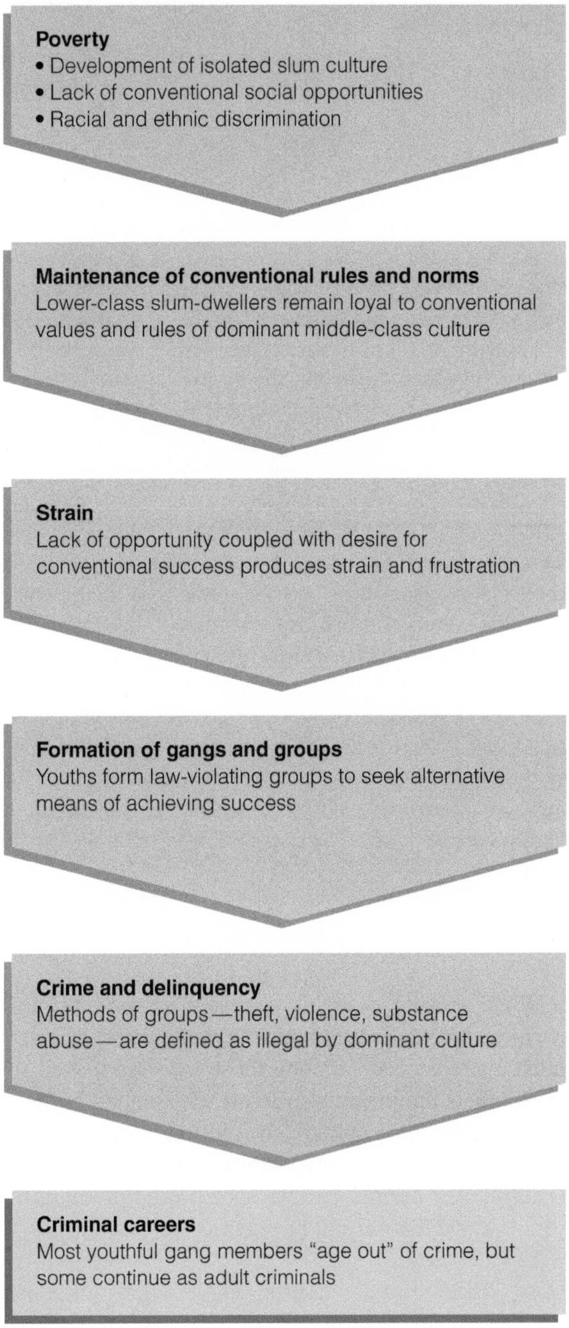

Anomie Theory

The roots of strain theories can be traced to Emile Durkheim's notion of anomie (from the Greek *a nomos*, "without norms"). Anomie occurs when norms of behaviour are broken down during periods of rapid social change. Anomie is most likely to occur in societies that are moving from a pre-industrial model held together by traditions, shared values, and unquestioned beliefs. In industrial societies, which are highly developed and dependent on the division of labour, people are connected by their interdependent needs for one another's services and production. This shift in traditions and values creates social turmoil, and established norms begin to erode and lose meaning, a theme also used in disorganization theory. If a division occurs between what the population expects and what society can realistically deliver, frustration and normlessness occurs.

Society works to limit people's goals and desires. If a society becomes anomic, it can no longer maintain control over its population's wants and desires. Because people find it difficult to control their appetites, their demands become unlimited. Under these circumstances, obedience to legal codes may be strained, making alternative behaviour choices, such as crimes, inevitable.

Durkheim's ideas were applied to criminology by sociologist Robert Merton in his theory of anomie.[82] Merton found that two elements of culture interact to produce potentially

Poverty
• Development of isolated slum culture
• Lack of conventional social opportunities
• Racial and ethnic discrimination

Maintenance of conventional rules and norms
Lower-class slum-dwellers remain loyal to conventional values and rules of dominant middle-class culture

Strain
Lack of opportunity coupled with desire for conventional success produces strain and frustration

Formation of gangs and groups
Youths form law-violating groups to seek alternative means of achieving success

Crime and delinquency
Methods of groups—theft, violence, substance abuse—are defined as illegal by dominant culture

Criminal careers
Most youthful gang members "age out" of crime, but some continue as adult criminals

FIGURE 7.5
The Basic Components of Strain Theory

anomic conditions: culturally defined goals and socially approved means for obtaining them. For example, modern societies stress the goals of acquiring wealth, success, and power, and the socially permissible means of achieving those goals, which include hard work, education, and thrift.

Merton argued that the legitimate means to acquire wealth are not available to all. Those with little formal education, for example, find that they are denied the ability to legally acquire wealth, the pre-eminent success symbol.

Famous Canadian Criminals
Women Who Kill Their Children

Before the 20th century, killing an infant was classed as murder and the current conception of postpartum depression did not exist. In the 18th century, the main offence under which women were charged was concealment of birth. And if a "bastard" child was born dead, it was assumed that the mother had killed the baby. Given the circumstances, juries were often unwilling to convict. In 1867, infanticide was formally added to the *Criminal Code* as a form of murder, and in 1948, the mental component (postpartum depression) was added to the *Criminal Code*. However, even before those changes, it was commonly understood that some women lived lives of desperation that might result in them killing their babies. Contraception had been criminalized, abortion was not legally available, and single mothers were seen as deviant. Homes in which unwed mothers could have their babies and give them up for adoption were common.

Consider the case of Marie McCabe, who in 1880 came to Canada with the help of a charitable organization. When she was six, her mother died and her father suffered an industrial accident. The nine children were placed in an orphanage, but only Marie and her sister survived. Working as a chambermaid in a Quebec City hotel, she became pregnant by a local businessman, who promptly abandoned her. The local city welfare officials and private charity sources refused to help her, even after her child was born. In desperation, she struck a deal with a family who agreed to keep her and the baby, and then adopt the child at the age of one.

However, the deal was not a happy one, and when the baby was four months old, McCabe abandoned it in a cistern, where it drowned. The corpse was discovered six months later, and McCabe was charged by the police. She pleaded guilty at the coroner's inquest and then at the trial. She was sentenced to death in 1883; however, when her case was trumpeted in the local newspaper, calls for clemency resulted in the commutation of her death penalty, and she was eventually released in 1889.

Today, we recognize that emotional imbalance and social situations can have an effect on mothers. Very few cases of infanticide come forward in any year, and they are treated very differently now from the way they were in the past. Mothers are more likely to be seen as needing medical treatment rather than criminal punishment.

SOURCES: I am indebted to Frank Anderson's *A Dance with Death: Canadian Women on the Gallows, 1754–1954* (Saskatoon: Fifth House, 1996). Also Helen Boritch, *Fallen Women: Female Crime and Criminal Justice in Canada* (Toronto: ITP Nelson, 1997).

When socially desirable goals are uniform throughout society but access to legitimate means is bound by class and status, a strain occurs among those who are locked out of the legitimate opportunity structure. Consequently, they may develop criminal or delinquent solutions to the problem of attaining goals. So it is not as simple as people not being able to control their desires, but that society itself produces a situation of wants that cannot be realized.

Social Adaptations. Merton argued that some people have inadequate means of attaining success, and others who do have the means reject societal goals as being unsuited to them. His typology included five social goals and the means for getting them.

Conformity occurs when individuals both embrace conventional social goals and have the means at their disposal to attain those goals. In a balanced, stable society, conformity is the most common social adaptation. If a majority of people in a society did not practise conformity, the society would cease to exist.

Innovation occurs when an individual accepts the goals of society but is incapable of attaining them through conventional means. Many people desire material goods and luxuries but lack the financial ability to attain them. The resulting conflict forces them to adopt innovative solutions to their dilemma. Sometimes they become legitimate entrepreneurs. Other times they steal, sell drugs, or extort money. Of the five adaptations, innovation is most closely associated with criminal behaviour.

If successful, innovation can have serious, long-term social consequences. Criminal success helps convince otherwise law-abiding people that crime pays. "The process thus enlarges the extent of anomie within the system," claims Merton, "so that others, who did not respond in the form of deviant behavior to the relatively slight anomie which they first obtained, come to do so as anomie is spread and is intensified."[83] This statement explains why crime is created and sustained in certain low-income ecological areas.

Ritualism occurs when social goals are lowered in importance. Ritualists gain pleasure from the practice of traditional ceremonies that have neither a real purpose nor a goal. The strict set of manners and customs in religious orders, feudal societies, clubs, and fraternities and sororities encourage and appeal to ritualists, who have the lowest level of criminal behaviour because they have abandoned the success goal that is at the root of criminal activity.

Retreatists reject both the goals and the means of society. Merton suggested that people who adjust in this fashion are in the society but not of it, such as psychotics, outcasts, vagrants, vagabonds, tramps, chronic drunkards, and drug addicts. Such people attempt to escape their lack of success

What has caused the riots in London? The news reports have accounts of burning buildings, crowds throwing rocks at police, and groups of youths looting shops. The police have increased the number of officers on the streets, and the Home Secretary has said the rioters will face the consequences of their actions.

But what caused the riots? On August 6, 2011, CBS News reported that the gritty north London neighborhood of Tottenham exploded in anger after a young man was shot to death by police. A quiet demonstration to demand justice after the shooting turned ugly and violent.

On the first night, two patrol cars, a building, and a double-decker bus were put on fire. Rioters clashed with officers who took hours to contain the crowds, sometimes seen standing by as looters ransacked shops.

The *New York Times* recounted the looting, describing how the riot escalated into a pitched battle between lines of police officers, some on horses. The hundreds of mostly young Black men, in small gangs of four or five, had hooded sweatshirts pulled over their heads and bandannas over their faces.

The young men had arrived in small groups on foot, by bicycle, or on mopeds. They had apparently told each other where to gather through social media. Reporters also used social media to fill in details of the spectacle as it unfolded by the minute.

So what caused the riots? The police admitted they could have handled relations with the family of Mark Duggan, shot in a stop by the police, differently. A local woman quoted in HuffPost UK said: "There's a theory going on that the man who was shot had dropped his gun, but they still shot him."

This is the underside of the story. While papers post pictures of riots and describe scenes of destruction, the less covered story is that Tottenham is one of the most deprived areas in all of England, with half of all children living in poverty. The area has the capital's biggest Black population, with a history of racial tension and resentment against the police.

Anti-police feeling comes from the fact that Blacks are 29 times more likely to be stopped by police than whites. The riots echo clashes between police and residents in 1985, following the death of a woman whose heart failed after police raided her home. The current looting might be opportunistic, copycat crime, but it is rooted in distrust and social deprivation.

But that's a hard story to cover. It's much easier, as *Boston Globe*'s Big Picture did, to provide an endless run of burning buildings and gutted shops. It's harder to answer why someone yelled out during the mayor's comments to the media, "the police want to see this place burn down." It's much harder to ask why youths say they "hate the police."

The Metropolitan Police have struggled for years to cope with a 1999 inquiry into the death of a Black teenager that concluded the force was institutionally racist. But it is not just Black youth who feel resentment. A youth worker quoted in the *National Post* said there had been growing anger over stop-and-search practices by police by youth in general who are frustrated at the way the police are treating them.

However, speculation in *The Economist* on August 9 is that politicians will use the riots to crack down on crime and further harden attitudes against the classes from which the rioters are seen to come. If so, the need to ask harder questions will be lost.

Last April, Peter Walker, writing in *The Guardian* on the eve of the 30th anniversary of the Brixton riots, said community leaders were warning that similar tensions could spill over again. Rising youth unemployment, cuts to local services, and political resentment against rising tuitions and other cuts were fuelling frustration.

Riots spread to Brixton the second night, and have now spread further to other cities, as people find something to identify with. Is it thuggery and hooliganism?

Sure, but it's also protest.

SOURCE: Copyright Chris McCormick, published in the *Daily Gleaner* (Fredericton), August 11, 2011.

by withdrawing, either mentally or physically, which is itself a deviant behaviour.

Rebellion involves substituting an alternative set of goals and means for conventional goals and means. Revolutionaries who want to promote radical change in the existing social structure and who call for alternative lifestyles, goals, and beliefs are engaging in rebellion. Rebellion may be a reaction against a corrupt and hated government, or an effort to create alternative opportunities and lifestyles within the existing system, such as skateboarding to work.

Evaluation of Anomie Theory.   To resolve the goals–means conflict or relieve their sense of strain, some people innovate by stealing or extorting money; others retreat into drugs and alcohol, rebel by joining revolutionary groups, or get involved in ritualistic behaviour by joining a religious cult.

Merton's theory is influential because by linking deviance to the success goals that control social behaviour, it pinpoints the conflict that produces personal frustration and consequent criminality. Society unfairly distributes the means to achieving success, which explains the existence of high-crime areas and the predominance of delinquent and criminal behaviour among the lower class. By suggesting that social conditions, not individual personalities, produce crime, Merton greatly influenced the directions taken to reduce and control criminality during the last half of the 20th century.

However, several questions are left unanswered by anomie theory.[84] Merton did not explain why people differ in their choice of criminal behaviour. Why does one anomic person become a mugger while another deals drugs? And why do most young criminals desist from crime as adults? Do perceptions of anomie dwindle with age? Is anomie short-lived?

Critics have also suggested that people pursue numerous different goals, including educational, athletic, and social success. Juveniles may be more interested in immediate goals, such as being a good athlete, than in long-term achievements, such as monetary success. Other factors, including athletic ability, intelligence, personality, and family life, can also either hinder or assist goal attainment.[85] Any assumption that all people share the same goals and values is false. People who are members of ethnic minorities, for example, tend to subscribe to different goals from members of the ethnic majority.[86]

Strain theories fell out of favour when criminologists turned their attention to social-psychological views of criminality. However, in the 1990s, interest in strain and anomie resurged because of the economic displacement brought on by a shifting economy. Research turned to how the disadvantaged are at risk for both normlessness and high crime rates. For example, recent research on five historical periods shows that gangs respond to social changes, confirming that poverty is a significant precondition generating gang formation.[87] In addition, some researchers are now reexamining Merton's work[88] and conducting cross-cultural research to confirm the concepts of anomie.[89]

Criminologists are now producing newer versions of anomie. On the macro level, some say that North America's materialistic culture influences the nature and extent of the aggregate crime rate. Micro-level versions suggest that individuals who experience anomie are more likely to commit crime than are those who are immune to feelings of strain or goal conflict. Examples of both of these views are discussed next.

Institutional Anomie Theory

At the macro level, antisocial behaviour is seen as a function of cultural and institutional influences in society. As a goal, the North American dream involves the accumulation of material goods and wealth. As a process, it involves both socialization to the pursuit of material success and the belief that prosperity is an achievable goal. Anomic conditions occur because the desire to succeed at any cost drives people apart, weakens the collective sense of community, fosters ambition, and restricts the desirability of other kinds of achievement, such as a good name and respected reputation.

That we are conditioned to succeed at all costs should come as no surprise. Business people hold esteemed positions in society. What is distinct about modern North American society, and what most likely determines high national crime rates, is that anomic conditions have been allowed to develop

There is growing concern about squeegee kids who walk up to cars stopped in traffic and clean their windows. People are threatened by the tattoos, clothing, and hairstyle of these kids, who are often homeless. Some cities, such as Vancouver, Winnipeg, and Toronto, have either passed or are considering bylaws limiting public panhandling in an effort to control the "squeegees."

to such an extraordinary degree.[90] Institutions that might otherwise control the exaggerated emphasis on financial success have been rendered powerless or obsolete in three ways:

1. Performance in non-economic institutional settings—the family, school, or community—is assigned a lower priority than the goal of financial success.
2. When conflicts emerge, the schedules, routines, and demands of the workplace take priority over those of the home, the school, the community.
3. Economic terms become part of the common language, such as getting to the "bottom line," or when politicians run for office promising to "run the country like a business."

High crime rates in Western society can be explained at the cultural level because the desire for material goods cannot always be achieved by legitimate means. Anomie becomes a norm, and extralegal means (crime) become a strategy for attaining material wealth. At the institutional level, the dominance of economic concerns weakens informal social control exerted by the family, church, and school. These institutions have lost their ability to regulate behaviour and have instead become a conduit for promoting material success. For example, schools are not evaluated on their ability to convey knowledge, but for their ability to train students to get high-paying jobs.

Thus, crime rates may rise in a healthy economy because national prosperity heightens the attractiveness of monetary rewards, encouraging people to gain financial success by any means possible, including illegal means, while reducing the importance of social institutions and lessening their abilities to exert social control.

Supporting Research. However, areas with high levels of church membership, lower levels of divorce, and high voter turnouts also enjoy lower crime rates. Researchers have found that strong institutional controls (family, church, and polity) may counteract the influence of economic deprivation, a finding in sync with institutional anomie theory.[91] In an analysis of survey data, people who valued the North American dream but failed to achieve economic success were found to be crime-prone. The effect was more substantial for Caucasians, who may have greater expectations of material success than non-Caucasians. When Caucasians experience strain, they are more apt to react with anger and antisocial behaviour.[92]

The Messner-Rosenfeld version of anomie strain may be a blueprint for crime-reduction strategies: Some research points to the possibility that investing in social programs to protect individuals and groups from market forces can lower the violent crime rates.[93] This process is called *decommodification:* If citizens are provided with an economic safety net, they may be able to resist the influence of economic deprivation and commit less crime. Nations that provide such resources—welfare, pension benefits, healthcare—have significantly lower crime rates, even though some of their citizens are beset by income inequality.[94]

This version of anomie builds on Merton's macro-level views by trying to explain why the success goal has reached such a place of prominence in Western culture. The message "succeed by any means necessary" has become a national maxim.

Relative Deprivation Theory

Ample evidence shows that neighbourhood-level income inequality is a significant predictor of neighbourhood crime rates.[95] Income inequality increases both perceptions of strain and crime rates because divisions between the rich and poor create an atmosphere of envy and mistrust. Braithwaite says those societies in which income inequality flourishes are especially demeaning to people who are poor. Criminal motivation is fuelled by both perceived humiliation and the right to humiliate a victim in return.[96]

Areas in which those who are affluent live in close proximity to those who are indigent create **relative deprivation**, a concept developed by Blau and Blau.[97] Lower-class people who feel deprived because of their race or class and who reside in urban areas that also house people who are affluent eventually develop a sense of injustice and discontent. They feel blocked, and their constant frustration produces aggression, hostility, and, eventually, violence and crime.[98] Those people who are relatively enriched also feel threatened, but they retreat to gated communities.

Adolescents raised in inner-city poverty areas will experience this crime-producing relative deprivation, because their neighbourhoods are usually located close to the most affluent neighbourhoods.[99] Wage inequality may motivate young males to enter the drug trade, an endeavour that increases the likelihood that they will become involved in violent crimes.[100]

Testing Relative Deprivation. Crime rates increase under conditions of relative deprivation when contiguous neighbourhoods become polarized along class lines.[101] Income inequality predicts violent and general area crime rates, even during times of improvement in income level and educational attainment.[102] Crime can increase during times of relative affluence and declining unemployment: The standard of living may improve, but people may find that they are still losing ground in comparison with other groups. It is the perception of relative deprivation and not absolute poverty levels that ushers in higher crime rates.

Recent research comparing income inequality and homicide rates in Canada and the United States confirms inequality as a strong determinant of levels of lethal violence.[103] Research on homicide levels among Aboriginal Americans may apply to Canada's Aboriginal population. That research shows that both social and family disorganization influence the homicide rate.[104]

The weight of the evidence supports relative deprivation, which remains an important concept for understanding area crime rates.

Is Relative Deprivation "Relative"? Relative deprivation theory holds that people who live in deteriorated urban areas; who lack proper healthcare, decent clothing, and adequate shelter; and who reside in close proximity to those who enjoy the benefits of higher social position, will inevitably resort to such crimes as homicide, robbery, and aggravated assault.[105] Is this view restricted to the lower classes, or can it also be responsible for crimes of people who are affluent? In other words, is relative deprivation "relative"?

Even the most affluent North Americans will feel strain when they fail to achieve "unlimited goals."[106] No matter what their level of affluence, people may perceive strain because the goals they set for themselves can never be achieved or their expected standard of living or economic security may decline. (See the Famous Canadian Court Cases box on former MP Svend Robinson, for example.) Research indicates that residing in an economically integrated neighbourhood harms the children of the more affluent families, producing greater dropout rates and more out-of-wedlock births among the prosperous than among the indigent.[107]

Some affluent people may feel relatively deprived when they compare their accomplishments with those of their even more socially successful peers. The relatively affluent may then use illegal means to satisfy their own "unrealistic" success goals:

> Upper-class individuals ... are by no means shielded against frustrations, relative deprivation and anomie created by a discrepancy between cultural ends and

relative deprivation The condition that exists when people of wealth and people of poverty live in close proximity to one another, affecting crime rates.

Famous Canadian Court Cases
Svend Robinson

During a nationally televised news conference in April 2004, Member of Parliament Svend Robinson announced that he had committed theft and was embarking on a much-needed stress leave. The New Democrat, who had occupied the same Vancouver riding for 25 years, was highly respected by colleagues and popular among constituents. Robinson may not personify the disadvantaged individual who is turned into an offender by the tension of socio-economic constraints, but he is certainly not precluded from experiencing strain.

Because he pleaded guilty to the crime, Robinson's true motives for stealing a diamond ring, appraised at almost $65,000, might never be uncovered. However, anyone trying to understand the 52-year-old's actions should take into account his demanding public position as Canada's first openly gay Member of Parliament, his recent near-fatal hiking accident, and his sister's struggle with multiple sclerosis. Undoubtedly, another important piece of the puzzle is the suspicion that Robinson could not afford to buy a $10,000 ring that he had been eyeing for his partner just two days before the shoplifting incident.

The auction house that Robinson attended required patrons to sign a form and surrender a piece of identification on arrival, and they were also monitored by electronic surveillance. However, these security measures and his status as a well-known public figure were still not powerful enough to deter him from pocketing the ring. Over the next few days, spent at his cottage, Robinson wrestled with a desire to return the merchandise and the fear of being caught. He finally approached police when his efforts to contact the auction service company were unsuccessful. Meanwhile, RCMP officers had already visited the government official's home and office on two occasions.

The auction house declined to pursue the matter after receiving an apology, but a specially appointed prosecutor elected to press charges. Two months later, a judge ruled that the scales of justice were tipped in the defendant's favour after considering Robinson's contributions to society, the remorseful guilty plea, his support network, and the shame he had experienced. Robinson was spared the burden of a criminal record as long as he fulfilled the provisions of a one-year conditional sentence that required him to attend counselling and perform 100 hours of community service. Even someone that successful was not immune to social pressures.

available means, especially in the context of industrial societies, where the ends are renewed as soon as they are reached.[108]

Perhaps some of the individuals involved in Bay Street securities scandals or Wall Street insider-trading cases feel relatively deprived and socially frustrated when they compare the paltry few millions they have already accumulated with the hundreds of millions held by the truly wealthy, whom they envy.

As economic inequality decreases between ethnic groups, Caucasian crime rates increase. Although Caucasians maintain a distinct advantage in power and resources, some perceive the economic progress made by members of ethnic minorities as a step backward for themselves. Feelings of relative deprivation result in the rise of white power groups when lower-class Caucasians begin to feel threatened. Many countries have experienced waves of anti-immigrant violence, for example, which supports the model and indicates relative deprivation is quite complex.

General Strain Theory

Robert Agnew's **general strain theory (GST)** differs from the previously discussed models because of its focus on the micro-level, or individual, effects of strain, and not the macro-level (social) effects (see Exhibit 7.1). Whereas Merton tries to explain social class differences in the crime rate, Agnew focuses on why individuals who feel stress and strain are more likely to commit crimes. Agnew also attempts to offer a more general explanation of criminal activity among all elements of society rather than restrict his views to lower-class crime.[109]

Multiple Sources of Stress. Criminality is the direct result of **negative affective states**, such as anger and frustration produced by a variety of sources of strain:

1. *Strain caused by the failure to achieve positively valued goals.* This strain is a result of the disjunction between aspirations and expectations, for example, when a youth aspires to wealth and fame but, lacking financial and educational resources, assumes that such goals are impossible to achieve.

> **general strain theory (GST)** A micro-level analysis of how individuals who feel stress and strain are more likely to commit crimes.
>
> **negative affective states** The anger, depression, disappointment, fear, and other adverse emotions that derive from strain.

EXHIBIT 7.1

Community-Level Sources of Strain

Sources of Strain
- Residents are unable to achieve positively valued goals such as wealth, status, and justice.
- These communities also produce feelings of relative deprivation.
- Deprivation, family disruption, child abuse, overcrowding, and incivility are high.
- Residents witness friends and family enduring deprivations, known as "vicarious strain."
- Adverse community traits increase negative emotions, including anger and frustration.
- Residence increases interactions of frustrated individuals, increasing stress levels.

Reasons Strain Produces Crime
- Blocked opportunity for advancement makes legitimate goals impossible to attain.
- Densely populated communities make it impossible to keep problems private.
- Lack of privacy creates pressure to "save face" by acting tough or committing crimes.
- Subcultures blame others for their misfortunes, including aggressive illegal acts.
- Residents in deprived areas are less able to develop non-criminal coping strategies.
- Residents in disorganized areas are less able to gain social support from others.
- Residents have weakened educational, religious, recreational, and other social institutions.
- Deprived areas have weakened agencies of both formal and informal social control.
- Residents of deprived areas are likely to hold values and beliefs conducive to crime.
- The increased presence of criminal groups heightens the chance strain will lead to crime.
- Such groups serve as models and also reinforce criminal responses.

SOURCE: Robert Agnew, "A Macro-Strain Theory of Community Differences in Crime Rates." Paper presented at the American Society of Criminology meeting, San Diego, 1997.

2. *Strain caused by the disjunction of expectations and achievements.* This strain is produced when people compare themselves with peers who are doing better financially or socially (or making more money or getting better grades), resulting in adverse reactions, such as vandalism.

3. *Strain as the removal of positively valued stimuli from the individual.* The strain experienced as a result of the loss, for example, of a girlfriend or boyfriend, the death of a loved one, moving to a new neighbourhood or school, and the divorce or separation of parents. A person may try to prevent the loss, to retrieve what has been lost, to obtain substitutes, or to seek revenge against those responsible for the loss.

4. *Strain as the presentation of negative stimuli.* The presence of negative stimuli, such as child abuse and neglect, crime victimization, physical punishment, family and peer conflict, school failure, and stressful life events ranging from verbal threats to air pollution.

Although these sources of strain are independent of one another, they may, in reality, overlap and be cumulative. For example, insults from a teacher may be viewed as an unfair application of negative stimuli, which may then interfere with a student's academic aspirations. The greater the intensity and frequency of strain experiences, the greater their impact and the more likely they are to cause delinquency.

Each type of strain will increase the likelihood of experiencing such negative emotions as disappointment, depression, fear, and, most important, anger. Anger increases perceptions of being wronged, produces a desire for revenge, and lowers inhibitions.

Because strain produces these emotions, it can be considered a predisposing factor for crime when it is chronic and repetitive and creates a hostile, suspicious, and aggressive attitude. Individual strain episodes may serve as a situational event or trigger that produces criminality, such as when a particularly stressful event ignites a violent reaction (see Figure 7.6).

Coping with Strain. Not all people who experience strain become criminals. Some marshal their emotional, mental, and behavioural resources to cope with anger and frustration. Some defences are cognitive, as when individuals rationalize frustrating circumstances, such as saying that not getting the career they desire is "just not that important." Others seek behavioural solutions by running away or seeking revenge. Some will try to regain emotional equilibrium with techniques ranging from physical exercise to drug abuse.

The GST acknowledges that the ability to cope with strain varies with personal experiences over the life course. Youths who lack economic means are less likely to have the resiliency to cope than those who have sufficient financial resources at their command. Also significant are personal temperament, prior learning of criminal attitudes and behaviours, and association with criminal peers who reinforce anger. When individuals can identify a target to blame for their problems, they are more likely to respond with retaliatory action, as in "Sneaky Joe stole my girl by lying about me, so I beat him up!" When individuals internalize blame, they are less likely to engage in criminal behaviour, as in "I lost my girlfriend because I was unfaithful; it's all my fault." Sometimes the source of strain is difficult to pinpoint, as in "I feel depressed because my parents got divorced." This last type of strain is ambiguous and unlikely to produce an aggressive response.[110]

Tracey Peter (Manitoba), Teresa LaGrange (Cleveland), and Robert Silverman (Queen's University) surveyed over 2,000 adolescents in a western Canadian city to look at the effect of self-control and strain on involvement in delinquent behaviour. Self-control and strain are often seen as complementary explanations for crime and delinquency. Strain precipitates deviance in the absence of sufficient self-control,

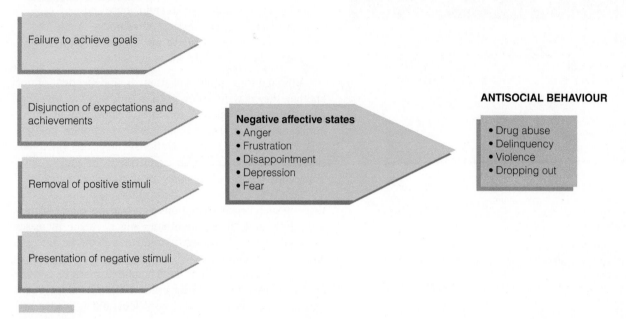

SOURCES OF STRAIN

Failure to achieve goals

Disjunction of expectations and achievements

Removal of positive stimuli

Presentation of negative stimuli

Negative affective states
- Anger
- Frustration
- Disappointment
- Depression
- Fear

ANTISOCIAL BEHAVIOUR
- Drug abuse
- Delinquency
- Violence
- Dropping out

FIGURE 7.6
Elements of General Strain Theory (GST)

and Gottfredson and Hirschi made the assumption that self-control acts as a barrier to criminal behaviour. Peter and colleagues hypothesize that individuals with high self-control would be able to mediate the effects of strain and refrain from engaging in delinquent activities; also, adolescents with low self-control may not be equipped with the necessary constraints to abstain from delinquency. They conclude that both self-control and strain are important, but the former doesn't condition the latter; it is simply a factor in its own right.[111]

Strain and Criminal Careers. How does GST explain both chronic offending and the stability of crime over the life course? GST recognizes that certain people have traits that may make them particularly sensitive to strain. These traits include having a difficult temperament, being overly sensitive or emotional, having a low tolerance for adversity, and having poor problem-solving skills. Kids who suffer from this form of "negative emotionality" are much more likely to engage in antisocial behaviours, especially if they also lack self-control.[112] These traits, which are linked to aggressive and antisocial behaviour, seem to be stable over a person's life cycle.[113]

CONNECTIONS

Cohort studies show that criminal behaviour begins early in life, and then remains stable over the life course. Considering that strain-producing interactions are not constant, explaining the stability of chronic offending is an important task, as discussed in Chapter 3.

Aggressive people who have these traits are likely to have poor interpersonal skills and are more likely to be treated negatively by others; their combative personalities make them feared and disliked. They are likely to live in families whose caretakers share similar personality traits. They are also more likely to reject conventional peers and join deviant groups. Such individuals are more likely to be subjected to a high degree of strain over the course of their lives.

Crime peaks during late adolescence, which is a period of social stress (and possibly opportunity) caused by the weakening of parental supervision and the development of relationships with a diverse peer group. Many kids going through the trauma of family break-up and frequent changes in family structure find themselves under stress and react with involvement in precocious sexuality and substance abuse. Young women of any social class are more likely to bear out-of-wedlock children if they themselves experienced an unstable family life.[114] In adolescence, hormone levels peak and the behaviour-moderating aspects of the brain are not fully developed, which make adolescent males susceptible to environmental sources of strain.[115]

As teens mature, their expectations increase, and some are unable to meet their academic and social demands. Adolescents are concerned about their standing with peers, and some become social outcasts. Feelings of strain and being overwhelmed become magnified as individuals attempt to comply with peer group demands. Kids may, for example, get involved in a shoplifting spree to pay for drugs.[116] In adulthood, these sources of strain are reduced, and as new sources of self-esteem emerge, adults are able to bring their goals in line with reality.

Crime in the News
When Profiling Targets Entire Communities

In August 2011, the *New York Times* reported that a judge rejected an effort to dismiss a case against the New York Police Department. The Center for Constitutional Rights alleged that the police department's "stop and frisk" policy was not based on reasonable suspicion but was in fact a program of racial profiling.

At face value, it looks like there is a case. Although Blacks and Hispanics make up a minority of the city's population, they make up 85 percent of recorded police stops. The police commissioner, on the other hand, says that the racial profile of stops represents the racial profile of crimes.

In 2010, over 600,000 people were stopped by police, more than in any previous year. In 2011, the department was on track for over 700,000. However, crime rates were at their lowest for decades, and it is for reasons separate from policing, such as changes in the population and in the economy.

The judge upheld the lawsuit and based her ruling in part on recordings of station house roll-calls. If there were predetermined quotas for stops, this would rule out the claim that suspicion was the only relevant factor at the time of being stopped.

Forward to February 2012, and *Time* magazine reports on "secret" NYPD documents it had obtained through the Associated Press that showed members of the Muslim community being investigated and profiled solely on the basis of their religion.

An intelligence unit of the NYPD had moved into minority neighbourhoods to engage in "human mapping," using undercover officers, informants, and allegedly CIA agents. One group singled out for investigation was Pakistani taxi drivers and food cart vendors, who were then subject to "voluntary" interrogations.

To make it worse, the mayor of New York City had to explain why the police commissioner had appeared in what was called a "scare-mongering" documentary that identified Muslim radicalization as a threat to America. The film was shown to 1500 police officers.

Moustafa Bayoumi, writing in *The Nation*, also comments on the allegations of profiling conducted by "rakers" in bookstores, cafes, bars, and nightclubs. Officers posing as activists, lawyers, and journalists subjected citizens to surveillance despite their having done nothing wrong. Furthermore, student associations were under surveillance at various universities and colleges.

In the 1960s, files were created on a million people using similar police operations. However, a 1971 federal lawsuit eventually resulted in the 1985 so-called Handshu guidelines, which preserve constitutional rights against police surveillance of those not committing criminal acts. Under Handshu, the current surveillance wouldn't have been possible, but those rights were weakened after 9/11.

The Nation's article says that one part of the joint NYPD/CIA program was to stop vehicles in minority neighbourhoods for "speeding, broken tail lights, running stop signs, whatever," and use that as an excuse for looking for outstanding warrants and other violations.

This sort of fishing expedition approach to law and order policing was adopted in the much-touted 1990s "broken windows" approach to social disorder. That was also a quota-based approach, which did not reduce crime but arguably alienated the population wherever it has been adopted, most notably in the lead-up to the London riots.

Now the New York Civil Liberties Union is suing the police over its new stop-and-frisk policy. This policy also seems to target mostly Blacks and Latinos. As part of the so-called Clean Halls program, it targets large apartment buildings with a problem of drug trafficking. An article in the *Village Voice* quotes a resident who says, "I'm a Black male, I look suspicious."

Such ideas should be impossible in a society based on openness and freedom. Such thinly disguised fishing expeditions are not intelligence-policing, a term much touted in the research on policing.

Rather, such practices are discriminatory policing in a new world, a world ready to sacrifice liberties, especially those of other people, for a putative security.

SOURCE: Copyright Chris McCormick, published in the *Daily Gleaner* (Fredericton), February 23, 2012.

Evaluating GST. Agnew's work is important because it both clarifies the concept of strain and directs future research into how social and life history events influence offending patterns. Because sources of strain vary over the life course, crime rates vary, too.

CONNECTIONS

Explaining continuity and change in offending rates over the life course is looked at in the analysis of latent trait and life-course theories in Chapter 8.

Recent research on GST using longitudinal survey data found that adolescents who score high on scales measuring perceptions of strain labelled "life hassles," (for example, "My classmates do not like me," adults and friends "don't respect my opinions"), and "negative life events" (such as being a victim of crime, the death of a close friend, serious illness), are the ones most likely to engage in crime.[117]

Other research efforts show that indicators of strain—family break-up, unemployment, moving, feelings of dissatisfaction with friends and school—are positively related to criminality.[118] Middle-class youth who drop out of school are more likely to engage in criminal behaviour because

Strain Theories

Theory	Major Premise	Strengths	Research Focus
Anomie Theory	People who adopt the goals of society but lack the means to attain them seek alternatives, such as crime.	Points out how competition for success creates conflict and crime. Suggests that social conditions and not personality can account for crime. Explains high lower-class crime rates.	Frustration; anomie; effects of failure to achieve goals.
Institutional Anomie Theory	Material goods pervade all aspects of North American life.	Explains why crime rates are so high in North American culture.	Frustration; effects of materialism.
General Strain Theory	Strain has a variety of sources. Strain causes crime in the absence of adequate coping mechanisms.	Identifies the complexities of strain in modern society. Expands on anomie theory. Shows the influence of social events on behaviour over the life course. Explains middle-class crimes.	Strain; inequality; negative affective states; influence of negative and positive stimuli.

removing this positive stimulus has a greater strain on those who are expected to succeed.[119]

Adolescents who report feelings of stress and anger are more likely to interact with delinquent peers and to engage in criminal behaviours.[120] Persistent drug abusers report feeling a great deal of life stress and associate with peers who are themselves substance users.[121] This criminal interaction may serve as an effective coping mechanism that helps relieve feelings of anger and resentment.[122]

In interviews with 200 male street youth, Stephen Baron (Queen's University) explored how their perceptions of unemployment are linked to criminal behaviour. He found that those who remained bonded to conventional society and believed in the dominant idea of getting ahead responded with depression and guilt, which led to being withdrawn and inhibited criminal behaviour. In contrast, those youth who dismissed the idea of getting ahead felt that criminal activities were superior to available employment.[123]

Baron has published an extensive selection of research on street youth. He has examined a high-risk sample of homeless street youth, focusing on labour-market strain to predict violent and property crime and substance use;[124] the role that self-control plays in the generation of crime and drug use, and its link to negative social consequences;[125] how specific forms of strain, such as abuse, homelessness, victimization, and unemployment lead to crime and drug use; how strain is conditioned by deviant peers, deviant attitudes, external attributions, self-esteem, and self-efficacy;[126] how relative deprivation and unemployment are conditioned by objective economic situations;[127] how low self-control influences the way street youth react to criminal events and the likelihood that they would become an offender or victim, with learned repertoires for aggression and situational dynamics mediating the effects of low self-control;[128] and how relative deprivation is differentially linked to property and violent crime depending on gender.[129]

GST and Gender.   GST doesn't explain gender differences in the crime rate. Compared with males, females experience as much or more strain, frustration, and anger, yet their crime rate is much lower. Is it possible that gender differences exist either in the relationship between strain and criminality or in the ability to cope with the effects of strain? For example, some research shows that males may be more deeply affected by interpersonal stress,[130] while other studies show that stressful life events have a similar impact on delinquency and drug abuse for both males and females.[131]

If stress is experienced equally by males and females and produces criminal behaviour in both, how can we explain the much greater male crime rate? It is possible that females use different coping mechanisms to deal with strain.[132] Females may be socialized to internalize stress, blaming themselves for their problems; males can relieve strain by deflecting criticism with aggression. Only those females who face overwhelming stress may succumb to criminality.[133]

Concept Summary 7.2 reviews strain theory.

CULTURAL DEVIANCE THEORY

The third branch of social structure theory combines the effects of social disorganization and strain to explain how people living in deteriorated neighbourhoods collectively react to social isolation and economic deprivation. Although middle-class culture stresses hard work, delayed gratification, formal education, and caution, the lower-class subculture stresses excitement, toughness, risk taking, fearlessness, immediate gratification, and "street smarts." The lower-class subculture is an attractive alternative because the urban poor find it impossible to meet the behavioural demands of middle-class society. Unfortunately, subcultural norms often clash with conventional values (see Figure 7.7).

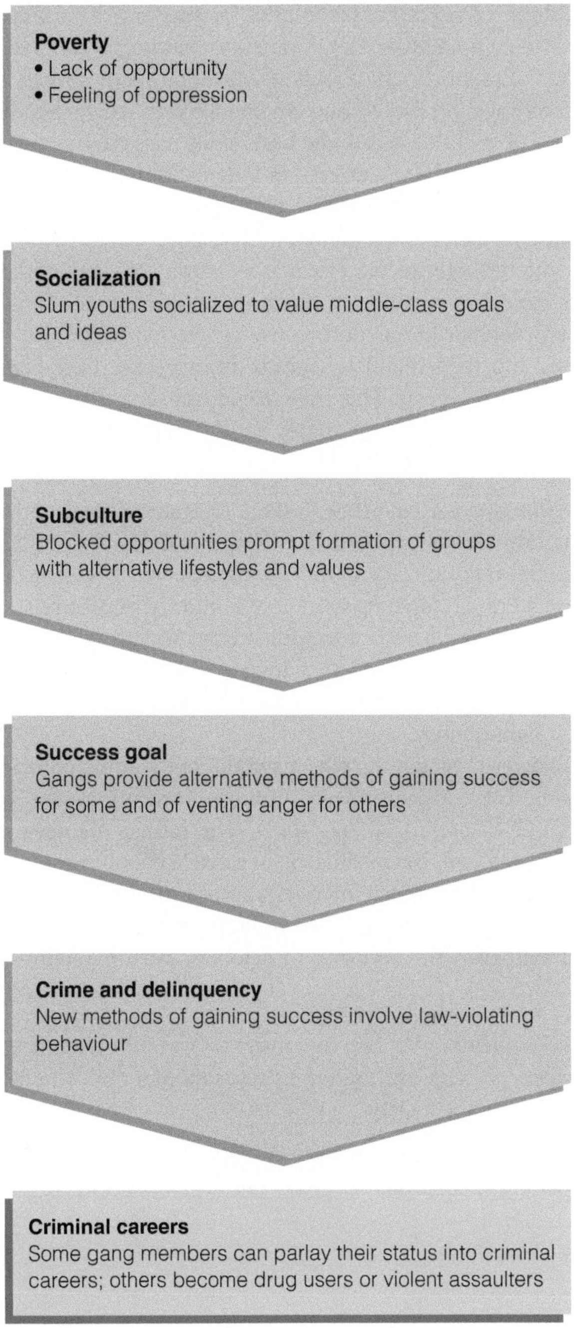

Poverty
• Lack of opportunity
• Feeling of oppression

Socialization
Slum youths socialized to value middle-class goals and ideas

Subculture
Blocked opportunities prompt formation of groups with alternative lifestyles and values

Success goal
Gangs provide alternative methods of gaining success for some and of venting anger for others

Crime and delinquency
New methods of gaining success involve law-violating behaviour

Criminal careers
Some gang members can parlay their status into criminal careers; others become drug users or violent assaulters

FIGURE 7.7
Elements of Cultural Deviance Theory

Conduct Norms

The concept that the lower class develops a unique culture in response to strain can be traced to Thorsten Sellin's classic 1938 work, *Culture Conflict and Crime*.[134] The criminal law was seen as an expression of the dominant culture, creating a clash between conventional, middle-class rules and those excluded from the social mainstream. A conflict of norms exists when divergent rules of conduct govern the specific life situation in which a person may find himself or herself. For example, **culture conflict** occurs when the rules expressed in the criminal law clash with the demands of group **conduct norms**. To make his point, Sellin cited the case of a Sicilian father in New Jersey who killed the 16-year-old seducer of his daughter, and then expressed surprise at being arrested; he had merely defended his family honour in a traditional way. Conduct norms are universal; they are not the product of one group, culture, or political structure.

Focal Concerns

In his classic 1958 paper, "Lower-Class Culture as a Generating Milieu of Gang Delinquency," Walter Miller identified the unique value system that defines lower-class culture.[135] Obedience is maintained to certain values that have evolved specifically to fit conditions in poor areas, as shown in Exhibit 7.2.

According to Miller, clinging to lower-class **focal concerns** promotes behaviour that often runs afoul of the law. Toughness may mean displaying fighting prowess; street smarts lead to drug deals; excitement may result in drinking, gambling, or drug abuse. It is this obedience to the prevailing cultural demands of lower-class society that causes urban crime, not alienation from conventional society.

Sociologist Elijah Anderson says lower-class areas have competing value systems.[136] One value system that he labels *decent* is committed to family and middle-class values; the other is an oppositional culture of *the streets,* whose norms are opposed to those of mainstream society. At the heart of the code is respect, which is the need to be treated with deference. Respect is hard won but easily lost, and so must constantly be guarded.

culture conflict A condition when the rules and norms of an individual's subcultural affiliation conflict with role demands of conventional society.

conduct norms Behaviours expected of social group members, which conflict with those of the general culture; as a result, group members may be outcast as criminals.

focal concerns The value orientations of lower-class culture include the needs for excitement, trouble, smartness, fate, and personal autonomy.

EXHIBIT 7.2

Miller's Lower-Class Focal Concerns

Trouble In lower-class communities, people are evaluated by their involvement in making trouble, such as fighting, drinking, and sexual misconduct. Dealing with trouble can confer prestige—for example, when a man establishes a reputation for being able to handle himself well in a fight. Not being able to handle trouble makes a person look foolish and incompetent.

Toughness Lower-class males want local recognition of their physical and spiritual toughness. They refuse to be sentimental or soft and instead value physical strength, fighting ability, and athletic skill. Those who cannot meet these standards risk getting a reputation for being weak, inept, and effeminate.

Smartness Members of the lower-class culture want to maintain an image of being streetwise and savvy, with the ability to outfox and out-con the opponent. Though formal education is not admired, knowing essential survival techniques, such as gambling, conning, and outsmarting the law, is a requirement.

Excitement Members of the lower class search for fun and excitement to enliven an otherwise drab existence, such as by gambling, fighting, getting drunk, and having sexual adventures. In between, the lower-class citizen may simply "hang out" and "be cool."

Fate Lower-class citizens believe their lives are in the hands of strong spiritual forces that guide their destinies. Getting lucky, finding good fortune, and hitting the jackpot are all slum dwellers' daily dreams.

Autonomy Being independent of authority figures, such as the police, teachers, and parents, is required; losing control is an unacceptable weakness, incompatible with toughness.

Lower-class focal concerns seem as relevant today as when first identified by Miller 50 years ago. These views of a lower-class subculture formed by strain inspired some formal theories that predicted the onset of gang delinquency in lower-class areas. The two best known are the theory of delinquent **subcultures** and the theory of **differential opportunity**.

Theory of Delinquent Subcultures

In his classic 1955 book, *Delinquent Boys*,[137] Albert Cohen said the delinquent behaviour of lower-class youths is a protest against the norms and values of the middle-class culture. Because legitimate success is difficult, lower-class youths experience **status frustration**. As a result, many of them join gangs and engage in behaviour that is non-utilitarian, malicious, and negativistic.

Cohen viewed the gang as a subculture, possessing an oppositional value system that takes its norms from the larger culture but turns them upside down. The delinquent's conduct is normal in the context of the subculture because it is deviant according to the norms of the larger cultures. For example, recent research based on interviews with inmates shows that transactions involving illegal firearms take place through informal, personal networks, despite the weight of gun control legislation.[138]

Accordingly, the development of the delinquent subculture is a consequence of socialization practices found in a poor environment. Deficient socialization renders lower-class kids unable to achieve conventional success. Cohen suggests that lower-class parents are incapable of teaching children the necessary techniques for entering the dominant middle-class culture. Developmental handicaps suffered by lower-class kids include lack of education, poor speech and communication skills, and an inability to delay gratification. These children lack the basic skills necessary to achieve social and economic success in a demanding "credentialist" society, which, unfortunately, is perpetuated by their socialization in the school system.

Interestingly, recent research by Baron shows that homeless male street youth are much more likely than are males in the general population to use aggression to resolve disputes and to demand reparation from people they believe have harmed them. This trait would not serve them well in an office environment perhaps, but it is highly adaptable and functional on the street.[139]

Middle-Class Measuring Rods. One significant handicap that lower-class children face is the inability to positively impress middle-class authority figures, such as teachers, employers, or supervisors. These authority figures set standards that are based on middle-class measuring rods. The conflict and frustration that lower-class youths experience when they fail to meet these standards are a primary cause of their delinquency.

Lower-class youths who have difficulty adjusting to the middle-class measuring rods of one institution may find themselves prejudged by others. The ratings are reviewed and magnified by records: a negative school record may be reviewed by juvenile court authorities; a juvenile court record may be opened by the military; and a military record can influence the securing of a job. A person's status and

---

subculture A group that maintains a unique set of values, beliefs, and traditions resistant and oppositional to dominant society.

differential opportunity The concept that all people share the same success goals, but some have limited means of achieving those goals and seek alternatives, such as joining with like-minded peers and pursuing criminal activity.

status frustration The clash created when lower-class youths are incapable of achieving success legitimately, which results in behaviour that is non-utilitarian, malicious, and negativistic.

esteem in the community are determined by judgments that reflect the traditional values of mainstream society.[140] Negative evaluations become part of a permanent file that follows an individual for the rest of his or her life. When he or she wants to improve, evidence of prior failures is used to discourage advancement.

What do such boys do, when together, they fail individually?

The Formation of Deviant Subcultures. Cohen said that lower-class boys who suffer rejection by middle-class decision makers usually elect to join one of three existing subcultures: the corner boy, the college boy, or the delinquent boy.

The corner boy is not a chronic delinquent but engages in petty offences, such as recreational drug abuse. He is loyal to his peer group, which he depends on for support, motivation, and interest. His values, therefore, are those of the group with which he is in close personal contact. He is well aware of his failure to achieve the standards of the "dream," retreats into the comforting world of lower-class peers, and eventually becomes a stable member of the neighbourhood, holding a menial job, marrying, and remaining in the community.

The college boy embraces the cultural and social values of the middle class. Rather than scorning middle-class measuring rods, he strives to be successful according to those standards. Cohen views this type of youth as one who is embarking on an almost hopeless path, because he is ill-equipped academically, socially, and linguistically to achieve the rewards of middle-class life.

The delinquent boy adopts a set of norms in opposition to middle-class values, living for today and letting tomorrow take care of itself. Delinquent boys resist efforts by family, school, and authority to control their behaviour and join a gang because it is autonomous and independent. Because they are frustrated by their inability to succeed, these boys exhibit **reaction formation**, an exaggerated response disproportionate to the stimulus. This reaction takes the form of irrational and unaccountable hostility, causing these youth to overreact to any perceived threat or slight, making them more willing to take risks and violate the law.

Cohen's work helps explain how social factors, such as status frustration and middle-class measuring rods, promote a delinquent subculture. The corner boy–college boy–delinquent boy triad explains why many lower-class youths fail to become chronic offenders: more than one social path is open to poor youth.[141] His work is a skillful integration of strain and social disorganization theories.

Strain and Street Youths. In their application of strain theory, Baron and Kennedy look at the growing problem of youths under the age of 24 who have left school and hang out on the street. This population is usually underemployed or unemployed and homeless, with lives characterized by poverty and hunger.

For many of these youths, criminal activity is the primary way to gain material wealth. Their culturally produced feelings of failure and rejection lead to a sense of relative deprivation and thwarted ambition in a culture where hard work is the way to get ahead. Youths in this situation gravitate together and develop a new frame of reference in which status is attained and alternative routes to financial success organized. Together, they develop new norms, new standards, and new criteria for success that are more readily achieved.

Baron and Kennedy's study of 200 homeless male youths took place in the downtown business core of a city bordered by the local skid row. The area contained a mix of commercial and financial establishments surrounded by bars, pawnshops, hotels, shelters, detoxification centres, rooming houses, rundown residential units, and abandoned buildings.

Respondents reported an average legal income of $335 a month in the previous year. Respondents reported an average of more than 1,600 offences in the prior 12 months, mostly for selling illegal drugs. They also reported an average of 348 property offences and 48 robberies throughout the year, such as thefts from cars, shoplifting, and break and enters.

The youths reported that their failure to find employment destroyed their motivation and made them less likely to think that law-breaking is wrong: "Because I could make more money selling drugs than working for five bucks an hour"; "'Cause I don't feel guilty about it 'cause I hate flipping burgers. If you're going to have a job you might as well be doing something you like, like robbing people."

Crime not only gave them money but also provided a structure to their day and a sense of doing something.[142] This research also shows how it is discourse that constitutes the grounds for resistance and accommodation.

Theory of Differential Opportunity

In *Delinquency and Opportunity*, Cloward and Ohlin portray the gang-sustaining criminal subculture by combining strain and social disorganization principles to describe how delinquent activity is a requirement for fitting in.[143]

Youth gangs are an important part of the delinquent subculture. Delinquent gangs spring up in disorganized areas where youths lack the opportunity to gain success through conventional means. True to strain theory principles, slum kids are individuals who want to conform to middle-class values but lack the means to do so; reaching out for socially approved goals under conditions that made it impossible to achieve them may become a prelude to deviance. Ignoring those goals is difficult; resisting them causes difficulties.

Differential Opportunities. The centrepiece of the theory is the concept of differential opportunity, in which people share the same success goals; however, those in the lower class have limited means of achieving those goals. People

---

reaction formation The rejection of goals and standards that seem impossible to achieve.

who perceive themselves as failures within conventional society will seek alternative or innovative ways to gain success, joining with like-minded peers. Gang members provide the emotional support to handle the shame, fear, or guilt they may develop while engaging in illegal acts. The youth who is considered a failure at school and is only qualified for a menial job at a minimum wage can earn thousands of dollars plus the respect of peers by joining a gang and engaging in drug deals or armed robberies.

The opportunity for success in either conventional or criminal careers is limited. In stable areas, adolescents may be recruited by professional criminals, drug traffickers, or organized crime groups. Unstable areas cannot support flourishing criminal opportunities, so adult role models are absent and young criminals have few opportunities to join established gangs or learn the fine points of professional crime. Cloward and Ohlin's most important finding is that all opportunities for success, both illegal and conventional, are closed for the most truly disadvantaged youth. Because of differential opportunity, kids are likely to join one of three types of gangs:

1. *Criminal gangs.* Criminal gangs exist in stable but poor areas in which close connections among adolescent and adult offenders create an environment for successful crime. Youths are recruited into established criminal gangs that provide training in criminal knowledge and skills. During this apprenticeship stage, older, more experienced members of the criminal subculture hold youthful trainees on tight reins, limiting activities that might jeopardize the gang's profits, so new recruits can learn the techniques and attitudes of the criminal world. To become fully accepted, novices must prove themselves reliable and dependable. They are introduced to the intermediaries—drug importers, fences, pawnshop operators—and to legal connections—crooked police officers and shady lawyers.

2. *Conflict gangs.* Conflict gangs develop in communities unable to provide either legitimate or illegitimate opportunities, usually highly disorganized areas marked by transient residents and physical deterioration. Crime is individualistic, unorganized, petty, and unprotected because successful adult criminal role models are missing, so violence is a means of gaining status. Swaggering toughs fight with weapons to win respect from rivals and engage in unpredictable and destructive assaults on people and property to protect their gang's honour to gain admiration from their peers. Conflict gangs help get the scarce resources for adolescent pleasure and opportunity in underprivileged areas.

3. *Retreatist gangs.* Retreatists are double failures, unable to gain success through legitimate means and unwilling to do so through illegal means. Retreatists have tried crime or violence but are too clumsy, too weak, or too scared to be accepted in criminal or violent gangs, so they retreat into the fringes and search for ways of getting

According to Cloward and Ohlin's theory of differential opportunity, those who perceive themselves as failures within conventional society or who conclude they have little hope for advancement by legitimate means may join with like-minded peers to form a gang.

high with alcohol, pot, heroin, unusual sexual experiences, or music. To feed their habits, retreatists develop a "hustle"—pimping, conning, selling drugs, and committing petty crimes. Personal status is derived from peer approval.

Analysis of Differential Opportunity Theory. Cloward and Ohlin's theory is important because of its integration of cultural deviance and social disorganization variables, and its recognition of different modes of criminal adaptation. The fact that criminal cultures can be supportive, rational, and profitable seems to be a more realistic reflection of the actual world of the criminal gang than was Cohen's original view of purely negativistic, destructive criminal youths who oppose all social values. The tripartite model of urban delinquency also relates directly to the treatment and rehabilitation of delinquents. Although other social structure theorists portray delinquent youths as having values and attitudes in opposition to middle-class culture, Cloward and Ohlin suggest that many delinquents share the goals and values of the general society but lack the means to obtain success. This position suggests that delinquency prevention can be achieved by providing youths with the means for obtaining the success they truly desire without the need to change their basic attitudes and beliefs.[144]

A study prepared for the Canadian Research Institute for Law and the Family reported that in the western provinces, both the number of gangs and gang-related activity are increasing. Further, youth at risk contribute to the complexity of gang structures and the reasons why youth gangs exist. Recent federal crime statistics support this increasing concern, given the noticeable increase in homicides and drug incidents. They conclude that in some jurisdictions, gang-related activity seems to have outpaced current anti-gang programs; however, programs that prevent Canadian youth

Cultural Deviance Theories

Theory	Major Premise	Strengths	Research Focus
Miller's Focal Concern Theory	Citizens who obey the street rules of lower-class life (focal concerns) find themselves in conflict with the dominant culture.	Identifies the core values of lower-class culture and shows their association to crime.	Cultural norms; focal concerns.
Cohen's Theory of Delinquent Gangs	Status frustration of lower-class boys, created by their failure to achieve middle-class success, causes them to join gangs.	Shows how the conditions of lower-class life produce crime. Explains violence and destructive acts. Identifies conflict of lower class with middle class.	Gangs; culture conflict; middle-class measuring rods; reaction formation.
Cloward and Ohlin's Theory of Opportunity	Blockage of conventional opportunities causes lower-class youths to join criminal, conflict, or retreatist gangs.	Shows that even illegal opportunities are structured in society. Indicates why people become involved in a particular type of criminal activity. Presents a way of preventing crime.	Gangs; cultural norms; culture conflict; effects of blocked opportunity.

from being involved with gangs that are criminally active provide a starting point to develop anti-youth gang strategies.[145]

CONNECTIONS

Chapter 13 looks at gangs in Canada and their relationship to members of ethnic minority groups.

Gang activity has increased because of the involvement of youth gangs in the distribution and sale of illegal drugs, replacing traditional organized crime families as the dominant supplier of illegal substances. The introduction of crack cocaine, which provides a cheap and powerful, albeit short-term, high, helped open new markets in the drug trade.[146]

A report on female gang association in Manitoba supports social structure theories and differential opportunity theory in particular. Female gang members typically come from poor socio-economic backgrounds, survive dysfunctional childhoods, and are predominantly Aboriginal. Gang life provides a sense of family and acceptance, supplies them with money and drugs, and gives them a sense of power.[147]

Gang formation may be the natural consequence of the evolution of Western society from a manufacturing economy to a low-wage service economy.[148] The modern city, which traditionally required a large population base for its manufacturing plants, now faces economic stress as these plants shut down. Only about 20 percent of the workforce is unionized. In this uneasy economic climate, gangs form and flourish in areas where the moderating influence of successful adult role models and stable families declines and where adolescents face constrained choices and weak social controls.[149] Gang

activity provides members with a stable income, so from this perspective, youth gangs are a response to the economy.

Two social conditions predicted by opportunity theory are the rise of gang memberships in a declining industrial market and the development of drug profits as an alternative or innovative method of financial success. The prevalence of gang activity in urban North American society provides staunch support for the social structure approach.

For an overview of cultural deviance theories, see Concept Summary 7.3.

EVALUATION OF SOCIAL STRUCTURE THEORIES

The social structure approach has influenced both criminological theory and crime-prevention strategies. Its core concepts seem valid in view of the high crime and delinquency rates and the gang activity occurring in the deteriorated inner-city areas of large cities. The public's image of inner cities includes roaming bands of violent teenage gangs, drug users, prostitutes, muggers, and similar frightening examples of criminality. All of these are present today in urban areas.

Each branch of the general structural model supports and amplifies others. Some theorists, such as Sampson and Wilson, suggest that these concepts are actually interdependent.[150] Factors that cause strain, such as lack of access to legitimate economic opportunities and economic inequality, also produce social disorganization. Stress leads to alcohol abuse and unprotected sex, causing an increase in dysfunctional families, urban hostility, and the deterioration of informal social controls.

Critics might say that lower-class culture and residence in urban areas are not sufficient to cause people to violate the law. They say that lower-class crime rates are due to bias in the criminal justice system. Lower-class areas seem to have higher crime rates because residents are arrested and prosecuted by the police.[151] Class bias is coupled with discrimination against minority-group members, who have long suffered at the hands of the justice system.

Even if the higher crime rates recorded in lower-class areas are valid, it is still true that most members of the lower class are not criminals. The discovery of the chronic offender indicates that a significant majority of people living in lower-class environments are not criminals and that a relatively small proportion of the population commits most crimes. If social forces alone can be used to explain crime, how can we account for the vast number of urban poor who remain honest and law-abiding? However, it is important to resist the temptation to say that law violators must be motivated by some individual mental, physical, or social process or trait.[152]

Whether a distinct lower-class culture actually exists is questionable. Several researchers have found that gang members and other delinquent youths value as highly as do middle-class youths such concepts as sharing, earning money, having an education, and respecting the law.[153] Opinion polls show that most lower-class citizens maintain middle-class values, such as tougher drug laws, more police protection, and greater control over criminal offenders. These opinions seem similar to conventional middle-class values rather than representative of an independent, deviant subculture. Thus, income does not seem to be a good predictor of youth delinquency.

Although this evidence contradicts some of the central ideas of social structure theory, a close association between crime rates and social class position is supported by stable patterns of lower-class crime, high crime rates found in disorganized inner-city areas, and the rise of teenage gangs and groups.

SOCIAL STRUCTURE THEORY AND SOCIAL POLICY

Social structure theory has significantly influenced social policy. If the cause of criminality is viewed as a separation between lower-class individuals and conventional goals, norms, and rules, it seems logical that alternatives to criminal behaviour can be provided by giving those who are deprived opportunities a chance to share in the rewards of conventional society.

One approach is to give poor people direct financial aid through welfare and to give aid to dependent children. Crime rates are reduced when families receive supplemental income through public assistance payments.[154]

Efforts have been made to reduce crime rates by directly applying the concepts suggested by social structure theories to social policy, such as Shaw's Chicago Area Project, which attempted to organize existing community structures to develop social stability in otherwise disorganized slums. The project sponsored recreation programs for children in the neighbourhoods, including summer camps. It campaigned for community improvements in education, sanitation, traffic safety, physical conservation, and law enforcement. Project members also worked with police and court agencies to supervise and treat gang youth and adult offenders. A 25-year assessment of the project successfully demonstrated the feasibility of creating youth welfare organizations in high-delinquency areas.[155]

Social structure concepts have been a critical ingredient in social reform projects, particularly those that sought to attack the crime-producing structures of poor areas. The crime-prevention effort called Mobilization for Youth was designed to provide teacher training to help educators deal with problem youth, create work opportunities through a youth job centre, organize neighbourhood councils and associations, provide street workers to deal with teen gangs, and set up counselling services and assistance to neighbourhood families. Subsequent programs included the Job Corps, Head Start, Upward Bound (educational enrichment programs), and Neighbourhood Legal Services. Such programs sought to reduce crime by developing community pride in poverty areas and providing educational and job opportunities for crime-prone youths.

Since then, the tendency has been to adopt more selective crime-prevention policies.

CONNECTIONS

Across Canada, more than 100 Head Start projects have been instituted. Designed as an early intervention strategy for Aboriginal people and non-Aboriginals alike, and funded by more than $20 million annually from the federal government, these projects are designed to increase self-esteem and develop a positive sense of self. This initiative is described in more detail in Chapter 8.

SUMMARY

Sociology has been a main orientation of criminologists because crime rates vary among social classes, society goes through changes that affect crime, and social interaction relates to criminality. Social structure theories suggest that a person's place in the socio-economic structure of society influences their chances of becoming a criminal. Poor people are more likely to commit certain crimes because they are unable to achieve monetary or social success in any other way.

Social structure theory has three schools of thought: social disorganization theory, strain theory, and cultural deviance theory (summarized in Concept Summary 7.4).

Social disorganization theory suggests that poor urban dwellers violate the law because they live in areas in which social control has broken down. The origin of social

Social Structure Theories

Theory	Major Premise	Strengths
Social Disorganization Theory		
Shaw and McKay's Concentric Zone Theory	Crime is a product of transitional neighbourhoods that manifest social disorganization and value conflict.	Identifies why crime rates are highest in slum areas. Points out the factors that produce crime. Suggests programs to help reduce crime.
Social Economy Theory	The conflicts and problems of urban social life and communities, including fear, unemployment, deterioration, and siege mentality, influence crime rates.	Accounts for urban crime rates and trends.
Strain Theory		
Anomie Theory	People who adopt the goals of society but lack the means to attain them seek alternatives, such as crime.	Points out how competition for success creates conflict and crime. Suggests that social conditions and not personality can account for crime. Can explain middle- and upper-class crime.
General Strain Theory	Strain has a variety of sources. Strain causes crime in the absence of adequate coping mechanisms.	Identifies the complexities of strain in modern society. Expands on anomie theory. Shows the influences of social events on behaviour over the life course.
Institutional Anomie Theory	Material goals pervade all aspects of Canadian life.	Explains why crime rates are so high in North American culture.
Relative Deprivation Theory	Crime occurs when the wealthy and poor live in close proximity to each other.	Explains high crime rates in deteriorated inner-city areas located near more affluent neighbourhoods.
Cultural Deviance Theory		
Sellin's Culture Conflict Theory	Obedience to the norms of their lower-class culture puts people in conflict with the norms of the dominant culture.	Identifies the aspects of lower-class life that produce street crime. Adds to Shaw and McKay's analysis. Creates the concept of culture conflict.
Miller's Focal Concern Theory	Citizens who obey the street rules of lower-class life (local concerns) find themselves in conflict with the dominant culture.	Identifies the core values of lower-class culture and shows their association to crime.
Cohen's Theory of Delinquent Gangs	Status frustration of lower-class boys, created by their failure to achieve middle-class success, causes them to join gangs.	Shows how conditions of lower-class life produce crime. Explains violence and destructive acts. Identifies conflict of lower class with middle class.
Cloward and Ohlin's	Blockage of conventional opportunities causes lower-class youths to join criminal, conflict, or retreatist gangs.	Shows that even illegal opportunities are structured in society. Indicates why people become involved in a particular type of criminal activity. Presents a way of preventing crime.

disorganization theory can be traced originally to Shaw and McKay, who concluded that disorganized areas marked by divergent values and transitional populations produce criminality. This research was also conducted at McGill University in Canada, as part of a larger process of social reform. Modern social ecology theory looks at such neighbourhood issues as community fear, unemployment, siege mentality, and deterioration.

Strain theories comprise the second branch of the social structure approach. They view crime as a result of the anger people experience over their inability to achieve legitimate social and economic success. Strain theories hold that most people share common values and beliefs, but the ability to achieve them is differentiated throughout the social structure. The best known strain theory is Merton's theory of anomie, which describes what happens when the means people have at their disposal are not adequate to satisfy their goals. This theory was subsequently developed by others to show that strain has multiple sources.

Cultural deviance theories hold that a unique value system develops in lower-class areas. Lower-class values approve of such behaviours as being tough, never showing fear, and defying authority. People perceiving strain will bond together in their own groups or subcultures for support and recognition. Cohen links the formation of subcultures to the failure of lower-class citizens to achieve recognition from middle-class decision makers, such as teachers, employers, and police officers. Cloward and Ohlin have argued that crime results from lower-class people's perception that their opportunity for success is limited. Consequently, youths in low-income areas may join criminal, conflict, or retreatist gangs.

In summary, then, what we have are a set of theories that describe destabilizing forces in society (disorganization), which have an effect on the individual (strain), who then associates with others who experience the same dislocations in the same circumstances (culture).

THINKING LIKE A CRIMINOLOGIST

You are a criminologist at a university and are serving as an adviser to the mayor of Central City, a capital city with a population of 150,000. The mayor wants to initiate a project to show that government can reduce vandalism, petty crime, and disturbances in an area suffering from a disorganized community structure. Efforts by the police to reduce public disorder and crime rates are not working.

Delinquent youths run free at night, vandalizing property and committing minor thefts. The school system is unable to do anything, and public education campaigns seem fruitless. Residents feel little can be done to bring the neighbourhood back to life.

A recently published research report suggests that the key to reducing neighbourhood crime is to create a sense of *collective efficacy* in city neighbourhoods. The report defined collective efficacy as "cohesion among neighbourhood residents combined with shared expectations for informal social control of public space."

The basic premise is that when people mistrust one another, they are unlikely to take action against disorder and crime. However, when cohesion and mutual trust exist among neighbours, the likelihood is greater that they will share a willingness to intervene for the common good. The report found that in neighbourhoods whose sense of collective efficacy was strong, rates of violence were low, regardless of neighbourhood composition or socioeconomic conditions. Collective efficacy also appeared to deter disorder: Where it was strong, observed levels of physical and social disorder were low.

The mayor wants to apply these concepts to Central City. She asks you to come up with a plan for increasing the collective efficacy of local neighbourhoods and to determine whether such measures can actually reduce crime. You can bring any public or private element to bear on this overwhelming problem.

Your problem is twofold: (1) How can collective efficacy be improved? (2) What test will show whether improvements in collective efficacy levels are responsible for lower violent crime rates?

KEY TERMS

at-risk p. 214
Chicago School p. 200
concentration effect p. 212
conduct norms p. 225
cultural deviance theory p. 204
cultural transmission p. 206
culture conflict p. 225
culture of poverty p. 202
differential opportunity p. 226

focal concerns p. 225
general strain theory (GST) p. 220
income inequality p. 212
natural areas p. 200
negative affective states p. 220
reaction formation p. 227
relative deprivation p. 219
siege mentality p. 209
social disorganization theory p. 204

social ecologists p. 208
social injustice p. 212
social structure theory p. 203
status frustration p. 226
strain theory p. 204
subculture p. 226
transitional neighbourhood p. 205
underclass p. 202
value conflict p. 207

DOING RESEARCH ON THE WEB

For an RCMP feature on youth gangs in Canada, see www .rcmp-grc.gc.ca/pubs/ccaps-spcca/gangs-bandes-eng .htm. Another good resource is the National Youth Gang Center at www.iir.com/nygc/faq.htm#.

CRITICAL THINKING QUESTIONS

1. Is there a transitional area in your town or city? Does the crime rate remain constant in this neighbourhood, regardless of the racial, ethnic, or cultural composition of its residents?
2. Do you believe a distinct lower-class culture exists? Do you know anyone who has the focal concerns Miller talks about? Did you experience elements of these focal concerns while you were in high school? Will emerging forms of communication, such as the Internet, reduce cultural differences and create a more homogeneous society, or are subcultures resistant to such influences?
3. Do you agree with Agnew that there is more than one cause of strain? If so, are there other sources of strain that he did not consider?
4. How would a structural theorist explain the presence of middle-class crime?
5. How would biosocial theories explain the high levels of violent crime in lower-class areas?

NOTES

1. Steven Messner and Richard Rosenfeld, *Crime and the American Dream* (Belmont, CA: Wadsworth, 1994), 11.
2. Robert Park, "The City: Suggestions for the Investigation of Behavior in the City Environment," *American Journal of Sociology* 20 (1915): 579–583.
3. Robert Park, Ernest Burgess, and Roderic McKenzie, *The City* (Chicago: University of Chicago Press, 1925).
4. Harvey Zorbaugh, *The Gold Coast and the Slum* (Chicago: University of Chicago Press, 1929); Frederic Thrasher, *The Gang* (Chicago: University of Chicago Press, 1927); Louis Wirth, *The Ghetto* (Chicago: University of Chicago Press, 1928).
5. Daniel Bell, *The Coming of Post-Industrial Society* (New York: Basic Books, 1973).
6. See, generally, Stephen Cernkovich and Peggy Giordano, "Family Relationships and Delinquency," *Criminology* 25 (1987): 295–321; Paul Howes and Howard Markman, "Marital Quality and Child Functioning: A Longitudinal Investigation," *Child Development* 60 (1989): 1044–1051.
7. Emilie Andersen Allan and Darrell Steffensmeier, "Youth, Underemployment, and Property Crime: Differential Effects of Job Availability and Job Quality on Juvenile and Young Adult Arrest Rates," *American Sociological Review* 54 (1989): 107–123.
8. Edwin Lemert, *Human Deviance, Social Problems and Social Control* (Englewood Cliffs, NJ: Prentice-Hall, 1967).
9. "Almost 900,000 Canadian Children Living in Poverty, StatsCan finds," Canadian Press, May 1, 2008.
10. Stephen W. Baron and Timothy F. Hartnagel, "Street Youth and Labour Market Strain," *Journal of Criminal Justice* 30 (2002): 519–533; "Double Spending on Child Poverty, Campaign Asks," *Canadian Medical Association Journal* 3 (2003): 168–174; John M. Bolland, "Hopelessness and Risk Behaviour among Adolescents Living in High-Poverty Inner-City Neighbourhoods," *Journal of Adolescence* 26 (2003): 145–158.
11. Jonathan Crane, "The Epidemic Theory of Ghettos and Neighborhood Effects on Dropping Out and Teenage Childbearing," *American Journal of Sociology* 96 (1991): 1226–1259; see also Rodrick Wallace, "Expanding Coupled Shock Fronts of Urban Decay and Criminal Behavior: How U.S. Cities Are Becoming 'Hollowed Out,'" *Journal of Quantitative Criminology* 7 (1991): 333–355.
12. Kevin J.P. Craib et al., "Risk Factors for Elevated HIV Incidence among Aboriginal Injection Drug Users in Vancouver," *Canadian Medical Association Journal* 1, 168 (2001): 19–24.
13. Carol LaPrairie, "Aboriginal Over-Representation in the Criminal Justice System: A Tale of Nine Cities," *Canadian Journal of Criminology* 4 (2002): 181–208.
14. "Domestic Violence. Low-Income Native American Women Suffer High Rates of Domestic Abuse," *Women's Health Weekly*, June 10, 2004, 51–52; "Raise Welfare Rates to Help Women Leave Abusive Relationships: Study," Canadian Press, April 5, 2004.
15. Oscar Lewis, "The Culture of Poverty," *Scientific American* 215 (1966): 19–25.
16. Gunnar Myrdal, *The Challenge of World Poverty* (New York: Vintage Books, 1970); Ken Auletta, *The Under Class* (New York: Random House, 1982).
17. Herbert Gans, "Deconstructing the Underclass: The Term's Danger as a Planning Concept," *Journal of the American Planning Association* 56 (1990): 271–277.
18. David Brownfield, "Social Class and Violent Behavior," *Criminology* 24 (1986): 421–438; Charles Tittle and Robert Meier, "Specifying the SES/Delinquency Relationship," *Criminology* 28 (1990): 271–295.
19. Ruth Kornhauser, *Social Sources of Delinquency* (Chicago: University of Chicago Press, 1978), 75.
20. Clifford R. Shaw and Henry D. McKay, *Juvenile Delinquency and Urban Areas*, rev. ed. (Chicago: University of Chicago Press, 1972).
21. Anthony Platt, *The Child Savers: The Invention of Delinquency* (Chicago: University of Chicago Press, 1968).
22. For a discussion of these issues, see Robert Bursik, "Social Disorganization and Theories of Crime and Delinquency:

Problems and Prospects," *Criminology* 26 (1988): 521–539.

23. Robert Sampson, "Effects of Socioeconomic Context of Official Reaction to Juvenile Delinquency," *American Sociological Review* 51 (1986): 876–885; Jeffrey Fagan, Ellen Slaughter, and Eliot Hartstone, "Blind Justice? The Impact of Race on the Juvenile Justice Process," *Crime and Delinquency* 33 (1987): 224–258; Merry Morash, "Establishment of a Juvenile Police Record," *Criminology* 22 (1984): 97–113.

24. Bernard Lander, *Towards an Understanding of Juvenile Delinquency* (New York: Columbia University Press, 1954); David Bordua, "Juvenile Delinquency and 'Anomie': An Attempt at Replication," *Social Problems* 6 (1958): 230–238; Roland Chilton, "Continuities in Delinquency Area Research: A Comparison of Studies in Baltimore, Detroit, and Indianapolis," *American Sociological Review* 29 (1964): 71–73.

25. For a general review, see James Byrne and Robert Sampson, eds., *The Social Ecology of Crime* (New York: Springer Verlag, 1985).

26. Christopher T. Lowenkamp, Francis T. Cullen, and Travis C. Pratt, "Replicating Sampson and Groves' Test of Social Disorganization Theory: Revisiting a Criminological Classic," *Journal of Research in Crime and Delinquency* 40, no. 4 (2003): 351–373.

27. William Spelman, "Abandoned Buildings: Magnets for Crime?" *Journal of Criminal Justice* 21 (1993): 481–493.

28. Keith Harries and Andrea Powell, "Juvenile Gun Crime and Social Stress: Baltimore, 1980–1990," *Urban Geography* 15 (1994): 45–63.

29. Steven Messner and Kenneth Tardiff, "Economic Inequality and Levels of Homicide: An Analysis of Urban Neighborhoods," *Criminology* 24 (1986): 297–317.

30. Travis C. Pratt, and Timothy W. Godsey, "Social Support, Inequality, and Homicide: a Cross-National Test of an Integrated Theoretical Model," *Criminology* 41, 3 (2003): 611–644.

31. G. David Curry and Irving Spergel, "Gang Homicide, Delinquency, and Community," *Criminology* 26 (1988): 381–407.

32. Jennifer L. Schulenberg, "The Social Context of Police Discretion and Young Offenders: An Ecological Analysis," *Canadian Journal of Criminology and Criminal Justice* 4 (2003): 127–157.

33. Per-Olof Wikstrom and Lars Dolmen, "Crime and Crime Trends in Different Urban Environments," *Journal of Quantitative Criminology* 6 (1990): 7–28.

34. Robert Sampson and W. Byron Groves, "Community Structure and Crime: Testing Social Disorganization Theory," *American Journal of Sociology* 94 (1989): 774–802.

35. Steven Messner, Lawrence Raffalovich, and Richard McMillan, "Economic Deprivation and Changes in Homicide Arrest Rates for White and Black Youths, 1967–1998: A National Time Series Analysis," *Criminology* 39 (2001): 591–614.

36. Darrell Steffensmeier and Dana Haynie, "Gender, Structural Disadvantage, and Urban Crime: Do Macrosocial Variables Also Explain Female Offending Rates?" *Criminology* 38 (2000): 403–438; Richard McGahey, "Economic Conditions, Organization, and Urban Crime," in *Communities and Crime*, eds. Albert Reiss and Michael Tonry, 231–270 (Chicago: University of Chicago Press, 1986).

37. Richard McGahey, "Economic Conditions, Organization, and Urban Crime," in *Communities and Crime*, eds. Albert Reiss and Michael Tonry, 231–270 (Chicago: University of Chicago Press, 1986); Scott Menard and Delbert Elliott, "Self-Reported Offending, Maturational Reform, and the Easterlin Hypothesis," *Journal of Quantitative Criminology* 6 (1990): 237–268.

38. Elijah Anderson, *Streetwise: Race, Class and Change in an Urban Community* (Chicago: University of Chicago Press, 1990), 243–244.

39. Pamela Wilcox Rountree and Kenneth Land, "Burglary Victimization, Perceptions of Crime Risk, and Routine Activities: A Multilevel Analysis Across Seattle Neighborhoods and Census Tracts," *Journal of Research in Crime and Delinquency* 33 (1996): 147–180.

40. Randy LaGrange, Kenneth Ferraro, and Michael Supancic, "Perceived Risk and Fear of Crime: Role of Social and Physical Incivilities," *Journal of Research in Crime and Delinquency* 29 (1992): 311–334.

41. Catherine E. Ross, John Mirowsky, and Shana Pribesh, "Powerlessness and the Amplification of Threat: Neighborhood Disadvantage, Disorder, and Mistrust," *American Sociological Review* 66 (2001): 568–580.

42. Ralph Taylor and Jeanette Covington, "Community Structural Change and Fear of Crime," *Social Problems* 40 (1993): 374–392.

43. Wesley Skogan, "Fear of Crime and Neighborhood Change," in *Communities and Crime*, eds. Albert Reiss and Michael Tonry, 191–232 (Chicago: University of Chicago Press, 1986).

44. Stephanie Greenberg, "Fear and Its Relationship to Crime, Neighborhood Deterioration and Informal Social Control," in *The Social Ecology of Crime*, eds. James Byrne and Robert Sampson, 47–62 (New York: Springer Verlag, 1985).

45. Anderson, *Streetwise: Race, Class and Change in an Urban Community*, 245.

46. Finn Aage-Esbensen and David Huizinga, "Community Structure and Drug Use: From a Social Disorganization Perspective," *Justice Quarterly* 7 (1990): 691–709; Allen Liska and Paul Bellair, "Violent-Crime Rates and Racial Composition: Convergence over Time," *American Journal of Sociology* 101 (1995): 578–610; Wesley Skogan, *Disorder and Decline: Crime and the Spiral of Decay in American Neighborhoods* (New York: Free Press, 1990), 15–35.

47. Ralph Taylor and Jeanette Covington, "Neighborhood Changes in Ecology and Violence," *Criminology* 26 (1988): 553–589.

48. Leo Scheurman and Solomon Kobrin, "Community Careers in Crime," in *Communities and Crime*, eds. Albert Reiss and Michael Tonry, 67–100 (Chicago: University of Chicago Press, 1986).

49. Robert Bursik, "Delinquency Rates as Sources of Ecological Change," in *The Social Ecology of Crime*, eds. Byrne and Sampson, 63–77; Janet Heitgerd and Robert Bursik, "Extracommunity Dynamics and the Ecology of Delinquency," *American Journal of Sociology* 92 (1987): 775–787.

50. Siu Kwong Wong, "Disorganization Precursors, the Family and Crime: A Multi-Year Analysis of Canadian Municipalities," *Western Criminology Review* 8, 1 (2007): 48–68.

51. Jeffrey Morenoff, Robert Sampson, and Stephen Raudenbush, "Neighborhood Inequality, Collective Efficacy, and the Spatial Dynamics of Urban Violence," *Criminology* 39 (2001): 517–560.

52. Karen Parker and Matthew Pruitt, "Poverty, Poverty Concentration, and Homicide," *Social Science Quarterly* 81 (2000): 555–582.

53. Carolyn Rebecca Block and Richard Block, *Street Gang Crime in Chicago* (Washington, DC: National Institute of Justice, 1993), 7.

54. Barbara Warner and Glenn Pierce, "Reexamining Social Disorganization Theory Using Calls to the Police as a Measure of Crime," *Criminology* 31 (1993): 493–519.

55. Marc Ouimet, "Aggregation Bias in Ecological Research: How Social Disorganization and Criminal Opportunities Shape the Spatial Distribution of Juvenile Delinquency in Montreal," *Canadian Journal of Criminology*, 42, 2 (2000): 135–156.

56. Donald Black, "Social Control as a Dependent Variable," in *Toward a General Theory of Social Control*, ed. D. Black (Orlando, FL: Academic Press, 1990).

57. Rodney Stark, "Deviant Places: A Theory of the Ecology of Crime," *Criminology* 25 (1987): 893–911.

58. Delbert Elliott, William Julius Wilson, David Huizinga, Robert Sampson, Amanda Elliott, and Bruce Rankin, "The Effects of Neighborhood Disadvantage on Adolescent

Development," *Journal of Research in Crime and Delinquency* 33 (1996): 389–426.

59. Robert Bursik and Harold Grasmick, "Economic Deprivation and Neighborhood Crime Rates, 1960–1980," *Law and Society Review* 27 (1993): 263–278.

60. Robert Sampson and W. Byron Groves, "Community Structure and Crime: Testing Social Disorganization Theory," *American Journal of Sociology* 94 (1989): 774–802; Denise Gottfredson, Richard McNeill, and Gary Gottfredson, "Social Area Influences on Delinquency: A Multilevel Analysis," *Journal of Research in Crime and Delinquency* 28 (1991): 197–206.

61. Felton Earls, *Linking Community Factors and Individual Development* (Washington, DC National Institute of Justice, 1998).

62. Robert J. Sampson and Stephen W. Raudenbush, *Disorder in Urban Neighborhoods: Does It Lead to Crime?* (Washington, DC: National Institute of Justice, 2001).

63. Robert J. Sampson, Jeffrey Morenoff, and Felton Earls, "Beyond Social Capital: Spatial Dynamics of Collective Efficacy for Children," *American Sociological Review* 64 (1999): 633–660.

64. Donald Black, "Social Control as a Dependent Variable," in *Toward a General Theory of Social Control*, ed. D. Black (Orlando: Academic Press, 1990).

65. Paul Bellair, "Informal Surveillance and Street Crime: A Complex Relationship," *Criminology* 38 (2000): 137–170.

66. Robert Sampson and W. Byron Groves, "Community Structure and Crime: Testing Social Disorganization Theory," *American Journal of Sociology* 94 (1989): 774–802; Denise Gottfredson, Richard McNeill, and Gary Gottfredson, "Social Area Influences on Delinquency: A Multilevel Analysis," *Journal of Research in Crime and Delinquency* 28 (1991): 197–206.

67. Fred Markowitz, Paul Bellair, Allen Liska, and Jianhong Liu, "Extending Social Disorganization Theory: Modeling the Relationships between Cohesion, Disorder, and Fear," *Criminology* 39 (2001): 293–320.

68. Robert Bursik and Harold Grasmick, "The Multiple Layers of Social Disorganization," paper presented at the annual meeting of the American Society of Criminology, New Orleans, November 1992; also, Robert Bursik and Harold Grasmick, "Economic Deprivation and Neighborhood Crime Rates, 1960-1980," 27 *Law and Society Review* (1993): 263.

69. Ruth Peterson, Lauren Krivo, and Mark Harris, "Disadvantage and Neighborhood Violent Crime: Do Local Institutions Matter?" *Journal of Research in Crime and Delinquency* 37 (2000): 31–63.

70. Maria Velez, "The Role of Public Social Control in Urban Neighborhoods: A Multi-Level Analysis of Victimization Risk," *Criminology* 39 (2001): 837–864.

71. David Klinger, "Negotiating Order in Patrol Work: An Ecological Theory of Police Response to Deviance," *Criminology* 35 (1997): 277–306.

72. Rodney Stark, "Deviant Places: A Theory of the Ecology of Crime," *Criminology* 25 (1987): 893–911.

73. Robert Bursik and Harold Grasmick, "Economic Deprivation and Neighborhood Crime Rates, 1960–1980," *Law and Society Review* 27 (1993): 263–278.

74. Delbert Elliott, William Julius Wilson, David Huizinga, Robert Sampson, Amanda Elliott, and Bruce Rankin, "The Effects of Neighborhood Disadvantage on Adolescent Development," *Journal of Research in Crime and Delinquency* 33 (1996): 389–426.

75. Walter S. DeKeseredy, Martin D. Schwartz, and Shahid Alvi, "Perceived Collective Efficacy and Women's Victimization in Public Housing," *Criminal Justice* 3, 1 (2003): 5–27.

76. Robert Sampson, Jeffrey Morenoff, and Felton Earls, "Beyond Social Capital: Spatial Dynamics of Collective Efficacy for Children," *American Sociological Review* 64 (1999): 633–660.

77. Thomas McNulty, "Assessing the Race–Violence Relationship at the Macro Level: The Assumption of Racial Invariance and the Problem of Restricted Distribution," *Criminology* 39 (2001): 467–490.

78. Mitchell Chamlin and John Cochran, "Social Altruism and Crime," *Criminology* 35 (1997): 203–228.

79. Travis C. Pratta, and Timothy W. Godseyb, "Social Support and Homicide: A Cross-National Test of an Emerging Criminological Theory," *Journal of Criminal Justice* 30, 6 (2002): 589–601.

80. Vincent F. Sacco, and M. Reza Nakhaie, "Fear of School Violence and the Ameliorative Effects of Student Social Capital," *Journal of School Violence* 6, 1 (2007): 3–25.

81. Carla Cesaroni, "Releasing Sex Offenders into the Community Through 'Circles of Support'—A Means of Reintegrating the 'Worst of the Worst,'" *Journal of Offender Rehabilitation* 34, 2 (2001): 85–98.

82. Robert Merton, *Social Theory and Social Structure*, enlarged ed. (New York: Free Press, 1968); for an analysis, see Richard Hilbert, "Durkheim and Merton on Anomie: An Unexplored Contrast in Its Derivatives," *Social Problems* 36 (1989): 242–256.

83. Richard Hilbert, "Durkheim and Merton on Anomie: An Unexplored Contrast in Its Derivatives," *Social Problems* 36 (1989): 243.

84. Albert Cohen, "The Sociology of the Deviant Act: Anomie Theory and Beyond," *American Sociological Review* 30 (1965): 5–14.

85. See Robert Agnew, "The Contribution of Social Psychological Strain Theory to the Explanation of Crime and Delinquency," in *Advances in Criminological Theory* 6 (1995): 113–122.

86. Stephen A. Cernkovich, Peggy C. Giordano, and Jennifer L. Rudolph, "Race, Crime, and the American Dream," *Journal of Research in Crime and Delinquency* 37, 2 (2000): 131–170.

87. Martin Sanchez-Jankowski, "Gangs and Social Change," *Theoretical Criminology* 7, 2 (2003): 191–216.

88. Scott Menard, "A Developmental Test of Mertonian Anomie Theory," *Journal of Research in Crime and Delinquency* 32 (1995): 136–174.

89. John Hagan, Hans Merkens, and Klaus Boehnke, "Delinquency and Disdain: Social Capital and Control of Right-Wing Extremism among East and West Berlin Youth," *American Journal of Sociology* 100 (1995): 1028–1052.

90. Steven Messner and Richard Rosenfeld, "An Institutional-Anomie Theory of the Social Distribution of Crime," in *Readings in Contemporary Criminological Theory,* eds. L. Siegel and P. Cordella, 143–148 (Boston: Northeastern University Press, 1996).

91. Mitchell Chamlin and John Cochran, "Assessing Messner and Rosenfeld's Institutional Anomie Theory: A Partial Test," *Criminology* 33 (1995): 411–429.

92. Stephen Cernkovich, Peggy Giordano, and Jennifer Rudolph, "Race, Crime, and the American Dream," *Journal of Research in Crime and Delinquency* 37 (2000): 131–170.

93. Gary Jensen, "Institutional Anomie and Societal Variations in Crime: A Critical Appraisal," *International Journal of Sociology and Social Policy* 22, 7/8 (2002): 45–74; Candice Batton and Gary Jensen, "Decommodification and Homicide Rates in the 20th-Century United States," *Homicide Studies* 6, 1 (2002): 6–38.

94. Jukka Savolainen, "Inequality, Welfare State and Homicide: Further Support for the Institutional Anomie Theory," *Criminology* 38 (2000): 1021–1042.

95. Jeffrey Morenoff, Robert Sampson, and Stephen Raudenbush, "Neighborhood Inequality, Collective Efficacy, and the Spatial Dynamics of Urban Violence," *Criminology* 39 (2001): 517–560.

96. John Braithwaite, "Poverty Power, White-Collar Crime and the Paradoxes of Criminological Theory," *Australian and New Zealand Journal of Criminology* 24 (1991): 40–58.

97. Judith Blau and Peter Blau, "The Cost of Inequality: Metropolitan Structure and Violent Crime," *American Sociological Review* 147 (1982): 114–129.

98. Peter Blau and Joseph Schwartz, *Crosscutting Social Circles* (New York: Academic Press, 1984).

99. Scott South and Steven Messner, "Structural Determinants of Intergroup Association," *American Journal of Sociology* 91 (1986): 1409–1430; Steven Messner and Scott South, "Economic Deprivation, Opportunity Structure and Robbery Victimization," *Social Forces* 64 (1986): 975–991.

100. Richard Fowles and Mary Merva, "Wage Inequality and Criminal Activity: An Extreme Bounds Analysis for the United States, 1975–1990," *Criminology* 34 (1996): 163–182.

101. Taylor and Covington, "Neighborhood Changes in Ecology and Violence," 582; Richard Block, "Community Environment and Violent Crime," *Criminology* 17 (1979): 46–57; Robert Sampson, "Structural Sources of Variation in Race-Age-Specific Rates of Offending Across Major U.S. Cities," *Criminology* 23 (1985): 647–673; Richard Rosenfeld, "Urban Crime Rates: Effects of Inequality, Welfare Dependency, Region and Race," in *The Social Ecology of Crime*, eds. James Byrne and Robert Sampson, 116–130 (New York: Springer Verlag, 1985).

102. Fowles and Merva, "Wage Inequality and Criminal Activity"; Ruth Peterson and William Bailey, "Rape and Dimensions of Gender Socioeconomic Inequality in U.S. Metropolitan Areas," *Journal of Research in Crime and Delinquency* 29 (1992): 162–177; Gary LaFree, Kriss Drass, and Patrick O'Day, "Race and Crime in Postwar America: Determinants of African-American and White Rates, 1957–1988," *Criminology* 30 (1992): 157–188.

103. Martin Daly, Margo Wilson, and Shawn Vasdev, "Income Inequality and Homicide Rates in Canada and the United States," *Canadian Journal of Criminology* 4 (2001): 219–236.

104. Christina Lanier, and Lin Huff-Corzine, "American Indian Homicide. A County-Level Analysis Utilizing Social Disorganization Theory," *Homicide Studies*, 10, 3 (2006): 181–194.

105. Kenneth Land, Patricia McCall, and Lawrence Cohen, "Structural Covariates of Homicide Rates: Are There Any Invariances across Time and Social Space?" *American Journal of Sociology* 95 (1990): 922–963; Robert Bursik and James Webb, "Community Change and Patterns of Delinquency," *American Journal of Sociology* 88 (1982): 24–42.

106. See, for example, Robert Agnew, "Delinquency as a Creative Enterprise: A Review of Recent Evidence," *Criminal Justice and Behavior*, 1989, 16, 1 98–113

107. Jeanne Brooks-Gunn, Greg Duncan, Pamela Klato Klebanov, and Naomi Sealand, "Do Neighborhoods Influence Child and Adolescent Development?" *American Journal of Sociology* 99 (1993): 353–395.

108. See, for example, Nikos Passas, "Anomie, reference groups, and relative deprivation," *The Future of Anomie Theory* (1997): 62–94.

109. Robert Agnew, "Foundation for a General Strain Theory of Crime and Delinquency," *Criminology* 30 (1992): 47–87.

110. Paul Mazerolle and Alex Piquero, "Linking Exposure to Strain with Anger: An Investigation of Deviant Adaptations," *Journal of Criminal Justice* 26, 3 (1998): 195–211.

111. Tracey Peter, Teresa C. LaGrange, and Robert A. Silverman, "Investigating the Interdependence of Strain and Self-Control," *Canadian Journal of Criminology and Criminal Justice* 45, 4 (2003): 431–464.

112. Robert Agnew, Timothy Brezina, John Paul Wright, and Frances Cullen, "Strain, Personality Traits, and Delinquency: Extending General Strain Theory," *Criminology* 40 (2002): 43–72.

113. Robert Agnew, "Stability and Change in Crime over the Life Course: A Strain Theory Explanation," in *Advances in Criminological Theory*, vol. 7: *Developmental Theories of Crime and Delinquency*, ed. Terence Thornberry (New Brunswick, NJ: Transaction Books, 1995), 113–137.

114. Lawrence Wu, "Effects of Family Instability, Income and Income Instability on the Risk of Premarital Birth," *American Sociological Review* 61 (1996): 386–406.

115. Anthony Walsh, "Behavior Genetics and Anomie/Strain Theory," *Criminology* 38 (2000): 1075–1108.

116. George E. Capowich, Paul Mazerolle, and Alex Piquero, "General Strain Theory, Situational Anger, and Social Networks: An Assessment of Conditioning Influences," *Journal of Criminal Justice* 29 (2001): 445–461.

117. Robert Agnew and Helene Raskin White, "An Empirical Test of General Strain Theory," *Criminology* 30 (1992): 475–499.

118. John Hoffman and Alan Miller, "A Latent Variable Analysis of General Strain Theory," *Journal of Quantitative Criminology* 14 (1998): 83–110; Raymond Paternoster and Paul Mazerolle, "General Strain Theory and Delinquency: A Replication and Extension," *Journal of Research in Crime and Delinquency* 31 (1994): 235–263.

119. G. Roger Jarjoura, "The Conditional Effect of Social Class on the Dropout–Delinquency Relationship," *Journal of Research in Crime and Delinquency* 33 (1996): 232–255.

120. Teresa Lagrange and Robert Silverman, "Perceived Strain and Delinquency Motivation: An Empirical Evaluation of General Strain Theory," paper presented at the American Society of Criminology meeting, Boston, November 1995.

121. Thomas Ashby Wills, Donato Vaccaro, Grace McNamara, and A. Elizabeth Hirky, "Escalated Substance Use: A Longitudinal Grouping Analysis from Early to Middle Adolescence," *Journal of Abnormal Psychology* 105 (1996): 166–180.

122. Timothy Brezina, "Adapting to Strain: An Examination of Delinquent Coping Responses," *Criminology* 34 (1996): 39–61.

123. Stephen W. Baron, "Street Youth Labour Market Experience and Crime," *Canadian Review of Sociology and Anthropology* 38, 2 (2001): 189–216.

124. Stephen W. Baron, and Timothy F. Hartnagel, "Street youth and labor market strain," *Journal of Criminal Justice*, 30, 6 (2002): 519–533.

125. Stephen W. Baron, "Self-Control, Social Consequences, and Criminal Behavior: Street Youth and the General Theory of Crime," *Journal of Research in Crime and Delinquency*, 40, 4 (2003): 403–425.

126. Stephen W. Baron, "General Strain, Street Youth and Crime: A Test of Agnew's Revised Theory," *Criminology* 42, 2 (2004): 457–484.

127. Stephen W. Baron, "Street Youth, Strain Theory, and Crime," *Journal of Criminal Justice* 34, 2 (2006): 209–223.

128. Stephen W. Baron, David R. Forde, and Fiona M. Kay, "Self-control, Risky Lifestyles, and Situation: The Role of Opportunity and Context in the General Theory," *Journal of Criminal Justice* 35, 2 (2007): 119–136.

129. Stephen W. Baron, "Street Youth, Gender, Financial Strain, and Crime: Exploring Broidy and Agnew's Extension to General Strain Theory," *Deviant Behavior* 28, 3 (2007): 273–302.

130. Lisa Broidy, "A Test of General Strain Theory," *Criminology* 39 (2001): 9–36; Robert Agnew and Timothy Brezina, "Relational Problems with Peers, Gender and Delinquency," *Youth and Society* 29 (1997): 84–111.

131. John Hoffman and S. Susan Su, "The Conditional Effects of Stress on Delinquency and Drug Use: A Strain Theory in Assessment of Sex Differences," *Journal of Research in Crime and Delinquency* 34 (1997): 46–78.

132. Lisa Broidy, "The Role of Gender in General Strain Theory," paper presented at the American Society of Criminology meeting, Boston, November 1995.

133. Robbin Ogle, Daniel Maier-Katkin, and Thomas Bernard, "A Theory of Homicidal Behavior among Women," *Criminology* 33 (1995): 173–193.

134. Thorsten Sellin, *Culture Conflict and Crime*, bulletin no. 41 (New York: Social Science Research Council, 1938).

135. Walter Miller, "Lower-Class Culture as a Generating Milieu of Gang Delinquency," *Journal of Social Issues* 14 (1958): 5–19.

136. Elijah Anderson, *Code of the Street: Decency, Violence, and the Moral Life of the Inner City* (New York: Norton, 2000).

137. Albert Cohen, *Delinquent Boys* (New York: Free Press, 1955).

138. Carlo Morselli, "The Relational Dynamics of Illegal Firearm Transactions," *Canadian Journal of Criminology* 44, 3 (2002): 255–277.

139. Stephen W. Baron, David R. Forde, and Leslie W. Kennedy, "Rough Justice: Street Youth and Violence," *Journal of Interpersonal Violence* 16, 7 (2001): 662–678.

140. Clarence Schrag, *Crime and Justice American Style* (Washington, DC: U.S. Government Printing Office, 1971), 74.

141. J. Johnstone, "Social Class, Social Areas, and Delinquency," *Sociology and Social Research* 63 (1978): 49–72; Joseph Harry, "Social Class and Delinquency: One More Time," *Sociological Quarterly* 15 (1974): 294–301.

142. Stephen Baron and Leslie Kennedy, "Deterrence and Homeless Male Street Youths," *Canadian Journal of Criminology* 40 (1998): 27–52.

143. Richard Cloward and Lloyd Ohlin, *Delinquency and Opportunity* (New York: Free Press, 1960).

144. Christopher Uggen, "Work as a Turning Point in the Life Course of Criminals: A Duration Model of Age, Employment and Recidivism," *American Sociological Review* 65 (2000): 529–546.

145. Brian Mellor, Leslie MacRae, Monica Pauls, and Joseph P. Hornick, *Youth Gangs In Canada: A Preliminary Review of Programs and Services* (Calgary: Canadian Research Institute for Law and the Family, 2005).

146. Finn-Aage Esbensen and David Huizinga, "Gangs, Drugs, and Delinquency in a Survey of Urban Youth," *Criminology* 31 (1993): 565–591; Malcom Klein, Cheryl Maxson, and Lea Cunningham, "Crack, Street Gangs, and Violence," *Criminology* 29 (1991): 623–650; see also Irving Spergel, "Youth Gangs: Continuity and Change," in *Crime and Justice*, vol. 12, eds. Michael Tonry and Norval Morris, 171–277 (Chicago: University of Chicago Press, 1990).

147. Melanie Nimmo, *The "Invisible" Gang Members: A Report on Female Gang Association in Winnipeg* (Ottawa: Canadian Centre for Policy Alternatives, 2001).

148. Felix Padilla, *The Gang as an American Enterprise* (New Brunswick, NJ: Rutgers University Press, 1992); see also Jeffery Fagan, "The Political Economy of Drug Dealing Among Urban Gangs," in *Drugs and the Community*, eds. Robert Davis, Arthur Lurigio, and Dennis Rosenbaum, 19–54 (Springfield, IL: Charles C. Thomas, 1993).

149. Pamela Irving Jackson, "Crime, Youth Gangs, and Urban Transition: The Social Dislocations of Postindustrial Economic Development," *Justice Quarterly* 8 (1991): 379–397.

150. Robert Sampson and William Julius Wilson, "Toward a Theory of Race, Crime and Urban Inequality," in *Crime and Inequality*, eds. John Hagan and Ruth Peterson, 37–54 (Stanford, CA: Stanford University Press, 1995).

151. Charles Tittle, "Social Class and Criminal Behavior: A Critique of the Theoretical Foundations," *Social Forces* 62 (1983): 334–358.

152. James Q. Wilson and Richard Herrnstein, *Crime and Human Nature* (New York: Simon & Schuster, 1985).

153. Kenneth Polk and F. Lynn Richmond, "Those Who Fail," in *Schools and Delinquency*, eds. Kenneth Polk and Walter Schafer, 67 (Englewood Cliffs, NJ: Prentice-Hall, 1974).

154. James DeFronzo, "Welfare and Burglary," *Crime and Delinquency* 42 (1996): 223–230.

155. Solomon Kobrin, "The Chicago Area Project—25-Year Assessment," *Annals of the American Academy of Political and Social Science* 322 (1959): 20–29.

Social Process Theories

Learning Objectives

After reading this chapter, you will be able to:

1. Understand the scope of social process theories.
2. Be familiar with the difference between this and structure theory.
3. Know the elements of labelling theory.
4. Discuss some new developments in integrating developmental models.
5. Explain different policy strategies developing out of this approach.

Newsmaker of the year, Toronto's mayor, Rob Ford, fought allegations of drug abuse, and then spent two months in a rehabilitation facility in Ontario.

© Fernando Morales/ *The Globe and Mail*

Many criminologists question whether a person's place in the social structure can alone control the onset of criminality. After all, the majority of people residing in the nation's most deteriorated urban areas are law-abiding citizens who hold conventional values and compensate for their lack of social standing and financial problems by working hard, living frugally, and looking to the future. Conversely, self-report studies tell us that many members of the privileged classes engage in theft, drug use, and other crimes.

Even if it is assumed that all criminals come from the lower classes (which they don't), the great majority of even the poorest Canadians do not commit criminal acts.[1] The U.S. National Crime Victimization Survey estimated that about two million people could account for most of 26 million serious crimes that occurred in 2000.[2] Using that same factor, less than 200,000 people, or less than one-half of one percent of Canadians, could be responsible for the 2.5 million crimes that occurred in 2006.

Neighbourhood deterioration and disorganization by itself cannot explain why, out of two individuals living in the same environment, one person commits crime while the other obeys the law, gets an education, and has a legitimate job.[3] Relatively few delinquent offenders living in the most deteriorated areas remain persistent, chronic offenders, despite the continuing pressure of social decay. Some other social forces must be at work to explain why the majority of at-risk individuals do not become persistent criminal offenders.

To explain this situation, attention has focused on social-psychological processes and interactions common to all people. **Social process theories** hold that criminality is a function of **socialization**, and these theories draw attention to the interactions people have with others. As we pass through life, we are influenced by our familial relationships, peer group associations, educational experiences, and interactions with authorities, such as teachers and employers. If our relationships are positive and supportive, we will be able to succeed within the rules of society. However, if these relationships are dysfunctional and destructive, conventional success is more difficult.

Social process theories share one basic concept: All people, regardless of race, class, or gender, have the potential to become either delinquent or law-abiding citizens. Although many have the burden of poverty, racism, poor schools, and disrupted family lives, these social forces may be counteracted by positive peer relations, a supportive family, and educational success. However, even the best people may turn to antisocial behaviour if their life experiences are destructive. An example is described in the Criminology Research box later in the chapter, which looks at the drift of Aboriginal youth into gangs.

Social process theorists focus attention on the socialization of youths to identify the supportive developmental factors—family relationships, peer influences, educational attainment, self-image development—that can lead to a successful life. However, if these developmental factors are dysfunctional, they can result in antisocial behaviours.

The influence of social process theories has endured. Most people refrain from criminal activity, and few of those who do commit crimes remain persistent, chronic offenders in their adulthood. If poverty were the sole cause of crime, for example, poor adults would be as criminal as would be poor teenagers, so it is apparent that class position alone cannot explain crime rates.[4]

Research shows that even in the most deteriorated areas, criminality is controlled by the quality of interpersonal interactions with parents, peers, and schools.[5] Socialization is as important as social structure to understanding crime.

CONNECTIONS

In Chapter 3, the analysis of the class–crime relationship showed why that relationship is still a hotly debated topic. Although serious criminals may be disproportionately found in lower-class areas, self-report studies show that criminality cuts across class lines. The discussion of drug use in Chapter 13 also shows that many members of the middle class engage in recreational substance abuse, an indication that many law violators are not economically motivated.

SOCIAL PROCESSES AND CRIME

Criminologists study the critical elements of socialization, such as family, peer group, and school, to determine how those elements contribute to the development of a criminal career. It is a toss-up as to which variable has garnered more research, but the family probably wins. Research techniques used to gather this information are more likely to be delinquency self-reports than official statistics.

Family Relations

As a result of research going back several decades, evidence is well established that parenting factors play a critical role in

social process theories Approaches that look at the operation of formal and informal social institutions, such as socialization within family, peer groups, schools, and legal system.

socialization The process of human development and enculturation. Primary socialization takes place in the family, and secondary socialization takes place in institutions.

determining whether individuals misbehave as children and as adults.[6] Youths who grow up in a household characterized by tension, where familial love and support are lacking, and discipline is inconsistent or abusive, will be susceptible to the crime-promoting forces in the environment, placing them at higher risk.[7]

Children possessing disruptive characteristics at an early age are more likely to engage in later risky behaviour, adolescent delinquency, and adult crime. However, during a window of opportunity, between the ages of four and nine, the quality of parental intervention is significant.[8] Even those children living in high-crime areas will be better able to resist the temptations of the streets if they receive fair discipline, care, and support from parents who provide them with strong, positive role models.[9]

Nonetheless, living in a disadvantaged neighbourhood places a strain on family functioning, especially in single-parent families experiencing social isolation from relatives, friends, and neighbours. Kids who are raised within such distressed families are at risk for delinquency.[10] The relationship between family structure and crime is critical, especially considering the high rates of divorce and single parenthood.

The percentage of children living in homes headed by married couples is declining. While the double-parent family is not necessarily the best kind of family,[11] such trends are important when we consider that since 1960, the number of single-parent households in the population has been significantly related to arrest rates, probably due to social and economic stress.[12]

For example, a prospective longitudinal survey of 411 South London males from age 8 to age 46 by Juby (Montreal) and Farrington (Cambridge), called the Cambridge Study in Delinquent Development, found that delinquency rates were higher among boys living in permanently disrupted families compared with boys in intact families. Delinquency rates were similar in disrupted families and in intact high-conflict families, with disruptions caused by parental disharmony more damaging than disruptions caused by their parent's death. However, boys from disrupted families who continued living with their mothers had the same rate of delinquency as boys from intact harmonious families.[13] Other research has also found that family disruption is associated with an increase in delinquency.[14]

At one time, growing up in a so-called broken home was considered a primary cause of criminal behaviour because single-parent or divorced families were themselves considered deviant. However, nowadays, criminologists discount any easy association between family structure and the onset of criminality, claiming that family conflict and discord are more important determinants of behaviour than is family structure.[15] Wilson and Herrnstein claim that single mothers and fathers face difficulties in making up for the loss of a second parent, increasing their chances of failure.[16] Single parents may also find it difficult to provide adequate supervision, and they offer less help with schoolwork. The children may be more prone to rebellious acts, such as running away and truancy.[17] As well, children in two-parent households are more likely to want to go on to post-secondary education than are kids in single-parent homes, and poor school achievement and limited educational aspirations have been associated with delinquent behaviour.[18]

Because many divorced mothers face reduced incomes in the aftermath of marital break-up, they may be forced to move to residences in deteriorated neighbourhoods, which places their children at risk for crime and drug abuse.[19] However, new research complicates the picture. A mother's delinquency before marriage has been found not only to predict her future divorce but also to account for the behaviour problems of her children after divorce.

The U.S. National Longitudinal Survey of Youth showed that an adolescent mother's delinquent behaviour in 1980 (abusing drugs and being delinquent at school) predicted both her divorced status in 1994 and whether her child was antisocial, anxious, or depressed. Thus, parents' personal behaviour and personality characteristics have a greater impact on their children's behaviour than does their married, never-married, or divorced status.[20]

Remarriage does not mitigate the effects of divorce on youths: Children living with a step-parent exhibit as many problems as youths in divorce situations and considerably more problems than those living with both biological parents.[21]

However, new research again complicates the picture. Although crime rates for adolescents from two-parent families are lower than for teens from single-parent families, evidence suggests that divorce will have an effect on delinquency only when a two-parent family structure is not reestablished.

Data on 1,169 boys and girls between the ages of 13 and 19 showed that having two adult caretakers in a household allows less opportunity for delinquency. Although children from single-parent families face a higher risk of delinquency than do those from two-parent families, having an intact family structure seems to be the important factor.

The family structure–delinquency relationship was also gender based. The difference in delinquent behaviour between girls from one-parent families and girls from two-parent families was greater than was the difference in delinquency for boys.[22]

Kerr and Beaujot (University of Western Ontario) found in general that family type is more important than low income in predicting behavioural, emotional, and psychological difficulties. While low income has an impact on childhood difficulties in lone-parent and stepfamilies, it didn't in intact families. And family functioning had less impact on children's outcomes in stepfamilies than in intact or lone-parent families.[23]

When income makes a difference, it may be the result of larger structural factors. Researchers at Statistics Canada and the University of British Columbia looked at the relationship between neighbourhood characteristics on the verbal and behavioural abilities of 3,350 Canadian preschoolers. They found that children's verbal ability scores were higher when residing in affluent neighbourhoods and lower when residing in poor neighbourhoods. Behaviour problem scores were higher in poor neighbourhoods that had high unemployment rates and low cohesion.[24]

The advantage of combining an analysis of family dynamics and neighbourhood characteristics is shown in research that used Canadian national longitudinal data to examine how neighbourhood socio-economic conditions affected the verbal and behavioural outcomes of 3,528 children. The same researchers mentioned previously used social disorganization theory and family stress models together. They found that neighbourhood disadvantage in the form of lower neighbourhood cohesion was associated with maternal depression and family dysfunction. The result was less consistent, less stimulating, and more punitive parenting behaviours, and, ultimately, poorer child outcomes.[25]

Other family factors include inconsistent discipline, poor supervision, and the lack of a warm, loving, supportive parent–child relationship.[26] Parents who are supportive and control their children in a non-coercive fashion (parental efficacy) are more successful,[27] as are parents who provide a structure that supports children while giving them the ability to assert their individuality and regulate their own behaviour.[28] Children who have warm ties to their parents report greater levels of self-esteem beginning in adolescence and extending into their adulthood, where low self-esteem is related to criminal behaviour.[29]

Parental deviance, such as growing up in homes in which parents have a mental impairment are at risk for delinquency.[30] Even at age two, the children of drug abusers exhibit personality defects, such as excessive anger and negativity.[31] And they are more likely to become persistent substance abusers,[32] and to engage in law-violating behaviour.[33]

A link also exists between child abuse, neglect, sexual abuse,[34] and serious self-reported and official delinquency.[35] Victims of child abuse are more likely to mature into abusing and violent adults,[36] and this cycle of violence means that children who are physically victimized and who witness interparental violence have an increased risk of becoming adults who abuse their children and partners. Same-gender modelling meant that men's risk was increased by exposure to father-to-mother violence, and women's risk for being in an abusive relationship was increased by childhood victimization.[37]

Childhood sexual abuse victims also report twice as many sexual assaults, four times more self-inflicted harm, higher rates of domestic violence, and more significant lifetime traumas.[38] Child abuse is most prevalent among families living in socially disorganized neighbourhoods, explaining in part the association between poverty and violence.[39]

Results from interviews with parents in the National Longitudinal Survey of Children and Youth indicate that 8 percent of children between the ages of four and seven had witnessed some type of physical violence in the home, with one-third of those children witnessing it sometime, and 5 percent, often. Witnessing violence in the home is related to short-term and long-term behavioural problems, such as aggression and anxiety. Furthermore, rates of violence in the home are on the rise.[40]

The cycle of violence is not automatic, and the most typical outcome for individuals exposed to violence in their families is to be non-violent in their adult lives.

CONNECTIONS

The cycle of violence is also discussed in Chapter 4, and shows how victims of violence can become perpetrators themselves.

The effect of the family on delinquency has also been observed in other cultures. For example, research on Chinese families shows that those who provide firm support inhibit delinquency, whereas families who experience parental deviance are more likely to contain youths involved in antisocial behaviours.[41]

Educational Experience

Adolescent achievement in school has also been linked to criminality. Children who do poorly in school, lack motivation, and feel alienated are the most likely to engage in criminal acts.[42] Although Caucasian children and males seem more deeply influenced by school failure, all children who fail in school offend more frequently, commit more serious and violent offences, and persist in their offending into adulthood.[43] Students who do well are less likely to deviate, because successful performance is an insulating factor.[44]

The Canadian Centre for Justice Statistics found that children's social relationships at school are related to aggression. Figure 8.1 demonstrates that when children feel unsafe and bullied at school, they are more likely to be involved in

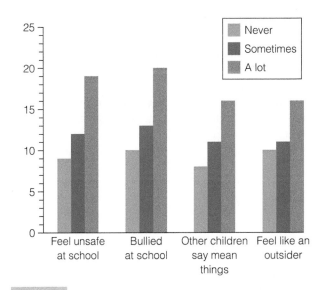

FIGURE 8.1

Percentage of Children Aged 12 to 13 Reporting High Levels of Aggressive Behaviour as a Function of School Relationships

Source: Adapted from the Statistics Canada publication "Children Witnessing Family Violence," 2001, *Juristat*, Catalogue 85-002, vol. 21, no. 4, June 12, 2001.

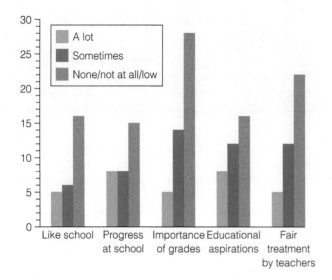

FIGURE 8.2

Percentage of Children Aged 12 to 13 Reporting High Levels of Delinquent Acts Involving Property as a Function of Relative Academic Ability and Aspirations

Source: Adapted from the Statistics Canada publication "Children Witnessing Family Violence," 2001, *Juristat*, Catalogue 85-002, vol. 21, no. 4, June 12, 2001.

aggressive behaviours. Children are also more likely to be aggressive when other children say mean things, or when they are bullied and feel like an outsider. Rather than aggression being simply a problem in itself, it is also a reaction to others.

Furthermore, a relationship exists between property offences and school risk factors (Figure 8.2). Of children who reported liking school a lot, 5 percent were involved in high numbers of property offences, compared with 16 percent of those who did not like school. Those children who scored higher on reading achievement tests were less likely to be involved in delinquent acts.[45] Children who do not like school, whose school progress is poor, and who think grades are unimportant are also more likely to be involved in property offences. In addition, children who have lower educational aspirations and who skip classes are more likely to report being involved in high levels of property offences. Does poor school performance cause delinquency, or is it simply co-related?

Jane Sprott (Ryerson University), conducted research recently to test the idea that classroom climate would have an important effect on children's perceptions and behaviours. *Climate* was conceptualized as either emotional or instrumental support provided at the levels of both the classroom and the school. Previous research has shown that classroom-based emotional support is important for some high-risk children; however, little research has focused on emotional support and delinquency. Using two years of the Canadian National Longitudinal Survey of Children and Youth, the study showed that an emotionally supportive classroom when the children were 10 to 13 years old was related to lower levels of violence

two years later. A classroom that focused on academics (instrumental support) was related to lower property offending.[46]

Schools also help contribute to criminality when they label problem youths, setting them apart from conventional society. A streaming system that identifies some students as university-bound and others as academic underachievers acts to **stigmatize** youths.[47] Research indicates that many school dropouts, especially those who have been expelled, face a significant chance of entering a criminal career.[48] In contrast, doing well in school and developing feelings of attachment to teachers have been linked to resistance to crime.[49]

Davies (McMaster University) and Tanner (University of Toronto) test labelling theory to see whether contact with school and justice system authorities has long-term, negative effects on a student's success in the labour market. Using the National Longitudinal Survey of Youth, they examined whether experiences ranging from school suspension to incarceration between ages 15 and 23 have an effect on occupational status, income, and employment later on in life. They find that severe forms of labelling, such as sentencing and incarceration, obviously have the strongest negative effects; although among females, suspension or expulsion from school also has a negative effect. Given that labelling can reduce employment chances,[50] diversion from formal punishment might be a better approach.

It is not surprising that the school system has been the subject of criticism concerning its methods, goals, and objectives. However, educational systems are often underfunded and understaffed, and despite the best efforts of teachers, reading and math ability levels are in question. These trends do not bode well for the crime rate. Most important, surveys indicate that much youth crime occurs within the schools themselves. In 2006, about 10 percent of youth crimes occurred on school property, with the most prevalent offences being assaults (27 percent) and drugs (18 percent). Weapons were present in about 7 percent of school crimes, but firearms were involved in only 1 percent of all school crimes.[51]

Peer Relations

The peer group has a powerful psychological effect on human conduct, influencing decision making and behaviour choices, an effect observed in many cultures.[52]

Early in children's lives, parents are the primary source of influence. However, between the ages of 8 and 14, children seek out a stable peer group. Soon, friends begin to have a greater influence over decision making than do parents.[53] By their early teens, children report their friends give them emotional support when they are feeling bad, and they can confide intimate feelings without their confidences being

stigmatize To create an enduring label that taints a person's identity and changes him or her in the eyes of others.

betrayed. As they go through adolescence, children form small groups of friends who share activities, confidences, and interests. They share intimate knowledge and activities, such as sports, religion, or hobbies. Although bonds in this wider circle of friends may not be intimate, kids learn a lot about themselves and their world while navigating through these relationships, some of it good, some of it negative.[54]

For example, research by the Department of Community Health and Epidemiology at Queen's University with a sample of 5,749 boys and girls aged 11 to 16 found that obese children and teenagers are more likely to be bullied. The research, part of a 35-country World Health Organization survey, found that one in seven overweight children was bullied and that the behaviour grew intensely more violent as the kids aged. Boys were more likely to be the victims of physical bullying, while girls were victims of relational bullying.[55]

In this example, we see how peer approval has a major impact on socialization. Popular youths do well in school and are socially astute. In contrast, children rejected by their peers are more likely both to display aggressive behaviour and to disrupt group activities through bickering or other antisocial behaviour.[56]

Peer relations are a significant aspect of maturation. In a self-report study of 526 students in Grades 8 and 9, researchers looked at interparental violence and peer-dating violence, and found that the latter was a good predictor of adolescent dating violence.[57] Similarly, in a study of 336 boys, researchers at the University of Montreal found that negative experiences with parents and with peers each predicted subsequent violence, dating-related violence, and more delinquency in general.[58]

The influence of peers is both negative and positive. On the one hand, peers pressure youths to conform to group values. However, peers also help them learn to share and cooperate, cope with aggressive impulses, and discuss feelings they would not dare bring up at home. With peers, youths can compare their experiences, learn that others have similar problems, and realize they are not alone. It is no surprise, then, that much adolescent criminal activity begins as a group process.[59]

Delinquent peers exert influence on behaviour and beliefs.[60] In every level of the social structure, youths who fall in with a bad crowd become more susceptible to criminal behaviour patterns.[61] Deviant peers provide friendship networks that support delinquency and drug use.[62] Riding around, staying out late, and partying with deviant peers provide youths with the opportunity to commit deviant acts.[63] And because delinquent friends are not easily lost, peer influence may continue through the lifespan.[64] Even though many groups are short-lived and transitory, being exposed to deviant influences in multiple groups helps explain why deviant group membership is highly correlated with personal rates of offending.[65]

In research on stressors experienced by young Mi'kmaq women living on reserve in Nova Scotia, women said:

"Peer pressure is the most important cause of stress because they want you to do something that you don't want to do."

"Peer pressure, we have nothing to do, there is nothing else to do but to do drugs."

"Drugs cause stress, there is peer pressure to drink, smoke and use drugs. Your friends make a deal with you. If you drink, then they'll do something."[66]

Institutional Involvement and Belief

People with strong moral values and beliefs who have learned to distinguish right from wrong and who regularly attend religious services are also less deviant. Religion binds people together and forces them to confront the effect their behaviour has on others. Therefore, it's no surprise that in studying bullying behaviour, researchers have found that children who engage in such positive social activities as going to church are generally less likely to be violent.[67] Religion is a traditional form of social control.

The association between religious attendance and delinquent behaviour was once thought to be negligible.[68] However, recent research shows attendance at religious services has a significant impact on crime.[69] For example, kids living in disorganized high-crime areas who attend religious services are better able to resist illegal drug use.[70] However, disorganized neighbourhoods are more likely to have deteriorating social services, such as lack of churches and service associations. Obviously, ongoing participation is a more significant inhibitor of crime than is the mere holding of religious beliefs and values.[71]

In an examination of the association between addicts' reductions in drug and alcohol use and their level of religiosity, results indicated that church attendance was associated with a reduction both in alcohol use and in cocaine use.[72] Cross-national research shows that countries with high rates of church membership and attendance have the lowest crime rates.[73]

CONNECTIONS

Arousal theory would also predict that church attendance is inversely correlated with crime rates because criminals are people who need large amounts of stimulation, and they would be unlikely to be able to sit through religious services. See Chapter 6 for more about arousal theory.

BRANCHES OF SOCIAL PROCESS THEORY

To criminologists, the elements of socialization just described are chief determinants of criminal behaviour. People living in even deteriorated urban areas can successfully resist crime if

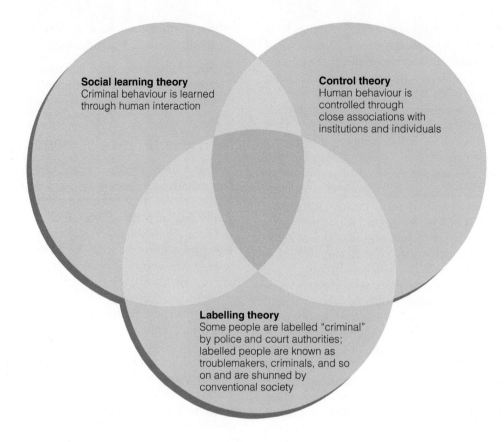

Social learning theory
Criminal behaviour is learned through human interaction

Control theory
Human behaviour is controlled through close associations with institutions and individuals

Labelling theory
Some people are labelled "criminal" by police and court authorities; labelled people are known as troublemakers, criminals, and so on and are shunned by conventional society

FIGURE 8.3

The Complex Web of Social Processes That Control Human Behaviour

they have a good self-image, have learned moral values, and have the support of parents, peers, teachers, and neighbours. The girl with a positive self-image who is chosen for a university scholarship, has the warm, loving support of her parents, and is viewed by her friends as someone who is "going places" is less likely to be delinquent than is another adolescent who is abused at home, who lives with criminal parents, and whose bond to the school and peer group is shattered because she is labelled as a troublemaker.[74]

Like social structure theory, the social process approach has several independent branches (see Figure 8.3). The first, **social learning theory**, suggests that people learn the techniques and attitudes of crime from close relationships with criminal peers: crime is a learned behaviour. The second branch, **control theory**, maintains that most people are controlled by their bond to society: crime occurs when the forces that bind people are weakened or broken. The third branch, **labelling theory**, says that people become criminals when significant members of society label them as such and they accept those labels as a personal identity.

Put another way, social learning theory assumes that people are born good and learn to be bad; control theory assumes that people are born bad and must be controlled to be good; labelling theory assumes that whether good or bad, people are controlled by the reactions of others.

Social Learning Theory

According to social learning theorists, crime is a product of learning the norms, values, and behaviours associated with criminal activity. Social learning can involve both the actual techniques of crime—how to hot-wire a car or roll a joint—and the psychological aspects of criminality—how to deal with the guilt or shame associated with illegal activities.

social learning theory The view that behaviour is modelled through observation of human interactions, either directly from observing others or indirectly through the media. Rewarded interactions are copied; punished interactions are avoided.

control theory An approach that looks at the ability of society and its institutions to control, manage, restrain, or direct human behaviour; sometimes called *social control theory.*

labelling theory The view that society creates deviance through the designation of individual behaviour as deviant. The stigmatized individual feels unwanted and accepts the label as an identity.

This section briefly reviews the three most prominent forms of social learning theory: differential association theory, differential reinforcement theory, and neutralization theory.

CONNECTIONS

In the late 19th century, Gabriel Tarde's theory of imitation held that criminals imitate superiors they admire and respect. Tarde's work, discussed in Chapter 6, is thus a precursor to modern learning theories.

Differential Association Theory

Edwin H. Sutherland (1883–1950) first put forth the **differential association (DA) theory** in 1939 in *Principles of Criminology*.[75] It remains one of the most enduring explanations of criminal behaviour.

Sutherland's research on white-collar crime and professional theft led him to dispute the notion that crime is a function of the inadequacy of people in the lower classes.[76] In Sutherland's view, criminality stemmed from neither individual traits (see Chapter 6) nor socio-economic position (see Chapter 7); instead, he believed it to be a function of a learning process that could affect anyone.

A few ideas are basic to the theory of differential association.[77] A primary idea is that the acquisition of behaviour is a social learning process, and criminal skills and motives are learned as a result of contacts with pro-crime values. Also, the political definition of crime by government may be rejected by some groups of people because of their acceptance of criminal definitions.

Principles of Differential Association. The basic principles of differential association are as follows:[78]

1. Crime is learned in the same manner as any other behaviour, such as writing, painting, or reading.
2. Crime is learned in interaction with other persons, not by living in a criminogenic environment or by having personal characteristics, such as low IQ or family problems.
3. Learning crime occurs within intimate personal groups, such as family, friends, and peers;[79] thus, social support overrides dominant social controls.
4. Learning crime includes techniques, such as picking a lock, shoplifting, or using narcotics, and learning supporting motives, rationalizations, and attitudes.
5. Because the reaction to social rules is not uniform across society, people come into contact with others who maintain different views on whether to obey the legal code. This conflict of social attitudes is the basis for the concept of differential association.
6. A criminal perceives more benefits than unfavourable consequences to violating the law (see Figure 8.4) when their acquaintances have definitions that are favourable toward criminality and are isolated from counteracting forces.

7. Differential associations vary in frequency, duration, priority, and intensity. Whether a person learns to obey the law or to disregard it is influenced by whether that person's social interactions are frequent or are influenced by a person who is respected.
8. Learning definitions favourable to criminality produces illegal behaviour because the motives for criminal behaviour are not the same as for conventional behavior; otherwise, the criminal would simply get a better education or work harder on a job.

In sum, DA theory says that people learn criminal attitudes and behaviour as adolescents from close and trusted relatives and companions. A criminal career develops if learned antisocial values and behaviours are not exceeded by conventional attitudes and behaviours. Criminal behaviour is learned in a process similar to learning any other human behaviour.

Testing Differential Association. Despite its importance, social scientists find it difficult to evaluate vague concepts such as "definition toward criminality." It is also difficult to follow people over time, establish precisely when definitions toward criminality begin to outweigh pro-social definitions, and determine whether this imbalance produces criminal behaviour.

However, one important area of research is the friendship patterns of delinquent youths. DA theory implies that criminals maintain close and intimate relations with deviant peers.[80] For example, institutionalized youths often have close associations with delinquent youths before their law-violating acts.[81] Thus, the delinquent friendship patterns predict youth crime.[82]

Law violators maintain close relationships with deviant peers,[83] and antisocial kids who maintain delinquent friends over a long duration are more likely to persist in delinquent behaviour. Curiously, recently cultivated friendships have a greater influence on criminality than friends acquired earlier in life, which is relevant in explaining the onset of both substance abuse and a career in the drug trade.[84] For example, an interview study of low-level drug dealers found many novices were tutored by more experienced dealers who helped them make connections with buyers and sellers:

> I had a friend of mine who was an older guy and he introduced me to selling marijuana to make a few dollars. I started selling a little and made a few dollars. For a young guy to be making a hundred dollars or so, it was a lot of money. So I got kind of tied up in that aspect of selling drugs.[85]

differential association (DA) theory According to Sutherland, the principle that criminal acts are related to a person's exposure to an excess amount of antisocial attitudes and values.

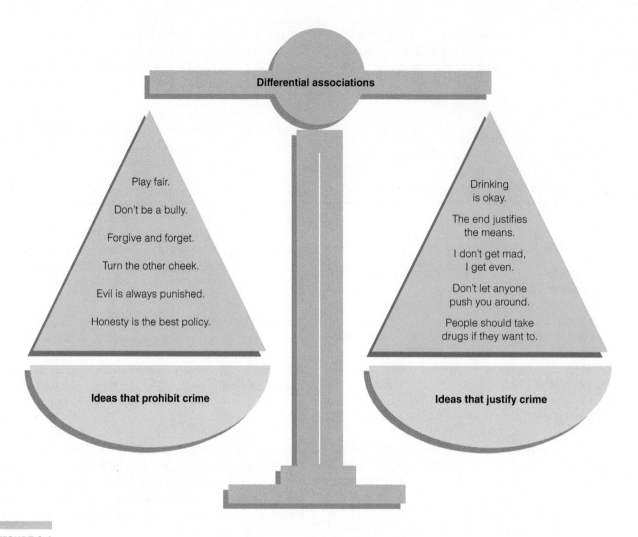

FIGURE 8.4

Differential Association Theory Assumes That Criminal Behaviour Will Occur When the Reasons For Crime Outweigh the Arguments Against Crime

Making connections is an important part of the dealer's world. Adolescent drug users are likely to have intimate relationships with a peer friendship network that supports their substance abuse.

Another assumption is that people who have assimilated pro-crime attitudes are likely to engage in criminal activity.[86] A cross-cultural study conducted in Hong Kong found that DA items were the most significant predictor of delinquent behaviour in a sample of secondary-school students.[87]

Self-report research must be interpreted cautiously. Because subjects are usually asked simultaneously about their peer relations, learning experiences, perceptions of differential associations, and criminal behaviours, it is impossible to determine whether differential associations were the cause or the result of criminal behaviour. Youths may learn about crime and then commit it, but experienced delinquents may also seek out like-minded peers after they engage in antisocial acts, internalizing deviant attitudes after, rather than before, crime.[88]

Researchers must develop more valid measures of differential associations.[89] Longitudinal analysis might be used to measure subjects over time to determine the effect of exposure to excess definitions toward deviance to see whether people who continually break the law develop a group of like-minded peers who support their behaviour, or if innocent people are seduced into crime.

Another approach may be to follow a cohort over time to see if repeated exposure escalates deviance. Adolescents who acquire criminal friends are also likely to eventually engage in criminal behaviour. Criminal friends are hard to shake, locking people into antisocial behaviour patterns through their life course. People who maintain deviant friendships are likely to persist in their offending careers, counteracting the crime-reducing effects of the aging-out process.[90]

Analysis of Differential Association Theory. Misconceptions about DA theory have produced some unwarranted criticisms. For example, if the theory is concerned solely

Circle of Hope Has Changed Lives, but Federal Cash about to Run Out

By Mary Agnes Welch, *The Winnipeg Free Press*

They ran drugs and weapons, did joyriding and assaults and were budding members of some of the city's best-known gangs.

Now the teens do aboriginal drumming, clean up the broken bottles in the park across the street and either attend school or hope to. One teen has missed only two days of programming in two years and virtually none has committed any new crimes since they started in the Circle of Courage program.

"I almost got stabbed at a house party when I was drinking," said one 16-year-old from Elmwood. "Ever since then, I wanted to get out. I didn't want to get killed or stabbed or anything."

Circle of Courage is one of four inner-city anti-gang programs shutting at the end of March when their federal funding runs out. Four teens, who spoke on condition their names wouldn't be published, said Circle of Courage kept them busy and out of trouble. They were warily hopeful they could stay out of trouble if the program, run out of a house on Pacific Avenue, ends.

About 65 youths are about to be cut loose, and city councillors, the provincial government and opposition MPs have lobbied for the programs to continue.

But Winnipeg's Conservatives MPs have been mum.

The federal government says it's been clear from the start the funds were finite.

Public Safety Minister Vic Toews was not available for an interview Thursday. His spokesman, Chris McCluskey, repeated word for word the statement Public Safety Canada staff emailed to the *Free Press* earlier this week.

"We cannot speculate on the contents of Budget 2011 before it is announced, however, we will continue to support programs that demonstrate results that help at-risk individuals develop positive life skills and avoid a life of crime," wrote McCluskey in an email.

Staff in the offices of Winnipeg South MP Rod Bruinooge and Charleswood-St. James-Assiniboia MP Steven Fletcher referred calls about anti-gang funding to McCluskey.

Kildonan-St. Paul MP Joy Smith was tied up in meetings Thursday as was St. Boniface MP Shelly Glover.

Like Circle of Courage, the programs mentor young people, mostly males, who have been linked to gangs or already have criminal records. They get help with schooling, housing, jobs, and the child-welfare and court system while structured recreational programs or aboriginal cultural programs keep them busy and off the streets all day and many evenings and weekends.

Ottawa has hinted new money may be available in the upcoming budget. But staff at inner-city agencies like Ndinawe and New Direction, which run the programs, say it's more likely the federal government will create a new fund, with slightly different parameters. That gives Ottawa a splashy new initiative to announce, but forces agencies with good programs to shoehorn them in to new criteria, said Liz Wolff, the program manager at New Directions, which runs an anti-gang program for refugees.

Often there's a long delay from the time money is announced to the time it actually flows, meaning programs fold and teens backslide in the interim.

If there's a spring election following the budget, as many believe there will be, that could delay things even more.

When agencies applied for the original funding, the paperwork alone took the Spence Neighbourhood Association four months. Then, when the SNA's outreach program got federal approval, it was almost a year until the anti-gang money arrived.

An independent evaluation on the five original programs is almost complete. It includes interviews with staff and students and data on things like attendance rates.

SOURCE: Excerpted from "Freed from gangs, but program in peril," by Mary Agnes Welch, January 28, 2011. Reprinted with permission from The Winnipeg Free Press.

---

with the number of a delinquent person's personal contacts and associations,[91] those people most likely to become criminals would be police, judges, and correctional authorities because they are constantly associating with criminals. Sutherland stressed "excess definitions toward criminality," not mere association with criminals. Juvenile justice system personnel have extensive associations with criminals, but these associations are counterbalanced by their associations with law-abiding citizens.

Another misconception is that definitions toward delinquency are acquired only from learning the values of a deviant subculture. However, some people become criminals because they have been either socialized into a deviant culture or improperly socialized into the normative culture.[92]

Although DA theory stresses an excess of definitions toward delinquency, these definitions need not come solely from the lower class. Law-abiding parents can encourage delinquent behaviour by their own drinking or family violence, and all youths are exposed to media images that express open admiration for violent heroes who take the law into their own hands. The influence of differential association is not affected by social class, because deviant learning can affect both middle-class and lower-class youths.[93]

Sutherland's work is criticized for not explaining why one youth who is exposed to delinquent definitions succumbs to them, while another living under similar conditions doesn't.[94] Another criticism of DA theory is its assumption that criminal and delinquent acts are rational and systematic, ignoring spontaneous acts of violence, such as isolated psychopathic killings, which are virtually unsolvable because of the killer's anonymity and lack of criminal associations.

The most serious criticism is the vagueness of terms, such as an "excess of definition toward criminality." How can we determine whether an individual actually has a pro-criminal imbalance of these definitions or a majority of definitions toward criminality?

Despite these criticisms, DA theory maintains an important place in the study of criminal behaviour by providing a consistent explanation of criminal behaviour. This theory is not limited to looking at lower-class gang activity but also accounts for criminal behaviour in middle- and upper-class areas, where youths are exposed to pro-criminal definitions from such sources as overly opportunistic parents and friends. Because criminal friends tend to be "sticky," differential association might be a key to explaining deviance through the life course.

Differential Reinforcement Theory

Differential reinforcement (DR) theory (social learning theory) also explains crime as a type of learned behaviour. First proposed by Akers and Burgess, it is a version of the social learning view that combines differential association concepts with elements of psychological learning theory.[95]

The same process is involved in learning both deviant and conventional behaviour. People do not learn to be "all deviant" or "all conforming," but rather strike a balance between the two.[96]

Various learning processes shape behaviour. *Direct conditioning* occurs when behaviour is either rewarded or punished during interaction with others. *Differential association* involves learning from direct or indirect interaction with others. *Imitation* occurs from observational learning experiences, such as from watching TV and films. People also learn *cognitive definitions,* which are attitudes that are favourable or unfavourable toward a behaviour and can either stimulate or extinguish that behaviour.

Behaviour is reinforced when positive rewards are gained or when punishment is avoided (negative reinforcement). It is weakened by negative stimuli (punishment) and loss of reward. Whether deviant or criminal behaviour is begun or persists depends on the degree to which it has been rewarded or punished and the rewards or punishments attached to its alternatives.

In a shocking study of reinforcement, researchers in Toronto found that correctional staff in juvenile institutions allowed and encouraged peer violence. Juvenile offenders interviewed reported that staff ignored violence by inmates and saw guards offering incentives to inmates to intimidate or assault others.[97]

People evaluate their behaviour through interaction with significant others who control sources of reinforcement, define behaviour as right or wrong, and model behaviours.

The more individuals learn to justify their behaviour, the more likely they are to engage in it. For example, kids in a peer group whose members value drugs and alcohol, encourage their use, and provide opportunities to use drugs, will be encouraged through this social learning experience to use drugs themselves.

The principal influence on behaviour comes from groups that control individuals' reinforcement and punishment,[98] such as peer and friendship groups, schools, churches, and similar institutions. Within the context of these groups, criminality is expected to the extent that it has been differentially reinforced over alternative behaviour and is defined as desirable or justified. Once people are initiated into crime, their actions are reinforced by exposure to deviant models, association with deviant peers, and lack of negative sanctions from parents or peers. The deviant behaviour, originated by imitation, is sustained by social support, thereby establishing criminal careers and explaining persistent criminality.

Akers surveyed 3,065 male and female adolescents on drug- and alcohol-related activities and their perception of variables related to social learning and DR theory. Included were respondents' perception of peers' attitudes toward drug and alcohol abuse, people they admired who used controlled substances, and whether people they admired would reward or punish them for substance abuse. A strong association between drug and alcohol abuse and social learning variables was found: Kids who believed they would be rewarded for deviance by those they respect were those most likely to engage in deviant behaviour.[99]

Learning experience continues within a deviant group because behaviour both is influenced by and exerts influence over group processes. For example, kids may learn to smoke because of social reinforcement by peers; over time, smoking influences friendships and peer-group memberships.[100]

DR theory is an important view of how socialization conditions crime, and how negative reinforcements can produce criminal results. For example, research shows that parental deviance is related to adolescent antisocial behaviour.[101] This finding fits well with rational choice theory because they both suggest that people learn the techniques and attitudes necessary to commit crime through experience. After considering the outcome of their past experiences, potential offenders decide which criminal acts will be profitable and which are dangerous and should be avoided.[102] People make rational choices about crime because they have learned to balance risks against the potential for criminal gain.

> **differential reinforcement theory**   In social learning theory, the view that crime is a type of learned behaviour, combining differential association with elements of psychological learning.

Neutralization Theory

Neutralization theory is the most interesting social learning theory and is identified with Sykes and Matza, who also viewed the process of becoming a criminal as a learning experience.[103] While such theorists as Sutherland and Akers look at the learning of deviant techniques, values, and attitudes as necessary for performing criminal acts, Sykes and Matza maintain that most delinquents and criminals actually hold conventional values and attitudes but master techniques that enable them to neutralize these values and drift between illegitimate and conventional behaviour.

Matza said **subterranean values** exist alongside conventional values, which, although condemned in public, may be practised in private, such as viewing pornographic videos. People commonly hold both subterranean and conventional values—few people are "all good" or "all bad."

Even the most committed criminals and delinquents are not involved in criminality all the time. They go to work, they attend school and family functions, and their behaviour falls along a continuum between total freedom and total restraint. They **drift** between deviance and constraint. Learning **techniques of neutralization** allows a person to rationalize their behaviour.[104]

For example, in a study of poaching, descriptive accounts obtained from surveys and in-depth interviews with wildlife law violators and conservation officers revealed widespread use of rationalizations, with denial of responsibility being the most common. What is interesting is that the neutralization process is a "cognitive dissonance reduction" strategy: individuals use this technique to alleviate their guilt associated with law-violating behaviour, *if they cared about that guilt,* by neutralizing any definition of themselves as criminals, as in the following example:

> I was cited for fishing with two 12-year-old boys at Cave Run Lake. They were not my children but a situation where children had no one to take them fishing. I also had a foreign Chinese student with me. I am a 55-year-old lady and I was trying to provide an enrichment experience for some folks who would not usually get to go fishing. I had not fished for 15 years probably and did not remember that I needed a fishing license or that my Chinese friend needed one. . . . I wasn't even interested in them catching fish—just having an afternoon out.[105]

In this case, the explanation sounds innocent enough, and demonstrates both a rationalization and the recognition that she would have obeyed the law if she could. Which then leads to a different question: why couldn't the enforcement officer exercise discretion?

Techniques of Neutralization. Sykes and Matza suggest that offenders develop a distinct set of justifications for law-violating behaviour. First, they voice a sense of guilt over their illegal acts. Second, offenders frequently respect and admire honest, law-abiding persons, such as sports figures, priests, parents, teachers, and neighbours. Third, criminals draw a line between those whom they can victimize and those whom they cannot. Finally, criminals are not immune to the demands of conformity, participating in the same social functions as law-abiding people.

Because of these factors, criminality is seen as the result of the neutralization of accepted social values through the learning of a standard set of techniques that allow people to counteract the moral dilemmas posed by illegal behaviour. Sykes and Matza identify the following techniques of neutralization used by offenders:

1. *Deny responsibility.* Illegality was not their fault but due to forces beyond their control.
2. *Deny injury.* The harm is neutralized by denying the wrongfulness of an act.
3. *Deny the victim.* The victim of crime had it coming, so doesn't deserve sympathy.
4. *Condemn the condemners.* The world is corrupt, so it is unfair to condemn misconduct.
5. *Appeal to higher loyalties.* Justify illegality as due to being loyal to their own peers.

Five additional neutralization techniques were subsequently introduced after Sykes and Matza's original study by Minor, Klockars, and Coleman:

6. *The defense of necessity.* Something is morally wrong, but okay if it is necessary.
7. *The metaphor of the ledger.* The balance of good qualities make up for the bad.
8. *The denial of the law's necessity.* The law itself is not fair or just.
9. *The claim that everybody else is doing it.* A criticism of being singled out.
10. *The claim of entitlement.* The individual feels they are entitled to the gains of crime.[106]

In sum, the theory of neutralization presupposes a condition in which such slogans as "I didn't mean to do it," "I didn't really hurt anybody," "They had it coming to them," "Everybody's picking on me," and "I didn't do it for myself" are used

---

neutralization theory A view that offenders adhere to conventional values while drifting into periods of crime by neutralizing those values.

subterranean values In neutralization theory, immorality that is entrenched in the culture but is otherwise publicly condemned.

drift According to Matza, the movement of youth in and out of delinquency because their lifestyles can embrace both conventional and deviant values.

techniques of neutralization A strategy of cognitive dissonance used by deviants to counteract moral constraints so they may drift into criminal acts.

FIGURE 8.5
Techniques of Neutralization

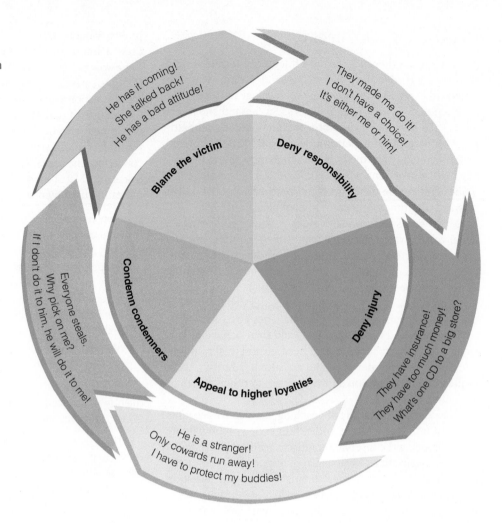

by offenders to neutralize conventional norms and values, which they care about, so that they can drift into criminal modes of behaviour (see Figure 8.5)

Testing Neutralization Theory. A test of neutralization theory would have to show that a person neutralized his or her moral beliefs and then drifted into criminality. Otherwise, people who commit crime could later attempt to rationalize their behaviour. It is also possible that criminals and non-criminals have different moral values and that neutralizing them is therefore unnecessary.[107] The validity of the model depends on showing that all people share similar moral values and must neutralize them first to engage in criminal behaviour. Research tries to empirically verify those assumptions.[108]

Agnew indicates that delinquents do not value or condone violent behaviour and that they justify their aggressive activities by using neutralizations, such as "It is all right to physically beat up people who call you names."[109] Research also shows that institutionalized youths excuse deviant behaviours to a significantly greater degree than the general population does.[110] People who commit criminal acts also have learned to rationalize their guilt. One study found that psychotherapists accused of sexually exploiting their clients

express neutralizations for their behaviour, blaming the victim for "seducing them" or claiming the sexual encounter caused little injury.[111]

Are Social Learning Theories Valid?

Social learning theories make a significant contribution to our understanding of the onset of criminal behaviour. Nonetheless, the general learning model has been subject to some criticism.

Learning theories imply that people learn techniques that allow them to be active and successful criminals, but these theories don't explain spontaneous acts of violence and other expressive crimes that have little utility or purpose. Is it possible that a random shooting is caused by an excess of deviant definitions? An estimated 70 percent of all people arrested were under the influence of drugs and alcohol when they committed their crime. Do addicts pause to neutralize their moral inhibitions before mugging a victim? Do drug-involved kids stop to consider what they have learned about moral values?

Learning theories have an important place in the study of delinquent and criminal behaviour because they can explain criminality across class structures. Even corporate executives are exposed to a variety of pro-criminal definitions and learn to neutralize their moral constraints.

For example, if we want to explain patterns of environmental crime by corporations, why would these crimes have to be rationalized when they take place within a political economy?[112] In some ways, such crimes would be a normal part of doing business.

In this way, social learning theories have the potential to be applied to a wide assortment of criminal activity.

SOCIAL CONTROL THEORIES

Social control theories maintain that all people have the potential to violate the law and that modern society presents many opportunities for illegal activity. Criminal activities, such as drug abuse or shoplifting, are often exciting and hold the promise of immediate reward and gratification.

Considering the attractions of crime, the question control theorists pose is, "Why do people obey the rules of society?" To a choice theorist, the answer is fear of punishment; to a structural theorist, obedience is due to access to legitimate opportunities; to a learning theorist, obedience is acquired through contact with law-abiding parents and peers.

In contrast, control theorists argue that people obey the law because behaviour and passions are controlled by internal and external forces. Some have a strong moral sense that renders them incapable of hurting others and violating social norms. Some maintain self-control because they have a **commitment to conformity**—a reason to obey the rules of society.[113] Perhaps they believe that being caught in a criminal activity will hurt a dearly loved parent or jeopardize their chance at a university scholarship, or perhaps their job will be forfeited if they get in trouble with the law. In other words, a person's behaviour is controlled by attachment and commitment to conventional institutions, individuals, and processes. If that commitment is absent, people are free to violate the law and engage in deviant behaviour; the "uncommitted" are not deterred by the threat of legal punishments.[114]

Self-Concept and Crime

Early control theory speculated that low self-control was a product of weak self-esteem. Youths who felt good about themselves could maintain a positive attitude and were able to resist the temptations of delinquency. Reiss described how delinquents had weak "ego ideals" and lacked the "personal controls" to produce conforming behaviour.[115] Others noted that youths who believe criminal activity would damage their self-image and their relationships with others will be most likely to conform to social rules; they have a commitment to conformity. In

contrast, those less concerned about their social standing are free to violate the law.

Empirical research indicates that an important association exists between self-image and delinquency.[116] Kaplan found that youths with poor self-concepts are the ones most likely to engage in delinquent behaviour and that successful participation in criminality helped raise their self-esteem.[117] Youths who perceive **self-rejection** ("I feel I do not have much to be proud of"; "I feel useless at times") are the ones most likely to engage in deviant behaviours.[118] Youths who maintain both the lowest self-image and the greatest need for approval are the ones most likely to seek self-enhancement from delinquency.[119]

Kids who are having problems in school feel better if they drop out and join a gang. However, this decision is a self-defeating strategy that usually hurts the individual in the long run.

Containment Theory

In an early effort to describe how self-image controls criminal tendencies, Reckless argued that youths growing up in even the most criminogenic areas can insulate themselves from crime if they have sufficiently positive self-esteem. He referred to the factors that enhance the individual's ability to resist criminal inducements through **containments**, the most important of which are a positive self-image and ego strength.[120] Kids with these traits can resist crime-producing "pushes and pulls." A strong self-image can counteract the following crime-producing forces:

- *Internal pushes.* Internal pushes include such personal factors as restlessness, discontent, hostility, rebellion, mental conflict, anxieties, and need for immediate gratification.
- *External pressures.* External pressures are adverse living conditions that influence deviant behaviour, such as poverty, unemployment, minority status, and limited opportunities.
- *External pulls.* External pulls are represented by deviant companions, membership in criminal subcultures or other deviant groups, and such influences as mass media and pornography.

commitment to conformity   A positive orientation to the rules of society, whereby the individual internalizes those rules.

self-rejection   The consequence of successfully being labelled, whereby the negative stigma is internalized.

containments   Internal and external factors that insulate youths from delinquency-promoting situations, such as strong self-concept and positive support from parents and teachers.

After testing containment theory in a school setting, Reckless concluded that the ability of youths to resist crime depends on their maintaining a positive self-image in the face of environmental pressures toward delinquency. This set the stage for following the idea that people are controlled by their feelings about themselves and others with whom they are in contact. In general, control theory maintains that although all people perceive inducements to crime, some are better able to resist them than are others.

For example, researchers in the Child and Youth Studies department at Brock University worked with focus groups of secondary-school students to investigate their perceptions of school conduct codes and their application. Obviously, the students supported the "big" rules such as no weapons, but were more critical of the minor rules. What the researchers propose is that although students challenge school rules, they are already caught within the dominant language that frames the rules.[121] Their acceptance of rules reflects school conduct codes, and students here speak to the role that rules play in preparing them to become employees:

Liz: They're trying to prepare you for the real world!

Bee: Yeah, people are judgmental and they're just trying to tell you that the clothes that you're wearing, as soon as you walk outside, what do you think? These people are talking behind your back. And you don't want that.

Liz: If you went to a job interview, would you wear like a short little miniskirt to let your butt show?

Social Control Theory

Social control theory, originally articulated by Travis Hirschi in his influential 1969 book, *Causes of Delinquency*, replaced containment theory as the dominant version of control theory.[122]

Hirschi linked the onset of criminality to the weakening of ties that bind people to society. Hirschi assumed that all individuals are potential law violators but are kept under control because they fear that illegal behaviour will damage their relationships with others. Without these social ties or bonds, a person is free to commit criminal acts. Most people are aware of the prevailing moral and legal code; however, people vary in their responses to conventional social rules and values.

Elements of the Social Bond. The social bond a person maintains with society is divided into four main elements: attachment, commitment, involvement, and belief (see Figure 8.6).

Attachment refers to a person's sensitivity to and interest in others. Psychologists believe that without a sense of attachment, a person loses the ability to relate coherently to others. The development of a social conscience depends on caring for other human beings. Parents, peers, and schools are the important social institutions with which a person should maintain ties. Attachment to parents and family is primary, leading later to feelings of respect for secondary others and for those in authority.

Commitment involves the time, energy, and effort expended in conventional lines of action, such as getting an education and saving money for the future. If people build a strong involvement in life, property, and reputation, they will be less likely to engage in acts that will jeopardize their positions.

Heavy involvement in conventional activities leaves little time for illegal behaviour. Involvement in school, recreation, and family insulates a person from the potential lure of criminal behaviour, whereas idleness enhances the temptation of crime.

It is the interrelationship of elements of the social bond that controls behaviour. For example, people who feel kinship and sensitivity to parents and friends are more likely to adopt legitimate goals and to work toward them. Conversely, a person who rejects social relationships lacks commitment to conventional goals. Similarly, people who are highly committed to conventional acts and beliefs are more likely to be involved in conventional activities.

Testing Social Control Theory. Hirschi tested social control theory by giving a self-report survey to more than 4,000 high-school students in Grades 11 and 12. The survey found the following evidence to support the theory:

- Youths who were strongly attached to their parents were less likely to commit crime.
- Commitment to conventional values, such as striving to get a good education and refusing to drink and "cruise around," was related to conventional behaviour.
- Youths involved in conventional activity, such as homework, were less likely to engage in crime.
- Youths involved in unconventional behaviour, such as smoking and drinking, were more delinquency-prone.
- Delinquent youths maintained weak and distant relationships with people, while non-delinquent youths were attached to their peers.
- Delinquent and non-delinquent youths shared similar beliefs about society.

Supporting Research. Because of its importance, social control theory has been the focus of much research. Associations among indicators of attachment, belief, commitment, and involvement with measures of delinquency have tended to be inversely related and significant.[123] Research indicates that family detachment, including intra-family conflict, abuse of children, and lack of affection, supervision, and family pride, are predictive of delinquent conduct.[124] Youths who are detached from the educational experience are at risk of criminality.[125] Lack of attachment to family, peers, and school has been found to predict delinquency in cross-cultural samples of youths.[126]

High peer tolerance of deviance and low parental empathy are also linked to offending, as are low academic achievement and low parental monitoring.[127] Conversely, high levels of parental attachment and individual self-reliance are associated with higher social and coping competencies,

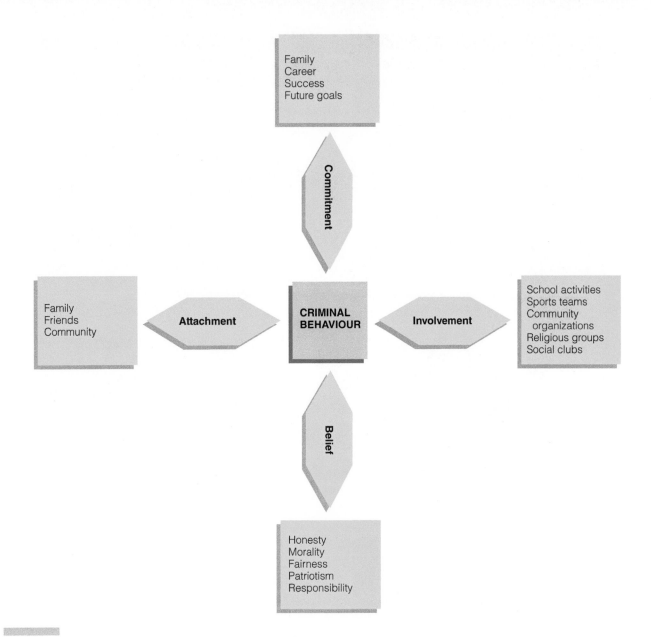

FIGURE 8.6
Elements of the Social Bond

lower levels of marijuana use, and fewer problems associated with substance use.[128] These findings point to the importance of social control in predicting youth delinquency.[129]

Other research has shown that positive beliefs are inversely related to criminality. Children who are involved in religious activities and hold conventional religious beliefs are less likely to become involved in substance abuse.[130] Similarly, youths who are involved in conventional leisure activities, such as supervised social activities and non-competitive sports, are less likely to engage in delinquency.[131]

In their research into the strength of school bonds, Sprott (of Ryerson University), Jenkins, and Doob (both from the University of Toronto) used longitudinal data to study what they call its protective effect against violent and non-violent

delinquency. When the researchers measured the strength of school bonds two years into their study, they found that, for children who had early aggression, a strong school bond had protected them from being violent. A strong school bond also acted as a protective factor against the influence of peers who committed non-violent delinquency. They conclude that because of the insulating effects of school, zero-tolerance policies that use suspensions or expulsions are counterproductive.[132]

In a study of youths in Edmonton, Alberta, parental attachment was the strongest predictor of delinquent or law-abiding behaviour.[133] Teens who are attached to their parents may develop the social skills that equip them both to maintain harmonious social ties and to escape life stresses, such as school failure.[134]

According to Hirschi, potential law violators are normally kept under control because they fear that illegal behaviour will damage their social relationships. Without such social ties, a person may feel free to commit criminal acts. Kids who commit crimes with their friends may appear attached, but they actually have few emotional commitments to their deviant peers.

Overall, the strength of attachments to conventional others and to institutions appears to be a control against criminality. As Sacco (of Queen's University) and Nakhaie (of the University of Windsor) found in their study of the relationship between students' social connections and their feelings of vulnerability to criminal danger, a "social capital" is found in relationships with parents, friends, and teachers.[135]

Opposing Views. Many attempts have been made to corroborate social control theory by replicating Hirschi's original survey techniques.[136] Although significant empirical evidence supports the model, some critics question some or all of its elements.

One criticism concerns the contention that delinquents are detached loners who have broken their bonds to family and friends. Since delinquents maintain relationships with deviant peers and are influenced by members of their deviant peer group,[137] they may not be "lone wolves" whose only personal relationships are exploitive. Their friendship patterns seem close to those of conventional youths.[138] For example, in one study, young male drug abusers maintained more intimate relations with their peers than non-abusers did, characterized by strong social ties and high levels of intimacy.[139]

Second, research shows that high levels of involvement, which Hirschi suggested should reduce delinquency, may actually increase delinquent behaviour. The more kids are involved in unsupervised, and possibly illegal, behaviours outside the home, the less contact they have with parental supervision and the greater the opportunity they have to commit crime.[140] Research with younger children found that the concepts of "involvement" and "belief" had relatively little influence over their behaviour patterns.[141]

Hirschi's conclusion that benefits stem from any form of social attachment, even attachment to deviant peers and to deviant parents, has also been disputed. For example, Hindelang found that attachment to delinquent peers escalated rather than restricted criminality.[142] Furthermore, youths who are attached to their drug-abusing parents are more likely to become drug users themselves.[143] And in an Edmonton study of dropouts, Samuelson, Hartnagel, and Krahn found that attachment to deviant peers helped motivate dropouts to commit crime and helped facilitate their delinquent acts.[144] Finally, attachment to delinquent friends is a powerful predictor of delinquency, strong enough to overcome the controlling effect of positive family relationships.[145]

Third, can social control theory explain all modes of criminality, or is it restricted to particular groups or forms of criminality? A survey of 3,065 high-school students in Grades 11 and 12 found that control variables were better able to explain female delinquency than male delinquency. It was also better

The life of Tyrone William Conn was not an easy one. Given up for adoption at the age of three, he spent eight years with abusive adoptive parents before being returned to the state in 1978. After that, he went from one group home to another, experiencing abandonment and deprivation.

He went from breaking into houses to eventually holding up a bank at the age of 16. In his criminal career, he was charged with almost 30 criminal offences. At the age of 25, he was ordered to serve 47 years in jail and would not be eligible for release until 2032. In prison, he completed his high-school education and took university-level sociology and psychology courses.

In 1989, at the age of 22, Conn escaped while on medical leave from Millhaven Penitentiary in Kingston, Ontario, and remained at large for 68 days. In 1991, he broke out of the Collins Bay Penitentiary and remained free for 46 days. Police found him in an apartment building in Ottawa, where he evaded escape for 90 minutes by climbing between fourth-floor balconies. By this time, Conn was suffering from anxiety caused by having been confined in prisons.

In 1999, at the age of 32, Conn became the first inmate to break out of Kingston Penitentiary in 40 years, causing a media frenzy. He visited his mother in Belleville, and then later robbed a bank in Colborne, the same bank he had robbed many years earlier. To his credit, Conn never caused physical harm to anyone during his career as an armed robber.

Conn spent his last hours in a dingy basement apartment in Toronto, listening to a police scanner. On May 20, 1999, at 10:30 p.m., after a standoff with police that began around 9 p.m., Conn called a CBC producer who had interviewed him years before. Conn had met producer Theresa Burke and broadcaster Linden MacIntyre while MacIntyre was working on a story about the effects of child abuse. At Conn's request, Burke phoned high-profile defence attorney Clayton Ruby. She then tried to get Conn to surrender, but the police set off a flash grenade to incapacitate him. When they entered the apartment, Conn was dead, apparently from a self-inflicted shotgun blast. His hard life had finally ended.

able to explain minor delinquency, such as alcohol and marijuana abuse, than more serious criminal acts.[146] Other school-based research also found gender differences, such as social control variables being more predictive of female behaviour than of male behaviour.[147] Perhaps girls are more deeply influenced by the quality of their bond to society than are boys.

Social bonds also seem to change over time. For example, in a sample of 12-, 15-, and 18-year-old boys, researchers found age differences in the perceptions of the social bond: Mid-teens are surprisingly likely to be influenced by their parents and teachers; boys in the other two age groups are more deeply influenced by their deviant peers.[148] This finding can be attributed to the problems of mid-adolescence, in which teens have a great need to develop "psychological anchors" to conformity. It is possible, then, that at one age level, weak bonds (to parents) lead to delinquency, while at another, strong bonds (to peers) lead to delinquency.

Finally, sociologist Robert Agnew claims that Hirschi miscalculated the direction of the relationship between criminality and a weakened social bond.[149] Although Hirschi says a weakened bond leads to delinquency, Agnew suggests the chain of events may flow in the opposite direction: Kids who break the law find their bond to parents, schools, and society is attenuated. Weakened social bonds are a consequence of criminality, not the reverse.[150]

In another test of the theory, Peter, LaGrange, and Silverman evaluated the interdependence of self-control and strain theories. These perspectives are usually seen as opposite explanations for crime and delinquency. Based on Gottfredson and Hirschi's assumption that self-control acts as a barrier to criminal behaviour, they suggest that the two theories are actually complementary in explaining participation in delinquency: Individuals with high self-control can mediate the effects of strain and refrain from engaging in delinquent activities, while adolescents with low self-control are not equipped with the necessary constraints to abstain from delinquency. Using a sample of 2,000 adolescents attending junior and senior high schools in a western Canadian city, Peters and colleagues suggest that both self-control and strain are important contributors to delinquency, but in an additive, not in an interactive, way.[151]

Despite these criticisms, the overall weight of evidence supports control theory, which has emerged as a dominant theory.[152] For many criminologists, control theory is perhaps the most important way of understanding the onset of criminal misbehaviour.

LABELLING THEORY

Labelling theory explains criminal career formation in terms of destructive social interactions and encounters. Its roots are in the **symbolic interaction theory** of sociologists Charles Horton Cooley, George Herbert Mead, and Herbert Blumer.[153]

Symbolic interaction theory says that people communicate via symbols, such as gestures, signs, words, or images to let others know how well they are doing and whether they are liked and appreciated. People interpret these symbolic gestures from others and incorporate them into their self-image. How people then view reality depends on the content of the messages, the contexts within which the messages occur, the subjective interpretation they use, and the consequences for how the interpretation of those messages shapes future behaviour.

In this view, no simple objective reality exists. People interpret the actions of others, and this interpretation defines meaning.

Throughout their lives, people are given a variety of symbolic labels in their interactions with others, such as *mental disorder*,[154] *difficult patient*,[155] or even *victim*,[156] as Kenney (of Memorial University) shows in his analysis of homicide survivors. These labels imply a variety of characteristics, and they define not just one trait but the whole person. For example, people labelled *insane* are also assumed to be dangerous and unstable. Labels such as *smart*, *honest*, and *hard worker* suggest overall competence. People given a positive trait, such as *attractive*, are assumed to have other positive traits, such as *intelligence*.[157] In contrast, negative labels, such as *troublemaker* and *stupid*, stigmatize people and reduce their self-image.

Both positive and negative labels entail subjective interpretations. Being called a *troublemaker* need not be based on any objective proof that the person is actually a troublemaker. A label can also be beneficial, as in the case of being labelled as having a learning disability, which then makes possible alternative forms of interaction.[158] The main point, however, is that even though a label may be a function of rumour or innuendo, or may be founded in fact or fiction, its impact can be immense.

A devalued status can cause permanent harm when conferred by a significant other, such as a teacher, police officer, elder, parent, or valued peer. Being perceived as a **social deviant** may affect a person's treatment at home, at work, at school, and in other social situations. School officials may limit social deviants to classes for students with behaviour problems. Adults labelled *criminal*, *ex-con*, or *drug addict* may find their employment possibilities severely restricted. If the label is the result of conviction for a crime, the labelled person may be subject to official sanctions, ranging from a mild reprimand to incarceration. Research on 16,636 Canadian youth court cases found that prior dispositions were a significant factor in both stabilizing and escalating dispositions, showing support for societal-reaction theory.[159]

CONNECTIONS

Fear of stigma has prompted efforts to reduce the impact of criminal labels through such programs as pre-trial diversion and community treatment programs. In addition, some criminologists have called for non-coercive "peacemaking" solutions to interpersonal conflict. This peacemaking or restorative justice movement is reviewed in Chapter 9.

Labelling also means that a person will have an increasing commitment to a deviant career and will be more likely to turn to others similarly stigmatized for support and companionship. Isolated from conventional society, they may identify themselves as members of an outcast group and become locked into deviant careers.

Because stigmatization is an interactive process, control institutions, such as the police, courts, and correctional agencies, produce the stigmas that are so harmful to the very people they are trying to help, treat, or correct. Thus, these institutions, rather than reducing deviant behaviour (as they were designed to do), actually help maintain and amplify criminal behaviour (see Figure 8.7).

FIGURE 8.7
The Labelling Process

symbolic interaction theory The view that people communicate meaning and interpret reality on the basis of their interpretation of symbols.

social deviant A person who has been labelled as an outsider at home, at work, at school, and in other social situations.

In March 2011, the people running various anti-crime programs were not sure whether federal funding for five initiatives would continue after the federal election. Despite an announcement that bridge funding of $900,000 had been approved for five Winnipeg agencies, the organizations' directors were told that continued funding under the Youth Gang Prevention Fund was in doubt. As a result, staff were laid off and kids dropped out, often back into the gang lives from which they were trying to escape.

The organizations involved were Ndinawemaaganag Endaawaad Inc.'s Turning the Tides, the Spence Neighbourhood Association Inc.'s Youth Outreach Project, the Ka Ni Kanichihk Inc.'s Circle of Courage, the New Directions' Project O.A.S.I.S., and the Broadway Neighbourhood Centre's Just TV Pilot Project.

The O.A.S.I.S. program works with high-risk young men who are refugees to Canada, and Ka Ni Kanichihk's Circle of Courage program works with Aboriginal boys between 12 and 17 years old. Such programs are a critical part of a strategy called Crime Control through Social Development, and attempt to make up for the lack of protective factors for Aboriginal youth susceptible to gang recruitment.

Risk factors for Aboriginal youths include racist discrimination, poverty, structural inequality and lack of opportunity. The sparse research done on Aboriginal gangs has made a distinction between street gangs, "wannabe" gangs, and organized crime gangs. The gangs have become popularized in the media: Redd Alert, Indian Posse, Alberta Warriors, and the Native Syndicate.

Through open-ended interviews with ex-gang members and with police officers, Jana Grekul of the University of Alberta looked at the personal experiences of being in a gang, and leaving it. The following is a quotation she elicited (2008: 66), from a man who grew up in the inner city of Edmonton:

> When I look around [at the place I grew up]...this was the community league for the hood—this is where gang members came, the drug dealers, the drunks, drug addicts, the people from the street...[When I was 10] that was a hard thing to deal with—having Mom taking off and not being there...you get up in the morning, sometimes she would be there, sometimes she wouldn't. When she was there, she wouldn't be up to get us ready for school, to cook us breakfast. I would slap something together for me and my little brother, get my little brother dressed, and away we went. [That's how I grew up], seeing my mother and step-father fight a lot—that's how they handled their problems, by yelling, swearing, screaming, and physically assaulting one another. So I thought, OK, that's how I deal with things.

The family plays an important role in gang involvement, first in terms of dysfunction, and second as a place of recruitment. The gang acts as a substitute family for youth who are scarred by violence, crime, and substance abuse.

The statistics are alarming: 29 percent of Edmontonians have not completed high school compared to 43 percent of Aboriginal people. Aboriginal people earn on average one-third less than the average Canadian. Having experienced ethnic marginalization, domestic violence, and missing fathers, Aboriginal youth are at prime risk for recruitment into gangs.

Prevention groups play a key preventive role in diverting youths from Aboriginal gangs. For example, the Hobbema Community Cadet Corps, run by two volunteer police officers, draws youths from four Cree nations—the Samson, Louis Bull, Montana, and Ermineskin—and has about 1,000 members. The group emphasizes leadership, discipline, education, self-esteem, teamwork, positive choices, and life skills.

In Hobbema, the unemployment rate is about 70 percent, more than 50 percent are under the age of 18, and on-reserve crime rates are three times higher than off the reserve. About 250 youths are in six different gangs, and in response, the government has adopted get-tough responses, including increased police and prosecution resources. The community, however, has created a safe community task force, and a citizen's action group, which has removed graffiti, imposed curfews, and held seminars on youth gang involvement.

When youth crime can be identified as a result of poor parenting, lack of education, and the presence of peers supporting crime, effective solutions can include reducing child poverty, illiteracy, and family violence. Research cited by Irwin Waller shows such solutions can lead to a 65 percent reduction in youth arrests, a 30 percent reduction in school expulsion, and a 16 percent reduction in overall crime.

What is interesting about this research is that it is not simply an analysis of a debased adolescent peer group, but situates youth gangs in a political economy of poverty, exclusion, and illegitimate opportunity. This is important research.

SOURCES: Jana Grekul and Kim Sanderson, "'I Thought People Would Be Mean and Shout.' Introducing the Hobbema Community Cadet Corps: A Response to Youth Gang Involvement," *Journal of Youth Studies*, 14, 1 (2011): 41–57; Jana Grekul and Patti LaBoucane-Benson, "Aboriginal Gangs and Their (Dis)placement: Contextualizing Recruitment, Membership, and Status," *Canadian Journal of Criminology and Criminal Justice*, 50, 1 (2008): 59–82.

Crime and Labelling Theory

As sociologist Kai Erikson said, "Deviance is not a property inherent in certain forms of behaviour, it is a property conferred upon those forms by the audience which directly or indirectly witnesses them."[160] This definition was amplified by Edwin Schur, who stated the following:

> Human behavior is deviant to the extent that it comes to be viewed as involving a personally discreditable

departure from a group's normative expectation, and it elicits interpersonal and collective reactions that serve to "isolate," "treat," "correct" or "punish" individuals engaged in such behavior.[161]

Crime and deviance are defined by the social audience's reaction to a person's behaviour and the subsequent effects of that reaction; they are not defined by the moral content of the illegal act itself. As difficult as it sounds, even a crime such as murder, is bad because it is labelled as such. After all, the difference between an excusable act and a criminal one is a matter of legal definition. A killing can be a murder, an execution, an accident, an act of self-defence, or a legitimate act in war. Such acts as abortion, marijuana use, possession of a handgun, and gambling have all been legal at some points and places in history, and illegal at others. What's important is who does the labelling.

Howard Becker refers to people who create rules as **moral entrepreneurs**. In a famous statement in his book *The Outsiders,* he summed up their effect as follows:

> Social groups create deviance by making rules whose infractions constitute deviance, and by applying those rules to particular people and labeling them as outsiders. From this point of view, deviance is not a quality of the act a person commits, but rather a consequence of the application by others of rules and sanctions to an "offender." The deviant is one to whom the label has successfully been applied; deviant behavior is behavior that people so label.[162]

Differential Enforcement

An important principle of labelling theory is that the law is differentially applied, benefiting those who hold economic and social power and penalizing the powerless. The probability of being brought before legal authority is a function of a person's race, wealth, gender, and social standing. For example, police officers are more likely to arrest males, minority-group members, and those in the lower class than more favoured groups.[163]

Similarly, members of minority groups and people living in poverty are more likely to be prosecuted for criminal offences and receive harsher punishments when convicted.[164] This evidence shows that personal characteristics and social interactions are actually more important variables in the criminal career formation process than is the mere violation of the law.

Labelling theorists also argue that the content of the law reflects power relationships in society. White-collar crimes are most often punished by a relatively small fine and rarely result in prison sentences, but long prison sentences are given to those convicted of street crimes, such as burglary or car theft.[165] For example in 2013, HSBC, the world's largest bank, pled guilty to money laundering, and in a deferred settlement paid $1.9 billion in fines. No one was incarcerated,

compared to the large numbers of those in prison for non-violent drug offences.

In sum, a major premise of labelling theory is that the law is differentially constructed and applied. It favours the powerful members of society who direct its content and penalizes people whose actions represent a threat to those in control.[166]

In this manner the micro-social approach of labelling theory has an affinity with the macro-social approach of conflict theory.

Becoming Labelled

Labelling theorists are not especially concerned with explaining why people originally engage in acts that result in their being labelled.[167] Crime may be a result of greed, personality, social structure, learning, or control, but labelling's concern is with criminal career formation, the reaction to the behaviour, and its consequence to the sequential development of deviance.

Labelling suggests that the less personal power and fewer resources a person has, the greater the chance of becoming labelled. In this view, a person is labelled as deviant primarily as a consequence of the **social distance** between the labeller and the person labelled. Race, class, and ethnic differences influence the likelihood of labelling. For example, a teenager who is from a poor family or is a member of a minority group may run a greater chance than a wealthy Caucasian youth of being officially processed for criminal acts by police, courts, and correctional agencies.

Of course, not all labelled people have chosen to engage in crime. Some labels are bestowed on people for behaviours over which they have little control, such as *mentally ill.* The probability of being labelled may depend on the visibility of the person in the community, the tolerance of the community for diversity, and the person's own power to combat labels.

Consequences of Labelling

Criminologists are most concerned with two effects of labelling: the creation of stigma and the effect on self-image. The social outcast may be prevented from enjoying higher

---

moral entrepreneurs   Interest groups that attempt to control social life and the legal order for the purpose of promoting their own set of moral values.

social distance   A person can be labelled as deviant because of the differences in power between the labeller and the person labelled; such differences are typically those of race, class, and ethnicity.

education, well-paying jobs, and other social benefits. Public condemnation is an important part of the label-producing process and is accomplished in "degradation ceremonies," such as a hearing in which a person is found to have a mental illness or a trial in which an individual is convicted of crime.[168] A public record of the deviant acts causes the denounced person to be ritually separated from citizens of good standing.

The label redefines the whole person: for example, the label *ex-con* connotes a person who is dangerous and dishonest, even though a person who has been in prison may not possess those traits. People react to the **master status** of the label and what the label signifies, and not necessarily to actual behaviour. In addition, the past of the labelled person is often reviewed retrospectively and reevaluated to fit his or her current outcast status. For example, boyhood friends of an assassin or killer are interviewed by the media, and report that the suspect was withdrawn and negativistic as a youth. This information appears to explain the offender's current behaviour, confirming the label as accurate.[169]

Labels become the basis of personal identity, prompting negative feedback from law enforcement agencies, parents, friends, and teachers to amplify the force of the original label and leading stigmatized offenders to reevaluate their own identities. Frank Tannenbaum referred to this process as the **dramatization of evil**:

> The process of making the criminal, therefore, is a process of tagging, defining, identifying, making conscious and self-conscious; it becomes a way of stimulating, suggesting and evoking the very traits that are complained of. If the theory of relation of response to stimulus has any meaning, the entire process of dealing with the young delinquent is mischievous insofar as it identifies him to himself or to the environment as a delinquent person. The person becomes the thing he is described as being.[170]

Primary and Secondary Deviance

One well-known view of the labelling process is Edwin Lemert's concept of primary and secondary deviance.[171]

Primary deviance involves norm violations that have little influence on the actor and can be quickly forgotten. For example, a university student takes a "five-finger discount" at the campus bookstore. He successfully steals a textbook, uses it to get an A in a course, goes on to graduate, is admitted into law school, and later becomes a famous judge. Because his shoplifting goes unnoticed, it is a relatively unimportant event that has little bearing on his life.

In contrast, **secondary deviance** occurs when a deviant event comes to the attention of those who apply a negative label. The newly labelled offender then reorganizes his or her behaviour and personality around the consequences of the deviant act. The shoplifting student is caught by a security

guard and expelled from university. With his law school dreams dashed and future cloudy, his options are limited; people who know him say he "lacks character," and he begins to share their opinion. He eventually becomes a drug dealer and winds up in prison, where he commits suicide. One little act begins a slippery slide.

If successful, secondary deviance involves resocialization into a deviant role. The deviance amplification effect results in offenders feeling isolated from the mainstream of society. They become firmly locked into their deviant role and seek out others similarly labelled to form deviant groups. They become locked into an escalating cycle of deviance, apprehension, more powerful labels, and identity transformation. This effect is the core of labelling theory: deviance is a process in which a person's identity is transformed. Efforts to control the offenders, whether by treatment or punishment, simply solidify them in a deviant role.

Numerous attempts have been made to formulate theories of deviant career formation using a labelling perspective. What follows is a discussion of two such efforts.

General Theory of Deviance

Howard Kaplan's general theory of deviance begins with the assumption that people who cannot conform to social group standards face negative sanctions. They are considered failures either because they lack desirable physical, social, or psychological traits, or because they fail to behave according to group expectations.

Those exposed to negative social sanctions experience self-rejection and a lower self-image. The experience of self-rejecting attitudes (e.g., "At times, I think I am no good at all") results in both a weakened commitment to conventional values and behaviours, and the acquisition of motives to deviate from social norms. Facilitating this attitude and value transformation is the bond that social outcasts form

---

master status   An identity that overrides all others, such as drug dealer being a more important status than citizen.

dramatization of evil   In Tannenbaum's pioneering study of labelling, the process whereby the reaction to deviance sets up a feedback effect that the individual internalizes.

primary deviance   According to Lemert, deviant acts that go undetected or unsanctioned, and thus do not help redefine the self and public image of the offender.

secondary deviance   According to Lemert, deviant acts that are sanctioned, after which the deviant label becomes a basis for personal identity.

According to Lemert's theory, if these kids are caught and labelled as "druggies," they may become secondary deviants, taking on an identity associated with their negative label, and enter a life of crime. If their actions go undetected, their behaviour remains primary, and their drug use remains nothing more than an easily forgotten youthful indiscretion.

with similarly labelled peers.[172] Membership in a deviant subculture involves conforming to group norms that conflict with those of conventional society. Deviant-group membership then encourages criminality and drug abuse.

Deviant behaviours that defy conventional values can serve several purposes. Some acts are defiant, showing contempt for the source of the negative labels, while others are planned to distance the target from further contact with the source of criticism (for example, an adolescent runs away from critical parents).[173]

Kaplan has found that imposing social sanctions on adolescents leads to self-rejection, deviant peer associations, and eventual deviance amplification.[174] This model is important because it accounts for the creation of labels, their impact on self-image, and the long-term effect they have on criminal careers. Negative sanctions also have a labelling effect if they help undermine conventional relationships and encourage deviant peer-group memberships.

Differential Social Control

Heimer and Matsueda's theory of differential social control says that self-evaluations reflect actual or perceived appraisals made by others.[175] Kids who view themselves as delinquents are giving an inner voice to their perceptions of how parents, teachers, peers, and neighbours feel about them. For example, kids who believe that others view them as troublemakers will expect to be rejected. Labelled youths may then join with similarly outcast delinquent peers who facilitate their behaviour. Eventually, antisocial behaviour becomes habitual and automatic. This effect is a self-fulfilling prophecy, and the process has been linked to delinquent behaviour and other social problems, including depression.[176]

This **reflective role-taking** is affected by families, schools, and peers, who can either help control kids and dissuade them from crime or encourage and sustain their deviance. When these groups are dysfunctional, such as when parents use drugs, they encourage, rather than control, antisocial behaviour.

Empirical research supports the core of the model. **Reflected appraisal** as a rule violator has a significant

reflective role-taking The experience in which youths who view themselves as delinquent give an inner-voice to their perceptions of how significant others feel about them.

reflected appraisal According to Matsueda and Heimer, a youth's self-evaluation that is based on his or her perceptions of how others evaluate him or her.

effect on delinquency: Kids who believe that their parents and friends consider them troublemakers are the ones most likely to engage in delinquency and to engage in risk-taking behaviours.[177]

This work is important because it is an alternative to traditional labelling theory and focuses on social control and symbolic interaction.

Research on Labelling Theory

Research on labelling theory can be classified into two distinct categories. The first says that offenders who are chosen for negative labels are likely to be powerless people unable to defend themselves. The second type of research attempts to discover the effects of being labelled.

Who Gets Labelled? It is widely believed that poor and powerless people are victimized by the law and justice system, and that labels are not equally distributed across class and racial lines. Although substantive and procedural laws govern almost every aspect of the criminal justice system, discretionary decision making also comes into play. From the police officer's decision on whom to arrest, to the prosecutor's decisions on whom to charge, or the court's decision on whom to release or for whom to permit bail, to the judge's decision on the length of the sentence, discretion works against members of minority groups. A meta-review of 30 years of research on minority-group members in the juvenile justice system found that race bias adversely influences decision making.[178] Contemporary research also supports this conclusion.[179]

> ### CONNECTIONS
>
> In Chapter 9, we look at some of the ways in which the powerless are discriminated against by the criminal justice system and how it is necessary to develop a critical perspective to analyze that process. In a multicultural society, ethnic discrimination is a very important topic.

Another example of how interpretations influence the labelling process is evident in what happens when protestations of innocence are made by suspects accused of socially undesirable acts. For example, people accused of child abuse are routinely defined as non-credible when they deny accusations of abuse and are only believed when they confess their guilt. In contrast, victims are believed when they make accusations but are considered "non-credible" when they claim the suspect is innocent.[180]

These consequences of labelling do not mean the justice system is inherently unfair and biased. Such procedures as arrest, prosecution, and sentencing are usually made on the basis of legal factors, such as prior record and crime

seriousness, rather than on personal characteristics, such as class and race.[181]

The Effects of Labelling. Empirical evidence suggests that negative labels have a dramatic influence on the self-image of offenders, leading to self-labelling and deviance amplification. Parents negatively label their children, who suffer a variety of problems, including antisocial behaviour and school failure.[182] Once labelled as troublemakers, adolescents begin to reassess their self-image in a process of deviance amplification, causing parents to become alienated from their child, further reducing the child's self-image and increasing delinquency.[183]

> ### CONNECTIONS
>
> Chapter 5 looked at Braithwaite's research on how parental attributions that are negative are linked to bullying.

Intensive official labelling can produce self-labelling and damaged identities.[184] Kids labelled as troublemakers in school are the students most likely to drop out, which has been linked to delinquent behaviour.[185] Male drug users labelled as addicts by social control agencies eventually became self-labelled and increase their drug use.[186] People arrested in domestic violence cases with a low "stake in conformity"—that is, who were jobless and unmarried—often increase their offending after being given official labels. This outcome could be seen as a mischievous or perverse effect.

Labelling and Criminal Careers. Until recently, scant attention has been paid to the fact that stigmatization and negative labels may sustain chronic offending and criminal careers.[187]

Although labels may not cause adolescents to initiate criminal behaviours, experienced delinquents are significantly more likely to continue offending if they believe their parents and peers view them in a negative light.[188] Labelling thus sustains criminality over time.

In sum, considerable evidence exists that people who are labelled by parents, schools, and the criminal justice system stand a good chance of getting involved in deviance. The labelling effect and other personal and social factors that cause the labelling to occur are interwoven.

Is Labelling Theory Valid?

Those who criticize labelling theory point to its inability to specify the conditions that must exist before an act or individual is labelled deviant—that is, why some people are labelled while others remain "secret deviants."[189] Critics also say labelling theory fails to explain differences in crime rates; if crime is a function of stigma and labels, why are crime rates higher in some parts of the country at particular times of the year? Labelling theory also ignores the onset of deviant behaviour and does not deal with the decision to forgo a deviant career.[190]

In addition, others question whether deviance is relative. They argue that some crimes, such as rape and homicide, are universally sanctioned.[191] Furthermore, crime is situationally motivated and depends more on ecological and personal conditions than on labels and stigma. Some charge that the focus on deviance all too often focuses on "nuts, sluts, and perverts" and ignores the root causes of crime.[192]

With the "discovery" of the chronic offender, many believed that labelling theory would receive renewed interest because the chronic offender is defined as someone who has been repeatedly labelled by the justice system.[193] However, Tittle found little evidence that stigma produces crime.[194] He claims that many criminal careers occur without labelling, that labelling often follows rather than precedes chronic offending, and that criminal careers may not follow even after labelling has taken place. If criminal careers begin early in life, those who go on to a life of crime are burdened with so many social, physical, and psychological problems that negative labelling may be a relatively insignificant event.[195]

Although criticisms of labelling theory exist, these criticisms come from different theoretical perspectives with different research questions. Labelling still has utility and contributes in the following ways to the study of criminality:[196]

1. The labelling perspective identifies the role played by social control agents in the process of crime causation.
2. Labelling theory recognizes that criminality is not a disease or pathological behaviour. It focuses attention on the social interactions and reactions that shape individuals.
3. Labelling theory distinguishes between criminal acts (primary deviance) and criminal careers (secondary deviance), showing that these concepts require different views.

Labelling theory is also important because of its focus on interaction and the situation of crime. Rather than view the criminal as an automaton whose actions are predetermined, it recognizes that crime is often the result of complex interactions and processes. The decision to commit crime involves the actions of a variety of people, including peers, the victim, the police, and other key characters. Labels may expedite crime because they guide the actions of all parties in criminal interactions. Actions deemed innocent when performed by one person are considered provocative when engaged in by a person labelled as a deviant. Similarly, labelled people may be quick to judge, take offence, or misinterpret behaviour because of their past experience. They experienced conflict in the past, so why not now?

NEW DIRECTIONS IN AN INTEGRATED DEVELOPMENTAL THEORY

Many reasons account for the current popularity of integrated theory. One reason is practical. Because of the development of computerized databases and software that can facilitate statistical analysis, theory integration is now possible. Criminologists of an earlier era simply did not have the tools to conduct the sophisticated computations necessary.

Another reason is substantive. Single-factor theories focus on the onset of crime, dividing the world into those who have a crime-producing condition and those who do not. For example, people who feel anomie become deviant, while those who do not feel anomie remain law-abiding; people with high testosterone levels are violent, while people with low levels are not.

CONNECTIONS

The issue of age and crime and the "desistance" phenomenon was discussed in Chapter 3. Crime rates peak in the teenage years and then decline over the life course. Explaining this decline has become an important focus of criminology.

The view that criminality is stable over one's lifetime is now being challenged. Criminologists today are concerned not only with the onset of criminality but also with its termination: Why do people age out of or desist from crime? If, for example, criminality is a function of intelligence, as some criminologists claim, why do most delinquents fail to become adult criminals? It seems unlikely that intelligence level increases as young offenders mature. If the onset of criminality can be explained by a person's intelligence level, then some other factor must explain its termination.

Why do some offenders escalate their criminal activities, while others decrease such activities? Why do some offenders specialize in a particular crime, while others become generalists? Why do some criminals reduce their criminal activity and then resume it later? Research now shows that some offenders begin their criminal career at a very early age, while others begin at a later point in their lives. The approach that seeks to explain early and late-onset criminality is sometimes referred to as **developmental criminology**.[197]

developmental criminology An approach that examines change in a criminal career over the life course, by looking at biological, social, and psychological factors involved in desistance, resistance, escalation, and specialization.

CONNECTIONS

As you may recall from Chapter 3, the Philadelphia cohort studies conducted by Wolfgang and his associates identified the existence of a relatively small group of chronic offenders who committed a significant amount of all serious crimes and persisted in criminal careers into their adulthood.

Single-factor theories struggle to explain why relatively few of the many individuals exposed to criminogenic influences in the environment actually become chronic offenders. For example, structural theories make a convincing case for linking crime to neighbourhood disorganization, but why do so many underprivileged youths resist crime despite their exposure to social disorganization? More than a single reason may be needed to explain why one person engages in criminal behaviour, whereas another person, living under similar circumstances, can avoid a criminal career.

Criminologists attempt to answer such complex questions by integrating a variety of ecological, socialization, psychological, biological, and economic factors into a coherent structure. This section summarizes these integrated theories.

OVERVIEW OF INTEGRATED THEORIES

Integrated theories can be divided into three groups on the basis of their view of human development and change: multifactor theories, latent trait theories, and life-course theories.

The earliest integrated theories are called multifactor theories, which combine variables that have been used in structural, socialization, conflict, choice, and trait theories. This approach explains both criminal career formation and desistance from crime. Although many youths are at risk, relatively few face the complete set of hazards that result in a criminal career, including an impulsive personality, a dysfunctional family, a disorganized neighbourhood, deviant friends, and school failure. For example, a model that is based on the concept of traits may explain the flow of crime over the life cycle, by looking at personal attributes or characteristics that control the inclination to commit crimes.[198] **Latent traits** may be present at birth and remain stable over time, such as defective intelligence, impulsive personality, and genetic abnormalities. Those who carry these latent traits are in danger of becoming career criminals. Latent traits affect the behaviour choices of all people equally, regardless of their gender or personal characteristics.[199]

The positive association between past and future criminality, as found in the cohort studies of career criminals, may

reflect the presence of underlying criminogenic traits. That is, if low IQ causes delinquency in childhood, it should also cause the same people to offend as adults because intelligence is usually stable over the lifespan. Similarly, people who are antisocial during their adolescence are more likely to be persistent criminals throughout their lifespan.

Because latent traits are stable, fluctuations in offending over time reflect criminal opportunities and not the propensity to commit crime. For example, assume that a stable latent trait, such as low IQ, causes some people to commit crime. Teenagers have more opportunity to commit crime than do adults of equal intelligence; therefore, adolescent crime rates are higher. As low-IQ teens mature, they will commit fewer crimes because they have fewer criminal opportunities. Although the propensity to commit crime is stable, the opportunity to commit crime fluctuates. Latent trait theories thus integrate concepts usually associated with trait theories (personality and temperament) with rational choice theories (criminal opportunity and suitable targets).

Another approach that has emerged is **life-course theory**. In contrast to the latent trait view, life-course theories hold that the propensity to commit crimes is not stable and does change over time. Some career criminals may desist from crime for a while, only to resume later. Some commit offences at a steady pace, while others escalate their rate of criminal involvement. Offenders may specialize in one type of crime or become generalists who commit a variety of illegal acts. Criminals may be influenced by family matters, financial needs, and changes in lifestyle and interests. Although latent traits may be important, they alone neither control the direction of criminal careers nor ensure that criminal acts are predetermined at birth or soon afterward.

Life-course theories also recognize that as people mature, the factors that influence their behaviour change.[200] At first, family relations may be most influential; in later adolescence, school and peer relations predominate; in adulthood, vocational achievement and marital relations may be the most critical. For example, antisocial kids who get into trouble as adolescents may manage to find stable work and maintain intact marriages as adults, which helps them to desist from crime. In contrast, those who are less fortunate may have arrest records, may find only menial jobs, and are at risk for criminal careers. Social forces that are critical at one stage of life may have little meaning or influence at another stage.

Multifactor theories, latent trait theories, and life-course theories share some common ground.[201] The criminal career

latent traits   Stable features, characteristics, properties, or conditions that are present at birth or soon after and that lead some people to be crime-prone over their life course.

life-course theory   Criminal offending patterns change over a person's life, influenced by conditions or events that occur at various stages in life.

Famous Canadian Court Cases
John Martin Crawford

Among the ranks of Canadian serial killers, John Crawford's name probably does not come to mind. However, he was convicted of slaying four women and the prime suspect in at least three other brutal murders and disappearances.

Born to a young, unwed mother in 1962 in Manitoba, he was severely burned in an accident, and other children teased him about his scars. With an alcoholic stepfather and sexually abusive babysitters while he was growing up, he had behavioural problems and failing grades. This glue-sniffing runaway who was picked on by his peers transformed into a drug-abusing car thief who bullied other kids. Crawford's deviant sexual tendencies first emerged at the age of 13, when he paid a younger girl for sex. He soon began to hear voices and display other psychotic symptoms.

By the age of 19, Crawford had become a sadistic predator and his first victim was Mary Jane Serloin in Lethbridge, Alberta. After pleading guilty to manslaughter, he served seven years of a decade-long sentence. Crawford's coping difficulties followed him to prison, where they manifested as anxiety and self-mutilation.

Crawford's appetite for sex, drugs, and violence escalated on his release from prison in 1989. While living with his then-divorced mother in Saskatoon, he was charged with sexual assault. In 1992, Crawford savagely raped, tortured, and killed Calinda Waterhen, Shelly Napope, and Eva Taysup, whose remains were not discovered until 1994.

With the aid of an informant paid $15,000 by the police, he was eventually convicted of one first-degree and two second-degree murders. The judge imposed three concurrent life sentences with no chance of parole. Professing her son's innocence, Crawford's mother hired lawyers to push the case forward. A higher Saskatchewan court rejected their appeal in 1999, as did the Supreme Court of Canada in 2000.

Crawford is now housed in a Prince Albert penitentiary, and his conviction record is surpassed only by Clifford Olson. However, his trial was under-reported compared to Paul Bernardo in 1995. This indifference has been attributed to the same systematic racism and sexism that allowed Robert Pickton to evade authorities for more than a decade: Crawford and Pickton preyed on Aboriginal women with high-risk lifestyles. As the sister of Crawford's first victim lamented, "It seems any time a Native is murdered, it isn't a major case. It's just another dead Indian."

---

is a passage along which people travel, and their journey is influenced by events and circumstances such as the following:

- Structural factors: income and status
- Socialization factors: family and peer relations
- Biological factors: size and strength
- Psychological factors: intelligence and personality
- Opportunity factors: free time, inadequate protection, easily stolen merchandise

Life-course and multifactor theories stress the influence of changing interpersonal and structural factors, whereas latent trait theories assume that change occurs not in people but in their criminal opportunities.

These perspectives differ in their view of human development: Do people change, as life-course theories suggest, or are people stable, constant, and changeless, as the latent trait view indicates? Does a dominant key control human destiny, or do multiple influences affect human behaviour? Are the social and personal factors that influence people stable, or do they change as a person matures?

In this section, we briefly discuss some integrated theories that address the development and sustenance of a criminal career.

Multifactor Theories

Multifactor theories integrate a range of variables into a cohesive explanation of criminality. These theories recognize that factors that appear later in life, such as peer relations, exert an important influence on people.

Efforts to create multifactor theories are not new. For example, according to Daniel Glazer's differential anticipation theory, "A person's crime or restraint from crime is determined by the consequences he anticipates from it."[202] According to Glazer, people commit crimes when the expectations of gain exceed the expectations of losses (rational choice). This decision is tempered both by the quality of social bonds (control theory) and by prior learning experiences (learning theory).

A few prominent examples of integrated theory are discussed next, including two important new developments.

The Social Development Model (SDM)

The **social development model (SDM)** attempts to integrate social control, social learning, and structural models (see Figure 8.8).

---

multifactor theories   Views that attempt to integrate individual factors and independent concepts into complex, coherent explanations of criminality.

social development model (SDM)   The attempt to integrate social control, social learning, and structural models of crime.

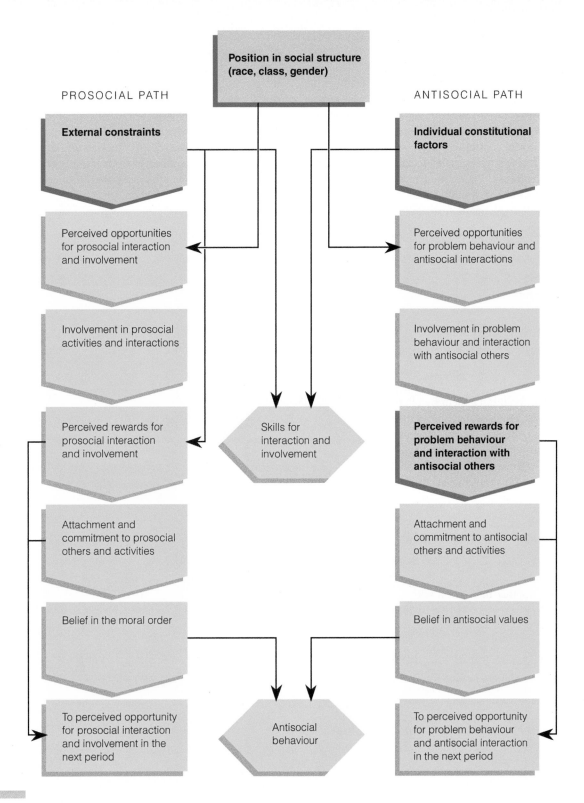

PROSOCIAL PATH

ANTISOCIAL PATH

Position in social structure
(race, class, gender)

External constraints

Individual constitutional
factors

Perceived opportunities
for prosocial interaction
and involvement

Perceived opportunities
for problem behaviour and
antisocial interactions

Involvement in prosocial
activities and interactions

Involvement in problem
behaviour and interaction
with antisocial others

Perceived rewards for
prosocial interaction
and involvement

Skills for
interaction and
involvement

Perceived rewards for
problem behaviour
and interaction with
antisocial others

Attachment and
commitment to prosocial
others and activities

Attachment and
commitment to antisocial
others and activities

Belief in the moral order

Belief in antisocial values

To perceived opportunity
for prosocial interaction
and involvement in the
next period

Antisocial
behaviour

To perceived opportunity
for problem behaviour
and antisocial interaction
in the next period

FIGURE 8.8

The Social Development Model of Antisocial Behaviour

Source: Adapted from J. David Hawkins, Karl G. Hill, Richard F. Catalano, Rick Kosterman, and Robert Abbot, *Seattle Social Development Project* (University of Washington).

Accordingly, several community-level "risk factors" make some people susceptible to developing antisocial behaviours. For example, in a low-income, disorganized community, families are under great stress, educational facilities are inadequate, fewer material goods are available, and respect for the law is weak. Crime rates are high, leading to greater opportunities for law violation, which increases the strain on the agencies of social control.

As a child matures, elements of socialization control the developmental process. Pre-existing risk factors are either reinforced or neutralized through socialization. Children are socialized and develop bonds to their family through four routes:

1. Their perceived opportunities for involvement in activities and interactions with others
2. Their degree of involvement and interaction with others
3. Their development of skills needed to participate in these interactions
4. Their perceived reinforcement (feedback) as a result of their participation

A child must maintain **pro-social bonds**, developed within the context of family life, which provide pro-social opportunities and reinforce them by offering consistent and positive feedback. Parental attachment affects a child's behaviour throughout the life course, determining both school experiences and personal beliefs and values. For those with strong family relationships, school will be a meaningful experience marked by academic success and commitment to education. Such youths are more likely to develop conventional beliefs and values, become committed to conventional activities, and form attachments to conventional others.

Children's antisocial behaviour also depends on the quality of their attachments to others. Unlike Hirschi's control theory, which assumes that all attachments are beneficial, the SDM suggests that interaction with antisocial peers and adults promotes participation in delinquency and substance abuse over the life course.[203] Whereas Hirschi maintains that early family attachments are the key determinants of future behaviour, the SDM suggests that later involvement in pro-social or antisocial behaviour determines the quality of attachments. Adolescents who perceive opportunities and rewards for deviance will form deep attachments to deviant peers, will become committed to delinquency, and will develop antisocial values and behaviour. In contrast, those who perceive opportunities and rewards for normalcy will be involved in conventional activities, form attachments to pro-social others, and develop moral beliefs.

The SDM thus holds that commitment and attachment to conventional institutions, activities, and beliefs work to insulate youths from the criminogenic influences of their environment, inhibiting deviance by strengthening bonds to pro-social others and activities.

When tested empirically,[204] the SDM seems to provide an accurate picture of the onset and continuation of violent and antisocial behaviour both for early onset offenders who engage in antisocial acts in childhood and later-onset offenders who begin offending in their teens.[205] The SDM also predicts the onset and continuation of delinquency and drug abuse, where both social learning and control bonding predict gang membership.[206] Youth who learn deviant attitudes and who have weak ties to conventional institutions are more likely to engage in criminal behaviours. Those youth who maintain antisocial opportunities and involvement, and who perceive deviant acts as both easy to get away with and rewarding, are the youths most likely to engage in crime.[207] Treatment interventions, then, promote the development of strong bonds to family and school to help youth resist the motivation to take drugs and engage in delinquency.[208]

Elliott's Integrated Theory

Another attempt at theory integration combines the features of strain, social learning, and control theories into a single theoretical model.[209]

According to this view (see Figure 8.9), adolescents who live in socially disorganized areas (A), who are improperly socialized (B), face a significant risk of perceiving strain (C).

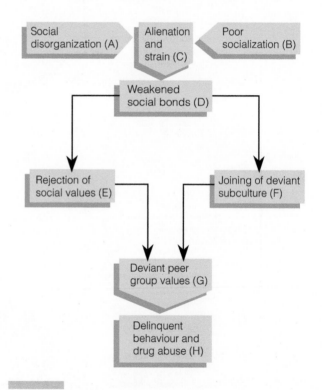

FIGURE 8.9
Elliott's Integrated Theory

pro-social bonds In the social development model, the bonds developed within the context of a family life that provide pro-social opportunities and consistent, positive feedback.

Their perceptions of strain then lead to weakened bonds with conventional groups, activities, and norms (D). Weak conventional bonds and high levels of perceived strain lead some youths to reject conventional social values (E) and seek out deviant peer groups (F). From these delinquent associations come positive reinforcements and role models for deviance (G). Attachment to delinquent groups, when combined with weak bonding to conventional groups and norms, leads to a high level of delinquent behaviour and drug abuse (H).

Social Factors. Elliott's integrated theory is similar to the SDM, with the addition of the concept of strain. Living in a disorganized neighbourhood, feeling hopeless and unable to get ahead, and becoming involved in petty crimes can eventually lead to a condition of declining conventional social values and weakened respect for the social order. A deviant peer group becomes an acceptable substitute; consequently, attitudes that support delinquency are amplified. The result is early experimentation with drugs, leading to delinquency as a way of life. According to both the SDM and Elliott's integrated theory, involvement with delinquent friends is assumed to increase the risk of crime.

Testing Integrated Theory. In a national survey of 1,800 youths interviewed over three years, the results supported integrated theory. However, some subjects who did not reject conventional values reported developing strong bonds to delinquent peers, which suggests that youths living in disorganized areas may join law-violating youth groups simply because conventional groups don't exist. Moreover, initial experimentation with drugs predicted joining a teenage law-violating peer group. Another national survey of more than a thousand youths also found that bonding to a delinquent peer group escalates criminal activity.[210]

Integrated Structural Marxist Theory

A multifactor theory developed to integrate conflict concepts with structural and process factors is the **integrated structural Marxist theory**, illustrated in Figure 8.10.[211]

Crime is a result of family relationships marked by conflict and despair, and is influenced by the quality of a person's work experience. Wage earners who occupy an inferior position are more likely to experience negative relationships with supervisors and employers. This experience can then create strain and alienation within the family, especially when discipline is inconsistent and overly punitive. Juveniles in such families become alienated from their parents and experience adjustment problems in school. They are more likely to attend underfunded schools, to perform poorly on standardized tests, and to be placed in slow-learner tracks, all of which correlate with delinquent behaviour.

FIGURE 8.10
Integrated Structural Marxist Theory

Negative social relations at home and school result in strain, which is reinforced by alienated peers and results in patterns of violent behaviour or economic crime. In the integrated structural theory, a crime control policy is needed to address root causes.[212]

THE GLUECK RESEARCH

Sheldon and Eleanor Glueck researched the life cycle of delinquent careers in longitudinal research studies by following the careers of known delinquents to determine the factors that predicted persistent offending.[213] In their research, the Gluecks made extensive use of interviews and records.[214]

Integrated structural Marxist theory An integrated approach that looks at the influence of a person's position within the relations of material production.

This life-course research focused on **early onset** of delinquency as a harbinger of a criminal career: The deeper the roots of childhood maladjustment, the smaller the chance of adult adjustment. Offending careers were also found to be stable: Children who are antisocial early in life are likely to continue their offending careers into adulthood.

Of personal and social factors related to persistent offending, the most important is the nature of family relations, such as the quality of discipline and emotional ties with parents.

As well, biological and psychological traits, such as body type, intelligence, and personality, have been found to play important roles. Children with low intelligence, with a background of mental illness, and with a powerful physique (i.e., mesomorphs) were most likely to become persistent offenders.

This research was ignored for nearly 30 years, as the study of crime and delinquency shifted almost exclusively to a focus on the social and social-psychological factors (poverty, neighbourhood deterioration, socialization) that formed the nucleus of structural and process theories.

Life Course Emerges

The rediscovery of the Gluecks's research has led to a renewed interest in criminal careers[215] and a revived interest in asking the following basic questions about how a criminal career unfolds over a person's life:[216]

1. Why do people begin committing antisocial acts?
2. Why do some stop or desist while others continue or persist?
3. Why do some escalate the severity of their criminality while others de-escalate?
4. If some terminate their criminal activity, what, if anything, causes them to begin again?
5. Why do some specialize in certain types of crime while others are generalists?

See also the next Criminology Research box on the follow-up to the Gluecks's study.

Criminogenic influences change and develop over time. Studies on delinquency prevention have found that poor discipline and monitoring by parents are key to the onset of criminality in early childhood. Then, in middle childhood, social rejection by conventional peers and academic failure sustain antisocial behaviour. In later adolescence, commitment to a deviant peer group creates a training ground for crime. Youths who are improperly socialized by unskilled parents are the youths most likely to rebel by wandering the streets with their deviant peers.[217] The onset of a criminal career is a function of poor parenting skills; its maintenance and support are related to social relations that emerge later in life.

Similar results have been obtained from longitudinal analyses of elementary school-aged boys that indicate a correlation between early onset and social withdrawal, depression, deviant peers, and family problems, while later onset (at ages 13 or 14) is related to low educational motivation.[218]

From these studies, an important observation of crime has emerged that incorporates personal change and growth. The factors that produce crime and delinquency at one point in the life cycle may not be relevant at another; as people mature, the social, physical, and environmental influences on their behaviour are transformed.

In summary, criminologists have tried combining different theoretical models into integrated theories of crime, by using multiple factors derived from structural and process theories. According to the social development model, social position controls life events, and living in a disorganized area helps weaken social bonds, leading to the development of deviant peer group associations.

Life-course theories argue that events that take place over the life course influence criminal choices and constantly change as people mature. The family, the peer group, marriage, and career are critical as pathways to crime. Crime may be part of a garden variety of social problems, including health, physical, and interpersonal troubles.

AN EVALUATION OF SOCIAL PROCESS THEORY

The branches of social process theory, social learning, social control, and labelling, are compatible because they suggest that criminal behaviour is part of the socialization process. Criminals are people who have troubled and disturbed interactions with critically important social institutions and processes—family, schools, the justice system, peer groups, employers, and neighbours. Although disagreement surrounds the relative importance of those influences, little question remains that social interactions shape the behaviour, beliefs, values, and self-image of the offender.

People who have learned deviant social values, who find themselves detached from conventional social relationships, or who are the subject of stigma and labels from significant others will be the most likely to fall prey to the attractions of criminal behaviour. These negative influences can affect anyone, beginning in youth and continuing into adulthood. The major strength of the social process view is the vast body of empirical data showing that delinquents and criminals often grew up in dysfunctional families, experienced troubled childhoods, and failed at school, at work, and in marriage. Prison data show that these characteristics are typical of inmates. Furthermore, integrated approaches help us understand more of the interconnections of different variables.

> **early onset** A term for how people who are deviant at a very young age are likely to persist in a criminal career throughout their lifetime.

Criminology Research
Shared Beginnings, Divergent Lives

Why are some delinquents destined to become persistent criminals as adults? Laub and Sampson conducted a follow-up to the Gluecks's study that matched 500 delinquent boys with 500 non-delinquents. Sampson and Laub located the survivors of the delinquent sample, the oldest, 70 years old, and the youngest, age 62, and re-interviewed this cohort.

Persistence and Desistance

Laub and Sampson find that delinquency and other forms of antisocial conduct in childhood are strongly related to adult delinquency and drug and alcohol abuse. Former delinquents also suffer consequences in other areas of social life, such as school, work, and family life. They are less likely to finish high school, more likely to be unemployed, to receive welfare, and experience divorce.

Laub and Sampson address one of the key questions posed by life-course theories: Is it possible for delinquents to turn their lives around as adults? They find that most antisocial children do not remain antisocial as adults. For example, of men in the study cohort who survived to age 50, 24 percent had no arrests for delinquent acts of violence and property after age 17; 48 percent had no arrests after age 25; 60 percent had no arrests after age 31; and 79 percent had no arrests after age 40. They conclude that desistance is the norm for most, if not all, serious delinquents.

Why Do Delinquents Desist?

Laub and Sampson interviewed 52 men as they approached age 70. The follow-up showed a dramatic drop in criminal activity as the men aged: Between ages 17 and 24, 84 percent had committed violent crimes; in their 30s and 40s, participation in violent crime dropped to 14 percent; and fell to 3 percent when the men were in their 60s and 70s.

Laub and Sampson's research showed that building social capital through marriage and jobs was key to desistance. Men who desisted were rooted in routines and had strong social ties to family and community. Drawing on the men's own words, they found that one important element for "going straight" was the "knifing off" of individuals from their immediate environment, which offered the men a new script for the future. Joining the military can provide this effect, as does marriage or changing one's residence. One former delinquent (age 69) told the researchers:

I'd say the turning point was, number one, the Army. You get into an outfit, you had a sense of belonging, you made your friends. I think I became a pretty good judge of character. In the Army, you met some good ones, you met some foul balls. Then I met the wife. I'd say probably that would be the turning point. Got married, then naturally, kids come. So now you got to get a better job, you got to make more money. And that's how I got to the Navy Yard and tried to improve myself.

Former delinquents who "went straight" put structure into their lives, and disassociated from delinquent peers. As one wife of a former delinquent said, "It is not how many beers you have, it's who you drink with." Even multiple offenders who did time in prison were able to desist with the help of a stabilizing marriage. Former delinquents acquired maturity by taking on family and work responsibilities, and were more likely than other former delinquents to find new direction and meaning in life.

However, although many former delinquents desisted from delinquency, they still faced the risk of an early and untimely death. Thirteen percent died by violence and suicide, compared with 6 percent of the non-delinquent subjects. By age 65, 29 percent of the delinquent subjects and 21 percent of the non-delinquent subjects had died from natural causes.

The strongest predictors of an early and unnatural death were frequent delinquent involvement during adolescence and alcohol abuse.

Policy Implications

Youth problems—delinquency, substance abuse, violence, dropping out, teen pregnancy—often share common risk characteristics. Intervention strategies need to consider how early prevention efforts to reduce delinquency will probably also reduce incidents of alcohol abuse, drunk driving, drug abuse, sexual promiscuity, and family violence. The best way to achieve these goals is through four significant life-changing events: marriage, joining the military, getting a job, and changing one's environment or neighbourhood. What is important about these processes is that they involve a knifing off of the past from the present, provide both supervision and new opportunities of social support, and offer the opportunity for transforming identity.

Critical Thinking

1. Are the factors that influenced the men in the original Glueck sample still relevant for making changes today? For example, is it possible for previously delinquent men to join the military today?
2. Would a universal service program be beneficial and help people turn their lives around?

SOURCES: John Laub and Robert Sampson, *Shared Beginnings, Divergent Lives: Delinquent Boys to Age 70* (Cambridge, MA: Harvard University Press, 2003); John Laub and Robert Sampson, "Understanding Desistance from Delinquency," in *Delinquency and Justice: An Annual Review of Research*, vol. 28, ed. Michael Tonry (Chicago: University of Chicago Press, 2001), pp. 1–71; John Laub and George Vaillant, "Delinquency and Mortality: A 50-Year Follow-Up Study of 1,000 Delinquent and Nondelinquent Boys," *American Journal of Psychiatry* 157 (2000): 96–102.

Criminology Research
Desisting from Crime

In other research on understanding desistance, called *Making Good: How Ex-Convicts Reform and Rebuild Their Lives,* criminologist Shadd Maruna interviewed a group of serious criminals to see how they could be reformed. These men had been in trouble for most of their lives, but were able to turn their lives around although their background suggested otherwise.

Maruna found that desistance was a process, not an instantaneous event. Desisters undergo a long-term cognitive change, during which they begin to see themselves as a "new person" or gain a new outlook on life. They begin to understand their past and develop insights into why they behaved the way they did, and why and how things went wrong. Desisters begin to feel a sense of fulfillment when engaging in productive behaviours and become agents of their own change. They start feeling in control of their future and have a newfound purpose in life. Importantly, rather than run from their past, they view their prior history as a learning experience.

Sociologists Giordano, Cernkovich, and Rudolph also link desistance to a process of cognitive change. For example, changes in some people's environment help to construct a kind of psychic "scaffolding" that makes it possible to create significant life change. They must discard their old bad habits and begin the process of crafting a different way of life, moving toward, or selecting the various environmental catalysts for change.

Cognitive Transformations

Certain positive life experiences help people turn their lives around, and if they can manage to seize the right opportunity, the former offender may undergo a *cognitive transformation*—a process by which the person reshapes their thought and behaviour patterns into a more conventional and rewarding lifestyle. Giordano and her associates have identified four critical cognitive transformations as key to the healing process:

1. *A shift in the actor's basic openness to change.* The person must be ready and willing to change.
2. *Exposure to a particular hook or set of hooks for change.* An environmental catalyst must be available to "hook on to" that can be seen as a positive development (for example, a high attachment to a spouse).
3. *A willingness to establish a "new identity."* The person must be able to envision and begin to fashion an appealing and conventional *replacement self* to substitute for the older, damaged identity. The new identity must serve as a basis for decision making, as the person moves into new and novel situations: "I may have smoked pot as a kid, but now that I am a husband, the new me would never take the risk." This is critical when facing stressful life circumstances, such as divorce or unemployment, and the person is forced to make decisions that differ from destructive choices made in the past.
4. *A transformation in the way the actor views the deviant behaviour, or lifestyle, itself.* The desistance process can be seen as complete when the actor no longer sees the past life and behaviours as positive, viable, or even personally relevant. The person's past behaviour is viewed as having been foolish and destructive: "It is no longer cool to get high, but selfish and destructive."

The desistance process proceeds using these cognitive shifts from an overall "readiness" to change, to encountering environmental hooks for change, to a shift in identity, and finally to the maintenance of a positive identity that decreases the desirability of former behaviour.

These views were tested by using data collected from incarcerated delinquent youth first interviewed in 1982 and re-interviewed in 1995. Youths who desisted from crime as adults experienced cognitive transformations. However, the hooks that led them to change were varied. For males, going to prison was a life-transforming event. For many females, having a religious conversion or having children helped them reform. Some desisters said having a romantic relationship was a key factor in their personal turnaround because supportive partners helped them raise their self-esteem: "He said I didn't belong where I was at." By seeking out conventional partners, desisters demonstrate a cognitive shift ("I am the type of person who wants to associate with this respectable man/woman"). The potential desister, tired of being dishonest, is helped when he or she is able to connect with someone who demonstrates the benefits of being honest on a daily basis.

This research helps us to better understand the life-transforming processes that lead some people to desist from crime.

Critical Thinking

Many of the women told the researchers that they had crafted highly traditional replacement selves (such as being a child of God, the good wife, or an involved mother), and that these new identities helped them with their successful exits from criminal activities. Giordano fears that latching on to these identities might be helpful in the short term but may be highly repressive and cut into women's becoming economically self-sustaining and independent in the long term. Do you agree?

SOURCES: Shadd Maruna, *Making Good: How Ex-Convicts Reform and Rebuild Their Lives* (Washington, DC: American Psychological Association, 2000); Peggy Giordano, Stephen Cernkovich, and Jennifer Rudolph, "Gender, Crime, and Desistance: Toward a Theory of Cognitive Transformation," *American Journal of Sociology* 107 (2002): 990–1,065.

However, these theories also have trouble accounting for some of the patterns and fluctuations in the crime rate. For example, people in the western provinces must be socialized differently from those in the eastern provinces because people from the eastern regions tend to have much lower crime rates. How can the fact that crime rates are lower in October than in July be explained if crime is a function of learning or control? How can social processes explain why criminals escalate their activity or why they desist from crime? Once a social bond is broken, how can it be "reattached"? Once crime is "learned," how can it be "unlearned"?

SOCIAL PROCESS THEORY AND SOCIAL POLICY

Social process theories have had a major influence on social policy since the 1950s. Learning theories have influenced concepts of treatment of the offender, especially young offenders, who are viewed as being more salvageable than are hardened criminals. Advocates argue that if people become criminal by learning definitions and attitudes toward criminality, they can "unlearn" them by being exposed to definitions toward conventional behaviour. This philosophy has been used in numerous treatment facilities, which use group interaction sessions to attack the criminal behaviour orientations held by residents (e.g., being tough, using alcohol and drugs, believing that school is for "sissies") while promoting conventional lines of behaviour (e.g., going straight, saving money, giving up drugs).

Today, many residential and non-residential programs offer such treatment programs. They teach kids to say no to drugs, to forgo delinquent behaviour, or to stay in school. Celebrities even return to their old neighbourhood to tell kids to stay in school or off drugs. After Ben Johnson was banned from international competition for using steroids, for example, he gave talks to school kids on the value of being drug-free. If learning did not affect behaviour, such exercises would be futile.

Making changes in how the system reacts can be an important part of the solution. All over the country, youth diversion programs are springing up. Their aim is to force offenders to be more accountable to the community. For minor crimes, offenders make restitution, apologize, and do volunteer work. Research shows that intervening early, in a non-judicial way, does work for delinquents. However, catching problems before they develop is also important. In Ontario, new spending was announced to help students in danger of dropping out of school. In British Columbia, early intervention initiatives began in high schools to encourage

Aboriginal students to attend university, which is key to them finding better jobs.[219]

Control theories have also influenced criminal justice and other social policymaking. Programs have been developed to improve people's commitments to conventional lines of action and to create and strengthen bonds early in life before the onset of criminality. The educational system has been the scene of numerous programs designed to improve basic skills and create an atmosphere in which youths will develop a bond to their schools. The Head Start program is one of the largest and best-known attempts to solidify social bonds and increase social capital, and is discussed in detail in the Comparative Criminology box.

Given the diversion emphasis of the new *Youth Criminal Justice Act,* restorative justice options are being explored. Extra-legal, community-oriented approaches, such as family group conferencing and sentencing circles, are being developed as a way to strengthen the relationships among offender, family, and community. Changes to emphasize on non-custodial programs and services also help to shift the balance in youth justice toward a community-based model.[220]

An approach that has proved effective in other countries is multisystemic therapy (MST). This home-based treatment for juveniles addresses the relationships among family, peers, school, and community. MST targets chronic, violent, and substance-abusing juveniles who are at high risk. The aim is to empower parents with the skills and resources needed to help their children cope. In one study, families reported increased cohesion and decreased conflict. The overall rate of recidivism was 22 percent, compared with 71 percent in a control group. The program has been estimated to have paid for itself more than eight times over in terms of savings in criminal justice. Results in family court in London, Ontario, are not optimistic, but the program has the promise of avoiding some of the deleterious effects of incarceration.[221]

Control theory's focus on the family has been put into operation in programs designed to repair and strengthen the bond between parent and child. Examples of this approach are the career, work furlough, and educational opportunity programs being developed in prisons. These programs are designed to help inmates maintain a stake in society so that they will be less willing to resort to criminal activity on their release. An important change and a good example of social process theory informing social policy was the establishment of federal guidelines on the use of conditional sentencing. Offenders serve their time in the community, reducing incarceration costs and making reintegration easier.

However, labelling theorists caution against too much intervention. Rather than asking social agencies to attempt to rehabilitate people who are having problems with the law, theorists argue that "less is better." Put another way, the more institutions try to help people, the more these people will be stigmatized and labelled. For example, a special education

Head Start is probably the best-known effort to help lower-class youths achieve proper socialization and, in so doing, reduce their potential for future criminality.

Head Start programs were first instituted in the 1960s, as a two-month summer program providing comprehensive programming and promoting physical and mental health. It worked to improve social and emotional development, self-image, and interpersonal relationships. Preschoolers were provided with an enriched educational environment to develop their learning and cognitive skills. They were given the opportunity to use materials that middle-class children take for granted—pegs and pegboards, puzzles, toy animals, and so forth.

Today, services have been expanded beyond the two-month summer program, with over 36,000 classrooms in the United States servicing 740,000 children and their families. Learning experiences appropriate to the child's age and development focus on reading books, understanding cultural diversity, and the expression of feelings and play with their peers. Students are guided in developing gross and fine motor skills and self-confidence. Healthcare is also an issue, and most children enrolled in the program receive comprehensive health screening, physical and dental examinations, and appropriate follow-up. Many programs provide meals and, in so doing, help children receive proper nourishment.

In addition, some programs allow parents to enrol in classes that cover parenting, literacy, nutrition, domestic violence prevention, and other social issues. Social

services, health, and education services are also available.

Early evaluation of Head Start found initial gains seemed to evaporate during the elementary school years, and by Grade 3 the performance of the Head Start children was no different from that of their peers. However, recent research has produced dramatically different results. One report found that by age five, children who experienced the enriched daycare offered by Head Start averaged more than 10 points higher on their IQ scores than did their peers who did not participate in the program. Other research that carefully compared Head Start children with similar youths who did not attend the program found that the former made significant intellectual gains. Head Start children were less likely to be placed in classes for slow learners; they outperformed peers on achievement tests; and they were more likely to graduate from high school. Head Start kids also had better health and enhanced emotional characteristics.

Research also shows that the Head Start program can have important psychological benefits for the mothers of participants, decreasing their depression and anxiety, and increasing their feelings of life satisfaction.

If, as many experts believe, a close link exists between school performance, family life, and crime, such programs as Head Start can help some potentially criminal youths avoid problems with the law. By implication, their success indicates that programs that help socialize youngsters can be used to combat urban criminality.

In Canada, the federal Aboriginal Head Start (AHS) program is aimed at children 3 to 6 years of age and focuses on school readiness, healthy living, life skills training, social support, and Aboriginal language and culture. Beginning in 1995, this program is oriented to high-risk children, such as single-parent families, special needs, low income, or those whose caregivers have low education levels. Funded by Health Canada, AHS now has 9000 children enrolled in 300 sites.

More than 70 percent of the children come from families in which the parents have Grade 12 education or less. Children identified as high risk are less likely to have both parents in the same household and are more likely to have a history of family violence. Other relevant factors are parents who have had histories of drug or alcohol abuse or who were survivors of residential school. In a 1998 evaluation report, success was reported in identifying those with risk factors, in retention through the whole program, and in addressing their needs.

SOURCES: Carol L. McAllister, Patrick C. Wilson, Beth L. Green, and Jennifer L. Baldwin, "'Come and Take a Walk': Listening to Early Head Start Parents on School-Readiness as a Matter of Child, Family, and Community Health," *American Journal of Public Health* 95, 4 (2005): 617–625; Annual Report, Public Health Agency of Canada, Alberta/Northwest Territories Region, 2006–2007; J. Ball, "Early Childhood Care and Development Programs as 'Hook' and 'Hub' for Inter-sectoral Service," *Journal of Aboriginal Health* 1, 2 (2005): 36–50; Aboriginal Head Start on Reserve, at www.hc-sc.gc.ca/fniah-spnia/famil/develop/ahsor-papa_intro-eng.php.

program designed to help problem readers may cause them to be labelled by themselves and others as slow or stupid; similarly, a mental health rehabilitation program created with the best intentions may cause clients to be labelled as crazy or dangerous.

The influence of labelling theory can be viewed in the development of diversion and restitution programs

designed to remove offenders from the criminal justice process by placing them in programs designed for rehabilitation. For example, a university student whose drunk driving causes injury to a pedestrian may, before a trial occurs, be placed for six months in an alcohol treatment program. If he or she successfully completes the program, the charges will be dismissed. Often, diversion programs offer counselling; vocational, educational, and family services; and medical advice. Another label-avoiding innovation that has gained popularity is restitution. Rather than face the stigma of a formal trial, an offender is asked either to pay back the victim of the crime for any loss incurred or to do some useful work in the community in lieu of receiving a court-ordered sentence.

Stigma-reducing programs have been criticized for substituting one kind of stigma for another—for instance, attending a mental health program in lieu of a criminal trial. Also, little hard evidence supports a reduced recidivism rate of people who have attended alternative programs compared with the rate of people who have been involved in the traditional criminal justice process. However it does show the influence of thinking in new ways.

SUMMARY

Social process theories view criminality as a function of people's interaction with society's various organizations, institutions, and processes. Everyone has the potential to become a criminal if he or she maintains destructive social relationships. Social process theory has three main branches: Social learning theory stresses that people learn how to commit crimes; control theory analyzes the failure of society to control criminal tendencies; and labelling theory maintains that negative labels produce criminal careers. These theories are summarized in Concept Summary 8.1.

CONCEPT SUMMARY 8.1

Social Process Theories

Theory	Major Premise	Strengths	Research Focus
Social Learning Theories			
Differential association theory	People learn to commit crime from exposure to antisocial definitions.	Explains onset of criminality. Explains the presence of crime in all elements of social structure. Explains why some people in high-crime areas refrain from criminality. Can apply to adults and juveniles.	Measuring definitions toward crime; influence of deviant peers and parents
Differential reinforcement theory	Criminal behaviour depends on the person's experiences with rewards for conventional behaviours and punishment for deviant ones. Being rewarded for deviance leads to crime.	Adds psychological learning theory principles to differential association theory. Links sociological and psychological principles.	Cause of criminal activity; ability of the content of socialization to condition crime
Neutralization theory	Youths learn ways of neutralizing moral restraints and periodically drift in and out of criminal behaviour patterns.	Explains why many delinquents do not become adult criminals. Explains why youthful law violators can participate in conventional behaviour.	Whether people who use neutralizations commit more crimes; the relationship between beliefs, values, and crime
Social Control Theory			
Hirschi's control theory	A person's bond to society prevents the violation of social rules. If the bond weakens, the person is free to commit crime.	Explains the onset of crime; can apply to both middle- and lower-class crime. Explains its theoretical constructs adequately so that they can be measured. Has been empirically tested.	The association between commitment, attachment, involvement, belief, and crime
Social Reaction Theory			
Labelling theory	People who have been labelled for their acts enter into law-violating careers and organize their personalities around the labels.	Explains the role of society in creating deviance. Explains why some juvenile offenders do not become adult criminals. Develops concepts of criminal careers.	Self-concept and crime; differential application of labels; effect of stigma

Social process theories have had a great influence on social policy. They have influenced both treatment orientations and community action policies.

The social learning branch of social process theory suggests that people learn criminal behaviours much as they learn conventional behaviour. Differential association theory, formulated by Edwin Sutherland, holds that criminality is a result of a person perceiving an excess of pro-crime definitions over definitions that uphold conventional values. Ronald Akers has reformulated Sutherland's work using psychological learning theory. He calls his approach differential reinforcement theory. Sykes and Matza's theory of neutralization stresses youths' learning of behaviour rationalizations that enable them to overcome societal values and norms, and engage in illegal behaviour.

Control theories maintain that all people have the potential to become criminals but that our bonds to conventional society prevent most of us from violating the law. Walter Reckless's containment theory suggests that a person's self-concept aids his or her commitment to conventional action. Travis Hirschi describes the social bond as containing elements of belief, commitment, attachment, and involvement. Weakened bonds allow youths to become active in antisocial behaviour.

Labelling theory holds that criminality is promoted by becoming negatively labelled by significant others. Such labels as *criminal*, *ex-con*, and *junkie* serve to isolate people from society and lock them into lives of crime. Labels create expectations that the labelled person will act in a certain way; so-labelled people are always watched and suspected. Eventually, these people begin to accept their labels as personal identities, locking them further into lives of crime and deviance. Edwin Lemert has said that people who accept labels are involved in secondary deviance.

THINKING LIKE A CRIMINOLOGIST

The federal government is considering a bill that requires the names of people convicted of certain offences, such as vandalism, soliciting a prostitute, or non-payment of child support, to be posted in local newspapers under the heading "For Shame." Those who favour the bill cite the situation in Boston, where men arrested for soliciting prostitutes are forced to clean streets. In Dallas, shoplifters are made to stand outside stores with signs stating their misdeeds. In some states, convicted sex offenders have been required to put signs on their lawn stating their offence.

The Canadian Civil Liberties Union opposes the idea, stating, "It's simply needless humiliation of the individual." They argue that public shaming is inhumane and further alienates criminals who already have little stake in society, further ostracizing them from the mainstream. For the one-time offender, shaming damages their reputation and puts them at risk of further offending.

This "liberal" position is challenged by those who believe that convicted lawbreakers have no right to conceal their crimes from the public. Shaming penalties seem attractive as cost-effective alternatives to imprisonment. These critics ask what could be wrong with requiring a teenage vandal to apologize personally at the school and wear a shirt with a big "V" on it while cleaning up the mess. Similarly, drunk drivers should have a big "D" placed on their car. If you do something wrong, they argue, you should have to pay the consequences.

As a social process theorist, you believe criminal attitudes and behaviours are learned. Weak ties to parents and families, poor school performance, and so on, influence the actions of the individual. Considering these effects, do you believe a "get tough" program could actually work, or does it miss the underlying causes of the behaviour? You have been asked to address the Justice Committee on the issue of whether shaming could deter crime. What would you say?

KEY TERMS

commitment to conformity p. 251
containments p. 251
control theory p. 244
developmental criminology p. 262
differential association (DA)
   theory p. 245
differential reinforcement (DR)
   theory p. 248
dramatization of evil p. 259
drift p. 249
early onset p. 268
integrated structural Marxist
   theory p. 267

labelling theory p. 244
latent traits p. 263
life-course theory p. 263
master status p. 259
moral entrepreneurs p. 258
multifactor theories p. 264
neutralization theory p. 249
primary deviance p. 259
pro-social bonds p. 266
reflected appraisal p. 260
reflective role-taking p. 260
secondary deviance p. 259
self-rejection p. 251

social development model
   (SDM) p. 264
social deviant p. 256
social distance p. 258
socialization p. 239
social learning theory p. 244
social process theories p. 239
stigmatize p. 242
subterranean values p. 249
symbolic interaction theory
   p. 256
techniques of neutralization
   p. 249

DOING RESEARCH ON THE WEB

Go to Restorative Justice Online, a non-partisan source of information on restorative justice, to begin researching your answer to the Thinking Like a Criminologist box on page 274: www.restorativejustice.org.

The Centre for Restorative Justice, at Simon Fraser University in British Columbia, in partnership with individuals, the community, and justice agencies, exists to support and promote the principles and practices of restorative justice by providing education, training, evaluation, and research. Visit the centre's website at www.sfu.ca/crj.

CRITICAL THINKING QUESTIONS

1. Do negative labels cause crime? Or, do people who commit crime become negatively labelled? That is, are labels a cause of crime or a result?

2. Once weakened, can a person's bonds to society become reattached? What social processes might help reattachment?

3. Can you devise a test of Sutherland's differential association theory? How would you go about measuring an excess of definitions toward criminality?

4. Can you think of ways you may have supported your peers' or siblings' antisocial behaviour by helping them learn criminal techniques or attitudes?

5. Do you recall neutralizing any guilt you might have felt for committing a criminal or illegal act? Did your neutralizations come before or after you committed the act in question?

NOTES

1. See, for example, James Q. Wilson and Allan Abrahamse, "Does Crime Pay?" *Justice Quarterly* 9 (1992): 359–378.

2. Callie Marie Rennison, *Criminal Victimization 2000. Bureau of Justice Statistics Changes 1999–2000 with Trends 1993–2000* (Washington, DC: Bureau of Justice Statistics, 2001).

3. Alan Lizotte, Terence Thornberry, Marvin Krohn, Deborah Chard-Wierschem, and David McDowall, "Neighborhood Context and Delinquency: A Longitudinal Analysis," in *Cross-National Longitudinal Research on Human Development and Criminal Behavior*, eds. E.M. Weitekamp and H.J. Kerner (Stavernstr, Netherlands: Kluwer, 1994), 217–227.

4. Charles Tittle and Robert Meier, "Specifying the SES/Delinquency Relationship," *Criminology* 28 (1990): 271–299.

5. Lizotte, Thornberry, Krohn, Chard-Wierschem, and McDowall, "Neighborhood Context and Delinquency: A Longitudinal Analysis," 217–227.

6. Denise Kandel, "The Parental and Peer Contexts of Adolescent Deviance: An Algebra of Interpersonal Influences," *Journal of Drug Issues* 26 (1996): 289–315; Ann Goetting, "The Parenting Crime Connection," *Journal of Primary Prevention* 14 (1994): 167–184; Sheldon Glueck and Eleanor Glueck, *Unraveling Juvenile Delinquency* (Cambridge, MA: Harvard University Press, 1950); Ashley Weeks, "Predicting Juvenile Delinquency," *American Sociological Review* 8 (1943): 40–46.

7. For general reviews of the relationship between families and delinquency, see Alan Jay Lincoln and Murray Straus, *Crime and the Family* (Springfield, IL: Charles C. Thomas, 1985); Rolf Loeber and Magda Stouthamer-Loeber, "Family Factors as Correlates and Predictors of Juvenile Conduct Problems and Delinquency," in *Crime and Justice, An Annual Review of Research*, vol. 7, eds. Michael Tonry and Norval Morris, 29–151 (Chicago: University of Chicago Press, 1986); Goetting, "The Parenting Crime Connection."

8. David J. Pevalin, Terrance J. Wade, and Augustine Brannigan, "Precursors, Consequences and Implications for Stability and Change in Pre-adolescent Antisocial Behaviours," *Prevention Science* 4, 2 (2003): 123–136.

9. Joseph Weis, Katherine Worsley, and Carol Zeiss, *The Family and Delinquency: Organizing the Conceptual Chaos* (Seattle: Center for Law and Justice, University of Washington, 1982).

10. Susan Stern and Carolyn Smith, "Family Processes and Delinquency in an Ecological Context," *Social Service Review* 37 (1995): 707–731.

11. General Social Survey on Families, 2011, Statistics Canada, www.statcan.gc.ca/daily-quotidien/130419/dq130419c-eng.htm.

12. Jukka Savolainen, "Relative Cohort Size and Age-Specific Arrest Rates: A Conditional Interpretation of the Easterlin Effect," *Criminology* 38 (2000): 117–136.

13. Heather Juby and David P. Farrington, "Disentangling the Link between Disrupted Families and Delinquency, Sociodemography, Ethnicity and Risk Behaviours," *The British Journal of Criminology* 41 (2001): 22–40.

14. Tracy R. Nicholsa, Julia A. Graberb, Jeanne Brooks-Gunnc, and Gilbert J. Botvina, "Sex Differences in Overt Aggression and Delinquency among Urban Minority Middle School Students," *Journal of Applied Developmental Psychology* 27, 1 (2006): 78–91.

15. Lawrence Rosen and Kathleen Neilson, "Broken Homes," in *Contemporary Criminology*, eds. Leonard Savitz and Norman Johnston, 126–135 (New York: Wiley, 1982).

16. James Q. Wilson and Richard Herrnstein, *Crime and Human Nature* (New York: Simon & Schuster, 1985), 249.

17. L. Edward Wells and Joseph Rankin, "Families and Delinquency: A Meta-Analysis of the Impact of Broken Homes," *Social Problems* 38 (1991): 71–90.

18. Nan Marie Astone and Sara McLanahan, "Family Structure, Parental Practices and High School Completion," *American Sociological Review* 56 (1991): 309–320.

19. Mary Patricia Traxler, Male role models' influence on inner-city, high-risk, African-American boys' development. Diss. University of Illinois at Chicago, 1993.

20. Robert E. Emery, Mary C. Waldron, Jeffrey Aaron, and Katherine M. Kitzmann, "Delinquent Behavior, Future Divorce or Nonmarital Childbearing, and Externalizing Behavior among Offspring: A 14-Year Prospective Study," *Journal of Family Psychology* 13, 4 (1999).

21. Paul Amato and Bruce Keith, "Parental Divorce and the Well-Being of Children: A Meta-Analysis," *Psychological Bulletin* 110 (1991): 26–46.

22. Cathy Keen, "UF Study: Delinquency Risk no Greater in Families with Stepparents," *University of Florida News*, November 4, 1998.

23. Don Kerr and Roderic Beaujot, "Family Relations, Low Income, and Child Outcomes: A Comparison of Canadian Children in Intact-, Step-, and Lone-Parent Families," *International Journal of Comparative Sociology* 43, 2 (2002): 134–152.

24. Dafna E. Kohen, Jeanne Brooks-Gunn, Tama Leventhal, and Clyde Hertzman, "Neighborhood Income and Physical and Social Disorder in Canada: Associations with Young Children's Competencies," *Child Development* 73, 6 (2002): 1844–1860.

25. Dafna E. Kohen, Tama Leventhal, V. Susan Dahinten, and Cameron N. McIntosh, "Neighborhood Disadvantage: Pathways of Effects for Young Children," *Child Development* 79 (1): 156–169.

26. Joseph Rankin and L. Edward Wells, "The Effect of Parental Attachments and Direct Controls on Delinquency," *Journal of Research in Crime and Delinquency* 27 (1990): 140–165.

27. John Paul Wright and Francis Cullen, "Parental Efficacy and Delinquent Behavior: Do Control and Support Matter?" *Criminology* 39 (2001): 677–706.

28. Carter Hay, "Parenting, Self-Control, and Delinquency: A Test of Self-Control Theory," *Criminology* 39 (2001): 707–736.

29. Robert Roberts and Vern Bengston, "Affective Ties to Parents in Early Adulthood and Self-Esteem across 20 Years," *Social Psychology Quarterly* 59 (1996): 96–106.

30. Robert Johnson, S. Susan Su, Dean Gerstein, Hee-Choon Shin, and John Hoffman, "Parental Influences on Deviant Behavior in Early Adolescence: A Logistic Response Analysis of Age- and Gender-Differentiated Effects," *Journal of Quantitative Criminology* 11 (1995): 167–192.

31. Judith Brook and Li-Jng Tseng, "Influences of Parental Drug Use, Personality, and Child Rearing on the Toddler's Anger and Negativity," *Genetic, Social and General Psychology Monographs* 122 (1996): 107–128.

32. Thomas Ashby Wills, Donato Vaccaro, Grace McNamara, and A. Elizabeth Hirky, "Escalated Substance Use: A Longitudinal Grouping Analysis from Early to Middle Adolescence," *Journal of Abnormal Psychology* 105 (1996): 166–180.

33. John Laub and Robert Sampson, "Unraveling Families and Delinquency: A Reanalysis of the Gluecks' Data," *Criminology* 26 (1988): 355–380.

34. Richard Famularo, Karen Stone, Richard Barnum, and Robert Wharton, "Alcoholism and Severe Child Maltreatment," *American Journal of Orthopsychiatry* 56 (1987): 481–485; Richard Gelles, "Child Abuse and Violence in Single-Parent Families: Parent Absence and Economic Deprivation," *American Journal of Orthopsychiatry* 59 (1989): 492–501; Cecil Willis and Richard Wells, "The Police and Child Abuse: An Analysis of Police Decisions to Report Illegal Behavior," *Criminology* 26 (1988): 695–716; Carolyn Webster-Stratton, "Comparison of Abusive and Nonabusive Families with Conduct-Disordered Children," *American Journal of Orthopsychiatry* 55 (1985): 59–69.

35. Carolyn Smith and Terence Thornberry, "The Relationship between Childhood Maltreatment and Adolescent Involvement in Delinquency," *Criminology* 33 (1995): 451–479.

36. Herman Daldin, "The Fate of the Sexually Abused Child," *Clinical Social Work Journal* 16 (1988): 20–26; Gerald Ellenson, "Horror, Rage and Defenses in the Symptoms of Female Sexual Abuse Survivors," *Social Casework: The Journal of Contemporary Social Work* 70 (1989): 589–596.

37. Richard E. Heyman and Amy M. Smith Slep, "Do Child Abuse and Interpersonal Violence Lead to Adulthood Family Violence?" *Journal of Marriage and Family* 64 (2002): 864–870.

38. Jennie G. Noll, Lisa A. Horowitz, George A. Bonanno, Penelope K. Trickett, and Frank W. Putnam, "Revictimization and Self-Harm in Females Who Experienced Childhood Sexual Abuse: Results from a Prospective Study," *Journal of Interpersonal Violence* 18, 12 (2003): 1452–1471.

39. Susan Zuravin, "The Ecology of Child Abuse and Neglect: Review of the Literature and Presentation of Data," *Violence and Victims* 4 (1989): 101–120.

40. Jodi-Anne Brzozowski, *Family Violence in Canada: A Statistical Profile 2004* (Ottawa: Statistics Canada, 2004).

41. Lening Zhang and Steven Messner, "Family Deviance and Delinquency in China," *Criminology* 33 (1995): 359–387.

42. *The Forgotten Half: Pathways to Success for America's Youth and Young Families* (Washington, DC: William T. Grant Foundation, 1988); Lee Jussim, "Teacher Expectations: Self-Fulfilling Prophecies, Perceptual Biases, and Accuracy," *Journal of Personality and Social Psychology* 57 (1989): 469–480.

43. Eugene Maguin and Rolf Loeber, "Academic Performance and Delinquency," in *Crime and Justice: A Review of Research*, vol. 20, ed. Michael Tonry, 145–264 (Chicago: University of Chicago Press, 1996).

44. Valerie Pottie Bunge, Holly Johnson and Thierno Balde, "Exploring Crime Patterns in Canada," Crime and Justice Research Paper Series, Canadian Centre for Justice Statistics, 2005.

45. Jane B. Sprott, Anthony N. Doob, and Jennifer M. Jenkins, "Problem Behaviour and Delinquency in Children and Youth," *Juristat* 21, 4 (2001).

46. Jane Sprott, "The Development of Early Delinquency: Can Classroom and School Climates Make a Difference?" *Canadian Journal of Criminology and Criminal Justice* 46, 5 (2004): 553–572.

47. Jeannie Oakes, *Keeping Track: How Schools Structure Inequality* (New Haven, CT: Yale University Press, 1985); Marc LeBlanc, Évelyne Vallières, Pierre McDuff, "The Prediction of Males' Adolescent and Adult Offending from School Experience," 35 *Canadian Journal of Criminology* 459 (1993).

48. G. Roger Jarjoura, "Does Dropping Out of School Enhance Delinquent Involvement? Results from a Large-Scale National Probability Sample," *Criminology* 31 (1993): 149–712; Terence Thornberry, Melanie Moore, and R.L. Christenson, "The Effect of Dropping Out of High School on Subsequent Criminal Behavior," *Criminology* 23 (1985): 3–18.

49. Carolyn Smith, Alan Lizotte, Terence Thornberry, and Marvin Krohn, *Resilient Youth: Identifying Factors That Prevent High Risk Youth from Engaging in Delinquency and Drug Use* (Albany, NY: Rochester Youth Development Study, 1994), 19–21.

50. Scott Davies, and Julian Tanner, "The Long Arm of the Law: Effects of Labeling on Employment," *The Sociological Quarterly* 44, 3 (2003): 385–404.

51. "Youth Crime 2006," *The Daily*, Friday, May 16, 2008.

52. Irving Janis, *Groupthink: Psychological Studies of Policy Decisions and Fiascoes* (Boston: Houghton Mifflin, 1982); Lening Zhang and Steven Messner, "Family Deviance and Delinquency in China," *Criminology* 33 (1995): 359–387.

53. Thomas Berndt, "The Features and Effects of Friendships in Early Adolescence," *Child Development* 53 (1982): 1447–1469; Thomas Berndt and T.B. Perry, "Children's Perceptions of Friendships as Supportive Relationships," *Developmental Psychology* 22 (1986): 640–648; Spencer Rathus, *Understanding Child Development* (New York: Holt, Rinehart and Winston, 1988), 462.

54. Peggy Giordano, "The Wider Circle of Friends in Adolescence," *American Journal of Sociology* 101 (1995): 661–697.

55. André Picard, "Obese Girls and Boys Bullied More Often, Research Finds," *The Globe and Mail*, May 3, 2004; see also, Ian Janssen, Wendy M. Craig, William F. Boyce, William Pickett, "Associations Between Overweight and Obesity With Bullying Behaviors in School-Aged Children," *Pediatrics*, 113, 5, 2004 pp. 1187–1194.

56. Delbert Elliott, David Huizinga, and Suzanne Ageton, *Explaining Delinquency and Drug Use* (Beverly Hills, CA: Sage, 1985); Helene Raskin White, Robert Padina, and Randy LaGrange, "Longitudinal Predictors of Serious Substance Use and Delinquency," *Criminology* 6 (1987): 715–740.

57. Ximena B. Arriaga and Vangie A. Foshee, "Adolescent Dating Violence: Do Adolescents Follow in their Friends', or Their Parents', Footsteps?" *Journal of Interpersonal Violence* 19, 2 (2004): 162–184.

58. Mara Brendgen, Frank Vitaro, Richard E Tremblay, and Brigitte Wanner, "Parent and Peer Effects on Delinquency-related Violence and Dating Violence: A Test of Two Mediational Models," *Social Development* 11, 2 (2002): 225–244.

59. See, generally, John Hagedorn, *People and Folks: Gangs, Crime and the Underclass in a Rustbelt City* (Chicago: Lakeview Press, 1988).

60. Scott Menard, "Demographic and Theoretical Variables in the Age-Period Cohort Analysis of Illegal Behavior," *Journal of Research in Crime and Delinquency* 29 (1992): 178–199.

61. Patrick Jackson, "Theories and Findings about Youth Gangs," *Criminal Justice Abstracts* 6 (1989), 313–327.

62. Marvin Krohn and Terence Thornberry, "Network Theory: A Model for Understanding Drug Abuse among African-American and Hispanic Youth," in *Drug Abuse among Minority Youth: Advances in Research and Methodology*, eds. Mario De La Rosa and Juan-Luis Recio Adrados (Washington, DC: U.S. Department of Health and Human Services, 1993).

63. D. Wayne Osgood, Janet Wilson, Patrick O'Malley, Jerald Bachman, and Lloyd Johnston, "Routine Activities and Individual Deviant Behavior," *American Sociological Review* 61 (1996): 635–655.

64. Mark Warr, "Age, Peers, and Delinquency," *Criminology* 31 (1993): 17–40.

65. Mark Warr, "Organization and Instigation in Delinquent Groups," *Criminology* 34 (1996): 11–35.

66. Lynn McIntyre, Fred Wien, Sharon Rudderham, Loraine Etter, Carla Moore, Nancy MacDonald, Sally Johnson, and Ann Gottschall, *An Exploration of the Stress Experience of Mi'kmaq On-Reserve Female Youth in Nova Scotia*. Dalhousie University, Maritime Centre of Excellence for Women's Health, 2001.

67. Marc Bertucco, "Bad Behaviour: Aggressive Children Are Also Unhappy," *Psychology Today* 34, 3 (2001): 28.

68. Travis Hirschi and Rodney Stark, "Hellfire and Delinquency," *Social Problems* 17 (1969): 202–213.

69. Colin Baier and Bradley Wright, "If You Love Me, Keep My Commandments: A Meta-Analysis of the Effect of Religion on Crime," *Journal of Research in Crime and Delinquency* 38 (2001): 3–21; Byron Johnson, Sung Joon Jang, David Larson, and Spencer De Li, "Does Adolescent Religious Commitment Matter? A Reexamination of the Effects of Religiosity on Delinquency," *Journal of Research in Crime and Delinquency* 38 (2001): 22–44.

70. Sung Joon Jang and Byron Johnson, "Neighborhood Disorder, Individual Religiosity, and Adolescent Use of Illicit Drugs: A Test of a Multilevel Hypothesis," *Criminology* 39 (2001): 109–144.

71. T. David Evans, Francis Cullen, R. Gregory Dunaway, and Velmer Burton, Jr., "Religion and Crime Reexamined: The Impact of Religion, Secular Controls, and Social Ecology on Adult Criminality," *Criminology* 33 (1995): 195–224.

72. Alan J. Richard, David C. Bell, and Jerry W. Carlson, "Individual Religiosity, Moral Community, and Drug User Treatment," *Journal for the Scientific Study of Religion* 39, 2 (2000): 240–246.

73. Lee Ellis and James Patterson, "Crime and Religion: An International Comparison among Thirteen Industrial Nations," *Personal Individual Differences* 20 (1996): 761–768.

74. Walter Miller, *Violence by Youth Gangs and Youth Groups as a Crime Problem in Major American Cities* (Washington, DC: U.S. Government Printing Office, 1975).

75. Edwin Sutherland, *Principles of Criminology* (Philadelphia: Lippincott, 1939).

76. See, for example, Edwin Sutherland, "White-Collar Criminality," *American Sociological Review* 5 (1940): 2–10.

77. This section is adapted from Clarence Schrag, *Crime and Justice: American Style* (Washington, DC: U.S. Government Printing Office, 1971), 46.

78. See Edwin Sutherland and Donald Cressey, *Criminology*, 8th ed. (Philadelphia: Lippincott, 1970), 77–79.

79. For example, see Sandra Brown, Vicki Creamer, and Barbara Stetson, "Adolescent Alcohol Expectancies in Relation to Personal and Parental Drinking Patterns," *Journal of Abnormal Psychology* 96 (1987): 117–121.

80. Ross Matsueda and Karen Heimer, "Race, Family Structure and Delinquency: A Test of Differential Association and Social Control Theories," *American Sociological Review* 52 (1987): 826–840.

81. James Short, "Differential Association as a Hypothesis: Problems of Empirical Testing," *Social Problems* 8 (1960): 14–25.

82. Albert Reiss and A. Lewis Rhodes, "The Distribution of Delinquency in the Social Class Structure," *American Sociological Review* 26 (1961): 732.

83. Douglas Smith, Christy Visher, and G. Roger Jarjoura, "Dimensions of Delinquency: Exploring the Correlates of Participation, Frequency, and Persistence of Delinquent Behavior," *Journal of Research in Crime and Delinquency* 28 (1991): 6–32.

84. Denise Kandel and Mark Davies, "Friendship Networks, Intimacy, and Illicit Drug Use in Young Adulthood: A Comparison of Two Competing Theories," *Criminology* 29 (1991): 441–467.

85. Kenneth Tunnell, "Inside the Drug Trade: Trafficking from the Dealer's Perspective," *Qualitative Sociology* 16 (1993): 361–381.

86. Charles Tittle, *Sanctions and Social Deviance* (New York: Praeger, 1980).

87. Yuet-Wah Cheung and Agnes M.C. Ng, "Social Factors in Adolescent Deviant Behavior in Hong Kong: An Integrated Theoretical Approach," *International Journal of Comparative and Applied Criminal Justice* 12 (1988): 27–44.

88. Robert Burgess and Ronald Akers, "A Differential Association–Reinforcement Theory of Criminal Behavior," *Social Problems* 14 (1966): 128–147.

89. Ross Matsueda, "The Current State of Differential Association Theory," *Crime and Delinquency* 34 (1988): 277–306.

90. Graham Ousey and David Aday, Jr., "The Interaction Hypothesis: A Test Using Social Control Theory and Social Learning Theory," paper presented at the American Society of Criminology meeting, Boston, November 1995.

91. These misconceptions are derived from Donald Cressey, "Epidemiologies and Individual Conduct: A Case from Criminology," *Pacific Sociological Review* 3 (1960): 47–58.

92. Ronald Akers, "Is Differential Association/ Social Learning Cultural Deviance Theory?" *Criminology* 34 (1996): 229–247; for an opposing view, see Travis Hirschi, "Theory Without Ideas: Reply to Akers," *Criminology* 34 (1996): 249–256.

93. Craig Reinerman and Jeffrey Fagan, "Social Organization and Differential Association: A Research Note from a Longitudinal Study of Violent Juvenile Offenders," *Crime and Delinquency* 34 (1988): 307–327.

94. Sue Titus Reed, *Crime and Criminology*, 2nd ed. (New York: Holt, Rinehart and Winston, 1979), 234.

95. See, for example, Albert Bandura, *Social Learning and Personality Development* (New York: Holt, Rinehart and Winston, 1963).

96. Ronald Akers, *Deviant Behavior: A Social Learning Approach*, 2nd ed. (Belmont, CA: Wadsworth, 1977).

97. Michele Peterson-Badali and Christopher J. Koegl, "Juveniles' Experiences of Incarceration: The Role of Correctional Staff in Peer Violence," *Journal of Criminal Justice* 30 (2002): 41–49.

98. Ronald Akers, Marvin Krohn, Lonn Lonza-Kaduce, and Marcia Radosevich, "Social Learning and Deviant Behavior: A Specific Test of a General Theory," *American Sociological Review* 44 (1979): 638.

99. Marvin Krohn, William Skinner, James Massey, and Ronald Akers, "Social Learning Theory and Adolescent Cigarette Smoking: A Longitudinal Study," *Social Problems* 32 (1985): 455–471.

100. Ronald Akers and Gang Lee, "A Longitudinal Test of Social Learning Theory: Adolescent Smoking," *Journal of Drug Issues* 26 (1996): 317–343.

101. Gary Jensen and David Brownfield, "Parents and Drugs," *Criminology* 21 (1983): 543–554.

102. Ronald Akers, "Rational Choice, Deterrence and Social Learning Theory in Criminology: The Path Not Taken," *Journal of Criminal Law and Criminology* 81 (1990): 653–676.

103. Gresham Sykes and David Matza, "Techniques of Neutralization: A Theory of Delinquency," *American Sociological Review* 22 (1957): 664–670; David Matza, *Delinquency and Drift* (New York: Wiley, 1964).

104. Sykes and Matza, "Techniques of Neutralization," 664–670; see also David Matza, "Subterranean Traditions of Youths," *Annals of the American Academy of Political and Social Science* 378 (1961): 116.

105. Stephen L. Eliason, "Illegal Hunting and Angling: The Neutralization of Wildlife Law Violations," *Society & Animals* 11, 3 (2003): 225–243.

106. W.W. Minor, "Techniques of Neutralization: A Reconceptualization and Empirical Examination," *Journal of Research in Crime and Delinquency*, 18, 1981: 295–318; C.B. Klockars, *The Professional Fence* (New York: The Free Press: 1974); J.W. Coleman, *The Criminal Elite: The Sociology of White Collar Crime* (New York: St. Martin's Press, 1994).

107. Michael Hindelang, "The Commitment of Delinquents to Their Misdeeds: Do Delinquents Drift?" *Social Problems* 17 (1970): 509.

108. Robert Regoli and Eric Poole, "The Commitment of Delinquents to Their Misdeeds: A Reexamination," *Journal of Criminal Justice* 6 (1978): 261–269.

109. Robert Agnew, "The Techniques of Neutralization and Violence," *Criminology* 32 (1994): 555–579.

110. Robert Ball, "An Empirical Exploration of Neutralization Theory," *Criminologica* 4 (1966): 22–32. For a similar view, see M. William Minor, "The Neutralization of Criminal Offense," *Criminology* 18 (1980): 103–120.

111. Mark Pogrebin, Eric Poole, and Amos Martinez, "Accounts of Professional Misdeeds: The Sexual Exploitation of Clients by Psychotherapists," *Deviant Behavior* 13 (1992): 229–252.

112. David Simon, "Corporate Environmental Crimes and Social Inequality: New Directions for Environmental Justice Research," *American Behavioral Scientist* 43, 4 (2000): 633–645.

113. Scott Briar and Irvin Piliavin, "Delinquency: Situational Inducements and Commitment to Conformity," *Social Problems* 13 (1965–1966): 35–45.

114. Lawrence Sherman and Douglas Smith, with Janell Schmidt and Dennis Rogan, "Crime, Punishment, and Stake in Conformity: Legal and Informal Control of Domestic Violence," *American Sociological Review* 57 (1992): 680–690.

115. Albert Reiss, "Delinquency as the Failure of Personal and Social Controls," *American Sociological Review* 16 (1951): 196–207.

116. John McCarthy and Dean Hoge, "The Dynamics of Self-Esteem and Delinquency," *American Journal of Sociology* 90 (1984): 396–410; Edward Wells and Joseph Rankin, "Self-Concept as a Mediating Concept in Delinquency," *Social Psychology Quarterly* 46 (1983): 11–22.

117. Howard Kaplan, *Deviant Behavior in Defense of Self* (New York: Academic Press, 1980); Howard Kaplan, "Self-Attitudes and Deviant Response," *Social Forces* 54 (1978): 788–801.

118. Howard Kaplan, Robert Johnson, and Carol Bailey, "Self-Rejection and the Explanation of Deviance: Refinement and Elaboration of a Latent Structure," *Social Psychology Quarterly* 49 (1986): 110–128.

119. L. Edward Wells, "Self-Enhancement through Delinquency: A Conditional Test of Self-Derogation Theory," *Journal of Research in Crime and Delinquency* 26 (1989): 226–252.

120. See, generally, Walter Reckless, *The Crime Problem* (New York: Appleton-Century-Crofts, 1967). Among the many research reports are Walter Reckless, Simon Dinitz, and Ellen Murray, "Self-Concept as an Insulator Against Delinquency," *American Sociological Review* 21 (1956): 744–746; Walter Reckless, Simon Dinitz, and Ellen Murray, "The Good Boy in a High Delinquency Area," *Journal of Criminal Law, Criminology, and Police Science* 48 (1957): 18–25; Walter Reckless, Simon Dinitz, and Barbara Kay, "The Self-Component in Potential Delinquency and Potential Nondelinquency," *American Sociological Review* 22 (1957): 566–570; Walter Reckless and Simon Dinitz, "Pioneering with Self-Concept as a Vulnerability Factor in Delinquency," *Journal of Criminal Law, Criminology, and Police Science* 58 (1967): 515–523.

121. Rebecca Raby and Julie Domitrek, "Slippery as Fish…But Already Caught? Secondary Students' Engagement with School Rules," *Canadian Journal of Education* 30, 3 (2007): 931–958.

122. Travis Hirschi, *Causes of Delinquency* (Berkeley, CA: University of California Press, 1969).

123. Marc LeBlanc, "Family dynamics, adolescent delinquency, and adult criminality," *Psychiatry: Interpersonal and Biological Processes*, 55, 4, 1992, 336–353.

124. Patricia Van Voorhis, Francis Cullen, Richard Mathers, and Connie Chenoweth Garner, "The Impact of Family Structure and Quality on Delinquency: A Comparative Assessment of Structural and Functional Factors," *Criminology* 26 (1988): 235–261.

125. M. LeBlanc, E. Vallières, and P. McDuff, "Adolescents' School Experience and Self-Reported Offending: A Longitudinal Test of a Social Control Theory," *International Journal of Adolescence and Youth* 3, 3–4 (1992): 197–247.

126. Marianne Junger and Wim Polder, "Some Explanations of Crime among Four Ethnic Groups in the Netherlands," *Journal of Quantitative Criminology* 8 (1992): 51–78.

127. Margit Wiesner and Rainer K. Silbereisen, "Trajectories of Delinquent Behaviour in Adolescence and Their Covariates: Relations with Initial and Time-Averaged Factors," *Journal of Adolescence* 26 (2003): 753–771.

128. Ji-Min Lee, and Nancy J. Bell, "Individual Differences in Attachment-Autonomy Configurations: Linkages with Substance Use and Youth Competencies" *Journal of Adolescence* 26 (2003): 347–361.

129. Christopher A. Kierkus, and Douglas Baer, "A Social Control Explanation of the Relationship between Family Structure and Delinquent Behaviour," *Canadian Journal of Criminology* 44, 4 (2002): 425–459.

130. John Cochran and Ronald Akers, "An Exploration of the Variable Effects of Religiosity on Adolescent Marijuana and Alcohol Use," *Journal of Research in Crime and Delinquency* 26 (1989): 198–225.

131. Robert Agnew and David Peterson, "Leisure and Delinquency," *Social Problems* 36 (1989): 332–348.

132. Jane B. Sprott, Jennifer M. Jenkins, and Anthony N. Doob, "The Importance of School. Protecting At-Risk Youth From Early Offending," *Youth Violence and Juvenile Justice* 3, 1 (2005): 59–77.

133. Josine Junger-Tas, "An Empirical Test of Social Control Theory," *Journal of Quantitative Criminology* 8 (1992): 18–29.

134. Teresa Lagrange and Robert Silverman, "Perceived Strain and Delinquency Motivation: An Empirical Evaluation of General Strain Theory," paper presented at the American Society of Criminology meeting, Boston, November 1995.

135. Vincent F. Sacco and M. Reza Nakhaie, "Fear of School Violence and the Ameliorative Effects of Student Social Capital," *Journal of School Violence* 6, 1 (2006).

136. Kimberly Kempf, "The Empirical Status of Hirschi's Control Theory," in *Advances in Criminological Theory*, eds. Bill Laufer and Freda Adler (Piscataway, NJ: Transaction Publishers, 1992).

137. Richard Lawrence, "Parents, Peers, School—and Delinquency," paper presented at the American Society of Criminology meeting, Boston, November 1995; see also Richard Lawrence, *School, Crime and Juvenile Justice*, Oxford, 1998.

138. Peggy Giordano, Stephen Cernkovich, and M.D. Pugh, "Friendships and Delinquency," *American Journal of Sociology* 91 (1986): 1170–1202.

139. Denise Kandel and Mark Davies, "Friendship Networks, Intimacy, and Illicit Drug Use in Young Adulthood: A Comparison of Two Competing Theories," *Criminology* 29 (1991): 441–467.

140. Velmer Burton, Francis Cullen, T. David Evans, R. Gregory Dunaway, Sesha Kethineni, and Gary Payne, "The Impact of Parental Controls on Delinquency," *Journal of Criminal Justice* 23 (1995): 111–126.

141. Kimberly Kempf Leonard and Scott Decker, "The Theory of Social Control: Does It Apply to the Very Young?" *Journal of Criminal Justice* 22 (1994): 89–105.

142. Michael Hindelang, "Causes of Delinquency: A Partial Replication and Extension," *Social Problems* 21 (1973): 471–487.

143. Gary Jensen and David Brownfield, "Parents and Drugs," *Criminology* 21 (1983): 543–554. See also M. Wiatrowski, D. Griswold, and M. Roberts, "Social Control Theory and Delinquency," *American Sociological Review* 46 (1981): 525–541.

144. Leslie Samuelson, Timothy Hartnagel, and Harvey Krahn, "Crime and Social Control among High School Dropouts," *Journal of Crime and Justice* 18 (1990): 129–161.

145. Mark Warr, "Parents, Peers, and Delinquency," *Social Forces* 72 (1993): 247–264.

146. Marvin Krohn and James Massey, "Social Control and Delinquent Behavior: An Examination of the Elements of the Social Bond," *Sociological Quarterly* 21 (1980): 529–543.

147. Jill Leslie Rosenbaum and James Lasley, "School, Community Context, and Delinquency: Rethinking the Gender Gap," *Justice Quarterly* 7 (1990): 493–513.

148. Randy LaGrange and Helene Raskin White, "Age Differences in Delinquency: A Test of Theory," *Criminology* 23 (1985): 19–45.

149. Robert Agnew, "Social Control Theory and Delinquency: A Longitudinal Test," *Criminology* 23 (1985): 47–61.

150. Alan E. Liska and M.D. Reed, "Ties to Conventional Institutions and Delinquency: Estimating Reciprocal Effects," *American Sociological Review* 50 (1985): 547–560.

151. Tracey Peter, Teresa C. LaGrange, and Robert A. Silverman, "Investigating the Interdependence of Strain and Self-Control," *Canadian Journal of Criminology and Criminal Justice,* 45, 4 (2003): 431–464.

152. Michael Wiatrowski, David Griswold, and Mary K. Roberts, "Social Control Theory and Delinquency," *American Sociological Review* 46 (1981): 525–541.

153. George Herbert Mead, *Mind, Self and Society* (Chicago: University of Chicago Press, 1934); George Herbert Mead, *The Philosophy of the Act* (Chicago: University of Chicago Press, 1938); Charles Horton Cooley, *Human Nature and the Social Order* (New York: Schocken, 1964, originally published 1902); Herbert Blumer, *Symbolic Interactionism: Perspective and Method* (Englewood Cliffs, NJ: Prentice Hall, 1969).

154. Bruce Link, Elmer Streuning, Francis Cullen, Patrick Shrout, and Bruce Dohrenwend, "A Modified Labeling Theory Approach to Mental Disorders: An Empirical Assessment," *American Sociological Review* 54 (1989): 400–423.

155. Marilyn MacDonald, "Seeing the Cage: Stigma and Its Potential to Inform the Concept of the Difficult Patient," *Clinical Nurse Specialist,* 17, 6 (November 2003): 305–310.

156. J. Scott Kenney, "Victims of Crime and Labeling Theory: A Parallel Process?" *Deviant Behavior* 23, 3 (2002): 235–265.

157. Linda Jackson, John Hunter, and Carole Hodge, "Physical Attractiveness and Intellectual Competence: A Meta-Analytic Review," *Social Psychology Quarterly* 58 (1995): 108–122.

158. Keith Macmaster, Leslie A. Donovan, and Peter D. Macintyre, "The Effects of Being Diagnosed with a Learning Disability on Children's Self-Esteem," *Child Study Journal* 32 (2002): 101–108.

159. Anthony Matarazzo, Peter J. Carrington, and Robert D. Hiscott, "The Effect of Prior Youth Court Dispositions on Current Disposition: An Application of Societal-Reaction Theory," *Journal of Quantitative Criminology* 17, 2 (2001): 169–200.

160. Kai Erikson, "Notes on the Sociology of Deviance," *Social Problems* 9 (1962): 397–414.

161. Edwin Schur, *Labeling Deviant Behavior* (New York: Harper & Row, 1972), 21.

162. Howard Becker, *Outsiders: Studies in the Sociology of Deviance* (New York: Macmillan, 1963), 9.

163. Christy Visher, "Gender, Police Arrest Decision, and Notions of Chivalry," *Criminology* 21 (1983): 5–28.

164. Marjorie Zatz, "Race, Ethnicity and Determinate Sentencing," *Criminology* 22 (1984): 147–171.

165. Roland Chilton and Jim Galvin, "Race, Crime and Criminal Justice," *Crime and Delinquency* 31 (1985): 3–14.

166. Joan Petersilia, "Racial Disparities in the Criminal Justice System: A Summary," *Crime and Delinquency* 31 (1985): 15–34.

167. Walter Gove, *The Labeling of Deviance: Evaluating a Perspective* (New York: Wiley, 1975), 5.

168. Harold Garfinkle, "Conditions of Successful Degradation Ceremonies," *American Journal of Sociology* 61 (1956): 420–424.

169. John Lofland, *Deviance and Identity* (Englewood Cliffs, NJ: Prentice-Hall, 1969).

170. Frank Tannenbaum, *Crime and the Community* (New York: Columbia University Press, 1938), 19–20.

171. Edwin Lemert, *Social Pathology* (New York: McGraw-Hill, 1951).

172. See, for example, Howard Kaplan and Hiroshi Fukurai, "Negative Social Sanctions, Self-Rejection, and Drug Use," *Youth and Society* 23 (1992): 275–298.

173. Howard Kaplan, *Toward a General Theory of Deviance: Contributions from Perspectives on Deviance and Criminality* (College Station: Texas A&M University, n.d.).

174. Howard Kaplan and Robert Johnson, "Negative Social Sanctions and Juvenile Delinquency: Effects of Labeling in a Model of Deviant Behavior," *Social Science Quarterly* 72 (1991): 98–122; Howard Kaplan, Robert Johnson, and Carol Bailey, "Deviant Peers and Deviant Behavior: Further Elaboration of a Model," *Social Psychology Quarterly* 30 (1987): 277–284.

175. Karen Heimer and Ross Matsueda, "Role-Taking, Role-Commitment and Delinquency: A Theory of Differential Social Control," *American Sociological Review* 59 (1994): 400–437.

176. Stacy DeCoster and Karen Heimer, "The Relationship between Law Violation and Depression: An Interactionist Analysis," *Criminology* 39 (2001): 799–837.

177. Karen Heimer, "Gender, Race, and the Pathways to Delinquency: An Interactionist Explanation," in *Crime and Inequality*, ed. John Hagan and Ruth Peterson (Stanford, CA: Stanford University Press, 1995).

178. Carl Pope and William Feyerherm, "Minority Status and Juvenile Justice Processing," *Criminal Justice Abstracts* 22 (1990): 327–336; see also Carl Pope, "Race and Crime Revisited," *Crime and Delinquency* 25 (1979): 347–357.

179. Michael J. Leiber, and Kristin Y. Mack, "The Individual and Joint Effects of Race, Gender, and Family Status on Juvenile Justice Decision-Making," *Journal of Research in Crime and Delinquency*, 40, 1 (2003): 34–70; Carl E. Pope, Rick Lovell, and Heidi M. Hsia, "Disproportionate Minority Confinement: A Review of the Research Literature From 1989 Through 2001," www.ojjdp.ncjrs.gov/dmc/pdf/dmc89_01.pdf; John M. MacDonald, and Meda Chesney-Lind, "Gender Bias and Juvenile Justice Revisited: A Multiyear Analysis," *Crime & Delinquency* 47, 2 (2001): 173–195.

180. Leslie Margolin, "Deviance on Record: Techniques for Labeling Child Abusers in Official Documents," *Social Problems* 39 (1992): 58–68.

181. Charles Corley, Stephen Cernkovich, and Peggy Giordano, "Sex and the Likelihood of Sanction," *Journal of Criminal Law and Criminology* 80 (1989): 540–553.

182. Ruth Triplett, "The Conflict Perspective, Symbolic Interactionism, and the Status Characteristics Hypothesis," *Justice Quarterly* 10 (1993): 540–558.

183. Ross Matsueda, "Reflected Appraisals, Parental Labeling, and Delinquency: Specifying a Symbolic Interactionist Theory," *American Journal of Sociology* 97 (1992): 1577–1611.

184. Suzanne Ageton and Delbert Elliott, *The Effect of Legal Processing on Self-Concept* (Boulder, CO: Institute of Behavioral Science, 1973).

185. Christine Bowditch, "Getting Rid of Troublemakers: High School Disciplinary Procedures and the Production of Dropouts," *Social Problems* 40 (1993): 493–507.

186. Melvin Ray and William Downs, "An Empirical Test of Labeling Theory Using Longitudinal Data," *Journal of Research in Crime and Delinquency* 23 (1986): 169–194.

187. Charles Tittle, "Two Empirical Regularities (Maybe) in Search of an Explanation: Commentary on the Age/Crime Debate," *Criminology* 26 (1988): 75–85.

188. Douglas Smith and Robert Brame, "On the Initiation and Continuation of Delinquency," *Criminology* 4 (1994): 607–630.

189. Jack Gibbs, "Conceptions of Deviant Behavior: The Old and the New," *Pacific Sociological Review* 9 (1966): 11–13.

190. Ronald Akers, "Problems in the Sociology of Deviance," *Social Problems* 46 (1968): 463.

191. Charles Wellford, "Labeling Theory and Criminology: An Assessment," *Social Problems* 22 (1975): 335–347.

192. Alexander Liazos, "The Poverty of the Sociology of Deviance: Nuts, Sluts, and Perverts," *Social Problems* 20 (1971): 103–120.

193. Paul Lipsett, "The Juvenile Offender's Perception," *Crime and Delinquency* 14 (1968): 49; Jack Foster, Simon Dinitz, and Walter Reckless, "Perception of Stigma Following Public Intervention for Delinquent Behavior," *Social Problems* 20 (1972): 202.

194. Charles Tittle, "Labeling and Crime: An Empirical Evaluation," in *The Labeling of Deviance: Evaluating a Perspective*, ed. Walter Gove, 157–179 (New York: Wiley, 1975).

195. David Farrington, "Early Predictors of Adolescent Aggression and Adult Violence," *Violence and Victims* 4 (1989): 79–100.

196. Raymond Paternoster and Leeann Iovanni, "The Labeling Perspective and Delinquency: An Elaboration of the Theory and an Assessment of the Evidence," *Justice Quarterly* 6 (1989): 358–394.

197. Gerald Patterson and Karen Yoerger, "Developmental Models for Delinquent Behavior," in *Mental Disorder and Crime*, ed. Sheilagh Higdins, 150–159 (Newbury Park, CA: Sage, 1993).

198. David Rowe, D. Wayne Osgood, and W. Alan Nicewander, "A Latent Trait Approach to Unifying Criminal Careers," *Criminology* 28 (1990): 237–270.

199. David Rowe, Alexander Vazsonyi, and Daniel Flannery, "Sex Differences in Crime: Do Means and Within-Sex Variation Have Similar Causes?" *Journal of Research in Crime and Delinquency* 32 (1995): 84–100.

200. G. R. Patterson, Barbara DeBaryshe, and Elizabeth Ramsey, "A Developmental Perspective on Antisocial Behavior," *American Psychologist* 44 (1989): 329–335.

201. Kenneth Land and Daniel Nagin, "Micro-Models of Criminal Careers: A Synthesis of the Criminal Careers and Life-Course Approaches via Semiparametric Mixed Poisson Regression Models with Empirical Applications," *Journal of Quantitative Criminology* 12 (1996): 163–190.

202. Daniel Glazer, *Crime in Our Changing Society* (New York: Holt, Rinehart and Winston, 1978).

203. Julie O'Donnell, J. David Hawkins, and Robert Abbott, "Predicting Serious Delinquency and Substance Use among Aggressive Boys," *Journal of Consulting and Clinical Psychology* 63 (1995): 529–537.

204. Julie O'Donnell, J. David Hawkins, and Robert Abbott, "Predicting Serious Delinquency and Substance Use among Aggressive Boys," *Journal of Consulting and Clinical Psychology* 63 (1995): 534–536; Richard Catalano, Rick Kosterman, J. David Hawkins, Michael Newcomb, and Robert Abbott, "Modeling the Etiology of Adolescent Substance Use: A Test of the Social Development Model," *Journal of Drug Issues* 26 (1996): 429–455.

205. Todd Herrenkohl, Bu Huang, Rick Kosterman, J. David Hawkins, Richard Catalano, and Brian Smith, "A Comparison of Social Development Processes Leading to Violent Behavior in Late Adolescence for Childhood Initiators and Adolescent Initiators of Violence," *Journal of Research in Crime and Delinquency* 38 (2001): 45–63.

206. D. Brownfield; K.M. Thompson; A.M. Sorenson, "Correlates of Gang Membership: A Test of Strain, Social Learning, and Social Control Theories," *Journal of Gang Research*, 4, 4, 1997: 11–22; see also David Eitle, Steven Gunkel, and Karen Van Gundy, "Cumulative Exposure to Stressful Life Events and Male Gang Membership," *Journal of Criminal Justice*, 32, 2 (2004): 95–111.

207. Bu Huang, Rick Kosterman, Richard Catalano, J. David Hawkins, and Robert Abbott, "Modeling Mediation in the Etiology of Violent Behavior in Adolescence: A Test of the Social Development Model," *Criminology* 39 (2001): 75–107.

208. J. David Hawkins, Richard Catalano, Diane Morrison, Julie O'Donnell, Robert Abbott, and L. Edward Day, "The Seattle Social Development Project," in *The Prevention of Antisocial Behavior in Children*, ed. Joan McCord and Richard Tremblay, 139–160 (New York: Guilford, 1992).

209. Delbert Elliott, David Huizinga, and Suzanne Ageton, *Explaining Delinquency and Drug Use* (Beverly Hills, CA: Sage, 1985).

210. Scott Menard and Delbert Elliott, "Delinquent Bonding, Moral Beliefs, and Illegal Behavior: A Three Wave–Panel Model," *Justice Quarterly* 11 (1994): 173–188.

211. Mark Colvin and John Pauly, "A Critique of Criminology: Toward an Integrated Structural-Marxist Theory of Delinquency Production," *American Journal of Sociology* 89 (1983): 513–551.

212. Steven Messner and Marvin Krohn, "Class, Compliance Structures, and Delinquency: Assessing Integrated Structural-Marxist Theory," *American Journal of Sociology* 96 (1990): 300–328.

213. See, generally, Sheldon Glueck and Eleanor Glueck, *500 Criminal Careers* (New York: Knopf, 1930); Sheldon Glueck and Eleanor Glueck, *One Thousand Juvenile Delinquents* (Cambridge, MA: Harvard University Press, 1934); Sheldon Glueck and Eleanor Glueck, *Predicting Delinquency*

and *Crime* (Cambridge, MA: Harvard University Press, 1967), 82–83.

214. Sheldon Glueck and Eleanor Glueck, *Unraveling Juvenile Delinquency* (Cambridge, MA: Harvard University Press, 1950).

215. See, generally, John Laub and Robert Sampson, "The Sutherland-Glueck Debate: On the Sociology of Criminological Knowledge," *American Journal of Sociology* 96 (1991): 1402–1440; John Laub and Robert Sampson, "Unraveling Families and Delinquency: A Reanalysis of the Gluecks' Data," *Criminology* 26 (1988): 355–380.

216. Rolf Loeber and Marc LeBlanc, "Toward a Developmental Criminology," in *Crime and Justice*, vol. 12, ed. Norval Morris and Michael Tonry, 375–473 (Chicago: University of Chicago Press, 1990).

217. G.R. Patterson, L. Crosby, and S. Vuchinich, "Predicting Risk for Early Police Arrest," *Journal of Quantitative Criminology* 8 (1992): 335–355.

218. Rolf Loeber, Magda Southamer-Loeber, Welmoet Van Kammen, and David Farrington, "Initiation, Escalation and Desistance in Juvenile Offending and Their Correlates," *Journal of Criminal Law and Criminology* 82 (1991): 36–82.

219. Gillian Livingston, "Justice Program for Youths to Expand," Canadian Press, June 14, 2004; Neena Chowdhury, "Youth Justice Program Moves to Malvern," Canadian Press, June 15, 2004; James McCarten, "Ontario Spends $39M to Lower Dropout Rate," Canadian Press, June 8, 2004; Sarah Schmidt, "Campus Camps Reach out to Native Students," CanWest, August 3, 2004; Craig Dowden and D.A. Andrews, "Does Family Intervention Work for Delinquents? Results of a Meta-Analysis," *Canadian Journal of Criminology and Criminal Justice*, July 2003, 327–342.

220. Doug Hillian and Marge Reitsma-Street, "Parents and Youth Justice," *Canadian Journal of Criminology* 45, 1 (2003): 19–42.

221. *Multisystemic Therapy: Treating Violent and Chronic Juvenile Offenders* (Canberra: Australian Institute of Criminology, 2000); "Multisystemic Therapy," American Youth Policy Forum, n.d.; *Effective Interventions for Young Offenders: Interim Results of a Four-Year Randomized Study of Multisystemic Therapy in Ontario, Canada* (London, ON: London Family Court Clinic, 2002); Allan Cunningham, *Lessons Learned from a Randomized Study of Multisystemic Therapy in Canada* (London, ON: Centre for Children and Families in the Justice System, London Family Court Clinic, 2002).

Social Conflict Theory

Chapter Outline

Learning Objectives

After reading this chapter, you will be able to:

1. Understand the background of social conflict theory.
2. Be familiar with different theorists who use this approach.
3. Know the various types of Marxist criminology.
4. Discuss the difference between this and other approaches.
5. Explain new directions in critical criminology.

Dozens of peaceful protestors in Rexton, New Brunswick, were arrested in a confrontation with police over the development of shale gas.

© THE CANADIAN PRESS/Andrew Vaughan

It would be unusual to pick up the morning paper and not see headlines loudly proclaiming renewed strife between countries, between union negotiators and company attorneys, or between citizens and police authorities. The world is filled with conflict. Conflict is destructive when it leads to war, violence, and death, but conflict can also result in positive social change. Those who view crime as a function of social and economic conflict are referred to as the conflict, critical, Marxist, or radical criminologists (see Figure 9.1 on the branches of social conflict theory).

The goal of social conflict theorists is to explain crime within economic and social contexts, and to express the connections among social class, crime, and social control.[1] Social conflict theorists are concerned with such issues as the role government plays in creating a criminogenic environment, the relationship of personal or group power in controlling and shaping the criminal law, the role of bias in the operations of the justice system, and the relationship between a capitalist economy and crime rates.

Conflict theorists view crime as the outcome of class struggle. Conflict promotes crime by creating a social atmosphere in which the law is a mechanism for controlling dissatisfied members of society while maintaining the position of the powerful. The conflict view of crime explains why crimes of the wealthy, such as illegal corporate activities, are sanctioned much more leniently than are

FIGURE 9.1

The Branches of Social Conflict Theory

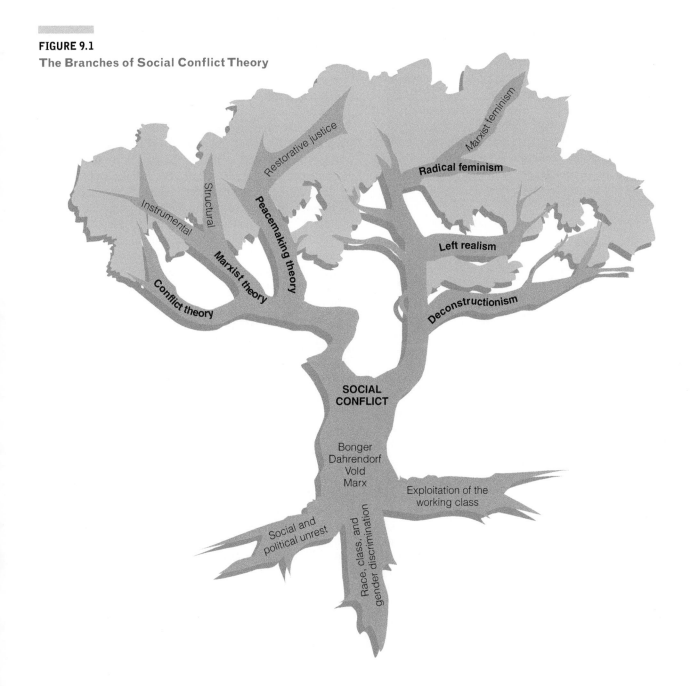

such crimes as burglary, which are considered lower-class activities.

Conflict theorists reject the notion that law is designed to maintain a tranquil and fair society, and that criminals are simply violent and predatory people. Rather, the "true crimes" are considered to be racism, sexism, imperialism, unsafe working conditions, inadequate childcare, substandard housing, pollution of the environment, and war. However, the crimes of the powerless, such as burglary, robbery, and assault, are more likely to be prosecuted.[2]

This chapter reviews criminological theories that analyze criminal behaviour as a function of conflict in the unfair distribution of wealth and power in society. The social conflict perspective has several independent branches. One branch, simply called **conflict theory**, assumes that crime is caused by the intergroup rivalry that exists in every society. A second branch focuses more directly on the crime-producing traits of capitalist society; the various schools of thought in this area of scholarship include critical, radical, and Marxist criminology. Other sections are devoted to feminist, new realist, and peacemaking criminology.

This chapter covers issues usually not discussed very well in introductory criminology textbooks relating to critical/radical perspectives. Recent developments in critical criminology such as critical feminism, left realism, peacemaking criminology, and postmodern criminology, in particular, are often omitted from contemporary criminology textbooks.[3]

CONNECTIONS

As discussed in Chapter 1, the philosophical and economic analysis of Karl Marx forms the historical roots of the conflict perspective of criminology.

MARXIST THOUGHT

Karl Marx lived in an era of unrestrained capitalist expansion.[4] By 1850, the tools of the Industrial Revolution, mechanized factories, the use of coal to drive steam engines, and modern transportation had become regular features of society. Production had shifted from cottage industries to large factories. Conditions in industrial factories were atrocious, and trade unions were ruthlessly suppressed by owners and government agents.

Marx had found his early career as a journalist interrupted by government suppression of the newspaper where he worked because of its liberal editorial policy. He then moved to Paris, where he met Friedrich Engels (1820–95), who became his friend and economic patron. By 1847, Marx and Engels had joined with a group of primarily German socialist revolutionaries known as the Communist League.

Productive Forces and Productive Relations

Marx believed the economic conditions of capitalism had put workers at the mercy of their capitalist employers. For example, young children worked in mines and factories from dawn to dusk with no protection under the labour law. Analysis of these and other such conditions led Marx to conclude that this method of developing and producing material goods was oppressive.

Production has two components: (1) productive forces, which include technology, energy sources, and material resources, and (2) relations of production, which exist among the people producing goods and services. The most important relationship in industrial culture is between the owners of the means of production and the people who do the actual labour. Throughout history, society has been organized this way: first, master–slave, then lord–serf, and now capitalist–proletarian. Capitalism is subject to the development of a rigid class structure: the capitalist bourgeoisie at the top and the working proletariat, who actually produce goods and services, at the bottom (see Figure 9.2).

The term *class* denotes position in relation to others. Thus, having a particular amount of wealth or prestige is not necessary; more important is having the power to exploit others economically, legally, and socially. The political and economic philosophy of the dominant class influences all aspects of life, as people's lives revolve around the means of production.[5]

Marx believed that societies change through slow evolution or sudden violence because of contradictions or conflicts present in a society. If these social conflicts are not resolved, they tend to destabilize society, leading to social change.

Marx on Crime

Marx viewed crime as the product of law enforcement policies akin to a labelling process theory. He also saw a connection between criminality and inequality, stating:

> There must be something rotten in the very core of a social system which increases in wealth without diminishing its misery, and increases in crime even more rapidly than in numbers.[6]

In *The Condition of the Working Class in England in 1844*, Engels portrayed crime as a function of social demoralization: workers, demoralized by capitalist society, are caught up in a process that leads to crime and violence.[7] Working people commit crime because their choice is a slow death of starvation or a speedy one at the hands of the law.

---

conflict theory   A general approach that sees criminal behaviour as caused by economic inequality, and criminal law defined by those in power.

The owners of production
Capitalist bourgeoisie

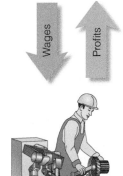

Wages

Profits

The worker
Proletariat

The nonproductive
Lumpen proletariat

FIGURE 9.2
The Marxist View of Class

DEVELOPING A SOCIAL CONFLICT THEORY OF CRIME

Conflict theory was first applied to criminology by Willem Bonger, Ralf Dahrendorf, and George Vold.

Willem Bonger

Bonger believed that society is divided into have and have-not groups, not on the basis of people's innate ability, but because of the system of production that is in force. In every society that is divided into a ruling class and an inferior class, penal law serves the will of the ruling class. Even though criminal laws may appear to protect members of both classes, hardly any act is punished that does not injure the interests of the dominant ruling class. Crimes, then, are considered to be antisocial acts because they are harmful to those who have the power at their command to control society. Under capitalism, the legal system discriminates against people who are poor by defending the actions of people who are wealthy. Because the proletariat are deprived of the materials that are monopolized by the bourgeoisie, they are more likely to violate the law.

Ralf Dahrendorf

Dahrendorf argued that modern society is organized into what he called *imperatively coordinated associations*. These associations comprise two groups: those who possess authority and use it for social domination, and those who lack authority and are dominated. Society is a plurality of competing interest groups. Dahrendorf proposed a unified conflict theory of human behaviour, which can be summarized as follows:

- Every society is at every point subject to processes of change; social change is everywhere.
- Every society displays at every point dissent and conflict; social conflict is everywhere.
- Every element in a society renders a contribution to its disintegration and change.
- Every society is based on the coercion of some of its members by others.

George Vold

Vold argued that laws are created by politically oriented groups, who seek the government's assistance to help them defend their rights and protect their interests. If a group can marshal enough support, a law will be created to hamper and curb the interests of some opposition group. For example, a capitalist might ask the government for help in breaking a strike because it hampers production. This creates conflict, and perpetuates the very inequality the union was seeking to mitigate in the first place. Every stage of the process—from passing the law to prosecuting the case to developing relationships between inmate and guard, parole agent and parolee—is marked by conflict. Criminal acts are a consequence of direct contact between forces struggling to control society.

MODERN CONFLICT THEORY

Criminologists did not adopt a Marxist perspective right away. However, in the late 1950s, self-report studies suggested that crime and delinquency were much more evenly distributed through the social structure than shown by the official statistics.[8] If this were true, then middle-class participation in crime was going unrecorded, while the lower class was the subject of discriminatory law enforcement practices.

Criminologists began to view the justice system as a mechanism to control the lower class and maintain the status quo, rather than as the means of dispensing fair and even-handed justice.[9] The publication of important labelling perspective works, such as Lemert's *Social Pathology* and Becker's *Outsiders,* also contributed to the development of the conflict model.[10] Labelling theorists rejected the notion that crime is morally wrong and studied the interaction among crime, criminal, victim, and social control agencies.[11]

A group of criminologists began to produce scholarship and research directed at (1) identifying "real" crimes in society, such as profiteering, sexism, and racism; (2) evaluating how the criminal law is used as a mechanism of social control; and (3) turning the attention of citizens to the inequities in society.[12] David Greenberg comments on the scholarship that was produced:

> The theme that dominated much of the work in this area was the contention that criminal legislation was determined not by moral consensus or the common interests of the entire society, but by relative power of groups determined to use the criminal law to advance their own special interests or to impose their moral preferences on others.[13]

This movement was aided by the general and widespread social and political upheaval of the late 1960s and early 1970s: political demonstrations against the Vietnam War, counterculture movements advocating changes in consumer society, and lobby groups based around environmentalism, women's rights, and liberation movements (for gay people, Aboriginal people, and members of minority groups). Conflict theory flourished within this framework because it provided a systematic basis for challenging the legitimacy of the government and for questioning the imbalance of power in society. However, the crackdown on political dissidents by agents of the federal government, the prosecution of draft resisters, and the infiltration of rights movements by the RCMP all seemed designed to maintain control in the hands of political power brokers.[14]

Conflict Criminology

In the early 1970s, conflict theory began to have a significant influence on criminology. Chambliss and Seidman wrote *Law, Order and Power,* which documented how the justice system operates to protect the rich and powerful:

> To maintain the existing legal system requires a choice ... between maintaining a legal system that ... supports the existing economic system with its power structure and developing an equitable legal system

accompanied by the loss of "personal freedom." But the old question comes back to plague us: Freedom for whom? Is the black man who provides such a ready source of cases for the welfare workers, the mental hospitals, and the prisons "free"? Are the slum dwellers who are arrested night after night for "loitering," "drunkenness," or being "suspicious" free?[15]

The objectives of conflict criminology are to describe how the control of the political and economic system affects the administration of criminal justice, to show how the definitions of crime favour those who control the justice system, and to show how justice in society is skewed so that those who deserve to be punished the most (wealthy white-collar criminals whose crimes cost society millions of dollars) are actually punished the least, while those whose crimes are relatively minor and committed out of economic necessity (petty, lower-class thieves) receive the stricter sanctions.[16]

Power Relations.   The unequal distribution of power and wealth produces conflict. People use power to shape public opinion to meet their personal interests, and crime is defined by those in power. This power differential can create criminogenic situations where no absolute standard of right and wrong exists, even though the law appears to reflect universal interests.[17]

The power to control people is exemplified by the relationship between the justice system and members of minority groups. For example, in policing, women represent only 13 percent of public police officers and 20 percent of security guards. Visible minorities constitute 10 percent of the paid labour force but only 3 percent of the public police force in Canada. Only in Aboriginal policing has Native representation exceeded the national average because of self-administered police services in Aboriginal communities. These types of under-representation affect the ability of the police to address the needs of these groups.[18]

The subtle ways that the justice system victimizes members of ethnic minorities have been well documented.[19] Socio-economic conditions that favour Caucasians create an environment in which members of minority groups commit crimes that get them processed by the system. Discretionary decisions by law enforcement officers have them charged with more serious offences; they are less likely to be advised to speak to a lawyer; they are shunted into the criminal courts and not diversion programs. Busy public defenders too often give their clients short shrift and force them into plea bargains that ensure early criminal records; and members of ethnic minorities are more likely to be encouraged to plead guilty.

Healthcare workers and teachers report suspected violent acts to the police, resulting in frequent and early arrests of minority-group adults and youths. Police departments routinely use policies of searching, questioning, and detaining males who are members of minority groups if a violent criminal has been described as non-Caucasian. And media accounts create the image of pervasive minority-group criminality by

Protestors demonstrate over the death of Dudley George, who was killed in 1995 by police at an occupation of the Stony Point Reserve in Ontario.

TABLE 9.1 Propositions of the Social Reality of Crime

1. Crime is a definition of human conduct created by politically authorized agents.
2. Criminal definitions describe behaviours that conflict with the interests of those that have the power to shape public policy.
3. Criminal definitions are applied by those that have the power to shape the enforcement and administration of the criminal law.
4. Behaviour is structured in segmentally organized society in relation to criminal definitions, and persons engage in actions that have relative probabilities of being defined as criminal.
5. Conceptions of crime are constructed and diffused in society by various means of communication.
6. The social reality of crime is constructed by the construction of criminal conceptions, the application of criminal definitions, and the development of behaviour to criminal definitions.

SOURCE: Adapted from Richard Quinney, *The Social Reality of Crime* (Boston: Little, Brown, 1970), pp. 15–23.

mentioning race when it concerns a Black or Aboriginal suspect, but not when it concerns a Caucasian suspect. When this stereotyping is coupled with unfair treatment, those in power further alienate members of minority groups from the mainstream, perpetuating a class- and race-divided society in which minority-group members are more likely to perceive "criminal injustice."[20] (See the nearby Criminology Research box for a discussion of the relations between Aboriginal people and the Canadian criminal justice system.)

The Social Reality of Crime. Richard Quinney integrated his beliefs about power, society, and criminality into a theory called the **social reality of crime**. The theory's six propositions are contained in Table 9.1.[21] Criminal definitions (law) represent the interests of those who hold power in society. Where conflict exists between social groups—for example, between those who are wealthy and those who are poor—the people who hold power will create laws to benefit themselves. Thus, harsh punishments for property crime are designed to help those who already have wealth to keep it in their possession; in contrast, the lenient sanctions attached to corporate crimes are designed to give the already powerful a free hand at economic exploitation.

Quinney wrote that criminal definitions are based on such factors as (1) changing social conditions; (2) emerging interests; (3) increasing demands that political, economic, and religious interests be protected; and (4) changing conceptions of public interest. Quinney pulled together these ideas to say that concepts of crime are controlled by the powerful, and that the criminal justice system works to secure the needs of the powerful. Criminal definitions are a constantly changing set of concepts that mirror the political organization of society. Criminals are people who have come up short in the struggle for success and are seeking alternative means of achieving wealth, status, or even survival.[22] Consequently, law violations can be viewed as political or even quasi-revolutionary acts.[23]

For example, in 2004, arson, vandalism, and other disturbances occurred in Kanesatake, an Aboriginal community outside Montreal, bringing back memories of violence in 1990 when police and Aboriginal people were locked in the deadly Oka land claims standoff. Part of the underlying conflict relates to norm resistance because for years the official policy toward Aboriginal people was assimilation. Today, Aboriginal communities react more in protest to threats of outside interference.[24]

Howard Ramos, a political sociologist at Dalhousie University, wanted to see how Canadian Aboriginal protests between 1951 and 2000 could be explained. He argues that the strongest influences on protest are the founding of new organizations, federal monies, media attention, and successful resolution of land claims.

social reality of crime Quinney's conflict theory regarding the interrelationships between power, society, and criminality.

CHAPTER 9 | **Social Conflict Theory**   287

- In the 1930s, Aboriginal workers were used at Port Radium to bag and haul uranium ore; they were not allowed to use the showers that were reserved for Caucasian workers to clean themselves of the poison.
- An Aboriginal woman taken to a Vancouver Island residential school in the 1950s when she was six years old suffered 12 years of degradation, abuse, and rape.
- In 1989, Ontario's task force on policing and race relations heard testimony from Aboriginal people about beatings, racial slurs, and neglect by police on northern reserves.
- In 1993, six Innu children were found in an unheated shack in Davis Inlet, sniffing gasoline and saying that they wanted to die.
- Militant loggers from the Listuguj reserve in Quebec blockaded a road for three weeks in the summer of 1998 in a protest to improve Aboriginal logging rights.
- In 2001, two Saskatchewan police officers were convicted of abandoning Aboriginal men outside of Saskatoon in the middle of the winter without proper clothing.

Stories like these are just the tip of the iceberg in the study of relations between Aboriginal people and the Canadian criminal justice system. Research into the issue could take many directions. We could look at the socio-economic conditions of Aboriginal people in Canada: the poverty rates they experience, their higher than normal rate of suicide, the violence and despair that are felt by those living in isolated reserves and in large cities. We could also question why Aboriginal people are overrepresented in prisons in Western Canada, why they are more likely to experience discrimination by the police, and why they are more likely to be advised to plead guilty and be sent to prison than are Caucasians.

We need only look at the case of Donald Marshall, Jr. for a prominent and clear example of how Aboriginal people are treated by the justice system. On May 28, 1971, Marshall, a 17-year-old Mi'kmaq, and Sandy Seale, a 17-year-old Black teenager, were walking through Wentworth Park in Sydney, Nova Scotia. There they met Roy Ebsary and Jimmy MacNeil. When they asked Ebsary for money, he responded by fatally stabbing Seale and wounding Marshall. The police officers who responded to the incident did not cordon off the crime scene, search the area, or question witnesses. The sergeant of detectives subsequently accused Marshall of stabbing Seale during an argument and pressured two youths to claim that they had witnessed the attack. Information from MacNeil was discounted by the police, as was that provided by Ebsary's daughter. Marshall was charged with murder and spent 11 years in jail for a murder he didn't commit. The RCMP reopened the case in 1982. Then Justice Minister Jean Chrétien referred the case to the Nova Scotia Court of Appeal, which acquitted Marshall in 1983 but concluded that he was partly to blame for his misfortune.

In 1989, a royal commission investigating the wrongful conviction and incarceration of Donald Marshall, Jr. concluded that the criminal justice system had failed him at every turn.

The commission's seven-volume report did not whitewash problems in the criminal justice system; it commissioned research to show that Aboriginal people and Black minorities were discriminated against by the system. In this larger context, what happened to Donald Marshall was certainly not an isolated case.

In 1999, Donald Marshall was in the news again in another case that put Aboriginal people in conflict with the law on different grounds, when the Supreme Court of Canada heard a case on appeal from Nova Scotia. In 1993, in a case called *R. v. Marshall* [1999, 3 S.C.R.], Marshall had been charged and convicted of three offences set out in the federal fishery regulations: the selling of eels without a licence, fishing without a licence, and fishing during the closed season with illegal nets. Marshall admitted he had caught and sold 463 pounds (210 kg) of eels worth $787.10, without a licence and with a prohibited net within closed times, but he argued that he possessed a treaty right to catch and sell fish under the treaties of 1760–61. In its decision, the Supreme Court overturned the two lower court decisions. It specifically concluded that prohibitions on catching, retaining, and selling fish without a licence, and on fishing during the closed time, as set out in Maritime Provinces Fishery Regulations, were inconsistent with the treaty rights of Aboriginal people.

The federal government, through its Department of Fisheries and Oceans (DFO), subsequently set out to negotiate interim agreements with Aboriginal bands throughout the Maritime region, but the Burnt Church reserve decided to develop its own management scheme and to fish for lobster independently. The DFO declared that the Aboriginal people were acting in defiance of the law and moved in. With the RCMP looking on, the DFO, with their boats and helicopters, conducted surveillance and seized traps and gear. Aboriginal people are now more likely to challenge discrimination in the criminal justice system and to press for their rights under historic treaties. However, change will be slow.

Critical Thinking

1. How do economic inequalities contribute to Aboriginal people's conflict with the laws?
2. How was Donald Marshall a pivot for turning points in the law, not once, but twice?

SOURCES: Royal Commission on the Donald Marshall, Jr., Prosecution, Digest of Findings and Recommendations (Province of Nova Scotia: King's Printer, 1989); *R. v. Marshall*, Supreme Court of Canada 1999.

Rima Wilkes at the University of British Columbia has also looked at how levels of deprivation are associated with participation by First Nations in collective action. Using data obtained from newspapers and the Canadian Census of Population, she showed that some forms of deprivation (unemployment) and resources (socio-economic status) were related to First Nation mobilization and protest.[25]

CONNECTIONS

Quinney has changed his theoretical outlook over his long and distinguished career. He is now a leader of the Zen-inspired peacemaking movement, which seeks to remove violence and coercion from the criminal justice system and promotes healing or restorative justice. See the section on peacemaking later in this chapter.

Norm Resistance. Other writers, such as Austin Turk, write that social conflict is inevitable when authorities in society are in conflict with those who are controlled by, but have little ability to control, the law. Conflict is inherent because both groups have their own sets of cultural norms (those that express ideals and values) and social norms (actual group behaviours). Interaction between authorities and subjects eventually produces **norm resistance**, or open conflict, which is highest under certain conditions:

- Authorities and subjects are both committed to opposing cultural norms.
- People with group support will be resistant to authority or change.
- Assessing the strengths, weaknesses of opponents helps avoid conflict with authorities.[26]

Research on Conflict Theory

Testing conflict theory is different from evaluating consensus models. Similar methodologies are often used, but conflict-centred research more specifically attempts to show that conflict principles hold up under empirical scrutiny. Areas of interest include comparing the crime rates of members of powerless groups with those of members of the elite classes, examining the operation of the justice system to uncover bias and discrimination, charting the historical development of the criminal law, and identifying laws created to preserve the power of the elite classes at the expense of the poor.

Conflict theorists say that such crimes as burglary and larceny are a means of social and economic survival, and others, such as assault, homicide, and drug use, are a means of expressing rage, frustration, and anger. This is not to excuse crime, but rather to see its economic origins.

Crime rates also vary according to indicators of poverty and need. For example, over a 50-year period, a comparison of homicide rates with infant mortality rates (which are considered an efficient measure of poverty) found that the two rates were significantly interrelated.[27] Other data collected by ecologists show that crime is strongly related to income level, deteriorated living conditions, and relative economic deprivation.[28] Crime then is not simply a rational choice, or due only to psychological processes, but is related to the stage of production and material relations of production.

In a 2005 update, research by public health and anthropology scientists showed that income inequality is strongly associated with both adolescent birth rates and general homicide rates internationally, and with inequality. Because they found no association with absolute income, they suggest that "violence and births to adolescents may reflect gender-differentiated responses to low social status and could be reduced by reducing income inequality."[29]

Another area of research focuses on the criminal justice system. For example, American states with significant poverty levels were also the most likely to have the largest number of fatal shootings by police, suggesting that police act more forcefully in areas of class conflict.[30] Similarly, an examination of criminal cases processed by the Chicago criminal courts found that members of powerless groups are the most likely to receive prejudicial sentences in criminal courts.[31] Other research shows that both Caucasian and Black offenders are more likely to receive stricter sentences in criminal courts if their personal characteristics (single, young, urban, male) give them the appearance of being a member of the **dangerous classes**.[32]

Studies of bail hearings show moral assessments by police have a strong influence on decisions to remand those suspected of crimes. Pretrial detention is important because it can be used to encourage (or coerce) guilty pleas from accused persons. Those accused who are not held in pretrial custody are more likely to have their charges withdrawn by the prosecution. The over-policing of stigmatized groups is related to views held by the police that create a conservative and authoritarian culture.

The Royal Commission on Aboriginal People found that Aboriginal people are more likely to be denied bail, to be subjected to pretrial detention, and to plead guilty without knowing the consequences of doing so. While Blacks are

norm resistance A concept referring to the interaction between authorities and subjects that produces open conflict between the two groups.

dangerous classes The idea that personal characteristics such as being single, young, urban, male, and ethnic can result in harsher treatment in the criminal justice system.

In 2002, the *Toronto Star* published a series of articles on race and crime, based on a data set of about 800,000 charges going back to 1996. What they showed was that Blacks are overrepresented in certain crimes, for example, drug possession. Furthermore, Blacks are more likely to be arrested, to be detained after arrest, and to be held in custody for a bail hearing.

The allegation was that the difference in how Blacks and Caucasians were treated represented the presence of racial profiling.

The police chief, the police association, the police civilian oversight board, and the mayor's office all denied that racial profiling was involved in police work. However, they did not demonstrate that the data could be read to represent anything else until they had hired a Toronto sociologist to reanalyze the data.

He claimed that no racial profiling had occurred.

Research in Britain has well established that racial profiling occurs. Research shows that Blacks are eight times more likely to be stopped by the police than Caucasians. As well, recent research in Toronto shows that Black students are more than twice as likely to be stopped by police, especially if they spend their leisure time in public places.

Furthermore, racial differences in stop and search practices were greatest among those with low levels of criminal behaviour, suggesting that they did nothing untoward to bring themselves to the attention of the police. For this reason, Black students were eight times more likely to be stopped and almost five times more likely to be searched despite not being engaged in criminal activity.

Obviously, then, because of the apparent racial profiling, when Blacks do engage in crime, they are more likely to be caught. Of all drug dealers surveyed, 65 percent of Blacks said they had been arrested, compared with 35 percent of the Caucasian drug dealers.

The original analysis done by the *Toronto Star* focused on racial differences in four types of offences: drug possession, the specific possession of cocaine, so-called out-of-sight traffic offences, and violence. Out-of-sight traffic violations refers to such offences as driving without a license or without insurance, which can only be detected after the police have stopped a driver.

In the analysis of the *Star*'s data, University of Toronto criminologists found that, across all police divisions, Blacks are almost four times as likely as Caucasians to incur out-of-sight driving offences. This means that they had not been stopped for a criminal offence originally.

When they looked at 52 Division specifically, an area with only a small Black residential population, not only were Blacks overrepresented in all offence categories, but they were more than seven times as likely to be represented in out-of-sight traffic offences.

This high rate is explained as due to the fact that Blacks are "out of place" and thus more visible for aggressive police enforcement.

In a follow-up study published in 2010, the *Toronto Star* showed the practice of filling out information cards on citizens stopped by the police or sometimes even on those persons requesting assistance from the police builds up an extensive police database. Using six years of contact information, the *Star* was able to show that race, age, and gender matter a lot in terms of who gets stopped.

Although Blacks make up about 8 percent of Toronto's population, they account for three times as many contact cards, more than twice the rate for Caucasian males of the same age. While the carding is an effective crime-detection tool, the *Star*'s analysis found most people documented by police had not been charged criminally in the previous six years, and four out of five did not show up in a criminal database in 2008.

The original articles on racial profiling by the *Star* prompted an inquiry by the Ontario Human Rights Commission into the impacts of racial profiling. However, the 2010 repeat of that analysis looking at arrest and charge data from 2003 to 2008 shows those results have changed little, says the *Star*.

Racial profiling or routine policing? A good question.

SOURCE: Copyright Chris McCormick, published in the *Daily Gleaner* (Fredericton), May 5, 2011.

shown to be over-policed in the United States, in Canada ethnic minorities in general, and natives in particular, are more subject to discrimination.

Bryan Hogeveen (of the University of Alberta) looked at this question in light of the implementation of the *Youth Criminal Justice Act* and warned of the risk of continued differential treatment of Aboriginal people,[33] whether being subjected to pretrial detention or being wrongfully convicted.[34]

The Commission on Systemic Racism in the Ontario Criminal Justice System found that Blacks were more likely than were Caucasians to be stopped by the police. In addition, research by Gail Kellough (of York University) and Scot Wortley (of the University of Toronto) found that Caucasians were more likely to be granted bail.[35] When the Toronto police were accused in 2002 of racial profiling, much controversy ensued over whether the facts supported that conclusion.[36] The police launched a $2.7 billion lawsuit in their own defence. This is discussed in more detail in the Crime in the News exhibit. Lately, they have been shown to use the controversial "stop and frisk" more on ethnic minorities than whites.

Conflict theorists show that the criminal justice system is quick to take action when the victim of crime is wealthy, Caucasian, and male, but is uninterested when the victim is

Famous Canadian Court Cases
R. v. Gladue

On Jamie Gladue's 19th birthday in 1996, she took her partner's life during a domestic dispute and changed her own forever. In the process, this young Cree woman from Alberta set the stage for a legal drama that has significantly affected the lives of Aboriginals across the country.

When Gladue was charged with second-degree murder, she pleaded guilty to a reduced count of manslaughter. On entering the disposition phase of the proceedings, a newly enacted *Criminal Code* provision was automatically invoked. Section 718.2(e) compels adjudicators to consider all available and reasonable sanctions other than imprisonment, paying particular attention to the circumstances of Aboriginal offenders. The presiding judge questioned the relevance of this provision to the matter at hand, noting that the couple lived in an urban area off-reserve. Gladue was handed a three-year prison term.

When Gladue challenged her disposition before the British Columbia Court of Appeal, targeting the lower court's reading of section 718.2(e), his decision was defended. Ultimately, the higher court agreed that there was no basis for a special focus on the appellant's heritage in this particular situation.

However, the battle reached a climax in 1999, when the Supreme Court of Canada evaluated both the Gladue case and the *Criminal Code* provision. The concern that due consideration had not been given to Gladue's Aboriginal background was legitimated, but her sentence was upheld yet again. Although the defendant was defeated in one sense, the judgment was successful in other respects. First and foremost, the Supreme Court validated section 718.2(e). Principles were also established to guide the proper interpretation and application of this provision.

The legal effects of the Gladue decision have proven to be far-reaching. For example, three provinces have established Aboriginal-only courts.

Not everyone is receptive to the Supreme Court decision, however. Some complain that Aboriginal offenders are treated too leniently. Others criticize the government for concentrating on sentencing practices when the overrepresentation of Aboriginals in prison stems from socio-economic inequalities.

---

poor, a member of a minority group, and female, indicating how power positions affect justice.[37] It is not surprising that an analysis of national population trends and imprisonment rates shows that as the percentage of minority-group members increases, the imprisonment rate does likewise.[38] This outcome may be a function of society becoming "less tolerant of nonwhite populations and/or feeling more threatened by them."[39] Data showing racial and class discrimination by the justice system support the conflict theory.

One reason for discrimination may be the attitudes of decision makers. For example, justice professionals who express racist values are also more punitive, believe that courts should be stricter, and believe that the death penalty is an effective deterrent.[40] Race has varying and subtle effects on decision making in the juvenile justice system.[41] Critical thinkers say that the powerless need a greater voice to express their needs and concerns, if these inequities are to be addressed.[42] More research is also needed, for example, on police–citizen encounters in domestic disputes.[43]

Social policy stems directly from such research. For example, a pilot project developed in New Brunswick to serve the Aboriginal population found that providing legal aid services in an Aboriginal person's first language reduced adjournments and resulted in a higher rate of not guilty pleas.[44] In Nova Scotia, a needs assessment by Don Clairmont (of Dalhousie University) of Nova Scotia's Mi'kmaq community examined their experiences with the court and policing systems. It recommended greater emphasis on community policing and cultural awareness of the police, and increased efforts to recruit Aboriginal peoples, especially women.[45]

The significance of being sensitive to the plight of members of minority groups when they come in conflict with the criminal justice system is illustrated in a Famous Canadian Court Case, *R. v. Gladue,* and as discussed by Savarese (of St. Thomas University).[46] Another, less well-known case, is that of Lisa Neve, who was only the second woman to be designated a dangerous offender in Canada. Between the ages of 15 to 21, she had been convicted for 22 offences and was finally sentenced to an indeterminate sentence for robbery. Her designation as a dangerous offender was eventually overturned. The reason for her treatment was probably not only her behaviour, but also the fact that she was an Aboriginal person, a woman, and a prostitute, and that she had a defiant attitude.[47]

Analysis of Conflict Theory

Conflict theorists identify power relations in society and their role in promoting criminal behaviour. They reject the view that the law represents the values of the majority or that legal codes create a just society and criminals are simple predators. Some criminologists disagree, suggesting instead that crime is a matter of rational choice made by offenders motivated more by greed and selfishness than by poverty and hopelessness.[48] Critics also say that crime is less likely to be a function of poverty and class conflict than a product of personal needs, socialization, or some other related factor.[49]

Similarly, studies of police discretion, criminal court sentencing, and correctional policy have not always found indicators of class or race bias, an outcome predicted by conflict theory.[50] An examination of the prison sentences of 10,488 inmates in three southeastern American states concluded that socio-economic status was unrelated to the length of prison terms assigned by the courts.[51] Sentencing decisions in California also found little evidence of race bias; Black Americans were neither more likely to be sent to prison than were Caucasian offenders, nor more likely to receive longer prison terms.[52]

Cross-cultural research indicates that crime rates are not reduced when a free-market system is replaced by a less competitive economic model. Analysis of crime in Tanzania found that when the free-enterprise system was replaced by a socialist system, the crime rate actually increased. New crimes, such as theft by public servants and corruption, also appear to increase.[53]

Other research looking at the relationship between inequality and violent crime across a variety of countries found a general relationship, but it was strongly influenced by cultural differences.[54]

However, despite these contradictory results, other research seems convincing, and more radical versions of the general conflict model have developed, to which we now turn.

MARXIST CRIMINOLOGY

Above all, Marxism is a critique of capitalism. Capitalism produces haves and have-nots, each engaging in a particular branch of criminality.[55] Street crime might be the province of the poor, but suite crime is committed by the rich. More importantly, those in political power also control the definition of crime.[56]

The only crimes available to the poor are the severely sanctioned "street crimes": rape, drugs, theft, and mugging. Members of the middle class cheat on their taxes and engage in petty corporate crime, acts that generate social disapproval but are rarely punished severely. The wealthy are involved in acts that should be described as crimes but are not, such as corporate crime. Though regulatory laws control business activities, these are rarely enforced, and violations are lightly punished. Laws regulating corporate crime are window dressing designed to create the impression that the justice system is fair.[57]

For example, when Bill C-45 was passed, it included revisions to the *Criminal Code of Canada* aimed at strengthening corporate criminal liability. The bill, passed in 2003, came after the deaths of 26 workers at Westray in 1993. This disaster was caused by unsafe working conditions in a coal mine inadequately regulated by provincial law. Through an examination of parliamentary committee hearings, Steven Bittle (of the Department of Justice) and Laureen Snider (of Queen's University) explored the potential of Bill C-45 to hold corporations to account and argued that conservative ideas of corporate liability limited the reform options that were considered by the committee. They say the legislation does little to challenge the underlying structural conditions that result in culpable workplace injury and death.[58]

CONNECTIONS

Chapter 12 looks at the case of Westray in more detail.

The Development of a Radical Criminology

Modern radical theory can be traced to the National Deviancy Conference (NDC) of 1968 in Britain. Members were critical of the positivist criminology being taught in British and American universities. They rejected the conservative stance of criminologists and their close financial relationship with government funding agencies. They investigated the concept of deviance from a labelling perspective, looking at how social control might be a cause of, rather than a response to, antisocial behaviour.

Radical theory was given a powerful boost when Taylor, Walton, and Young published *The New Criminology*, followed by *Critical Criminology*, which criticized existing concepts in criminology as **correctionalist**.[59] Those books became important resources for scholars critical of both the field of criminology and the existing legal process.

Meanwhile, American scholars began to follow a new radical approach to criminology at the University of California. These scholars, and others, such as Richard Quinney and William Chambliss, were influenced by social criticism of the Vietnam War, prison struggles, and the civil rights and feminist movements. Mainstream criminology was criticized as conservative, pro-government, and anti-human. Critical criminologists scoffed when their fellow scholars used statistical analysis of computerized data to describe criminal and delinquent behaviour:

> Many of our scientific heroes of the past, upon rereading, turned out to be racists or, more generally, apologists for social injustice. In response to the

correctionalist The concept that social science seeks to correct criminal behaviour rather than see it as rooted in economic relations.

widespread protests on campuses and throughout society, many of the contemporary giants of social science emerged as defenders of the status quo and vocally dismissed the claims of the oppressed for social justice.[60]

Marxists did not meet with widespread approval. The criminology school at Berkeley was eventually closed for what many believe were political reasons. Even today, conflict exists between critical thinkers and mainstream academics. The prestigious Harvard Law School and other law centres have been the scenes of conflict, including charges of purges and of tenure denials because some professors held critical views of law and society, victimized by "academic McCarthyism."[61]

In the ensuing years, new branches of a radical criminology were developing elsewhere. In the early 1980s, the left realism school was started by scholars affiliated with the Middlesex Polytechnic and the University of Edinburgh in Great Britain. In the United States, scholars influenced in part by the pioneering work of Dennis Sullivan and Larry Tifft created the peacemaking movement.[62]

At the same time, feminist scholars began to apply critical analysis to the relationships among gender, power, and criminality. Theorists rediscovered a radical potential in Canadian political economics and sociology. These movements have coalesced into a rich and complex criminological tradition.

Fundamentals of Marxist Criminology

Marxist criminologists ignore formal theory construction, with its heavy emphasis on empirical value-free testing, arguing that criminological scholarship should have a political and ideological basis.[63] Crime and criminal justice must be viewed in a historical, social, and economic context. Leftist criminologists see the definition of crime as being designed to protect the power and position of the upper classes at the expense of the poor. Part of the radical agenda, then, is to make the public aware that crimes of power are crimes just as much as are burglary and robbery.[64]

Criminals are not social misfits but rather a product of the society and its economic system in which they reside. Capitalism has always produced a relatively high level of crime and violence. Three implications follow from this view:

1. Each society will produce its own types and amounts of crime.
2. Each society will have its own distinctive ways of dealing with criminal behaviour.
3. Each society gets the amount and type of crime that it deserves.

Criminals are not outsiders who can be controlled by an increase in law enforcement. Criminality is a function of the social and economic organization of society. To control crime and reduce criminality is to end the social conditions that promote crime.

Economic Structure and Surplus Value

Marxist criminology's general theme is the relationship between crime and the ownership and control of private property in a capitalist society.[65] That ownership and control, according to sociologist Gregg Barak, is the principal basis of power in capitalist society.[66] Social conflict is fundamentally related to the historical and social distribution of productive private property and surplus value (profit).

One important aspect of capitalism is the effect of **surplus value**, which refers to the value resulting from production when the cost of labour is less than the cost of the goods it produces. The profit can be shared with workers, reinvested in technology, or used to enrich the owners. To increase the rate of surplus value, workers can be made to work harder for less pay, be made more efficient, or be replaced by "labour-saving" technology (see Figure 9.3). In modern times, surplus value has been increased through globalization as production shifts to regions of the world with lower wages and fewer restrictions, such as environmental laws, or unions.

Unfortunately, as surplus value increases, more people are displaced from productive relationships, and the size of the marginal population swells. As corporations downsize to increase profits, high-paying labour and managerial jobs are lost to computer-driven machinery. Displaced workers are forced into service jobs at minimum wage or become temporary employees without benefits or a secure position.

As more people are thrust outside the economic mainstream through marginalization, a larger portion of the population is forced to live in areas conducive to crime. Once people are marginalized, commitment to the system declines, producing another criminogenic force: a weakened bond to society.[67] The nature of capitalism, then, is inherently destabilizing, and the proletariat becomes the "precariat," the worker living in precarious times.

This effect has also been observed in former socialist republics that have converted to free-market economies. Both China and the former Soviet Union have experienced an upsurge in gang activity as they embrace market economies; Russia may now have a murder rate higher than that of the United States.

surplus value The Marxist view that the labouring classes produce wealth that far exceeds their wages and goes to the capitalist class as profits.

FIGURE 9.3
Surplus Value

Worker produces goods that exceed wages in value → Profit → Capitalist keeps profits → Uses profits to buy machines and replace workers → Workers make less and buy less → **Economic crisis**

Several schools of thought exist within the radical literature. Some of these different approaches are discussed in further detail in the following sections.

Instrumental Marxism

Instrumental Marxists view the criminal law and criminal justice system solely as an instrument for controlling the poor; the state is the tool of the capitalists. Accordingly, capitalist justice serves the powerful and enables them to impose their morality on the entire society.[68]

People who are poor may or may not commit more crimes than the people who are rich do, but they certainly are arrested and punished more often. People who are poor are driven to crime because, as we saw with anomie theory, a natural frustration exists in a society in which affluence is well publicized but unattainable. The difference between strain theory and Marxist theory is that the frustration is generalized to a whole social strata. When class conflict becomes unbearable, frustration can spill out in riots, such as the one that occurred in Los Angeles on April 29, 1992, described as a "class rebellion of the underprivileged against the privileged."[69]

Because of class conflict, hostility is generated among members of the lower class toward the social order. The focus of conventional criminology on social conditions that cause crime, such as family structure, intelligence, peer relations, and school performance, serves to keep the lower classes servile by showing why its members are more criminal, less intelligent, and more prone to school failure and family problems than are members of the middle class.

Rather, the goal of criminology should be to show how law in capitalist society works to preserve ruling-class power, summarized here as follows:

- society is based on an advanced capitalist economy;
- the state is organized to serve the interests of the dominant economic class;

- the criminal law is a state instrument used to maintain the existing social and economic order;
- crime control occurs through institutions established and administered by the elite class;
- contradictions in capitalism require that lower classes remain oppressed by the legal system;
- the collapse of capitalism and creation of a society based on socialism will solve crime.[70]

Concepts of Instrumental Marxism. Legal relations underpin the infrastructure required by capitalism, and maintain the family and school structure so as to secure the labour force. The system may at times serve the interests of the working class, for example, to protect collective bargaining. Yet legal relations maintain patterns of individualism and selfishness and perpetuate a class system characterized by anarchy, oppression, and crime.[71]

At its core, **instrumental Marxism** defines the state, the law, and the ruling class as a single entity. The law is shaped by the economic, social, and political interests of the ruling class and is used by the ruling class to its own advantage; the definition of crime deflects attention from social injustice.[72]

Privilege. Barry Krisberg has linked crime to the differentials in **privilege**, which include such rights as life, liberty, and happiness; such traits as intelligence, sensitivity, and humanity; and such material goods as monetary wealth, luxuries, land, and the like. The effective use of violence and

> **instrumental Marxism** The view that the law is designed to specifically advance the interests of particular groups or organizations.
>
> **privilege** The concept that the wealth and prestige enjoyed by some, puts them in conflict with those in society who are less well off.

coercion is the major factor in determining which social group ascends to the position of defining and holding privilege.

Class discrimination that is based on privilege can be quite subtle, as when, for example, the Ontario government announced that it was going to require mandatory drug testing and treatment for welfare recipients suspected of having a substance abuse problem. Another move criticized for being an attack on the poor is the *Safe Streets Act* introduced in British Columbia in 2004, modelled on Ontario legislation, which makes it illegal to solicit money in a threatening manner, to panhandle within five metres of an automated bank machine, and to solicit money from vehicles that are stopped or parked, eliminating the market for window-washing squeegee kids. Such laws tend not to meet with widespread resistance because they are targeted at people who are marginal and powerless.

Conversely, criminologists such as Laureen Snider (of Queen's University) argue that corporate crime has virtually disappeared through decriminalization, deregulation, and downsizing of enforcement capability. As she says:

> While punishment for corporate criminals was being eliminated, incarceration rates for traditional, blue-collar criminals were doubling and tripling. Increasing penality—through criminalizing behaviours previously tolerated, through the "war on drugs," by abolishing parole and statutory remission, lengthening minimum sentences, instituting compulsory urinalysis for "at risk" populations—became a growth business in the 1980s and 1990s.[73]

More recently, the federal government has introduced mandatory minimum sentences, for example, in an effort to get tough on crime. This comes at a time when crime is at its lowest since the 1960s.

Furthermore, some say criminology itself helps support state repression:

> Criminology has serviced domestic repression.... This system has been used to repress and maintain the powerlessness of poor people, people of colour, and young people. In the past, we have been constrained by a legal definition of crime which restricts us to studying and ultimately helping to control only legally defined "criminals." We need a more humanistic definition of crime, one which reflects the reality of a legal system based on power....A human rights definition of crime frees us to examine imperialism, racism, sexism, capitalism, exploitation, and other political or economic systems which contribute to human misery.[74]

Despite such critical observations, Michael Lynch says that instrumental Marxist theory may be limited simply because it is based on incorrect assumptions: The law always operates in the interests of the ruling class, members of the ruling class conspire to control society, and what benefits one member of the ruling class benefits them all. In reality, some laws benefit the lower classes, and capitalists compete with one another rather than conspire. Because of these deficiencies, some radicals have turned from instrumental theory and embraced structural Marxism.

Structural Marxism

Structural Marxism disagrees with the view that the relationship between law and capitalism always works for people who are rich and against people who are poor.[75]

The law is not the exclusive domain of the rich. However, the law is used to maintain the long-term interests of the capitalist system and to control members of any class who pose a threat to its existence, which perhaps explains why the sponsorship scandal in Quebec became such a boondoggle: the favouring of Liberal-friendly companies threatened the legitimacy of the whole system.

On the other hand, if law and justice were purely instruments of the capitalist class, why would society create and enforce laws controlling corporate crimes, such as price fixing, false advertising, and illegal restraint of trade?

To a structuralist, the law is designed to keep the capitalist system operating in an efficient manner, and anyone who "rocks the boat" will be sanctioned. For example, antitrust legislation is designed to prevent both any single capitalist from dominating the system and others from "playing the game." Therefore, the law works more to legitimate the system, despite its obvious inequalities.

In Stephen Spitzer's Marxian theory of deviance, he says that law defines as deviant any person who disturbs, hinders, or calls into question any of the following:[76]

- Capitalist modes of appropriating the product of human labour
- The conditions under which capitalist production takes place (for example, wage labour)
- Patterns of consumption (for example, using drugs for escape rather than adjustment)
- The process of socialization for production (for example, schooling youths to conformity)
- The ideology that supports the functioning of capitalist society

Capitalism has special ways of dealing with those who oppose its operation. One way is to normalize formerly illegal acts—for example, through legalizing abortions. Another is conversion, which refers to co-opting deviants by making them part of the system—for example, a gang leader may be recruited to work with younger delinquents. Containment involves segregating deviants into isolated geographic areas

> **structural Marxism** The view that the law maintains the capitalist system, and individuals who threaten social stability will be sanctioned.

Criminology Research
How Capitalism Influences Rape

Herman and Julia Schwendinger's classic study of rape provides an excellent example of Marxian critical analysis. In looking at why women who are raped often feel guilty, the researchers came to believe that a rape victim has internalized discriminatory norms because she has been raised in a sexist society. Women have traditionally been viewed as the weaker sex, dependent on parents or husbands, so rape was seen as a property crime against those men.

During the early stages of capitalism, families underwent strain when industry demanded a labour force of men, only infrequently supplemented by single women. The role of father was strained as men were separated from their households. The woman's role became more narrowly defined as child-bearer and child-raiser. The limited economic role of women helped define them as dependants. Married women were viewed as non-productive, because they did not participate in commodity markets and earn money.

In reality, women's household productivity must be viewed as an essential contribution to the family and the economy. A woman may be dependent on her husband's wage to buy things for the family, and her sense of self-worth reflects her dependency. Negative evaluations, such as those created by a rape experience, are likely to be turned inward by the woman, creating unwarranted self-recrimination and remorse.

In addition, schools and the media traditionally reinforce dependency in the curriculum. Textbooks once stereotyped the woman's role: girls were depicted as helpless and frightened. Vocational tests provide fewer opportunities for girls. In media presentations, women are usually depicted as housewives and mothers. When women are portrayed on television commercials, they seem "concerned mainly with clean floors and clean hair—housework and their personal appearance."

Although women have made great advances, their labour is often in low-paid, low-mobility occupations and does little to improve their economic dependency. For these reasons, women often blame themselves for being raped. The Schwendingers imply that women feel they have "let down" the people they depend on when they are trapped in a rape encounter. This self-blame for the attack prevents a woman from focusing on the true culprits: the rapist and the capitalist system whose economic structure results in a rape-producing climate in which women are undervalued. The Schwendingers' research approach illustrates the effect of material economic conditions.

It is not accidental that rape was traditionally seen as a crime of property.

SOURCES: Herman Schwendinger and Julia Schwendinger, *Rape and Inequality* (Newbury Park, CA: Sage, 1983); Herman Schwendinger and Julia Schwendinger, "Rape Victims and the False Sense of Guilt," *Crime and Social Justice* 13 (1980): 4–17.

A member of the police providing security at the 2010 G20 summit in Toronto rose to video fame after threatening a protestor with arrest if any bubbles touched him.

© Steve Russell/GetStock.com

so that they can easily be controlled—for example, by conducting a crackdown on prostitution so the trade moves to another area. Finally, capitalist society actively supports some criminal enterprises, such as organized crime through money laundering, for example.

Research on Marxist Criminology

Marxist criminologists rarely use standard social science methodologies.[77] Marxists believe that the research conducted by mainstream liberal/positivist criminologists is designed to unmask powerless members of society so that they can be better dealt with by the legal system—a process called correctionalism. They are particularly offended by purely empirical studies, such as those showing that minority-group members have lower IQs than the Caucasian majority, or that the inner city is the site of the most serious crime while middle-class areas are relatively crime-free. The result has been much more empirical research within conventional criminology than within radical studies.

However, empirical research is not totally incompatible with Marxist criminology, and some important efforts have been made to test its assumptions.[78] For example, early research by Alan Lizotte has shown that the property crime rate reflects a change in the level of surplus value; the capitalist system's emphasis on excessive profits accounts for the need of the working class to commit property crime.[79] Lizotte also studied the relationship between economic inequality and police function, the influence of extra-legal factors of sentencing, and the influence of the extraction of surplus value on imprisonment and crime rates.[80] Marxist research tends to be historical and analytical. Social trends are interpreted to understand how capitalism has affected human interaction: how the accumulation of wealth affects crime rates and the effect of criminal interactions on individuals. Of particular importance is the analysis of the historical development of capitalist social control institutions, such as the criminal law, police agencies, courts, and prison systems.

Crime, the Individual, and the State. Marxists study the relationships among crime, victims, the criminal, and the state. Two common themes emerge: (1) Crime and its control are a function of capitalism, and (2) the justice system is biased against the working class and favours upper-class interests. Marxian analysis of the criminal justice system is designed to identify the processes that exert control over people's lives.[81]

Marxists might show how sentencing in a juvenile court is a function of social class,[82] how power relationships help undermine any benefit the lower class gets from sentencing reforms,[83] how the justice system is class biased,[84] or the relationship between capitalism and rape.[85] Conflict theorists are not surprised that police brutality complaints are highest in neighbourhoods where most residents are minority-group

members. Critical research of this sort is designed to reinterpret commonly held beliefs about society within the framework of Marxist social and economic ideas.[86] The goal is to show that capitalism creates an environment in which crime is inevitable.

In addition to conducting studies showing the relationship between crime and the state, some critical researchers have attempted to show how capitalism influences the distribution of punishment. For example, research shows that over two decades, the rate of imprisonment grew substantially in those American states with (1) the highest revenues, (2) the highest unemployment rates, and (3) the largest Black populations.[87] In wealthier states, where income is concentrated in the hands of a few affluent people, those in power will be willing to spend enormous sums to keep people who are poor and minority-group members under state control.

An increasing prison population masks unemployment rates. Many inmates were chronically unemployed before their imprisonment. When the large numbers of people who are on probation and parole and who must maintain jobs are added to the mix, the correctional system is now playing an ever-more important role in suppressing wages and maintaining the profitability of capitalism.[88]

Historical Analysis. A second type of Marxist research focuses on the historical background of commonly held institutional beliefs and practices, to show how changes in the criminal law corresponded to the development of a capitalist economy.

For example, the Highland Clearances involved burning townships and dispossessing feudal peasants, all for the sake of clearing land for sheep. In Canada, capitalism had already been imported from Europe, but resistance from Aboriginal people, Métis, and then later trade unions had to be suppressed in the interests of economic reform.[89]

Analysis of historical records shows that law reform in 19th-century England was largely a response to pressure from the business community to make the punishment for property law violations more acceptable.[90]

Another topic of importance is the development of modern police agencies. Police often play an active role in putting down labour disputes and controlling the activities of political dissidents. Prominent examples include research on the history of private police and historical analysis of police excesses in the repression of an early union, the International Workers of the World.[91] Analysis of the development of modern policing shows how police developed as an anti-labour force that provided muscle for industrialists at the turn of the 20th century.[92]

For example, one interpretation of the development of the North-West Mounted Police is that they were sent west to prevent U.S. annexation and whisky smuggling to the Aboriginal people. Another interpretation is that they were to quell uprisings and to secure a western market for central Canadian goods. An example is discussed in the nearby Famous Canadian Criminals box on Louis Riel.

In 1869, the newly confederated Dominion of Canada was in the process of purchasing Rupert's Land from the Hudson's Bay Company, causing the Métis of Manitoba to worry about their land rights and the preservation of their culture. As a result, they proclaimed a provisional government and appointed as its secretary Louis Riel, a young Métis lawyer. During the Red River Rebellion of 1869, an armed group representing the committee seized Upper Fort Garry and ordered the lieutenant governor of the North-Western Territory not to enter the territory. In addition, Riel issued the "Declaration of the People of Rupert's Land and the North-West" and became head of the provisional government of Red River.

In an attempt to overthrow Riel, a group of men travelled from Portage la Prairie to Fort Garry, but they were captured and imprisoned. The Métis tried and sentenced one of the men, Thomas Scott, to death for insubordination in captivity. They executed him by firing squad. Responding to appeals from a bishop, they then released the remaining prisoners. After land negotiations between the federal government and the Métis were completed, the government sent a military force on a "mission of peace" to Red River. Riel, fearing its true purpose, fled to the United States.

Although the federal government preferred that Riel stay in the United States—the province of Ontario considered him a murderer—his supporters in Manitoba and Quebec persuaded him to run for election in Canada. He was elected a Member of Parliament three times, but when he attempted to take his seat in 1874, he was expelled from the House of Commons. In 1875, he was exiled for five years. In the winter of 1878–79, Riel tried to assemble a coalition of Métis and Indians to invade Western Canada, but Poundmaker and Sitting Bull refused. He even wrote to Ulysses S. Grant, asking for his help in an invasion of Western Canada. In 1884, he was asked to become political leader of a Métis movement in Saskatchewan, and the North-West Rebellion ensued. Riel seized a church at Batoche in 1885, but after less than two months of fighting, he surrendered.

He was taken to Regina rather than stand trial before a 12-member mixed-race jury in Winnipeg. His six-member jury was English, Caucasian, and Protestant, presided over by a part-time magistrate. The Criminal Code of Canada did not yet exist, so the charge was laid under the British Statute of Treasons. Riel pleaded not guilty to the charge of treason, although his lawyer wanted him to plead insanity. On August 1, 1885, he was found guilty with a recommendation for mercy. After appeals to the Manitoba Court of Appeal and to the Privy Council in London failed, Riel was hanged on November 16, 1885. The Métis dream was over.

Relations between the North-West Mounted Police and the Aboriginal residents eroded after the establishment of the federal Department of Indian Affairs in the early 1880s and the official policy of total assimilation and segregation on reserves.

One hundred and twenty years later, the federal government announced it would review Riel's case and look into pardoning him.

SOURCES: The Northwest Resistance 1885, "Louis Riel," University of Saskatchewan Library, http://library.usask.ca/northwest/background/riel.htm (accessed May 15, 2005); Canadian Encyclopedia (Toronto: McClelland and Stewart, 1988).

Critique of Marxist Criminology

As mentioned before, Marxist criminology has met with criticism.[93] Some mainstream criminologists argue that Marxist theory is the old tradition of helping the underdog, such as Robin Hood stealing from the rich to help feed the poor. In reality, they claim, most theft is for luxury, not survival. Moreover, they dispute the idea that the crimes of the rich are more reprehensible and less understandable than crimes of those who live in poverty. Criminality and immoral behaviour occur at every social level, but those who are relatively disadvantaged contribute disproportionately to crime and delinquency rates.

Other critics charge that Marxists ignore the varied interest groups that exist in a pluralistic society and focus unilaterally on class differentials.[94] For example, if social reforms are disguised attempts to control the underclass, is it logical to believe that giving people more rights is a trick to allow greater control to be exerted over them? Consider the right to a jury, the rights of free speech, free press, free association, public trial, habeas corpus, and so on.

The problems of Marxist theory are summarized in the following statements:

- Marxist criminologists ignore the problems of socialist countries, such as the gulags and purges of the Soviet Union under Stalin.
- Capitalism is blamed for every human vice and for predatory and personal crime.
- Marxist criminology doesn't explain criminality existing in states that have abolished private ownership of the means of production, such as Cuba.
- Marxists overlook distinctions that exist between people in different classes.
- Marxists attempt to explain issues that are obvious, such as politicians who are corrupt and businesspeople who are greedy.

- Marxists suspect even those practices and freedoms that most people cherish as the cornerstones of democracy (e.g., the right to trial, free press, religious freedom, and so on).

In response, Marxist scholars charge that critics rely on traditional variables, such as class and poverty, in their analysis of radical thought. Although important, these concepts do not reflect the key issues in the structural and economic process. In fact, like crime, they, too, may be the outcome of the capitalist system.[95]

Although radical criminologists dispute criticisms, they have also responded by creating new theoretical models that incorporate Marxist ideas in an innovative manner. In the following section, we discuss some recent forms of radical theory in detail.

NEW DIRECTIONS IN CRITICAL CRIMINOLOGY

Mainstream criminology has been criticized for focusing too much on crimes committed by working-class, poor, or unemployed people. They are the most easy to subject to surveillance, they are the least likely to know their rights, and they are least able to afford a defence.

However, various branches of critical criminology look at crimes of the powerful and view crime as a consequence of unequal power relations in society. In particular, left realism explains and measures street crime that victimizes working class communities, and proposes short-term solutions.

Left Realism

Some radical scholars are troubled by the emergence of a strict "law and order" philosophy that places crime control as more important than due process. The Crime in the News box provides an example where some think that bad urban planning helped fuel crime; what makes the difference is people changing the community from the inside.

At the same time, the focus of most left-wing scholarship, the abuse of power by the ruling elite, is sometimes seen as too narrow. Is it wrong to ignore the problem of inner-city gang crime and violence, which all too often targets indigent people?[96] Those who share these concerns are referred to as left realists.[97]

Left realism is connected to British scholars Lea and Young, especially their 1984 work, *What Is to Be Done about Law and Order?* They rejected utopian views of Marxists they called idealistic, who portrayed street criminals as revolutionaries, and themselves took the self-named "realistic" approach that street criminals prey on the poor and disenfranchised, thus making them doubly abused,

---

EXHIBIT 9.1

Basic Principles of Left Realism

- Crime is a symbol of the antisocial nature of capitalism.
- The relationship between the police and the public determines the efficacy of policing.
- The relationship between the victim and the offender determines the impact of crime.
- The relationship between the state and the offender is a major factor in recidivism.
- Relative deprivation leads to discontent; discontent plus lack of political solutions leads to crime.
- Local crime surveys provide the best measure of crime in any one area.
- Anti-crime strategies should be short term and avoid crime-control solutions, such as more police.

---

first by the capitalist system and then by members of their own class.[98] Lea and Young's view of crime causation closely resembles the relative deprivation approach. As they put it,

> The equation is simple: relative deprivation equals discontent; discontent plus lack of political solution equals crime.

In Canada, *Realist Criminology: Crime Control and Policing in the 1990s* came onto the scene in 1992 with a left realist approach to crime control and law enforcement. In line with left realism and critical criminology, they felt it important to assert the centrality of the victim in the development of a progressive criminology. **Left realism**, also called critical realism, recognized the seriousness of street crime for its victims, recognized public support for law, and advocated that criminology turn itself to criminal justice reform and crime prevention strategies (see Exhibit 9.1). At the time, even local crime surveys to measure patterns of victimization and policing were just being developed in Canada. This book, and others like it, were based in a tradition of critical scholarship in Canada, and would go on to have implications for studies of prostitution, corporate law, environmentalism, feminism, and victimology.[99]

Left realists argue that crime victims in all classes need protection, and crime control reflects community needs. The police and courts are not inherently evil tools of capitalism whose tough tactics alienate the lower classes. These institutions would, in fact, offer life-saving public services if their use of force could be reduced and their sensitivity to the public increased.[100]

---

left realism A theory that crime is a social problem experienced by the lower classes, and criminologists should develop crime prevention strategies.

Pinecrest-Highfield Park was designed and built so poorly that it was fated to become the city's most crime-ridden neighbourhood. But dedicated community activists are working to rebuild the broken social fabric, with promising results.

by Geoff Bird, Brittney Teasdale and Lily Sangter, The Coast

"There's a lot of quiet desperation in this neighbourhood," says Kees Zwanenburg.

The priest of Holy Trinity Emmanuel church, Zwanenburg's one of the most qualified to gauge the state of the souls who live in the north end of Dartmouth.

Just a stone's throw from the church is Victoria Road, and across that busy thoroughfare is Pinecrest-Highfield Park. Bound by Victoria on the west, Highway 111 on the north, and Albro Lake Road to the south, it's an area that has long been in crisis. Packed with apartment buildings, the neighbourhood is a literal and figurative dead end.

Pinecrest-Highfield Park remains one of the poorest neighbourhoods in the city. Most homes are rented, people move frequently, incomes are near rock-bottom, a disproportionate percentage of families are led by single parents—mostly women— and there are high rates of government assistance. Many people live in shoddy housing.

And the police are there a lot.

Analysis of police call data by University of King's College journalism students shows that seven percent of all police calls for serious incidents from 2005 to 2010 are to the area that includes Highfield-Pinecrest. Among the most common incidents: assaults; robberies; drug use; weapons and attempted suicides.

Donald MacLean, the outgoing East Division commander for the Halifax Regional Police Service, attributes many of the neighbourhood's woes to the high-density apartments on Highfield Park and Pinecrest Drives. "What we see is the type of housing situation that contributes to the transient nature of the community, which probably plays a part in some of this."

The apartments are the legacy of planning decisions that zoned the area for apartment buildings, first on the semi-urban Pinecrest and later in the brand-new community of Highfield Park, built starting in the 1980s on the site of a former naval radio base.

The result was cramming thousands of low- to middle-income people into the same area, a recipe for the area's problems today....

Highfield Park went from an empty field to a forest of apartments in less than a decade. "That area, that came out of nowhere," says Hughes. "There was no history, no buildings existed, there was no one living there."

Foster MacKenzie, former president of the Nova Scotia Association of Architects, says during Highfield Park's development, he predicted the neighbourhood would quickly turn into a high-density slum: "Start erecting these high-density housing units, four and five storeys, very close together with very few amenities, and you start putting low- to middle-income families in those areas with lots of children, you're going to end up with problems."...

While it would be tempting to write off the area that many call The Dark Side, there is another side to Highfield-Pinecrest: a small band of community activists fighting the decades of neglect that have created a place where many fear to go out at night.

Zwanenburg, the priest, runs several outreach programs out of the basement of his small, white-painted, cinderblock church on Alfred Street. One is Youth United, which attracts up to 40 teenagers every Friday to play games, watch movies, eat, and just hang out. "We're not talking

---

Schwartz and DeKeseredy point out that another approach would be to develop **pre-emptive deterrence**, in which community organization efforts eliminate or reduce crime before it becomes necessary to use police force. This tactic aims at reducing the number of marginalized youth, those who feel they are not part of society and have nothing to lose by committing crime.[101]

They point out that as left realism moves in this direction, an analysis is needed of the left realist position on crime control. In addition, left realists need to respond to issues raised by feminists,[102] and to suggest responses critical criminologists might explore, such as those proposed by peacemaking criminology.

Street crime is real, and the fear of violence among the lower classes has allowed the right wing to seize law and order as a political issue. Most gang kids prey on members of their own race and class, and are happy to keep the proceeds for themselves. Gang kids are capitalists, hustling their way to obtain coveted symbols of success.

Left realists want crime-control policy to build on the work of strain theorists, social ecologists, and other mainstream views. Community-based efforts seem to hold the most promise as crime control techniques.

Left realism has been critiqued as legitimizing the existing power structure: By supporting existing definitions of law and justice, left realism suggests that the deviant and not the capitalist system is the cause of society's problems. However, left realists say it is unrealistic to think even a socialist state would lack a police force or system of laws and justice. While the *Criminal Code* represents relations of power in society, it also represents public opinion.

> **pre-emptive deterrence** An approach in left realism in which community organization efforts can reduce crime before it becomes necessary to use police force.

about saints," he says of the adults who work with the kids.

"We're talking about regular ordinary people that show respect and affection and affirmation."

"Most communities can learn from people up in this area," says police constable Randy Wood. "It's a very vibrant community that's sometimes not portrayed properly."...

Wood's job is to help residents any way he can. He doesn't normally make arrests or detain people; his role is simply to assist the community however he sees fit. One Wednesday a month, he ferries people from the local food bank to their apartments, via a police SUV filled with grocery bags....

MacLean oversaw the Highfield Park area for the last five years and knows the challenges facing the community. The community response officer model was piloted in Highfield Park, and its success led to implementation in other troubled Halifax areas.

MacLean says that while drugs, weapons, and violent crime are prevalent in the area, it's problematic to blanket it with that characterization because those crimes are committed by a small fraction of the population.

Most people just mind their own business.

Georgina Lee, 52, watched as the first apartments on Pinecrest Drive went up, and then the development of Highfield Park Drive. She moved to the neighbourhood with her infant son because, "It was cheaper rent than any place else."...

But while she sees all that is good in the neighbourhood, she has also seen the decline. "At one time, this neighbourhood, you could walk the street two, three, four o'clock in the morning and wouldn't think twice about it," she says. "But now you wouldn't. By the time, nine, 10 o'clock comes, you're not outside, because of the things going on in the area."

She knows her neighbourhood is labelled as a slum. "And that's the way it's going to stay."

But not if Sylvia Anthony has her way. Sometimes called "the mayor of Dartmouth North," the 71-year-old is a tireless volunteering machine, emblematic of the passion many have toward the area, where she has spent her entire life....

She also started a community paper, the *North Dartmouth Echo*, seven years ago, that focuses solely on good news stories from the area. She's providing a bit of positive bi-monthly counter-spin. "I mean you can't expect a community to be perfect. Nobody's perfect, nothing's perfect," says Anthony. "You couldn't find a better place to live in for resources, helping and caring individuals."...

On a Friday in early spring, back in the basement of the Holy Trinity Emmanuel church, dozens of young teenagers have come out for another night of Youth United. In the past, they've gone out for bowling, swimming at the Sportsplex, and for a night at the movies.

"We have a total enrolment of 48 kids now, which is pretty good seeing how the junior high only has 210 students," says Jenifer Fitzsimmons, creator of Youth United. "If they form that pride in their community, then they'll help make it a better place and maybe people will stand up and listen."

"At least we're not out roaming the streets looking for something to do, or out at the mall by ourselves," says Megan Vance, 15, who has come to the Friday night group since it started in September....

Read more about the King's investigation of police calls and take a multimedia tour of Highfield Park-Pinecrest at 902911 .kingsjournalism.com.

SOURCE: University of King's College Investigative Workshop comprising Ezra Black, Alex Boates, Tim van der Koii, Geoff Bird, Andrei Deszi, Lily Sangster, Schenley Brown, Brittney Edelman, Corbett Hancey, Dane Butler, and Patrick Odell.

Feminist Theory

Like so many theories in criminology, most of the efforts of radical theorists have been devoted to explaining male criminality.[103] To remedy this imbalance, feminist writers explain the cause of crime, gender differences in the crime rate, and the exploitation of female victims from a gendered perspective. Scholars usually hold one of two related philosophical orientations: **Marxist feminism** or radical feminism.

Marxist Feminism. The first group views gender inequality as stemming from the unequal power of men and women in a capitalist society. Gender inequality is a function of the exploitation of females by fathers and husbands; women are considered a commodity worth possessing, like land or money.[104] The origin of gender differences can be traced to the development of private property and male domination over the laws of inheritance.

Bernard Schissel, for example, says that violence by male youth against female youth originates largely within the confines of patriarchal, profit-driven culture. The subsequent feelings of powerlessness and depression increase the likelihood of violence against women, who are considered easy victims in an alienated culture.[105]

In this way, Marxist feminists link criminal behaviour patterns to the gender conflict created by the economic and social struggles common in post-industrial societies. Messerschmidt argues in *Capitalism, Patriarchy, and Crime* that capitalist society is marked by both patriarchy and class conflict. Capitalists control the labour of workers, while men control women

marxist feminism The view that gender inequality stems from the unequal power of men and women in capitalism, based on private property, male domination, and the exploitation of women.

both economically and biologically.[106] This "double marginality" explains why females in a capitalist society commit fewer crimes than males do: They are isolated in the family, with fewer opportunities to engage in elite deviance, and denied access to male-dominated street crimes.[107] Because capitalism renders women powerless, they are forced to commit less serious, non-violent, self-destructive crimes, such as drug abuse.

Powerlessness also increases the likelihood that women will become the target of violent acts,[108] as lower-class males shut out of the economic opportunity structure improve their self-image through acts involving violence or abuse of women. A significant percentage of female victims are attacked by a spouse or an intimate partner.

In *Masculinities and Crime,* Messerschmidt suggests that in every culture, males try to emulate what are considered to be ideal masculine behaviours,[109] which, in Western culture, means being authoritative, in charge, combative, and controlling. Failure to adapt to these roles leaves men feeling effeminate and unmanly. Crime is a good way for men to "do gender" because abusers believe it separates them from the weak and allows them to demonstrate physical bravery.

Radical Feminism.   In contrast, **radical feminism** views the cause of female crime as originating with the onset of male supremacy (patriarchy), the subsequent subordination of women, male aggression, and the efforts of men to control females sexually.[110] Radical feminists focus on social forces that shape women's lives and experiences to explain female criminality.[111] For example, the sexual victimization of girls is a function of male socialization because so many young males learn to be aggressive and exploitive of women in same-sex peer groups. On university campuses, peers encourage sexual violence against women whom they define as *teasers*, *pickups*, or *sluts*; a code of secrecy then protects the aggressors from retribution.[112] Sexual and physical exploitation of young girls may cause the girls to run away or abuse substances, both of which are labelled as deviant behaviour.[113]

A survey conducted by the Center for Research on Women at Wellesley College in Massachusetts found that 90 percent of adolescent girls are sexually harassed in school, almost 30 percent report having been pressured to "do something sexual," and 10 percent said they were forced to do something sexual.[114]

In a sense, the female criminal is a victim herself. Feminists have struggled to have youth prostitution looked at as a form of child abuse, and the prosecution of prostitution as re-victimizing young women. And in one notorious case, former judge David Ramsay was sentenced in 2004 for taking advantage of and molesting young Aboriginal girls. He knew his victim: The typical female inmate is Aboriginal, without skills, and a single mother who has a history of illegal drug dependency and childhood sexual abuse.[115]

The Wellesley survey of sexual harassment found that teachers and school officials ignore about 45 percent of complaints made by female students; school officials responded to reports of sexual harassment by asking the young victim,

"Do you like it?" and saying, "They must be doing it for a reason." Because agents of social control often choose to ignore reports of abuse and harassment, young girls may feel trapped and desperate.

Accordingly, exploitation acts as a trigger for the onset of delinquent and deviant behaviour. When female victims run away and abuse substances, reacting to abuse at home and school, their attempts at survival are labelled deviant, and victim blaming occurs. Research shows that a significant number (86 percent) of girls who had been sent to the hospital emergency room to be treated for sexual abuse later reported engaging in physical fighting as a teen or as an adult; also, many of these abused girls later formed a romantic attachment with an abusive partner. Many girls involved in delinquency, crime, and violence have themselves been the victims of violence in their youth and later as adults.[116]

One criticism is that radical feminism focuses on the problems and viewpoints of Caucasian, middle-class, heterosexual women, without taking into account the special interests of lesbians and women of colour.[117] It has been argued that the future of feminist criminology lies in developing a Marxist framework that recognizes the multiple, intersecting inequalities of gender, race, and class.[118]

How the Justice System Penalizes Women.   Radical feminists have said that the justice system contributes to the onset of female delinquency. From its inception, the juvenile justice system has viewed female delinquents as sexually precocious girls who need to be brought under control.

For example, writing on the "girl problem," Ruth Alexander described how working-class young women desiring autonomy and freedom in the 1920s were considered delinquents and placed in reformatories. These young girls were considered outlaws in a male-dominated society because they flouted the rules of appropriate behaviour applied to females in Victorian society. Girls who rebelled against parental authority or who engaged in inappropriate sexual behaviour were incarcerated to protect them from a career in prostitution.[119]

In fact, young women were much more likely to be prosecuted for sexual promiscuity under the *Juvenile Delinquents Act* than were young men, even though these girls had to be promiscuous with someone.

According to Steven Bittle, the current attempts to redefine how youth prostitution is dealt with under "secure care" legislation in various provinces can also be criticized for not dealing with the unequal power relations that give rise to the youth sex trade.[120] The pull of addiction, pimps/boyfriends, and peers, coupled with the lack of non-custodial alternatives, results in higher incarceration rates for these young women.[121]

> **radical feminism**   The view that female crime is caused by male patriarchy, and the subordination and control of women by men.

In a similar vein, a study of the early Los Angeles Juvenile Court found that in 1920, so-called delinquency experts identified young female "sex delinquents" as a major social problem. Civic leaders who were concerned about immorality mounted a eugenics and social hygiene campaign that identified the "sex delinquent" as a moral and sexual threat to society. These experts advocated a policy of eugenics, or sterilization, to prevent these inferior individuals from having children. Female police officers were hired to deal with girls under arrest and female judges to hear girls' cases in juvenile court; they also established a female detention centre and a girls' reformatory.

The majority of these delinquent girls were petitioned for either suspected sexual activity or behaviour that placed them at risk of sexual relations. Despite the limited seriousness of these charges, the majority of girls were detained before their trials and given a compulsory pelvic exam. Girls adjudged sexually delinquent on the basis of the exam were segregated from the merely incorrigible girls to prevent moral corruption. Those testing positive for venereal disease were confined in the Juvenile Hall hospital for usually from one to three months. More than 29 percent of these female adolescents were eventually committed to custodial institutions.[122]

Similar procedures were in place in Ontario under the *Female Refuges Act,* as women were incarcerated in the Belmont Refuge and the Mercer Reformatory for Women. In these institutions, they were subject to psycho-surgery, drug therapy, and confinement, often for the crime of being vagrant or drunk in public.

Looking at the judicial victimization of female delinquents, Meda Chesney-Lind has written extensively on how police in Honolulu were more likely both to arrest female adolescents for sexual activity (74 percent), and to ignore the same behaviour among male delinquents (27 percent).[123] The length of girls' detention was three times that of the boys, and girls were more likely both to be sent to a detention facility before trial and to undergo physical examinations (70 percent versus 15 percent). Because female adolescents have a much narrower range of acceptable behaviour than do males, any sign of misbehaviour in girls is seen as a substantial challenge to authority and perpetuates the double standard of sexual inequality. Female delinquency is viewed as relatively more serious than male delinquency, and therefore is more likely to be severely sanctioned.

Power-Control Theory.   Although the power-control theory is a control-based theory, John Hagan created a radical feminist model that uses class and gender differences to explain the onset of criminality. The most significant statements are expanded in Hagan's 1989 book, *Structural Criminology.*

Crime and delinquency rates are a function of two factors: (1) class position (power) and (2) family functions (control).[124] Within the family, parents reproduce the power relationships they hold in the workplace. The class position and work experiences of parents influence the criminality of children.[125] A position of dominance at work is equated with control in the household.

In **paternalistic** families, fathers assume the traditional role of breadwinners, while mothers have menial jobs or remain at home to supervise domestic matters. Within the home, mothers are expected to control the behaviour of their daughters while granting greater freedom to their sons. In such a home, the parent–daughter relationship can be viewed as a preparation for the "cult of domesticity," while boys are freer to deviate because they are not subject to maternal control. Consequently, male siblings exhibit a higher degree of delinquent behaviour than do their sisters.

Conversely, in **egalitarian** families—those in which the husband and the wife share similar positions of power at home and in the workplace—daughters gain a kind of freedom that reflects reduced parental control. These families produce daughters whose law-violating behaviour mirrors that of their brothers. Ironically, these kinds of relationships also occur in female-headed households with absent fathers. Similarly, when both fathers and mothers hold equally valued managerial positions, the similarity between the rates of their daughters' and sons' delinquency is greatest.

By implication, middle-class girls are the most likely to violate the law because they are less closely controlled than their lower-class counterparts. In homes in which both parents hold positions of power, girls are more likely to have the same expectations of career success as their brothers. Consequently, siblings of both sexes will be socialized to take risks and engage in other behaviour related to delinquency. Power-control theory, then, implies that middle-class youth of both sexes will have higher overall crime rates than their lower-class peers (although lower-class males may commit the more serious crimes).

Power-control theory has received a great deal of attention in criminology because it encourages studying gender differences, class position, and the structure of the family. Some evidence supports the view that parental power and control in the workplace increases male antisocial behaviour, and that in more egalitarian families, female crime rates are higher, a key element of power-control theory: Females in paternalistic households have been socialized to fear legal sanctions more than their brothers have.[126]

Not all research is as supportive.[127] Although its basic premises have not yet been thoroughly tested, some critics have questioned the assumption that power and control variables can explain crime.[128] More specifically, critics fail to replicate the finding that upper-class kids are more likely to deviate than are their lower-class peers or that class and power interact to produce delinquency.[129]

> **paternalistic**   The characterization of leaders in government or organizations as father figures, while others are treated as children.
>
> **egalitarian**   The description of an equal sharing of authority and power, for example, between the two partners in a family.

However, empirical testing may produce further refinement of the theory. For example, Kevin Thompson found few gender-based supervision and behaviour differences in worker-, manager-, or owner-dominated households.[130]

However, parental supervision practices were quite different in families headed by parents who are chronically unemployed, and these findings conformed to the power-control model. The research indicates that the concept of class used by Hagan may need to be reconsidered: Power-control theory may actually explain criminality among the truly disadvantaged and not among the working class.

Deconstructionism

Radical criminologists often use **deconstructionism**, which focuses on the critical analysis of communication and language in legal codes. Rules and regulations are analyzed to determine whether they contain language and content that institutionalizes relations of power: gender, ethnicity, and social class.

Deconstructionists rely on various types of discourse analysis, such as **semiotics**, to conduct their research efforts. Semiotics refers to seeing language as signs that indicate more than the mere meaning of words. For example, sports rely very heavily on the use of signs, and to become a sports expert means becoming familiar with terminology, such as *blitzing the quarterback* and *scoring a hat trick*. These terms convey meaning that is far greater than the words themselves and provide images to sports fans familiar with the signs that would be lost on others.

Deconstructionists believe that language is value-laden and contains the same sorts of inequities present in the rest of the social structure.[131] For example, in deconstructing relations of gender and power, anthropologist Shirley Lee (of the University of Manitoba) used women's narratives to understand their perceptions of menstrual cycle changes. She found that most women accepted the premenstrual syndrome (PMS) label and interpreted their experience within the realm of sickness. However, a small group of women conceptualized their cyclic changes in a more positive way and resisted interpreting their experience as sickness. They tended to be more critical of society's labelling.[132]

However, while there is a class of symptoms labelled Premenstrual Dysphoric Disorder (PMDD), PMS might be the product of deviant stereotyping. Psychologists Offman and Kleinplatz, argue that PMDD is a socially constructed diagnosis rather than a psychiatric disorder. This deconstruction of physiological experience as pathology is investigated for its ability to create a discourse that medicalizes and deviantizes women's experiences of sexuality.[133]

Similarly, we can apply an analysis of discourse to various social issues for the purpose of dissecting power relations. Certain groups are defined as dangerous, as in racial profiles that result in discriminatory enforcement. The police are able to use discourse to create constructions of street gangs, for example, which are often based on race and gender stereotypes.[134] The resulting discrimination reinforces the racism

and inequality that drove Aboriginal youth to gangs in the first place, as Jana Grekul of the University of Alberta shows.[135]

Gladys Symons (of the University of Quebec) also conducted intensive interviews with police, this time in Montreal, where police routinely deal with ethnic gangs. What she found was that police personnel rarely raised the racial/ethnic dimension in conversation, using discursive strategies to deny the significance of the racial/ethnic question for the street gang phenomenon. Said one policeman, "For myself it was very clear, the police did not apprehend a black, they arrested a thief. I had to get that into everyone's head."[136]

Discourse on critical social issues is also a way in which the state legitimates social policy, as Kathryn Campbell and her colleagues at the University of Ottawa show. For example, since the mid-1980s, successive federal governments debated amendments to the *Young Offenders Act*, and in the process constructed the problem of youth crime.[137] The significance of this is evident when the conceptualization of youth crime is looked at historically. In the early 20th century, youth crime was seen as more of a welfare problem, and the whole family context was seen as part of the solution. By the 1980s, however, youth crime comes to be seen more punitively, first with changes to the *Young Offenders Act*, and then the development of the *Youth Criminal Justice* Act in the early 21st century.

Restorative Justice

As an outgrowth of critical criminology, restorative justice is based on a social view of crime as an injury to personal and community relations. Accordingly, **restorative justice** theorists and practitioners emphasize the need for a holistic response to crime, rather than a focus on abstract legal violation and punishments of individual actions.

In his pioneering work on how the retributive and restorative justice models can be distinguished from each other, Howard Zehr stated that crime is a violation of relationships: "Justice involves the victim, the offender, and the community in a search for solutions which promote repair, reconciliation, and reassurance."[138]

Zehr's emphasis on viewing criminal behaviour as a violation of relationships serves as the basis of restorative justice programming throughout Canada. Distinct from the legal

deconstructionism The critical analysis of language in legal codes and regulations to see how content causes racism or sexism to become institutionalized.

semiotics Language comprising a set of signs that describe the world by conveying meanings understood by their audience.

restorative justice Mediation and conflict resolution as an alternative to the formal court system to heal personal injury and community relations.

definition of crime, restorative justice rests on understanding the causes of conflict, and then exercising compassion when responding to criminal justice and social justice issues.

According to the legal view, society consists of an aggregation of people over which the state has jurisdiction. Legally, this aggregation possesses group qualities: common meanings and values, sustained interaction, and symbolic bonds. In the restorative view, the bureaucratic nature of society is not capable of manifesting such social qualities. It is only in smaller, less formal, and more cohesive social groups, such as families, congregations, and residential communities that such qualities are found. Therefore, the potential for restoring social relations damaged by crime is to be found not in the state but in social groups, in the community.

Restorative justice theorists, such as Sullivan and Tifft, and practitioners such as Mark Umbreit, are critical of the traditional role that the state has played in the criminal justice system.[139] The needs of victims, offenders, and communities are not met except in smaller, less formal, and more cohesive social groups. Only in groups where strong interpersonal communication is facilitated and encouraged to take place can social justice–related issues be successfully addressed. The potential for restoring social relationships damaged by crime is to be found not in the state, but in communities.[140]

In small northern Aboriginal communities where most inhabitants know each other, sentencing circles are usually held in a band hall or a church. The setting is informal, with participants, including the judge, in casual attire. The space is free from the ritualistic legal language and furniture of the regular courtroom. Participants usually include the offender; the victim; their families, friends, and support systems; others from the community (e.g., alcohol/drug treatment specialists); and the judge, prosecutor, and defence attorney.[141] In this way, collective life draws its strength not from threat, coercion, and fear, but from motivation, based on trust, participation, and support.[142]

In the restorative view, the state and formal legal institutions inhibit qualities that encourage healing and harmony. In addition, proponents say that individuals who are typically marginalized by the state and the formal legal institutions, individuals who hold little or no power or economic clout, will be included in the criminal justice process.

Restorative justice is in opposition to the adversary system, whose response to crime has been almost exclusively punitive. In attempting to ensure equal protection under the law, the procedural design of the adversarial system limits consideration of the unique personal and social qualities of particular crimes. As a result of the adversarial system's preoccupation with the protection of individual rights, it encourages the accused to deny, justify, or excuse his or her actions rather than accept responsibility.

In addition, the central role of trained professionals in the adversarial process, such as prosecution and defence attorneys, severely limits the possibility of direct exchanges

---

EXHIBIT 9.2

The Basic Principles of Restorative Justice

- Crime is an offence against human relationships.
- Victims and the community are central to justice processes.
- The first priority of justice processes is to assist victims.
- The second priority is to restore the community.
- The offender has a responsibility to victims and the community for crimes committed.
- Stakeholders share responsibilities through partnerships for action.

SOURCE: Adapted from Anne Seymour, National Victim Assistance Academy, *Restorative Justice/Community Justice* (Washington DC; National Victim Assistance Academy, 2001).

---

between the victim and the offender. Because the adversaries are narrowly defined as the "accused" and the "state," little consideration can be given to community concerns and participation. Restorative justice is a direct response to the inadequacies of the adversarial process.

Restorative justice is guided by three principles: (1) community ownership of conflict (including crime), (2) material and symbolic reparation for victims and the community, and (3) social reintegration of the offender (see Exhibit 9.2). The restorative process begins by redefining crime in terms of a conflict among the offender, the victim, and the affected constituencies, such as families, schools, workplaces, and so on. Therefore, the resolution takes place within the context in which the conflict originally occurred rather than being transferred to a specialized institution that has no social connection to the community. By maintaining ownership over the conflict, the community is able to express its shared outrage about the offence, which can be communicated to the offender. The victim is given a chance to voice his or her story, and the offender can directly communicate the need for social reintegration and treatment.

The restoration process depends on encouraging people to discuss problems, and developing an informal communicative exchange among victim, offender, and community. Although restorative processes differ in structure and style, they include a recognition of the injury to personal and social relations, a determination and acceptance of responsibility (ideally accompanied by a statement of remorse), a commitment to both material and symbolic reparation (e.g., an apology), and a determination of community support and assistance for both victim and offender. The intended result of the restorative process is to repair injuries suffered by the victim and the community while ensuring reintegration of the offender.

One of the first contemporary victim–offender mediation programs in the world was established in Kitchener, Ontario, in 1974, and since then, an explosion of restorative

Comparative Criminology
Practising Restorative Justice Abroad

The restorative justice philosophy is catching on and is widely practised abroad, as evidenced here in a discussion of just a few of the many programs found around the world.

South Africa

After 50 years of oppressive white rule in South Africa, the race-dividing apartheid policy was abolished in the early 1990s, and Nelson Mandela, leader of the African National Congress (ANC), was elected president. Some Black leaders wanted revenge for the political murders carried out during the apartheid era, but Mandela established the Truth and Reconciliation Commission. Rather than seeking vengeance for the crimes, this government agency investigated the atrocities with the mandate of granting amnesty to those individuals who confessed their roles in the violence and could prove that their actions served some political motive and were not based on personal factors such as greed or jealousy. Supporters of the commission believed that this approach would help heal the nation's wounds and prevent years of racial and ethnic strife. Mandela, who had been unjustly jailed for 27 years by the regime, had reason to desire vengeance. Yet, he wanted to move the country forward after first establishing the truth of what had happened in the past. Though many South Africans, including some ANC members, believe that the commission is too lenient, Mandela's attempts at reconciliation have prevailed. The commission is a model of restoration over revenge.

Australia

The justice system in Australia makes use of the conferencing process to divert offenders from the justice system. This process offers offenders the opportunity to attend a conference to discuss and resolve their offence instead of being charged and appearing in court. (Those who deny guilt are not offered conferencing.) The conference, normally lasting one to two hours, is attended by the victims and their supporters, the defendant and his or her supporters, and other concerned parties. The conference coordinator focuses the discussion on condemning the act without condemning the character of the actor. Offenders are asked to tell their side of the story, what happened, how they have felt about the crime, and what they think should be done. The victims and others are asked to describe the physical, financial, and emotional consequences of the crime. This discussion may lead the offenders, their families, and their friends to experience the shame of the act, prompting an apology to the victim. A plan of action is developed and signed by key participants. The plan may include the offender paying compensation to the victim, doing work for the victim or the community, or similar solutions. It is the responsibility of the conference participants to determine the outcomes that are most appropriate for these particular victims and these particular offenders.

Ireland

The Nenagh Community Reparation Project is managed by a local committee representing different community interests in partnership with the Probation and Welfare Service. It began on the initiative of Judge Michael Reilly, who, with the cooperation of the community and various agencies, has sought to use reparation in his court. In cases where an offender has admitted guilt, judges can use their discretion to offer the offender the choice of either the normal course of jail or participation in the community reparation project. At this point, the court adjourns for approximately 30 minutes while the probation officer explains the project to the offender. If the offender decides to participate in the project, a meeting will be called in the near future.

This meeting is attended by the offender, two panel members representing the community, the police officers who have been involved in the case, and the probation officer. If the crime involves victims, they are also invited to attend the meeting, although their participation is not mandatory. At the meeting, offenders are asked to explain the circumstances of the offence, why it happened, how they felt about it then, and how they feel about their actions now. Together, the group decides how the offender might make reparation to the victim and/or the community for the damage caused by the offence.

Once agreement is reached about the form of the reparation, a contract is drawn up that sets out treatment courses the offender will be expected to take (for example, treatment for alcoholism, substance abuse, anger management, and so on, as appropriate). Reparation may include letters of apology to the victim, monetary restitution, and other proportionate and appropriate activities. Contracts generally cover a period of approximately six months and are monitored by the probation officer. If the terms of the contract are successfully completed, the record of the offence will be dropped. If the terms are not met, the case will go back to court and proceed in the normal manner.

Critical Thinking

Restorative justice may be the model that best serves alternative sanctions. How can this essentially humanistic approach be sold to the general public that now supports more punitive sanctions? For example, would it be reasonable to expect that using restorative justice with non-violent offenders frees up resources to deal with the relatively few dangerous people in the criminal population? Explain.

SOURCES: Leena Kurki, *Incorporating Restorative and Community Justice into American Sentencing and Corrections* (Washington, DC: National Institute of Justice, 1999); Australian Government, Australian Institute of Criminology, "Restorative Justice: An Australian Perspective," www.aic.gov.au/rjustice/australia.html. Accessed August 4, 2004; Restorative Justice in Ireland, Nenagh Community Reparation Project, Co. Tipperary: www.extern.org/restorative; John W. De Gruchy, *Reconciliation: Restoring Justice* (Minneapolis: Fortress, 2002).

justice programs has occurred around the world.[143] The continued growth of mediation programs in Canada is due to restorative principles of sentencing incorporated into the *Criminal Code* as part of the fundamental purpose of sentencing (section 718), as well as alternative measures also incorporated into the Code (section 717).

However, although widespread agreement exists among proponents of restorative justice as to what constitutes restoration, not all believe that restorative justice can be achieved within the context of the existing social structure.

Canadian legal theorist Robert C. Depew states that in some non-Aboriginal community settings, traditional Aboriginal restorative justice practices may not be suitable.[144] Additionally, in Aboriginal communities where traditional cultural practices have been lost, it may be impossible to follow an Aboriginal restorative model. In her criticism of restorative justice, Ruth Morris states that for restorative practices to be truly successful, individuals must address structural issues that promote racism and classism, and that significant social structural changes must occur for the true potential of restorative justice to be realized.[145]

Some argue that the social qualities of the group can be recreated within such processes as family group conferencing, victim–offender reconciliation, and sentencing circles. The latter suggest that such social qualities cannot be effectively recreated; rather, they must exist before the restorative process begins.

The effectiveness of restorative justice ultimately depends on the stake a person has in the community or a particular social group. Persons who do not value group membership will be unlikely to accept responsibility, show remorse, or repair the injuries caused by their actions. Existing restorative justice programs, such as mediation programs, will be unable to reach effectively those persons who are disengaged from all community institutions. Therefore, the relative effectiveness of existing restorative justice programs provides us with a measurement of the need for structural change.[146]

Exhibit 9.3 summarizes concerns that some victim advocacy groups have voiced about the focus of restorative justice programs, and the previous Comparative Criminology box discusses a few international restorative justice initiatives.

Peacemaking Criminology

One of the newer movements in radical criminological theory is **peacemaking** criminology, which is based on principles that promote increased understanding and a return to a condition of wholeness.[147] The transformation of human beings and the transformation of the Canadian criminal justice system are actively promoted.[148] Peacemaking criminology theorists believe that the main purpose of criminology is to promote a peaceful and just society. Peacemaking draws its inspiration from religious and philosophical teachings ranging from Quakerism to Zen.

EXHIBIT 9.3

Victim Concerns about Restorative Justice

- Victims are props in a drama focused on the offender.
- A victim may press a blaming rather than restorative shaming agenda.
- Criminal defendants have more rights than victims in the legal process.
- Listening to the offender's story offends a victim's claim not to be "victimized by the process."
- Some victims just want to put the incident behind them and retrieve their stolen property.
- Active participation is more emotionally demanding than that of witness in a conventional trial.

SOURCE: Adapted from Michael E. Smith, *What Future for "Public Safety" and "Restorative Justice" in Community Corrections* (Washington, DC: National Institute of Justice, 2001).

Moving to a culture of cooperation and peacemaking shifts the focus from violence and repression to non-violence and emancipation.[149] Peacemakers view the efforts of the state to punish and control as crime-encouraging rather than crime-discouraging:

> The violent punishing acts of the state and its controlling professions are of the same genre as the violent acts of individuals. In each instance, these acts reflect an attempt to monopolize human interaction.[150]

Sullivan suggests that correcting and punishing criminals in the context of our conflict-ridden society is a futile act and instead promotes the idea that mutual aid rather than coercive punishment is the key to a harmonious society. In *Restorative Justice,* Sullivan and Tifft reaffirm their belief that society must seek humanitarian forms of justice without resorting to brutal punishments:

> By allowing feelings of vengeance or retribution to narrow our focus on the harmful event and the person responsible for it—as others might focus solely on a sin committed and the "sinner"—we tell ourselves we are taking steps to free ourselves from the effects of the harm or the sin in question. But, in fact, we are putting ourselves in a servile position with respect to life, human growth, and the further enjoyment of relationships with others.[151]

Mutual aid rather than coercive punishment is the key to a harmonious society. Today, advocates of the peacemaking movement, such as Pepinsky and Quinney, try to find

peacemaking A branch of conflict theory that stresses humanism, mediation, and conflict resolution as a means to end crime.

Social Conflict Theories

Theory	Major Premise	Strengths
Conflict theory	Crime is a function of class conflict. The definition of the law is controlled by people who hold social and political power.	Accounts for class differentials in the crime rate. Shows how class conflict influences behaviour.
Marxist theory	The capitalist means of production creates class conflict. Crime is a rebellion of the lower class. The criminal justice system is an agent of class warfare.	Accounts for the associations between economic structure and crime rates.
Instrumental Marxist theory	Criminals are revolutionaries. The real crimes are sexism, racism, and profiteering.	Broadens the definition of crime and demystifies or explains the historical development of law.
Structural Marxist theory	The law is designed to sustain the capitalist economic system.	Explains the existence of white-collar crime and business control laws.
Radical feminist theory	The capitalist system creates patriarchy, which oppresses women.	Explains gender bias, violence against women, and repression.
Power-control theory	Gender differences in crime are a function of economic power (class position, one- versus two-earner families) and parental control (paternalistic versus egalitarian families).	Encourages a new approach to the study of criminality, one that includes gender differences, class position, and the structure of the family.
Left realism	Crime is a function of relative deprivation; criminals prey on the poor.	Represents a compromise between conflict and traditional criminology.
Deconstructionism	Language controls the meaning and use of the law.	Provides a critical analysis of meaning.
Peacemaking	Peace and humanism can reduce crime; conflict resolution strategies can work.	Offers a new approach to crime control through mediation.

humanist solutions to crime and other social problems.[152] Rather than punishment and prison, they advocate such policies as mediation and conflict resolution, closely related to the principles of restorative justice.

True justice will be attained only when victims are understood in a holistic way that promotes connectedness and positive growth.[153] This process requires that individuals develop and utilize strong communication skills, resist **marginalization**, challenge existing social structures that promote violence, and make the administration of justice more compassionate.

Today, advocates of the peacemaking movement try to find and apply humanist solutions to violence or conflict situations, encouraging active communication and positive conflict resolution, responding to the experiential and subjective realities shaping people's perspectives and needs.[154]

The Canadian criminal justice system must therefore respond to conflict situations in ways that promote greater understanding among those who have been harmed by crime. Sustainable peace can be established. Violent conflict situations cannot be avoided; however, what can change are the ways that individuals and communities respond to unjust and harmful occurrences. Much literature has been developed in this area, and it constitutes a significant new direction in critical criminology.[155]

SUMMARY

Social conflict theorists view crime as a function of the conflict that exists in society. Social conflict has its theoretical basis in the works of Karl Marx, as interpreted by Willem Bonger, Ralf Dahrendorf, and George Vold. Conflict theorists suggest that crime in any society is caused by class conflict. Laws are created by those in power to protect their rights and interests. All criminal acts have political undertones. Richard Quinney has called this concept the social reality of crime. One of conflict theory's most important premises is that the justice system is biased and designed to protect the wealthy. Research has not been unanimous in supporting this point.

Marxist criminology views the competitive nature of the capitalist system as a major cause of crime. The poor commit crimes because of their frustration, anger, and need. The wealthy engage in illegal acts because they are used to competition and because they must do so to keep their positions in

marginalization When people live in areas conducive to crime, which leads to decreased commitment, and a weakened bond to society.

society. Marxist scholars have attempted to show that the law is designed to protect the wealthy and powerful and to control the poor, have-not members of society. Branches of radical theory include instrumental Marxism and structural Marxism (see Concept Summary 9.1 for a summary of these theories).

Research on Marxist theory focuses on how the system of justice was designed and how it operates to further class interests. Quite often, this research uses historical analysis to show how the capitalist classes have exerted their control over the police, courts, and correctional agencies. Both Marxist and conflict criminology have been heavily criticized by consensus criminologists.

During the 1990s, new forms of conflict theory emerged. Feminist writers drew attention to the influence of patriarchal society on crime; left realism took a centrist position on crime by showing crime's rational and destructive nature; peacemaking criminology brought a call for humanism to criminology; and deconstructionism looked at the symbolic meaning of law and culture.

THINKING LIKE A CRIMINOLOGIST

A local school board has just announced a plan to have police officers patrol schools daily with drug-sniffing dogs. Despite the lack of evidence of a drug problem, the dogs will be sniffing lockers, gym bags, and people. If any drugs are found, criminal charges may be filed against students. You are a lawyer and a member of the British Columbia Civil Liberties Association. Concerned students come to you for advice. They want you to answer the following questions:

1. Are civil liberties being violated? If so, which ones? Provide some details.
2. What type of legal or other action would you advise your clients to take? Estimate their chances of success.

SOURCE: Adapted from Rights Talk: Students and Civil Liberties at School, "Legal Rights: Search and Seizure," B.C. Civil Liberties Association, http://bccla.org/our_work/rightstalk/ (accessed May 15, 2005).

KEY TERMS

conflict theory p. 284
correctionalist p. 292
dangerous classes p. 289
deconstructionism p. 304
egalitarian p. 303
instrumental Marxism p. 294
left realism p. 299

marginalization p. 308
Marxist feminism p. 301
norm resistance p. 289
paternalistic p. 303
peacemaking p. 307
pre-emptive deterrence p. 300
privilege p. 294

radical feminism p. 302
restorative justice p. 304
semiotics p. 304
social reality of crime p. 287
structural Marxism p. 295
surplus value p. 293

DOING RESEARCH ON THE WEB

Before you answer the questions in the Thinking Like a Criminologist box above, you might want to think about the victims of predatory criminals.

Should we use harsh punishments to bring down the crime rate? Would they work with chronic offenders?

The National Center for Policy Analysis has a conservative take on this issue: see www.ncpa.org/pub/bg148.

CRITICAL THINKING QUESTIONS

1. How would a person with conservative views reply to a call for more restorative justice? How would a restorative justice advocate respond to a conservative person's call for more prisons?
2. How would a power-control theorist explain recent drops in the crime rate?

3. If Marx were alive today, what would he think about the prosperity enjoyed by the working class in industrial societies? Might he alter his vision of the capitalist system?
4. How can restorative justice be sold as an alternative sanction when the public supports more

punitive sanctions? For example, is it feasible for people to believe that using restorative justice with non-violent offenders frees up resources for the relatively few dangerous people in the criminal population? Explain.

NOTES

1. Michael Lynch, "Rediscovering Criminology: Lessons from the Marxist Tradition," in *Marxist Sociology: Surveys of Contemporary Theory and Research*, ed. Donald McQuarie and Patrick McGuire (New York: General Hall Press, 1994).

2. Michael Lynch and W. Byron Groves, *A Primer in Radical Criminology*, 2nd ed. (Albany, NY: Harrow and Heston, 1989), 32–33.

3. Richard A. Wright, "Left Out? The Coverage of Critical Perspectives in Introductory Criminology Textbooks, 1990–1999," *Critical Criminology* 9, 1–2 (2000): 101–122.

4. See, generally, Karl Marx and Friedrich Engels, *Capital: A Critique of Political Economy*, trans. E. Aveling (Chicago: Charles Kern, 1906); Karl Marx, *Selected Writings in Sociology and Social Philosophy*, trans. P.B. Bottomore (New York: McGraw-Hill, 1956). For a general discussion of Marxist thought, see Lynch and Groves, *A Primer in Radical Criminology*, 6–26.

5. Karl Marx, *Grundrisse: Introduction to the Critique of Political Economy*, trans. Martin Nicolaus (New York: Vintage, 1973), 106–107.

6. Karl Marx, "Population, Crime and Pauperism," in Karl Marx and Friedrich Engels, *Ireland and the Irish Question* (Moscow: Progress, 1859, reprinted 1971), 92.

7. Friedrich Engels, *The Condition of the Working Class in England in 1844* (London: Allen & Unwin, 1950).

8. James Short and F. Ivan Nye, "Extent of Undetected Delinquency: Tentative Conclusions," *Journal of Criminal Law, Criminology, and Police Science* 49 (1958): 296–302.

9. For a general view, see David Friedrichs, "Crime, Deviance and Criminal Justice: In Search of a Radical Humanistic Perspective," *Humanity and Society* 6 (1982): 200–226.

10. Edwin Lemert, *Social Pathology* (New York: McGraw-Hill, 1951); Howard Becker, *Outsiders: Studies in the Sociology of Deviance* (New York: Macmillan, 1963).

11. Alexander Liazos, "The Poverty of the Sociology of Deviance: Nuts, Sluts and Perverts," *Social Problems* 20 (1972): 103–120.

12. See, generally, Robert Meier, "The New Criminology: Continuity in Criminological Theory," *Journal of Criminal Law and Criminology* 67 (1977): 461–469.

13. David Greenberg, ed., *Crime and Capitalism* (Palo Alto, CA: Mayfield Publishing, 1981), 3.

14. Steve Hewitt, *Spying 101: The RCMP's Secret Activities at Canadian Universities, 1917–1997* (Toronto: University of Toronto Press, 2002); S. Hewitt, "'Information Believed True': RCMP Security Intelligence Activities on Canadian University Campuses and the Controversy Surrounding Them, 1961–71," *Canadian Historical Review* 81, 2 (2000): 191–228; Gary Kinsman, Dieter K. Buse, and Mercedes Steedman, eds., *Whose National Security? Canadian State Surveillance and the Creation of Enemies* (Toronto: Between the Lines 2000); Steve Hewitt, "Reforming the Canadian Security State: The Royal Canadian Mounted Police Security Service and the 'Key Sectors' Program," *Intelligence and National Security* 17, 4 (2002): 165–184.

15. William Chambliss and Robert Seidman, *Law, Order and Power* (Reading, MA: Addison-Wesley, 1971), 503.

16. John Braithwaite, "Retributivism, Punishment and Privilege," in *Punishment and Privilege*, eds. W. Byron Groves and Graeme Newman, 55–66 (Albany, NY: Harrow and Heston, 1986).

17. Austin Turk, "Class, Conflict and Criminology," *Sociological Focus* 10 (1977): 209–220.

18. Karen Swol, "Private Security and Public Policing in Canada," *Juristat* 18 13, 1998.

19. Daniel Georges-Abeyie, "Race, Ethnicity, and the Spatial Dynamic: Toward a Realistic Study of Black Crime, Crime Victimization, and Criminal Justice Processing of Blacks," *Social Justice* 16 (1989): 35–54.

20. John Hagan and Celesta Albonetti, "Race, Class and the Perception of Criminal Injustice in America," *American Journal of Sociology* 88 (1982): 329–355.

21. Richard Quinney, *The Social Reality of Crime* (Boston: Little, Brown, 1970), 15–23.

22. Austin Turk, *Criminality and Legal Order* (Chicago: Rand McNally, 1969), 58.

23. Lynch and Groves, *A Primer in Radical Criminology*, 2nd ed., 38.

24. Andrea McCalla and Vic Satzewich, "Settler Capitalism and the Construction of Immigrants and 'Indians' as Racialized Others," in *Crimes of Colour: Racialization and the Criminal Justice System in Canada*, eds. Wendy Chan and Kiran Mirchandani (Peterborough, ON: Broadview Press, 2002); "Mediation Offered in Kanesatake Standoff," *The Globe and Mail*, June 15, 2004; "Fire Damages Kanesatake Police Station," Canadian Press, June 11, 2004.

25. Howard Ramos, "What Causes Canadian Aboriginal Protest? Examining Resources, Opportunities and Identity, 1951–2000," *The Canadian Journal of Sociology* 31, 2 (2006): 211–234; Rima Wilkes, "First Nation Politics: Deprivation, Resources, and Participation in Collective Action," *Sociological Inquiry* 74, 4 (2004): 570–589; see also A.J. Orkin, "When the Law Breaks Down: Aboriginal Peoples in Canada and Governmental Defiance of the Rule of Law," *Osgoode Hall LJ* 41 (2003): 445.

26. Austin Turk, *Criminality and Legal Order* (Chicago: Rand McNally, 1969).

27. David McDowall, "Poverty and Homicide in Detroit, 1926–1978," *Victims and Violence* 1 (1986): 23–34; see also David McDowall, "Firearm Availability and Homicide Rates in Detroit, 1951–1986," *Social Forces* (1991) 69 (4): 1085–1101.

28. Judith Blau and Peter Blau, "The Cost of Inequality: Metropolitan Structure and Violent Crime," *American Sociological Review* 147 (1982): 114–129; Richard Block, "Community Environment and Violent Crime," *Criminology* 17 (1979): 46–57; Robert Sampson, "Structural Sources of Variation in Race-Age-Specific Rates of Offending across Major U.S. Cities," *Criminology* 23 (1985): 647–673.

29. Kate E. Pickett, Jessica Mookherjee, and Richard G. Wilkinson, "Adolescent Birth Rates, Total Homicides, and Income Inequality in Rich Countries," *American Journal of Public Health* 95, 7 (2005): 1181–1183.

30. David Jacobs and David Britt, "Inequality and Police Use of Deadly Force: An Empirical Assessment of a Conflict Hypothesis," *Social Problems* 26 (1979): 403–412.

31. Alan Lizotte, "Extra-Legal Factors in Chicago's Criminal Courts: Testing the Conflict Model of Criminal Justice," *Social Problems* 25 (1978): 564–580.

32. Terance Miethe and Charles Moore, "Racial Differences in Criminal Processing: The Consequences of Model Selection on Conclusions about Differential Treatment," *Sociological Quarterly* 27 (1987): 217–237.

33. Bryan Hogeveen, "Toward 'Safer' and 'Better' Communities?: Canada's Youth Criminal Justice Act, Aboriginal Youth and the Processes of Exclusion," *Critical Criminology* 13, 3 (2005): 287–305.

34. Myriam S. Denov and Kathryn M. Campbell, "Criminal Injustice. Understanding the Causes, Effects, and Responses to Wrongful Conviction in Canada," *Journal of Contemporary Criminal Justice* 21, 3 (2005): 224–249.

35. Gail Kellough and Scot Wortley, "Remand for Plea: Bail Decisions and Plea Bargaining as Commensurate Decisions," *British Journal of Criminology* 42 (2002): 186–210; Yasmin Jiwani, "The Criminalization of 'Race,' the Racialization of Crime," in *Crimes of Colour:*

Racialization and the Criminal Justice System in Canada, ed. Wendy Chan and Kiran Mirchandani (Peterborough, ON: Broadview Press, 2002).

36. Ron Melchers, "Do Toronto Police Engage in Racial Profiling?" *Canadian Review of Criminology and Criminal Justice* 7 (2003): 347–366; Scot Wortley and Julian Tanner, "Data, Denials, and Confusion: The Racial Profiling Debate in Toronto," *Canadian Review of Criminology and Criminal Justice* (2003): 367–389; Alan D. Gold, "Media Hype, Racial Profiling, and Good Science," *Canadian Review of Criminology and Criminal Justice* (2003): 391–399.

37. Douglas Smith, Christy Visher, and Laura Davidson, "Equity and Discretionary Justice: The Influence of Race on Police Arrest Decisions," *Journal of Criminal Law and Criminology* 75 (1984): 234–249.

38. Thomas Arvanites, "Increasing Imprisonment: A Function of Crime or Socioeconomic Factors?" *American Journal of Criminal Justice* 17 (1992): 19–38.

39. Nancy Wonders, "Determinate Sentencing: A Feminist and Postmodern Story," *Justice Quarterly* 13 (1996): 610–648.

40. Michael Leiber, Anne Woodrick, and E. Michele Roudebush, "Religion, Discriminatory Attitudes and the Orientations of Juvenile Justice Personnel: A Research Note," *Criminology* 33 (1995): 431–447.

41. Michael Leiber and Katherine Jamieson, "Race and Decision Making Within Juvenile Justice: The Importance of Context," *Journal of Quantitative Criminology* 11 (1995): 363–388.

42. Dragan Milovanovic, "Postmodern Criminology: Mapping the Terrain," *Justice Quarterly* 13 (1996): 567–610.

43. Richard Greenleaf and Lonn Lanza-Kaduce, "Sophistication, Organization and Authority-Subject Conflict: Rediscovering and Unraveling Turk's Theory of Norm Resistance," *Criminology* 33 (1995): 565–585.

44. Ab Currie, *Research Report: The New Brunswick Aboriginal Duty Counsel Project* (Ottawa: Department of Justice, 2000).

45. For a summary of this and other recommendations, see Shelley Trevethan, Nancy Steele, and Lil Krstic, *Selected Annotated Bibliography: Aboriginal Justice and Corrections Research*. Research Branch Correctional Service of Canada, June 2004, Aboriginal Justice Implementation Commission (2001); *Aboriginal Justice Implementation Commission Final Report*. www.csc-scc.gc.ca/text/rsrch/briefs/b30/b30-eng.shtml.

46. J. Savarese, "Gladue Was a Woman: The Importance of Gender in Restorative-based Sentencing," in *New Directions in Restorative Justice. Issues, Practice, Evaluation*, eds. Elizabeth Elliott and Robert M. Gordon, 134–152. (Cullompton, UK: Wilan, 2005).

47. Matthew Yeager, "Ideology and Dangerousness: The Case of Lisa Colleen Neve," *Critical Criminology* 9, 1–2 (2000): 9–21.

48. Jackson Toby, "The New Criminology Is the Old Sentimentality," *Criminology* 16 (1979): 513–526.

49. Kenneth Land and Marcus Felson, "A General Framework for Building Dynamic Macro Social Indicator Models: An Analysis of Changes in Crime Rates and Police Expenditures," *American Journal of Sociology* 82 (1976): 565–604.

50. See, generally, William Wilbanks, *The Myth of a Racist Criminal Justice System* (Monterey, CA: Brooks/Cole, 1987).

51. Theodore Chiricos and Gordon Waldo, "Socioeconomic Status and Criminal Sentencing: An Empirical Assessment of a Conflict Proposition," *American Sociological Review* 40 (1975): 753–772.

52. Stephen Klein, Joan Petersilia, and Susan Turner, "Race and Imprisonment Decisions in California," *Science* 247 (1990): 812–816.

53. Basil Owomero, "Crime in Tanzania: Contradictions of a Socialist Experiment," *International Journal of Comparative and Applied Criminal Justice* 12 (1988): 177–189.

54. Eric Neumayer, "Inequality and Violent Crime: Evidence from Data on Robbery and Violent Theft," *Journal of Peace Research* 42, 1 (2005): 101–112.

55. This section borrows heavily from Richard Sparks, "A Critique of Marxist Criminology," in *Crime and Justice*, vol. 2, eds. Norval Morris and Michael Tonry (Chicago: University of Chicago Press, 1980), 159–208.

56. Jeffery Reiman, *The Rich Get Richer and the Poor Get Prison* (New York: Wiley, 1984), 43–44.

57. For a general review of Marxist criminology, see Lynch and Groves, *A Primer in Radical Criminology*, 2nd ed.

58. Steven Bittle, Laureen Snider, "From Manslaughter to Preventable Accident: Shaping Corporate Criminal Liability," *Law & Policy* 28, 4 (2006): 470–496.

59. Ian Taylor, Paul Walton, and Jock Young, *The New Criminology: For a Social Theory of Deviance* (London: Routledge and Kegan Paul, 1973); Ian Taylor, Paul Walton, and Jock Young, eds., *Critical Criminology* (London: Routledge and Kegan Paul, 1975).

60. Barry Krisberg, *Crime and Privilege: Toward a New Criminology* (Englewood Cliffs, NJ: Prentice-Hall, 1975), 167.

61. David Friedrichs, "Critical Criminology and Critical Legal Studies," *Critical Criminologist* 1 (1989): 7.

62. See, for example, Larry Tifft and Dennis Sullivan, *The Struggle to Be Human: Crime, Criminology and Anarchism* (Orkney Islands, Over-the-Water-Sanday: Cienfuegos Press, 1979); Dennis Sullivan, *The Mask of Love* (Port Washington, NY: Kennikat Press, 1980).

63. R.M. Bohm, "Radical Criminology: An Explication," *Criminology* 19 (1982): 565–589.

64. R.M. Bohm, "Beyond Employment: Toward a Radical Solution to the Crime Problem," *Crime and Social Justice*, 1984, 21–22:213–222.

65. W. Byron Groves and Robert Sampson, "Critical Theory and Criminology," *Social Problems* 33 (1986): 58–80.

66. Gregg Barak and Robert M. Bohm, "The Crimes of the Homeless or the Crime of Homelessness? On the Dialectics of Criminalization, Decriminalization, and Victimization," *Crime, Law and Social Change* 13, 3 (1989): 275–288.

67. Michael Lynch, "Assessing the State of Radical Criminology: Toward the Year 2000," paper presented at the annual meeting of the American Society of Criminology, Phoenix, AZ, November 1993; see also Michael J. Lynch; Raymond J. Michalowki; W. Byron Groves, New Primer in Radical Criminology: Critical Perspectives on Crime, Power and Identity, Third Edition, Criminal Justice Press, 2000.

68. Gresham Sykes, "The Rise of Critical Criminology," *Journal of Criminal Law and Criminology* 65 (1974): 211; David Jacobs, "Corporate Economic Power and the State: A Longitudinal Assessment of Two Explanations," *American Journal of Sociology* 93 (1988): 852–881.

69. Deanna Alexander, "Victims of the L.A. Riots: A Theoretical Consideration," paper presented at the annual meeting of the American Society of Criminology, Phoenix, AZ, November 1993.

70. Richard Quinney, "Crime Control in Capitalist Society," in *Critical Criminology*, eds. Ian Taylor, Paul Walton, and Jock Young, 199 (London: Routledge and Kegan Paul, 1975).

71. Herman Schwendinger and Julia Schwendinger, "Delinquency and Social Reform: A Radical Perspective," in *Juvenile Justice*, ed. Lamar Empey, 246–290 (Charlottesville: University of Virginia Press, 1979).

72. Michael Lynch, Raymond Michalowski, and W. Byron Groves, *The New Primer in Radical Criminology: Critical Perspectives on Crime, Power, and Identity*, 3rd ed. (Monsey, NY: Criminal Justice Press, 2000), 45; herein cited as *The New Primer*; Malcolm Homes, "Minority Threat and Police Brutality: Determinants of Civil Rights Criminal Complaints in U.S. Municipalities," *Criminology* 38 (2000): 343–368.

73. Laureen Snider, "The Sociology of Corporate Crime: An Obituary," *Theoretical Criminology* 4, 2 (2000): 169–206.

74. Elliott Currie, "A Dialogue with Anthony M. Platt," *Issues in Criminology* 8 (1973): 28.

75. John Hagan, *Structural Criminology* (New Brunswick, NJ: Rutgers University Press, 1989), 110–119.

76. Stephen Spitzer, "Toward a Marxian Theory of Deviance," *Social Problems* 22 (1975): 638–651.

77. Roy Bhaskar, "Empiricism," in *A Dictionary of Marxist Thought*, ed. T. Bottomore, 149–150 (Cambridge: Harvard University Press, 1983).

78. Byron Groves, "Marxism and Positivism," *Crime and Social Justice* 23 (1985): 129–150; Michael Lynch, "Quantitative Analysis and Marxist Criminology: Some Old Answers to a Dilemma in Marxist Criminology," *Crime and Social Justice* 29 (1987): 110–117.

79. Alan Lizotte, James Mercy, and Eric Monkkonen, "Crime and Police Strength in an Urban Setting: Chicago, 1947–1970," in *Quantitative Criminology*, ed. John Hagan, 129–148 (Beverly Hills, CA: Sage, 1982).

80. Francis T. Cullen, John Paul Wright, and Kristie R. Blevins, eds., *Taking Stock: The Status of Criminological Theory*, Advances in Criminological Theory, vol. 15 (Piscataway, NJ: Transaction Publishers, 2006).

81. William Chambliss, "The State, the Law and the Definition of Behavior as Criminal or Delinquent," in *Handbook of Criminology*, ed. D. Glazer, 7–44 (Chicago: Rand McNally, 1974).

82. Timothy Carter and Donald Clelland, "A Neo-Marxian Critique, Formulation and Test of Juvenile Dispositions as a Function of Social Class," *Social Problems* 27 (1979): 96–108.

83. David Greenberg, "Socio-Economic Status and Criminal Sentences: Is There an Association?" *American Sociological Review* 42 (1977): 174–175; David Greenberg and Drew Humphries, "The Co-optation of Fixed Sentencing Reform," *Crime and Delinquency* 26 (1980): 206–225.

84. Steven Box, *Power, Crime and Mystification* (London: Tavistock, 1984); Gregg Barak, *In Defense of Whom? A Critique of Criminal Justice Reform* (Cincinnati: Anderson Publishing, 1980); for an opposing view, see Franklin Williams, "Conflict Theory and Differential Processing: An Analysis of the Research Literature," in *Radical Criminology: The Coming Crisis*, ed. J. Inciardi, 213–231 (Beverly Hills, CA: Sage, 1980).

85. Herman Schwendinger and Julia Schwendinger, "Rape Victims and the False Sense of Guilt," *Crime and Social Justice* 13 (1980): 4–17.

86. For more of their work, see Herman Schwendinger and Julia Schwendinger, *Adolescent Subcultures and Delinquency* (New York: Praeger, 1985); Herman Schwendinger and Julia Schwendinger, "The Paradigmatic Crisis in Delinquency Theory," *Crime and Social Justice* 18 (1982): 70–78; Herman Schwendinger and Julia Schwendinger, "The Collective Varieties of

Youth," *Crime and Social Justice* 5 (1976): 7–25; Herman Schwendinger and Julia Schwendinger, "Marginal Youth and Social Policy," *Social Problems* 24 (1976): 184–191.

87. David Greenberg and Valerie West, "State Prison Populations and Their Growth, 1971–1991," *Criminology* 39 (2001): 615–654.

88. Robert Weiss, "Repatriating Low-Wage Work: The Political Economy of Prison Labor Reprivatization in the Postindustrial United States," *Criminology* 39 (2001): 253–292.

89. W. Gordon West and Ruth Morris, *The Case for Penal Abolition* (Toronto: Canadian Scholar's Press, 2000).

90. Michael Rustigan, "A Reinterpretation of Criminal Law Reform in Nineteenth-Century England," in *Crime and Capitalism*, ed. D. Greenberg (Palo Alto, CA: Mayfield Publishing, 1981), 255–278; Rosalind Petchesky, "At Hard Labor: Penal Confinement and Production in Nineteenth-Century America," in *Crime and Capitalism*, ed. D. Greenberg, 341–357; Paul Takagi, "The Walnut Street Jail: A Penal Reform to Centralize the Powers of the State," *Federal Probation* 49 (1975): 18–26.

91. Steven Spitzer and Andrew Scull, "Privatization and Capitalist Development: The Case of the Private Police," *Social Problems* 25 (1977): 18–29; Dennis Hoffman, "Cops and Wobblies," Ph.D. dissertation, Portland State University, 1977.

92. Sidney Harring, "Policing a Class Society: The Expansion of the Urban Police in the Late Nineteenth and Early Twentieth Centuries," in *Crime and Capitalism*, ed. D. Greenberg, 292–313.

93. Jack Gibbs, "An Incorrigible Positivist," *Criminologist* 12 (1987): 2–3.

94. Carl Klockars, "The Contemporary Crises of Marxist Criminology," in *Radical Criminology: The Coming Crisis*, ed. J. Inciardi, 92–123 (Beverly Hills, CA: Sage, 1980).

95. Michael Lynch, W. Byron Groves, and Alan Lizotte, "The Rate of Surplus Value and Crime: A Theoretical and Empirical Examination of Marxian Economic Theory and Criminology," *Crime, Law and Social Change* 1 (1994): 1–11.

96. Anthony Platt, "Criminology in the 1980s: Progressive Alternatives to 'Law and Order,'" *Crime and Social Justice* 21–22 (1985): 191–199.

97. See, generally, Roger Matthews and Jock Young, eds., *Confronting Crime* (London: Sage, 1986); for a thorough review of left realism, see Martin Schwartz and Walter DeKeseredy, "Left Realist Criminology: Strengths, Weaknesses and the Feminist Critique," *Crime, Law and Social Change* 15 (1991): 51–72.

98. John Lea and Jock Young, *What Is to Be Done About Law and Order?* (Harmondsworth, England: Penguin, 1984).

99. J. Lowman and B.D. MacLean, eds., *Realist Criminology: Crime Control and Policing in the 1990s* (Toronto: University of Toronto Press, 1992).

100. Richard Kinsey, John Lea, and Jock Young, *Losing the Fight against Crime* (London: Blackwell, 1986).

101. Martin Schwartz and Walter DeKeseredy, *Contemporary Criminology* (Belmont, CA: Wadsworth, 1996), 249.

102. Martin D. Schwartz and Walter S. DeKeseredy, "Left Realist Criminology: Strengths, Weaknesses and the Feminist Critique," *Crime, Law and Social Change* 15, 1 (1991): 51–72.

103. For a general review of this issue, see Kathleen Daly and Meda Chesney-Lind, "Feminism and Criminology," *Justice Quarterly* 5 (1988): 497–538; Douglas Smith and Raymond Paternoster, "The Gender Gap in Theories of Deviance: Issues and Evidence," *Journal of Research in Crime and Delinquency* 24 (1987): 140–172; Pat Carlen, "Women, Crime, Feminism, and Realism," *Social Justice* 17 (1990): 106–123.

104. Julia Schwendinger and Herman Schwendinger, *Rape and Inequality* (Beverly Hills, CA: Sage, 1983).

105. Bernard Schissel, "Boys against Girls. The Structural and Interpersonal Dimensions or Violent Patriarchal Culture in the Lives of Young Men," *Violence Against Women* 6, 9 (2000): 960–986.

106. James Messerschmidt, *Capitalism, Patriarchy and Crime* (Totowa, NJ: Rowman and Littlefield, 1986); for a critique of this work, see Herman Schwendinger and Julia Schwendinger, "The World According to James Messerschmidt," *Social Justice* 15 (1988): 123–145.

107. Kathleen Daly, "Gender and Varieties of White-Collar Crime," *Criminology* 27 (1989): 769–793.

108. Jane Roberts Chapman, "Violence against Women as a Violation of Human Rights," *Social Justice* 17 (1990): 54–71.

109. James Messerschmidt, *Masculinities and Crime: Critique and Reconceptualization of Theory* (Lanham, MD: Rowman and Littlefield, 1993).

110. For a review of feminist theory, see Sally Simpson, "Feminist Theory, Crime and Justice," *Criminology* 27 (1989): 605–632.

111. Suzie Dod Thomas and Nancy Stein, "Criminality, Imprisonment, and Women's Rights in the 1990s," *Social Justice* 17 (1990): 1–5.

112. Walter DeKeseredy and Martin Schwartz, "Male Peer Support and Woman Abuse: An Expansion of DeKeseredy's Model," *Sociological Spectrum* 13 (1993): 393–413.

113. Daly and Chesney-Lind, "Feminism and Criminology." See also Drew Humphries and Susan Caringella-MacDonald,

"Murdered Mothers, Missing Wives: Reconsidering Female Victimization," *Social Justice* 17 (1990): 71–78.

114. Center for Research on Women, *Secrets in Public: Sexual Harassment in Our Schools* (Wellesley, MA: Wellesley College, 1993).

115. Sandy Cook and Susanne Davies, eds., *Harsh Punishment. International Experiences of Women's Imprisonment* (Boston: Northeastern University Press, 1999).

116. Jane A. Siegel, "Aggressive Behavior among Women Sexually Abused as Children," *Violence and Victims* 15, 3 (2000): 235–255.

117. Susan Ehrlich Martin and Nancy Jurik, *Doing Justice, Doing Gender* (Thousand Oaks, CA: Sage, 1996), 27.

118. Amanda Burgess-Proctor, "Intersections of Race, Class, Gender, and Crime. Future Directions for Feminist Criminology," *Feminist Criminology* 1, 1 (2006): 27–47.

119. Ruth Alexander, *The "Girl Problem": Female Sexual Delinquency in New York, 1900–1930* (Ithaca, NY: Cornell University Press, 1995).

120. Steven Bittle, "When Protection is Punishment: Neo-liberalism and Secure Care Approaches to Youth Prostitution," *Canadian Journal of Criminology* 44, 3 (2002): 317–351.

121. Raymond R. Corrado, Candice Odgers, and Irwin M. Cohen, "The Incarceration of Female Young Offenders: Protection for Whom?" *Canadian Journal of Criminology* 42, 2 (2000): 189–208.

122. Mary Odem and Steven Schlossman, "Guardians of Virtue: The Juvenile Court and Female Delinquency in Early 20th-Century Los Angeles," *Crime and Delinquency* 37 (1991): 186–203.

123. Meda Chesney-Lind, "Judicial Enforcement of the Female Sex Role: The Family Court and the Female Delinquent," *Issues in Criminology* 8 (1973): 51–69; see also Meda Chesney-Lind, "Women and Crime: The Female Offender," *Signs: Journal of Women in Culture and Society* 12 (1986): 78–96; Meda Chesney-Lind, "Female Offenders: Paternalism Reexamined," in *Women, the Courts, and Equality*, eds. Laura L. Crites and Winifred L. Hepperle, 114–139 (Newbury Park, CA: Sage, 1987); Meda Chesney-Lind, "Girls' Crime and a Woman's Place: Toward a Feminist Model of Female Delinquency," paper presented at a meeting of the American Society of Criminology, Montreal, 1987.

124. John Hagan, A.R. Gillis, and John Simpson, "The Class Structure and Delinquency: Toward a Power-Control Theory of Common Delinquent Behavior," *American Journal of Sociology* 90 (1985): 1151–1178; John Hagan, John Simpson, and A.R. Gillis, "Class in the Household: A Power-Control Theory of Gender and Delinquency," *American Journal of Sociology* 92 (1987): 788–816.

125. John Hagan, Bill McCarthy, and Holly Foster, "A Gendered Theory of Delinquency and Despair in the Life Course," *Acta Sociologica* 45 (2002): 37–47.

126. Brenda Sims Blackwell, "Perceived Sanction Threats, Gender, and Crime: A Test and Elaboration of Power-Control Theory," *Criminology* 38 (2000): 439–488.

127. Christopher Uggen, "Class, Gender, and Arrest: An Intergenerational Analysis of Workplace Power and Control," *Criminology* 38 (2000): 835–862.

128. Gary Jensen, "Power-Control versus Social-Control Theory: Identifying Crucial Differences for Future Research," paper presented at the annual meeting of the American Society of Criminology, Baltimore, November 1990.

129. Gary Jensen and Kevin Thompson, "What's Class Got to Do with It? A Further Examination of Power-Control Theory," *American Journal of Sociology* 95 (1990): 1009–1023. For some critical research, see Simon Singer and Murray Levine, "Power Control Theory, Gender and Delinquency: A Partial Replication with Additional Evidence on the Effects of Peers," *Criminology* 26 (1988): 627–648.

130. Kevin Thompson, "Gender and Adolescent Drinking Problems: The Effects of Occupational Structure," *Social Problems* 36 (1989): 30–38.

131. Dragan Milovanovic, *A Primer in the Sociology of Law* (New York: Harrow and Heston, 1988) 127–128.

132. Shirley Lee, "Health and Sickness: The Meaning of Menstruation and Premenstrual Syndrome in Women's Lives," *Sex Roles* 46, 1–2 (2002): 25–35.

133. Alia Offman and Peggy J. Kleinplatz, "Does PMDD Belong in the DSM? Challenging the Medicalization of Women's Bodies," *The Canadian Journal of Human Sexuality* 13 (2004).

134. Gladys L. Symons, "Police Constructions of Race and Gender in Street Gangs," in *Crimes of Colour: Racialization and the Criminal Justice System in Canada*, eds. Wendy Chan and Kiran Mirchandani (Peterborough, ON: Broadview Press, 2002).

135. Jana Grekul and Patti LaBoucane-Benson, "Aboriginal Gangs and Their (Dis)placement: Contextualizing Recruitment, Membership, and Status," *Canadian Journal of Crime and Criminal Justice*, January 2008.

136. Symons, Gladys L., "Racialization of the Street Gang Issue in Montreal: A Police Perspective," *Canadian Ethnic Studies* 31, 1 (1999): 124–139.

137. Kathryn Campbell, Martin Dufresne, and Richard MacLure, "Amending Youth Justice Policy in Canada: Discourse, Mediation and Ambiguity," *The Howard Journal* 40, 3 (2001): 272–284.

138. Howard Zehr, *Changing Lenses* (Scottdale, PA: Herald Press, 1990), 181.

139. Dennis Sullivan and Larry Tifft, *Restorative Justice: Healing the Foundations of Our Everyday Lives* (Monsey, NY: Willow Tree Press, 2001), 49.

140. John L. McKnight, "Redefining Community," *Social Policy*, Fall–Winter (1992): 56–62.

141. Robin J. Wilson, Bria Huculak, and Andrew McWhinnie, "Restorative Justice Innovations in Canada," *Behavioural Science and the Law* 20 (2002): 363–380.

142. Bas Van Stokkom, "Moral Emotions in Restorative Justice Conferences: Managing Shame, Designing Empathy," *Theoretical Criminology* 6 (2002): 339–360.

143. Alan N. Young, *Victims of Crime: The Role of the Victim in the Criminal Process: A Literature Review—1989 to 1999* (Ottawa: Department of Justice Canada, 2001), 60.

144. Robert C. Depew, "Popular Justice and Aboriginal Communities," *Journal of Legal Pluralism* 36 (1996): 21–67.

145. Ruth Morris, *Stories of Transformative Justice* (Toronto: Canadian Scholar's Press, 2000).

146. Peter Cordella, *Restorative Justice* (unpublished paper, Manchester, NH: St. Anselm College, 1997); see also Herbert Bianchi, *Justice as Sanctuary* (Bloomington, IN: Indiana University Press, 1994); Nils Christie, "Conflicts as Property," *The British Journal of Criminology* 17 (1977): 1–15; L. Hulsman, "Critical Criminology and the Concept of Crime," *Contemporary Crises* 10 (1986): 63–80.

147. Richard Quinney, "The Way of Peace: On Crime, Suffering and Service," in *Criminology as Peacemaking*, eds. Harold Pepinsky and Richard Quinney (Bloomington: Indiana University Press, 1991), 8–9.

148. John Paul Lederach, *Building Peace: Sustainable Reconciliation in Divided Societies* (Washington, DC: United States Institute of Peace Press, 1997); Denise Breton and Stephen Lehman, *The Mystic Heart of Justice* (West Chester, PA: Chrysalis Books, 2001); Harold Pepinsky and Richard Quinney, eds., *Criminology as Peace-Making* (Indianapolis, IN: Indiana University Press, 1991), 10.

149. Gregg Barak, *Violence and Nonviolence: Pathways to Understanding* (Thousand Oaks, CA: Sage Publications, 2003), 120.

150. See, for example, Tifft and Sullivan, *The Struggle to Be Human*; and Sullivan, *The Mask of Love*.

151. Dennis Sullivan and Larry Tifft, *Restorative Justice* (Monsey, NY: Willow Tree Press, 2001).

152. Richard Quinney, "The Way of Peace: On Crime, Suffering and Service," in *Criminology as Peacemaking*, eds. Harold Pepinsky and Richard Quinney, 8–9 (Bloomington, IN: Indiana University Press, 1991). To read about the evolution of Quinney's work, see Kevin Anderson, "Richard Quinney's Journey: The Marxist Dimension," *Crime and Delinquency* 48 (2002): 232–243.

153. Denise Breton and Stephen Lehman, *The Mystic Heart of Justice* (West Chester, PA: Chrysalis Books, 2001), 181–182.

154. John Paul Lederach, *Building Peace: Sustainable Reconciliation in Divided Societies* (Washington, DC: United States Institute of Peace Press, 2002), 24.

155. For more resources on restorative justice and peacemaking, see Gene Stephens, "The Future of Policing: From a War Model to a Peace Model," in *The Past, Present, and Future of American Criminal Justice*, ed. Brendan Maguire and Polly Radosh, 77–93 (Dix Hills, NY: General Hall, 1996); Kay Pranis, "Peacemaking Circles: Restorative Justice in Practice Allows Victims and Offenders to Begin Repairing the Harm," *Corrections Today* 59 (1997): 74; Carol LaPrairie, "The 'New' Justice: Some Implications for Aboriginal Communities," *Canadian Journal of Criminology* 40 (1998): 61–79; David R. Karp and Beau Breslin, "Restorative Justice in School Communities," *Youth and Society* 33 (2001): 249–272; Paul Jesilow and Deborah Parsons, "Community Policing as Peacemaking," *Policing and Society* 10 (2000): 163–183; Gordon Bazemore and Curt Taylor Griffiths, "Conferences, Circles, Boards, and Mediations: The 'New Wave' of Community Justice Decision Making," *Federal Probation* 61 (1997): 25–37; John Braithwaite, "Setting Standards for Restorative Justice," *British Journal of Criminology* 42 (2002): 563–577; David Altschuler, "Community Justice Initiatives: Issues and Challenges in the U.S. Context," *Federal Probation* 65 (2001): 28–33; Lois Presser and Patricia Van Voorhis, "Values and Evaluation: Assessing Processes and Outcomes of Restorative Justice Programs," *Crime and Delinquency* 48 (2002): 162–189; Sharon Levrant, Francis Cullen, Betsy Fulton, and John Wozniak, "Reconsidering Restorative Justice: The Corruption of Benevolence Revisited?" *Crime and Delinquency* 45 (1999): 3–28.

Crime Typologies

Regardless of the reasons that people commit crime in the first place, their actions are defined by law as falling into particular crime categories. Criminologists often seek to group individual criminal offenders or behaviours so that they may be more easily studied and understood. These groupings are referred to as offender typologies.

In this section, crime patterns are clustered into four groups: violent crime (Chapter 10); property crime (Chapter 11); crimes involving white-collar criminals or criminal organizations (Chapter 12); public order crimes such as moral offences (Chapter 13); and crimes of the 21st century, such as terrorism and cybercrime (Chapter 14). These groupings focus our attention on crimes of physical harm to others, the misappropriation of other people's property, crimes requiring the exercise of power, public morals offences, and modern crimes symptomatic of life in late modern capitalism.

Typologies can be useful in classifying large numbers of criminal offences or offenders into easily understood categories. This text has grouped offences and offenders on the basis of (1) their legal definitions; (2) their collective goals, objectives, and consequences; and (3) societal reaction. In this way, we can better understand the patterns of crime, predict their occurrence, and work to prevent them.

Violent Crime

Learning Objectives

After reading this chapter, you will be able to:

1. Understand the various factors involved in violent crime.
2. Be familiar with different major violent crimes.
3. Know the elements of sexual assault, murder, and robbery.
4. Discuss the different patterns of violent crimes.
5. Explain some preventive approaches to violent crime.

Riot police walk by a burning police car in downtown Toronto during anti-G20 protests in the summer of 2010. In the most expensive summit ever, police engaged in mass arrests of people in peaceful protest.

© THE CANADIAN PRESS/Frank Gunn

In our society, people are afraid of becoming crime victims. TV news stories and newspaper articles feature grisly accounts of mass murder, child abuse, and serial rape. However, the police-reported crime rate in 2012 dropped 3 percent from 2011 to its lowest level since 1972. About 2 million criminal incidents were reported to police, with a decrease in the violent offences of assault and robbery. The overall crime severity index continued to drop in 2012 to more than 25 percent lower than it was in 2006, the ninth consecutive decrease since 2003.[1] In 2012, approximately 415,000 violent incidents occurred in Canada, down 3 percent since 2011 to its lowest level since 1987. Most crimes of violence decreased, although increases were reported in attempted murders, extortion, firearms offences, and sexual violence against children.

Are the downward trends due to getting tough on crime? Probably not. Will they reassure people that society is becoming safer? Probably not.

Many people have personally experienced violence or have a friend who has been victimized. More importantly, almost everyone has heard about someone having been robbed, beaten, or killed; riots and violent protests have recently made the headlines; *hate crime* has become a common phrase; assassination has claimed the lives of political, religious, and social leaders all over the world; and *terrorism* has become a household word. We live in a mediated world, and our perception of our experiences is influenced by what we read, see, and hear in the media.

Because of such events, politicians try to persuade us that the government should take a get-tough approach to violent crime, especially when the perpetrators are young offenders. However, many Canadians have the perception that youth criminal legislation, reflected in the *Youth Criminal Justice Act,* might not go far enough. In Canada, many people believe that society is becoming more violent and that things are not as they were in the "good old days." And maybe they are right—since 1962, the rate of violent crime has increased from 221 per 100,000 people to 1,190 in 2012. However, is longing for the serenity of earlier days appropriate, considering that violence has been a long-standing feature of social life? Perhaps we are just hearing more highly publicized accounts of violent crime, or perhaps more violent crime is being reported to the police.

Theories we have looked at suggest various explanations: that violence originates in a relatively small number of

CONNECTIONS

As discussed in Chapter 6, biosocial theorists link violence to biological irregularities, including genetic influences and inheritance, hormones, neurotransmitters, brain structure, and diet. Psychologists link violent behaviour to observational learning from violent TV shows, traumatic childhood experiences, low intelligence, mental illness, impaired cognitive processes, and abnormal (psychopathic) personality structure.

inherently violence-prone individuals who themselves may have been the victims of physical violence or who may have psychological abnormalities; that violence and aggression are inherently human traits; and that there are violence-prone subcultures within society whose members value force and routinely carry weapons.[2]

This chapter surveys the nature and extent of violent crime. First, we briefly review some hypothetical causes of violence. Then, we turn our attention to specific types of interpersonal violence: rape, homicide, assault, and robbery. Finally, we look at political violence, state-sponsored violence, and terrorism.

THE ROOTS OF VIOLENCE

What causes people to behave violently? Numerous competing explanations attempt to make sense of public incidents of violent behaviour, such as the following Canadian examples (see also the nearby Famous Canadian Criminals box):

- In 1984, Denis Lortie opened fire in Quebec's National Assembly with a machine gun, killing three and wounding 13 others; he pleaded guilty by reason of insanity.
- In 1989, Marc Lepine killed 14 women and wounded 12 others at the École Polytechnique in Montreal; a suicide note found on his body blamed feminists for having spoiled his life.
- In 1992, Valery Fabrikant killed three professors at Concordia University's engineering department; the university had asked the police not to approve Fabrikant's gun permit.
- On Boxing Day 2005, two gangs were involved in a shooting spree that killed a teenage girl and injured six others in a packed downtown Toronto area.
- In 2006 at Dawson College, Kimveer Gill shot one victim and injured another 19 in a widely publicized incident recorded on cellphone cameras.
- In 2008, Vince Li sat down next to Tim MacLean on a bus travelling from Winnipeg to Edmonton, and then killed and beheaded him, eating some of his body parts.

Bizarre outbursts, such as these acts of mass violence, exacerbate our worst fears that we could be victimized by brutal, random crime committed by strangers in public places. Fear distorts the experience of living in modern society. But fear, and the reality it is based on, is a relative thing.

For example, Canada's homicide rate was 1.8 homicides per 100,000 people in 2007 compared with England and Wales, at 1.6; France, at 1.6; and Germany, at 1.0. However, the homicide rate in El Salvador was 55 per 100,000, South Africa's, 41; Russia's, 17; and even the United States was at 5.7. The Canadian homicide rate is low, and furthermore, it varies. In Aboriginal communities, the suicide rate is three

Few people would have otherwise recognized his name. He was considered a loser, unable to keep a girlfriend, and ineligible for the military because of his mental instability and antisocial personality. Then, on December 6, 1989, Marc Lepine, dressed in military fatigues, hid his guns under his coat and went to the École Polytechnique. He went into an engineering classroom and ordered all the men out, after which he shot the women while cursing them for being feminists. He walked through the school systematically shooting women until he turned the gun on himself.

Was he a lunatic or part of the wider continuum of violence against women? Was this act an isolated one or the extreme end of everyday misogyny?

A letter found on his body said that he had decided to kill women because they had ruined his life. He had tried to enter the Polytechnique as a student but was turned down. He admired Denis Lortie for

going into the legislature and shooting politicians and wanted to emulate him.

The initial reaction to the Montreal Massacre was incredulity and anger. How could a person be in possession of such weapons? Why did the police take so long to respond? Why did Lepine single out women?

Now, years later, this event has come to symbolize wider patterns of violence against women in society.

When Suzanne Lapointe-Edward speaks about what happened to her daughter, she calls Lepine "the killer." She believes that the media made Lepine an anti-hero while the women became nameless victims. Lapointe-Edward lectures across the country to promote action and healing with respect to violence against women, advocating stricter gun control legislation.

Women are usually killed by men they know, after withstanding repeated assaults. That night in Montreal, the women were selected because of their gender. They

had done nothing to Lepine and nothing to deserve what happened to them.

Not all men are violent, but most violence is committed by men—a fact that is hard to overlook. However, men and women have joined together in trying to overcome a legacy of gendered violence and to work for change.

And then in 2006, another man fascinated by guns and wanting notoriety started shooting at Montreal's Dawson College. The perpetrator was Kimveer Gill, who advertised his intentions on the Internet. He began shooting outside the entrance to the school, and moved into the atrium on the main floor. He killed one victim and injured another 19. The toll would have been higher but police were on the scene immediately and, following a new policy of rapid intervention, cornered Gill. The shooter then committed suicide after being shot in the arm by police. This was the fourth fatal school shooting in Montreal.

times higher than the average for Canada, and violent crime is more than three times the Canadian average rate. Our society can't prevent the victimization of women and children, and we have many instances of police and prison violence.

Figure 10.1 shows some of the known sources of violence.

Personal Traits

Some see a link between violence and personal traits. More than 35 years ago, Laura Bender examined convicted juveniles who had killed their victims and concluded that they suffered from abnormal electroencephalogram (EEG) readings, learning disabilities, and psychosis.[3]

More recent research has found that murderous youths suffer signs of major neurological impairment (abnormal EEGs, multiple psychomotor impairment, and severe seizures), low intelligence, and psychotic symptoms, such as paranoia, illogical thinking, and hallucinations.[4] Similarly, studies of male batterers indicate that abnormal personality structure, including depression, borderline personality syndrome, and psychopathology, is associated with various

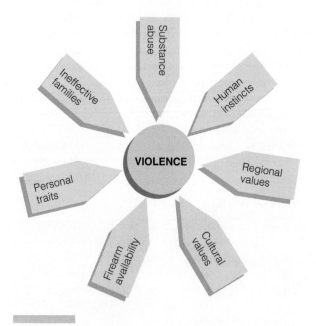

FIGURE 10.1
Sources of Violence

forms of spousal and family abuse.[5] However, other theories have also been proposed.

Ineffective Families

In 1990, residents of Gainesville, Florida, were shocked when five young students were brutally murdered. Newspaper accounts told how the victims had been stabbed dozens of times and raped, and how their mutilated bodies had been posed in sexually suggestive positions.[6] Danny Harold Rolling was convicted for committing these horrible crimes, and the jury recommended the death penalty. During sentencing, Rolling pleaded for mercy and claimed his behaviour was a result of emotional and physical abuse by his father.

Research linking violence to ineffective, abusive, or inadequate parenting shows that parents reinforce a child's coercive behaviour by failing to set adequate limits or use proper and consistent discipline. Such factors are all linked to persistent violent offending.[7]

The Canadian Centre for Justice Statistics (CCJS) confirms this pattern. As part of the National Longitudinal Survey of Children and Youth, more than 20,000 children or their caregivers are interviewed every two years until they are 25 years of age. A key finding is that children who are exposed to fighting in the home are more likely to be physically aggressive themselves. Figure 10.2 shows that almost three times as many children who witness violence are likely to be violent compared with those who don't witness violence. There is also a direct relationship among seeing violence; being hyperactive, anxious, or depressed; and committing property crimes.

Abused Kids. Victims of childhood abuse later engage in violent delinquent behaviour at a rate greater than do non-abused children.[8] Samples of convicted murderers contain a high percentage of seriously abused youths.[9] Abuse is a factor in many cases when parents have been killed by their children.[10] And children who are physically punished are the ones most likely to physically abuse a sibling and later engage in spouse abuse.[11]

This effect is called the **brutalization process**. Case studies of violent criminals show that antisocial careers are created in stages, beginning with brutal episodes during early adolescence. In the first stage, abusive parents or caretakers cause the young victim to develop a belligerent, angry demeanour. When confronted at home, at school, or on the street, these youths respond with hostility. The success of their confrontations provides them with a sense of power. In the virulency stage, these youth develop a violent identity that makes them feared; they enjoy intimidating others. This process takes now-violent youths full circle, from being the victim of aggression to being its initiator; they are now the same person they grew up despising, ready to begin the process with their own children.[12]

Research on schizophrenia, for example, finds that people may behave violently for reasons not directly related to their mental illness. Medical treatment for psychotic symptoms alone may not eliminate the risk of violence because numerous factors contribute to violence independently from the person's schizophrenia, such as childhood conduct problems, substance abuse, having been the victim of past violent acts, and poverty.[13]

However, although evidence shows the association between abuse and violent crime, many offenders have not suffered abuse, and many abused youths do not grow up to become persistent adult offenders.[14]

Evolutionary Factors/Human Instinct

It is possible that violent responses are inherent in all humans and need only the right trigger to emerge. Freud believed human aggression and violence were produced by instinctual drives.[15] Freud said that humans have two opposing instinctual drives that control behaviour: **eros**, the life instinct, drives people to self-fulfillment and enjoyment; **Thanatos**,

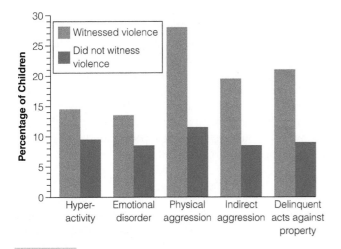

FIGURE 10.2

Child Behavioural Outcomes in Homes where Children Witnessed Violence

Source: Adapted from Statistics Canada, "Children Witnessing Family Violence," *Juristat*, Catalogue no. 85-002-XIE, Vol. 21, no. 6, 2001; retrieved from: http://www.statcan.ca/english/freepub/85-002-XIE/0060185-002-XIE.pdf.

brutalization process The first stage in a violent career, during which parents victimize children, causing them to develop a belligerent, angry demeanour.

eros According to Freud, of the two opposing instinctual drives that interact to control behaviour, eros is the life instinct, which drives people to self-fulfillment and enjoyment.

Thanatos According to Freud, of the two instinctual drives, Thanatos is the death instinct, which drives people toward aggression, violence, and self-destruction.

the death instinct, produces self-destruction. Thanatos can be expressed externally (as violence and sadism) or internally (as suicide, alcoholism, or other self-destructive habits).

Biologists and anthropologists also speculate that instinctual violence-promoting traits may be common to the human species, the results of instincts inborn in all animals. Konrad Lorenz[16] argues that aggressive energy is produced by instincts independent of environmental forces. In the animal kingdom, aggression serves a productive purpose—for example, leading members of grazing species to spread out over available territory to ensure an ample food supply and the survival of the fittest.

Lorenz felt that humans have some of the same aggressive instincts as animals but without some important inhibitions. For example, among lower species, aggression is rarely fatal; when a conflict occurs, the winner is determined through a test of skill or endurance. Animals' inhibition against killing members of their own species protects them from self-extinction.

Evolutionary theories suggest that violence may have become instinctual because of the long-term influences of reproductive behaviour: Males who are sexually aggressive are the ones most likely to produce children. Over time, male aggression has become predominant.[17] On the other hand, males that are good providers and caretakers are more likely to have children that live to reproduce themselves. The theory of evolution is about ideology as well as science.

Cultural Values

Explanations of the cause of violent behaviour that focus on the individual fail to account for larger patterns of societal violence. Is interpersonal violence more common in large, urban, inner-city areas? Are violent crime rates linked to socially disorganized areas?[18]

Subculture of Violence. To explain the existence of areas and groups with disproportionately high violence rates, Marvin Wolfgang suggests the existence of a subculture of violence.[19] The subculture's norms are separate from society's central, dominant value system, and violence becomes a way to solve conflicts.[20]

Ganging. Empirical evidence shows that violence is highest in those urban areas where subcultural values support teenage gangs who embrace the use of violence.[21] Gang members are more likely to own guns and other weapons.[22] Gang violence may be used to retaliate against rivals and to protect turf from incursions by outsiders.[23] The number of gang-related killings has increased significantly in recent years.[24]

In Canada, increasing attention is being paid to Aboriginal, Chinese, and Vietnamese gangs, and to outlaw motorcycle gangs.[25]

Regional Values

Do regional values promote violence?[26] Research in the southern United States attributed high homicide rates to a culture that stresses a frontier mentality, mob violence, personal vengeance, and easily available firearms.[27] However, not all criminologists agree with these conclusions.[28]

Police data and victimization surveys in Canada show that western provinces have historically had a higher overall rate of violent crime. This pattern is consistent for property and violent crime, with provincial and territorial variations due to age, sex, urban concentration, and social disorganization.[29] However, Kennedy and Silverman suggest that crime rates increase, moving from low rates in the East and gradually increasing in a westward direction because of relative disadvantage. That is, crime is likely to be higher in the West, which has a broader range of social inequality. In areas of absolute disadvantage, as in much of Eastern Canada, citizens have little animosity because there is little societal difference among individuals.[30]

Substance Abuse

Violence can also be linked to substance abuse, which influences violence in three ways: through the actual effects of drugs, out of the need to obtain drugs, and in relation to drug trafficking.[31]

The relationship is **psychopharmacological** when it is the direct consequence of ingesting mood-altering substances. Drugs such as PCP and amphetamines produce violence and aggression. Alcohol abuse is also associated with violence, especially because drinking reduces cognition.[32]

Drug ingestion may result in economic compulsive behaviour when drug users resort to violence to gain funds to support their habit. In a Corrections Canada survey of 6,000 offenders entering federal institutions, 48 percent admitted to having used a drug on the day of their offence, and 30 percent said they had used cocaine in the six months before arrest. The U.S. Drug Use Forecasting (DUF) survey shows that 80 percent of people arrested for violent crimes test positively for drugs.[33] Surveys of American prison inmates show a majority report being under the influence of drugs and alcohol at the time of their offence.[34]

A bond between violent crime and substance abuse is also forged by the activities of drug-trafficking gangs whose members sell and use drugs. Drug-related deaths are motivated by drug trafficking and interpersonal conflict brought on by drug abuse; relatively few people are killed by drug users trying to get drug money.[35]

Firearm Availability

Although firearm availability is not in itself a cause of violence, it is certainly a facilitating factor: An argument can escalate

> **psychopharmacological**   The type of effect of a mood-altering substance such as alcohol, PCP, or amphetamines, which can produce a violent change in behaviour.

into a fatality if one party has a handgun, but in Canada, only about 2 percent of violent victimizations involve a firearm. The long-term trend in firearm-related homicides shows that the rate has declined from the 1970s to less than half in 2006. Handguns are used in three-quarters of all firearm homicides.[36] In 2012, there were 5,600 victims of firearm-related crime, 1,800 fewer than in 2009. This represents a rate of 21 victims per 100,000 population, down from a rate of 29 in 2009. Also, the rate of firearm-related violent crime has fallen faster than non-firearm-related violent crime.

Statistics Canada reports that one of the major changes in robbery over the past decade has been a decrease in the use of weapons. In 2009, robberies with a firearm accounted for only 15 percent of all robberies, down 5 percent since 1999. Robberies committed with knives have also declined, from 36 percent in 1999 to 30 percent in 2009. Shootings (33 percent) and stabbings (31 percent) remain the most common methods of committing homicide. The overall rate of firearm-related homicide was down 61 percent from 1975. When compared to other countries, Canada's firearm-related homicide rate is .49 per 100,000 population, low when compared to the United States at 3.5, but high when compared to Japan's in 2008 at .01 per 100,000.

Shootings are a major cause of death for police officers who are killed, and the presence of firearms in the home significantly increases suicide, regardless of how carefully the guns are secured or stored.[37] In 2004, three-quarters of all firearm-related deaths in Canada were suicides. Exhibit 10.1 provides more details about weapons and violent crime in Canada.

Between 1970 and 1995, probably as a result of more stringent firearms regulations, the use of firearms for suicide and homicide decreased. Unintentional firearms deaths have also decreased.[38]

CONNECTIONS

Some criminologists have focused on "violent" business or corporate crimes, such as the release of toxic pollutants into the environment. Because these acts are linked to business organizations, they will be covered in the sections on corporate crime in Chapter 13.

Although gun control is a hotly debated topic in Canada, we have had a gun registry since the 1930s for handguns and from the early 1940s for long guns, both being initiated during wartime. Changes to the law in the form of Bill C-51 in 1979, Bill C-17 in 1991, and Bill C-68 in 1995 occurred during peacetime.[39] Canadians face many obstacles to acquiring a gun: firearm acquisition certificate screening, penalties for gun-related offences, strengthened prohibition orders, and provisions for safe handling and storage. Following the Montreal Massacre, carbines and high-capacity magazines became restricted.

EXHIBIT 10.1

Quick Facts about Weapons and Violent Crime, Various Years

- Attempted murder and homicide are the violent crimes that most frequently involve the use of weapons: a firearm is used against approximately one-third of victims.
- Firearm-related violent crime rates are higher in Western Canada than in Eastern Canada.
- About 2 percent of all violent-crime victims encounter firearms.
- Shootings increased to 172 in 2012, accounting for 33 percent of all homicides.
- Youth accused of a violent offence are more likely than adults to use a firearm, and strangers rather than acquaintances.
- Beginning in the 1990s to the present, handguns are the most common firearms involved in shootings.
- In 2004, three out of every four firearm-related deaths were due to suicides; homicides accounted for 20 percent, and 5 percent were classified as accidents.
- Firearm-related homicides are three times more likely to be unsolved compared with other homicides.
- Persons convicted of firearm-related offences are sentenced to an average of four years in prison, double the sentence of those convicted of non-firearm-related violent offences.

SOURCES: Statistics Canada, "Firearms and Violent Crime," *Juristat*, Catalogue no. 85-002-XIE, Vol. 28, no. 2, 2008, www.statcan.ca/english/freepub/85-002-XIE/85-002-XIE2008002.pdf; *Homicide in Canada, 2012*, Jillian Boyce and Adam Cotter, Statistics Canada; Firearms and Violent Crime in Canada, *The Daily*.

In an analysis of Canadian Bill C-17, health education professor Stephen Bridges investigated the effect of firearm control laws in the use of firearms for suicide and homicide in the periods prior to and after the passing of the bill. He found a significant decrease in the rates of suicides and homicides involving firearms, and also in the percentage of suicides using firearms after the passage of Bill C-17. This finding provides support for the position that restricting the availability of firearms will help reduce the numbers of suicides and homicides.[40]

Other legislative changes have involved mandatory reporting of gunshot wounds and firearm mandatory registration.[41] The gun registry was again revamped in 2004 to focus more on the criminal use of guns and to decriminalize registry offences, although it was eventually scrapped by the Conservative government less than a decade later. Public opinion was widely divided on the necessity of gun registration: a majority of Canadians favoured stricter laws for gun ownership in 2001, and then supported scrapping the gun registry in 2002.[42] Those who see crime as being motivated by internal factors are less likely to support gun registration than are those who believe that access to guns facilitates crime.[43]

So far, we have reviewed a few of the factors suspected to be causes of violent crime. In the remainder of the chapter, we turn our attention to the individual acts that comprise violent crime in our society. When violence is directed toward strangers, it is said to be an instrumental crime, such as armed robbery, which is designed to improve the financial position of the criminal; such violence is sometimes called **crime-related violence**. In contrast, **expressive violence** is designed to vent rage, anger, or frustration, as when a romantic triangle results in a murder, sometimes called **conflict-related violence**.

Among the common-law violent crimes are rape, murder, assault, and robbery. Newly recognized forms of violence are directed at specific targets. Included within this category are workplace crimes. In addition, violent, politically motivated crimes are commonly referred to as acts of terrorism.

SEXUAL ASSAULT

Rape is defined under common law as "carnal knowledge of a female forcibly and against her will."[44] Under traditional common law, rape involved non-consensual sexual intercourse performed by a male against a female he is neither married to nor cohabiting with,[45] and until recently, Canadian law provided an exemption for husbands accused of raping their wives (see Exhibit 10.2). This definition was removed in 1983 as part of a series of sweeping changes to sexual assault laws. The situation is different in some countries, however. In 1993, for example, Italy's Supreme Court accepted a husband's argument that he raped his wife to save their marriage.[46]

Traditionally, rape has been viewed as a sexual offence. Even today, some men view rape as a sexual act, including one Tennessee judge who in 1994 released an accused rapist after stating that all the man needed was a girlfriend and telling the public defender's office to arrange for a dating service.[47]

Criminologists now consider rape to be a violent, coercive act of aggression, and the term has been changed to *sexual assault*. The campaign to alert the public to the seriousness of rape, to initiate help for victims, and to change legal definitions to facilitate the prosecution of rape offenders has increased the reported rate of sexual assault because victims feel less reluctant to come forward and report the crime to police.

History of Rape

In early civilization, rape was common. Men staked a claim of ownership on women by forcibly abducting and raping them. This activity was part of male domination of women. In *Against Our Will*, Susan Brownmiller says the criminalization of rape occurred after the development of a monetary economy.[48] Thereafter, the violation of a virgin caused an economic hardship on her family, who was expected to pay a significant dowry for her hand in marriage. In Babylonian and Hebraic law, the rape of a virgin was a crime punishable by death. However, if the victim was a married woman, both she and her attacker were equally to blame. Unless her husband chose to intervene, the victim and her attacker were put to death.

During the Middle Ages, ambitious men commonly abducted and raped wealthy women to force them into marriage. "Heiress stealing" illustrates how feudal law gave little protection to women and equated them with property. Only in the 15th century was forcible sex outlawed, and then only if the victim was of the nobility. Raped peasant women and raped married women were not considered rape victims until well into the 16th century. A woman who was raped was suspected of having contributed to her attack.

Sexual Assault and the Military

In 1998, allegations began to surface of sexual assault in the Canadian military. Although such stories are not new, what was shocking were accounts of women going to their superiors only to have their complaints discounted, to be told nothing could be done, or to hear it suggested that *they* were to blame for the incidents.

EXHIBIT 10.2

Quick Code: Sexual Assault Law in Canada before 1983

143. A male person commits rape when he has sexual intercourse with a female person who is not his wife,

a. Without her consent, or

b. With her consent if the consent
   i. Is extorted by threats or fear of bodily harm,
   ii. Is obtained by personating her husband, or
   iii. Is obtained by false and fraudulent representations as to the nature and quality of the act

SOURCE: C. Boyle, "Sexual Assault: A Case Study of Legal Policy Options," in *Canadian Criminology: Perspectives on Crime and Criminality*, ed. M. Jackson and C. Griffiths (Toronto: Harcourt Brace, 1991), p. 101.

---

crime-related violence   Violence, usually between strangers, is committed during the course of another crime.

expressive violence   Violence that is designed not for profit but to vent anger or frustration; also called conflict-related violence.

conflict-related violence   An expressive crime of passion involving acquaintances.

CBC News; last updated Wednesday, July 2, 2008

Reprinted with the permission of the Calgary Police Service

Police released a sketch of a man wanted in a sexual assault in November 2007.

A woman who was seriously injured after a vicious sexual assault in Calgary's Beltline neighbourhood has given police enough information for them to release an updated sketch of her attacker.

The 23-year-old woman was walking alone last November at about 2:30 a.m. when she was approached by a man who tried to engage her in a friendly conversation.

She refused to respond. He then violently attacked and sexually assaulted her in a parking lot on the north side of 10th Avenue, west of 6th Street S.W., said police.

Calgary police released a sketch of the suspect Wednesday and described him as about 25 years old with a thin build and a medium skin tone, perhaps of Indo-Canadian descent. He was about five feet six inches tall with short dark brown hair.

Police said they have reason to believe the attacker was from Ontario and was looking for work in Calgary around the time of the assault.

Crime Stoppers also filmed a re-enactment on Wednesday, hoping it will generate tips from the public.

The woman was new to Calgary and investigators said alcohol was not involved in the attack.

Police reminded people to take safety precautions, such as attending festivals and functions in groups, and to stay in well-lit areas when alone.

Police said sexual assaults in Calgary tend to increase in the summer months, and that drugs and alcohol are often involved and may increase a victim's vulnerability.

SOURCE: Reprinted with the permission of the Canadian Broadcasting Corporation (www.CBC.ca).

Rape is associated with warfare, as conquering armies have long considered rape of their enemies' women one of the spoils of war. Among the ancient Greeks, rape was socially acceptable and well within the rules of warfare. During the Crusades, even knights and pilgrims, who were bound by vows of chivalry and Christian piety, raped as they marched toward Constantinople.

The practice has continued, from the Crusades through the war in Vietnam, to more recent conflicts. The systematic rape of Bosnian women by Serbian army officers during the civil war in Yugoslavia, part of an official policy of genocide, horrified the world. In Haiti, the rape of politically involved women became a norm in the wake of the 1991 military coup that ousted President Jean-Bertrand Aristide. In the former Yugoslavia, victims told of rape camps set up for soldiers with captured women. In Darfur, in the Sudan, thousands of women and girls have been raped since 2003, when an armed conflict began. In 2014, more than 200 young girls were abducted from their school in northern Nigeria by a radical Islamic group, to be sold into sexual slavery or marriage in protest against their attending western-style schools.

Incidence of Sexual Assault

How many sexual assaults occur each year, and what is known about rape patterns? In 2012, about 21,900 sexual assaults

occurred in Canada, a slight decrease from the previous year. These statistics represent an overall general downward trend over the years. However, sexual assault has a very low report rate, as we know from victimization surveys. It also tends to have a lower clearance rate than crimes of violence in general. The good news is that the rate of sexual assault reported to the police has continued to increase over the years.

Because of the low report rate of acquaintance-related sexual assault, and because of the difficulty of solving stranger-related cases, the police often call on the public for assistance in solving cases, as the Crime in the News box illustrates. After a violent sexual assault by a stranger in public, the police issued a crime re-enactment and released a composite photo of the subject.

Population density influences the rape rate: Metropolitan areas have a rape rate significantly higher than in rural areas. Nonetheless, urban areas have experienced a much higher drop in rape reports than rural areas. Rape is also a warm-weather crime, usually occurring during July and August, with the lowest rates occurring during December, January, and February.

Data must be interpreted cautiously because sexual assault is frequently under-reported by victims. In Canada, of all personal victimizations studied by the General Social Survey, only 8 percent of sexual assault victims report the crime to the police.[49] Many are embarrassed, believe nothing can be done, or blame themselves. In a now older, but important American study of campus date rape, researchers found that only

27 percent of the women whose sexual assault met the legal definition of rape thought of themselves as rape victims.[50]

Males are victims of sexual assault too, although not nearly to the extent women are. However, male victims experience similar effects: depression, self-blame, low self-esteem, anger, anxiety, and sexuality problems.[51] Although most sexual assault perpetrators are male, females are responsible for between 1 percent and 4 percent of offences against youths.[52]

Official data often reflect reporting practices. Chapter 3 refers to this phenomenon as report-sensitive crime. At least 20 percent of adult women, 15 percent of university-aged women, and 12 percent of adolescent girls have experienced sexual abuse or assault sometime during their lifetime, so it is evident that both the official and the victimization statistics significantly undercount rape.[53] In Canada, 39 percent of women over 18 years of age report having experienced sexual assault in their adult lifetime, 5 percent in the previous year.[54] An independent study of sexual contact between physicians and patients conducted by the Ontario College of Physicians and Surgeons estimated that the rate of sexual abuse by doctors was nearly 10 percent.[55] Exhibit 10.3 provides additional detail about sexual assault in Canada.

A large continuum of violence against women exists in our society, ranging from date rape and sexual assault to wife abuse and domestic violence. The fact that such crimes are examples of **gendered violence** should be obvious from the proportion of female victims and male offenders.

Types of Rapists

Some rapes are planned, others are spontaneous; some focus on a particular victim, while others occur during the commission of other crimes, such as burglary.[56] Some rapists are one-time offenders, while others engage in multiple or serial rapes. Some attack their victims without warning ("blitz rapes"); others try to "capture" their victims by striking up a conversation or by offering them a ride; others use a personal relationship to gain access to their target.[57]

One of the best-known attempts to classify the personality of rapists was made by Groth, a psychological expert on classification of sex offenders. He said every rape encounter contains three elements: anger, power, and sexuality:[58]

- *Anger rape.* This rape occurs when sexuality becomes a means of expressing and discharging pent-up anger and rage. The rapist uses far more brutality than would have been necessary if his real objective had been simply to have sex with his victim. His aim is to hurt his victim as much as possible; the sexual aspect of rape may be an afterthought.
- *Power rape.* This type of rape involves an attacker who does not want to harm his victim as much as he wants to possess her sexually. His goal is sexual conquest, and he uses only the amount of force necessary to achieve his objective. The power rapist wants to be in control, to be able to dominate women, and have them at his mercy.
- *Sadistic rape.* This type of rape involves both sexuality and aggression. The sadistic rapist is bound up in ritual—he may torment his victim, bind her, or torture her. In the rapist's view, his victims are usually related to a personal characteristic that he wants to harm or destroy.

About 55 percent of rapists are of the power type; 40 percent, the anger type; and 5 percent, the sadistic type. The key issue is that rape is a crime of violence and not a sexual act. Rape might be committed during the course of another crime or might be caused by intense anger toward women, but it is almost always a gendered crime committed by men against women.[59]

gendered violence The concept that some forms of violence tend to be committed against women, by men, such as sexual assault, stalking, and domestic violence.

EXHIBIT 10.3

Quick Facts about Sexual Assault

- As with other violent crimes, sexual assault continues a downward trend.
- The most common sexual assault offence is sexual assault level one, which is committed without a weapon or extra violence.
- Most victims are female, usually between 15 and 25 years of age, single, working or student, living in a rural area, participating in many evening activities, and from a variety of income groups.
- Most sexual assaults take place in or around residences, with only a minority occurring in public places.
- One-quarter of victimizations surveyed by the GSS result in an injury; however, the incidence of injury is higher for the offences of physical assault (31 percent) and robbery (30 percent), than for sexual assault (7 percent).
- A third of child victims are male, compared to 10 percent of adult and youth victims.
- Victimization rates are highest for female teenagers; rates of offending highest for males.
- Provincial and territorial rates vary from a high in the North to a low in the East.
- Of all offences, sexual offences are least likely (about 10 percent) to be reported to police.
- Reasons for not reporting include the belief it is a personal matter, the person not wanting the police involved, and the victim fearing revenge.
- Sexual offences are the least likely violent crime to be founded and to result in charges.

SOURCES: "Impacts and Consequences of Victimization, GSS 2004," by Kathy AuCoin and Diane Beauchamp, *Juristat* 27, 1, 2007; "Crime Statistics in Canada, 2012," by Samuel Perreault, Statistics Canada 2013.

Types of Rape

Criminologists also divide rapes into two categories: stranger rapes and acquaintance rapes. The former involve two people who have never met; the latter involve someone known to the victim, even a family member or friend. So-called date rape, which involves acquaintances, has a low report rate.

It is difficult to estimate the ratio of rapes involving strangers to those in which victim and assailant were in some way acquainted, as women are more reluctant to report acts involving acquaintances. Official police statistics usually show that 90 percent of sexual assaults involved strangers. However, the 2009 GSS reported the percentage of stranger sexual assaults at 37 percent, and acquaintance assaults at 51 percent.[60]

Date Rape. Many sexual assaults involve a friend or acquaintance.[61] Because women are less likely to report crimes involving acquaintances, it is possible that acquaintance rape, referred to as **date rape**, constitutes the bulk of sexual assaults.

Some date rapes occur on first dates, others after a relationship has been developing, and still others after the couple have been involved. The male may feel he has invested so much time and money in his partner that he is owed sexual relations or that sexual intimacy is an expression that the involvement is progressing.[62]

A survey of Canadian college and university women found that about one-third had experienced an episode of physical, verbal, or psychological sexual coercion; 25 percent said they had experienced unwanted sexual relations during the previous year.[63]

The incidence of date rape may be even higher than surveys indicate because many victims blame themselves and do not recognize the incident as a rape, saying, for example, "I should have fought back harder," or "I should not have gotten drunk." Some victims do not report because they do not view their experiences as a "real rape," which they believe involves a strange man "jumping out of the bushes"; others are too embarrassed or frightened to report the crime.[64]

To fight back, some campus women's groups wrote on bathroom walls the names of men accused of date rape as a way to alert potential victims about men they might consider trustworthy friends.[65] One disturbing phenomenon is campus gang rape, in which a group of men attack a defenceless or inebriated victim, while another is the growing number of women reporting that they have been raped while sedated by the "date rape drug," Rohypnol.[66]

Marital Rape. Some women are raped by their husbands as part of an overall pattern of spousal abuse, often accompanied by brutal and sadistic beatings.[67]

Until recently, a legally married husband could not be charged with raping his wife, referred to as the **marital exemption**. This legal doctrine can be traced to the 16th-century pronouncement of Matthew Hale, England's chief justice, who wrote, "The husband cannot be guilty of rape committed by himself upon his lawful wife, for by their mutual matrimonial consent and contract the wife hath given up herself in this kind unto the husband which she cannot retract."[68] The exemption was abolished in Canada in 1983. In 1980, only three American states had laws against marital rape; today almost every state recognizes marital rape as a crime.

The Cause of Rape

What factors cause rape? The answers formulated by criminologists are varied; however, most explanations can be grouped into a few categories.

Evolutionary/Biological Factors. Evolutionary/biological aspects of the male sexual drive may have once served the purpose of maximizing offspring. Some believe that males still have a natural sexual drive that encourages them to have intimate relations with as many women as possible.[69] Men who are sexually aggressive may have the reproductive edge over their more passive peers; however, women are more cautious and want stable partners who are willing to make a long-term commitment to child rearing. This difference produces sexual tension that causes men to use forceful copulatory tactics, especially when the chances of punishment are quite low.[70]

However, one important evolutionary criticism is that less aggressive males who devote time to child rearing may also have children who are less likely to deviate and more likely to reach adulthood and to reproduce.

Male Socialization. In contrast, some researchers argue that rape is a function of male socialization.[71] Boys are taught to be aggressive, to separate sexual feelings from love and affection, and to think of sexual inexperience as a mark of shame. Similarly, sexual insecurity may lead some men to commit rape to bolster their self-image and masculine identity.

If rape is an expression of male anger and the devaluation of women, men socialized into traditional sex-role stereotypes are more likely to be sexually aggressive (see also the nearby Criminology Research box on masculinity and sexual violence among the urban poor).

> **date rape** A form of sexual assault that occurs between acquaintances; of all sexual assaults, it has the lowest level of reporting.
>
> **marital exemption** The practice in some jurisdictions of prohibiting the prosecution of husbands for the rape of their wives.

In an important work, Walter DeKeseredy, Shahid Alvi, Martin Schwartz, and E. Andreas Tomaszewski studied the lives of people whose economic circumstances force them to live in urban housing projects. They found that as the economy of North America shifts from manufacturing to services, a greater percentage of working-class men and women end up in urban public housing.

Unable to care for their families and live up to their culturally defined role as breadwinner, socially and economically excluded men experience high levels of stress because their normal paths for personal power and prestige are blocked. Stress prompts them to seek support from male peers with similar problems. Peer group support may be helpful, but it has consequences. Socially and economically excluded males in and around public housing complexes view wife beating, rape, and other forms of male-to-female victimization as legitimate and effective means of repairing their damaged masculinity. Keeping women under control helps shore up their fragile self-identity.

Compounding the problem, many male public housing residents are not emotionally attached to women and have little interest in marriage and family. These single, unemployed inner-city men become heavily integrated into peer groups that pressure them to be sexually active, brag about their sexual encounters, and reward them for breaching the sexual defences of women. Young males in this culture are expected to have high or exaggerated levels of sexual involvement, which, for most men, regardless of their social class position, is almost impossible to achieve. If their peers see them as failures with women, they will face group ridicule and experience sexual frustration. Sexual violence and rape may be an outcome of peer pressure to constantly prove one's manhood.

DeKeseredy and his colleagues note that poor urban women are not simply passive victims of this patriarchal domination and control. A growing number of them are creating autonomy for themselves and their "sisters." When they make the financial decisions for the household and put the lease for the car in their own name, their actions are perceived by their mates as an assault on their masculinity. Some men deal with their partner's economic autonomy by leaving them, while others use violence as a means of sabotaging women's attempts to gain economic independence. For example, women who have obtained better economic resources through welfare reform are at greater risk of being abused because the male partner fears that the woman will be able to leave him or will meet a more attractive, financially secure man in the workplace.

Social service providers are now hearing many reports of women who are stalked or assaulted in their workplaces by their economically disenfranchised partner as a means of making them lose their job and, thereby, their economic independence. Male violence deters women from participating in the paid labour market. Many abused female public housing residents, like other poor battered women, are forced to return to their violent partner out of economic necessity.

Critical Thinking

1. Discuss the following statement: Some men assault and/or rape women in a misguided attempt to deflect accusations that they are weak and passive around women.

2. Is sexual assault used as a means of keeping women in their place so that they will not challenge male economic superiority?

SOURCES: Walter S. DeKeseredy, Shahid Alvi, Martin D. Schwartz, and E. Andreas Tomaszewski. *Under Siege: Poverty and Crime in a Public Housing Community* (New York: Lexington Books, 2003); Walter S. DeKeseredy and Martin D. Schwartz, "Theorizing Public Housing Women Abuse as a Function of Economic Exclusion and Male Peer Support," *Women's Health & Urban Life: An International and Interdisciplinary Journal* 1 (2002): 26–45.

CONNECTIONS

In Chapter 9, we discussed Messerschmidt's view that men's need to prove their masculinity helps them to justify their abuse of women. Men who are sexually violent need to prove that they are not effeminate.

Psychological Views. Another view is that rapists have some type of personality disorder or mental illness. Many incarcerated rapists often exhibit psychotic tendencies, and some have hostile and sadistic feelings toward women.[72]

Social Learning. Men often learn to commit rapes from, and are influenced by, watching violent or pornographic films featuring women who are beaten, raped, or tortured.[73]

In one case, a 12-year-old boy in Providence, Rhode Island, sexually assaulted a 10-year-old girl on a pool table after watching TV coverage of a case in which a woman was similarly raped.[74] (The case was made into a film, *The Accused*, starring Jodie Foster.)

CONNECTIONS

The social learning view is explored further in Chapter 13, where the issue of pornography and violence is analyzed in greater detail. Most research does not link watching pornographic films to sexual violence, but a link may exist between sexual aggression and viewing movies whose theme is sexual violence.

Sexual Motivation.   Most current views of rape hold that it is a violent act. Yet, some rapes might still have a sexual motive.[75] Although older criminals may be raping for motives of power and control, younger offenders are seeking sexual gratification.

In sum, rape is the product of many social, cultural, and psychological forces.[76] Although some experts view rape as a normal response to an abnormal environment, others view it as the product of a disturbed mind and deviant life experiences.

Rape and the Law

Women are reluctant to report this crime because of how rape victims are often treated by police, prosecutors, and court personnel. In the past, police were reluctant to make arrests, and courts reluctant to convict, in cases where the woman was not beaten seriously or in which she had previously known her attacker. Laws made rape so difficult to prove that women believed the chances of their attacker being convicted were insufficient to warrant their participation in the prosecutorial process.

However, police and courts have become more sensitive and are now just as likely to investigate "acquaintance" rapes as they are "aggravated" rapes involving multiple offenders, weapons, and victim injuries. The justice system is more willing to take rape cases seriously and to not ignore those assaults in which the victim and attacker had a prior relationship or those that did not involve serious injury.[77]

Proving Rape.   Proving guilt in a rape case is challenging because some psychiatrists still maintain that women create false accusations.

Sexism has created a cultural suspicion of women. Consequently, some people attempt to shift the burden to the woman and prove that she provoked the rape. Jurors are sometimes swayed by the insinuation that the rape was victim-precipitated, thus shifting blame from rapist to victim. To get a conviction, prosecutors must establish that the act was forced and that voluntary compliance did not exist.

Rape represents a major legal challenge.[78] One issue is **consent**. Proving victim dissent is not a requirement in any other violent crime (robbery victims do not have to prove they did not entice their attacker by flaunting expensive jewellery); yet, in rape cases, defence counsel can try to create a reasonable doubt about the woman's credibility under sections 265.4 and 276.1 of the *Criminal Code*. A defence attorney might try to introduce suspicion in the minds of the jury that the woman may have consented to the sexual act and later regretted her decision.

Law Reform.   Because of the difficulty victims have had in receiving justice in rape cases, legislation in Canada has undergone significant change since 1983. Efforts for reform have included changing the language of statutes, dropping the conditions of recent complaint and corroboration, and developing **shield laws** to protect women from being questioned about their sexual history unless it is judged to have a direct bearing on the case. These changes are quickly becoming an international standard.[79]

In addition to requiring evidence that consent was not given, the common law of rape required **corroboration** that the crime of rape actually took place. This requirement involved the need for independent or third-party evidence from police officers, physicians, and witnesses that the accused was actually the person who committed the crime, that sexual penetration took place, and that force was present and consent absent.[80] Current law does not require corroboration, intercourse, or a complaint to be filed immediately.

In the early 1990s, consent also became legally required, and it is now considered impossible for consent to be given when the victim is too drunk to know what is happening. Section 273.1 of Canada's *Criminal Code* requires that sexual activity be voluntary. No consent is obtained, where

- the agreement is expressed by someone else;
- the victim is incapable of consenting to the activity (e.g., unconscious);
- the accused induces the victim by abusing a position of trust, power, or authority;
- the victim expresses, by words or conduct, a lack of agreement to engage in the activity; or
- the victim, having consented, expresses by words or conduct, a lack of agreement to continue.

Therefore, sexual assault laws make illegal any type of forcible or non-consensual sex. However, the credibility of sexual assault victims is still more likely to be challenged than is testimony of victims of non-sexual assault.[81]

For example, a psychologist found that judges tend to characterize sexual assault as erotic rather than as violent, that the consent laws are not applied uniformly, and that only when the victim resists an unwanted advance will the court recognize lack of consent.[82] Clearly, more efforts are needed to improve the prosecution rate in sexual assault cases.

consent   The agreement of the victim to have sexual relations with another person, the lack of which is a legal element in the charge of sexual assault; cannot be extinguished by drunkenness.

shield laws   Legislation designed to protect rape victims by prohibiting the defence attorney from inquiring about their previous sexual relationships.

corroboration   The backing up of a claim of sexual assault by a third party, which before 1983, was required in a charge alleging sexual assault; no longer required.

MURDER

There are different degrees of murder, from accidental manslaughter to premeditated homicide, and each requires different levels of proof. To prove first-degree murder, it has to be demonstrated that the act was planned and premeditated. Prosecutors must prove that the accused intentionally desired the death of the victim. In second-degree murder, while prior intent is not an issue, malice might be. Malice is assumed to exist when someone kills another in the absence of apparent provocation. Implied malice exists when death results from negligent behaviour; even though the perpetrator did not want to kill the victim, the killing was the result of a dangerous act and is considered a form of murder.

Degrees of Murder

Murder is defined in the common law as "the unlawful killing of a human being with malice aforethought." Exhibit 10.4 details some facts about homicide in Canada.

There are different levels or degrees of homicide. This categorization came about with the abolition of capital punishment in 1976. (The Famous Canadian Court Cases box on page 335 discusses the last executions in Canada.) Murder in the first degree occurs when a person kills after deliberation. **Premeditation** means that the killing was considered beforehand, and that it was more than an act of impulse.

Second-degree murder requires the actor to have malice but not premeditation, and it occurs when disregard for the victim or the desire to inflict serious bodily harm results in the loss of life.

An unlawful homicide without malice is called manslaughter. Voluntary manslaughter refers to a killing committed in the heat of passion or during a sudden quarrel with sufficient provocation to produce violence; although intent may be present, malice is not. Involuntary or negligent manslaughter refers to a killing that occurs when a person's acts are negligent and without regard for the harm that such actions may cause others. Most involuntary manslaughter cases involve motor vehicle deaths, as when a drunk driver causes the death of a pedestrian. However, people can be held criminally liable for the death of another in any instance in which the actor's disregard of safety causes the death. Infanticide involves the killing of an infant, and has a long and changing history under the law. And a recent category, workplace homicide, involves a death caused by something a corporation did or failed to do at work.

The Nature and Extent of Murder

The Homicide Survey details information on all homicide offences in Canada since 1961. Homicide is relatively rare in Canada, with only 543 offences in 2012, for a rate of

EXHIBIT 10.4

Quick Facts about Homicide in Canada

- Police reported 543 homicides in Canada in 2012, down from 598 in 2011.
- Shooting (34 percent) accounted for most deaths in 2005, followed by stabbing (30 percent), beating (22 percent), strangulation (7 percent), and shaken baby syndrome (2 percent).
- Homicide rates increase from east to west, with Prince Edward Island having the lowest rate (0), compared with Manitoba (4.1), in 2012.
- Highest ranked homicide rates were in Thunder Bay, Winnipeg, Regina, and Halifax.
- Gang-related homicides remained stable in 2012, with 95 incidents.
- Males are more likely to be homicide victims (73 percent) and accused (90 percent).
- Most victims knew their killer. Of 454 homicides solved by police in 2009, 14 percent were killed by spouse, other family member (19 percent), 39 percent by acquaintance, 9 percent by someone known through criminal relationship, and 18 percent by a stranger.
- In child murder cases, the killer is often a parent (39 percent), and, of all parents who kill, 54 percent are mothers.
- Homicides committed by strangers are at their lowest in 40 years in 2012, and account for 16 percent of solved homicides compared to someone known (84 percent).
- Two-thirds of adults accused of homicide and half of adult victims had a criminal record.
- Spousal-related homicides account for 20 percent of solved homicides in 2012.
- Canada's homicide rate ranked fifth among comparable countries.
- Aboriginal people account for 3 percent of the population, 17 percent of homicide victims, and 23 percent of those accused of homicide.
- The largest decrease in homicides for any age group in 2012 was 18- to 24-year-olds.
- Canada's homicide rate was 1.6 in 2012, compared to 4.67 in the United States.

SOURCES: "Homicide in Canada, 2005," *Juristat* 26, 6, 2006; *Homicide in Canada*, 2012, Jillian Boyce and Adam Cotter, Statistics Canada; "Police-reported Crime Statistics, 2012," Statistics Canada, 2013.

murder Colloquially refers to the killing of one person by another; homicide is separated into the categories of first-degree and second-degree murder, manslaughter, and infanticide.

premeditation The thinking out and planning of a crime; must be proven by the prosecution to have occurred to qualify for the charge of first-degree homicide.

It reads like a movie, and at any point as it played out I could have said I didn't believe it. In April 2008, Nicole Ryan was charged with trying to hire a hit man to murder her husband. She was a 38-year-old schoolteacher in Digby, Nova Scotia, and her husband was a member of the armed forces.

After she was arrested, she was given a psychiatric evaluation and found fit to stand trial.

An undercover RCMP officer said he had been paid $10,000 to arrange the death, and she readily admitted that she had done so. The surprise came in 2010 when the trial judge said that she was innocent of attempted murder because she had been under duress at the time.

The defense of duress requires proving that a criminal act was committed in order to avoid a larger evil, such as harm against oneself or one's family, for example. I have heard of self-defense used in spousal homicide cases, but never duress. The fact that she claimed duress suggested that she feared for her safety or perhaps the safety of someone else.

Given that possibility, but also knowing how the justice system worked, I wasn't surprised when I found out that the Crown was appealing the acquittal on the basis that hiring a hit man was an excessive response to the duress she felt she was under. They did not deny the facts but rather the application of that point of law.

In a similar case over 25 years ago, this was also the decision in the Angelique Lynn Lavallee case, where, when threatened with harm, the victim turned on her attacker and killed him. She also was initially acquitted and the case ended up in the Supreme Court. That appeal eventually became the basis for the battered wife defense in Canada.

Nicole Ryan, it turns out, also lived in a battered relationship. It appears that for years, her husband threatened her and her daughter, and said he would kill her if she ever left him. News reports now show that when she turned to authorities for help, they said there was nothing they could do.

She testified that her husband threatened her with a gun and said he would burn the house down. The defense said that as a result, she was in imminent fear of her life, but the prosecution doubted the imminent threat, pointing out that there had been a four-month lapse between being threatened and paying the undercover police officer.

While the appeal was being heard, her daughter was in interim custody with the father in Ontario, while she lived with her sister. The wait must have seemed interminable. And then finally, in April 2011, the Nova Scotia Court of Appeal agreed in what has been called a landmark decision that she was acting under duress.

The Crown has now appealed that decision, in a display of throwing good money after bad, and she is now case number 34272 in the Supreme Court of Canada. The heart of the matter is that it seems duress has never been used in this way before. The fact that the Supreme Court is hearing the case is evidence that it also considers the case novel, because it only hears a fraction of the cases that are submitted to it.

However, as others have pointed out, while the appeal will test the law, there are also questions in the case that will likely go unanswered. Why was the husband allowed to have guns? Why was it that her requests for assistance went unanswered? Why did the police set out to arrest her in what seems to be a sting operation?

These questions provide drama in a movie but should have no part in real life.

SOURCE: Copyright Chris McCormick, published in the *Daily Gleaner* (Fredericton), October 20, 2011.

1.6 per 100,000. This represents a decrease of 10 percent from 2011, and the lowest rate since 1966.

What else do the official crime statistics tell us about murder today? Murder is gendered, with most crimes committed by males, and the victims tend to be males over 18 years of age. Murder, like many crimes, also tends to be an intraracial crime, committed by people against members of their own ethnic group. Most homicides involve a single victim, and most are solved by the police. Violent crimes tend to have a high clearance rate, and homicide is no exception, with about three-quarters solved by the police. Most people are killed by acquaintances, and few people are killed by a stranger. Most are killed during a conflict, not during the course of another crime. Youths account for a growing percent of all accused persons.

The next section explores the relationship between social and ecological factors and murder.

Murderous Relations

The relationship between the murderer and the victim has received a great deal of attention from criminologists. They separate murders into those involving strangers— typically stemming from a crime, such as a robbery or drug deal—and those involving acquaintance homicides, which typically result from disputes between family, friends, and acquaintances.

CONNECTIONS

In a discussion of victim precipitation theory in Chapter 4, we mentioned the argument made by some criminologists that murder victims help create the "transaction" that leads to their death.

Criminology Research
The Death of James Bulger

On February 12, 1993, the security cameras at a shopping centre near Liverpool, England, recorded two-year-old James Bulger being abducted by two strangers. He was taken on a long walk, cruelly tortured, sexually abused, beaten to death, and abandoned on the railroad tracks. Jon Venables and Robert Thompson, his murderers, were 10 years old. When arrested and questioned, they each denied their role in the murder and blamed the other.

Jon's psychological profile showed that he was generally well behaved but sometimes hyperactive. His mother thought that Jon was the victim of bullies at school. Jon's parents had repeatedly split up and reunited, undermining the family as a source of stability. Jon seemed to have low self-esteem and was defensive about

his family. He had a history of self-inflicted violence: banging his head against the wall and cutting himself with scissors. He was also destructive at school. Both his siblings had developmental problems, and his parents had histories of clinical depression. His mother had, on occasion, physically and verbally assaulted Jon.

Robert's psychological profile showed that he was intelligent and had no sign of mental illness or depression. However, he was often assaulted by his older brothers and alcoholic mother. His father beat his wife and eventually abandoned the family. Both his mother and father came from abusive families. One of his brothers had been placed in protective services after he had been abused. Another was a thief, and another was an arsonist

and suspected of sexually abusing young children.

An important issue in the trial was whether the boys knew the difference between right and wrong. The concept of *doli incapax* was established to protect innocent children from punishment, and dates back to Roman law. If a child cannot grasp the consequences of his or her actions, he or she is legally incapable of wrongdoing. Jon and Robert's teachers and psychiatrists testified that they believed the defendants knew the severity of their crime. The interviews recorded by the police also revealed that the boys understood the charges against them.

The judge addressed the boys: "The killing of James Bulger was an act of unparalleled evil and barbarity. This child of two

---

Spousal Relations. Women are more likely to be killed by their mates than are men. In Canada since 1974, three-quarters of victims who were killed by someone they had an intimate relationship with were women. Although the number of unmarried men killed by their partners declined in the late 1990s, the rate of women killed by the men they lived with increased dramatically.

Men kill their spouses because they fear losing control and power. Because people who live together without marriage have a legally and socially more "open" relationship, cohabiting males are more likely to feel loss of control and exert their power by using violence. In contrast, research indicates that females who kill their mates do so after suffering repeated violent attacks.[83]

Recent research by Geris Serran and Philip Firestone, respectively a psychologist and a psychiatrist at the University of Ottawa, looks at intimate partner homicide and the differences that exist in the motivation behind the homicide. They propose the male proprietariness theory and the self-defence theory as a means of understanding the gender differences in spousal homicide. These theories suggest that dynamics of the relationship play an important role in the increasing violence, which can eventually result in homicide.[84]

Between 1991 and 2000, separated women aged 15 to 24 were killed at a rate 10 times higher than the homicide rate for separated women aged 55 years and older. Women have a heightened risk of homicide after separation, and the motive is most often male jealousy.[85]

Women Who Kill. Statistics Canada data show that although the killing of children represents a small proportion of the total number of homicides in Canada, it represents the largest proportion of killing done by women. Infanticide is usually committed by very young women, and the vast majority of accused are single. Many of these women have a mental illness, and, in fact, that is how the law against infanticide has been defined since the 1940s.[86]

Children Who Kill. The rate of homicide committed by youths rises as youth approach 18 years of age, and half of all homicides committed by youth involve more than one offender. Weapons are often involved, and common targets are friends and acquaintances. Research by Silverman and Meloff shows that younger children's victims are more likely to be family members, whereas older children are more likely to kill in the commission of other crimes, and are more likely to kill strangers (see also the nearby Criminology Research box on the murder of James Bulger in the United Kingdom).[87]

Stranger Relations. The likelihood of stranger-homicide is fairly low. Most stranger-related homicides occur during the commission of other offences, such as assault, robbery, and sexual assault. Very few murders are random or motiveless, such as would occur if a homeowner told a motorist to move his car because it is blocking the driveway and in the ensuing argument got a pistol and killed the motorist.[88]

How do murderous relations develop between two people who have never met? Luckenbill's study of murder was taken from his mother on a journey of over two miles and then, on the railway line, was battered to death without mercy. Then his body was placed across the railway line so it would be run over by a train in an attempt to conceal his murder. In my judgment your conduct was both cunning and very wicked."

With their conviction for the murder of James Bulger, Jon Venables and Robert Thompson became the youngest convicted murderers in Britain in 250 years. Their original sentence of 15 years was overturned when the European Court of Human Rights decreed in 1999 that the boys had not received a fair trial and mandated their release after eight years in jail. In a newspaper phone poll, 96 percent of the British public protested that the boys

had been released. Because of the public outcry over the killing, Jon and Robert have been given false identities for their own safety.

SOURCES: Blake Morrison, "Children of Circumstance," *The New Yorker*, February 14, 1994, 48–60; Shirley Lynn Scott, "Death of James Bulger," Court TV's Crime Library, www.crimelibrary.com/notorious_murders/young/bulger/1.html.

Preacher Spells out Britain's Moral Decline

By Victoria Combe, Churches Correspondent

The American evangelist Morris Cerullo yesterday took two full-page adverts in broadsheet newspapers, costing more than £40,000, to outline Britain's "rapid moral and spiritual decline". . . .

Mr. Cerullo claimed Britain's laws, formerly a model of Christian principles for other governments, had been "eroded" since the 1960s by "atheists, rationalists and confused spiritual leaders". . . .

Listing disasters such as Hillsborough, Lockerbie and the Jamie Bulger killing, he said Britain was in a state of "rapid decline morally, spiritually and materially". [The] British people want political leaders who tell them the truth. Men and women who live honestly. They want unconfused Church leaders. "The nation wants men of integrity who lead by what God of the Bible has to say, not what they think may be politically acceptable."

SOURCE: Excerpted from "Preacher Spells Out Britain's Moral Decline," by Victoria Combe, July 29, 1996. © *The Daily Telegraph*.

---

transactions found common sequential patterns of behaviour in the transaction between killer and victim: The victim makes what the perpetrator considers an offensive move, the perpetrator typically retaliates in a verbal or physical manner, and in the ensuing fight, the victim is slain or injured (see Figure 10.3 on page 332).[89] Research shows that the person who initiates a conflict with a stranger in public is usually the one to get hurt.

Conversely, Kennedy and Silverman found that seniors are likely to be the victims of theft-based homicide, by strangers, in their homes. Even though routine activities theory would suggest that seniors are least likely to be victimized by homicide, in cases of household theft, they stand a high risk because the house is usually the intended victim of the crime, and the seniors are victimized during the course of the crime.[90]

Youths living on the street, however, experience violence certainly as a result of the activities they engage in and almost as a part of their culture.[91]

Homicide Networks

Although some murders may be the result of violence by a stranger, others involve a social interaction between people who know each other and whose destructive social interaction leads to death.[92] These seemingly senseless deaths often mask an underlying cause: revenge, dispute resolution, jealousy, bad drug deals, racial bias, or threats to identity or status.[93] Perpetrators and victims are joined in a "homicide network" that links victims, suspects, and witnesses together.

Often a prior act of violence, motivated by profit or greed, generates revenge killings. The instigator of one criminal act becomes the victim in another. Those individuals who are most isolated from conventional society are those most likely to seek "street justice." Witness the battle between the Hells Angels and the Rock Machine motorcycle gangs in Quebec. The combatants take the victimization of family and friends seriously, killing the people they feel are responsible.[94]

Types of Murderers

Other forms of stranger homicides take a toll on society. **Thrill killings** involve impulsive violence motivated by the killer's decision to kill a stranger as an act of daring or recklessness.

Gang killings involve members of gangs who make violence part of their group activity. Some of these gangs engage

thrill killings Impulsive violent murders motivated by the killer's decision to kill a stranger as an act of daring or recklessness.

gang killings Murders committed by gangs who make violence part of their group activity; often committed as part of warfare over territory or control of the drug trade.

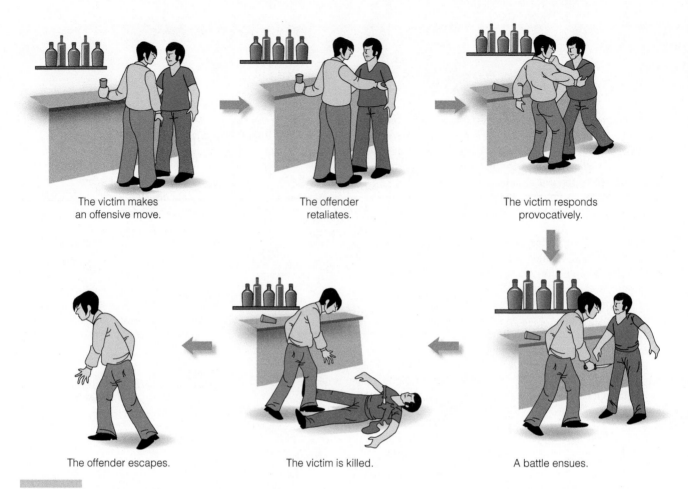

The victim makes an offensive move.

The offender retaliates.

The victim responds provocatively.

A battle ensues.

The victim is killed.

The offender escapes.

FIGURE 10.3
Murder Transactions

in warfare over territory or control of the drug trade; in drive-by shootings, enemies are killed and strangers are sometimes caught in the crossfire.

Cult killings occur when members of religious cults are ordered to kill by their leaders, and examples include the killings in Jonestown, Guyana, and those by the Solar Temple cult. On some occasions, the cult members kill peers who deviate from the leader's teachings. Other crimes involve random violence out of the misguided belief that the strangers are a threat to the cult's existence. In Matamoros, Mexico, police uncovered the grave of a 21-year-old American college student who had served as a human sacrifice for members of a Mexican drug ring that practised *palo mayombe,* a form of black magic; killing the youth was believed to bring immunity from bullets and criminal prosecution.[95]

In 1994, bodies were recovered in homes belonging to the Order of the Solar Temple cult in Switzerland and Montreal. Some members of the apocalyptic cult were murdered, while others committed suicide. The cult combined teachings from medieval orders, such as the Knights Templar, and the leaders appropriated their followers' wealth for their own personal gain. Police speculated the cult's leaders were also involved in an international money-laundering and arms-smuggling operation.

Some murders blamed on Satanism are not carried out by members of an organized group but are perpetrated by individuals who have visions of the Devil. In 1993, a 15-year-old Houston boy killed his mother after hearing the Devil tell him to "kill all the Christians"; law enforcement officials linked the boy's passion for heavy metal music to the crime.[96]

Serial Murder

Donald Harvey was described as pleasant and normal by those who knew him best. However, his co-workers in a Cincinnati-area hospital where he worked as a nurse's aide referred to Harvey as the "angel of death" because so many patients died in his ward. An investigation led to Harvey

cult killings Murders committed by members of religious cults who are ordered to kill as part of the cult's rituals.

being convicted of killing at least 21 patients.[97] This is not our typical image of a serial killer.

However, some serial murderers, such as Ted Bundy, fit the stereotype more easily, as he roamed the country seemingly killing at random. Others terrorize a city, such as the Green River Killer, believed to have slain more than four dozen young women in Seattle; and the Hillside Stranglers who tortured and killed 10 women in the Los Angeles area. Others, such as Donald Harvey and Milwaukee cannibal Jeffrey Dahmer, kill so cunningly that many victims are dispatched before the authorities even realize the deaths can be attributed to a single perpetrator.

In 2007, Robert Pickton, a Canadian pig farmer, was charged and convicted of murdering six women who had gone missing from the Vancouver area. He lured women to his farm, where he assaulted and killed them. Because he is suspected of killing many more, perhaps up to 50, he is probably Canada's worst serial killer.

Serial killers operate over a long period and can be distinguished from the **mass murderer**, who kills many victims in a single, violent outburst, such as Thomas Hamilton's outburst in Dunblane, Scotland, or James Huberty's murder of 21 people in a McDonald's restaurant in San Ysidro, California. In Canada, the most infamous mass murder occurred at the Montreal Polytechnique in 1989.

Types of Serial Murderers.   Research shows that serial killers have long histories of violence, beginning in childhood with the targeting of other children, siblings, and small animals.[98] They maintain superficial relationships with others, have trouble relating to the opposite sex, and have guilt feelings about sex. Despite these commonalities, there is no single distinct type of serial killer.

Possible contributing factors include mental illness, sexual frustration, neurological damage, child abuse and neglect, smothering relationships with mothers, and childhood anxiety. However, most experts view serial killers as sociopaths who, from early childhood, demonstrate bizarre behaviour, such as torturing animals, who are immune to their victims' suffering, and who bask in the media limelight.

However, Philip Jenkins's study of serial murder in England identified offenders who had no apparent personality problems until late in their lives, were married and respectable, and even had careers in the armed services and police.[99]

Holmes and DeBurger have studied serial killers and found that they can be divided into at least four types:

- *Visionary killers*, who commit psychotic murders in response to an inner voice or vision
- *Mission-oriented killers*, who want to kill persons considered undesirable, e.g., prostitutes
- *Hedonistic killers*, thrill-seekers who get excitement and sexual pleasure from their acts
- *Power/control-oriented killers*, who enjoy having complete control over their victims[100]

Other types of serial killers include the sadistic child killer, who gains sexual satisfaction from torturing and killing children; the psychopathic killer, who is motivated by a character disorder that results in their being unable to experience feelings of shame, guilt, or other normal human emotions; and professional hit killers, who assassinate complete strangers for economic, political, or ideological reasons (terrorists and organized crime figures fall within this category). Professional killers are not usually considered as "serial killers," by definition.

When the Serial Killer Is a Woman.   An estimated 10 percent to 15 percent of serial killers are women.[101] Female killers are older, usually abuse both alcohol and drugs, and often are diagnosed as having histrionic, bipolar, borderline, dissociative, and antisocial personality disorders. The typical female serial killer smothers or poisons someone she knows, suffered herself from abuse in a disrupted family, has a low education level, and if she is employed, works in a low-status position.

Controlling Serial Killers.   Police are often at a loss to control random killers who leave few clues, constantly move, and have little connection with their victims. In the 1980s, because of a series of high-profile serial homicides that encompassed multiple jurisdictions, a better way for police to share information was proposed. The "automated case linkage system," called ViCLAS (Violent Crime Linkage Analysis System), helps police profile cases and identify potential suspects. It was modelled on the computerized information service developed by the FBI, called the Violent Criminal Apprehension Program (VICAP), which gathers information and matches offence characteristics on violent crimes around the country.[102]

Philip Jenkins reports the number of victims per criminal and the savagery of killings has increased since the 1960s. Jenkins attributes the increase to a permissive, drug-abusing culture and a mental health system so overcrowded that potentially dangerous people are released without supervision.[103]

ASSAULT

Assault is the most common form of violent crime. The Canadian Centre for Justice Statistics reported that 223,000 nonsexual assaults occurred in 2012. All forms of assault were down over the previous year, and level 1 assault, which is less serious but the most common, was 20 percent lower

> **serial killer**   One who kills more than three people over a period of time.
>
> **mass murderer**   One who kills a large number of people in a single incident.

than it was a decade before. Assaults tend to have a high clearance rate of around 75 percent because the majority involve acquaintances. They tend to be committed by males, and in 9 out of 10 cases are committed by adults.

Assault in the Home

One of the most frightening aspects of assault is the incidence of violent attacks in the home. Exhibit 10.5 displays some facts about violence against children. Intrafamily violence is a serious social problem, and one area that has received media attention is **child abuse**. This term describes any physical or emotional trauma to a child for which no reasonable explanation, such as an accident, can be found.[104]

Some people believe that ordinary disciplinary practices, such as spanking, are abuse, but spanking is protected under Section 43 of the *Criminal Code*, which allows parents and teachers to use reasonable force when correcting a child.

Child abuse can involve actual physical beatings to a child or shaken baby syndrome. Another form of abuse results from neglect—not providing a child with proper care and shelter. According to the 1998 *Canadian Incidence Study of Reported Child Abuse and Neglect,* the main reasons for child maltreatment investigations are neglect (40 percent), physical abuse (31 percent), emotional maltreatment (19 percent), and sexual abuse (10 percent).[105]

In Canada, 6 percent of the victims of violent crime are children under the age of 12, while 20 percent are aged 12 to 19. In general, boys and girls are equally likely to be the victims of violent crimes. Boys, however, are more likely to be the victims of homicide, while girls are more likely to be sexually abused.[106] A classic study by Gelles and Straus found that in the United States, more than one million children a year suffer physical abuse from their parents.[107] It is also rarely a one-time event.

Another aspect of the abuse syndrome is **sexual abuse**, which includes rape, incest, and molestation. Child sexual abuse is the exploitation of children by the same means, often committed by parents or other adults. It is difficult to estimate the incidence of sexual abuse. Many allegations of sexual impropriety have been made against religious figures and leaders, such as priests and Boy Scout leaders.[108] Many Canadian organizations that use the services of volunteers now require their applicants to be screened by the police for a criminal record.

One survey found that 38 percent of women had experienced intrafamilial or extrafamilial sexual abuse by the time they reached age 18.[109] A survey of students in Grades 6, 9, and 12 found about 2 percent of males and 7 percent of females had experienced incest, while 4 percent of males and 13 percent of females had suffered extrafamilial sexual abuse. Other research indicates that one in five girls suffers sexual abuse.[110]

These results likely underestimate the incidence of sexual abuse. Young victims might not understand their abuse or might have repressed their memories of the incidents. One study found that more than half of children referred to a clinic because they had sexually transmitted diseases claimed not to have been molested despite this irrefutable physical

---

EXHIBIT 10.5

Quick Facts about Family Violence in Canada

In 2011, police reported nearly 95,000 victims of family violence, a rate of 279 victims for every 100,000 individuals in the population.

- Children under age 18 are overrepresented as sexual offence victims.
- Physical assault victims tend to be male; sexual assault victims tend to be female.
- In 2011, about half of victims (49 percent) were married to the accused, 18 percent were victimized by their parent, 13 percent by an extended family member, 11 percent by a sibling, and 9 percent by a child, most often a grown child.
- Males are typically the offenders in physical assault (78 percent) and sexual assault (98 percent).
- About one-third of sexual assaults are committed by family members (30 percent).
- There were 344 murder-suicides in Canada between 2001 and 2011, of which more than three-quarters (77 percent) involved at least one victim that was related to the accused.
- In 2011, police reported approximately 18,300 child victims of family violence, representing a rate of 267 child victims for every 100,000 Canadians under the age of 18.
- In physical assault by a family member, the perpetrator is a parent (67 percent), sibling (18 percent), and extended family member (8 percent).
- In cases of non-stranger kidnapping/abduction of children, parents are usually the perpetrators in cases involving boys, compared to friends in cases involving girls.
- Overall, in cases of kidnapping/abduction, strangers are usually around 25 percent.
- The lowest rate of family violence involves seniors, often assaults by children.

SOURCES: *Family Violence in Canada: A Statistical Profile, 2011,* by Maire Sinha, Canadian Centre for Justice Statistics, June 25, 2013; Catherine Trainor, ed., *Family Violence in Canada: A Statistical Profile 2002* (Ottawa: Canadian Centre for Justice Statistics, 2002); CCJS, "Children and Youths as Victims of Violent Crimes," *Juristat* 15, 15, 1995.

---

child abuse   Any physical, emotional, or sexual trauma to a child; includes neglecting to give proper care and attention to a young child.

sexual abuse   A form of violence, usually by a family member or relative, which involves rape, incest, and molestation, and can occur in wife abuse, child abuse, and elder abuse.

The exact number of Canadian executions for capital offences is unknown because the government began systematically recording information only after Confederation in 1867. Although the identities of many Canadians condemned to death will never be uncovered, Ronald Turpin and Arthur Lucas will likely always be remembered as the final two to be executed in 1962, before the abolition of capital punishment.

Compared to earlier times, Lucas and Turpin lived during a time when the only crimes warranting the death penalty were certain types of murders: those that were planned and deliberate, those occurring during the commission of violent crimes, and those involving on-duty police and corrections officers. The days were long over when people could be executed for almost any offence, like one unfortunate man hanged in Halifax in 1795 for stealing a few potatoes. Lucas and Turpin

had the right to secure legal counsel, give evidence on their own behalf, and appeal their death sentence, unlike many of their predecessors.

Lucas had murder on his mind when he drove to Toronto to confront Therland Carter, a pimp and material witness in a pending American narcotics trial. He stabbed Carter to death on November 17, 1961, along with Carol Newman, a prostitute who was with Carter at the time of the altercation. On February 12, 1962, Turpin shot and killed Metropolitan Toronto police constable Frederick Nash when he was pulled over for a broken taillight. Not only was Turpin wanted for questioning in relation to a shooting that transpired the year before, but he had also just robbed the Red Rooster Restaurant of $632.84. Turpin shot Nash in the chest with a .32 calibre handgun before attempting to flee in the slain officer's cruiser.

Lucas and Turpin came from different walks of life, but they shared the same fate. Both were arrested, tried, convicted, and executed within 14 months. They were represented by the same defence counsel and ate the same last meal. At the ages of 54 and 29, Lucas and Turpin were hanged at Toronto's Don Jail while an angry crowd protested outside the prison gates. They were buried side by side in unmarked graves. Although Lucas and Turpin were shown no mercy by the governor general, all remaining death sentences in Canada were thereafter commuted to life imprisonment. In July 1976, capital punishment officially met its end when Parliament passed a bill to abolish the practice by a meagre six votes. The government rejected a motion to reinstate the death penalty 11 years later by 148 votes to 127, but the debate over capital punishment continued for some time.

evidence. Parental response significantly influences reporting abuse: Kids whose caretakers admitted the possibility of abuse were 3.5 times more likely to report abuse than those whose parents denied any possibility that their children had been victims.[111]

The growing incidence of sexual abuse is of particular concern when its long-term impacts are considered. Abused kids experience fear, post-traumatic stress disorder, behaviour problems, sexualized behaviour, and poor self-esteem. They are also more likely to be abusers themselves. The amount of force used, its duration, and its frequency are all related to the extent of the long-term effects and the length of time needed for recovery.[112]

Causes of Child Abuse

Why do parents physically assault their children? Child abuse is a highly complex problem, cutting across ethnic, religious, and socio-economic lines. Abusive parents come from all walks of life.

However, one common factor associated with systematic child abuse is familial stress. Abusive parents are unable to cope with life crises—divorce, financial problems, alcohol and other drug abuse, poor housing conditions. This inability leads them to maltreat their children. A higher rate of assault

on children occurs among lower economic classes; however, this doesn't mean that parents from lower classes are more abusive than those in the upper classes. Low-income people are often subject to greater levels of environmental stress and have fewer resources to deal with it. Second, abuse among poor families is more likely to be dealt with by public agencies and therefore is more frequently counted in official statistics.[113]

Other characteristics that are related include the presence of a step-parent in the household, young parents, poor parenting skills, marital violence, alcohol or other drug abuse, large family size, poverty, unemployment, and disability in the child.[114]

Also, parents who themselves suffered abuse as children tend to abuse their own children; and, isolated and alienated families tend to become abusive. Potentially or actually abusing parents live in states of alienation, cut off from contact with other people in the neighbourhood and lacking close relationships with people who could provide help and support.

A cyclical pattern of family violence is perpetuated from one generation to another. A large number of abused and neglected children grow into adolescence and adulthood with a tendency to engage in violent behaviour. The behaviour of abusive parents can be traced to negative experiences in their own childhood—physical abuse, lack of love, emotional neglect, and incest. These parents become unable to separate their own childhood traumas from their relationships with their children. They have unrealistic perceptions of the appropriate stages of childhood development. Thus, when their children cry, throw food, or strike their parents, the parents may react in an abusive manner: "A fussy baby can be the lighted match."[115]

Public concern about child abuse has led to the development of programs designed to prevent and deter it. The reporting of child abuse by doctors, social workers, and other such persons is mandated by law. As well, Human Resources Development Canada (HRDC) implemented the National Longitudinal Survey of Children and Youth in 1994, which follows 25,000 children as they grow to adulthood, for the purpose of collecting data about child welfare in Canada.

Spouse Abuse

On the evening of June 23, 1993, John Wayne Bobbitt came home and, according to his wife, Lorena, committed a marital rape. Afterward, while he slept, Lorena used a 30-centimetre (12-inch) kitchen knife to slice off two-thirds of his penis, which she then threw into a field. Police officers recovered the penis, and it was surgically reattached, and he went on to a career as a porn star.

Bobbitt was acquitted on charges of sexual assault, and Lorena was found not guilty by reason of insanity on a charge of malicious wounding. No longer considered a threat (at least to anyone other than her former husband), she was released.

Although highly publicized, this case is misleading: Spouse abuse usually involves a physical assault in which a wife is injured by a husband.[116] There are indeed some cases of husband battering, but they typically involve a defensive measure taken by a previously abused spouse, according to Schwartz and DeKeseredy.[117]

CONNECTIONS

In Chapter 4, the case of Angelique Lyn Lavallee is considered in relation to victimization theory.

Spouse abuse has occurred throughout recorded history. During the Roman era, men had the legal right to beat their wives for drinking wine or walking outdoors with their faces uncovered, while adultery was punishable by death. However, by the 4th century, excessive violence on the part of husband or wife could be used as sufficient grounds for divorce. During the Middle Ages, the wife was guarded jealously and could be punished severely for violations of duty. A husband was expected to beat his wife for misbehaviour and might himself be punished in the cuckold's court if he failed to do so.

By the mid-19th century, severe wife beating had fallen into disfavour, and accused wife beaters were subject to public ridicule. By the 20th century, England had outlawed wife beating, yet the tradition of husbands' domination over wives made physical coercion difficult to control. Even after World War II, some English courts found domestic assault to be a reasonable punishment for a disobedient wife.[118]

Brinkerhoff and Lupri, in their study of family violence, found that both women and men are the agitators of violence, and that much abuse goes unreported. Furthermore, if one violent episode had occurred, another was likely to occur. Violent couples came from all socio-economic classes, and occupational/educational attainment had an insignificant role in predicting interspousal violence.[119]

Tragically, family members convicted of violent crimes against spouses are less likely than other violent offenders to get prison terms.

The Nature and Extent of Spouse Abuse. Statistics Canada's National Survey on Violence Against Women estimated that 29 percent of women who have ever been married have been assaulted. The rate was highest in British Columbia (36 percent) and lowest in Newfoundland and Labrador (17 percent). In cases of previous marriages, 48 percent of the women had been assaulted, while 15 percent of currently married women reported having been assaulted.[120] In a national survey of college and university students, more than 20 percent of the females had experienced violence during their dating and courtship relationships.[121]

Characteristic traits of the wife assaulter include excessive alcohol abuse, hostility and dependency that are based on resentment, and brooding over a wife's behaviour. Other factors include being under economic stress, serving in the military, being given to sudden bursts of anger, and having been battered as a child (see Exhibit 10.6).[122]

Is Spouse Abuse Intergenerational? Although it is generally agreed that child abuse is intergenerational, do the same patterns apply to spouse abuse? Although there is little conclusive evidence that spouse abusers grew up in homes where spouses were abused, some research indicates that abused children later act abusively toward their own children and their spouses.[123]

According to one view, children learn the role of parent/ spouse through observation, and those who grow up in abusive households believe that harsh parenting and violent behaviour are normal in the typical family. A second view is that harsh and incompetent parenting produces children who have behavioural problems. People who have experienced abusive and incompetent parenting are more likely to use drugs and commit crimes. The relationship between deviant behaviour and physical punishment is constant across race, ethnic origin, and socio-economic status.

Support given to battered women includes transition houses and shelters. Police departments have made enforcement of domestic abuse laws a top priority with presumptive

EXHIBIT 10.6

Factors That Predict Spousal Abuse

- Excessive alcohol use may turn otherwise docile husbands into wife abusers.
- Perpetrator's access to a gun and previous threat with a weapon may lead to abuse.
- Having a stepchild may provoke abuse because the step-parent may have a more limited bond to the child.
- Estrangement from a controlling partner and subsequent involvement with another partner.
- Some husbands are hostile because of dependence on their wives; linked to sexual inadequacy.
- Excessive brooding over a wife's behaviour, however trivial, can result in violent assaults.
- Some males believe society approves of spouse abuse; peer support helps shape their attitudes.
- Men who fail as providers are under economic stress and may take frustrations out on their wives.
- A significant amount of family violence results from a sudden burst of anger after a verbal dispute.
- Spouse abuse among men who have served in the military is extremely high.

- Husbands who assault their wives were generally battered as children.
- Batterers are unpredictable, and difficult to prevent from battering once an argument has begun.

SOURCES: Christine Sellers, John Cochran, Kathryn Branch, "Social Learning Theory and Partner Violence: A Research Note," *Deviant Behavior* 26 (2005) 379–395; Jacquelyn Campbell, Daniel Webster, Jane Koziol-McLain, Carolyn Block, Doris Campbell, Mary Ann Curry, Faye Gary, Nancy Glass, Judith McFarlane, Carolyn Sachs, Phyllis Sharps, Yvonne Ulrich, Susan Wilt, Jennifer Manganello, Xiao Xu, Janet Schollenberger, Victoria Frye, and Kathryn Laughon, "Risk Factors for Femicide in Abusive Relationships: Results from a Multisite Case Control Study," *American Journal of Public Health* 93 (2003): 1089–1097; Neil Jacobson and John Mordechai Gottman, *When Men Batter Women: New Insights into Ending Abusive Relationships* (New York: Simon & Schuster, 1998); Kenneth Leonard and Brian Quigley, "Drinking and Marital Aggression in Newlyweds: An Event-Based Analysis of Drinking and the Occurrence of Husband Marital Aggression," *Journal of Studies on Alcohol* 60 (1999): 537–541.

arrest policies, where charges are laid when reasonable grounds exist to believe an offence has been committed. Exhibit 10.7 includes a summary of a public attitude survey on family violence.

EXHIBIT 10.7

Public Attitudes toward Family Violence

- Those who agree that insulting family members will eventually move to slapping and punching: 59 percent.
- Those who say people who are violent with family members are not responsible for their actions: 23 percent.
- Those who agree that spousal violence involving hitting is a crime: 86 percent.
- Those who say stress due to lack of money and unemployment is a cause of violence in families: 54 percent.
- Those who believe the greatest impact on individuals is negative psychological effects: 44 percent.
- Those who believe that children raised in violent homes are more likely to be bullies: 79 percent.
- Those who believe that living with family violence affects people's health: 81 percent.
- Those who believe that the media has overstated the problem: 17 percent.
- Those who say that the problem is more serious than it was 10 years ago: 62 percent.
- Those who say family violence does not occur in their own community "very often": 39 percent.

SOURCE: EKOS Research Associates Inc., *Public Attitudes Towards Family Violence: A syndicated Study,* Final Report (Ottawa: Author, 2002).

ROBBERY

The common-law definition of **robbery** is taking anything of value from the custody or control of a person by force or threat or by putting the victim in fear. A robbery differs from a theft because robbery involves the use of force and personal contact. Robbery is punished severely because the victim's safety is put in jeopardy. The amount of force used and not the value of the items taken determines the level of punishment.

Robbery is another serious form of violent crime, and in 2012 it reached its lowest level in 30 years. Only a small minority of robberies involve firearms. Most are committed by adults, and because robberies are usually stranger-related, generally only a third are solved by police.[124]

The Ecology of Robbery

The ecological pattern for robbery is similar to that of other violent crimes. Robbery is most often a public crime. The public nature of robbery has greatly influenced people's behaviour. Because most people believe that the most serious instances of violent crimes occur in large cities, many choose to move to suburban communities. However, in cities larger than 500,000, the rate can vary, for example, from a high of 272 in Winnipeg to a low of 62 in Quebec City. Provincially,

robbery A crime of violence involving the use of force to obtain money or goods.

Criminology Research
Armed Robbers in Action

Criminologists Richard Wright and Scott Decker have identified and interviewed a sample of 86 active armed robbers in St. Louis, Missouri. Their sample, primarily young Black men, helped provide an in-depth view of armed robbery that had been missing from the criminological literature.

Wright and Decker found that most armed robberies are motivated by a pressing need for cash, and an endless quest for stimulation and thrills. Interviewees told of how they partied, gambled, drank, and abused substances until they were broke. Their partying not only provided excitement but also helped generate a street reputation as a "hip" guy who can "make things happen." Robbers had a "here and now" mentality, which required a constant supply of cash to fuel their appetites. Those interviewed showed little long-range planning or commitment to the future, and few of the robbers were able to obtain or keep legitimate employment.

Armed robbery also provided a psychic thrill. It was a chance to hurt or humiliate victims, or to get even with someone who may have wronged them in the past. As one robber explained, "This might sound stupid, but I [also] like to see a person get scared, be scared of the pistol . . . . You got power. I come in here with a big old pistol and I ain't playing."

Robbers show evidence of being highly rational offenders. Many choose victims who themselves are involved in illegal behaviour, most often drug dealers. Ripping off a dealer kills three birds with one stone, providing both money and drugs while at the same time targeting victims who are quite unlikely to call the police. One told them why he chose to be a robber:

I feel more safer doing a robbery because doing a burglary, I got a fear of breaking into somebody's house not knowing who might be up in there . . . . On robbery I can select my victims, I can select my place of business. I can watch and see who all work in there or I can rob a person and pull them around in the alley or push them up in a doorway and rob them. (p. 52)

Others target non-criminal victims. They like to stay in their own neighbourhood, relying on their intimate knowledge of streets and alleys to avoid detection. Although some range far afield seeking affluent victims, others believe that residents in the city's poorest areas are more likely to carry cash (wealthy people carry credit cards). Because they realize that

the rate of robbery also varies widely across the country, for example, from a low of 17 in Prince Edward Island to a high of 182 in Manitoba.

Statistics Canada reports that robbery is lower than average in the territories, despite violent crime rates usually being higher in the territories than in the rest of Canada. In 2009, as in previous years, robbery rates in the Northwest Territories, Yukon, and Nunavut were among the lowest in the country. Decreases in 2012 were fuelled by large drops in Quebec (15 percent) and Montreal (18 percent), and in Alberta (11 percent) and Calgary (23 percent).

Robber Typologies

Criminologists classify and explain the nature and dynamics of robbery, identifying the following:[125]

- robbery in places where money is exchanged: banks, jewellery stores
- robbery in open areas: muggings and purse snatchings, in streets, parking lots, on public transit
- robbery on private premises, such as breaking into homes
- robbery in the aftermath of a chance meeting, such as at a bar or a party
- robbery after previous association of some duration between the victim and offender

In addition, robbers can also be categorized into the following specialties:[126]

- Professional robbers committed to crime as a livelihood because it is fast and very profitable usually operate in groups, and they typically steal large amounts from commercial establishments.
- Opportunist robbers steal small amounts of money from accessible and vulnerable targets: cab drivers, drunks, and seniors; usually involves little planning and juvenile gangs.
- Addict robbers stealing to support drug habits have a low commitment to robbery because of its danger but they need the funds; usually more cautious than other robbers, tend not to use weapons, choose their targets on the basis of risk.
- Alcoholic robbers steal to get money to buy liquor and have no commitment to robbery as a way of life; their crimes are random, with little thought to victim or escape—making them the robbers most likely to be caught.

As these typologies indicate, the typical armed robber is unlikely to be a professional who carefully studies targets while planning a crime. Convenience stores, gas stations, and people walking along the street are much more likely to be the target of robberies than are banks or other highly secure environments. Robbers, therefore, seem to be diverted by modest defensive measures, such as having more than one clerk in a store or locating stores in strip malls rather than in stand-alone isolation.[127]

The Criminology Research box discusses a classic criminological study of armed robbery in the United States.

the risk of detection and punishment is the same whether the victim is carrying a load of cash or is penniless, experienced robbers use discretion in selecting targets. People whose clothing, jewellery, and demeanour mark them as carrying substantial amounts of cash make suitable targets; people who look like they can fight back are avoided. Some station themselves at cash machines to spot targets who are flashing rolls of money.

Robbers have racial, gender, and age preferences in their selection of targets. Some Black robbers prefer white targets because they believe they are too afraid to fight back. As one interviewee revealed, "White guys can be so paranoid [that] they just want to get away . . . . They're not . . . gonna argue with you." Likewise, intoxicated victims in no condition to fight back were favoured targets. Some robbers tend to target women because they feel they are easy subjects; however, others avoid them because they believe they will get emotionally upset and bring unwanted attention. Most agree that the elderly are less likely to put up a fuss than younger, stronger targets.

Some robbers choose commercial targets, such as convenience stores or markets that are cash businesses open late at night. Gas stations are a favourite victim. Security is of little consequence to experienced robbers, who may bring an accomplice to subdue guards.

Once they choose their targets, robbers carefully orchestrate the criminal incidents. They immediately impose their will on their chosen victims, leaving little room for the victims to manoeuvre and making sure the victims feel threatened enough to offer no resistance. Some approach from behind so that they cannot be identified, and others approach victims head-on, showing that they are tough and bold. By convincing the victims of their impending death, the robber takes control.

Critical Thinking

1. It is unlikely that punishment can deter robbery (most robbers don't think about getting caught), but would a cashless society end the threat, or would innovative robbers find new targets?
2. Based on what you know about how robbers target victims, how can you better protect yourself from robbery?

SOURCE: Based on Richard Wright and Scott Decker, *Armed Robbers in Action, Stickups and Street Culture* (Boston: Northeastern University Press, 1997).

EVOLVING FORMS OF VIOLENCE

Assault, rape, robbery, and murder are traditional forms of interpersonal violence. However, criminologists have recognized new categories within these crime types, such as serial murder, date rape, and hate crime. In this section, we briefly discuss a new crime concern: workplace violence.

CONNECTIONS

Hate crimes are another "newly discovered" form of violence, discussed in the context of passive precipitation theory in Chapter 4 on victimization.

Workplace Violence

In August 1992, after a long history of disciplinary problems and increasingly erratic behaviour, Dr. Valery Fabrikant walked into the engineering department at Concordia University and opened fire, killing three people and wounding two others because he had been denied a tenured position.[128]

In 1999, a former employee at the Ottawa bus terminal took a high-powered rifle to work and shot six employees in the parts department (see the Crime in the News box). He allegedly had a history of mental illness.

As of April 2005, Canada was ranked as the fourth-worst country in the world for violence in the workplace, just behind Argentina, Romania, and France, according to the International Labour Organization (ILO). In the United States, the Bureau of Labour Statistics notes that workplace homicide is the third-most frequent cause of employee deaths after highway accidents and falls.[129]

It has become commonplace to read of irate employees or former employees attacking co-workers or sabotaging machinery and production lines. Workplace violence is now considered the third-leading cause of occupational injury or death in the United States.[130] A majority of respondents in a Canadian survey felt that workplace violence was increasing, and significant sources are psychological violence and aggression. Canada ranks fourth in the world when it comes to workplace aggression.

The typical offender is a middle-aged Caucasian male who faces losing his job. In businesses, long-term employees fear job loss because of automation and reorganization. The common phrase for this type of mass violence is "going postal," due to some high-profile shootings by postal employees in 1986.

Crime in the News
Pierre Lebrun

One of the most tragic examples of workplace violence in Canada unfolded at Ottawa's largest bus depot in April 1999. Former city transit worker Pierre Lebrun fatally shot four co-workers with a high-powered rifle and wounded two others before turning the gun on himself. Exactly what triggered Lebrun's murderous rampage and subsequent suicide may never be known, but it is clear that any social ties he had at the time of the incident were little more than dangling threads.

Lebrun's rocky career with the Ottawa-Carleton Transpo began in 1986. He took on a garage attendant position after a five-year stretch of bus driving, which rates as one of the most stressful occupations, according to Statistics Canada. Not only

did Lebrun have to deal with the routine hassles of this job, but he was also relentlessly ridiculed by colleagues. His status as an unmarried, middle-aged man with a speech impediment made him a vulnerable target.

The harsh treatment Lebrun received at work and his history of depression proved to be a volatile combination. Several complaints and transfers later, he finally retaliated by assaulting another employee. Lebrun was promptly fired, then reinstated and shuffled yet again into an isolating, non-union position as an audit clerk. He decided to resign in January 1999, citing personal reasons, and virtually disappeared for three months before ambushing the station.

The case of this 40-year-old with no criminal record turned mass murderer warranted a coroner's inquest. Witnesses depicted Lebrun as "a quiet, withdrawn loner who often slept during his breaks or buried his head in newspapers." In a letter introduced as evidence, Lebrun described himself as "tired, exhausted and completely backed against the wall." City transit employees either denied or downplayed the harassment Lebrun suffered, but his anguish and thirst for revenge resounded in a suicide note left to his parents. The product of this six-week hearing was a list of 77 recommendations to various agencies, the majority of which addressed workplace violence and harassment issues.

Another cause may be leadership styles. Some companies have authoritarian management styles that demand performance from employees above all else. Managers who are unsympathetic and unsupportive may help trigger workplace violence.

Not all workplace violence is caused by an injustice by management. In some incidents, co-workers have been killed because they refused a romantic relationship with the assailant or had reported him for sexual harassment; others have been killed because they got a job the assailant coveted. In a few cases, irate clients and customers have killed because of poor service or perceived slights.

Workplace "provocations" can also lead to a variety of responses. Some former employees attack supervisors to punish the company that dismissed them. Others sabotage company equipment. Over time, if a conflict remains unresolved, some other events may eventually cause an eruption.

In his study of workplace violence in British Columbia's healthcare industry, Neil Boyd found more than 70 percent of nurses in British Columbia reported some form of violence at work, and 20 percent of these involved physical injury from an attack. Female workers were far more likely to experience violence at work than were males, probably because 80 percent of workers in healthcare are female. Cutbacks have increased both workload and tensions, and have decreased the standard of medical care expected by many patients.[131]

Can workplace violence be controlled? Dispute resolution may help, and some researchers argue for aggressive job retraining, continued medical coverage in case of layoffs, and due process guarantees to thwart unfair terminations.

SUMMARY

We seem to live in an extremely violent time, with new forms of violence being identified and publicized more than ever before. Among the various explanations for violent crimes are personal traits, ineffective families, a subculture of violence that stresses violent solutions to interpersonal problems, substance abuse, and the availability of firearms.

Interpersonal violent crime can take many forms. Sexual assault has been known throughout history, and at one time it was believed that a woman was as guilty as her attacker was for her rape. At present, it is estimated that less than 10 percent of all sexual assaults are reported to police each year, it has a relatively low clearance rate for violent crime, and it is a difficult charge to prove.

Murder is the unlawful killing of a human being. Murders are classified into different degrees, and their punishments vary accordingly. One important characteristic of murder is that the victim and criminal often know each other. This

Criminology Research
Violence in Healthcare

Workplace violence has gradually come to be recognized as a problem in many areas of work, highlighting what for some is an everyday concern. For example, workplace violence is now recognized as a widespread public health concern among healthcare workers such as doctors and nurses.

Researchers at Thompson Rivers University and at the universities of Alberta, British Columbia, Manitoba, and Calgary looked at the experiences of violence among registered nurses in Alberta and British Columbia. They found that nurses experienced many incidents of violence in the workweek, particularly in the emergency, psychiatric, and surgical wards.

While it may be predictable that most violent acts are perpetrated by patients, a significant portion of violence and abuse was found to be committed by hospital co-workers. This finding is the result of the definition of violence having been broadened enough to accommodate emotional abuse and sexual harassment. Most of this workplace violence was not reported.

The amount and type of violence varied greatly across nursing units. Nurses working in emergency and psychiatry experienced the highest incidence of violence, while nurses in critical care units experienced the lowest.

Across the board, patients were the main source of violence, particularly when it came to threats and physical assault. Family and visitors also made up a smaller portion of violent perpetrators, particularly in emergency units.

However, hospital staff such as physicians and nursing co-workers were more often said to be the source of non-physical violence, such as emotional abuse and verbal sexual harassment. These incidents were especially pronounced in the critical care units. While patients were the largest proportion of perpetrators overall, hospital co-workers were responsible for 57 percent of all emotional abuse and 54 percent of all verbal sexual harassment in the critical care setting.

While the majority of nurses who experienced a violent episode did not report it, psychiatric nurses were more likely to report an incident than any other group. Interestingly, all groups were less likely to report violence if a co-worker was the source. Violence by patients' family members and other visitors or by patients was most likely to be reported (42 percent and 34 percent, respectively). On the other hand, only 28 percent of violence caused by physicians and only 19 percent of violence by other nurses was reported.

Non-reporting of co-worker violence is even more prevalent for emotional abuse and verbal sexual harassment.

The researchers sought to find an explanation for the phenomena at a structural level. They suggest that hospital units are faced with increasingly acutely ill patients, and yet have to manage them with shortened hospital stays to free up monetary resources. They suggest this situation has put a lot of pressure on human resources. They argue that under-resourced staff members are more likely to experience violence from patients, patients' families, and co-workers who are frustrated with the hospital not having enough staff and resources to provide quality care.

That conclusion is not unreasonable, and they go further to suggest that the "soft" emotional abuse should be seen as a warning sign. Using the idea from broken windows theory—that soft signs of disrepair encourage harder forms of violence—they suggest that emotional abuse may create an environment where other forms of violence, such as physical and sexual assault, are more likely to be accepted.

They suggest that by conceptualizing why workplace violence occurs in this manner, new violence prevention policies and strategies can be developed. Essentially, everything from physical assaults down to insults or humiliation must be treated seriously to prevent workplace violence. This approach is also positive in that it needs to focus on fostering a work environment where courtesy, civility, and decency are expected and displayed at all levels in everyday practice.

They believe that if such an effort is launched at a systemic level, with support from all levels of the hospital, then these workplaces will become less tolerant of violence and more of a positive place to work.

SOURCES: Susan M. Duncan, Kathryn Hyndman, Carole A. Estabrooks, Kathryn Hesketh, Charles K. Humphrey, Jennifer S. Wong, Sonia Acorn, Phyllis Giovannetti, "Nurses' Experience of Violence in Albert and British Columbia Hospitals," *Canadian Journal of Nursing Research* 32, 4 (2001): 57–78.

fact has caused some criminologists to believe that murder is a victim-precipitated crime. Murder victims and offenders both tend to be young and male.

Assault is another serious interpersonal violent crime. One important type of assault occurs in the home and includes child abuse and spouse abuse. It has been estimated that many children are abused by their parents each year, and a significant proportion of families report husband–wife violence. A trend is also developing toward violence between dating couples on university and college campuses.

Robbery involves theft by force, usually in a public place. Types of offenders include professional, opportunist, addict, and alcoholic robbers.

Violence is an important topic facing society today, and the tasks of criminology are to identify and explain it and to work toward solutions. It is also the task of criminology to show that because we live in an information age, we are also more sensitive to reports of violent crime, especially crimes committed seemingly randomly, by strangers, in public places.

The provincial government has hired you to prepare a report on what used to be called "statutory rape," that is, sex with an underage youth. The government is concerned because of the growing number of underage girls who have been impregnated by adult men. Studies reveal that many teenage pregnancies result from affairs that underage girls have with older men, with age gaps ranging up to 10 years. The girl typically drops out of school and goes on social assistance. Some outraged parents want the provincial government to more strictly enforce the law.

However, some critics suggest that implementing statutory rape laws to punish males who have relationships with minor girls does not solve the problems of teenage pregnancies and out-of-wedlock births. Liberals dislike the idea of using the criminal law to solve social problems because it does not provide for the girls and their young children, and focuses only on punishing offenders.

In contrast, conservatives fear that such laws give the state the power to prosecute people for victimless crimes, thereby adding to the government's ability to control people's private lives. Not all cases involve much older men, and critics ask whether we should criminalize the behaviour of 17-year-old boys and their 15-year-old girlfriends.

As a criminologist with expertise on rape and its effects, what would you recommend regarding implementation of the law?

KEY TERMS

brutalization process p. 319
child abuse p. 334
conflict-related violence p. 322
consent p. 327
corroboration p. 327
crime-related violence p. 322
cult killings p. 332
date rape p. 325

eros p. 319
expressive violence p. 322
gang killings p. 331
gendered violence p. 324
marital exemption p. 325
mass murderer p. 333
murder p. 328
premeditation p. 328

psychopharmacological p. 320
robbery p. 337
serial killer p. 333
sexual abuse p. 334
shield laws p. 327
Thanatos p. 319
thrill killings p. 331

DOING RESEARCH ON THE WEB

For more information on workplace violence, see "OSH Answers," occupational health and safety answers, at www .ccohs.ca/oshanswers/psychosocial/violence.html.

CRITICAL THINKING QUESTIONS

1. Should different types of rape receive different legal sanctions? For example, should someone who rapes a stranger be punished more severely than someone who is convicted of marital rape or date rape?

2. There have been significant changes in rape laws regarding issues, such as corroboration and shield laws. What other measures would you take to protect the victims of rape when they are forced to testify in court?

3. Should hate crimes be punished more severely than crimes motivated by greed, anger, or revenge?

Why should crimes be distinguished by the motivations of the perpetrator? Is hate a more heinous motivation than revenge?

4. Crime rates were exceedingly high in the 19th century before TV, movies, and rap videos had been created. What, if anything, does this say about the effect of media on crime? What were some of the other factors that provoked violence in the 19th century? Do you think that these factors still cause violence today?

5. It is unlikely that the threat of punishment can deter robbery, but

eliminating cash and relying on debit and credit cards may be the most productive method to reduce robbery. Although this strategy seems far-fetched, our society is becoming progressively more cashless; it is now possible to buy both gas and groceries with credit cards and debit cards. Would a cashless society end the threat of robbery, or would innovative robbers find new targets?

6. Based on what you know about how robbers target victims, how can you better protect yourself from robbery?

NOTES

1. The sources for data cited in this chapter, unless otherwise noted, are annual statistics publications, such as Warren Silver, "Crime Statistics in Canada, 2006," *Juristat* 27, 5, 2007; Mia Dauverge, "Crime Statistics in Canada, 2007," *Juristat* 28, 7, 2008; and Samuel Perreault, "Crime Statistics in Canada, 2012," Statistics Canada, 2013.

2. Robert Nash Parker and Catherine Colony, "Relationships, Homicides, and Weapons: A Detailed Analysis," paper presented at the annual meeting of the American Society of Criminology, Montreal, November 1987; also see Robert Nash Parker, "Poverty, Subculture of Violence, and Type of Homicide," Social Forces (1989) 67 (4): 983–1007.

3. Laura Bender, "Children and Adolescents Who Have Killed," *American Journal of Psychiatry* 116 (1959): 510–516.

4. Dorothy Otnow Lewis, Ernest Moy, Lori Jackson, Robert Aaronson, Nicholas Restifo, Susan Serra, and Alexander Simos, "Biopsychosocial Characteristics of Children Who Later Murder," *American Journal of Psychiatry* 142 (1985): 1161–1167.

5. Amy Holtzworth-Munroe and Gregory Stuart, "Typologies of Male Batterers: Three Subtypes and the Differences Among Them," *Psychological Bulletin* 116 (1994): 476–497.

6. "Jury Recommends Death for Florida Killer of Five," *New York Times*, March 25, 1994, A14.

7. Deborah Capaldi and Gerald Patterson, "Can Violent Offenders Be Distinguished from Frequent Offenders? Prediction from Childhood to Adolescence," *Journal of Research in Crime and Delinquency* 33 (1996): 206–231; see also, Pamela Lattimore, Christy Visher, and Richard Linster, "Predicting Rearrest for Violence Among Serious Youthful Offenders," *Journal of Research in Crime and Delinquency* 32 (1995): 54–83.

8. Robert Scudder, William Blount, Kathleen Heide, and Ira Silverman, "Important Links between Child Abuse, Neglect, and Delinquency," *International Journal of Offender Therapy* 37 (1993): 315–323.

9. Dorothy Lewis et al., "Neuropsychiatric, Psychoeducational, and Family Characteristics of 14 Juveniles Condemned to Death in the United States," *American Journal of Psychiatry* 145 (1988): 584–588.

10. Charles Patrick Ewing, *When Children Kill* (Lexington, MA: Lexington Books, 1990), 22.

11. Murray Straus, "Discipline and Deviance: Physical Punishment of Children and Violence and Other Crime in Adulthood," *Social Problems* 38 (1991): 133–154.

12. Lonnie Athens, *The Creation of Dangerous Violent Criminals* (Urbana, IL: University of Illinois Press, 1992), 27–80.

13. Duke University Medical Center (2008, July 2). "Violence Declines with Medication Use in Some with Schizophrenia." *ScienceDaily*, www.sciencedaily.com/releases/2008/07/080701083527.htm.

14. Cathy Spatz Widom, "Child Abuse, Neglect, and Violent Criminal Behavior," *Criminology* 27 (1989): 251–271; Beverly Rivera and Cathy Spatz Widom, "Childhood Victimization and Violent Offending," *Violence and Victims* 5 (1990): 19–34.

15. Sigmund Freud, *Beyond the Pleasure Principle* (London: Inter-Psychoanalytic Press, 1922).

16. Konrad Lorenz, *On Aggression* (New York: Harcourt Brace Jovanovich, 1966).

17. See, generally, Lee Ellis and Anthony Walsh, "Gene-Based Evolutionary Theories in Criminology," *Criminology* 35 (1997): 229–276.

18. Paul Joubert and Craig Forsyth, "A Macro View of Two Decades of Violence in America," *American Journal of Criminal Justice* 13 (1988): 10–25; M. Dwayne Smith and Victoria Brewer, "A Sex-Specific Analysis of Correlates of Homicide Victimization in United States Cities," *Violence and Victims* 7 (1992): 279–285.

19. Marvin Wolfgang and Franco Ferracuti, *The Subculture of Violence* (London: Tavistock, 1967).

20. David Luckenbill and Daniel Doyle, "Structural Position and Violence: Developing a Cultural Explanation," *Criminology* 27 (1989): 419–436.

21. Steven Messner, "Regional and Racial Effects on the Urban Homicide Rate: The Subculture of Violence Revisited," *American Journal of Sociology* 88 (1983): 997–1007; Steven Messner and Kenneth Tardiff, "Economic Inequality and Levels of Homicide: An Analysis of Urban Neighborhoods," *Criminology* 24 (1986): 297–317.

22. Beth Bjerregaard and Alan Lizotte, "Gun Ownership and Gang Membership," *Journal of Criminal Law and Criminology* 86 (1995): 37–58.

23. Scott H. Decker ed., *Policing Gangs and Youth Violence* (Belmont, CA: Wadsworth, 2003); see also J. Miller and S.H. Decker, "Young Women and Gang Violence: Gender, Street Offending, and Violent Victimization in Gangs," *Justice Quarterly* 18, 1 (2001): 115–140.

24. Carolyn Rebecca Block, "Chicago Homicide from the Sixties to the Nineties: Have Patterns of Lethal Violence Changed?" paper presented at the annual meeting of the American Society of Criminology, Baltimore, November 1990; also see Carolyn Rebecca Block, "Race/Ethnicity and Patterns of Chicago Homicide 1965 to 1981," *Crime & Delinquency*, 1985, 31, 1 104–116.

25. Vincent F. Sacco and Leslie W. Kennedy, *The Criminal Event*, 2nd ed. (Toronto: ITP Nelson, 1998).

26. See, generally, Kirk Williams and Robert Flewelling, "The Social Production of Criminal Homicide: A Comparative Study of Disaggregated Rates in American Cities," *American Sociological Review* 53 (1988): 421–431.

27. Raymond Gastil, "Homicide and the Regional Culture of Violence," *American Sociological Review* 36 (1971): 12–27; Keith Harries, *Serious Violence: Patterns of Homicide and Assault in America* (Springfield, IL: Charles C. Thomas, 1990).

28. Howard Erlanger, "Is There a Subculture of Violence in the South?" *Journal of Criminal Law and Criminology* 66 (1976): 483–490; Colin Loftin and Robert Hill, "Regional Subculture of Violence: An Examination of the Gastil-Hackney Thesis," *American Sociological Review* 39 (1974): 714–724; Raymond Gastil, "Comments," *Criminology* 16 (1975): 60–64; F. Frederick Hawley and Steven Messner, "The Southern Violence Construct: A Review of Arguments, Evidence, and the Normative Context," *Justice Quarterly* 6 (1989): 481–511.

29. T.F. Hartnagel, "The Effect of Age and Sex Compositions of Provincial Populations on Provincial Crime Rates," *Canadian Journal of Criminology* 20 (1978): 28–33; C. Lindsay, "Trends in the Crime Rate in Canada, 1970–1985," *Canadian Social Trends* (Autumn 1986): 33–38; L.W. Kennedy, R.A. Silverman, and D.R. Forde, "Homicide in Urban Canada," *Canadian Journal of Sociology* 16 (1991): 397–410; for the United States, see Gregory Kowalski and Thomas Petee, "Sunbelt Effects on Homicide Rates," *Sociology and Social Research* 76 (1991): 73–79.

30. Leslie Kennedy, Robert Silverman, and David Forde, "Homicide in Urban Canada: Testing the Impact of Economic Inequality and Social Disorganization," *Canadian Journal of Sociology* 16 (1991): 397.

31. Paul Goldstein, Henry Brownstein, and Patrick Ryan, "Drug-Related Homicide in New York: 1984–1988," *Crime and Delinquency* 38 (1992): 459–476.

32. James Collins and Pamela Messerschmidt, "Epidemiology of Alcohol-Related Violence," *Alcohol Health and Research World* 17 (1993): 93–100.

33. Thomas Feucht, *Drug Use Forecasting 1995* (Washington, DC: National Institute of Justice, 1996).

34. Christopher Innes, *Profile of State Prison Inmates 1986* (Washington, DC: Bureau of Justice Statistics, 1988).

35. Paul Goldstein, Patricia Bellucci, Barry Spunt, and Thomas Miller, "Volume of Cocaine Use and Violence: A Comparison between Men and Women," *Journal of Drug Issues* 21 (1991): 345–367; Paul J. Goldstein, Henry H. Brownstein, Patrick J. Ryan, Patricia A. Bellucci, "Crack and Homicide in New York City, 1988: A Conceptually Based Event Analysis," *16 Contemporary Drug Problems.* 651 (1989); Goldstein, Brownstein, and Ryan, "Drug-Related Homicide in New York: 1984–1988," 473.

36. Mia Dauverge and Leonardo de Socio, "Firearms and Violent Crime," *Juristat* 28, 2, 2008; Josée Savoie, "Homicide in Canada, 2002," *Juristat* 23, 8, 2003; "Firearms and Violent Crime in Canada, 2012," The Daily.

37. David Brent, Joshua Perper, Christopher Allman, Grace Moritz, Mary Wartella, and Janice Zelenak, "The Presence and Accessibility of Firearms in the Home and Adolescent Suicides," *Journal of the American Medical Association* 266 (1991): 2989–2995.

38. David Lester, "Gun Availability and the Use of Guns for Suicide and Homicide in Canada," *Canadian Journal of Public Health* 91, 3 (2000): 186; "Unintentional Firearm Deaths: Can They Be Reduced by Lowering Gun Ownership Levels?" *Canadian Journal of Public Health* 92, 5 (2001): 396–398.

39. Philip C. Stenning, "Long Gun Registration: A Poorly Aimed Longshot," *Canadian Journal of Crime and Criminal Justice* 10 (2003): 479–488; Neil Boyd, "Gun Control: Placing Costs in Context," *Canadian Journal of Crime and Criminal Justice* 10 (2003): 473–478.

40. F.S. Bridges, "Gun Control Law (Bill C-17), Suicide, and Homicide in Canada," *Psychological Reports* 94, 3 Part 1, (2004): 819–826; also see F.S. Bridges, and J.C. Kunselman, "Gun Availability and Use of Guns for Suicide, Homicide, and Murder in Canada," *Perceptual and Motor Skills* 98, 2 (2004): 594–598.

41. "Gunshot Wounds: The New Public Health Issue," *Journal of the American Medical Association* 3 (2004): 170–175; "Shooting Ourselves in the Foot: Why Mandatory Reporting of Gunshot Wounds Is a Bad Idea," *Canadian Medical Association Journal* 4 (2004): 170–178; "Why Mandatory Reporting of Gunshot Wounds Is Necessary," *Canadian Medical Association Journal* 4 (2004): 170–178.

42. "More Canadians Oppose Gun Ownership by General Public, but Majority Still Favours Stricter Gun Laws," Gallup Canada, November 28, 2001; "Majority of Canadians Say Gun Registry Should Be Scrapped," Ipsos Reid poll, December 13, 2002.

43. Timothy Hartnagel, "Gun Control in Alberta: Explaining Public Attitudes Concerning Legislative Change," *Canadian Journal of Criminology* 44, 4 (2002): 403–424; see also Thomas Gabor, "Universal Firearm Registration in Canada: Three Perspectives," *Canadian Journal of Crime and Criminal Justice* 10 (2003): 465–471; Thomas Gabor, "The Federal Gun Registry: An Urgent Need for Independent, Non-Partisan Research," *Canadian Journal of Crime and Criminal Justice* 10 (2003): 489–498.

44. William Green, *Rape* (Lexington, MA.: Lexington Books, 1988), 5.

45. Susan Randall and Vicki McNickle Rose, "Forcible Rape," in *Major Forms of Crime*, ed. Robert Meyer (Beverly Hills, CA: Sage, 1984), 47.

46. As cited in Chris McCormick, "Contemporary Sociological Thought," in *Canadian Criminology: Perspectives in Crime and Criminality*, 2nd ed., eds. Margaret A. Jackson and Curt T. Griffiths (Toronto: Harcourt Brace, 1995), 129.

47. Associated Press, "Judge Who Told Rape Suspect to Get a Girlfriend Orders Him into Custody," *Manchester Union Leader*, February 19, 1994, 2.

48. Susan Brownmiller, *Against Our Will: Men, Women and Rape* (New York: Simon & Schuster, 1975).

49. Maire Gannon and Karen Mihorean, "Criminal Victimization in Canada, 2004," *Juristat* 25, 7, 2005.

50. Robin Warshaw, *I Never Called It Rape: The Ms. Report on Recognizing, Fighting, and Surviving Date and Acquaintance Rape* (New York: Harper and Row, 1988), 26.

51. Elisa Romano and Rayleen V. De Luca, "Male Sexual Abuse: A Review of Effects, Abuse Characteristics, and Links with Later Psychological Functioning," *Aggression and Violent Behaviour* 6 (2001): 55–78.

52. Myriam S. Denov, "A Culture of Denial: Exploring Professional Perspectives on Female Sex Offending," *Canadian Journal of Criminology* 43, 3 (2001): 303–330.

53. Angela Browne, "Violence against Women: Relevance for Medical Practitioners," *Journal of the American Medical Association* 267 (1992): 3184–3189.

54. Julian Roberts, "Criminal Justice Processing of Sexual Assault Cases," *Juristat* 14, 7, 1994.

55. *The Final Report of the Task Force on Sexual Abuse of Patients* (Toronto: Ontario College of Physicians and Surgeons, 1991).

56. Mark Warr, "Rape, Burglary and Opportunity," *Journal of Quantitative Criminology* 4 (1988): 275–288.

57. James LeBeau, "Patterns of Stranger and Serial Rape Offending Factors Distinguishing Apprehended and At-Large Offenders," *Journal of Criminal Law and Delinquency* 78 (1987): 309–326.

58. A. Nicholas Groth and Jean Birnbaum, *Men Who Rape* (New York: Plenum Press, 1979).

59. Raymond Knight, "Validation of a Typology of Rapists," in *Sex Offender Research and Treatment: State-of-the-Art in North America and Europe*, eds. W.L. Marshall and J. Frenken (Beverly Hills, CA: Sage, 1997).

60. Rebecca Kong, Holly Johnson, Sara Beattie, and Andrea Cardillo, "Sexual Offences in Canada," *Juristat* 23, 6, 2003.

61. Maire Gannon and Karen Mihorean, "Criminal Victimization in Canada, 2004," *Juristat* 25, 7, 2005.

62. R. Lance Shotland, "A Model of the Causes of Date Rape in Developing and Close Relationships," in *Close Relationships*, ed. C. Hendrick, 247–270 (Newbury Park, CA: Sage, 1989).

63. Walter DeKeseredy, Martin Schwartz, and Karen Tait, "Sexual Assault and Stranger Aggression on a Canadian Campus," *Sex Roles* 28 (1993): 263–277; Thomas Meyer, "Date Rape: A Serious Campus Problem That Few Talk About," *Chronicle of Higher Education* 29 (December 1984): 15.

64. Martin Schwartz, "Humanist Sociology and Date Rape on the College Campus," *Humanity and Society* 15 (1991): 304–316.

65. Mark Starr, "The Writing on the Wall," *Newsweek*, November 26, 1990, 64.

66. Peggy Reeves Sanday, *Fraternity Gang Rape: Sex, Brotherhood, and Privilege on Campus* (New York: New York University, 1990); Sarah Elton, "McMaster: Rohypol [sic] and Sexual Assault," *The Brunswickan*, March 13, 1998, 4.

67. David Finkelhor and K. Yllo, *License to Rape: Sexual Abuse of Wives* (New York: Holt, Rinehart and Winston, 1985).

68. Cited in Diana Russell, "Wife Rape," in *Acquaintance Rape: The Hidden Crime*, eds. A. Parrot and L. Bechhofer (New York: Wiley, 1991).

69. Donald Symons, *The Evolution of Human Sexuality* (Oxford: Oxford University Press, 1979).

70. Lee Ellis, "A Synthesized (Biosocial) Theory of Rape," *Journal of Consulting and Clinical Psychology* 39 (1991): 631–642.

71. Diana Russell, *The Politics of Rape* (New York: Stein & Day, 1975).

72. Paul Gebhard, John Gagnon, Wardell Pomeroy, and Cornelia Christenson, *Sex Offenders: An Analysis of Types* (New York: Harper & Row, 1965), 198–205; Richard Rada, ed., *Clinical Aspects of the Rapist* (New York: Grune & Stratton, 1978), 122–130.

73. See, generally, Edward Donnerstein, Daniel Linz, and Steven Penrod, *The Question of Pornography* (New York: Free Press, 1987); Diana Russell, *Sexual Exploitation* (Beverly Hills, CA: Sage, 1985), 115–116; Neil Malamuth and John Briere, "Sexual Violence in the Media: Indirect Effects on Aggression Against Women," *Journal of Social Issues* 42 (1986): 75–92.

74. Associated Press, "Trial on TV May Have Influenced Boy Facing Sexual-Assault Count," *Omaha World Herald*, April 18, 1984, 50.

75. Richard Felson and Marvin Krohn, "Motives for Rape," *Journal of Research in Crime and Delinquency* 27 (1990): 222–242.

76. Larry Baron and Murray Straus, "Four Theories of Rape: A Macrosociological Analysis," *Social Problems* 34 (1987): 467–489.

77. Julie Horney and Cassia Spohn, "The Influence of Blame and Believability Factors on the Processing of Simple versus Aggravated Rape Cases," *Criminology* 34 (1996): 135–163.

78. Gerald Robin, "Forcible Rape: Institutionalized Sexism in the Criminal Justice System," *Crime and Delinquency* 23 (1977): 136–153.

79. *Michigan v. Lucas* 90–149 (1991); Comment, "The Rape Shield Paradox: Complainant Protection Amidst Oscillating Trends of State Judicial Interpretation," *Journal of Criminal Law and Criminology* 78 (1987): 644–698.

80. Andrew Karmen, *Crime Victims* (Pacific Grove, CA.: Brooks/Cole, 1990), 252.

81. See, generally, Gary LaFree, "Official Reactions to Rape," *American Sociological Review* 45 (1980): 842–854; Martin Schwartz and Todd Clear, "Toward a New Law on Rape," *Crime and Delinquency* 26 (1980): 129–151; Susan Caringella-MacDonald, "The Comparability in Sexual and Nonsexual Assault Case Treatment: Did Statute Change Meet the Objective?" *Crime and Delinquency* 31 (1985): 206–223.

82. Linda Coates, "Causal Attributions in Sexual Assault Trial Judgments," *Journal of Language and Social Psychology* 16 (1997): 287–296; Linda Coates, Janet Bavelas, and James Gibson, "Anomalous Language in Sexual Assault Trial Judgments," *Discourse and Society* 5 (1994): 189–206.

83. Angela Browne and Kirk Williams, "Gender, Intimacy, and Lethal Violence: Trends from 1976 through 1987," *Gender and Society* 7 (1993): 78–98. See also, Linda Saltzman and James Mercy, "Assaults between Intimates: The Range of Relationships Involved," in *Homicide, The Victim/Offender Connection*, ed. Anna Victoria Wilson (Cincinnati: Anderson Publishing, 1993), 65–74; Angela Browne and Kirk Williams, "Exploring the Effect of Resource Availability and the Likelihood of Female-Perpetrated Homicides," *Law and Society Review* 23 (1989): 75–94; Joseph A. Kuypers, *Man's Will to Hurt: Investigating the Causes, Supports and Varieties of His Violence* (Halifax: Fernwood, 1992).

84. Geris Serran, and Philip Firestone, "Intimate Partner Homicide: A Review of the Male Proprietariness and the Self-defense Theories," *Aggression and Violent Behavior* 9, 1 (2004): 1–15.

85. Valerie Pottie Bunge, "National Trends in Intimate Partner Homicides, 1974–2000," *Juristat* 22, 5, 2002; Tina Hotton, "Spousal Violence After Marital Separation," *Juristat* 21, 7, 2001; Myrna Dawson, *Examination of Declining Intimate Partner Homicide Rates* (Ottawa: Department of Justice, 2001).

86. Robert Silverman and Leslie Kennedy, "Women Who Kill Their Children," *Violence and Victims* 3 (1988): 113.

87. Robert Silverman and William Meloff, "Canadian Kids Who Kill," *Canadian Journal of Criminology*, January (1992): 15.

88. Margaret Zahn and Philip Sagi, "Stranger Homicides in Nine American Cities," *Journal of Criminal Law and Criminology* 78 (1987): 377–397.

89. David Luckenbill, "Criminal Homicide as a Situational Transaction," *Social Problems* 25 (1977): 176–186.

90. Leslie Kennedy and Robert Silverman, "The Elderly Victim of Homicide: An Application of the Routine Activities Approach," *Sociological Quarterly* 31 (1990): 308.

91. Stephen Baron and Leslie Kennedy, "Routine Activities and a Subculture of Violence: A Study of Violence on the Street," *Journal of Research in Crime and Delinquency* 30 (1993): 88.

92. Michael Hazlett and Thomas Tomlinson, "Females Involved in Homicides: Victims and Offenders in Two Southern States," paper presented at the annual meeting of the American Society of Criminology, Montreal, November 1987; rev. 1988.

93. Scott Decker, "Deviant Homicide: A New Look at the Role of Motives and Victim-Offender Relationships," *Journal of Research in Crime and Delinquency* 33 (1996): 427–449.

94. Scott Decker, "Exploring Victim–Offender Relationships in Homicide: The Role of Individual and Event Characteristics," *Justice Quarterly* 10 (1993): 585–613.

95. James A. Fox and Jack Levin, *Mass Murder*, 2nd ed. (New York: Plenum Press, 1991).

96. Cindy Horswell, "Teen Held in Mom's Shooting Death: 'The Devil Made Me Do It,'" *Houston Chronicle*, May 19, 1993, 1.

97. Thomas Palmer, "A Doctor Smelled Arsenic, Leading to Arrest of Serial Killer," *Boston Globe*, August 20, 1987, 3.

98. Ronald Holmes and Stephen Homes, *Murder in America* (Thousand Oaks, CA: Sage, 1994), 6.

99. Philip Jenkins, "Serial Murder in England, 1940–1985," *Journal of Criminal Justice* 16, 1 (1988): 1–15.

100. Ronald Holmes and James DeBurger, *Serial Murder* (Newbury Park, CA: Sage, 1988), 58–59.

101. Belea Keeney and Kathleen Heide, "Gender Differences in Serial Murderers: A Preliminary Analysis," *Journal of Interpersonal Violence* 9 (1994): 37–56.

102. Royal Canadian Mounted Police, "Violent Crime Linkage Analysis System (ViCLAS)," www.rcmp-grc.gc.ca/viclas/viclas_e.htm; Jennifer Browdy, "VI-CAP System to Be Operational This Summer," *Law Enforcement News*, May 21, 1984, 1.

103. Philip Jenkins, "A Murder 'Wave'? Trends in American Serial Homicide 1940–1990," *Criminal Justice Review* 17 (1992): 1–18.

104. See, generally, Joel Milner, ed., "Special Issue: Physical Child Abuse," *Criminal Justice and Behavior* 18 (1991); see, generally, Ruth S. Kempe and C. Henry Kempe, *Child Abuse* (Cambridge, MA: Harvard University Press, 1978).

105. Catherine Trainor, *Family Violence in Canada: A Statistical Profile 2002* (Ottawa: Canadian Centre for Justice Statistics, 2002).

106. Holly Johnson, "Children and Youths as Victims of Violent Crimes," *Juristat* 15, 1995; for the United States, see David Wiese and Deborah Daro, *Current Trends in Child Abuse Reporting and Fatalities: The Results of the 1994 Annual Fifty-State Survey* (Chicago: National Committee to Prevent Child Abuse, 1995).

107. Richard Gelles and Murray Straus, "Violence in the American Family," *Journal of Social Issues* 35 (1979): 15–39.

108. Steve Geissinger, "Boy Scouts Dismissed 1,800 Suspected Molesters from 1971–91," *Boston Globe*, October 15, 1993, 3.

109. Diana Russell, "The Incidence and Prevalence of Intrafamilial and Extrafamilial Sexual Abuse of Female Children," *Child Abuse and Neglect* 7 (1983): 133–146; see also David Finkelhor, *Sexually Victimized Children* (New York: Free Press, 1979), 88.

110. Glenn Wolfner and Richard Gelles, "A Profile of Violence Toward Children: A National Study," *Child Abuse and Neglect* 17 (1993): 197–212.

111. Louanne Lawson and Mark Chaffin, "False Negatives in Sexual Abuse Disclosure Interviews," *Journal of Interpersonal Violence* 7 (1992): 532–542.

112. For a thorough review, see Kathleen Kendall-Tackett, Linda Meyer Williams, and David Finkelhor, "Impact of Sexual Abuse on Children: A Review and Synthesis of Recent Empirical Studies," *Psychological Bulletin* 133 (1993): 164–180.

113. Brandt Steele, "Violence within the Family," in *Child Abuse and Neglect: The Family and the Community*, eds. R. Helfer and C.H. Kempe, 12 (Cambridge, MA: Ballinger Publishing, 1976).

114. M. O'Keefe, "Predictors of Child Abuse in Maritally Violent Families," *Journal of Interpersonal Violence* 10 (1995): 3–25; as cited in Johnson, "Children and Youths as Victims of Violent Crimes."

115. Ruth Inglis, *Sins of the Fathers: A Study of the Physical and Emotional Abuse of Children* (New York: St. Martin's Press, 1978), 68.

116. Russell Dobash, R. Emerson Dobash, Margo Wilson, and Martin Daly, "The Myth of Sexual Symmetry in Marital Violence," *Social Problems* 39 (1992): 71–86; Martin Schwartz and Walter DeKeseredy, "The Return of the 'Battered Husband Syndrome': Typification of Women as Violent," *Crime, Law and Social Change* 8 (1993): 11–27.

117. Schwartz and DeKeseredy, "The Return of the 'Battered Husband Syndrome.'"

118. R. Emerson Dobash and Russell Dobash, *Violence against Wives* (New York: Free Press, 1979); Julia O'Faolain and Laura Martines, eds., *Not in God's Image: Women in History* (Glasgow: Fontana/Collins, 1974); Laurence Stone, "The Rise of the Nuclear Family in Modern England: The Patriarchal Stage," in *The Family in History*, ed. Charles Rosenberg, 53 (Philadelphia: University of Pennsylvania Press, 1975). See also John Braithwaite, "Inequality and Republican Criminology," paper presented at the annual meeting of the American Society of Criminology, San Francisco, November 1991, 20.

119. Merlin Brinkenhoff and Eugene Lupri, "Interspousal Violence," *Canadian Journal of Sociology* 13 (1988): 407.

120. Karen Rodgers, "Wife Assault: The Findings of a National Survey," *Juristat* 14, 1994.

121. James Makepeace, "Social Factor and Victim-Offender Differences in Courtship Violence," *Family Relations* 33 (1987): 87–91.

122. Graeme Newman, *Understanding Violence* (New York: Lippincott, 1979), 145–146.

123. Gerald Hotaling and David Sugarman, "An Analysis of Risk Markers in Husband to Wife Violence," *Violence and Victims* 1 (1986): 101–124; Ronald Simons, Chyi-In Wu, Christine Johnson, and Rand Conger, "A Test of Various Perspectives on the Intergenerational Transmission of Domestic Violence," *Criminology* 33 (1995): 141–171.

124. Canadian Centre for Justice Statistics, *Canadian Crime Statistics 2003* (Ottawa: Statistics Canada, 2004), catalogue 85-205-XPE.

125. F.H. McClintock and Evelyn Gibson, *Robbery in London* (London: Macmillan, 1961), 15.

126. John Conklin, *Robbery and the Criminal Justice System* (New York: Lippincott, 1972), 1–80.

127. James Calder and John Bauer, "Convenience Store Robberies: Security Measures and Store Robbery Incidents," *Journal of Criminal Justice* 20 (1992): 553–566.

128. John Scott Cameron, Lessons from the Fabrikant File: A Report to the Board of Governors of Concordia University, May 1994.

129. "Health and Safety Canada 2005—Violence in the Workplace Spotlighted at Canada's Largest Health and Safety Conference," Canada Newswire Group, www.newswire.ca/en/releases/archive/April2005/01/C1083.html.

130. James Alan Fox and Jack Levin, "Firing Back: The Growing Threat of Workplace Homicide," *Annals* 536 (1994): 16–30.

131. Neil Boyd, "Violence in the Workplace in British Columbia: A Preliminary Investigation," *Canadian Journal of Criminology*, October (1995): 491.

Property Crimes

Chapter Outline

Learning Objectives

After reading this chapter, you will be able to:

1. Understand the scope of property crime.
2. Be familiar with different types of property crime.
3. Know the new types of property crime that are evolving.
4. Discuss the implications of certain crimes on the victim.
5. Explain different strategies for combatting property crime.

With the growing theft and distribution of classified material, the group Anonymous has become an important advocate for cyber-freedom.

Economic crimes are acts in violation of the criminal law designed to bring financial reward to an offender. In our society, the range and scope of criminal activity motivated by financial gain are tremendous.

Whereas average citizens may be puzzled and enraged by violent crimes, they often view economic crimes with ambivalence. Although it is true that society generally disapproves of crimes involving theft and corruption, the public seems quite tolerant of romanticized crime and gentlemen bandits, even to the point of admiring such figures. They pop up as characters in popular myths and legends—Robin Hood, Jesse James, Bonnie and Clyde, and Edwin Alonzo Boyd. They are the semi-heroic subjects of books and films, such as *48 Hours, Pulp Fiction, Ocean's Eleven,* and *Heat.*

A Ponzi scheme architect, such as Earl Jones, who operated a massive investment fraud for 20 years and took in over $50 million, might even seem enviable to some. However, he was sentenced to 11 years in jail in 2010.

How can such ambivalence toward criminality be explained? For one thing, tolerance toward economic criminals may be prompted by the fact that almost everybody has been involved in economic crime. Even law-abiding people may have at one time engaged in petty theft, cheated on their income taxes, stolen a textbook from a university bookstore, or pilfered from their place of employment. Property crimes tend not to be seen as crimes of victimization in the way that, say, assault is.

Similarly, people may also be more tolerant of economic crimes because these crimes never seem to seriously hurt anyone—banks are insured, large businesses pass along losses to consumers, stolen cars can be replaced. Convicted offenders, especially business people who commit white-collar crimes involving millions of dollars, are often punished lightly. However, we fail to realize how great the cost of economic crime is. In Nova Scotia, for example, a GPI Atlantic study found that crime costs $550 million a year in economic losses to victims, including public spending on police, courts, and prisons, and private spending on burglar alarms, security guards, electronic surveillance, and theft insurance. When unreported crimes, such as insurance fraud, are added, the cost is $1.2 billion a year, or $1,250 per person. As long as it doesn't happen to us and we aren't forced to pay for it directly, then it registers pretty low on the radar. But if somebody came to the door and demanded we pay, it would be a different situation.

This chapter is the first of two that review the nature and extent of economic crime in our society. It is divided into two principal sections. The first deals with the concept of professional crime and focuses on different types of professional criminals, including the **fence**, a buyer and seller of stolen merchandise. The chapter then turns to the second section, a discussion of common theft-related offences, or **street crimes**. These offences include the major forms of common theft: shoplifting, auto theft, theft by false pretences, bad cheques, credit card fraud, and embezzlement. Next, the chapter discusses a more serious form of theft—burglary, or break and enter—that involves forcible entry into a person's home or place of work for the purpose of theft. Finally, arson is discussed briefly.

In Chapter 12, attention will be given to white-collar crimes and economic crimes that involve organizations devoted to criminal enterprise.

SOME BASIC PATTERNS

Official information from Statistics Canada indicates that the ratio of property crimes to violent crimes was one to three, or 25 percent and 75 percent of the total, respectively. Because the likelihood of violent crime is so much smaller than the rate of property crime, we might not even realize we have been the victims of theft, for example, just because we are so sensitized to the possibility of violent crime.

Between 2002 and 2012, total crime decreased from 2,355,332 incidents to 1,949,160. This was a decrease of 26 percent. However, the property crime rate decreased 33 percent in the same time period. Break-ins decreased by 43 percent, and motor vehicle theft decreased by 57 percent over the decade. Identity theft has increased, but counterfeiting decreased by 84 percent.

Among other trends worth noting are self-report studies showing that property crime among the young of every social class is widespread, but youths make up a small percentage of those charged in property offences. Youth crime overall was also down in 2012.

The rate of property crime varies by region. For example, the rate of robbery is lowest in Prince Edward Island (17 per 100,000) and the highest in the Prairies (Manitoba's rate is 168 per 100,000). Ontario's rate of 79 is exactly the country's average. Outside Yukon and the Northwest Territories, Saskatchewan continued to have the highest break and enter rate (790), and Saskatchewan moved ahead of Manitoba to have the highest motor vehicle theft rate, at 401. These interprovincial variations are influenced by many factors, as we saw in Chapter 3.

Property crime does not vary so much by city size as where the city is located. Toronto usually has a lower crime severity index rating of any census metropolitan area,

---

economic crimes   Acts designed to bring financial gain to the offender, as opposed to violent crimes, which are often conflict-related.

fence   A buyer and seller of stolen merchandise.

street crimes   Crime-related acts that prey on the public through theft, damage, and violence.

while Regina, Saskatoon, and Edmonton usually have the highest.

Furthermore, property crime cuts across all social classes. They might be called corporate or white-collar crimes when they are committed by the rich, or a political scandal when committed by the powerful, but property crime is widespread in society.

A BRIEF HISTORY OF THEFT

Theft is known throughout recorded history. The Crusades of the 11th century inspired peasants and downtrodden noblemen to leave their estates to prey on passing pilgrims.[1] The Crusaders felt it within their rights to appropriate the possessions of any infidels, Greeks, Jews, or Muslims they encountered during their travels. By the 13th century, returning pilgrims, not content to live as serfs on feudal estates, gathered in the forests of England to poach on game that was the rightful property of their lord or king, and to steal from passing strangers.

By the 14th century, many highwaymen and poachers were full-time livestock thieves, stealing cattle and sheep. Interestingly enough, the origin of the vagrancy statutes are rooted in the need to control people who wandered about with no lawful occupation and preyed on travellers. The first statutes allowed a vagrant to be apprehended and sometimes forced into servitude. Now, however, vagrancy is seen as a much less serious offence.

The 15th century brought hostilities between England and France in the Hundred Years' War. Foreign mercenary troops roamed the countryside, and their looting and pillaging were viewed as part of their pay. Theft became more professional with the rise of the city and the establishment of a class of urban poor.[2] By the 18th century, three separate groups of property criminals were active. In larger cities, such as London and Paris, groups of skilled thieves, pickpockets, forgers, and counterfeiters operated freely. As noted in the nearby Criminology Research box, some of the earliest organized police operated in London.

Thieves congregated in **flash houses**, typically public meeting places, such as taverns, which were headquarters for gangs. Deals were made, crimes plotted, and the sale of stolen goods negotiated. There were also smugglers, who moved freely in sparsely populated areas and transported goods without paying tax or duty. The third group were poachers, who lived in the country and supplemented their diet and income with game that belonged to a landlord. By the 18th century, professional thieves in larger cities had banded into gangs to protect themselves, increase their activities, and dispose of stolen goods.

EN AMÉRIQUE
VOYAGEURS ATTAQUÉS DANS UN TRAIN PAR DES BANDITS MASQUÉS

Train robbery flourished toward the end of the 19th century because professional robbers considered trains to be easy pickings. Law enforcement was decentralized, and robbers could escape over the border to a neighbouring province or state to avoid detection. Security was minimal, so robbers could stop a train, board it, and loot the passengers with little fear of capture. In this 19th-century French lithograph designed to depict the dangers of the Wild West, masked and armed train robbers frighten passengers on the Rocky Mountain Line.

Sometimes the difference between cop and criminal was difficult to see. Jack Wild, London's most famous thief and thief-taker, perfected the process of buying and selling stolen goods and gave himself the title of "Thief-Taker General of Great Britain and Ireland." Before he was hanged, Wild controlled numerous gangs and dealt harshly with any thief who violated his strict code of conduct.[3] During this period, individual theft-related crimes began to be defined by the common law. The most important of these categories are still used today.

> **flash houses** In the 18th century, the taverns where skilled thieves and pickpockets congregated and which served as headquarters for gangs.

Criminology Research
Catching Thieves in 18th-Century England

By the 18th century, the Industrial Revolution had lured thousands from the English countryside to work in the factory towns. The swelling population of urban poor, whose minuscule wages could hardly sustain them, increased the crime rates. In the London area, law enforcement was provided by thief-takers—organized groups of private police who earned a living by catching thieves and collecting rewards for their capture. Between 30 and 40 thief-takers were active in London by the mid-18th century.

Most thief-takers started as prison turnkeys, constables, court bailiffs, or other minor court officers. They were called *monied police* because they made a living not only from catching and informing on criminals, but also from receiving stolen property, stealing, perjury, and blackmail.

Typically corrupt, they took hush money and stolen goods from prisoners, gave perjured evidence, swore false oaths, and operated extortion rackets. Petty debtors were easy targets for those who combined thief-taking with the keeping of taverns. The health and safety of incarcerated prisoners was entirely at the whim of the keepers/thief-takers, who were free to charge what their prisoners could pay for board and other necessities.

Thief-takers' use of violence was notorious. Among the most infamous violent thief-takers was Jack Wild. He pursued armed thieves and was prepared to maim or kill. Before he was hanged in 1725, Wild had two fractures in his skull, and his bald head was covered with silver plates. He had 17 wounds in various parts of his body from swords, daggers, and gunshots, and

his throat had been cut in the course of his duties.

Henry Fielding sought to clean up the thief-taking system. As a city magistrate in 1748, Fielding operated his own group of monied police from Bow Street in London, deploying them throughout the city, deciding which cases to investigate and what streets to protect. Fielding's "Bow Street Runners" were an improvement over earlier monied police because their administrative structure improved record-keeping and investigative procedures, and they were instructed on legitimate duties. However, by the 19th century, state police officers were needed, ushering in the need for modern policing.

To read more about Jack Wild and his times, go to the website of the Old Bailey Court in England: www.oldbaileyonline.org.

Modern Thieves

Hundreds of thousands of property-related crimes occur each year. In 2012, Canada logged more than 496,781 thefts under $5,000, 77,939 auto thefts, and about 175,712 break and enters. Most property-related crimes are committed by occasional criminals who act opportunistically and are not committed career criminals; other theft-offenders are skilled, professional criminals. The following sections review these two orientations toward property crime.

Occasional Criminals

The majority of economic crimes are the work of amateur criminals whose decision to steal is spontaneous and whose acts are unskilled, unplanned, and haphazard. These offences do not involve the threat of violence, and many occur at domestic residences. Those accused are disproportionately youths.

Millions of theft-related crimes likely occur each year, and most are not reported to police agencies. In 2009, the General Social Survey (Canada's most recent national victimization study) found that the thefts reported to the police represented only 28 percent of all thefts of personal property, 23 percent of all household thefts, and 50 percent of all motor vehicle thefts.[4] Reporting has steadily decreased

between 1993, when the survey just began, to today. In 2009, just 31 percent of criminal incidents were reported to the police. Of those crimes not reported, 68 percent were felt to be not important enough; in 59 percent of cases, victims felt that the police couldn't do anything; 42 percent dealt with it another way; and 36 percent felt it was too personal. About one-quarter of Canadians reported being victimized in 2009.

Most school-aged youths who commit thefts won't enter a criminal career, and their behaviour drifts between conventional and criminal behaviour. Added to the pool of amateur thieves are millions of adults whose behaviour may occasionally violate the criminal law, such as shoplifters, pilferers, and tax cheats, but whose main source of income comes from conventional means and whose self-identity is non-criminal. Added together, their behaviours form the bulk of theft crimes.

According to routine activity theory, occasional property crime occurs when there is a **situational inducement** to commit crime.[5] Opportunities are available to members of all classes, but the upper class can engage in crimes of price fixing, bribery, and embezzlement, which are closed to the lower classes; and lower-class individuals are overrepresented

situational inducement The opportunity that influences the decision to commit crimes, such as occasional property crime.

in street crime. Situational inducements are short-run influences on a person's behaviour that increase risk taking. These include psychological factors, such as financial problems, and social factors, such as peer pressure.

Seasonality also contributes to the opportunity to commit crime, with almost 10 percent more crime occurring in the summer than in the winter. Opportunity and situational inducements are not the cause of crime; rather, they are occasions for crime—hence, the term **occasional criminal**.[6]

Opportunity and inducements are not randomly situated, and vary by age, class, and gender. Young persons, single women, high-income earners, urbanites, and homeowners are at greatest risk.[7]

Occasional offenders are not professionals. They do not rely on special skills to commit their crimes, and they are not committed to crime as a way of life. Unlike professionals, occasional criminals do not receive peer group support for their crimes. They will deny any connection to a criminal lifestyle and view their transgressions as being out of character. They see their crimes as being motivated by necessity, but because of their lack of commitment, they may be the most likely to respond to general deterrence.

Professional Criminals

In contrast, **professional criminals** make a significant portion of their income from crime. They don't believe their acts are impulsive, nor do they use rationalizations to excuse the harmfulness of their action. Consequently, professional criminals pursue their craft with vigour, learning from experienced criminals the techniques that will earn them the most money with the least risk. Although few in number, professional criminals produce the greater losses to society and cause significant social harm.

Professional theft is non-violent criminal behaviour undertaken with a high degree of skill for monetary gain that maximizes financial opportunities and minimizes the possibilities of apprehension. The most typical forms include pocket-picking, burglary, shoplifting, forgery and counterfeiting, extortion, sneak theft, and confidence swindling.

Three patterns emerge in the career patterns of professional criminals: (1) Youths come under the influence of older, experienced criminals who teach them the trade; (2) juvenile gang members continue their illegal activities at a time when most of their peers have "dropped out" to marry, raise families, and take conventional jobs; and (3) youths sent to prison for minor offences learn the techniques of crime from more experienced thieves. For example, this professional thief relates this story of his entry into crime:

> It was while I was at this parental school that I learned that some of the kids had been committed there by the court for stealing bikes. They taught me how to steal and where to steal them and where to sell them. Incidentally, some of the "nicer people" were the ones

FIGURE 11.1

Sutherland's Typology of Professional Thieves

Source: Edwin Sutherland and Chic Conwell, *The Professional Thief* (Chicago: University of Chicago Press, 1937).

who bought bikes from the kids. They would dismantle the bike and use the parts: the wheels, chains, handlebars, and so forth.[8]

Edwin Sutherland used the term *professional criminal* to refer to thieves who do not use force or physical violence in their crimes and live solely by their wits and skill.[9] However, some criminologists use the term to refer to any criminals who identify with a criminal subculture, make their main living from crime, and possess skill in their chosen trade.[10] Thus, one can become a professional safecracker, burglar, car thief, or fence.

Sutherland's Professional Criminal. What we know about the lives of professional criminals has come to us through journals, diaries, autobiographies, and first-person accounts given to criminologists. The best-known account is Edwin Sutherland's in *The Professional Thief*.[11] This concept of professional theft has two dimensions. First, professional thieves engage in limited types of crime, which are described in Figure 11.1.

Second, professional thieves rely exclusively on their wits, a believable demeanour, and their talking ability. Manual dexterity and physical force are of little importance. Professional areas of activity include bank robbery, car theft, burglary, and safecracking.

occasional criminal An offender who does not derive much income from crime but when there's an opportunity is more likely to drift in and out of crime.

professional criminals Those offenders who make a significant portion of their income from crime; less likely to drift in and out of crime.

Professional thieves acquire status in their profession on the basis of their technical skills (see, for example, the Criminology Research box, "Transforming Theft: Train Robbers and Safecrackers," on page 362), financial standing, and connections. Sutherland and Conwell say that professional thieves have common feelings, sentiments, and behaviours, none more important than the code of honour of the underworld; even under threat of the most severe punishment, a professional thief must never inform on his fellows.

Professional Criminals: The Fence. This view of the professional thief may be outdated because modern thieves often work alone and are not part of a criminal subculture.[12] However, Sutherland's principles certainly apply to the professional fence, a person who earns a living solely by buying and reselling stolen merchandise. In 2012, Canada had approximately 17,359 cases of people being in possession of stolen goods (see Exhibit 11.1), a decrease of 48 percent over the last decade, but still a rate of 50 per 100,000. Certainly some would involve professional fences.

The fence's critical role in criminal transactions has been recognized since the 18th century. Fences act as intermediaries who purchase stolen merchandise, ranging from diamonds to outboard motors, and then resell these goods to merchants who market them to legitimate customers. Much of what is known about fencing comes from three in-depth studies.[13]

Klockars's study of the fence Vincent Swaggi found that this highly professional criminal had developed techniques that made him almost immune to prosecution. During the course of a long and profitable career, Vincent spent only four months in prison because of his sophisticated knowledge of the law of stolen property. To convict someone of receiving stolen goods, the prosecution must prove that the accused was in possession of the goods and knew that the goods had been stolen. Vincent had the skills to make sure that these factors could never be proved. He maintained close ties with influential members of the justice system, helping them purchase items at below-cost, bargain prices. He also helped authorities recover stolen goods, which suggests that fences customarily cheat their thief-clients and at the same time cooperate with the law.

In another study, the fence Sam Goodman also purchased stolen goods from a wide variety of thieves and suppliers, including burglars, drug addicts, shoplifters, dockworkers, and truck drivers. According to Sam, a successful fence must meet the following conditions:

1. *Upfront cash.* All deals are cash transactions, so a fence must have ready cash on hand.
2. *Knowledge of dealing: learning the ropes.* The fence must develop a "larceny sense": learning to buy at good prices, avoiding getting caught, making the right contacts, and knowing how to wheel and deal.
3. *Connections with suppliers of stolen goods.* The successful fence engages in long-term relationships with reliable suppliers; the warehouse worker is preferred over the narcotics addict.
4. *Connections with buyers.* The successful fence must have continuing access to buyers of stolen merchandise who are inaccessible to the common thief and who will sometimes "place orders."
5. *Complicity with law enforcers.* The fence must work out a relationship with law enforcement; perhaps bribing officials, or acting as an informer to help police recover goods and arrest thieves.

Fences handle products from televisions to cigarettes, stereo equipment, watches, cars, and cameras. They operate through many legitimate fronts, including art dealers, antique stores, furniture and appliance retailers, remodelling companies, salvage companies, trucking companies, and jewellery stores. When deciding what to pay for goods, the fence uses a pricing policy. Professional thieves who steal high-priced items are given the highest amounts, 30 percent to 50 percent of wholesale price. For example, furs valued at $5,000 may be bought for $1,200. However, the amateur thief or drug addict who is not in a good bargaining position may receive only 10 cents on the dollar.

Fencing contains many elements of professional theft as described by Sutherland: Fences live by their wits, never engage in violence, depend on their skill in negotiating, and maintain community standing based on connections and power. The only divergence between Sutherland's thief and the fence is the code of honour; the fence is more willing to cooperate with authorities than are professional criminals.

EXHIBIT 11.1

Quick Code: Possession of Stolen Property

Section 354. (1) Every one commits an offence who has in his possession any property or thing or any proceeds of any property or thing knowing that all or part of the property or thing or of the proceeds was obtained by or derived directly or indirectly from

(a) the commission in Canada of an offence punishable by indictment; ...

Section 355. Every one who commits an offence under section 354

(a) is guilty of an indictable offence and is liable to imprisonment for a term not exceeding ten years, where the subject-matter of the offence is a testamentary instrument or the value of the subject-matter of the offence exceeds five thousand dollars; ...

[Other relevant sections: 356, 357, 358, 359, and 360]

SOURCE: *The Criminal Code of Canada*, Section 354.

In a striking twist on an old trade, fencing stolen merchandise has now hit the World Wide Web. The National Fraud Information Center, (at www.fraud.org), has information on a lot of different frauds, and says that online auction frauds account for 78 percent of all frauds and cost more than $300 each.

The Nonprofessional Fence

Professional fences are the thieves who have attracted the attention of criminologists. Yet fencing is also performed by amateur or occasional criminals. The guy who steals an outboard motor and sells it out of the back of a truck in the parking lot of a coffee shop is unlikely to be making that his steady occupation, but is most likely to get caught. That diamond ring for sale for $50 in the neighbourhood bar is a deal too good to be true.

In interviews with convicted thieves, fences, and people who bought stolen property, criminologists discovered that novice burglars, such as juveniles and drug addicts, often find it so difficult to establish relationships with professional fences that they turn instead to non-professionals to unload their stolen goods.[14]

One type of occasional fence is the part-timer who, unlike professional fences, has other sources of income. Part-timers are often legitimate businesspeople who integrate the stolen merchandise into their regular stock. For example, the manager of a local video store buys stolen DVD players and DVDs, then rents them along with his legitimate merchandise and obviously does not report the income for tax purposes. Or perhaps it's cigarettes, or car stereos, or antique jewellery.

Some merchants become actively involved in theft either by specifying the merchandise they want the burglars to steal or by fingering victims, such as the car owner in to get a stereo installed. Some businesspeople sell merchandise to people, and then describe the customers' homes and vacation plans to known burglars so that they can steal it back!

Some amateur fences barter stolen goods for services rendered. These *associational fences* typically have legitimate professional dealings with known criminals and include bail bonds agents, police officers, and attorneys. One lawyer bragged of getting a $12,000 Rolex watch from one client in exchange for legal services. Bartering for stolen merchandise avoids taxes and becomes a transaction in the underground economy.

Neighbourhood hustlers buy and sell stolen property as one of many ways they make a living; they keep some of the booty for themselves and sell the rest in the neighbourhood.

Amateur receivers can be complete strangers approached in a public place by someone offering a great deal on valuable commodities. Anyone buying a diamond ring for $50 cash should suspect it has been stolen. The amateur receivers who make a habit of buying merchandise at reasonable prices from a so-called trusted friend may account for a great deal of criminal receiving.

The Toronto and Regional Crime Stoppers is one of dozens of similar programs across the country responsible for recovering millions of dollars in stolen property every year. Recently, the program redesigned its website to incorporate a new logo.

Common theft falls into several categories linked together because they involve the intentional misappropriation of property for personal gain. In such cases as fencing, the property is bought from another who is in illegal possession of the goods. In the case of embezzlement or burglary, the property is taken through stealth, while in such cases as bad cheques, fraud, and false pretenses, property is obtained through deception. Some of the major categories of common theft offences are discussed in detail in the rest of this chapter.

THEFT

Theft was one of the earliest common-law crimes defined by English judges as acts in which one person took for his or her own use the property of another.[15] In common law, **larceny** was defined as "the trespassory taking and carrying away of the personal property of another with intent to steal." Today, definitions of theft include such acts as shoplifting and other

larceny Usually known as theft, the taking of property, one of the oldest common-law crimes.

theft offences that do not involve using force or threats on the victim or forcibly breaking into a person's home or place of work. (The former is robbery; the latter, break and enter.)

Originally, larceny involved only taking property that was in the possession of the rightful owners. For example, it would have been considered larceny for someone to go secretly into a farmer's field and steal a cow. Thus, the original common-law definition required a "trespass in the taking," which meant that goods must have been taken from the physical possession of the owner.

In creating this definition, English judges were more concerned with disturbance of the peace than they were with loss of property because if someone stole property from another's possession, the act could eventually lead to a confrontation. Consequently, the original definition did not include crimes in which the thief had come into the possession of the stolen property by trickery or deceit. For example, if someone entrusted with another person's property decided to keep it, it was not considered larceny.

Greater protection for private property was an outcome of the growth of manufacturing and the development of the free enterprise system. Commercial enterprise often required that property be entrusted to another for legitimate means, such as leaving a watch with a jeweller to be repaired or taking a car to a mechanic.

To get around the element of "trespass in the taking," English judges created the concept of **constructive possession**, which applied to situations in which persons voluntarily and temporarily gave up custody of their property but still believed that the property was legally theirs. For example, if a person gave a jeweller a watch for repair, that person would believe that he or she owned the watch, although it was handed over to the jeweller. Similarly, when a person misplaces his or her wallet and someone else finds it and keeps it, although identification of the owner can be plainly seen, the concept of constructive possession makes the person who has kept the wallet guilty of larceny.

Theft Today

The criminal justice system now separates theft into two classes according to the value of the goods involved: theft over and under $5,000. The former involves small amounts of money or property and accounts for the majority of thefts in Canada. The latter is more likely to be punished by a sentence in prison. In 2012, Canada had about 15,000 cases of theft over $5,000, and just under 500,000 thefts under $5,000. The latter includes bicycles, shoplifted goods, and goods taken from motor vehicles.

Theft under $5,000 is the most common criminal offence, accounting in 2012 for about 40 percent of all property crime in Canada. Such thefts cost billions of dollars in lost revenues to broadcasters, artists, and actors, and in property loss to residents and store owners. It also has a soft cost, in loss of both trust and feelings of safety. Theft has steadily increased over the last several decades as society has become

EXHIBIT 11.2

Quick Facts about Theft in Canada, Various Years

- In 2012, theft was the largest property crime category, with over 500,000 offences.
- There were almost 80,000 thefts of motor vehicles in 2012.
- The rate of motor vehicle theft has decreased 57 percent from 10 years earlier.
- In 2009, large decreases in motor vehicle theft were reported in Manitoba (28 percent), while an increase was reported in Newfoundland and Labrador (4 percent).
- For "other theft," British Columbia was 176 percent of the national average in 2006.
- The 15- to 24-year-old age group is about 10 times as likely to be victimized as those over 65 years of age.
- The proportion of female youth charged with minor theft was nearly twice that of males.
- In 2012, theft represented about 40 percent of all cases of property crime.
- The most common form of youth crime is theft under $5,000, usually shoplifting.
- In 2004, those earning $60,000 were three times as likely to be victimized as those earning $15,000.
- The highest theft rate occurs from June to August, and the lowest from December to February.
- The clearance rate for property crime is around 25 percent, compared to 75 percent for violent crime.
- In 2003, the most likely single item to be stolen was a motor vehicle (20 percent); firearms were the least likely (0.2 percent).
- A motor vehicle is more likely to be stolen from a parking lot than from a residence.
- Thefts are highest from commercial establishments.
- The General Social Survey shows that personal theft in 2009 was 44 percent higher than in 1999.

SOURCES: Statistics Canada, Canadian Crime Statistics 2006 (Ottawa: Canadian Centre for Justice Statistics, 2007); Andrea Taylor-Butts and Angela Bressan, "Youth Crime in Canada, 2006," Juristat 28, 3, 2008; "Criminal Victimization in Canada, 2004," Juristat 25, 7, 2005; "Youth Court Statistics, 2006/07," Juristat 28, 4, 2008; Dianne Hendrick, "Theft," in Crime Counts: A Criminal Event Analysis, ed. Leslie W. Kennedy and Vincent F. Sacco (Toronto: ITP Nelson, 1996); Samuel Perreault and Shannon Brennan, "Criminal Victimization in Canada, 2009," Juristat 30, 2, 2010; Mia Dauvergne and John Turner, "Police-reported Crime Statistics in Canada, 2009," Juristat 30, 2, 2010 "Police Reported Crime in 2012," Statistics Canada.

more affluent, and people have spent less time at home. As a result, our personal property has increased, and our guardianship of property has decreased, leading to opportunities for theft continuing to climb.[16] (Exhibits 11.2 and 11.3 offer additional detail about theft in Canada.) In 2012, however, theft showed about a 30 percent decrease since 2002.

constructive possession In larceny, the temporary physical custody of property given up willingly by the owner.

CONNECTIONS

Chapter 5 looks at routine activities theory and how situational variables affect crime rates.

CONNECTIONS

The Criminology Research exhibit in Chapter 9 looks at rape and its relationship to capitalism as a property crime.

Shoplifting

Shoplifting is a common form of theft that involves taking goods from stores. The Retail Council of Canada estimates that inventory shrinkage costs businesses several billions of dollars a year. The shoplifter is usually thought of as trying to snatch goods—jewellery, clothes, DVDs, appliances—when store personnel are otherwise occupied. The so-called *five-finger discount* is an extremely common form of crime.[17] Retail security measures add to the already high cost of this crime, which is passed on to the consumer. Shoplifting incidents have increased dramatically in the past 20 years, and retailers now expect an annual increase of 10 percent to 15 percent. Some studies estimate that about one in every nine shoppers steals from department stores. Discount stores have a minimum of sales help and depend on highly visible merchandise displays to attract purchasers, which make the merchandise vulnerable to shoplifters.

The Shoplifter. Only 10 percent of all shoplifters are professionals who derive the majority of their income from shoplifting.[18] Sometimes called **boosters**, or *heels*, professional shoplifters resell stolen merchandise to pawnshops or fences, usually at half the original price.

The majority of shoplifters are amateurs. These **snitches** are usually respectable persons who do not conceive of themselves as thieves but are systematic shoplifters who steal merchandise for their own use. They are not simply seized by an uncontrollable urge to take something that attracts them; they come equipped to steal. Usually, they have never been apprehended before, lack criminal experience, and lack association with a criminal subculture. Drifting into criminality because of situational inducements, they are unlikely to think of themselves as criminals.

Shoplifters are likely to reform if apprehended because they are not part of a criminal subculture. Getting arrested has a traumatic effect, and they will likely not risk a second offence.[19] Apprehension sometimes has a labelling effect that can result in repeated offending, but youths who are apprehended for shoplifting are usually deterred by the official processing of their offence.[20] A first offence is often the only offence.

However, in addition to the customer who shoplifts are employees who are responsible for a significant percentage of company theft. Thinking the employer owes them something, they steal inventory or from the till. For example, undercover investigators are often hired to see whether bartenders are stealing.

Controlling Shoplifting. One major problem associated with combatting shoplifting is that many customers who observe pilferage are reluctant to report it to security agents. Store employees themselves often hesitate to get involved in apprehending a shoplifter. For example, in a controlled experiment, customers observed only 28 percent of staged shoplifting incidents that had been designed to get their attention. Furthermore, less than one-third of people who said they had observed an incident reported it to store employees.

In another controlled experiment using staged shoplifting incidents, less than 10 percent of shoplifting was detected by store employees, and customers appeared unwilling to report even serious cases.[21] Even in stores with an announced policy of full reporting and prosecution, only 70 percent of the shoplifting detected by employees was actually reported to managers, and only 5 percent was prosecuted. Recent immigrants, adults, and blue-collar workers were disproportionately represented among those officially punished. The store owner's decision to prosecute shoplifters

---

booster A professional shoplifter; also known as a *heel*.

snitches Amateur pilferers who think of themselves as respectable people.

is based on the value of the goods stolen, the nature of the goods stolen, and the manner in which the theft was realized. For example, shoplifters who planned their crime by using a concealed apparatus, such as a bag pinned to the inside of their clothing, were more apt to be prosecuted than were those who had impulsively put merchandise into their pockets.[22]

To aid in the arrest of shoplifters, some jurisdictions have passed merchant privilege laws that are designed to protect retailers and their employers from litigation stemming from improper or false arrests of suspected shoplifters.[23] These laws protect but do not immunize merchants from lawsuits. Stores can also detain persons suspected of shoplifting under "defence of property" laws, which require that arrests be made on reasonable grounds or probable cause, detention be of short duration, and store employees or security guards conduct themselves in a reasonable fashion.

Prevention Strategies. Retail stores are now initiating many strategies designed to reduce or eliminate shoplifting. Security devices are just one way to combat shoplifting.

Target removal strategies involve using dummy goods on display while the real merchandise is kept under lock and key. Some stores sell from a catalogue while keeping merchandise in stockrooms. In one incident at the Bay, a shopper stole a box that he believed to contain a VCR from a display; unfortunately, the box was full of bricks. He was caught when he returned it for a refund.

Target hardening strategies involve locking goods into place or having them monitored by electronic systems. Clothing stores may use racks designed to prevent large quantities of garments from being slipped off easily. Expensive goods such as leather coats and bicycles are sometimes chained to displays.

Situational measures place the most valuable goods in the least vulnerable places, use warning signs to deter potential thieves, and use closed-circuit cameras. Goods may be tagged with devices that give off an alarm or spray a dye if they are taken out of the shop.

Exhibit 11.4 describes some of the steps retail insurers recommend to reduce the incidence of shoplifting.

Private Justice. Efforts to control the spread of shoplifting have prompted some retail chains to establish loss prevention units, which are private justice systems that work parallel to but independent of the public justice system. Private security officers have many of the law enforcement powers granted to municipal police officers, including the arrest of suspects and search and seizure.[24]

Because private police now outnumber public police in Canada, municipal police forces often work in conjunction with private security to detect and control crime.

Shoplifters may also be required to compensate store owners for the value of the goods they attempted to steal, costs incurred because of their illegal acts, and punitive damages. Some major Canadian retailers practise this form of "cost recovery" but with some controversy, especially when

---

EXHIBIT 11.4

How to Stop Shoplifting: Some Useful Tips

- Train employees to watch for suspicious behaviour, such as a shopper loitering over a trivial item.
- Have employees watch for shoppers wearing baggy clothes and carrying their own bag.
- Develop a call code to summon security when employees suspect that a customer is shoplifting.
- Because products on lower floors face the greatest risk, relocate more expensive products to other floors.
- Use smaller exits and avoid placing the most expensive merchandise near these exits.
- Design traffic patterns within stores to make theft less tempting and to funnel customers toward cashiers.
- Locate service departments (credit and packaging) to create supervision near areas where shoplifters work.
- Restrict and supervise areas where electronic tags can be removed; avoid blind corners.

SOURCE: Based on Marcus Felson, "Preventing Retail Theft: An Application of Environmental Criminology," *Security Journal* 7 (1996); 71–75.

---

they attempt to sue the parents of a youth who steals. The availability of civil damages can affect decision making, such as when store owners go after affluent shoplifters for civil recovery and ship poor or working-class shoplifters to the public criminal justice system for prosecution.

Sometimes, defending a store against shoplifting can get the merchant into trouble. In one highly publicized case in Toronto, Chinatown merchant David Chan apprehended a shoplifter and threw him into the back of a van until police arrived. When Chan was arrested and charged with confinement and assault, the public outcry was understandable.

Auto Theft

In 2012, 77,939 motor vehicles were stolen, down 7 percent from the previous year and down 57 percent from a decade earlier. That's a rate of 223 per 100,000, or over a hundred a year for a city with a population of 50,000.

And, of course, the pattern ranges across the country, from a low of 81 in Kingston, Ontario, to a high of 473 in Regina, Saskatchewan. The lowest provincial rate was 99 in Newfoundland and Labrador to a high of 401 in Saskatchewan, pushing out Manitoba for top place. The Northwest Territories and Nunavut had much higher rates, but they are difficult to compare to the provinces. With a Canadian average of 223 per 100,000 we see there is considerable interprovincial variation. These numbers mean that more than one person out of two thousand will have his or her car stolen, and the likelihood of recovery is low, especially in a province like Quebec.

More than 10 percent of all *Criminal Code* property offences in 2012 involved the theft of a car. See Exhibit 11.5 for some quick facts on Canadian auto thefts. However, the 2009 General Social Survey (GSS) reports 453,000 cases of motor vehicle or parts theft, for a rate of 34 per 1,000. So the odds increase from one out of two thousand to three out of a hundred. And these numbers don't include trucks or motorcycles.

The 2000 International Crime Victimization Survey (ICVS) estimated that car vandalism was the most prevalent crime measured, with 7 percent of the population having been a victim of this crime.

EXHIBIT 11.5

Quick Facts about Auto Theft in Canada, Various Years

- In 2012, motor vehicle theft reported to the police had decreased 57 percent in 10 years.
- Canada ranked fifth for risk of car theft in the 1999 International Crime Victimization Survey.
- In 2009, 108,000 motor vehicles were stolen, an average of almost 300 each day, decreasing to 77,939 in 2012, or one every seven minutes.
- Cars are most commonly stolen, but SUV theft increased 59 percent between 1991 and 2001.
- In 2007, most vehicles were stolen from public places, such as parking lots or streets, while only about one-third of motor vehicles were taken from a private residence.
- One-quarter of all stolen vehicles are never recovered, sold for resale, exported, or chopped; the highest rate of non-recovery is in Montreal.
- Motor vehicle thefts have low clearance rates: 13 percent in 2001, and about the same in 2012.
- In 2007, vehicle theft was disproportionately highest among 15- to 18-year-olds.
- Thefts from vehicles increased 11 percent in 2001 over the previous year, the first increase in 10 years (audio equipment is taken most often).
- More vehicle thefts (38 percent) occur between 6:00 a.m. and noon than in any other six-hour period.
- About one-quarter of vehicle thefts are linked to organized crime.
- Vehicle theft costs to insurers (e.g., repairing and replacing stolen vehicles), police, and healthcare and court systems add up to over $1 billion annually.
- Motor vehicle theft costs Canadians over $900 million per year in insurance claims, healthcare, court time, and police response.
- Canadian consumers have financial losses of over $3,000 for each instance of automobile theft.

SOURCES: CCJS, "Motor Vehicle Theft in Canada, 2001," *Juristat* 23, 1 (2003); CBC Marketplace, "Vehicles Grand Theft Auto Facts & Figures Broadcast," Oct 28, 2003; Mia Dauvergne, "Motor Vehicle Theft in Canada, 2007," *Juristat*, 28, 10, 2008; Insurance Board of Canada; Frank Mazilli, Gerry Martiniuk, "Auto Theft: The Human Costs," Ontario Crime Control Commission, 2001; "Crime Statistics in Canada 2012," Statistics Canada; "Clearance Rates for Crime in Canada, 2012," Statistics Canada.

Research shows that while improvements in vehicle security have reduced the opportunities for auto theft, auto thieves have adapted to these changes by illegally obtaining keys. Research with offenders found that while some of them simply found keys left in cars, many relied on such strategies as burglary, robbery, or fraud to acquire keys. Some thieves are opportunistic and easily prevented; however, others exhibit a higher degree of reasoning when offending.[25]

To add to the injury, the likelihood of getting a car back after it is stolen is low. Thirty years ago, 95 percent of the cars were recovered, but this figure dropped to 72 percent some years ago. The clearance rate in auto theft is low, typically at 10 percent. In the past, the typical car thief was out for a joyride; today, however, the car is stolen for resale or to be chopped into parts.[26] But that is itself dependent on where the car is stolen, as cars stolen in the west are more likely to be stolen for transportation or a joyride, while those in the east are more likely to be stolen for parts or to be sold overseas.

Understanding the patterns of car theft is important for providing clues for its control. One typology uncovered five categories of auto theft transactions:[27]

1. *Joyriding:* Motivated by teenagers' desire to acquire power and prestige, joyriders do not steal cars for profit but to experience the benefits of having an automobile.
2. *Short-term transportation:* Auto theft for short-term transportation involves the theft of a car to drive to another place, and then perhaps another theft to continue the journey.
3. *Long-term transportation:* Stealing cars for long-term transportation means keeping the car; usually older and lower class, may paint and disguise cars to avoid detection.
4. *Profit:* Auto theft is motivated by monetary gain; organized professionals resell expensive cars after altering identification numbers; amateur auto strippers steal batteries, tires, and wheel covers to sell them or equip their own cars.
5. *Commission of another crime:* A small portion of auto thieves steal cars to use in other crimes, such as robberies and thefts.

Once we understand the patterns of crime, we can better implement crime prevention. However, Rick Linden of the University of Manitoba, suggests crime prevention programs must analyze the crime problems in their community context, involve a broad group of people and organizations, consider a diverse range of prevention strategies, carefully implement the programs most suited to a particular community, and assess the results.[28] (See also the Crime in the News box on auto theft prevention.)

For example, at one time, joyriding was the predominant motive for auto theft, and most cars were taken by relatively affluent, Caucasian, middle-class teenagers looking for excitement.[29] However, this pattern has shifted: Fewer cars are being taken today while, concomitantly, fewer stolen cars

The latest crime statistics show that the rate of auto theft in Canada is about 321 thefts per 100,000 people. This is down 15 percent from the previous year, and down significantly from the early 2000s.

The last time I saw a cost fixed to it, it was about $1 billion per year: $600 million for insurance premiums and $400 million for criminal justice and healthcare.

Part of the decrease in motor vehicle theft may be due to the increased use of anti-theft devices such as vehicle immobilizers and car alarms. Police have used targeted initiatives such as a "bait car" in high-theft areas, and youth prevention programs and specialized task forces to tackle organized crime have resulted in significant decreases.

An interesting pattern is that the highest rates are out west, in Regina, Winnipeg, Edmonton and Kelowna, at twice the national average. In eastern Canada, however, the rate can be a third of the national average.

In Canada, vehicles are most likely to be stolen from parking lots, followed by streets, home garages, and driveways. Thefts are most frequent in low-income, high-crime communities because of the higher number of motivated offenders, less guardianship, and more vulnerable targets. The availability of older cars that are easy to steal and a lack of private parking facilities mean that the poor are the main victims of vehicle theft.

While about 75 percent of stolen vehicles are recovered in Canada, the rate of recovery varies across the country. At one point, for example, the recovery rate varied from 56 percent in Montreal to 97 percent in Regina. The high recovery rate cannot be credited to policing but rather to the fact that cars are stolen for different reasons in different parts of the country.

In eastern Canada, professional vehicle theft is more prevalent. This is the reason for the lower recovery rate. If a car is stolen professionally, it's gone, put into a container, and shipped out. Or it's taken to another province and sold using a vehicle identification number taken from a salvaged vehicle.

Joyriding, on the other hand, is more prevalent in the west. Some older cars are easier to steal, and in Winnipeg about one in 12 older Dodge Caravans and Plymouth Voyagers are stolen each year because they are easier to break into. In other parts of Canada, older Hondas and Toyotas have high theft rates. These older vehicles are more likely to be owned by poorer people living in low income neighbourhoods.

Most vehicle thefts are reported, and, as a result, we know a lot about the victims. However, we know less about the thieves, because the low clearance rate means we cannot be sure that those who are arrested are representative of all those who steal motor vehicles.

However, it seems that youths make up a higher proportion for vehicle theft than for any other offence, and it is also a precursor offence. This means that youths who are first arrested for vehicle theft are more likely to continue their criminal behaviour than for any other offence.

We also know that most vehicle thefts are committed by males, and a large proportion of vehicle thefts are committed by small groups of chronic offenders, whether they are joyriders or professional vehicle thieves.

When cars are being stolen for joyriding rather than for profit, there is evidence that stealing cars is part of the youth culture in some inner city schools. Joyriding is usually committed in the company of peers, and interviews with incarcerated young offenders have shown that their primary motivation for stealing cars is excitement rather than profit.

Research has also found that joyriders are more likely to have an adversarial relationship with the community, to feel excluded by dominant institutions and culture, and to be poorly supervised by their parents. They report low rates of participation in sports and other recreation, and high rates of school truancy.

Targeting youth through recreation and other prevention programs might help solve the problem.

SOURCE: Copyright Chris McCormick, published in the *Daily Gleaner* (Fredericton), September 22, 2011.

are being recovered. Part of the reason is the increase in the number of professional car thieves who are linked to "chop shops" or export rings.

A 2004 Statistics Canada study found that Montreal has both the largest problem of organized vehicle theft in the country and the highest proportion of vehicles not recovered, which, at 44 percent, is more than twice that of the next highest jurisdiction (Halifax). Vehicles stolen from private homes have a higher probability of not being recovered (34 percent) than vehicles stolen from streets (10 percent) and parking lots (15 percent). More importantly, 41 percent of vehicles stolen from car dealerships are not recovered, which indicates that organized groups are very selective in the vehicles they target.[30]

Export of stolen vehicles has become a global problem, and the emergence of capitalism in Eastern Europe has increased the demand for Western-made cars.[31]

In 2001, INTERPOL reported that more than three million cars were stolen in the world annually. The value of vehicles stolen from 45 countries in Europe, North America, Africa, and Asia was estimated at US$21 billion per year. INTERPOL's Automated Search Facility database for stolen motor vehicles contains records for more than 2.5 million stolen cars from 59 countries and is used by police forces worldwide to track stolen vehicles. INTERPOL alleges that profits from smuggling stolen cars are used to fund terrorist organizations.[32]

Longer Sentences Won't End Car Theft Scourge

It is often said in politics that to be effective, politicians must not only do, they must be seen to be doing. Unfortunately, it is sometimes the case that political leaders are seen to be doing something when, in reality, they are doing nothing at all.

Prime Minister Stephen Harper was seen in Winnipeg Monday, and seen to be doing something important to battle auto theft, one of the most chronic crimes plaguing Winnipeg and many other large urban centres. Harper's pledge Monday was to introduce tougher laws to crack down on the trafficking of stolen vehicles and parts.

The problem is that the changes he outlined will do precious little to help the situation here, where auto theft is less about organized syndicates and more about a bunch of teenagers out for a dangerous joyride.

When this observation was made at Harper's news conference, the prime minister indicated the measures announced Monday were not "the be-all and end-all" of his government's attack on auto theft. There is a private-member's bill currently before the Senate that would make auto theft its own crime, with tougher penalties. And Harper hinted there would be changes to the *Youth Criminal Justice Act*.

There shouldn't be any mystery about what the federal government is going to do.

As is the case with adult offenders, the Conservative government intends to apply harsher sentences to youth offenders as a deterrent. This approach to fighting crime is probably the best example of not actually doing anything while creating the impression something is being done.

The so-called "war" on crime is often about being seen to be addressing the problem, while ignoring the root causes that lurk below the public's radar, and seemingly outside of the grasp of politicians.

Manitoba's NDP government supported Harper's announcement, even though it has introduced measures here that are much more effective at curbing auto theft than new *Criminal Code* measures.

Some may still resent it, but the immobilizer program has successfully frustrated car thieves. It was risky and expensive, but ultimately more effective than harsher penalties.

Then last week, the province announced an additional $500,000 to hire recreation directors at inner-city community centres. Professionalizing the management of recreation in needy areas of the city where such activity is a proven way of keeping kids away from crime and gang activity is a simple but effective way of combatting all youth crime, auto theft in particular.

Supporters of harsher penalties will argue that they are just one part of an effective campaign, meant to work in concert with enhanced social programs and anti-theft initiatives. The reality is that tougher laws with longer sentences tend to eclipse those other initiatives.

Longer sentences mean more people in remand, on trial and in jail, which means significant increases in the costs of administering the courts and of incarceration. That leaves less money for social programs that divert potential auto thieves to more wholesome activities. As more young people experience prison—we already incarcerate youth at 10 times the rate of European countries—society can boast more graduates of what is essentially a post-secondary education in crime.

A large constituency embraces the idea of harsher penalties for all types of crimes because it satisfies a hunger to punish, and creates an illusion that we are in control. This is why politicians love to be seen changing laws and toughening sentences.

And therein lies the greatest irony. While lawmakers are content to be seen doing something, the criminals are the ones actually doing. And longer sentences aren't likely to change that equation.

SOURCE: Dan Lett, "Longer sentences Won't End Car Theft Scourge," *Winnipeg Free Press*, April 15, 2008. Reprinted with permission from The Winnipeg Free Press.

Apparently, high-ranking members of the Hezbollah, an Iranian-backed terrorist group, favoured the $70,000 Lincoln Navigator, which was often stolen in Ontario!

Which Cars Are Taken Most? Car thieves show signs of rational choice when they make their target selections. Luxury cars and utility vehicles are popular for resale, and older Japanese models are more valuable because of the interchangeability of their parts.

Among the top 10 stolen vehicles in Canada in 2013 continued to be the 2000 Honda Civic, the 2002 Cadillac Escalade, the 2006 Chevrolet Trailblazer, the 2005 Acura RSX and 1997 Acura Integra 2-door, and the 2006 and 2007 Ford 250 and 350 four-wheel-drive models.

Car models that have been in production for a few years without many design changes stand the greatest risk of theft. The Camry made between 1988 and 1991 is attractive because it has parts that are most valued in the secondary market, which is a similar problem for Toyotas ten years later. Luxury cars typically experience a sharp decline in their theft rate soon after a design change. Older cars are also more likely to be uninsured, and demand for stolen used parts is higher for these vehicles.

The economics of auto theft are interesting. The Insurance Board of Canada estimates that an organized theft ring will pay between $150 and $500 for a stolen Jeep Grand Cherokee. The vehicle identification number (VIN) from a wrecked model purchased for $2,000 will be placed on the

FIGURE 11.2

Carjacking Compared with Risks of Other Life Events

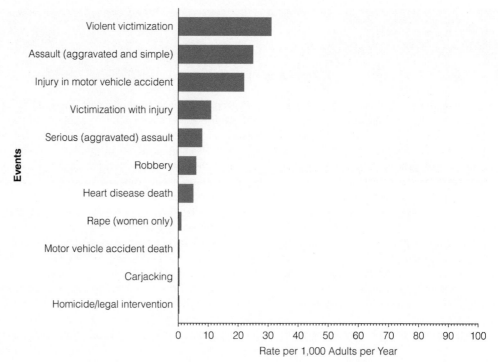

Events (y-axis):
- Violent victimization
- Assault (aggravated and simple)
- Injury in motor vehicle accident
- Victimization with injury
- Serious (aggravated) assault
- Robbery
- Heart disease death
- Rape (women only)
- Motor vehicle accident death
- Carjacking
- Homicide/legal intervention

Rate per 1,000 Adults per Year (x-axis: 0 10 20 30 40 50 60 70 80 90 100)

Source: Highlights from 20 years of Surveying Crime Victims, October 1993, NCJ-144525. Online: http://www .ojp.usdoj.gov/bjs/pub/ascii/c.txt (U.S. Dept. of Justice).

stolen SUV for a cost between $500 and $1,500. It can then be sold "legitimately" in another jurisdiction to an unsuspecting buyer for about $45,000, creating a profit of about $40,000. If it is sold in Eastern Europe, the profit could be as high as $95,000!

CONNECTIONS

Chapter 5 discusses the rational choice view of car theft. As you may recall, cars with expensive radios and parts are more often the target of rational thieves.

Carjacking. You may have read about armed offenders approaching an occupied car and forcing the owner to give up the keys; in some cases, people have been killed when they reacted too slowly. This type of auto theft has become common enough that it has its own name: **carjacking**.[33] Carjacking is considered a type of robbery because it involves the use of force.

Carjacking is a new form of crime that some have dubbed urban terrorism. Such high-profile crime attracts widespread media coverage. In Florida, for example, the killing of tourists in out-of-state rental cars received international attention several years ago. In a form of carjacking, called the "bump and grab," cars are stolen when they are hit from behind and the driver pulls off to the side of the road.

In another form of urban terrorism, called a home invasion, armed robbers force their way into a home while the residents are there and extort money by force.[34] Such crimes

strike at the heart of our safest places, our homes, and cause a lot of concern. In two-thirds of home invasions, all the accused are strangers to the homeowners, half of the home invasions involve a weapon, seniors are most frequently the victims, and the rates of home invasions have remained stable at about 23 per 100,000 population.[35]

However, home invasions and carjacking are relatively rare. Figure 11.2 shows the risk of carjacking compared with other life events.

Combatting Auto Theft. Because of its commonality and high loss potential, auto theft has been a target of situational crime prevention efforts.[36] One approach has been to increase the risk of apprehension. Information hotlines offer rewards for information leading to the arrest of car thieves. Another approach has been to place fluorescent decals on windows that indicate that the car is never used between 1 a.m. and 5 a.m.; if police spot a car with the decal being operated during this period, they know it is stolen.

Some cars have also been equipped with radio transmitters. The LoJack system involves a tracking device installed in the car that gives off a signal, enabling the police to pinpoint the car's location.

Other prevention measures make it more difficult to steal cars. The most common method of stealing a car is by using

carjacking Stealing a car by forcing the driver out of the car; it has a low likelihood of occurring but a high news value.

the keys (43 percent), as most cars in Canada are stolen using the keys left in them.[37] The last decade has seen an increase in break and enters to steal vehicle keys. Parking lots have been equipped with theft-deterring closed-circuit TV cameras and barriers. Manufacturers have installed more sophisticated steering-column locking devices and other security systems that make theft harder. Improved security measures, such as lighting and patrols, probably deter auto crime but likely displace it to other areas.[38]

A study by the Highway Loss Data Institute (HLDI), however, found that most car theft prevention methods, especially alarms, have little effect on theft rates. The most effective methods appear to be devices that immobilize a vehicle by cutting off the electrical power needed to start the engine. Alternatively, a person can choose to drive a car that nobody would want to steal, which is actually a very successful option.

In 2008, the federal government introduced new amendments to the *Criminal Code* to combat organized auto theft rings. The provisions included making it a crime to alter, destroy, or remove a VIN; expanding the criminal definition of trafficking in stolen property to include stolen cars and car parts; and giving the Canada Border Services Agency authority to search containers suspected of being used for shipping stolen vehicles.[39] In 2010, the federal government passed Bill S-9, *Tackling Auto Theft and Property Obtained by Crime Act*, which gives Canada Border Services Agency the authority to seize stolen vehicles intended for export.

False Pretences or Fraud

False pretences, or **fraud**, involves misrepresenting a fact to cause a victim to willingly give his or her property to the wrongdoer, who keeps it.[40] The definition of false pretences was created by the English Parliament in 1757 to cover an area of law left untouched by larceny—statutes. The first false pretences law punished people who "knowingly and designedly by false pretense or pretenses, [obtained] from any person or persons, money, goods, wares or merchandise with intent to cheat or defraud any person or persons of the same."[41] The offence of false pretences differs from traditional larceny because the victims willingly give their possessions to the offender.

An example of false pretences is an unscrupulous merchant who sells a chair by claiming it was an antique, but knowing all the while that it was a cheap copy. Another example is a phony healer selling a victim a bottle of coloured sugar water as an elixir that will cure a disease. One report estimated that hazardous fake products now commonly found include cosmetics laced with toxins, toys made with contaminated material, and faulty electrical switches. The total cost of lost revenue from the sale of counterfeit products was estimated to be in the billions of dollars.[42]

Exhibit 11.6 illustrates some facts and trends about fraud in Canada in recent years.

Confidence games are run by swindlers and usually involve getting a "mark" interested in some get-rich-quick scheme, which may have illegal overtones. The criminal's hope is that when victims lose their money, they will be too embarrassed and afraid to call the police. There are hundreds of varieties of con games. One of the most common is called the pigeon drop.[43] A package or wallet containing money is found by a con

false pretences   Illegally obtaining money, goods, or merchandise by fraud or misrepresentation.

fraud   Taking possessions through deception, such as selling a desk as an antique that is really a copy.

confidence games   A fraud in which the victim, or *mark*, is persuaded to trust the criminal.

According to Neal Shover, the activities of professional thieves began to be influenced by technology before the 20th century. For example, train robberies flourished toward the end of the 19th century because professional robbers considered them easy pickings. Law enforcement was decentralized, and robbers could escape over the border to a neighbouring jurisdiction to avoid detection. Security arrangements were minimal, and robbers could stop, board, and loot trains with little fear of capture. However, technological improvements were initiated in an effort to deter would-be robbers:

- Plainclothes officers placed on trains rode unobtrusively among the passengers.
- Baggage cars carried horses that could be used to immediately pursue bandits.
- Cars were made with finer precision and strength to make them impregnable.
- Forensic science and improved communication made it easier to capture and identify robbers.

As a result of these innovations, the number of train robberies decreased, and by 1920, train robbers had all but disappeared. U.S. federal involvement in train protection also extended law enforcement beyond the county or state in which the robbery occurred.

Safecracking also underwent a dramatic change due to technological changes in the design of safes. In the early 1900s, safes were made of manganese steel because it was resistant to drilling and was fireproof. With the invention and distribution of acetylene torches in the latter part of the 19th century, safes constructed of manganese became vulnerable and encouraged safecrackers to commit bold crimes. Safe manufacturers fought back by constructing safes with alternative sheets of copper and steel. The copper diffused heat and made the safe resistant to being torched. In response, safecrackers shifted their approach to attacking safes' locks and locking mechanisms. They developed mechanical devices that either dismantled or destroyed locks. Some burglars developed methods of peeling the laminated layers of the safe apart.

After World War II, safecrackers began using carbide and then diamond drill bits, which tore through metal. Safe manufacturers responded by lining safes with new metals designed to chip or break drill bits. They also developed sophisticated security systems featuring light beams, which would trip an alarm if the beam was interrupted by an intruder. When thieves learned how to neutralize these alarms, they were supplanted by motion detectors and ultrasonic systems, which fill space with sound waves and set off alarms when they are disturbed. Though these systems can be defeated, it requires expensive electronic gear, which most criminals can neither afford nor operate. As a result, the crime of safecracking is now relatively rare.

Critical Thinking

Technology changes the nature and extent of theft crimes. For example, using bogus credit cards and stealing from automated banking machines (ABMs) has increased in number and value. What other crime patterns have been created by technological change?

SOURCE: Neal Shover, *Great Pretenders, Pursuits, and Careers of Persistent Thieves* (Boulder, CO: Westview Press, 1996), pp. 50–51.

---

man or woman. A passing victim is asked for advice about what to do because the wallet contains no identification. Another supposed stranger, who is actually part of the con, approaches and enters the discussion. The three decide to split the money. But first, one of the swindlers goes off to consult a lawyer; on return, the swindler says the money can be split up, but each must have the means to reimburse the original owner. The victim is asked to give some good-faith money for the lawyer to hold. When the victim goes to the lawyer's office to pick up a share of the loot, the address is bogus and the money is gone.

Compared with this clumsy and laborious con, con games in the 1990s were appropriated by corrupt telemarketers, who contacted people, typically seniors, over the phone to defraud them. The Federal Bureau of Investigation (FBI) estimates that illicit telephone pitches cost $3 billion to $40 billion a year in the United States and $80 million to $100 million in Canada.[44] In one scam, a salesman tried to get $500 from a 78-year-old woman by telling her the money was needed as a deposit to make sure she would get $50,000 cash she had supposedly won in a contest. A Las Vegas-based telephone con game defrauded people out of more than $1.3 million by soliciting donations for families of those killed in the Oklahoma City bombing. The Phone Busters unit of the Ontario Provincial Police estimates that one Canadian per week loses more than $5,000 in such schemes. Some common telemarketing scams are detailed in Exhibit 11.7.

In another study of fraud, a study, conducted for the Insurance Board of Canada's investigative division by a team at St. Francis Xavier University, determined that 26 percent of 4,000 closed personal injury claims were fraudulent. Opportunistic fraud, such as inflating medical expenses, was the most common type of fraudulent crime. The rate was highest in Ontario and lowest in Alberta. It also tends to be higher in major cities and metropolitan areas.

In one case, an organized ring of 25 people were sued for staging car accidents and defrauding the Insurance

EXHIBIT 11.7

Telemarketing Scams

The Toronto Police Service published the following list of common telemarketing scams in a community handbook aimed specifically at seniors.

1. *The lottery scam:* The caller wants you to be part of a syndicate, or group that is buying a large number of lottery tickets, usually in a foreign lottery. Being part of a group purchase will better your chances of winning. The caller sometimes claims to be able to decrease your odds from millions to one down to as low as six to one, making you almost a sure winner.
   Response: No matter what the caller says, the odds per ticket remain the same, usually millions to one. Do not buy lottery tickets from a telephone solicitation.
2. *The prize scam:* The caller tells you that you have won a valuable prize or prizes, but you must first submit a payment to cover such things as taxes, transportation, customer's insurance, legal fees, etc.
   Response: When you're a winner, you do not have to pay for your prize. Do not send any money.
3. *The advance fee loan scam:* This scam usually starts with an advertisement for an "easy loan" appearing in a local newspaper. The victim is usually someone whose credit history may prohibit him or her from getting a traditional loan from a bank. The victim calls the number in the advertisement and is told that he or she has been approved for the amount being sought. However, the lending company representative advises the victim that an advance fee is required, usually about 10 percent of the amount to be borrowed.
   Response: It is illegal in Ontario to ask for an advance fee for a loan. Do not deal with any lender who charges a fee

in advance for a loan. Report this scam to the Ministry of Consumer Services, Ontario.
4. *Vacation scams:* The caller offers incredible savings and sometimes even free travel to popular destinations. Certificates are issued in the victim's name, representing a reservation.
   Response: You do not get something for nothing. If you try to take advantage of this golden opportunity, you will undoubtedly end up paying the original cost of the vacation. Do not buy a vacation through a telephone sales pitch. When travelling, deal with a reputable agent.
5. *Charity scams:* The caller appears to be soliciting for what is clearly a worthy cause, although you do not recall ever hearing the exact name of the charity before. Many scams are successful because the name of the charity being used in the scam is similar to an easily recognized charity.
   Response: There are so many charities that it is almost impossible to know them all. Do not try. True charitable causes are worthwhile and should be supported. They are frequently listed in the telephone book. Arrange to have your contribution delivered to them directly. Using this approach ensures that your donation goes to the charity you wish to support. Do not send money to an unfamiliar charity.

With the growth of direct-mail marketing and 1-900 telephone numbers that charge callers more than $2.50 per minute for conversations with beautiful and willing sex partners, new confidence games will increase. However, 64 percent of fraud offences were cleared in 1995—most likely a small percentage of all swindlers, scam artists, and frauds.

SOURCE: Toronto Police Service, www.TorontoPolice.on.ca.

Corporation of British Columbia of $400,000. They staged the accidents between 9:30 p.m. and midnight, in an area where they were assured no witnesses would be, and then submitted claims for about $30,000.

In 2004, several sellers on eBay were fined and ordered to pay restitution for fraudulently bidding up prices to unsuspecting buyers of motor vehicles.

Identity Theft

A new form of fraud or false pretences is identity theft. The Canadian Council of Better Business Bureaus estimates that identity theft takes $2.5 billion out of the Canadian economy annually.

Now that fake driver's licences are available on the Internet, illegitimate identities are much easier to build. A jump in counterfeiting was a significant factor in the increase in the crime rate in 2003. In the same year, it was reported that hundreds of social insurance numbers (SINs) were stolen at Canada Customs. SINs allow access to databases that include employment records, and allow a person to apply for employment insurance, credit cards, and social assistance.

Identity theft occurs when a person's private and personal information is stolen, enabling the thief to access confidential information, often for the purpose of financial gain. The use of the Internet has turned identity theft into a type of cybercrime that has grown at surprising rates over the past few years (see the Crime in the News box on page 366).

Identity theft can destroy people's lives by manipulating their credit records or stealing from their bank accounts. Identity thieves use a variety of techniques to steal information. They may fill out change of address cards at the post office to obtain another person's credit card bills and bank statements. They may then call the credit card issuer and, pretending to be the victim, ask for a change in address on the account. They can then charge numerous items over the Internet and have the merchandise sent to the new address. It may take months for the victim to realize the fraud because the victim is not receiving bills from the credit card company.

> **identity theft**   The fraudulent acquisition of another person's private and personal information.

Famous Canadian Criminals
Albert Johnson Walker

After his company defrauded 30 clients of more than $3 million from pension and investment funds, Albert Walker, a financial adviser, fled to England in 1990 with his daughter Sheena, age 15. With an arrest warrant issued for him in Woodstock, Ontario, he was soon on INTERPOL's most wanted list. If he had stayed in Canada, he would have faced more than three dozen fraud-related charges, including money laundering.

When Walker was arrested in 1996 in a tiny village northwest of London, he was living with his daughter and her two children. However, he was living under the name of David Davis. His daughter posed as his wife, Noel Davis. The paternity of the children was described as "unknown."

Through his personal secretary, Walker had met a man named Ronald Platt and arranged to use his identity in exchange for money. However, in 1996, Walker killed Platt, dumped his body in the ocean, and then assumed Platt's identity completely. Police were able to trace Walker's whereabouts on the day Platt was killed from information retrieved from his Global Positioning System (GPS) device. In 1998, Walker was found guilty of murder and sentenced to life in prison without parole for 15 years. In 2000, he asked for a transfer to a Canadian prison, but was flatly turned down.

Albert Walker still faced multiple charges in Canada. His offence was a fraud of magnificent proportions, made possible because of his privileged position. Walker came back to Canada in late February 2005 to serve the rest of his sentence and was sentenced to four years in jail on fraud-related charges. Years on the run came full circle.

Some identity theft schemes are extremely elaborate. For example, in one case, 19 people were indicted on charges that they had created an organization called Shadowcrew to provide stolen credit card numbers and identity documents through an online marketplace. The stolen account numbers were contributed by approved "vendors" who had been granted permission to sell on the Shadowcrew site after being vetted through a complex review process. Shadowcrew members allegedly trafficked in at least 1.7 million stolen credit card numbers and caused total losses in excess of $4 million.[45]

Phishing.   Some identity thieves create false emails or false websites, or both, which look legitimate but are designed to gain illegal access to a victim's personal information; this activity is known as **phishing** (or *carding* and *spoofing*).

Some phishers send out emails that look like they come from a credit card company or online store, informing victims of a problem with their account credit or balance. To fix the problem and update their account, they are asked to submit their name, address, phone numbers, personal information, and credit card numbers. Alternatively, the email may direct victims to a phony website that purports to be a legitimate company or business enterprise. Once a victim accesses the website, he or she is asked to provide personal information or financial account information so that the problem can be fixed.

Once phishers have a victim's personal information, they can do three things with it: (1) gain access to pre-existing accounts—bank cards and credit cards—and purchase goods with those accounts; (2) use the information to open new bank and credit card accounts without the victim's knowledge; (3) implant viruses into their software that forwards the phishing email to other recipients once one person responds to the original email, thereby luring more potential victims in the net. Some common phishing scams are listed in Exhibit 11.8.

EXHIBIT 11.8

Phishing Scams

A common form of email fraud is called "phishing," where the sender tries to convince the recipient that their bank account has been hacked, for example. Using the brand's logo, the sender asks for them to log in to verify their account information, or to change their password. Sometimes the message says that their account has been suspended until that action has been taken. There is often a sense of urgency, and usually a lot of misspellings.

Other information that the fraudster might want to obtain are names, social insurance numbers, address, credit card information, and so on. This information can then be used to create bank accounts, arrange loans, debit credit cards, hide criminal activity, or obtain a passport.

The use of a logo makes the email look authentic, and is called "spoofing" or "branding." However, banks never contact customers through email, and it is important not to reply to such messages. The RCMP says that if you receive one of these messages, it should be reported to the financial institution or info@antifraudcentre.ca.

To learn about this and other online scams, you can go to getcybersafe.gc.ca. An organization that does a lot of online transactions, it can also educate consumers about online safety. Here you will find other characteristics to look for, such as fake email addresses. And if you receive a message from PayPal, for example, you can send it to spoof@paypal.com, and they will investigate it.

---

phishing   Creating false emails or websites that look legitimate but are designed to gain illegal access to a victim's personal information.

Criminology Research
Credit Card Fraud

Philip Arcand and his wife, Roberta Galway, lived a life of luxury. They owned two homes, one in British Columbia and one in Las Vegas. They had a Mercedes, Corvette, and Ferrari in their driveways. They took frequent trips around the world. All this without having a job. How did they do it? Through credit card fraud!

Arcand wrote high-pressure scripts to lure victims, arranged for telemarketing companies to make the pitch, and set up front businesses to process the illegal monies. The telemarketers claimed to be from a credit card company. They told victims how easy it is to steal a credit card number, especially over the Internet. They offered to sell protection policies that would insure that the buyer would not have to pay if thieves ran up a huge tab on their account. The telemarketers told the victims that if they did not get this protection, they would have to foot the bill for any unauthorized charges made if their credit cards were stolen. After making their pitch, the victims were asked: "May we have your credit card number, please?" Later, a charge of between $199 and $389 appeared on their account, even if they did not sign up for the service.

The scheme was bogus, illegal, and entirely unnecessary because most major credit card companies will protect consumers from fraudulent charges. Still, thousands of people were victimized by this scam—the overwhelming majority of victims were senior citizens who lived across the United States, from Massachusetts and West Virginia to California and Hawaii. In all, they were defrauded of more than $12 million.

Arcand and Galway were ultimately caught when some of the victims reported their suspicions and complaints to authorities. Because they were Canadian citizens, a joint partnership of Canadian and U.S. law enforcement agencies—including the Royal Canadian Mounted Police (RCMP), the FBI, and the Federal Trade Commission (FTC)—pursued the case, which was called Project Emptor. In August 2002, the couple was arrested by FBI agents while living in Las Vegas, and on November 17, 2003, Arcand was sentenced to 10 years in federal prison; his wife Roberta Galway pleaded guilty and was sentenced to six months in jail. The couple also paid a $100,000 civil judgment in a case initiated by the FTC.

Critical Thinking

1. Should a person such as Arcand be sentenced to 10 years in prison for credit card fraud? Is this sentence too severe for someone whose victims actually lost relatively little money on an individual basis?
2. Should it be a crime to sell people services they are unaware of, but are already eligible to receive? Is this fraud or merely taking advantage of the uninformed?

SOURCE: Federal Bureau of Investigation, "Credit Card Con: Canadian Man Gets 10 Years for $12 Million Telemarketing Scam," http://www2.fbi.gov/page2/nov03/credit112803.htm. Accessed April 29, 2011.

Phishing emails and websites have become even more of a problem now that cybercriminals can easily copy brand names, corporate letterheads, and company logos directly into the email. The look may be so authentic that victims do not doubt that the email comes from the advertised company. Most phishers send out spam emails to a large number of recipients, knowing that some of those recipients will likely have accounts with the company they are impersonating.

To meet the increasing threat of phishing and identity theft, many jurisdictions have passed laws against knowingly transferring or using, without lawful authority, a means of identification with the intent to commit any unlawful activity.[46]

Furthermore, committing identity fraud while engaged in crimes associated with terrorism—such as aircraft destruction, arson, airport violence, or kidnapping top government officials—will receive a mandatory sentence enhancement of five years.[47]

Bad Cheques

An older form of fraud is cashing a bank cheque drawn on a non-existent or underfunded bank account. Cheque fraud accounted for 68 percent of all reported frauds in 1979, but had declined in 2003 to 21 percent. This form of fraud had a high clearance rate: 55 percent in 2003, higher than for non-cheque fraud (44 percent) and for property crime (20 percent).

Edwin Lemert found that the majority of "naive" cheque forgers are amateurs who do not believe their actions will hurt anyone.[48] They come from middle-class backgrounds and have little identification with a criminal subculture. They cash bad cheques because of a financial crisis—perhaps they have lost money gambling and have some pressing bills to pay. Often socially isolated, they are unsuccessful in their relationships and are risk-prone when faced with a situation that is unusually stressful. The willingness of stores and other commercial establishments to cash cheques with a minimum of fuss so they can attract business encourages the cheque forger to risk committing a criminal act.

Lemert found that a few professionals, known as **systematic forgers**, make a substantial living by passing

systematic forgers Fraud artists who make a substantial living by passing bad cheques; a dying profession.

Identity Theft a Nightmare

I stole a car today. And I used your credit card.

I walked into the car rental shop, and in five minutes drove out with a new minivan. I went shopping, bought a DVD player, a digital camera, some sports equipment, and a computer, which I promptly hawked. On the way to Montreal, I stayed in motels, bought meals, and received cash advances, all with your credit card. I sold the car for $5,000, which went into a cargo container destined for a foreign country. All told, you're on the hook for $10,000. Your credit rating will be ruined.

This is called identity theft.

The RCMP says that with your name, address, date of birth, and social insurance number, a thief can take over your financial accounts, open new bank accounts, transfer money between accounts, apply for loans or credit cards, all the things that you can do yourself. Except you are no longer yourself.

In fact, the basic information needed to apply for credit, to receive cellphone service, to rent an apartment, to purchase goods online, could be used to steal your identity.

Maybe it started with stealing your purse in the grocery store, or the gym, or out of your car. I found your driver's licence, credit cards, social insurance card, and your employee identification card. Have you checked your wallet lately to see how much personal information is there? We carry a lot of plastic, and credit card fraud is the most common type of identity theft complaint. Or maybe I simply found your credit card invoice in the garbage, or your blue box, and took that information. Or perhaps I found a letter soliciting re-approval of your credit card in the mailbox after you moved.

Identity theft is simple.

I could redirect all your mail to a new address, or fill out a pre-approved credit card application in your name. There is

no guarantee that even a legitimate company's database is invulnerable to infiltration. Maybe you ordered something online through an unsecured website, or over the phone using a credit card number. Today's business practices involve collecting a lot of personal information to ensure more effective marketing. However, creating intensive consumer profiles also leaves consumers susceptible to identify theft.

It is unfortunate, but you will spend hundreds of hours, and thousands of dollars trying to clear your name, and it will probably never come to trial. The Ontario government is introducing new legislation to deal with what it calls the fastest growing and most serious consumer crime in North America. We are not yet sure how good that legislation will be. The PhoneBusters organization estimates that the number of identity theft victims grew 8 percent in 2003 over the previous year, and that the losses increased by 60 percent. This is definitely the tip of the iceberg. Most victims probably don't realize they've been taken, or don't report the crime if they are. The three major credit bureaus estimate the problem to be very large, not the 8,000 cases reported by PhoneBusters, but at least 20,000 cases a year. This shows a shocking non-report rate of staggering dimensions. All told, identity theft costs consumers, banks, credit card firms, and business at least $2.5 billion per year.

The cost to society will include money spent by the business community, costs to you for legal assistance from lawyers, costs to the government for judicial and law enforcement, investigation, and prosecution. And we are at an infancy in terms of estimating the costs. The FBI estimates the average cost for this type of crime investigation is $20,000, and for prosecution, a minimum of

$10,000. There is the cost of the theft itself, the cost of time to deal with the problem personally, the cost of policing and professional assistance, and most importantly, the cost of the loss of public trust.

The Privacy Rights Clearing House estimates the average victim spends 175 hours to restore their identity, if they know of the theft. You might eventually be cleared of fault, but in the intervening period, the debts appear on your credit record.

What can you do? Well, it's quite simple. Most people are worried about the misuse of personal information, even at the same time as they are increasingly unable to control that information. So, first, only carry as much plastic as you need. Second, keep your eye on your mail if it's delivered to an unsecured place; and make sure the change of address works. Third, never give personal information over the phone, over the Internet, or to someone who has no need to know. Fourth, if someone calls wanting to know personal banking information, you should call the police. Fifth, know your payment cycles on your credit card, and call if the bill is late. If a change of address is requested for your credit card billing, it might be a while before you notice not receiving a bill. And then it's too late.

The U.S. National Center for Victims of Crime estimates that 12 months pass between the first misuse of the victim's identity and its discovery. There are other estimates that are even higher. If research shows that it may be over a year before you even realize that your identity and financial security have been compromised—you may never do so.

To report an incident of identity theft, contact your local RCMP.

SOURCE: Copyright Chris McCormick, published in the *Daily Gleaner* (Fredericton), June 24, 2004.

---

bad cheques. However, professionals constitute a relatively small segment of the total population of cheque forgers. The 15,000 known incidents of cheque forgery in 1993 resulted in an estimated loss of $100 million. Some stores and banks may choose not to press charges because the effort to collect the money due them is often not worth their while. It is also difficult to separate the true cheque forger from the neglectful shopper.

Today, far more important than bad cheques is using computers to commit fraud.

Computer Fraud

In 2004, Jessica Sabathia, age 31, a California woman, pled guilty to counts of computer fraud for using her computer to embezzle more than $875,000 from North Bay Health Care Group. Sabathia, an accounts payable clerk for North Bay, used her computer to access North Bay's accounting software without the authority of her employer and issued approximately 127 cheques payable to herself and others. To conceal the fraud, she then altered the electronic cheque register to make it appear that the cheques had been payable to North Bay's vendors. Jessica cashed several of the cheques, deposited many in her bank account and the accounts of others, and used some money for personal expenses.[49]

This crime falls under the general category of computer fraud. Computer fraud is not a unique offence but rather a common-law crime committed using contemporary technology. Consequently, many computer crimes are prosecuted under such traditional criminal statutes as larceny or fraud, which often groups them with phone crimes. Some of these crimes are listed in Exhibit 11.9.

There are numerous recent trends in computer frauds. Internal attacks are now outgrowing external attacks at the world's largest financial institutions. According to a recent global security survey (2005), 35 percent of financial institutions encountered attacks from inside their organization within a 12-month period, compared with 26 percent from external sources.[50] The shift from external to internal attacks may be explained by improved security technologies that make it more difficult for people unfamiliar with the system to misuse it for personal gain. It has now become easier for disgruntled employees to attack the company's computers than for outsiders to breach their defences.

A growing trend has been to commit fraud using devices that rely on information technology (IT) for their operations. For example, automated bank machines (ABMs) are now attracting the attention of cybercriminals looking for easy profits.[51] One criminal approach is to use a thin, transparent-plastic overlay on an ABM keypad that captures a user's identification code as it is entered. Though the plastic covering looks like some sort of cover to protect the keys, in fact it contains microchips that record every keystroke. Another transparent device inside the card slot captures card data. While the client completes the transaction, a computer attached to the overlay records all the data necessary to clone the card.

EXHIBIT 11.9

Examples of Phone and Computer Fraud

The Canadian Anti-Fraud Centre identifies many types of computer fraud, including

- 900 Scams—a phone scam that says you have won huge prizes
- Advanced Fee Letter Fraud (419 / Nigerian Letters)—an email scam promising huge dividends for setting up an overseas bank account
- Advanced Fee Loans—asked to pay an upfront fee for a loan that never materializes
- Anti-Virus Scam—a phone scam to fix a computer remotely; usually involves downloading malware or keylogging programs
- Bomb Threat—a demand for money to deactivate a bomb placed at a business, apparently from an insider
- Cheque Overpayment Fraud—receiving a cheque for goods in excess of the amount requested; the excess is returned and the cheque is returned as counterfeit
- Dead Air Calls—automatic dialing used by telemarketers to determine when you are home
- Emergency Scam—a pretend call from a relative that they need money immediately, usually while travelling
- Extortion Scam—a demand for money by an alleged hit man, or to remove computer malware
- False Charities—phone, door, or emails which ask for donations to non-existent charities
- Identity Theft—an extensive form of fraud, used to set up fake bank accounts, lines of credit, and loans
- Inheritance—similar to the 419 scam; involves an offer of large amounts of money to set up a bank account to deposit funds
- Job—paid by a counterfeit cheque, a person is selected to be a mystery shopper and asked to wire back a portion of the money

- Lottery Emails—the false promise to claim a lottery by paying an upfront fee or tax
- Office Supplies / Directory—targeting businesses, a telemarketer offers discount supplies
- Phishing—an email scam to gather financial information
- Phone Number Spoofing—creating a false number to mask a caller's identity
- Prize Pitch—similar to the lottery scam, a fee must be paid to collect the prize
- Puppy Scam—using classified ads to sell non-existent dogs
- Pyramid Schemes—investors are promised a huge return on their money, which is paid by late investors
- Recovery Pitch—a caller who promises to get back your money after you fall for one of the other scams
- Romance Scam—that sincere email from the Russian girl who is looking for true love, and your credit card
- Service Scam—offering non-existent services, similar to the home repair scam
- Travel—a phone scam offering travel packages, etc.
- Vacation—similar to the travel scam, too good to be true
- Vehicle Warranty Package—an unsolicited offer for extra warranty coverage

In general, "buyer beware" and "is it too good to be true" are the best guides when receiving unsolicited offers by email, phone, or at the door.

SOURCE: Adapted from "Scam Types," Canadian Anti-Fraud Centre, http://www.antifraudcentre-centreantifraude.ca/english/recognizeit.html. Reprinted with permission.

Famous Canadian Court Cases
GST Fraud Ring

In 1991, the Canadian government introduced a goods and services tax (GST). This move generated a new opportunity for criminal gain. Loopholes in GST rebate procedures gave some ideas on ways to exploit the system.

To promote business, the government reimburses Canadian companies for certain GST payments. However, weaknesses in the administration of these tax breaks have managed to boost illicit activity. Authorities rely on self-reports of GST payment amounts, and they tend to issue refunds before verifying any submitted paperwork. Both real and phony companies have defrauded the government by fabricating business transactions and forwarding bogus tax claims.

In a very complex and lucrative GST rebate scam in 1998, a ring of swindlers staged thousands of sales involving vehicles that were sometimes non-existent. This "Cadillac of GST frauds" was exposed through Project Phantom, a police probe that lasted 10 months. Investigators from the Halton Regional Police Service, the Royal Canadian Mounted Police, the Ontario Provincial Police, the Ontario Motor Vehicle Industry Council, and Revenue Canada joined forces in the operation.

Although an estimated $50 million in rebates were illegally obtained, the legal value of this scheme was capped at $20 million. Auditors were able to track this amount through flagged bank accounts. Most of the money disappeared before it could be seized, so Revenue Canada only recovered a few thousand dollars. Regardless, 219 fraud-related charges were laid against 18 suspects and one car dealership.

Although many counts were processed separately, seven accused were tried together in 2002. Their fate was decided after a court in Milton, Ontario, considered seven months of testimony and more than 100,000 exhibits. Five years after the crackdown, 11 convictions had been registered. The penalties imposed varied between an 18-month conditional sentence and a five-year prison term, accompanied by restitution orders ranging from $15,000 to $1 million.

It has been said that death and taxes are the only two certainties in life. Judging by the tremendous risks that some people take to get rich quick, greed may very well qualify as a third.

Here we can see the significant differences between common-law crime and cyber-crime: Rather than rob an ABM user at gunpoint, the cybercriminal relies on stealth and technological skill to commit the crime.

Credit Card Theft

The use of stolen credit cards has become a major problem. Every year, credit card companies sustain millions of dollars of loss due to credit card fraud. Many credit cards used fraudulently were lost or stolen; counterfeit or forged cards account for the rest.[52]

Most credit card abuse is the work of amateurs who acquire stolen cards through theft and then use them for two days. However, members of professional credit card rings get jobs as clerks in stores, where they collect names and credit card numbers of customers. Gang members buy plain plastic cards and have the names and numbers embossed on them. The gang then creates a fictitious wholesale jewellery company, receives authorization to accept credit cards from the customers, and uses the phony cards to charge non-existent jewellery purchases on the accounts of the people whose names and card numbers they had collected. The thieves withdraw the money from their business account and leave town. Recently, organized crime gangs have come to dominate credit card crime, described more in the next chapter.

Embezzlement

The crime of **embezzlement** was observed in early Greek culture when Aristotle alluded to theft by road commissioners and other government officials.[53] It was first codified into law by the English Parliament during the 16th century to fill a gap in the larceny law.[54] Until then, to be guilty of theft, a person had to take goods from the physical possession of another. However, as explained earlier, this definition did not cover instances in which one person willingly gave another temporary custody of his or her property. For example, in everyday commerce, store clerks, bank tellers, brokers, and merchants gain lawful possession but not legal ownership of other people's money.

Embezzlement occurs when someone trusted with property fraudulently keeps it for his or her own use, distinguished from fraud on the basis of when the criminal intent was formed. The mere act of moving property without the owner's consent, or damaging it or using it, is not considered embezzlement. However, using it up, selling it, pledging it, giving it away, or holding it against the owner's will is held to be embezzlement.

> **embezzlement** A type of larceny that involves taking the possessions of another that have been placed in possession for safekeeping, e.g., a stockbroker rifling a customer's account.

It is probably impossible to know how many embezzlement incidents occur annually. However, it seems that (1) employees are willing to steal from their employers, (2) employers are willing to report instances of embezzlement, and (3) law enforcement officials are willing to prosecute embezzlers.

In an interesting case of theft from employers, in Hollinger and Clark's classic 1983 self-report study, questionnaires were administered to low- and middle-level staff in a broad range of business and government organizations. Subjects were asked whether they had committed acts such as stealing money or goods, faking illness, or covering an unauthorized absence of another employee. The authors coined the term "theft of time" to describe employee behaviours such as coming back late from breaks, conducting personal business on the job, or loafing around while pretending to be working. They claimed that employee theft was widespread, due to job dissatisfaction, to perceived need, and to youth.[55] The nearby Famous Canadian Court Cases box refers to a lucrative effort to defraud the government.

BREAK AND ENTER

Under common law, the crime of **break and enter**, sometimes called *burglary*, is defined as "the breaking and entering of a dwelling house of another in the nighttime with the intent to commit a felony within." Burglary is more serious than theft, because it involves entering another's home, which increases the threat of harm even though the premises may be unoccupied.

The legal definition of burglary has undergone considerable change since its common-law origins. When laws against burglary were first created by English judges during the late Middle Ages, they were designed to protect people whose homes might be set upon by wandering criminals. Including the phrase "breaking and entering" in the definition protected people from unwarranted intrusions; if an invited guest stole something, it would not be considered a burglary. Similarly, the requirement that the crime be committed at nighttime was added because evening was considered the time when honest people might fall prey to criminals.[56]

The Extent of Break and Enter

The definition of burglary includes any unlawful entry into a structure to commit an indictable offence. Break and enter is categorized into those against businesses, those against residences, and others (see Exhibit 11.10). According to Statistics Canada, there is a break and enter in Canada every three minutes. While it is one of the most commonly reported property offences in Canada, it has

been on a steady decline over the last decade. The rate of break and enter was 43 percent lower in 2012 than 10 years earlier. This decrease was not even, or even across the board. While it fell 4 percent on average, it fell 11 percent in Newfoundland, and rose 20 percent in Prince Edward Island. There were 175,712 incidents in 2012, for a rate of 504 per 100,000. Most burglaries are of residences, and about a quarter are business-related. Break and enter victims suffered losses of billions of dollars a year, with an average loss in the thousands. The insurance industry pays out millions a year in claims for residential and commercial break and enters.

On the other hand, the GSS reported that 630,000 Canadian households were victimized by break and enters in 2009, with one of the highest rates of reporting to the police (54 percent), but down from 1999 (62 percent). Overall, household crimes were reported more frequently than were personal crimes (see Exhibit 11.11). Part of the reason that people report household crimes to the police is to be able to make insurance claims. The greater the damage or loss, the more likely people are to report to police.

Those most likely to be burgled live in rented dwellings in urban areas and have the lowest incomes.

> **break and enter** Unlawful entry into a house to commit theft; sometimes called burglary.

EXHIBIT 11.10

Quick Code: Break and Enter

Section 348. (1) Every one who

(a) breaks and enters a place with intent to commit an indictable offence therein,

(b) breaks and enters a place and commits an indictable offence therein, or

(c) breaks out of a place after
  (i) committing an indictable offence therein, or
  (ii) entering the place with intent to commit an indictable offence therein, is guilty of an indictable offence and liable

(a) to imprisonment for life, if the offence is committed in relation to a dwelling-house, or

(b) to imprisonment for a term not exceeding fourteen years, if the offence is committed in relation to a place other than a dwelling-house ...

[Other relevant sections: 321, 349, 350, 351, 352]

SOURCE: *Criminal Code of Canada*, Section 348 (1).

Quick Facts about Break and Enter in Canada, Various Years

- Break and enters accounted for 15 percent of property crime in 2012.
- This single crime accounts for about 9 percent of incidents reported to the police.
- There were 175,712 reported cases in 2012, 43 percent lower than 2002.
- The majority of adult suspects charged are male.
- Youths charged decreased overall by 4 percent between 2008 and 2009, but increased in Prince Edward Island (34 percent), New Brunswick (26 percent), and Yukon (30 percent).
- In 1993, the perpetrator was known in 60 percent of cases: a friend (38 percent), an ex/spouse (17 percent), or a family member (5 percent).
- In 2009, 60 percent of break-ins occurred at a residence, 30 percent at a business, and 10 percent at another location, such as a shed or detached garage.
- Residential break-ins decreased by 2 percent in 2009, compared with 2008, while business break-ins declined by 9 percent.
- The rate of victimization (GSS) was 47 per 1,000 in 2009, up from 39 in 2004.
- Break and enters are more likely to be urban (434) than rural (72).
- In 2002, two-thirds of residential robberies involved a weapon (firearm, 33 percent; knife, 30 percent).
- In 2012, robbery decreased to its lowest point in 30 years.
- Persons aged 60 and older were victimized in 15 percent of such incidents, compared with 4 percent for all violent crimes.
- The clearance rate for break and enters in 2003 was 15 percent; for property crimes, it was 20 percent; in 2010, the rates were 16 percent and 25 percent, respectively.

SOURCES: Statistics Canada, *Canadian Crime Statistics 2003, 2006* (Ottawa: Canadian Centre for Justice Statistics, 2004, 2007); Statistics Canada, *Canadian Crime Statistics 1999* (Ottawa: Canadian Centre for Justice Statistics, 2000); "Canadian Crime Statistics, 1996," *Juristat* 17, 1997; Rosemary Gartner and Anthony N. Doob, "Trends in Criminal Victimization: 1988–1993," *Juristat* 14, 1994; Criminal Victimization in Canada, 2004, *Juristat* 25, 7, 2005; Peter Greenberg, "Break and Enter," in *Crime Counts: A Criminal Event Analysis*, eds. Leslie W. Kennedy and Vincent F. Sacco (Toronto: ITP Nelson, 1996); "Breaking and Entering in Canada, 2002," *Juristat* 24, 5, 2004; "Police reported crime statistics in Canada, 2012," Daniel Perreault, Statistics Canada, 2012; Police-reported Clearance Rates in Canada, 2010, Tina Hotton Mahoney and John Turner, *Juristat*, 2012.

CAREERS IN BURGLARY

Within the ranks of burglars are crude thieves who will smash a window and enter a vacant home or structure. However, because burglary involves planning, risk, and skill, it has been a crime long associated with professional thieves. The burglar must learn the craft. For example, one experienced professional burglar describes how another educated him in the craft of burglary when the two were serving time in prison:

> Never wear deodorant or shaving lotion; the strange scent might wake someone up. The more people there are in a house, the safer you are. If someone hears you moving around, they will think it's someone else.... If they call, answer in a muffled sleepy voice.... Never be afraid of dogs, they can sense fear. Most dogs are friendly; snap your finger, they come right to you.[57]

However, despite his elaborate preparations, Hoheimer spent many years in confinement, so perhaps his advice is not the best.

Burglars on the Job

Burglars must master the skills of their trade, learning to spot environmental cues that non-professionals fail to notice.[58] In *Burglars on the Job,* Richard Wright and Scott Decker describe the working conditions of active burglars.[59] Most are motivated by the need for cash so they can get high; they want to enjoy the good life without the need for working. Although, as Exhibit 11.12 shows, they approach their "job"

Burglars on the Job

According to active burglars, they tend to abide by the following guidelines:

- Most avoid occupied residences, considering them high-risk targets.
- Most are not deterred by alarms and elaborate locks; in fact, these devices tell them that something inside is worth stealing.
- Some call occupants from a pay phone; if the phone is still ringing when they arrive, they know no one is home.
- Once having entered a residence, anxiety turns to calm as they first turn to the master bedroom for money and drugs. They also search kitchens, believing that some people keep money in a mayonnaise jar.
- Most work in groups, one serving as a lookout while another ransacks the place.
- Some dispose of goods through a professional fence; others try to pawn the goods. Some exchange goods for drugs; some sell goods to friends and relatives; and a few keep the stolen items for themselves, especially guns and jewellery.
- Many approach a target home by masquerading as workers, such as carpenters or house painters.
- Tipsters help the burglars select attractive targets.
- Drug dealers are favoured targets because they tend to have a lot of cash and drugs and are unlikely to call the police.
- Some stake out residences to learn the occupants' routines.
- Targets are often acquaintances.

SOURCE: Richard Wright and Scott Decker, *Burglars on the Job: Streetlife and Residential Break-Ins* (New Hampshire: University Press of New England). © University Press of New England, Lebanon, NH. Reprinted with permission.

in a rational fashion, and their lives are controlled by their culture and environment. Unskilled and uneducated, urban burglars make the choices they do because they have had few conventional opportunities for success.

The Good Burglar.   This characterization is applied by professional burglars to colleagues who have distinguished themselves by their (1) technical competence, (2) maintenance of personal integrity, (3) specialization in burglary, (4) financial success at crime, and (5) ability to avoid prison sentences.[60]

To receive recognition as good burglars, novices must learn the skills needed to commit lucrative burglaries, such as how to gain entry into homes and apartment houses; how to select targets with high potential payoffs; how to choose items with a high resale value; the proper way to open safes without damaging their contents; and the proper use of equipment, including cutting torches, electric saws, explosives, and metal bars. Second, the good burglar must be able to team up to form a criminal gang. Choosing trustworthy companions is essential if the obstacles to completing a successful job—police, alarms, secure safes—are to be overcome. Third, the good burglar must have inside information. Without knowledge of what awaits them inside, burglars can spend a tremendous amount of time and effort on empty safes and worthless jewellery boxes. Finally, the good burglar must cultivate fences, or buyers for stolen wares. Once the burglar gains access to people who buy and sell stolen goods, he or she must also learn how to successfully sell these goods for a profit.

The process of becoming a professional burglar is similar to the process Sutherland described in his theory of differential association. A person becomes a good burglar through learning the techniques of the trade from older, more experienced burglars. The older burglar teaches the novice how to deal with defence attorneys, bail bond agents, and other agents of the justice system. Consequently, the opportunity to become a good burglar is not open to everyone. Apprentices must have the appropriate character before they are taken under the wing of the older professional. Usually, the opportunity to learn burglary comes as a reward for being a highly respected juvenile gang member, from knowing someone in the neighbourhood who has made a living at burglary, or more often, from having built a reputation for being solid while serving time in prison.

The Burglary "Career Ladder."   Burglars progress through stages of career development.[61] They begin as young novices who learn the trade from older, more experienced burglars, often relatives. They continue to get this tutoring as long as they can develop their own markets (fences) for stolen goods. After their education is over, novices enter the journeyperson stage, characterized by careful planning and by forays in search of lucrative targets; they develop reputations as experienced, reliable criminals. Finally, they become professional burglars when they have developed advanced skills and organizational abilities that give them the highest esteem among their peers; they plan and execute their crimes after careful deliberation.

These burglars display rational decision making, carefully evaluating potential costs and benefits. They follow this pattern in their choice of burglary sites, preferring corner houses because they are easily observed and offer the maximum number of escape routes. Other issues are occupancy and accessibility. They look for houses that show evidence of long-term care and wealth. Although people may erect fences and other barriers to deter burglars, these devices may actually attract crime because they protect something worth stealing: If there were nothing valuable inside, why go to so much trouble to secure the premises?[62]

The researchers also found that many burglars had serious drug habits and that their criminal activity was in part aimed at supporting their substance abuse.

CONNECTIONS

According to the rational choice approach discussed in Chapter 5, burglars make rational and calculated decisions before committing crimes. If circumstances and culture dictate their activities, can their decisions be considered a matter of choice?

Repeat Burglary.   Research suggests that burglars may return to the scene of the crime to repeat their offences. One reason is that many burgled items are deemed indispensable (such as televisions and VCRs), so it is safe to assume they will be quickly replaced.[63] Other reasons include the following:

- It takes less effort to burgle a home or apartment known to be a suitable target than it does to burgle an unknown or unsuitable residence.
- The burglar is already aware of the target's layout.
- The ease of entry of the target has probably not changed, and escape routes are known.
- The lack of both protective measures and nosy neighbours has probably not changed.
- Goods were observed that could not be taken the first time.[64]

CONNECTIONS

Chapter 4 discussed repeat victimization. As you may recall, certain people and places are commonly the target of numerous predatory crimes.

The Female Burglar

While relatively little is known about female burglars, their offending patterns are similar to those of males, and they have typically engaged in other thefts, such as shoplifting and assault. The major difference between male and female burglars is that females tend to avoid auto theft.[65] Another difference is that females almost always work with a partner, but only 40 percent of males do. Females commit fewer offences and have a lesser chance of doing time.

Criminology Research
Are There Gender Differences in Burglary?

Does gender play a role in shaping burglary careers? Are there differences in the way professional male and female burglars approach their craft? Do gender roles influence the burglar lifestyle? Christopher Mullins and Richard Wright used interviews with 18 active female burglars and 36 males, matched approximately for age. Their findings indicate that significant gender-based differences exist in the way males and females begin and end their offending careers and how they carry out their criminal tasks.

There were similarities in the way most offenders, male or female, were initiated into residential burglary. Both became involved via interaction in intimate groups, such as older friends, family members, or street associates. One told them:

> [M]e and my brother, we wanted to, you know, he came and got me and say he know where a house at to break into. And, uhm, we go there and uh, we just do it ... me and my brother, he and some more friends.

But there was one key difference between the male and female offenders: The men typically became involved in burglary with male peers; women more often were introduced to crime by their boyfriends. Males are more likely to bring their male peers and family members into their offending networks and resist working with women except their girlfriend or female relative. And when they do include women, they put them in a subservient role, such as a lookout.

Why do they get involved in a burglary career in the first place? Both males and females generally said they got involved in break-ins to finance a party lifestyle centred on drug use and to buy bling bling like designer clothing and jewellery. There were some differences: Males reported wanting money to pursue sexual conquests; female burglars were far more likely to say that they needed money to buy necessities for their children.

When asked what they were looking for in a prospective residential burglary target, the male and female offenders expressed similar preferences; both wanted to find a dwelling that was (a) unoccupied and (b) contained something of value. Both the men and the women wanted to know something about the people who lived in the residence, be familiar with their day-to-day routine, and to have an idea of the target's valuables. Male offenders used their legitimate jobs as home remodellers, cable television installers, or gardeners to scout potential burglary targets. Female burglars who lacked legitimate entry had to rely on information generated by the men in their immediate criminal social network. Some used sexual attraction to gain the victim's confidence and gather information.

Mullins and Wright also found that men preferred to commit residential burglaries by themselves, while women most often worked with others. Males seemed unwilling to trust accomplices and were also unwilling to share the proceeds. Females, on the other hand, reported that they lacked the knowledge or skills needed to break into a dwelling on their own and were therefore more willing to work with a team.

Finally, when asked what it would take to make them stop committing crime, both male and female offenders claimed that a good job that paid well and involved little or no disciplined subordination to authority would be required to get them to give up their careers in crime. Men also claimed they would probably give up burglary once they settled down and started a family. Because they were dependent on male help, female burglars needed to sever their relationships with criminally involved males in order to reduce their offending. Female burglars were also more sensitive than the males to shaming and ostracism at the hands of their relatives and might quit under family pressure.

Mullins and Wright found that residential burglary is a significantly gender-stratified offence; the processes of initiation, commission, and potential desistance are heavily structured by gender. Women have to negotiate the male-dominated world of burglary to accomplish their crimes. Gender, they find, plays a significant role in shaping opportunity (such as initiation) and the events leading up to residential burglaries (for example, information gathering), while playing a lesser but still important role in moulding actual offence commission.

Critical Thinking

Do gender differences in burglary reflect gender differences found in other segments of society?

SOURCE: Based on Christopher Mullins and Richard Wright, "Gender, Social Networks, and Residential Burglary," *Criminology* 41 (2003): 813–839.

Female burglars who work as accomplices feel compelled to commit crimes for different reasons: because of a relationship, a lack of legitimate employment, drug dependency, or alcohol problems. Most male and female burglars report substance abuse problems, including cocaine, heroin, and marijuana use.

Accomplices exercised little control over their crimes and commonly acted as a lookout or driver, as discussed in the nearby Criminology Research box about gender differences among burglars. However, in planning their crimes, partners displayed many of the characteristics of the rational criminal: They helped spot targets and planned entries. As one female burglar stated:

> That's one reason why we got so many youngsters in jail today. I see this, so let's go make a hit. No, no, no. If they see this and it looks good, then it's going to be there for a while. So the point is, you have to case it

and make sure you know everything. I want to know what time you go to work, the time the children go to school. I know there's no one coming home for lunch. So plan it with somebody else. We'll take the new dishwasher, washing machine, and this other stuff. We just put it in the truck. Do you know when people rent a truck, nobody ever pays that any attention? They think you're moving [but] only if you rent a truck.

In conclusion, most female burglars maintain roles and identities quite similar to those of their male colleagues. Although some gender-based differences are evident (males more often work alone; women almost always work with others), both male and female burglars plan crimes for many of the same reasons. This research shows that for the majority of both male and female burglars, criminal careers may be a function of economic need and role equality, a finding that supports a feminist view of crime. It also illustrates that repeat criminals use rational choice in planning their activities.

ARSON AND VANDALISM

Arson is the willful and malicious burning of a home, public building, vehicle, or commercial building. UCR statistics for 2012 show about 11,040 arsons were known to the police, increasing 5 percent from 2011, but down 23 percent since 2002. Arson is a very difficult crime to solve, with a clearance rate usually below 20 percent. Of those charged, about half are youths and most are males. (Exhibits 11.13 and 11.14 provide some more factual data about arson.)

Studies show that juvenile arsonists can be classified in one of four categories,[66] as shown in the Criminology Research box, "What Motivates Juvenile Fire Setters?"

Adult arson may also be a function of severe emotional turmoil. Some psychologists view fire starting as a function of a disturbed personality, and thus as a mental health problem and not a criminal act.[67]

Arsonists often experience sexual pleasure from starting fires, and then observing their destructive effects.[68] It is equally likely that fires are started by angry people looking for revenge against property owners or by teenagers out to vandalize property.

Other arsons are set by "professional" arsonists who engage in arson for profit. Such acts are often related to arson fraud, in which a business owner burns his or her property or hires someone to do it to escape financial problems.[69] Over the years, investigators have found that businesspeople are willing to become involved in arson to collect fire insurance or for the following reasons:

- to obtain money during a period of financial crisis
- to dispose of outdated or slow-moving inventory
- to destroy outmoded machines and technology
- to pay off legal and illegal debt

EXHIBIT 11.13

Quick Facts about Arson in Canada, Various Years

- In 1990, 57 people were killed and 551 injured in fires, costing $244 million.
- Arson is an under-reported crime, but 11,040 incidents were reported in 2012.
- The percentage of arson cases in which an accused was identified dropped from 30 percent in 1974 to 16 percent in 2003.
- Fifty percent of all fires with losses of more than $500,000 in 1989 had an unknown cause.
- The peak for arson in the 1980s coincided with an economic recession.
- Adults accounted for 58 percent of all arson charges in 2003, 85 percent of whom were male.
- The most favoured locations are homes (31 percent) and commercial locations (20 percent).
- Arson was redefined in 1990, with the maximum penalty increased to life in prison.
- Arson is a difficult crime to investigate, often requiring forensic analysis.

SOURCES: Statistics Canada, *Canadian Crime Statistics 2003* (Ottawa: Canadian Centre for Justice Statistics, 2004); Statistics Canada, *Canadian Crime Statistics 1999* (Ottawa: Canadian Centre for Justice Statistics, 2000); Statistics Canada, *Canadian Crime Statistics 1995* (Ottawa: Canadian Centre for Justice Statistics, 1996); Lee Wolff, "Arson in Canada," *Juristat* 12, 1992; John L. McMullan and Peter D. Swan, "Social Economy and Arson in Nova Scotia," *Canadian Journal of Criminology* 31 (1989): 281–308; "Police-reported crime in Canada, 2012," Daniel Perreault, Statistics Canada, 2013.

EXHIBIT 11.14

Quick Code: Arson

Section 433. Every person who intentionally or recklessly causes damage by fire or explosion to property, whether or not that person owns the property, is guilty of an indictable offence and liable to imprisonment for life where

(a) the person knows that or is reckless with respect to whether the property is inhabited or occupied
(b) the fire or explosion causes bodily harm to another person.

[Other relevant sections: 434, 435, 436, 437]

SOURCE: *Criminal Code of Canada,* Section 433.

arson The intentional burning of a home, structure, or vehicle because of psychological issues or for criminal purposes, such as profit, revenge, insurance fraud, or crime concealment.

What motivates young people to commit arson? According to research by sociologist Wayne Wooden, juvenile arsonists can be classified in one of four categories:

- *The "playing with matches" fire setter:* The youngest fire starter, usually aged 4 to 9, who sets fires because parents are careless with matches and lighters; fire safety lessons can help prevent fires.
- *The "crying for help" fire setter:* A 7- to 13-year-old with stress due to family conflict, divorce, death, or abuse; has difficulty expressing sorrow or anger; uses fire for stress relief or revenge.
- *The "delinquent" fire setter:* Sets fire to school property to retaliate for a slight experienced at school; may break into school to vandalize property, and then set a fire to cover up their activities.

- *The "severely disturbed" fire setter:* Obsessed with fires, dreams about them in "vibrant colours"; the most disturbed type, most likely to set numerous fires with potential for death, damage.

Other research, by Eileen M. Garry, concluded that juvenile fire setters fall into three general groups. The first is made up of children under 7 years of age. Generally, fires started by these children are the result of accidents or curiosity. In the second group of fire setters are children ranging in age from 8 to 12. Although the fire setting of some of these children is motivated by curiosity or experimentation, a greater proportion of their fire setting represents underlying psychosocial conflicts. The third group comprises adolescents between the ages of 13 and 18. These youth tend to have a long history of undetected fire play and fire-starting behaviour. Their current fire-setting episodes are usually either the result of psychosocial conflict and turmoil or intentional criminal behaviour.

Critical Thinking

How is it possible to identify a problem with someone fascinated with fire? Are there other signs that might be relevant?

SOURCES: Wayne Wooden, "Juvenile Firesetters in Cross-Cultural Perspective: How Should Society Respond?" in *Official Responses to Problem Juveniles: Some International Reflections*, ed. James Hackler (Onati, Spain: Onati Publications, 1991), pp. 339–348; Eileen M. Garry, *Juvenile Firesetting and Arson* (Washington, DC: Office of Juvenile Justice and Delinquency Prevention, 1997).

- to relocate or remodel a business
- to take advantage of government funds available for redevelopment
- to apply for government money, to avoid making repairs, and claim that fire destroyed all
- to plan bankruptcies to eliminate debts, after merchandise supposedly destroyed has been secretly sold
- to eliminate business competition by burning out rivals
- to use extortion schemes to demand that victims pay or the rest of their property will be burned
- to show displeasure during labour–management problems
- to conceal another crime, such as embezzlement

Some recent technological advances may help prove that many alleged arsons were actually accidental fires. For example, a flashover occurs during the course of an ordinary fire, and heat and gas at the ceiling of a room can reach 1,093°C. This temperature causes clothes and furniture to burst into flame, duplicating the effects of an arsonist's gasoline or explosives. Many suspected arsons may actually be the result of flashover.[70]

However, arson is a difficult crime to investigate and prosecute because of the tendency on the part of the public to see arson as a "victimless" crime or to feel compassion for the defendant.

Because arson is a form of vandalism, in this last section we look at the special case of *cybervandalism*, the use of computers to damage property. Many of the same psychological explanations that explain arson also explain cybervandalism: curiosity, boredom, stress, and psychological imbalances.

CONNECTIONS

Cyber crime of various sorts is also discussed in more detail in Chapter 14.

Cybervandalism: Crime with Malicious Intent

On September 8, 2005, an unnamed Massachusetts juvenile pled guilty in federal court and was sentenced to 11 months' detention in a juvenile facility, to be followed by two years of supervised release. During his periods of detention and supervised release, the juvenile was barred from possessing or using any computer, cellphone, or other electronic equipment capable of accessing the Internet.

The basis for the charges was criminal conduct over a 15-month period beginning in March 2004, when the juvenile sent an email to a Florida school with the caption, "this is URGENT!!!" The text of the email read as follows:

your all going to perish and flourish ... you will all die

we're going to have a "blast"

Wiebo Ludwig was convicted in 2001 of charges related to vandalism against gas installations he said were poisoning his family, after numerous farm animals died and women experienced stillborn births.

hahahahahaha wonder where I'll be? youll all be destroyed. im sick of your [expletive deleted] school and piece of [expletive deleted] staff, your all gonna [expletive deleted] die you pieces of crap!!!!

Die Mother [expletive deleted] Im gona blow all you up and myself

All you Nazi loving Mexican Faggot Bitches are Dead

As a result of this bomb threat, the school was closed for two days, while a bomb squad, a canine team, the fire department, and Emergency Medical Services were called in.

The juvenile engaged in numerous other acts. In January 2005, he gained access to the internal computer system of a major telephone service provider, an act that allowed him access to account information of the company's customers. He used this computer system to discover key information about an individual who had an account with the telephone service. He then accessed the information stored on this individual's mobile telephone and posted the information on the Internet.[71]

Some cybercriminals, such as the boy in Massachusetts, may not be motivated by greed or profit, but by the desire for revenge, destruction, and to achieve a malicious intent. Cybervandalism ranges from sending destructive viruses and worms to terrorist attacks designed to destroy important computer networks. Cybervandals are motivated more by malice than by greed:

- Some cybervandals target computers and networks, seeking revenge for a perceived wrong.
- Some desire to exhibit their technical prowess and superiority.
- Some wish to highlight the vulnerability of computer security systems (see Exhibit 11.15).
- Some spy on other people's private financial and personal information ("computer voyeurism").
- Some destroy computer security because they believe in open access to systems and programs.[72]

SUMMARY

Economic crimes are designed to bring financial reward to the offender. The majority of economic crimes are committed by opportunistic amateurs. However, economic crime has also attracted professional criminals who earn the bulk of their income from crime, view themselves as criminals, and have skills that aid them in their lawbreaking. Edwin Sutherland's *The Professional Thief* is perhaps the most famous portrayal of professional crime, showing how professionals live by their

Agencies Making Little Progress against Cybervandalism

By Ethan Butterfield, July 29, 2005

Two Men Sentenced to Prison Time, Fined for Breaking into Federal Sites

Three years after a pair of hackers broke into several federal agency computers and defaced Web sites, industry experts said not enough has been done to prevent further attacks.

"Usually they don't have a lot of money, or time and resources, or the ability a lot of times to go out and secure these things," said Caleb Sima, founder and chief technical officer of SPI Dynamics of Atlanta, an Internet security firm.

In April 2002, Robert Lyttle of San Francisco and Benjamin Stark of St. Petersburg, Fla., hacked into a computer at NASA's Ames Research Center in Moffett Field, Calif., and stole information about members of the agency's Astrobiology Institute, said assistant U.S. attorney Kyle Waldinger, who prosecuted the case.

"He used that information, which was in the form of a spreadsheet, to deface the home page of the NASA Astrobiology Institute," Waldinger said. "In addition, he and his co-conspirator posted their mission statement."

Calling themselves "The Deceptive Duo," Lyttle and Stark stated that their attacks were intended to demonstrate vulnerabilities in the government's computer security systems. The pair also hacked into the Defense Department's Defense Logistics Information Service Web site and the agency's Office of Health Affairs.

Lyttle pleaded guilty to the attacks in March and the U.S. District Court in Oakland, Calif., sentenced him in June to four months in prison, a payment of restitution of $71,181 and three years of probation. Stark, who also pleaded guilty, was sentenced in January to two years of probation and to pay restitution of $29,006.

NASA officials declined to discuss the specifics of the case, but said security is something they have improved since the attacks in 2002.

"We take security very seriously, and over the last couple of years have worked to coordinate our IT security operations, keep them up to date and ensure that people have access to the tools and training they need to do their jobs," said NASA spokesman Brian Dunbar.

But even with these improvements, private cybersecurity experts said the government still needs to do more to improve security.

"I think they know there's a problem," said Pete Allor, director of intelligence at Internet Security Systems of Atlanta. "It's a matter of focus. In the entire government infrastructure there's a lack of focus."

But as new protection technologies are developed, hackers are creating and sharing new infiltration techniques and technologies. Allor said that a buffer override prevention program, which still is in development, already is being tested for weaknesses by the hacking community.

Sharing knowledge of how to illegally access government computers and Web sites has become big business, said Chris Sonderby, chief of the Computer Hacking and Intellectual Property Unit for the U.S. Attorney's office in San Francisco.

"There are hacker Web sites," Sonderby said. "There are chat forums. There are networks of individuals who traffic in information in efforts to gain this type of unauthorized access."

wits and never resort to violence. A good example of the professional criminal is the fence who buys and sells stolen merchandise. There are also occasional thieves whose skill level and commitment fall below the professional level.

Common theft offences include larceny, fraud, embezzlement, and burglary. These are common-law crimes, created by English judges to meet social needs. Theft involves taking the legal possessions of another and is divided into thefts over and under $5,000. The crime of false pretences, or fraud, is similar to larceny because it involves the theft of goods or money, but it differs because the criminal tricks victims into voluntarily giving up their possessions. Embezzlement is another larceny crime. It involves people taking something that was temporarily entrusted to them, such as bank tellers taking money out of the cash drawer and keeping it for themselves.

Newer larceny crimes have also been defined to keep abreast of changing social conditions: passing bad cheques,

stealing or illegally using credit cards, shoplifting, stealing autos to sell on the international underground market, and Internet fraud. The top Internet fraud in 2001 was online auctions. Overall losses topped $6 million.[73]

Burglary, a more serious theft offence, was defined in the common law as the "breaking and entering of a dwelling house of another in the nighttime with the intent to commit a felony within." Today, the definition of burglary includes theft from any structure at any time of day. Because burglary involves planning and risk, it attracts professional thieves. The most competent have technical competence and personal integrity, specialize in burglary, are financially successful, and avoid prison sentences.

Arson is another serious property crime. Although many arsonists are teenage vandals, professional arsonists specialize in burning commercial buildings for profit. And finally, we look at how computers have enabled shifts in traditional crimes, where those criminally predisposed can commit identity theft or cybervandalism.

To reduce the risk of loss during the Christmas holidays, the Association of Household Insurers (AHI) suggests that you don't display presents where they can be seen from a window or doorway and that you put gifts in a safe place before leaving the house or taking a trip. Moreover, closing drapes or blinds during even short trips away from home is a good habit.

To safeguard your home, people need to trick burglars into believing someone is home. If you are away, the AHI suggests putting lights on timers, stopping mail and newspaper delivery, and arranging, if possible, to have the walkways shovelled and have a car parked in the driveway as additional security measures. Other suggestions include installing a good deadbolt lock with at least a 2.5 cm (one-inch) throat into a solid wood or a steel door that fits securely into a sturdy frame, keeping doors locked, putting a chain-link fence around a yard, getting a dog, and having police inspect the house for security. Putting a mannequin in a chair by the window might be a good idea, too. Also, buy a weighted safe deposit box to secure items that can't be replaced, and engrave your driver's licence number and province or territory of residence on your property to give police a way to contact you if your home is burglarized and the stolen items are later found.

Con artists may take advantage of people's generosity during the holidays by making appeals for non-existent charities. Always ask for identification from solicitors.

As a criminologist, can you come up with any new ideas that the Association of Household Insurers failed to cover?

KEY TERMS

arson p. 373
booster p. 355
break and enter p. 369
carjacking p. 360
confidence games p. 361
constructive possession p. 354
economic crimes p. 348

embezzlement p. 368
false pretences p. 361
fence p. 348
flash houses p. 349
fraud p. 361
identity theft p. 363
larceny p. 353

occasional criminal p. 351
phishing p. 364
professional criminals p. 351
situational inducement p. 350
snitches p. 355
street crimes p. 348
systematic forgers p. 365

DOING RESEARCH ON THE WEB

Before you answer the questions in the Thinking Like a Criminologist box, you may want to see the suggestions of the Metropolitan Police Service, by far the largest of the police services that operate in greater London. Go to www .met.police.uk/crimeprevention/burglary.htm.

The Burglary Prevention Council offers advice at www .burglaryprevention.org.

CRITICAL THINKING QUESTIONS

1. Differentiate between an occasional and a professional criminal. Which would be more likely to resort to violence? Which would be more easily deterred?

2. What crime occurs when a person who owns an antique store sells a client an "original" Tiffany lamp that the seller knows is a fake? Is it still a crime if the seller had not been aware that the lamp was a fake? As an antique dealer, should the seller have a duty to determine the authenticity of the products he or she sells?

3. You have been the victim of repeat burglaries. What can you do to reduce the chances of future victimization? (Hint: buying a gun is not an option!)

4. Technology changes the nature and extent of theft crimes. Although train robbing and safe-cracking may be rare today, using bogus credit cards and stealing from ABMs have increased in both number of crimes and value. What other crime patterns have been created by technological innovation?

5. If you knew of someone who frequently tampered with matches to the point of causing you concern, how would you handle this situation? What other danger signs would you look for?

NOTES

1. Andrew McCall, *The Medieval Underworld* (London: Hamish Hamilton, 1979), 86.
2. J.J. Tobias, *Crime and Police in England, 1700–1900* (London: Gill and Macmillan, 1979).
3. Marilyn Walsh, *The Fence* (Westport, CT: Greenwood Press, 1977), 18–25.
4. Sandra Besserer and Catherine Trainor, "Criminal Victimization in Canada, 1999," *Juristat* 20, 10, 2000: Figure 3; Rosemary Garter and Anthony N. Doob, "Trends in Criminal Victimization: 1988–1993," *Juristat* 14, 13, 1994: Table 7.
5. John Hepburn, "Occasional Criminals," in *Major Forms of Crime*, ed. Robert Meier, 73–94 (Beverly Hills, CA: Sage, 1984).
6. P.F. Cromwell, J.N. Olson, and D.W. Avary, *Breaking and Entering: An Ethnographic Analysis of Burglary* (Newbury Park, CA: Sage, 1991).
7. Dianne Hendrick, "Theft," in *Crime Counts: A Criminal Event Analysis*, eds. Leslie W. Kennedy and Vincent F. Sacco (Toronto: ITP Nelson, 1996).
8. Harry King and William Chambliss, *Box Man: A Professional Thief's Journal* (New York: Harper & Row, 1972), 24.
9. Edwin Sutherland, "White-Collar Criminality," *American Sociological Review* 5 (1940): 2–10.
10. Gilbert Geis, "Avocational Crime," in *Handbook of Criminology*, ed. D. Glazer (Chicago: Rand McNally, 1974), 284.
11. Edwin Sutherland and Chic Conwell, *The Professional Thief* (Chicago: University of Chicago Press, 1937).
12. See, for example, Edwin Lemert, "The Behavior of the Systematic Check Forger," *Social Problems* 6 (1958): 141–148.
13. Carl Klockars, *The Professional Fence* (New York: Free Press, 1976); Darrell Steffensmeier, *The Fence: In the Shadow of Two Worlds* (Totowa, NJ: Rowman and Littlefield, 1986); Walsh, *The Fence*, 25–28.
14. Paul Cromwell, James Olson, and D'Aunn Avary, "Who Buys Stolen Property? A New Look at Criminal Receiving," *Journal of Crime and Justice* 16 (1993): 75–95.
15. This section depends heavily on a classic book: Wayne LaFave and Austin Scott, *Handbook on Criminal Law* (St. Paul, MN: West Publishing, 1972).
16. L.E. Cohen and M. Felson, "Social Change and Crime Rate Trends: A Routine Activity Approach," *American Sociological Review* 44 (1979): 588–608.
17. Paul McPhie, "Fraud," in *Crime Counts: A Criminal Event Analysis*, eds. Leslie W. Kennedy and Vincent F. Sacco (Toronto: Nelson, 1996).
18. Mary Owen Cameron, *The Booster and the Snitch* (New York: Free Press, 1964).
19. Lawrence Cohen and Rodney Stark, "Discriminatory Labeling and the Five-Finger Discount: An Empirical Analysis of Differential Shoplifting Dispositions," *Journal of Research on Crime and Delinquency* 11 (1974): 25–35.
20. Lloyd Klemke, "Does Apprehension for Shoplifting Amplify or Terminate Shoplifting Activity?" *Law and Society Review* 12 (1978): 390–403.
21. D. Hartmann, D. Gelfand, B. Page, and P. Walder, "Rates of Bystander Observation and Reporting of Contrived Shoplifting Incidents," *Criminology* 10 (1972): 248.
22. Michael Hindelang, "Decisions of Shoplifting Victims to Invoke the Criminal Justice Process," *Social Problems* 21 (1974): 580–595; Erhard Blankenburg, "The Selectivity of Legal Sanctions: An Empirical Investigation of Shoplifting," *Law and Society Review* 11 (1976): 109–129.
23. George Keckeisen, *Retail Security versus the Shoplifter* (Springfield, IL: Charles C. Thomas, 1993), 31–32.
24. Melissa Davis, Richard Lundman, and Ramiro Martinez, Jr., "Private Corporate Justice: Store Police, Shoplifters, and Civil Recovery," *Social Problems* 38 (1991): 395–408.
25. Heith Copes and Michael Cherbonneau, "The Key to Auto Theft. Emerging Methods of Auto Theft from the Offenders' Perspective," *British Journal of Criminology* 46, 5 (2006): 917–934.
26. "Challenges and Champions," Canadian Coalition against Insurance Fraud, April 2001.
27. Charles McCaghy, Peggy Giordano, and Trudy Knicely Henson, "Auto Theft," *Criminology* 15 (1977): 367–381.
28. Rick Linden and Renuka Chaturvedi, "The Need for Comprehensive Crime Prevention Planning: The Case of Motor Vehicle Theft," *Canadian Journal of Criminology and Criminal Justice* 47, 2 (2005): 251–270.
29. Donald Gibbons, *Society, Crime and Criminal Careers* (Englewood Cliffs, NJ: Prentice-Hall, 1977), 310.
30. Marnie Wallace, "Exploring the involvement of organized crime in motor vehicle theft," Statistics Canada, 2004, Catalogue no. 85-563-XIE.
31. Kim Hazelbaker, "Insurance Industry Analyses and the Prevention of Motor Vehicle Theft," in *Business and Crime Prevention*, eds. Marcus Felson and Ronald Clarke, 283–293 (Monsey, NY: Criminal Justice Press, 1997).
32. "Vehicle Crime Profits Can Be Used to Support Terrorist Organizations, Interpol's Chief Says," Interpol press release, November 19, 2000, http://www.interpol .int (accessed May 24, 2001).
33. Michael Rand, *Carjacking* (Washington, DC: Bureau of Justice Statistics, 1994), 1.
34. Frederick J. Desroches, *Force and Fear: Robbery in Canada* (Toronto: ITP Nelson, 1995).
35. Melanie Kowalski, "Home Invasions," Canadian Centre for Justice Statistics, *Bulletin*, June 2002.
36. Ronald Clarke and Patricia Harris, "Auto Theft and Its Prevention," in *Crime and Justice: An Annual Review*, eds. N. Morris and M. Tonry (Chicago: University of Chicago Press, 1992).
37. R. Light, C. Nee, and H. Ingham, *Car Theft: The Offender's Perspective*, Home Office Research Study No. 130 (London: Home Office, 1993); R.V. Clarke and P.M. Harris, "Auto Theft and Its Prevention," in *Crime and Justice: A Review of Research*, ed. M. Tonry (Chicago: University of Chicago Press, 1992).
38. P.J. Brantingham and P.L. Brantingham, *Patterns in Crime* (New York: Macmillan, 1984).
39. "PM Announces New Legislation That Targets Auto Theft and Property Crime," April 14, 2008, Ottawa, Ontario, http:// pm.gc.ca/eng/media.asp?id=2071.
40. LaFave and Scott, *Handbook on Criminal Law*, 655.
41. 30 Geo. III, C.24 (1975).
42. Michael Friscolanti, "Canada Fails to Combat Counterfeits," *National Post*, May 4, 2004; James McCarten, "Ontario Driver's Licenses Sell for $90US on Internet," Canadian Press, June 8, 2004; "Stronger ID-Theft Laws Needed, CBA Says," Canadian Press, August 23, 2004.
43. As described in Charles McCaghy, *Deviant Behavior* (New York: Macmillan, 1976), 230–231.
44. Susan Gembrowski and Tim Dahlberg, "Over 100 Here Indicted after Telemarketing Fraud Probe around the U.S.," *San Diego Daily Transcript Online*, December 8, 1995.
45. These sections rely on "Phishing Activity Trends Report, June 2005," Anti-Phishing Working Group. www.ncjrs.org/spotlight/ identity_theft/publications.html#phishing; U.S. Department of Justice, Criminal Division, "Special Report of 'Phishing' (2004)." www.ncjrs.org/spotlight/identity _theft/publications.html#phishing.
46. U.S. Department of Justice, Press Release, "Nineteen Individuals Indicted in Internet 'Carding' Conspiracy," October 28, 2004.
47. Identity Theft and Assumption Deterrence Act, as amended by Public Law 105-318, 112 Stat. 3007 (October 30, 1998).
48. Edwin Lemert, "An Isolation and Closure Theory of Naive Check Forgery," *Journal of Criminal Law, Criminology and Police Science* 44 (1953): 297–298.

49. Department of States Attorney, Eastern District of California, Press Release, "Vallejo Woman Admits to Embezzling More than $875,035: Not-for-Profit Organization Victim of Computer Fraud," www.cybercrime.gov.

50. Deloitte & Touche, 2005 Global Security Survey www.deloitte.com/dtt/cda/doc/content/Deloitte+2005+Global+ Security +Survey.pdf.

51. Chris Richard, "Guard Your Card: ATM Fraud Grows More Sophisticated," *Christian Science Monitor* 95 (July 21, 2003):15.

52. Canadian Bankers' Association, www .cba.ca.

53. Jerome Hall, *Theft, Law and Society* (Indianapolis, IN: Bobbs-Merrill, 1952), 36.

54. LaFave and Scott, *Handbook on Criminal Law*, 644.

55. Laureen Snider, "Theft of Time: Disciplining through Science and Law," *Osgoode Hall Law Journal* 40, 1 (2002): 89–113.

56. E. Blackstone, *Commentaries on the Laws of England* (London: 1769), 224.

57. Frank Hoheimer, *The Home Invaders: Confessions of a Cat Burglar* (Chicago: Chicago Review, 1975).

58. Richard Wright, Robert Logie, and Scott Decker, "Criminal Expertise and Offender Decision Making: An Experimental Study of the Target Selection Process in Residential Burglary," *Journal of Research in Crime and Delinquency* 32 (1995): 39–53.

59. Richard Wright and Scott Decker, *Burglars on the Job: Streetlife and Residential Break-Ins* (Boston: Northeastern University Press, 1994).

60. See, generally, Neal Shover, "Structures and Careers in Burglary," *Journal of Criminal Law, Criminology and Police Science* 63 (1972): 540–549.

61. Paul Cromwell, James Olson, and D'Aunn Wester Avary, *Breaking and Entering: An Ethnographic Analysis of Burglary* (Newbury Park, CA: Sage, 1991), 48–51.

62. See M. Taylor and C. Nee, "The Role of Cues in Simulated Residential Burglary: A Preliminary Investigation," *British Journal of Criminology* 28 (1988): 398–401; Julia MacDonald and Robert Gifford, "Territorial Cues and Defensible Space Theory: The Burglar's Point of View," *Journal of Environmental Psychology* 9 (1989): 193–205.

63. Roger Litton, "Crime Prevention and the Insurance Industry," in *Business and Crime Prevention*, eds. Marcus Felson and Ronald Clarke, 162 (Monsey, NY: Criminal Justice Press, 1997).

64. Graham Farrell, Coretta Phillips, and Ken Pease, "Like Taking Candy, Why Does Repeat Victimization Occur?" *British Journal of Criminology* 35 (1995): 384–399.

65. Scott Decker, Richard Wright, Allison Redfern, and Dietrich Smith, "A Woman's Place Is in the Home: Females and Residential Burglary," *Justice Quarterly* 10 (1993): 143–163.

66. Eileen M. Garry, *Juvenile Firesetting and Arson* (Washington, DC: Office of Juvenile Justice and Delinquency Prevention, 1997).

67. Nancy Webb, George Sakheim, Luz Towns-Miranda, and Charles Wagner, "Collaborative Treatment of Juvenile Firestarters: Assessment and Outreach," *American Journal of Orthopsychiatry* 60 (1990): 305–310.

68. Vernon Quinsey, Terry Chaplin, and Douglas Unfold, "Arsonists and Sexual Arousal to Fire Setting: Correlations Unsupported," *Journal of Behavior Therapy and Experimental Psychiatry* 20 (1989): 203–209.

69. Leigh Edward Somers, *Economic Crimes* (New York: Clark Boardman, 1984), 158–168.

70. Michael Rogers, "The Fire Next Time," *Newsweek*, November 26, 1990, 63.

71. U.S. Department of Justice, District of Massachusetts, Press Release, "Massachusetts Teen Convicted for Hacking into Internet and Telephone Service Providers and Making Bomb Threats to High Schools in Massachusetts and Florida," September 8, 2005, www .cybercrime.gov.

72. Anne Branscomb, "Rogue Computer Programs and Computer Rogues: Tailoring Punishment to Fit the Crime," *Rutgers Computer and Technology Law Journal* 16 (1990): 24–26.

73. National Fraud Information Center, "2001 Internet Fraud Statistics," www.fraud.org.

Crimes of Power: White-Collar, Corporate, and Organized Crime

12

Chapter Outline

Learning Objectives

After reading this chapter, you will be able to:

1. Understand the factors that make crimes of power possible.
2. Be familiar with different types of corporate crime.
3. Know the elements of trying to control crimes of power.
4. Discuss different types of organized crime.
5. Explain attempts to control organized crime enterprises.

© POOL/Reuters/Landov

A small community, Lac-Mégantic, Quebec, was the scene of a horrific train crash and explosion in 2013, when brakes failed on an unmanned crude oil transport. Almost four dozen people were killed after the train rolled into town late at night and crashed.

In 2008, Conrad Black lost his appeal of his conviction on fraud and obstruction of justice. At issue were phony "non-compete fees" that Black gave himself in the sell-off of Hollinger's community newspapers and the removal of items from his office in defiance of a court order. The offences amounted to a multimillion-dollar corporate fraud scheme, and the removal of boxes was caught on videotape.

His publishing career began in 1969 with the acquisition of the *Sherbrooke Record*, and two years later expanded with the acquisition of a string of local papers across Canada. By 1986, Black's company, Hollinger, owned more than 100 newspapers, including Britain's *Daily* and *Sunday Telegraph*. In 2004, the U.S. Securities and Exchange Commission (SEC) charged Hollinger with falsifying documents and making illicit payments to executives amid allegations that Black had been looting millions from Hollinger.

Black served several years of a six-and-a-half-year prison sentence in Florida as federal prisoner 18330-424, before successfully appealing the law that was used to convict him. Two of the three charges of fraud were overturned, but he returned to jail in 2011 to serve time for one count of mail fraud and obstruction of justice.

Black's case is complicated, but we have a person who is able to exploit an opportunity for profit within an organization. It has similarities to another case, that of Christopher Horne. In 1996, RBC Dominion Securities Inc. was fined $250,000 for failing to properly supervise former vice-president and stockbroker Christopher Horne. A Toronto-based broker, Horne defrauded elderly clients of millions of dollars over a 10-year period. He quit his job with RBC Dominion Securities in 1994, but in 1996 he was charged with fraud and theft. The Royal Bank, which owned RBC Dominion, reimbursed more than $5 million to his victims.

Horne had misappropriated millions of dollars from client accounts, channelling the money into the Toronto and Grand Cayman bank accounts of a shell company, International Haven Services, which he had founded in Panama City in 1980. Horne had sat on the board of the Art Gallery of Ontario and had used his ill-gotten gains to finance his own art collection, worth more than $4 million. Sentenced to five years in prison in August 1996, his collection of paintings, photographs, and sculptures was seized to pay back creditors.

The Cayman Islands is a tax haven where individuals and corporations pay no taxes and benefit from absolute secrecy. The Bahamas is another tax haven with no personal or corporate taxes. It is well established, with more than 400 banks and US$320 billion on deposit. More than 44,000 offshore companies are registered in the Bahamas. Because of its unique financial position, money laundering is a problem there.

Our global economy has made it easy to use illegal tactics to make profit. We refer to these crimes of the marketplace as **enterprise crimes**, and divide these crimes into three categories. **White-collar crime** involves the illegal activities of people and institutions whose acknowledged purpose is profit through legitimate business transactions. Related to white-crime is green-collar crime, a newly defined category that includes some old crimes. **Green criminology** involves crimes against the environment, usually for profit.

Two related crimes are cybercrime and organized crime. **Cybercrime** involves people using the instruments of modern technology for criminal purposes and is discussed more in Chapter 14, while **organized crime** involves the illegal activities of people and organizations whose acknowledged purpose is profit through illegitimate business enterprise.

These enterprise crimes involve all phases of illegal commercial activity. Organized crime involves individuals or groups who use illegal marketing techniques (threats, extortion, and smuggling) and outlawed or controlled product lines (drugs, sex, gambling, and loan sharking). White-collar crimes include the use of illegal business practices (embezzlement, price-fixing, and bribery) to market what are ordinarily legitimate commercial products. Green-collar criminals might engage in environmental dumping to increase corporate profits. Cyber criminals use technical expertise for criminal misappropriations, behaviour that is defined as illegal by society:

> White-collar crime is not simply a dysfunctional aberration. Organized crime is not something ominously alien to the … economic system. Both are made criminal by laws declaring that certain ways of doing business, or certain products of business, are illegal. In other words, criminality is not an inherent characteristic either of certain persons or of certain business activities but rather, an externally imposed evaluation of alternative modes of behaviour and action.[1]

Enterprise crime is a spectrum of acts;[2] however, the basic underlying similarity is the sale of illegal goods and services to customers who know these goods and services are illegal.[3]

Although organizational practices may be desirable to many consumers (for example, the sale of narcotics) or an efficient way of doing business (such as the dumping of

enterprise crimes Illegal acts of opportunity that involve breaking regulatory rules but not personal victimization for the purpose of financial gain.

white-collar crime Illegal acts that capitalize on a person's status in the marketplace, including embezzlement, fraud, market manipulation, restraint of trade, and false advertising.

green criminology The study of crimes against the environment, usually for profit.

cybercrime Illegal acts that use computer technology both for illicit gain, such as fraud, and for moral crimes, such as child pornography and stalking.

organized crime Illegal acts committed by a gang, such as drug trafficking.

hazardous wastes), society tries to regulate or outlaw these behaviours. However, corporate crime is not prosecuted criminally in the same way that street crime is.

The *Corporate Crime Reporter* compiled a list of the top 100 corporate criminals of the 1990s, using only corporations that had pled guilty to crimes and had been criminally fined. They found that corporate criminals fell into 14 categories: environmental (38), antitrust (20), fraud (13), campaign finance (7), food and drug (6), financial crimes (4), false statements (3), illegal exports (3), illegal boycott (1), worker death (1), bribery (1), obstruction of justice (1), public corruption (1), and tax evasion (1). Experts claim that 200,000 or more occupational deaths occur each year and that corporate violence annually kills and injures more people than all street crimes combined.[4]

Exhibit 12.1 has more detail about the impact of corporate crime in Canada.

Some criminal enterprises involve both organized and white-collar crime. Organized criminals may seek out legitimate enterprises to launder money, diversify their sources of income, and gain and enhance respectability.[5] Legitimate businesspeople may turn to organized criminals to help them with problems of an economic nature (such as breaking up a strike or dumping hazardous waste products) or to stifle or threaten competition. The distinction between organized crime and white-collar and corporate criminals often overlap, as we see in Figure 12.1.

EXHIBIT 12.1

Quick Facts about the Cost of Corporate Crime in Canada

- Between 1972 and 1981, more than 10,000 Canadians died from work-related injuries.
- Canada has about 500 homicides per year, but about 15,000 die from corporate inaction.
- Failure to remit payroll deductions costs more than bank robbery, extortion, and kidnapping.
- Occupational deaths are the third leading cause of death, after heart disease and cancer.
- Hundreds of thousands of workers are exposed to radioactive and chemical pollutants every year.
- In 1993, the Canadian Union of Public Employees (CUPE) estimated that 61 percent of workers were victimized; 43 percent said no action was taken.
- Canadian Labour Congress (1993) reports that deaths from workplace disease are largely uncompensated.
- Of those killed in fatal workplace accidents, 97 percent are men.
- Women are at risk of reproductive health hazards due to exposure to toxic substances.

SOURCES: John L. McMullan, *Beyond the Limits of the Law: Corporate Crime and Law and Order* (Halifax: Fernwood, 1992); Brian MacLean, ed., *The Political Economy of Crime* (Scarborough, Ont.: Prentice Hall, 1986).

FIGURE 12.1

Enterprise Crimes: The Linkage among White-Collar Crime, Cybercrime, and Organized Crime

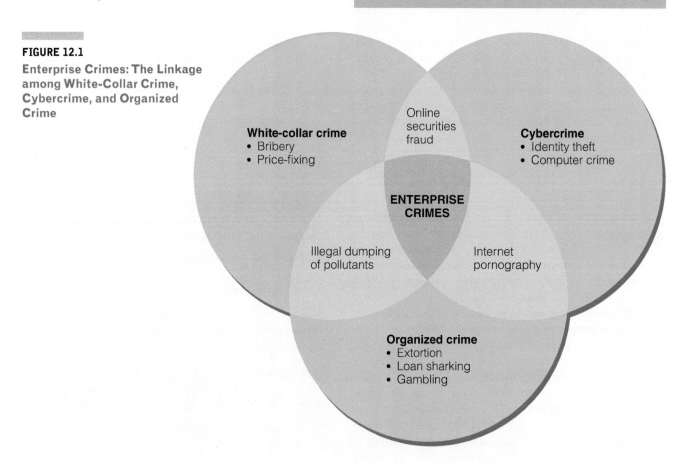

White-collar crime
- Bribery
- Price-fixing

Online securities fraud

Cybercrime
- Identity theft
- Computer crime

ENTERPRISE CRIMES

Illegal dumping of pollutants

Internet pornography

Organized crime
- Extortion
- Loan sharking
- Gambling

Some forms of white-collar crime may be more like organized crime than others.[6] Although some corporate executives cheat to improve their company's position in the business world, others are motivated purely by personal gain. It is this latter group, people who engage in ongoing criminal conspiracies for their own profit, that most resembles organized crime.[7]

WHITE-COLLAR CRIME

Edwin Sutherland first used the term *white-collar crime* to describe criminal activities of the rich and powerful.[8]

Sutherland said that white-collar crime involved conspiracies by the wealthy to use their position for personal gain without regard for the law. All too often, these actions were handled by civil courts because injured parties were more concerned with recovering their losses than with seeing the offenders punished criminally. Yet the financial cost of white-collar crime is many times greater than street crime, and moreover, leads to damage to social relations. White-collar crimes violate trust between consumers and corporations, clients and professionals, citizens and their government. The effect is a lowering of social morale; in contrast, other types of crimes produce relatively little effect on social institutions or social organization.[9]

Redefining White-Collar Crime

Modern criminologists have developed Sutherland's work and broadened their definition of white-collar crime. Edelhertz described it as "an illegal act committed by nonphysical means to obtain money or property or to obtain business or personal advantage."[10] Because that definition encompasses crimes with little connection to business enterprise,[11] the following definition is more specific:

> White-collar crime consists of the illegal or unethical acts that violate fiduciary responsibility or public trust, committed by an individual or organization, usually during the course of legitimate occupational activity by persons of high or respectable social status for personal or organizational gain.[12]

Today's definition of white-collar crime includes all individuals who use the marketplace for their criminal activity, from middle-income Canadians to corporate titans.[13]

Included in this definition are "middle-class" acts such as income tax evasion, credit card fraud, and bankruptcy fraud. White-collar individuals use their positions of trust in business or government to commit crimes such as pilfering, soliciting bribes or kickbacks, and embezzlement. Some white-collar criminals victimize the public in land swindles, securities thefts, and medical or health frauds. Some become involved in criminal conspiracies designed to improve the market share or profitability of their corporations, such as antitrust violations, price-fixing, and false advertising.

Criminologists also study state–corporate crimes, which are illegal or socially injurious actions resulting from cooperation between governmental and corporate institutions.[14]

The White-Collar Crime Problem

Despite the cost of white-collar crime being difficult to estimate,[15] experts place the cost at hundreds of billions of dollars, far outstripping any other crime. For example, **occupational crime** alone, such as loss due to employee theft from businesses, amounts to billions of dollars per year.[16] Employee fraud can include inflated expense accounts, false invoices, and personal use of company supplies.

A 2002 KPMG survey of 881 large Canadian corporations pointed to several issues that create opportunities for fraud: high turnover of middle-level managers, too much financial authority invested in a few senior people, inadequate channels for reporting fraud, and a failure to perceive reasons for being unhappy at work. In their words, "Underpaid employees are more inclined to look for ways to create their own bonuses."[17]

A study by Statistics Canada found that many banking and insurance businesses experience fraud, but they seldom call police because the frauds are too minor and they are able to deal with it themselves.

White-collar crimes also involve property damage and loss of human life, violations of safety standards, environmental pollution, and industrial accidents due to negligence. The potential impact ranges from acute environmental catastrophes, such as the collapse of a dam, to the chronic effects of diseases resulting from industrial pollution.[18]

Gilbert Geis says white-collar crime is much more serious than is street crime:

> It destroys confidence, saps the integrity of commercial life and has the potential for devastating destruction. Think of the possible results if nuclear regulatory rules are flouted or if toxic wastes are dumped into a community's drinking water supply.[19]

occupational crime Crime committed by employees for personal gain using the structural advantage provided by their employment.

Society has begun to recognize the seriousness of white-collar crimes, such as a judge taking a bribe in return for a light sentence, a doctor cheating on medical insurance claims, and a factory owner knowingly disposing of waste in a way that pollutes the water supply.[20] However, white-collar criminals generally face monetary fines and relatively short sentences; judges and prosecutors are reluctant to incarcerate offenders who do not fit the image of "common criminals," as discussed in the nearby Criminology Research box.

International White-Collar Crime

White-collar crime also occurs in other countries. In China, cases of corruption account for a high percentage of all cases of economic crime and have been the subject of extreme crackdowns. Despite death being the penalty for corruption in China, most people involved in corruption and bribery are state personnel. However, of 170,000 Communist party members disciplined for wrongdoing in 2004, only 3 percent were prosecuted, and 52 percent of officials convicted from 2003 to 2005 received suspended sentences.[21]

North American companies are also suspected of being targets of white-collar criminals overseas. Agents have been inserted into companies abroad to steal trade secrets and intellectual property, such as computer programs and technology. Offences can be grouped into four categories:[22]

1. *corporate crime,* in which legitimate companies commit crime in the course of their usual business, fostered by a strongly competitive environment
2. *government crime,* which includes illegal acts committed either by government officials or with their knowledge and support, as well as cover-ups of other persons' crimes
3. *occupational crime,* which involves people making extra money by bending or breaking the rules, perhaps because of business-related problems
4. *organized/professional crime,* which involves people or groups of people whose primary source of income is illegal

Crimes can amount to billions of dollars of losses each year. For example, fraud in the agricultural sector, which ranges from evasion of taxes and deceitful claims to phantom operations and false or forged documentation, may amount to $8 billion per year.[23]

Components of White-Collar Crime

White-collar crimes involve individuals acting within a business structure. The victims can be the public, the organization that employs the offender, or a competing

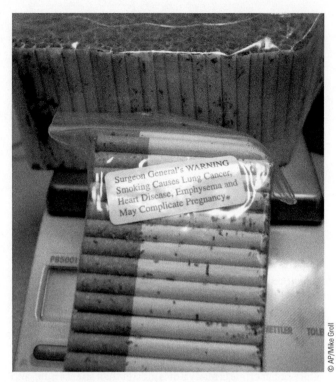

Top tobacco executives were charged with conspiracy for sending cigarettes to smugglers in 2003, defrauding the Canadian government of more than $1 billion in tax revenue. The cigarettes were sent to organized crime units in the United States, and then were smuggled back into Canada through Aboriginal reserves. For more information, see the Famous Canadian Court Cases box, "Tobacco Smuggling," later in this chapter.

organization. Clinard and Quinney divide white-collar crime into an occupational category (offences committed both by individuals in the course of their occupation and by employees against their employers) and into corporate crime (offences committed by corporate officials for the corporation, and the offences of the corporation itself).[24] Edelhertz divides white-collar criminality into four categories:

1. *ad-hoc violations,* committed for personal profit, such as welfare or tax fraud
2. *abuses of trust,* committed against an organization, such as embezzlement or bribery
3. *collateral business crimes,* committed to protect business, such as concealing pollution
4. *con games,* committed to cheat clients, such as fraudulent land sales

Edelhertz's typology captures the diverse nature of white-collar criminality and illustrates how both individuals and institutions can be the victims of, and the offenders in, a white-collar crime. A different type of typology is shown in Exhibit 12.2, a way of characterizing the various victims of corporate crime.

Christopher Horne committed an outrageous fraud while at RBC Securities. In a case on a grander scale,

Criminology Research

Tyco, Enron, and WorldCom: Enterprise Crime at the Highest Levels

The Tyco Case

Tyco International Ltd. is a gigantic corporation that operates in over 100 countries and employs more than 250,000 people. Despite its great success, its chief executive officer, L. Dennis Kozlowski, and chief financial officer, Marc Swartz, were indicted on a variety of fraud and larceny charges, including misappropriating $170 million in company funds by hiding unauthorized bonuses and secretly forgiving loans to themselves. Kozlowski and Swartz were also accused of making more than $430 million by lying about Tyco's financial condition in order to inflate the value of their stock.

During the first trial in 2004, the government tried to establish a motive by showing jurors elements of Kozlowski's extravagant lifestyle. He spent more than $2 million on a party for his wife on the Italian island of Sardinia. He also spent $15 million to furnish an $18 million Tyco-owned apartment on Fifth Avenue in New York City; his expenses included a $15,000 umbrella holder, a $2,200 gilt metal trash basket, and a $6,000 shower curtain.

The defence claimed the two were merely highly paid executives and that everything they received had been approved by Tyco's board of directors. Because there was no stealth, there could be no embezzlement. However, before the jury could decide on the matter, the judge declared a mistrial after a juror revealed that she had been the subject of threats.

At the second trial, Kozlowski was convicted for misappropriation of Tyco's corporate funds: $150 million in unauthorized bonuses, and fraud of more than $400 million against the company shareholders.

The Enron Case

Enron Corporation, an oil and gas trading firm, was one of the largest companies in the United States before it collapsed and cost thousands of employees their life savings and millions of investors their hard-earned money. Enron's share price collapsed when word got out that the company had been concealing debts so they would not show up in company accounts.

In one incident, six Enron executives negotiated complex deals in which they made $42 million on personal investments totalling $161,000, all the while knowing that the limited partnerships they sold to retirement plans and private foundations were collapsing in value. Enron's auditors shredded key documents to keep them out of government hands. One partner, who was head of the team that audited Enron, agreed to serve as a government witness after pleading guilty to obstruction of justice.

In the aftermath of the Enron collapse, chairman Kenneth L. Lay was charged with conspiracy, securities fraud, wire fraud, bank fraud, and making false statements. Enron CEO Jeffrey K. Skilling and former Enron chief accounting officer Richard Causey were also charged with money laundering and conspiracy.

What had motivated the head of one of the nation's largest companies to commit fraud? Greed: Between 1998 and 2001, Lay had received approximately $300 million from the sale of Enron stock options and restricted stock, and made over $217 million in profit; he was also paid more than $19 million in salary and bonuses.

The WorldCom Case

In 2005, WorldCom CEO Bernie Ebbers was found guilty and received a 25-year sentence for falsifying the company's financial statements by more than $9 billion; WorldCom was forced to file for the largest bankruptcy in U.S. history. One of the most important elements of the case was the more than $400 million that WorldCom either loaned or guaranteed to loan Ebbers at an interest rate of 2.15 percent.

When the market collapsed in 2000, WorldCom was heavily in debt and losing money. In 2002, WorldCom announced that it had illegally treated $3.8 billion in ordinary costs as capital expenditures. The bottom dropped out of the stock, and creditors sued. The company admitted to having overstated profits by a whopping $74.4 billion between 2000 and 2001, including at least $10.6 billion that the firm attributed to accounting "errors" and to "improper" and "inappropriate" accounting.

Critical Thinking

1. Considering various theories of criminal behaviour, how would you explain the criminal behaviour of millionaires such as Kozlowski, Ebbers, and Lay? Are they impulsive? Do they lack self-control? Do they have a personality deficit?
2. Should white-collar criminals be punished with a prison sentence, or would society be better served if all their ill-gotten gains were confiscated?

SOURCES: Lynne W. Jeter, *Disconnected: Deceit and Betrayal at WorldCom* (New York: Wiley, 2003); Bethany McLean and Peter Elkind, *Smartest Guys in the Room: The Amazing Rise and Scandalous Fall of Enron* (New York: Penguin, 2003); Kurt Eichenwald, "Ex-Andersen Partner Pleads Guilty in Record-Shredding," *New York Times,* 12 April 2002, p. C1; John A. Byrne, "At Enron, the Environment Was Ripe for Abuse," *Business Week* (25 February 2002):12; Peter Behr and Carrie Johnson, "Govt. Expands Charges against Enron Execs," *Washington Post,* 1 May 2003, p.1; Associated Press, "Ex-Tyco CEO Dennis Kozlowski Found Guilty," MSNBC, 17 June 2005, www.msnbc.msn.com/id/8258729.

EXHIBIT 12.2

A Typology of Corporate Crime

Victim	Crime
Consumer	False advertising, harmful products, price gouging
Environment	Pollution, resource mismanagement, destruction of way of life
Worker	Unsafe work conditions, pension fund abuse, benefit fraud
Competitors	Price-fixing, illegal takeovers, industrial espionage
State	Fraudulent billing, tax evasion, bribing of politicians

SOURCES: Adapted from John L. McMullan, *Beyond the Limits of the Law: Corporate Crime and Law and Order* (Halifax: Fernwood, 1992); C. Goff and C. Reasons, "Organizational Crimes against Employees, Consumers, and the Public," in *The Political Economy of Crime: Readings for a Critical Criminology*, ed. B. Maclean (Scarborough, ON: Prentice Hall, 1986).

German financier Wolfgang Stolzenberg of Montreal-based Castor Holdings used a Ponzi scheme, a pyramid scam in which money raised from new investors was used to pay off earlier investors, to defraud investors of $200 million. It was one of the largest fraud investigations ever conducted by the Royal Canadian Mounted Police (RCMP), second only to the inquiry into the failure of mining company Bre-X Minerals Ltd.

TYPES OF WHITE-COLLAR CRIME

Mark Moore's typology of white-collar crime ranges from an individual using a business enterprise to commit theft-related crimes, to individuals using their place within a business for illegal gain, to business enterprises collectively engaging in crime.[25] This typology tries to encompass the complex array of acts possible in white-collar crime.

As we can see in the Famous Canadian Criminals box, the attractions are high.

Stings and Swindles

Swindling is stealing through deception by individuals whose entire purpose is to bilk people out of their money. Offences range from the door-to-door sale of faulty merchandise to the passing of millions of dollars in counterfeit stock certificates to established brokerage firms. If caught, white-collar swindlers are usually charged with common-law crimes, such as embezzlement or fraud.

swindling Stealing through deception by individuals who try to bilk people out of their money, e.g., door-to-door sales of faulty merchandise.

Famous Canadian Criminals
The Senate Scandal

The Canadian Senate expenses scandal involves the expense claims of certain Canadian senators. In 2012, Senators Mike Duffy, Mac Harb, Pamela Wallin, and Patrick Brazeau were accused of claiming travel and housing expenses from the Senate for which they were allegedly not eligible. The RCMP opened an investigation, as did the Auditor General of Canada. Despite their claims of innocence Duffy, Wallin, and Harb eventually repaid the ineligible amount. Harb retired a few months into the scandal, and in 2013, Duffy, Wallin, and Brazeau were suspended from the Senate without pay. Wallin and Duffy were criticized for claiming travel expenses to and from Saskatchewan and Prince Edward Island, respectively. While senators are allowed to claim travel to and from their primary residence, Wallin had a condo in Toronto and Duffy had a house in Ottawa. Duffy repaid $90,000 in illegitimate expense claims, and Wallin over $120,000.

Elected to Senate by the government of the day, senators enjoy a long career with many perks. While there is oversight of their expenses and rules regarding their claims, senators also enjoy the advantages of their political connections. Wallin, for example, earned more than a million dollars in stock options and fees serving on corporate boards during her time as a senator.

Were these crimes? There were no charges, no trials, and no convictions. Yet they were declared to have abused the rules and they were ousted as a result. Most people will never enjoy such opportunities.

CONNECTIONS

In Chapter 11, the crime of fraud was discussed in the context of individual-level crimes that involve con games. Although similar, swindles here involve organizations that are devoted to fleecing the public.

Financial Swindles. Although swindlers are often considered petty thieves, swindles can run into millions of dollars.[26] For example, the collapse of the Bank of Credit and Commerce International (BCCI) is a swindle that cost depositors billions of dollars. BCCI was the world's seventh-largest private bank, with assets of about $23 billion. Bank officials made billions in unsecured loans to confederates, and also used false accounting methods to defraud depositors. Its clients included Colombian drug cartel leaders and dictators Saddam Hussein and Ferdinand Marcos, who financed terrorist organizations, smuggled illegal arms, and laundered money for narcotics traffickers.[27]

In another example, in 2003, Ken Lay quit as CEO of Enron, the seventh-largest corporation in the United States. The bankruptcy of Enron cost thousands their jobs and became the largest collapse in corporate history. Accused of hiding billions of dollars in debts, the accounting firm that audited Enron was complicit in masking the problem and shredding important documents. The two biggest banks in the United States were required to pay $236 million to compensate victims of the fraud.

Religious Swindles. One investment scam used religion to steal from trusting investors. TV evangelist Jim Bakker was convicted of defrauding followers of $3.7 million when he oversold "lifetime partnerships" at his Heritage USA religious retreat. Bakker used ministry funds to buy vacation homes, a houseboat, expensive cars, and an air-conditioned doghouse. Bakker was sentenced to 45 years in prison.

It is estimated that swindlers using fake religious identities bilk people out of millions of dollars.[28] Religious swindlers use religious television and radio shows to sell their product and are tough to guard against because they are promoted in the same manner as legitimate religious fundraising.

Chiselling

Chiselling, the second category of white-collar crime, refers to cheating an organization or its consumers. Chisellers look to make quick profits, so might charge for bogus auto repairs or home repairs. Corporations can engage in large-scale chiselling when they misrepresent products or alter their content. In a classic case, Beech-Nut Nutrition Corporation paid a $2 million fine for illegally selling a product labelled "apple juice" that was nothing more than sweetened water.[29]

Professional Chiselling. Professionals such as pharmacists can alter prescriptions or substitute low-cost generic drugs for more expensive name brands.[30] Lawyers chisel clients out of millions of dollars by forging signatures on compensation cheques and tapping escrow accounts and other funds for personal investments.[31]

Securities Fraud. In the commodity and stock markets, **churning** of a client's account by an unscrupulous stockbroker involves repeated and unnecessary buying and selling of stock with the intent to defraud the client.[32] The organization that deals with stock market regulation in Canada is the Toronto Stock Exchange, a non-profit organization overseen by the Ontario Securities Commission, which investigates rules regarding insider trading or market manipulation. The Vancouver Stock Exchange has been plagued with improprieties involving stock trading and insider trading, which is the use of a position of trust to gain inside information, giving the trader an unfair advantage over the public.

It is illegal for corporate employees with direct knowledge of market-sensitive information to use it for their own benefit—for example, by buying stock in a company that they have learned will be taken over. In recent years, the definition of **insider trading** has been expanded to include employees of financial institutions, such as law firms or banks, who use confidential information to purchase stock in a company.[33]

In a now famous case, Dr. Samuel Waksal, founder of a biotech company called ImClone Systems, pleaded guilty in 2002 to charges of securities fraud, perjury, and obstruction of justice. The charges were the result of an investigation into the dumping of stock by Waksal, his friends, and his family shortly before the company announced that the U.S. Food and Drug Administration had rejected its application for approval of a cancer drug. The announcement would have depressed the value of company shares.

As part of his guilty plea, Dr. Waksal read a detailed description of how he had phoned his daughter, urging her to sell her stock ahead of the critical announcement about the cancer drug, and how he directed her to cover up those conversations when she was questioned by government

chiselling Cheating an organization or its customers.

churning A white-collar crime in which a stockbroker makes repeated trades to fraudulently increase his or her commissions.

insider trading Illegal buying of stock in a company on the basis of information provided by someone in the company, such as an employee, attorney, or accountant of the firm.

investigators. Waksal's friend, Martha Stewart, dumped her shares just before the announcement and was also investigated.[34] The ending is now well known, with Stewart going to jail for obstructing justice.

Interpretations of what constitutes insider trading vary widely. In the most celebrated insider trading cases, billionaires Ivan Boesky and Michael Milken, two of Wall Street's most prominent **arbitrage** experts, were convicted and sentenced to prison. Arbitragers speculate on the stock of companies that are rumoured to be takeover targets, and then profit on the difference between current stock prices and the price the acquiring company is willing to pay. Boesky was ordered to pay $100 million in penalties. Milken received a billion-dollar fine; his 10-year sentence was reduced in return for his cooperation with authorities.[35]

Internet Securities Fraud. Jonathan Lebed, age 15, was charged with securities fraud by the SEC after he repeatedly bought low-cost, thinly traded stocks, and then spread hundreds of false and misleading messages concerning them—generally baseless price predictions. After their values were artificially inflated, Lebed sold the securities at an exaggerated price. His smallest one-day gain was $12,000, and on one particular day he made $74,000. Lebed questioned whether he had done anything wrong.[36] There are two major types of Internet securities fraud:

- *Market manipulation:* In a "pump and dump" scheme, erroneous information is first posted online to get unsuspecting investors to become interested in a stock, and then the previously purchased stock is sold at an inflated price. The "cyber smear" can also work in reverse: Negative information is spread online about a stock, driving down its price, enabling people to buy it at an artificially low price.[37]
- *Fraudulent offerings of securities:* A criminal creates websites designed to fraudulently sell securities by inflating the value of assets, overstating returns, and understating risks. Investors are promised abnormally high profits on their investments, and early investors are paid returns with the investment money received from the later investors. The system usually collapses.

An example of fraudulent security offerings occurred when Tri-West Investment solicited investments in "prime bank notes."[38] Visitors to the firm's website were promised an annualized rate of return of 120 percent plus return of their principal at the end of a year. The website contained testimonials describing instant wealth from early investors. Investors contributed $60 million in funds to Tri-West, some dividends were paid from new investments, and most of the cash was siphoned off by the schemers.

Individual Exploitation of Institutional Position

In this third type of white-collar crime, individuals can exploit their power to take advantage of others; for example, a fire inspector can demand that a restaurant owner pay him to be granted an operating licence. This type of offence occurs when the victim has a clear right to expect a service and the offender threatens to withhold the service unless an additional payment or bribe is paid.

Exploitation in Government. Throughout history, political and government figures have used their positions to profit from bribes and kickbacks.[39] On the local level, such scandals can involve liquor licence board members, food inspectors, and fire inspectors wanting "consideration."[40] Even powerful politicians have been implicated in corrupt practices, such as Conservative senator Michel Cogger, who was sentenced to pay a $3,000 fine for peddling his influence to a Montreal businessman.[41] (See the Famous Canadian Criminals exhibit for a more current example.)

Exploitation in Industry. Purchasing agents in large companies can demand a kickback for awarding contracts to suppliers and distributors, such as the J.C. Penney employee who received $1.4 million from a contractor who did $23 million of business with the company,[42] or the purchasing agent for American Chiclets who received a $300,000 kickback from the makers of the supermarket wire display racks.

Influence Peddling and Bribery

In this fourth type of white-collar crime, individuals in important institutional positions can sell power, influence, and information to outsiders, such as government employees taking kickbacks from contractors in return for awarding them contracts.

In an investigation into the sale of British Columbia's publicly owned railway to CN Rail, the RCMP raided the provincial legislature to collect documents and later alleged that at least two officials were offered personal benefits for their cooperation.[43] In a scandal in Toronto in 2004, police officers were charged with breach of trust, fraud, and obstructing justice after demanding cash for receiving tips about liquor inspectors. Six members of the now-disbanded drug squad were charged after a corruption probe by the RCMP.[44]

Also in 2004, the RCMP laid charges against a retired bureaucrat and the president of an advertising firm for their involvement in the sponsorship scandal, a deal that saw lucrative government contracts be awarded to firms

> **arbitrage** The practice of buying large blocks of stock in companies that are believed to be the target of corporate buyouts or takeovers.

by Adrian Humphreys

The government of the world's smallest republic, branded a gangster's paradise because of its lax banking laws, says international pressure can be eased now that it has strengthened anti-money laundering regulations.

The Republic of Nauru amended legislation on banking and corporate secrecy in a bid to avoid sanctions by the Financial Action Task Force (FATF), an agency supported by about 30 countries, Mathew Batsiua, the island's Chief Secretary, said yesterday.

Nauru is a desolate South Pacific island of 24 square kilometres and with a population of 12,088. Money laundering specialists say the island is home to more shell corporations and banks than people.

For years, its use by the Russian mafia, tax dodgers, and other gangsters to hide money has enraged banks, police, and tax collectors around the world. However, attempts to shame the tiny country into tightening regulations have failed.

SOURCE: Adrian Humphreys, "Nauru Gets Tough on Illicit Banking," *National Post*, December 8, 2001: A16.

friendly to the Liberal government. The RCMP alleged that contracts worth about $100 million were awarded non-competitively and that work was not done before payments were made.[45]

One major difference distinguishes influence peddling from exploitation of an institutional position: Exploitation involves forcing victims to pay for services to which they have a right, while influence peddlers and bribe-takers use their position to grant favours and sell information to which their co-conspirators are not entitled.

Influence Peddling in Government. In 1995, a scandal erupted in Canada over kickbacks in the airline industry. It was alleged that former Prime Minister Brian Mulroney, along with former Premier of Newfoundland Frank Moores, had accepted payments from a private company in return for procuring a lucrative contract with the federal government to supply passenger airplanes. Franz Schreiber had set up a shell company, International Airlines, to influence Air Canada to purchase the Airbus 330. A *Fifth Estate* documentary on the CBC alleged that $20 million was paid in kickbacks. The allegations were unproved, and Mulroney won $1 million when he sued.

In a classic case, senior Pentagon officials received bribes for granting contracts for military clothing. The $1 billion scandal touched some of the largest defence contractors in the United States, including Raytheon, Litton Industries, and Lockheed.[46]

Corruption in the Criminal Justice System. Corruption in the criminal justice system is disturbing because society expects a higher standard of moral integrity from people empowered to uphold the law. The credibility of the justice process is weakened when officials who hold power over other people engage in criminal behaviour.

In 2001, the RCMP was called in to investigate the drug squad of Toronto's police. Officers were suspected of corruption and theft of money from the squad's "fink fund." The way the fraud worked was that officers would send out users to buy drugs from traffickers. They would attribute the source as a police informant, requisition money to pay them, and pocket the cash instead. More than 100 court cases were compromised.

In 2008, two Toronto police constables were charged with offences relating to organized crime, including running a marijuana-cultivation operation involving dozens of grow houses, participating in an offence for the benefit of a criminal organization, breach of trust, conspiracy to produce marijuana, obstruction of justice, and laundering the proceeds of crime.

The interest in studying criminal justice system corruption comes from a now-classic case: The Knapp Commission found that police corruption was widespread, ranging from patrol officers accepting small gratuities from local businesspeople to senior officers receiving payoffs from gamblers and narcotics violators.[47] Construction firms paid police to ignore violations of city ordinances, such as obstruction of sidewalks. Bar owners paid police to allow them to operate after hours. Police kept money and narcotics confiscated during drug raids.

Such cases show how eradicating police corruption requires changing police operations so that they have more oversight and better public complaints procedures.

Influence Peddling in Business. In the 1970s, revelations were made that multinational corporations regularly made payoffs to foreign officials and businesspeople to secure business contracts. Gulf Oil executives admitted paying $4 million to the South Korean ruling party. Burroughs Corporation admitted paying $1.5 million to foreign officials. McDonnell

Douglas Aircraft Corporation was indicted for paying $1 million in bribes to officials of Pakistani International Airlines to secure orders. In 1995, executives of Lockheed Aircraft pleaded guilty to bribery in the sale of transport aircraft to the Egyptian government.[48] And in 2010, after the Deepwater Horizons oil rig exploded, there were allegations that the regulatory agencies and the industry were too "well connected" (focus of the following Crime in the News exhibit).

Embezzlement and Employee Fraud

The fifth type of white-collar crime involves individuals' use of their positions to embezzle company funds or appropriate company property for themselves. Here, the company or organization that employs the criminal is the victim of the white-collar crime.

Blue-Collar Fraud. Employee theft can reach all levels of the organizational structure. Blue-collar employees have been involved in systematic theft of company property, commonly called **pilferage**:

- Piece workers zip completed garments into their clothing and take them home.
- Cashiers ring up lower prices on single-item purchases and pocket the difference.
- Clerks sell untagged sale merchandise at its original cost, pocketing the difference.
- Receiving clerks obtain duplicate keys to storage facilities, returning later to steal.
- Truck drivers make fictitious purchases of fuel, splitting the gains with the truck stop.
- Employees hide items in garbage pails or under trash heaps for retrieval later.[49]

In one study, 35 percent of employees surveyed reported involvement in pilferage.[50] Employee theft can be explained by factors related to the work setting, such as job dissatisfaction and the neutralization belief that employees are being exploited by employers. It has been estimated that pilferage can amount to losses of billions of dollars annually.[51]

Management Fraud. Management-level fraud includes (1) converting company assets for personal benefit, (2) fraudulently receiving increases in compensation (such as raises or bonuses), (3) fraudulently increasing personal holdings of company stock, (4) retaining a position within the company by manipulating accounts, and (5) concealing unacceptable performance from stockholders.[52] An example of management fraud is overstating company profits, which pays off if bonuses are tied to company profits.

Of the 300 American companies in the 2003 KPMG Fraud Survey, 75 percent had experienced fraud, ranging from employee fraud ($464,000) to financial reporting fraud ($258 million). In the 2007 study of fraud against businesses in Canada, about half of retail businesses reported being victimized, with most incidents committed by non-employees.[53]

EXHIBIT 12.3

The Bre-X Scandal

In March 1997, Mike de Guzman, the top geologist of the Bre-X mine in Busang, Indonesia, leapt to his death from a helicopter. De Guzman had been credited with helping Calgary-based Bre-X discover what was believed to be the world's biggest gold deposit at the Busang mine.

The site was alleged to contain 200 million ounces of gold. However, suspicions surfaced that Bre-X's core samples had been "salted" with alluvial gold to increase the gold content. Tests conducted by Barrick Gold, a Toronto-based gold mining corporation, in 1996 showed no gold in 148 out of 150 samples. When news leaked out that the massive gold discovery was a fraud, Bre-X shares dropped substantially from a high of $286.50. Shortly after, trading in the company was halted by regulators at the Toronto Stock Exchange until an independent audit of drilling tests was completed.

The executive chief geologist of the company, Jon Felderhof, was sued for $3 billion by Bre-X's receiver-manager, Deloitte and Touche. Felderhof is believed to have made at least $70 million trading in Bre-X stock. The total amount acquired by company insiders was estimated to be $150 million. Approximately 40,000 Canadian investors lost more than $3 billion investing in Bre-X, looking for that lucky strike.

SOURCES: Glen Whelon, "Felderhof Hit by Suit," *Calgary Sun,* December 31, 1997; Sandra Roubin, "Bre-X Board Told in Late 1996 Tests Showed No Busang Gold," *Financial Post,* April 13, 1998.

A serious violation of the public trust occurred in the Bre-X scandal in 1996, involving insider trading, stock manipulation, and management fraud on a scale hardly ever accomplished in Canada, as shown in Exhibit 12.3.

A Case in Point: The Savings and Loan Scandal. This case of management fraud in the savings and loan (S&L) industry cost $500 billion and saw 1,700 banks collapsed. In 1980, the American federal government allowed the S&Ls to expand their business operations so that they could get involved in high-risk commercial real estate lending, offering high interest rates to encourage investors to pour billions of dollars into the banks.

The government insured all deposits, while the banks made irresponsible and fraudulent loans to commercial real estate developers, sometimes involving kickbacks. Other related criminal activity was embezzlement, siphoning funds for personal gain. For example, Erwin Hansen took over Centennial Savings and Loan of California, and then threw a Christmas party for 500 friends and their guests at a cost of $148,000. He travelled in the bank's private airplanes,

pilferage   Theft by employees through stealth or deception.

purchased antiques, refurbished his home at a cost of more than $1 million, bought a fleet of luxury cars, and built an extensive art collection. The commissioner of the California Department of Savings and Loans said in 1987, "The best way to rob a bank is to own one."

Other practices involved outright fraud. Land was "flipped" between conspirators, driving up the price before it was sold for more than it was worth to a bank owned by a co-conspirator. Another method was reciprocal lending in which bank insiders would lend each other money that was never paid back, and then trade the bad loans back and forth to delay discovery of the fraud.

In the aftermath of these white-collar crimes, owners tried to cover up their crimes by using shady accounting practices or fabricated income statements; some of the offenders were respected businesspeople with political connections. For example, when the collapse of Denver-based Silverado Banking Savings and Loan cost taxpayers $1 billion, President George Bush Sr.'s son Neil, who was on Silverado's board of directors, was called to testify before the U.S. House Banking Committee. There he was questioned on his relationships with developers, one of whom had given Bush $100,000 to invest with the condition that they share in the profits but not the losses. Even Neil Bush admitted, "I know it sounds a little fishy."

The crimes were difficult to detect because they revolved around seemingly innocent loans and mortgages made to associates for investment purposes. The investments later turned out to be worthless, and the government was forced to take over the banks.

The S&L crisis was a result of the unregulated finance capitalism that dominated the American economy in the 1980s. Because nothing is produced or sold, financial institutions are ripe for fraud. Their business is the manipulation of money, and the line between smart business practices and white-collar crime is often thin.[54]

So, in 2008, it was like seeing history repeat itself. Perhaps the worst economic crisis since the Depression, it threatened the collapse of financial institutions, banks and major corporations, and the stability of the stock market. Brought on in part by policies that encouraged home ownership, and mortgages that people couldn't afford to pay back, the collapse threatened the stability of the world's economy. By all accounts, the crisis was avoidable, brought on by a lack of regulation and corporate greed. While illegal and unethical acts were identified in the aftermath, no one was ever charged or convicted for their role.

Client Frauds

A sixth component of white-collar crime is theft by a client from an organization that advances credit to its clients. Included in this category are insurance fraud, credit card fraud, welfare and medical insurance fraud, and tax evasion. These offences are grouped together because they involve theft from organizations that have many individual clients who may take advantage of their positions of trust to steal from the organizations.

Healthcare Fraud. Client frauds may be common even among upper-income people.[55] Some physicians have been caught cheating the federal government out of health insurance payments, such as the Toronto chiropractor caught billing the government $65,000 in services he never delivered. Other abusive practices include such techniques as unnecessarily referring patients to other physicians in the same office, billing for multiple services when a single service was rendered, and directing patients to specific pharmacies owned by colleagues.[56]

Of a more serious nature are fraudulent acts designed to cheat both the government and the consumer, such as billing excessive amounts, setting up kickback schemes, and providing false identification on reimbursement forms. For example, an undercover operation in New York State netted 20 professionals who were fraudulently overbilling insurance companies. One doctor saw a patient 11 times and billed for 150 office visits; another treated a patient once and sent in 90 claims. One of the chiropractors was secretly videotaped coaching a patient on how to fake injuries when examined by physicians evaluating his insurance claim.[57]

Bank Fraud. Bank fraud can encompass such diverse schemes as cheque kiting (see Exhibit 12.4), cheque forgery, false statements on loan applications, money laundering, sale of stolen cheques, bank credit card fraud, unauthorized use of automated bank machines (ABMs), auto title frauds, and illegal transactions with offshore banks. For example, a car

EXHIBIT 12.4

Cheque Kiting

Cheque kiting is a scheme in which a client with accounts in two or more banks takes advantage of the time required for cheques to clear to obtain unauthorized use of bank funds. For example, a person has $5,000 on account in a bank and cashes a cheque for $3,000 from an account in another bank in which he or she has no funds. The bank cashes the cheque because this person is already a customer. The fraudster then closes his original account before the bad cheque is discovered or writes cheques on his account that total $5,000, which clear because he has funds in his account. In some instances, the kiter expects the bank to cover a withdrawal before a cheque is presented to another bank for collection: He simply wants a short-term interest-free loan. Others have no intention of ever covering the transaction, but instead want to take cash out of the system after building accounts to artificially high amounts. Kiting can be a multimillion-dollar offence involving cheques written and deposited in banks in two or more provinces or territories and sometimes among banks in multiple countries.

dealership could commit bank fraud by securing loans on titles to cars it no longer owns. Similarly, a real estate owner would be guilty of fraud if a falsely high appraisal were made on property with the intention of obtaining a bank loan in excess of the property's worth.

Tax Evasion. Another important client fraud is tax evasion. Many citizens regularly under-report their income, but it is difficult to separate honest error from deliberate tax evasion. To prove tax fraud, the government must find both that the taxpayer either under-reported or did not report taxable income, and that the taxpayer has purposely attempted to evade or defeat a tax payment. The temptation lures those who provide services under the table and off the books. In Canada, the value of the underground economy is estimated to be as high as 3 percent of the gross national product (GNP). In 2011, the underground economy in Canada was estimated at $41 billion. Illegal activities such as drug trafficking are not included. Industries that were included were construction (28 percent), finance (13 percent), retail (12 percent), and accommodation and food services (12 percent).[58]

If the temptation is high, the likelihood of getting caught is low. In the United States, for example, the number of tax audits has declined, and despite some well-publicized cases, such as a $16 million judgment against singer Willie Nelson, the U.S. Internal Revenue Service has been accused of targeting middle-income taxpayers and ignoring the upper classes and large corporations.

Corporate Crime

The final component of white-collar crime is corporate representatives violating laws that restrain these institutions from doing social harm, known as **corporate crime**, or organizational crime.

Interest in corporate crime emerged in the 1900s, when writers targeted the unscrupulous business practices of John D. Rockefeller and other corporate business leaders.[59] And in 1907, sociologist E.A. Ross described the *criminaloid*, a business leader who victimized an unsuspecting public. Edwin Sutherland further developed the subject in the 1940s.

Corporate crimes are socially injurious acts committed by companies to further their business interests (see Exhibit 12.5). The target of their crimes can be the general public, the environment, or even their own workers (see Exhibit 12.2). The victims of corporate crime can range from the thousands of women with immune system disorders from breast implants, to the 26 miners who died in the Westray coal mine, or the 47 who died in the train explosion in Lac-Mégantic, discussed later. In the Firestone Tire case, the company was sued after 100 people were killed when the tread separated from their tires, causing their vehicles to crash, a problem that could have been fixed for as little as 90 cents a tire.

What makes corporate crimes unique is that the corporation is not an individual, but is what is termed a *legal fiction*. That is, although the corporation may be accused of a corporate crime, in reality company employees or owners commit corporate crimes and ultimately benefit through career advancement or greater profits. Some of the acts included in corporate crime are price-fixing and illegal restraint of trade, false advertising, and company practices that violate environmental protection statutes. The variety of crimes contained within this category is great, and the damage they cause is vast. The following subsections will examine some of the most important offences.

corporate crime A legal violation by a corporate entity, such as price-fixing, restraint of trade, hazardous waste dumping, unfair advertising, or monopolistic practices.

Illegal Restraint of Trade and Price-Fixing.   Restraint of trade involves a contract or conspiracy designed to stifle competition, create a monopoly, artificially maintain prices, or otherwise interfere with competition. A good example of restraint of trade is **price-fixing**, an act that usually takes one of four forms:[60]

- *Predation.* Large firms agree to sell below market prices to drive out weaker firms.
- *Identical bidding.* Competitors agree to submit high identical bids for each contract.
- *Dividing territory.* One member bids a low bid, while conspirators either refrain from bidding or bid high.
- *Rotational bidding.* The opportunity to submit a winning bid is decided by conspirators in advance, often with each conspirator winning a bid in turn at a higher than normal price.

False Claims and Advertising.   Executives in corporations are sometimes caught in the position in which the expectation of profits demands that sales be increased. However, if these executives make product claims that cannot be justified by actual performance, the line between clever, aggressive sales techniques and fraudulent claims may be a fine line in business but a much larger one morally. For example, showing a delivery service vehicle taking off into outer space is not fraudulent; however, knowingly and purposely advertising a product as possessing qualities that it does not have constitutes an illegal claim.

In a classic case in 1991, the third-largest-selling breakfast drink in the United States, Citrus Hill, had billed itself as "pure squeezed" despite being made from concentrate.[61] Orange juice might seem like a minor example; however, what about a car manufacturer's claim that a car yields higher gas mileage than it really does, or a mouthwash maker's claim that its product can cure colds?

In the pharmaceutical industry, medicines are commonly advertised as cures for previously incurable diseases.[62] Such medicines include alleged cures for cancer and arthritis, and drugs advertised to give energy and sexual potency. Competing companies market similar products, and their competitive drive for profits leads to the falsification of data and unethical sales promotions.[63]

Authorities find it difficult to police such violations of the public trust. The most serious consequence is usually an order that the company refrain from using the misleading advertising or that it withdraw the advertising claims.

GREEN-COLLAR CRIME

We can begin thinking about green crime by using the example of environmental crime, which has many types, from endangering the lives of workers because of unsafe conditions in plants and mines, to exposing workers to hazardous materials while on the job. For example, the asbestos industry was inundated with lawsuits after environmental scientists found a close association between exposure to asbestos and the development of cancer.

Another type of environmental crime is illegal pollution of the environment. In 1984, leaking methyl isocyanate from a Union Carbide plant in Bhopal, India, killed an estimated 5,000 to 20,000 people, and injured 60,000.

In another case, the tanker *Exxon Valdez* ran aground on a reef off the coast of Alaska in 1989, dumping 500 million litres of crude oil and fouling 1,100 km of shoreline. Rather than face trial, Exxon agreed to pay $1 billion in criminal and civil fines, then the largest amount paid as a result of environmental pollution, but now overshadowed by the penalty assessed against BP Oil for the rig blowout and subsequent oil spill in the Gulf in 2010. Under U.S. law, BP employees or subcontractors could be held legally responsible if they had lied in the process of acquiring permits, tried to cover up the extent of the spill, or engaged in negligence that resulted in the spill. This event is the feature of the Crime in the News exhibit.

Some other environmental disasters in the news illustrate the fine line between an accident and a crime. At the Canadian-owned Los Frailes mine in Spain, five million cubic metres of toxic mine waste spilled through a break in a mine tailings pond, contaminating thousands of hectares of farming land. In another example, the Canadian-owned Omai gold mine in Georgetown, Guyana, was the site of a massive cyanide spill from a tailings pond. The mine was developed by Canadian Robert Friedland, who had been sued by the American government for a huge environmental spill of cyanide at the Summitville gold mine in Colorado.

Could these disasters have been prevented by adequate environmental safeguards? Are they more likely to happen in poor countries that are heavily dependent on resource extraction? Some question remains whether environmental legislation can be enforced well enough to deter environmental crime. Lack of effective regulation was certainly an issue at the Westray mine. In 2004, the Westray bill came into effect, making organizations and senior officers liable for criminal acts related to workplace safety, but such was not the case in 1992. See Exhibit 12.6 for more about the Westray Mine disaster, and its parallels more than 20 years later in the Lac-Mégantic train disaster.

Move forward about twenty years. On July 6, 2013, a 73-car freight train rolled into Lac-Mégantic carrying crude oil. It was unmanned and had been parked overnight. There had been a small fire on the train earlier that day, and it was alleged that it was not properly secured afterward. When it

price-fixing   A form of corporate crime, where companies conspire together to artificially inflate the price of goods.

CHAPTER 12 | **Crimes of Power: White-Collar, Corporate, and Organized Crime**

News from the United States says federal prosecutors are considering whether to charge BP managers for their role in the Gulf of Mexico oil well explosion last year.

That explosion killed 11 workers and caused the biggest offshore spill in history.

The explosion occurred aboard the Deepwater Horizon rig on April 20, 2010. London-based BP, formerly named British Petroleum, leased the rig from Transocean Ltd. of Switzerland.

Under U.S. law, those involved in the spill can face a fine, a civil lawsuit, or criminal sanctions.

Pursuing sanctions against those involved would be done in the interests of punishment, but also for general deterrence. Since decisions to compromise safety are, in the short term, profitable, a message has to be sent to large companies that they are not outside the law.

A civil lawsuit is already ongoing, and it has been estimated that the fine could run as high as $10 billion, far higher than that paid by Exxon after the Valdez oil tanker ran aground off the coast of Alaska in 1989. In addition, BP has already paid out $4 billion in compensation and cleanup costs.

The difficulty of pursuing certain charges is the scope of penalties that are possible. Under the *Clean Water Act* and the *Migratory Bird Act*, penalties are low because they are misdemeanours. What the government needs is a stick large enough to convince people that taking such risks are unconscionable.

The risks taken were predictable, and the result preventable. The allegation is that managers made decisions that sacrificed safety in favour of speed and profit.

Corporate records and executive emails have been investigated to see whether executives minimized known risks and whether they knew about them prior to the explosion.

Investigators also want to determine if they whitewashed their testimony at hearings before the U.S. Congress last June in an attempt to minimize their liability.

It's now known that because the rock formation around the well drill hole kept cracking and collapsing, changes were made repeatedly to the well plan. In addition, the presidential commission investigating the disaster identified 11 choices that were made that saved time but increased risks.

These managerial decisions included operating without recommended equipment, not running tests to ensure the well's stability, ignoring warnings that the well design could allow leaks, misreading tests, and not using the recommended number of stabilizers for cement in the well.

As a result, in the interest of rushing to production, steps were taken and decisions were made that allowed natural gas to leak to the oil rig. The resulting explosion killed 11 workers.

The risk was predicted, the risk could have been prevented. It was not.

In some cases of corporate crime, there have been what are called deferred prosecutions, where the companies involved have been able to avoid prosecution by paying large fines.

However, in this case, such a route would not be politically attractive. So lawsuits are up and running, and criminal charges are probably pending.

What is interesting about the criminal charges is that they will probably be for negligence on the part of those working both on and off shore. These charges will be involuntary manslaughter or seaman's manslaughter.

Seaman's manslaughter is an offence created in 1838, and then revised in 1852, which allows for the prosecution of those who failed to take action to protect the lives of those on steamboats. These boats were highly flammable and thousands of people died over the years.

The most notable case was the General Slocum of 1904, when more than a thousand people died in a single event. The investigation showed that fire drills were not practised, and the firehoses and life jackets were rotten. The ship's captain, company executives, and an inspector were all indicted, and the captain was convicted of manslaughter.

The seaman's manslaughter charge does not require showing intent to harm, rather that there is negligence to prevent harm. It's an old tool that has been dusted off for a new use, to prosecute environmental violations and to punish workplace homicide.

It's an old tool and a little blunt, but it can deliver a strong wallop.

SOURCE: Copyright Chris McCormick, in the *Daily Gleaner* (Fredericton), April 7, 2011.

rolled into the small town in Quebec, it derailed and caught on fire. The resulting fireball destroyed 30 buildings and businesses, and 47 people were dead or missing. Subsequent inquiries found thousands of derailments, incomplete manifests for cargo, and insufficient supervision of dangerous cargo. Was this an accident or a corporate crime? Westray was a crime against workers, but no one was charged and no one was convicted.

Lac-Mégantic was a crime against the public, and in 2014 it was announced that 47 charges of negligence were to be laid against three employees and the company, U.S.-based Montreal Maine and Atlantic (MMA) Railway. The employees were the train's engineer, the manager of train operations, and the traffic controller. The MMA Railway is now defunct, so it is unclear where charges against it will go. The train crash was the worst in 150 years, and was the subject of intense scrutiny. Canada's Transport Agency said that the type of car involved in the crash must be taken out of service or retrofitted because they were known to be prone to rupturing. An accident waiting to happen? So it would seem.

EXHIBIT 12.6

The Tragedy of Westray

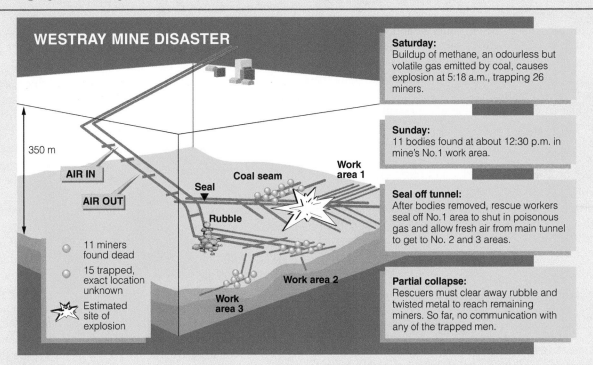

WESTRAY MINE DISASTER

350 m

AIR IN

AIR OUT

Coal seam

Seal

Rubble

Work area 1

Work area 2

Work area 3

○ 11 miners found dead

○ 15 trapped, exact location unknown

☆ Estimated site of explosion

Saturday:
Buildup of methane, an odourless but volatile gas emitted by coal, causes explosion at 5:18 a.m., trapping 26 miners.

Sunday:
11 bodies found at about 12:30 p.m. in mine's No.1 work area.

Seal off tunnel:
After bodies removed, rescue workers seal off No.1 area to shut in poisonous gas and allow fresh air from main tunnel to get to No. 2 and 3 areas.

Partial collapse:
Rescuers must clear away rubble and twisted metal to reach remaining miners. So far, no communication with any of the trapped men.

FIGURE 12.2
Westray Mine Disaster Map

Source: *The Toronto Star*, May 11, 1992, p. A1. Reproduced with permission of Torstar Syndication Services.

In 1987, the Nova Scotia government was looking for someone to take over the stalled Westray mine in Plymouth, Pictou County. Clifford Frame of Curragh Mining agreed to develop the mine, despite studies pointing out dangers such as the high concentrations of methane gas.

A deal brokered with provincial and federal politicians was announced three days before the provincial election in 1988. Westray was to receive $85 million in the form of a federal loan guarantee, plus a $12 million provincial loan. A lucrative 15-year contract was signed with Nova Scotia Power, despite the availability elsewhere of cleaner, cheaper coal.

Labour Department inspection reports showed that between 1991 and 1992, the mine's owners were cautioned about methane gas levels, improper storage of flammable materials, and the use of unauthorized equipment. No charges were laid. Despite cave-ins and a roof collapse, mining began in 1991, and changes were made to the mine's design without the knowledge or approval of the Department of Natural Resources.

On May 9, 1992, at 5:18 a.m., a methane explosion ignited a build-up of coal dust in the mine, and 26 miners were killed. As Figure 12.2 shows, the explosion happened deep underground, making it impossible for workers to escape.

The RCMP launched a criminal investigation, and a provincial inquiry was commissioned to determine whether neglect had contributed to the disaster. In October, the Nova Scotia Department of Labour charged Curragh and four mine managers with 52 violations of the *Occupational Health and Safety Act*; the maximum penalty was $10,000. In November 1992, the Supreme Court of Nova Scotia quashed the inquiry, and in December the safety charges were dropped. In April 1993, Curragh and two underground managers were charged with manslaughter and criminal negligence, but charges were thrown out for being too vague. Curragh went into receivership, and charges were relaid against the two managers.

In 1995, the criminal trial began, but four months later the proceedings were stayed by the judge, who ruled that the prosecution did not properly disclose evidence. In December, the Nova Scotia Court of Appeal subsequently quashed the appeal, and the likelihood that anyone would face criminal charges looked increasingly grim. In March 1997, the Supreme Court of Canada upheld the new trial order.

By 1998, six years had elapsed since the explosion. The Government of Nova Scotia announced it would not pursue criminal charges, Curragh was bankrupt, and Frame wouldn't testify before the provincial inquiry. The inquiry's report, based on 17,000 pages of oral testimony, was released, citing extensive problems with government regulation. The John T. Ryan Trophy Committee of the Canadian Institute of Mining, Metallurgy and Petroleum, which had declared the Westray mine the safest colliery in Canada a month before it exploded, announced that it would adopt measures to ensure that companies do not fudge accident statistics. The miners' families decided that they must move on, and the province announced that it would dismantle the Westray minehead.

SOURCES: Shaun Comish, *The Westray Tragedy: A Miner's Story* (Halifax: Fernwood, 1993); Dean Jobb, *Calculated Risk: Greed, Politics, and the Westray Tragedy* (Halifax: Nimbus, 1994); *The Westray Story: A Predictable Path to Disaster,* Report of the Westray Mine Public Inquiry (Halifax, 1997).

Oil spills and other such disasters are just part of the green crime problem. Environmental activists have long called attention to a variety of ecological threats that they feel should be deemed criminal, although politicians might disagree. Green crimes involve a wide range of actions and outcomes that harm the environment and stem from decisions about what is produced, where it is produced, and how it is produced. Global warming, overdevelopment, population growth, and other changes will continue to bring these issues front and centre.

While crimes targeting the environment have received scant attention in the criminological literature, recent events have shifted attention to what is variously called green crime, green criminology, and green-collar crime. The Gulf Coast disaster in 2010 is a powerful and tragic example of how environmental destruction and green crimes may be linked to enterprise systems: the need for corporate profit may outweigh attention to safety, with subsequent catastrophic consequences to the environment.

Defining Green Crime

The concept of green crimes has several different definitions:

- *Legalist*. In this perspective, environmental crimes are violations of existing criminal laws designed to protect people, and the environment. This definition includes occupational health and safety crimes, and laws designed to protect nature and the environment.
- *Environmental justice*. According to this view, limiting environmental crimes to actual violations of the criminal law is too narrow. A great deal of environmental damage occurs in poorer areas willing to give mining and oil companies a free hand to develop resources. In addition, corporations can manipulate environmental laws, for example, through public relations and advertising campaigns that suggest they respect the environment and therefore don't need government regulation.
- *Biocentric*. According to this approach, environmental harm is viewed as any human activity that disrupts a biosystem, destroying plant and animal life. This more radical approach would criminalize any intentional or negligent human activity or manipulation that negatively affects Earth's natural resources, resulting in trauma to those resources. Environmental harm is much greater than what current law defines as environmental crimes, which are typically oriented toward protecting humans and their property and have a limited interest in protecting animals and plants. Environmental laws protect animal and fish processing plants that treat "nature" and "wildlife" simply and mainly as resources for human exploitation. Human beings are the cause of environmental harm and need to be controlled.

Forms of Green Crime

Green-collar crime can take many different forms, ranging from deforestation and illegal logging to violations of worker safety. A few of the most damaging forms are set out below.

Illegal Logging. Illegal logging involves harvesting, processing, and transporting timber or wood products in violation of existing laws and treaties. It is a universal phenomenon, occurring in major timber producing countries, especially in developing countries, where enforcement is lax. Logging violations include taking trees in protected areas such as national parks, exceeding legally prescribed logging quotas, processing logs without acquiring licences, and exporting logs without paying export duties. By sidestepping the law, loggers can create greater profits than can be generated through legal methods.

The situation is serious because illegal logging can have severe environmental and social impact. Illegal logging in central Africa is destroying the habitats and threatening the survival of the great apes. It causes deforestation, which can lead to flash floods and landslides. By reducing forest cover, illegal logging impairs the ability of land to absorb carbon emissions and each year costs billions of dollars in government revenue, impairing the ability to provide needed social services. It creates unsustainable economic devastation in the poorest countries. Vietnam, for example, has lost a third of its forest cover, while in nearby Cambodia, illegal logging is at least 10 times the size of the legal harvest. These rates of extraction are clearly unsustainable, destroying valuable future sources of both employment and export revenues. The substantial revenues from illegal logging fund national and regional conflict. In Cambodia, Khmer Rouge insurgents were sustained for several years, primarily by the revenue from logging areas under their control.

While the scale of illegal logging is difficult to estimate, more than half of all logging activities in the world's most vulnerable forest regions—southeast Asia, central Africa, South America, and Russia—is believed to be conducted illegally. Worldwide, estimates suggest that illegal activities may account for over a tenth of the total global timber trade, representing products worth at least $15 billion per year.

Illegal Wildlife Exports. The smuggling of wildlife across national borders includes illicit commodities such as tiger parts, caviar, elephant ivory, rhino horn, and exotic birds and reptiles. Wildlife contraband may include live pets, hunting trophies, fashion accessories, cultural artifacts, ingredients for traditional medicines, wild meat for human consumption (or bush meat), and other products. Illegal profits can be immense.

Poachers imperil endangered species and threaten them with extinction, and create the potential for introducing pests and diseases into formerly unaffected areas. They import non-native species, which could harm the receiving habitats. Illegal wildlife traders range from independent one-person operations that sell a single item, to complex, multi-ton, commercial-sized consignments shipped all over the world. Adding all these sources together, the global trade in illegal wildlife is estimated to be between $5 billion and $20 billion annually.

Illegal Fishing.
Unlicensed and illegal fishing can take on many forms and may involve highly different parties, such as huge factory ships operating on the high seas that catch thousands of tons of fish on each voyage. When such catches are not reported by the fishing vessels, their illegal fishing can have a detrimental effect on species: because government regulators have no idea how many species have been caught, stocks can become depleted and species endangered. In addition, illegal fishing techniques, including fishermen using the wrong-sized nets or fishing in prohibited areas, can damage fragile marine ecosystems, threatening coral reefs, turtles, and seabirds. In underdeveloped nations, regulators may look the other way because the need for short-term economic, social, or political gains is given more weight than long-term sustainability. As a result, species of whales, abalone, groundfish, and lobsters have become endangered.

Illegal Dumping.
Some green-collar criminals want to skirt restrictions on dumping dangerous substances in the environment. Illegally dumped wastes are discarded in an effort to avoid either disposal fees or the time and effort required for proper disposal. Two substances commonly disposed of illegally are motor oil and waste from construction sites.

A growing problem is the disposal of millions of tons of obsolete high-tech electronics, called e-waste, such as televisions, computers and computer monitors, laptops, VCRs, and so on. In some jurisdictions, in an effort to avoid recycling costs, e-waste is sent abroad to developing nations for recycling, but the extent of the e-waste can overwhelm recycling plants and may end up being dumped in local villages near people and water sources. Such illegal dump sites have been documented in Nigeria, Ghana, China, the Philippines, Indonesia, Pakistan, and India, where they pose severe threats to both human health and the natural environment.

Illegal Polluting.
As mentioned above, prior to the BP spill, the most notorious environmental disaster occurred when the oil tanker *Exxon Valdez* hit a reef in Prince William Sound and devastated Prudhoe Bay on the coast of Alaska. The spill released more than 500 million litres of crude oil, which fouled 1,100 km of shoreline. The resulting water pollution killed 250,000 sea birds, 2,800 sea otters, 300 harbour seals, 250 bald eagles, up to 22 orcas, and billions of salmon and herring eggs. Exxon Mobil was fined $150 million; paid an additional $100 million as restitution for damage caused to fish, wildlife, and land; and agreed to pay $900 million in 10 annual installments to civil claimants. In 1994, a jury found that Exxon acted recklessly and awarded victims $5 billion in punitive damages. The U.S. Supreme Court cut the amount to $507.5 million in June 2008, hardly a day's pay for the largest company on Earth.

Because of the *Exxon Valdez* disaster and other environmental crimes, much attention is now paid to intentional or negligent environmental pollution caused by many large corporations.

Enforcing Environmental Laws.
In 1971, the Canadian government established a new federal department, Environment Canada, to protect the environment. Environment Canada uses various acts and regulations to enforce its mandate, including legislation regarding environmental protection, migratory birds, species at risk, fisheries, pest control, and so on. In addition, the provinces and territories have their own network of regulations covering pesticides, transportation of dangerous goods, fish and wildlife, and so on. Legal constraints on green-collar crime are complex, sometimes vague, and often difficult to enforce. Sanctions can be levied for non-compliance, negligence, and violations of the law. Green-collar offences are increasingly seen as important to control, as evidenced by governments imposing new environmental restrictions and civil lawsuits forcing the adoption of new environmental standards. Green-collar crime is an important new focus for criminology.

THE CAUSE OF WHITE-COLLAR CRIME

When Ivan Boesky pleaded guilty to security fraud, he paid a fine of $100 million, the largest at that time in U.S. SEC history. How, many asked, can people with so much disposable wealth get involved in a risky scheme to produce even more, a question made even more obvious when we look at the nearby Comparative Criminology box on white-collar crime in Britain.

Offenders who engage in business crime convince themselves that their behaviour is not criminal because the acts involved do not resemble street crimes. For example, a banker who uses a position of trust to lend an institution's assets to a company he secretly controls may see himself as doing shrewd business. A pharmacist who chisels customers on prescription drugs may rationalize that it does not really hurt anyone. Businesspeople feel justified in committing white-collar crimes because they believe that government regulators do not understand the problems of competing in the free enterprise system. Because "everyone" breaks the law, it is not bad if they do so themselves. Neutralizing their greed is a common trait of white-collar criminals not unlike those justifications used by other criminals. It is just a matter of scale.

Greedy or Needy?

Executives tamper with company books because they feel the need to keep or improve their jobs and satisfy their egos.

Comparative Criminology
Snakes and Ladders: Confronting White-Collar Crime in Britain

How do otherwise law-abiding people cope with the emotional turmoil created when they are cast as white-collar criminals? This issue was explored by Sara Willott, Christine Griffin, and Mark Torrance through a series of interviews they conducted with groups of working-class and professional men in Great Britain who had been convicted of white-collar offences.

Willott and her colleagues found that members of both groups used linguistic devices to justify their behaviour. The working-class men argued that they were forced by dire economic circumstances to commit crime. Their crimes were not for personal gain but simply to feed their families. They also viewed themselves as modern-day Robin Hoods who were taking from the rich to help the poor, in this case their own families. Rather than accept blame, they positioned themselves as decent men who were forced to commit crimes: It was not their fault but the government's for failing to provide them with a safety net during a time of financial crisis. And, having been forced into crime by an unfair system, the men claimed they were revictimized and humiliated when sent to prison. They viewed themselves as the bottom of life's barrel, as pawns similar to the ones used in the children's game Snakes and Ladders. They were being kept in place by powerful forces beyond their control.

The professional men used some similar linguistic tools to justify their behaviour. They also saw themselves as breadwinners who used other people's money to help their families. But, unlike the blue-collar workers, they saw their professional responsibilities as adding to their burden. As businesspeople, they saw themselves as protectors of a wider circle of dependants, including their employees and their families. They did not steal but were "digging into funds" when the need arose. They were careful to point out that they did not use the funds to support an extravagant lifestyle but to shoulder the responsibility they had been socialized to carry. The professionals were aware of the high social standing demanded by their profession and lifestyle. Along with power come the obligations of power, and they were forced to violate the law to meet these obligations.

Some of the professional men viewed themselves as victims of bureaucrats who relentlessly pursued them to enhance their careers in government. They viewed law enforcers, many of whom had lower-class backgrounds, as ruthlessly ambitious people who used the prosecutions as stepping stones to success. Class envy, then, was responsible in part for their current dilemma.

The businesspeople believed the conditions that produced their descent were not of their doing and were beyond their control. Economic decline and recession had pushed them down the slippery slope. And, once in the system, their entire world was rocked to its very foundations. They were aliens in a strange land of courts and correctional facilities: They complained that as professionals they had fallen out of the structures of our lives. And even though they viewed themselves as competent professionals in the business world, their amateurism as criminals helped get them into their current predicament. They sought to distinguish themselves as being morally superior to both working-class criminals and the justice officials who led them to their disgrace.

Critical Thinking

Willott and her colleagues found that both working-class and professional-class white-collar offenders created elaborate justifications for their behaviour. They were pawns in an economic and social system beyond their control. Do their findings seem similar to Cressey's earlier research, which indicates that white-collar criminals are more likely to view themselves as victims than predators?

SOURCE: Based on Sara Willott, Christine Griffin, and Mark Torrance, "Snakes and Ladders: Upper-Middle-Class Male Offenders Talk about Economic Crime," *Criminology* 39 (2001): 441–466.

Many white-collar crimes involve relatively trivial amounts: Women convicted of white-collar crime typically work in lower-echelon positions, and their acts are motivated more by economic survival than by greed and power.[64] Sometimes, perhaps, even people in the upper echelons of the financial world, such as Ivan Boesky, may be working from a more basic emotional insecurity.

Embezzlement is caused by a "nonshareable financial problem"[65] and may, for example, be the result of offenders living beyond their means and piling up gambling debts. Solving personal financial problems through criminal means begins by using the rationalizations that society has developed for white-collar crime, as in these typical phrases: "Many people get their start in life by using other people's money"; "in real estate, there is nothing wrong with using deposits before the deal is closed"; "anybody will steal if they get in a tight spot." Rationalizations allow offenders' financial needs to be met without compromising their values.

Of the many theories of white-collar crime, we next examine two of the more prominent ones: corporate culture theory and the self-control view.

Corporate Culture Theory

Some business organizations promote white-collar criminality in the same way that lower-class culture encourages the development of juvenile gangs and street crime. Business enterprises cause crime by placing excessive demands on employees while maintaining a business climate tolerant of employee deviance. New employees learn the attitudes and techniques needed to commit white-collar crime from their business peers in a learning process similar to how gang members learn the techniques of drug dealing and burglary from older youths through differential association.

Criminologists use corporate culture and structure to explain white-collar crime. For example, business organizations will encourage employee criminality when firms encounter difficulties in attaining goals, especially making profits. Some organizations will create cost-reduction policies that inspire lawbreaking and corner-cutting to become norms passed on to employees. When new employees balk at violating business laws, they are told: "This is the way things are done here, don't worry about it." A business's organizational environment influences white-collar crime. Conditions for corporate crime are maximized when market conditions are weak, competition intense, law enforcement lax, and managers are willing to stress success at any cost.[66]

Corporate culture theory is analogous to the cultural deviance approach, suggesting that crime occurs when obedience to subculture norms and values causes people to break the rules of conventional society. However, cultural deviance theory was originally directed at lower-class slum boys, not business executives. However, the same crime-producing forces may be operating in both socio-economic groups.

Corporate Climate.
John Braithwaite, in his writings on white-collar crime, has said that businesspeople in any society may find themselves in a situation where their organization's stated goals cannot be achieved through conventional business practices.[67] For example, executives may find that their profit ratios are below par and that illegitimate opportunities are the only solution to their problem. Thus, when a government official is willing to take a bribe to overlook costly safety violations, the bribe is gratefully offered. Similarly, when insider trading can increase profits, the investment banker may leap at the chance. But how can traditionally law-abiding people overcome the ties of conventional law and morality?

If corporations contain an employee subculture that resists government regulation and socializes new workers in the skills and attitudes necessary to violate the law, junior executives may learn from seniors how to meet with competitors to fix prices. When governmental agencies are viewed as uncooperative and resistant to change, corporations will be more likely to develop clandestine, law-violating subcultures. A positive working relationship with governmental overseers will reduce the need for a secret, law-violating infrastructure to develop. Illegal corporate behaviour can exist only in secrecy; public scrutiny brings the shame of a criminal label to people whose social life and community standing rests on their good name and character.

Shame of Discovery.
The shame of discovery has an important moderating influence. Its source may be external: the community, peers, or government regulatory agencies. The source of shame and disapproval can also be internal:

Bernie Madoff leaves a bail hearing in 2009, after being accused of running a US$50 billion Ponzi scheme through his investment company.

corporate policies that admonish employees to obey the rule of law. For example, some corporations encourage whistleblowing by co-workers to sanction workers who violate the law and cause embarrassment. In a sense, corporations that maintain an excess of definitions unfavourable to violating the law will be less likely than those that don't to contain deviant subcultures and business violations. In contrast, corporate crime thrives in organizations that isolate people within spheres of responsibility, where lines of communication are blocked, thereby allowing deviant subcultures to develop.

Thus, corporate culture theorists would view the 2008 financial collapse as a prime example of what happens when people work in organizations whose cultural values stress profit over fair play, where government scrutiny is limited and regulators are viewed as the enemy, and where senior members encourage newcomers to believe that greed is good.

The Self-Control View

Hirschi and Gottfredson take exception to the idea that white-collar crime is a product of the corporate culture.[68] If that were true, society would experience much more white-collar crime, and criminals would not be embarrassed. Instead, the motives that produce white-collar crimes are the same motives that produce any other crime: the desire for quick, certain benefit with minimal effort. Hirschi and Gottfredson's general theory holds that criminals lack self-control. White-collar criminals are people with low self-control who follow momentary impulses without consideration of long-term costs. White-collar crime is rare because executives hire people with self-control, limiting the number of potential white-collar criminals.

Data show that the demographic distribution of white-collar crime is similar to that for other crimes. For example,

CHAPTER 12 | **Crimes of Power: White-Collar, Corporate, and Organized Crime** gender, race, and age ratios are the same for such crimes as embezzlement and fraud as they are for street crimes, such as burglary and robbery.

Business executives and corporate executives may seem to be people who would have above-average self-control.[69] However, some white-collar criminals are repeat offenders, sharing characteristics with street criminals (such as being impulsive and egocentric), although they begin their careers later in life.[70]

Even if this view is accurate, white-collar offenders may manifest a wide range of self-control, which determines the path they take to crime. People with low self-control of their impulsivity commit fraud and other crimes in self-interest, as do common criminals. Others with high self-control pursue ego gratification in an aggressive and calculating fashion. In the middle are offenders who take advantage of criminal opportunities to satisfy an immediate personal need; in them, self-control becomes overwhelmed by special problems. Self-control is a variable that interacts with need and opportunity to produce white-collar crimes.[71]

CONTROLLING WHITE-COLLAR CRIME

Conflict theorists argue that, unlike lower-class street criminals, white-collar criminals are rarely prosecuted and, when convicted, receive relatively light sentences.[72] Physicians who engage in medical insurance fraud are rarely prosecuted, and when they are, judges are reluctant to severely punish them. As one official explained, "When we convicted a guy, I wanted to see him do hard time. But what the hell, seeing what's going on in prisons these days and things like that, I think to put one of these guys in prison for hard time doesn't make any sense."[73] An analysis of 477 corporations found that only 1 in 10 serious and 1 in 20 moderate violations resulted in sanctions. When white-collar statutes are enforced, the tendency is to investigate, prosecute, and penalize small, powerless businesses while treating the market leaders more leniently.[74]

Many reasons explain the leniency afforded white-collar criminals. Although white-collar criminals may produce millions of dollars of losses and endanger human life, some judges believe they are not "real criminals" but businesspeople just trying to make a living. Businesspeople seek legal advice, are well aware of the loopholes, and can claim that they had sought legal advice and had believed they were in compliance with the law. White-collar criminals are often considered non-dangerous offenders because they are respectable, older citizens who have families to support.

These pillars of the community are not seen in the same light as a teenager who breaks into a drugstore to steal a few dollars. Their public humiliation at being caught is usually deemed punishment enough; a prison sentence seems unnecessarily cruel.

Judges and prosecutors may identify with the white-collar criminal because of shared background and worldviews.[75] Another factor complicating white-collar crime enforcement is that many legal business and governmental acts seem as morally tinged as those made illegal by government regulation. It may seem unfair to prosecutors and judges to penalize some government and business officials for actions not too dissimilar from those applauded on Bay Street or in pages of the *Financial Post,* or the *Globe and Mail's* Report on Business.

Finally, some corporate practices that result in death or disfigurement are treated as civil actions in which victims receive monetary damages. The Dalkon Shield intrauterine device (IUD) caused massive trauma to hundreds of thousands of women, including pelvic disease, infertility, septic abortions, and a suspected 20 deaths. The company went bankrupt and set up a multibillion-dollar trust for the survivors. Bristol Myers Squibb set up a trust fund to compensate victims who suffered because their products used in breast implant surgery were deemed defective and dangerous. Leading American tobacco companies agreed to set up a multibillion-dollar trust to compensate smokers and their families for illness and death related to smoking. Although these cases involve much more serious injury than, say, insider trading, they are not considered criminal matters.

White-Collar Law Enforcement Systems

The detection of white-collar crime is primarily in the hands of government inspectorates and agencies.[76] Usually, the decision to pursue criminal rather than civil violations is based on the seriousness of the case.

For example, provincial and territorial departments of labour have their own investigators, and enforcement is both reactive (generated by complaints) and proactive (involving ongoing investigations or the monitoring of activities). In Canada, the RCMP has made enforcement of white-collar laws one of its top three priorities (along with combating foreign counterintelligence and organized crime); see the nearby Criminology Research box, "Why the Mounties Can't Get Their Man."

Prosecutors will pursue white-collar criminals more vigorously if they are part of a team effort that includes a network of law enforcement agencies.[77] However, local prosecutors might not consider white-collar crimes particularly serious. They are more willing to prosecute cases if the offence caused substantial harm and other agencies failed to take action.

A growing number of people believe upper-class criminals are not above the law. However, funds and staff needed for white-collar prosecutions are often scarce. Crimes considered more serious, such as drug trafficking, usually take precedence over corporate violations. However, concern over the environment may encourage prosecutors to take action against those who violate pollution and antidumping laws.

Corporate Policing

White-collar crime law enforcement is often left to business organizations themselves. However, corporate structures can be crime facilitative or crime inhibiting. Corporations spend hundreds of millions of dollars each year on internal audits that help unearth white-collar offences:

- *Security strategies* employ security personnel who guard merchandise and conduct surveillance (using closed-circuit TV, or CCTV); passive security includes passes and key cards to restrict access.
- *Screening and education strategies* use screening, background checks, and personality and integrity tests to screen applicants; employees are taught to report problems.
- *Whistle-blowing strategies* create hotlines so that employees can report theft anonymously; however, employees may be reluctant to report fellow workers.[78]

James Williams, a sociologist at the University of Windsor, suggests that private agencies control white-collar crime through internal policing in the form of forensic accounting, marking a division of public and private networks of risk and security.[79]

White-Collar Control Strategies: Compliance

If white-collar criminals avoid prosecution, and those who are prosecuted receive lenient punishments, what efforts have been made to bring violators of the public trust to justice? White-collar enforcement typically involves two strategies designed to control organizational deviance: compliance and deterrence.[80]

Compliance strategies aim for conformity without the necessity of detecting or penalizing violators. They seek cooperation and self-policing within the business community, creating conformity by providing economic incentives to companies to obey the law. Compliance depends on the threat of economic sanctions or civil penalties to control violators, such as the risk of being prosecuted for securities violations.

Administrative agencies can oversee business activity, with legislation spelling out penalties for violating regulatory standards. This approach has been used to control environmental crimes, by levying heavy fines that are based on the quantity and the quality of pollution released into the environment.[81] Sometimes, people and businesses are barred from receiving government contracts if they are found to have engaged in fraudulent practices, such as bribing public officials.[82] Strict enforcement of penalties under the *Occupational Health and Safety Act* can significantly reduce workplace injuries.[83]

In sum, compliance strategies attempt to create a marketplace incentive to obey the law; for example, the more a company pollutes, the more costly and unprofitable that pollution becomes. Compliance strategies limit individual blame and avoid stigmatizing and shaming businesspeople by focusing on the act rather than on the actor.[84]

Economic sanctions have limited value because penalties are imposed after crimes have occurred, and often amount to only a slap on the wrist.[85] Compliance is particularly difficult to achieve if the federal government adopts a pro-business, anti-regulation policy that encourages economic growth by removing controls over business. It is also difficult to achieve when multinational corporations have sufficient resources not only to resist prosecution but also to use the courts to their own advantage.

Corporations hit with fines and regulatory fees can pass the costs on to consumers in the form of higher prices or reduced services. Shareholders who had little to do with the crime may see their stock dividends cut or share prices fall. Fines and penalties may also be insignificant for a company doing billions of dollars in annual business. For a large Canadian brokerage company, such as First Marathon, a fine of millions of dollars represents a small fraction of its total revenue. Similarly, when Baxter International was banned from bidding on new federal contracts, the punishment was a blow to its corporate reputation, but its total annual revenue still amounted to $8.5 billion.[86]

Because of these problems, the punishment of white-collar crimes should contain a retributive component similar to that used in common-law crimes. White-collar crimes, after all, are immoral activities that have harmed social values and deserve commensurate punishment.[87] Furthermore, corporations can get around economic sanctions by moving their rule-violating activities overseas, where legal controls over injurious corporate activities are lax or non-existent.[88]

> **compliance** A white-collar enforcement strategy that encourages law-abiding behaviour through both the threat of economic sanctions and the promise of rewards for conformity.

Criminology Research
Why the Mounties Can't Get Their Man

Canada has been the setting for some spectacular frauds: John C. Doyle and Canadian Javelin Limited; Lenny Rosenberg, Bill Player, and Ontario's $500-million Cadillac Fairview apartment flip; the collapse of the Principal Group of companies in Alberta; and most recently, the Bre-X gold stock scam. Some of the swindles have been stunningly well planned and daringly executed. Toronto stockbroker Christopher Horne, for example, built a world-class art collection with money he embezzled from clients. Montreal-based Castor Holdings sucked as much as $1.8 billion from victims around the world in a 15-year Ponzi scheme, a pyramid scam where money raised from new investors was used to pay off earlier investors.

Toronto has achieved the distinction of many experts as the North American capital of organized criminal fraud, surpassing even such hotbeds of white-collar crime as south Florida, Houston, Orange County in California, and the suburbs of New York City. Extradition laws that make it difficult to expel white-collar crooks are part of the problem. Cutbacks in the justice system have forced compromises in both law enforcement and prosecution. Crown attorneys across the country have been given extraordinary powers to choose cases to prosecute, and police forces deploy resources to address the concerns of interest groups. These factors, combined with Canada's lax banking and securities laws, tough privacy legislation, increasing constitutional restrictions on the police, and a disinclination by politicians to declare all-out war on white-collar crime, have created fertile ground for fraudulent business practices to flourish.

Some experts say that the conditions are close to ideal. "If a fraud is committed against a bank or a Fortune 500 company, the police aren't interested," says Toronto forensic accountant Tedd Avey. "The big companies are on their own. All the police want to deal with are investment scams, widows and orphans and, perhaps, government as victims." Twenty years ago the RCMP was internationally renowned for its success in putting fraud artists behind bars. "Today," he says, "criminals know it's pretty well open season in Canada. They know they're not going to go to jail."

Others agree. "There's so much fraud that the police can't keep up," says Pat McKernan, a commercial crime officer who left the Mounties in 1995 and now heads security for Western Canada at Imperial Oil Ltd. in Calgary. A veteran RCMP officer says that if a crook wants to commit fraud, "Canada is the place to come and do it." Added the Mountie: "Over the years, we have lost the ability and will to investigate fraud. As a result, the criminals have no fear of the police. It's a terrible situation."

So what are the authorities doing to combat white-collar crime? The answer, according to police and civilian experts, is that financially strapped police forces across the country—following the lead of the RCMP—are getting out of commercial crime investigation. Metropolitan Toronto police have a two-year backlog of fraud investigations—and will not even look at scams involving less than $1 million....

Over the years, the RCMP has attempted to adjust to the changing demands of its political masters. It has made itself less militaristic, promoted bilingualism, opened its ranks to women, recruited members of visible minorities, hired civilians for non-policing jobs, decentralized administration and operations, and embraced advanced technology. It has even learned to act more like a business, generating revenue for the government by, among other things, confiscating the assets of drug dealers and other criminals.

Despite its efforts to modernize, however, the RCMP keeps running up against one immutable fact—there are not enough resources available for the force to carry out its panoply of federal, provincial, and municipal policing tasks, let alone keep

White-Collar Control Strategies: Deterrence

Deterrence strategies involve detecting criminal violations, determining who is responsible, and penalizing them to deter future violations. Punishment serves as a warning to potential violators who might break the rules. Deterrence systems are oriented toward apprehending violators and punishing them rather than creating conditions that induce conformity to the law.

Deterrence strategies should work because white-collar crime is a rational act whose perpetrators are extremely sensitive to the threat of criminal sanctions. In numerous instances, prison sentences for corporate crimes have produced a significant decline in white-collar activity. The perceptions of detection and punishment for white-collar crimes appear to be powerful deterrents to future law violations.[89]

Punishing White-Collar Criminals. Some dramatic examples of deterrence strategies have been used by federal,

> **deterrence** The act of preventing crime before it occurs by means of the threat of criminal sanctions; the perception that the pain of punishment outweighs the criminal gain or profit.

pace with today's sophisticated criminals. Since 1992, the number of RCMP officers has declined 4.2 percent, to 14,997 from 15,661, while the population has grown 6.3 percent. And over the same period, far from seeing an increase in their annual budget—$1.8 billion this year—the Mounties have had to absorb cutbacks of $173 million. Wages have been frozen for five years, with the result that RCMP officers now earn barely half as much as their counterparts in U.S. federal police agencies do. Because the force will not pay housing allowances, even Mounties with 20 years' experience find they cannot afford to live in high-cost centres like Vancouver and Toronto. Restrictions on overtime are so tight that in some places policing has become essentially a 9-to-5 operation. Police sources say that in Hamilton, shift changes and a ban on overtime caused the RCMP to refuse to respond in two cases—one involving the sale of guns, the other a cocaine shipment....

The part of the RCMP's operations that has been most affected by budget cuts and policy changes is the investigation of white-collar crime. In the mid-1960s, partly in response to a series of gruesome murders in Quebec linked to a phony bankruptcy scheme—a case known as the limepit murders—the Mounties pioneered a new approach to commercial crime investigation. Until then, fraud had generally been treated as a civil matter. But when it was evident that organized crime was making inroads into the business world, the RCMP felt it had to establish a powerful presence.

As a result, the Mounties created the specialized Commercial Crime Branch, which quickly attracted some of the force's best and brightest investigators. Widely copied in other countries, the elite branch had some high-profile successes in the late 1960s and 1970s. As a result of its investigations, the criminal-infested Canadian Stock Exchange in Montreal was shut down, and charges were brought against leading businessmen and companies in the patronage and fraud scandals related to the dredging of the Hamilton harbour and the licensing of airport kiosks called Sky Shops.

In 1997, however, the branch was downgraded and incorporated into a much larger operation called Federal Services, which has borne the brunt of the budget cutbacks. Commercial crime investigators, especially, are starved for resources and manpower. This year, the Mounties will spend just $36.7 million investigating commercial crime of all types in all parts of the country. That is barely 2 percent of the RCMP's overall budget and less than half of the amount—$83 million—that Canadian businesses lost last year to just one form of commercial crime: credit-card fraud.

The Mounties have largely taken themselves out of the business of investigating white-collar crime—except where the government itself is the victim or there is money to be recovered for the treasury. Today, if a corporation is targeted by criminals, it has little choice but to hire forensic accountants and other private investigators—at rates that can run as high as $600 per hour—to root out the crooks. Sonny Saunders, director of corporate security at the Royal Bank of Canada, says that budget cutbacks have caused most police forces in Canada to give low priority to fraud investigations. "Violent crime takes priority," Saunders said. "I don't think anybody would argue against that. But it means increasingly that most corporations are going to do their own fraud investigations. Every day there seems to be more and more withdrawal of police services."

For better or worse, Canada now has a two-tier system of law enforcement: The Mounties look after the interests of the state, and businesses look after themselves.

SOURCE: Reprinted with permission from Paul Palango.

provincial, and territorial justice systems to prevent white-collar crime. For example, it is not extraordinary to hear of corporate officers receiving long prison sentences for their corporate crimes. Corporate executives have even been charged with murder because of the actions of their companies.[90] However, in other cases prosecution fails, as in the Westray mine explosion.

Are such stiff penalties the norm, or do they represent infrequent instances of government resolve? A classic survey found that white-collar crimes accounted for 6 percent of arrests; of those, 88 percent were prosecuted, and 74 percent were subsequently convicted. Although 60 percent of those convicted were incarcerated, relatively few white-collar offenders received a prison term of more than a year.[91]

Is the Tide Turning? The new get-tough deterrence approach appears to be affecting all classes of white-collar criminals. Although the prevailing wisdom is that the affluent corporate executive usually avoids serious punishment, high-status offenders are now more likely to be punished.[92] Public displeasure with highly publicized white-collar crimes may produce a backlash resulting in more frequent use of prison sentences. Governments may be going overboard in their efforts to punish white-collar criminals, especially for crimes that result from negligent

Comparative Criminology
Russian Organized Crime

In the years since the collapse of the Soviet Union, criminal organizations in Russia and other former Soviet republics such as the Ukraine have engaged in a variety of crimes: drugs and arms trafficking, stolen automobiles, trafficking in women and children, and money laundering. No area of the world seems immune to this menace.

Unlike Colombian, Italian, Mexican, or other well-known forms of organized crime, Russian organized crime is not primarily based on ethnic or family structures. Instead, Russian organized crime is based on economic necessity that was nurtured by the oppressive Soviet regime. Here, a professional criminal class developed in Soviet prisons during the Stalinist period that began in 1924—the era of the gulag. These criminals adopted behaviours, rules, values, and sanctions that bound them together in what was called the thieves' world, led by the elite *vory v zakone,* criminals who lived according to the "thieves' law." This thieves' world, and particularly the *vory,* created and maintained the bonds and climate of trust necessary for carrying out organized crime.

The following are some specific characteristics of Russian organized crime in the post- Soviet era:

- Russian criminals make extensive use of the state governmental apparatus to protect and promote their criminal activities. For example, businesses in Russia—legal, quasi-legal, and illegal—must operate with protection, provided by police or security officials employed outside their official capacities. In other cases, officials are silent partners in criminal enterprises that they, in turn, protect.

- The criminalization of the privatization process has resulted in the massive use of state funds for criminal gain. Valuable properties are purchased through insider deals for much less than their true value and then resold for lucrative profits.
- Criminals have been able to directly influence the state's domestic and foreign policy to promote the interests of organized crime, either by attaining public office themselves or by buying public officials.

Russian organized crime also shares other characteristics common to organized crime elsewhere:

- Systematic use of violence, including both the threat and the use of force
- Hierarchical structure
- Limited or exclusive membership
- Specialization in types of crime and a division of labour
- Military-style discipline, with strict rules and regulations for the organization
- The use of high-tech equipment, military weapons, threats, blackmail, and violence

As a result of these activities, the following consequences emerge:

- Homicide rates are 20 times those of Western Europe, similar to a country in civil war.
- Russian organized crime is active in Europe, Africa, Asia, and North and South America.
- Massive money laundering is common, in some cases tied to terrorist funding.

The organized crime threat to Russia's national security is now becoming a global threat. Russian organized crime operates both on its own and in cooperation with foreign groups. The latter cooperation often comes in the form of joint money-laundering ventures. Russian criminals have become involved in killings for hire in Central and Western Europe, Israel, Canada, and the United States.

However, in the United States, with the exception of extortion and money laundering, Russians have had little or no involvement in some of the more traditional types of organized crime, such as drug trafficking, gambling, and loan sharking. Instead, these Russian criminal groups are extensively engaged in a broad array of frauds and scams, including healthcare fraud, insurance scams, stock frauds, antiquities swindles, forgery, and fuel tax–evasion schemes. Recently, for example, Russians have become the main purveyors of credit card fraud in the United States. Legitimate businesses, such as the movie business and textile industry, have become targets of criminals from the former Soviet Union and are often used for money laundering.

Critical Thinking

The influence of new immigrant groups in organized crime seems to suggest that illegal enterprise is a common practice in certain countries. What factors allow for organized crime to exist?

SOURCES: Louise I. Shelley, "Crime and Corruption: Enduring Problems of Post-Soviet Development," *Demokratizatsiya* 11 (2003): 110–114; James O. Finckenauer and Yuri A. Voronin, *The Threat of Russian Organized Crime* (Washington, DC: National Institute of Justice, 2001).

business practices rather than intentional criminal conspiracy.[93] Nonetheless, relatively few white-collar offenders are prosecuted, and when they are convicted, many escape serious punishment.

One reason may be a group's ties to power, as shown in the nearby Comparative Criminology box on Russian organized crime.

ORGANIZED CRIME

The second branch of criminality discussed here is organized crime, ongoing criminal groups whose purpose is economic gain through crime. A structured enterprise system is set up to supply consumers with merchandise and services banned by criminal law but for which a ready market exists: prostitution, some kinds of pornography, some gambling, and narcotics—the classic victimless crimes. The system may even resemble a legitimate business, employing assistants, staff attorneys, and accountants.

Because of secrecy, power, and wealth, a growing mystique has surrounded organized crime. Legendary leaders, such as Al Capone, have been the subjects of books and films. The famous *Godfather* films popularized organized crime figures, and the media all too often glamorize them.[94] Most citizens believe that organized criminals are capable of taking over legitimate business enterprises if given the opportunity. Almost everyone is familiar with such synonyms as *the mob*, *the underworld*, *the Mafia*, *the syndicate*, or *La Cosa Nostra*. This section briefly defines organized crime, reviews its history, and discusses its economic effect and control, and its similarity to corporate crime.

Characteristics of Organized Crime

Organized crime has some of the following general traits:

- *Organized crime is a conspiratorial activity* involving the planning and execution of illegal acts, requiring commitment and specialized skills.
- *Organized crime has economic gain as its primary goal*, through selling illegal goods and services, including drugs, gambling, some types of pornography, and prostitution.
- *Organized crime activities often work through legitimate activities*, such as laundering illegal money through legitimate businesses.
- *Organized crime employs predatory tactics*, such as intimidation, violence, and corruption to accomplish its objectives and preserve its gains.
- *Organized crime disciplines its members*, associates, and victims, to the extent that deviation from organizational rules can prompt a reduction in rank to death.
- *Organized crime is not synonymous with the stereotypical Mafia*, but has evolved through different regional and ethnic gangs and organizations.
- *Organized crime does not include terrorists* dedicated to political change, although violent acts are a major tactic of organized crime.

Activities of Organized Crime

Traditionally, organized crime income comes from providing illicit materials, narcotics distribution, loan-sharking, and prostitution.[95] The annual gross income from criminal activity can outstrip most major industries. In 2004, the RCMP estimated the drug trade and organized crime have made money laundering the second-largest global industry with the circulation of "dirty" money estimated at $3 trillion worldwide.

In some cases, organized criminals have infiltrated labour unions, taking control of their pension funds and dues.[96]

Hijacking of shipments and cargo theft are other sources of income, as is the fencing of high-value items. In recent years, organized criminals have branched into computer crime and other white-collar activities.

Organized Crime and Legitimate Enterprise

Outside of criminal enterprises, billions are earned by organized crime figures who force or buy their way into legitimate businesses for profit, such as garbage collection, which operates in markets where increases in price will not result in reduced demand.

Stephen Schneider of St. Mary's University looked at how the financial proceeds of organized criminal activity are laundered through the Canadian real estate market. Using cases from the RCMP, he shows how real estate is an attractive place to invest criminal proceeds because it provides both a home for the offender and a site for the cultivation of marijuana. The criminal source of funds is often difficult to unearth because nominees, fake mortgages, solicitor–client privilege, and legal trust accounts can make it difficult to trace the origin of funds.[97]

Organized criminals today become involved in legitimate enterprise in five ways: (1) business activity that supports illegal enterprise by providing a front, (2) predatory exploitation in which protection money is demanded, (3) organization of monopolies or cartels to limit competition, (4) unfair advantages gained by such practices as manipulation of labour unions and corruption of public officials, and (5) illegal manipulation of legal vehicles, particularly stocks and bonds.[98]

These traits show how organized crime is more similar to a business enterprise than to a confederation of criminals. Furthermore, controlling organized crime today involves a cooperative relationship among big business, politicians, and racketeers.

THE CONCEPT OF ORGANIZED CRIME

The term *organized crime* conjures up images of strong men in dark suits, machine-gun-toting bodyguards, and professional gangland killings. Criminologists refer to this view as the **alien conspiracy theory** concept of organized crime, the belief that organized crime is a direct offshoot of the

alien conspiracy theory The view that organized crime was imported from Europe, and that crime cartels restrict their membership to people of their own ethnic background.

Mafia that first originated in Italy and Sicily. A major premise is that the Mafia is centrally coordinated by a national committee that settles disputes, dictates policy, and assigns territory.[99]

Not all criminologists believe in this narrow concept of organized crime.[100] Instead, many criminologists characterize organized crime as a group of ethnically diverse gangs or groups who independently compete for profit in the sale of illegal goods and services or who use force and violence to extort money from legitimate enterprises.

The Development of a Syndicate

According to the alien conspiracy theory, organized crime really consists of a national syndicate of Italian-dominated crime families, La Cosa Nostra.[101]

The first organized gangs consisted of Irish immigrants who made their home in the slum districts of New York City.[102] The first New York gang members with a definite acknowledged leadership were muggers, thieves, and pickpockets on the Lower East Side of Manhattan from the 1820s to just before the Civil War. Around 1890, Italian immigrants began forming gangs modelled after the Mafia, called the Black Hand. Prohibition created a multimillion-dollar bootlegging industry overnight, and bloody wars for control of rackets and profits became common. However, the problems of supplying liquor to thousands of illegal drinking establishments required organization and an end to open warfare.

The end of Prohibition required a new source of profits, so narcotics and horse racing created a national network of gang-dominated bookmakers. After World War II, organized crime families began using their profits from liquor, gambling, and narcotics to buy into legitimate businesses, such as the entertainment industry, legal gambling in Cuba and Las Vegas, hotel chains, restaurants, and taverns. By paying off politicians, police, and judges, and by using blackmail and coercion, organized criminals became almost immune to prosecution. The machine-gun-toting gangster had given way to the businessman-racketeer. Gang activity expanded into legitimate businesses.

The Cosa Nostra version of organized crime is fanciful, heavily influenced by media accounts.[103] In an alternative view, Philip Jenkins studied organized crime in Philadelphia and found little evidence that it was controlled by an Italian-dominated crime family.[104] Organized crime is a loosely constructed social system, comprising relationships that bind professional criminals, politicians, law enforcers, and various entrepreneurs. The social world of organized crime is often chaotic because of the constant power struggle between competing groups.

Some criminologists view the world of professional criminals as one shaped by the political economy. Madams, drug distributors, and bookmakers are workers in the world of illegal enterprise. This world of organized crime is dominated by business leaders, politicians, and union leaders who work hand in hand with criminals. The violent, chaotic social world of power struggles does not lend itself to a tightly controlled syndicate.

Organized Crime Groups

Organized crime is a loose confederation of ethnic and regional crime groups, bound together by a commonality of economic and political objectives. Canada has four or five main organized crime groups.[105] They commit a variety of offences, as shown in Figure 12.3.

Asian-Based Organized Crime. These groups are extensively involved in trafficking cocaine and ecstasy; the production, trafficking, and exporting of marijuana; and the importation and distribution of Southeast Asian heroin. They are also involved in large-scale illegal migrant smuggling. Based primarily in Vancouver, Calgary, Edmonton, Toronto, and Montreal, these groups include criminal youths and members of street gangs. They are involved in home invasions, kidnapping, theft, shoplifting, prostitution, assaults, illegal gambling, loan-sharking, and the production and distribution of counterfeit currency, software,

FIGURE 12.3

Crimes Committed by Organized Crime Groups in Canada

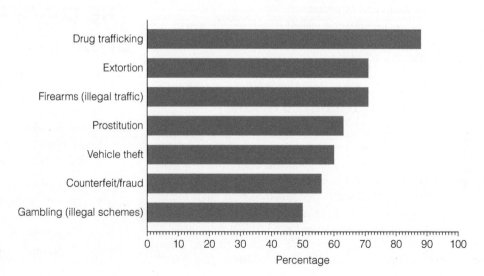

Source: Adapted from the Statistics Canada publication "Organized Crime Activity in Canada: A Pilot Survey of 16 Police Services," 1998, Catalogue 85-548, no. 01, May 20, 1999.

Famous Canadian Court Cases
Tobacco Smuggling

Tobacco companies are notorious for generating two things: smoke and controversy. They have been condemned for manufacturing lethal products, misleading the public about the dangers of smoking, and aggressively marketing cigarettes to youth. At the root of all this criticism, the burning question seems to be one of legality rather than of morality. Are industry executives criminal conspirators? Canadian courts may soon provide an answer. Currently, cigarette makers are at the centre of the largest corporate fraud case ever filed in this country.

Ottawa tried to encourage smokers to kick the habit by doubling tobacco taxes in 1991. However, these barriers to smoking soon buckled under a flood of contraband. Federal and provincial or territorial governments lost more than $10 billion in total revenue after nearly $1 billion of cigarettes were smuggled into Canada. Struggling to curb the black market tobacco trade, politicians were forced to backpedal. Taxes were slashed in 1994, but began to surge again five years later when one of America's top cigarette manufacturers came under investigation.

As the allegations stand, R.J. Reynolds Tobacco spearheaded an elaborate smuggling ring. Plants in Montreal and Puerto Rico shipped loads of Export A cigarettes to the United States. Much of the merchandise was funnelled through Northern Brand International (NBI), a shell company created by RJR to avert suspicion. In turn, the goods were leaked into Canada through Mohawk reserves along the New York–Ontario border and sold at discount prices.

Ironically, while the corporation evaded cigarette taxes, RJR officials lobbied the government for tax relief to help combat the smuggling problem. RJR managed to hide behind this smokescreen for some time after the scandal was exposed. A New York court indicted more than 20 people in 1997, none of them employed in the tobacco business. All were eventually convicted, along with NBI and the sham company's sales director, while the industry giant remained untouched.

RJR finally came under fire in December 1999. Following an RCMP investigation that lasted more than four years, the Canadian government decided to recoup some of its losses. Ottawa refused a $100 million settlement, filing a $1 billion civil racketeering case in New York instead. Authorities accused RJR, its Canadian subsidiary RJR-Macdonald, several other affiliated companies, and the Canadian Tobacco Manufacturers' Council of plotting to stock the black market on this side of the border.

Hopes for legal redress almost went up in smoke after the United States Supreme Court rejected Ottawa's claim in November 2002. Fortunately, the case was dismissed on technical grounds alone. An American rule of law regarding jurisdiction presented the problem, so authorities brought the matter home. In February 2003, fraud and conspiracy charges were laid against RJR, a number of its affiliates, and eight senior executives. A trial was not expected until the fall of 2005. Meanwhile, the federal government is suing the tobacco companies for $1.5 billion in an Ontario Court.

Update: In 2008, Canada's two largest tobacco manufacturers pleaded guilty to aiding the smuggling of cigarettes in the 1980s and 1990s, and agreed to pay penalties of more than $1.1 billion to settle criminal and civil cases. Imperial Tobacco Canada and Rothmans Inc. paid the "largest criminal fines and civil settlements in Canadian history"; however, RJR-Macdonald was not part of the agreement.

The federal revenue minister said that the level of the fine assured that the companies did not benefit financially from the smuggling.

No executives were charged.

---

manufactured goods, and credit and debit cards. They are also involved in the laundering of criminal proceeds and the investment of laundered money into legitimate businesses. An investigation by the RCMP in 2004 concluded that more than $200 million was laundered in one cross-border operation.

East European–Based Organized Crime. Groups from Eastern Europe continue to expand, particularly in larger urban centres. They are well-connected to established criminal organizations around the world, and exploit technology to commit sophisticated financial and Internet-based frauds. These organized crime groups from the former Soviet Union engage in crimes ranging from petty theft to sophisticated fraud. They typically use legitimate business ventures as fronts for their illegal activities, which are most frequently reported to be financial frauds, prostitution, theft, contraband

smuggling, illicit drug importation, vehicle theft and illegal export (such as the stolen vehicles discussed in Chapter 11), and money laundering. They also engage in activities that are made easier by the Internet, such as credit card skimming, e-commerce site hacking, and fraudulent credit card purchases.

Traditional (Italian-Based) Organized Crime. The traditional organized crime associated with Italy remains a threat and includes the Sicilian Mafia, which has ties to clans in Venezuela, the United States, and Italy. They participate in joint criminal ventures, such as importing illegal narcotics, laundering drug proceeds, drug trafficking, illegal gaming, extortion, and loansharking. Illegal gaming activities include backroom gambling, sports betting, and illegal video lottery gaming terminals. Profits from these criminal activities are invested in legitimate commercial enterprises.

Aboriginal-Based Organized Crime. Various Aboriginal gangs have emerged, including the Manitoba Warriors, Indian Posse, Redd Alert, and Native Syndicate. Aboriginal-based street gangs are generally involved in street crime, such as trafficking marijuana, cocaine and crack, and meth-amphetamines. They are also involved in prostitution, break and enters, robberies, assaults, intimidation, vehicle theft, and illicit drug debt collection. The gangs' capability to plan sophisticated or large-scale crimes is low, but they are very violent, using handguns that have been stolen or smuggled.[106] Some experts say gangs comprising minority-group members will have a tough time developing a network of organized corruption similar to that enjoyed by traditional crime families, which involves working with government officials and unions.[107]

Organized Crime at Marine Ports. Marine ports are used by organized crime groups to move illegal commodities into Canada for sale and for export. Officials at marine ports have seized such drugs as cocaine, heroin, hashish, and ecstasy; tobacco; alcohol; and firearms. Criminal associates are placed within the port, where they access information on the movement of commercial cargo from the vessels and through the port environment. Conspirators take contraband from marine containers before inspection, while other containers may simply disappear.

Outlaw Motorcycle Gangs. Motorcycle gangs use violence to accomplish their goals, which involve money laundering, intimidation, assaults, attempted murder, murder, fraud, theft, counterfeiting, loansharking, extortion, prostitution, escort agencies, strip clubs, illegal booze cans, and the possession and trafficking of illegal weapons, stolen goods, contraband, alcohol, and cigarettes. Members of the Hells Angels are involved in the cultivation and exportation of high-grade marijuana; and the production and trafficking of cocaine, methamphetamine, ecstasy, and other synthetic illicit drugs. The Hells Angels are the largest and most criminally active outlaw motorcycle gang (OMG) in the country. The RCMP says that members of OMGs comprise the largest proportion of people on the annual Strategic Threat Assessment list.[108]

One important recent change in organized crime is the interweaving of ethnic groups. Asian racketeers and Aboriginal gangs now collaborate or compete with more traditional groups, such as the Hells Angels, overseeing the distribution of drugs, prostitution, and gambling in a symbiotic relationship with old-line racketeers. Eastern European gangs cooperate in narcotics trafficking, fencing, money laundering, and other crimes.[109]

Part of the evolution of organized crime is created by patterns of law enforcement. Pressure on traditional organized crime encouraged the Hells Angels to become the leading distributor of narcotics in Canada. A series of bombings erupted in Montreal as part of a turf war between the Hells Angels and the Rock Machine, another motorcycle gang. Chinese criminal gangs have taken over the dominant role in New York City's heroin market from the traditional Italian-run syndicates.[110] In Canada, Chinese Triad gangs traditionally relied on extortion as a source of illegal wealth and have extended their activity to include the sale of drugs. Unlike the hierarchical structure of the traditional Mafia, they operate in cells to ensure that no one member knows the whole picture.

Overall, organized crime is estimated to generate more than $20 billion a year in Canada, half from the sale of drugs alone; the rest from auto thefts, money laundering, smuggling, fraud, prostitution, and violent crime. Selling restricted weapons, providing access to illicit toxic waste dumps, and selling high-technology secrets are also profitable. Most experts agree it is simplistic to view organized crime as a national syndicate that controls illegitimate rackets, ignoring the variety of gangs and groups, their membership, and their relationship to the outside world.

Mafia-type groups might be traditional, but they are not the only organized criminals.[111]

CONTROLLING ORGANIZED CRIME

George Vold argued that the development of organized crime parallels early capitalist enterprises. Organized crime uses ruthless and monopolistic tactics to maximize profits; it is also secretive and protective of its operations and defensive against any outside intrusion.[112] Consequently, controlling its activities is extremely difficult, and, until recently, little has been done to combat organized crime.

One measure aimed directly at organized crime in the United States was implementing the *Organized Crime Control Act* and the *Racketeer Influenced and Corrupt Organization Act* (RICO). RICO did not create new categories of crimes but rather new categories of offences in racketeering activity, such as murder, kidnapping, gambling, arson, robbery, bribery, extortion, and narcotics violations, and such federally defined crimes as bribery, counterfeiting, transmission of gambling information, prostitution, and mail fraud.

In Canada, attempts to control organized crime include Bill C-69, which gives the police more power to seize goods suspected of being purchased with the proceeds of crime. Section 312 of the Canadian *Criminal Code* makes it an offence to possess property derived from an indictable offence. During the confrontation between rival bike gangs in Montreal, the RCMP and the Montreal Urban Community Police made significant arrests and seized explosive devices, including a thousand sticks of dynamite. In addition, the Canadian Security Intelligence Service (CSIS) asked that the $1,000 bill be eliminated and that the movement of large sums of money be reported by financial institutions. Bill

C-24, created after September 2001, freed up $200 million over five years to give police new measures to fight organized crime.

New developments in the enforcement of laws designed to control organized crime include police anti-drug-profiteering units, joint Canada–United States agreements on sharing the proceeds of crime, and joint investigations into organized crime. For example, a money-laundering operation broken in Montreal with cooperation from American authorities involved the seizure of $1 million.

Some provincial police organizations have their own anti-biker squads, and the *Witness Protection Program Act* was designed to encourage witnesses to come forward to report on crime. The National Action Plan to Combat Smuggling resulted in $2 billion of smuggled goods confiscated.

Human smuggling and trafficking in humans continues to be a problem linked to organized crime. The former involves assisting those wanting to illegally immigrate to Canada, while the latter involves the transportation of people by means of coercion or violence. Most of these victims are women and children forced into illegal activities, such as labour, slavery, and prostitution. Legislation to combat these crimes includes the *UN Convention against Transnational Organized Crime*, the *Immigration and Refugee Protection Act*, and the *Anti-Smuggling Initiative*.

Exhibit 12.7 has more information about fighting organized crime in Canada.

THE FUTURE OF ORGANIZED CRIME

Indications are that the traditional organized crime syndicates are in decline. Active government enforcement policies have reduced the membership in organized crime from 20 years ago, and high-ranking leaders have been imprisoned. Additional pressure comes from newly emerging ethnic gangs that want to muscle in on traditional syndicate activities. For example, Chinese Triad gangs have been active in the drug trade, loansharking, and labour racketeering. Other ethnic crime groups include Black and Colombian drug cartels and the Sicilian Mafia.

Caucasian, ethnic, inner-city neighbourhoods, once the locus of Mafia power, have been reduced in size as families have moved to the suburbs. Organized crime groups have consequently lost their political and social base of operations. In addition, the code of silence, which served to protect Mafia leaders, is now being broken by younger members who turn informer rather than face prison. For example, the reign of John Gotti, the most powerful mob boss in New York, was ended by testimony given at

---

EXHIBIT 12.7

The Fight against Organized Crime

In 2007, the Criminal Intelligence Service reported the following:

- Canada had about 950 organized crime groups in 2007, up from 800 groups in 2006.
- Drug crime involves 80 percent of all crime groups, particularly as street-level traffickers.
- Mortgage fraud costs hundreds of millions of dollars annually.
- Credit card fraud losses cost $185 million, debit card skimming cost $94.6 million.
- The International Monetary Fund estimates $22 billion to $55 billion is laundered annually.
- Counterfeit products, such as entertainment-based software, generate billions of dollars.
- The Canadian Police Information Centre says 44,000 stolen firearms are restricted.

In recent years, steps against organized crime include the following:

- The Anti-Smuggling Initiative targets smuggling, distribution networks at the border; the Integrated Proceeds of Crime (RCMP, Customs, accountants) target and seize assets.
- Legislation makes participation in a criminal organization an indictable offence; the Witness Protection Program Act protects those who assist police investigations.
- Forums bring together police, government, business, legal counsel, and academics.
- Coordinating committees cooperate to combat organized crime; CPIC is modernized to improve information sharing.
- 2010, PROJECT CORRAL: 1000 police from 20 Ontario jurisdictions executed 105 simultaneous search warrants against three criminal organizations—the Falstaff Crips, the Five Point Generals, and the Jamaican Shower Posse, arresting 71 individuals, seizing $314,000 in proceeds of crime, 15 firearms, and drugs including cocaine, crack cocaine, marijuana, hashish oil and more than 10,000 ecstasy pills. The Shower Posse imported cocaine from the United States, the Dominican Republic, and Panama, and distributed to the Falstaff Crips and the Five Point Generals for street-level distribution in the Toronto area, who were involved in their own conflicts over territory, with a number of violent clashes.

SOURCES: 2010, Report on Organized Crime, CISC, www.cisc.gc.ca; *2007 Annual Report on Organized Crime in Canada*, Criminal Intelligence Service Canada, 2008.

---

his murder trial by his one-time ally, Sammy "The Bull" Gravano.

Jay Albanese, a leading expert on organized crime, predicts that pressure by government will encourage organized crime figures to engage in safer activities, such as credit card and airline ticket counterfeiting and illicit toxic waste disposal. Instead of running illegal enterprises, established families may be content with financing younger entrepreneurs and channelling or laundering profits through their legitimate business enterprises. In the future, organized criminals may make greater efforts to infiltrate legitimate business enterprises to obtain both access to money for financing and the means to launder illicitly obtained cash. In the past, their favourite targets have been labour unions and the construction industry.[113]

Although government pressures are considered a major blow to Italian-dominated organized crime cartels, they are unlikely to stifle criminal entrepreneurship. As long as vast profits can be made from selling narcotics, producing pornography for the Internet, or taking illegal bets, many groups stand ready to fill the gaps and reap the profits of providing illegal goods and services.

CONNECTIONS

The future of organized crime might be transnational, discussed in more detail in Chapter 14.

SUMMARY

White-collar and organized criminals are similar because they both use ongoing illegal business enterprises to generate personal profits.

There are several types of white-collar crime. Stings and swindles involve the use of deception to bilk people out of their money. Chiselling customers, businesses, or the government on a regular basis is a second common type of white-collar crime. Surprisingly, many professionals engage in chiselling offences. Other white-collar criminals use their positions in business and the marketplace to commit economic crimes, involving illegal payments, embezzlement, employee pilferage, fraud, client fraud, influence peddling, and bribery. Further, corporate officers sometimes violate the law to improve the position and profitability of their businesses, which might include price-fixing, false advertising, and environmental offences. More recently, computers have been used to commit high-tech crimes, such as counterfeiting, or variations on old crimes, such as libel.

So far, little has been done to combat white-collar crimes. Most offenders do not view themselves as criminals and therefore do not seem to be deterred by criminal statutes. Although thousands of white-collar criminals are prosecuted each year, their numbers are insignificant compared with the magnitude of the problem. Law enforcement strategies to combat white-collar crime involve deterrence, which uses punishment to frighten potential abusers, and compliance, which creates economic incentives to obey the law.

A new focus for criminology is crimes against the environment, discussed in the section on green-collar crime. Again, when profits are to be made, green-collar criminals can fall prey to the many incentives to compromise on safety and environmental protection.

Similarly, the demand for illegal goods and services has produced a symbiotic relationship between the public and an organized criminal network. Organized crime supplies many goods to the public, including alcohol, smuggled tobacco, gambling, drugs, prostitutes, and some types of pornography. Members of organized crime groups are immune from prosecution because of public apathy and because of their own strong political connections. Organized criminals used to be members of European ethnic groups—Jews, Italians, and Irish—but today Blacks, Hispanics, Asians, and other minority groups have become involved in organized crime activities. The old-line families are more likely to use their criminal wealth and power to buy into legitimate businesses.

Much debate surrounds the control of organized crime. Efforts to control organized crime have been stepped up. But as long as vast profits can be made, illegal enterprises will continue to flourish. In this way, they might function in a way similar to that of corporate crime. This idea is taken up more fully in Chapter 14.

THINKING LIKE A CRIMINOLOGIST

People who commit computer crime are found in every segment of society. They range in age from 10 to 60, and their skill level runs from novice to professional. They are otherwise average people, not supercriminals possessing unique abilities and talents. Any person of any age with even a little skill is a potential computer criminal. Most studies indicate that employees represent the greatest threat to computers. Almost 90 percent of computer crimes against businesses are inside jobs. Ironically, as advances continue in remote data processing, the threat from external sources will probably increase. With the networking of systems and the adoption of more user-friendly software, the sociological profile of the computer offender may change. For example, computer criminals may soon be members of organized crime syndicates who use computer systems to monitor law enforcement activities. In the 21st-century organized crime family, the recruit will need to develop knowledge of the equipment used for audio surveillance of law enforcement communications: computers with sound cards or microphones, modems, and software programs for the remote operation of the systems.

Which theories of criminal behaviour best explain the actions of computer criminals, and which ones fail to account for computer crime?

KEY TERMS

alien conspiracy theory p. 405
arbitrage p. 388
chiselling p. 387
churning p. 387
compliance p. 401
corporate crime p. 392

cybercrime p. 381
deterrence p. 402
enterprise crimes p. 381
green criminology p. 381
insider trading p. 387
occupational crime p. 383

organized crime p. 381
pilferage p. 390
price-fixing p. 393
swindling p. 386
white-collar crime p. 381

DOING RESEARCH ON THE WEB

Before answering the question posed in the Thinking Like a Criminologist box on page 410, visit the American Civil Liberties Union website: www.aclu.org/Privacy/PrivacyMain.cfm. The ACLU states:

"The United States is at risk of turning into a full-fledged surveillance society. The tremendous explosion in surveillance-enabling technologies, combined with the ongoing weakening in legal restraints that protect our privacy, mean that we are drifting toward a surveillance society. The good news is that it can be stopped. Unfortunately, right now the big picture is grim."

You may also want to look at the website of the Center for Democracy and Technology (CDT), a non-profit public policy organization dedicated to promoting the democratic potential of today's open, decentralized global Internet. The CDT's mission is to conceptualize, develop, and implement public policies to preserve and enhance free expression, privacy, open access, and other democratic values in the new and increasingly integrated communications medium: www.cdt.org.

CRITICAL THINKING QUESTIONS

1. How would you punish a corporate executive whose product killed people if the executive had no knowledge that the product was potentially lethal? Would the situation be different if the executive had been aware of the product's capacity to harm?

2. Is organized crime inevitable as long as immigrant groups seek to become part of the North American dream?

3. Does the media glamorize organized crime? Does it paint an inaccurate picture of noble crime lords fighting to protect their families?

4. Apply traditional theories of criminal behaviour to white-collar and organized crime. Which theory best predicts why someone would engage in these behaviours?

NOTES

1. Dwight Smith, Jr., "White-Collar Crime, Organized Crime and the Business Establishment: Resolving a Crisis in Criminological Theory," in *White Collar and Economic Crime: A Multidisciplinary and Crossnational Perspective*, eds. P. Wickman and T. Dailey, 53 (Lexington, MA: Lexington Books, 1982).

2. See, generally, Dwight Smith, Jr., "Organized Crime and Entrepreneurship," *International Journal of Criminology and Penology* 6 (1978): 161–177; Dwight Smith, Jr., "Paragons, Pariahs, and Pirates: A Spectrum-Based Theory of Enterprise," *Crime and Delinquency*

26 (1980): 358–386; Dwight Smith, Jr. and Richard S. Alba, "Organized Crime and American Life," *Society* 16 (1979): 32–38.

3. Mark Haller, "Illegal Enterprise: A Theoretical and Historical Interpretation," *Criminology* 28 (1990): 207–235.

4. Nancy Frank and Michael Lynch, *Corporate Crime, Corporate Violence* (Albany, NY: Harrow and Heston, 1992), 7.

5. Nikos Passas and David Nelken, "The Thin Line between Legitimate and Criminal Enterprises: Subsidy Frauds in the European Community," *Crime, Law and Social Change* 19 (1993): 223–243.

6. For a thorough review, see David Friedrichs, *Trusted Criminals* (Belmont, CA: Wadsworth, 1996).

7. Kitty Calavita and Henry Pontell, "Savings and Loan Fraud as Organized Crime: Toward a Conceptual Typology of Corporate Illegality," *Criminology* 31 (1993): 519–548.

8. Edwin Sutherland, *White-Collar Crime: The Uncut Version* (New Haven, CT: Yale University Press, 1983).

9. Edwin Sutherland, "White-Collar Criminality," *American Sociological Review* 5 (1940): 2–10.

10. See, generally, Herbert Edelhertz, *The Nature, Impact and Prosecution of White-Collar Crime* (Washington, DC: U.S. Government Printing Office, 1970), 73–75.

11. James Coleman, "What Is White Collar Crime? New Battles in the War of Definitions," in James Helmkamp, Richard Ball, and Kitty Townsend, *Proceedings of the Academic Workshop, Definitional Dilemma: Can and Should There Be a Universal Definition of White Collar Crime?* (Morgantown, WV: National White Collar Crime Center, 1996), 77–86.

12. James Helmkamp and Richard Ball, "Progress in the Definition and Exploration of White-Collar Crime," paper presented at the annual meeting of the American Society of Criminology, Chicago, November 1996, 9.

13. David Weisburd and Kip Schlegel, "Returning to the Mainstream," in *White-Collar Crime Reconsidered*, eds. Kip Schlegel and David Weisburd, 352–365 (Boston: Northeastern University Press, 1992).

14. Ronald C. Kramer, Raymond J. Michalowski, and David Kauzlarich, "The Origins and Development of the Concept and Theory of State-Corporate Crime," *Crime & Delinquency* 48, 2 (2002): 263–282.

15. Elizabeth Moore and Michael Mills, "The Neglected Victims and Unexamined Costs of White-Collar Crime," *Crime and Delinquency* 36 (1990): 408–418.

16. Stuart Traub, "Battling Employee Crime: A Review of Corporate Strategies and Programs," *Crime and Delinquency* 42 (1996): 244–256.

17. KPMG Fraud and Misconduct Diagnostic Survey, 2002, www.kpmg.ca/en/services/advisory/forensic/fmdSurvey2002.html.

18. Laura Schrager and James Short, "Toward a Sociology of Organizational Crime," *Social Problems* 25 (1978): 415–425.

19. Gilbert Geis, "White-Collar and Corporate Crime," in *Major Forms of Crime*, ed. Robert Meier, 145 (Beverly Hills, CA: Sage, 1984).

20. Bureau of Justice Statistics, *The Severity of Crime* (Washington, DC: U.S. Government Printing Office, 1984).

21. Minxin Pei, "The Tide of Corruption Threatening China's Prosperity," *Financial Times*, September 27, 2006.

22. Nikos Passas and David Nelkin, "The Fight against Fraud in the European Community: Cacophony Rather Than Harmony," *Corruption and Reform* 6 (1991): 237–266.

23. Nikos Passas, "European Integration, Protectionism, and Criminogenesis: A Case Study on Farm Subsidy Frauds," *Mediterranean Quarterly* 5 (1994): 66–84.

24. Marshall Clinard and Richard Quinney, *Criminal Behavior Systems: A Typology* (New York: Holt, Rinehart and Winston, 1973), 117.

25. Mark Moore, "Notes Toward a National Strategy to Deal with White-Collar Crime," in *A National Strategy for Containing White-Collar Crime*, eds. Herbert Edelhertz and Charles Rogovin, 32–44 (Lexington, MA: Lexington Books, 1980); For a general review, see John Braithwaite, "White-Collar Crime," *Annual Review of Sociology* 11 (1985): 1–25.

26. Scott Paltrow, "Goldblum Now in Consulting and on Parole," *Wall Street Journal*, March 22, 1982, 25.

27. Nikos Passas, "Structural Sources of International Crime: Policy Lessons from the BCCI Affair," *Crime, Law and Social Change* 19 (1994): 223–231; Nikos Passas, "Accounting for Fraud: Auditors' Ethical Dilemmas in the BCCI Affair," in *The Ethics of Accounting and Finance*, eds. W. Michael Hoffman, Judith Brown Kamm, Robert Frederick, and Edward Petry, 85–99 (Westport, CT: Quorum Books, 1996).

28. Earl Gottschalk, "Churchgoers Are the Prey as Scams Rise," *Wall Street Journal*, August 7, 1989, C1.

29. Diana Henriques, "10 Percent of Fruit Juice Sold in U.S. Is Not All Juice, Regulators Say," *New York Times*, October 31, 1993, 1.

30. Richard Quinney, "Occupational Structure and Criminal Behavior: Prescription Violation of Retail Pharmacists," *Social Problems* 11 (1963): 179–185; see also John Braithwaite, *Corporate Crime in the Pharmaceutical Industry* (London: Routledge and Kegan Paul, 1984).

31. Amy Dockser Marcus, "Thievery by Lawyers Is on the Increase, with Duped Clients Losing Bigger Sums," *Wall Street Journal*, November 26, 1990, B1.

32. James Armstrong et al., "Securities Fraud," *American Criminal Law Review* 33 (1995): 973–1016.

33. *Carpenter v. United States*, 484 U.S. 19 (1987); also see John Boland, "The SEC Trims the First Amendment," *Wall Street Journal*, December 4, 1986, 28.

34. Constance Hays, "ImClone Founder Pleads Guilty to 6 Charges," *New York Times*, October 16, 2002, A1.

35. Tim Metz and Michael Miller, "Boesky's Rise and Fall Illustrate a Compulsion to Profit by Getting Inside Track on Market," *Wall Street Journal*, November 17, 1986, 28; Wade Lambert, "FDIC Receives Cooperation of Milken Aide," *Wall Street Journal*, April 25, 1991, A3.

36. This section is based on Richard Walker and David M. Levine, "'You've Got Jail': Current Trends in Civil and Criminal Enforcement of Internet Securities Fraud," *American Criminal Law Review* 38 (2001): 405–430.

37. Jim Wolf, "Internet Scams Targeted in Sweep: A 10-Day Crackdown Leads to 62 Arrests and 88 Indictments," *Boston Globe*, 22 May 2001, p. A2.

38. U.S. Department of Justice, "Alleged Leaders of $60 Million Internet Scam Indicted on Fraud and Money Laundering Charges Massive Internet Investment Fraud Case Involves 15,000 Investors from 60 Countries," press release, January 3, 2003.

39. This section depends heavily on Frank Browning and John Gerassi, *The American Way of Crime* (New York: Putnam, 1980), 151.

40. Edward Ranzal, "City Report Finds Building Industry Infested by Graft," *New York Times*, November 8, 1974, 1.

41. Rod Macdonell, "Tory Senator Must Pay Fine," *Halifax Daily News*, July 8, 1998.

42. Marshall Clinard and Peter Yeager, *Corporate Crime* (New York: Free Press, 1980), 166–167.

43. "Rail Deal Debate Heats Up: Provincial Government Reveals Billion-Dollar Operational Lease for BC Rail Could Last a Lot Longer Than 90 Years," *Penticton Herald*, April 20, 2004; "Furor in British Columbia Grows over Bribery Probe," Mark Hume, *The Globe and Mail*, March 4, 2004.

44. "More Charges Laid in Police Scandal," Canada.com, October 15, 2004; Oliver Moore, "Toronto Police Officers Charged," *The Globe and Mail*, May 3, 2004; Jonathan Fowlie, "Toronto Officers Charged in 'Shakedown' Case," *The Globe and Mail*, May 4, 2004; Steve Fairbairn, "Outside Force Won't Probe Toronto Cops," Canadian Press, April 27, 2004.

45. Daniel Leblanc, Campbell Clark, and Ingrid Peritz, "Pair Held in Sponsorship Scandal," *The Globe and Mail*, May 11, 2004; Jack Aubry, "Ex-Adman Alleges Liberal Kickback Scheme," *Ottawa Citizen*, April 8, 2004; "Judicial Inquiry into Scandal Officially Begins," Canadian Press, May 7, 2004.

46. Edward Pound, "Honored Employee Is a Key in Huge Fraud in Defense Purchasing," *Wall Street Journal*, March 2, 1988, 1.

47. *The Knapp Commission Report on Police Corruption* (New York: George Braziller, 1973), 1–3, 170–182.

48. "Newsbreaks," *Aviation Week and Space Technology*, July 10, 1995, 19.

49. Charles McCaghy, *Deviant Behavior* (New York: Macmillan, 1976), 178.

50. John Clark and Richard Hollinger, *Theft by Employees in Work Organizations* (Washington, DC: U.S. Government Printing Office, 1983), 2–3.

51. "Business Fraud Prevails, May Worsen, Study Says," *Wall Street Journal*, August 17, 1993, A4.

52. J. Sorenson, H. Grove, and T. Sorenson, "Detecting Management Fraud: The Role of the Independent Auditor," in *White-Collar*

Crime, Theory and Research, eds. G. Geis and E. Stotland, 221–251 (Beverly Hills, CA: Sage, 1980).

53. "Fraud against Businesses in Canada: Results from a National Survey, 2007-2008," Andrea Taylor-Butts and Damuel Perreault, Statistics Canada, 2009; "KPMG Fraud Survey, 2003," www.kpmg.com/aci/docs/Fraud%20Survey_040855_R5.pdf.

54. Henry Pontell, Kitty Calavita, and Robert Tillman, *Fraud in the Savings and Loan Industry: White-Collar Crime and Government Response* (Report to the National Institute of Justice, Washington, DC, 1994); Robert Tillman and Henry Pontell, "Organizations and Fraud in the Savings and Loan Industry," *Social Forces* 73 (1995): 1439–1463; Kitty Calavita and Henry Pontell, "Savings and Loan Fraud as Organized Crime: Toward a Conceptual Typology of Corporate Illegality," *Criminology* 31 (1993): 519–548; Kitty Calavita and Henry Pontell, "'Heads I Win, Tails You Lose': Deregulation, Crime, and Crisis in the Savings and Loan Industry," *Crime and Delinquency* 36 (1990): 309–341; Rich Thomas, "Sit Down Taxpayers," *Newsweek*, June 4, 1990, 60; John Gallagher, "Good Old Bad Boy," *Time*, June 25, 1990, 42–43; L. Gordon Crovitz, "Milken's Tragedy: Oh, How the Mighty Fall before RICO," *Wall Street Journal*, May 2, 1990, A17.

55. See Kristine DeBry, Bonny Harbinger, and Susan Rotkis, "Health Care Fraud," *American Criminal Law Review* 33 (1995): 818–838.

56. Henry Thomas Stelfox and Donald A. Redelmeier, "An Analysis of One Potential Form of Health Care Fraud in Canada," *Canadian Medical Association Journal* 7 (2003): 169–171; Moe Litman, "Self-Referral and Kickbacks: Fiduciary Law and the Regulation of 'Trafficking in Patients,'" *Canadian Medical Association Journal* 3 (2004): 170–177.

57. Bruce Lambert, "12 Chiropractors among 20 Arrested in Insurance Fraud Sting," *New York Times*, May 22, 1997, A30; Laura Johannes and Wendy Bounds, "Corning Agrees to Pay $6.8 Million to Settle Medicare Billing Charges," *Wall Street Journal*, February 22, 1996, B2.

58. Alan Murray, "IRS in Losing Battle against Tax Evaders Despite Its New Gear," *Wall Street Journal*, April 10, 1984, 1; "The Police Perspective on Organized Crime," *RCMP Gazette*, n.d.; Canadian Taxpayers Federation, "The Oldest Profession, the Underground Economy and Swiss Cheese," February 28, 2002, www.taxpayer.com/main/news.php?news_id=110; "The Underground economy in Canada, 2011," *The Daily*, July 30, 2014.

59. Nancy Frank and Michael Lynch, *Corporate Crime, Corporate Violence* (Albany, NY: Harrow and Heston), 12–13.

60. Michael Maltz and Stephen Pollack, "Suspected Collusion Among Bidders," in *White-Collar Crime, Theory and Research*, eds. G. Geis and E. Stotland, 174–198 (Beverly Hills, CA: Sage, 1980).

61. Bruce Ingersoll and Alecia Swasy, "FDA Puts Squeeze on P&G over Citrus Hill Labeling," *Wall Street Journal*, April 25, 1991, B1.

62. John Conklin, *Illegal but Not Criminal* (Englewood Cliffs, NJ: Prentice-Hall, 1972), 45–46.

63. For an analysis of false claims, see Jonathan Kaye and John Patrick Sullivan, "False Claims," in *Eighth Survey of White-Collar Crime, American Criminal Law Review* 30 (1993): 643–657.

64. Kathleen Daly, "Gender and Varieties of White-Collar Crime," *Criminology* 27 (1989): 769–793.

65. Donald Cressey, *Other People's Money: A Study of the Social Psychology of Embezzlement* (Glencoe, IL: Free Press, 1973).

66. Ronald Kramer, "Corporate Crime: An Organizational Perspective," in *White-Collar and Economic Crime: A Multidisciplinary and Crossnational Perspective*, eds. P. Wickman and T. Dailey, 75–94 (Lexington, MA: Lexington Books, 1982).

67. John Braithwaite, "Toward a Theory of Organizational Crime," paper presented at the annual meeting of the American Society of Criminology, Montreal, November 1987.

68. Travis Hirschi and Michael Gottfredson, "Causes of White-Collar Crime," *Criminology* 25 (1987): 949–974.

69. Michael Gottfredson and Travis Hirschi, *A General Theory of Crime* (Stanford, CA: Stanford University Press, 1990), 191.

70. David Weisburd, Ellen Chayet, and Elin Waring, "White-Collar and Criminal Careers: Some Preliminary Findings," *Crime and Delinquency* 36 (1990): 342–355.

71. Michael Benson and Elizabeth Moore, "Are White-Collar and Common Offenders the Same? An Empirical and Theoretical Critique of a Recently Proposed General Theory of Crime," *Journal of Research in Crime and Delinquency* 29 (1992): 251–272.

72. David Simon and D. Stanley Eitzen, *Elite Deviance* (Boston: Allyn & Bacon, 1982), 28.

73. Paul Jesilow, Henry N. Pontell, and Gilbert Geis, "Physician Immunity from Prosecution and Punishment for Medical Program Fraud," in *Punishment and Privilege*, eds. W. Byron Groves and Graeme Newman, 7–22 (New York: Harrow and Heston, 1986).

74. Peter Yeager, "Structural Bias in Regulatory Law Enforcement: The Case of the U.S.

Environmental Protection Agency," *Social Problems* 34 (1987): 330–344.

75. See, generally, Stanton Wheeler, David Weisburd, Elin Waring, and Nancy Bode, "White-Collar Crimes and Criminals," *American Criminal Law Review* 25 (1988): 331–357.

76. This section relies on Daniel Skoler, "White-Collar Crime and the Criminal Justice System: Problems and Challenges," in *A National Strategy for Containing White-Collar Crime*, eds. Herbert Edelhertz and Charles Rogovin, 57–76 (Lexington, MA: Lexington Books, 1980).

77. Michael Benson, Francis Cullen, and William Maakestad, "Local Prosecutors and Corporate Crime," *Crime and Delinquency* 36 (1990): 356–372.

78. Traub, "Battling Employee Crime: A Review of Corporate Strategies and Programs," 248–252.

79. James W. Williams, "Reflections on the Private Versus Public Policing of Economic Crime," *British Journal of Criminology* 45, 3 (2005): 316–339.

80. This section relies heavily on Albert Reiss, Jr., "Selecting Strategies of Social Control over Organizational Life," in *Enforcing Regulation*, eds. Keith Hawkins and John M. Thomas, 25–37 (Boston: Klowver Publications, 1984).

81. John Braithwaite, "The Limits of Economism in Controlling Harmful Corporate Conduct," *Law and Society Review* 16 (1981–1982): 481–504; "EPA Sues Sherwin-Williams: Pattern of Pollution at Paint Factory Is Alleged," *Wall Street Journal*, July 19, 1993, 1; "Making Firms Liable for Cleaning Toxic Sites," *Wall Street Journal*, March 9, 1988, 29.

82. Rhonda Rundle, "Computer Sciences Will Pay $2.1 Million to Settle Charges by U.S. Government," *Wall Street Journal*, July 19, 1993, B8.

83. Wayne Gray and John Scholz, "Does Regulatory Enforcement Work? A Panel Analysis of OSHA Enforcement," *Law and Society Review* 27 (1993): 177–191.

84. Michael Benson, "Emotions and Adjudication: Status Degradation Among White-Collar Criminals," *Justice Quarterly* 7 (1990): 515–528; John Braithwaite, *Crime, Shame and Reintegration* (Sydney: Cambridge University Press, 1989).

85. John Braithwaite and Gilbert Geis, "On Theory and Action for Corporate Crime Control," *Crime and Delinquency* 28 (1982): 292–314.

86. James Miller, "U.S. Ban on Baxter International Bids Hurt Reputation More Than Business," *Wall Street Journal*, August 16, 1993, A3.

87. Kip Schlegel, "Desert, Retribution and Corporate Criminality," *Justice Quarterly* 5 (1988): 615–634.

88. Raymond Michalowski and Ronald Kramer, "The Space Between Laws: The Problem of Corporate Crime in a Transnational Context," *Social Problems* 34 (1987): 34–53.

89. Steven Klepper and Daniel Nagin, "The Deterrent Effect of Perceived Certainty and Severity of Punishment Revisited," *Criminology* 27 (1989): 721–746.

90. Bill Richards and Alex Kotlowitz, "Judge Finds Three Corporate Officials Guilty of Murder in Cyanide Death of Worker," *Wall Street Journal*, June 17, 1985, 2.

91. Donald Manson, *Tracking Offenders: White-Collar Crime* (Washington, DC: Bureau of Justice Statistics, 1986); Kenneth Carlson and Jan Chaiken, *White-Collar Crime* (Washington, DC: Bureau of Justice Statistics, 1987); Robert Bennett, "Foreword: Eighth Survey of White-Collar Crime," *American Criminal Law Review* 30 (1993).

92. David Weisburd, Elin Waring, and Stanton Wheeler, "Class, Status, and the Punishment of White-Collar Criminals," *Law and Social Inquiry* 15 (1990): 223–243.

93. Mark Cohen, "Environmental Crime and Punishment: Legal/Economic Theory and Empirical Evidence on Enforcement of Federal Environmental Statutes," *Journal of Criminal Law and Criminology* 82 (1992): 1054–1109.

94. Frederick Martens and Michele Cunningham-Niederer, "Media Magic, Mafia Mania," *Federal Probation* 49 (1985): 60–68.

95. Alan Block and William Chambliss, *Organizing Crime* (New York: Elsevier, 1981).

96. Alan Block, *East Side/West Side* (New Brunswick, NJ: Transaction Books, 1983), vii, 10–11; G.R. Blakey and M. Goldsmith, "Criminal Redistribution of Stolen Property: The Need for Law Reform," *Michigan Law Review* 81 (August 1976): 45–46.

97. Stephen Schneider, "Organized Crime, Money Laundering, and the Real Estate Market in Canada," *Journal of Property Research* 21, 2 (2004): 99–118.

98. Merry Morash, "Organized Crime," in *Major Forms of Crime*, ed. Robert Meier, 198 (Beverly Hills, CA: Sage, 1984).

99. Donald Cressey, *Theft of the Nation* (New York: Harper and Row, 1969).

100. Dwight Smith, Jr., *The Mafia Mystique* (New York: Basic Books, 1975).

101. *Organized Crime Today*, 489; Robert Rhodes, *Organized Crime: Crime Control versus Civil Liberties* (New York: Random House, 1984).

102. This section borrows heavily from Browning and Gerassi, *The American Way of Crime*, 288–472; and August Bequai, *Organized Crime* (Lexington, MA: Lexington Books, 1979).

103. Jay Albanese, "God and the Mafia Revisited: From Valachi to Frantianno," paper presented at the annual meeting of the American Society of Criminology, Toronto, 1982.

104. Philip Jenkins and Gary Potter, "The Politics and Mythology of Organized Crime: A Philadelphia Case Study," *Journal of Criminal Justice* 15 (1987): 473–484.

105. Based on the 2001 Report on Organized Crime in Canada, Criminal Intelligence Service of Canada, www.cisc.gc.ca.

106. Criminal Intelligence Service Canada, *2004 Annual Report on Organized Crime in Canada* (Ottawa: Criminal Intelligence Service Canada, 2004).

107. Robert Kelly and Rufus Schatzberg, "Types of Minority Organized Crime: Some Considerations," paper presented at the annual meeting of the American Society of Criminology, Montreal, November 1987.

108. Chad Skelton, "Losing the War on Bikers," *Vancouver Sun*, October 9, 2004; Adrian Humphreys, "Forces Fear Bikergang Infiltration," *National Post*, August 30, 2004.

109. Omar Bartos, "Growth of Russian Organized Crime Poses Serious Threat," *CJ International* 11 (1995): 8–9; Francis Ianni, *Black Mafia: Ethnic Succession in Organized Crime* (New York: Pocket Books, 1975).

110. Peter Kerr, "Chinese Now Dominate New York Heroin Trade," *New York Times*, August 9, 1987, 1; Ian McDermid Gomme, *The Shadow Line: Deviance and Crime in Canada*, 2nd ed. (Toronto: Harcourt Brace, 1998).

111. William Chambliss, *On the Take* (Bloomington, IN: Indiana University Press, 1978).

112. George Vold, *Theoretical Criminology*, 2nd ed., rev. Thomas Bernard (New York: Oxford University Press, 1979).

113. Jay Albanese, *Organized Crime in America*, 2nd ed. (Cincinnati: Anderson, 1989), 68.

Public Order Crimes: Legislating Morality

Learning Objectives

After reading this chapter, you will be able to:

1. Understand the history of public order offences.
2. Be familiar with the scope of illegal sexuality.
3. Know the extent of drug use and abuse.
4. Discuss the different strategies for the control of drugs.
5. Explain new areas of public order offences and their control.

Casinos came on the scene in the late 1980s and early 1990s. They play a role in provinces and territories realizing huge profits from legalized gambling.

In 2008, Marc Emery, Vancouver's so-called Prince of Pot, faced extradition to the United States over charges of money laundering and selling marijuana seeds. He offered to serve his five-year sentence in Canada, but in the end he was deported.

He and two others were arrested in 2005 at the request of the United States and charged, even though prosecutors in Canada have not enforced the law against selling pot seeds. Stores selling cannabis seeds can be found in Vancouver, Toronto, and other major Canadian cities.

In fact, when Emery was convicted in Canada of selling pot seeds in 1998, he was given a $2,000 fine. He has openly violated the law for more than a decade, pays taxes, has run in various elections, and has championed the cause of legal marijuana at parliamentary hearings. Moreover, the crime he committed is a victimless, non-violent crime.

In 2010, he was extradited to the United States, jailed for five years for selling mail-order marijuana seeds, and subsequently denied transfer to a Canadian prison.

As one commentator suggests, perhaps Emery has angered the anti-drug law-enforcement community. However, despite enforcement, more marijuana is on our streets than ever, and even the 1970s Le Dain Commission urged legalization, so maybe it's time to retract the hypocrisy.[1]

Societies have always limited behaviours *believed* to run contrary to social norms, customs, and values. These acts are referred to as **public order crimes**, or *victimless crimes*.[2] Public order crimes usually include acts that offend our moral sense of how people should act. Put another way, although such common-law crimes as rape or robbery are considered *mala in se*, inherently evil and wrong, other offences are known as *mala prohibitum* crimes, which are behaviours outlawed because they conflict with social policy, moral sensibilities, and current public opinion.

Laws to uphold public order usually prohibit the distribution of morally questionable items, such as erotic material and mood-altering drugs. These laws may also ban acts that some people holding political power consider immoral, such as abortion, prostitution, marijuana use, or assisted suicide. These acts are controversial because law-abiding citizens sometimes engage in them. However, the line between good and bad behaviour is often a thin one.

This chapter is divided into four main sections: (1) the relationship between law and morality, (2) public order crimes of a sexual nature, (3) drug and alcohol abuse, and (4) emerging issues, such as the decriminalization of gambling and euthanasia.

LAW AND MORALITY

The legislation of moral issues is a continual source of frustration. The purpose of the criminal law is to protect society and reduce social harm, so when a store is robbed or a child assaulted, it is easy to condemn the social harm done to the victim.

However, identifying the victim is more difficult in the case of immoral acts such as prostitution because the parties involved may be willing participants. Or, as the example opening this chapter shows, what if the crime is the buying and selling of marijuana seeds? If there is no victim, can there be a crime? Should acts be made illegal merely because they violate prevailing moral standards? And, if so, who defines morality? The absolute letter of the law might be unrealistically strict, might reflect conservative standards not accepted by the majority, and might be based on an outdated morality.

Should a person be punished for providing a service for which other people are willing to pay? If people willingly pay to purchase sexual services, are they crime victims? Many, but not all, prostitutes willingly engage in sexual activity for money, and their income is far higher than they would have earned in legitimate jobs. Although their behaviour is considered immoral, should a prostitute and her or his clients be considered criminals for engaging in this victimless crime?

We might first consider whether there is actually a victim in victimless crimes. Some participants may have been forced into their acts, for example, some women involved in adult films.[3] Young runaways can be coerced into a life on the streets, where they are cruelly treated and held as virtual captives.[4] Asian girls are trafficked into Canada and sold into debt bondage to brothels. Although less than 20 percent of prostitutes are juveniles, a majority of street prostitutes interviewed had become sex trade workers before the age of 18.[5]

Society as a whole should consider the victims of these crimes.

Conversely, when consenting behaviour between adults is criminalized, it sends out a message that repression is an acceptable way to enforce conformity. People often feel that the state has no business regulating the private sexual relationships of consenting adults.[6]

Debating Morality

Some argue that pornography, prostitution, and drug use erode the moral fabric of society and should be punished by law because of a collective feeling of revulsion toward certain acts, even if they are not dangerous.[7] In his classic statement on the function of morality in the law, Sir Patrick Devlin stated:

CONNECTIONS

Chapter 2 discusses the difference between *mala in se* and *mala prohibitum* offences.

---

public order crimes   Sometimes called *victimless* crimes, these acts interfere with public order, such as loitering for the purposes of prostitution..

Without shared ideas on politics, morals, and ethics no society can exist…. If men and women try to create a society in which there is no fundamental agreement about good and evil, they will fail; if having based it on common agreement, the society will disintegrate. For society is not something that is kept together physically; it is held by the invisible bonds of common thought. If the bonds were too far relaxed, the members would drift apart. A common morality is part of the bondage … which is part of the price of society; and mankind, which needs society, must pay its price.[8]

Accordingly, some argue, criminal law must express public morality and prohibit victimless crimes.[9]

Some argue that basing criminal definitions on moral beliefs is an impossible task: Who defines morality? Are we not punishing differences rather than reducing social harm? If morals are really the expression of the majority, should they be the basis for regulating the conduct of all? Are photographs by Robert Mapplethorpe art or obscenity? As U.S. Supreme Court Justice William O. Douglas put it, "What may be trash to me may be prized by others."[10]

In the Puritan society of Salem, Massachusetts, women were burned at the stake as witches because their behaviour seemed strange. We know now that the witch craze occurred during a time of societal change, and it scapegoated individuals in a process of salving social anxiety. What if moral panics are "anxiety panics"?

In parts of Africa today, female circumcision is performed to ensure virginity and make girls suitable for marriage. Critics of this practice consider it an act of mutilation and torture, and a restriction of women's sexuality. However, others argue that this ancient custom should be left to the discretion of people who consider it part of their culture. Can an outsider define the morality of another culture?[11] Or, in a democracy, should a majority dictate how all should live?

A "game" unfolds nightly on the streets and alleys of downtown Canadian cities—a picture of prostitution that masks the hidden world of pimps and johns.

Gusfield says that the outlawing of behaviour shows the moral superiority of those who condemn the acts over those who commit them. The legislation of morality "enhances the social status of groups carrying the affirmed culture and degrades groups carrying that which is condemned as deviant."[12]

Legislating morality thus creates insiders who are normal and outsiders who are deviant. However, the question of whether taking such a stand is legitimate remains open.

Criminal or Immoral?

Acts that we might feel are immoral are not necessarily criminal. No law legislates against pride, sloth, lust, gluttony, wrath, avarice, or envy, although they are considered the seven deadly sins.

Violations of conventional morality may even be tolerated because they serve a useful social function. For example, watching sexually explicit films is thought to release tension; immoral behaviour may even provide benefits to legitimate enterprises.[13]

Some acts also seem well intentioned, but are still criminal in Canada, such as killing a loved one who is suffering from an incurable disease (euthanasia), stealing to feed a poor family (theft), or marrying many women (polygamy) in conforming to religious beliefs.[14]

It might be possible to settle this argument by saying that immoral acts become crimes if they are harmful to the public. Yet some acts that cause social harm are legal, such as the use of tobacco and alcohol, and driving vehicles that can accelerate to more than 160 km per hour. More people die each year from alcohol-, tobacco-, and auto-related deaths than from all drug-related deaths combined. Should drugs be legalized and fast cars outlawed?

Even if an act were outlawed, the law might prove difficult to enforce if the public was divided. For example, assisted suicide may be against the law because it causes social harm, but prosecutors have failed to gain convictions in assisted suicide cases because so many people view it as a humanitarian act and refuse to convict. Although Sue Rodriguez failed in her request to the Supreme Court of Canada for legal assisted suicide, many people were sympathetic to her cause (see the Famous Canadian Court Cases box, later in this chapter).

When asked whether they favour or oppose legalized euthanasia, 49 percent of people surveyed said they were in favour, while 37 percent were opposed, and 14 percent were undecided.[15]

Moral Crusades

Canada doesn't have the wild west history of the United States, where vigilance committees were set up in boomtowns to pursue cattle rustlers and stagecoach robbers.

However, Canada does have a largely unknown history of "popular justice." These vigilantes held to a strict standard of morality, punishing moral transgressions such as sexual deviance, drunkenness, severe wife beating, and adultery. The popularity of such vigilante movements diminished with the growth of state institutions and the development of the police.[16]

The avenging vigilante is an important part of North American popular culture, enforcing the law and social customs. From Superman to Captain Canada, the righteous **vigilante** goes on **moral crusades** without authorization from legal authorities. Popular targets of moral crusaders are abortion clinics, pornographers, gun dealers, and logging companies. What else but moral issues could explain the thousands of acts of violence against abortion clinics over the last 30 years?

Howard Becker has labelled such people **moral entrepreneurs**, who operate with an absolute certainty that their way is right and that any means are justified to get their way; "the crusader is fervent and righteous, often self-righteous."[17]

Moral crusades are directed against people defined as evil by a segment of the population. For example, anti-smut campaigns attempt to ban an author's books from the library or to prevent a controversial figure from speaking at a university. One way to accomplish their goal is to prove that their target is evil, polarizing people into bad guys and good guys, while creating a climate where the good are deified while the bad are demonized.[18]

Categorizing people as all good or all bad creates crime control policies that may be overly punitive. For example, the death penalty is justified if murderers are bad guys—unrepentant monsters who commit serial murders and mutilate their victims. If, instead, murderers were seen as disturbed victims of child abuse and neglect, then considering the death penalty would be out of the question.

Enforcement of morally tinged statutes has become a significant problem for law enforcement agencies. In Vancouver, several stores selling marijuana paraphernalia have been raided, and pipes and seeds were seized under section 462.2 of the *Criminal Code of Canada* (CCC).[19] If laws governing marijuana use are enforced too vigorously, local authorities are branded as reactionaries who waste time on petty issues. But if the authorities confiscate marijuana destined for alleviating pain, they risk being seen as insensitive. However, if police agencies ignore public order crimes, they are accused of being soft on immorality.

"Society would be a lot better off," the argument goes, "if the cops cracked down on 'those people.'" Who "those people" are and what should be done about them is a matter of great public debate.

Let us now turn to specific examples of public order crimes.

ILLEGAL SEXUALITY

One type of public order crime relates to what conventional society considers deviant sexual practices, such as paraphilia, prostitution, and pornography.

Paraphilia

In 1996, 250,000 Belgians took to the streets to protest the government's inept handling of a case involving the deaths of four children at the hands of a pedophile ring led by convicted rapist, Marc Dutroux. Two of the victims (8-year-old girls) had been imprisoned and molested for months in Dutroux's home. They starved to death when he was arrested and sent to jail on an unrelated charge. Other children had been kidnapped, raped, tortured, and sold into sexual slavery by the ring.

The case of Marc Dutroux is an extreme example of **paraphilia**, abnormal sexual practices involving recurrent sexual urges focused on (1) non-human objects (underwear, shoes, leather); (2) humiliation or the experience of receiving or giving pain (sadomasochism, bondage); or (3) children or others who cannot grant consent.[20] Some acts of paraphilia, such as wearing clothes normally worn by the opposite sex (transvestitism), can be engaged in by adults in the privacy of their homes and do not involve a third party. Others, however, present a risk of social harm and are subject to criminal penalties, such as exposure of genitals in public (indecent exposure, section 173 CCC), and sexual interference with a person under the age of 14 (section 153 CCC). Voyeurism is handled under trespassing (section 177 CCC), or stalking (section 264 CCC).

In paraphilia that involve unwilling or underage victims, the victim and offender often have a prior relationship as

---

vigilante   Someone who takes the law into their own hands, and acts outside the law in the interest of justice.

moral crusades   Efforts by interest groups to stamp out behaviour they find objectionable; typically public order crimes, such as drug use or pornography.

moral entrepreneurs   Interest groups that attempt to control social life for the purpose of promoting their own personal set of moral values.

paraphilia   Abnormal sexual practices that may involve recurrent sexual urges focused on objects, humiliation, or children.

family members, intimates, or acquaintances. Generally, family members are involved in about a quarter of sexual assaults and a third of other sexual offences, while acquaintances commit about half. Many will involve a child under 12 years of age. The offender is typically older than other violent offenders, heterosexual, and more likely to be related to or known by the victim and exploiting a position of authority.[21] This picture of the sex offender is very different from an earlier image of sexual danger.

In the 1950s and 1960s, hundreds of suspected gay men and lesbians lost their jobs, were demoted from high-security positions in the Canadian civil service, or were purged from the military (see the nearby Famous Canadian Criminals box about the case of Everett Klippert). By the late 1960s, the RCMP had collected the names of 9,000 suspected lesbians and gay men.[22] The government also funded research into a means to detect homosexuals, known as the "fruit machine." However, homosexuality was dropped from the list of deviant sexualities by the Canadian Psychological Association in the late 1970s, and 20-some years later, same-sex marriage became legal in Canada.

The recognition of homosexuality as a legitimate sexual choice and the resultant decline of legal persecution probably rank as major accomplishments of the latter 20th century.

Prostitution

The earliest record of prostitution appears in ancient Mesopotamia, where priests engaged in sex to promote fertility in the community. All women were required to do temple duty, and passing strangers were expected to make donations to the temple after enjoying its services.

Modern commercial sex has its roots in ancient Greece, where Solon established licensed brothels in 500 BCE. The earnings of Greek prostitutes helped pay for the temple of Aphrodite, where famous men went to enjoy intellectual, aesthetic, and sexual stimulation.

Although some early Christian religious leaders, such as St. Augustine and St. Thomas Aquinas, were tolerant of prostitution, this attitude disappeared after the Reformation. Lutheran doctrine depicted prostitutes as emissaries of the devil who were sent to destroy the faith.[23]

In more recent times, prostitution was tied to the rise of English brewery companies during the early 19th century. The breweries employed prostitutes in saloons to attract patrons and encourage them to drink.

Today, **prostitution** is defined as the consensual exchange of sex for money, and money for sex. This exchange itself is not illegal, although it is virtually impossible not to break some part of the law. For example, section 213 of the *Criminal*

Famous Canadian Criminals
The Case of Everett Klippert

In 1965, during a police investigation, a man named Everett Klippert said he was homosexual. At the time, a man having sex with men was categorized as gross indecency under the criminal law. Sentenced to three years in prison, he was interviewed by two psychiatrists who identified that, under Canada's law, Klippert fit the profile of a dangerous sexual offender, simply because he was likely to repeat his behaviour. Klippert was incarcerated for life, a sentence confirmed by the Supreme Court of Canada in 1967.

Reaction to the judgment was swift. An editorial in the *Toronto Star* called the decision "a return to the Middle Ages," and Pierre Elliott Trudeau, then justice minister, said that "the state has no place in the bedrooms of the nation."

Two years later, in 1969, Bill C-150, an omnibus bill dealing with offences from gross indecency through abortion to gambling, decriminalized homosexuality by suggesting that sexual acts between consenting adults in private were legal. The bill caused heated debate in the House of Commons. John Diefenbaker, recorded in the *Hansard Debates* of January 27, 1969, said, "I am opposed to these homosexuality amendments. I think they are wrong.... I know there is no individual more subject to intimidation and threat by the USSR as it endeavours to obtain information detrimental to the security of Canada than those who are believed to be homosexuals."

Trudeau said, "It's certainly the most extensive revision of the *Criminal Code* since the 1950s and...I feel that it has knocked

down a lot of totems and overridden a lot of taboos.... It's bringing the laws of the land up to contemporary society.... The view we take here is that there's no place for the state in the bedrooms of the nation.... What's done in private between adults doesn't concern the *Criminal Code*. When it becomes public, this is a different matter, or when it relates to minors, this is a different matter."

On July 20, 1971, Everett Klippert was released from prison.

SOURCES: Anne Vassal, John Fisher, Ralf Jürgens, and Robert Hughes, "Gay and Lesbian Issues and HIV/AIDS, A Discussion Paper," Canadian HIV/AIDS Legal Network and Canadian AIDS Society, July 1997, www.aidslaw.ca/Maincontent/issues/gaylesbian/07p2bE.html; Owen Wood, "The Fight for Gay Rights: Canada Timeline," *Pride News*, www.caw2002tca.ca/e/pride.htm.

Code of Canada (CCC) makes it illegal to either ask for or offer a money–sex exchange in public. This law has been challenged on constitutional grounds as violating the constitutionally protected right to communication; however, the Supreme Court ruled that the law is a "reasonable infringement" on civil liberties, because of the nuisance caused by the public solicitation of sex for money.[24]

However, as Simon Fraser University criminologist John Lowman notes, the Special Committee on Pornography and Prostitution, which is charged with reviewing prostitution law in light of the "nuisances" created by street prostitution, concluded that the law itself was responsible for the increase of street prostitution. It recommended sweeping changes to the *Criminal Code*, including regulation; however, in 1985, the street prostitution law was rewritten to make convictions easier to obtain.

The new communicating law prohibits communicating in a public place for the purpose of buying or selling sexual services. As a result, the street trade was forced to relocate, exposing sex trade workers to more violence. In British Columbia, for example, 11 prostitutes were murdered in the 25-year period before the introduction of the communicating law, as compared with approximately 100 in the 15-year period immediately after.[25]

The definition of the offence of prostitution is gender neutral, because prostitutes can, of course, be male or female, straight or gay. Other sections of the code include "Keeping a common bawdy-house" (section 210 CCC), "Transporting person to bawdy-house" (section 211 CCC), and "Procuring," otherwise known as pimping (section 212 CCC). The most usual offence for which a person is charged under prostitution law is section 213, "Communicating for the purposes of prostitution" (see also Exhibit 13.1).

In 1990, Metropolitan Toronto Police charged *NOW* magazine with "Communicating for the purposes of prostitution" because some of its classified advertising offered sexual services for sale. The charges, laid by morality bureau officers despite the lack of official approval by the attorney general's office, were subsequently dropped.[26]

The commercial sexual transaction usually involves activity with sexual significance for the customer: intercourse, exhibitionism, sadomasochism, oral sex; an economic transaction: money or drugs are exchanged for the activity; and emotional indifference: the interaction has nothing to do with affection.[27]

Incidence of Prostitution. Of the 2,077 prostitution-related offences (PROs) recorded in 2012, most were for communication (90 percent in 2009). This was a decline of 3 percent over the previous year, but an increase of 91 percent over the previous decade. However, because communication is an enforcement-related crime, it is difficult to know whether prostitution or policing is responsible for the increase. Only 21 youths were charged with prostitution in 2007.

Of adults charged, the split is usually about 50-50 male-female. While initially these statistics seem to portray gender equity, it is actually a gender imbalance in charging; one

---

---

prostitute will service hundreds of different clients each year. These statistics provide clear evidence that johns are undercharged in relation to prostitutes, and more resources are put into arresting prostitutes than arresting clients. The clearance rate is usually very high, but only because prostitutes and their clients are caught by undercover officers. Of the people convicted in 2003 and 2004, 30 percent received a fine, almost half received probation, and less than a quarter went to prison.

Types of Prostitution. Prostitutes who work the streets are called hustlers, hookers, or streetwalkers. Although glamorized by the Julia Roberts character in the film *Pretty Woman* (who winds up with multimillionaire Richard Gere), streetwalkers are considered the least attractive, lowest-paid, most vulnerable women and men in the profession. Streetwalkers wear bright clothing and makeup and take their customers to hotels or cars.[28] Streetwalkers are most likely to be members of ethnic minorities, to live in poverty and suffer from addictions. Many are young runaways who gravitate to major cities to find an exciting life and escape from sexual and physical abuse at home.[29] Of all prostitutes, streetwalkers have the highest incidence of drug abuse and larceny arrests.

Bar girls (B-girls) spend their time in bars, drinking and waiting to be picked up by customers. B-girls work out an arrangement with the bartender so that they are served diluted

---

prostitution The buying and selling of sex, not illegal in Canada, although prostitution-related offences are illegal, such as pimping, brothel-keeping, and public communication of such an exchange.

---

drinks or water coloured with dye or tea, for which the customer is charged an exorbitant price. It is common to find B-girls in towns with military bases and large transient populations.

Brothels flourished in the 19th and early 20th centuries. They are establishments run by **madams** that house several prostitutes. The owner, or madam, employs and supervises the prostitutes and takes a cut of the prostitutes' earnings. The owner's role may include recruiting women into prostitution and socializing them in the trade.[30] Many jurisdictions in the world today have some form of legalized or regulated prostitution; however, the international sex trafficking of women and girls is important for organized crime.

The aristocrats of prostitution are **call girls**. They charge customers thousands of dollars per encounter and may net more than $100,000 per year. Some gain clients through employment in escort services, while others develop independent customer lists. Many call girls come from middle-class backgrounds and service upper-class customers. Working exclusively via telephone "dates," call girls get their clients by word of mouth or by making arrangements with bellhops, cab drivers, and so on. They either entertain clients in their own apartments or make outcalls to clients' hotels and apartments. Call girls are at risk by being alone with strangers, so they might request the business cards of their clients to make sure they are dealing with upstanding citizens.

In the adult entertainment zones of large cities are *rap booths*. Here, the prostitute and her customer occupy booths that are separated by a glass wall, and they talk via telephone for as long as the customer is willing to pay. The more money he spends, the more she engages in sexual banter and disrobing. No actual touching takes place, and sex is through masturbation.

Some prostitutes have substance abuse problems, and prostitution supports their drug habits. Not all drug-addicted prostitutes barter sex for drugs, but those who do report more frequent drug abuse and physical violence than do other prostitutes.[31]

Some sex trade work is based in **massage parlours**, where prostitutes provide oral sex and manual stimulation. Photography studios and escort services are other possible covers for commercial sex. Stag party girls will service all-male parties and groups by putting on shows and having sex with participants. In years past, many hotels had live-in prostitutes, while today's hotel prostitute makes a deal with the bell captain or manager to refer customers to her for a fee.

Becoming a Prostitute.

Why does someone turn to prostitution? Both male and female prostitutes often come from troubled homes marked by extreme conflict, where divorce or death has split the family.[32] Many prostitutes have long histories of sexual exploitation and abuse.[33]

For example, a youth prostitution survey done for the Department of Justice in 2002 found that 82 percent of females and 100 percent of males had a background of sexual abuse before living on the street.[34] This finding was significant in terms of getting police and policy-makers to rethink juvenile prostitution as sexual exploitation.

A 2005 study, which interviewed 100 women prostituting in Vancouver, found an extremely high prevalence of lifetime violence and post-traumatic stress disorder (PTSD). Fifty-two percent were Aboriginal women, a significant overrepresentation in prostitution compared with their representation in Vancouver generally (1.7 to 7 percent). Eighty-two percent reported childhood sexual abuse, 72 percent reported childhood physical abuse, 90 percent had been physically assaulted in prostitution, and 78 percent had been raped in prostitution. Seventy-two percent met the American Psychiatric Association's *Diagnostic and Statistical Manual of Mental Disorders, 4th edition (DSM-IV)* criteria for PTSD. Furthermore, 86 percent reported current or past homelessness, and 82 percent expressed a need for treatment for drug or alcohol addictions.[35]

Conflict with school authorities, poor grades, and drug abuse are often contributing factors.[36] Other personal characteristics include growing up in a slum neighbourhood, living in a single-parent home, being a member of a gang, and being unemployed. No evidence suggests that people become prostitutes because of psychological problems. Money, drugs, and survival seem to be greater motivations, a combination of rational choice and structural inequality.

Pimps may convince girls to become prostitutes through flattery and promises, but relatively few kidnap or coerce kids into prostitution. It is more likely that friends or relatives introduce kids to prostitution.[37]

Child Prostitution.

Child prostitution is a worldwide problem. Girls from Latin America are sold for sex in Europe and the Middle East. Southeast Asian girls wind up in Northern Europe and the Middle East, and Russian and Ukrainian girls are sold in Hungary, Poland, and the Baltic States. An estimated one million children are part of the sex trade in Asia. Thailand is the leader, but child prostitution is also a problem in India, Bangladesh, and the Philippines. Sex tours are a common practice in these nations, and Canada now has laws to prosecute sex tourism with minors. In some Asian nations, such as Thailand, most young girls are forced into prostitution because they are poor.

---

brothel   A house of prostitution, typically run by a madam who sets prices and handles the business arrangements.

madam   The traditional name for a woman who runs a brothel; more common today is the male pimp.

call girls   Prostitutes who make dates via the phone, and then service steady clientele in hotel rooms or apartments.

massage parlours   Seemingly legitimate businesses where men can buy sex under the guise of massage therapy; one of the more hidden sides of prostitution.

Pimps. A pimp derives his livelihood from the earnings of a prostitute. The pimp helps steer customers to the prostitute, stays on the alert for police, posts bail, and protects his prostitutes from unruly customers. Pimps can pick up established working girls or they can turn out young girls who have never been in the life. Occasionally, they pick up young runaways, buy them clothes and jewellery, and turn them into street prostitutes.

The role of the pimp is changing. The decline of the brothel, the development of independent prostitutes, and the control of prostitution by organized crime have decreased the number of full-time pimps. Many prostitutes are drug-dependent, and in some areas, drug dealers have replaced pimps as the controlling force in prostitution.[38] Pimps are often reluctant to work with younger prostitutes because of the risk of more severe penalties if they are caught running juveniles.[39]

Johns. It is primarily men who buy the sexual services of both male and female prostitutes, although little research has been done on the topic. The men are virtually invisible as attention is focused on the female prostitute. Johns are usually between 20 and 40 years old, married, and consider themselves heterosexual, even if they pick up young men. Their reasons for seeking out prostitutes are as varied as the desire for discreet sex to wanting sexual services they are unable to obtain elsewhere.[40]

The customers need to be included in the debates surrounding prostitution because, though prostitution seeking is often treated as a natural part of masculine sexual experience, most men do not pursue prostitutes, and very few are regular users.[41]

Legalize Prostitution? Prostitution is a minor offence, punishable by a fine or a short jail sentence. In some jurisdictions, johns must attend "john school," where they listen to stories of women forced to work in prostitution. John schools originated in San Francisco in 1995, and today more than a dozen john school programs operate successfully in Canada. They focus on educating offenders on the legal ramifications of prostitution, the health risks, and the effects of prostitution on women. The john school started in Vancouver by the John Howard Society is a precharge diversion program. Offenders arrested in the course of police undercover sting operations for communication are screened by police and offered the option of attending a Prostitution Offender Program. The cost of attending is $400, and during the day, the john will hear various speakers, including community members, legal experts, former sex trade workers, police officers, and health professionals.

To some feminists, women are victims of male dominance, and in patriarchal societies, prostitution is a clear example of gender exploitation.[42] For other feminists, prostitution should be a matter of free choice. Advocates of both sides argue that the penalties for prostitution should be reduced. Decriminalization would relieve already desperate women of the additional burden of severe legal punishment.

Pornography

The term **pornography** derives from the Greek *porne*, meaning "prostitute," and *graphein*, meaning "to write." Pornographic books, magazines, films, and websites that depict explicit sex acts are widely available. Opponents of pornography argue that pornographers exploit their models, who may include underage children or victims of physical and psychological coercion.

One problem of controlling pornography is its relation to **obscenity**, which is defined as material deeply offensive to morality or decency. Police and law enforcement officials can legally seize only material that is judged obscene. But who is to judge what is obscene? For example, the novel *Tropic of Cancer* by Henry Miller was once banned in the United States because it was considered obscene, but today it is considered a work of great literary value. Books destined for gay bookstores used to be detained at the Canadian/American border. Today, it is doubtful this would get a second thought.

Child Pornography Rings. Many of the hard-core pictures that find their way into hands of collectors are the work of pornographic rings that exploit children and adolescents for sex. A typical ring comprises from 3 to 11 children, predominantly males, some of preschool age. Adults who control the ring use a position of trust to recruit the children, and then exploit them through material and psychological rewards.

Solo sex rings involve several children and a single adult often in a position of trust (counsellor, teacher, Boy Scout leader) who uses this relationship to recruit children into sexual activity. Transition rings are impromptu groups set up to sell and trade photos and sex, whereas syndicated rings are well structured and create extensive networks of customers who desire sexual services.[43] The sexual exploitation involved causes physical and psychological problems of a variety of forms.

Given the frequency with which child pornography is now traded over the Internet, Parliament debated passing a law prohibiting the intentional viewing of any child pornography. Previously, a person had to possess pornography to be charged.[44]

Does Pornography Cause Violence? Serial killer Ted Bundy claimed that his murderous rampage was fuelled by reading pornography. However, what evidence exists that viewing sexually explicit material has an effect on behaviour? An American national commission on pornography could find no relationship between pornography and violence.[45]

> **pornography** Depiction of sex acts in a variety of forms, such as books, magazines, films, and websites.
>
> **obscenity** Sexually explicit material, for example, open sexual behaviour, masturbation, and genital exhibition banned in most communities.

Another commission called for legal attacks on hard-core pornography and condemnation of all sexually related material, but also found little evidence that obscenity is a cause of antisocial behaviour.

How can we account for this surprisingly insignificant association? In Denmark, research showed that sex offences actually declined shortly after pornography was decriminalized in 1967.[46] Other research found that sex offenders report less exposure to pornography than non-offenders.[47]

Viewing pornography may have the side effect of satisfying erotic impulses that otherwise might result in more sexually aggressive behaviour. Although some criminologists believe that a relationship exists between pornography and rape, others say that people exposed to violent material are likely to become sexually aggressive.[48] Laboratory experiments have found that men exposed to violence in pornography are more likely to act aggressively toward women.[49] Adult-only books and films often have sexually violent themes, such as rape, bondage, and mutilation. Many also feel that violent pornography leads to a greater acceptance of rape myths and violence against women, and to more tolerance of sexual aggression.

Pornography and the Law.   In Canada, it is an offence to publish or circulate any obscene "thing" (section 163 CCC), where "obscenity" is defined as the undue exploitation of sex and crime, horror, cruelty, and violence. The key question is whether the material violates community standards. Our society has a high level of tolerance for adult nudity in magazines, but not for pictures of adult–child sex.

The Supreme Court of Canada, in the 1992 *Butler* decision, identified the objective of this section of the *Criminal Code* as the protection of society from harm caused by exposure to obscene materials. Under section 163(8) of the *Criminal Code* and the federal *Customs Act,* officers had been in the habit of detaining materials bound for gay bookstores, so in 1998 the Little Sisters Bookstore in Vancouver challenged the law. The court found the law constitutional, but that it had been enforced in a discriminating way.

When *NOW* magazine was charged for running sex ads in its business personals section, community support rallied for the magazine but not for the police. Similarly, in Halifax in 1998, some police officers took it upon themselves to contact businesses that advertised in *The Coast* and urge them to withdraw their advertising because of the nature of the "Savage Love" advice column. The column had been investigated by the morality section in 1996 and found not to be obscene, but this ruling didn't prevent the police from trying to enforce what they thought were community standards but, in this case, were their standards.

The punishment of pornographers often creates moral and legal dilemmas, as in the posthumous 1990 exhibition of the work of photographer Robert Mapplethorpe in Cincinnati. The exhibition was heavily criticized by conservative politicians because it included images of nude children and of men in homoerotic poses. Obscenity charges were brought against the exhibition's director, but he was acquitted. The actions taken against the Mapplethorpe exhibit brought protests from not only artists and performers but also from civil libertarians, who fear government control over art, music, and theatre.

Obviously, a plebiscite cannot be held to determine the community's attitude for every trial concerning the sale of pornography. However, works that are considered obscene in Orillia might be considered acceptable in Toronto.

Distributing Illegal Sexual Material

The information technology revolution has revitalized the porn industry. The Internet is an ideal venue for selling and distributing obscene material, and the computer is an ideal device for storing and viewing it. It is difficult to estimate how many websites feature sexual content, including nude photos, videos, live sex acts, and web-cam strip sessions, among other forms of "adult entertainment."[50] However it has been said that pornography pays for the Internet.

N2H2, a Seattle-based web-filtering company, estimates that the number of pornographic Web pages has soared during the past six years and that now over 1.3 million sites contain approximately 260 million pages of erotic content—all aimed at cashing in on the billions in revenue spent annually on Internet porn.[51] The number of visits to pornographic sites surpasses those made to Internet search engines; some individual sites report as many as 50 million hits per year. How do adult sites operate today?[52]

While some sites cater to adult tastes, others cross the legal border by peddling access to obscene material. In one well-known case, Landslide Productions of Fort Worth, Texas, operated as a highly profitable Internet-based pornography ring, taking in as much as $1.4 million in one month.[53] To its 250,000 subscribers worldwide, it offered access to websites that advertised themselves with such names as Cyber Lolita. Landslide provided a credit card verification service that acted as an electronic gateway to the pictures and movies of minors engaging in sexually explicit conduct. Internet customers were required to provide a credit card number and a charge authorization to gain access to the pornographic productions on the websites. Landslide charged each customer approximately $29.95 per month per site for access to these pornographic images of minors and was the only gateway to these child pornography websites.[54] The sites, off limits to U.S. control because they were located in Russia and Indonesia, had a fee-sharing arrangement with Landslide's owners who earned millions, but were eventually sentenced to life in prison for their crimes.

Despite this successful prosecution, controlling Internet pornography has been difficult. Filtering devices used extensively in schools and libraries fail to block out much obscene material. Any law enforcement efforts are unlikely to put a dent in the Internet porn industry.

Controlling Sex for Profit

Sex for profit predates Western civilization, and law enforcement crusades can make sex-related goods and services a relatively scarce commodity, driving up prices. The threat of government regulation may also convince some participants in the sex-for-profit industry to police themselves. Fear of government control probably influences mainstream sex magazines to alter their content rather than risk provoking public officials. Fewer controls exist for Internet-based material.

Technological change will challenge the sex-for-profit industry as people buy or rent DVDs from local stores to play in their homes. Adult DVDs are now a staple of the computer industry. Internet sex services (cybersex) include live, interactive stripping and sexual activities. Governments have moved to control the broadcast of obscene films via satellite and other technological innovations. Police have also moved to control Internet-based pornography.

SUBSTANCE ABUSE

The problem of substance abuse is widespread in modern societies. Large urban areas are beset by drug-dealing gangs, drug users who engage in crime to support their habits, and alcohol-related violence. Rural and coastal areas are important staging centres for the shipment of drugs across the country, and the production of synthetic drugs and marijuana farming form significant portions of the underground economy.[55]

Another indication of the concern about drugs is simply the volume of cases. In 2012, there were 109,455 total drug crimes known to the police, a decrease of 5 percent over the previous year, but a 6 percent increase since 2002. Cannabis possession accounts for more than half of the total cases. Less than 10 percent of cases were for the possession of cocaine, and about a third overall were for trafficking. Most of those charged are adults; however, half of the youth accused of crime were accused of theft of $5,000 or under, mischief, level 1 assault, or cannabis possession.

Given that drug offences are enforcement sensitive, the number of cases is highly dependent on the willingness of the police to detect and to want to deter the crime. It is difficult to know, then, whether the increase represents an increase in drug activity or an increase in policing.

Similar to drug-related crimes (such as possession), the number of impaired driving offences reported by police is influenced by many factors: legislative changes, enforcement practices such as increased use of roadside suspensions, local police resources and initiatives, shifts in demographics, and changing attitudes on drinking and driving. In 2012, Canada had about 84,000 cases of impaired driving, a decrease of 7 percent over the previous year, and the rate of impaired driving has been declining in general over the past 25 years.

Generally, the drug problem is argued to be a victimless crime. The Canadian Centre on Substance Abuse (CCSA) says that penalties for marijuana possession have done nothing to enhance public safety and health. This view represents one side of the debate: that drug use is a private matter and that drug control is simply the government's intrusion into people's private lives. People with this view are said to support decriminalization. Furthermore, legalization could reduce the profit of selling illegal substances and drive suppliers out of the market.[56]

Others see these substances as dangerous, believing that the criminal activity of users makes the term *victimless* nonsensical. Still another position favours limited regulation: that the possession and use of all drugs and alcohol should be legalized, but that the sale and distribution of drugs should be heavily penalized. People with this view would punish those profiting from drugs, and would enable users to be helped without fear of criminal punishment.

When Did Drug Use Begin?

The use of chemical substances to change reality and provide stimulation or relaxation has gone on for thousands of years. In Mesopotamia, opium was known 4,000 years ago as the "plant of joy."[57] The ancient Greeks knew of drug use, and during the Crusades, Arabs used marijuana. In the West, natives of Mexico and South America chewed coca leaves for endurance and used "magic mushrooms" in their religious ceremonies.[58] In fact, the coca leaf aids in the uptake of oxygen in the thin air of the Peruvian Andes. Drug use was also accepted in Europe well into the 20th century. Recently uncovered pharmacy records circa 1900 to 1920 showed sales of cocaine and heroin solutions to members of the British royal family. Winston Churchill, then a member of Parliament, bought a cocaine solution while staying in Scotland in 1912.

In the early years of Canada and the United States, opium-based drugs were used in various patent medicine cure-alls. Morphine was used extensively to relieve the pain experienced by wounded soldiers. By the turn of the 20th century, many citizens were opiate users.

Several factors precipitated the stringent drug laws in force today. The rural religious creeds of the 19th century—for example, those of the Methodists, Presbyterians, and Baptists—emphasized individual human toil and self-sufficiency while designating the use of intoxicating substances as an unwholesome surrender to the evils of urban morality. The medical literature of the late 19th century began to designate the use of morphine and opium as a vice and a disease. Late 19th-century and early 20th-century police literature described drug users as habitual criminals. Moral crusaders defined drug use as evil and urged lawmakers to outlaw the sale and possession of drugs. Some well-publicized research efforts categorized drug use as highly dangerous.[59] Foreign immigrants who were recruited to work in factories and mines were the focus of early anti-drug legislation.[60]

In Canada, a flood of Asian immigrants, brought in by industrialists in the 19th century, were used as a pool of cheap labour. Asian workers, paid one-half to two-thirds what European workers received, were single men who planned to return to their home country, and they kept to themselves. Their habits of gambling and opium smuggling, although legal in Canada, were thought to be immoral. By 1907, many of these workers were no longer needed for large construction projects, and they began to compete more directly for other jobs. This competition created political and labour unrest. In 1907, the Asiatic Exclusion League and its supporters rioted in downtown Vancouver. An estimated 20,000 people caused extensive damage to the shops of Chinese and Japanese people.

Deputy Minister of Labour Mackenzie King was appointed to investigate and settle Chinese property damage claims. He discovered the use of opium among the Chinese population and decided that the only way to eliminate the civil unrest was to eliminate the Chinese. He based his report, "The Need for the Suppression of Opium Traffic in Canada," on sensational newspaper stories depicting the ruin of Caucasian women caused by opium use. The *Opium Narcotic Act* of 1908 criminalized opium; and in 1911, the *Opium and Drug Act* expanded the list of prohibited drugs, made simple use and possession of the prohibited drugs an offence, and widened police powers of search and seizure.[61]

In 1920, one year before Mackenzie King became prime minister of Canada, the Opium and Drug Branch was established by the Department of Health and was charged with enforcing narcotics legislation. *Maclean's* magazine ran a series of articles about the illicit drug trade written by Emily Murphy, a police magistrate and judge of the Juvenile Court in Edmonton, under the pen name "Janey Canuck." They were later compiled into a larger book, *The Black Candle*.[62] Murphy's articles were biased and sensational. In one oft-quoted section, a Los Angeles County Chief of Police is quoted:

persons using this narcotic smoke the dry leaves of the plant, which has the effect of driving them completely insane. The addict loses all sense of moral responsibility. Addicts to this drug, while under its influence, are immune to pain. While in this condition they become raving maniacs and are liable to kill or indulge in any forms of violence to other persons, using the most savage methods of cruelty without, as said before, any sense of moral responsibility.

When *The Black Candle* was released in 1922, it aroused public opinion and resulted in pressure on the government to create stricter drug laws. Cannabis hemp was made illegal under the *Opium and Narcotic Drug Act* of 1923 with little discussion. The film *Reefer Madness* in 1936 reinforced this opinion. It was not until the Le Dain Commission of 1969–1971 that marijuana was recommended for decriminalization.

Alcohol and Its Prohibition

The history of alcohol and the law has also been controversial and dramatic. At the turn of the 20th century, a drive was mustered to prohibit the sale of alcohol. The **temperance movement** was fuelled by the belief that the purity of agrarian culture was being destroyed. The growth of the city was viewed as a threat to the lifestyle of people living on farms and in villages. The Anti-Saloon League, led by Carrie Nation, the Woman's Christian Temperance Union, and the Protestant clergy of the Baptist, Methodist, and Congregationalist faiths, viewed the growing city, filled with newly arriving Irish, Italian, and Eastern European immigrants, as centres of degradation and wickedness. The propensity of these ethnic people to drink heavily was viewed as the main force behind their degenerate lifestyle.[63]

Prohibition turned out to be a failure. Organized crime was only too happy to supply illicit liquor. Law enforcement agencies were inadequate, and officials were more than likely to be corrupted by wealthy bootleggers. The smuggling of alcohol from Canada into the United States was especially lucrative. However, one unanticipated consequence of Prohibition in Canada between 1921 and 1929 was the growth of provincial and territorial police forces, as shown by John Phyne (St. Francis Xavier University).[64]

Commonly Used and Abused Drugs

A wide variety of drugs are available to drug abusers, only some of which are addictive. Various effects include hallucinations, depression, relaxation, and exhilaration. These drugs were controlled by two statutes until 1996, the *Food and Drugs Act* and the *Narcotic Control Act*, when they were replaced by the *Controlled Drugs and Substances Act*. The following are some of the most widely used illegal drugs.[65]

temperance movement An organized effort to prohibit the sale of liquor, largely seen as unsuccessful.

The film *Reefer Madness* (1936) came to symbolize the danger of marijuana: the life of a promising young man brought to ruin, madness, and murder.

© Bettman/CORBIS

Anesthetics. Anesthetic drugs are nervous system depressants. They act on the brain to produce a generalized loss of sensation or unconsciousness. The most widely abused anesthetic drug is phencyclidine (PCP), known as *angel dust*. PCP can be sprayed on marijuana and smoked, or it can be drunk or injected. PCP is an animal tranquillizer and causes hallucinations.

Volatile Liquids. Volatile liquids that are easily vaporized and inhaled include lighter fluid, paint thinner, cleaning fluid, and model airplane glue. The psychological effect is a short-term sense of excitement and euphoria followed by disorientation, slurred speech, and drowsiness. Amyl nitrates (known as *poppers*) are sold in capsules that are broken and inhaled, often to be used during sexual activity to prolong and intensify the experience.

Barbiturates. These hypnotic-sedative drugs depress the central nervous system into a sleeplike condition. Prescribed by doctors as sleeping pills, on the illegal market, they are called *downers* and are known by the colour of the capsules—"reds" (Seconal), "blue dragons" (Amytal), and "rainbows" (Tuinal). They create relaxed, sociable, and good-humoured feelings, but are probably the major cause of drug overdose deaths.

Tranquillizers. Tranquillizers have the ability to reduce anxiety, easing tension. Ampazine, Thorazine, Pacatal, and Sparine are used by people with mental illness who experience psychoses, aggressiveness, and agitation. Valium, Librium, Miltown, and Equanil are used by the average citizen to combat anxiety, tension, fast heart rate, and headaches. These mild tranquillizers are obtained by prescription; however, they can lead to addiction and painful withdrawal.

Amphetamines. Known as *uppers*, these synthetic drugs stimulate the central nervous system to produce elevated blood pressure, increased breathing rate, and elevated mood. Psychological effects include increased confidence, euphoria, fearlessness, impulsivity, and appetite loss. Uppers include Benzedrine ("bennies"), Dexedrine ("dex"), Dexamyl, Bephetamine ("whites"), and Methedrine ("meth," "speed," "crystal meth," "ice"). Speed is the most widely used and the most dangerous. Swallowed in pill form or injected, long-term heavy use can result in exhaustion, anxiety, prolonged depression, and hallucinations.

Cannabis (Marijuana). "Pot," "grass," "ganja," "maryjane," or "dope" is produced from the leaves of *Cannabis sativa* or *indica*, a hemp plant grown throughout the world. Hashish is made from resin gathered from the female plant. Various effects include changes in auditory and visual perceptions of time and space, excitement, drowsiness, and increased appetite. Marijuana is not addictive. Its use has been decriminalized in Canada for medical use, and the penalty for minor possession has been decreased.

In 1972, the Le Dain Commission into the non-medical use of drugs concluded that the Canadian marijuana market was free of professional criminal involvement. However, the RCMP now says that almost every large-scale grow operation is linked to organized crime. In the past, outlaw motorcycle gangs ran most operations, but now Asian-based criminal gangs predominate. As was the case with Prohibition and alcohol, criminalization has probably made the problem worse by driving it underground. Recently, several U.S. states have moved to decriminalize and regulate marijuana instead.

Technological developments and the use of cloning methods have led to a rise in the potency of the drug. Marijuana with a tetrahydrocannabinol (THC) content of 2 percent was considered high quality in 1965, whereas THC can now exceed more than 10 percent. When grown hydroponically, the potency can go as high as the mid-teens.[66]

Cannabis is often referred to as the gateway drug, whose use leads to progressively more serious drug abuse. However, this idea has been disproven.[67]

Hallucinogens. Hallucinogens, either natural or synthetic, produce vivid sensory distortions without greatly disturbing consciousness. Some produce hallucinations, while others cause psychotic behaviour. One common hallucinogen is mescaline, which occurs naturally in the peyote cactus. Mescaline produces vivid hallucinations, a feeling of depersonalization, and out-of-body sensations. Alkaloid compounds, either natural or made in the laboratory, include dimethyltryptamine (DMT), morning glory seeds, and psilocybin. Transformed into D-lysergic acid diethylamide-25 (LSD), this substance (800 times more potent than mescaline) stimulates cerebral sensory centres to produce visual hallucinations, intensifies hearing, increases sensitivity, and induces euphoria.

Cocaine. Cocaine is a derivative of the coca leaf first isolated in 1860 by Albert Niemann of Göttingen, Germany. Originally considered a medicinal breakthrough that could relieve fatigue and depression, it was endorsed by psychologists such as Sigmund Freud and used in popular patent medicines. When pharmacist John Styth Pemberton first brewed his new soft drink in 1886, he added cocaine to act as a "brain tonic" and called the drink Coca-Cola; this secret ingredient was taken out in 1906.

When cocaine's addictive qualities and dangerous side effects became apparent, its use was controlled by such legislative bills as Ontario's Anti-Cocaine Bill, an act to amend the *Pharmacy Act* of 1908. Awareness was growing of the dangerous effects of cocaine, and physicians and pharmacists were trying to control "medications" in a wider climate of moral reform. For example, the following claim appeared in a flyer issued by the Children's Aid Society of Montreal:

> The cocaine habit must be stamped out of Canada. It is undermining our boyhood and cutting away the moral fibre of our girls. It is turning our young people into criminals and imbeciles.... Will YOU help the Children's Aid Society fight cocaine? You can do so by asking your clergyman to preach about it, [and] by writing to your member of parliament.[68]

Until the 1970s, cocaine remained underground, used by artists, jazz musicians, beatniks, and jetsetters. Cocaine produces euphoria and excitement. Overdoses cause delirium, increased reflexes, violent manic behaviour, and respiratory failure. Cocaine can be sniffed, or snorted, into the nostrils or injected. Mixing cocaine and heroin is called *speedballing*; this practice is highly dangerous and is alleged to have killed comedian John Belushi. When cocaine is treated with a liquid to remove the hydrochloric acid, the resultant *freebase* is dissolved in a solvent such as ether and crystallized, producing a high more powerful than cocaine but dangerous to make. The creation of **crack cocaine** also involves using ammonia or baking soda to remove the hydrochlorides and create a crystalline form of cocaine base that can then be smoked.[69]

The use of crack and other cocaine derivatives is not widespread. However, because crack cocaine is relatively cheap, its use is concentrated among the poor and lower classes, who are susceptible to this powerful and inexpensive

drug. So, although crack may not be the national epidemic among the middle class as some thought it would become, its use has had a powerful effect in the inner city, where it was credited with the rise and fall of crime in the 1980s.[70]

Narcotics. These drugs produce insensibility to pain, relieve anxiety, and create sedation. Users experience euphoria, reduced fear, apprehension, and tension. Narcotics can be injected under the skin, into a muscle, or directly into the bloodstream (mainlining). Some narcotics come in pill form.

The most common narcotics are derivatives of opium, produced from the opium poppy. Chinese users popularized the habit of smoking or chewing opium extract to produce euphoric feelings. Morphine (from Morpheus, the Greek god of dreams), a derivative of opium, is about 10 times as strong and is used legally by physicians to relieve pain. Heroin was first produced as a painkilling alternative to morphine in 1875 because, although 25 times more powerful, it was considered non-addictive by its creator, Heinrich Dreser. The drug's name derives from it having been originally considered heroic because of its painkilling ability.

Heroin is today a commonly used narcotic, although less than 2 percent of all drug offences are for heroin. Dealers cut it with neutral substances such as sugar, and it is often only 1 percent to 4 percent pure. Users can build up a tolerance, so larger doses or a changed method of ingestion are needed. Withdrawal symptoms include irritability, depression, extreme nervousness, abdominal pain, and nausea. Heroin abuse is generally considered a lower-class phenomenon.[71] The popularity of heroin in the 1990s has been linked to its relatively low cost, ready supply, and the effect of government efforts to control other substances such as crack cocaine. Although the popularity of heroin increased among the middle class, heroin addiction is still commonly associated with youths who are minority-group members living in lower-class, inner-city neighbourhoods.

In 2003, a class-action suit was announced against Purdue Pharma, the makers of OxyContin, a powerful, highly addictive medication, nicknamed *hillbilly heroin* because of its popularity in poor regions.

Other opium derivatives include codeine, Dilaudid, Percodan, and Prinadol. Synthetics include Demerol, Methadone, Nalline, and Darvon.

Steroids. Anabolic steroids are used to gain muscle bulk and strength for athletics and bodybuilding. Although not physically addictive steroids are dangerous because of the significant health problems associated with long-term use: liver ailments, tumours, hepatitis, kidney problems, sexual dysfunction, hypertension, and depression. Steroid users often share needles, which puts them at high risk for contracting human immunodeficiency virus (HIV).

---

crack cocaine A smokable form of purified cocaine that provides an immediate and powerful high.

CHAPTER 13 | **Public Order Crimes: Legislating Morality**

After Canadian sprinter Ben Johnson tested positive for steroid use at the 1988 Olympic Games, the Dubin Inquiry found widespread use of steroids among professional athletes, who used the performance-enhancing drugs to stay competitive.[72] In 1998, a scandal rocked the Tour de France bicycle race after athletes were tested for banned substances, including synthetic hormones. In 2013, another scandal erupted after bike racer Lance Armstrong admitted to doping.

Designer Drugs. **Designer drugs** are chemical substances made in small batches that induce mood-altering effects. They include MDMA ("ecstasy"), which combines an amphetamine-like rush with hallucinogenic experiences, the hallucinogens DMT and 2c-B or "Nexus," and the steroid substitute gamma-hydroxybutyric acid (GHB), which causes drowsiness.

Alcohol. Although the sale and purchase of alcohol is legal today, excessive alcohol consumption is considered a major substance abuse problem. The cost of alcohol abuse is high and has been associated with homicides, suicides, and deaths resulting from motor vehicle accidents.[73]

Alcohol reduces tension, diverts worries, enhances pleasure, improves social skills, and transforms experiences for the better.[74] However, higher doses act as a sedative and depressant. Long-term use has been linked to depression, heart disease, cirrhosis of the liver, and a diminished sexual response.[75] Moderate drinking has been linked to a reduced probability of heart attack.

The Extent of Substance Abuse

Surveys. When surveying drug use, self-report evidence is subject to error. Although the possibility of error from self-reports is true for any criminal act, it is especially likely for those crimes with high social disapproval levels. Drug users may boastfully overinflate the extent of their substance abuse, under-report out of fear, or simply be unaware or forgetful.

Another problem is that surveys can overlook important segments of the drug-using population: for example, people who are homeless, in prison, in drug rehabilitation clinics, or in acquired immune deficiency syndrome (AIDS) clinics. A survey can miss youth who are institutionalized and those who have dropped out of school.[76] Numerous studies indicate that serious abusers under-report their drug use in surveys.[77]

Despite these weaknesses, surveys can get at information that would be difficult to collect otherwise, for example, on student drug use, with most provinces and territories administering self-report surveys.

Patterns. Despite a continuing effort to control the use of mood-altering substances, their use persists. Despite the media attention given to the incidence of drug abuse, controversy surrounds the extent of drug use. National surveys show that drug use is not substantially greater than it was two decades ago. Drug possession offences declined during the 1980s, except for cocaine, which tripled from 1985 to 1991. Drug offences were up in the 1990s, but almost 70 percent of that increase was for marijuana, which is very sensitive to police enforcement.[78]

Health Canada reports that cannabis use was 6.5 percent in 1989, 7.4 percent in 1994, and more than 12 percent in 2002.[79] Overall, 2.4 percent of Canadians surveyed had used one of cocaine/crack, ecstasy, LSD, amphetamines, or heroin.

The continued trend in drug abuse among adolescents indicates that the drug problem has not gone away and may be on the increase. When drug use declined in the 1980s, one reason may have been changing perceptions about the harmfulness of drugs, such as cocaine and marijuana; as people come to view these drugs as harmful, their use of them tends to wane. Considering the widespread publicity linking drug use, needle sharing, and the AIDS virus, it comes as no surprise that people began to see drug taking as dangerous and risky. In the 1990s, however, the perceived risk of drugs was on the decline.

A survey of almost 5,000 Manitoba high school students found that about 40 percent smoked tobacco, 81 percent had consumed alcohol in the past year, and 33 percent drank once a week or more. Of those who drink, 30 percent do so in cars and 15 percent at school. About 38 percent of students used cannabis, the most commonly used drug. In Ontario, a survey on student drug use conducted by the Centre for Addiction and Mental Health showed that alcohol use had increased to 67 percent of all students surveyed, cannabis use had more than doubled to 29 percent, and 28 percent of students smoked tobacco.[80] A New Brunswick Student Drug Use Survey found an increase in cannabis, Ritalin, and psilocybin use, a decrease in tobacco and LSD use, and stable patterns in alcohol use.

The longest ongoing survey, the Ontario Student Drug Use Survey, found a significant amount of alcohol and drug use, as shown in Figure 13.1. However, across the board, drug use was on the decline.

Overall, research shows that when drug use declines, youths report greater disapproval of drug use among their friends, and peer pressure may contribute to lower use rates. In the 1990s, the number of youths disapproving of drugs remained in the majority. It is no surprise that a cohort of young people who perceive little peer rejection for drug use, who consider drugs risk-free and easily available, and whose parents either ignore or condone drug use, will increase the frequency of their substance abuse.

Drug-Involved Youths Who Continue to Commit Crimes as Adults. Although about two-thirds of substance-abusing youths continue to use drugs after they reach adulthood, about half desist from other criminal activities.

---

designer drugs Chemical substances made and distributed in relatively small batches for the purpose of inducing mood-altering effects.

Percentage

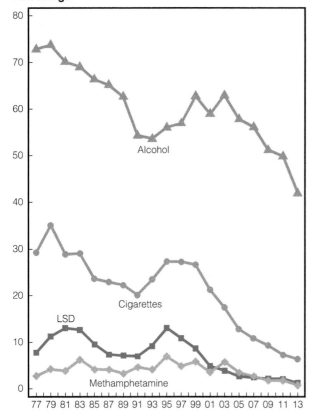

Note: estimates for LSD and methamphetamine exclude Grade 7 students

Percentage

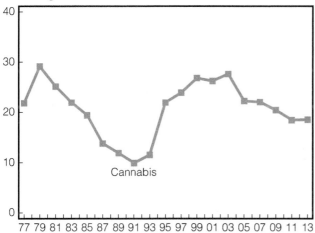

Percentage

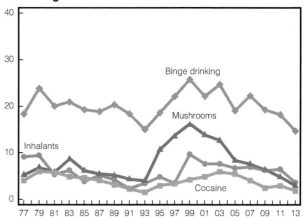

Notes: (1) binge drinking refers to drinking 5 or more drinks on one occasion at least once in the past month;
(2) estimates for mushrooms and cocaine exclude grade 7 students

Percentage

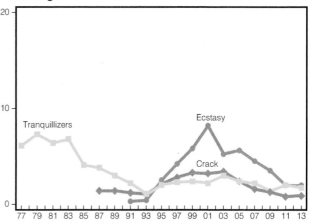

Notes: (1) estimates exclude Grade 7 students;
(2) crack not asked about prior to 1987;
(3) ecstasy not asked about prior to 1991

FIGURE 13.1

Long-Term Drug Use among Ontario Students (1977–2013)

Source: *Drug Use Among Ontario Students 1977–2013*, "Pattern 1: Long-term drug use trends, 1977–2013." Centre for Addiction and Mental Health. Reprinted with permission; *Drug Use Among Ontario Students 1977–2013*, "Pattern 2: Long-term drug use trends, 1977–2013." Centre for Addiction and Mental Health. Reprinted with permission; *Drug Use Among Ontario Students 1977–2013*, "Pattern 3: Long-term drug use trends, 1977–2013." Centre for Addiction and Mental Health. Reprinted with permission; *Drug Use Among Ontario Students 1977–2013*, "Pattern 4: Long-term drug use trends, 1977–2013." Centre for Addiction and Mental Health. Reprinted with permission.

Those adults who persist in both substance abuse and crime tend to come from poor families, have other criminals in the family, have done poorly in school, started using drugs and committing delinquent acts at a young age, and have few opportunities in late adolescence to participate in legitimate and rewarding adult activities.

Some evidence also exists that these drug-using persisters have low nonverbal IQs and poor physical coordination. Nonetheless, little scientific evidence is available to indicate why some drug-abusing kids drop out of crime while others remain active into their adulthood.

Smugglers. Smugglers import drugs into the country. They are generally middle-aged men who have strong organizational skills, established connections, capital to invest, and a willingness to take large business risks. There is a constant flow of people in and out of the business as some sources become the target of law enforcement activities, new drug sources become available, older smugglers become dealers, and former dealers become smugglers.

Adult Predatory Drug Users. Many users who abuse substances early in adolescence will continue their life in drugs and crime in adulthood. Getting arrested, doing time, using multiple drugs, and committing predatory crimes become a way of life for them. These users typically have few skills, did poorly in school, and have a long criminal record specializing in robberies, burglaries, thefts, and drug sales. They filter in and out of the justice system and begin committing crimes as soon as they are released.[81]

However, some drug users commit hundreds of crimes each year but are rarely arrested. Known for committing calculated violence, they plan their crimes carefully. They often work with partners and are more likely to use recreational drugs, such as coke and pot, than the more addicting heroin or opiates. Some may become high-frequency users and risk apprehension and punishment. But for the lucky few, their criminal careers can stretch for up to 15 years without interruption by the justice system.

AIDS and Drug Use

Drug use is linked to the risk of contracting HIV.[82] Since monitoring of the spread of AIDS began in 1981, about one-fourth of all adult AIDS cases reported to the Centers for Disease Control in Atlanta have occurred among intravenous (IV) drug users.[83]

In Canada, the percentage of HIV-positive cases among injection drug users reached its peak in 1997 at 34 percent. In comparison, 17 percent of HIV-positive cases were attributable to heterosexual contact, and 40 percent could be traced to homosexual contact. Women are more likely to be exposed to HIV through injection drug use (IDU) than are men. In 2000, 40 percent of 226 HIV-positive females and 17 percent of 1,085 HIV-positive males were due to IDU.[84]

One reason for the AIDS–drug use relationship is the widespread habit among IV users of needle sharing without disinfecting.[85] Because HIV is spread through blood transfer, sharing HIV-contaminated needles is the primary mechanism for transmitting AIDS among the drug-using population. Any attempt to control drugs by outlawing the sale of hypodermic needles has the unfortunate consequence of promoting needle reuse and sharing. Consequently, legal jurisdictions have developed outreach programs to help these drug users; others have made an effort to teach users how to clean their needles and syringes; and some have gone so far as to provide addicts with sterile needles.[86]

In 2002, the most common forms of exposure to HIV for youths aged 15 to 19 were heterosexual contact (55 percent) and injection drug use (36 percent). Half of all new infections worldwide are occurring among young people, with youths aged 15 to 29 accounting for 28 percent of all positive HIV test reports in Canada.[87]

Statistics Canada reports that since 1981, the exposure to HIV through homosexual contact has decreased from 80 percent of all HIV-positive test reports to 40 percent, exposure through IDU has increased to 30 percent, and exposure through heterosexual contact has increased to almost 25 percent.[88]

Drug users also have a significant exposure to AIDS because they tend to have multiple sex partners, some of whom may be engaging in prostitution to support a drug habit.[89] Further complicating the link among prostitution, drug use, and AIDS is that women are more likely to contract HIV from men than the reverse. This was especially true in the early 1990s, when the main risk for women was heterosexual sex; however, by 2000, the main risk was injection drug use.[90]

In Vancouver's Downtown Eastside, a public health emergency was declared among the estimated 6,000 to 10,000 heroin addicts who live in poor housing, share needles, and engage in prostitution. In 1993, 356 people died of drug overdoses at the peak of the epidemic. More alarming is the area's HIV transmission rate of 19 percent, the highest rate in the developed world, with 40 percent of HIV-positive addicts lending needles despite needle exchange programs. British Columbia's chief coroner proposed the federal government decriminalize heroin so that the issue can be dealt with in a medical rather than a criminal manner.[91]

In 2003, North America's first supervised safe injection site opened in Vancouver. As many as 800 addicts a day were expected to use the site, out of the 5,000 injection drug users estimated to live in the neighbourhood.[92] Health Canada provided some money for research, and an exemption was granted under the Controlled Drugs and Substances Act. Current evidence shows that the safe injection site has decreased the spread of HIV and contributed to a decrease in drug use.[93] However, the federal government wants to shut it down.

According to the evidence from countries such as Portugal, where much drug use is now legal, treating drug addiction as a medical matter rather than a criminal matter is beneficial to society in the long term.

Although the threat of AIDS may be having an impact on the drug-taking behaviour of recreational and middle-class users, drug use may be increasing among the poor, high-school dropouts, and other disadvantaged groups.

The Cause of Substance Abuse

What causes people to abuse drugs? Although many views attempt to explain the causes of drug use, most view the onset of an addictive career as either an environmental or a personal matter.

Subcultural View. Those who view drug abuse as having an environmental basis concentrate on lower-class addictions. Because many drug abusers are poor, the onset of drug use can be tied to their devalued identities, low self-esteem, and poor socio-economic status.

Alienated youths living in depressed areas will come in contact with established drug users, who teach them that narcotics can relieve their feelings of personal inadequacy and stress.[94] Youths will join with peers to learn techniques of drug use and receive social support for their habit within the subculture.[95] However, upward mobility is available to only a few.[96]

Psychodynamic View. Yet not all drug abusers reside in lower-class slum areas; the problem of middle-class substance abuse is very real. Some have linked substance abuse to emotional problems that can strike people in any class. This explanation of substance abuse suggests that drugs help youths control or express their unconscious needs and impulses. Drinking alcohol may also be associated with dependence and depression. A young teen may resort to drug abuse to reduce the emotional turmoil of adolescence. Addicts might have personality disorders characterized by a weak ego, low frustration tolerance, anxiety, and fantasies of omnipotence. Some research also shows an association between mental illness and drug abuse.

Genetic Factors. Substance abuse may have a genetic basis. The biological children of alcoholics reared by non-alcoholic adoptive parents develop alcohol problems more often than do the biological children of the same adoptive parents.[97] Studies comparing alcoholism between identical twins and fraternal twins have found that the likelihood of both siblings behaving identically is twice as high among the identical twin groups. However, identical twins are more likely to be treated similarly than fraternal twins are, and therefore are also more likely to be influenced by environmental conditions.

Taken as a group, people whose parents were alcoholic or drug dependent have a greater chance of developing a similar problem than do children of non-abusers. Nonetheless, most children of abusing parents do not become drug dependent, suggesting that even if drug abuse is heritable, environment and socialization play a role in the onset of abuse.[98]

Social Learning. Social psychologists suggest that drug abuse patterns may result from the observation of parental drug use. Parental drug abuse begins to have a damaging effect on children as young as two years old, especially when parents manifest drug-related personality problems, such as depression or poor impulse control.[99]

People who learn that drugs provide pleasurable sensations may be the most likely to experiment with illegal substances; a habit may develop if the user experiences lower anxiety, fear, and tension levels.[100] Having a history of family drug and alcohol abuse has been found to be a characteristic of violent teenage sexual abusers.[101] Heroin abusers report an unhappy childhood, which included harsh physical punishment and parental neglect and rejection.[102] Drinking with an adult present, presumably a parent, was also a significant precursor of future substance abuse and delinquency.[103]

Problem Behaviour Syndrome (PBS). For many people, substance abuse is just one of many problem behaviours. Longitudinal studies show that drug abusers are maladjusted, alienated, and emotionally distressed.[104] A deviant lifestyle begins early and is punctuated with criminal relationships, a family history of substance abuse, educational failure, alienation, and low commitment to religious values. Research on problem behaviour syndrome (PBS) has found

support for the connection among problem drinking, drug abuse, delinquency, precocious sexual behaviour, school failure, family conflict, and other similar social problems.[105]

Rational Choice. Some people choose to use drugs and alcohol because they want to enjoy the effects: get high, relax, improve creativity, escape reality, and increase sexual responsiveness. Adolescent alcohol abusers believe that getting high will make them powerful, increase their sexual performance, and facilitate their social behaviour; they care little about negative future consequences.[106] Research on middle-class, drug-abusing women shows that most were introduced to drug use by friends or lovers in the context of just having some fun.[107]

Substance use/abuse, then, may be a function of the rational belief that drugs can be of benefit to the user. The decision to use drugs involves evaluating personal consequences (addiction, disease, legal punishment) and the expected benefits of drug use (peer approval, positive affective states, heightened awareness, relaxation).[108]

Constructionist. Not all theories of drugs and crime start from the presupposition that drug use is automatically bad or that it leads to crime. The social constructionist position looks at who is in a position to influence the ideological characterization of drugs. In the example discussed in the section "When Did Drug Use Begin?" earlier in this chapter with regard to the criminalization of opium, labour leaders and politicians were able to trade on the prejudice against Asians prevalent in British Columbia to successfully outlaw opium at the turn of the 20th century. The criminalization of cocaine around the same time turned on a fear promoted by police officers and religious leaders that Black men addicted to cocaine were corrupting Caucasian women. People who are able to influence public opinion in such a manner are called **claimsmakers**.[109]

In sum, many views suggest the reasons why people take drugs, and no one theory has proved to be an adequate explanation of all forms of substance abuse. However, research does show that drug users tend to suffer a variety of family and socialization difficulties, have addiction-prone personalities, and are generally at risk for many other social problems.[110]

DRUGS AND CRIME

One reason for the criminalization of particular substances is the association believed to exist between drug abuse and crime. Many criminal offenders have extensive experience

> **claimsmakers** People in a position to influence the social construction of crime images in the media, such as the police, politicians, and journalists.

In 1975, Brian O'Dea, a marijuana smuggler and a pilot, flew a decrepit DC-6 to a town in Colombia, where they were to pick up eight tonnes of high-grade pot. Shortly before touchdown, the plane's nose gear failed, and the four-engine aircraft plunged through a fence and into a field of cacti. When the plane took off again, it was with one less engine.

When they were about a mile out over the water, a second engine died, and they crash-landed in the water.

After he was picked up by U.S. authorities, O'Dea received a 10-year sentence for importing marijuana into the United States. This was only one dramatic incident in a life lived outside the law.

By February 2001, out of jail and wanting to put his criminal past behind him, O'Dea decided to try his hand at a different career. He placed an ad in the *National Post* featuring the fact that he had been a marijuana smuggler and showing how this had given him business experience. The response was phenomenal. His ad circulated on the Internet, drawing mail from Egypt, China, and Australia. Talent agents, script brokers, and movie producers called from New York, Los Angeles, and Vancouver. His face turned up in the *Financial Times* and the *National Enquirer*. He appeared on *Good Morning America* and Court TV. *Playboy*

wanted an interview. So did the *Wall Street Journal*.

There were a few job offers, too, though mostly from cold-call sales outfits and people operating on the fringes of the law. One man asked O'Dea to join what he described as an "offshore organ transplant" business.

O'Dea has survived a troubled childhood, a cocaine addiction, and numerous encounters with the world's most dangerous drug lords. He has served time in federal penitentiaries in Canada and the United States, and lived to tell his story. Now he needs a job, and telling that story is turning out to be it.

Part of O'Dea's new life is as a motivational speaker for the Congress of Canadian Student Associations to talk about his journey into the drug world.

At a conference centre in downtown Calgary, this is what he might say: "Good morning, I'm Brian O'Dea. For much of my life, if you'd asked me my name, I would have told you something different. I'm going to teach you how to smuggle drugs. I ended up with way too much money and way too few brains, and way too big a coke habit … that's what cocaine is. It wants everything from you, and it takes it."

O'Dea was born in St. John's, Newfoundland, in 1948. When he was 11, his parents enrolled him in St. Bonaventure's school, a Roman Catholic institution run by the Christian Brothers. O'Dea says he endured two years of

sexual abuse at the hands of a senior staff member there, a fact he kept to himself until he was 40. He downplays the impact, but admits it affected his sense of self-worth. He became a people-pleaser, often stealing from his parents to impress his friends.

By the time he reached his second year of university, in 1968, at St. Mary's in Halifax, O'Dea was using the tuition money his parents gave him to buy marijuana and hashish. Soon, he started dealing for most of his income. Within a couple of years, he was circumventing his expensive Toronto suppliers by taking buying trips to Britain. In 1972, when he mailed himself a half-kilogram of hash from England through the mail, Canada Customs intercepted the package and notified the RCMP. He received 18 months.

Eighteen hours after his release from prison, O'Dea booked a ticket to Bogotá, Colombia, and bought 55 grams of coke. That was the first of many trips to Colombia. But by the end of the 1970s, a string of failures had driven him to the brink of bankruptcy.

Then an old acquaintance came to him with news of an abandoned shipyard on Anacortes Island, near Seattle, that was an ideal landing spot for marijuana shipments. With William and Christopher Schaffer, two brothers from Los Angeles with legendary marijuana-growing connections, O'Dea undertook what turned out to be a lucrative marijuana smuggling business.

with drug use, and drug users do in fact commit an enormous amount of crime (for one well-known example, see the Famous Canadian Criminals box on page 434, about Brian O'Dea). Alcohol abuse has also been linked to criminality and appears to be an important precipitating factor in domestic assault and homicide cases.[111] Arrestees who test positive for drugs are also more likely than non-users to recidivate.[112]

However, whether the relationship between drug abuse and crime is causal is uncertain, as many users had a history of criminal activity before the onset of their substance abuse.[113] As well, many people use drugs recreationally without ever committing other crimes. If drug use is not a cause of crime, perhaps it can amplify the frequency and seriousness of criminality.

Research Methods

Two approaches have been used to study the relationship between drugs and crime. One has been to survey known addicts to assess the extent of their law violations; the other has been to survey known criminals to see whether they were or are drug users.

User Surveys. Research on the criminal activity of drug users shows that people who take drugs have extensive involvement in crime. Alcohol abuse has been linked to serious, violent offending patterns. Although research indicates that drug use is not an initiator of crime (because many users had committed crime before turning to drugs), strong evidence suggests that the amount and value of crime increased proportionately with the frequency of the subjects' drug involvement.[114]

O'Dea started by creating SeaCal Fisheries, an Alaska-based salmon-packing company, to land, vacuum-pack, and conceal the marijuana among its boxes of fresh fish. He hired five tractor-trailer units under the auspices of a friend's company to pick up the pot in Washington State and transport it to California. And to ensure that every state trooper and weigh-scale operator on U.S. Interstate 5 should believe his company was legitimate, he set up a phantom roofing company to provide his trucks with cargo and waybills. For 12 months, one of his semis drove up and down the highway with the same load of cedar shingles, just to create cover.

The first load of dope arrived on Forrester Island, a speck of rock off southern Alaska, on August 25, 1986, and made its way south without a hitch. According to prosecutors, the organization made more than $26 million from the deal. The second shipment ran into trouble. A disgruntled former group member had alerted the U.S. Drug Enforcement Agency (DEA) to the group's plans. U.S. authorities and the RCMP were watching as the shipment arrived off Alaska with 42 tonnes of marijuana.

Although the DEA and RCMP continued to have O'Dea and his outfit under observation, they were not able to get concrete evidence. In 1989, however, the U.S. Attorney's office in Seattle started squeezing confessions out

Employment Wanted

Former Marijuana Smuggler

Having successfully completed a 10-year sentence, incident-free, for importing 75 tonnes of marijuana into the U.S., I am now seeking a legal and legitimate means to support myself and my family.

Business Experience: Owned and operated a successful fishing business—multi-vessel, one airplane, one island, and processing facility. Simultaneously owned and operated a fleet of tractor-trailer trucks conducting business in the western U.S. During this time I also co-owned and participated in the executive level management of 120 people worldwide in a successful pot-smuggling venture with revenues in excess of US$100 million

annually. I took responsibility for my own actions, and received a 10-year sentence in the U.S. while others walked free for their cooperation.

Attributes: I am an expert in all levels of security; I have extensive computer skills, am personable, outgoing, well-educated, reliable, clean, and sober. I have spoken in schools to thousands of kids and parent groups over the past 10 years on "the consequences of choice," and received public recognition from the RCMP for community service. I am well-travelled and speak English, French, and Spanish. References available from friends, family, the U.S. District Attorney, etc.

Please direct replies to
Box 375, National Post Classified,
1450 Don Mills, ON, M3B 3R5

of deckhands from O'Dea's boats, gradually working its way up the chain of command. "There was no way," says O'Dea, "they were going to walk away from $100 million worth of drugs."

By the time DEA officers arrived, in April 1990, to search his house, O'Dea was living in a spartan apartment, surviving on fruit juice and natural foods. He had sworn off drugs and alcohol and dedicated his life to good works. The turning point had come on the eve of his

40th birthday, he says, when he suffered a near-fatal drug overdose.

When he reflects on the changes in his life, he believes nothing he did was morally wrong. "I think the laws against marijuana are bad laws. So how do you change bad laws? Through Parliament? No way. Bad laws only get changed if somebody breaks them."

SOURCE: Charlie Gillis, "You're Gonna Love This," *National Post*, December 8, 2001. Material reprinted with the express permission of the *National Post*, a CanWest Partnership.

A survey of 144 untreated illicit opiate users in Toronto found a high rate of property and drug-related offences for income-generating purposes.[115] This finding is significant, given that Canada has an estimated 60,000 to 90,000 illicit opiates users.

Surveys of Known Criminals. In the second method used to link drugs and crime, known criminals are tested to determine the extent of their substance abuse. A survey of prison inmates disclosed that most (80 percent) had engaged in a lifetime of drug and alcohol abuse, more than one-third claimed to have been under the influence of drugs when they committed their last offence, and 62 percent claimed to have used drugs such as heroin, cocaine, PCP, or LSD, on a regular basis before their arrest.[116] This finding supports the association between substance abuse and serious crime.

The drug–crime relationship may thus be explained in three ways: Some may commit crime to support a drug habit; others may become violent while under the influence of drugs or alcohol, which lowers inhibitions and increases aggression levels; or the drug–crime connection may be a function of the violent world of drug distributors, who regularly use violence to do business.[117]

In sum, research testing both the criminality of known narcotics users and the narcotics use of known criminals produces a strong association between drug use and crime (see Exhibit 13.2 on page 436). Even if the crime rate of drug users were actually half that reported in the research literature, users would be responsible for a significant portion of total criminal activity.

The Cycle of Addiction

The drug–crime connection may also be mediated by the amount of drugs that users require and their ability to support their habit through conventional means. Occasional users are people just beginning their addiction, who use small amounts and whose habit can be supported by income from conventional jobs. In contrast, stabilized users have learned the skills needed to purchase and process larger amounts of drugs. Their addiction enables them to maintain their normal lifestyles, although they may turn to drug dealing to create contacts with drug suppliers. Full-time working people involved in drugs typically commit more crime than drug users who are unemployed. Employment does not reduce their criminal activity.[118]

If stable users make a score through a successful drug deal, they may increase their drug use, destabilizing their lifestyle, destroying family and career ties. Addiction is not a unidimensional process. The career of a hard-drug user has various stages, and criminal activity may vary according to the user's drug lifestyle. Perhaps crime is a "drug facilitator," enabling addicts to increase their drug consumption according to the success of their criminal careers.

Drugs and the Law

Early in the 20th century, both Canada and the United States initiated legal action to curtail the use of some drugs. Canada criminalized opium before 1910; in the United States, the 1914 *Harrison Narcotics Act* restricted the importation, manufacture, sale, and dispensing of narcotics. Marijuana was criminalized in Canada in 1923, and in the United States the *Marijuana Tax Act* of 1937 required registration and payment of a tax by all persons who imported, sold, or manufactured marijuana.

In later years, other federal laws were passed to clarify existing drug statutes and revise penalties. For example, psilocybin, a chemical component of some mushrooms, was criminalized in Canada before 1982. This criminalization is a good example of the social constructionist position, in which the reaction defines the crime. Although no research has demonstrated a link between the consumption of psilocybin and the commission of crime, psilocybin is classified as a restricted drug under the U.S. *Food and Drug Act* (FDA). Sometimes police are accused of enforcing drug laws too zealously. In 1971, a royal commission was established in Vancouver under the *Public Inquiries Act* to inquire into the circumstances surrounding a police intervention at a marijuana smoke-in. The inquiry established that the police officers had acted with unwarranted and excessive force when they charged a peaceful crowd by using horses and riot gear.[119]

Alcohol Abuse

Although drug control laws have been enacted on both the federal and the provincial or territorial levels, provincial and territorial legislatures have also acted to control alcohol-related crimes. One of the more serious problems is the alarming number of highway fatalities linked to drunk driving. Governments created more stringent penalties for drunk driving, for example, and in 2008, the courts ruled that drivers could also be tested for drug use. Mothers Against Drunk Driving continues to campaign to have the legal limit for blood alcohol reduced from 0.08 percent to 0.05 percent.

One caution in interpreting the success of drug control programs, such as those designed to control drunk driving, is that they are sensitive to levels of enforcement; if the number of roadside checks is reduced, the number of offences will appear to drop, although the reduction might simply reflect the level of policing.

CONNECTIONS

In Chapter 3, we talked about how crime rates can reflect changes in actual crimes, in levels of reporting by the public, and in reaction to policing activity.

DRUG CONTROL STRATEGIES

Substance abuse remains a major social problem, sometimes leading politicians looking for a campaign issue to call for a "war on drugs."[120] Yet can illegal drug use be eliminated or controlled?

Drug control strategies have varying degrees of success. Some aim at deterring drug use by stopping the flow of drugs into the country, apprehending and punishing dealers, and cracking down on street-level drug deals. Others focus on preventing drug use by educating potential users to the dangers of substance abuse ("just say no") and by organizing community groups to work with the at-risk population in their area. Still another approach is to treat known users so that they can control their addictions.

Source Control

One approach to drug control is to apprehend large-volume drug dealers. Source control involves destroying overseas crops and arresting members of drug cartels in Central and South America, Asia, and the Middle East, where drugs are grown and manufactured. However, drug lords are able to fight back and will use violence and assassination to protect their interests. The United States invaded Panama with 20,000 troops in 1989 to stop its leader, General Manuel Noriega, from dealing cocaine, and then tried to suppress evidence that the CIA had been involved in the cocaine smuggling.

Comparative Criminology
Drug Courts

The mission of drug courts is to stop the abuse of alcohol and other drugs and related criminal activity by offenders. Drug courts handle cases involving drug-addicted offenders through an extensive supervision and treatment program. In exchange for successful completion of the program, the court may dismiss the original charge, reduce or set aside a sentence, offer some lesser penalty, or offer a combination of these. The aim is to place non-violent first offenders into intensive treatment programs rather than in jail or prison. The drug court movement began in Florida to address the state's growing problem of prison overcrowding due in large part to an influx of drug-involved offenders. Today, about 2,500 drug courts operate in the United States. In 2009, Justice Canada announced funding to expand Canada's drug courts from Toronto and Vancouver to Edmonton, Regina, Winnipeg, and Ottawa. In these courts, participants receive counselling and medications such as methadone.

Drug courts address the overlap between the public health threats of drug abuse and crime: crimes are often drug related; drug abusers are frequently involved with the criminal justice system. Drug courts provide an ideal setting to address these problems by linking the justice system to health services and drug treatment providers while easing the burden on the already overtaxed correctional system.

Are drug courts effective? The jury is still out. Research by Denise Gottfredson and her associates conducted in the Baltimore City Drug Treatment Court (BCDTC) found that drug courts did seem to work for reducing crime in a population of offenders who were severely drug addicted. In one study conducted with Lyn Exum, Gottfredson used a carefully designed experimental model in which cases were randomly sent either to the drug court or a traditional court. The researchers found that drug court judges actually impose harsher sentences, but suspended these sentences conditional to compliance with the drug court regimen in drug testing and treatment and attending status hearings. Most importantly, within a 12-month period, 48 percent of drug treatment court clients were arrested for new offences, compared with 64 percent of the people handled in traditional courts. Among the more serious cases heard, 32 percent of drug court clients were rearrested versus 57 percent of clients in the control group. All things considered, offenders whose cases were handled in a traditional court suffered rearrests at a rate nearly three times that of offenders who attended drug treatment court.

Not all drug courts are equal, and some are more effective than others. One reason may be clientele: drug courts with the lowest recidivism rates (10 percent or less) tend to accept offenders with the least severe problems, mostly alcohol or marijuana charges, and who are classified by the drug courts as having "minimal" drug problems. In contrast, the drug courts with the highest recidivism rates are willing to handle the more difficult cases involving people addicted to heroin and/or cocaine.

Critical Thinking

1. Are drug courts inherently coercive? Should drug users be forced to go into treatment?
2. Are drug treatment programs doomed to failure because of so many different types of drug abusers who have entirely different motivations?

SOURCES: C. West Huddleston III, Douglas B. Marlowe, and Rachel Casebolt, "Painting the Current Picture: A National Report Card on Drug Courts and Other Problem-Solving Court Programs in the United States," Bureau of Justice Assistance, www.ojp.usdoj.gov/BJA/pdf/12902_PCP_fnl.pdf; J. Scott Sanford and Bruce Arrigo, "Lifting the Cover on Drug Courts: Evaluation Findings and Policy Concerns," *International Journal of Offender Therapy and Comparative Criminology* 49 (2005): 239–259; John Goldkamp, "The Impact of Drug Courts," *Criminology and Public Policy* 2 (2003): 197–206; Denise Gottfredson, Stacy Najaka, and Brook Kearley, "Effectiveness of Drug Treatment Courts: Evidence from a Randomized Trial," *Criminology and Public Policy* 2 (2003): 171–197; Denise Gottfredson and Lyn Exum, "The Baltimore City Drug Treatment Court: One-Year Results from a Randomized Study," *Journal of Research in Crime and Delinquency* 39 (2002) 337–357; John Roman, Wendy Townsend, and Avinash Singh Bhati, "Recidivism Rates for Drug Court Graduates: Nationally Based Estimates, Final Report" (Washington, DC: Urban Institute, 2003), www.ncjrs.gov/pdffiles1/201229.pdf.

However, *The Economist* says that "there is no sign that government intervention has cut supply, although it may sometimes divert it ... instead the drug's purity seems to have increased."[121]

The amount of narcotics produced each year is so vast that even if three-quarters of the opium crop were destroyed, the Canadian market would still require only a small portion of the remainder to sustain its drug trade.[122] Drug users in North America and Europe are willing to pay more for drugs than are any other users in the world, so if the supply were reduced, whatever drugs existed would find their way to these countries. One study of the impact of supply-side control of illicit drugs found that even a massive heroin seizure had no effect on availability, use, or price. This finding is significant, given that 93 percent of the $500 million spent on Canada's drug strategy is devoted to efforts to reduce that supply.[123]

Adding to control problems is the drug trade's importance as a source of revenue for many countries; destroying the drug trade would likely undermine the economies of some developing nations. Many people in Peru, Bolivia, Colombia, Burma, Thailand, and Laos are engaged in cultivating and processing drugs. Even if one nation cooperates in drug suppression, suppliers in other nations, eager to cash in

The Drug–Crime Relationship

Dependence on Illicit Drugs and Alcohol

- In the male federal inmate population, 38 percent are dependent on alcohol or drugs.
- In the provincial prison population, 43 percent are rated as drug dependent.
- Of all arrestees, 54 percent are judged by police to be abusers of alcohol or drugs.

Relationship of Dependency to Type of Offence

- Alcohol-dependent federal inmates are more likely to have committed a violent crime.
- Drug-dependent inmates are more likely to have committed a gainful crime.

Use and Dependency as They Relate to Volumes of Crimes Committed

- Inmates who used neither drugs nor alcohol committed 1.7 crimes per week.
- Inmates who used one or more substances committed 3.3 crimes per week.
- Inmates who were dependent on drugs or alcohol committed 7.1 crimes per week.

Intoxication at the Time of Committing a Crime

- Police report 51 percent of arrestees were under the influence of psychoactive substance.
- Thirty-nine percent of assault offenders were under the influence of alcohol.
- Thirty-two percent of thefts were committed under the influence of drugs.

Proportion of Crimes Attributable to Drugs and Alcohol

- Forty-nine percent of violent crimes, 50 percent of gainful crimes, and 24 percent of drug crimes are attributed to alcohol and/or illicit drugs.

SOURCE: Kai Pernanen, Marie-Marthe Cousineau, Serge Brochu, and Fu Sun, *Proportions of Crimes Associated with Alcohol and Other Drugs in Canada* (Ottawa: Canadian Centre on Substance Abuse, 2002). Reproduced with permission from the Canadian Centre on Substance Abuse.

on the seller's market, would be encouraged to turn more acreage over to coca or poppy production.

The difficulty of source control is illustrated by the pursuit, capture, and slaying in 1993 of billionaire drug lord Pablo Escobar. His Medellin drug cartel controlled more than 80 percent of the cocaine imported into North America. While he was in hiding, his drug empire was replaced by that of his competitors, the Cali cartel. When the Colombian government put pressure on the drug cartels, even more powerful Mexican organizations emerged to take over the drug trade. In 1997, Mexico's government announced that it had arrested General Jesus Gutierrez Rebello, its top anti-narcotics enforcer, for his suspected links to drug traffickers.

Eradication efforts in one country may encourage crop development in another. For example, the Bolivian government's voluntary coca eradication program kept cultivation levels from significantly expanding, and reduced potential coca leaf production. Unfortunately, this decline was more than offset by an increase in both coca cultivation and production in Colombia, despite an aggressive aerial eradication program by authorities. Colombian coca cultivation tripled, and source control efforts convinced the Colombian drug cartels of the importance of controlling all facets of production.[124]

The drug trade remains a dynamic force: its wealth, power, and organization exceed the resources of many governments. Hundreds of tonnes of cocaine flow to North America, Western Europe, Latin America, Asia, Africa, and the countries of the former Soviet Union. The lines between cocaine-consuming and heroin-consuming countries are blurring. Colombian cocaine syndicates have established distribution centres on virtually every continent, and recently, large Mexican drug organizations have gained control of much of the cocaine traffic formerly dominated by the Colombians.

Synthetic drugs have been gaining in popularity. Methamphetamines (MDMA or "ecstasy") may be displacing cocaine as the stimulant of choice on the world drug market. Mexico is one of the principal suppliers, but other centres of methamphetamine production are located in Poland, Japan, Burma, and the Philippines. Easily produced in kitchen labs from ordinary household ingredients, it is a hard-to-control, dangerous drug.

Law Enforcement Strategies

Law enforcement efforts to intercept drug supplies entering the country involve border patrols and military personnel using sophisticated hardware. However, homegrown marijuana and laboratory-made drugs, such as "ice," LSD, and PCP, could become the drugs of choice. Their easy availability and relatively low cost are increasing their popularity among the at-risk population.

Law enforcement agencies have tried to direct efforts at large-scale drug rings. However, the long-term consequence has been to decentralize drug dealing and encourage younger independent dealers to become major suppliers. Because drug-dealing gangs are difficult to infiltrate and prosecute, some non-traditional groups have broken into the drug trade. For example, the Hells Angels motorcycle club has become one of the primary distributors of cocaine and amphetamines.[125]

Police can also target, intimidate, and arrest street-level dealers and users in an effort to make drug use so much of a hassle that consumption is cut back and the crime rate reduced. Approaches that have been tried include "reverse stings" in which undercover agents pose as dealers to arrest users who approach them for a buy. Police have attacked fortified crack houses by using heavy equipment to breach their defences. Special police task forces have used undercover operations and drug sweeps to discourage both dealers and users.[126]

Police have also used "asset forfeiture" laws to seize the assets of known dealers. Under section 462.37 of the *Criminal Code,* property can be seized if it is believed to have been derived from the proceeds of crime. Because the wealth generated from drug sales can be so immense, dealers need to make their wealth seem legitimate. Buying real estate, investing in legitimate businesses, and transferring money internationally are all preferred methods of hiding illegally gained wealth. Such methods of concealing the proceeds of crime, called *money laundering,* require sophisticated expertise.

Although street-level enforcement efforts have had success, drug cases have clogged courts and correctional facilities with petty offenders while proving a costly drain on police resources. Some people suspect that a displacement effect occurs: Stepped-up efforts to curb drug dealing in one area or city simply encourage dealers to seek out friendlier "business" territory.[127] However, occasionally, law enforcement strategies do succeed: In the summer of 1998, the RCMP busted the Cuntrera-Caruana crime empire in Montreal. Described by some as the largest, most powerful drug-smuggling and money-laundering organization in the world, the Cuntrera-Caruanas acted as intermediaries between the Colombians and the Mafia.[128]

Community Strategies

Citizen-sponsored programs attempt to restore a sense of community in drug-infested areas, to reduce fear, and to promote conventional norms and values.[129] These efforts can be classified into one of four distinct categories.[130] The first involves law enforcement efforts, which may include block watches, cooperative police–community efforts, and citizen patrols. Some of these citizen groups are non-confrontational, willing to simply observe or photograph dealers, take down a licence plate number, and then notify police. On occasion, telephone hotlines have been set up to take anonymous tips on drug activity. Some of these community-based efforts are homegrown, while others attract outside organizations, such as the Guardian Angels. Area residents have gone as far as contracting with private security firms to conduct neighbourhood patrols.

Another tactic is to use the civil justice system to harass offenders. Landlords have been sued for owning properties that house drug dealers; neighbourhood groups have formed and have scrutinized drug houses for building code violations. Information acquired from these sources is turned over to police and housing agencies for more formal action.

In community-based treatment efforts, citizen volunteers participate in self-help support programs, such as Narcotics Anonymous or Cocaine Anonymous. Other programs provide youths with martial arts training, dances, and social events as an alternative to the drug life. Healing centres and treatment facilities, often organized around a theme, such as Aboriginal healing, also operate to counter the effects of drug abuse.

Community drug prevention efforts are designed to enhance the quality of life, improve interpersonal relationships, and upgrade the neighbourhood's physical environment. Activities might include the creation of drug-free school zones, demonstrations and marches to publicize the drug problem, and better police protection or tougher laws. Residents have cleaned up streets, fixed broken streetlights, and planted gardens in empty lots to broadcast the message that they have local pride and do not want drug dealers in their neighbourhood.

While community crime-prevention efforts seem appealing, little conclusive evidence supports their effectiveness as a drug control strategy. Most residents do not participate in programs, and they tend to work best in stable, middle-income areas. Although these findings are discouraging, some studies have also found the opposite: that deteriorated areas can sustain successful anti-drug programs.[131]

Drug Testing Programs

Drug testing of private employees, government workers, and criminal offenders is believed to prevent people from involvement in substance abuse. Employees are tested to enhance on-the-job safety and productivity. In some industries, such as mining and transportation, drug testing is considered essential because abuse can pose a threat to the public. Mandatory drug testing programs are common in government and industry.

Drug testing is not without legal controversy, however. For example, the Canadian Civil Liberties Association filed a complaint with the Canadian Human Rights Commission over the Toronto-Dominion Bank's drug-testing policy. New bank employees were required to submit to a drug test within 48 hours of being offered a job; refusal to do so would be grounds for dismissal. A federal human rights tribunal ruled the bank's policy was intrusive and an invasion of privacy, and the Canadian Federal Court of Appeal ruled that the bank's policy of testing new employees for drugs constituted a violation under the *Human Rights Act.* Key to the decision was the lack of demonstrable evidence linking traces of drugs in a person's system to a lower job performance.[132]

In another incident, doctors and nurses working in neonatal units of Toronto hospitals surreptitiously tested infants' hair for traces of cocaine. Acting on suspicion of mothers' drug use, staff sent samples to the Hospital for Sick Children for analysis, and positive results were sent to the Children's Aid Society. The director of the clinical pharmacology and toxicology program at the Hospital for Sick Children was quoted as saying that physicians had a right to know such information. The co-chairperson of the reproductive technology committee of the National Action Committee on the Status of Women criticized the practice as an invasion of the mother's privacy.[133]

CHAPTER 13 | **Public Order Crimes: Legislating Morality**

Legalization

Despite the massive effort to control drugs through prevention, deterrence, education, and treatment strategies, the fight against substance abuse has not proved successful. It is difficult to get people out of the drug culture because of the enormous profits involved in the drug trade: 500 kg of coca leaves, worth $4,000 to a grower, would yield about eight kilograms of street cocaine, once valued at about $300,000, and probably worth more in today's market.

Considering these problems, some commentators have called for the legalization or decriminalization of restricted drugs. Legalization is warranted, according to Ethan Nadelmann, because the use of mood-altering substances is customary in almost all human societies.[134] Banning drugs serves to create networks of manufacturers and distributors, many of whom use violence as part of their standard operating procedures. Although some may charge that drug use is immoral, some question whether it is really any worse than the unrestricted use of alcohol and cigarettes, both of which are addictiveand unhealthy. Far more people die each year because they abuse these legal substances than are killed in drug wars or from abusing illegal substances.

Prohibition failed to stop the flow of alcohol in the 1920s, while at the same time it increased the power of organized crime. When drugs were legal and freely available earlier in this century, the proportion of people using drugs was not much greater than today; most users managed to lead normal lives, probably because of the legal status of their drug use.[135]

If drugs were legalized, price and distribution could be controlled by government, reducing addicts' cash requirements, and bringing down crime rates as users would no longer need the same cash flow to support their habit. Drug-related deaths would decline because government control would reduce needle sharing and the spread of AIDS, and drugs would not be cut with other toxic substances. Legalization would also destroy the drug-importing cartels and gangs. Because drugs would be bought and sold openly, the government would receive tax revenue both on the sale of drugs and from the income taxes paid by drug dealers on profits that are now part of the hidden economy. Of course, drug distribution would be regulated, like alcohol, keeping it out of the hands of adolescents, public servants such as police and airline pilots, and known felons. Those who favour legalization point to the experience in the Netherlands, which legalized drugs and remains relatively crime-free.[136]

As mentioned earlier, in 2001, Portugal became the first European country to officially abolish criminal penalties for personal possession of drugs, including marijuana, cocaine, heroin, and methamphetamines. Because incarceration is expensive, people found guilty of possession are interviewed by a panel made up of a psychologist, social worker, and legal adviser. They recommend treatment, which can be refused. In the five years since decriminalization, drug use has declined, as has the rate of HIV transmission. Portugal's rate of marijuana use is now 10 percent, compared with America's 40 percent.

Stephen Easton of the Fraser Institute looked at the cultivation, production, and consumption of marijuana in British Columbia, specifically focusing on the issue of legalization versus prohibition. Because the prohibition on marijuana production fuels organized crime, he argues that removing the prohibition would provide an additional source of revenue for government capital. He says that in the long term, the prohibition of marijuana cannot be sustained because marijuana is too easily produced and exported to be controlled by the tools available to law enforcement in a free society.[137]

However, if drugs were legalized and freely available, drug users might significantly increase their daily intake. In countries such as Iran and Thailand, where drugs are cheap and readily available, the rate of narcotics use is high. Historically, the availability of cheap narcotics has preceded drug use epidemics, as was the case when British and American merchants sold opium in 19th-century China.[138]

Efforts to control legal use would likely backfire. If juveniles, criminals, and members of other at-risk groups were forbidden to buy drugs, wouldn't such controls create an underground market almost as vast as the current one? If the government tried to raise money by taxing legal drugs, as it now does for liquor and cigarettes, would drug smuggling be encouraged to avoid tax payments?

What effect would a policy of partial decriminalization (for example, legalizing small amounts of marijuana) have on drug use rates? Would a get-tough policy help "widen the net" of the justice system and actually deepen some youths' involvement in substance abuse? Can society provide alternatives to drugs that will reduce teenage drug dependency?[139]

The various efforts at drug control are summarized in Figure 13.2.

EMERGING ISSUES

A chapter on the legislation of morality would not be complete without looking at issues that have become the focus of debate in contemporary society. Euthanasia and gambling are two issues that continue to evolve and be debated: euthanasia because it is still illegal to assist or contribute to the death of another despite public opinion otherwise, and gambling because, as we will see, some unknowns surround its social and personal costs.

Euthanasia

Euthanasia tests the moral resolve of a society interested in protecting human rights while also respecting human dignity.

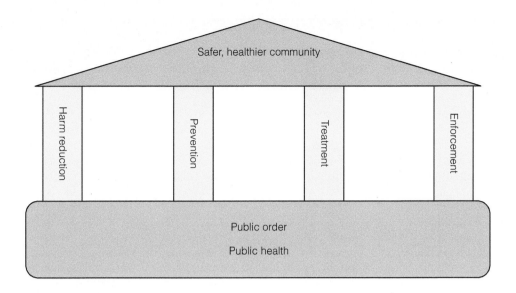

FIGURE 13.2

Strategies for Controlling Drugs

In 2005, Vancouver adopted the "four pillars" approach as a drug strategy. Developed in Europe and pioneered in cities around the world, the strategy combines public order and public health. Prevention aims to reduce the onset and harm of psychoactive substance abuse. Treatment involves addiction services and assistance housing. Harm reduction has been successful in reducing overdose deaths, the spread of HIV, and the open drug scene. Enforcement orients to reduce public disorder and the fear of crime. Taken together, these four pillars comprise a humanitarian approach to substance use and addiction.

Source: http://vancouver.ca/people-programs/four-pillars-drug-strategy.aspx.

Euthanasia has two types: passive and active. The difference is whether a patient is capable of making a decision to end his or her life.

In Quebec in 1991, Nancy B petitioned the court to allow her doctor and the hospital to disconnect her life-support equipment. The judge said he had to respect the patient's right to choose to discontinue treatment and ruled that doing so would not make the physician guilty of euthanasia.[140]

However, when Sue Rodriguez petitioned the Supreme Court of Canada in 1993 for the right to assisted suicide, her request was denied (see the Famous Canadian Court Cases box on page 442). Her famous quote was, "whose life is it anyway?" She subsequently got the medical assistance she needed, illegally, and no one was ever charged.

In 1997, a Halifax doctor was charged with first-degree murder when she gave a patient suffering from terminal cancer an injection to ease his pain. However, because this charge requires proof of premeditation, it was subsequently thrown out of court for lack of evidence. In Canada everyday, patients with terminal illnesses with severe pain are given life-ending doses of morphine, effectively euthanasia through palliative care.

Currently, a challenge to Canada's assisted suicide law is before the courts in British Columbia on the basis that the current law is unconstitutional (see the Crime in the News exhibit). Will this court case succeed 20 years after Sue Rodriguez?

In an update on this case, a B.C. lower court ruled that Canada's assisted suicide law violates a person's Charter rights. This ruling was overturned by the British Columbia Court of Appeal in October 2013, citing the 1993 Rodriguez case as upholding the law. However, in January 2014, the Supreme Court agreed to hear an appeal of the decision. Many feel that the current law is out of date, and that the Rodriguez decision needs to be revisited.

Gambling

Gambling is a good example of decriminalization, in which the law gradually changes to allow a behaviour previously prohibited. Gambling is also a behaviour that receives widespread public support.

A hundred years ago, gambling was illegal in Canada. In 1900, an exemption was granted for religious and charity bazaars to hold small raffles under $50. This charitable exemption opened the door for gambling in Canada. In 1910, an amendment was passed allowing parimutel betting at fairs to encourage horse breeding, and in 1952, games of chance were allowed at agricultural fairs to promote the rural economy.

Lotteries were legalized in 1969, and a national lottery helped finance the 1976 Olympic Games in Montreal. By 1985, exclusive control over lotteries had passed to the provinces and territories, regulated by provincial and territorial Crown monopolies, such as the Atlantic Lottery Commission. Revenues from these lotteries are used for the benefit of all citizens.

Crime in the News

Euthanasia on Public Agenda Again

In 1993, Sue Rodriguez petitioned the Supreme Court of Canada to hear her case for assisted suicide. The court agreed and the justices listened carefully, but at the end of the day, they ruled against her in a 5-4 decision.

Ms. Rodriguez was suffering from amyolateral sclerosis, or Lou Gehrig's disease, a terminal progressively debilitating disease. She wanted the court to recognize her right to choose to end her life in dignity.

When the court refused, she exercised that right anyway without their blessing, aided by an anonymous physician.

Many Canadians thought the court was wrong, and then justice minister Allan Rock appointed a special Senate committee on euthanasia and assisted suicide that heard from witnesses all across Canada.

It considered hundreds of letters and briefs, but when it finally delivered its long-awaited report in 1995, the committee also recommended that both euthanasia and assisted suicide remain illegal.

Now euthanasia might be on the public agenda again. A Quebec provincial commission called Dying with Dignity has begun public hearings this week on assisted suicide and the ethics of euthanasia. It has already heard from the professionals, and now it wants to hear from the public.

While the province can't change criminal law, it has been argued that medical care falls under provincial jurisdiction. Furthermore, the administration of justice is a provincial matter, and whether someone is charged for assisted suicide is up to provincial prosecutors, not federal politicians.

This loophole could be a way of opening up the public debate, especially since the federal government is unlikely to want to stir up this hornet's nest.

A constitutional challenge could be a way to argue that the federal law against euthanasia violates the province's healthcare and administration-of-justice responsibilities.

However, the debate is unlikely to get that far.

In British Columbia, for example, there's already a quiet way of dealing with the matter. That province takes a selective stand on whether to prosecute assisted suicide cases, and palliative sedation is a recognized end-of-life treatment option.

Other jurisdictions such as Belgium, the Netherlands, Oregon, and Washington go further and allow assisted suicide and euthanasia under strict guidelines.

Public opinion is probably in line with a change, although the Canadian Medical Association doesn't support euthanasia or assisted suicide. Given an ethical mandate to uphold life, it's sometimes difficult to manage that mandate at bedside.

However, it's significant that two polls—one of Quebec medical doctors and the other the public—found that three-quarters of those surveyed were in favour of euthanasia.

Muddying the waters are medical practices that skirt the definition of euthanasia. The practice of palliative sedation, for example, has been called a form of euthanasia by some, or the relief of distress by others. But as a way of managing end-of-life distress, it's widespread.

In Britain, for example, one-sixth of all deaths take place after continuous deep sedation, usually with benzodiazepine. A study of palliative sedation in the Netherlands found that as its use increased, the rate of euthanasia declined, a relationship that must show how interrelated these two practices are.

Lining up to debate these questions are various groups that have their agendas for or against euthanasia. And, typically, media reports, such as one in the Montreal Gazette a few weeks ago, present both sides antagonistically, as if they're equal.

However, it was hard watching an archive video of Ms. Rodriguez preparing her statement to the Supreme Court, and to think that the two sides are equal.

Presenting both sides of this story doesn't get at the truth. We've come a long way from when we prosecuted people for suicide or even attempted suicide, and maybe we should move further along in allowing assisted suicide in law as it already is in practice.

After all, as Ms. Rodriguez said, "Whose life is this, who owns my body?"

SOURCE: Copyright Chris McCormick, in the *Daily Gleaner* (Fredericton), September 9, 2010.

Casinos came on the scene in the late 1980s and early 1990s. By 1995, Quebec, Ontario, and Manitoba had large casinos, while Alberta, British Columbia, Nova Scotia, and Saskatchewan allowed video lottery terminals. Provincial and territorial governments can realize huge profits from legalized gambling. The Windsor Casino in Ontario, for example, generated more than $200 million in profits in its first year, while Montreal's casino made more than $70 million in its first six months.[141] Statistics Canada estimates that gambling is a significant percentage of provincial revenue.[142]

In addition to the various types of gambling options now available at convenience stores, from sports lotteries to break-open tickets, are video lottery machines. These machines are controversial because they create both problem gamblers and new opportunities for crime.[143]

Canadians spend hundreds of dollars per year per capita on gambling. People also tend to under-report the amount they spend on gambling because of the perceived stigma attached to it. In all provinces and territories, people spend the most on lotteries, followed by bingo, horseracing, and other forms of gaming.

Lotteries are regulated under section 207 of the *Criminal Code,* which gives provinces and territories the lawful right to "manage a lottery scheme," as shown in Exhibit 13.3. The *Criminal Code of Canada* also prohibits, among other gambling activities, keeping a common gaming or betting house (section 201), betting or bookmaking (section 202),

Famous Canadian Court Cases
Sue Rodriguez

Until recently in Canadian society, suicide was more than taboo; it was a crime punishable by law. The state could charge, prosecute, and incarcerate individuals for trying to take their own life. Although attempted suicide was stricken from the *Criminal Code* in 1972, aiding and abetting suicide remains illegal. Assisted suicide is illegal under section 214(b) of the Code with punishment of up to 14 years in prison. Major debate persists on whether this legislation is unconstitutional. Sue Rodriguez's Supreme Court case challenged this prohibition, and although she may not have won her case, it helped fuel the debate.

Sue Rodriguez was diagnosed in 1992 with the debilitating terminal illness amyotrophic lateral sclerosis (ALS), also known as Lou Gehrig's disease. As her condition worsened and her life expectancy shortened to mere months, Rodriguez decided that she would prefer to take her own life, which is legally permitted in Canada. However, due to her disease, she was unable to commit suicide without assistance. Rodriguez challenged the law prohibiting assisted suicide at the Supreme Court of Canada on the grounds that it violated her constitutional rights.

Under section 7 of the *Canadian Charter of Rights and Freedoms*, every person has the right to life, liberty, and security of the person. This right can only be deprived in accordance with fundamental justice. Rodriguez used this section of the Charter to frame her case, believing that she was being denied autonomy and personal liberty. However, the Supreme Court ruled that the deprivation of her rights was not violating fundamental justice. However, in her 1993 appearance, the ruling was split 5 to 4, perceived to be a major break in the battle for the decriminalization of assisted suicide. With their ruling, the Supreme Court justices urged Parliament to deal with this issue. Despite having lost her case, Sue Rodriguez committed suicide in 1994 with the assistance of a doctor and then-parliamentarian Svend Robinson.

The government has not yet dealt with the issue, but some provinces, such as British Columbia, have a very high tolerance for not prosecuting such cases.

Since the 1970s, a movement has been growing to change assisted suicide legislation. What has made the right-to-die debate so controversial is that it is charged with religious beliefs. Although religion has no place in the formation of legislation, pro-life groups have used the suggestion that suicide is morally wrong to sway Parliament. Some fear that assisted suicide will be abused by those taking care of the terminally ill. Conversely, pro-choice groups believe that individuals should be able to control the time and circumstances of their own deaths.

In 2010, surveys showed that 75 percent of the public and a similar proportion of physicians support euthanasia. Assisted suicide remains illegal in Canada today, but Sue Rodriguez's case, and her death, have helped frame the debate.

EXHIBIT 13.3

Quick Code: Permitted Lotteries

207.

(1) Notwithstanding any of the provisions of this Part relating to gaming and betting, it is lawful

(a) for the government of a province, either alone or in conjunction with the government of another province, to conduct and manage a lottery scheme in that province, or in that and the other province, in accordance with any law enacted by the legislature of that province;

(b) for a charitable or religious organization, pursuant to a licence issued by the Lieutenant Governor in Council of a province or by such other person or authority in the province as may be specified by the Lieutenant Governor in Council thereof, to conduct and manage a lottery scheme in that province if the proceeds from the lottery scheme are used for a charitable or religious object or purpose;

(c) for the board of a fair or of an exhibition, or an operator of a concession leased by that board, to conduct and manage a lottery scheme in a province where the Lieutenant Governor in Council of the province or such other person or authority in the province as may be specified by the Lieutenant Governor in Council thereof has

(i) designated that fair or exhibition as a fair or exhibition where a lottery scheme may be conducted and managed, and

(ii) issued a licence for the conduct and management of a lottery scheme to that board or operator;

(d) for any person, pursuant to a licence issued by the Lieutenant Governor in Council of a province or by such other person or authority in the province as may be specified by the Lieutenant Governor in Council thereof, to conduct and manage a lottery scheme at a public place of amusement in that province if

(i) the amount or value of each prize awarded does not exceed five hundred dollars, and

(ii) the money or other valuable consideration paid to secure a chance to win a prize does not exceed two dollars....

by CTV.ca News Staff

A lawsuit has been filed on behalf of a B.C. family who travelled to Switzerland last year to help an aging family member end her life, because laws in Canada would have made the act illegal.

The lawsuit alleges that laws that prohibit assisted suicide deny people the right to make choices about their own physical and emotional dignity.

The B.C. Civil Liberties Association filed the suit in B.C. Supreme Court Tuesday in an attempt to reverse the current laws banning doctor-assisted suicide.

The BCCLA wants to see changes to the Criminal Code that would allow mentally competent adults with incurable diseases the right to seek medical help to end their lives.

"We want every Canadian to have a choice to have what they consider to be a good death," Grace Pastine, litigation director for the BCCLA, told reporters at a Vancouver press conference.

"Inflicting unbearable suffering on individuals, on dying patients who wish to end their lives, is unjust, unacceptable, and unconstitutional."

The lawsuit was filed on behalf of Lee Carter and her husband Hollis Johnson, of Fort Langley, B.C. They travelled with Carter's 89-year-old mother, Kay, to Switzerland last year to help her end her life.

Before she left, Kay Carter told CTV News why she was making her decision. She said she suffered from spinal stenosis, which left her in chronic pain and almost immobile. She could do little for herself, was confined to a bed or wheelchair, and was losing her sight and hearing.

"As far as I can see it, there is absolutely no quality of life in this at all," she told CTV in September, 2009.

So in January, 2010, she travelled to Switzerland, where assisted suicide and euthanasia are legal, and sought the help of an assisted suicide group called Dignitas.

She died from a lethal dose of sodium pentobarbital on Jan. 15, 2010, after writing a farewell letter to friends.

Now Carter and Johnson are moving ahead with this legal challenge in hopes that it will allow mentally competent adults the right to medical assistance to hasten death.

They plan to argue that Criminal Code provisions against physician assisted-dying are unconstitutional because they deny individuals the right to have control over choices that are fundamental to their physical, emotional, and psychological dignity.

"My mother, Kay, was a lifelong supporter of the dying with dignity movement. She lived her life with passion, independence, and resolve, and her independence extended to insisting that she would have choice and control over how she would leave this world," Lee Carter said in a release.

"I feel that I'm honouring her memory by participating in this legal challenge."

Victoria physician Dr. William Soichet is also named as a plaintiff in the suit. He treats patients suffering from diseases like cancer, Huntington's disease, and multiple sclerosis, and says he would be willing to help patients end their lives.

"Dr. Soichet considers the ability to participate in physician-assisted dying on request, in appropriate circumstances and where there are all the necessary safeguards in place, an important component of the provision of health care to grievously and irremediably ill patients," the lawsuit reads.

The Attorney General of Canada will have 21 days after being served with the claim to file a response.

The BCCLA's claim is one of two right-to-die suits filed this month in B.C. Supreme Court. The Farewell Foundation for the Right to Die filed a claim on Apr. 8, also contesting the laws against assisted suicide.

SOURCE: CTV News, "B.C. Family Sues Over Assisted Suicide Laws," April 27, 2011, from http://www.ctvnews.ca/b-c-family-sues-over-assisted-suicide-laws-1.636458. Reprinted with permission.

---

placing bets on behalf of others (section 203), promoting lotteries (section 206), and cheating at play (section 209). A new concern is whether the law can adapt to handle the increasing interest in gambling on the Internet, where overhead costs are low and the potential for profits is high.

Much controversy surrounds the link between gambling and crime. When the Nova Scotia government announced its plans to open a casino in Halifax, widespread opposition was voiced by the police, citizens' groups, and church groups. Three government commissions advised against it, and 40,000 people signed petitions in opposition. Police predicted an increase in prostitution, drug abuse, organized crime, and other spinoff crimes from gambling.[144]

John McMullan and Jason Mullen of Saint Mary's University looked at print media coverage of casino and electronic gambling between 1992 and 1997. The content analysis of 234 gambling stories indicated that pro-gambling sources, both corporate and political, constructed a powerful public rhetoric in support of new gambling services and institutions. They found that the media helped create expectations favourable to gambling. Other discourses, however, such as concerns about law and order, and moral and medical issues were subordinated in news coverage. While moral narratives were a pervasive secondary theme, at the end of the day, the press produced a "politics of truth" that legitimated gambling.[145]

Research has shown that the social costs of gambling are high. Problem gamblers tend to have a high involvement in other drug and alcohol abuse, higher rates of suicide, more absenteeism from work, lower productivity, and higher rates of job loss due to gambling. Problem and pathological gamblers tend to turn to crime to support their habits, such as stealing from work, friends, and family. Although men are more likely to be problem

In 2004, researchers with specialties in mood and anxiety disorders, psychiatry, community, and public health at the University of Manitoba, and in psychology at Laval University in Quebec, undertook an examination of gambling problems in Canada.

In the 1990s, new forms of legalized gambling were expanded widely in Canada. Video lottery terminals (VLTs) were introduced into community settings such as bars, gas stations, and restaurant lounges. In addition, permanent casinos were developed in several provinces.

However, as the authors note, no national survey has been done of gambling problems. Gambling has been introduced as a significant revenue source for provincial and territorial governments with little understanding of its psychological consequences. This research then is an important step in understanding gambling problems across the 10 Canadian provinces and the three territories.

Using the Canadian Problem Gambling Index, the researchers investigated the prevalence of gambling problems over a 12-month period in the Canadian Community Health Survey. This survey looks at mental health and well-being, an important issue in understanding the quality of life in Canada. The survey is a large random sample of 34,770 community-dwelling respondents aged 15 years and over. They were interviewed, which accounts for the high response rate of 77 percent.

Of interest to the researchers was the relationship of gambling problems to the availability of VLTs per 1,000 people and with the presence of permanent casinos for each province. The researchers found that people with the highest self-reported gambling problems were living in provinces with the highest concentration of VLTs and permanent casinos.

Specifically, Manitoba and Saskatchewan had rates of 2.9 percent, the highest prevalence of gambling problems. These two provinces had significantly higher levels than the two provinces with the lowest prevalence of gambling problems: Quebec (1.7 percent) and New Brunswick (1.5 percent). When the figures are averaged out, the 12-month prevalence of gambling problems in Canada was 2 percent, yet with significant inter-provincial variability.

The highest prevalence of gambling problems in areas with high concentrations of VLTs combined with permanent casinos should be troubling from a public health point of view. The rapid and prolific expansion of new forms of legalized gambling is associated with a considerable public health cost, whose effects linger long after those governments that reaped the short-term benefits have gone.

SOURCE: Based on Brian J. Cox, Nancy Yu, Tracie O. Afifi, and Robert Ladouceur, "A National Survey of Gambling Problems in Canada," *Canadian Journal of Psychiatry* 50, 4 (2005): 213–217.

gamblers than are women, women gamblers are more likely to be young, single, and unemployed, and to have less than a high-school education. Women are "escape" gamblers, while men are "excitement" gamblers. Canada has done little research on the effects of gambling, as discussed in the Criminology Research box.

The amount spent on lottery tickets per household varies by social class (see Figure 13.3). While households with incomes less than $20,000 buy fewer lottery tickets than those with incomes of more than $60,000, low-income households spend more of their income on lotteries. A survey of the Montreal casino found that the typical visitor was from Montreal (85 percent), had a high-school education (47 percent), and had a household income of less than $40,000 (48 percent). Industry profiles suggest that the online gambler tends to be in the lowest income demographic, similar to other forms of gambling.

Recent research also shows that the more people feel their income is low compared with others, the more likely they will buy lottery tickets. In some cases, the likelihood doubles.[146]

Internet gambling is developing quickly, and organized crime families are getting involved. In addition, Aboriginal reserves are also getting into online gambling, in some cases in violation of provincial law.

The amount of money involved makes Internet gambling attractive as a criminal opportunity. Cryptologic, the creator of encryption technology used in online gambling, processed more than US$5 billion in transactions in 2000.[147]

SUMMARY

Public order crimes are acts considered illegal because they conflict with social policy, accepted moral rules, and public opinion. Great debate usually surrounds public order crimes. Some charge that they are not really crimes at all and that it is foolish to try to legislate morality. Others view such morally tinged acts as prostitution, gambling, and drug abuse as harmful and therefore subject to public control.

Prostitution is a sex-related public order crime that has been practised for thousands of years. There are several kinds of prostitutes, including streetwalkers, B-girls, and call girls. Prostitutes often come from poor, troubled families and have abusive parents. However, little evidence suggests that prostitutes are emotionally disturbed, addicted to drugs,

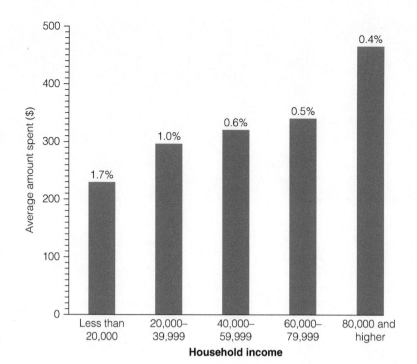

FIGURE 13.3

Lottery Play Is Tied to Household Income

Source: Adapted from Statistics Canada "Lottery play is tied to household income" Chart B, from *A Sure Bet Industry* by Katherine Marshall, Autumn 1996 PERSPECTIVES - Catalogue no. 75-001-XPE sourced at URL: http://www.statcan.ca/english/freepub/75-001-XIE/pdf/topics/gambling1996.pdf.

or sexually abnormal. Although the exchange of money for sex, and sex for money is legal, society and its laws make it virtually impossible.

Pornography involves the sale of sexually explicit material intended to sexually excite paying customers. The depiction of sex and nudity is not illegal, but it does violate the law when it is judged to be obscene. Obscenity is a legal term that is defined as material offensive to community standards. Thus, the decision of what pornographic material is obscene is somewhat open to debate. A growing problem is the exploitation of children in obscene materials. No hard evidence links pornography to crime or aggression, but data suggest that sexual material with a violent theme is related to sexual violence by those who view it.

Substance abuse is another type of public order crime. Debate continues over the legalization of drugs, usually centring on such non-addicting drugs as marijuana. However, the federal government outlaws a wide variety of drugs, including narcotics, amphetamines, barbiturates, cocaine, hallucinogens, and marijuana. One of the main reasons for the continued ban on drugs is their relationship to crime. Numerous studies have found that drug addicts commit enormous amounts of property crime.

Many strategies are used to control substance abuse, ranging from source control to treatment. So far, no single method seems effective. Although legalization is frequently debated, the fact that so many people already take drugs and that drug abuse is associated with crime make legalization unlikely in the near future.

Gambling is one of the more interesting "victimless crimes" discussed in this chapter because it illustrates the process of decriminalization. As governments increasingly

come to depend on income from gaming revenues, gambling will become an expanding province- or territory-run business.

However, euthanasia is more controversial, as the attempt by individuals to control the time of their own death seems more problematic to claimsmakers than letting the elderly and sick weaken and die in nursing homes and hospitals.

THINKING LIKE A CRIMINOLOGIST

According to data from a 1997 national school survey, high-school boys who have been physically or sexually abused are at least twice as likely as non-abused boys are to drink, smoke, or use drugs. The survey was an in-class questionnaire completed by 3,162 boys in Grades 5 to 12 at a nationally representative sample of 265 public, private, and parochial schools from December 1996 to June 1997. The survey included roughly equal samples of adolescent boys in Grades 5 to 8 and 9 to 12. All responses were weighted to reflect grade, region, race and ethnicity, and gender.

Thirteen percent of boys in Grades 9 to 12 said that they had been physically or sexually abused. Thirty percent of abused boys reported that they drank frequently, and 34 percent reported that they had used drugs in the past month, compared with 16 percent and 15 percent, respectively, of non-abused boys. Abused boys were also nearly three times more likely to smoke frequently (27 percent versus 10 percent).

As a criminologist, what is your interpretation of these data? What is the association between child abuse and substance abuse?

KEY TERMS

DOING RESEARCH ON THE WEB

To learn more about the association between mental illness and drug abuse, check out the website of the National Alliance on Mental Illness: www.nami.org/helpline/dualdiagnosis.htm.

You may also want to check out research at a Substance Abuse and Mental Health Services Administration website: www.samhsa.gov.

CRITICAL THINKING QUESTIONS

1. Alcohol is highly related to violence, while marijuana is not. Under what circumstances, if any, might the legalization or decriminalization of drugs be beneficial to society?

2. Do TV shows and films glorify drug usage and encourage youths to enter the drug trade? Should all images on TV of drugs and alcohol be banned?

3. Is prostitution really a crime? Should a man or woman have the right to sell and buy sexual favours if they so choose?

4. Do you believe greater controls should be placed on the distribution of sexually explicit material on the Internet? Would you approve of the online sale of sexually explicit photos of children if they were artificial images created by computer animation?

5. Are there objective standards of morality? Does the existing *Criminal Code of Canada* reflect contemporary national moral standards? Or are laws banning sexual behaviours and substance abuse the product of a relatively few "moral entrepreneurs" who seek to control other people's behaviours?

6. Some researchers conclude that if pornography consumption per se is not a cause of aggression toward women, it may still be a contributing factor. Is it possible that sexually aggressive men are drawn to the images in pornography because it reinforces their pre-existing hostile orientation to sexuality?

7. The findings suggest the need for increased research attention on the use and impact of pornography in men at elevated risk for sexual aggression. Given the potential for problems, should Internet pornography be strictly controlled or banned until conclusive research is conducted?

NOTES

1. "Emery agrees to 5 years in Canadian prison," Ian Mulgrew, *Vancouver Sun*, January 14, 2008.

2. Edwin Schur, *Crimes without Victims* (Englewood Cliffs, NJ: Prentice-Hall, 1965).

3. Andrea Dworkin, quoted in "Where Do We Stand on Pornography," *Ms*, January–February 1994, 34.

4. Jennifer Williard, *Juvenile Prostitution* (Washington, DC: National Victim Resource Center, 1991).

5. The Committee on Sexual Offences against Children and Youth (the Badgley Committee), 1984; and the *Report of the Special Committee on Pornography and Prostitution* (the Fraser Committee), 1985.

6. The Royal Commission on the Criminal Law Relating to Criminal Sexual Psychopaths, 1956.

7. Morris Cohen, "Moral Aspects of the Criminal Law," *Yale Law Journal* 49 (1940): 1017.

8. Sir Patrick Devlin, *The Enforcement of Morals* (New York: Oxford University Press, 1959), 20.

9. See Joel Feinberg, *Social Philosophy* (Englewood Cliffs, NJ: Prentice-Hall, 1973).

10. *United States v. 12 200-ft Reels of Super 8mm Film*, 413 U.S. 123 (1973) at 137.

11. David Kaplan, "Is It Torture or Tradition?" *Newsweek*, December 20, 1993, 124.

12. Joseph Gusfield, "On Legislating Morals: The Symbolic Process of Designating

Deviancy," *California Law Review* 56 (1968): 58–59.

13. E. Hatfield, S. Sprecher, and J. Traupman, "Men and Women's Reactions to Sexually Explicit Films: A Serendipitous Finding," *Archives of Sexual Behavior* 6 (1978): 583–592; Henry Lesieur and Joseph Sheley, "Illegal Appended Enterprises: Selling the Lines," *Social Problems* 34 (1987): 249–260.

14. Wayne LaFave and Austin Scott, Jr., *Criminal Law* (St. Paul, MN: West Publishing, 1986), 12.

15. Bill Curry, "Canadians Back Legalized Euthanasia: Numbers down from Past Polls, Yet Half Still Support MD-Assisted Suicide," *Ottawa Citizen*, September 7, 2003.

16. Tina Loo and Lorna McLean, *Historical Perspectives on Law and Society in Canada* (Toronto: Copp Clark, 1994); Bryan D. Palmer, "Discordant Music: Charivaris and White-Capping in Nineteenth-Century North America," *Labour/Le Travail* 3 (1978): 5–62.

17. Howard Becker, *Outsiders* (New York: Macmillan, 1963), 13–14.

18. Daniel Claster, *Bad Guys and Good Guys, Moral Polarization and Crime* (Westport, CT: Greenwood Press, 1992), 28–29.

19. "Amsterdam Cafe Raided," *Cannabis Culture Magazine Online*, May 15, 1998, archived at http://www.cannabisculture.com.

20. See, generally, Spencer Rathus and Jeffery Nevid, *Abnormal Psychology* (Englewood Cliffs, NJ: Prentice-Hall, 1991), 373–411.

21. *Canadian Crime Statistics 2000* (Ottawa: Canadian Centre for Crime Statistics, 2001).

22. G. Kinsman, "'Character Weaknesses' and 'Fruit Machines': Towards an Analysis of the Anti-homosexual Security Campaign in the Canadian Civil Service," *Labour/Le Travail* 35 (1995): 133–161; Gary Kinsman and Patrizia Gentile, "'In the Interests of the State': The Anti-gay, Anti-lesbian National Security Campaign in Canada," unpublished report.

23. See, generally, V. Bullogh, *Sexual Variance in Society and History* (Chicago: University of Chicago Press, 1958), 143–144; Spencer Rathus, *Human Sexuality* (New York: Holt, Rinehart and Winston), 463; Annette Jolin, "On the Backs of Working Prostitutes: Feminist Theory and Prostitution Policy," *Crime and Delinquency* 40 (1994): 60–83.

24. "The Court and the Soliciting Law," *The Globe and Mail*, June 6, 1990; Richard Barnhorst, Sherrie Barnhorst, and Kenneth Clarke, *Criminal Law and the Canadian Criminal Code* (Toronto: McGraw-Hill Ryerson, 1992).

25. John Lowman, "Commentary. Reconvening the Federal Committee on Prostitution Law Reform," *Canadian Medical Association Journal* 171, 2 (2004): 147–148.

26. "NOW Charges Dropped. Alright!" *NOW*, September 27, 1990; "Crown Finds No Legal Basis, Drops NOW Charges," *NOW*, September 27, 1990, 15.

27. Charles McCaghy, *Deviant Behavior* (New York: Macmillan, 1976), 348–349.

28. Information for the following section draws on various sources, including Charles Winick and Paul Kinsie, *The Lively Commerce* (Chicago: Quadrangle Books, 1971); Jennifer James, "Prostitutes and Prostitution," in *Deviants: Voluntary Action in a Hostile World*, eds. E. Sagarin and F. Montanino (New York: Scott, Foresman, 1977).

29. Mark-David Janus, Barbara Scanlon, and Virginia Price, "Youth Prostitution," in *Child Pornography and Sex Rings*, ed. Ann Wolbert Burgess, 127–146 (Lexington, MA: Lexington Books, 1989).

30. Paul Goldstein, "Occupational Mobility in the World of Prostitution: Becoming a Madam," *Deviant Behavior* 4 (1983): 267–279.

31. Paul Goldstein, Lawrence Ouellet, and Michael Fendrich, "From Bag Brides to Skeezers: A Historical Perspective on Sex-for-Drugs Behavior," *Journal of Psychoactive Drugs* 24 (1992): 349–361; Lisa Maher and Kathleen Daly, "Women in the Street-Level Drug Economy: Continuity or Change?" *Criminology* 34 (1996): 465–491.

32. D. Kelly Weisberg, *Children of the Night: A Study of Adolescent Prostitution* (Lexington, MA: Lexington Books, 1985), 44–55.

33. Gerald Hotaling and David Finkelhor, *The Sexual Exploitation of Missing Children* (Washington, DC: U.S. Department of Justice, 1988).

34. Carolyn McIntyre, *Strolling Away* (Ottawa: Department of Justice, 2002). See also, Steven Bittle, *Youth Involvement in Prostitution: A Focus on Intrafamilial Violence. A Literature Review* (Ottawa: Department of Justice, n.d.); and Steven Bittle, *Youth Involvement in Prostitution: A Literature Review and Annotated Bibliography* (Ottawa: Department of Justice, Research and Statistics, 2002).

35. Melissa Farley, Jacqueline Lynne, and Ann J. Cotton, "Prostitution in Vancouver: Violence and the Colonization of First Nations Women," *Transcultural Psychiatry* 42, 2 (2005): 242–271.

36. N. Jackman, Richard O'Toole, and Gilbert Geis, "The Self-Image of the Prostitute," in *Sexual Deviance*, eds. J. Gagnon and W. Simon, 152–153 (New York: Harper & Row, 1967).

37. Paul Gebhard, "Misconceptions about Female Prostitutes," *Medical Aspects of Human Sexuality* 3 (July 1969): 28–30.

38. Reuters, "UN Cites Sharp Rise in Child Labor, Prostitution," *Boston Globe*, November 12, 1996, A6.

39. Dorothy Bracey, *"Baby Pros": Preliminary Profiles of Juvenile Prostitutes* (New York: JohnJay Press, 1979).

40. A. Brannigan, L. Knafla, and C. Levy, *Street Prostitution. Assessing the Impact of the Law: Calgary* (Ottawa: Department of Justice, 1989); N. Crook, *A Report on Prostitution in the Atlantic Provinces*, Working Papers on Pornography and Prostitution, Report No. 12 (Ottawa: Department of Justice, 1984); J. Lowman, *Vancouver Field Study of Prostitution*, Working Papers on Pornography and Prostitution, Report No. 8 (Ottawa: Department of Justice, 1984).

41. Martin A. Monto, "Female Prostitution, Customers, and Violence," *Violence Against Women* 10, 2 (2004): 160–188.

42. Andrea Dworkin, *Pornography* (New York: Dutton, 1989).

43. Albert Belanger et al., "Typology of Sex Rings Exploiting Children," in *Child Pornography and Sex Rings*, ed. Ann Wolbert Burgess, 51–81 (Lexington, MA: Lexington Books, 1984).

44. "Battling Child Porn," *Maclean's*, April 8, 2002, 55.

45. *The Report of the Commission on Obscenity and Pornography* (Washington, DC: U.S. Government Printing Office, 1970).

46. Berl Kutchinsky, "The Effect of Easy Availability of Pornography on the Incidence of Sex Crimes," *Journal of Social Issues* 29 (1973): 95–112.

47. Michael Goldstein, "Exposure to Erotic Stimuli and Sexual Deviance," *Journal of Social Issues* 29 (1973): 197–219.

48. John Court, "Sex and Violence: A Ripple Effect," *Pornography and Aggression*, eds. Neal Malamuth and Edward Donnerstein (Orlando, FL: Academic Press, 1984); also see Edward Donnerstein, Daniel Linz, and Steven Penrod, *The Question of Pornography* (New York: Free Press, 1987).

49. Edward Donnerstein, "Pornography and Violence against Women," *Annals of the New York Academy of Science* 347 (1980): 277–288; E. Donnerstein and J. Hallam, "Facilitating Effects of Erotica on Aggression against Women," *Journal of Personality and Social Psychology* 36 (1977): 1270–1277; Seymour Fishbach and Neil Malamuth, "Sex and Aggression: Proving the Link," *Psychology Today* 12 (1978): 111–122.

50. *United States v. 12 200-ft Reels of Super 8mm Film*, 413 U.S. 123 (1973) at 137.

51. "N2H2 Reports Number of Pornographic Web Pages Now Tops 260 Million and Growing at an Unprecedented Rate," *PRNewswire*, September 23, 2003.

52. John Franks, "The Evaluation of Community Standards," *Journal of Social Psychology*, 139 (1999): 253–255.

53. Information provided by Hitwise, Inc. June 4, 2004; www.hitwise.com.

54. Irving Kristol, "Liberal Censorship and the Common Culture," *Society* 36 (September 1999): 5.

55. Ralph Weisheit, "Studying Drugs in Rural Areas: Notes from the Field," *Journal of Research in Crime and Delinquency* 30 (1993): 213–232.

56. Arnold Trebach, *The Heroin Solution* (New Haven, CT: Yale University Press, 1982).

57. James Inciardi, *The War on Drugs* (Palo Alto, CA: Mayfield, 1986), 2.

58. See, generally, David Pittman, "Drug Addiction and Crime," in *Handbook of Criminology*, ed. D. Glazer, 209–232 (Chicago: Rand McNally, 1974); Board of Directors, National Council on Crime and Delinquency, "Drug Addiction: A Medical, Not a Law Enforcement,

Problem," *Crime and Delinquency* 20 (1974): 4–9.

59. James Inciardi, *Reflections on Crime* (New York: Holt, Rinehart and Winston, 1978), 15.

60. William Bates and Betty Crowther, "Drug Abuse," in *Deviants: Voluntary Actors in a Hostile World*, eds. E. Sagarin and F. Montanino, 269 (New York: Foresman and Co., 1977).

61. A. Elizabeth Comack, "The Origins of Canadian Drug Legislation: Labelling versus Class Analysis," in *The New Criminologies in Canada*, ed. Brian Fleming, 65–86 (Toronto: Oxford, 1985).

62. Emily Murphy, *The Black Candle* (Toronto: Thomas Allen, 1922).

63. Inciardi, *Reflections on Crime*, 8–10; see also A. Greeley, William McCready, and Gary Theisen, *Ethnic Drinking Subcultures* (New York: Praeger, 1980); Joseph Gusfield, *Symbolic Crusade* (Urbana: University of Illinois Press, 1963), Chapter 3.

64. John Phyne, "Prohibition's Legacy: The Emergence of Provincial Policing in Nova Scotia, 1921–1932," *Canadian Journal of Law and Society* 7 (1992): 157–184.

65. This section relies heavily on the descriptions in Kenneth Jones, Louis Shainberg, and Curtin Byer, *Drugs and Alcohol* (New York: Harper & Row, 1979), 57–114.

66. "Drug Situation in Canada—2002," Organized Crime Analysis Section, Royal Canadian Mounted Police, Ottawa, July 2003.

67. Cannabis: Our Position for a Canadian Public Policy. Report of the Special Senate Committee on Illegal Drugs (Ottawa: Senate Committee, 2002).

68. Glenn F. Murray, "Cocaine Use in the Era of Social Reform: The Natural History of a Social Problem in Canada, 1880–1911," *Canadian Journal of Law and Society* 2 (1987): 29–43; Jeffrey Fagan and Ko-Lin Chin, "Initiation into Crack and Powdered Cocaine: A Tale of Two Epidemics," *Contemporary Drug Problems* 16 (1989): 579–617.

69. Thomas Mieczkowski, "The Damage Done: Cocaine Methods in Detroit," *International Journal of Comparative and Applied Criminal Justice* 12 (1988): 261–267.

70. John Hagedorn, "Homeboys, Dope Fiends, Legits, and New Jacks," *Criminology* 32 (1994): 197–220.

71. Charles Winick, "Physician Narcotics Addicts," *Social Problems* 9 (1961): 174–186.

72. *Commission of Inquiry into the Use of Drugs and Banned Practices Intended to Increase Athletic Performance* (Ottawa: Supply and Services Canada, 1990).

73. Addiction Research Foundation, "Deaths Due to Alcohol," Statistical Information Service.

74. D.J. Rohsenow, "Drinking Habits and Expectancies about Alcohol's Effects for Self Versus Others," *Journal of Consulting and Clinical Psychology* 51 (1983): 752–756.

75. Spencer Rathus, *Psychology*, 4th ed. (New York: Holt, Rinehart and Winston, 1990), 161.

76. Eric Wish, *Drug Use Forecasting Program, Annual Report 1990* (Washington, DC: National Institute of Justice, 1990).

77. Thomas Gray and Eric Wish, *Maryland Youth at Risk: A Study of Drug Use in Juvenile Detainees* (College Park, MD: Center for Substance Abuse Research, 1993); Eric Wish and Christina Polsenberg, "Arrestee Urine Tests and Self-Reports of Drug Use: Which Is More Related to Rearrest?" paper presented at the annual meeting of the American Society of Criminology, Phoenix, AZ, November 1993.

78. "Canadian Crime Statistics, 1996," *Juristat* 17, 8, 1997; "Drug Offences in Canada," *Juristat* 10, 11, 1990.

79. Michael Tjepkema, "Use of Cannabis and Other Illicit Drugs," *Statistics Canada Health Reports* 15, 4 (2004).

80. David Patton, David Brown, Brian Broszeit, and Jastej Dhaliwal, "Substance Abuse among Manitoba High School Students, 2001," Addiction Foundation of Manitoba, http://www.crystalrecovery .com/Research/Manitoba.pdf (accessed May 24, 2005); E.M. Adlaf, A. Pagli, and F.J. Ivis, *Drug Use Among Ontario Students 1977 to 1999: Findings from the Ontario Student Drug Use Survey* (Toronto: Centre for Addiction and Mental Health, 1999).

81. Hilary Saner, Robert MacCoun, and Peter Reuter, "On the Ubiquity of Drug Selling among Youthful Offenders in Washington, DC, 1985–1991: Age, Period, or Cohort Effect?" *Journal of Quantitative Criminology* 11 (1995): 362–373.

82. See, generally, Mark Blumberg, ed., *AIDS: The Impact on the Criminal Justice System* (Columbus, OH: Merrill Publishing, 1990).

83. Scott Decker and Richard Rosenfeld, "Intravenous Drug Use and the AIDS Epidemic: Findings for a Twenty-City Sample of Arrestees," paper presented at the annual meeting of the American Society of Criminology, Baltimore, November 1990.

84. *HIV and AIDS in Canada. Surveillance Report to June 30, 2000* (Ottawa: Health Canada, 2000), http://publications.gc.ca/ site/eng/446192/publication.html.

85. Douglas Longshore, "Prevalence and Circumstances of Drug Injection at Los Angeles Shooting Galleries," *Crime and Delinquency* 42 (1996): 21–35.

86. Mark Blumberg, "AIDS and the Criminal Justice System: An Overview," in *AIDS: The Impact on the Criminal Justice System*, 11.

87. Aids Committee of Toronto, "HIV/AIDS Statistics—Youth," July 23, 2004.

88. *Estimates of HIV Prevalence and Incidence in Canada, 2002* (Ottawa: Health Canada, 2003).

89. Bruce Johnson, Andrew Golub, and Jeffrey Fagan, "Careers in Crack, Drug Use, Drug Distribution, and Nondrug Criminality," *Crime and Delinquency* 41 (1995): 275–295.

90. "Women's AIDS Blamed on Men," *Toronto Star*, September 30, 1994, A1.

91. "Where Death Gets a Double Shot. The Call to Clean Up a Hotbed of Heroin and HIV in Canada's Poorest Ghetto," *The Globe and Mail*, October 8, 1997.

92. "Safe Injection Site Opens," Vancouver CBC, September 15, 2003. See also "Potential Use of Safer Injecting Facilities among Injection Drug Users in Vancouver's Downtown Eastside," *Canadian Medical Association Journal* 10 (2003): 169–177.

93. "Vancouver's Safe Injection Site Successful: Study. Top AIDS Researcher Suggests Harper Government Has 'Profound Bias' against Site," CBC, November 20, 2006.

94. C. Bowden, "Determinants of Initial Use of Opioids," *Comprehensive Psychiatry* 12 (1971): 136–140.

95. Marvin Krohn, Alan Lizotte, Terence Thornberry, Carolyn Smith, and David McDowall, "Reciprocal Causal Relationships among Drug Use, Peers, and Beliefs: A Five-Wave Panel Model," *Journal of Drug Issues* 26 (1996): 205–428; R. Cloward and L. Ohlin, *Delinquency and Opportunity: A Theory of Delinquent Gangs* (Glencoe, IL: Free Press, 1960).

96. Kellie Barr, Michael Farrell, Grace Barnes, and John Welte, "Race, Class, and Gender Differences in Substance Abuse: Evidence of Middle-Class/Underclass Polarization among Black Males," *Social Problems* 40 (1993): 314–326.

97. D.W. Goodwin, "Alcoholism and Genetics," *Archives of General Psychiatry* 42 (1985): 171–174.

98. For a thorough review of this issue, see John Petraitis, Brian Flay, and Todd Miller, "Reviewing Theories of Adolescent Substance Use: Organizing Pieces in the Puzzle," *Psychological Bulletin* 117 (1995): 67–86.

99. Judith Brooks and Li-Jung Tseng, "Influences of Parental Drug Use, Personality, and Child Rearing on the Toddler's Anger and Negativity," *Genetic, Social and General Psychology Monographs* 122 (1996): 107–128; Thomas Ashby Wills, Donato Vaccaro, Grace McNamara, and A. Elizabeth Hirky, "Escalated Substance Use: A Longitudinal Grouping Analysis from Early to Middle Adolescence," *Journal of Abnormal Psychology* 105 (1996): 166–180.

100. Denise Kandel and Mark Davies, "Friendship Networks, Intimacy and Illicit Drug Use in Young Adulthood: A Comparison of Two Competing Theories," *Criminology* 29 (1991): 441–471.

101. J.S. Mio, G. Nanjundappa, D.E. Verlur, and M.D. DeRios, "Drug Abuse and the Adolescent Sex Offender: A Preliminary Analysis," *Journal of Psychoactive Drugs* 18 (1986): 65–72.

102. D. Baer and J. Corrado, "Heroin Addict Relationships with Parents during Childhood and Early Adolescent Years," *Journal of Genetic Psychology* 124 (1974): 99–103.

103. James Inciardi, Ruth Horowitz, and Anne Pottieger, *Street Kids, Street Drugs, Street Crime: An Examination of Drug Use and Serious Delinquency in Miami* (Belmont, CA: Wadsworth, 1993), 43.

104. John Wallace and Jerald Bachman, "Explaining Racial/Ethnic Differences in

Adolescent Drug Use: The Impact of Background and Lifestyle," *Social Problems* 38 (1991): 333–357.

105. John Donovan, "Problem-Behavior Theory and the Explanation of Adolescent Marijuana Use," *Journal of Drug Issues* 26 (1996): 379–404.

106. A. Christiansen, G.T. Smith, V. Roehling, and M.S. Goldman, "Using Alcohol Expectancies to Predict Adolescent Drinking Behavior after One Year," *Journal of Counseling and Clinical Psychology* 57 (1989): 93–99.

107. Claire Sterck-Elifson, "Just for Fun? Cocaine Use among Middle-Class Women," *Journal of Drug Issues* 26 (1996): 63–76.

108. Icek Ajzen, *Attitudes, Personality and Behavior* (Homewood, IL: Dorsey Press, 1988).

109. Lester Grinspoon and James B. Bakalar, *Cocaine: A Drug and Its Social Evolution*, rev. ed. (New York: Basic Books, 1985).

110. Judith Brook, Martin Whiteman, Elinor Balka, and Beatrix Hamburg, "African-American and Puerto Rican Drug Use: Personality, Familial, and Other Environmental Risk Factors," *Genetic, Social, and General Psychology Monographs* 118 (1992): 419–438.

111. Carolyn Rebecca Block and Antigone Christakos, "Intimate Partner Homicide in Chicago over 29 Years," *Crime and Delinquency* 41 (1995): 496–526.

112. Douglas Smith and Christina Polsenberg, "Specifying the Relationship between Arrestee Drug Test Results and Recidivism," *Journal of Criminal Law and Criminology* 83 (1992): 364–377.

113. George Speckart and M. Douglas Anglin, "Narcotics Use and Crime: An Overview of Recent Research Advances," *Contemporary Drug Problems* 13 (1986): 741–769; Charles Faupel and Carl Klockars, "Drugs-Crime Connections: Elaborations from the Life Histories of Hard-Core Heroin Addicts," *Social Problems* 34 (1987): 54–68.

114. Helene Raskin White and Stephen Hansell, "The Moderating Effects of Gender and Hostility on the Alcohol-Aggression Relationship," *Journal of Research in Crime and Delinquency* 33 (1996): 450–470; James Inciardi, "Heroin Use and Street Crime," *Crime and Delinquency* 25 (1979): 335–346; see also W. McGlothlin, M. Anglin, and B. Wilson, "Narcotic Addiction and Crime," *Criminology* 16 (1978): 293–311; M. Douglas Anglin and George Speckart, "Narcotics Use and Crime: A Multisample, Multimethod Analysis," *Criminology* 26 (1988): 197–235; David Nurco, Ira Cisin, and John Ball, "Crime as a Source of Income for Narcotics Addicts," *Journal of Substance Abuse Treatment* 2 (1985): 113–115.

115. Benedikt Fischer, Wendy Medved, Maritt Kirst, Jurgen Rehm, and Louis Glicksman, "Illicit Opiates and Crime: Results of an Untreated User Cohort Study in Toronto," *Canadian Journal of Criminology* 43, 2 (2001): 197.

116. Allen Beck, Darrell Gilliard, Lawrence Greenfeld, Caroline Harlow, Thomas Hester, Lewis Jankowski, Tracy Snell, James Stephen, and Danielle Morton, *Survey of State Prison Inmates, 1991* (Washington, DC: Bureau of Justice Statistics, 1993).

117. Paul Goldstein, "The Drugs-Violence Nexus: A Tripartite Conceptual Framework," *Journal of Drug Issues* 15 (1985): 493–506.

118. Charles Faupel, "Heroin Use, Crime and Unemployment Status," *Journal of Drug Issues* 18 (1988): 467–479.

119. Royal Commission on Disturbances in a Portion of the City of Vancouver known as "Gastown," as cited in *Royal Commissions and Commissions of Inquiry in British Columbia, 1943–1980* (B.C. Legislative Library, 1982).

120. Eric Jensen, Jurg Gerber, and Ginna Babcock, "The New War on Drugs: Grass Roots Move-ment or Political Construction?" *Journal of Drug Issues* 21 (1991): 651–667.

121. "Just Say Maybe," *The Economist* 366, 8318 (2003): 72–73.

122. *RCMP National Drug Intelligence Estimate, 1994* (Ottawa: Minister of Supply and Services, 1994).

123. "Impact of Supply-Side Policies for Control of Illicit Drugs in the Face of the Aids and Overdose Epidemics: Investigation of a Massive Heroin Seizure," *Canadian Medical Association Journal* 1 (2003): 168–170.

124. Bureau for International Narcotics and Law Enforcement Affairs, *International Narcotics Control Strategy Report, 1996* (Washington, DC: U.S. Department of State, 1997).

125. Walter Shapiro, "Going After the Hell's Angels," *Newsweek*, May 13, 1985, 41.

126. David Hayeslip, "Local-Level Drug Enforcement: New Strategies," *NIJ Reports*, March/April 1989.

127. Mark Moore, *Drug Trafficking* (Washington, DC: National Institute of Justice, 1988).

128. "Why It Took 30 Years to Bust a Crime Family," *Globe and Mail*, July 17, 1998, A1.

129. Robert Davis, Arthur Lurigio, and Dennis Rosenbaum, eds., *Drugs and the Community* (Springfield, IL: Charles C. Thomas, 1993), xii–xv.

130. Saul Weingart, "A Typology of Community Responses to Drugs," in *Drugs and the Community*, eds. Davis, Lurigio, and Rosenbaum, 85–105.

131. Bureau of Justice Statistics, *Drugs, Crime and the Justice System* (Washington, DC: Bureau of Justice Statistics, 1992), 109–112.

132. "TD's Drug-Testing Policy Wrong, Court Rules," *Globe and Mail*, July 25, 1998, A3; "Drug Testing in the Workplace," *Daily News*, August 21, 1994, 19; "Just Say No to Testing," *Toronto Star*, August 23, 1994, A12; "Submission on Mandatory Drug Testing in the Workplace," Canadian Civil

Liberties Association, http://ccla.org/wordpress/wp-content/uploads/2008/10/2005-03-08-police-drug-testing.pdf.

133. "Infants' Hair Tested without Moms Knowing," *Toronto Star*, April 15, 1995, A1.

134. Ethan Nadelmann, "America's Drug Problem," *Bulletin of the American Academy of Arts and Sciences* 65 (1991): 24–40.

135. Ethan Nadelmann, "Should We Legalize Drugs? History Answers Yes," *American Heritage* (February/March 1993): 41–56.

136. See, generally, Ralph Weisheit, *Drugs, Crime and the Criminal Justice System* (Cincinnati: Anderson, 1990).

137. Stephen T. Easton, "Marijuana Growth in British Columbia," Fraser Institute, *Public Policy Sources*, 74, 2004.

138. David Courtwright, "Should We Legalize Drugs? History Answers No," *American Heritage* (February/March 1993): 43–56; James Inciardi and Duane McBride, "Legalizing Drugs: A Gormless, Naive Idea," *Criminologist* 15 (1990): 1–4.

139. Kathryn Ann Farr, "Revitalizing the Drug Decriminalization Debate," *Crime and Delinquency* 36 (1990): 223–237.

140. "Nancy B's Gift," *Mail Star*, January 8, 1992, C1; "Nancy B.'s Right to Die," *Montreal Gazette*, January 7, 1992, B2; "Exercising the Right to Die," *The Globe and Mail*, November 29, 1991, A18.

141. "The Government as Bookie," *The Globe and Mail*, May 23, 1995, A18.

142. "Bernie Bets Big on Gambling Gains," *Halifax Herald*, April 12, 1995, A1; "A Sure Bet Industry," *Perspectives* 8 (1996): 3–6.

143. John L. McMullan, and David C. Perrier, "Controlling Cyber-Crime and Gambling: Problems and Paradoxes in the Mediation of Law and Criminal Organization," *Police Practice and Research* 8, 5 (2007): 431–444.

144. "RCMP Fears Fuel N.S. Casino Debate," *The Globe and Mail*, April 27, 1994, A3; "Casino Will Boost Crime, Windsor Police Report Says," *The Globe and Mail*, August 4, 1993, A4; "Mobsters Bet on Niagara Falls to Win Casino," *Toronto Star*, May 16, 1994, A1.

145. John McMullan and Jason Mullen, "What Makes Gambling News?" *Journal of Gambling Studies* 17, 4 (2001): 321–352.

146. Emily Haisley, Romel Mostafa, and George Loewenstein, "Subjective Relative Income and Lottery Ticket Purchases," *Journal of Behavioral Decision Making*, 21 (2008): 283–295.

147. Robin Kelley, Peter Todosichuk, and Jason Azmier, *Gambling@Home: Internet Gambling in Canada* (Calgary: Canada West Foundation, 2001). See also "Gambling@Home: Internet Gambling in Canada Background," Ontario Problem Gambling Research Centre Home Page, www.gamblingresearch.org.

Crimes in the 21st Century

14

Chapter Outline

Learning Objectives

After reading this chapter, you will be able to:

1. Understand the scope of new crimes currently developing.
2. Be familiar with characteristics of transnational organized crime.
3. Know the elements of political crime and terrorism.
4. Discuss the responses to terrorism and political crime.
5. Explain some challenges to confronting state crime.

© Barton Gellman/Getty Images

In 2010, WikiLeaks founder Julian Assange published 400,000 classified documents on the Iraq war. Shortly after, in 2013, Edward Snowden, shown here, flew to Japan where he met with journalists. Formerly employed by the CIA and the NSA, he revealed thousands of documents detailing a massive global surveillance operation. Unable to return to the United States, where he was charged with espionage, he was granted asylum in Russia.

In 2010, people around the world became very familiar with a previously unknown website called WikiLeaks, created by an international organization of the same name that publishes classified and secret documents submitted by unnamed and anonymous sources. Launched in 2006 and run by Julian Assange, an Australian who immigrated to Sweden, WikiLeaks has supporters around the globe. In April 2010, the site began to post videos and documents that had been illegally appropriated from U.S. diplomatic and military computers by unknown hackers. For example, one video showed a 2007 incident in which Iraqi civilians and journalists were killed by U.S. forces in helicopters. It also leaked more than 76,000 classified war documents from Afghanistan. In November 2010, WikiLeaks released U.S. State Department cables. In the aftermath of the leaks, Army Specialist Bradley Manning, 22, was arrested after an informant told federal authorities that he had overheard him bragging about giving WikiLeaks a video of a helicopter assault in Iraq plus more than 260,000 classified U.S. diplomatic cables taken from government computers. Both the U.S. and foreign governments were embarrassed when the confidential cables hit the Net.[1]

Similarly, when Snowden, a former employee of the CIA and the National Security Agency, disclosed thousands of classified documents to journalists, he was charged with espionage. The scope of the revelations was shocking, uncovering massive international surveillance programs run by the U.S. government. Key in the debate is the balance of security over privacy, and whether the surveillance and collection of communications metadata and images violates people's constitutional rights.

This chapter is about new directions and issues that affect Canadian society in the 21st century. Some of these topics might seem old, but some of these crimes have changed over the years. For example, organized crime has evolved to become a force that Al Capone might not recognize. Similarly, terrorism has moved a long way since the Middle Ages, and even since the 1960s, when the Front de Libération du Québec (FLQ) terrorized Quebec. Likewise, computer technology has evolved and today enables the commission of surveillance on a massive scale.

HIGH-TECH CRIME

The Moore typology of white-collar crime organized the analysis of traditional entrepreneurial crime into several distinct elements. However, high-tech crimes are emerging that contain combined elements of fraud, theft, swindles, and false claims. The crimes are difficult to categorize because they can be committed by corporations and individuals, can be singular or ongoing, and can involve the theft of information, resources, or funds. High-tech crimes

cost consumers billions of dollars each year and will increase dramatically. They are also difficult to detect and police.

Just a few years ago, complex, global incidents involving the leaking of classified documents could not have been contemplated, let alone transacted. Innovation brings change and with it new opportunities to commit and expose crime. The technological revolution has provided new tools to misappropriate funds, damage property, sell illicit material, or conduct warfare, espionage, and terror. It has created **cybercrime**, a new breed of offences that can be singular or ongoing, but typically involve the mis/use of information, resources, or funds through the use of computers, networks, and the Internet. With new tools and opportunities, organized criminals have morphed from local gangs into transnational criminal organizations whose illegal activities cross borders. Drug gangs and human traffickers may ply their trade across continents. The Internet age also raises questions about what is considered a cybercrime. Is leaking classified government documents, as Assange and Snowden did, a violation of legal rules or actions protected by constitutional rights to free speech? Do we need new regulations to control the content of the Internet and regulate its usage?

Criminals are becoming more technologically sophisticated, routinely using the Internet to carry out their criminal conspiracies. The widespread use of computers and the Internet has ushered in the age of **information technology (IT)** and made it an intricate part of daily life in most industrialized societies. It is the key to the economic system and will become more important as major industries shift their manufacturing plants to areas of the world where production is much cheaper. In the process, **globalization** creates transnational markets, politics, and legal systems—in other words, a global economy.

Magnifying the importance of the Internet is the fact that many critical infrastructure functions are now conducted online. This vast network has become a target for illegal activities and enterprise. Some cybercriminals use modern technology to sell illegal goods and services, or conversely, to illegally appropriate legitimate products and services. **Cybertheft** schemes range from the illegal copying of copyrighted material to using technology to commit traditional theft-based offences such as larceny and fraud.

cybercrime The theft or destruction of information using computers, networks, and the Internet.

information technology (IT) The use of computer networks and communications for education and commerce.

globalization The creation of international markets, politics, and legal systems.

cybertheft The use of computer technology to commit traditional crimes, such as fraud, and modern offences, such as identity theft.

Another type of cybercriminal is motivated less by profit and more by the urge to commit **cybervandalism** or technological destruction. These cybercriminals aim their malicious attacks at disrupting, defacing, and destroying technology that they find offensive.

A third type of cybercrime, **cyberwar**, is political, involving spying, espionage, and even **cyberterrorism**, which refers to acts aimed at undermining the social, economic, and political system of an enemy nation by destroying its electronic infrastructure and disrupting its economy. This crime can be state against state, as when China was accused in 2014 of cyber-spying on U.S. solar and nuclear technology companies; or it can be state against citizens, as when the National Security Agency (NSA) collects communications metadata.

In sum, some cybercriminals are high-tech thieves while others are high-tech vandals; the property they destroy is electronic rather than physical. Some cybercriminals may create transnational networks that integrate IT into their plans to carry out criminal schemes while confounding law enforcement agents who seek to disrupt their criminal efforts.

This new array of crimes presents a compelling challenge for the justice system and law enforcement community because (a) these new crimes are rapidly evolving with new schemes being created daily, (b) they are difficult to detect through traditional law enforcement channels, and (c) their control demands that agents of the justice system develop technical skills that match those of the perpetrators. Instead of robbing a bank at gunpoint, a new group of contemporary thieves finds it easier to hack into accounts and transfer funds to offshore banks. Instead of shoplifting from a brick-and-mortar store, the contemporary cyberthief devises clever schemes to steal from etailers. Instead of limiting their criminal escapades to the local population, transnational gang members now face a whole world of opportunity.

Cyber and transnational crimes also present a significant challenge for criminologists because they defy long-held assumptions about the cause of crime. How can we say that crime is a function of social forces, the social environment, or the social structure, when these contemporary criminals are typically highly educated and technologically sophisticated people who commit their crimes in places far removed from their victims? These criminal conspiracies demand a high degree of self-control and dedication, characteristics that a truly impulsive or mentally unstable person would have difficulty achieving.

This chapter considers the importance of cybercrime and transnational crime, both theoretically and practically, and reviews their various forms.

Internet Crimes

Millions of people worldwide are on the Internet, and the number entering cyberspace is growing rapidly. This vast pool of people represent targets for high-tech crimes.

In some cases, adults have solicited teenagers in Internet chat rooms, distributed obscene material, or allowed right-wing hate groups to publish on the Internet. Other illegal acts include downloading pirated software, bogus get-rich-quick schemes, weight-loss scams, and investment swindles pitched on the Internet. In some cases, these fraudulent acts can be dangerous to clients (see Exhibit 14.1).

Some other examples include using spam email to steal credit card numbers, and phishing, whereby fake email messages are sent to bank clients asking them to verify their account numbers and personal identification number (PIN) information. An estimated 16 percent of attacks on businesses are in the ecommerce area.[2]

> **CONNECTIONS**
>
> In Chapter 11, we looked at ordinary forms of fraud. Because of the amount of power corporations have in the information age, they can commit larger frauds than ever before.

Computer Crimes

Computer-related thefts are a new trend in employee theft and embezzlement. The widespread use of computers for business transactions has encouraged people to also use them for illegal purposes, such as the following:[3]

1. theft of services or using the computer for unauthorized purposes
2. use of data in a computer system for personal gain
3. unauthorized use of computers employed for financial processing to obtain assets
4. theft of property by computer for personal use or conversion to profit
5. use of a computer as the object of a crime, such as spreading a computer virus

Several techniques used by computer criminals are so common that experts have created their own jargon to describe the theft styles and methods:

> **cybervandalism**   The use of computer technology for malicious purposes, such as bringing down business networks.
>
> **cyberwar**   The use of computer technology and communications to disrupt networks of foreign governments.
>
> **cyberterrorism**   An effort by covert forces to disrupt the intersection between the virtual electronic reality of computers and the physical world.

EXHIBIT 14.1

Common Internet Fraud Schemes

Hitman Scam

The victim receives an email from a member of an organization such as the "Ishmael Ghost Islamic Group." The emailer claims to have been sent to assassinate the victim and the victim's family members. The emailer asserts that the reason for the impending assassination resulted from an alleged offence, by the victim, against a member of the emailer's gang. In a bizarre twist, however, the emailer reveals that upon obtaining the victim's information, another member of the gang (purported to know a member of the victim's extended family) pleaded for the victim's pardon. The emailer alleges that an agreement was reached with the pleading gang member to allow the victim to avoid assassination if he or she takes some action, such as sending $800 to a receiver in the United Kingdom for the migration of Islamic expatriates from the United States. Victims of this email are typically instructed to send the money via Western Union or MoneyGram to a receiver in the United Kingdom. The emailer often gives the victim 72 hours to send the money or else pay with his or her life.

Economic Stimulus Scam

Another popular scam involves unsolicited calls regarding fraudulent government stimulus money. The Internet Crime Complaint Center (IC3) received numerous complaints from victims receiving unsolicited telephone calls that include a recorded message. The recorded voice message reportedly sounds very much like President Barack Obama discussing alleged government funds available for those who apply. Victims are warned that the offer is available only for a limited time and are instructed to visit certain websites to receive their money. These sites require victims to enter personal identifying information after which they are directed to a second page to receive their notification of eligibility. Upon completion of an online application and payment of small fees, victims are guaranteed to receive a large sum of stimulus money, but they never do.

Pet Scams

A self-proclaimed breeder posts an online ad (along with a cute picture or even a streaming video) offering to sell a pet. The breeder asks the buyer to send money, plus a little extra for delivery costs. But the buyer never gets the pet; the scam artist simply takes the money and runs.

Secret Shoppers and Funds Transfer Scams

Individuals are hired via the Web to rate their shopping or dining experiences. They are paid by cheque and are asked to wire a percentage of the money to a third party. The cheque they are sent then bounces, and they are out the money they sent to the third party. As part of the scam, the fraudsters often use the real logos of legitimate companies.

Adoption and Charity Fraud

A person is sent an email that tugs on his or her heartstrings, asking for a pressing donation to a charity and often using the subject header, "Urgent Assistance Is Needed." The name of a real charity is generally used, but the information provided sends the money to a con artist. One set of scams used the name of a legitimate British adoption agency to ask for money for orphaned or abandoned children.

Romance Fraud

A person encounters someone in an online dating or social networking site who lives either far away or in another country. That person strikes up a relationship with the victim and then wants to meet, but needs money to cover travel expenses. Typically, that's just the beginning—the person may then claim to have been taken ill or injured during the journey and ask for additional money to pay the hospital expenses. What is obvious is that the Internet magnifies the proportion of the crime.

SOURCES: FBI, "Internet Crime Report 2008 and 2009," www.ic3 .gov/media/annualreport/2009_IC3Report.pdf (accessed November 9, 2010); www.fbi.gov/page2/april08/ic3_report040308.html (accessed November 9, 2010).

1. *the Trojan horse*: one computer is used to reprogram another for illicit purposes
2. *the salami slice*: a dummy account is used to steal from customers' accounts
3. *super-zapping*: a maintenance program orders cheques issued to a private account
4. *the logic bomb*: a virus program is attached to the company's computer system
5. *impersonation*: unauthorized use of an authorized user's identity to gain access
6. *data leakage*: illegally obtaining data from a system by leaking it in small amounts

Although most of these crimes involve using computers for personal gain, spreading a computer virus is motivated more by malice than by profit. Computer criminals are typically motivated by (1) revenge for some perceived wrong, (2) a need to exhibit their technical prowess and superiority, (3) a desire to highlight the vulnerability of computer security systems, (4) a need to spy on other people's private financial and personal information, and (5) the desire to assert a philosophy of open access to all systems and programs.[4]

An accurate accounting of computer crime is not possible because many offences go unreported. Sometimes company managers refuse to report the crime to police lest they display their incompetence to stockholders, or because it involves so-called low-visibility acts, such as illegally copying computer software.

Distributing Illicit or Illegal Services and Material. The Internet has become a prime source for the delivery of illicit or legally prohibited material. Included within this market are distribution of pornography and obscene material, including kiddie porn, and the distribution of dangerous drugs. In 2008 an international child pornography ring was broken when investigators confiscated more than 400,000 pictures, video files, and other images showing children engaged in sexual behaviour. Some of the child victims were as young as 5 years old; many displayed innocent characteristics, such as wearing their hair in pigtails. The ring was begun in Australia and recruited pornographers all over the world, including England, Canada, and Germany.

Though the ring was first discovered and infiltrated in 2006, it took more than two years to get indictments because of the ring's technical sophistication, which included the use of encryption, background checks, and other security measures. The accused were charged with engaging in a child exploitation enterprise; illegally posting notices seeking to receive, exchange, and distribute child porn; obstruction of justice; and producing the pornography.[5]

The IT revolution has revitalized the porn industry. The Internet is an ideal venue for selling and distributing obscene material, and the computer is an ideal device for storage and viewing. It is difficult to estimate the vast number of websites featuring sexual content, including nude photos, videos, live sex acts, and webcam strip sessions among other forms of "adult entertainment."[6]

The number of visits to pornographic sites surpasses those made to Internet search engines; some individual sites report as many as 50 million hits per year. How do adult sites operate today? Many different schemes operate, including the following:[7]

- A large firm sells annual subscriptions in exchange for unlimited access to content.
- Password services charge an annual fee to deliver access to hundreds of small sites, which share the subscription revenues.
- Large firms provide free content to smaller affiliate sites which post the free content and channel visitors to the large sites, receiving a percentage of fees paid by those who sign up.
- Webmasters forward traffic to another porn site in return for a small per-consumer fee, often involuntarily, a practice known as *mousetrapping*, where the Web page loads automatically dozens of times, causing users to panic and restart their computers.
- Adult sites cater to niche audiences looking for specific kinds of adult content, either legal sexually related material or illegal obscene material, or even kiddie porn.

Despite some successful prosecutions, electronic pornography is difficult to control. Filtering devices are used in schools and libraries to block obscene material. However, any law enforcement efforts are unlikely to put a dent in the Internet porn industry.

Distributing Dangerous Drugs. In addition to the distribution of sexual material, the Internet has become a prime purveyor of prescription drugs, some of which can be dangerous. One national survey found, in a single year (2006–07), a 135 percent increase in websites advertising these drugs and a 7 percent increase in sites offering to sell them over the Net.[8]

While the sites selling prescription drugs are booming, relatively few require the patient provide a doctor's prescription, and of those that do, only about half require that an original prescription be provided. Thus for many of these websites, the prescriptions can be faxed, giving buyers the opportunity to make multiple purchases with a single scrip. Of those sites, a third required no prescription, and one-half offered an "online consultation" that allowed users to acquire a prescription, which they were then able to fill.

Youth are especially at risk, as teens have abused illegal drugs, including ecstasy, cocaine, crack, and methamphetamines. With access to a credit card, they can order opioid-based drugs (e.g., codeine, Demerol, OxyContin, Percocet, and Darvon), depressants (e.g., Xanax, Librium, and Valium), and stimulants (e.g., Adderall, Dexedrine, and Ritalin).[9]

A different type of computer crime involves the installation in a computer system of a virus that disrupts existing programs and networks. This high-tech vandalism is the work of hackers, many of whom consider their efforts to be pranks. Some of these are detailed in Exhibit 14.2.

Denial-of-Service Attack. In the aftermath of the WikiLeaks scandal, many service providers cut off WikiLeaks and refused it services. In retaliation, hackers who support WikiLeaks launched attacks and crashed the websites of several businesses, including credit card firm MasterCard, which had blocked donations to WikiLeaks.[10] The web activists (calling themselves Anonymous) threatened to launch similar attacks.

The methods used by the Anonymous group are collectively known as a **denial-of-service attack**, typically designed to harass or extort money from legitimate users of an Internet service by threatening to prevent the user having access to the service.[11] While the WikiLeaks attacks were aimed at vengeance, denial-of-service typically involves cyberextortion. Examples of cyberextortion include

- attempts to flood a computer network, thereby preventing legitimate network traffic
- attempts to disrupt a computer network, thereby preventing access to a service
- attempts to prevent a particular individual from accessing a service
- attempts to disrupt service to a specific system or person

denial-of-service attack An assault triggered when computers bombard a server with so many requests for service that it shuts down, usually as a result of computer bots controlled by viruses.

EXHIBIT 14.2

A Short History of Computer Viruses and Attacks

1945: Rear Admiral Grace Murray Hopper refers to a moth trapped between relays in a Navy computer as a *bug*, a term used since the late 19th century to refer to problems with electrical devices.

1964: AT&T monitors telephone calls to discover identities of phone *phreaks* who use tone generators to make free phone calls; monitors 33 million calls and scores 200 convictions by 1970.

1972: John Draper discovers that the plastic whistle in a box of breakfast cereal reproduces a 2600-hertz tone that can be used to unlock AT&T's phone network, allowing free calls.

1979: Engineers at Xerox Palo Alto discover the computer *worm*, a program that scours a network for idle processors—the ancestor of modern worms that alter or erase data on computers.

1983: The FBI busts the 414s, a group of young hackers who break into several U.S. government networks using only an Apple II+ computer and a modem.

1983: University of Southern California doctoral candidate Fred Cohen coins the term *computer virus* to describe a computer program that can "modify computer programs to copy itself."

1986: One of the first PC viruses ever created, The Brain, is released in Pakistan, infecting computers in the West the next year; it is the first bootable virus.

1988: Programmer Robert Morris unleashes a worm that invades ARPANET (forerunner of the Internet), disabling 6,000 computers by flooding them with copies of itself; Morris is fined $10,000.

1990: The first polymorphic virus, Chameleon, is released.

1991: Symantec releases its Norton anti-virus software.

1994: Inexperienced email users dutifully forward an email hoax warning people not to open any message with the phrase "Good Times" in the subject line.

1995: Windows 95 is released, infecting Microsoft Word documents.

1996: The Laroux virus infects Microsoft Excel spreadsheets.

1998: Intruders infiltrate and take control of more than 500 military, government, and private-sector computer systems; first thought to have originated in Iraq, the intrusions were actually committed by two California teenagers.

1999: The Melissa virus infects thousands of computers, causing $80 million in damages, sending copies of itself to recipient's Outlook address book; in 2002, virus author David Smith, is sentenced to 20 months in prison.

2000: The I Love You virus infects millions of computers, sending computer passwords and usernames to the virus's author, who goes free because the Philippines has no laws against spreading computer viruses.

2000: Yahoo, eBay, Amazon, and Datek are knocked offline following a series of distributed denial-of-service attacks, in which a system is disabled by traffic from hundreds of computers simultaneously.

2001: The Anna Kournikova virus emails itself to everyone listed in a victim's Microsoft Outlook address book; believed to have been written using a software toolkit that even inexperienced programmers can use.

2001: The Code Red worm infects tens of thousands of computer systems, causing $2 billion in damages; programmed to use the power of all infected machines against the White House website.

2001: Days after September 11, the Nimda virus infects computers around the world; considered one of the most sophisticated, with up to five methods of infecting systems and replicating itself.

2002: The Klez worm sends copies of itself to all of the email addresses in the victim's Microsoft Outlook directory.

2002: A denial-of-service attack hits the 13 servers for almost all Internet communications.

2003: The Slammer worm infects hundreds of thousands of computers in less than three hours, wreaking havoc on businesses worldwide, knocking cash machines offline, and delaying airline flights.

2004: Santy, the first webworm is launched; uses Google to find new targets, infecting 40,000 sites.

2005: Sony BMG purposefully infects music CDs with a rootkit to prevent illegal copying of music.

2006: A low-threat Trojan horse is discovered, the first-ever malware for Mac OS X.

2007: Storm Worm, an email spamming threat from Russia, infects 1.7 million computers and compromises up to 10 million more by disguising itself as a news email containing a film about bogus news stories.

2008: Jason Milmont, 19, is arrested on charges that he modified LimeWire to be the first to use peer-to-peer sharing to control zombie computers.

2009: Daprosy Worm is discovered, a Trojan horse that steals online-game passwords in Internet cafés, making it dangerous by infecting B2B (business-to-business) systems.

2010: Stuxnet is detected, suspected of targeting Iranian nuclear facilities.

2011: Anti-Spyware 2011 disables security-related anti-virus programs and blocks access to the Internet to prevent updates.

2012: Skywiper malware is discovered; used for cyber espionage in Middle Eastern countries; said to be the most complex malware ever found.

SOURCES: Adapted from Brian Krebs, "A Short History of Computer Viruses and Attacks," *Washington Post*, February 14, 2003, www.washingtonpost.com; "Timeline of Notable Computer Viruses and Worms," en.wikipedia.org/wiki/Timeline_of_notable_computer_viruses_and_worms; "The History of Computer Viruses," Virus Scan Software, www.virus-scan-software.com/virus-scan-help/answers/the-history-of-computer-viruses.shtml; and "History of Malicious Programs," Viruslist.com, www.viruslist.com/en/viruses/encyclopedia?chapter=153280684.

A denial-of-service attack may involve threatening or actually flooding an Internet site with millions of bogus messages or orders so that the services will be tied up and unable to perform as promised. Unless the site operator pays extortion, the attackers threaten to keep up the interference until real consumers become frustrated and abandon the site. Even so-called respectable businesspeople have been accused of launching denial-of-service attacks against rival business interests.[12]

Online gambling casinos—a $7 billion a year industry—have proven particularly vulnerable to attack. Hundreds of attacks have been launched against online casinos located in Costa Rica, the Caribbean, and Great Britain. If the attack coincides with a big sporting event such as the Super Bowl, the casinos may give in and make payments rather than lose revenue and fray customer relations.[13]

The Extent of Computer Crime. How prevalent is computer crime? A survey of more than 500 computer security practitioners in corporations, government agencies, financial institutions, medical institutions, and universities indicated an increasing threat from computer crime and other information security breaches. Financial losses, theft of proprietary information, and software piracy were among the reported problems.

In 2011, the McAfee security firm reported that it had detected a hacking scheme from a "single-state operator," reportedly China, which had targeted government computer systems, defence firms, and private industries.

Exhibit 14.2 presents a brief history of computer viruses.

Illegal Copyright Infringement. Groups of individuals sometimes work together to illegally obtain software and then "crack" or "rip" its copyright protections, before posting the software on the Internet for other members of the group to use; this practice is called **warez**. Frequently, these new pirated copies reach the Internet days or weeks before the legitimate product is commercially available. It is a crime in many countries now to circumvent the antipiracy measures built into most commercial software and also outlaws the manufacture, sale, or distribution of code-cracking devices used to illegally copy software.[14]

Another form of illegal copyright infringement involves file-sharing programs that allow Internet users to download music and other copyrighted material without paying the artists and record producers their rightful royalties. Theft through the illegal reproduction and distribution of movies, software, games, and music costs billions of dollars worldwide each year. A 2005 decision in the United States, where the software market is many times bigger than in Canada, held that software distributors such as Grokster could be sued for inducing copyright infringement if they market file-sharing software that might induce people to illegally copy protected material, even if that software could also be used for legitimate purposes. As a result, Grokster announced it would suspend its file-sharing service; it was also forced to pay $50 million to the music and recording industries.

Internet Securities Fraud. Fifteen-year-old Jonathan Lebed was charged with securities fraud by the U.S. Securities and Exchange Commission (SEC) after he repeatedly bought low-cost, thinly traded stocks, and then spread hundreds of false and misleading messages concerning them—mostly baseless price predictions. After their values had been artificially inflated, Lebed sold the securities at their inflated price. His smallest one-day gain was $12,000, and one day he made $74,000. Lebed said he had done nothing wrong.[15]

Such actions are considered Internet fraud because they involve using the Internet to intentionally manipulate the securities marketplace for profit. Internet securities fraud usually takes the form of one of three major types:

- *Market manipulation.* This occurs when an individual tries to control the price of stock by interfering with the natural forces of supply and demand. This crime has two principal forms: the "pump and dump" and the "cybersmear." In a pump-and-dump scheme, erroneous and deceptive stock information is posted online to pique the interest of unsuspecting investors while those spreading the information sell their previously purchased stock at an inflated price. The cybersmear is a reverse pump and dump: negative information is spread online about a stock, driving down its price and enabling people to buy it at an artificially low price before rebuttals by the company's officers reinflate the price.[16]
- *Fraudulent offerings of securities.* Some cybercriminals create websites specifically designed to fraudulently sell securities. To make the offerings look more attractive than they are, assets may be inflated, expected returns overstated, and risks understated. In these schemes, investors are promised abnormally high profits on their investments. No investment is actually made. Early investors are paid returns with the investment money received from the later investors, similar to the Ponzi scheme discussed in Chapter 12. The system usually collapses: the later investors do not receive dividends and lose their initial investment.
- *Illegal touting.* This crime occurs when individuals make securities recommendations and fail to disclose that they are being paid to disseminate their favourable opinions. If those who tout stocks fail to disclose their relationship with the company, the information misleads investors into believing that the speaker is objective and credible rather than bought and paid for.

Identity Theft. This crime occurs when a person uses the Internet impersonate the victim to open a new credit card account or conduct some other financial transaction. Identity thieves use a variety of techniques to steal information, such as hacking a company's account and stealing credit card information. It may take months for the victim to realize the fraud, if they ever do.

---

warez The practice of illegally copying software and posting it on the Internet for others to use.

CHAPTER 14 | **Crimes in the 21st Century** 455

What are the most common goals of credit card thieves? One 2009 survey found that opening new lines of credit remains the most frequently occurring use for a victim's identity, followed by using personal information to make charges on stolen credit cards and debit cards, obtaining utilities, applying for bogus personal loans and business loans, and cheque fraud.[17]

However, relatively little is known about the extent of identity theft. Further research is required to better understand this growing cybercrime.[18]

Phishing. Some identity thieves create false emails or websites that look legitimate but are designed to gain illegal access to a victim's personal information; this practice is known as **phishing** (also known as *carding* and *spoofing*).

Some phishers send out emails that look like they come from a credit card company or online store informing victims of a problem with their account credit or balance. To fix the problem and update their account, the victims are asked to submit their name, address, phone numbers, personal information, credit card account numbers, and social insurance number (SIN). Alternatively, the email may direct the victims to a phony website that purports to be a legitimate company or business enterprise. Once victims access the website, they are asked to provide personal information or financial account information so the problem can be fixed.

Once phishers have a victim's personal information, they can do three things. They can gain access to pre-existing accounts, debit cards, and credit cards, and then buy goods using those accounts. Phishers can also use the information to open brand new banking accounts and credit cards without the victim's knowledge. Finally, the phishers can implant viruses into the software that forwards the phishing email to other recipients once one person responds to the original email, thereby luring more potential victims.

Phishing emails and websites have become even more of a problem now that cybercriminals can easily copy brand names, logos, and corporate personnel insignia directly into the email. The look is so authentic that victims believe the email comes from the advertised company (such as a bank). Most phishers send out spam emails to a large number of recipients knowing that some of those recipients will have accounts with the company they are impersonating.

Vishing. Voice over Internet Protocol (VoIP) is a technology that allows people to make voice calls using a broadband Internet connection instead of a regular phone line. Some VoIP services allow subscribers to call only other people who also use the same service, but others allow subscribers to call anyone who has a telephone number. Cyberthieves have already employed this technology in identity theft schemes known as **vishing**.

In one version, the victim receives an email that provides a phone number to call. Those who call this customer service number (a VoIP account, not a real financial institution) are led through a series of voice-prompted menus that ask for account numbers, passwords, and other critical information. In another version, the victim is contacted over the phone instead of by email. The call is either a live person or a recorded message

that directs the victim to take action to protect a personal account. The visher may have collected some personal information, including account or credit card numbers, which can create a false sense of security for the victim.

Etailing Fraud. New fraud schemes are evolving to take advantage of the billions of dollars in goods sold on the Internet each year. **Etailing fraud** can involve both illegally buying and selling merchandise on the Net.

Not only do etail frauds involve selling merchandise, they can also involve buyer fraud. One scam involves purchasing top-of-the-line electronic equipment over the Net, and then purchasing a second, similar looking but cheaper model of the same brand. The cheaper item is then returned to the etailer after switching bar codes and boxes with the more expensive unit.

In another tactic, called *shoplisting*, a person obtains a legitimate receipt from a store either by buying it from a customer or finding it in the trash, and then returns to the store and, casually shopping, picks up an identical product. He then takes the product and receipt to the returns departments and attempts to return it for cash, store credit, or a gift card. The thief then sells the gift card on the Internet at a discount for quick cash. Not surprisingly, the underground market for receipts has been growing, as many stores have liberalized their return policies.

CYBERCRIME

As mentioned in Chapter 11, cybercrime is of increasing importance in the modern world, due to a whole new breed of high-tech crimes that cost consumers billions of dollars and are difficult to police. In this section, we continue that theme, looking at cybertheft, cybervandalism, and forms of cyberwarfare.

Cybertheft: Cybercrimes for Profit

Ironically, technological breakthroughs since the dawn of the Industrial Revolution—such as telephones and automobiles—not only brought with them dramatic improvements for society but also created new opportunities for

phishing The setting up of phony websites to gain access to people's personal information.

vishing Similar to phishing, this practice uses Voice over Internet Protocol (VoIP) software to access personal information.

etailing fraud The selling of illegal or intentionally misrepresented goods over the Internet.

Comparative Criminology
The Nigerian 419 Email Scam

The Nigerian 419 email scam is so called because it violates Section 419, the fraud section of the Nigerian criminal code.

Beginning in the 1980s as an investment scam, it typically involved an initial letter on stolen official letterhead apparently from an important person. Today, it is an email, but the form and content are the same. The tone is polite, almost Victorian, as the sender requests the assistance of the recipient to arrange the transfer of funds out of the sender's country.

For example, here is an email (verbatim) from Prince Johnson Weah:

My dear friend,

Compliments of the day and happy new year in arrears. My name is prince Prince Johnson weahjr), the chief security officer to Charles Taylor the formar President of Liberia. As a matter of fact, he has been forced to step down from power due to presures from the united nation governments and other african leaders, so far he is presently in assylum in Nigeria while he is been sought to come and face war criminal charges in sirra leone where he has been indicted by the war crime tribunal on human right abuse/violations.

If the recipient replies to such a message, and 1 to 2 percent do, requests begin for a series of payments to prepare documents, secure stamps, and so on. The requests for payments escalate, and victims lose an average of $3,000 to $4,000. Some have lost tens of thousands of dollars. Overall, Canadians have lost $30 million, and scammers defrauded individuals and organizations of an estimated $3 billion in 2005. In Britain alone, these advance fraud fees scams cost £150 million annually.

Overall, at least 250,000 scammers worldwide send thousands of messages daily to email addresses that have been harvested, email addresses accessed through illegally purchased lists, and email addresses gleaned from public sites and discussion boards.

The letters play on appeals to pity, trust, and avarice, as Prince Weah continues:

Well dear friend I need your assistance to secure this fund for proper use in your country, this can be done through your a/c no, based on my present statue in liberia, the government has begun to seize all mr. Taylor's assets as well as those of his past associates including this (25m) hence I am making this move in order to safeguide this my little assets. I have decided to make you my partner who will help me safeguide this fund untill I arrive your country after the fund is released to you in person. I am hundred percent sure that you are going to help me, incuding my wife and our children....

The amount is (USD$15.6 million) in a Security firm in EUROPE. All that is needed is for me to instruct the company to release the funds to you. I will compersate you with 25% of the total funds released to you as compensation for your assistance, five percent (5%) would be set aside to take care of all expenses we may incure during the transaction while i will rechannel the 70% into profitable investments in and within your country.

The structure of the advance fee fraud is instantly identifiable. First comes the contact, then the request for assistance in moving funds out of the country, the stressed need for secrecy, an obstacle for which fees must be paid, requests that escalate, and in some cases only ends when the recipient spends thousands of dollars only to realize he or she has been scammed. In some cases, recipients of the 419 message have gone to Nigeria, only to be kidnapped and assaulted.

The history of the scam dates back to the 16th century when it was called "the Spanish prisoner"; the recipient was asked to pay a fine for the release of a wealthy captive, upon which they would be paid a wealthy reward. It also involved the same scam within a scam, which meant tricking the letter's recipient into thinking that he or she was involved in a plan to trick the authorities.

The reason that these scams succeed cannot be explained simply on the basis of the gullibility of victims or bare greed, although these vulnerabilities do play a part. Rather, the scams play on the hope that chance can be controlled, that the world is ruled by mysterious events and magical thinking, and above all, that capitalism can be the source of happiness even at the same time as the products it sells are destined to wither away just as surely as the ruse will be exposed.

SOURCES: Marilyn Dryud, "'I Brought you a Good News'. An Analysis of Nigerian 419 Letters," Proceedings of the 2005 Association for Business Communication Annual Convention; Andrew Smith, "Nigerian Scam E-Mails and the Charms of Capital," *Cultural Studies* 2008; RCMP, 2003, Nigerian letter scam, www.rcmp-grc.gc.ca/faq/Nigeria e.html.

criminal wrongdoing: criminals use the telephone to place bets or threaten victims; cars can be stolen and sold for big profits. The same pattern is now occurring during the IT revolution. The computer and Internet provide opportunities for socially beneficial endeavours—such as education, research, commerce, and entertainment—while at the same time serving as a tool to facilitate illegal activity. Cyberthieves now have the luxury of remaining anonymous, living in any part of the world, conducting their business anytime, working alone or in a group, while at the same time reaching a much wider number of potential victims than ever before. No longer is the con artist or criminal entrepreneur limited to fleecing victims in a particular geographic locale. The technology revolution has opened novel methods for cybertheft, ranging from the unlawful distribution of computer software to Internet security fraud.

Cyberthieves conspire to use cyberspace to either distribute illegal goods and services or to defraud people for quick profits. Some of the most common methods are discussed here.

Theft from ATMs. Automatic teller machines (ATMs) attract the attention of cybercriminals looking for easy profits, using stealth and technological skill to commit the crime. One approach is to use a thin, transparent-plastic overlay on an ATM keypad that captures a user's identification code as it is entered. Though the plastic covering looks like some sort of cover to protect the keys, in fact microchips in the device record every keystroke. Another transparent device inside the card slot captures card data. While the client completes the transaction, a computer attached to the overlay records all the data necessary to clone the card. The skimming devices and cameras are removed from the ATMs and the stolen information is downloaded to create false bank debit cards by encoding cards with magnetic strips containing the stolen banking information. Using these false cards and the victims' PINs, the thieves can withdraw funds from ATMs.

Cyberwarfare: Cybercrime with Political Motives

Because the developed world is totally dependent upon electronic communication, protecting technological infrastructure is important for national defence. Some cybercriminals are politically motivated. They may be employed by intelligence agencies to penetrate computer networks at an enemy nation's most sensitive military bases, defence contractors, and aerospace companies for the purpose of stealing important data. In one well-known case of **cyberespionage**, Chinese agents were able to penetrate computers, enter hidden sections of a hard drive, zip up as many files as possible, and transmit the data to way stations in South Korea, Hong Kong, and Taiwan before sending them to mainland China. The spy ring, known as Titan Rain, compromised networks ranging from NASA to the World Bank. Hundreds of military computer systems were penetrated, and similar attacks have been launched against classified systems in Britain, Canada, Australia, and New Zealand.[19] In 2008, the Pentagon issued a report on China's "Cyberwarfare Capabilities," acknowledging that hackers in China had penetrated the Pentagon's computer system and that the intrusions apparently from China into computer networks used "many of the skills and capabilities that would also be required for computer network attack." Whether the hackers acted alone or were backed by the Chinese military was not clear; however, ample evidence pointed to Chinese interest in cyberespionage as part of their long-term strategy.[20]

In another well-known cyber attack, the secretary general of the International Atomic Energy Agency announced that on November 23, 2010, Iran had been forced to shut down its main uranium enrichment plant at Natanz for seven days after it was targeted by the Stuxnet computer worm. Experts believe that Stuxnet was specifically designed to attack systems at the plant that control the speed at which the enrichment centrifuges spin. The source of the attack remains unknown, but suspects include the United States and Israel security agencies.[21]

Cyberterrorism. Attacks that integrate terrorist goals with cyber capabilities are called cyberterrorism, used by covert forces to disrupt the intersection where the virtual electronic reality of computers meets the physical world.[22] FBI expert Mark Pollitt defines cyberterrorism as "the premeditated, politically motivated attack against information, computer systems, computer programs, and data which results in violence against noncombatant targets by subnational groups or clandestine agents."[23]

Terrorist organizations are beginning to understand the power that cybercrime can inflict on their enemies, and agencies of the justice system have to be ready for a sustained attack on the nation's electronic infrastructure.

Cyberspace is a handy battlefield for the terrorist because an attack can strike directly at a target that bombs won't affect: the economy, or communications. Because technological change plays a significant role in the development of critical infrastructures, they are particularly vulnerable to attack. And because of rapid technological change, and the interdependence of systems, it is difficult to defend against efforts to disrupt services.[24]

Cyberterrorists have many advantages. Criminals can operate from countries where cyber laws barely exist, making them almost untouchable.[25] Thus, they avoid risking loss of life and do not need to infiltrate enemy territory. Terrorists can commit crimes from anyplace in the world, and the costs are minimal. Also, terror organizations do not lack skilled labour to mount cyber attacks: a growing number of highly skilled computer experts are available at reasonable costs in developing countries. Cyberterrorism may result in a battered economy in which the government is forced to spend more on the military and cut back on social programs and education.

While it may be difficult to separate the damage caused by hackers from deliberate attacks by terrorists, the Center for Strategic and International Studies has uncovered attacks on the National Security Agency, the Pentagon, and a nuclear weapons laboratory.[26] The financial service sector is also a prime target and has been victimized by information warfare. One survey found that, in a single year, financial service firms received an average of 1,018 attacks per company, and 46 percent of these firms had at least one server attack during the period.[27]

> **cyberespionage** The use of computer networks and communications to commit espionage, such as hacking into military, government, and industry computer systems.

Computers can be used by terrorist groups to remain connected and to communicate covertly with agents around the world. Networks are a cost-effective tool for planning and striking.[28] They enable terror groups to plan and carry out a variety of Internet-related attacks, such as the following possible scenarios:

- implanting logic bombs in an enemy's computer, which can go undetected for years
- using programs to enter supposedly secure systems, and then disrupt the network
- using conventional weapons to overload a network's electrical system[29]
- breaching the computer system of a corporation whose welfare is vital to national security
- attacking systems used to manage basic infrastructure needs, such as an oil pipelines

Cyberterrorists may directly attack the financial system. In ever-increasing numbers, people are spending and investing their money electronically, using online banking, credit card payment, and online brokerage services. The banking/financial system transacts billions of dollars each day through a complex network of institutions and systems. Efficient and secure electronic functioning is required if people are willing to conduct credit and debit card purchases, money transfers, and stock trading.[30]

One attack method is to release a *botnet* or software robot, also known as a zombie or drone, which allows an unauthorized user to remotely take control of a host computer without the victim's knowledge or permission.[31] Infected computers can be used to launch denial-of-service attacks, send spam and spyware, or commit cyber extortion. In one attack, a global telecommunications company with a business unit in Central America experienced several unusual problems, including multiple network outages—some lasting up to six hours—which disrupted businesses and national connectivity, and took automated teller machines offline for extended periods of time. A botnet-based distributed denial-of-service attack had crippled the country's infrastructure.[32]

Funding Terrorist Activities. Terrorist groups have used the Internet to conduct white-collar crimes to raise funds to buy arms and carry out operations.[33] One method of funding is through fraudulent charitable organizations claiming to support a particular cause, such as disaster relief or food services. Using bogus charities to raise money is particularly attractive to cyberterrorists because these organizations face far less scrutiny from the government than do for-profit corporations and individuals.

Bogus companies have also been used by terrorist groups to receive and distribute money. These shell companies may engage in legitimate activities to establish a positive reputation in the business community but produce bills for non-existent products that are "paid" by another party with profits from illegal activities, such as insurance fraud or identity theft.[34] If a shell company generates revenues, funds can be distributed by altering financial statements to hide profits, and then depositing the profits in accounts that are used directly or indirectly to support terrorist activities and organizations, such as Hamas.

Another source of terrorist funding, which is discussed less often in the literature, is intellectual property (IP) crime. The illegal sale of counterfeited goods and illegal use of IP to commit other crimes, such as stock manipulation, have been used to support terrorist activities.[35]

The Extent and Costs of Cybercrime. How common are cybercrimes, and how costly are they to industry and to the general public? The Internet has become a vast engine for illegal profits and criminal entrepreneurs. An accurate accounting of cybercrime will probably never be possible because so many offences go unreported, but the incidence of cybercrime is undoubtedly growing rapidly.

Though thousands of breaches occur each year, most are not reported to authorities. Some cybercrime goes unreported because it involves low-visibility acts—such as copying computer software in violation of copyright laws—that simply never get detected.[36] Some businesses choose not to report cybercrime because they fear revealing the weaknesses in their network security systems. However, the information available indicates that the profit in cybercrime is vast and continually growing.[37] Losses are now in the billions and rising with the continuing growth of e-commerce.

The proliferation of cybercrime and its cost to the economy have created the need for new laws and enforcement processes specifically aimed at controlling its emerging formulations. Because technology evolves so rapidly, the enforcement challenges are particularly vexing. Numerous organizations have been set up to provide training and support for law enforcement agents. In addition, new laws have been aimed at particular areas of high-tech crimes.

International Treaties. Because cybercrime operates essentially in a global manner, international cooperation is required for its control. The Convention on Cybercrime (2006) was the first international treaty to address the definition and enforcement of cybercrime. Now signed by 43 nations, this treaty focuses on improving investigative techniques and increasing cooperation. The convention includes a list of crimes that each signatory state must incorporate into its own law, including such cyber offences as hacking, distribution of child pornography, and protection of intellectual property rights. Under this convention, law enforcement agencies are granted new powers, including the ability to require that an Internet service provider monitor a user's online viewing and search choices in real time. The convention also requires signatory states to cooperate whenever possible in the investigations and prosecution of cybercriminals. The vision is that a common legal framework will eliminate jurisdictional hurdles to facilitate the law enforcement of borderless cybercrimes.[38]

Carrying out this mandate may be difficult to achieve, given the legal rights afforded citizens in western countries that may not be realized by residents of other nations.

For example, constitutional protections that restrict the definition of pornography and obscenity in the west may not apply overseas. It is not surprising that watchdog institutions such as the American Civil Liberties Union (ACLU) have condemned the treaty.[39]

Cybercrime Enforcement. Over the last several years, law enforcement has made remarkable strides in dealing with identity theft as a crime problem. For example, local police departments are now creating special units to crack down on cybercriminals. In Toronto, the police department's child-exploitation section concentrates on cracking high profile and difficult cases of Internet child pornography, using inventive and aggressive investigative methods. The unit looks for even the smallest clues to lead them to perpetrators. In one well-known case, investigators homed in on a computer keyboard where the character ñ—unique to the Spanish language—was visible. In the same series of pictures, they noticed what appeared to be a European train ticket being held in a child's hand. By sharing the information with Interpol, the international police consortium led to the break-up of a sadistic child-porn ring operating south of Madrid, led by a man who had been using his position as a babysitter to gain access to small children.[40]

TRANSNATIONAL ORGANIZED CRIME

On June 10, 2010, more than 2,200 individuals were arrested on narcotics-related charges.[41] The two-year investigation, involving more than 3,000 U.S. federal agents and officers, targeted the transportation infrastructure of Mexican drug trafficking organizations. Overall, Project Deliverance led to the seizure of approximately $154 million in U.S. currency and approximately 572 kg of methamphetamine, 2.3 tonnes of cocaine, 640 kg of heroin, 63 tonnes of marijuana, 501 weapons, and 527 vehicles.

The scope of the operation gives a glimpse into the global reach of transnational organized crime. These criminal conspiracies involve ongoing criminal enterprise groups whose ultimate purpose is personal economic gain through illegitimate means. Here a structured enterprise system is set up to continually supply consumers with merchandise and services banned by criminal law, but for which a ready market exists: prostitution, pornography, gambling, and narcotics. The system may resemble a legitimate business run by an ambitious chief executive officer, complete with assistants, staff attorneys, and accountants, and thorough, efficient accounts receivable and complaint departments.[42]

This section briefly defines organized crime, reviews its history, and discusses its economic effect and control.

Origins of Organized Crime

Organized crime itself is not a recent phenomenon. In the 1600s, London was terrorized by organized gangs that called themselves Hectors, Bugles, Dead Boys, and other colourful names. In the 17th and 18th centuries, English gang members wore distinctive belts and pins marked with serpents, animals, stars, and the like.[43] The first mention of youth gangs in America occurred in the late 1780s, when prison reformers noted the presence of gangs of young people hanging out on Philadelphia's street corners. By the 1820s, New York's Bowery and Five Points districts, Boston's North End and Fort Hill, and the outlying Southwark and Moyamensing sections of Philadelphia were the locales of youth gangs with such colourful names as the Roach Guards, the Chichesters, the Plug Uglies, and the Dead Rabbits.[44]

At the turn of the 20th century, La Mano Nera (the Black Hand), an offshoot of Sicilian criminal groups, established its presence in northeastern urban centres. Gangsters demanded payments from local businessmen in return for protection; those who would not pay were beaten and their shops vandalized. Eventually, the Black Hand merged with gangs of Italian heritage to form larger urban-based gangs and groups.

A turning point in the development of organized gangs occurred with Prohibition. Until then, gangs had remained relatively small and local, but now the national and international market for controlled substances opened the door to riches. What emerged was a national syndicate, referred to as Cosa Nostra, or the Mafia, which was centrally coordinated and whose various component gangs worked cooperatively to settle disputes, dictate policy, and assign territory.[45] Despite efforts at cooperation and control, numerous and bloody gang wars and individual vendettas were common.

The Mafia remains one of the largest organized crime groups, gaining huge profits through the manufacture and sale of illegal goods and services. Recently, however it has been in decline, as have other traditional organized crime groups. What has caused this alleged erosion of Mafia power? First, many of the reigning family heads are aging, in their 80s and older, prompting some law enforcement officials to dub them "the Geritol gang."[46] A younger generation of mob leaders stepped in to take control of the families, but they seem to lack the skill and leadership of the older bosses. In addition, active government enforcement policies have halved what the estimated mob membership was 25 years ago, and a number of the highest-ranking leaders have been imprisoned.

The Mafia was also hurt by changing values in society. Caucasian, ethnic, inner-city neighbourhoods, which were the locus of Mafia power, have been shrinking as families move to the suburbs. Organized crime groups lost their urban-centred political and social base of operations. In addition, the code of silence that protected Mafia leaders is now broken regularly by younger members who turn informer rather than face prison terms. It is also possible that their success has hurt organized crime families: younger family members are better educated than their forebears and are equipped to seek their fortunes through legitimate enterprise.[47]

While traditional organized crime families may be shrinking in size, the demand for the services they provide remains constant. To fill the void, a new type of organized crime operation has developed—**transnational organized crime**. Based in Asia, Eastern Europe, and North, South, and Latin America, this new breed of organized crime uses the Internet and other IT devices to facilitate their operations across nations and continents.

Organized Crime Abroad

Many countries confront the problem of organized criminal gangs. The Cali and Medellin drug cartels in Colombia are world famous for both their vast drug trafficking profits and their use of violence to achieve their objectives.

Japan also has a long history of organized criminal activity by Yakuza gangs. In 1993, officials of the Kirin Brewery, Japan's largest beer maker, resigned after allegations were made that they had paid more than 33 million yen in *sokaiya* (extortion money) to racketeers who threatened their business.[48] In China, organized gangs use violence to enforce contracts between companies, serving as an alternative to the legal system. They also help smuggle many of the 100,000 people who leave mainland China each year.[49]

Since the break-up of the Soviet Union, Russia has been beset by organized crime activity and now has an estimated 3,000 active criminal gangs. Bloody shootouts have become common as gangs stake out territory and extort businesses.

Computer and communications technology has fostered international cooperation among crime cartels. East European and Russian gangs sell arms seized from the former Soviet Army to members of the Sicilian Mafia; Japanese and Italian mob members meet in Paris; drug money from South America is laundered in Canada and England.

Characteristics of Transnational Organized Crime

A precise description of the characteristics of transnational organized crime is difficult to formulate, but here are some of its general traits:[50]

- Transnational organized crime is a conspiratorial activity, involving the coordination of numerous people in the planning and execution of illegal acts or in the pursuit of a legitimate objective by unlawful means (e.g., threatening a legitimate business to get a stake in it).
- An offence is transnational if
  - it is committed in more than one state.
  - it is committed in one state, but its preparation and control takes place in another.
  - it is committed in one state, but involves an organized criminal group that engages in criminal activities in more than one state.
  - it is committed in one state, but has substantial effects in another state.[51]
- Transnational organized crime involves continuous commitment by primary members, although individuals with specialized skills may be brought in as needed. Organized crime is usually structured along hierarchical lines—a chieftain supported by close advisers, lower subordinates, and so on.
- Transnational organized crime has economic gain as its primary goal, although power and status may also be motivating factors. Economic gain is achieved through global supply of illegal goods and services, including drugs, sex slaves, arms, and pornography.
- In addition to providing illegal material such as narcotics, contemporary global syndicates engage in business-related crimes such as laundering illegal money through legitimate businesses, land fraud, and computer crime.
- Transnational criminal syndicates employ predatory tactics, such as intimidation, violence, and corruption.
- Transnational organized crime groups are quick and effective in controlling and disciplining their members, associates, and victims, and will not hesitate to use lethal violence against those who flout organizational rules.
- Transnational crime depends heavily on the instruments of the IT age: the Internet, global communications, rapid global transportation systems, the universal banking system, and global credit card and payment systems.
- Transnational organized crime groups do not include terror organizations, though the two groups may have some overlap. Some terror groups are involved in criminality to fund their political objectives, and some have morphed from politically motivated organizations to organizations solely involved in for-profit criminal activity. Transnational criminal organizations may aid terror groups with transportation and communication.

Activities of Transnational Organized Crime

What are the main activities of organized crime? The traditional sources of income are derived from providing illicit materials and using force to first enter into legitimate businesses and to then maximize profits. Most organized crime

> **transnational organized crime** Unlike traditional organized crime, organized crime that operates across international boundaries, transporting people and stolen goods.

In the popular 2008 film *Taken*, Bryan Mills, a former CIA agent (played by Liam Neeson) uses his special combat skills to save his daughter Kim after she is abducted while on a trip to Paris. Almost as soon as she arrives in town, Kim and a friend are kidnapped, drugged, and forced into the slave trade by a gang of Albanian mobsters. As Bryan searches frantically for his beloved daughter, he uncovers a scheme, protected by corrupt police, in which young women are being kidnapped and sold into the sex trade. Because she is a virgin, Kim is spared prostitution: she is to be auctioned off to a millionaire wishing to buy a concubine for his personal use. In pursuit, Bryan Mills kills about 100 sex traffickers, saves his daughter in the nick of time, and returns her safely home to the United States.

Can these dreadful images be based on reality? While few fathers are like Bryan Mills, international sex trafficking is all too real. Every year, hundreds of thousands of women and children—primarily from Southeast Asia and Eastern Europe—are lured by the promise of good jobs, and then end up forced into brothels or as circuit travellers in labour camps. Most go to wealthy industrialized countries. Japan now has more than 10,000 commercial sex establishments with 150,000 to 200,000 foreign girls trafficked into the country each year. India has experienced a large influx of foreign sex workers who are believed to be the source of the HIV epidemic that is sweeping the country.

It is believed that traffickers import up to 50,000 women and children every year into the United States despite legal prohibitions (in addition to prostitution, some are brought in to work in sweatshops). U.S. federal law defines *trafficking* as

1. sex trafficking in which a commercial sex act is induced by force, fraud, or coercion, or in which the person induced to perform such an act has not attained 18 years of age; or
2. the recruitment, harbouring, transportation, provision, or obtaining of a person for labour or services, through the use of force, fraud, or coercion for the purpose of subjection to involuntary servitude, peonage, debt bondage, or slavery.

Global trafficking gangs use force, fraud, or coercion to exploit a person for profit. Victims are subjected to labour and/or sexual exploitation. Trafficking for labour exploitation, the form of trafficking claiming the greatest number of victims, includes traditional slavery, forced labour, and holding people in bondage until they can pay off debts. Trafficking for sexual exploitation may include involvement in prostitution or pornographic films. The use of force or coercion can be direct and violent or psychological.

How great is the problem? The International Labour Organization (ILO)—the United Nations agency charged with addressing labour standards, employment, and social protection issues—estimates that at any given time, at least 12 million adults and children live in forced labour, bonded labour, and commercial sexual servitude. Of these victims, the ILO estimates that at least 1.39 million of them, 56 percent female, are victims of commercial sexual servitude, both transnational and within countries.

Human traffickers prey on the weak, by targeting vulnerable men, women, and children. They use creative and ruthless ploys designed to trick, coerce, and win the confidence of potential victims. Very often, these ruses involve promises of a better life through employment, educational opportunities, or marriage.

Although films such as *Taken* depict sex traffickers as almost entirely men, the UN report found that sex traffickers are often women, many of whom began as sex workers themselves. They are encouraged by their recruiter/ trafficker to return home and recruit other women, often under the scrutiny of people working for the trafficker to make sure they don't try to escape.

income comes from such activities as human trafficking, narcotics distribution, illegal gambling, theft rings, Internet pornography, and cargo theft. The international trade in human trafficking and prostitution is the subject of the Comparative Criminology feature, "International Trafficking in Persons."

Contemporary organized crime cartels have also branched out into securities fraud. They target small cap or micro cap stocks, over-the-counter stocks, and other types of thinly traded stocks that can be easily manipulated and sold to seniors or inexperienced investors. The conspirators use offshore bank accounts to conceal their participation in the fraud scheme and to launder the illegal proceeds in order to avoid paying income tax.[52]

Contemporary Transnational Crime Groups

Emerging transnational crime syndicates are primarily located in nations whose governments are too weak to present effective opposition. If these syndicates believe that

Because human trafficking is a global enterprise, it attracts a great deal of cooperation, so that in Eastern Europe a single gang may include Russians, Moldavians, Egyptians, and Syrians. Cooperation allows sex slaves to be trafficked not only to neighbouring countries, but all around the globe. The UN found that victims from East Asia were detected in more than 20 countries in regions throughout the world, including Europe, the Americas, the Middle East, Central Asia, and Africa.

Contributing Factors

Human trafficking is facilitated by social problems and disorder, such as disruptions in the global economy, war, and social unrest. Economic crisis hits young women especially hard. Female victims are often poor and aspire to a better life. They may be forced, coerced, deceived, and psychologically manipulated into industrial or agricultural work, marriage, domestic servitude, organ donation, or sexual exploitation. Some traffickers exploit victims' frustration with low salaries in their home countries, while others prey upon a crisis in victims' families that requires them to make money abroad. The traffickers then promise to take victims abroad and find them traditionally female service-sector jobs, such as waitress, salesperson, domestic worker, or au pair/babysitter.

While victims often come from poorer countries, the market for labour and sex is found in wealthier countries or in countries that, while economically poor, cater to the needs of citizens from wealthy countries, of corporations, or of tourists.

Combatting Trafficking

The United States has made stopping the trafficking of women a top priority. In 1998, the "Memorandum on Steps to Combat Violence Against Women and the Trafficking of Women and Girls" was issued, which directed the secretary of state, the attorney general, and the president's Interagency Council on Women to expand their work against violence against women to include work against the trafficking of women.

In the Russian Federation, prevention education projects are aimed at potential victims of trafficking, and nongovernmental organizations have established hotlines for victims or women seeking information about the risks of accepting job offers abroad.

The UN report found that the number of convictions for human trafficking is increasing, especially in a handful of countries. Nonetheless, most countries' conviction rates rarely exceed 1.5 per 100,000 people, which is even below the level normally recorded for rare crimes such as kidnapping. As of 2007–08, two out of every five countries covered by the United Nations Office on Drugs and Crime (UNODC) report had not recorded a single conviction for sex trafficking, so the problem still remains.

Critical Thinking

1. If you were put in charge, what would you do to slow or end the international sex trade? Before you answer, remember the saying that prostitution is the oldest profession, which implies that curbing it may prove very difficult.

2. Should men who hire prostitutes who are obviously involved in the sex trade against their will be punished more severely to deter them from getting involved in the exploitation of these vulnerable young women? Or is it unfair to expect someone to know the reasons their sex partner was involved in prostitution?

SOURCES: Shannon Devine, "Poverty Fuels Trafficking to Japan," *Herizons* 20 (2007): 18–22; Jay Silverman, Michele Decker, Humka Gupta, Ayonija Maheshwari, Vipul Patel, and Anita Raj, "HIV Prevalence and Predictors Among Rescued Sex-Trafficked Women and Girls in Mumbai, India," *JAIDS: Journal of Acquired Immune Deficiency Syndromes* 43 (2006): 588–593; David Enrich, "Trafficking in People," *U.S. News and World Report* 131 (2001): 34; Mark Lusk and Faith Lucas, "The Challenge of Human Trafficking and Contemporary Slavery," *Journal of Comparative Social Welfare* 25 (2009): 49–57; U.S. Department of State, "Trafficking in Persons Report 2009," www.state.gov/g/tip/rls/tiprpt/2009/123123.htm (accessed November 9, 2010); Linda Williams and Jennifer Ngo, "Human Trafficking," in *Encyclopedia of Interpersonal Violence,* eds. Claire Renzetti and Jeffrey Edelson (Thousand Oaks, CA: Sage Publications, 2007); Donna Hughes, "The 'Natasha' Trade: Transnational Sex Trafficking," *National Institute of Justice Journal* (January 2001), www.uri.edu/artsci/wms/hughes/natasha_nij.pdf.

the government is poised to interfere with their illegal activities, they will carry out a terror campaign, killing police and other government officials to achieve their goals. Easier international travel, expanded world trade, and financial transactions that cross national borders have enabled them to branch out of local and regional crime to target international victims and develop criminal networks within more prosperous countries and regions.[53] For example, Africa, a continent that has experienced political turmoil, has also seen the rise of transnational gangs. African criminal enterprises in Nigeria, Ghana, and Liberia have developed quickly since the 1980s due to the globalization of the world's economies and the great advances in communication technology. Nigerian criminal enterprises, primarily engaged in drug trafficking and financial frauds, are the most significant of these groups, operate in more than 80 countries, and cost billions of dollars each year.

Some of the most prominent transnational gang clusters are described in some detail in the following sections:

Eastern European Gangs.   Eastern gangs trace their origin to countries spanning the Baltics, the Balkans, Central and Eastern Europe, Russia, the Caucasus, and central Asia. For example, Albanian organized crime activities in the United

States include gambling, money laundering, drug trafficking, human smuggling, extortion, violent witness intimidation, robbery, attempted murder, and murder.[54]

Although these gangs are ethnically based, they work with other ethnic groups when perpetrating crimes. They operate a multibillion-dollar transnational crime cartel that trades in illegal arms, narcotics, pornography, and prostitution. Balkan organized crime groups have recently expanded into more sophisticated crimes such as real estate fraud.

Organized groups prey upon women in the poorest areas of Europe—Romania, the Ukraine, Bosnia—and sell them into sexual slavery. Many of these women are transported as prostitutes around the world, some finding themselves in North America.

Russian Transnational Crime Groups.   Since the collapse of the Soviet Union in 1991, criminal organizations in Russia and in other former Soviet republics, such as the Ukraine, have engaged in a variety of crimes: drugs and arms trafficking, stolen automobiles, trafficking in women and children, and money laundering.[55] No area of the world seems immune, certainly not North America, which is seen by many as the land of opportunity for unloading criminal goods and laundering dirty money.

Russian organized crime is not primarily based on ethnic or family structures. Instead, it is based on economic necessity that was nurtured by the oppressive Soviet regime. Here, a professional criminal class developed in Soviet prisons during the Stalinist period that began in 1924—the era of the gulag.

Contemporary Patterns in Russian Organized Crime.   The following are some specific characteristics of Russian organized crime in the post-Soviet era:

- Russian criminals make extensive use of the state governmental apparatus to protect and promote their criminal activities. For example, most businesses in Russia have protection provided by police or by security officials employed outside their official capacities for this purpose. In other cases, officials are silent partners in criminal enterprises.
- As Communism collapsed, the privatization of industry resulted in the massive use of state funds for criminal gain. Valuable properties are purchased through insider deals for much less than their true value, and then resold for lucrative profits.
- Criminals have been able to directly influence the state's domestic and foreign policy to promote the interests of organized crime, either by attaining public office themselves or by buying public officials.

Beyond these particular features, organized crime in Russia shares other characteristics common to organized crime elsewhere in the world:

- the systematic use of violence, including both the threat and use of force
- a hierarchical structure
- a limited or exclusive membership
- a specialization in types of crime and a division of labour
- a military-style discipline, with strict rules and regulations for the organization as a whole
- the possession of high-tech equipment, including military weapons; threats, blackmail, and violence are used to penetrate business management and to assume control of commercial enterprises or, in some instances, to found their own enterprises with money from their criminal activities

As a result of these activities, Russia has high rates of homicide that are now more than 20 times those in Western Europe, resembling a country in civil war. Furthermore, the corruption is globalized, with Russian organized crime active in Europe, Africa, Asia, and North and South America. Massive money laundering is now common, and in some cases is tied to terrorist funding. Russian criminals have become involved in killings for hire in central and Western Europe, Israel, Canada, and the United States.

However, with the exception of extortion and money laundering, Russians have had little or no involvement in some of the more traditional types of organized crime, such as drug trafficking, gambling, and loansharking. Instead, Russian criminal groups are extensively engaged in a broad array of frauds and scams, including healthcare fraud, insurance scams, stock frauds, antiquities swindles, forgery, and fuel-tax evasion schemes. Legitimate businesses, such as the movie business and textile industry, have become targets of criminals from the former Soviet Union, and they are often used for money laundering and extortion.

The first significant conviction against the Russian mob occurred in 1996 when Vyacheslav Kirillovich Ivankov was convicted on extortion and conspiracy charges in the United States. Ivankov led an international criminal organization that operated mainly in New York, Toronto, London, Vienna, Budapest, and Moscow, specializing in extorting Russian business interests. While Ivankov's conviction was a setback, Russian groups continue to thrive, engaging in Internet crimes, extortion, and white-collar crimes.

Latin American and Mexican Drug Cartels

Transnational crime cartels operate freely in South American nations such as Peru and Colombia. Caribbean nations such as Jamaica, the Dominican Republic, and Haiti are the home to drug and gun-smuggling gangs. The money inflows from illicit trade strengthen and enlarge the gangs, enabling them to increase their involvement in intraregional and transnational dealing to gain more money. Furthermore, drug trafficking has contributed to a sharp increase in the availability and usage of firearms.[56]

The Mexican drug cartels are of greatest concern. These transnational gangs have become large-scale suppliers of narcotics, marijuana, and methamphetamines, making Mexico a drug-producing and transit country. Although Mexican drug cartels, or drug trafficking organizations, have existed for quite some time, they have become more powerful since Colombia was able to crack down on the Cali and Medellín cartels in the 1990s. Mexican drug cartels now dominate the wholesale illicit drug market and are wholesale launderers of drug money. Mexican and Colombian trafficking organizations annually smuggle an estimated $8 billion to $25 billion in drug proceeds into Mexico for laundering.

Numerous drug cartels operate in Mexico: the main ones are Gulf, Tijuana, Sinaloa, Juárez, Millennium, Oaxaca, and Colima. Some are dominant in local regions, while the major gangs—Gulf, Sinaloa, and Juárez—are present throughout all of Mexico. In recent years, new cartels have formed and others have become allies, in a constantly shifting landscape of drug activity. For example, La Familia Michoacana cartel was an independent drug trafficking organization and later allied itself with the Gulf cartel. La Familia is a heavily armed cartel that has utilized violence to support its narcotics trafficking business, including murders, kidnappings, and assaults.

Asian Transnational Crime Groups

Asian-based transnational crime groups are also quite active in such areas as human trafficking, narcotics, and money laundering.[57] Chinese gangs are involved in importing heroin from the neighbouring Golden Triangle area and distributing it throughout the country. They are also involved in gambling and prostitution, activities that had all but disappeared under the former Communist regime. The two leading organized crime problems in Cambodia are drug production/trafficking and human trafficking. Drug traffickers also use Cambodia as a transit country and traffic Cambodian women into Thailand for sexual activities. In Taiwan, the number one organized crime problem is the penetration of mobsters into the legitimate business sector and the political arena. Gangs are now heavily involved in the businesses of bid-rigging, waste disposal, construction, cable television networks, telecommunications, stock trading, and entertainment. Further, starting in the mid-1980s, many criminals have successfully run for public office to protect themselves from police crackdowns. Taiwan gangs are also involved in gambling, prostitution, loansharking, debt collection, extortion, and gang violence; kidnapping for ransom is also a serious concern. Among the best-known Asian crime groups are the following:

- *Yakuza.* A Japanese criminal group often involved in multinational criminal activities, including human trafficking, gambling, prostitution, and undermining legitimate businesses.
- *Fuk Ching.* A Chinese organized criminal group involved in smuggling, street violence, and human trafficking.
- *Triads.* Underground Hong Kong-based criminal societies that control secret markets and bus routes, often involved in money laundering and drug trafficking.
- *Heijin.* Taiwanese gangsters who are often executives in large corporations. They are often involved in white-collar crimes, such as illegal stock trading and bribery, and sometimes run for public office.

- *Jao Pho.* An organized crime group in Thailand that is often involved in illegal political and business activity.
- *Red Wa.* Gangsters from Thailand that are involved in manufacturing and trafficking methamphetamine.[58]

Controlling Transnational Crime

Efforts to control transnational organized crime are typically in the hands of federal agencies. One approach is to form international working groups to collect intelligence, share information, and plot unified strategies among member nations, such as the Eurasian Organized Crime Working Group. Established in 1994, this group meets to discuss and jointly address the transnational aspects of Eurasian organized crime that affect member countries and the international community in general. The member countries are Canada, Great Britain, Germany, France, Italy, Japan, the United States, and Russia. These groups discuss cooperative investigative matters, such as the growing presence of Russian and other Eurasian organized criminals, and work to establish lines of communication and to develop strategies to address transnational organized crime. They are important as ways to share information and support specialized task forces for countering transborder crimes such as the trafficking of people, drugs, and cars; smuggling; financial crimes; and terrorism.

While international cooperation is now common, and law enforcement agencies are willing to work together to fight transnational gangs, these criminal organizations are extremely difficult to eradicate. The gangs are ready to use violence and are well equipped to carry out their threats. It has proven difficult for law enforcement to combat the drug cartels because they employ enforcer gangs to both protect them and intimidate their enemies. For example, Mexico's Gulf cartel has its own paramilitary force known as the Zetas, whose core members are alleged to be former members of the Mexican military. The Zetas are able to carry out complex operations and use sophisticated weaponry, acting as assassins, trafficking arms, kidnapping, and collecting payments for the cartel on its drug routes. In addition to defending the cartel's terrain in northern Mexico, Zetas are believed to control trafficking routes along the eastern half of the U.S.–Mexico border.[59]

Adding to control problems is the fact that the drug trade is an important source of foreign revenue, and destroying the drug trade undermines the economies of third-world nations. Even if the government of one nation were willing to cooperate in vigorous drug suppression efforts, suppliers in other nations, eager to cash in on the sellers' market, would be encouraged to turn more acreage over to coca or poppy production. Today, almost every Caribbean country is involved with narcotics trafficking; illicit drug shipments in the region are worth more money than the top five legitimate exports combined. Drug gangs are able to corrupt the political structure and destabilize countries. Drug addiction and violent crime are now common in Jamaica, Puerto Rico, and even on small islands such as St. Kitts. The corruption of the police and other security forces has reached a crisis

The focal point of illicit drug production and trafficking in Southeast Asia is known as the Golden Triangle, a rugged, mountainous region that overlaps the borders of Burma (Myanmar), Laos, and Thailand. Although the tri-border region accounts for the majority of heroin production in Southeast Asia, the amount of heroin produced in the area has decreased by approximately 70 percent in the past five years. In 2004, Burma and Laos accounted for nearly all heroin produced in the region. Eradication efforts and the enforcement of poppy-free zones have combined to depress cultivation levels.

However, the decline in heroin production is being offset by an increase in the production of amphetamine-type stimulants (ATS). Methamphetamine is cheaper and easier to produce than heroin; it entails a simple process that starts with ephedrine, the principal alkaloid of ephedra, a shrub that grows wild on vast expanses of the nearby Chinese province of Yunnan.

Much of the heroin produced in the Golden Triangle reaches markets through southern China, although increased law enforcement pressure by Chinese authorities has forced some traffickers to seek new routes through Thailand. In Laos, the Mekong River is a major conduit for heroin trafficking and is patrolled in only a few areas. Many key drug areas, particularly in the north, are virtually inaccessible to Laotian officials. According to Interpol, "ethnic Chinese traffickers control the heroin trade in Oceania (often with Vietnamese criminal organizations), Malaysia, and the few remaining markets in Canada and the United States."

Hong Kong's position as a key port city and its proximity to the Golden Triangle and mainland China have made it a natural transit point for heroin moving from Southeast Asia to global markets. Although the amount of heroin transiting through Hong Kong appears to be diminishing, drug traffickers continue to use it as a base of operations.

SOURCE: James O. Finckenauer and Ko-lin Chin, *Asian Transnational Organized Crime* (Washington, DC: National Institute of Justice, 2007), www.ncjrs.gov/pdffiles1/nij/214186.pdf (accessed November 9, 2010).

point, where an officer can earn the equivalent of half a year's salary by simply looking the other way on a drug deal.[60] Some indications suggest that the drug syndicates may be planting a higher-yield variety of coca and have refined their techniques to replace crops lost to government crackdowns.

Little change has occurred in some key drug-producing areas, such as Taliban-held Afghanistan and Myanmar (formerly Burma). War and terrorism also may make gang control strategies problematic. After the United States toppled Afghanistan's Taliban government, the remnants began to grow and sell poppy to support their insurgency; Afghanistan now supplies 90 percent of the world's opium.[61] And while the Colombian guerrillas may not be interested in joining or colluding with crime cartels, they finance their war against the government by aiding drug traffickers and by "taxing" crops and sales.[62] Considering these problems, it is not surprising that transnational gangs continue to flourish.

POLITICAL CRIME

Although terrorism now occupies the focal point of public concern, it is merely one of many different types of politically motivated crimes. The term **political crime** is used to signify illegal acts that are designed to undermine an existing government and threaten its survival.[63] Political crimes can include both violent and nonviolent acts and range in seriousness from dissent, treason, and espionage, to terrorism and assassination.[64]

When an act becomes a political crime and when an actor is considered a political criminal are often extremely subjective. In highly repressive nations, any form of non-sanctioned political activity, including writing a newspaper article critical of the regime, may be considered a political crime, punishable by a prison term or even death. For example, in the central Asian nation of Azerbaijan, Amnesty International says harassment and ill treatment of opposition journalists by police and other government officials has become routine. The government is bent on silencing these journalists through arrest and imprisonment on dubious charges or by levying heavy fines following trials for criminal defamation. In contrast, no instances have been recorded of attacks on pro-government journalists in Azerbaijan.[65] Similarly, people whom some label as terrorists and insurrectionists are viewed by others as freedom fighters and revolutionaries.

The Nature of Political Crimes

The political criminals and their political crimes may stem from religious or ideological sources. Because their motivations shift between selfish personal needs and selfless, noble,

> **political crime** Depending on the country, any action critical of, or in opposition to, the state.

or altruistic desires, political crimes often occupy a grey area between conventional and outlawed behaviour. Interpersonal violent crimes such as rape or murder are easy to condemn because their goals are typically selfish and self-centred (e.g., motivated by revenge or profit). In contrast, political criminals may be motivated by conviction rather than by greed or anger. Although some political crime involves profit (such as selling state secrets for money), most political criminals do not consider themselves antisocial but instead patriotic and altruistic. They are willing to sacrifice themselves for what they consider to be the greater good. While some concoct elaborate schemes to hide or mask their actions, others are quite brazen, hoping to provoke the government to overreact in their zeal to crack down on dissent. Because state authorities may engage in a range of retaliatory actions that result in human rights violations, even those who support the government may begin to question its activities: maybe the government is corrupt and authoritarian? On the other hand, if the government does nothing, it appears weak and corrupt and unable to protect citizens.

Even those political criminals who profit personally from their misdeeds, such as someone who spies for an enemy nation for financial payoffs, may believe that such acts are motivated by a higher calling than common theft. "My ultimate goal is to weaken or overthrow a corrupt government," they reason, "so selling secrets to the enemy is justified." Political criminals may believe that their acts are criminalized only because the group holding power fears them and wants to curtail their behaviour. And while the general public voices little objection to laws that control extreme behaviours, such as plotting a bloody revolution, they may have questions when a law criminalizes ordinary political dissent or bans political meetings in order to control suspected political criminals.

The Goals of Political Crimes

On August 24, 2010, another in a very long series of bombings took place in Iraq. While the population has gotten used to these attacks, this bombing was clearly designed to undermine public confidence in the nation's security forces. The bombers wanted to exploit political uncertainty and undermine the public's trust in Iraq's political parties to form a government. One survivor told reporters, "There may be a state, there may be a government. But what can that state do? What can they do with all the terrorists? Are they supposed to set up a checkpoint in every house?" The bombers may have succeeded in their efforts to create an atmosphere of intimidation and fear designed to oust the government.[66]

While common criminals may be motivated by greed, vengeance, or jealousy, political criminals have a different agenda. Rather than personal profit, their acts are aimed at achieving a different set of goals:

- *Intimidation*: to threaten an opponent who does not share their political orientation or views

- *Revolution*: to overthrow the existing government and replace it with one more acceptable
- *Profit*: selling state secrets or trafficking in stolen arms and munitions
- *Conviction*: believe crimes will benefit society
- *Pseudo-conviction*: conceal criminal motivations behind a mask of conviction and altruism[67]

Becoming a Political Criminal

Why does someone become a political criminal? There is no set pattern or reason; their motivations vary widely. Some use political crime as a stepping stone to public office, while others use it as a method to focus their frustrations. Others hope they can gain respect from their friends and family. Although the motivations for political crime are complex and varied, some regularity appears in the way ideas are formed. Political crime expert Randy Borum finds that this pattern takes the form of a series of cognitive stages:

- Stage 1: *"It's not right."* A dissatisfied individual identifies an undesirable event or condition, either economic (e.g., poverty, unemployment, poor living conditions), social (e.g., government-imposed restrictions on individual freedoms, lack of order, or morality), or personal ("I am being cheated of what is due me"). While the conditions may vary, those involved perceive the experience as "things are not as they should be."
- Stage 2: *"It's not fair."* The prospective criminal concludes that the undesirable condition is a product of injustice that does not apply to everyone. A government worker may feel their low pay is not right and that corporate workers with less skill are making more money and getting more benefits. At the same time, government workers are portrayed as lazy and corrupt. For those who are deprived, this facilitates feelings of resentment and injustice.
- Stage 3: *"It's your fault."* Someone or some group must be held accountable for the extremist's displeasure. For example, the underpaid worker may become convinced that minorities get all the good jobs while the underpaid worker continues to suffer financially. Extremist groups spread this propaganda to attract recruits.
- Stage 4: *"You're evil."* Because good people would not intentionally hurt others, targeted groups are appropriate choices for revenge and/or violence. The disaffected government worker concludes that since his country has let him down, it is only fair to sell state secrets to foreign nations for profit or to join a terrorist group or both. Aggression becomes justifiable when aimed against bad people, particularly those who intentionally cause harm to others. Second, by casting the target as evil, it is dehumanized, which makes justifying aggression even easier.[68]

Types of Political Crimes

Considering this cognitive thought that produces political crime and terrorism, what are the specific crimes and what form do they take?

Election Fraud. Some political criminals want to shape elections to meet their personal needs. In some instances, their goal is altruistic: the election of candidates who reflect their personal political views. In others, their actions are motivated by profit: they are paid by a candidate to rig the election.

Whatever the motive, **election fraud** is illegal interference with the process of an election. Acts of fraud tend to involve affecting vote counts to bring about a desired election outcome, whether by increasing the vote share of the favoured candidate, depressing the vote share of the rival candidates, or both. In the last Canadian federal election, there were allegations of fraud when robo-calls were made to electors, misinforming them of where polling stations were.

In some third-world dictatorships, election fraud is the norm: after party members have counted the votes, it is common for the ruling party to announce that it has been returned to office with an overwhelming majority. Sometimes, allegations of voter fraud by ruling juntas can have disastrous consequences. Take, for instance, the parliamentary elections that took place in Kenya on December 27, 2007. When it was announced that President Mwai Kibaki had won the presidential election over opposition candidate Raila Odinga, fighting broke out, tearing this African nation apart. More than 1,200 Kenyans were reported killed, thousands more injured, and hundreds of thousands made homeless; more than 40,000 houses, farms, and businesses were looted or destroyed.[69] Despite the post-election chaos, Kibaki retained his victory and his power.

Election fraud, a feature of political life since Roman times, includes a variety of behaviours designed to give a candidate or his or her party an unfair advantage:

- *Intimidation:* Scaring voters away through threats or intimidation, such as having armed guards posted at polling places, or obtaining lists of registered voters and making threatening calls before the election.
- *Disruption:* Bomb threats can be called into voting places in areas that are known to heavily favour the opposing party, with the goal of suppressing the vote. An outright sabotage may occur of polling places, ballots, and ballot boxes.
- *Misinformation:* Voters registered with the opposition party are sent flyers containing misleading information, such as the wrong election date or an announcement that rules have been changed about who is eligible to vote.
- *Registration fraud:* Shaping the outcome of an election by bussing in ineligible voters from other districts, providing conspirators with "change of address" forms to allow them to vote in a particular election, when in fact no actual change of address has occurred.
- *Vote buying.* And, lastly, is the age-old problem of securing votes by payment or other rewards. It is difficult to know how much vote buying still exists.

Treason. Few people can forget the image of John Walker Lindh, the so-called *American Taliban*, when he was captured during the American invasion of Afghanistan. Lindh had converted to Islam and wound up in an al-Qaeda training camp, and then fought with the Taliban on the front lines in Afghanistan. He was captured in 2001 by Afghan Northern Alliance forces, and questioned by CIA agents. Later that day, a violent uprising occurred in the prison where he was being held, and during the attack, a CIA agent was killed. Walker escaped only to be recaptured seven days later. At his trial, he apologized for fighting alongside the Taliban, saying, "Had I realized then what I know now ... I never would have joined them." The 21-year-old said Osama bin Laden is against Islam and that he "never under- stood jihad to mean anti-American or terrorism." "I understand why so many Americans were angry when I was first discovered in Afghanistan. I realize many still are, but I hope in time that feeling will change." After a plea agreement, John Walker Lindh was sentenced to 20 years in prison.[70]

Because treason is considered such a heinous crime, and to deter would-be traitors, many nations apply or have applied the death penalty to those convicted of attempting to overthrow the existing government. Treason was considered particularly loathsome under English common law, and until the 19th century, it was punishable by being "drawn and quartered," a method of execution that involved hanging the offender, removing the intestines while the offender was still living, and finally cutting the offender into four pieces for public display. William Wallace, the Scottish patriot made famous in the film *Braveheart*, was so displayed after his execution.

Acts can be considered treasonous for the purpose of stifling political dissent. In 18th-century England, merely criticizing the king or his behaviour was considered a treasonous act.

election fraud Practices designed to undermine the fair procedures of a democratic election, such as buying votes.

After World War II, two women, Iva Ikuko Toguri D'Aquino, a Japanese American born in Los Angeles and known as Tokyo Rose, and Mildred Elizabeth Gillars, born in Portland, Maine, and known as Axis Sally, served prison terms for broadcasting for the Axis powers in an effort to demoralize American troops.

Espionage. Robert Hanssen was a counterintelligence agent for the FBI, assigned to detect and identify Russian spies. A former Chicago police officer, Hanssen's assignment required him to have access to sensitive top-secret information. In one of the most shocking cases in U.S. history, Hanssen volunteered to become a paid spy for the KGB during the Cold War, and over a period of 15 years received at least $1.4 million in cash and diamonds. He was arrested on February 18, 2001, after leaving a package of classified documents for his Russian handlers under a footbridge in a park outside Washington. During his years as a double agent, Hanssen not only provided more than 6,000 pages of documents to the Soviet Union, but also caused the death of two U.S. double agents whose identities were uncovered with the aid of his secret documents. The Hanssen case was the subject of the 2007 film *Breach*, which starred Chris Cooper as the corrupt agent.[71]

Espionage (more commonly called "spying") is the practice of obtaining information about a government, organization, or society that is considered secret or confidential without the permission of the holder of the information. Espionage traditionally involved obtaining the information illegally by covertly entering the area where the information is stored, secretly photographing forbidden areas, or subverting through threat or payoff people who know the information and will divulge it through subterfuge.[72]

Today it is probably more likely to involve electronic means of theft.

Espionage is typically associated with the spying on potential or actual enemies by a foreign agent who is working for his or her nation's intelligence service. With the end of the Cold War, the threat of espionage seemed reduced until 2010, when a major Russian spy group was unravelled and 10 people arrested. These spies were sleeper agents who had spent decades fitting seamlessly in their new environment. Neighbours were shocked to find out they were actually spies. The case was settled when the Russians were exchanged for four American spies being held in Russian prisons.

Not all spies are foreign nationals. Many homegrown spies are motivated by misguided altruism or belief. Perhaps the most famous international case involved a group of five upper-crust students recruited during the Cold War at prestigious Cambridge University in England by Russia's foreign intelligence service, the KGB. The five were motivated by the belief that capitalism was corrupt and that the Soviet Union offered a better model for society. After graduation, they secured sensitive government posts that gave them access to valuable intelligence that they then passed on to the Soviet Union. Most famously, Kim Philby, who had worked as a high-level

intelligence agent, defected to Russia in 1963, but not before passing on information that cost hundreds of lives.[73]

While some spies, like the Cambridge Five, are motivated by ideology, others, like FBI agent Robert Hanssen and CIA operative Harold Nicholson, were looking for profit. In 1997, Nicholson was convicted of selling U.S. intelligence to Russia for $180,000 and was sentenced to 23.5 years imprisonment; Nicholson was the highest-ranking CIA official ever convicted for spying for a foreign country. Hanssen sold American secrets to Russia for more than $1.4 million in cash and diamonds over a 22-year period; he is currently serving a life sentence.[74]

Industrial Espionage. The concept of espionage has been extended to spying involving corporations, referred to as industrial espionage. This type of espionage involves such unethical or illegal activities as bribing employees to reveal trade secrets, including computer codes or product formulas. The traditional methods of industrial espionage include recruiting agents and inserting them into the target company, or breaking into an office to take equipment and information. It can also involve surveillance and spying on commercial organizations to determine the direction of their new product line or even what bid they intend to make on a government contract. Such knowledge can provide vast profits when it allows a competitor to save large sums on product development or to win an undeserved contract by underbidding.[75]

Foreign Industrial Espionage. Not all corporate espionage is homegrown, and some attacks have been carried out by foreign agents. A report of the National Counterintelligence Center lists biotechnology, aerospace, telecommunications, computer software, transportation, advanced materials, energy research, defence, and semiconductor companies as the top targets for foreign economic espionage.[76] Espionage enables foreign militaries to acquire sophisticated capabilities that might otherwise have taken years to develop. Such efforts also undercut the economy by making it possible for foreign firms to gain a competitive economic edge over domestic companies.

Numerous factors have combined to facilitate private-sector technology theft. Globalization has given foreigners unprecedented access to sensitive technologies. A proliferation of devices have made it easy for private-sector experts to illegally retrieve, store, and transfer massive amounts of information, including trade secrets and proprietary data; such devices are increasingly common in the workplace.

In addition to private citizens conducting espionage, foreign government organizations also mount their own operations, including

espionage Spying against a foreign government, designed to undermine its industry or political system.

- targeting defence firms for technology that would strengthen defence capabilities
- posting personnel at military bases to collect classified information
- employing commercial firms in a covert effort to target and acquire technology
- recruiting students, professors, scientists, and researchers to collect technology
- making direct requests for classified, sensitive, or export-controlled information
- forming ventures in the hope of gaining access to sensitive technologies

State Political Crime.   While some political crimes are committed by people who oppose the state, others are perpetrated by state authorities against the people they are supposed to serve; such a crime is referred to as **state political crime**. Critical criminologists argue that rather than political crime being committed by disaffected people, a great deal of this crime arises from the efforts of the state to maintain governmental power. In industrial society, the state will do everything to protect the property rights of the wealthy while opposing the real interests of the poor, even as far as going to war to support the capitalist classes who need the wealth and resources of other nations. The desire for natural resources such as rubber, oil, and metals was one of the primary reasons for Japan's invasion of China and other Eastern nations that sparked their entry into World War II, and said by some to be the reason for the United States invading Iraq in the first Persian Gulf War.

TERRORISM

Violent crime can be motivated by conflict or monetary gain, but it also involves acts that have a political motivation, such as terrorism. Political crime has been with us throughout history.[77]

To be a political crime, an act must carry with it the intent to disrupt and change the government and not simply a common-law crime committed for reasons of greed. Perpetrators believe their actions will benefit society and are necessary to create social changes.

The political crime that many people are most concerned with is terrorism, and the remainder of this chapter focuses on the history, nature, and extent of terrorism and the methods employed for its control. Despite terrorism's long history, it is often difficult to precisely define terrorism and to separate terrorist acts from interpersonal crimes of violence. For example, in the 1960s, the FLQ (Front de Libération du Québec) robbed banks and credit companies to obtain funds for its revolutionary struggles, making it more than common bank robbery. In this instance, to be considered

terrorism, which is a political crime, an act must carry with it the intent to disrupt and change the government and must not be merely a common-law crime committed for greed or egotism.

Because of its complexity, an all-encompassing definition is difficult to formulate, although most experts agree that the term *terrorism* usually means premeditated, politically motivated violence perpetrated against non-combatant targets by subnational groups or clandestine agents to influence an audience. The term *international terrorism* refers to terrorism involving either the citizens or the territory of more than one country.

Terrorism usually involves a type of political crime that emphasizes violence as a mechanism to promote change. Whereas some political criminals sell secrets, spy, and the like, terrorists systematically murder and destroy or threaten such violence to terrorize individuals, groups, communities, or governments into conceding to the terrorists' political demands.[78] Because terrorists lack large armies and formidable weapons, their use of subterfuge, secrecy, and hit-and-run tactics is designed to give them both a psychological advantage and the power to neutralize the physical superiority of their opponents.

However, assuming that terrorists have political goals may be erroneous. Some may try to bring about what they consider to be social reform—for example, by attacking women wearing fur coats or sabotaging property during a labour dispute. Terrorism must also be distinguished from conventional warfare because it requires secrecy and clandestine operations to exert social control over large populations.[79] So terrorist activities may be aimed at promoting an ideology other than political change.

Terrorism generally involves the illegal use of force against innocent people to promote political change,[80] differentiating them from other political criminals.[81] Terrorism is distinguished from conventional warfare because it requires secret operations.[82]

The term *terrorist* is sometimes used interchangeably with *guerrilla*. The latter term, meaning "little war," developed out of the Spanish rebellion against French troops after Napoleon's invasion in 1808. Guerrillas are often located in rural areas, and the objects of their attacks include the military, the police, and government officials.[83] Guerrillas can often become effective military organizations, as the Russians learned when occupying Afghanistan in the 1980s, or the Americans found in Iraq.

state political crime   Illegal actions by a state against its population or other sovereign governments.

terrorism   A wide variety of violent acts that have a political motivation; can be committed both against a state and by a state.

Comparative Criminology
Transnational Terrorism

In 1998, terrorism expert Harvey Kushner wrote: "Today, international terrorists likely to target the United States are individuals.... The greatest threat to the security of the U.S. in the next millennium will come from the hands of the freelancer."

The traditional image of the armed professional terrorist group with a clear-cut goal, such as nationalism or independence, is giving way to a new breed of terrorist with diverse motives. They do not have a unified central command, they are not located in any particular area, and they are capable of attacking anyone at any time with great destructive force. They may employ any number of weapons.

The new terrorist is more lethal, with fatalities steadily increasing in recent years. Terrorism expert Bruce Hoffman believes this greater lethality is due to the rise of religiously motivated terrorist groups, such as al-Qaeda. Religiously inspired terrorist attacks are more likely to result in higher casualties because they are motivated not by efforts to obtain political freedom, but by conflicting cultural values. Maintaining a differing value system allows the perpetrators to justify the deaths of large numbers of people: "For the religious terrorist, violence is a divine duty ... executed in direct response to some theological demand ... and justified by scripture."

The al-Qaeda network is the paradigm of the new value-oriented terrorist organization. The September 11, 2001, attack was not designed to restore a homeland or bring about a new political state, but to have a value structure adopted by Muslim nations. Osama bin Laden's attack may have been designed to create a military invasion of Afghanistan, which he hoped to exploit for revolution. According to Michael Scott Doran, bin Laden believed his acts would reach the audience that concerned him the most: the *umma*, or universal Islamic community. The media would show Americans killing innocent civilians in Afghanistan, and the *umma* would find it shocking. The ensuing outrage would open a chasm between the Muslim population of the Middle East and the ruling governments in such states as Saudi Arabia, which were allied with the West. On October 7, 2001, bin Laden made a broadcast in which he said that the Americans and the British "have divided the entire world into two regions—one of faith, where there is no hypocrisy, and another of infidelity, from which we hope God will protect us."

Accordingly, his aim was to cause an Islamic revolution within the Muslim world. His attack was designed to force those governments to choose: You are either with the idol-worshipping enemies of God, or you are with the true believers. The attack on the United States was designed to help his brand of extremist Islam survive and flourish among the believers who could bring down these corrupt governments.

This new generation of terrorists is especially frightening because its members are willing to engage in suicide missions to achieve their goals, and willing to martyr themselves because they consider themselves true believers surrounded by blasphemers.

SOURCES: Michael Scott Doran, "Somebody Else's Civil War," *Foreign Affairs* 81 (2002): 22–25; Bruce Hoffman, "Change and Continuity in Terrorism," *Studies in Conflict and Terrorism* 24 (2001); Harvey Kushner, *Terrorism in America, A Structured Approach to Understanding the Terrorist Threat* (Springfield: Charles C. Thomas, 1998); Ian Lesser, Bruce Hoffman, John Arquilla, David Ronfeldt, and Michele Zanini, *Countering the New Terrorism* (Washington, DC: Rand, 1999); Jessica Stern, *The Ultimate Terrorists* (Cambridge, Mass.: Harvard University Press, 1999).

Historical Perspective on Terrorism

Terrorism is known throughout history, becoming widespread in the Middle Ages, when political leaders were assassinated by their enemies. The word *assassin* is derived from an Arabic term meaning *hashish eater* and refers to members of a drug-using Muslim terrorist organization that carried out plots against prominent Christians and other religious enemies.[84]

European states have encouraged terrorism against enemies. For example, Queen Elizabeth I empowered Francis Drake to carry out attacks against the Spanish fleet. These privateers would have been considered pirates, but they operated with government approval. American privateers operated against the British during the Revolutionary War and the War of 1812. Contra-revolutionaries operated in El Salvador with the backing of the U.S. government in the 1980s. History can turn terrorists into heroes, depending on which side wins. (For more about transnational terrorism, see the Comparative Criminology box.)

The term *terrorist* became popular during the French Revolution. From the fall of the Bastille in 1789 until 1794, thousands suspected of counter-revolutionary activity went to their deaths on the guillotine. The end of the terror was signalled by the death of its prime mover, Robespierre, who was executed on the same guillotine to which he had sent almost 20,000 people to their deaths.

In the hundred years after, the world saw the Hur Brotherhood in India, the Internal Macedonian Revolutionary Organization in Turkey, and the Black Hand in Serbia. The Irish Republican Army battled British forces from 1919 to 1923, culminating in the southern part of Ireland's gaining independence.

Between the world wars, right-wing terrorism existed in Germany, Spain, and Italy. Russian left-wing revolutionary activity led to the death of the czar in 1917 and the rise of the Marxist state. During World War II, resistance to Germans was common throughout Europe; these terrorists are now considered heroes. In Palestine, three Jewish terrorist groups—the Haganah, Stern Gang, and Irgun, (the latter once led by Menachim Begin, who later became prime minister)—waged war against the British to force them to allow Jewish survivors of the Holocaust to settle in their traditional homeland. Today, Palestinian and Islamic terrorist groups carry out violent political action against the Israeli state.

Forms of Terrorism

Today, the term *terrorism* is used to describe many behaviours and goals. We will briefly describe some of the more common forms.[85]

Terrorist and Insurgent. As the term is commonly used, an *insurgency* differs from both guerrilla warfare and terrorism. The typical goal of an insurgency is either to confront the existing government for control of all or a portion of its territory, or to force political concessions in sharing political power by competing with the opposition government for popular support.[86] **Insurgents** are organized into covert groups who engage in an organized campaign of extreme violence, which may appear to be random and indiscriminate, such as causing the death of innocent civilians, but has a distinct political agenda. [87]

While insurgents may engage in violence, they can also use nonviolent methods or political tactics. For example, they may set up food distribution centres and schools in areas where they gain control so they can provide the population with needed services while contrasting their benevolent rule with the government's incompetence and corruption. Apparently, this is the role of the PLO in Lebanon.

Insurgents' use of violence is designed to inspire support and gain converts while at the same time destroying the government's ability to resist. Supporters are easy to recruit once the population believes that the government is incapable of fighting back. On the other hand, some members of the insurgency might shun violence and eventually create non-violent splinter groups, which can then operate openly, claiming to sympathize with the violent wing of their organization, but not being part of its structure. They may seek external support from other nations to bring pressure on the government. A terror group, in contrast, neither requires nor has active support or sympathy from a large percentage of the population.

Terrorist and Revolutionary. A revolution (from the Latin *revolutio*, "a revolving," and *revolvere*, "turn, roll back") is generally seen as a civil war fought either between nationalists and a sovereign power that holds control of the land, or between the existing government and local groups over issues of ideology and power. Historically, revolutions occur as a struggle between nationalistic groups and an imperialistic overseas government. Classic examples of ideological rebellions are the French Revolution, which pitted the middle class and urban poor against the aristocracy, and the Russian Revolution of 1917, during which the Czarist government was toppled by the Bolsheviks. More recent ideological revolutions have occurred in China, Cuba, Nicaragua, and Chile, to name but a few. It also characterizes the so-called Arab Spring revolutions in the recent Middle East.

While some revolutions rely on armed force, terror activities, and violence, others can be nonviolent, depending on large urban protests and threats. Such was the case when the Shah Mohammad Reza Pahlavi was toppled in Iran in the 1979 revolution that transformed Iran into an Islamic republic under the rule of Ayatollah Ruhollah Khomeini. Similar events unfolded in Egypt in early 2011 in the effort to topple the government of Hosni Mubarak that had been in power for 30 years.

In Europe, a German Marxist group, called the Baader-Meinhof group, conducted a series of robberies, bombings, and kidnappings in the 1980s. After reunification, terrorist actions were believed over, yet in 1991, the Red Army Faction claimed credit for assassinating the head of the government agency charged with rebuilding the East German economy. In Italy, the Red Brigade kidnapped and executed a former Italian president and abducted an American general, who was later rescued.

In the Middle East, the Palestine Liberation Organization (PLO) has directed terrorist activities against Israel. More radical splinter groups include Abu Nidal, the Popular Front for the Liberation of Palestine, Hamas, and the Iranian-backed Hezbollah group. When the World Trade Center in New York City was bombed in 1993, the group responsible was demonstrating its hatred of American policies in the Middle East. And again, on September 11, 2001, when the World Trade Center towers were brought down by hijacked airliners, it was a Middle Eastern group, al-Qaeda, that was responsible.

Numerous tragic incidents have occurred, but several stand out because of the large loss of life: Agents of the pro-Iranian Islamic Jihad used a truck bomb to blow up the U.S. Marine compound in Beirut, Lebanon, on April 18, 1983, killing 241; Libyan agents are the main suspects in the Christmas Day 1988 bombing of PanAm Flight 103 over Lockerbie, Scotland, which killed 270 people; and the August 7, 1998, bombings of American embassies in Kenya and Sudan by agents of Osama bin Laden killed at least 250 and injured more than 4,000.

The attacks on September 11 killed approximately 3,000 people. The 2001 Tel Aviv nightclub bombing killed 140 people; Chechen rebels held 800 people hostage in 2002; the Madrid train bombings in 2004 killed 191 and injured 1,755; the London subway bombings launched one of the most intensive surveillance investigations in modern history.

> **insurgents** People acting against their government, seeking to secure a revolution or disruption of the state.

Political Terrorism. In 1996, after an 11-month federal investigation had resulted in their indictment on fraud charges, members of the U.S. Freemen movement held federal officers at bay in a month-long standoff before surrendering. Heavily armed, the Freemen are one of many right-wing groups who have conducted or plan to conduct anti-government activities. Their peaceful surrender prevented another in a long line of bloody engagements between federal agents and right-wing militants, such as the 1992 siege at Ruby Ridge, Idaho, or the infamous standoff in Waco, Texas, which resulted in the fiery deaths of followers of Branch Davidian leader David Koresh.

Political terrorism is directed at those who oppose the terrorists' political ideology or against those whom terrorists define as outsiders. Political terrorists in the United States tend to be heavily armed groups organized around white supremacy, Nazism, militant tax resistance, and religious revisionism. Groups include the Aryan Republican Army, Aryan Nation, Posse Comitatus, and the traditional Ku Klux Klan organizations. Some have formed their own churches; for example, the Church of Jesus Christ Christian claims that Jesus was born an Aryan rather than a Jew, and that white Anglo-Saxons are the true chosen people. Some groups commit crimes such as bank robberies to fund their activities. The Oklahoma City bombing in 1995 may have been the most tragic example of such activities.

Nationalistic Terrorism. Nationalistic terrorism promotes the interests of minority ethnic or religious groups that feel they have been persecuted under majority rule. In India, Sikh radicals assassinated Indian Prime Minister Indira Gandhi in 1984 in retaliation for the government's storming of their Golden Temple religious shrine. In Egypt, fundamentalist Muslims have attacked foreign tourists in an effort to wreck the tourist industry, topple the secular government, and turn Egypt into an Islamic state. In Algeria, fundamentalist Muslim groups have waged a decade-long battle against the government. The best-known nationalistic terrorist group is the Provisional Irish Republican Army (IRA), dedicated to unifying Northern Ireland with the Republic of Ireland under home rule.

A Canadian nationalist terrorist group, the Front de Libération du Québec (FLQ) or Quebec Liberation Front, planted bombs, robbed banks, and raided military armouries for weapons in the 1960s. Thought to have begun the modern age of terrorism, they had suspected links with the Black Panthers, Cuba's revolutionary government, and radical groups in Algeria. On October 5, 1970, James Cross, a British trade official, was kidnapped by the FLQ. The group demanded $500,000, the release of political prisoners, and safe passage to Cuba. The Quebec premier refused to negotiate and asked the federal government to send in troops. On October 10, Quebec cabinet minister Pierre Laporte was also abducted and murdered a week later. The imposition of the *War Measures Act* resulted in the arrest without warrant of 450 people, of which few were ever charged with a crime. When asked to justify his use of such extreme legal measures

to fight terrorism, then prime minister Pierre Trudeau said: "There's a lot of bleeding hearts who don't like to see people with helmets and guns ... but it is more important to keep law and order in society."[88]

Non-political Terrorism. Terrorist activity also involves groups that espouse a particular social or religious cause and use violence to address their grievances. For example, anti-abortion groups have sponsored demonstrations at abortion clinics, and some members have gone so far as to attack clients, bomb offices, and kill doctors who perform abortions.

Animal rights organization members have harassed and thrown blood at people wearing fur coats. It has also become common for environmental groups to resort to terror tactics to sabotage their enemies' ability to harm the environment. One of the biggest targets is the livestock and research animal–producing industry. Members of such groups as the Animal Liberation Front (ALF) and Earth First! have attacked ranches and packing plants. ALF members free animals, such as by raiding turkey farms before Thanksgiving and rabbit farms before Easter.

Eco-terrorism. The most active left-leaning domestic political terror groups today are involved in violent actions to protect the environment. Of these groups, the Earth Liberation Front (ELF) is perhaps the best known. Founded in 1994 in Brighton, England, by members of the Earth First! environmental movement, ELF has been active for several years in the United States and abroad. Operating in secret, ELF cells have conducted a series of actions intent on damaging individuals or corporations that they consider a threat to the environment. On October 19, 1998, ELF members claimed responsibility for fires that were set atop Vail Mountain, a luxurious ski resort in Colorado, claiming that the action was designed to stop the resort from expanding into animal habitats (especially that of the mountain lynx); the fires caused an estimated $12 million in damages. On August 22, 2003, members of ELF claimed responsibility for fires that destroyed about a dozen sport utility vehicles at a Chevrolet dealership in West Covina, California.[89] Fires have also been set in government labs where animal research is conducted. Spikes have been driven into trees to prevent logging in fragile areas. Members have conducted arson attacks on property ranging from a Nike shop in a mall north of Minneapolis to new homes on Long Island, New York. On February 7, 2004, ELF group members targeted construction equipment at a 30-acre development site in Charlottesville, Virginia.[90] ELF is believed to have burnt a row of luxury homes in Seattle on March 2, 2008, causing $7 million in damage. While the multimillion-dollar homes used green technology such as formaldehyde-free materials, energy-efficient appliances, and landscaping that included native plants in their construction, the development had drawn opposition because of fear that septic systems could damage critical wetlands needed to protect an aquifer used by about 20,000 people in the area and could harm streams used by Chinook salmon.[91]

The World Trade Center towers collapsed after a terrorist attack on September 11, 2001.

for example. In the Crime in the News exhibit, the legal rationale for resisting shale gas mining is discussed. Violent confrontations developed over this issue in 2013, which pitted environmental activists against the police.

State-Sponsored Terrorism. State-sponsored terrorism occurs when a repressive government oppresses its citizens and stifles political dissent. Death squads and the use of government troops to destroy political opposition parties are associated with political terrorism in Latin America,[94] and now also in Africa.

Some governments have been accused of using terrorist-type actions to control political dissidents. For example, in the first 18 months of its deployment, members of the Haitian National Police allegedly executed 15 political opponents of the regime. In the lead-up to a national election in Zimbabwe in 2008, pro-government police and army personnel were allegedly committing acts of violence against opponents of the incumbent president, Robert Mugabe.

Much of what we know about state-sponsored terrorism comes from the efforts of human rights groups. London-based Amnesty International maintains that tens of thousands of

Another group, the Animal Liberation Front (ALF) focuses their efforts on protecting animals from being used as food, in clothing, or as experimental subjects. Their philosophy is that animals are entitled to the moral right to possess their own lives and control their own bodies, while rejecting the view that animals are merely capital goods or property intended for the benefit of humans and can be bought, sold, or killed by humans. ALF members conduct actions against scientists who conduct animal research, vandalizing their homes and cars, attacking labs, and setting animals free. They also conduct actions against animal breeding farms and food processing plants. ALF members have raided turkey farms before Thanksgiving and rabbit farms before Easter. Their activities have had significant impact on the commercial aspects of scientific testing, driving up the price of products, such as drugs, which rely on animal experimentation.[92]

Not surprisingly, the FBI and other law enforcement agencies have targeted eco-terror groups such as ELF and ALF. On January 20, 2006, the FBI announced that its Operation Backfire had led to the arrest of 11 people who were accused of 17 attacks, including the $12 million arson of the Vail Ski Resort in 1998, and the sabotage of a high-tension power line near Bend, Oregon, in 1999.[93]

However, these are also extreme examples. Far more common are low-level protests against resource development,

A soldier stands guard at Parliament Hill. Security was stepped up because of terrorist kidnappings in Montreal during the FLQ crisis.

Crime in the News

Environmental Action on the Agenda for 2013?

When protest erupted over shale gas exploration, there were demonstrations at the legislature, petitions were circulated and signed, and thumper trucks were blockaded in Stanley.

The government pledged proper regulations to develop the industry safely. However, other jurisdictions such as Quebec, with more than half of its exploratory wells leaking, have banned or imposed a moratorium on hydraulic fracturing due to environmental and health issues.

Reports have been written, speeches have been made, and fracking is a fractious topic on social media. It has been pronounced a game-changer, and a danger.

However, in order to extract gas in New Brunswick's hard shale geology, hydraulic fracturing with horizontal drilling will be required. This new process has implications for air and water quality, uses massive amounts of fresh water, and produces huge volumes of toxic waste water.

There is a growing body of evidence suggesting negative impacts on human health, and lawsuits in states such as Pennsylvania are based on a lack of government and corporate accountability.

In a presentation at the Health Effects of Shale Gas Extraction 2012 conference at the University of Pittsburgh, Karen White (New Brunswick Department of Health) said, "... a key question regarding the shale gas development that to the best of our knowledge hasn't been answered yet—and maybe someone here today can tell me—but will be there be a net benefit to public health? Or will be there be a net harm?"

Relying on regulations to contain the environmental threat is costly and difficult to enforce.

In addition, natural resource extraction has caused a 'boomtown effect' in some places, with higher crime rates, stress, substance abuse, and depression. In Fort McMurray, policing research has found increased rates of driving under the influence, and interpersonal violence.

However, natural gas development is more similar to offshore oil production, and a boomtown model is less appropriate. Some researchers use a 'social dislocation' model because of smaller changes in population and jobs linked to shale gas development.

In Texas, researchers interested in dislocation caused by Barnett Shale energy development found the public perceived that corporations were not responsible citizens, and that politicians were influenced by the oil and gas industry.

Research published in the *Journal of Rural Social Sciences* and the *International Journal of Rural Criminology* recommended residents take an active role to become informed if unconventional natural gas development was to occur in their area.

Getting involved increases social capital and social control.

An article in the *Journal of Conflict Resolution* on the Marcellus Shale region of New York compares citizens to David confronting the Goliath of energy development, and warns of the importance of public participation and consultation.

However, while government can resist involving the public in the decision-making process, citizens will organize themselves.

Using Fractracker, for example, users can post information to a geographic information system, sharing information and research.

Furthermore, the methods and rights of protestors are expanding. A Utah court ruled that the use of satire in fake press releases is legal if it is non-commercial in nature. A Dutch court has upheld the right of Greenpeace to protest outside Shell property as in the public's interest.

In Canada, researchers discussing the use of civil disobedience to confront natural gas development argue that the defence of necessity could be applied for civil disobedience in environmental activism.

Specifically, if there is a clear danger posed by development that could have been mitigated through public consultation, which the government disallowed, and which activism can reasonably correct, the defence of 'necessity' may be successful. It has been successfully used in Britain.

In Canada, civil disobedience in response to shale gas development is not hypothetical. In 2011, citizen groups in Quebec said they would target exploration company equipment. Feeling ignored by government, they opted for direct action. Before the issue could come to a head, the government imposed a moratorium.

The defence of necessity is based on the legal recognition that sometimes acting outside of the law is necessary. It challenges the law's credibility in defining what is for the greater good.

SOURCE: Copyright Chris McCormick, published in the *Daily Gleaner* (Fredericton), December 27, 2012.

---

people continue to become victims of security operations that result in disappearances and extrajudicial executions.[95] Political prisoners are tortured, and people have disappeared because of government-sponsored death squads. Countries known for encouraging violent control of dissidents include Brazil, Colombia, Guatemala, Honduras, Peru, Iraq, Zimbabwe, and the Sudan. When Túpac Amaru rebels seized and held hostages at the Japanese ambassador's villa in Peru in 1996, Amnesty International charged that the

action came in response to a decade-long campaign of human rights violations by national security forces and extensive abuses against opposition groups. Between 1983 and 1992, Amnesty documented at least 4,200 cases of people who had "disappeared" in Peru following detention by security forces. Thousands more were killed by government forces in extrajudicial executions.[96]

While structural violence is imposed by a state against its own people (poverty, malnutrition, poor sanitation, and

Criminology Research
Genocide

The most extreme form of political violence is genocide—the attempt to eliminate a whole group of people defined by their race, religion, ethnicity, or political beliefs. Genocidal episodes have included the attempted destruction of European Jews by the Nazis during the Holocaust, the killing of the Armenians in Turkey at the beginning of the 20th century, the annihilation of native tribes during the Spanish conquest of Latin America, the "ethnic cleansing" that occurred during the recent wars in the former Yugoslavia, and the horrifying military attacks against civilians throughout Darfur since 2003.

A framework for understanding how these unimaginable outbreaks of political mass murder can occur in a civilized society must include conditions that have preceded the onset of genocide in Western society, such as the following:

- *Difficult life conditions:* Basic physical and material needs are not being met, and social groups lack a sense of positive identity, effectiveness, and control.
- *Scapegoating:* A group is identified as the cause of life's problems, which affirms the group identity by diminishing individual responsibility for problems.
- *New ideology:* Ideologies emerge that offer the hope of a better life. The scapegoated group is seen as a roadblock to its fulfillment.
- *Devaluation:* Members of a scapegoated group who are devalued can be harmed at will. The perpetrators become increasingly prone to act aggressively.
- *"Just world" thinking:* As members of the scapegoated group are harmed, both perpetrators and bystanders believe the people who suffer deserve their fate.

- *Commitment:* As harm increases, so does commitment to group process and ideology. The more harm they cause, the less likely perpetrators are to be willing to change.
- *Passive bystanders:* Bystanders within and outside the society remain passive, affirming the perpetrators' belief that they are right to victimize the outcast group.
- *Authority orientation:* Groups with unquestioning respect for authority are more prone to group violence and less likely to oppose leaders.
- *Monolithic culture:* A limited set of cultural values inhibits intergroup relations; non-members are kept from important cultural and professional offices, and from the legal process they could use to speak out against or halt destructive practices.
- *Group self-concept:* Shared belief that a group is either superior or inferior; life's difficulties become more frustrating when they conflict with a group's feelings of superiority. Frustrated feelings of superiority combined with feelings of weakness and vulnerability lead to the embrace of destructive ideologies and scapegoating.
- *History of aggression:* Some cultures have a long history of violence and aggression. Using aggressive tactics to solve problems thus may seem normal, appropriate, and even desirable.

How does this model fit 20th-century genocides, such as the Holocaust, and those that have occurred since? The Germans had a long history of violence and aggression. Their culture was monolithic and featured such values as loyalty, obedience, and order.

Life conditions in Germany were difficult after World War I, and the Jews were scapegoated as being responsible for the economic catastrophe that followed. The Nazi ideology promised a better tomorrow that would elevate the Germans as the purest race and that conditions could be improved by eliminating lesser races. The Nazi ideology was appealing, with its emphasis on the superiority of the German people, nationalism, and unquestioning obedience to a leader.

Because the Jews were relatively successful, they could easily be portrayed as dishonest and manipulative, enhancing their devalued status. Although a progression of anti-Semitic actions followed Hitler's coming to power, non-aligned Germans distanced themselves from Jews, and the rest of the world stood idly by, attending the Berlin Olympics in 1936. American corporations conducted business in Germany throughout the 1930s. These conditions provoked an escalating round of violence that eventually led to genocide and mass destruction.

By setting out the factors that support genocide, we can get some insight into how the risk of political mass murder can be avoided. For example, societies must stress inclusion rather than exclusion, including education about other cultures in school curricula, to lay the groundwork for understanding and acceptance.

SOURCES: Ervin Staub, "Cultural-Societal Roots of Violence," *American Psychologist* 51 (1996): 117–32; Ervin Staub, *The Roots of Evil: The Origins of Genocide and Other Group Violence* (New York: Cambridge University Press, 1989); Eric Reeves, "Unnoticed Genocide," *Genocide Watch*, http://www.genocidewatch.org/

high infant mortality),[97] state-sponsored terrorism is also directed at people and governments outside the state's borders. Particularly disturbing is the possibility that an outlaw state, such as North Korea, will carry out a nuclear-based attack against a nation viewed as the enemy.[98] Although special expertise is needed to build such a bomb, because so many nuclear bombs are in the hands of unstable Eastern European states, nuclear terrorists might be able to purchase what they need to build a bomb. If the World Trade Center had been attacked with a low-yield nuclear device rather than chemical explosives, as many as 50,000 people would have been killed. Instead, the towers were brought down by airliners flown by hijackers armed with box cutters.

The extreme form of state-sponsored terrorism occurs when a government seeks to wipe out a minority group within the jurisdiction it controls, referred to as **genocide** (see the Criminology Research box on this subject). The Holocaust during World War II is the most notorious example of genocide, but more recent atrocities have taken place in Cambodia, Rwanda, and Bosnia.

Criminal Terrorism. In 2001, six men were arrested by Russian security forces as they were making a deal to sell weapons-grade uranium. Some of the men were members of the Balashikha criminal gang, who were in possession of almost one kilogram of top-grade radioactive material, which can be used to build weapons. They were asking $30,000 for the deadly merchandise.[99] Since 1990, a half dozen cases have involved theft and transportation of nuclear material, and other cases have involved people who offered to sell agents material that was not yet in their possession. These are the known cases.

In some instances, organized criminal groups work in close cooperation with guerrillas. For example, the Revolutionary Armed Forces of Colombia (FARC) imposes a tax on Colombian drug producers, but cooperates with the top drug barons. In some cases, the line between being a terrorist organization with political support and vast resources, and being an organized criminal group engaging in illicit activities for profit can be confusing for counterterrorism authorities: Are they dealing with convictional criminals or criminals for profit? For example, financially motivated terrorists are more likely to follow through on their end of a kidnapping negotiation than is a traditionally motivated political terrorist.[100]

Cult Terrorism. In 1995, members of Aum Shinrikyo, a radical religious cult, set off poison gas in a Tokyo subway, killing 12 and injuring more than 3,000.[101]

Such cults may be classified as *cult terror* groups because their leaders demand that followers prove their loyalty through violence or intimidation.[102] Members typically follow a charismatic leader who may be viewed as having godlike powers or being the reincarnation of an important religious figure. The leader and his or her lieutenants commonly enforce loyalty by severe discipline and by physically preventing members from leaving the group. They may go through doomsday drills and maintain a siege mentality, stockpiling weapons and building defensive barricades. The cult may openly or tacitly endorse individual killings or mass murder, which may be accompanied by mass suicide, either as a further symbolic instrument of their cause or, more commonly, as what they perceive to be justified self-defence, a last resort when the hostile world starts closing in and the leader's authority is threatened.[103]

How Are Terrorist Groups Organized?

Terror Cells. Regardless of what organizational structure is used, most groups subdivide their affiliates into **terror cells** for both organizational and security purposes. To enhance security, each cell may be functionally independent so that each member has little knowledge of other cells, their members, locations, and so on. However, individual cell members provide emotional support to one another and maintain loyalty and dedication. Because only the cell leader knows how to communicate with other cells and/or a central command, capture of one cell does not then compromise other group members.

Terror cell formations may be based on location, employment, or family membership. Some are formed on the basis of function: some are fighters, others political organizers. The number of cells and their composition depend on the size of the terrorist group: local or national groups will have fewer cells than international terrorist groups that may operate in several countries, such as the al-Qaeda group.

Terrorists often have an urban focus. Operating in small bands, or cadres, of three to five members, they target the property or persons of their enemy, such as members of the ruling class.[104] However, terrorists may not have political ambitions, and their actions may be aimed at stifling or intimidating other groups who oppose their political, social, or economic views. For example, terrorists who kill abortion providers to promote their pro-life agenda are not aiming for regime change. Guerrillas, on the other hand, are armed military bands that attack military, police, and government officials in an effort to destabilize the existing government. Their organizations can grow quite large and eventually take the form of a conventional military force. Guerrilla bands are typically located in rural areas, but some infiltrate urban areas (urban guerrillas). For the most part, guerrillas are a type of insurgent band.

Newer terrorist organizations can also be formed as **networks**, loosely organized groups located in different parts of a city, state, or country (or worldwide) that share a common theme or purpose, but have a diverse leadership and command structure, and are only in intermittent communication with one another. These groups have few resources and little experience, so it is critical that they operate under cover and with as little public exposure as possible.

When needed, networked groups can pull factions together for larger-scale operations, such as an attack on a military headquarters, or conversely, they can readily splinter off into smaller groups to avoid detection when a

---

genocide An extreme form of state-sponsored terrorism, in which a government seeks to wipe out a minority group within the jurisdiction it controls.

terror cells A structure often used by modern terrorist organizations, whereby no one member knows all the other members of the group.

networks Loosely organized terrorist organizations that lack a specific organizational structure.

counterterrorism operation is underway. The advent of the Internet has significantly improved communications among networked terror groups.

As terror organizations evolve and expand, they may eventually develop a hierarchical organization with a commander at the top, captains, local area leaders, and so on. Ideological and religious groups tend to gravitate toward this model since a common creed or dogma controls their operations, and a singular leader may be needed to define and disseminate group principles and maintain discipline. In a hierarchical model, the leader has the power to increase or decrease levels of violence for political purposes (i.e., the leader may order followers to initiate a bombing campaign to influence an election). Schools may be off limits so that the population is not antagonized, or schools may become a target to show that the government cannot protect their children.

What Motivates Terrorists?

In the aftermath of the September 11, 2001, destruction of the World Trade Center in New York City, people asked what could motivate someone like Osama bin Laden to order the deaths of thousands of innocent people.

Some experts believe that the attacks had a political basis and were an outgrowth of America's Middle East policies. Others saw a religious motivation: The terrorists were radical Muslims at war with the liberal religions of the West. Another view was that bin Laden's rage was fuelled by deep-rooted psychological problems.

On the surface, Osama bin Laden, the favoured son of a wealthy Saudi Arabian family, financed his terrorist activities from an inheritance of more than $300 million.[105] Although bin Laden may have had a mental disorder, he once said that his father wanted his sons to fight against the enemies of Islam. After his father's death, bin Laden was mentored by a Jordanian named Abdullah Azzam, who was killed in 1989 by a car bomb in Pakistan. He vowed to carry on Azzam's "holy war" against the West, and threw himself into the Afghan conflict against the Soviet Union.

Osama bin Laden's motivations will probably never be fully understood, especially now that he is dead, but is it possible that his violent urges stemmed from the same web of emotions that fuel the thousands of predatory criminals who prowl society looking for unwary victims? If so, his actions, although extreme, are certainly not unique. Many people have personally experienced violence or have a friend who has been victimized. Almost everyone has heard about someone being robbed, beaten, or killed. Riots and mass disturbances have ravaged urban areas; racial attacks plague schools and university campuses; assassination has claimed the lives of political, religious, and social leaders all over the world.

What motivates these individuals to risk their lives and those of innocent people? If terrorists are emotionally disturbed, acting out their psychosis within violent groups, their violence is not so much a political instrument as it is the result of psychopathology. Terrorists act out of emotional problems, including self-destructive urges, disturbed emotions, and problems with authority.[106] As terrorism expert Jerrold M. Post puts it, "Political terrorists are driven to commit acts of violence as a consequence of psychological forces ... their special psychology is constructed to rationalize acts they are psychologically compelled to commit."[107]

Terrorists hold extreme ideological beliefs that prompt their behaviour. They have heightened perceptions of oppressive conditions, believing that they are being victimized by some group or government, and conclude they must resort to violence to encourage change. "Successful" terrorists believe that their "self-sacrifice" outweighs the guilt created by harming innocent people.

Ironically, Osama bin Laden was a multimillionaire and at least some of his followers were highly educated and trained. The acts of the modern terrorist—using the Internet; planning logistically complex and expensive assaults; and writing and disseminating formal critiques, manifestos, and theories—require the training and education of the social elite, not the poor and oppressed.

In some instances, terrorists may be motivated by feelings of alienation and failure to comprehend technological society. Japanese novelist Haruki Murakami interviewed members of the Aum Shinrikyo, a radical religious group that released poison gas into a Tokyo subway in 1995, killing 12 and injuring 5,000.[108] Murakami found that the terrorists thought modern society was too complex, with few clear-cut goals and values. Some were relatively ordinary people, but others were highly educated professionals. All seemed alienated, and some felt that a suicide mission would cleanse them from the corruption of the modern world. One told him that since he had been a child, he had realized that everything in life was heading straight for destruction and there was no turning back. Once he joined the terrorist group, he was on a path to salvation and once again life had meaning.

Cyberterrorism: Crime with Political Motives

The justice system must now also be on guard against attacks that integrate terrorist goals with cyber capabilities. Cyberterrorism is an effort by covert forces to disrupt the intersection between the virtual electronic reality of computers and the physical world.[109] It has been defined as "the premeditated, politically motivated attack against information, computer systems, computer programs, and data which result in violence against noncombatant targets by subnational groups or clandestine agents."[110] Cyberterrorism may involve use of computer network tools to shut down critical national infrastructures or to coerce or intimidate a government or civilian population.[111]

Terrorist organizations are now beginning to understand the power that cybercrime can inflict on their enemies, even though, ironically, they come from regions where computer databases and the Internet are not widely used. Terrorist organizations are now adapting IT into their arsenal, and agencies of the justice system have to be ready for a sustained attack on the nation's electronic infrastructure.

Common examples of infrastructure at risk for attacks are water treatment plants, hydro plants, dams, oil refineries, and nuclear power plants. These industries all provide vital services to society by allowing people to go about their daily lives. Terrorist computer hackers could make a dam overflow or cause property damage to oil refineries or nuclear plants by shutting down safeguards in the system that prevent catastrophes.

Why Terrorism in Cyberspace? Cyberspace is a handy battlefield for terrorists because an attack can strike directly at a target that bombs will not affect: the economy. Terror attacks designed to cripple the enemy nation may be aimed at destroying or reducing its economic growth, creating an inflationary economy. Battered by cyberterrorist attacks, the enemy's staggered economy will not be able to fund existing social programs while at the same time devoting adequate sums to the military and security to keeps the terrorists at bay.[112]

Cyberterrorism is more efficient and less dangerous than more traditional forms of terrorism, with no loss of life and no need to infiltrate enemy territory. Cyberterrorists can commit crimes from any place in the world, and the costs are minimal. Nor do terror organizations lack for skilled labour to mount cyber attacks. A growing number of highly educated experts are available at reasonable costs in developing countries in the Middle East and former Soviet Union.

Cyber Attacks. Has Western society already been the target of cyber attacks? The Center for Strategic and International Studies claims to have uncovered attacks on the National Security Agency, the Pentagon, and a nuclear weapons laboratory; security breaches disrupted operations in each of these sites.[113] The financial service sector is a prime target and has been victimized by information warfare. In 2002, financial service firms received an average of 1,018 attacks per company, and 46 percent had at least one server attack.[114]

Here are some possible scenarios for future cyber attacks:

- Logic bombs are implanted in a computer and wait until they are instructed to overwhelm a computer.
- Programs are used to allow terrorists to enter secure systems and disrupt or destroy the network.
- Using conventional weapons, terrorists overload a network's electrical system.[115]
- Computers allow terrorist groups to communicate covertly with agents around the world.[116]
- The computer system of a corporation vital to national security is breached and disrupted.
- Internet-based systems used for basic infrastructure, such as power dams, are disrupted.

- Cyberterrorists attack the financial system, interrupting billions of dollars of transactions.[117]
- The Internet is used to recruit new members, disseminate information, broadcast anti-Western slogans, and to solicit funds.

Is Cyberterrorism a Real Threat? Some experts question the existence of cyberterrorism, claiming that not a single case of cyberterrorism has yet been recorded, that cybervandals and hackers are regularly mistaken for terrorists, and that cyber defences are more robust than is commonly supposed. James Lewis of the Center for Strategic and International Studies points out that fears of cyberterrorism may be exaggerated or misplaced for a number of important reasons:[118]

- The infrastructure that would be the target of cyber attacks is not easy to hack into.
- Infrastructure services are not all connected and do not share a common computer network.
- Power outages with infrastructure in the past have not resulted in mass panic or physical damage.
- Cyber attacks would most likely be in conjunction with a more traditional physical attack.

Because terrorists seek to complete their political goals by inflicting psychological and physical damage, they are unlikely to spend extra time trying to orchestrate cyber attacks that would cause neither death nor widespread destruction. A greater fear is that terrorist organizations would hack into economic or military sites in an attempt to steal money for their attacks or to gain intelligence information. The weaknesses of computer systems, including systems that control a nation's national security, are prime targets for terrorist organizations that need to collect information on targets. These organizations need to be as hidden as possible in the attempt to gather as much intelligence as possible.

So far we have had no reports of major widespread cyberterrorism attacks. Even so, the potential threat is still there, is likely to increase, and steps must be taken to address the dangers ahead.[119]

The Extent of Terrorism

The number of international terrorist incidents has decreased in recent years. However, Iran, Iraq, and North Korea continue their policy of giving logistic and financial support to groups committing terrorism.

Terrorists engage in criminal activities, such as bombings, shootings, and kidnappings. One view of their motivation is that they have heightened perceptions of oppressive conditions—they feel relative deprivation.[120] The terrorists conclude that they must resort to violence to encourage change. The cause justifies the need for violence.[121]

According to Austin Turk, terrorists tend to come from upper-class rather than lower-class backgrounds.[122] Because their position in the class structure gives them the feeling they can influence society, upper-class citizens are more likely to seek confrontations with authorities. Class differences are also manifested in different approaches to political violence. The violence of the lower class is more often associated with spontaneous demonstrations and collective riots. Higher-class violence tends to be more calculated and organized. Revolutionary cells, campaigns of terror and assassination, logistically complex and expensive assaults, and writing and disseminating formal critiques, manifestos, and theories are typically acts of the socially elite.

Responses to Terrorism since September 11, 2001

Governments have tried various responses to terrorism. Law enforcement agencies have infiltrated terrorist groups, offered rewards for information leading to the arrest of terrorists, and held elections to discredit terrorists' complaints that the state is oppressive. Most western nations have anti-terrorist legislation for terrorist acts, acts that ban fundraising to support terrorist organizations, and acts that allow officials to deport terrorists and to bar terrorists from entering in the first place.

In Canada, various antiterrorism measures have been taken,[123] which give the police broad new powers of arrest without warrant, increase the period for which a person can be detained, and enable the government to place a ban on the release of information related to terrorist investigations. As an omnibus bill, it included acts to amend the *Criminal Code of Canada,* the *Official Secrets Act,* the *Canada Evidence Act,* the *Proceeds of Crime (Money Laundering) Act,* and other acts. The federal government could designate an area vital to national security, after which the military could compel everyone to leave and seal it off. These bills came under heavy fire for violating civil rights. Canada's own *Anti-terrorism Act* was tested in the Supreme Court in 2004, which ruled that someone could be compelled to testify in investigative hearings and that these court hearings could not be held in private. Furthermore, there was a challenge to the so-called Security Certificate in 2014, but it was upheld by the Supreme Court as constitutional.

However, challenges are expected to continue. For example, the American antiterrorism bill, the *Patriot Act,* allows the FBI to monitor Internet traffic, which civil libertarians call a violation of civil rights.[124]

Some countries have specially trained antiterrorist squads. The American military, for example, has created the renowned Delta Force, made up of members from the four service areas. Delta Force activities are generally secret, but it is known that the force saw action in Iran (1980), Honduras (1982), Sudan (1983), and during the Grenada invasion (1983), and it was prepared to take action against the hijacking of the ship *Achille Lauro* in 1985. The American government's counterrevolutionary study, Project Camelot, had a branch studying the secession movement in Quebec.

The World Trade Center attack forever changed American policy on terrorism. What have been some of the major efforts to combat terrorist groups?

Legal Efforts. In the wake of the September 11 attacks, the United States moved to freeze the financial assets of groups engaging in, or supporting, terrorist activities. For example, the assets of the Holy Land Foundation for Relief and Development were frozen because the foundation was suspected of funding Hamas. The United States blocked more than $27 million in assets of the Taliban and al-Qaeda; and to help monitor terrorist assets, the Foreign Terrorist Asset Tracking Center was founded. Legislation was passed in many countries giving law enforcement agencies a freer hand to investigate and apprehend suspected terrorists.[125]

Traditional tools of surveillance have been expanded, such as wiretaps, search warrants, and subpoenas to check and monitor phone, Internet, and computer records without first needing to demonstrate that these systems were being used by a suspect or target of a court order.

Although law enforcement agencies may applaud these new laws, civil libertarians are troubled because they view the laws as eroding civil rights. The new and sweeping authority might not be limited to true terrorism investigations but might actually cover a much broader range of activity involving reasonable political activities. Increased security also creates its own problems, such as congested border crossings, which cost more than $8 billion a year.

The fight against terrorism makes it easy to seek to tighten up the law and restrict important rights. Ontario's "terror czar" wanted the power to ban travel, destroy property, and search and seize property without a warrant, actions that would have been impossible without the threat of terrorism. Transport Canada decided to check into the backgrounds of 130,000 airport workers. Under the new *Public Safety Act,* the Canadian Security Intelligence Service would create a no-fly list of passengers banned from domestic flights.[126]

We will be living with this new reality for some time.

SUMMARY

In this chapter, we look at issues that are of particular importance at the beginning of the 21st century: cybercrime, transnational organized crime, and terrorism.

Cybercrime is the name of a new breed of offences that involve the theft and/or destruction of information. Cybercrime presents a challenge for the justice system because it is rapidly evolving, it is difficult to detect through traditional law enforcement channels, and its control demands that agents of the justice system develop technical skills that match those of the perpetrators. Cybercrime has grown because information technology (IT) has become part of daily life in most industrialized societies.

The growth of cybercrime and its cost to the economy have created the need for new laws and enforcement processes specifically aimed at controlling its new and emerging forms. Specialized enforcement agencies have been created to crack down on cybercriminals, especially as they are related to terrorist organizations. Terrorism continues to evolve to effect political change through promoting instability, and violence. Whereas some political criminals sell secrets, spy on the enemy, and the like, terrorists systematically murder and destroy or threaten violence to terrorize individuals, groups, communities, or governments into conceding to the terrorists' political demands.

In conclusion, the problem of organized crime has evolved today to become transnational in operation. With the aid of the Internet and instant communications, groups are operating on a global scale to traffic drugs and people, to launder money, and to sell arms. Eastern European crime families are active abroad. Russian organized crime has become a major problem for law enforcement agencies.

Mexican and Latin American groups are active in the drug trade; Asian crime families are involved in smuggling and other illegal activities.

These developments will be a challenge for criminology to understand and for criminal justice to control.

THINKING LIKE A CRIMINOLOGIST

On July 16, the hacktivist group Anonymous posted a video to YouTube announcing that on November 5, 2011, it would shut down Facebook. The loosely organized group had already gone after websites operated by PayPal, MasterCard, Visa, and the Church of Scientology. The group claims that Facebook privacy settings are an illusion and that private information on people is being sold to huge corporations. Your mission: determine the truth of the claim that Facebook knows more about you than your family.

KEY TERMS

cybercrime p. 450
cyberespionage p. 458
cyberterrorism p. 451
cybertheft p. 450
cybervandalism p. 451
cyberwar p. 451
denial-of-service attack p. 453
election fraud p. 468

espionage p. 469
etailing fraud p. 456
genocide p. 477
globalization p. 450
information technology p. 450
insurgents p. 472
networks p. 477
phishing p. 456

political crime p. 466
state political crime p. 470
terror cells p. 477
terrorism p. 470
transnational organized crime p. 461
vishing p. 456
warez p. 455

DOING RESEARCH ON THE WEB

Read more about transnational terrorism by going to www.transnationalterrorism.eu, the site for Transnational Terrorism, Security, and the Rule of Law.

CRITICAL THINKING QUESTIONS

1. Which theories of criminal behaviour best explain the actions of cybercriminals? Which theories fail to explain cybercrime?
2. How would you punish a Web page defacer who placed an antiwar message on a government site? Prison? Fine?
3. What guidelines would you recommend for the use of IT in law enforcement?
4. Are we creating a Big Brother society, and is the loss of personal privacy worth the price of safety?
5. What can be done to reduce the threat of transnational organized crime?

NOTES

1. John F. Burns and Ravi Somaiya, "WikiLeaks Founder on the Run, Trailed by Notoriety," *New York Times*, October 23, 2010, www.nytimes.com/2010/10/24/world/24assange.html (accessed December 15, 2010).

2. Shirley Won and Simon Avery, "Hackers Step up E-Commerce Attacks," *The Globe and Mail*, September 20, 2004; Jack Kapica, "Cyber Threats on Rise: Report," *The Globe and Mail*, July 28, 2004.

3. M. Swanson and J. Terriot, "Computer Crime: Dimensions, Types, Causes and Investigations," *Journal of Political Science and Administration* 8 (1980): 305–306; Donn Parker, "Computer-Related White-Collar Crime," in *White-Collar Crime, Theory and Research*, eds. G. Geis and E. Stotland, 199–220 (Beverly Hills, CA: Sage, 1980).

4. Anne Branscomb, "Rogue Computer Programs and Computer Rogues: Tailoring Punishment to Fit the Crime," *Rutgers Computer and Technology Law Journal* 16 (1990): 24–26.

5. Associated Press, "International Child Porn Ring Uncovered," Goldstein Report, 2008, http://goldsteinreport.com/article.php?article=4145.

6. Andreas Philaretou, "Sexuality and the Internet," *Journal of Sex Research* 42 (2005): 180–181.

7. Jeordan Legon, "Sex Sells, Especially to Web Surfers: Internet Porn a Booming, Billion-Dollar Industry," CNN, December 11, 2003, http://articles.cnn.com/2003-12-10/tech/porn.business_1_adult-content-sites-avn-online.

8. National Center on Addiction and Substance Abuse at Columbia University, "'You've Got Drugs!' IV: Prescription Drug Pushers on the Internet," May 2007, http://www.casacolumbia.org/addiction-research/reports/youve-got-drugs-perscription-drug-pushers-internet-2008.

9. Ibid.

10. Reuters, "WikiLeaks Supporters Attack MasterCard Site," December 8, 2010, www.reuters.com/article/idUSTRE6B72G620101208.

11. This section relies heavily on CERT® Coordination Center, "Denial of Service Attacks," www.cert.org/tech_tips/denial_of_service.html (accessed November 10, 2010).

12. Saul Hansell, "U.S. Tally in Online-Crime Sweep: 150 Charged," *New York Times*, August 27, 2004, C1.

13. Stephen Baker and Brian Grow, "Gambling Sites, This Is a Holdup," *BusinessWeek*, August 9, 2004, 60–62.

14. *The Digital Millennium Copyright Act,* Public Law 105–304 (1998).

15. This section is based on Richard Walker and David M. Levine, "'You've Got Jail': Current Trends in Civil and Criminal Enforcement of Internet Securities Fraud," *American Criminal Law Review* 38 (2001): 405–430.

16. Jim Wolf, "Internet Scams Targeted in Sweep: A 10-Day Crackdown Leads to 62 Arrests and 88 Indictments," *Boston Globe*, May 22, 2001, A2.

17. Linda Foley, Karen Barney, and Jay Foley, "Identity Theft: The Aftermath 2009," Identity Theft Resource Center (ITRC), http://www.idtheftcenter.org/images/surveys_studies/Aftermath2009.pdf.

18. Michael White and Christopher Fisher, "Assessing Our Knowledge of Identity Theft: The Challenges to Effective Prevention and Control Efforts," *Criminal Justice Policy Review* 19 (2008): 3–24.

19. Nathan Thornburgh, Matthew Forney, Brian Bennett, Timothy Burger, and Elaine Shannon, "The Invasion of the Chinese Cyberspies (and the Man Who Tried to Stop Them)," *Time*, September 5, 2005, 10.

20. Andrew Gray "Chinese Hackers Worry Pentagon," Virusinfo, March 9, 2008, http://virusinfo.info/showthread.php?t=19455.

21. Ken Timmerman, "Computer Worm Shuts Down Iranian Centrifuge Plant," Newsmax.com, November 29, 2010, www.newsmax.com/KenTimmerman/iaea-stuxnet-computer-worm/2010/11/29/id/378288.

22. Barry C. Collin, "The Future of CyberTerrorism: Where the Physical and Virtual Worlds Converge," http://www.crime-research.org/library/Cyberter.htm.

23. Mark Pollitt, "Cyberterrorism—Fact or Fancy?" FBI Laboratory, http://www.researchgate.net/publication/222596729_Cyberterrorism_fact_or_fancy.

24. Tomas Hellström, "Critical Infrastructure and Systemic Vulnerability: Towards a Planning Framework," *Safety Science* 45 (2007): 415–430.

25. Mathieu Gorge, "Cyberterrorism: Hype or Reality?" *Computer Fraud and Security* 2 (2007): 9–12.

26. Daniel Benjamin, *America and the World in the Age of Terrorism* (Washington, DC: CSIS Press, 2005), 1–216.

27. General Accounting Office (now Government Accountability Office), "Critical Infrastructure Protection: Efforts of the Financial Services Sector to Address Cyber Threats," January 2003.

28. Michael Whine, "Cyberspace—A New Medium for Communication, Command, and Control by Extremists," Informaworld, http://www.tandfonline.com/doi/pdf/10.1080/105761099265748.

29. Yael Shahar, "Information Warfare," IWS: The Information Warfare Site, www.iwar.org.uk/cyberterror/resources/CIT.htm.

30. General Accounting Office, "Critical Infrastructure Protection: Efforts of the Financial Services Sector to Address Cyber Threats."

31. Frank Hayes, "Botnet Threat," *Computerworld* 40 (2006): 50.

32. Gale Reference Team, "McAfee Reports Botnets Threaten National Security," *Computer Security Update*, December 1, 2006, 2–4.

33. This section leans heavily on Kane and Wall, "Identifying the Links between White-Collar Crime and Terrorism."

34. Kane and Wall, "Identifying the Links between White-Collar Crime and Terrorism."

35. Napoleoni, Modern Jihad: Tracing the Dollars behind the Terror Networks.

36. Clyde Wilson, "Software Piracy: Uncovering Mutiny on the Cyberseas," *Trial* 32 (1996): 24–31.

37. Deloitte, "2006 Global Security Survey," www.deloitte.com/view/en_MK/mk/industries/financialservices/42b88e6bc220e110VgnVCM100000ba42f00aRCRD.htm.

38. U.S. State Department Fact Sheet, September 29, 2006, The Council of Europe Convention on Cybercrime, www.state.gov/r/pa/prs/ps/2006/73354.htm; Council of Europe Convention on Cybercrime, CETS No. 185, https://cs.brown.edu/courses/csci1950-p/sources/lec16/Vatis.pdf.

39. ACLU Memo on the Council of Europe Convention on Cybercrime, June 16, 2004, www.aclu.org/privacy/gen/15746leg20040616.html.

40. Steven Frank, "Toronto's Child Porn Sleuths: A Canadian Team Leads the Way in Tracking Down Global Perpetrators of Grisly Internet Child Pornography," *Time Canada* 166 (2005): 30.

41. Department of Justice Press Release, "'Project Deliverance' Results in More than 2,200 Arrests During 22-Month Operation, Seizures of Approximately 74 Tons of Drugs and $154 Million in U.S. Currency Joint Effort with Mexican Law Enforcement Results in Arrest of High Priority Target," June 10, 2010, www.justice.gov/opa/pr/2010/June/10-ag-680.html.

42. See, generally, President's Commission on Organized Crime, *Report to the President and the Attorney General, The Impact: Organized Crime Today* (Washington, DC: U.S. Government Printing Office, 1986).

43. James O. Finckenauer and Ko-lin Chin, *Asian Transnational Organized Crime* (Washington, DC: National Institute of Justice, 2007), www.ncjrs.gov/pdffiles1/nij/214186.pdf (accessed November 10, 2010).

44. Christopher Adamson, "Defensive Localism in White and Black: A Comparative History of European-American and African American Youth Gangs," *Ethnic and Racial Studies* 23 (2000): 272–298.

45. Donald Cressey, *Theft of the Nation* (New York: Harper & Row, 1969).

46. Selwyn Raab, "A Battered and Ailing Mafia Is Losing Its Grip on America," *New York Times*, October 22, 1990, 1.

47. Ibid., B7.

48. Yumiko Ono, "Top Kirin Brewery Executives Resign amid Reports of Paying off Racketeers," *Wall Street Journal*, July 19, 1993, A6.

49. Michael Elliott, "Global Mafia," *Newsweek*, December 13, 1993, 22–29.

50. President's Commission on Organized Crime, *Report to the President and the Attorney General*.

51. James O. Finckenauer and Ko-lin Chin, *Asian Transnational Organized Crime* (Washington, DC: National Institute of Justice, 2007), www.ncjrs.gov/pdffiles1/nij/214186.pdf.

52. "Statement for the Record of Thomas V. Fuentes, Chief, Organized Crime Section, Criminal Investigative Division, Federal Bureau of Investigation, Organized Crime, before the House Subcommittee on Finance and Hazardous Materials," September 13, 2000.

53. FBI, "African Criminal Enterprises," www.fbi.gov/about-us/investigate/organizedcrime/african

54. FBI, "Balkan Organized Crime," www.fbi.gov/about-us/investigate/organizedcrime/balkan.

55. Louise I. Shelley, "Crime and Corruption: Enduring Problems of Post-Soviet Development," *Demokratizatsiya* 11 (2003): 110–114; James O. Finckenauer and Yuri A. Voronin, *The Threat of Russian Organized Crime* (Washington, DC: National Institute of Justice, 2001).

56. Bilyana Tsvetkova, "Gangs in the Caribbean," *Harvard International Review*, June 2009, http://hir.harvard.edu/index.php?page=article&id=1863.

57. This section leans heavily on James O. Finckenauer and Ko-lin Chin, *Asian Transnational Organized Crime*.

58. National Institute of Justice, "Major Transnational Organized Crime Groups, 2010," www.ojp.usdoj.gov/nij/topics/crime/transnational-organized-crime/major-groups.htm.

59. William Booth, "Mexican Azteca Gang Leader Arrested in Killings of 3 Tied to U.S.," *Washington Post*, March 30, 2010, www.washingtonpost.com/wp-dyn/content/article/2010/03/29/AR2010032903373.html.

60. Orlando Patterson, "The Other Losing War," *New York Times*, January 13, 2007.

61. Office of National Drug Control Policy, 2010 National Strategy, www.whitehousedrugpolicy.gov/strategy.

62. Francisco Gutierrez, "Institutionalizing Global Wars: State Transformations in Colombia, 1978–2002: Colombian Policy Directed at Its Wars, Paradoxically, Narrows the Government's Margin of Maneuver Even as It Tries to Expand It," *Journal of International Affairs* 57 (2003): 135–152.

63. Jeffrey Ian Ross, *The Dynamics of Political Crime* (Thousand Oaks, CA: Sage, 2003).

64. Ibid.

65. Amnesty International press release, "Azerbaijan: Rising Tide of Persecution against Independent Journalism," January 24, 2007, http://www.amnesty.org/en/library/asset/EUR55/005/2007/ru/f064d4a4-fd71-4a39-bd3a-8fe4c44f9643/eur550052007en.html.

66. Stephen Farrell and Anthony Shadid, "Dozens Killed in Wave of Attacks Across Iraq," *New York Times*, August 25, 2010, www.nytimes.com/2010/08/26/world/middleeast/26iraq.html.

67. Stephen Schafer, *The Political Criminal, The Problem of Morality and Crime* (New York: Free Press, 1974), 154–157.

68. Randy Borum, "Understanding the Terrorist Mind-Set," *FBI Law Enforcement Bulletin* 72 (2003): 7–10.

69. Amnesty International, "Kenya: Amnesty International Concerned at Police Killings in Election Protests," December 31 2007, www.amnesty.org/en/for-media/press-releases/kenya-amnesty-international-concerned-police-killings-election-protests.

70. "Profile of John Walker Lindh," BBC News, January 24, 2002, news.bbc.co.uk/2/hi/americas/1779455.stm.

71. CNN, "Accused FBI Spy Hanssen Pleads Not Guilty," May 31, 2001, http://archives.cnn.com/2001/LAW/05/31/hanssen.arraignment.02/index.html.

72. David Owen, *Hidden Secrets: The Complete History of Espionage and the Technology Used to Support It* (Toronto: Firefly Books, 2002).

73. BBC News, "Key Cases in Soviet-UK Espionage," January 23, 2006, http://news.bbc.co.uk/2/hi/europe/4639130.stm.

74. Lawrence Schiller, *Into the Mirror: The Life of Master Spy Robert P. Hanssen* (Darby, PA: Diane Publications, 2004).

75. Hedieh Nasheri, *Economic Espionage and Industrial Spying* (Cambridge, England: Cambridge University Press, 2004).

76. Office of the National Counterintelligence Executive, "Annual Report to Congress on Foreign Economic Collection and Industrial Espionage, 2005," www.fas.org/irp/ops/ci/docs/2005.pdf.

77. Stephen Schafer, *The Political Criminal* (New York: Free Press, 1974), 1.

78. Paul Wilkinson, *Terrorism and the Liberal State* (New York: Wiley, 1977), 49.

79. Jack Gibbs, "Conceptualization of Terrorism," *American Sociological Review* 54 (1989): 329–340, at 330.

80. Robert Friedlander, *Terrorism* (Dobbs Ferry, NY: Oceana Publishers, 1979); Walter Laquer, *The Age of Terrorism* (Boston: Little, Brown, 1987), 72; National Advisory Commission on Criminal Justice Standards and Goals, Report of the Task Force on Disorders and Terrorism (Washington, DC: U.S. Government Printing Office, 1976), 3.

81. Paul Wilkinson, *Terrorism and the Liberal State* (New York: Wiley, 1977), 49.

82. Jack Gibbs, "Conceptualization of Terrorism," *American Sociological Review* 54 (1989): 329–340.

83. Daniel Georges-Abeyie, "Political Crime and Terrorism," in *Crime and Deviance: A Comparative Perspective*, ed. Graeme Newman, 313–333 (Beverly Hills, CA: Sage, 1980).

84. This section relies heavily on Friedlander, *Terrorism*, 8–20.

85. For a general view, see Jonathan White, *Terrorism* (Pacific Grove, CA: Brooks/Cole, 1991).

86. "Differences between Terrorism and Insurgency," www.terrorism-research.com/insurgency.

87. Andrew Silke, "Holy Warriors: Exploring the Psychological Processes of Jihadi Radicalization," *European Journal of Criminology* 5 (2008): 99–123.

88. "Ottawa Is Prepared to Go Any Distance to Stop FLQ, Trudeau Says," *Globe and Mail*, October 14, 1970.

89. Jocelyn Parker, "Vehicles Burn at Dealership: SUV Attacks Turn Violent," *Detroit Free Press*, August 23, 2003, 1.

90. "Brutal Elves in the Woods," *The Economist* 359 (2001): 28–30.

91. Steve Miletich, "Hunt Is On: Who Torched the Street of Dreams?" *Seattle Times*, March 4, 2008, http://seattletimes.com/html/snohomishcountynews/2004258337_arson04m.html.

92. Fiona Proffitt, "Costs of Animal Rights Terror," *Science* 304 (2004): 1731–1739.

93. Department of Justice, "Eleven Defendants Indicted on Domestic Terrorism Charges, Group Allegedly Responsible for Series of Arsons in Western States, Acting on Behalf of Extremist Movements," January 20, 2006, www.usdoj.gov/opa/pr/2006/January/06_crm_030.html.

94. Ted Robert Gurr, "Political Terrorism in the United States: Historical Antecedents and Contemporary Trends," in *The Politics of Terrorism*, ed. Michael Stohl (New York: Dekker, 1988); Martha Crenshaw, ed., *Terrorism, Legitimacy, and Power* (Middletown, CT: Wesleyan University Press, 1983), 1–10.

95. Amnesty International, *Annual Report, 1992* (Washington, DC), released July 1993.

96. This report on state action in Peru can be obtained on the Amnesty International

website at_www.amnesty.org/ailib/ aipub/1996/AMR/2460396.html.

97. Ronald Kramer, "Structural Violence and State Terrorism: Neglected Forms of Criminal Violence," paper presented at the annual meeting of the American Society of Criminology, Phoenix, AZ, November 1993.

98. Dick Ward, "The Nuclear Terror Threat," *Crime and Justice International* 12 (1996): 1–4.

99. Jeffrey Kluger, "The Nuke Pipeline: The Trade in Nuclear Contraband Is Approaching Critical Mass. Can We Turn Off the Spigot?" *Time*, December 17, 2001, 40.

100. Chris Dishman, "Terrorism, Crime, and Transformation," *Studies in Conflict and Terrorism* 24 (2001): 43–56.

101. Haruki Murakami, *Underground* (New York: Vintage Books, 2001).

102. Lawrence Miller, "The Terrorist Mind: A Psychological and Political Analysis, Part II," *International Journal of Offender Therapy and Comparative Criminology* 50 (2006): 255–268.

103. Ibid.

104. Daniel Georges-Abeyie, "Political Crime and Terrorism," in *Crime and Deviance: A Comparative Perspective*, ed. Graeme Newman (Beverly Hills, CA: Sage, 1980), 313–333.

105. Peter L. Bergen, *Holy War, Inc.: Inside the Secret World of Osama bin Laden* (New York, Free Press, 2001), 41–50; Yonah Alexander and Michael S. Swetnam, *Usama bin Laden's al-Qaida: Profile of a Terrorist Network* (New York: Transnational Publishers, 2001); Michael Kranish and Anthony Shadid, "Bin Laden Zeal for Stature Used Psychology, Religion," *Boston Globe*, November 19, 2001, 3.

106. Mark Jurgensmeyer, *Terror in the Mind of God* (Berkeley and Los Angeles, CA: University of California Press, 2000).

107. Jerrold M. Post, "Terrorist Psycho-Logic: Terrorist Behavior as a Product of Psychological Forces," in *Origins of Terrorism: Psychologies, Ideologies, Theologies, States of Mind*, ed. Walter Reich (Cambridge: Cambridge University Press, 1990), 12.

108. Haruki Murakami, *Underground* (New York: Vintage Books, 2001).

109. Barry C. Collin, "The Future of CyberTerrorism: Where the Physical and Virtual Worlds Converge," 2004. http://www.crime-research.org/library/Cyberter.htm.

110. Mark Pollitt, "Cyberterrorism—Fact or Fancy?" FBI Laboratory. http://www.researchgate.net/publication/222596729_Cyberterrorism_fact_or_fancy.

111. James Lewis, "Assessing the Risks of Cyber Terrorism, Cyber War, and Other Cyber Threats," Center for Strategic and International Studies, Washington DC, 2002.

112. Sanjeev Gupta et al., "Fiscal Consequences of Armed Conflict and Terrorism in Low- and Middle-Income Countries," *European Journal of Political Economy* 20 (2004): 403–421.

113. Daniel Benjamin, *America and the World in the Age of Terrorism* (Washington, DC: CSIS Press, 2005), 1–216.

114. General Accounting Office, "Critical Infrastructure Protection: Efforts of the Financial Services Sector to Address Cyber Threats Reports to the Technology Committee" (Washington, DC: January 2003).

115. Yael Shahar, "Information Warfare: The Perfect Terrorist Weapon," Institute for Counter-Terrorism, 1997. www.ict.org.il/articles/infowar.htm.

116. Michael Whine, "Cyberspace—A New Medium for Communication, Command, and Control by Extremists," Institute for Counter-Terrorism, 1999. www.ict.org.il/articles/articledet.cfm?articleid=76.

117. General Accounting Office, "Critical Infrastructure Protection: Efforts of the Financial Services Sector to Address Cyber Threats."

118. Lewis, "Assessing the Risks of Cyber Terrorism, Cyber War, and Other Cyber Threats."

119. Gabriel Weimann, "Cyberterrorism: The Sum of All Fears?" *Studies in Conflict and Terrorism* 28 (2005): 129–150.

120. Theodore Gurr, *Why Men Rebel* (Princeton, NJ: Princeton University Press, 1970).

121. M. Cherif Bassiouni, "Terrorism, Law Enforcement, and Mass Media: Perspectives, Problems and Proposals," *Journal of Criminal Law and Criminology* 72 (1981): 1–51.

122. Austin Turk, "Political Crime," in *Major Forms of Crime*, ed. R. Meier, 119–135 (Beverly Hills, CA: Sage, 1984).

123. "Chapter 3: National Security in Canada—The 2001 Anti-Terrorism Initiative," *Report of the Auditor General of Canada to the House of Commons* (Ottawa: Office of the Auditor General, 2004); Ronald J. Daniels, Patrick Macklem, and Kent Roach, eds., *The Security of Freedom: Essays on Canada's Anti-Terrorism Bill* (Toronto: University of Toronto Press, 2001).

124. The Special Senate Committee on the Subject-Matter of Bill C-36, 2001; "Justice Minister Preparing for Possible Changes to Anti-terrorism Bill," *National Post*, November 15, 2001.

125. "Hunting Terrorists Using Confidential Informant Reward Programs," *The FBI Law Enforcement Bulletin* 71 (2002): 26–28; Sara Sun Beale and James Felman, "The Consequences of Enlisting Federal Grand Juries in the War on Terrorism: Assessing the USA Patriot Act's Changes to Grand Jury Secrecy," *Harvard Journal of Law and Public Policy* 25 (2002): 699–721.

126. "Ottawa Compiles 'No-Fly' List of Banned Passengers," *The Globe and Mail*, September 3, 2004; "Terror Czar Demands More Power," *Ottawa Citizen*, June 24, 2004; "Top Court Backs Sun Challenge of Secret Air India Hearings," *CanWest News Services*, June 24, 2004; "Slow Border 'Dire' for Canada," *Financial Post*, June 7, 2004; "Crime Link Probe on at Airports," *National Post*, May 10, 2004.

Glossary

acquaintance-related crime A crime committed by an offender who has had a prior relationship with the victim; date rape is such a crime (p. 95)

active precipitation The aggressive behaviour of victims, which provokes a reaction (p. 101)

actus reus An illegal act, such as taking money or shooting someone; also a failure to act, such as not taking proper precautions while driving a car (p. 39)

aggravating factor A circumstance that makes a crime more serious; for example, racism makes an assault more serious, resulting in a harsher sentence as a hate crime (p. 102)

aging out Individuals reduce the frequency of offending as they age; also known as spontaneous remission, aging out occurs among all groups of offenders (p. 77)

alien conspiracy theory The view that organized crime was imported from Europe, and that crime cartels restrict their membership to people of their own ethnic background (p. 405)

androgens Male sex hormones, which have been linked to criminality (p. 167)

anomie Rapidly shifting moral values produce normlessness, where the individual has little guide to what is socially acceptable; usually associated with Robert Merton (p. 11)

antisocial personality Synonymous with psychopathy, the antisocial personality is characterized by a lack of normal responses to life situations, the inability to learn from punishment, and violent reactions to non-threatening events (p. 186)

arbitrage The practice of buying large blocks of stock in companies that are believed to be the target of corporate buyouts or takeovers (p. 388)

arousal theory The view that people with a high arousal level seek powerful stimuli to maintain an optimal level of arousal; often associated with violence, aggression, and sociopathy (p. 174)

arson The intentional burning of a home, structure, or vehicle because of psychological issues or for criminal purposes, such as profit, revenge, insurance fraud, or crime concealment (p. 373)

assisted suicide The practice of seeking help from a physician in committing suicide; not legal in Canada (p. 47)

atavistic anomalies The physical characteristics of "born criminals" that indicate they are throwbacks to primitive people (p. 10)

at-risk The susceptibility of people to criminal activity as a result of a "culture of poverty" passed from one generation to the next; marked by apathy, cynicism, and mistrust of social institutions (p. 214)

attention deficit hyperactivity disorder (ADHD) A condition in which a child shows a developmentally inappropriate lack of attention, impulsivity, and hyperactivity (p. 172)

attrition The number of cases decreases as they make their way through the criminal justice system; the number of cases investigated by police that result in convictions is a small percentage of the total (p. 57)

behaviour modelling In modern society, the process of learning aggressive acts from three principal sources: family members, environmental experiences, and the mass media (p. 181)

behaviour theory The approach that human actions are developed through a variety of learning experiences over the course of a lifetime (p. 181)

blameworthy The amount of culpability or guilt a person maintains for participating in a particular criminal offence (p. 153)

booster A professional shoplifter; also known as a *heel* (p. 355)

bourgeoisie In Marxist theory, the owners of the means of production; the capitalist ruling class (p. 12)

break and enter Unlawful entry into a house to commit theft; sometimes called burglary (p. 369)

brothel A house of prostitution, typically run by a madam who sets prices and handles the business arrangements (p. 421)

brutalization effect The outcome of capital punishment having created an atmosphere of brutality, which reinforces the view that violence is an appropriate response to provocation (p. 142)

brutalization process The first stage in a violent career, during which parents victimize children, causing them to develop a belligerent, angry demeanour (p. 319)

call girls Prostitutes who make dates via the phone, and then service steady clientele in hotel rooms or apartments (p. 421)

capable guardians In routine activities theory, the presence of police, homeowners, neighbours, and others, which can have a deterrent effect on crime (p. 131)

career criminal A person who repeatedly violates the law, devotes much of their life to criminality, and commits a large portion of the total crime in a community (p. 82)

carjacking Stealing a car by forcing the driver out of the car; it has a low likelihood of occurring but a high news value (p. 360)

Chicago School Pioneering research on the social ecology of the city and urban crime developed in the early 20th century by sociologists at the University of Chicago (p. 11; p. 200)

child abuse Any physical, emotional, or sexual trauma to a child; includes neglecting to give proper care and attention to a young child (p. 334)

chiselling Cheating an organization or its customers (p. 387)

chivalry hypothesis The idea that low female crime and delinquency rates are a reflection of the leniency with which police treat female offenders (p. 81)

choice theory The view that delinquent behaviour is a rational choice made by a motivated offender who perceives the chances of gain as outweighing any perceived punishment or loss (p. 126)

chronic offender The small percentage of those who are arrested five or more times before age 18, who will become adult criminals, and are

responsible for more than half of all serious crimes (p. 82)

churning A white-collar crime in which a stockbroker makes repeated trades to fraudulently increase his or her commissions (p. 387)

claimsmakers People in a position to influence the social construction of crime images in the media, such as the police, politicians, and journalists (p. 431)

classical criminology The theory that people have free will, choose to commit crime for reasons of greed or need, and can be controlled only by the fear of criminal sanctions (p. 9; p. 126)

cleared Refers to crimes that are determined to be founded, which are then solved or cleared away by the police; do not necessarily result in charges or convictions (p. 57)

Code of Hammurabi The first written criminal code, developed in Babylonia about 2000 BCE (p. 29)

cognitive school (perspective) A theory that studies our perceptions of reality and of the mental processes required to understand the world we live in (p. 182)

cohort A sample of subjects whose behaviour is followed over a period (p. 20)

commitment to conformity A positive orientation to the rules of society, whereby the individual internalizes those rules (p. 251)

common law Early English law that was developed by judges and incorporated Anglo-Saxon tribal custom, feudal rules and practices, and the everyday rules of behaviour of local villages. Common law became the standardized law of the land in England, and eventually formed the basis of criminal law in Canada (p. 31)

community notification Legislation that requires convicted sex offenders to register with local police when they move into an area or neighbourhood (p. 50)

compliance A white-collar enforcement strategy that encourages law-abiding behaviour through both the threat of economic sanctions and the promise of rewards for conformity (p. 401)

concentration effect The outcome when middle-class families flee inner-city poverty areas, taking with them institutional resources and support, which leads to the most disadvantaged people being consolidated in urban ghettos (p. 212)

conduct norms Behaviours expected of social group members, which conflict with those of the general culture; as a result, group members may be outcast as criminals (p. 225)

confidence games A fraud in which the victim, or *mark*, is persuaded to trust the criminal (p. 361)

conflict-linked crime or violence An expressive crime or an act of expressive violence involving people who know each other and who may be under the influence of drugs (p. 143)

conflict-related violence An expressive crime of passion involving acquaintances (p. 322)

conflict theory A general approach that sees criminal behaviour as caused by economic inequality, and criminal law defined by those in power (p. 284)

consent The agreement of the victim to have sexual relations with another person, the lack of which is a legal element in the charge of sexual assault; cannot be extinguished by drunkenness (p. 327)

constructive intent The finding of criminal liability for an unintentional act that is the result of negligence or recklessness (p. 40)

constructive possession In larceny, the temporary physical custody of property given up willingly by the owner (p. 354)

containments Internal and external factors that insulate youths from delinquency-promoting situations, such as strong self-concept and positive support from parents and teachers (p. 251)

continuity of crime The view that crime begins early in life and continues throughout the life course. Thus, the best predictor of future criminality is past criminality (p. 83)

control theory An approach that looks at the ability of society and its institutions to control, manage, restrain, or direct human behaviour; sometimes called *social control theory* (p. 244)

corporate crime A legal violation by a corporate entity, such as price-fixing, restraint of trade, hazardous waste dumping, unfair advertising, or monopolistic practices (p. 392)

correctionalist The concept that social science seeks to correct criminal behaviour rather than see it as rooted in economic relations (p. 292)

corroboration The backing up of a claim of sexual assault by a third party, which before 1983, was required in a charge alleging sexual assault; no longer required (p. 327)

crack cocaine A smokable form of purified cocaine that provides an immediate and powerful high (p. 427)

crackdown The concentration of police resources on a particular problem area, such as street-level drug dealing, to eradicate or displace criminal activity (p. 141)

crime displacement An effect of crime prevention efforts, in which efforts to control crime in one area shift illegal activities to another area (p. 128)

crime funnel The phenomenon in which, as cases move farther into the justice system, the number of cases being dealt with gradually drops (p. 57)

crime rate The number derived by calculating the ratio of crimes in the whole population expressed as per 100,000 people, providing the relative likelihood of crime occurring (p. 56)

crime-related violence Violence, usually between strangers, committed during the course of another crime (p. 322)

criminal anthropology Early efforts to discover a biological basis to crime through physical measurements, usually associated with Cesare Lombroso (p. 10)

criminal justice system The stages through which the offender passes, including police, courts, and corrections (p. 3)

criminological enterprise The totality of criminology, which includes many fields or subareas of study (p. 13)

criminologist One who brings objectivity and method to the study of crime and its consequences (p. 4)

criminology The scientific study of the nature, extent, cause, and control of criminal behaviour (p. 4)

crisis intervention A form of program provided to victims of crime, many of whom are feeling isolated, vulnerable, and in need of immediate services such as counselling (p. 114)

cross-sectional research Surveys that use data from all age, race, gender, and income segments of the population (p. 20)

cult killings Murders committed by members of religious cults who are ordered to kill as part of the cult's rituals (p. 332)

cultural deviance theory Criminal behaviour is in conformity to lower-class subcultural values that develop in disorganized neighbourhoods due to strain and values in conflict with conventional social norms (p. 204)

cultural transmission The cultural passing down of conduct norms from one generation to the next, which become stable and predictable (p. 206)

culture conflict A condition when the rules and norms of an individual's subcultural affiliation conflict with role demands of conventional society (p. 225)

culture of poverty The lower class culture, characterized by values and norms in conflict with conventional society (p. 202)

cybercrime Illegal acts that use computer technology both for illicit gain, such as fraud, and for moral crimes, such as child pornography and stalking (p. 381); the theft or destruction of information using computers, networks, and the Internet (p. 450)

cyberespionage The use of computer networks and communications to commit espionage, such as hacking into military, government, and industry computer systems (p. 458)

cyberstalking The use of the Internet, email, or other electronic communication devices to stalk another person (p. 50)

cyberterrorism An effort by covert forces to disrupt the intersection between the virtual electronic reality of computers and the physical world (p. 451)

cybertheft The use of computer technology to commit traditional crimes, such as fraud, and modern offences, such as identity theft (p. 450)

cybervandalism The use of computer technology for malicious purposes, such as bringing down business networks (p. 451)

cyberwar The use of computer technology and communications to disrupt networks of foreign governments (p. 451)

cycle of violence The phenomenon of child victims of abuse becoming adult criminals due to their early abusive experiences (p. 95)

dangerous classes The idea that personal characteristics such as being single, young, urban, male, and ethnic, can result in harsher treatment in the criminal justice system (p. 289)

date rape A form of sexual assault that occurs between acquaintances; of all sexual assaults, it has the lowest level of reporting (p. 325)

deconstructionism The critical analysis of language in legal codes and regulations to see how content causes racism or sexism to become institutionalized (p. 304)

decriminalization Reducing the penalty for a criminal act, and its illegality (p. 5)

defensible space The principle that crime prevention can be achieved through modifying the physical environment to reduce the opportunity individuals have to commit crime (p. 137)

definition-sensitive crimes Crimes sensitive to legislative activity—gambling has seen a loosening of criminal sanctions around gaming (p. 55)

degradation Shaming occurs when the offender is branded as evil and cast out of society through a ritual exclusion, such as a school disciplinary hearing or a criminal court trial (p. 149)

denial-of-service attack An assault triggered when computers bombard a server with so many requests for service that it shuts down, usually as a result of computer bots controlled by viruses (p. 453)

designer drugs Chemical substances made and distributed in relatively small batches for the purpose of inducing mood-altering effects (p. 428)

desistance The process by which crime rate declines with the perpetrator's age; synonymous with the aging-out process (p. 77)

deterrence The act of preventing crime before it occurs by means of the threat of criminal sanctions; the perception that the pain of punishment outweighs the criminal gain or profit (p. 402)

developmental criminology An approach that examines change in a criminal career over the life course, by looking at biological, social, and psychological factors involved in desistance, resistance, escalation, and specialization (p. 262)

deviant behaviour Behaviour that departs or doesn't conform to social norms, but isn't defined as a crime by the law (p. 5)

deviant place hypothesis The theory that suggests there are natural areas for crime, which are poor, densely populated, highly transient neighbourhoods in which commercial and residential property exist side by side (p. 108)

differential association (DA) theory According to Sutherland, the principle that criminal acts are related to a person's exposure to an excess amount of antisocial attitudes and values (p. 245)

differential opportunity The concept that all people share the same success goals, but some have limited means of achieving those goals and seek alternatives, such as joining with like-minded peers and pursuing criminal activity (p. 226)

differential reinforcement (DR) theory In social learning theory, the view that crime is a type of learned behaviour, combining differential association with elements of psychological learning (p. 248)

diffusion of benefits An effect that occurs when an effort to control one type of crime has the unexpected benefit of reducing the incidence of another type of crime (p. 140)

disclosure A principle established in *R. v. Stinchcombe* (1991), where the prosecution must give all evidence gathered by police to the defendant in order to make a complete defence to the charges (p. 46)

discouragement The effect when efforts made to eliminate one type of crime also control other types of crime by limiting access to desirable targets and thereby reducing the value of the criminal activity (p. 140)

displacement The effect when heavy law enforcement in one area drives crime to another, less well-enforced area, thus making this policing strategy ineffective overall (p. 116)

dramatization of evil In Tannenbaum's pioneering study of labelling, the process whereby the reaction to deviance sets up a feedback effect that the individual internalizes (p. 259)

drift According to Matza, the movement of youth in and out of delinquency because their lifestyles can embrace both conventional and deviant values (p. 249)

duress One of the grounds that excuse an accused from responsibility from an act, if it can be shown that the accused was forced or compelled by someone else to commit a criminal act (p. 42)

early onset Description of people who are deviant at a very young age and who are most likely to persist in crime, if their criminal career begins early in life (p. 78; p. 268)

economic crimes Acts designed to bring financial gain to the offender, as opposed to violent crimes, which are often conflict-related (p. 348)

egalitarian The description of an equal sharing of authority and power, for example, between the two partners in a family (p. 303)

election fraud Practices designed to undermine the fair procedures of a democratic election, such as buying votes (p. 468)

electroencephalograph (EEG) A device that can record the electronic impulses given off by the brain, commonly called brain waves (p. 171)

embezzlement A type of larceny that involves taking the possessions of another that have been placed in possession for safekeeping, e.g., a stockbroker rifling a customer's account (p. 368)

enterprise crimes Illegal acts of opportunity that involve breaking regulatory rules but not personal victimization for the purpose of financial gain (p. 381)

entrapment A criminal defence maintaining that the police initiated the criminal action (p. 44)

moral entrepreneurs Interest groups that attempt to control social life and the legal order for the purpose of promoting their own set of moral values (p. 258)

equipotentiality The concept that individuals are equal at birth and thereafter are influenced by their environment (p. 166)

equivalent group hypothesis The view that victims and criminals share similar characteristics, and their lifestyle exposes them to increased levels of victimization risk (p. 106)

eros According to Freud, of the two opposing instinctual drives that interact to control behaviour, eros is the life instinct, which drives people to self-fulfillment and enjoyment (p. 319)

espionage Spying against a foreign government, designed to undermine its industry or political system (p. 469)

etailing fraud The selling of illegal or intentionally misrepresented goods over the Internet (p. 456)

expressive crimes Illegal activities with no instrumental purpose, such as shooting someone during the course of an argument (p. 76)

expressive violence Violence that is designed not for profit but to vent anger or frustration; also called conflict-related violence (p. 322)

extinction The phenomenon in which a crime prevention effort has an immediate impact that dissipates as criminals adjust to new conditions (p. 140)

false pretences Illegally obtaining money, goods, or merchandise by fraud or mis-representation (p. 361)

fence A buyer and seller of stolen merchandise (p. 348)

flash houses In the 18th century, the taverns where skilled thieves and pickpockets congregated and which served as headquarters for gangs (p. 349)

focal concerns The value orientations of lower-class culture include the needs for excitement, trouble, smartness, fate, and personal autonomy (p. 225)

folkways Customs with no moral values attached, such as not interrupting people who are speaking (p. 37)

founded Crimes reported to police that are believed to be real; otherwise known as *actual* (p. 56)

fraud Taking possessions through deception, such as selling a desk as an antique that is really a copy (p. 361)

gang killings Murders committed by gangs who make violence part of their group activity; often committed as part of warfare over territory or control of the drug trade (p. 331)

gendered violence The concept that some forms of violence tend to be committed against women, by men, such as sexual assault, stalking, and domestic violence (p. 324)

general deterrence Measures, such as long prison sentences for violent crimes, aimed at convincing the potential law violator that the pains associated with crime outweigh its benefits (p. 38; p. 140)

general strain theory (GST) A micro-level analysis of how individuals who feel stress and strain are more likely to commit crimes (p. 220)

genocide An extreme form of state-sponsored terrorism, in which a government seeks to wipe out a minority group within the jurisdiction it controls (p. 477)

globalization The creation of international markets, politics, and legal systems (p. 450)

green criminology The study of crimes against the environment, usually for profit (p. 381)

hypoglycemia A biochemical condition, in this case a deficiency of sugar, which influences antisocial behaviour and criminality (p. 167)

inchoate crimes Incomplete or contemplated crimes such as solicitation or criminal attempts (p. 32)

incidence The number of crimes reported to the police in a given time period (p. 55)

incident-based data Compared with aggregate (UCR) crime data, incident-based data provides data on specific factors, such as the location of the offence and the relationship between the offender and the victim (p. 55)

income inequality The differences in personal income that create structural inequalities in society, which may be at the root of crime (p. 212)

identity crisis A psychological state, identified by Erikson, in which youths face inner turmoil and uncertainty about life roles (p. 180)

identity theft The fraudulent acquisition of another person's private and personal information (p. 363)

indictable offence A serious offence, such as murder, which carries a serious penalty (p. 35)

inferiority complex A term used to describe the sense of inadequacy held by people who compensate for their feelings of inferiority with a drive for superiority; controlling others may help reduce their sense of personal inadequacies (p. 180)

informal sanctions The disapproval of parents, peers, and neighbours directed toward an offender, which may have a greater crime-reducing impact than the fear of formal legal punishments (p. 143)

information technology (IT) The use of computer networks and communications for education and commerce (p. 450)

insider trading Illegal buying of stock in a company on the basis of information provided by someone in the company, such as an employee, attorney, or accountant of the firm (p. 387)

instincts The mechanism by which routine actions and behaviour are known automatically without being learned (p. 166)

instrumental crimes Illegal activity, such as the sale of narcotics, committed for the purpose of obtaining desired goods that are unable to be attained through conventional means (p. 76; p. 134)

instrumental Marxism The view that the law is designed to specifically advance the interests of particular groups or organizations (p. 294)

insurgents People acting against their government, seeking to secure a revolution or disruption of the state (p. 472)

integrated structural Marxist theory An integrated approach that looks at the influence of a person's position within the relations of material production (p. 267)

intent Carrying out an act intentionally, knowingly, and willingly (p. 39)

intimate violence Crime that occurs in the context of familiarity, such as spousal abuse, child abuse, or elder abuse (p. 3)

just desert The philosophy of justice that asserts that those who violate the rights of others deserve to be punished, with severity commensurate with the seriousness of the crime (p. 153)

labelling theory The view that society creates deviance through the designation of individual behaviour as deviant. The stigmatized individual feels unwanted and accepts the label as an identity (p. 244)

larceny Usually known as theft, the taking of property, one of the oldest common-law crimes (p. 353)

latent delinquency The idea that a mental predisposition prepares youths psychologically for antisocial acts (p. 180)

latent traits Stable features, characteristics, properties, or conditions that are present at birth or soon after and that lead some people to be crime-prone over their life course (p. 263)

left realism A theory that crime is a social problem experienced by the lower classes, and criminologists should develop crime prevention strategies (p. 299)

lex talionis Punishment based on physical retaliation ("an eye for an eye"), a precursor of more abstract forms of retribution used today (p. 29)

liberal feminist theory An approach that focuses attention on the social and economic roles of women in society and their relationship to female crime rates (p. 81)

life-course theory Criminal offending patterns change over a person's life, influenced by conditions or events that occur at various stages in life (p. 263)

lifestyle theory The view that the lifestyle of the victim is a factor in the likelihood of a crime being committed, such as the number of times the victim goes out or the people the victim associates with (p. 108)

longitudinal research Research that tracks the development of a group of subjects over time (p. 20)

macro perspective A large-scale view that takes into account social and economic reasons to explain how and why things happen; relevant to Marxism and functionalism (p. 130)

madam The traditional name for a woman who runs a brothel; more common today is the male pimp (p. 421)

mala in se Crimes rooted in the core values inherent in our culture, deemed universal (p. 37)

mala prohibitum Crimes defined by current public opinion and social values, subject to change (p. 37)

marginalization When people live in areas conducive to crime, which leads to decreased commitment, and a weakened bond to society (p. 308)

marital exemption The practice in some jurisdictions of prohibiting the prosecution of husbands for the rape of their wives (p. 325)

Marxist feminism The view that gender inequality stems from the unequal power of men and women in capitalism, based on private property, male domination, and the exploitation of women (p. 301)

masculinity hypothesis The view that women who commit crimes have biological and psychological traits similar to those of men (p. 81)

massage parlours Seemingly legitimate businesses where men can buy sex under the guise of massage therapy; one of the more hidden sides of prostitution (p. 421)

mass murderer One who kills a large number of people in a single incident (p. 333)

master status An identity that overrides all others, such as drug dealer being a more important status than citizen (p. 259)

media-sensitive crimes Crimes sensitive to media attention—youth crime, when covered in the media, increases public concern, which increases reports to police, which makes the news (p. 55)

mens rea The intent to commit the criminal act, needed for most offences except strict liability (p. 39)

mental disorder A disease of the mind, includes an abnormal condition that impairs functioning, excluding self-induced states caused by alcohol and transitory states such as hysteria (p. 41)

micro perspective A small-scale view of events, looking at interaction to explain how and why things happen; relevant to interactionist studies of deviance and development (p. 130)

minimal brain dysfunction (MBD) An abnormality in cerebral structure that causes maladaptive behaviour and is linked to antisocial acts and an imbalance in urge-control (p. 172)

mitigating factor A circumstance that makes a crime less serious; for example, abused people react more when threatened, which may serve as a defence or may lead to a lighter sentence (p. 102)

M'Naghten rule In 1843, an English court established Daniel M'Naghten was not responsible for murder because delusions had caused him to act. The principle of criminal responsibility states that an accused cannot be held legally liable for their actions if they do not know what they are doing or cannot distinguish right from wrong (p. 41)

moral crusades Efforts by interest groups to stamp out behaviour they find objectionable; typically public order crimes, such as drug use or pornography (p. 418)

moral entrepreneurs Interest groups or individuals who are in a position to promote their own values onto others (p. 19); interest groups that attempt to control social life and the legal order for the purpose of promoting their own personal set of moral values (p. 258; p. 418)

mores Customs or conventions essential to a community, which often form the basis of criminal law (p. 37)

Mosaic Code By tradition, the covenant between God and the tribes of Israel in which they agreed to obey his law in return for God's special care and protection (p. 29)

motivated criminals The potential offenders in a population. According to rational choice theory, crime rates will vary according to the number of motivated offenders (p. 131)

motivated offenders The potential offenders in a population who exploit opportunities to commit crime (p. 109)

multifactor theories Views that attempt to integrate individual factors and independent concepts into complex, coherent explanations of criminality (p. 264)

murder Colloquially refers to the killing of one person by another; homicide is separated into the categories of first-degree and second-degree murder, manslaughter, and infanticide (p. 328)

natural areas Zones or neighbourhoods that develop as a result of social forces operating in urban areas, and become natural areas for crime (p. 200)

negative affective states The anger, depression, disappointment, fear, and other adverse emotions that derive from strain (p. 220)

networks Loosely organized terrorist organizations that lack a specific organizational structure (p. 477)

neurophysiology The study of brain activity that looks at neurological and physical abnormalities acquired during the fetal or perinatal stage, which are thought to control behaviour (p. 171)

neurosis A syndrome in psychodynamic theory whereby people suffer when they experience feelings of mental anguish and are afraid they are losing control of their personalities (p. 179)

neutralization theory A view that offenders adhere to conventional values while drifting into periods of crime by neutralizing those values (p. 249)

norm resistance A concept referring to the interaction between authorities and subjects that produces open conflict between the two groups (p. 289)

oath-helpers During the Middle Ages, groups of 12 to 25 people who would support the accused's innocence (p. 30)

obscenity Sexually explicit material, for example, open sexual behaviour, masturbation, and genital exhibition banned in most communities (p. 422)

occasional criminal An offender who does not derive much income from crime but when there is an opportunity is more likely to drift in and out of crime (p. 351)

occupational crime Crime committed by employees for personal gain using the structural advantage provided by their employment (p. 383)

offence-specific crime An illegal act committed by offenders reacting selectively to characteristics of particular offences, assessing opportunity and guardianship; relevant to routine activities theory (p. 128)

offender-specific crime An illegal act committed by offenders who do not usually engage in random acts of antisocial behaviour, but who evaluate their skill at accomplishing the crime (p. 129)

organized crime Illegal acts committed by a gang, such as drug trafficking (p. 381)

paraphilia Abnormal sexual practices that may involve recurrent sexual urges focused on objects, humiliation, or children (p. 418)

passive precipitation The view that personal and social characteristics of victims make them attractive targets for predatory criminals (p. 101)

paternalistic The characterization of leaders in government or organizations as father figures, while others are treated as children (p. 303)

peacemaking A branch of conflict theory that stresses humanism, mediation, and conflict resolution as a means to end crime (p. 307)

percentage change An increase or decrease in crime rates over a period of years so that criminologists can tell whether society is becoming more dangerous (p. 56)

perceptual deterrence The view that the perceived risk of being caught or the threat of severe punishments can deter active criminal offenders (p. 143)

personality The reasonably stable patterns of behaviour, thoughts, and emotions that distinguish one person from another; used to explain how

psychological conflict or underdevelopment might result in neurotic or psychotic behaviour patterns (p. 185)

phishing Creating false emails or websites that look legitimate but are designed to gain illegal access to a victim's personal information (p. 364; p. 456)

pilferage Theft by employees through stealth or deception (p. 390)

policing-sensitive crimes Crimes sensitive to law enforcement—drug crime is proactively investigated by police; otherwise, it would not be detected (p. 55)

political crime Depending on the country, any action critical of, or in opposition to, the state (p. 466)

pornography Depiction of sex acts in a variety of forms, such as books, magazines, films, and websites (p. 422)

positivism A branch of social science that sees behaviour as a product of social, biological, psychological, and economic forces (p. 9)

predatory crime A violent, opportunistic crime, not usually familiar-related, such as stealing brand-name clothing from strangers (p. 109)

pre-emptive deterrence An approach in left realism in which community organization efforts can reduce crime before it becomes necessary to use police force (p. 300)

premeditation The thinking out and planning of a crime; must be proven by the prosecution to have occurred to qualify for the charge of first-degree homicide (p. 328)

premenstrual syndrome (PMS) The biogenetic theory that several days prior to and during menstruation, females are beset by irritability and poor judgment as a result of hormonal changes, which places them at a greater risk for criminality (p. 170)

price-fixing A form of corporate crime, where companies conspire together to artificially inflate the price of goods (p. 393)

primary deviance According to Lemert, deviant acts that go undetected or unsanctioned, and thus do not help redefine the self and public image of the offender (p. 259)

privilege The concept that the wealth and prestige enjoyed by some, puts them in conflict with those in society who are less well off (p. 294)

professional criminals Those offenders who make a significant portion of their income from crime; less likely to drift in and out of crime (p. 351)

proletariat In Marxist theory, the working class, who provide the labour in capitalism (p. 12)

pro-social bonds In the social development model, the bonds developed within the context of a family life that provide pro-social opportunities and consistent, positive feedback (p. 266)

prostitution The buying and selling of sex, not illegal in Canada, although prostitution-related offences are illegal, such as pimping, brothel-keeping, and public communication of such an exchange (p. 419)

proximity hypothesis The view that people become crime victims because they live or work in areas with large criminal populations (p. 108)

psychodynamic (psychoanalytic) theory The branch of psychology that holds that the human personality is controlled by unconscious mental processes developed early in childhood (p. 178)

psychopathy A mental disorder, especially when manifested as antisocial behaviour. The term is often used interchangeably with *sociopathy* and *antisocial personality disorder* (p. 186)

psychopharmacological The type of effect of a mood-altering substance such as alcohol, PCP, or amphetamines, which can produce a violent change in behaviour (p. 320)

psychosis A syndrome in which people have lost total control and are dominated by their primitive id; their behaviour may be marked by bizarre episodes, hallucinations, and inappropriate responses to situations (p. 179)

public order crimes Sometimes called *victimless* crimes, these acts interfere with public order, such as loitering for the purposes of prostitution (p. 416)

radical feminism The view that female crime is caused by male patriarchy, and the subordination and control of women by men (p. 302)

rational choice theory The view that crime is a function of a decision-making process, in which the potential offender weighs the potential costs and benefits of an illegal act (p. 130)

reaction formation The rejection of goals and standards that seem impossible to achieve (p. 227)

reflected appraisal According to Matsueda and Heimer, a youth's self-evaluation that is based on his or her perceptions of how others evaluate him or her (p. 260)

reflective role-taking The experience in which youths who view themselves as delinquent give an inner-voice to their perceptions of how significant others feel about them (p. 260)

reintegrative shaming A method of correction that encourages offenders to confront their misdeeds, experience shame, and then be reincluded in society (p. 147)

relative deprivation The condition that exists when people of wealth and people of poverty live in close proximity to one another, affecting crime rates (p. 219)

report-sensitive crimes Crimes are sensitive to victims reporting them—if sexual assault is not reported, then it is unlikely that police will know about it (p. 55)

repression A process identified in psychodynamic theory, in which the unconscious mind contains feelings about sex and hostility; most people keep these feelings below the surface of consciousness (p. 178)

restorative justice Mediation and conflict resolution as an alternative to the formal court system to heal personal injury and community relations (p. 304)

r/K theory An evolutionary theory of crime that holds that K-oriented people are more cooperative and sensitive to others; r-oriented people are more cunning and deceptive (p. 176)

robbery A crime of violence involving the use of force to obtain money or goods (p. 337)

routine activities theory The view that crime is a normal function of the routine activities of modern living: a suitable, unprotected target will be identified as a target by motivated offenders (p. 109; p. 130)

schizophrenia A psychosis marked by bizarre behaviour, hallucinations, loss of thought control, and inappropriate emotional responses; types of schizophrenia include catatonic (impairment of motor activity), paranoid (delusions of persecution), and hebephrenic (immature behaviour and giddiness) (p. 179)

secondary deviance According to Lemert, deviant acts that are sanctioned, after which the deviant label becomes a basis for personal identity (p. 259)

seductions of crime According to Katz, the visceral and emotional appeal that the situation of crime has for those who engage in illegal acts (p. 135)

selective incapacitation The policy of creating enhanced prison sentences for the relatively small group of dangerous chronic offenders (p. 152)

self-rejection The consequence of successfully being labelled, whereby the negative stigma is internalized (p. 251)

self-report survey A research approach that requires subjects to reveal their own participation in delinquent or criminal acts (p. 61)

semiotics Language comprising a set of signs that describe the world by conveying meanings understood by their audience (p. 304)

serial killer One who kills more than three people over a period of time (p. 333)

sex offender registration Requirement that released offenders register and report to the police, and keep them informed of their whereabouts, including any change of address (p. 50)

sexual abuse A form of violence, usually by a family member or relative, which involves rape, incest, and molestation, and can occur in wife abuse, child abuse, and elder abuse (p. 334)

siege mentality A consequence and symptom of community disorganization, where fear causes the belief that the outside world is an enemy out to destroy the neighbourhood (p. 209)

situational crime prevention A method to eliminate or reduce particular crimes in narrow settings, such as increasing lighting and installing security alarms (p. 136)

situational inducement The opportunity that influences the decision to commit crimes, such as occasional property crime (p. 350)

shield laws Legislation designed to protect rape victims by prohibiting the defence attorney from inquiring about their previous sexual relationships (p. 327)

snitches Amateur pilferers who think of themselves as respectable people (p. 355)

social development model (SDM) The attempt to integrate social control, social learning, and structural models of crime (p. 264)

social deviant A person who has been labelled as an outsider at home, at work, at school, and in other social situations (p. 256)

social disorganization theory An approach that looks at neighbourhoods marked by culture conflict, lack of cohesiveness, transiency, and anomie (p. 204)

social distance A person can be labelled as deviant because of the differences in power between the labeller and the person labelled; such differences are typically those of race, class, and ethnicity (p. 258)

social ecologists Those whose approach looks at community-level indicators of social disorganization, such as disorder, poverty, alienation, and fear of crime (p. 208)

social injustice The perception of unfairness, which leads to anger, especially where the poor and wealthy live in close proximity, and people can see how poorly off they are (p. 212)

socialization The process of human development and enculturation. Primary socialization takes place in the family, and secondary socialization takes place in institutions (p. 239)

social learning theory The view that behaviour is modelled on observation of social interactions, direct observation of those who are close, or indirectly through the media. Interactions that are rewarded are copied, while those that are punished are avoided (p. 178; p. 244)

social process theories Approaches that look at the operation of formal and informal social institutions, such as socialization within family, peer groups, schools, and legal system (p. 239)

social reality of crime Quinney's conflict theory regarding the interrelationships between power, society, and criminality (p. 287)

social structure theory An approach that looks at the effects of class stratification in society (p. 203)

sociobiology The branch of science that views human behaviour as motivated by inborn biological urges and desires. The urge to survive and reproduce motivates human behaviour (p. 164)

sociopathy A mental disorder characterized by lack of warmth and affection, inappropriate responses, and an inability to learn from experience. The term is often used interchangeably with *psychopathy* and *antisocial personality disorder* (p. 186)

somatype An idea used in a system developed for categorizing people on the basis of their body build, associated with the work of William Sheldon (p. 164)

specific deterrence A punishment severe enough to convince convicted offenders never to repeat their crimes, which is based on the principle that an individual can be dissuaded from committing a crime if the cost outweighs the benefit (p. 38; p. 146)

stalking The criminal offence of following or harassing a victim even though no actual assault or battery has occurred (p. 49)

stare decisis The principle that the courts are bound to follow the law established in previously decided cases (precedent) unless the law was overruled by a higher authority (p. 31)

state political crime Illegal actions by a state against its population or other sovereign governments (p. 470)

status frustration The clash created when lower-class youths are incapable of achieving success legitimately, which results in behaviour that is non-utilitarian, malicious, and negativistic (p. 226)

stigmatization An enduring label that taints a person's identity and changes him or her in the eyes of others (p. 149)

stigmatize To create an enduring label that taints a person's identity and changes him or her in the eyes of others (p. 242)

strain theory An approach that looks at the conflict caused when people cannot achieve their goals through legitimate means, and are denied access to adequate educational opportunities and social support (p. 204)

stranger-related crime A crime committed by an offender who has had no prior relationship with the victim, such as most incidents of carjacking (p. 95)

street crimes Crime-related acts that prey on the public through theft, damage, and violence (p. 348)

strict-liability crimes Illegal acts with no need for intent, or *mens rea*; they are usually acts that endanger the public welfare, such as illegal dumping of toxic wastes or speeding (p. 40)

structural Marxism The view that the law maintains the capitalist system, and individuals who threaten social stability will be sanctioned (p. 295)

subculture A group that maintains a unique set of values, beliefs, and traditions resistant and oppositional to dominant society (p. 226)

subterranean values In neutralization theory, immorality that is entrenched in the culture but is otherwise publicly condemned (p. 249)

suitable target According to routine activities theory, a target for crime that is relatively valuable, easily transportable, and not capably guarded (p. 109)

summary offence A minor offence whose penalty is a maximum six months in jail, or a fine (p. 35)

surplus value The Marxist view that the labouring classes produce wealth that far exceeds their wages and goes to the capitalist class as profits (p. 293)

swindling Stealing through deception by individuals who try to bilk people out of their money, e.g., door-to-door sales of faulty merchandise (p. 386)

symbolic interaction theory The view that people communicate meaning and interpret reality on the basis of their interpretation of symbols (p. 256)

systematic forgers Fraud artists who make a substantial living by passing bad cheques; a dying profession (p. 365)

target hardening Making one's home and business crime-proof through the installation of locks, bars, alarms, and other devices (p. 116)

target reduction strategies Methods for reducing crime through the use of locks, bars, alarms, and other devices; based on the routine activities theory and its analysis of potential risk factors (p. 139)

techniques of neutralization A strategy of cognitive dissonance used by deviants to counteract moral constraints so they may drift into criminal acts (p. 249)

temperance movement An organized effort to prohibit the sale of liquor, largely seen as unsuccessful (p. 425)

terror cells A structure often used by modern terrorist organizations, whereby no one member knows all the other members of the group (p. 477)

terrorism A wide variety of violent acts that have a political motivation; can be committed both against a state and by a state (p. 470)

testosterone An androgen, or male hormone, which controls secondary sex characteristics and can alter behaviour (p. 167)

Thanatos According to Freud, of the two instinctual drives, Thanatos is the death instinct, which drives people toward aggression, violence, and self-destruction (p. 319)

thrill killings Impulsive violent murders motivated by the killer's decision to kill a stranger as an act of daring or recklessness (p. 331)

tort law The law of personal wrongs and damage, such as negligence, libel, and slander (p. 34)

trait theories These approaches look at the combination of biological or psychological attributes that might explain criminality (p. 163)

transferred intent An illegal yet unintended act results from the intent to commit a crime (p. 40)

transitional neighbourhood An area undergoing a shift in population and structure, usually from middle-class residential to lower-class mixed use (p. 205)

transnational organized crime Unlike traditional organized crime, organized crime that operates across international boundaries, transporting people and stolen goods (p. 461)

underclass A world cut off from society, its members lacking the education and skills needed to survive, which becomes a breeding ground for criminality (p. 202)

Uniform Crime Report (UCR) An aggregate census based on reports from police, which is the basis for criminological research (p. 55)

utilitarianism A view that punishment should be balanced and fair, and that crime is a rational choice (p. 8; p. 126)

vagrancy A summary offence crime, meant to prohibit homelessness, begging, and loitering (p. 38)

value conflict The clash of deviant values of teenage law-violating groups with middle-class norms, which demand obedience to the law (p. 207)

victim compensation Financial restitution to the victim of crime, usually provided by provinces and territories and funded by a surcharge levied in criminal cases (p. 113)

victimologist A researcher who studies the role of victims in the crime process (p. 100)

victimology The study of the victim's role in criminal transactions (p. 92)

victim precipitation The view that a victim's behaviour or characteristics, such as verbal abuse, or openly displaying wealth, can act as the spark that ignites the subsequent offence (p. 100)

vigilante Someone who takes the law into their own hands, and acts outside the law in the interest of justice (p. 418)

vishing Similar to phishing, this practice uses Voice over Internet Protocol (VoIP) software to access personal information (p. 456)

warez The practice of illegally copying software and posting it on the Internet for others to use (p. 455)

wergild Under medieval law, the money paid by the offender to compensate the victim and the state for a criminal offence (p. 29)

white-collar crime Crimes committed by those with power, such as embezzlement, false advertising, or stock market manipulation (p. 14); illegal acts that capitalize on a person's status in the marketplace, including embezzlement, fraud, market manipulation, restraint of trade, and false advertising (p. 381)

Index

murderers, 184, 330
  nature theory vs. nurture theory, 188–189
  peer relations, 242–243
  and poverty, 201
  social control theory, 252–255
  socialization, 266
  socialization and family relations,
    239–241
  who kill, 330
  as witnesses of violence, 319
China, 16, 17, 293, 384, 458, 461, 465
Chinese Triad gangs, 408, 465
Chiricos, Theodore, 21
chiselling, 387–388
chivalry hypothesis, 81
choice theory
  classical theory, development of,
    126–127
  crime pays, 127–128
  elimination of crime, 135
  emergence of, 127–133
  general deterrence, 140–145
  incapacitation strategies, 151–153
  introduction to, 126
  offence and offender specifications,
    128–130
  overview of theories, 154
  policy implications of, 153
  rational choice, 128
  rational choice and routine activities
    theories, 130–133
  rationality of crime, 133–135
  rethinking deterrence, 150–151
  situational crime prevention, 135–140
  specific deterrence, 146–150
  summary, 153–154
Chrétien, Aline, 187
Chrétien, Jean, 187, 288
Christopher's Law, 50
chronic offenders, 82–84, 147, 152–153
Chunn, Dorothy, 182
churning, 387
Circle of Courage program, 247, 257
Circles of Support, 214
civil law, 34–35
claimsmakers, 431
Clairmont, Don, 291
Clarke, Ronald, 137
class. See social class
class conflict, 294
class-crime controversy, 76–77
class-crime relationship, 76
class discrimination, 295
classical/choice perspective, 13
classical criminology, 8–9, 126
classical theory, 126–127
classroom climate, 242
Clean Water Act and the Migratory Bird
  Act, 394
clearance status, youth crime by, 59
cleared, 57
cleared otherwise, 57
client frauds, 391–392

climate, and crime, 74–75
closed-circuit television (CCTV) cameras,
  136, 137–138, 144–145
Cloward, Richard, 227–228
coal mine safety violations, 141
The Coast, 423
cocaine, 427
Cogger, Michel, 388
cognitive definitions, 248
cognitive dissonance reduction, 249
cognitive theory, 178, 182–184, 191
cognitive transformation, 270
Cohen, Albert, 226–227
Cohen Commission, 64, 105
cohort research, 20–21
Coles, Robert, 139
collateral business crimes, 384
collective efficacy, 213–214
Colombia, 16, 436, 461, 465
Commission on Systemic Racism, 64,
  70, 290
commissions of inquiry, 64–65
commitment to conformity, 251
common law, 30–33, 353–354, 468
community change, 212
community deterioration, 208–209
community fear, 209
community notification, 50
community organization, 117
community strategies to control drugs, 437
comparative research, 16–17, 142–143,
  148, 189–190
compensation for crimes, 29, 30
compliance, 401
complicity with law enforcement, 352
computer crimes
  copyright infringement, 455
  denial-of-service attack, 453, 454, 455,
    459
  distribution of dangerous drugs, 453
  distribution of illicit or illegal services
    and material, 452–453
  etailing fraud, 456
  extent of, 455
  fraud, 367–368
  identity theft, 363–365, 366, 455–456
  Internet fraud schemes, 452
  Internet securities fraud, 388, 455
  introduction to, 451–452
  phishing, 364, 456
  viruses and attacks, 454
  vishing, 456
computer worm, 454
Comte, Auguste, 9
concentration effect, 212
concentric zone theory, 205–208,
  214, 231
The Condition of the Working Class in England
  in 1844 (Engels), 284
conduct disorder (CD), 169–170
conduct norms, 225
confidence games, 361–362
conflict criminology, 12, 286–287, 289

conflict gangs, 228
conflict-linked crime, 143
conflict-oriented radical criminology, 12
conflict perspective, 13
conflict-related violence, 322
conflict resolutions, 43
conflict theory, 284, 308. See also social
  conflict theory
conflict view of crime, 18, 19
conformity, 216, 251
con games, 384
Conn, Tyrone, 255
conscientiousness, 185
consensus view of crime, 18, 19
consent, 327
Constitution Act, 45
constructionist view of substance
  abuse, 431
constructive intent, 40
constructive possession, 353–354
containments, 251
containment theory, 251–252
continuity of crime, 83–84
Controlled Drugs and Substances Act,
  425, 430
control theory, 244
conventional values, 249
Convention on Cybercrime, 459
conviction rates, 17
Cooley, Charles Horton, 18, 256
coping mechanisms, 186
copyright infringement, 455
corporal punishment, 147
corporate climate, 399
corporate crime, 51, 141, 382, 384, 386,
  392–393. See also white-collar crime
Corporate Crime Reporter, 382
corporate culture theory, 398–399
corporate policing, 401
Corrado, Raymond, 185
correctionalist, 292
Correctional Services Canada, 21, 84
Corrections and Conditional Release Act, 113
La Cosa Nostra, 406, 460
costs of crime, 92–93
court services, 113–114
court system, 32
crack cocaine, 73, 427
crackdowns, 142, 146
Crawford, John Martin, 264
Cream, Thomas Neill, 22
Creba, Jane, 4
credit card fraud, 365
credit card theft, 368
Cressey, Donald, 4, 15
crime
  costs of, 92–93
  vs. criminality, 129
  definition of, 19–20
  ecology of, 74–75
  elimination of, 135
  fear of, 60, 94, 209
  legal definition of, 39–40

Fourth Amendment, 136
fracking, 475
Frame, Clifford, 395
Frame Breaking Act, 33
Framework Decision, 115
France, 17, 317
fraud
 bank fraud, 391–392
 blue-collar fraud, 390
 charity fraud, 452
 cheque fraud, 365–366
 client frauds, 391–392
 credit card fraud, 365
 election fraud, 468
 employee fraud, 390–391
 etailing fraud, 456
 healthcare fraud, 391
 Internet fraud schemes, 452
 Internet securities fraud, 388, 455
 management fraud, 390
 overview of, 361–363
 registration fraud, 468
 romance fraud, 452
 securities fraud, 387–388, 455
fraudulent offerings of securities, 388, 455
Freedom of Information and Protection of Privacy Acts, 144
French, Kristen, 3, 22
Freud, Sigmund, 178, 180, 319–320, 427
Friedland, Robert, 393
Front de Libération du Québec (FLQ), 450, 470, 473
function creep, 144
funding of terrorist activities, 459
funds transfer scams, 452

Gabor, Thomas, 69, 140
Gagnon, Lysiane, 60
Gall, Franz Joseph, 9
Galway, Roberta, 365
gambling, 439–443
Gandhi, Indira, 473
The Gang (Thrasher), 11, 200, 206
ganging, 320
gang killings, 331–332
gangs, 72, 209, 215, 227–229, 247
gang violence, 320
Garfinkel, Harold, 148
Garofalo, Raffaele, 164
Garry, Eileen M., 374
Gartner, Rosemary, 94
Gault, Howard, 129
gay bashing, 106–107
Geis, Gilbert, 383
gender
 and burglary, 371–373
 and crime, 80–82
 differences in violence rates, 176
 family structure–delinquency relationship, 240
 general strain theory, 224
 murder, 329
 school bonds, 255

victim characteristics, 96–97, 98
 victims of crime, 93
gender differences, 81
gendered violence, 324
gender inequality, 301–302
general deterrence
 certainty of punishment, 141–142
 closed-circuit television (CCTV) and public surveillance, 136, 137–138, 144–145
 criminal behaviour, 38
 informal sanctions, 143–144
 introduction to, 140–141
 overview of, 154
 perception and, 143
 severity of punishment, 142–143
 strategies for, 135
 summary, 145
 youth crime, 46
General Social Survey (GSS), 58, 61–63, 70, 80, 92, 95–96, 104, 323, 350, 357
general strain theory (GST), 220–224, 231
general theory of deviance, 259–260
genetics and crime, 175–176, 431
genetic theory of crime, 166, 191
genocide, 476
George, Dudley, 287
Gesch, Bernard, 168
The Ghetto (Wirth), 11, 200
Gill, Kimveer, 317, 318
Gill, Nirmal Singh, 102
Gillars, Mildred Elizabeth, 469
Gladue, Jamie, 291
Glazer, Daniel, 264
globalization, 450
Glover, Shelly, 247
Glowatski, Warren, 79
Glueck, Eleanor, 267–268
Glueck, Sheldon, 267–268
goals, 215–216, 220, 222, 227–228
Goddard, Henry, 188
Gold Coast and the Slum (Zorbaugh), 11, 200
Goodman, Sam, 352
goods and services tax (GST), 368
Goring, Charles, 177
Gottfredson, Denise, 435
government, response to victims, 112–113
government crime, 384
Great Britain. *See* England; Scotland
Greater Vancouver Victimization Survey, 112
Greenberg, David, 286
green-collar crime, 393–397
green criminology, 381
Green River Killer, 333
Grekul, Jana, 257, 304
Griffin, Christine, 398
Grokster, 455
group self-concept, 476
Guardian Angels, 437
guardianship, 110, 112, 131, 137, 139
guerrillas, 470
Guido, Frank, 174
gun control debate, 72, 321

Hagan's Varieties of Deviance, 5, 6
Hale, Matthew, 325
hallucinogens, 426–427
Hamelin, Louise, 183
Hamilton, Thomas, 333
Handshu guidelines, 223
Hansen, Erwin, 390
Hanssen, Robert, 469
Harb, Mac, 386
Hare Psychopathy Checklist, 187
Harper, Stephen, 359
Harrison Narcotics Act, 434
Hartwell, Martin, 44
Harvey, Donald, 332–333
hate crimes, 93–94, 102–104, 106–107, 317
Hatewatch.org, 102
Head Start program, 271, 272
Health Canada, 5, 428, 430
healthcare, violence in, 341–342
healthcare fraud, 391
hedonistic killers, 333
"heiress stealing," 322
Hells Angels, 3, 22, 408
Henry, Janet, 22
heterosexual panic, 106–107
Hier, Sean, 144
Highland Clearances, 297
high-risk lifestyles, 104–105
high-risk professions, 105–106
high-tech crime, 450–456
Himmel, Susan, 23
"hindsight bias," 103
Hirschi, Travis, 252, 254, 255, 399
Hitchcock, Alfred, 163
HIV (human immunodeficiency virus) infection, 201, 430
The Hobo (Anderson), 11
Hoffman, Bruce, 471
Hogeveen, Bryan, 60, 290
home invasion, 360
homeless people, 93, 105, 108
home occupancy, 112
homicide. *See also* murder
 in Canada, 72–73
 and capital punishment, 142–143
 female, by country or territory, 66
 and income inequality, 219
 international rates of, 16
 male, by country or territory, 64
 by more common method, 73
 relationships of victim and offender, 98
 in various countries, 317
homicide networks, 331
Homicide Survey, 55, 328
Homolka, Karla, 3, 22, 94
Homolka, Tammy, 22
homosexuality, 38, 419
"homosexual panic defence," 107
Hopper, Grace Murray, 454
hormonal influences, 81, 167–170, 173
Horne, Christopher, 381, 384–385, 402
Huberty, James, 333

human development, 179
human instinct, 319–320
"human mapping," 223
Human Rights Act, 437
human trafficking, 16, 409, 462–463
hydraulic fracturing, 475
hypoglycemia, 167

id, 178
identical bidding, 393
identity crisis, 180
identity theft, 363–365, 366, 455–456
Idle No More rally, 15
ignorance as a defence, 40–41
illegal restraint of trade, 393
illegal sexuality, 418–424
illegal touting, 455
illicit banking, 389
imitation, 248
immigrants, 201
Immigration and Refugee Protection Act, 409
imperatively coordinated associations, 285
impersonation, 452
inalienable rights, 45
incapacitation strategies, 135, 154
incarceration, logic of, 151–152
incarceration rate, 151
inchoate (incomplete) offences, 32
incidence, 55
incident-based data, 55
income inequality, 77, 212, 219–220, 289
indictable offences, 35–37
indirect heredity, 10
indirect tactics, 103
individual constitutional factors, 265
individual exploitation of institutional position, 388
industrial espionage, 469
industrialization, 210
Industrial Revolution, 350
ineffective families, 319
inequality, 201–202
infanticide, 216
inferiority complex, 180
influence peddling, 388–390
informal control, 112
informal sanctions, 143–144
informal social control, 213
information processing, 184
information technology (IT), 367, 450
injuries and crime, 173
injury, denial of, 249
innovation, 216
insider trading, 387–388
instability, 185
instincts, 166
institutional anomie theory, 218–219, 224, 231
institutional controls, 219
institutional involvement and belief, 243
institutionalization of the criminally insane, 182–183
institutional racism, 212

institutional social control, 213
instrumental crimes, 76, 134
instrumental Marxism, 294–295, 308
insurgency, 472
integrated developmental theory, 262–263
integrated perspective, 13
integrated structural Marxist theory, 267
intelligence, 188–189
intent, 39–40
interactionist view of crime, 18–19
interactive effects, 131–132
Interagency Council on Women, 463
internal pushes, 251
International Atomic Energy Agency, 458
international crime trends, 16–17
International Crime Victimization Survey (ICVS), 16, 62, 63, 357
International Labour Organization (ILO), 339, 462
international terrorism, 470
international treaties, 459–460
International Youth Survey, 61
Internet crime, 451
Internet fraud schemes, 452
Internet securities fraud, 388, 455
INTERPOL, 16, 358, 364
intimate violence, 3, 98, 99
intimidation, 467, 468
intoxication, as a defence, 42
intravenous (IV) drug users, 430
introversion, 185
involuntary intoxication, 42
involuntary manslaughter, 328
IQ scores, 25, 188–189, 263
Iribarren, Carlos, 168
Italian-based organized crime, 407
Ivankov, Vyacheslav Kirillovich, 464

Jackson, "Tough Lennie," 129
Jackson, Willie "The Clown," 129
Jacobs, George, 8
James, William, 182
Janoff, Victor, 106–107
jaywalking, 146
Jeffery, C. Ray, 137
Jeffrey, Lesley Ann, 105
Jenkins, Philip, 333
Jessop, Christine, 47
John Howard Society, 422
johns, 422
Johnson, Ben, 428
Johnson, Clayton, 47
Johnson, Hollis, 442
Jones, Earl, 35, 348
Jones, Holly, 51
joyriding, 357–358
Judgment of the Glowing Iron, 30
The Jukes (Dugdale), 164
juries, 31
Juristat series, 61, 76
jury independence, 31
just desert, 153
Justice Canada, 435

justice policy, and crime trends, 74
justification, as a defence, 40
"just-world bias," 103
"just world" thinking, 476
juvenile delinquency. *See* youth crime
Juvenile Delinquents Act, 302

Kaglik, Herman, 47
Kaplan, Howard, 259–260
Keegstra, James, 105
Kelling, George, 142
Kellough, Gail, 290
Kennedy, Leslie, 116
Kesler, Stephen, 43
Kibaki, Mwai, 468
King, Mackenzie, 425
King, Rodney, 209
Kingston Penitentiary, 255
Klippert, Everett, 38, 419
Klippert v. The Queen, 38
Knapp Commission, 389
knowledge of dealing, 352
"known group" method, 61
Kohlberg, Lawrence, 182–184
KPMG Fraud Survey, 390
Krieger, Grant, 46
Krisberg, Barry, 294–295
Kushner, Harvey, 471

labelling process, 256
labelling theory, 242, 244, 256
    becoming labelled, 258
    consequences of, 258–259
    and crime, 257–258
    differential enforcement, 258
    differential social control, 260–261
    general theory of deviance, 259–260
    influence of, 272–273
    introduction to, 256
    primary and secondary deviance, 259
    research on, 261
    validity of, 261–262
LaChance, Leo, 64, 69
Lac Megantic train explosion, 393–394
Lacombe, Daniel, 106
Ladue case, 41
LaGrange, Teresa, 221–222, 255
Langlois case, 42
Lapointe-Edward, Suzanne, 318
Laporte, Pierre, 473
larceny, 353–354
latency stage, 179
latent delinquency, 180–181
latent traits, 263
Lavallee, Angelique Lynn, 44, 98, 99, 329
Lavater, J.K., 9
law, 34–37, 416–417
Law, Order and Power (Chambliss and Seidman), 286
law enforcement, 58, 400–401, 436–437
Lay, Kenneth L., 385, 387
learning, 166

Sprott, Jane, 95, 242
Spurzheim, Johann Kaspar, 9
squeegee kids, 218
stability, 185
Stack, Steven, 148
Stafford, Jane, 98
stalking, 49–51, 97, 180, 188, 418
standardized personality tests, 187
Standing Committee on Justice and Human Rights, 41
Stark, Benjamin, 376
state political crime, 470
state-sponsored terrorism, 474–477
statistics, 13–14
status frustration, 226
statutory law, vs. common law, 31–33
Steele, Tracey, 148
steering locks, 139
stigma-reducing programs, 273
stigmatization, 148–150, 242, 256, 258–259
Stinchcombe, William, 49
stings, 386–387
stink bomb, 34
stolen property, 134, 352
Stolzenberg, Lisa, 148
Stolzenberg, Wolfgang, 386
Stoppel, Barbara, 47
strain theory, 131, 204
    anomie theory, 215–218, 224, 231
    community-level sources of, 220–221
    general strain theory, 220–224
    general strain theory (GST), 231
    institutional anomie theory, 218–219, 224, 231
    vs. Marxist theory, 294
    overview of, 204, 224, 231
    poverty, 215
    relative deprivation theory, 219–220, 231
    sources of, 220–222
stranger-related crime, 95–96, 330–331
Strategic Threat Assessment, 408
stratification, 201
Street Corner Society (Whyte), 23
street crime, 133–134, 348, 351
street lighting, 137–138
streetwalkers, 420
street youth, 227
stress, 220–222
strict liability, 40
Structural Criminology (Hagan), 303
structural factors, and hate crimes, 102
structural Marxism, 295–297, 308
structural perspective, 13
structuring of crime, 129–130, 135
Stuxnet computer worm, 458
subcultural influences, 132
subcultural view of substance abuse, 430
subcultures, 225, 226–227, 320
substance abuse, 320
    AIDS and drug use, 430
    alcohol and prohibition, 425
    beginning of, 424–425

cause of, 430–431
commonly used and abused drugs, 425–428
cycle of addiction, 434
extent of, 428–430
and mental illness, 184
in self-report surveys, 61–62
subterranean values, 249
Suchan, Steve, 129
sugar and crime, 167
suicide, 14, 70
suicide rate, 317–318
suitable targets, 109, 110, 134
Sullivan, Dennis, 293
summary offences, 35–37
superego, 179, 181
supervision, lack of, 132
super-zapping, 452
Supreme Court of Canada, 23, 39, 41, 44, 45, 99
surplus value, 293–294
surveillance, 136, 144–145
surveillance through environmental design, 112
survey research, 20
surveys of known criminals, 433
Sutherland, Edwin, 4, 14, 15, 189, 245, 351–352, 371, 383, 392
Swaggi, Vincent, 352
Swain, Owen, 49
Swartz, Marc, 385
swindles, 386–387
symbolic interaction theory, 256
Symons, Gladys, 304
syndicate, development of, 406
systematic forgers, 365–366

Tackling Auto Theft and Property Obtained by Crime Act, 361
tactical crime displacement, 139
Tailing, Bertha, 183
Tannenbaum, Frank, 259
Tanner, Julian, 23
Tarde, Gabriel, 177
target antagonism, 100
target attractiveness, 110
target crime displacement, 139
target gratifiability, 100
target hardening, 112, 116, 137, 139, 355
target reduction strategies, 139
target removal strategies, 355
targets, 130–131, 137
target vulnerability, 100, 130–131
Taub, Richard P., 207
tax evasion, 392
Taysup, Eva, 264
Teasdale, Brittney, 300
techniques of neutralization, 249–250
teenage behaviour, 174
telemarketing scams, 362, 363, 365
"telescoping" events from the past, 62
temperance movement, 425
temperature, and crime, 75

temporal crime displacement, 139
terror cells, 477–478
terrorism, 317, 450
    cyberterrorism, 478–479
    extent of, 479–480
    forms of, 472–477
    historical perspective on, 471–472
    motivation, 478
    organization of terrorist groups, 477–478
    responses to since September 11, 2001, attacks, 480
tertiary prevention, 131
testosterone, 167–169
Thanatos, 319–320
theft
    from ATMs, 458
    auto theft, 356–361
    bad cheques, 365–366
    computer fraud, 367–368
    credit card theft, 368
    current state of, 354–355
    embezzlement, 368–369
    false pretences, 361–363
    fraud, 361–363
    GST fraud ring, 368
    history of, 349–353
    identity theft, 363–365, 366
    introduction to, 353–354
    modern thieves, 350
    nonprofessional fence, 353
    occasional criminals, 350–351
    professional criminals, 351–353
    shoplifting, 355–356
Thematic Apperception Test, 187
theory construction, 13, 14
There Goes the Neighborhood (Wilson), 207
Thinking About Crime (Wilson), 127
third-hand knowledge of crime, 4
Thomas, W.I., 18
Thompson, Kevin, 304
Thompson, Robert, 330–331
Thrasher, Frederic, 11, 200, 206
three-strikes-and-you're-out policy, 152–153
thrill killings, 331
Tifft, Larry, 293
Time magazine, 223
time-series studies, 21–22, 148
Titan Rain, 458
Titchener, Edward, 182
tobacco smuggling, 407
Todd, Amanda, 77
Toews, Vic, 247
Toft, Karl, 67
Tokyo Rose, 469
Tolson case, 41
Tomaszewski, E. Andreas, 326
Tong, Edmund, 129
Toronto Stock Exchange, 387
Torrance, Mark, 398
tort law, 34–35
Tortorici, Ralph, 180
torture, 127